THE SOCIOECONOMIC STRUCTURE

OF THE

TOKYO METROPOLITAN COMPLEX

To Dr. Norton Ginsberg.

From Takeo Yazaki

Nov. 25, 1970

THE SOCIOECONOMIC STRUCTURE

OF THE

TOKYO METROPOLITAN COMPLEX

by Takeo Yazaki

translated by MITSUGU MATSUDA

Social Science Research Institute
University of Hawaii
Honolulu

Cover Design by Karen Essene

Library of Congress Catalog Card Number: 72-631611

Translated from the Japanese edition © 1966 by Takeo Yazaki
Printed in Japan by Keio Tsushin Kabushikikaisha, Tokyo
Published by Masafumi Tomita

TABLE OF CONTENTS

TABLE OF CONTENTS (continued)

LIST OF FIGURES

LIST OF FIGURES (continued)

LIST OF TABLES

PUBLISHER'S FOREWORD

When Professor Yazaki (Professor of Sociology, Keio University) expressed the wish for an English edition of his book, *Shufuken no shakai keizai kōzō to sono kiso shiryō*, he was teaching urban sociology as a visiting professor at the University of Hawaii. Sophisticated and reliable analyses of contemporary Asian urban areas were relatively scarce; therefore, given the concern of the Social Science Research Institute with the study of socio-cultural change in Asia, it seemed most fitting for us to undertake translation and publication. Professor Yazaki, who is a noted authority in this field, generously gave approval to our suggestion that his work appear in an inexpensive format, accessible to students.

The socioeconomic analysis of change in contemporary Tokyo is a most relevant task, for as the largest city on earth it is the harbinger of what is to come for most of the highly industrialized nations of the world as well as those still in the early phase of development. To be placed in proper perspective, this present work should be read in conjunction with Professor Yazaki's other major works in English, *The Japanese City* and *Social Change and the City in Japan*. The former is a sociological analysis, while the latter provides more of a historical overview of urbanization in Japan. The present volume supplements the aforementioned by focusing exclusively on the Tokyo region and by providing basic data for further study and analysis.

The present work is no mere translation of Dr. Yazaki's original work, which was published in 1966. Indeed, that effort has been greatly enlarged by Dr. Yazaki, for the original contained but 25 pages of text while there has been a fourfold increase in the present volume. Moreover, an additional 100 tables and figures have been added to the original. The difficult task of translation was successfully carried out in his usual meticulous manner by the late Dr. Mitsugu Matsuda; without his persistence this task would not have been realized.

William P. Lebra, Director
Social Science Research Institute

PREFACE

The modern world is becoming urbanized at an unprecedented rate, and in Japan, population concentration in urban centers is taking place at a faster rate and on a greater scale than in any other country. This population concentration in Japan is particularly noticeable in such highly industrialized regions as the capital region, with metropolitan Tokyo as a nucleus; the Kinki region surrounding Osaka; the Nagoya-centered Chūkyō region; and north Kyūshū, with its clusters of urban centers. The concentrations and increases of populations and institutions in pivotal urban centers and the allied neighboring areas has been great. In the past, these metropolitan complexes were centripetally structured, with the central metropolises as nuclei, and each complex characteristically maintained an independent structure in relation to other metropolitan complexes. In the present situation, functional specialization characterizes metropolitan complexes, making them far more interdependent, and one gigantic megalopolis, with metropolitan Tokyo as its nucleus, is in the making. As a result, the isolation and exclusiveness of rural districts throughout Japan have been broken, and rural areas have become closely linked structurally to urban centers.

Generally, the sizes of metropolitan centers have varied in proportion to their distances from metropolitan Tokyo, the center of the whole structure. Each metropolis can no longer function within a limited geographical boundary: in Tokyo, the geographical area where people work and live far surpasses the administrative area of Tokyo as a metropolis; the area encompasses parts of the neighboring prefectures. This expanded area is characterized by the functional specialization and close structural relationships of its component districts, and the size of its population makes it perhaps the world's greatest metropolitan complex.

Needless to say, urban development is attendant upon the social and economic development of the whole society, and the rapid socioeconomic development of Japan has accounted for its high rate of urbanization. Social change as a whole does not, however, necessarily imply simultaneous, parallel changes in the various sectors of society, and in Japan, changes in social institutions have not conformed with the rapid increase of population and the social and economic activities. As a result, big cities are now confronted with many problems: traffic congestion, scanty and poor housing, water shortages, inadequate rubbish disposal, increasing exhaust fumes and smog, ground sinking, river and sea water pollution, shortage of parks and green tracts of land, land price rises, slums, insufficient educational facilities, worsening social environment, an increasing crime rate, and local financial difficulties.

The seriousness of urban problems has been publicized in the mass media and many urban theories have been advanced, but most of them are superficial and fragmentary and do not contribute to systematic analyses or solutions to the problems. To understand and solve the problems of the metropolitan centers, it is essential to analyze each metropolis on the basis of the data of its population, geography, economy, social conditions, transportation, administration, finance, etc. Then conceptualization of the problems and the various phenomena are possible. Finally, plans can be formulated to solve the problems--with ultimate goal of establishing a more democratic and modern society by promoting economic growth and the people's welfare. Plans formulated without a basic methodological background will be ineffective because one plan will only contradict another. Compilation of basic data and the formulation of an urban theory are indispensable for solving the pressing urban problems of today. Having a long tradition of scholarship in the social sciences and a long history of modern urban development, Western nations have demonstrated excellence in theory building, but in Japan, so far as I know, there has been little theorizing from analysis of actual conditions in the country. Especially lacking is a systematic compilation of basic data.

This volume presents a general description of social and economic conditions in the Tokyo metropolitan complex, pointing out characteristics of the region and basic problems in urban planning. Then, according to the method mentioned above, data are presented to facilitate as many and varied analyses as possible of the Tokyo metropolitan complex. The data should also permit comparison with conditions in other metropolitan complexes in Japan, as well as those in foreign countries. Four metropolitan area maps for 1960-1965, 1966, and 1967 precede Part I; they indicate the more recent population distribution patterns. These data have been compiled solely from national census materials, which can be used for many purposes, including comparative analyses of various districts of the country. To be sure, many more kinds of data than are presented here are necessary for total comprehension of conditions in the complex. All relevant data have been collected in the research, but because of space limitations, we include only the basic statistics in this volume. Ancillary data will be presented in later reports.

I would like to express my deep appreciation for the special considerations given me in the publication of this volume by William P. Lebra and the staff of the Social Science Research Institute, University of Hawaii.

Tokyo, Japan   Takeo Yazaki
June 10, 1967

A. Rate of Population Increase in the Tokyo Metropolitan Complex, 1960-1965

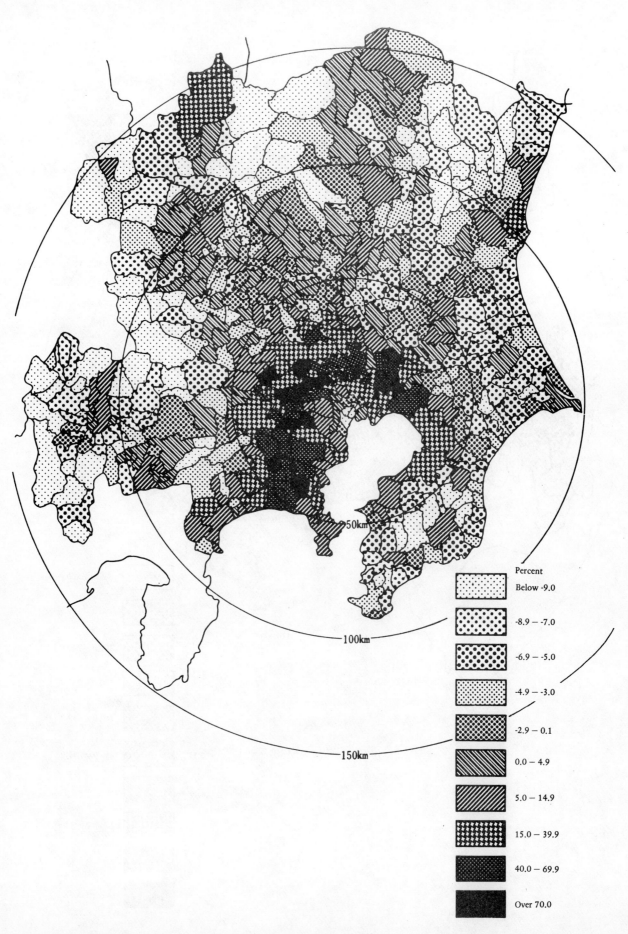

Percent

Below -9.0

-8.9 — -7.0

-6.9 — -5.0

-4.9 — -3.0

-2.9 — -0.1

0.0 — 4.9

5.0 — 14.9

15.0 — 39.9

40.0 — 69.9

Over 70.0

B. Population Density in the Tokyo Metropolitan Complex, 1965

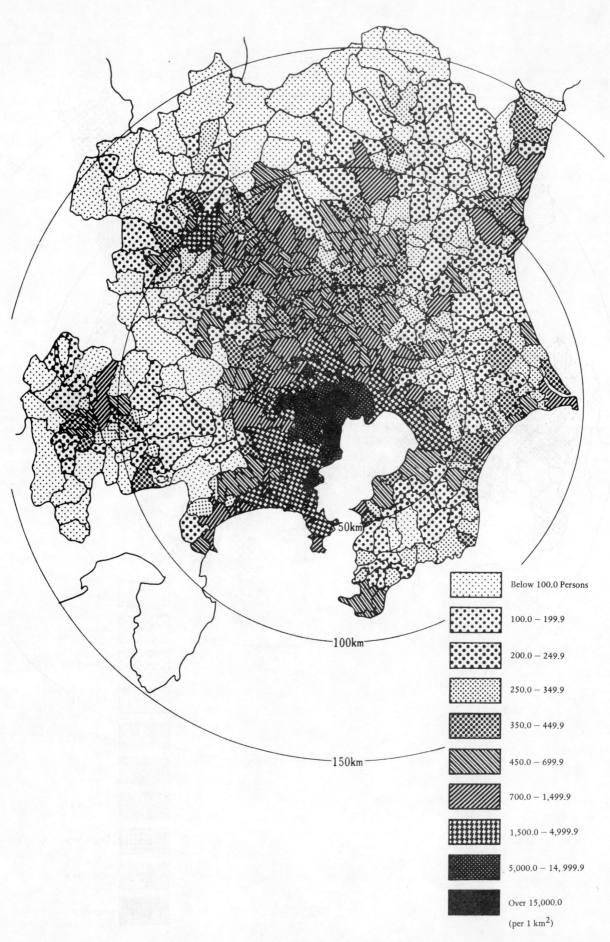

50km

100km

150km

Below 100.0 Persons

100.0 — 199.9

200.0 — 249.9

250.0 — 349.9

350.0 — 449.9

450.0 — 699.9

700.0 — 1,499.9

1,500.0 — 4,999.9

5,000.0 — 14, 999.9

Over 15,000.0

(per 1 km^2)

C. Land Utilization In and Around the Metropolis, 1966

Commercial Areas (Offices, Stores, Theaters, etc.)

Industrial Areas (Factories, Workshops, etc.)

Commercial-Industrial Areas

Residential Areas (Houses, Apartments, etc.)

Public Facilities Areas (Government Offices, Schools, Hospitals, Reservoirs, etc.)

Parks and Green Lands

Forests

Others (Farmlands, Farming Settlements, etc.)

National Railroads

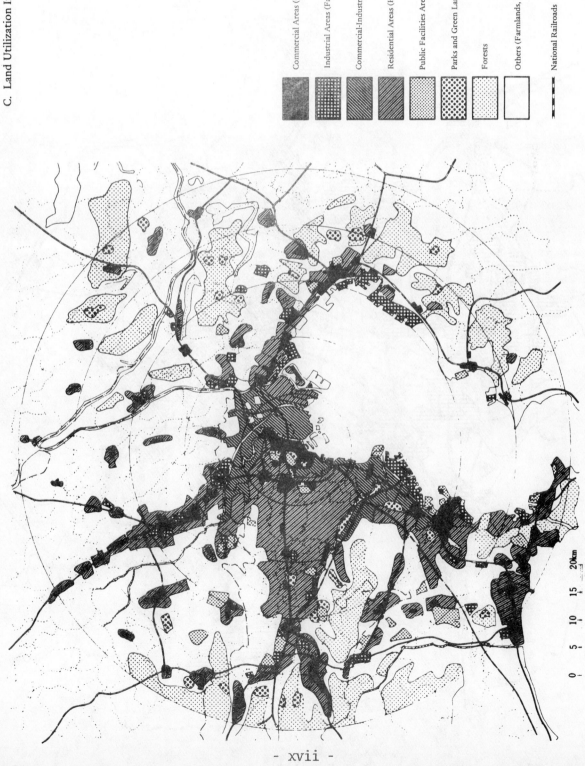

0   5   10   15   20km

D. Metropolitan plan, 1967

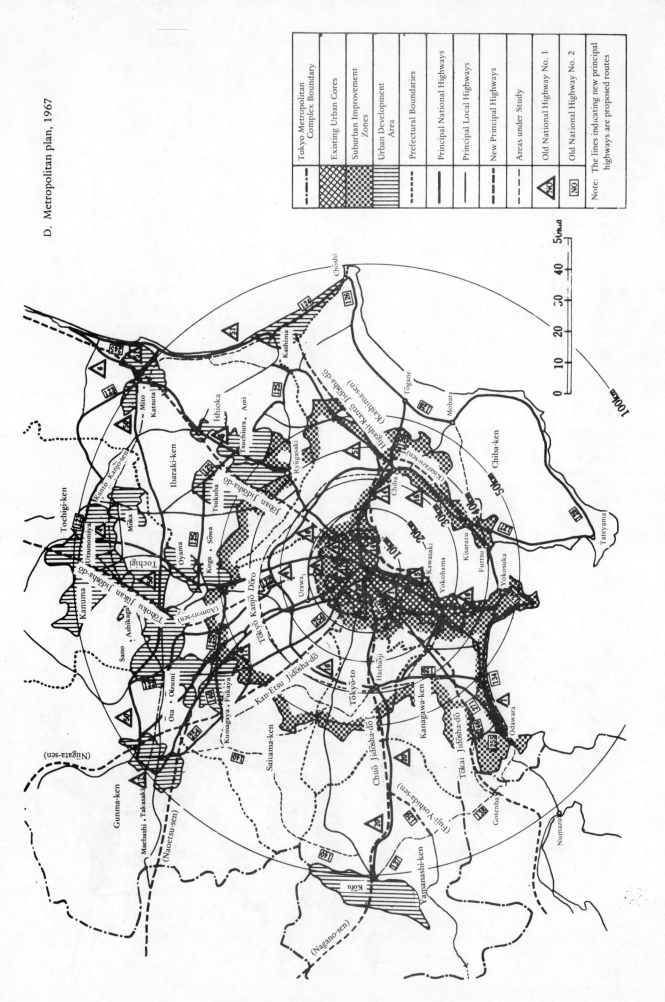

	Tokyo Metropolitan Complex Boundary
	Existing Urban Cores
	Suburban Improvement Zones
	Urban Development Area
	Prefectural Boundaries
	Principal National Highways
	Principal Local Highways
	New Principal Highways
	Areas under Study
	Old National Highway No. 1
	Old National Highway No. 2

Note: The lines indicating new principal highways are proposed routes

PART I

DISCUSSION AND DESCRIPTION

CHAPTER 1

URBANIZATION AND URBAN PROBLEMS IN JAPAN
IN RELATION TO WORLD URBANIZATION

World demographers describe today's rapid increase of population as a population explosion. In 1750, the world population stood at 750,000,000; by 1900 it had increased twofold to 1,500,000,000; and by 1965, the figures had increased more than twofold again to 3,300,000,000. World population projections for the end of the present century reach as high as 6,300,000,000.

Population increase and urbanization are closely related, but the urban concentration of population during the present century, or even during the last generation, took place faster than in all the previous centuries put together, and this tendency has been accelerating.

In 1800, only 2 percent of the world's people lived in cities of 20,000 or more, but in 1900 a total of 10 cities in the world had populations of more than 1,000,000: 5 were in Europe, 3 in North America, 1 in Asia, and 1 in Russia. At present, 20 percent of the world population live in cities of 20,000 or more, and a total of 61 cities have more than 1,000,000 people: 16 are in Europe, 5 in America, 38 in Asia, and 2 in Oceania. There are several big metropolises that have populations of 10,000,000, or thereabouts, including Tokyo, New York, London, Paris, Moscow, Shanghai, and Calcutta. On the basis of the past tendency towards urbanization, it is estimated by authorities that in the year 2000 approximately half the world population will be living in cities of 20,000 or more.

Urbanization progresses at different rates and takes different patterns in the various areas of the world. The growth of cities progresses in conformity with the social and economic development of the societies to which they belong, and the cities' structures depend upon that socioeconomic development, as well as the societies' national cultural histories. England developed preconditions for modernization takeoff in the eighteenth and the early nineteenth centuries, while other countries of Europe and the United States completed takeoff in the middle of the nineteenth century; Japan reached takeoff towards the end of the nineteenth century, and South America reached that point only recently. Countries in Asia and Africa have just begun to modernize. Generally speaking, the more belated the industrialization of a country, the faster the rate of its urbanization--10 to 30 percent of the population of such a country begin to live in cities of 100,000 or more shortly after industrialization. For example, it took 79 years for England and Wales to reach such a stage, 66 years for the United States, 48 years for Germany, 35 years for Japan, and 26 years for Australia.

The rate of urban growth reached the peak in Europe and America in the latter half of the nineteenth century, but in Asia and Africa it became greatest after the middle of the present century. In 1950, in Asia, where urbanization began late, the total population came to comprise one-third of the world population, but this fact does not mean that urbanization is well in progress now. Despite the increase of urban population in Asia, the proportion of the population living in cities of 100,000 or more increased from

2.1 percent in 1900 to 7.5 percent in 1950:   that is, an increase of only 5.6
percent, in comparison with 9.3 percent in Oceania, 22.6 percent in America,
and 19.9 percent in Europe. Together with Africa, where the increase was 5.2
percent, Asia still has a small percentage of its population living in cities.
Urbanization in less developed countries does not follow the same pattern
demonstrated by advanced countries.

The Process of Urbanization

It is well known from the history of the West that urbanization was
accelerated greatly by the Industrial Revolution. Based upon improvements in
agriculture and transportation technology, productive activities were expanded
and intensified through the development of overseas markets for trade, and
urban enterprises were developed and expanded with the development of factory
production, which was accelerated by the use of capitalistic methods of
production and by improved power supplies. People began to migrate from
agricultural communities where the rate of natural population increase was
high, but the income level was low, to cities where conditions were reversed.
Thus, urban growth was stimulated as a result of population migration.

In the West, during the migration to the cities, to cope with overpopula-
tion in the agricultural districts, attempts were made to control and adjust
land ownership, to promote capitalism, and to raise the income level; on the
other hand, efforts were made to improve capital accumulation, production
techniques, income level, and general living conditions in the urban areas
where problems such as housing, water shortages, and sanitation, were arising
in the midst of social change. Thus, unlike the Asian and African nations,
which are now undergoing change, the Western countries have been able to pay
attention to their rural and urban problems while going through the process
of urbanization.

Features common to Western societies, such as population movement from low-
income to high-income occupations, expansion of urban industries, and improvements in living conditions cannot be found in the underdeveloped and presently
urbanizing countries of Asia, Africa, and Latin America, in which three-
fourths of the human race live. In these underdeveloped countries, population
in cities of 10,000 or more increased over the ten-year period between 1950
and 1960 at a rate 30 percent faster than in industrialized countries. While
urban population in sixteen industrialized countries increased by 15 percent
in the ten-year period of the most rapid urbanization of the nineteenth century, urban population in forty underdeveloped countries increased by 20
percent over the recent ten-year period, and cities are growing at a startling
rate at present in these countries.

The major reason for this rapid increase in urban population in underdeveloped countries is not a shift of agricultural population into cities, as
was the case in Western society, but the very natural increase of population
both in rural and urban areas since 1940, which by far surpassed, perhaps
doubled, the population increase in industrialized countries. The rapid urban
growth was not accounted for by population migration from rural to urban
areas, but by this natural increase of population in general. The birth rate
in underdeveloped countries was about the same in cities as in villages, and
the death rate in cities, which had been high, gradually declined as health
and sanitation conditions improved.

- 4 -

Underdeveloped countries are now confronted with a serious dilemma: despite the rapid growth of cities, rural populations are increasing, with unemployment becoming serious, while in urban areas, industries are not fully developed, and the income level is low. The conditions in the cities are being aggravated by the natural increase of population, as well as by the continuing migration from the rural communities. Jobs are becoming hard to obtain and the newcomers to cities are spending their last savings. This type of urbanization is bringing the poverty of people into sharp focus. Urban administrative affairs are not being handled adequately, many facilities necessary for urban living are lacking, health and sanitation conditions are deplorable, many people are homeless, illegal holdings of land are increasing with big slum areas developing, and what employment one can hold assures him of only a subsistence-level living.

To be sure, in industrialized countries, urbanization was not a smooth and easy process, but it helped solve the problems of rural communities; the income level in the cities was high and employment conditions were relatively good. In underdeveloped countries, urbanization is progressing rapidly, but cities are laden with problems, and urbanization is not an answer to problems of rural areas.

In Japan, the most highly urbanized nation in Asia, the limited landspace and inadequate investment in rural areas, poor agricultural techniques, and low productivity have resulted in prevailing conditions of poverty, which have been responsible for population migration into the cities. The cities have had the ability to absorb such surplus population owing to their high degree of industrialization. Yet, compared with conditions in Western countries, wages are still low in Japan, and the number of people who are engaged in more than one type of work for their livelihood is increasing. Potential unemployment still exists, and although there are some excellent facilities for urban living, little has been accumulated from the past for the growth of truly modern cities. There are many barriers to adequate accommodations for the increasing population and to modern and efficient social and economic activities. Thus, Japan still lags behind Western nations in modernization and urbanization, in spite of her remarkable progress.

Urbanization had advanced to the greatest extent in the world's capitalistic countries, but urbanization and capitalism are not synonymous. In the Soviet Union, 32 percent of the population was urban in 1939, and by 1959, 48 percent of the population lived in cities; more than half of this urban population lived in cities of 100,000 or more. In mainland China, 40,000,000 people migrated from villages to cities during the period 1949 to 1956, leading to a great increase of urban population and a high degree of population concentration in big cities. In 1953, there were 103 cities with populations of more than 100,000, in which 63 percent of the total urban population lived. But the urban population is only 13 percent of the total Chinese population, and therefore urbanization in China has not reached its peak.

As we have seen above, although countries differ in social and cultural structures, urbanization is progressing rapidly in every country, regardless of the degree of industrialization. And of the Asian countries, Japan is attracting the attention of the world as she exhibits a high rate and degree of urbanization. Most Asian countries are "developing" countries, where urbanization is progressing, but at a low level; however, in Japan, the rapid development of urban industries and the relative poverty of rural districts has pushed urbanization at a rate and degree unprecedented in world history. In 1920, less than 25 percent of the Japanese population lived in cities of 20,000 or more, but in 1930 the figure was 33 percent, a higher proportion of city dwellers at the time than France had with 30 percent. By 1940 Japan's urban population surpassed the United States, which registered 42 percent. In 1950 the figure reached 60 percent, surpassing the 54 percent figure in the Netherlands and the 56 percent figure in Australia, both of which are highly urbanized countries. In 1960, Japan had 67 percent of her population living in cities of 20,000 or more, ranking closely behind Great Britain, which was the most highly urbanized country in the world, with the figure in the neighborhood of 70 percent. Moreover, there has been a strong tendency towards population concentration in big cities; there are now sixty-four cities with populations of 100,000 or more each, and the total population of these cities constitutes about one-fourth of the total Japanese population. Japan has become one of the most rapidly and highly urbanized countries in the world, although many unsolved problems have been created as a result.

Today cities are growing in size and number, and population concentration in big cities is particularly striking. In some underdeveloped countries, population concentration in big cities has been closely related to the countries' traditional socioeconomic structures, characterized by lowproductive and labor-intensive industry, and people usually crowd in one big city--often the capital city of the country, as evidenced in Bombay (population 4,420,000 in 1963), Cairo (3,410,000 in 1961), Rio de Janeiro (3,220,000 in 1960), Mexico City (3,550,000 in 1963), Buenos Aires (1,960,000 in 1963), and Djakarta (2,900,000 in 1961). In other cases, population concentration in big cities has been a result of the progress of industrialization and the subsequent concentration of political and economic activities in the cities; such activities, and similar activities in areas far and widely extending beyond the boundaries of the cities, further stimulated an increase in the number of urban activities.

The continuous concentration of population and activities in the big cities of industrial countries has transformed the centripetally structured urban society, setting off a dispersion of the concentrated population and institutions into the peripheral areas. This population dispersion is possible through improved transportation and communications facilities; organically structured metropolitan complexes are created, each covering a great expanse of space and each is closely linked to the others.

There are today four great metropolitan complexes in the world which were created as a result of industrialization, and the greatest of all is the Tokyo metropolitan complex (considering a 50-kilometer-radius circle with the Tokyo Central Station as its center) with a population of 15,780,000 in 1960. Next largest is the New York complex, including the northeastern part of New Jersey, which had a population of 14,000,000 in 1960. The third largest is the London metropolitan region with a population of 10,500,000 in 1956, and the last of the big four is the Moscow region which had 7,300,000 people in 1955.

The Tokyo metropolitan complex was legally delimited by the Tokyo Metropolitan Complex Improvement Act of 1956 to a 100-kilometer radius, with the Tokyo Central Station as its center, on the basis of the traffic mileage one truck covers in a day's work. This area had a population of 20,190,000 in 1955 and 24,300,000 in 1963. It registered 60 percent of the total national increase in population during that period, and its population constituted one-fourth of the total national population. During the same period, however, the 50-kilometer-radius region registered an increase of 6,440,000 people, while the circular belt region between 50 kilometers and 100 kilometers from the Tokyo Central Station registered a decrease of 2,330,000 people--mainly the result of a migration from the outer belt to the inner region. Thus, it became clear that the two regions had different characters, and it has been regarded more appropriate to take the 50-kilometer-radius region for metropol-itan planning. To be sure, there are other factors to be considered for the delimitation of a metropolitan planning zone, but as we shall see in more detail later, it appears feasible to take this smaller region as a unit of analysis and as a unit for planning.

It must be noted here that the 50-kilometer-radius region we have chosen for our analysis is not the same as the region delimited anew in 1966 by the government. In 1966, the Tokyo metropolitan complex was expanded to include metropolitan Tokyo and the seven neighboring prefectures (Kanagawa, Saitama, Chiba, Ibaragi, Tochigi, Gunma, and Yamanashi) because great discrepancies were found to exist between the original 1956 plan and the actual conditions ten years later in the size of population and industries; and also because the 100-kilometer-radius region cut the areas of some prefectures in half, causing administrative problems for the prefectures affected. The new 1966 region had a radius of approximately 130 kilometers, in which 26,930,000 people lived in 1965, representing 27.4 percent of the total national popu-lation, and the total area constituted 10 percent of the total national area.

Within the 130-kilometer radius, the area extending 50 kilometers from the center of Tokyo was divided into two parts which were respectively designated as the Existing Urban Cores Area (Kisei shigaichi) and the Suburban Improve-ment Zone (Kinkō seibi chitai), in which efforts were to be made to improve urban facilities and to provide and maintain green tracts of land. Pre-viously, efforts were made to create a New Urban Cores Development Area (Shigaichi kaihatsu kuiki), consisting of satellite and mainly industrial cities in order to alleviate the excessive concentration of people and industries in the Existing Urban Cores Area; but in 1966 the designation was changed to the new Urban Development Area (Toshi kaihatsu kuiki), with new plans for zone development and improvement. Educational and other activities were added to the original plans and fourteen industrial districts were designated in the area.

Metropolitan complexes in Japan not only have great proportions of the total national population, but they also occupy important roles in changing society because there is a close interplay of functions and structures between them and the national and international functions of society.

As we have seen already, urbanization is a common feature in the world today, regardless of the stages of national development. The concentra-tion of population and industries in big cities is particularly striking, and the tendency of cities to grow into big metropolises is now being accel-erated. Japan, especially, is undergoing rapid change in this respect. Urbanization in industrialized, advanced countries in the world has been closely related to countries' general industrialization, and urbanization in capitalistic countries has been related to the accelerating development of capitalism.

Capitalistic countries, with rationalistic attitudes and orientations, have been making efforts to improve production for greater profits through mechanized methods of production, and this rationalization has occurred not only in commodity production, but in transportation and communication; the influence of mass production is being felt in the commercial and agricultural sectors, whose structures have been altered. With the growth of mass production, both the absolute and relative numbers of people engaged in primary industry have declined, while the secondary and tertiary industrial population has increased.

Percentage distribution of population in various industries is said to indicate the degree of industrial development of a given nation. In 1965 in the developing countries of Asia, Africa, and Latin America, the primary industry population made up 50 percent or more (in average) of the total national population, while in Great Britain, those in primary industry constituted only 2 percent of the total population, and those in secondary industry, 45 percent, and in tertiary, 53 percent. In the United States in 1965, in primary, secondary and tertiary industries, the figures were 6 percent, 33 percent, and 61 percent, respectively; in West Germany 11 percent, 48 percent, and 41 percent in 1960; in France 20 percent, 37 percent, and 43 percent in 1962; in Italy 25 percent, 40 percent, and 35 percent in 1965; and in the Soviet Union 36 percent, 35 percent, and 29 percent in 1959.

In Japan, the only industrialized nation in Asia, the primary industry population stood at 54 percent in 1920 while the secondary and tertiary populations were 21 percent and 25 percent, respectively. This industrial population structure was drastically changed by 1965, when the percentages for three types of industrial activity were 25 percent, 32 percent, and 43 percent; the great decline in the primary industry population reflected Japan's economic growth. With the index for 1955 set at 100, the gross national product of the United States in 1965 was 139.2; Great Britain 133.4; France 161.8; Italy 170.1; West Germany 181.9; and the Soviet Union 197.3; Japan topped them all with 246.8. Japan's most striking feature is this rapid growth. The gross national product of Japan in 1965 was $84.7 billion, compared with $991 billion in the United States, $112.6 billion in West Germany, $98.3 billion in Great Britain, $94.8 billion in France, and $56.6 billion in Italy. If her rate of growth continues, before long Japan will surpass some of these wealthy Western countries. In 1961 Japan surpassed Great Britain in steel production and ranked fourth below West Germany, the Soviet Union, and the United States. Shipbuilding and the production of electrical tools and appliances, cameras, television sets, and radios have carried Japan near the top in world ranking.

Japan's rapid economic development represents a shift of population from low-income primary industry to secondary and tertiary industry. Per capita income of the gainfully employed people in 1950/1951 showed, with the average index of 100 for the whole, the index of 54 for the primary industry population, 147 for the secondary, and 140 for the tertiary. Judged from the standpoint of industry, this was an indication of: an increase and concentration of accumulated capital; an increase in the number and scale of enterprises; improved production techniques; a high degree of specialization; an increase in the number of employees in various enterprises; an increase in wages; an expansion of unit investment scale; a shift from light industry to heavy and to chemical industry; and an expansion of management and sales functions of enterprises.

In 1961, the 150 greatest firms of the world in terms of commodity sales were distributed as follows: 42 in the United States, 16 in West Germany, 12 in Great Britain, 5 each in France and Canada, and 4 in Japan, with the rest distributed to a few other countries. Thus, Japan ranked sixth in the world. As for the scales of manufacturing enterprises, the employers having 99 or fewer employees in the United States in 1958 constituted 23.2 percent of the total number of employers in manufacturing, those with 100 to 999 employees 40.4 percent, and those with 1,000 or more employees 36.4 percent. Great Britain in 1961 had 24.7 percent, 43.8 percent, and 32.5 percent in the respective categories, while West Germany in 1964 had the figures 40.4 percent, 32.1 percent, and 27.5 percent, respectively. In Japan, the figures were 52.8 percent, 30.2 percent, and 17.0 percent in 1965. Despite the growth of big corporations in Japan, there are still many petty enterprises, in contrast to the conditions in the United States where production techniques are advanced, productivity is high, and big enterprises that can stimulate industrial development and control markets exist in a great number.

With economic growth comes the tendency toward an increase of the population employed by big business and a decrease in the number of those who are self-employed or engaged in types of domestic work without pay. In 1965, 87.1 percent of the working population of the United States were industrial employees, 11.1 percent were self-employed, and 1.8 percent were domestic workers; comparative figures for West Germany in 1965 were 80.4 percent, 11.4 percent, and 8.2 percent; and for France in the same year, 72.6 percent, 18.9 percent, and 8.6 percent, respectively. In contrast, the percentages for Japan in 1965 were 58.7 percent, 20.4 percent, and 20.9 percent; thus, Japan has not yet emerged from a state of backwardness as far as population distribution according to occupational status is concerned.

As for productivity and wages in industries, setting the index numbers of productivity and wages in a big business firm employing 1,000 or more employees at 100 each, we derived the index numbers 90 for productivity and 84 for wages in an enterprise in the United States having 10 to 29 employees, while the numbers were 89 and 79 in Great Britain. Japan had the numbers 31 and 38 in contrast with those two countries. Furthermore, per capita annual national income in 1965 in the United States was $2,893; in Sweden $2,013; in the Soviet Union $1,893 (1964); in West Germany $1,186; in Canada $1,825; in Australia $1,620; in Great Britain $1,451; in France $1,436; in Italy $883; in Poland $876 (1964); in Brazil $217; and in the Philippines $219. In Japan the figure was $696, ranking it twenty-seventh in annual per capita income of the nations in the world.

Japanese society is characterized by a double structure in which, on the one hand, economic growth has been the fastest in the world with great strides made in heavy and chemical industries, and, on the other hand, petty agricultural and commercial activities still hold great importance in national economy. Japan's national income is still small, and great earning differentials exist according to individual occupations and statuses within industry. Therefore, in spite of the most rapid industrialization and urbanization in the world, Japan is still far from being a highly modernized and democratic nation.

Despite all of the above contradictions, Japan has achieved a high degree of economic development. The following reasons may be cited for this development: (1) the relatively weak traditional value system which did not militate against modernization of the various social and economic institutions; (2) the relative political stability which made planned development possible; (3) dissolution of the monopoly system after the war and the resulting keen competition among numerous enterprises, which led for cost reduction purposes to the introduction of advanced technology and managerial methods from overseas; (4) the continued expansion of heavy industry from prewar days, the supply of the majority of capital goods by domestic industry, and the multiplication of total industrial output; (5) a high educational level and diligence of the people, and the low wages of labor despite high productivity; (6) the dissolution of the traditional two-generation households into one-generation households, and the increased rate of savings for individual security, which in turn served to meet demands for capital for higher economic development; (7) expansion of enterprises through loans from banks; (8) the enormous economic assistance from the United States in the postwar periods, the Korean War, and the international cooperation for expansion of world trade, all of which favorably influenced the expansion of Japanese foreign trade; and (9) the fact that Japan is a peaceful and unarmed nation.

Aggregation: Causes and Effects

Since societies are made up of political, economic, cultural, and many other factors, it may not be accurate to single out just one factor to explain social phenomena, but it cannot be denied that a major motive for individual and corporate activity in capitalistic societies is the profit motive, and that the profit motive plays a significant role in determining their cities' community structures and the patterns of interrelationship between urban and rural communities. Non-capitalistic societies have traditional social and cultural structures that are transformed into a new structure when capitalistic practices and activities are introduced; and in modern societies, economic structures and activities are important factors in determining the whole social structure.

Each enterprise in a great capitalistic society built around metropolitan complexes seeks to operate rationally for effective profit making; the principal corporations rationalize management to expand their scale of operations, and gradually, the operations' geographical areas expand too. In the process, corporate competition expedites the gradation of corporations, according to their capital holdings and economic capabilities, and at the same time, competition leads to a high degree of corporate specialization and interdependence. This process is not a natural economic phenomenon, but represents a complex relationship between politics and economics. Therefore, it goes without saying that structural relationships between political power, culture, and economics in societies have to be closely studied.

At any rate, in the course of a society's economic development, corporations with big capital and managerial ability usually concentrate and expand their managerial functions, their factories, and their wholesale and retail operations in and around big cities. The big cities, in turn, begin to assume the role of integrating various operations and activities over vast geographical areas. The cities function as the network centers of closely interdependent regions, and the whole national society becomes enfolded in the big-city activities of big corporations. A high degree of specialization of functions develops throughout society and a single nationwide market emerges. To integrate their activities over wide geographical areas, corporations compete for the best locations possible and the best reciprocal corporate relationships for promoting their operations. The best corporate locations, so far as transportation and communication facilities are concerned, are the central sections, or hearts, of big cities. Capital investors with specialized staffs for their enterprising activities crowd into high rise buildings in these central locations, which causes a rise in land prices and invites further investments. Corporations also find good locations for operations in subcenters of big cities, which are the consumer zones for the city residents, as well as in the minor urban centers. Thus, the cities' central sections subordinate subcenters and minor urban centers, but occupy the central positions in integrating the cities' activities.

The structure of a nation's social and economic development is built around its big cities, and this is a result of both centralization and decentralization processes. As we have mentioned already, as corporations expand, they specialize managerial, sales, and operational functions. Managerial, sales, and procurement functions are performed, if possible, in the city's central area, which provides accessibility to the integrative activities of other corporations, to government agencies, and to financial institutions. However, easy access to raw materials, vast and cheap land, railroad and harbor facilities, industrial water supplies, gas, electricity, oil and other fuels supply, health and sanitation upkeep, the corporations begin to move their operational functions to peripheral areas of big cities, so long as the relocation does not jeopardize their accessibility to market and to sources of labor and technical skills, which is a prerequisite for managerial and sales functions as well. In relocating, corporations must also consider the need for coordination between their operational functions and their managerial and sales functions. Depending upon the types of industries, decentralization may lead to the creation of an industrial belt around each big city or to the formation of satellite cities, or kombinats, separate from the city proper.

These corporations can be regarded as the basic organizations that contribute to the formation and expansion of metropolises in modern capitalistic societies; the number and scale of the corporations and their operational and distributional patterns most directly represent the community structures of the big cities. These big cities, however, cannot be understood adequately from just a study of the production activities of the people and organizations within them. One must analyze the whole social structure in connection with the living patterns of the people who work in those organizations. Because the people supply skills and labor for the organizations, the organizations cannot function independently of them, and the corporations' operations are determined by the number and quality of the people.

People assume roles in various organizations as capitalists, managers, white- and blue-collar employees, technicians, wage laborers, and professionals, and some people also come to cities as merchants to supply daily necessities to those people.

Of utmost importance to all these people are the conveniences for commuting to their places of employment in the hearts and industrial areas of the cities --the very nerve centers for the cities' formation and development. The availability of adequate transportation conveniences increases the formation of residential districts around the cities' hearts, subcenters, and industrial areas, near the organizations supplying consumer goods. The character of each residential district is determined by the income level, the occupations, and the other cultural patterns of the residents. The whole structural and distribution patterns of these residential districts differ from each other according to the availability of technical skills in civil engineering, construction, transportation, and communications in each metropolis. The districts' structural patterns are also influenced by topographical and cultural conditions in the metropolis and by the degree of good or poor communication with the current political powers who are responsible for urban development plans. But generally speaking, the patterns are determined by the people's commuting distances, as measured in terms of time and costs.

As described above, the whole community structure of a metropolitan complex exhibits a high degree of specialization of functions among its component sectors, which are organically closely interrelated, and the whole complex functions as a unit. This is the basic community structure of a metropolitan complex in an industrialized country.

The formation of a metropolitan complex in an industrialized society represents at once a process of change in community structure and an overall rise in living standards. It also represents a process of structural changes in occupations, education, households, thoughts, and politics. Because urbanization and industrialization require proper adjustments to the corporations' demands for "brain-power" to develop new technical skills and to understand the highly advanced technical issues, not only compulsory general education but higher education must be improved, and the national level of education raised.

In prewar Japan, there were 160,000 people who had university educations and fifteen years of practical experience. Twenty years after the war, there were 650,000 people in that category. The more highly urbanized districts had higher levels of education, and the bigger cities had more people with higher educations. In 1960, the college graduates in all the rural communities in Japan constituted 2.8 percent of the total rural population, while 8.0 percent of the total urban population were college graduates. People with higher education offer their services to various big-city organizations and become the driving forces behind the development of new technical skills, or they become the operators or managers in technical firms, playing important roles in social change.

As for business enterprises, capital and management have separated, and their traditional status in society has become less determined by the family backgrounds of the management and has come to depend more on the technical and other abilities of the individuals involved. Most of the white- and blue-collar employees and wage laborers, whose numbers increase as cities grow in size, assume roles in, and receive compensations from, the organizations engaged in integrative activities in the hearts and industrial areas of such cities, and these people lead a consumer life in the residential areas in the suburbs. As their population and ability to consume increase, there will be more commercial and service people who cater to this employee population.

In Japan, urban families relinquish some of the traditional roles which have been expected of them in the past and family members depend upon specialized agencies for educational, religious, and recreational benefits; second- and third-generation households divide and subdivide into smaller units, which gradually lead to individual democratic household units of a single couple and their children. In a Japanese agricultural village in 1960, the households with members of a single generation cohabiting constituted 6.7 percent of the total households; those with members of two generations living together 52.5 percent; those with members of three generations 33.0 percent; single-family households 3.7 percent; and other types of households 4.0 percent. In contrast, a Japanese city had 12.8 percent one-generation households, 62.8 percent two-generation households, 16.8 percent three-generation households, 5.8 percent single-family households, and 1.9 percent of other descriptions. Thus, in cities, the number of three-generation households is smaller and single-family, one-generation, and two-generation households are more numerous.

As for thought systems, the traditional authoritarianism of the past, which was based on coherent value systems, has lost its force, and in its place has arisen democracy, which has been adopted as the spiritual mainstay of social integration and for the betterment of the national welfare through respect for human rights, promotion of technology, accumulation of capital, expansion of production, and other ideals. Greater portions of national and local budgets have been allocated to investments in social welfare, education, and public services, and the nation has begun to take on a welfare-state character. In this process, the traditional relationships between the employer and employee have been altered through improvements in customary and legal practices; instead they are contractual relationships between independent and free individuals--since labor has the rights to free organization, negotiation, and protest. With the expansion of industry, corporations in big cities have grown big and monopolistic, while the principles of liberty and equality for individuals have gradually permeated to society in general.

In postwar periods, each of the advanced countries registered greater national economic growth and showed greater economic activities than in pre-war days, and, moreover, government intervention in national economies in such forms as national management of industry, government investments, government subsidies, and social security increased after the war to a great degree, and national public finance took on a greater dimension. The cold war continues and national budgets for defense purposes have impelled advanced nations, excluding Japan, to build up industrial capital at the expense of social capital. To ameliorate the situation, these countries have begun to increase social capital, to emphasize science education, to develop human resources to meet new industrial needs, and to redistribute income for further equalization of income through public finance. All these countries have become more or less welfare states.

In the United States, national expenditure increased from $94.3 billion in 1960 to $122.4 billion in 1965 and $172.4 billion in 1968. The proportion of defense expenditure to the total national expenditure was higher than in any other country: 44.6 percent in 1960, 41.5 percent in 1965, and 44.5 percent in 1968. The actual figures were $45.9 billion in 1960 and $76.8 billion in 1968. The proportion of the expenditure for health, labor and social security benefits, which was next highest in priority in national budget, was

20.3 percent, 27.9 percent, and 27.0 percent, for the respective years, the amounts being $19.1 billion in 1960 and $46.6 billion in 1968.

In the highly advanced welfare state of Great Britain (although her economic growth is slack) the total national expenditure was Ł5,787 million in 1960 and Ł8,010 million in 1965, of which national health expenditure was 34.9 percent and the housing and insurance expenditure was 37.6 percent; the actual amount of increase was Ł986 thousands. Defense expenditure decreased in proportion from 28.6 percent in 1960 to 25.7 percent in 1965.

In West Germany, national finance was expanded greatly with the high rate of economic growth, and the total national expenditure, DM64.6 billion in 1965, was DM72.3 billion in 1967. National defense costs occupied 26.4 percent of the total 1965 budget and slightly decreased to 26.1 percent in 1967. Social security appropriations increased, however, from 26.2 percent in 1965 to 26.4 percent in 1967; the actual amount increased by DM1.6 billion.

The total national expenditure of Japan increased 2.26 times in ten years, from ¥1,089.7 billion (settled accounts) in 1956 to ¥4,314.3 billion (original budget) in 1966. Expenditures for land conservation and development increased from 12.9 percent of the total national expenditure in 1956 to 19.3 percent in 1966, or a sixfold increase in actual amounts. Over the same ten-year period, social security costs increased from 12.8 percent to 16.8 percent (the figure for 1966 was ¥530 million), grants for local administration are from 16.7 percent to 18.5 percent to 9.8 percent. Proportional decreases were seen in educational and cultural expenditures (12.4 percent to 12.2 percent), defense costs (12.8 percent to 7.9 percent), and costs for national agencies (10.8 percent to 7.5 percent). With relatively small expenditures for national defense, Japan has been able, with a high rate of economic development, to make up for deficiencies in social capital by making improvements in roads and streets, rivers, harbors, housing, water supplies, and sewers and to bolster social security programs; thus, the system for the major national goal of economic development is strengthened along with the promotion of the people's welfare.

According to a study made by the metropolitan Tokyo authorities in 1967, the gross national product in 1985 will be about ¥117 trillion, compared with the ¥30 trillion in 1965, assuming the average annual rate of economic growth in Japan to be at 7 percent, and the cumulative gross national product over the twenty-year period to be ¥1,320 trillion. If we further assume that 32 percent of that amount is earmarked for fixed investment, as that percentage was registered in 1955, the total amount of fixed investment, including public fixed investment, private installations investment, and individual housing investment, would reach ¥425 trillion. In 1985, the share in national economy of metropolitan Tokyo and the nine neighboring prefectures, considering a further concentration of economic activities and population and an increase in income in this region, would be between 36.8 and 43.0 percent-- about ¥184 trillion. Of that amount ¥81 trillion would be accrued in metropolitan Tokyo, ¥78 trillion in Kanagawa, Saitama, Chiba, and Shizuoka, and ¥25 trillion in Ibaragi, Tochigi, Gunma, Yamanashi, and Nagano. This means that in this region large-scale construction projects will continue to be undertaken, and they will proceed at a rate several times faster than before. As we shall discuss later, it becomes possible to take necessary measures for coping with problems arising in the process of urbanization and, at the same time, to formulate large-scale and long-term plans so far unimaginable.

The process of an industrialized society becoming a great metropolitan complex is not a simple and fixed-pattern process, as can be observed in Japan and several other countries which have attained industrialization, and the complexity of this process is made all the more unmanageable in actuality because of a close interplay between the pressures of industrial change and the unique cultural structure of each modern capitalistic society.

The socioeconomic structure of a metropolitan community in a capitalistic society is formed through a historical process, whether it is a long or a short one. When a metropolitan complex grows rapidly, as we have observed, the existing facilities and institutions become inadequate for new and developing social functions and activities and stand in the way of the new society's smooth development. The process causes many contradictions to arise.

Concentration of industry and high buildings in the heart of a metropolis causes traffic and communication congestion, health and sanitation problems, ground sinking, water shortages, and many other problems, unless counter-measures are taken in time to arrest them. These problems naturally impair the proper functions of the heart of the metropolis, and the surrounding industries need land space for production facilities, harbor facilities, surface transportation, industrial water supplies, and gas and electricity, as well as large and low-priced tracts of good-quality land for new factories. The development of these industrial zones also improves the welfare of the people who inhabit them. Measures have to be taken to combat dirt, smog, noise and vibrations, and unless these problems are successfully dealt with, adequate development of the industrial zones cannot be expected.

Many people who work in various corporations, whether they are in the heart of the metropolis or in industrial areas, must be provided with adequate housing units, and proper measures must be taken with respect to slums and low-income quarters, which are found in a capitalistic society. School buildings and facilities, facilities to meet consumer demands, gas and water supplies, sewerage, green tracts of land, street cleaning, and commuting facilities--all of these must be provided for the people. Each of these facilities must be up to date; otherwise sound urban development is hindered and serious social problems develop.

It is difficult for individuals alone to solve all these problems. The solutions depend upon the great financial ability of the national and local governments. Since the functions of a metropolis extend over vast geographical areas, most of the problems mentioned must be tackled by unified and systematic efforts, which entail reorganizing administrative areas and administrative and financial arrangements, a process which requires the strong cooperative efforts of the administrative units concerned.

The most significant of all the problems which affect the orderly development of modern cities is maintaining a balance between economic growth and the improvement of the people's welfare. The community consensus determines how this balance should be kept in a democratic society; however, it may become necessary for the political leadership to guide the way. In the latter case, the leadership must honor the social goals and norms which symbolize community consensus and strive to achieve these goals. In modern capitalistic and democratic societies, free individual and corporate enterprises are presupposed, but relationships between public welfare, individual, and corporate freedom take different forms in different societies. In their attempts to solve urban problems, it is difficult for national and local governments, public corporations, and citizens' organizations to formulate policies and plans which call for compulsory community compliance. Therefore, the planners must proceed with respect for free enterprises and activities and estimate the tendencies and changes in society; and if contradictions and obstacles arise to obstruct economic growth and the improvement of the people's welfare, adjustments in individual and corporate activities must be encouraged, perhaps in return for some favorable offer; or certain regulations may be formulated to help achieve social goals.

With the foregoing statements as our basis, we shall proceed to the next chapter for a discussion of the socioeconomic structure of the Tokyo metropolitan complex, its problems, and some suggestions for remedial policies and plans.

CHAPTER 2

THE POSITION OF THE TOKYO METROPOLITAN COMPLEX
IN THE PROCESS OF THE FORMATION OF A MEGALOPOLIS

As we have discussed already, in many countries of the world urbanization is progressing at a rapid rate, a striking concentration of population and institutions occurs in big cities, especially in the industrialized countries, and similar socioeconomic structures which have similar urban problems arise in these countries. In Japanese national society as a whole, industrialization has progressed well and some excellent features have emerged, but compared to conditions in industrialized Western societies it is still at a low level and the standards of living still lag behind. However, urbanization is progressing rapidly, and because there are few institutional improvements corresponding to the cities' rapid growth, there are many grave problems.

In studying the socioeconomic structure of the Tokyo metropolitan complex, we must bear in mind that this complex, among other metropolitan complexes in rapidly urbanizing Japan, is specially structured and occupies the overwhelmingly predominant position in the society. To make this point clear, we must proceed with a general description of the way traditional Japan has gone through industrialization and urbanization in modern times.

The Industrialization and Urbanization of Modern Japan

Many cities in Japan had their origins in feudal Japanese society, but it was only after the Meiji Restoration that those cities began taking on the character of modern cities. In our study of the structure and problems of the Tokyo metropolitan complex, we must begin with a review of the connections between the post-Restoration industrial revolution and the post-World War II political and economic conditions.

In feudal Japanese society, as far back as one hundred years ago, there was considerable urban growth: the development of castle towns as centers of feudal provinces, port towns, inn towns, temple and shrine towns, etc. Among these urban centers, Edo was the seat of the shogūnate (military government) power and the political and military center of the country, which had a population of 1,000,000, and Osaka was the center of national economic exchange and had a population of 300,000.

The structure of the post-Restoration Japanese society was determined by the political centralization devised and developed by the ex-samurai bureaucrats of the Imperial system; Tokyo was the base of activity for national integration, and this fact was responsible for the singular character of Tokyo in modern society.

Japanese capitalism did not develop among common people, as a society of common people had not yet emerged. Its development was a result of the activities of big merchant-businessmen who worked closely with the ex-samurai government bureaucrats; the bureaucrats established big industries and later transferred them to the merchants. The merchants expanded their operations in such big cities as Tokyo and Osaka under generous government protection. When the industrial revolution was accelerated in the 1890's with the growth of militarism and world trade, the big business enterprises grew bigger and came to dominate the national economy; Tokyo and Osaka were the major bases of operation. During this industrial development, Tokyo and Osaka changed their characters from bureaucratic urban centers to pivotal centers that controlled the political and economic life of the capitalistic nation, a new political and economic structure emerged--modern Japanese society.

In the course of the Industrial Revolution, cities were transformed from political and commercial centers where consumer economy prevailed to production centers where industrial activities predominated, and with the increased ability of these cities to absorb people, their populations increased rapidly. Tokyo and Osaka, taking advantage of modern advanced transportation facilities, expanded into gigantic metropolitan communities, together with their satellite cities. The need for foreign trade for raw materials import and finished products export impelled Japan to develop the regions with good harbor facilities and hinterlands, like the Tokyo-Yokohama, Osaka-Kōbe, Nagoya, and north Kyūshū areas, all of which became modern industrial regions where few feudal characteristics thrived. Compared with the growth of the industrial centers, the traditional inland cities lagged behind.

Under the postwar Constitution, the Emperor is the symbol of the nation and not the foundation of a national integrative value system, and government officials are public servants for the people, in whom sovereignty resides. Traditional monopolistic industries were liquidated, and in their place new enterprises developed with new structural patterns. Mass organizations developed, suffrage was extended, local autonomy established, the people's welfare emphasized, social security systems improved, and democratization of society advanced.

Accompanying the structural changes of national society as a whole, the structures and functions of cities changed also. Gradually the cities emerged out of the yoke of traditional cultural controls and more rationalistic economic activities began to be performed in them. Although still imperfect, these cities have become citizens' communities based upon democratic principles.

In the postwar economic reconstruction and development programs, the government has actively assisted, guided, and encouraged the development of the national economy, through financial investments and subsidies, corporation tax reductions, and grants for interest payments. After the outbreak of the Korean war and especially after 1955 to 1960 (as a result of technical improvements and the expansion of foreign trade), Japan's economy was not only restored but its 10 percent growth rate was the highest in the world. Industry has been rapidly expanded and its structure and geographical locations have changed; national living conditions have been improved and the living standards have been raised to a level near that of the Western nations. In short, Japan has become the only highly industrialized country in Asia.

The development of big corporations was expedited by the government, which provided them with positive assistance, and financial institutions gave priority to corporations over smaller enterprises in making loans to meet the ever-increasing need for capital. Thus, big corporations not only expanded their scale of operations, but improved their technical skills. The development of big corporations was followed by an increase and expansion of smaller corporations.

Japan's economic growth resulted in the further development of heavy and chemical industries and the physical expansion of many industrial facilities, which entailed the acquisition of great expanses of land and vast amounts of capital. Technological improvements sped automation and diversification which intensified the interdependence of various industries and the sectors of specific industries. The result has been a gradual but steady concentration of big corporations in certain localities.

Since trade with the Asian continent has been suspended, oil has been substituted for coal as fuel, and raw materials have begun to be imported from the free world to the eastern shores of Japan. Big corporations have determined the formation of gigantic industrial zones in the seacoast areas of southern Kantō, Hanshin (Osaka-Kōbe), Tōkai (centering around Nagoya), the Inland Sea, and northern Kyūshū.

The former industrial zones offered little room for further industrial expansion, and so new industries have been developed along the peripheral areas or the big metropolises, such as Tokyo, Osaka, Nagoya, and Kitakyūshū; public and private investments were poured into these areas and the external economy and benefited from the concentration of industries naturally exploited the operations. The overall result was the appearance of four major industrial regions in Japan; namely, the Tokyo metropolitan complex, Chūkyō complex, Keihinshin complex, and Kitakyūshū complex. Industrial development was seen not only in littoral districts where petroleum, steel, and steam-power plants and other types of fixed-installation industrial operations were located, but also in the hinterlands where labor-intensive industries which depend less on foreign trade for raw materials and fuel (such as electronics, automobile, and mechanical-equipment industries) could be established.

The four industrial regions accounted for 61.5 percent of the total number of factories in the nation in 1950, 67.2 percent of the total national industrial employee population, and 73.1 percent of the total finished products shipped. In 1963, the figures for the respective categories just mentioned were 64.3 percent, 72.0 percent, and 79.1 percent.

From 1950 to 1963, the total number of factories in Japan increased by 53 percent, but this increase was uneven from region to region. In the Tokyo metropolitan complex, where centralization tendencies began during World War II, the government encouraged consolidation of big corporations, and big corporations have been concentrated in the region; as a result, the general population and smaller corporations also crowded into this region. The shift in foreign trade orientation from continental China to America has also expedited the concentration of population and industry in the region. In 1950, the region accounted for 18.9 percent of the total number of factories in Japan, 19.6 percent of the total number of employees in industry, and 22.2 percent of the total amount of finished products. In 1963, however, the figures were 21.1 percent, 26.6 percent, and 30.3 percent, respectively, indicating the increased importance the region came to occupy in the national economy.

The Chūkyō region has many traditional small and medium industrial establishments within its boundaries and it has some advantages over the other
industrial regions: there is available, usable land; there are sources of
energy, water, etc., which are necessary for the expansion of the new heavy
and chemical industries and Chūkyō does not face the serious problems of
public nuisances that other regions suffer. During the last war, modern
industries gradually began to develop in the Chūkyō region, and during the
postwar period of economic growth there was a rapid development of heavy and
chemical industries in both the inland and coastal districts. In 1950, the
region accounted for 16.8 percent of the total number of factories in the
nation, 15.6 percent of the total industrial employee population, and 14.8
percent of the total amount of finished products; by 1963, great strides were
made which placed the Chūkyō region second only to the development of the
Tokyo area--the figures for the respective categories mentioned above stood at
17.5 percent, 16.5 percent, and 16.2 percent.

The Keihinshin industrial region, which once boasted the greatest productivity in the nation, generally thrived on "wholesale" industrial capital, and
its connections with governmental capital were weak even during wartime, which
caused a lag in the development of the heavy and chemical industries in the
region. Moreover, there is very limited land space for the modernization of
production facilities and equipment. The availability of land in other areas
of the nation determined the direction of the technological growth of the
postwar period. Keihinshin is out of date as an industrial region, and the
relative weight it carries in the national economy has been further reduced
because of the shift of the trade center--from the Chinese to the American
continent. In 1950, the number of factories in the region accounted for 17.2
percent of the national total, the number of employees for 20.8 percent, and
the amount of finished products for 24.0 percent. Compared with the figures
for 1963, which were 17.4 percent, 20.0 percent, and 23.2 percent, respectively,
there was relative stagnation, even retrocession, of the regional economy in
relation to the national economy.

Of all the regions, the Kitakyūshū region stands closest to the Asian continent and, traditionally, the steel and coal industries have been its mainstays.
The region lacks in the production of consumer goods, and since the close of
the Asian continental trade and the reduced importance of the coal industry,
it has registered a decrease in its relative economic importance in the nation.
For example, in 1950, of the nation's total number of factories, total
industrial employee population, and total finished products produced, the
Kitakyūshū region registered 8.7 percent, 11.1 percent, and 12.1 percent,
respectively, in comparison with the 1963 figures of 8.3 percent, 8.9 percent,
and 9.4 percent for the same categories.

Factories play an important role in the formation of cities, since they
depend upon cities as markets and induce an increase in the demand for labor
and consumer population. The managerial and sales functions for the factories'
operations are concentrated in cities and many tertiary-industrial enterprises
are located in them, as well. By looking at the tendencies of the enterprises'
distribution over various prefectures, we may obtain a clearer picture of
developmental tendencies of urban functions.

During the period of rapid economic growth in Japan, the distribution
pattern of enterprises underwent changes. The number of enterprises in Tokyo

accounted for 10.0 percent of the national total in 1954; in Osaka 6.0 percent; in Aichi 5.1 percent; in Hyōgo 3.9 percent; in Hokkaidō 3.8 percent; in Fukuoka 3.8 percent; in Shizuoka 3.2 percent; in Kyoto 3.0 percent; in Kanagawa 2.9 percent; and in Nīgata 2.7 percent. In 1963 the percentages were as follows: in Tokyo 11.7 percent; in Osaka 7.1 percent; in Aichi 5.4 percent; in Hokkaidō 4.2 percent; in Hyōgo 4.0 percent; in Fukuoka 3.7 percent; in Shizuoka 3.2 percent; in Kanagawa 3.2 percent; in Nīgata 2.7 percent; and in Kyoto 2.7 percent. In 1954, 44.4 percent of the total number of enterprises in the nation were found in the top ten prefectures, whereas the percentage for the same ten prefectures in 1963 was 47.9 percent. With the further concentration of enterprises in certain areas, the unbalanced distribution of enterprises became marked, as shown in the case of Hyōgo, Fukuoka, and Kyoto, where the distribution percentage decreased; in Tokyo, Osaka, and Aichi, and also in the peripheral areas of Shizuoka and Kanagawa, the percentages increased.

Enterprises are important in that they provide jobs for urban populations, and urban populations are important to enterprises in that they become consumers. Therefore, an analysis of the general characteristics of urban life must include a study of the population living over a wide area within and around each city. In fact, the population size--the increase or decrease-- and the population concentration pattern are the most important indices of an urbanization process.

Population changes in Japan in 1945-1950 were such that 43 prefectures registered population increases, while only 3 prefectures had population decreases. In 1950-1955, populations increased in 39 prefectures and decreased in 7; and in 1955-1960, populations increased in 20 prefectures and decreased in 26, which reflects a great population movement and concentration in cities over these years. In 1960-1965, 21 prefectures registered increases in their populations, and 25 showed decreases. Of those 21 prefectures registering increases, 7 were within the Tokyo metropolitan complex, 4 in the Chūkyō region, including Shizuoka, and 6 in the Keihinshin area. The populations in the Tokyo region (Tokyo and 7 neighboring prefectures), the Chūkyō area, and the Keihinshin regions, in 1965, represented 26.6 percent, 11.1 percent, and 16.0 percent, respectively, of the total national population, and the combined populations of the three regions accounted for 53.7 percent of the national total.

Enterprises and population have thus been concentrated in a gigantic belt of urban zones that stretches along the Pacific coast and the Tōkaidō route, extending some 500 kilometers from the Tokyo metropolitan complex through the Chūkyū complex to Hyōgo Prefecture in the Keihinshin complex; the differences between the prefectures within this belt and those outside it have become greater, and the prefectures in northern Kyūshū have experienced population losses.

Urbanization has been accelerated by the industrial development in Japan, and the cities that were administrative and commercial centers in former days have now assumed additional functions as production centers as well. The Keishin, Hanshin, Chūkyō, and Kitakyūshū industrial regions have emerged and developed, with centers located in Tokyo, Yokohama, Osaka, Kōbe, Nagoya, Fukuoka, and Kitakyūshū, and they bring within the sphere of their integrative activities all the areas around these cities. Thus, the great metropolitan complexes have been created.

A new era for Japanese cities was ushered in after the war. The high rate of economic growth and the accompanying technological improvements changed the industrial locations and structures. Not only did the industrial regions expand around big cities, but they developed as littoral regions in a chain along the Pacific coast. Highly developed transportation facilities served to intensify the specialization of various metropolitan complexes and their interdependence. These metropolitan complexes as a whole have become a diversified metropolitan region, or a megalopolis which occupies the central role in political, economic, technological, and cultural activities of the whole national society.

This process of a megalopolis in the making coincided with the process of expansion of the metropolitan complexes around Tokyo, Osaka, Nagoya, and other big cities; each of these complexes grew in scale and transformed its structure as the megalopolis developed. The Tokyo metropolitan complex far exceeds all the other metropolitan complexes in discharging political, economic, financial, and cultural functions, and it should not be considered as being on the same plane as other complexes, but as occupying the integrative role for the whole national society. The Japanese megalopolis is structured in such a fashion.

We find metropolitan complexes grown into belt-like regions in foreign countries. For example, there is a 1,000-kilometer belt of metropolitan centers on the eastern coast of the United States, extending from Boston through New York to Washington, and on a smaller scale, there is a belt in the Netherlands which includes Europort, Rotterdam, and Amsterdam, and another belt in West Germany covering such cities as Düsseldorf, Essen, and Cologne. The special feature of the Japanese belt, as distinguished from foreign belts of urban centers, is its highly organic structure under the overwhelming influence of Tokyo which acts as a unifying center for the whole region.

In 1960, the combined capital strength of the five prefectures of Tokyo, Osaka, Aichi, Hyōgo, and Kanagawa accounted for 77.3 percent of the total national capital, and Tokyo alone accounted for 47.89 percent, or almost half the national total, compared with 15.83 percent for Osaka, 2.16 percent for Hokkaidō, 1.41 percent for Hiroshima, and 1.30 percent for Kyoto. The number of corporations in Tokyo with capital of ¥5 million or more represented 37.1 percent of the total number of such corporations in the nation; the number with capital of ¥100 million or more accounted for 47.1 percent of the national total, while those with capital of ¥10 billion or more accounted for 49.0 percent. Thus, the bigger the corporations in terms of capital strength, the more they come to Tokyo, making the metropolis assume the preponderant functions for national economy.

In 1964, there were 214 corporations in the whole nation capitalized at ¥5 billion or more, and 123 of them had their main offices in Tokyo, while 44 had main offices in Osaka, 7 in Nagoya, and 5 in Kōbe. These big corporations spread networks of branch offices, factories, and subsidiaries all over the country, and financing and planning for their operations are performed by main offices located in Tokyo, which, in turn, absorb greater parts of the profits which accrued from branch operations. Thus, Tokyo's functions as the strategic location for corporate activities and as headquarters for the country have been greatly multiplied. The role of Tokyo as the center for production activities and corporate managerial and distribution functions has been increased: a special occupational structure has emerged in Tokyo, which exhibits high distributional percentages for those engaged in technical or professional, managerial, clerical, and sales activities.

Along with its important role as the center of economic activities, Tokyo has also come to assume a significant role in financing. A majority of the important banks in the country have main offices in Tokyo, and their networks of branch offices canvass the whole country. In 1964, 35.4 percent of the bank deposits in the country were in Tokyo, 16.1 percent in Osaka, and 6.4 percent in Aichi, while 42.0 percent of the bank loans were floated in Tokyo, 18.7 percent in Osaka, and 6.5 percent in Aichi. As for sales and stock purchases, 67.9 percent of the number of stock transactions in the country in 1962 were in Tokyo, 24.8 percent in Osaka, and 6.2 percent in Aichi, and in terms of stock prices 69.2 percent of the total sum was transacted in Tokyo, 24.6 percent in Osaka, and 3.6 percent in Aichi. As for bank clearings, 51.6 percent of the national total was registered in Tokyo, 26.6 percent in Osaka, and 6.2 percent in Aichi. Thus, Tokyo far exceeds other big cities and occupies a dominant position in the financial field.

The predominant role of Tokyo in the national economy is still minor when compared with its role in national and local finance and in cultural fields, which further surpasses the roles played by other big cities. As a welfare state, Japan has been witnessing increasing government activities in the national society, and these activities are mainly those of the national government.

In 1955 the total local government revenue was ¥1,120 billion, of which 16.2 percent represented national taxes levied for transfer or subsidies for local administrations, 24.9 percent represented national appropriations directly to local governments, and 58.9 percent came from locally levied taxes, or other sources. In 1966, the total local government revenue stood at ¥4,130 billion, of which 20.4 percent came from national taxes for transfer or subsidy, 28.9 percent from direct national appropriations, and 41.7 percent from local sources. Comparing the conditions in 1966 with those in earlier years, local finance has been greatly strengthened, with the increased rates of inhabitants' taxes, corporation taxes, and fixed asset taxes, but the weight of national grants and direct appropriations in local finance is still great. Under these circumstances in which the national government pours great amounts of money into local finance, local administration is bound to reflect the policy of the national government.

Revenues from taxes collected by the national government are redistributed to local districts according to standards set by the national government, so autonomous local governments must maintain constant contact with the national government if they expect national appropriations and grants-in-aid to execute their policies and programs. Each prefecture is obliged to station a liaison office in Tokyo to protect its interests, or to send petition groups from various areas to Tokyo whenever something important transpires.

Since Tokyo is the center and source of economic, social and cultural activities of both international and national import and also the source of information regarding these activities, such big newspapers as the Asahi, Mainichi, and Yomiuru, are there and cater to several million readers; there are other papers, such as the Sankei and Nikkei, that have their main offices in Tokyo and spread their communications networks over the country and abroad. Furthermore, international news agencies make Tokyo their most important source of news of Asia. Television and radio, which have increasing importance as mass communications media with increasing numbers of audiences in recent years are also gathering news and producing programs mainly in Tokyo. (TV sets were found in 80 percent of all the households in Japan in 1964.) Tokyo also has 76 percent of the total number of publishers in the nation. Patterns of thought and behavior, which are transmitted through these mass communications media, have a great influence over the whole nation.

Thronged into the advanced cultural environment of Tokyo are 33 percent of all the higher institutions of learning and 49 percent of all the students in higher-learning institutions for Tokyo has more academic stimulations of national and international origin and there are easier accesses to the services of able and competent people than in any other metropolis in Japan. Thus, there are many institutions and personnel of a high academic level, and professional and research institutes and specialized educational and cultural organizations find suitable locations in this city. The concentration of these institutes and organizations and, in turn, personnel spurs further concentration of other organizations and people in the city.

In short, the Tokyo metropolitan complex with Tokyo as its center has become a political, economic, and cultural organism with many and varied integrative activities over a vast expanse of land. The expansion of this complex has been the result mainly of the concentration, centralization, and expansion of the political, economic, and cultural institutions in the heart of the city and of the factories and educational facilities in the areas surrounding the heart of the city. People participate in the operations of these establishments by assuming various roles, and with the money they earn from their occupations they make their residences in the heart of the city, or in areas adjacent to the industrial establishments of Tokyo, and lead their lives as consumers in certain patterns, as determined by their occupational and income status or by environmental conditions. Retail stores, recreational establishments, and schools are distributed to meet different needs and tastes of these residents of Tokyo. The whole complex functions as an organism over a vast area which centers around the heart of the city and extends to the peripheral industrial regions and satellite cities; all the subsidiaries are organically interrelated and integrated. Therefore, the question of the geographical boundaries of the complex should be settled only on the basis of a consideration of the degree of integration within the organic structure just described.

Public Measures and Plans

So far we have reviewed changes in the social and economic structure of the country and discussed the status and functions of the Tokyo metropolitan complex in connection with those national structural changes. The present-day socioeconomic structure of the country or the structures of its cities do not undergo changes merely through processes of socioeconomic activities of individual citizens and corporations, but changes are effected consciously by the national and local governments, which take measures towards solutions of social and economic problems, or formulate plans for the creation of an ideal social order. Thus, it becomes necessary for an understanding of current changes in society to analyze those public measures and plans.

Cities and city regions in prewar days were of small scale, and urban problems and urban planning were not taken very seriously. Social and economic plans of prewar days emphasized the enhancement of the country's nationalistic and militaristic interests, but in postwar periods there has been increasing recognition of the phenomena of urban population and industrial concentration, growth of heavy and chemical industries, development of large-scale business enterprises and other institutions, and excessive urban congestion: all are considered problems of not only the individual cities concerned, but the wider regions of the national society as a whole. Emphasis in postwar planning has shifted to considerations of maximum benefit to the nation as a democratic and peaceful society.

The war destroyed urban and industrial regions of Japan and removed Korea, Taiwan, Manchuria, and Sakhalin from Japanese sovereignty. In Tokyo, a total of 32.94 million people, or 51 percent of the total population of the city, lost lives or property; 768 thousand houses, or 56 percent of the total number, were damaged; 11.2 thousand school buildings, or 36 percent of the total, were destroyed; 900 electric cars, or 30 percent of the total, went out of operation; and 150 thousand hospital beds, or 42 percent of the total, were lost.

As early as 1946, the national government announced national reconstruction and rehabilitation plans (Fukkō kokudo keikaku yōkō), which were designed to increase production of foodstuffs and reconstruct the devastated country. In those days of confusion and unrest, however, economic trends were hard to estimate, basic ideas for stabilization of the people's livelihood were lacking, and approaches to planning were inadequate. Most of the housing construction and food production activities were conducted by private hands.

In later years, however, rapid social and economic progress was achieved and national conditions underwent radical changes, which made nationwide systematic plans for development necessary. In 1950, the Ten-Year General National Development Act (Kokudo sogo kaihatsu ho) was passed to "effect a systematic utilization, development, and conservation of national land, with attention paid to general physical conditions of the nation and in consideration of possible social, economic, and cultural benefits to the people; to make proper adjustments in industrial locations; and to contribute to the promotion of social welfare." Multiple development plans were incorporated into a unified national plan, under which individual plans were to be coordinated. Under this integrated plan, four categories for planning were established: the whole nation, the individual prefectures, the individual local districts, and the special areas. The national government was responsible for taking care of the nation as a whole and the special areas, while the prefectural and local governments were given autonomy for formulating plans for their respective prefectures and localities, which were to be coordinated by the national government. This action by the national government in 1950 did much to contribute to the formulation of the principles of planning for general development and was highly valued when the government drove home to the nation the importance of such planning, and urged national support for the realization of plans. Yet, there were few substantial achievements under this national plan.

Japan's unprecedented economic growth since 1955 and the accompanying rapid industrialization and urbanization have made it difficult for the preexisting institutions and facilities to cope with the problems which resulted from excessive concentration of population and industry in the big metropolitan regions, such as Tokyo, Osaka, and Nagoya. In industrial regions, roadways, harbor facilities, transportation facilities, etc. became archaic and land and water were short in supply. In cities, land prices went up, houses were too few, traffic became congested and commuting difficult, and other problems like water shortage, ground sinking, and air and river water pollution became serious, making urban functions ineffective and the general environment unhealthy for living.

To combat these problems, systematic reforms in various facilities and systems over wider areas must be instituted and, in view of the magnitude of the problems, which cannot be handled by individual citizens and corporations, new and large organizations must be created and social capital investments made in great amounts.

In 1956, the Tokyo Metropolitan Complex Improvement Act (Shuto-ken seibi ho) was passed, for an area of a 100-kilometer radius with Tokyo as its center. It included a twenty-year basic development plan and a ten-year improvement plan. The main objectives of this law were to create satellite cities in the suburbs of Tokyo to absorb surplus populations and industrial establishments which overflowed from the central area of Tokyo and to make improvements in the existing urban cores of central Tokyo, where urban functions were stagnating and many public nuisances were arising. The concentration of population and industry in Tokyo continued at a higher rate than was originally anticipated, and the residential settlements and industrial locations did not agree with the planned systems of land utilization; the law has been amended accordingly.

In 1958, a new law, the Act Concerning the Improvement of the Urban Cores Development Region of the Tokyo Metropolitan Complex (Shuto-ken shigaichi kaihatsu chiku seibi ho), was promulgated, and in 1959 the Act Governing Industrial and Other Establishments in the Existing Urban Cores of the Tokyo Metropolitan Complex (Shuto-ken no kisei shigaichi ni okeru kōgyō tō no seigen ni kansuru hōritsu) was passed. Furthermore, the Metropolitan Freeways Corporation was organized specifically to handle roadway improvement projects. With these various measures, redevelopment programs for the complex have been carried out.

In 1963, the Kinki Metropolitan Complex Improvement Act was passed. This region has a complex variety of topographical features and, unlike the Tokyo area, has more than one big city as its basic center. With Osaka as the biggest and central unit, this region extends over a 100-kilometer radius, as delimited and governed by the above act. The objectives of the law included the improvement of the existing urban districts in the region and the development of urban centers in areas 50 kilometers or more from Osaka to absorb surplus population and industrial establishments and to relieve the pressure from the central cities.

As originally planned in the General National Development Act, the 1970 target was to control industrial production in the Tokyo metropolitan complex to 29 percent of the national production, but it reached 31 percent in 1961 and 36 percent in 1965, far in advance of the plan. Likewise, the industrial production of the Kinki Complex reached 25 percent in 1965, which was 5 percent beyond the goal set in the plan.

Concentration of population and industry is an inevitable process in modern society, and to redevelop the society and prevent the jeopardy of urban functions, plans are made to disperse surplus elements and relieve the cities from extreme pressure. At the same time, local public bodies demand special legislation to ensure smooth development of their respective localities and to prevent an increase in social and economic unbalance between their districts and other developing areas. Thus a series of legislative acts were passed, beginning with the Tōhoku Development Acceleration Act (Tōhoku kaihatsu sokushin hō) of 1957 and including similar acts for Kyūshū (1959) and for Shikoku, Chūgoku, and Hokuriku (1960).

A new plan was announced again in 1960--the Plan for Doubling National Income (Shotoku baizō keikaku)--designed to help raise national income two-fold in ten years. This was, however, not so much of a plan as a hopeful forecast of a national goal for the people to look forward to, and its significance lay in the official admission of lags in public investments to meet the conditions created by the rapid and large-scale concentration of population and industry and in the announcement of the national goal. As originally formulated, the plan would have given priority in public investment to strengthen the industrial foundations in the regions along the Pacific and Inland Sea coasts, where corporations concentrate because of the favorable conditions provided there for effective economic operation; but this plan did not materialize because of opposition from other regions of the country. Despite this opposition, the megalopolis stretching along the Pacific coast from the Tokyo area through Nagoya to the Osaka area has attained a far more remarkable social and economic progress and, at the same time, created more problems than were originally anticipated, as we have already pointed out. The condition of the megalopolis clearly indicates the extent to which government policies influence social and economic situations and the need to maintain a proper relationship between accurate assessment of trends in socioeconomic conditions and the formulation of broad government policies based upon socioeconomic conditions; it is also important that the people understand and cooperate in the execution of such government policies.

From the standpoint of a balanced development of democracy and national economy as a whole, the phenomenal growth of metropolitan complexes in any society will demand complex redevelopment of these complexes along with development of backward regions. Thus, in Japan, in 1962, a new plan, the Integrated National Plan, was formulated on the basis of the General National Development Act of 1950. This plan, in contrast to the Plan for Doubling National Income, took "note of the need for preventing excessive expansion of cities and reducing regional differences" and was designed "to effect a balanced development of all regions through a more effective utilization of natural resources and a more equitable redistribution of capital, labor, technical skills, and other resources over various regions." To attain this objective, while bearing in mind the advantages of industrial activities concentrated in cities, officials formulated a development plan for local districts around big cities which had favorable sites for business operation, high investment efficiency, and great potential influence over other areas. Under this plan, the whole country was divided into three classes of regions:

the excessively concentrated regions (kamitsu chiiki), such as the Tokyo and Osaka regions, in which the new establishment and expansion of factories were to be controlled, existing establishments were to be relocated elsewhere, and redevelopment programs were to be initiated; the improvement regions (seibi chiiki), which covered the areas around the outer rims of the excessively concentrated regions, and in which big and medium urban centers were to be developed to take over production functions from the concentrated regions; and the development regions in relatively backward areas, where positive measures were to be taken for development of industrial foundations at strategic points.

In 1963, "with a view to preventing excessive concentration of population and industry in big cities, lessening regional differences, and facilitating the stabilization of employment, and for the purpose of ensuring balanced national land and economic development," thirteen cities in relatively backward areas were designated as "new industrial urban centers [shin sangyō toshi] which . . . [were] to become the development nuclei of the areas with improved industrial location conditions and urban facilities." In 1965, six model industrial improvement zones (kōgyō seibi chiiki) were designated in the industrially advanced Pacific belt. The selection of these centers, into which economic functions of the problematic big cities will be redistributed, has been viewed as contributing to a balanced national economic development with reduced regional differences.

To be selected as new urban industrial centers, areas should have the very best conditions available for the future concentration of urban industries and for the individual industries' development. There is the problem of strong pressure being brought to bear upon the government by local districts interested in having their own areas designated as development programs, which results in having too many districts so designated, including those in which little can be expected in the way of development; investment is then divided by too many districts with only a nominal sum per district.

Some designated areas are also unattractive to big industries that have a promising future. Under present conditions where designation is not followed by effective measures to control rises in land prices, abnormal rises in land prices make it difficult to invite factory establishment. Moreover, local finance is being drained by public investment through local governments, which must precede industrial establishment. All these conditions militate against acceleration of production and public investment in any of the designated areas. Thus, there is a big gap between the goal envisioned and the reality.

According to the government plan, a total of 2.2 million people were to settle down in the designated new industrial urban centers and model industrial improvement zones between 1960 and 1970. By 1965, however, there was a 13 percent increase in industrial production in these areas, which was higher than the planned 12 percent increase, and the population increase was only 20 percent of the 2.2 million target, with 400,000. The plan to control concentration of population in big cities through the development of these areas had not materialized.

The basic idea behind these government policies and plans is to control the concentration of population and industry in big cities, which has jeopardized urban functions and healthy living environments, and at the same time, to develop new areas to accommodate excess populations and industry. Needless to say, the lag of development in areas other than big cities is accounted for by political, social, and cultural factors. These factors determine the locations of economic, political, and cultural institutions and the population settlement, which in turn determine the structures and functions of various areas of the country. Therefore, unless regional development plans are based upon analyses of locational patterns of various institutions and population settlement patterns and on the understanding of possible trends of change in these patterns, and unless these plans incorporate adequate measures for providing the best conditions of location for various institutions, they will create many contradictions and cannot be implemented fully.

CHAPTER 3

STRUCTURE AND FUNCTIONS OF THE HEART OF TOKYO

In chapters 1 and 2, we have reviewed the position of the Tokyo metropolitan complex in relation to the social and economic development of Japan and have discussed various problems relative to plans formulated in the development process. We shall now proceed with an analysis, based on human ecology, of each of the problems arising in the complex and a discussion of proper plans and programs needed for the solution of the pressing problems of today.

For a realistic and systematic understanding of a city in constant change, the following operations must be performed:

1. A structural and functional analysis of the political, economic, and cultural institutions that operate in the heart of the city. These institutions assume central integrative roles in metropolitan functions and positively determine the character of the city. They provide jobs for the city's residents and depend for their success on the residents' ability to consume. Since the institutions represent channels of circulation of goods for city consumers, they are distributed according to the distribution and migration patterns of the people.

2. A separate analysis of wholesale and retail business establishments which, being of different character than the integrative institutions, perform only passive functions for the formation of a metropolitan structure.

3. An analysis of the types of living patterns, distribution patterns, and social environments of the residents living in and around the city. All these items are determined by the types of occupations and income levels of the residents working in the central integrative institutions and by their levels of education, social consciousness, and cultural values.

4. An analysis of the factories located in areas of different character than those in the heart of the city, with respect to their structures and local conditions.

5. An analysis of change and urbanization in the suburban agricultural communities as brought about by urban expansion, which greatly affects the overall urban social structure, land use, and living patterns.

6. A discussion of redevelopment plans and wide-area administration for further economic development and public welfare in the Tokyo metropolitan complex. It must be remembered that a city grows not merely as a result of its citizens' free social and economic activities, but under positive public and private planning, and that it expands far beyond its original administrative boundary.

The Structure and Influence of Integrative Institutions in Japan

We have mentioned that basic determinants of urban and suburban structure and growth or decay are integrative political, economic, and cultural institutions. Especially in modern capitalistic societies, centrally located economic and financial institutions are most closely related to growth or decay, since they integrate activities over a wide area in and around the city.

Closely related to these institutions are political institutions.

Depending on what types of sociocultural structures exist in the society, various reasons can be given for the concentration and centralization of integrative institutions, which have mainly administrative, sales, and procurement functions. As far as metropolitan institutions in an industrialized and capitalistic country are concerned, the following reasons for their concentration and centralization may be given.

Whether their activities are political, economic, or cultural in character, integrative institutions need, for their most effective operation, locations that have the best accessibility (measured mainly by distance in terms of time and cost; that is, ecological distance) to the area in which their integrative activities are performed. Therefore, the institutions' directors select central locations that have short ecological distances from, and good communication with, the areas to be covered. These locations are determined from the consideration of the integrative institutions' various spheres of activities: political spheres, or administrative areas, or areas specifically delimited for various purposes, including health, school, and police administration; commercial spheres--telephone and telegraph service zones, television and radio zones, and shopping zones for convenience goods and luxury goods; economic spheres--storage and sales zones and wholesale and retail business zones; and industrial spheres--raw material and labor procurement zones, marketing zones, factory zones, and commuting and traveling zones. Locations with such accessibility do not exist naturally nor do they come into being through technological development alone. They develop through the application of new technology and political power to the existing natural conditions.

When Edo (Tokyo) became the political center of Japan in the Tokugawa period, it was made more accessible to all parts of the country than it had been through the development of five major highways and the creation of coastal navigation. In the Meiji period, when Tokyo was made the national capital, a nationwide railroad system was established with Tokyo as the center, and with the development of airways, Tokyo's accessibility became even greater. The accessibility was not evenly maintained for all parts of the nation; it was greatest for the areas where local structural and functional interrelationships were intensive. Thus, the megalopolitan region extending from Tokyo to Osaka has the shortest ecological distance and the greatest traffic volume--new express trains that run at 200 km per hour operate every fifteen minutes on regular days and carry 100,000 people each day (150,000 on holidays).

Social and economic development leads to an increase in the number of political, economic, financial, social, and cultural institutions performing integrative functions and to an increase in the size of the institutions themselves. There is also an expansion of the areas to be integrated and an increase in integrative activities of the institutions. In the process of economic monopolization, the number of enterprises decreases through amalgamation and absorption. At the same time, the number of new enterprises increases as existing enterprises undertake rationalization of their operations and, with increased volumes of transactions, specialization of their functions. Interrelationships or control-subordination relationships of enterprises are intensified, and networks of closely related enterprises spread over vast areas, each centering around a big city.

Among the nuclear integrative institutions, economic and political institutions occupy central positions. Their urban functions are usually those exercised by their main offices, which control branch offices, agencies, shops, and factories and integrate the activities of all these places of work; at the same time they maintain working relationships with the other main offices. The spheres of activities integrated by central institutions differ according to the types and sizes of the institutions. According to a survey made by Kiuchi Shinzō and others in 1963 on the existing urban cores of Tokyo, a corporation located in the city that operates with a capital of ¥10 billion or more has an average of 482 local establishments under its control, and it performs various activities of international, national, and local scope. In comparison, a smaller corporation, with a capital of ¥100-500 million, operates with about 7.5 local establishments under its control. Thus, the smaller the scale of operation, the fewer are the number of establishments under the control of a corporation.

In Tokyo, not all enterprises have large-scale structures. In some, there is no clear distinction of functions between the main office, the branch office, and the factory. A number of small- and medium-scale enterprises may congregate and take up various production and distribution functions individually; together they may appear as a big corporation.

As capitalism advances and politics becomes involved in economic activities through such programs as public investment and financing, corporations--especially big corporations--come under increasing influence of government investment, financing, and other economic measures. These large corporations, which have functions relative to management, negotiation, research and study, planning, information exchange, recording, and filing of records, find it necessary to locate themselves near government agencies (especially the Ministry of Finance and the Ministry of International Trade and Industry), financial, research, and information and communication centers, and lawyers' and accountants' offices.

The number of people directly participating in final decision-making in a large-scale corporation is small, but the processes leading to the decision-making involve much work that requires a vast bureaucratic structure. Lines of command are built on a hierarchical order, and functional specialization is achieved to a great extent, as the many technical and clerical employees occupy different roles and positions. All the administrative work is handled formally through indirect and objective communication, such as letters and memoranda. Employment in these corporations--and in organizations such as government agencies, financial institutions, research, information and communication, and cultural establishments--requires a high degree of special training and education; there is therefore an increasing number of highly-paid managerial, technical, clerical, and service employees.

Business corporations, which constitute a majority of all the integrative institutions, increase their capital, technical ability, and production, and this spurs mass production and mass consumption. Sales functions of these corporations become important, and their sales sector is expanded. The increase in the number of sales employees is accompanied by an increase in the number of those involved in transportation and communication functions of the corporations.

In the percentage distribution of people in different occupations in Tokyo in 1960, the number of skilled laborers, production process workers, and simple laborers is the greatest with 35.5 percent, followed by clerical workers with 18.3 percent, sales employees with 14.8 percent, those in services with 10.7 percent, technical and professional employees with 7.1 percent, supervisory employees with 5.5 percent, transportation and communications employees with 4.1 percent, farmers and fishermen with 2.2 percent, and mining employees with 0.1 percent. In the degree of concentration in Tokyo of several types of occupations, we find 21.8 percent of the national total of supervisory employees in the city, 18.6 percent clerical workers, 17.2 percent service workers, 15.1 percent sales employees, 13.8 percent skilled laborers, production process workers and simple laborers, 12.5 percent transportation and communications employees, 0.7 percent farmers and fishermen, and 0.5 percent mining employees. This makes clear the character of Tokyo as the city where supervisory functions predominate.

With the strengthening of political centralization, the closer relationships between politics and economy, and the increasing benefits of economic accumulation in Tokyo in postwar periods, the supervisory tendency has become even more marked. Big corporations that operate in other cities such as Osaka and Nagoya begin establishing branch offices in the heart of Tokyo in order to avail themselves of opportunities for easier contact with other large corporations and government agencies and for easier access to new information and other material essential for business operation. This condition has added greatly to the nationwide influence of Tokyo.

The Formation of the Heart of the City

Modern social life demands efficient performance of clerical work. As long as changes in the present-day structure of clerical work and in transportation and communication technology do not bring about changes in patterns of human relations, various institutions need to be in close physical proximity to one another. Thus, in the heart of Tokyo, contacts between institutions are maintained with the highest frequency. The population of the Tokyo metropolitan complex in 1962 was 16 percent of the national total, but its traffic volume accounted for 37 percent of the national total; in the Osaka-Kōbe area, the traffic volume was 19 percent of the national total when its population accounted for 10 percent of the total national population. Human and institutional interrelationships are more intense in urban than in rural areas, more intense in big cities than in small cities, and most intense in the heart of a big city.

Taking the distribution of interrelated corporations as an example, the 1963 survey of Kiuchi and others mentioned earlier shows that 69.2 percent of such corporations have their main offices in the three wards in the heart of Tokyo, 88.0 percent within the metropolitan boundary, and only 12.0 percent in various local areas outside that boundary. As for the distribution of sales and purchasing agencies for these corporations, 44.0 percent of the sellers are in the three wards in the heart of Tokyo, 36.0 percent in the other eighteen wards of the city, 3.4 percent in other areas of the city, 1.6 percent in the Kantō region, and 17.3 percent in other parts of Japan. As for the buyers, 13.3 percent of them are in the three wards and 15.8 percent in the other eighteen wards of Tokyo, 5.6 percent in other parts of Tokyo, 9.2 percent in three neighboring prefectures, 6.7 percent in the Kantō region, and

49.4 percent in other parts of Japan. It is clear from this distribution pattern that sellers are concentrated in Tokyo while buyers are scattered widely over the country.

When a regional structure is formed through the process of concentration of institutions in the heart of the city, a location within this region provides: better opportunities for interinstitutional relations, easy access to a big market, opportunities for effective and efficient management of the individual integrative institutions, and conveniences for the acquisition of capital, information, technical skills, and labor. This condition in turn makes it possible for these institutions to provide their employees with promising roles and satisfactory wages and salaries. Under these circumstances, concentration of people and integrative institutions is bound to be further stimulated.

The heart of a big capitalistic, accessible city provides a corporation with a favorable location inseparably connected with profit-making activities. The greater the accessibility of a location, the greater is the profit accrued in that location; therefore, institutions and individuals compete with each other for locations. Those with greater political and financial power obtain better locations with greater accessibility, and land prices in those locations rise sky-high. In the end, gigantic corporations that wield nationwide influence and control converge upon a tightly confined land space. In 1964, there were 97 corporations in the country that had a capital of ¥10 billion or more each, and 49 of them were operating with Tokyo as their base. Of these 49, 29 were found in one of the central wards of Tokyo, Chiyoda, and 10 and 5, respectively, in the other two central wards, Chuo and Minato. The fact that the number in Chiyoda Ward alone was greater than the number of such corporations in Osaka (26) clearly attests to the powerful centripetal force at work in Tokyo.

The survey of 1963 mentioned above shows, further, that in the heart of Tokyo there is an accumulated capital amounting to ¥879.6 billion per area of only one square kilometer; in the outskirts, the amount of capital accumulated per area of the same size ranges from ¥100 million to ¥3 billion only. This means that greatly capitalized corporations are located in the heart of the city, while small corporations operate outside it.

Integrative institutions and individual people in the heart of Tokyo exert efforts to make intensive use of land for public and private purposes as long as it promises a smoother exercise of urban functions and beneficial returns to them. National and local governments, as well as business corporations and private individuals, make investments in the construction and improvement of high-rise buildings, freeways, elevated railroads, subways, underground towns, and roads and streets. With these developments comes the development of radial and loopline transportation routes--both elevated and underground --that connect the area with its surrounding regions and make Tokyo the hub of national and international traffic.

This connection, in turn, increases the accessibility of the surrounding regions to Tokyo, promotes activities of integrative institutions, increases the number and size of these institutions, makes land prices rise, increases traffic volume, and necessitates the construction of new buildings and transportation routes.

Under the present state of clerical, communication, and transportation systems, areas with adequate conditions of accessibility are geographically limited, and intensive investment is made in these areas. Vertical development of everything takes place because of lack of land, and buildings become taller.

From the standpoint of corporations, the intensive use of space, both vertical and horizontal, in areas of great accessibility will assure them of better business operation. According to the survey by Kiuchi and others, those corporations which have their main office building in any of the three wards in the central area of Tokyo are usually capitalized at ¥10 billion or more each, and more than 96.0 percent of them house their offices in big buildings of six stories or higher. Those which can rent some space for their main office functions in big buildings in central Tokyo are the ones with capital ranging from ¥3 to ¥10 billion; corporations capable of renting limited space for their main offices in smaller buildings in central Tokyo are those medium-size corporations capitalized at ¥1 to ¥3 billion; and those which can have their main offices only in the areas outside the central area of the city are new corporations capitalized at ¥100 million to ¥1 billion. The smaller the corporations, the further away their main offices are from the heart of the city.

The types of trade engaged in by the corporations also determine the locations of their main offices. Corporations whose activities form nation-wide networks--such as those dealing with mining, pulp, textile, chemical products, finance, and real estate--are more concentrated in the heart of the city than corporations with relatively localized functions, like construction and transportation enterprises.

At any rate, large-scale corporations with great capital strength can themselves create conditions favorable to their operation, not only in the matter of locations, but in the use of open vertical space.

The Heart of Tokyo in Relation to the Surrounding Region

In Tokyo, the areas with high degrees of accessibility are Chiyoda Ward (its buildings average 3.49 stories in height), Chūō Ward (2.56 stories), and part of Minato Ward. The further the distance from these central wards of Tokyo, the less favorable are the conditions of accessibility: the further away from the center of the city, the lower are the land prices, the smaller the investments, the less intensive the land use, and the lower the height of the buildings (an average of 1.61 stories in the other wards of Tokyo). In terms of intensity of land use, population density, and land price, a gradual declining gradient can be drawn on a graph as the distance from the center of the city becomes greater.

This declining gradient does not, however, represent a smooth uniform curve for various indices. For instance, for the whole Tokyo metropolitan complex, the 1955 statistics show that the daily average of the number of people using various means of transportation was 14,050,000: 36 percent of them used national railroads, 23 percent private railroads, 16 percent surface trams, 15 percent buses, 7 percent cabs, 3 percent subways, and very few used private cars. In 1964, the daily average of the number of people using those means of transportation was 28,140,000, and the percentages were 32 percent, 24 percent, 7 percent, 21 percent, 9 percent, and 7 percent, respectively (no figure for private car users). The curves indicating the use of the mass transit systems of national and private railroads begin at a very high point on a graph corresponding to the center of the city, gradually taper off as the distance from the center becomes greater, and then rise slightly at points indicating subcenters of the city; they rise further at points indicating railroad-station-side towns, decline, rise again at points for satellite cities, and then continue to decline until they reach "rural-level" points. Thus, the curves are in an undulated declining form.

The population distribution pattern in the complex does not present a steady, declining curve either. Types of industries and occupations differ from one area to another, and daily population movements do not show a uniform pattern. In general, figures for all indices do not change a great deal and, as expressed on a curve, extend further along the Tōkaido Railroad Line. The next less declining curve may be seen for the Chūō Railroad Line, followed by the curves for the Tōhoku, Jōban, and Sōbu Lines, in that order.

The recent development of subway systems affiliated with suburban private railroad systems has broken the monopoly by the national railroad system of direct connections between the heart of Tokyo and its suburbs. New facilities were added, and more passengers were transported by private railroad and subway systems. Together with this condition, the increase in the number of buses, taxicabs, and private cars (the number of taxis and private cars increased fourfold in ten years to 920,000 in 1963) and the decline of usefulness of surface trams contributed to the gradual transformation of the distribution of residential districts. From the former octopus-feet pattern, which was largely determined by the national railroads, a cogwheel pattern emerged, spurred by the growth of loopline roadways.

As the preceding discussion shows, the influence of cities on the formation of regional structures is very important in modern capitalistic and urban society. However, it is wrong to assume that such patterns of regional structures are determined solely by the self-regulatory functions of those economic activities that have been described. The foregoing general statements are focused on those integrative institutions--such as government and business offices and financial establishments--that operate in the heart of Tokyo and have worldwide and nationwide functions. The heart of Tokyo is not a single-unit district. Institutions exercising similar functions tend to concentrate in given areas because of the availability of favorable conditions of location and the need for being physically close to one another. Various factors are involved in the selection of locations for these institutions.

The present locations of the Imperial Palace and government offices were determined by the social structure and values of Japan's feudal society. Edo Castle and the daimyo residences were established through the employment of feudal political power and the civil engineering techniques that were available. When Tokyo was being constructed as the new capital of the modern society, it inherited those feudal traditions. The national will, represented mainly by ex-samurai bureaucrats, made Edo Castle the residence of the deified emperor, and those ex-samurai bureaucrats under the emperor made the former daimyo residences their government offices. Furthermore, the present-day financial, retail, and wholesale business districts of Nihonbashi and Kyōbashi grew out of a feudal past. They had been designated by feudal political authorities as commercial districts, and to this foundation were added modern transportation facilities to make these districts what they are in modern Tokyo.

The traditional practice of retailers was to cater to a limited number of wealthy customers. As the customers' general living standards and abilities to consume increased, the scale of the retailers' business increased, and the business became more diversified. The retailers then advanced into the main streets of the city. Unlike retailers, wholesalers need connections only with specialized enterprises, and, as they become more modernized and large-scale, they need a vast space of land for warehousing goods and other operations. They begin moving back from the center of the city to where land price is cheap and conveniences of transportation are available. Thus the wholesalers present a sharp contrast to retailers in locational distribution.

The development of the office district of Marunouchi began during the industrial revolution of the Taishō period when corporations expanded and increased in number. National railroad systems developed, with Tokyo as the center, and the central and hillside railroad looplines were completed within Tokyo. This gave the Marunouchi district easy access to the areas that immediately surrounded Tokyo and to other parts of the country.

The gradual westward shift of the traditional business centers in the Nihonbashi and Kyōbashi areas to the Ginza area began at the time when Ginza, through the opening of the port of Yokohama and the establishment of the Shinbashi railroad station, became the front gate of Tokyo. The gradual development in the Ginza area of bustling business sections, which extended in a long belt from north to south between Nihonbashi and Ginza, and the development of a long strip of business districts from Yūrakuchō to Ginza were accounted for by the following factors: the shift of residential districts in Tokyo to the hillside areas of the southwest, the shift in importance from the Shinbashi railroad station to the Yūrakuchō station as a point of boarding off for the people going to Ginza, and the extension of business centers from the Marunouchi to the Tamura-chō area.

That Tokyo's residential districts did not fan out evenly--that is, in a concentric circle--from the center of the city to its suburbs may be explained by the fact that white-collar employees of the government agencies and business corporations operating in the center of the city began to be attracted by the cultural values found in the southwestern hillside areas and moved towards those areas. In the meantime, the accessibility of the southwestern areas to central Tokyo increased through new developments in transportation facilities, and subsequently, their positions as ideal residential areas was enhanced.

The reason for the slow residential development of the northeastern part of Tokyo, the area located beyond the traditional "downtown" commercial and industrial districts, may be found in the fact that traditional value judgments regarding lowland and industrial districts have underestimated this part of Tokyo as a residential area. The development of residential districts in the southwestern part of the city has almost reached its saturation point, and a gradual extension of residential areas into the northeastern section of the city is beginning. This new trend was influenced to no small degree by the recent public housing projects of the national and local governments in this area.

Thus, the regional structure of the Tokyo metropolitan complex has been determined not only by the economic activities that we have discussed earlier but by an interplay of such factors as organizational structures, political power, technology, and cultural patterns.

Changes and Problems Within the Central City

We have completed an examination of the basic problems of the regional structure of Tokyo thus far, emphasizing the formation of the heart of the city. With these findings, let us now discuss several problems within the heart of the city.

Structural change in the heart of a city seems to accompany change in the political and economic structure of both the nation and the city itself. In the case of Japan, where economic development has been very rapid in recent years, the heart of Tokyo saw the completion of ferro-concrete buildings with 14,394,000 square meters of floor space during the four years between 1958 and 1962. This represented 4.3 times the total floor space that was available in Tokyo in the past sixty years. Admitting that the buildings constructed in the past could not be taller than 31 meters, necessitated by consideration of earthquake-proof building construction and by the availability of construction technology, the construction of buildings had been rather slow. Considering Tokyo as the largest city in an industrialized nation, the intensity of land use was also low. With modern improvements in construction technology and greater needs for intensive use of land, the heights of buildings came to be governed by the capacity-based zone system (yōseki chiku sei), which took account of floor and ground space of the buildings. A number of buildings taller than 100 meters are now being constructed.

Under these circumstances, the heart of Tokyo has not yet reached its height of possible development. The need for redevelopment is acutely felt in the construction of buildings, in the widening of roads and streets, and in the construction of freeways, subways, underground towns, and parking lots. There is also a need for further vertical utilization of space in order to provide room for roads and lands for public use in the central area of the city and its surrounding zones. On the other hand, criticisms are being made that the tendency of the current urban planning of Japan is being directed only towards the improvement of the central area of Tokyo and the industrial production centers of the country--that is, that the tendency of urban planning is to serve only the interests of capitalists--at the expense of the people's welfare.

Although Tokyo is the city equipped with the best modern facilities in Japan, when compared with cities in Western countries it has only a short history as a modern city and lacks the accumulated facilities necessary for modern social living and activities. Furthermore, its rapid expansion and change make it hard for the national and metropolitan governments to cope with them.

According to the 1964 survey of the accumulated private and social capital in various prefectures of the country, the following facts are known. With the index for the national average of private fixed assets set at 100, Tokyo has 2,812, Osaka 1,877, Kanagawa 1,154, Aichi 453, Hyōgo 281, and Fukuoka 430.

With the national average of social capital set at 100, Tokyo had 768, Osaka 580, Kanagawa 496, Aichi 319, Hyōgo 163, and Fukuoka 247. Thus, the three prefectures of Tokyo, Osaka, and Kanagawa had accumulated great amounts of private and public capital. Per capita distribution of private capital shows Tokyo with 146, Osaka with 153, Kanagawa with 194, Aichi with 135, Hyōgo with 150, and Fukuoka with 134; per capita social capital was 40 in Tokyo, 49 in Osaka, 86 in Kanagawa, 97 in Aichi, 88 in Hyōgo, and 76 in Fukuoka. Per capita figures for private and social capital accumulation in Tokyo and Osaka are low, and this indicates that although social capital was accumulated in these areas in proportion to the accumulation of private capital, it was not distributed fast enough to the increased population.

The heart of Tokyo is the point where integrative institutions--including the Diet and other government agencies that serve not only Tokyo but the whole nation--are greatly concentrated, and the question of whether or not central Tokyo is smoothly functioning takes on national importance.

The increase and expansion of integrative institutions and the resulting problems in the heart of Tokyo are too broad a subject to be fully treated here, but we shall attempt to take some of these problems for consideration.

Integrative institutions perform their functions in close contact with each other and with individuals through transportation and communication channels; therefore, an increase in their number implies an increase in the volume of traffic and communication within the center of Tokyo and its surrounding areas. The wards with the character of residential districts around the heart of Tokyo--Suginami, Nerima, Setagaya, Meguro, Shibuya, and Toshima--sent out in 1960 more than 15.0 percent of their working and student population (of 15 years of age or older) to areas outside their own ward boundaries during the daytime. The three central wards, Chiyoda, Chūō, and Minato, increased their daytime population by 5.24 times, 3.90 times, and 1.08 times, respectively, over their nighttime population. The commuting workers and students in all the wards of Tokyo numbered 2,610,000 in 1960, of which 1,180,000 were destined for the three wards of Chiyoda, Chūō, and Minato. This number of people coming into the three central wards has been increasing each year, with an increase of 330,000, or 38 percent, registered over the years 1955-1960. This clearly adds to the pressure on the heart of the city.

We have already discussed the various means of transportation used by the people of the Tokyo metropolitan complex as a whole. The national railroads are used for long-distance transportation, and thus they are of far greater importance in terms of man-kilometers than was indicated above. The national railroads remain the principal means of transportation connecting the heart of the city with the outside; their stations also serve as terminals for bus lines and private railroads. Thus, even if people use other transportation systems on their way to central Tokyo, the national railroad system has the greatest number of users. The relative weight of the national railroads may be seen in the fact that, in 1960, 70.0 percent of the commuting population coming into the three central wards used the national railroads, while 23.0 percent used subways, 4.0 percent surface trams, and 2.0 percent buses.

As the urban population increases and is distributed over a wider area, the commuting distances increase as well as the size of the commuting population.

To cope with this situation, railroad lines have begun to speed up their operation, reduce the distance of travel each train makes, and increase the number of cars for passengers; staggered office hours have been introduced for the benefit of the commuters. All these measures, however, have not yet adequately solved the problem of the growing number of commuters, and large-scale surface and underground transportation routes are now being planned. At any rate, the present rush-hour use of the principal lines of the national railroads represents 300 percent more than their capacity, causing the world's worst traffic congestion.

Automobile traffic congestion is also marked. In 1967 Japan produced 23.5 percent of all the vehicles produced in the world--second to the 33.6 percent for the United States--and she ranked seventh in the production of passenger cars (with 690,000), behind the United States (9,300,000), West Germany, Great Britain, France, Italy, and Canada. The increase of automobiles in Tokyo has been appalling. In 1949, there was one car for every thirty-four individuals in all the wards of the city, but in 1958 there was one car for every eleven people. The availability was 43 percent of what it should be in ratio to the volume of automobile traffic, 26 percent in New York, 24 percent in Berlin, and 23 percent in London; in Tokyo it was as low as 11.6 percent, even in 1967. In Tokyo the available roadway per automobile is only 0.35 kilometers, compared with an average of 2.7 kilometers in twenty American cities. The number of automobiles in operation in Tokyo increased twofold between 1960 and 1967, but the roadway space increased only 1.5 times. Stagnated traffic lines, each extending several hundred meters, are found here and there; and complete traffic paralysis results. Traffic accidents are also numerous. Traffic deaths per 10,000 cars in 1963 were 2.9 in Chicago and 4.3 in New York, but in Tokyo there were 10.4, and in Yokohama 21.2.

To cope with these traffic problems, there have been a great many traffic control measures, such as enforcement of one-way traffic, speed limits, and prohibition of overpassing and parking at certain places. These measures, however, represent only negative approaches, and it must be recognized that the real problems are the concentration and increase of integrative institutions, the increase in the use of automobiles, and the inadequacy of the necessary accompanying facilities. It is imperative, then, that some of the integrative institutions be removed from the heart of the city. Networks of roads must be improved through the construction of multi-level crossings and new roads, parking lots must be provided, and vehicle and pedestrian roads should be separated --all through the efficient execution of carefully formulated plans.

The decline in importance of surface trams in the metropolitan transportation systems has been noted earlier. Despite the great increase in the number of people needing various means of transportation owing to the increase in population, geographical area, and activities in the metropolis, the importance of surface trams relatively declined. The average number of people transported by these trams per day decreased from 2.3 million in 1955 to 1.95 million in 1965. With the increase in automobile traffic, roads and streets became too narrow, and the speed limit for trams was reduced from 14.07 kilometers per hour in 1955 to 11.97 kilometers in 1965. The slow-moving trams lost attraction for people who were hurrying for various purposes, and they stood in the way of smooth traffic flow in the city. Traffic congestion reduced the number of round trips per 1 kilometer daily from 625 in 1955 to 524 in 1965.

As personnel costs went up, it became increasingly difficult to keep down the per-tram maintenance costs; the subsequent rise in fares, considered in relation to the ability and willingness of people to pay, caused deficit financing to become the rule. Thus, with management difficulties, they fell behind the times. These surface trams are now scheduled to be replaced entirely by subways and buses by 1971.

The expansion and increase of integrative institutions also cause an increase in consumer demands and in the volume of polluted water and garbage. Unless measures are to be taken to meet this condition, there will be more problems. For instance, the increase in the construction of large modern buildings means an increase in the volume of water used for drinking and cleaning; but because of the lower cost of well water as opposed to water from the water supply lines, some people dig wells and pump water for their cooling installations. This causes the ground to sink in areas where big buildings stand in the heart of Tokyo. Drainage from buildings, factories, and private homes is polluting the air and the river waters in the center of the city, causing problems not only in matters of beautification but in those of sanitation and the pleasantness of modern urban living. Exhaust gas from automobiles, noises, vibration, dust, lack of green tracts of land, and general beautification of the city environment are some of the many problems existing in the city.

The Need for Redevelopment

There are many such problems arising in central Tokyo, and redevelopment is needed to deal with these present and future changes. When land price is not controlled and rises to an extreme extent through speculation, it would be impossible to execute improvement plans with limited funds. Therefore, it becomes necessary for the public good to enforce measures that control land price and provide for the acquisition of land for improvement purposes. It is also particularly important that people be made fully aware of their responsibility of sharing the costs of improving public facilities.

This responsibility of the beneficiaries of various public facilities to share expenses for their improvement is easily recognized as a principle; but when it comes to the question of who shares what proportion of the necessary costs, no easy formula can be found. What should be the proper share of profit for those corporations or individuals who engage in public services, and what responsibilities should they assume for public nuisances caused by such service activities? One way to determine the proper shares of profit or responsibility may be through rationalization of government price policy with respect to public services, as was done in the case of transportation fares and water charges.

It must be borne in mind that urban redevelopment plans aim not so much to break a current impasse as to execute precedence investments. Accordingly, the shares of responsibility on the part of those corporations or individuals involved must be determined on the basis of the marginal costs rather than the average costs of given improvement projects. It must also be remembered that it is not always easy to establish definite connections between the problems that have arisen and the corporations or individuals who are to share expenses for improvements, and that too exorbitant a share of responsibility would drive those corporations or individuals to great profit losses. It may be more appropriate in this case to levy some kind of tax--perhaps an urban redevelopment tax. The opportunity for higher economic gains that is available in cities is one of the important reasons for excessive urban concentration of corporations and individuals; this is attested to by the high corporation and personal income levels in the cities. It must then be said that it is not too much to expect those individual and corporate inhabitants of the cities to pay higher taxes, such as those special taxes levied in Paris, than residents of other areas to help correct their own congested environmental conditions. This formula would help alleviate, to some extent, the urban conditions that were worsened by excessive concentration of population and industry.

Redevelopment of the heart of Tokyo to prepare for future growth costs a great deal of money, and there is a view favoring the transfer of some or all of the functions performed in the central wards to some other places. But it must be pointed out that the center of the city is part of the structure of the whole metropolitan complex, and that once its structural relations with the whole are severed it will not be able to function properly.

There is also the problem of various activities that are concentrated in the small central segment of Tokyo. The three central wards of Chiyoda, Chūō, and Taitō have 59 percent of all the wholesalers in Tokyo. There are also many warehouses and wholesale markets operating within their boundaries; 75 percent of the total loading and unloading operations in Tokyo are performed in these wards. There is an attempt now being made to relocate the wholesalers and markets, together with warehouses, truck terminals, and railroad stations-- whose functions are directed to relatively limited concerns--to areas along the freeways in the outskirts of the city which are directly supplied by those wholesalers and markets. It is hoped that these new areas will develop into circulation centers and that the whole attempt will help alleviate the crowded assembling and redistribution operations in the heart of Tokyo; the outskirt area would then contribute to the rationalization of the system of circulation of goods and services.

At any rate, as long as the core of modern urban life remains in the inter- relationships among various integrative institutions and between these insti- tutions and individual citizens--unless there are changes in the mechanisms of those interrelationships, viz., changes in transportation and communication patterns and in customary practices in human and institutional relations-- there will be constant and increasing pressures on the heart of Tokyo as it develops.

Technical improvements in central Tokyo are imperative. Efforts may be made, for instance, to prevent further concentration and congestion at the center point of the city and to facilitate its solid, shaped growth; to expedite the development of the area for more effective human and institutional contacts; and to disperse those institutions whose outside contacts are limited and which can make positive gains in peripheral areas.

The view favoring concentration of functions in the heart of Tokyo and the view favoring their dispersion should not be regarded as antinomy. The problem we must consider is the proper geographical distribution of social and economic functions so that the overall effectiveness of Tokyo will be ensured. According to the tenets of economics, private enterprises in capitalistic society tend to concentrate in certain areas as long as no laws or ordinances prohibit it; when this concentration process reaches a certain point, there will be such problems as the rise in transportation costs, a decline of labor productivity, the rise in land value, housing and water shortage, the rise in commodity prices, and the rise in wages. This will lead to a situation in which there will be more expenditures than profits for those private enterprises. If social capital is invested to relieve private enterprises of increasing burdens, the concentration may continue. Therefore, from the economic standpoint, the question of whether social capital should be invested for the redevelopment of big cities or for the development of other areas must be determined by the degree of per-unit investment efficiency that private and social capital have for development of the national economy as a whole.

Urban planning should include both long-range and short-range planning, and, of course, this balanced planning must take into account both current conditions and possible future changes in economic and other sectors of society.

CHAPTER 4

DISTRIBUTION (CIRCULATION) PATTERNS AND THE
PROCESS OF CHANGE OF CONSUMER GOODS DEALERS

We have thus far observed several principal integrative institutions in the
heart of Tokyo that are most significant in determining the prosperity or
decline of the city and its larger regional structure. Among them are administrative and business organizations, financial institutions, mass communication
media, higher and special educational institutions, and other cultural establishments. We have also discussed the ways in which they determine the structure of the center of the city and what bearing their functions have on the
formation of the whole metropolitan structure. But we have left out a discussion
of the wholesalers and retailers--those commercial institutions directly
related to consumer life in the city; in 1964, they accounted for 46.8 percent
of the total number of business enterprises in Tokyo. Manufacturing firms
constituted 20.4 percent, and 32.8 percent were service establishments.

The Characteristics and Functions of Wholesalers in Japan

Wholesalers and retailers act as distribution agencies, moving goods from
producers to consumers; they, like other business enterprises, undergo specialization of functions when the economy progresses. As business specialization
increases, wholesalers and retailers of sundry goods gradually specialize in
fewer goods. Under conditions of keen business competition, capital is
accumulated, and the concentration of business ownership and control into fewer
hands is accelerated. Furthermore, recent technological development and expansion of the scale of business has made mass sales of mass produced goods
necessary. This has led to the growth of mass sales agencies of the supermarket type, thereby cutting the costs incurred in the operation of interme-
diary institutions such as wholesalers. Concentration of control and mass
markets have also created the problem of producers performing direct sales
functions.

Some economists feel that wholesalers are nonproductive and thus useless.
Their raison d'etre is their handling of a great number of transactions for
retailers; without their services retailers would have to bear greater expenses.
They make it possible for retailers to maintain in stock the minimum amount of
goods to meet intermittent demands only, and they can, through their financial
functions, warehouse goods that are consumed only seasonally. Furthermore,
they serve as haulers, stockers, and transporters of goods; they can also
furnish information, give guidance on technical aspects of business operation,
provide financial aid, and promote standardization of goods for small and
medium producers before the goods are sold to retailers. The value of wholesalers is maintained, however, only as long as they contribute to the operation
of their dealers. Once defects develop in the functions of the wholesalers,
they may end up being absorbed by big corporations.

The number of wholesalers in Tokyo went up 11.8 percent between 1956 and 1964
(there were 34,422 wholesalers in 1964), the number of full-time employees increased
almost twofold, or 88.0 percent (543,395 employees in 1964), the total annual

sales was up three and a half times, or 248.8 percent (¥11,544,662 million in 1964), and the total annual sales per wholesaler increased about threefold, or 193.4 percent (¥2,934 million in 1964). The percentage distribution of the wholesalers by size of employment in 1962 was as follows: 1-2 employees, 15.2 percent; 3-4 employees, 21.2 percent; 5-9 employees, 31.0 percent; 10-19 employees, 18.5 percent; 20-29 employees, 6.1 percent; 30-49 employees, 4.2 percent; and 50 or more employees, 3.8 percent. Compared with the situation in 1950-1961, wholesalers with 9 or fewer employees steadily declined in number while those with 10 or more employees increased, which indicates the gradual expansion of scale of the business.

The wholesalers in Tokyo are mostly concentrated in the following central wards: 19.6 percent in Chūō Ward; 16.0 percent in Taitō; 10.6 percent in Chiyoda; and 5.9 percent in Minato. In terms of the number of employees, these four wards have, respectively, 30.0 percent, 12.4 percent, 17.2 percent, and 11.1 percent of the whole number in the city, while in the total sum of sales they represent 37.5 percent, 6.2 percent, 28.7 percent, and 14.1 percent, respectively. These central wards together have 52.1 percent of the total number of wholesalers in Tokyo, 71.5 percent of the employees, and 85.5 percent of the sales.

Taitō Ward, where small and medium enterprises concentrate, has smaller distribution percentages of wholesalers, employees, and sales than the other wards in the heart of the city. At any rate, many of the wholesalers operating in all these central wards exercise integrative functions by doing business with local retailers, wholesalers in areas of production, and other local wholesalers.

In 1964, the combined number of wholesalers in Tokyo, Osaka, and Aichi accounted for only 33.7 percent of the national total, but in the amount of sales the three prefectures registered 65.3 percent of the national total-- Tokyo registered 30.0 percent, Osaka 26.7 percent, and Aichi 9.6 percent. Each of the other prefectures in the country registered an average of 3.0 percent or less. Most integrative wholesale activities for the whole nation are carried on by these three big prefectures. Each prefecture in the nation is its own most important market and source of goods supply, but the next important market and source for each is either Tokyo, Osaka, or Aichi. For the supply of goods, for example, Hokkaido and the prefectures in Tōhoku and Kantō depend on Tokyo; Gifu and Mie Prefectures depend on Aichi; the prefectures in Hokuriku, Kinki, Chūgoku, and Shikoku rely on Osaka; and the prefectures in Kyūshū depend on Fukuoka. For market, Hokkaido and 18 prefectures in Tōhoku and Kantō, excluding Aomori and Miyagi, look to Tokyo; 12 prefectures in Kinki, Shikoku, and Hokuriku choose Osaka; and Yamaguchi and the prefectures of Kyūshū, excluding Miyazaki, choose Fukuoka. Thus, the role of Tokyo as the center of wholesale activities is clear.

Most wholesaling firms--which are the most numerous of all enterprises in the heart of Tokyo, whether they are dealing in industrial or consumer goods-- are comparatively modernized, and the business roads and other facilities used by them are generally in good condition. These wholesalers are concentrated in spots that have been traditionally reserved for them since the Edo period. Their scales of operation, however, have grown, and many transactions are done in the heart of the city. Managerial functions, warehousing, delivering, and hauling are performed in this area. Also, there are still many wholesalers who use a living-in system in which buildings are used both as places of work and as residences for the employees.

The volume of freight hauled by trucks and light vehicles is increasing in proportion to the expansion of the wholesale business. Of the goods brought into the heart of the city, 50 percent go to factories and department stores, 40 percent to wholesalers, and 10 percent to warehousing firms. Most of the goods are handled through the rear entrances of the wholesalers plant, facing narrow roads. During the period of loading and unloading, vehicles parked on these roads block traffic to an extreme degree; this condition, in turn, reduces work efficiency and raises operational costs of the enterprises affected. Furthermore, the congestion is detrimental to the safety of school children and to the general living environment by causing noise, dust, and exhaust gas hazards.

Some wholesalers have had management modernized considerably, but others adhere to traditions and remain behind the times. Because of the limited space, high prices of land, and transportation difficulties, it is well for the wholesalers in the central city to do their major warehousing and transacting in outer areas. Only sample goods should be handled in the heart of the city. Wholesalers must also modernize industrial relations management and separate their places of work from their residences. These courses of action are now being taken by some wholesalers.

According to the surveys made by the Tokyo metropolitan government and the Tokyo Chamber of Commerce, more than 80 percent of the wholesalers in the center of Tokyo want to move to other areas or to have their facilities made taller; 37 percent of the wholesalers and 50 percent of the warehousing firms want to have some general circulation and distribution centers established, complete with adequate facilities for wholesaling, warehousing, trucking, and other operations. In fact, plans are being made to establish such centers in the cities of Gotanda (Shinagawa Ward), Ōji (Kita Ward), and Chōfu City, each in a large lot--approximately 10,000 square meters in area--that has been vacated by factories.

The central wholesale markets of vegetables, fruits, and fish, which have the largest number of transactions in Tokyo are those of Kanda and Tsukiji; there are also big markets at Yodobashi, Toshima, and Ebara. The volume of transactions at these markets increases as the population increases in Tokyo and its vicinity. The spheres of wholesaling activity expands, and sites of the wholesalers then become too limited. For better and more modern circulation and distribution of vegetables, fruits, and fish, plans are being formulated for the construction of distribution centers in areas that are closely connected with areas of production.

Goods handled by central wholesale markets have a high rate of putrefaction, and they have to be disposed of as quickly as possible. Their demand is great, and their variety is large. Many of them are seasonal products. In the past these products were generally sold on a cash basis at auction, and then sold again to retailers through middlemen for various products. Because of this complex sales structure and the nature of the products handled, it was necessary for central wholesale markets to be located near consumer markets. At present, however, these locations and the sales structure of the markets must be reexamined to ensure more rational operation. The recent increase in demand for processed foodstuffs has made it necessary for central wholesale market operators to process and circulate foods by themselves.

The Characteristics and Functions of Retailers in Japan

As for the retail business in Tokyo, there were 120,294 retailers in 1964, who maintained a total of 467,142 employees; their total annual sales amounted to ¥1,495,894 million. The number of retailers in 1964 was up 6.3 percent from what it was in 1956, the employees were up 26.7 percent, and the sales were up 367.7 percent. The types of retailers doing most of the business included: those dealing with foods and beverages, 48.0 percent of the total; those selling drugs, cosmetics, books and stationery, watches and clocks, spectacles, tobacco and cigarettes, etc., 22.0 percent of the total; and those dealing with dry goods and articles of daily use, 19.0 percent of the total number of retailers.

Except for the large specialized stores in the heart of the city, most of the stores are very small in scale and domestic in style of operation. Fifty-four percent of them have only one or two employees each, and 27.3 percent have three to four employees each. These stores are distributed according to the distribution of the city's resident population and play only a passive role in urban formation. On the other hand, they constitute nuclear parts of the central city, subcenters, business sections in front of railroad stations, suburbs, and satellite cities. They also reflect the overall community structure of the metropolis. In this sense they hold significance on a different level from that of the major integrative institutions that we have discussed.

The relative position of retail business in the commercial activities of the whole metropolitan area is high, but not so high as wholesale business. Retail stores are distributed according to the population density of the metropolis, and those in the heart and subcenters of the city are operated on a large scale. In total sales, the stores in the wards of Chūō, Chiyoda, Minato, and Bunkyō in the central area of the city account for 28.5 percent of the total sales in the whole city; stores in the subcenter districts of Shibuya, Shinjuku, and Toshima (Ikebukuro) account for 20.0 percent. The sales by all of these stores together make up almost half of the total sales in the whole metropolis, which indicates the great role they play in consumer life.

In matters such as capital, management structure, employment scale, sales transactions of goods, and volumes of goods transacted, retail business--as represented in the center of the city by department stores, specialty and luxury stores, and general merchandise stores--is different from the business conducted by stores conveniently located near people's residences. The neighborhood shops are for items of daily consumption, such as rice, wine, fish and meat, groceries, drugs, and daily wear. Standing between the downtown and the neighborhood retail businesses is another type generally found in subcenters of the city and areas in front of railroad stations. Under the present conditions in Tokyo--where the use of private cars for shopping is rare--retail stores and shops must necessarily take into consideration the number of pedestrians and their buying habits. The pedestrians are from the surrounding neighborhood and also from other locales. These stores, then, prosper or decline according to the patterns of pedestrian flow, and they undergo character transformation in the process.

In the busiest central sections of Tokyo, such as Yurakuchō, Ginza, Kyōbashi, and Nihonbashi, where mass transit systems converge and accessibility to outer areas is high, there is a constant flow of masses of people. People coming from other parts of the country and from foreign nations, who have a high propensity and ability to buy, join those living in Tokyo. It is in these places that we find luxury-goods stores offering unstandardized, special goods such as jewels, objets d'art, and high quality dry goods. The unit prices are high, but the retailers obtain considerable margins on this merchandise. These stores have far greater capital strength than the small stores selling daily commodities that are conveniently located for people to drop in, but even small stores have a great amount of capital invested in them. They have close connections with manufacturers, and their employees have exact information about the quality and prices of the goods they handle. The names of these stores are well established and widely known to customers; thus, because they can attract customers from far, it is possible for them to operate even in wayside places far from busy sections of the city.

General merchandise stores occupy an important position in retail business in the heart of the city. Goods handled by these stores--including men's and women's dresses, dry goods, imported goods, quality confectionery, foodstuffs, shoes, musical instruments, watches and clocks, furniture, refrigerators, and cars--are not standardized to the extent of the goods sold by neighborhood stores, and their unit prices are relatively high (a common belief is that the higher the price the better is the quality of a commodity). They constantly strive to keep up with the current vogue and to set new styles and fashions. These stores are managed by big capital with extensive public relations.

The heart and subcenters of the city that have a great number of prospective customers make possible the development of large-scale department stores that meet the many and varied needs and tastes of those customers. Clothing and furniture constitute the major goods handled by these department stores, and general merchandise is also available in quantity. The department stores are retail business operations that have a large sectionalized organization and great capital and sales volumes. As the citizens' ability to consume has increased, these stores have made great strides; the quality of their goods and their trademarks have won wide social recognition and have attracted many customers. The stores make efforts to maintain the high quality of their merchandise. The total sales by the department stores of Tokyo in 1964 reached as high as 21.1 percent of the total retail sales in the area, and it represented about half the total department store sales in the nation. Moreover, the annual sales per employee in Tokyo's department stores amounted to ¥7,650,000, which far exceeded the sales per employee of the other types of retail stores (¥2,770,000). Thus, not only is the scale of operation great but their financial condition is much better than that of other retail stores.

With the development of the heart of the city, stores grow larger and more specialized, land prices rise, and the area becomes increasingly unfit to be a residential district. In the process, small stores and shops gradually disappear. To protect numerous small retail stores from extinction in their keen competition against big-capital department stores, legal measures have been taken to control the increase in number and scale of department stores and to let small stores develop as specialty and luxury goods stores. However, these small retail stores are also encouraged to deal with low-priced goods as well. At the present time, the clustering of retail stores in the city makes it possible for customers to choose many goods in one shopping outing; it also helps to make the large shopping areas widely known to the people. This clustering leads to the concentration of transportation facilities in these areas and accelerates the further growth of the stores. Ultimately, however, growth depends upon the relationships that these stores have with the hinterlands--that is, on the size and quality of the commercial spheres of the stores.

Profits that retailers can make in the center of the city are closely related to land prices. The more conveniently a store is located, the greater is the profit a retailer can make and the greater are the advantages he has; thus, competition to secure the good locations for business becomes keen among retailers. Land in Ginza 4-chome (fourth block) and its vicinity is sold for as high as ¥10 million per tsubo [36 square feet] or higher. Retailers making the greatest profits in Tokyo are located in areas where land prices are the highest, and the further removed they are from these areas, the lower are the prices of land.

In high-priced land areas, efforts are made to utilize land to the maximum. As high-rise buildings are built, the combination small store-residences, which we see in great numbers in central Tokyo and in other cities of the nation, gradually disappear. The number of stores and business buildings that are separate from the residences of their owners greatly increases as these stores expand and the number of employees increase. The traditional big household business operation is being dissolved, and nuclear and branch families are taking up residence in separate homes, apartments, and lodging houses in the suburbs. The traditional personal neighborhood relations that were built around living in the combined store-residences in business districts are gradually giving way. New functional ties are arising among business concerns with common interests in the socioeconomic development of the areas in which they operate.

The retail business districts in the heart and subcenters of Tokyo are in areas where there are great numbers of pedestrians, and many restaurants, tea rooms, beer parlors, bars, cabarets, delicatessens, and theatres-- compared with other types of retailers. Their numbers and sales are increasing with the expansion of the central urban area. The number of restaurants and snack bars in the heart of the city represents 24.9 percent of the total number of such establishments in the whole metropolis; in the subcenters the number accounts for 15.6 percent of the total. The sales of the establishments in the center of the city represents 43.1 percent of the total sales in the whole city, and in the subcenters represents 23.3 percent.

Among the reasons behind the large number of retail business establishments in the central city are the many employees in large-scale administrative and business institutions whose residences are in areas far from the heart of the city. A great majority are young unmarried people, and conveniences are available here for mutual contacts in social and economic activities as well as for shopping and recreational purposes. Similar establishments are found in numbers in the subcenters of the city and in the central sections and railroad-station-side business districts of the satellite cities. When compared with the retailers in central Tokyo and in the city subcenters, those in other parts of the metropolitan region are smaller in scale, have cheaper and less varied goods, and maintain more personalized relationships with customers.

On the rim of the central urban area where investments have not been made in quantity, the existing buildings and facilities are left unimproved owing to the anticipation of further urban redevelopment that might necessitate their demolition. Although land prices are rather high, these areas are basically low-rent housing districts. Their relative anonymity contributes to the development of small low-priced bars, cabarets, taverns, restaurants, theatres, movie houses, and hotels, and the areas often brew social evils.

As people and institutions in a big city move away from its center radially, and new consumer areas develop far from the existing centers of supply of goods, new commercial and transportation centers develop. New retailers begin concentrating for their business, and these centers, located in the outskirts, become subcenters of the city. The sphere of business activity of each of these subcenter retailers is far smaller than that of a retailer operating in the heart of the city. The commercial sphere of each subcenter fans out from the center of the city in a pie-shaped form. The process of dispersion of retail business functions accompanies the expansion of the city as a whole, an increase in traffic congestion, a relative decline in retail sales, and a relative decline in retail business as a whole in the heart of the city. Large-scale retailers, especially the well-established quality foods and confectionery stores that operate in subcenters, are owned and managed by the central-city retailers; they make up the chain stores.

After classifying the department stores in the ward section of Tokyo into three groups, we would like to observe comparative changes in the sales of each group; this operation is impossible, however, because of the legal proscriptions imposed to safeguard managerial secrecy. Therefore, we shall look at changes in the floor space of the department stores as surveyed in 1966 by the Planning Bureau of the Ministry of International Trade and Industry. The three groups of stores are: the centrally located stores (in Tokyo's three central wards), the "terminal" stores (located in the Shinjuku, Shibuya, Ikebukuro, and Asakusa transportation terminals), and the "near-terminal" stores (those in Sukiyabashi and Ōi that are near the transportation terminals).

In 1956, the total floor space of the six centrally located stores was 160,000 square meters, and the space of the six "terminal" and the nine "near-terminal" stores was 91,000 square meters and 79,000 square meters, respectively. In percentage, the first group of stores accounted for 48 percent of the total, the second, 27 percent, and the third, 23 percent. In 1966, the space changed as follows: 207,000 square meters for the first group, 213,000 square meters for the second, and 178,000 square meters for the third. With the index of the floor space of each group in 1956 being set at 100, the 1966 indices were 129 for the first group, 233 for the second, and 225 for the third. In percentage, the space of the first group dropped from 48.0 percent to 34.7 percent, but that of the second and third groups increased from 27.5 percent to 35.6 percent and from 23.9 percent to 29.8 percent, respectively. The relative decline of business in the central areas and the advance in outer areas form an interesting contrast.

According to the 1967 survey made by the Tokyo Chamber of Commerce on the shopping patterns of consumers in seventeen cities, excluding Yokohama, located within the 30-, 50-, 70-, and 100-kilometer limits from the Tokyo Central Station, the following facts are known. During the first half of the year, the people living in Kawasaki, Koganei, Kawaguchi, and Matsudo of the

30-kilometer limits who came out to Tokyo for shopping more than once represented 81 percent of the total number of households in those cities; the people in Atsugi, Kawagoe, Kasukabe, and Sakura of the 50-kilometer limits coming to Tokyo represented 58 percent of the total number of households in those cities; those of Odawara, Kumagaya, Furukawa, and Tsuchiura in the 70-kilometer limits constituted 44 percent of the total number of households in those cities; those of Mishima, Tochigi, and Chōshi in the 100-kilometer limits, 42 percent. The farther away the residences are from Tokyo, the less frequently do people come to Tokyo for shopping, but the dependence of people on Tokyo, even in areas 100 kilometers from the city, is considerable. The people in these seventeen cities who came to Tokyo twice or more represented 47 percent of the total number of households in the cities. Those who spent ¥10,000 or more each per shopping visit to Tokyo constituted 29 percent of all the people visiting; those spending ¥5,000-10,000, 21 percent; those spending ¥3,000-5,000, 19 percent; and those spending ¥1,000-3,000, 23 percent. Thus, those spending more than ¥5,000 represented half the total number of shoppers.

Among the shopping areas in Tokyo frequently visited by the people from the seventeen cities, Ueno draws the greatest number of visiting shoppers, representing 18 percent of the total number, then come Nihonbashi with 14 percent, Shinjuku with 11 percent, and Ikebukuro with 10 percent. The Ginza and Yūrakuchō areas, which are considered to be the most central sections of Tokyo, have only 6 percent of the shoppers visiting them. More than half of the shopping by the people, 57 percent to be exact, is done in department stores, indicating the relative importance of these stores in the heart and subcenters of Tokyo. The goods most frequently purchased include handbags, accessories, ladies' dresses, other front-running fashion goods, and quality trademark gift items. In comparison, standardized furniture and electrical appliances--such as TV sets and daily wear--are bought by these shoppers in their own local stores.

Since these consumer habits have become more prevalent, 56 percent of the households in the seventeen cities want to see the establishment of Tokyo-based department stores and supermarkets in their own cities. In Kawaguchi, Koganei, and Matsudo, department stores are especially desired; in Ichikawa, Atsugi, and Kawagoe, supermarkets are wanted most, and in Kasugabe, Sakura, and Mishima, dry goods stores are desired. When the sales in the heart of Tokyo continue to decline and consumption levels off, department stores will be established in numbers in the outlying areas, as can be seen in the United States.

Transportation Patterns and Consumer Life

At any rate, the heart and subcenters of Tokyo are directly related to consumer life in the Tokyo metropolitan complex as a whole. The big subcenters of Tokyo, such as Shinjuku, Shibuya, and Ikebukuro, are unique in size and development, unequalled in the major cities of the world. One of the reasons for this uniqueness is the traditional role that these places have played as points of transfer for users of the mass transit systems. There they have transferred from private railroad and bus lines to the national railroad lines that have monopolized the transportation networks connecting the heart of the city with outer districts. The recent establishment of direct connections between private railroad and subway lines, the latter penetrating into the heart of the city, has greatly ameliorated the conditions of the past. But the subcenters mentioned have grown into giant centers, independent of the center of the city--with a great many department stores, specialty goods stores, recreation establishments, and restaurants--that have a great ability to absorb consumers.

There have been attempts to relocate some institutions of the central city to subcenters, hoping to relieve urban congestion and confusion, but unless certain conditions are met, the institutions so relocated will not be able to function properly. Even if the redevelopment of the heart of the city is much more costly than that of subcenters, considerations must be given to the degree of accessibility to wide areas and to the availability of opportunities for the proper interinstitutional relationships that central location affords. Even if these conditions are met in subcenters, it would merely mean a contiguous extension and expansion of the heart of the city into these subcenters.

Large investments are needed to develop a wide-area region in which conditions are the same as those in central Tokyo, but it should be remembered that the wider the area in which investments are made, the less effective are such investments. Thus, relocation of institutions must consider redevelopment investments in light of whether they will hinder or promote institutional functions.

One of the most striking features of the structural change of the Tokyo metropolitan complex in recent times is the improvement of transportation facilities. This has resulted in the speed-up of traffic, the increase in transport capacity of national and private railroads, bus lines, and private cars, and the development of express highways, which directly connect the heart of the city with residential areas in the outskirts. This increased accessibility has made the central section of the city more important as the point from which integrative functions emanate. At the same time, the increase in suburban population and income and the gradual standardization of consumption habits have encouraged wholesalers and retailers to concentrate in subcenters and railroad-station-side business sections.

People living in the outskirts depend on the heart and subcenters of the city for their luxury goods and general merchandise, but their greatest needs are for unstandardized goods and fresh foodstuffs. In Japan it is still customary for women to go shopping for daily necessities on foot in the neighborhood; therefore, it is necessary that stores and shops be operated to meet these daily, small-volume needs. We see small stores and shops combined with the residences of their owners operating in centers of the residential areas; sometimes we find clusters of these stores located along main streets and roads, making ribbon-pattern business sections in the areas. Generally, these stores and shops are distributed in proportion to the population density, which is progressively lower as the distance from the heart of the city becomes greater. The distribution density of stores and shops is higher towards the center of the city, in contrast to the density of the residential population, but the settlement of residential population always precedes the concentration of retailers, and there has arisen the problem of a relative dearth of stores and shops in the suburbs of Tokyo.

Japanese cities, including Tokyo, are unlike cities in the advanced industrial nations of the West: more people are engaged in tertiary industry--domestic services and small-scale businesses with minimal capital--than in manufacturing and other secondary industrial activities; and small-scale stores and shops are more numerous per unit population than they are in Western cities. The Japanese cities are different from those in less developed countries, on the other hand, in that their stores and shops have a greater quantity and better quality of goods for sale, and there are better facilities for sanitation and other purposes.

Each of these small businesses usually caters to an average of 200 to 300 households located within a radius of one kilometer. The stores have the retailing advantage of being aware of individual consumer needs, owing to the close personal contacts that are established with regular customers. They place orders with and have goods delivered by the stores, although the recent shortage of labor is making it more difficult for the stores to provide such services. The total sales volume is not great, and unless small stores obtain as great a margin as possible, their management becomes strained. With low gross sales, their income is low, and it is difficult to accumulate capital.

Threatening the existence of small retailers at present is the low-price, mass-sale, self-service supermarkets that made their first appearance in Tokyo in 1953 with the backing of big capital. In 1962, in 113 cities in Japan that had a population of 100,000 or more each, there were a total of 383 self-service retail stores, each of which had an average annual sales of ¥100 million. In the following year there were 741 such stores in 126 cities. The total sales in supermarkets was estimated at ¥300 billion, or 44.0 percent of the total sales of the nation's department stores, which took several decades for development, and 5.0 percent of the total sales of all the other retail stores in the nation.

In 1964, there were 331 supermarkets in Tokyo, 80.0 percent of which were retailers of foodstuffs and beverages. Their total sales amounted to 4.4 percent of the total sales of all the retailers in the metropolis, and their annual sales per employee was ¥5,380,000, indicating far better business management than that of other retailers.

Supermarkets have penetrated into small retail business sections in local neighborhoods and station-side business districts with foodstuffs and other daily commodities as their principal goods; in the heart and subcenters of the city they have intruded into retail business sections principally with clothing. The custom of pedestrian shopping expeditions in the neighborhood limits the business sphere of supermarkets, however. Suburban Japanese supermarkets cannot be expected to become as large as supermarkets in America, with their huge parking lots. It goes without saying, however, that gigantic market complexes, each combining a number of supermarkets, are still growing in size as they resort to mass procurement and mass sales. The markets dealing with clothing in the heart and subcenters of Tokyo are successful in their mass sales, expansion of their chain markets, and accumulation of capital.

At any rate, when residential population is distributed more widely and the employment of women in various fields of work increases in Japan, the frequency of shopping trips will decrease, and cars will be used more for shopping purposes. Then it can be expected that clusters of small retailers in local neighborhoods and station-side business sections will undergo changes or be left behind the times.

The numerous petty retailers in Japan, which numbered 37.0 per 1,000 population in 1947, have been gradually liquidated or merged with one another; their number was reduced to 13.5 per 1,000 population in 1964. The present trend is towards a further decline in number and expansion in size despite a continuous increase in population. Even if they become large, they appear to suffer from disadvantages in management, which result from their former status as petty retailers. There remains a serious need for reorganization of these many traditional small business operations in order to fit them well into the new society.

The development of supermarkets was a blow to the small retail business of long standing. In order to meet the new competitive conditions, some of the retailers have begun cooperating with one another and have developed voluntary chain stores. This development was promoted to some extent by interest-free loans from the government's "cooperative retail business funds" ("tenpo kyōdōkin kashitsuke seido"). These voluntary chain stores, whether they are made up of retailers alone or include wholesalers or producers in their cooperative schemes, cooperate in the procurement and transporting of goods, advertising, financing, storing, cost accounting, employee training, and merchandising development. This cooperative venture is noteworthy in that it has the following advantages: it prevents sudden changes in the business management and operation of small retailing establishments that were formerly based on traditional domestic-type labor, since it is able to secure profits comparable to those enjoyed by big enterprises, and it is able to control the prices of commodities in society. However, when organization of retail business is simplified and margins are cut down through the cooperative procurement of goods and cooperative cost accounting, wholesalers also try to cut down their margins in order to induce individual retailers to purchase cheaper goods directly from them. This leads to the disorganization of the cooperative scheme; full function of the concentrated procurement of goods is obstructed, and, therefore, the savings in distribution costs is less directly beneficial to the consumers. There is also the danger that executives of a cooperative scheme may assume that since the venture basically represents a program of modernizing small- and medium-scale enterprises, the managerial and sales ability of voluntary chain stores are equal, or not much inferior, to the ability of wholesale enterprises. Thus, they do nothing towards the modernization of many petty enterprises.

As one way to compete with big organizations, retailers have gotten together and started so-called promiscuous department stores (yoriai hyakkaten) --big buildings in which individual shops are operated. For the construction of such buildings they receive financial aid from the Small- and Medium-Scale Enterprises Promotion Corporation (Chūshō Kigyō Shinkō Jigyōdan) through prefectural governments. Many of these retailers have jointly had their buildings made taller and have had parking lots and arcades constructed. Thus, they have made the places of their operations into modern business sections that attract more people and earn twice or three times as much income from sales as before.

It is apparent that in order to compete with such big enterprises as department stores and supermarkets by means of cooperative ventures, small retailers must form either voluntary chains or promiscuous department stores. Perhaps they will consider the following points: shops to be opened in a cooperative department store must be selected on the basis of their importance in the composition of the store and their excellence in business. Operational funds may be borrowed jointly from city banks or hypothec banks in order to enhance the significance of cooperative activity. A whole building may be rented for each department store in order to reduce per-shop cost for renting. With respect to the allocation of shops within each store, the chairman of the cooperative should make decisions that give due consideration to space locations in the store and the most effective ways to motivate masses of people to shop—for instance, giving central locations to the shops dealing with foodstuffs and clothing. Shop hours must be determined, and public relations must be conducted jointly. There have been cases where success was attained by some who adhered to these points of emphasis and gave people an image of the cooperative as being a reliable organization.

Japanese economy, which has already seen the liberalization of capital, soon will be facing its effect in the retail business sector. Foreign makers with more powerful capital strength, organization, greater skills, and ability in sales and advertising are expected to spread their networks in Japan. Many of the tradition-bound, and inefficient Japanese retailers must develop their abilities and strength to sustain themselves in keen competition among themselves and with such foreign business enterprises.

We have described how various integrative institutions that provide foundations for life and work in Tokyo are determining the whole structure of the metropolitan complex. Integrative institutions function with the base of their operation in and near the heart of the city and, at the same time, direct their attention to the geographical distribution of residential areas. Some of these institutions are located in central Tokyo. Others, especially those related to the supply of goods and services for daily consumption, find locations near urban centers that are distributed in concentric circles around the center of the city and along railroad lines and radial roads and streets. These institutions control their respective commercial spheres and share common cultural conditions and structural relationships with nearby urban centers. The greater the inaccessibility to the heart of the city, the smaller are the nuclei that are made up of such institutions, but large nuclei appear at places along the line. Such is the distribution pattern of integrative institutions.

Residents of Tokyo are related to the various integrative institutions for their work and consumption, and their geographical distribution is generally dependent on the distribution of nuclei of integrative institutions. This distribution of the resident population also determines the development and distribution of the institutions that provide goods and services for consumption, such as stores, shops, and recreational facilities.

Institutions of higher and special education and special hospitals—all of which can belong to the same category as the establishments that supply goods and services for consumption—need good natural and social environments as well as large spaces of land. Thus, their dispersion from the heart of the city tends to precede population movements for suburban settlement.

CHAPTER 5

HOUSING AND LIVING ENVIRONMENT

Housing is a most serious problem in any expanding major city in the world. Housing conditions in Japan are substandard for an industrialized, modern democratic nation. Handsome high-rise buildings in the hearts and subcenters of big metropolises and new gigantic industrial complexes in Japan make a sharp contrast with the indigent housing conditions of the nation.

Investments by private individuals in housing have been very inadequate owing to low individual income levels; there has also been a lack of investments for the development and improvement of transportation facilities, parks and green tracts of land, gas and water supply, and sewerage in the cities of Japan that are now inflated with heavy population concentration. Nor have the national and local governments and public corporations made adequate plans and investments for improvements in housing facilities and living environments, because, in the past, their major emphasis had been placed upon the national policy of industrialization--to make the nation physically strong. Therefore, very little has been accumulated in the way of facilities necessary for modern living. With the rapid inflow of mass population into cities and the fast subdivision of households in recent years, housing and general environmental conditions have become aggravated.

When a country is underdeveloped, there is a tendency to control the utilization of resources in the consumption sector of the economy (including housing) and to direct the resources, instead, to the expansion of production. This was the economic reason for the past investments in Japan for national industrialization and prosperity and strength. This situation has led in recent times to inadequate housing and environmental facilities and low social capital that are keenly felt as economic growth continues. Under this condition, sound national life has been obstructed and economic development impeded. As the economy progresses, however, and a stage is reached where supply surpasses demand, investments for improvements in housing and environmental conditions become effective in helping to produce more demands. Again, as a democratic social system matures, goals of economic growth come to include the promotion of labor efficiency and, ultimately, the public welfare as well as the accumulation of capital for production. In light of this, greater emphasis has been placed on welfare policy and programs.

Factors Related to Urban Housing Problems

When treating housing problems in cities, it is necessary to study the sex and age composition of the resident population, the industrial and occupational structures, the educational levels, the marital statuses, the households and household composition, and the personal incomes in relation to the locations and structures of residences and other environmental aspects of living.

Characteristics of an urban residential population differ from one city to another according to the types, structures, scales, and numbers of integrative organizations and institutions found in different cities; they also differ according to the size and structure of urban residential population change as the integrative institutions change. In Tokyo, as in other cities of the country, opportunities for employment have been more numerous for men than for women in the past, but more and more, women are finding occupations, as indicated by the sex ratio in employment which decreased from 107.1 (men for every 100 women) in 1960 to 105.9 (men to every 100 women) in 1964. This ratio in Tokyo, however, should be compared with 74.4 for Berlin in 1963, 89.3 for London in 1963, 91.5 for New York in 1960, and 92.8 for Rome in 1961--all lower than the Tokyo ratio. The ratio in Delhi is higher at 126.8 men to 100 women in 1961.

The sex ratio in the productive-age population, which constitutes a majority of the newcomers to cities, was a high 123.8 for the 20-29 age bracket in 1964 and 102.4 for those 30-39 years old; the ratios in New York, Chicago, Berlin and other Western cities were all below the mark of 100. In the Tokyo metropolitan complex, the sex ratio decreases as the distance from the center of the city becomes greater, and this is also true in the case of the ratio in the productive-age population.

During the recent rapid economic growth, the inflow of the productive-age population has become further marked. In 1950, population distribution by major industry showed 4.0 percent in primary industry, 37.5 percent in secondary industry, and 58.6 percent in tertiary industry; but in 1960, the percentages changed to 1.0 percent, 44.0 percent, and 55.0 percent, respectively, indicating a decrease in primary industry and an increase in secondary and tertiary industry. The special feature of Japanese cities is that secondary industry is not powerful enough to absorb the labor force; thus, the proportion of the tertiary industry population, which includes a big unproductive population--we may call it a potentially unemployed population--is greater than that of the secondary industry population.

All of these people make up families or households and live a consumer life. Their household compositions differ according to the types of integrative organizations and institutions in which they work or have some connection; that is, the household composition depends upon the members' occupations--they may be capitalists, managers, small and medium business operators, white-collar and blue-collar employees, merchants, service workers, day laborers, or civil service workers.

In cities, there has been a trend towards a reduction of the family size and the subdivision of families and the formation of democratic nuclear families. Various factors contribute to this trend, including the separation of place of work from residence, difficulties in the inheritance of family property or occupations, the decline of patriarchal authority, and other traditional familial customs and institutions; there has also been a penetration of democratic education and a reduction of the number of children in a family owing to the parents' aspirations for a higher standard of living and better education for the children.

During the five-year periods from 1955 to 1960 and from 1960 to 1965, the number of households in Tokyo increased by 38.8 percent and 24.4 percent, respectively, but the number of people in each household decreased (in average) from 4.47 in 1955 and 3.87 in 1960 to 3.50 in 1965. In 1960, the small household units of 2, 3, and 4 people each made up 49.3 percent of the total number of households in the metropolis. The geographical distribution of married and unmarried people in the metropolis shows a tendency towards a heavier concentration of married people in the suburbs and peripheral farming areas of the city and a greater concentration of unmarried youths in and near the heart of the city. Living accommodations in the city are more suited for single people who flow into the city in great numbers and housing for them is more readily available.

The expansion of a big city means an increase and expansion of the various integrative institutions that operate in the heart of the city. People who occupy various roles and positions in these integrative institutions earn their income and live different types of lives in different areas, according to their interests and tastes. For an understanding of the living conditions of Tokyo's residents, then, it is necessary to begin with an observation of their income levels as determined by the sources of their income and the types and scales of occupations and industries in which they work.

The sum total of personal incomes in Tokyo was about ¥3 trillion in 1963, of which 59.9 percent represented incomes from personal services, 17.3 percent from privately-owned businesses, 6.3 percent from leasing, 6.0 percent from interests, 5.1 percent from dividends, and 5.4 percent from transfers such as welfare aids. The per capita annual income of the whole population of Tokyo was ¥280,861, of which ¥250,000 was disposable; this was the highest in the whole nation, being 1.73 times the national average. This fact was one of the main reasons for the great inflow of population into the city and, at the same time, indicates the high cultural standard of life in the city.

Employment status has much to do with levels of income. The per capita annual income of the salaried employees and wage earners in private businesses in Tokyo was approximately ¥510,000 in 1963; the incomes of all types of employees was ¥430,000, compared with the per capita income of the company directors, which was ¥1,270,000. Sizes of business enterprises also determine income levels of employees. The per capita income among the employees of enterprises having 30 of more employees each is ¥470,000, while among employees of firms with 29 or fewer employees each the per capita income is ¥340,000, or about two-thirds of the income from the larger firms. These low income levels greatly determine the living patterns of the employees. Income levels are also determined by the types of businesses in which people work, the lengths of their work experiences, their educational backgrounds, sex, age, skills, and the composition of their families.

The average per capita annual income of private business operators in all types of business is ¥820,000, much higher than the ¥510,000 of the salaried employees and wage earners in private businesses as cited above. Their per capita income differs greatly from one type of business to another. The per capita annual income is highest in the mining industry at ¥1,210,000, followed by ¥1,120,000 in transportation and communications, ¥900,000 in services, ¥890,000 in manufacturing, ¥860,000 in wholesale and retail, ¥840,000 in real estate, ¥590,000 in construction, ¥540,000 in finance and insurance, ¥480,000 in forestry, ¥470,000 in fishery, ¥440,000 in agriculture, and ¥110,000 in household side work. The low levels of income in primary industry, including household side work, are conspicuous.

Business operators' incomes also differ according to the number of employees they have. The per capita income of those without any employee is ¥550,000; with 2-4 employees, ¥830,000; with 5-9 employees, ¥1,510,000; and with 10 or more employees, ¥2,340,000.

The income level distribution of salaried employees and wage earners in the wards of Tokyo shows that the greatest proportion (20.6 percent) earn ¥200,000-300,000 annually; the next largest group earns ¥300,000-400,000 (16.1 percent), and then there are those earning ¥100,000-200,000 (16.0 percent). Those workers who have an income of ¥500,000 or less annually constitute 69.6 percent of the total number of salaried employees and wage earners, and their aggregate income is only 38.5 percent of the income of the whole. Employees with an income of ¥1,000,000 or more constitute only 3.2 percent of the whole, but their aggregate income is 17.6 percent of the income of the whole--disproportionately high for their small number.

The income level distribution of private business operators shows a pattern similar to that of salaried employees and wage earners. The greatest proportion (17.9 percent) are those having an income of ¥200,000-300,000 annually, followed by those with income categories of ¥300,000-400,000 (17.7 percent), ¥100,000-200,000 (13.4 percent), and ¥400,000-500,000 (13.0 percent). Business owners who make less than ¥500,000 annually constitute 68.3 percent of all owners, and their combined income is 36.9 percent of the total. Those who make more than ¥500,000 make up about the same percentage as do the salaried employees and wage earners who earn more than ¥500,000. The only difference lies in the smaller proportion of the business operators making between ¥200,000 and ¥300,000, compared with the employees and wage earners making similar sums of income.

The income of Tokyo's citizens is the most important determinant of the location and structure of their residences. It influences people's ability to pay land prices and house rents and the distances they can and must travel to work. This economic factor, plus cultural and other factors, enters into people's choices of residence location and structure. Most people prefer their homes to be convenient to their daily work and life, in areas such as the heart and subcenters of the city, industrial zones, and station-side districts. All parts of the metropolitan complex are organically related to the life and work of all the Tokyo residents, and the whole complex functions under a system of functional specialization of the component areas.

The patterns of distribution of the resident population in a big city is basically determined by degrees of accessibility to the heart and industrial centers of the city. People congregate and segregate according to their similarities and differences in such matters as ability to pay land prices and house rents, land and home ownership, housing structures, sex and age compositions, household composition, educational levels, types of industries and occupations, income patterns and levels, social and political interests, and neighborhood structures. Their homes form separate residential zones, mainly around railroad stations, markets, and schools. These residential zones may be high, middle, or lower class in character, and they may include public and private apartments, foreign colonies, and those industrial and commercial settings where residences are not segregated from places of work. Such is the community structure of the consumer resident population.

The distributional pattern of different types of housing units in the total community structure of a metropolis in Japan is different from that seen in the West. Especially in the United States, aggregation and segregation occur according to similarities and differences in social, economic, and cultural status of people; these characterize different communities. In Japan, separation of residence from place of work is still incomplete. This is true even in Tokyo, except in the business office districts in the central area and in the city's big industrial zones. Although there are different residential areas characterized by different social levels of the residents, the areas marked by uniformity of the residents' living and general cultural standards are geographically limited, and houses of various sizes and kinds coexist.

Furthermore, Japan is yet to have census tracts established for statistical purposes. The statistical data presently available from the central and local governments, which are compiled in the big units of shi, ku, chō, and son, i.e., cities, wards, towns, and villages--each of which contains many elements--make it difficult to adequately classify various areas according to their characters and to get a clear picture of the changing conditions of each of these areas.

As we have pointed out, it is not income and other economic and demographic factors alone that determine residential patterns, structures, and locations. For an understanding of changes in housing structures and locations in the Tokyo metropolitan complex, it would be worthwhile to rank various unit areas of the complex (cities, wards, towns, and villages) on the basis of the following indices: income from wages and salaries and from business operations, residential land prices, population density, population change, commuting, age and sex compositions of population, marital status, size of households, ownership or renting of houses and rooms, sizes of residences in terms of the number of floor mats (tatami), educational levels, percentage distribution of employees by industry and occupation, and the number of dependents for each employee. The patterns of relationships among the rankings for various indices will make clear the characteristics of the various areas, while changes observed in such relationships over a period of time may lead to an understanding of structural changes of the areas. We must make note here that data on income distribution are available only for the wards of Tokyo and that what we present below are only summary statements about selected unit areas of Tokyo. The data on earned income and income from sales of goods and services and residential lands are for the year 1964, and the data on all the other indices are for 1960.

Regional Differences in Residential Patterns

In the traditional center of Tokyo, which includes the wards of Chūō, Chiyoda, Minato, and Taitō, the expansion and multiplication of business enterprises and high-rise buildings were accompanied by a rapid separation of residences from places of work in both the business office sections and the wholesale and retail business sections, where land prices have sharply increased. Neighborhood relationships between households changed from informal and personal ties to formal and occupational connections. We have observed decreases in the nighttime population (Chiyoda Ward registered a 4.7 percent decrease and Chūō Ward 5.8 percent in the last five years), in population density, and in the number of households, a result of an increase in the commuting day-workers who leave the heart of the city empty at night. This problem of vacancy at the center of the city is becoming increasingly serious because of the uneconomical utilization of the land. The buildings are not tall by the Western standards, and the area is relatively overpopulated; the land value is going up, the residential houses are overaged, the lack of playgrounds leave children at the mercy of traffic irregularities, and the shortage of facilities for daily life is becoming serious.

Of course, more people than just the number of residents in the four central wards of Tokyo are engaged in wholesale and retail business (45.3 percent of the total industrial population in Chiyoda, 43.4 percent in Chūō, 38.3 percent in Taitō, and 31.9 percent in Minato). Occupationally, the proportion of persons engaged in sales work is the greatest (28.0 percent in Chūō, 24.7 percent in Chiyoda, 23.6 percent in Taitō, and 15.8 percent in Minato). The educational standards in the wards of Chiyoda and Minato, where government and business offices are concentrated and high- and middle-class residences are found, rank about the middle of the scale for all the wards (graduates of colleges and universities constitute 11.5 percent of the total population in Chiyoda and 14.1 percent in Minato), but Chūō and Taitō Wards, which are areas of large and small wholesale and retail business, rank low on the scale (college graduates make up 7.7 percent in Chūō and 6.8 percent in Taitō).

Among the middle-aged and old people who run wholesale and retail businesses in the heart of the city, many combine their stores with residences (57.8 percent of the total number of such businesses in Chiyoda, 51.5 percent in Chūō, 50.3 percent in Taitō, and 47.4 percent in Minato). A majority of the people who are absorbed into the city, especially into its central section, are unmarried young people, especially men (57.5 percent of the total migrating population in Chiyoda, 55.7 percent in Chūō, 59.1 percent in Taitō, and 48.2 percent in Minato). Business firms that try to recruit these youths as a labor force provide nonprofit, nominal-rent housing units for them. These company housing units are numerous; they make up 14.9 percent of the total number of the housing units in Chiyoda, 10.7 percent in Chūō, and 12.2 percent in Minato. Only in Taitō Ward, where many small and medium businesses operate, is the percentage of housing units run by various companies low--3.3 percent. Many private rooming accommodations for these young people are also available: 5.5 percent of the houses in Chiyoda provide such accommodations, 7.4 percent in Chūō, 7.3 percent in Minato, and 8.3 percent in Taitō).

Therefore, the level of income from salaries and wages in this central area of Tokyo is very low. Chūō Ward ranks lowest of all the wards at ¥350,000 and Chiyoda Ward ranks third from the bottom. In terms of corporate income, however, Chiyoda ranks highest at ¥680,000, followed by Chūō, Kōtō, Minato, Taitō, Ōta, Setagaya, Shinjuku, and Shibuya in that order, which indicates the high corporate income level in central Tokyo. Furthermore, the average residential land price in this area (which has the greatest accessibility to places of work for the residents) is more than ¥200,000 per tsubo--the highest in the metropolitan complex. It occupies the highest point on a contour-line graph showing land prices in various places.

Almost all the areas surrounding the heart of the city lose their population during the day and gain at night because of the movement of commuters to work and school. The greatest number of commuters enter the center of the city, and the next largest groups go to the subcenters, satellite cities, and industrial zones on the periphery. The areas with the most fluid population, where more than 50 percent of the commuters go out of the boundaries of their respective areas of residence--that is, the areas having strong organic ties with other areas--include the following among the wards of Tokyo (which make up the 15-kilometer-radius region around the heart of the city). Suginami has 75.3 percent of its commuting population going out of the ward, 41.7 percent of which enter central Tokyo (Chūō, Chiyoda, Minato, and Taitō Wards); Nerima has 60.3 percent and 31.2 percent for the respective categories; Setagaya, 56.2 percent and 46.1 percent; Meguro, 54.6 percent and 43.6 percent; Shibuya, 52.9 percent and 50.1 percent; Toshima, 51.8 percent and 34.3 percent; and Kita, 50.7 percent and 40.2 percent. In areas outside the ward region, Hoya has 72.4 percent and 25.9 percent; Fukuoka, 68.2 percent and 34.4 percent; Koganei, 68.1 percent and 31.6 percent; Kokubunji, 64.9 percent and 23.1 percent; Komae, 64.7 percent and 24.0 percent; Musashino, 64.6 percent and 36.9 percent; Higashimurayama, 64.3 percent and 18.5 percent; Kunitachi, 63.6 percent and 21.4 percent; Tanashi, 60.8 percent and 20.9 percent; Kurume, 60.6 percent and 28.4 percent; Mitaka, 58.7 percent and 30.1 percent; Hino, 57.0 percent and 13.2 percent; Kodaira, 56.4 percent and 19.9 percent; Kamakura, 52.9 percent and 30.9 percent; and Chōfu, 50.9 percent and 30.7 percent. Most of these 23 municipalities outside the ward region of Tokyo, from which commuters come to central Tokyo, are located in the southwestern hillside region along the Chūō railroad line.

Looking at other districts outside Tokyo for similar trends, we find that central Yokohama (Naka Ward) receives the greatest number of commuters from five districts of Yokohama City: Isogo Ward, Hodogaya Ward, Nishi Ward, Minami Ward, and Tozuka Ward. Yokosuka receives from the three districts of Zushi, Hayama, and Kanazawa Ward; Kawasaki from the Kanagawa and Minatokita Wards of Yokohama City; Tachikawa from Akijima and Yamato; Kawaguchi from Warabi and Hodogaya; and Urawa from Yono.

Viewed from the standpoint of the commuter zones--we call them the primary area as a whole--the structure of the Tokyo metropolitan complex is under the predominant influence of the heart of Tokyo. This primary area extends some forty kilometers, from central Tokyo to the southwestern hillside region along the railroad lines and stretches even as far as Kamakura, although the areas under the direct influence of central Tokyo are not contiguous in this direction. To be sure, the heart of Tokyo is not the only center that dominates the whole metropolitan complex, and we find other important nuclei such as central Yokohama, Yokosuka, Kawasaki, Tachikawa, Kawaguchi, and Urawa.

Residential settlement takes place first in areas where integrative institutions concentrate, that is, in the areas that have easy access to places of work. Population density is greater in and near the central districts of Tokyo; the further removed from these central districts, the lower is the density. Therefore, as time goes by, areas with a high rate of population increase will be found further away from the central districts.

In 1950-1955, the area within 5 kilometers from the center of Tokyo had a 16.4 percent population increase, while the greatest was registered in the area between 5 and 10 kilometers from the center (33.9 percent), followed by the areas between 10 and 15 kilometers (30.2 percent), between 15 and 20 kilometers (28.5 percent), between 20 and 25 kilometers (26.0 percent), between 25 and 30 kilometers (19.4 percent), between 30 and 35 kilometers (15.2 percent), between 35 and 40 kilometers (9.5 percent), between 40 and 45 kilometers (2.4 percent), and between 45 and 50 kilometers (5.4 percent).

In 1955-1960, little population increase was registered in central Tokyo (a mere 2.5 percent; population actually decreased in Chiyoda and Chūō. The following increase was observed in different areas: 17.4 percent in the area between 5 and 10 kilometers, 27.4 percent in the 10-15 kilometer area, 35.4 percent in the 15-20 kilometer area (the greatest increase in Tokyo), 20.6 percent in the 20-25 kilometer area, 24.4 percent in the 25-30 kilometer area, 19.6 percent in the 30-35 kilometer area, and 11.1 percent in the 35-40 kilometer area. The area between 40 and 45 kilometers from the center of the city lost 0.1 percent of its population, while the area between 45 and 50 kilometers from the center registered a 3.1 percent increase (a smaller rate than in the previous period). These figures indicate a gradual decline in the rate of population increase in and near the heart of the city, reflecting the steady decline of the importance of the area as a residential district; the reverse trend is seen in the fringe areas of the city. Areas with a high rate of increase will be found further and further away from the center of Tokyo, and neighboring agricultural communities, beyond a certain distance from central Tokyo, begin to be characterized by outmigration of their population. The boundaries of the metropolitan region can be found somewhere between the sprawling city and the agricultural communities.

Competition for land ownership is staged as people move further away from the central sections of the city, and land price distribution takes a form similar to that of population density distribution. The land priced at ¥80,000 per tsubo can be found around the areas some 15 kilometers southwestward from central Tokyo, about 30 kilometers southward, and 8 kilometers in the northeastward direction. Distribution of the land valued at ¥30,000 per tsubo follows the pattern similar to that of population density and increase rate, which shapes up like the feet of an octopus along national railroad lines. These "feet" extend some 40 kilometers along the Keihin railroad line, 35 kilometers along the Chūō line, 30 kilometers along the Tōhoku line, and 20 kilometers along the Sōbu line. Thus, the extension of the ¥30,000 land is shortest in the eastward direction, longer towards the north, still longer towards the southwest, and longest towards the south, in the direction of Yokohama. The price of land in between these extension lines is generally cheaper, but in pivotal urban centers (satellite cities) on the fringe of Tokyo the prices are high again.

Industrial classification of the people living along the Chūō railroad line and in the hillside region of the southwest, where the greatest number of people commuting to central Tokyo reside, shows that a great number of them are engaged in manufacturing (20-30 percent) and wholesale and retail business (20-30 percent), as is the case in the metropolis as a whole. There is also a considerably greater number engaged in services (20-23 percent) and civil service (3-5 percent) than are found in other districts of the metropolis. Occupationally, many of the people are in clerical (20-28 percent) and sales (13-16 percent) positions. These two regions, especially, are characterized by a higher ratio of persons who exercise advanced technical duties (9-12 percent) and managerial functions (4-8 percent) than in other regions of Tokyo. They also have a greater percentage of persons with higher educational backgrounds (13-22 percent).

For the people in these two regions, residence and place of work are clearly separated, and the regions are relatively clearly demarcated. Therefore, aggregate corporate income in these regions ranks about the middle in the scale for the whole metropolis, but income from salaries and wages is relatively high. The highest level is found in Suginami Ward, followed by Setagaya, Minato, Meguro, Nerima, Shibuya, and Shinjuku, in that order.

As for the marital status of the people in these residential regions, the ratio of unmarried people is lower than in the heart of the city, but higher than in industrial and agricultural regions. The ratios of the middle-aged population and of the female population are higher here than in the heart of the city, while the ratio of the married population is high, second only to that in the agricultural region.

Viewing family size, the average household membership is 3.6 which represents the small nuclear household. In housing types, these regions have a greater population living in rented houses (35-52 percent) than in any other region, and the ratios of families living in employer-supplied housing units (4.6-9.4 percent) and in rented rooms (5.1-8.7 percent) are the second highest, following those in the heart of the city.

Living space is measured by the number of _tatami_ in the home. (A _tatami_ floor mat is about three feet by six feet, or approximately 18 square feet.) Given this unit of measure, 4.5 _tatami_ floor mats per person characterize areas within 15-20 kilometers of the heart of the city--more spacious than in other areas of the business sections of the city. Further away from the center of the city, the per capita space is about 3.5 _tatami_ or smaller, indicating that on the fringe of the city, houses are smaller in size and that low-income people have crowded residences. Living space increases in agricultural communities, where the average size of household space per person is 4 _tatami_ or larger. Rented houses provide an average of 3 _tatami_ per person, which is larger than the 2 to 2.5 _tatami_ space per person in the industrial region of the northeast. Space in employer-supplied housing units and in rented rooms is larger per person than in industrial regions, the former being an average of about 3.5 _tatami_ and the latter, an average of 2 to 4 _tatami_.

The areas in the Tokyo metropolitan complex that are recognized as residential districts are so designated in a relative sense only, and it is impossible at present to clearly demarcate residential areas in Tokyo. However, we can observe that, except for the city of Akijima and the town of Fukuo, the rate of population increase has fallen to 11 percent or below in the belt that is between 35 and 40 kilometers from the center of the metropolis. This belt includes such cities as Hachiōji. Likewise, the commuting population decreases in this belt, while the agricultural population increases. Beyond the 40-kilometer points there are areas where people outmigrate into the metropolis; their population decreases accordingly. That belt, then, may be seen as the approximate boundary line between the outer areas and the primary area of Tokyo that is directly involved in the life and activities within the ward section of the metropolis.

There are differences in residential situations between the industrial belt in the northeast and the big Keihin industrial region. The northeast region of small-scale factories encompasses the wards of Kōtō, Sumida, Arakawa, Edogawa, Katsushika, Adachi, and Kitaitabashi along the Arakawa River. In the Keihin region, which extends along the Tokyo Bay coast from Shinagawa through Yokohama to Yokosuka, mostly big-scale chemical and heavy industries are located. Towards the northeast, population density remains about the same along the Tōhoku, Jōban, and Sōbu railroad lines up to about the 15-kilometer points from central Tokyo; beyond these points the density drops sharply and takes on rural characteristics. This condition in the northeast makes a clear contrast to that in the southwest. Residential land prices exhibit a similar pattern. The contour line that indicates the distribution of land valued at ¥30,000 tsubo extends 30 kilometers along the Tōhoku railroad line and 25 kilometers along the Sōbu and Jōban lines, but in many areas between these railroad lines, the contour line extends only 15 kilometers from the center of Tokyo.

This northeastern part of the metropolitan complex is the most recently urbanized area. The industrial composition of its population shows that the greatest number of people are in manufacturing (45.8-55.0 percent), followed by those in wholesale and retail business (19.0-24.0 percent). The ratios of those in services and civil service are low (10.5-11.2 percent and 1.2-2.9 percent, respectively). Occupationally, skilled workers, production process workers, and semi-skilled laborers make up a little over half of the total number in all occupations (52.2-56.7 percent). Clerical and sales workers are fewer here than in other regions, and workers with advanced technical skills and managerial duties are especially few (2.8-4.4 percent and 2.2-3.7 percent, respectively). This reflects the low ratio of people with secondary and higher education backgrounds (4.7-6.6 percent, except in Kita Ward which is a semi-residential area and has the figure 9.8 percent).

As for income levels, all the wards in this region, except Kōtō and Sumida Wards, have the lowest levels of corporate income and income from salaries and wages among the wards of Tokyo. Kōtō Ward is nearest to the center of Tokyo and ranks third among the wards of the city in aggregate corporate income, and Sumida Ward ranks about middle on the scale. The lowest corporate income level is in Edogawa (¥370,000), and the lowest level of income from salaries and wages is in Arakawa (¥380,000). The ratios of the welfare grantees in Adachi, Itabashi, and Katsushika are the highest in the metropolis.

This northeastern region is a so-called town-factory region, where either homes and places of work are not separated, or homes and factories exist side by side. Because of this proximity of residences to work places, not many people in this region commute out of their districts, despite the region's proximity to central Tokyo. (The ratios of commuters to central Tokyo are 50.7 percent in Kita Ward, 41.8 percent in Edogawa, and 21.2 percent in Sumida.) To this extent, the region is isolated and characterized by its internal neighborliness.

The ratio of unmarried people in the northeastern region in areas that are near the center of Tokyo is high, second only to the ratio in the center of the city. The ratio of married people is high in areas further away in the region. Occupants of employer-supplied housing units and rented rooms are fewer in proportion here than in the central city and in the residential region of the southwest--4.0-5.4 percent in employer-supplied housing units, except in Kōtō Ward where the figure is 10.1 percent; and 4.6-5.8 percent in rented rooms, except in Kōtō which has 8.1 percent. The ratio of those who have their own houses is higher at 41.9-50.6 percent than in the southwestern region. Residential space per person, however, is smallest in this region for every type of housing: 3.0-3.5 tatami in owned houses, 2.1-2.4 in rented houses, 2.8 in employer-supplied houses, and 1.76-1.91 in rented rooms.

Because many residences and places of work are located in the same structure that serve factories as well, people are constantly vexed with noises, congested traffic, vibrations, inadequate sewerage, etc. The method of pumping up underground water, the cheapest industrial water supply, has caused the sinking of ground. The 37-square-kilometer area that includes Kōtō, Sumida, and Adachi Wards has sunk below sea level. To prevent floods from rivers and high tides, measures are being taken to control the pumping of underground water, to lay out industrial water supply lines, and to build seawalls. But, in the absence of necessary facilities, people are still pumping out rain water and other dirty waters that inundate their homes.

The statements above are a general description of the community structure of the northeastern region within the 15-kilometer limits from the center of Tokyo. Beyond this region are found extensions of the industrial belt region and residential areas built on terraces a little lower than those in the southwestern region.

In the area that lies beyond the northeastern region along the Tōhoku railroad line, which includes such places as Hatogaya, Warabi, and Kawaguchi, the rate of population increase is high at 45-50 percent. The commuting population is also large. Many go out to Kawaguchi, which has a great number of people working in manufacturing (44.4-54.4 percent of the total employee population) and many skilled workers, production process workers, and semi-skilled laborers (41.6-53.7 percent of the employee population). Residents also go out to industrial areas in the ward section of Tokyo. In the areas further away, between 20 to 30 kilometers from central Tokyo (such cities as Urawa and Ōmiya), the rates of population increase are low (16.0 percent and 17.6 percent, respectively) despite their roles as suburban centers. These cities, however, in comparison with the northeastern region, have a smaller proportion of their populations engaged in manufacturing (28.7 percent in Urawa and 29.8 percent in Ōmiya) and larger proportions in wholesale and retail business (20.7 percent and 17.5 percent, respectively), services (16.5 percent and 12.6 percent), and civil service (5.9 percent and 5.4 percent). Occupationally, more people are performing clerical and sales functions (37.7 percent and 29.7 percent) and managerial functions (9.1 percent and 5.5 percent). Educational levels are higher here (14.2 percent and 7.9 percent with higher education). More residents are also commuting to the center of Tokyo--to Chiyoda and Chūō Wards, for instance--going beyond the intervening region we have described above. Home ownership is rated high, and space per person in these owned houses is 4.15 tatami, which is just about as spacious as in the southwestern hillside region. These cities of Urawa and Omiya serve as bedroom towns for Tokyo.

The town of Kashiwa, which is located 30 kilometers from central Tokyo along the Jōban line, has an agricultural population accounting for one-third of its total population, but the rate of its population increase is high at 41.6 percent, and there are many commuters to the heart of Tokyo. This town is becoming a residential area.

Along the Sōbu line, the rate of population increase is not very high (26.1 percent in Matsudo, 15.0 percent in Ichikawa, and 17.5 percent in Funahashi), but the ratio of commuting populations is relatively high, and so is the ratio of educated people (higher education: 12.3 percent in Ichikawa, 9.5 percent in Matsudo, and 8.7 percent in Funahashi). Urban centers such as Matsudo, Ichikawa, and Funahashi are white-collar residential areas, and the industrial and occupational compositions of their populations are similar to those of Urawa. Home ownership is rated as high as in Urawa and Ōmiya (60 percent and above); this is higher than in the ward section of Tokyo. Tatami space per person, however, is small (3.7) except in Ichikawa (4.1), despite the fact that these centers are far from central Tokyo. Here again, the indication is that, like the composition of the southwestern region of Tokyo, low-income people reside in these fringe areas of the northeast.

Land in the areas surrounding the centers of Matsudo, Ichikawa, and Funahashi is generally priced at ¥30,000 per tsubo, but the general area encompassing all these places together represents a ¥50,000-per-tsubo area.

The city of Chiba, the prefectural capital some 30 kilometers from the heart of Tokyo, has a population of 240,000. The rate of its population increase is not very high despite its status as a suburban center (22 percent over the last five years). It is a self-regulating urban center with the population composition balanced between industrial and occupational. The commuting population is not as large as that of the cities mentioned above, but the fact that a great number of commuters go to the central wards of Chiyoda and Chūō in Tokyo indicate the special character of Chiba as a city directly under the influence of Tokyo.

Except for the city of Chiba and the town of Yachiyo with their relatively high rates of population increase, areas on the rim of the eastern region between 30 and 35 kilometers from central Tokyo are characterized by a low rate of population increase, a low ratio of commuting population, and a relatively high ratio of agricultural population--all indicating the low degree of urbanization. Beyond the 35-kilometer limit is an agricultural region with a declining population, and this limit may be taken as the boundary of the primary area of Tokyo in this direction.

The coastal region along the Keihin and Tōkaido railroad lines, which has many large-scale industrial establishments, a high population density, and a high rate of population increase, extends from Tokyo through Kawasaki and Yokohama to the Chūkyō (Nagoya) metropolitan region to the west along the Tōkaido line. The contour line representing the distribution of land valued at ¥30,000 per tsubo spreads from Tokyo to the 40-kilometer points in the westward direction along this national railroad line; after a break, the line further extends from the 45-kilometer mark to the 50-kilometer points along the Shōnan coast.

The percentage of the outcommuting population in this industrial region is higher than in the isolated industrial region of the northeast. The ward of Ōta, for instance, has 37.8 percent, and the cities of Kawasaki and Tsurumi 29.1 percent and 40.4 percent, respectively. Ōta Ward, which is near the heart of Tokyo and has a number of residential districts within its boundary, has many of its commuters going into the heart of Tokyo. The commuters from Kawasaki and Tsurumi mostly commute between these two cities.

The Keihin region is characterized by the coexistence of such large residential and industrial districts and different population groups, as are seen in Kawasaki and Ōta, for instance. Industrially, the region is best represented by the Kawasaki-Tsurumi area. Kawasaki's population in manufacturing accounts for 49.3 percent of its total industrial population, and in Tsurumi such a population makes up half its industrial population. In contrast to this overwhelming proportion of population in manufacturing, the wholesale and retail business population is small--Kawasaki has 14.9 percent and Tsurumi 16.3 percent. Occupationally, these cities have few residents with advanced technical skills (Kawasaki 5.4 percent; Tsurumi 6.7 percent) and managerial functions (2.1 percent and 3.7 percent, respectively); the proportion of clerical and sales people is also small. The proportion of skilled workers and production process workers is large (Kawasaki 23.9 percent; Tsurumi 27.2 percent), and so is the proportion of the semi-skilled labor population (47.8 percent and 49.2 percent).

The educational level of the region is lower than in the southwestern residential area of Tokyo (Ōta Ward has 12.3 percent with higher education, Kawasaki 8.0 percent, and Tsurumi 8.3 percent), but it is much higher than in the northeastern industrial region. The ratio of unmarried people in Shinagawa and Ōta Wards is high (43.8 percent and 42.2 percent, respectively), because of their proximity to central Tokyo. The big industrial districts of Kawasaki and Tsurumi have high ratios of married people (55.1 percent and 55.4 percent, respectively) and of home ownership (45.6 percent and 45.7 percent)--ratios comparing well with those in the southwestern residential region of Tokyo. Tsurumi, where large factories are located, also has a high ratio of people living in employer-supplied housing units (13.5 percent).

The contour line representing the distribution of land valued at ¥50,000 per tsubo extends far in this direction, reaching Kawasaki and Tsurumi and even the center of Yokohama, which is some 30 kilometers from central Tokyo. Competition for land ownership is very keen in this area. As for living space, per capita tatami space here would rank between the space available in the southwestern residential region and that in the northeastern industrial region.

The wards of Naka, Nishi, Minami and Isogo in Yokohama, which together make up the southern core of the Tokyo metropolitan complex, have relatively stable rates of population increase (16.7 percent in Naka, 3.7 percent in Nishi, 13.4 percent in Minami, and 9.5 percent in Isogo), and this area represents an urban center which has reached a saturation point in urbanization. Naka Ward's population in wholesale and retail business makes up a high 34.1 percent of the ward's total industrial population, and the ward absorbs many commuters from the outside. Naka is the heart of Yokohama. Nishi Ward has 24.5 percent of its industrial population engaged in wholesale and retail business, and Minami has 23.5 percent. In the central area of Naka Ward, the land price is ¥80,000 per tsubo, and the ¥50,000 contour line mentioned above surrounds this area.

There is an area adjoining this central Yokohama ward section which has a high rate of population increase; it includes Hodogaya (48.5 percent), Tozuka (38.3 percent), and Yamato (34.9 percent). A large proportion of residents commute to central Yokohama, and exert an influence on the expansion of the city.

The ratio of people with their own houses in Yokohama is high, next to that in the agricultural region; the highest is 65.6 percent, in Minatokita Ward, and the lowest 52.8 percent, in Naka Ward. The ratio of persons renting houses is accordingly low, but in the central wards of Yokohama (Naka, Nishi, and Minami) and in the industrial Kanagawa Ward, the ratios range from 7.1 percent to 9.4 percent, which are higher than central Tokyo. As for living space per person, individually owned houses have 3.21-3.98 tatami, rented houses 2.42-3.21, employer-supplied houses 3.04-4.09, and rented rooms 1.99-2.32. Thus, space in individually owned houses is greater here than in the northeastern industrial region but smaller than in the southwestern residential region, whereas space in rented and employer-supplied houses and in rented rooms compares well with the situation in the southwestern region.

Such centers along the Keihin railroad line as Kamakura, Zushi, and Hayama and the city of Fujisawa on the Tōkaido line all have low rates of population increase. Despite the long distance of 40-50 kilometers from Tokyo, these locations along the scenic Shōnan coast have been serving as bedroom towns for Tokyo since before the Tokyo area became a gigantic metropolitan complex. At present, however, Zushi and Hayama have most of their commuters going to Yokosuka, and the next largest group goes to central Tokyo.

The Kamakura-Zushi-Hayama area has 25-29 percent of its industrial population engaged in manufacturing, 18-21 percent in wholesale and retail business, and 21.2-24.5 percent in services. Its advanced technicians make up 7.2-11.6 percent of the employee population, and its managerial people 6.0-7.9 percent. As for the college-educated people, Kamakura has 17.8 percent, Zushi 15.0 percent, and Hayama 12.0 percent. All of these percentages compare favorably with the percentages in residential areas of Tokyo.

Home ownership ratios are high: 59.7 percent in Kamakura, 55.2 percent in Zushi, and 68.3 percent in Hayama. House rental ratios are accordingly low, at 26.6 percent, 32.6 percent, and 22.7 percent, respectively. People living in employer-supplied houses are few, and those renting rooms make up about the same percentage as those renting rooms in Tokyo's southwestern region. Living space in this area is the greatest of all the areas in the metropolitan complex. Owned houses have 5.02 tatami per person in Kamakura, 4.76 in Zushi, and 5.00 in Hayama. Rented houses have 3.72, 3.22, and 4.14, respectively, which represent the best conditions available near business centers of the metropolitan complex. The conditions are also good in employer-supplied houses, which provide 3.83, 4.08, and 4.34 tatami per person, respectively, in the three cities, and in rented rooms, the space is 2.40, 2.87, and 2.70 tatami, respectively. This area, plus the city of Fujisawa, represents a residential area where the ¥50,000 per tsubo land contour line runs along the coast.

Fujisawa has a high home ownership rate (55.7 percent) and low house and room rent and employer-supplied house rates (24.1 percent, 4.2 percent, and 5.9 percent, respectively). In terms of tatami space per person, owned houses have 4.51, rented houses 3.25, employer-supplied houses 3.75, and rented rooms 2.53, all of which are about the same as in Kamakura.

Areas beyond Fujisawa along the Tōkaido route make up part of the megalopolis, and they are undergoing urbanization in every respect.

This concludes the general description of regional differences in residential patterns and living environments. As residential areas and as personal environments, the regions have different problems that have to be solved.

Private and Public Housing

The total ordinary households in Tokyo was 2,530,000 in 1963, and the number has increased by 660,000 over the last five years. The number of houses--

2,510,000 in 1963--increased by 690,000 in five years. Owned houses constituted 94.1 percent of all the ordinary households in 1958 and 95.5 percent in
1963. Improvements have been made in the supply of housing units for the
increasing number of households, but the problem has been the numerical increase of low-quality houses.

The number of houses in Tokyo owned by the occupants who had them built or
bought them individually constituted 65.5 percent of all the houses in 1955
and 56.9 percent in 1958, but the proportion decreased to 44.7 percent in 1963.
On the other hand, the number of houses for rent increased in proportion from
22.6 percent in 1955 to 35.5 percent in 1958 and 47.4 percent in 1963, the
result of a great inflow of population and a rise in rent. As we have already
observed, the nearer the peoples' places of work and the heart of Tokyo are to
their residential areas, the greater is the proportion of rented houses to the
total housing units available.

Individually owned houses have gradually expanded in size, and the number
of those houses with 30 or more tatami each has increased. As the number of
high-income people increased under a developing economy, many houses within 5-20
kilometers from central Tokyo, especially in the southwestern hillside region,
began to have Western-style living rooms, bedrooms separate from living rooms,
and rooms for individual family members. Moreover, the kitchens are equipped
with stainless sinks, gas ranges, refrigerators, and built-in cupboards,
and flush toilets and garages have become common in many of the homes.

In areas nearer the heart of the city, within 5-10 kilometers, smart concrete high-rise apartment buildings with elevators (popularly called "mansions")
began to appear in numbers. Each of the units has several rooms, an air con-
ditioning system, and a parking stall. Some people buy these units for several
millions of yen or several tens of millions, and others rent them for some
tens or hundreds of thousand yen per month. Because of their convenient locations near the heart of Tokyo, some of these apartment units are also being
used as offices.

Most people want to live in places that are best suited for their work and
tastes. However, meager incomes, rapid rises in land prices--ten times during
the past ten years--and skyrocketing costs of construction have forced them to
make their residences in remote places where land is cheap but environmental
conditions are poor. Many houses for these people were constructed in areas
between 20 and 30 kilometers from central Tokyo in 1959, but in 1960 construction of these houses moved to areas between 40 and 50 kilometers. Very often,
approximately half the funds for construction of houses are spent for the
purchase of land. As we have seen in the fringe areas of Tokyo where settlement and the number of individually owned houses are increasing, many small-
size wooden houses are being built along narrow, unpaved roads. Often no
water and gas supply or sewerage is available. Such areas are sprawling far
and wide. The high costs of transportation to work and physical fatigue must
be counted as additional burdens on the low-income people who work long hours
and live in these areas. Whatever the reason, the size and number of individually owned houses has increased.

Rented houses are in poor condition; about 70 percent provide space of 9
tatami or less per household, and 77 percent (474,000) have no rooms for bath
and are provided with only community kitchens and toilets. The number of

rented houses has increased, but these houses are wooden structures with facilities for joint use by several households.

That housing standards in terms of tatami space in rented houses have improved is indicated by the figures of 2.9 tatami in 1955, 3.5 in 1960, and 3.9 in 1963, but many of these houses are still small and crowded. The average size of a rented house in Tokyo is 8.6 tsubo. A comparison of housing standards in terms of the number of occupants per room shows 0.64 persons in the United States (1960), 0.68 in Britain (1961), 1.01 in France (1954), 1.03 in Germany (1956), 1.07 in Italy (1961), and 1.40 in Japan (1958). The standards are thus lower in Japan than in Western countries. Though it is common in Western homes, it is rare in Japan that children of different sexes have separate rooms after they reach the age of ten or thereabouts. Under such circumstances, although the tendency is towards an increasing branching off of households, young people feel restrained about getting married.

Public housing units now being constructed for many low-income people are wooden-structured apartments with facilities similar to those provided in privately-operated rented rooms. The one-room-per-household units constitute 77 percent of all the units (68 percent have 4.5 tatami space each; 27 percent, 6 tatami; and 5 percent, 3 tatami). There is no room for the bath in each unit, and 88 percent of the units have community toilets. There is no play yard for children, and in some cases, the maximum number of children is prescribed for admission to the units. The rent is ¥1,200 or higher per tsubo. Entrances and exits are used jointly by several households, and partitions between units are usually thin walls of plywood that afford little privacy.

The ratio of households living in apartments for low-income tenants to the total number of households in the districts of Ikebukuro, Sugamo, Ōji, Nakano, and Ōmori--each of these cities under the jurisdiction of a separate police station--are 44 percent, 43 percent, 36 percent, 36 percent, and 29 percent, respectively. These apartments are most numerous in areas between 5 and 10-15 kilometers away from central Tokyo, and these areas are gradually sprawling. At present, approximately 25 percent of all the households in the metropolis are living in such public housing units.

Despite undesirable conditions, people keep moving to vast fringe areas where private and public investments have been inadequate, and they have to travel further to their work. Traffic volume also increases. In Tokyo, 43 percent of all the commuters using various means of transportation spend more than one hour commuting to their work. These means of transportation, whether they are national or private railroads, subways, or bus lines, are not equipped with adequate facilities for transporting a great number of people over a long distance. The use of principal railroad lines such as the Keihin, Tōhoku, Chūō, and Yamate in rush hours reaches the unimaginable rate of 300 percent, and this condition increases physical exhaustion and dangers to health, and decreases public confidence in transportation.

House rents and land prices in Tokyo are rising at an average rate of 16.0 percent each year. In 1965, persons making ¥20,000 or less per month spent 16.5 percent or more of their income for rent; those making ¥30,000 or less spent 16.0 percent or more; those making ¥40,000 or less, 10.0 percent or more; those making ¥50,000 or less, 8.2 percent; those making ¥60,000 or less, 14.5 percent; and those making ¥80,000 or more, 15 percent or less. Thus, the lower the income, the greater is the proportion of income spent for rent payment. Those with a relatively high income are also spending a large part of their income for rent. Very often, people have to pay high rents for very low-quality housing units. The fact that 77 percent of the households with housing problems are low-income people who make ¥30,000 or less per month each, especially calls for a formulation of drastic measures by national and local governments. This problem cannot be left for private citizens to handle.

The housing conditions described so far are those resulting from processes of economic and cultural selection among individuals and families. In the post-war periods, the national government and local public bodies have used their political power to formulate and execute large-scale housing projects. They began with the construction of simple emergency-relief structures for the people whose houses were damaged during the war, and proceeded to systematic urban planning. The construction of these public housing units should not be regarded as a burden on the national economy. It serves as an economic stimulant that helps to adjust the balance between supply and demand in time of oversupply, and through redistribution of resources it positively contributes to the promotion of social welfare, better social environments, and labor efficiency.

In housing construction in residential areas near the heart of the city, wooden-structure units, which constituted 91 percent of all the housing units in Tokyo in 1963, are being replaced mainly by sturdy and safe concrete buildings of medium heights. In suburban areas, apartment zones are being created that have spacious roads, open yards, and public facilities. Plans are being made for zoning and improving the quality of housing units so that new business sections might develop along with the residential areas. Groups of relatively low-income people are provided housing in units sponsored by local public bodies and supported by national grants-in-aid; relatively high-income groups are provided housing units by public corporations that have both public and private funds. The national government is also making use of the Public Housing Finance Funds to give long-term individual financial aids for use in PHFF housing units, subdivision units, and public housing corporation units. The government also leases houses and lands to the House Lots Development Company. All these measures are intended to alleviate housing conditions, and they are yielding good results.

Metropolitan Tokyo has formulated a plan to have 1,800,000 houses constructed over the ten-year period from 1961 to 1970, with a goal that every household would have a house of its own. Of that number 1,010,000 are to be built by individuals, and the remaining 790,000 by the national and metropolitan governments. Tokyo is also planning to establish a new model residential town of about 300,000 people in the hilly area of Minamitama, which has a total land area of 2,752 hectares and 80,000 public houses. There are a number of problems in executing such a plan, the most serious being the problem of land acquisition. The land in this area is very expensive. Tokyo must face the problem of making a drastic land price policy in this respect.

The standard unit in a Public Housing Corporation Zone apartment has two rooms of 6 tatami and 4 tatami space, a kitchen-dining room, a bath with a gas heater, and a flush toilet. This unit is called "2 DK" and rents for ¥5,700 to ¥10,000 per month. The Corporation must secure a revenue 5.5 times as much as the rents charged; therefore, the occupants are selected mostly from the families averaging 3.25 persons in size (in 1964), whose couples are middle-aged (males 20-40 years old, females 20-30 years old) and whose heads have higher education backgrounds. They are usually in some general clerical or technical occupation and make a monthly salary of ¥40,000 or higher. Very few old people, over 60 years of age, and few young people, between 10 and 24 years of age, are found in the apartments. As income and living standards are rising, it has become increasingly apparent that the 2 DK units are too small, and plans are being made to build only 3 DK or equivalent units in the future.

Other housing units of the Corporation are intended for people making less money than those described above. They are of two types: Class I units are for those making between ¥20,000 and ¥36,000 per month, and Class II units for those making less than ¥20,000. The size of a Class I unit is 12 tsubo, and that of a Class II unit 11 tsubo, but plans are now being made for units of 15 tsubo and 13 tsubo for Class I and Class II, respectively.

In Public Housing Corporation Zone apartments, the tendency has been for people of similar income levels, ages, occupations, social positions, household compositions, and social interests to conglomerate. These standardized apartments are found near such pivotal places as railroad stations, bus stations and stops, supermarkets, business centers, and schools. The people living in these apartments are commuters. Since they plan to have their own houses someday, their interest in apartment neighborhood affairs is very shallow, and there are few traditionally structured neighborhood organizations. These people do extend their cooperation for the solution of common problems such as traffic and school difficulties as they arise.

In the beginning, Public Housing Corporation Zone apartments were constructed near the heart of Tokyo, but as demands for land ownership increased (owing to the great inflow of population into the city and the subdivision of household units following the expansion of political, economic, and cultural functions of Tokyo), land prices rose far faster than private income and the prices of commodities. Moreover, when land became a subject for investment, its prices took a further upward trend, and it became difficult for the national and local governments to acquire land with their limited funds. Originally, many apartments were constructed in the southwestern region of Tokyo, which was suited for residential purposes, but new apartments began to gradually appear in industrial regions and in the northeast lowlands. Finally, such construction began in remote areas that extend into agricultural regions.

Thus, the construction of these apartments often stimulated a great increase in the population of towns and villages around the rim of Tokyo. Furthermore, large investments for the construction of new apartments encouraged investments for the construction of traffic and communication systems over wide areas. This situation has made it possible for the agricultural areas near the apartments that were built to enjoy easier access to the heart and industrial regions of the metropolis. The water and gas supply and sewerage has improved. Subdivision of agricultural lands for residential purposes and a rapid rise in land prices have in turn been stimulated.

On the other hand, the large-scale construction of apartments, unlike the construction of factories, has brought more burdens than benefits to the municipalities where they are located. They create new problems in traffic, water supply, sewage disposal, schools, street cleaning, and other public responsibilities. The increase in population that results from the construction of the apartments may be beneficial to the factories and offices in the cities where apartment dwellers work because it represents a new labor force, but the municipalities face new problems. There is now a need for coordinating mutual interests between these municipalities and Tokyo.

Despite governmental participation in projects to provide housing facilities for Tokyo's people, the facilities established by the national and metropolitan governments constituted only 24.5 percent of all the housing units constructed in Tokyo after the war. The remaining 75.5 percent have been built by private funds. Despite the increase in the number of these units, many of them are too small and are inadequately furnished. The number of high-rent houses is increasing, and individually owned houses are decreasing in proportion, as we have observed. Applications for admission to public housing units exceed the availability by tens and hundreds of times, and many of these applications come from low-income people. Under these circumstances, then, it is imperative for better housing conditions in Tokyo that public budgets be increased for more housing projects, especially for the benefit of low-income people. Stringent control must be exercised over the rise in land prices which threatens the economical and systematic utilization of land. The government should develop and create new residential lands and pour more money into housing construction projects and other projects for public facilities in these areas.

Needless to say, the rise in land prices, which presents the greatest obstacle in the planned reconstruction of Tokyo, is basically caused by the relative lack of land. Land is scarce because of the increasing concentration of industry and population that accompanies the development of the city. We do not mean to say that land is absolutely lacking. Land does not rot with time. It is only that land owners, knowing that land prices will go up as demands increase, do not sell until the prices rise; this speculation helps the prices to rise further. A great amount of land lies unused; this also contributes to a lack of land and a continuous upward trend of land prices. According to a study made by the Takayama Research Institute, the total area of unused lands in the 23-ward area of Tokyo was 110,000,000 square meters. Assuming that one house occupies an area of 165 square meters, this area of unused land was big enough to accommodate 680,000 households.

One reason for the existence of unused land is that the low assessment standards of the immediate postwar period have not yet been changed, a condition conducive to landowners. Even if a piece of land is currently valued at ¥60,000 or ¥70,000 per tsubo, it is legally assessed, for fixed asset taxation purposes, at ¥300 or thereabouts. In this respect, the current fixed asset taxation assessment must be reviewed in earnest.

The rise in land prices was especially stimulated during the period of prosperity in 1955 when capital investments were prevalent and when corporations, in concert with real estate firms, obtained funds from banks and bought as much land as they could for their industrial and housing projects. The prices of residential lands consequently increased tenfold by 1965, while wholesale prices of commodities, according to a Bank of Japan study, rose scarcely at all during the same period.

Another reason for the sharp rise in land prices in Tokyo was the lump purchase of legally uncontrolled lands by public corporations in 1965 for the construction of new roads and railroads in time for the Olympics. These public bodies went so far as to buy the lands at the prices offered by adamant landowners in order to complete the planned projects. It is a fact that 85 percent of the budget for the preparations for the Olympics was expended as compensations for landowners.

The people who benefited most by the rise in land prices were the farmers in the suburbs of Tokyo who, after the war, obtained farmlands from landowners for almost nothing. They are the ones who obtained large unearned incomes, and there are many such postwar landowners who are still holding lands in anticipation of a further rise in land prices.

Unlike other commodities, land is part of a nation, and its supply cannot be increased even if its price rises. For this reason, recognition of private ownership of land must presuppose the assurance that such ownership does not jeopardize the general interests of the nation and its citizens. Land must be put to best use. Thus, measures must be taken to prevent private land ownership from harming public interests.

There are views advocating the creation of a tax on land price increase and a tax on unused lands as measures to control the rise in land prices, but control through such tax measures cannot be exercised completely. Solutions must be found in improving the actual social and economic conditions of society which necessitate such tax measures. The many problems relative to lands that are most necessary for a sound reconstruction of the metropolis have resulted from the absence of an overall land policy in the public administration. This policy should be formulated on the basis of an analysis of the complicated functions that land can perform.

Basic to overall land utilization planning is the zoning of the metropolis and its surrounding areas. Zones should be able to withstand constant change in society, and they should be strongly controlled. Zoning aims to demarcate areas of different purposes, such as business sections, commercial and industrial zones, residential zones, parks, green lands, and farmlands. Such zoning will not only help to control land prices but will improve traffic, health, and other social environmental conditions. It will also prevent public nuisances, and help to develop recreational opportunities.

Generally, land becomes most expensive when it is used for commercial purposes, but when clearly marked zones exist, residential land may not be much affected by an increase in commercially used land. Unused lands can be clearly defined and become an easy subject for taxation. Moreover, making public announcements on prices of land in different zones would give guidelines for land assessment and wild speculation control.

After these measures have been taken, land may come increasingly into supply; this, in turn, would help stabilize land prices. When a land policy is formulated together with land utilization planning, great progress will be made in solving not only the housing problems that we have been discussing but other pressing problems as well--such as those of roads, streets, parks, and green belts that are indispensable for modern urban living.

In the principal cities of advanced countries, sewerage is almost 100 percent adequate, but in metropolitan Tokyo adequate sewerage is available only in the area extending 15 kilometers around the heart of the city (26 percent of the total area of the metropolis, and 32 percent of the total population). The condition is thus pre-modern. As for park area per resident, whereas Washington, D.C. has 56 square meters, the largest of all; Vienna has 27 square meters; even New York, where skyscrapers stand close together, has 12 square meters; and Paris has 8.9 square meters. In comparison, Tokyo has only 0.73 square meters. Chiyoda Ward in central Tokyo has 11.49 square meters, and Minato Ward 4.30 square meters, but 10 kilometers and beyond from the central city there is scarcely 0.5 square meters of park area for each resident. What few parks there are have little aesthetic harmony with their surroundings.

It is in the realm of common sense that national governments and local public bodies in modern societies should make efforts to buy as much necessary land as possible to demarcate industrial, business, and residential zones and to provide adequate parks, green lands, roads, adequate water, and sewerage. Governments would then not only prevent public nuisances, but would pay attention to the beautification of cities.

Residential zones must be created so that residents have easy access to their places of work. Especially, housing units for young working people must be constructed near the heart of Tokyo or its industrial zones. Buildings must be fireproof, and they must be tall, making room for the widening of roads and streets and for parks and green lands. Roads for vehicles and pedestrians must be separated. All these matters must be taken care of before Tokyo can, in fact, be called a modern metropolis.

For suburban areas of Tokyo, the green lands that are shrinking must be preserved. These lands may best be used as residential areas for relatively high-income people, whose houses are built low and edged with gardens. Whether to make Tokyo a compact metropolis or a loosely dispersed one should not be decided outright in one way or the other. Given the present conditions of the Tokyo metropolitan complex, the best way to proceed is to plan initially for the construction of a compact urban center by making adequate investments; then, gradually, concentrated investments may be shifted to principal points in outlying areas. This approach is the best one for building a better life for the residents of Tokyo, for the best anticipated effects of investments, for long-term planning designed to prevent wasteful investments, and for cumulative reconstruction of the metropolis.

CHAPTER 6

INDUSTRIAL LOCATIONS AND STRUCTURAL CHANGES

In the preceding chapters we have discussed the growth and development of metropolitan Tokyo, with central Tokyo and its nucleus. We have also discussed the structures, functions, and distribution of the integrative institutions that play a most important role in the community structure of the metropolis. In addition, we have pointed out some problems in metropolitan planning and delved into problems of housing and living environments for the inhabitants. Our focus has been on metropolitan administration and the circulation and consumption of goods and services in the metropolis; now let us discuss matters relative to the production sector of metropolitan Tokyo.

Manufacturing in Metropolitan Tokyo

There are 95,000 manufacturing firms in metropolitan Tokyo. This number accounts for 20.4 percent of all the various firms in the metropolis, which is second only to the 218,000 wholesale and retail businesses which account for 46.8 percent of all metropolitan firms. Manufacturing occupies a position of special importance in metropolitan industry, since it employs the largest number of employees--182,000, or 38.1 percent of the total industrial population. This far exceeds the second largest number--in wholesaling and retailing --which is 144,000, or 28.7 percent of the industrial population.

Various integrative institutions for administrative purposes and for circulation of goods and services have varying sizes of operations and spheres of influence. They all share the need for easy access to central Tokyo, city subcenters, or the heart of Yokohama. The more centrally located institutions have larger scales of operation, greater spheres of integrative activities, and greater geographical concentration of activities. Conversely, institutions further away from central locations have more varied kinds and structures of integrative institutions, smaller scales of operation, more limited spheres of integrative activities, and a less dense geographical concentration of activities.

Residences are generally distributed in patterns similar to those of institutions because of the premium placed on easy access to places of work by working people; this distribution of residence in turn determines the distribution of institutions dealing in consumer goods. As a whole, then, the distribution of institutions takes a concentric pattern; or it may take the form of a fan, wherein institutions spread out from central locations towards outskirts along the radially formed railroad lines and freeways in the metropolis. It may also take a cogwheel pattern when loop roads and highways develop around such central areas.

Conditions for factory location differ from those for the integrative institutions described above. A big city, with its heavy concentration of political, cultural, and economic institutions and people, is an important market for factories. Although a market may break up into smaller units under economic competition, factories must be so located that they have a favorable ecological distance (the distance in terms of time and cost for transportation) from the market for the purpose of transporting their finished products. Easy access to a big city also ensures the advantage of obtaining information about public demands for goods, price fluctuations, and new technical matters. It also promises a good supply of quality labor from the population of the city. All these factors encourage and induce factories to choose their locations near big cities.

In the meantime, the development of factories stimulates an increase in the demand for labor, and they can absorb working people from near and far. The areas around factories begin to be urbanized as the people settle down, and the existing cities near the factories expand. In areas where factories already exist in numbers, land and sea transportation facilities, supply of water, gas, electricity and other power sources, and sewerage are generally quite adequate; naturally, these areas offer choice locations for new factories. With the added advantages of external economy in such zones, concentration of factories is greatly stimulated. This concentration is further spurred under the favorable economic conditions that result from the concentration of industrial activities and permit closer structural and functional ties among various enterprises and more efficient production by each enterprise.

The establishment of factories also means additional revenues for the communities in which they are located because these factories pay fixed asset and corporation taxes. Part of the profits of the factories is also returned to the communities and their people through payments for raw materials purchased in the communities and through wages to the local people working in these factories. This contributes to the improvement of the standard of living. For these reasons, social capital is invested, tax exemptions are provided, cheap lands are offered, a labor supply is promised, and other favorable conditions are made available by communities wishing to lure factories into their areas. Population and consumption increases follow the establishment and concentration of factories, which further stimulates the development of wholesale and retail businesses, and new urban areas come into existence. When the scale of a factory expands, management and sales functions are usually performed in the heart of a big city at some distance from the production function, which tends to be located in an outlying area.

Depending upon the scale of operation and the types of products manufactured, a factory needs to be located where the size, availability, and price of land is advantageous, where there are sources and outlets for products, where raw materials and finished products can be conveniently transported, where there is access to related industries, to available capital, information, labor, technological skills, sources of power, land, and buildings. In modern Japanese society, the need is keenly felt to eradicate public nuisances that result from the concentrated operation of industry, and factory locations must also be chosen with this need in mind. Since conditions for industrial locations differ from those for administrative, sales, or service institutions, the pattern of industrial distribution naturally differs from the distribution of those institutions.

In Japan, industrial activities greatly depend upon the import of raw materials; as foreign trade expands, dependence on it increases, and as industrial activities expand and intensify, the problem of transportation costs looms large. For this reason, when choosing their locations, factories must also consider accessibility to deep harbors that are suited for mooring large, special vessels. In modern society, national and local governments as well as private organizations try to create conditions favorable for factories by investing money in the reclamation of lands and the improvement of facilities necessary for industrial activities.

In present-day Japan, where scientific analysis of current conditions is inadequate for predicting future developments and where political ability is insufficient for guiding effective advance investments, much time is being spent belatedly in meeting, through administrative and legislative measures, the problems that rapid and heavy urban concentration have caused. Especially near big cities, many factories are forced to move because of high land prices, congested traffic, increasing costs of production and transportation, lack of industrial water supply, ground sinking, the spread of smog, river water pollution caused by drains from industrial activities, noises and vibrations, and high costs of labor. The high prices of land, especially, make it imperative for a factory that needs to expand and improve to sell its current site and purchase a new site for more profitable operation.

The national and local governments have been paying attention to the adverse effects of the excessive concentration of factories and are attempting to control this concentration through a series of legal measures. Among them are the Public Nuisances Control Regulations (Kōgai bōshi jōrei), the Tokyo Metropolitan Complex Improvement Act, the Act Governing Financial Aids for the Development of Small- and Medium-Scale Industries (Chūshō kigyō shinkō shikin josei hō), and other laws regulating industrial establishments in the existing urban centers of the complex. Government bodies are also creating and leasing industrial sites in planned zones, providing services in industrial land acquisition and in the supply of labor, water, gas, and electricity, improving roads and other transportation facilities, and reclaiming lands along seacoasts. Furthermore, the local governments are offering temporary exemptions of fixed asset and corporation taxes and are extending interest-free loans for the purchase of industrial sites, the construction of factories, and the modernization of existing facilities and equipment. All these measures are intended to help relocate factories away from the present areas of concentration.

Structural Change in Industry, 1950-1962

Unlike consumer businesses, especially retail businesses, factories have positive roles to play in the formation and development of cities. Factory locations are more or less fixed at certain places, but they often change as changes take place in national and international economic and technological structures, social norms, goals, and plans, and political power structures. Therefore, problems relating to factories in the Tokyo metropolitan complex in its narrow sense (encompassing the prefectures of Tokyo, Kanagawa, Saitama, and Chiba) must be studied with special reference to changes in the industrial structures of the nation as a whole; it is necessary to relate these changes to the place and structure of the complex in the industrialization of the whole nation.

The postwar industrial development of Japan has been phenomenal. Between 1950 and 1962 the following changes were observed in Japan's industry. (For accurate comparison, statistics for the years up to 1962 were used, although statistics were available for the year 1965. The latter are based on a survey of the enterprises having 30 or more employees each, while the former are based on surveys of enterprises having 4 or more employees each.) The number of enterprises increased from 156,223 in 1950 to 187,112 in 1955; 238,320 in 1960; and 239,134 in 1962; representing a 53 percent increase over the twelve-year period. The number of employees increased from 3,860,814 in 1950 to 4,063,941 in 1955 to 7,601,963 in 1960 and to 8,665,212 in 1962--that is, a 124 percent increase over the period. The amount of goods shipped out in these respective years were ¥2,294,333 million; ¥6,564,427 million; ¥15,293,704 million; and ¥20,560,582 million--an increase of 752 percent over the period. In terms of values added, the figures for the respective years were ¥730,622 million; ¥2,099,095 million; ¥4,837,126 million; and ¥6,665,792 million--an increase of 839 percent.

Despite this rapid economic development, the proportion of the petty enterprises is quite high. The number of enterprises employing 4-29 people each constituted 79.7 percent of all the enterprises in 1950, 85.4 percent in 1955, 81.4 percent in 1960, and 81.7 percent in 1962. The number of employees in these petty enterprises made up 26.6 percent of all the employees in 1950, 34.9 percent in 1955, 29.0 percent in 1960, and 26.1 percent in 1962, while in amounts of goods shipped out the percentages were 14.7 percent, 19.7 percent, 14.6 percent, and 13.5 percent for the respective years. These percentage figures for the petty enterprises are becoming generally smaller each year, but the absolute figures continue to increase.

With a few fluctuations, enterprises of all sizes and employee capacities, as well as the amounts of goods shipped out and the values added, have continued to increase during the period from 1950 to 1962. An increase in these indices is proportionately greater for large-scale enterprises than for smaller ones; and in large-scale operations, there is a larger proportional increase in goods shipped out and values added than in the number of employees. This indicates the advantages enjoyed by large-scale enterprises, and the trend now is towards the expansion of the scale of industrial operations in general.

The ratio of the enterprises employing 500-900 people each to the total number of enterprises in various years was as follows: 0.3 percent (416 establishments) in 1950, 0.3 percent (540) in 1955, 0.4 percent (881) in 1960, and 0.3 percent (812) in 1962. The number of employees in these enterprises constituted 7.5 percent (288,618 employees) of the total number of employees in industry in 1950, 7.5 percent (375,316) in 1955, 8.0 percent (608,192) in 1960, and 6.6 percent (568,470) in 1962. As for the goods shipped out by the enterprises, the percentages were 10.9 percent (¥249,782 million) in 1950, 11.4 percent (¥749,672 million) in 1955, 12.6 percent (¥1,935,371 million) in 1960, and 8.5 percent (¥1,755,968 million) in 1962.

As for the enterprises employing 1,000 or more workers each, the ratio to the total number of enterprises in the country was as follows: 0.2 percent (339 establishments) in 1950, 0.2 percent (376) in 1955, 0.3 percent (618) in 1960, and 0.3 percent (680) in 1962. Their employees constituted 19.4 percent (750,277) of all in 1950, 16.2 percent (804,492) in 1955, 18.0 percent (1,373,748) in 1960, and 27.3 percent (2,368,308) in 1962. The percentage of the goods shipped out by these enterprises was 26.8 percent (¥615,879 million) in 1950, 24.2 percent (¥1,592,843 million) in 1955, 31.1 percent (¥4,759,950 million) in 1960, and 44.7 percent (¥9,182,801 million) in 1962.

As can be seen from the statistics, the importance of large-scale enterprises is increasing in Japan's industry in terms of number, number of employees, goods shipped out, and values added. On the other hand, many petty enterprises still exist in Japan and, under current industrial conditions, these small enterprises cannot be ignored.

By classifying industrial enterprises according to two major types--light and heavy industries--and looking at changes in 1950-1962 in various categories with respect to the number of enterprises and employees, amounts of goods shipped out, and values added, we find the following. (Light industries include enterprises dealing in food, textiles, clothing, lumber, furniture, pulp, printing, rubber, leather, and pottery; heavy industries produce or refine chemicals, petroleum and coal, iron and steel, nonferrous metals, fabricated metals, machinery, electrical appliances and equipment, transportation equipment, precision instruments, and weapons.)

In 1950, the number of textile enterprises was the greatest of all the light industries--they accounted for 18.6 percent of the total--followed by 16.8 percent for the food industry, 14.9 percent for the lumber industry, and 6.5 percent for the pottery industry. Among the heavy industries, those producing machinery topped the list with 7.5 percent, followed by 5.5 percent for the fabricated metal industry, 3.8 percent for the chemical industry, and 2.8 percent for the transportation equipment industry. In that year, 1950, the light industries made up 74.1 percent of all industries; the remaining 25.9 percent was accounted for by heavy industries.

There was little change in the rankings of these various enterprises up to 1962, but in that year the proportions of textile, food, clothing, and pottery industries were smaller than in previous years. Among the heavy industries, the proportions dealing in machinery, fabricated metals, and electrical appliances and equipment increased. The percentage of the light and heavy industries in 1962 was 70.4 percent and 29.6 percent, respectively, indicating the advance of heavy industries.

In 1950, the textile industry had the greatest number of employees in light industries (21.6 percent of the total), and this was followed by 9.0 percent for the food industry, 7.1 percent for the lumber industry, 5.1 percent for pottery, and 3.8 percent for printing. Among the heavy industries, the machinery producing enterprises had the largest number of employees (8.6 percent of the total); the next largest groups of employers were the chemical industry with 8.5 percent, the iron and steel and nonferrous metals industry with 8.0 percent, and the transportation equipment industry with 7.0 percent. The shares of light and heavy industries in terms of employee population were 58.1 percent and 41.9 percent, respectively. Changes made by 1962 show that the textile industry still had the greatest number of employees, but that its proportion to the total employee population in the light industries was down to 13.6 percent. The proportion of food industry employees increased a little to 9.9 percent, and those of the lumber and pottery industries decreased to 5.3 percent and 4.9 percent, respectively. As a whole, the total number of employees in the light industries decreased in proportion to the total industrial employee population (to 51.9 percent), whereas the proportion of the heavy industrial employee population increased to 47.8 percent of the total. In the heavy industries, an increase in proportion was registered in the machinery industry (to 10.1 percent) and the electrical appliances and equipment industry (to 9.5 percent), while a decrease occurred in the iron and steel and nonferrous metals industry (to 7.6 percent) and the transportation equipment industry (to 6.5 percent).

In amount of goods shipped out, the textile industry headed the list for the light industries in 1950, with 21.6 percent, followed by 12.5 percent for the food industry, 3.7 percent for lumber, 3.6 percent for pulp, and 3.3 percent for pottery. By 1962, however, the textile industry had dropped to second place, with 9.9 percent, behind the food industry, which had 11.9 percent, a figure smaller than in 1950. A slight increase was made in the pulp (3.8 percent) and pottery (3.5 percent) industries. The total output by light industries dropped in proportion to the total industrial output from 54.8 percent in 1950 to 42.4 percent in 1962. In the heavy industries, the greatest advance was made in the electrical appliances and equipment industry (9.3 percent). A decrease was registered in the iron and steel industry (9.3 percent) and the chemical industry (9.1 percent), but increases occurred in the transportation equipment industry (9.1 percent) and the general machinery industry (8.9 percent). The shares of heavy industry in the total industrial output of 1950 and 1962 was 45.2 percent and 57.6 percent, respectively, replacing light industry in importance.

In terms of values added, the chemical and heavy industries are still increasing in importance. Of the total values added for the heavy industries, the chemical industry in 1950 made up 14.8 percent of the total, followed by 12.3 percent for iron and steel and other metal industries, 6.7 percent for the machinery industry, and 5.6 percent for the transportation equipment industry. In 1962, electrical appliances and equipment industry topped the list with 11.7 percent, followed by 11.4 percent for the machinery industry, 10.2 percent for the chemical industry, 8.9 percent for the transportation equipment industry, and 8.9 percent for iron and steel and the other metals industry. Thus, the total values added in the heavy industries accounted for 59.2 percent of the values added in all industries, which is a greater proportion than their total outputs.

Of the light industries in 1950, the textile industry accounted for 18.9 percent of the total values added, compared with 8.1 percent for the food industry, 4.8 percent for printing, 4.4 percent for pottery, and 3.8 percent for pulp. But by 1962, the food industry values increased to 9.1 percent, dropping the textile industry to second place with 8.5 percent, while the proportions of pottery, printing, and pulp industries were 4.8 percent, 4.4 percent, and 3.3 percent, respectively. The light industries thus accounted for 40.8 percent of the total values added in all industries.

Between 1950 and 1962 the total number of industrial enterprises increased 1.5 times, the total number of employees increased 2.2 times, the total amount of goods shipped out increased 8.5 times, and the total values added increased 9.4 times. While many petty enterprises still exist, large-scale industries have increased their proportions of employees, outputs, and values added in the total industrial system of the country, and an increasing number of industries are becoming large-scale operations. The trend of change in industrial activities has been towards a proportional decrease of light industry and a proportional increase of heavy industry.

The industries contributing most to the economic growth of the country through increased outputs and rates of production include the following: the electrical appliances and equipment industry, whose production of television sets, radios, washers, and refrigerators increased 1.8 times, 6 times, and 5 times, respectively, between 1955 and 1963; the transportation equipment industry, in which an increase in production of trucks and cars for private use was particularly noticeable; and the machinery industry. Thus, light industry had a greater weight in the total industrial system of the country in the prewar periods. (Heavy industry generally represented capital goods, such as ships, trucks, trains, and electrical and construction equipment.) The emphasis in recent years has been not only on the production of installation machinery but on directly market-bound durable consumer goods. According to Rostow's scheme, Japan has reached the mass consumption stage of economic development, joining the Western industrial nations in this respect. This expansion of the consumer goods industry represents a balanced industrial structure that is common in advanced industrial nations.

A Regional Comparison of Industrial Development, 1950-1962

The rapid development and structural change of Japan's industry, as we have seen above, is not uniform throughout the country. Industrial development and change assumes different paces in different locations. Certain areas invite specific types of industries for better profit-making operations, and a concentration of those industries results. Concentration continues until the adverse effects, as well as restrictions imposed by public legal measures, are recognized by the industries. In other areas, the number of industrial establishments decreases owing to unfavorable conditions of location. The gap between areas of industrial concentration and sparseness becomes greater, and each locality undergoes further structural change, partly under the influences of various administrative measures taken for the benefit of national welfare.

Changes are taking place in the industrial structure of each region of the country. These industrial changes accompany social and economic structure changes in the regions, which, in turn, are closely related to one another. We shall now examine the changes in different regions with respect to the number of enterprises and employees, amounts of goods shipped out, and values added, with reference to the relative weight of light and heavy industries during the period 1950 to 1962. For comparison, we divide the whole country into 13 regions as follows: Hokkaidō, Tōhoku (including the prefectures of Aomori, Iwate, Miyagi, Akita, Yamagata, Fukushima, and Nīgata), Inland Kantō (Ibaragi, Tochigi, Gunma, Nagano, and Yamanashi), Coastal Kantō (Saitama, Chiba, Tokyo, and Kanagawa), Tōkai (Gifu, Shizuoka, Aichi, and Mie), Hokuriku (Toyama, Ishikawa, and Fukui), Inland Kinki (Shiga, Kyoto, and Nara), Coastal Kinki (Osaka, Hyōgo, and Wakayama), San'in (Tottori and Shimane), San'yō (Okayama, Hiroshima, and Yamaguchi), Shikoku (Tokushima, Kagawa, Ehime, and Kōchi), North Kyūshū (Fukuoka, Saga, Nagasaki, and Ōita), and South Kyūshū (Kumamoto, Miyazaki, and Kagoshima).

Assuming the index number for the total number of enterprises in the country in 1950 to be 100, the index numbers for the 13 regions were: 2.8 for Hokkaidō, 8.7 for Tōhoku, 8.9 for Inland Kantō, 18.9 for Coastal Kantō, 16.8 for Tōkai, 4.6 for Hokuriku, 4.5 for Inland Kinki, 14.4 for Coastal Kinki, 1.2 for San'in, 5.6 for San'yō, 4.6 for Shikoku, 5.7 for North Kyūshū, and 3.3 for South Kyūshū.

Thus, enterprises concentrate in Coastal Kantō, Coastal Kinki, and Tōkai, where the combined number of enterprises makes up 50.1 percent of the national total.

In 1962, index numbers decreased for 9 regions: 2.7 for Hokkaidō, 7.8 for Tōhoku, 7.8 for Inland Kantō (whose index for 1955 was also 7.8), 3.9 for Hokuriku, 1.1 for San'in, 5.2 for San'yō, 3.4 for Shikoku, 4.4 in North Kyūshū, and 2.6 for South Kyūshū. Index numbers increased for 4 regions: 23.1 for Coastal Kantō, 17.5 for Tōkai, 4.7 for Inland Kinki, and 16.0 for Coastal Kinki. The three regions of Coastal Kantō, Coastal Kinki, and Tōkai increased their combined index number from 50.1 in 1950 to 56.6 in 1962.

In the number of employees in Coastal Kantō, Coastal Kinki, and Tōkai also increased; their combined index number rose from 53.5 in 1950 to 56.0 in 1962. As for the amounts of goods shipped out, the three regions' combined index number was 58.3 in 1950 and 67.8 in 1962, and the index number for the values added was 56.9 in 1950 and 68.4 in 1962.

Looking more closely at the amounts of goods shipped out from Coastal Kantō, Coastal Kinki, and Tōkai, compared with other regions of the country, we find that the high index number of 21.9 for Coastal Kantō in 1950 further increased to 30.2 in 1962, and that Tōkai's index number was 14.8 in 1950 and 16.0 in 1962. The index number for Coastal Kinki remained at 21.6 for both 1950 and 1962, although there was an increase in the absolute figures for its outputs. Index numbers for the other regions all decreased, except for Inland Kantō where, under the influence of the rapidly expanding Coastal Kantō, an increase was registered, especially after 1960, as can be seen in the figures 4.4 in 1955 and 5.1 in 1962. Therefore, Coastal Kantō and Tōkai are the only regions that have shown a significantly steady increase in the amounts of goods shipped out since 1950. The combined amount of goods shipped out in Coastal Kantō (which is the core of the Tokyo metropolitan complex) and in the neighboring Inland Kantō region made up 26.4 percent of the national total in 1950 and increased to 35.3 percent by 1962. Their combined number of enterprises made up 31.3 percent of the national total in 1962, while their employee population and values added were 36.7 percent each of the national totals. Thus, the Tokyo metropolitan complex, which encompasses the Coastal and Inland Kantō regions, is steadily increasing in importance.

Concerning industrial changes in relation to regional structural changes, we find that in Japan the relative importance of so-called traditional, native light industries, or those whose locations are determined by the availability of resources, is decreasing. These industries include food products manufacturing, textiles, lumber and wood products manufacturing, and pulp and paper products manufacturing. Also decreasing is the relative importance of the regions of Hokkaidō, Tōhoku, Hokuriku, Shikoku, and Kyūshū, which still greatly depend on light industries.

Heavy industry has been developing at a remarkable rate, evidenced by the growth of the coastal industries of petroleum and oil products manufacturing, the chemical industry, and the iron and steel industry. Inland industries such as machine production, electrical appliances and equipment manufacturing, transportation equipment and machinery manufacturing, and precision instruments manufacturing have also advanced. The Tokaido megalopolis, which encompasses the Tokyo, Chūkyō, and Kinki metropolitan complexes and extends from the Chiba to Hyōgo prefectures along the Tōkaidō coast, has a great number of heavy and chemical industrial establishments. The position of the Tokyo metropolitan complex, especially, has become more preponderant in the industrial structure of the country, since it has a greater concentration of population and industry and a greater geographical area than any other metropolitan complex. Its various functions are being performed, and their influences are felt, over wide areas.

Considering the approximate agreement in geographical identity of the Coastal Kantō region with the highly urbanized, organically structured core of the Tokyo metropolitan complex, for the conveniences of using the statistical data, we shall refer to that region as being the core of the complex.

In Tokyo, the center of the core, the total amount of goods shipped out was ¥297,333 million in 1950 (12.8 percent of the national total), but it went up to ¥3,166,281 million by 1962 (15.4 percent of the national total). The employee population of Tokyo made up 15.2 percent of the national total in 1962. In comparison, the amount of goods shipped out and the employee population in Kanagawa Prefecture in 1962 was 10.5 percent and 6.4 percent of the national totals, while the percentages for Saitama were 2.8 percent and 3.5 percent, respectively, and for Chiba, 1.5 percent in each category. Thus, we can see the degree of the importance of Tokyo and Kanagawa in the industrial structure of the complex. In terms of rates of increase during the twelve-year period, however, Tokyo's employee population increased by 2.8 times, and its output of goods increased by 10.6 times. In Kanagawa the increases in the respective categories were 3.0 times and 15.2 times, in Saitama 3.2 and 13.4 times, and in Chiba 3.0 and 13.3 times. This shows a greater rate of increase in employee population and in output of goods in the fringe areas of the core of the complex than in the core (Tokyo).

In 1950, the output of Tokyo's chemical industry constituted 15.5 percent of the city's total output of goods, while the output of the printing and publishing industry made up 13.0 percent; the food industry, 9.8 percent; steel and other metals industry, 9.6 percent; metal products manufacturing, 7.4 percent; textile industry, 6.7 percent; the electrical appliances and equipment industry, 6.3 percent; and machinery manufacturing, 5.7 percent. In 1962, the figures were 13.2 percent for electrical appliances and equipment, 11.6 percent for machinery, 9.4 percent for printing and publishing, 9.0 percent for the food industry, 8.3 percent for the chemical industry, 7.7 percent for metal products, and 7.0 percent for transportation equipment. These statistics indicate that the principal reason for Japan's high economic growth was the great strides made in producing electrical appliances and equipment and general machinery.

The heavy industry of Tokyo increased its ratio to the city's total industrial activity from 52.9 percent to 61.9 percent during the twelve-year period from 1950 and 1962. Taking a look at the scales of the enterprises, however, we find that in the country as a whole the number of enterprises employing 3 or fewer workers each constituted 50.3 percent of the total number of enterprises. Those with 4-29 employees comprised 40.4 percent, those having 30-99 employees made up 7.0 percent, those with 100-299 employees constituted 1.7 percent, and those with 300 or more employees comprised 0.6 percent. In Tokyo, by contrast, the enterprises employing 3 or fewer people made up 31.6 percent of the city's total number of enterprises; those with 4-29 employees constituted 53.4 percent; those with 30-99 employees, 11.6 percent; those with 100-299 employees, 2.6 percent; and those with 300 or more employees, 0.8 percent.

These figures tell us that, despite the great development in heavy and chemical industrial establishments in Tokyo, many petty enterprises still remain.

The prefectures of Kanagawa, Saitama, and Chiba adjoin Tokyo and are tied to it through networks of transportation facilities; together they constitute the largest commercial, residential, and industrial community structure in the country. Tokyo and Kanagawa, above all, occupy the most important position in the industrial structure of the complex, constituting the compact Keihin industrial region.

During the period of economic growth from 1950 to 1962, the national average of the amounts of goods shipped out of various parts of the country increased by 9 times, but the amount in Tokyo increased by 10.6 times. The amount in Tokyo in 1962 represented 15.4 percent of the national total, which was the highest proportion in the country. The industrial development of Kanagawa Prefecture, which had a high rate of increase in heavy and chemical industrial production, was also remarkable. In 1950, Kanagawa Prefecture ranked fifth in the country in the amount of goods shipped out (6.1 percent of the national total), but during the twelve-year period the amount increased by 15.2 times (10.5 percent of the national total in 1962). The prefecture ranked third, close behind second-ranked Osaka whose output in 1950 and 1962 constituted 12.4 percent and 13.3 percent, respectively, of the national total. The prefectures of Saitama and Chiba likewise increased their output of goods--by 12.4 times in the former and 13.3 times in the latter.

These production increases in Tokyo's three neighboring prefectures can be properly understood when viewed in the light of the expansion of Tokyo's industrial activities, which has reached a saturation point. Furthermore, the rapid progress of industry in such inland prefectures as Ibaragi and Gunma can be explained as a process of absorption of those prefectures by the expanding core of the Tokyo metropolitan complex.

The prefecture of Kanagawa, which, together with Tokyo, constitutes the Keihin industrial region, includes the important industrial centers of Kawasaki City and the wards of Tsurumi and Kanagawa of Yokohama City. Its total output of goods amounted to ¥142,126 million in 1950, constituting 6.1 percent of the national total, and increased to ¥2,159,385 million in 1962; the share in the national total increased by 4.1 percent to 10.5 percent. Shares of various industries in the total output of the prefecture in 1950 were: 25.3 percent for the primary metal industry, 15.5 percent for precision instruments manufacturing, 14.3 percent for the chemical industry, 12.1 percent for the food industry, 10.3 percent for transportation equipment manufacturing, 4.3 percent for electrical appliances manufacturing, 3.9 percent for the petroleum products industry, and 3.8 percent for the pottery industry. Thus, the production of heavy industry was already high in 1950, constituting 76.3 percent of the total industrial production of the prefecture. By 1962, the percentage was still higher at 79.2 percent. In that year, 10.3 percent of the total industrial production was accounted for by the transportation equipment industry, 18.6 percent by the electrical appliances industry, 13.4 percent by the primary metal industry, 11.7 percent by the food industry, 8.0 percent by machinery manufacturing, 7.6 percent by the chemical industry, 6.4 percent by the petroleum industry, and 3.4 percent by the fabricated metal industry. Progress was particularly noticeable in the production of such durable consumer goods as electrical appliances and equipment and motor vehicles; this progress represented a major factor in the high rate of economic growth in Japan and for the change in its economic structure.

Even in this prefecture with advanced heavy industry, the ratio of the number of petty enterprises to the total number of enterprises is high. In 1962, the number of enterprises employing 3 or fewer people each made up 34.2 percent of the total number of enterprises; those employing 4-29 people comprised 56.2 percent; those employing 30-99 people, 12.8 percent; those with 100-299 people, 4.3 percent; and those with 300 or more, 2.5 percent. Thus, the proportion of medium-scale enterprises was relatively high, and the proportion of each of the various categories of enterprises mentioned was higher in this prefecture than in any other prefecture.

The total number of enterprises in the prefecture in 1962 constituted 2.8 percent of the total number of enterprises in the nation; the prefecture ranked eighth in this respect. The number of employees in all the enterprises of the prefecture was 6.4 percent of the national total, ranking fourth nationally, and the amount of goods shipped out and the amount of value added were each 10.5 percent of the national total, ranking third in the nation.

Located around large-scale parent assembly plants are many small factories producing parts for various products, and around wholesale manufacturing firms exist a number of petty subcontracting establishments. This is the industrial structure of this prefecture, which is basically noted for its heavy industrial activities. In many other industrial areas of the country, excepting kombinat zones, the more common structure is one with a more inflated bottom than was found in Kanagawa.

The inland industrial area stretching from northern Tokyo along the Arakawa River and the Tōhoku railroad line constitutes the Saitama industrial region, which includes such centers as Kawaguchi, Toda, and Warabi. The proximity of the region to the big consumer area of Tokyo, coupled with the fact that an increasing number of factories are being relocated here from the crowded Tokyo area, has greatly influenced the phenomenal development of industry in the region.

In 1950, Saitama's total amount of goods shipped out was ¥45,261 million, or 1.9 percent of the national total; it ranked 14th nationally in this respect. By 1962, however, the total output increased to ¥556,019 million, and its share in the national total increased to 2.8 percent (it ranked 8th). As for the shares of various industries in 1950, the textile industry produced 24.9 percent of the total prefectural output; the food industry, 15.1 percent; the clothing industry, 9.3 percent; transportation equipment manufacturing, 8.6 percent; the primary metals industry, 8.6 percent; the machinery industry, 5.8 percent; the chemical industry, 5.1 percent; and pottery, 4.6 percent. Light industries had greater weight than heavy industries.

By 1962, industrial production changed as follows: 14.3 percent for transportation equipment manufacturing, 13.3 percent for the primary metal industry, 11.3 percent for the food industry, 8.9 percent for the machinery industry, 8.4 percent for the textile industry, 6.3 percent for the electrical appliances and equipment manufacturing, 5.9 percent for pottery, and 5.2 percent for the fabricated metals industry. Heavy industry has been developing greatly. Particularly noteworthy is the development of inland-type industries--the manufacturing of transportation equipment and electrical appliances. Favored by the physical proximity to the expanding mass consumption area, food, clothing, and furniture industries are also making great strides.

As for the scales of enterprises and their ratios in Saitama Prefecture, the enterprises employing 3 or fewer people each made up 46.4 percent of the total number of enterprises in the prefecture; those with 4-29 employees had 42.9 percent; those with 30-99 employees, 8.9 percent; those with 100-299 employees, 2.2 percent; and those with 300 or more employees, 0.6 percent. These figures are larger than the national averages, but compared with Tokyo and Kanagawa there are more petty enterprises, especially the small enterprises that have 3 or fewer employees each. Thus, in 1962, Saitama's share in the total number of enterprises in the country was 3.3 percent (ranking 6th), and the shares in the total number of employees, in the total amount of goods shipped out, and the total values added were 3.5 percent (ranking 7th), 2.8 percent (ranking 8th), and 2.8 percent (ranking 7th), respectively.

The newly developed coastal industrial city of Chiba, which lies contiguous to Tokyo along the Tokyo Bay coast, had in 1950 a total output of products amounting to ¥23,143 million, or 1.0 percent of the national total, and ranked 27th in the nation. But in 1962 the amount reached ¥316,812 million, and the share in the national total increased by 0.5 percent to 1.5 percent; the prefecture passed twelve prefectures to rank 15th in the nation.

Shares of various industries in the total output of the prefecture in 1950 were as follows: 56.5 percent for the food industry, 13.9 percent for textiles, 4.5 percent for chemicals, 3.6 percent for machinery, 3.6 percent for lumber, 2.7 percent for primary metals, 2.5 percent for fabricated metals, and 2.4 percent for pulp. These figures show an overwhelmingly greater output by light industries than by heavy industries. In 1962, however, the industrial structure of the prefecture showed a heavier concentration of heavy industrial activities, as seen in the following shares of various industries: 28.2 percent for the primary metals industry, 26.4 percent for food, 8.2 percent for electrical equipment, 7.0 percent for chemicals, 6.5 percent for machinery, 5.5 percent for fabricated metals, 4.6 percent for pottery, and 3.1 percent for textiles. This expansion of heavy industry reflects the expansion of Tokyo's industries into the Chiba area in search of more land, water, and the conveniences of sea transportation. Particularly remarkable was the development of the iron and steel industry, the manufacturing of petroleum products, the chemical industry, and other coastal-type industries centering in the cities of Chiba, Goi, and Ichihara. The development of the iron and steel industry, spearheaded mainly by the Kawasaki Steel Corporation, was especially noteworthy, as shown by its production increase by 7.5 times over the twelve-year period.

Functional and Structural Classification of Industrial Areas: North

The preceding description of changes in the industrial structures of various prefectures was based on data on these prefectures as administrative units. Industrial plants are structurally and functionally related to one another, and owing to their connections with many elements in society, these plants are located in areas that have the economic, social, and cultural conveniences for their operation. Under these circumstances, then, the distribution of industrial plants does not usually follow local administrative boundaries. For this reason, it is necessary to classify industrial areas of the Tokyo metropolitan complex according to the types of functions and structures of various industries and to examine the structural relationships and changes of the various areas. There are several excellent studies on the subject, such as "Tokyo ni okeru kōgyō bunpu" [Industrial distribution in Tokyo] by Tsujimoto and others, "Kantō no kōgyō chiiki kubun" [Industrial zones of Kantō] by Itakura, "Keihin kōgyō chitai no chiiki kōzō" [Community structure of the Keihin industrial region] by Itakura and others, "Keihin kōgyō chitai" [The Keihin industrial region] by Sumiya and others, and "Nihon no kōgyō-ka" [Industrialization of Japan] by Kōda Seiki and others. I take the liberty of making use of these studies, and with the addition of my own research data, I now proceed to apply a human ecological approach to a study of the industrial structure of the Tokyo metropolitan complex and the process of its change.

It is difficult to select a proper standard out of the many standards available for delimiting geographical areas of industrial concentration. Industrial activities that produce daily consumer goods are complex in character. Many industrial enterprises exist that are said to represent traditional activities peculiar to certain areas, regardless of the degrees of urbanization of those areas. The main reason for the concentration of factories and the formation of industrial zones in the Tokyo metropolitan complex is the drive for the great profits that can be expected from such concentration of related industries. It seems most appropriate to use the distribution of the durable consumer goods industry as the standard for delimiting urban industrial zones, since its basic operation involves the procurement of many parts and assembling them into finished products. Thus, Itakura took the municipalities that produced values totaling ¥100 million each in 1960 and selected the ones whose durable consumer goods industry comprised more than a third of the total production. He presented the area around Tokyo that encompassed all those selected municipalities as the industrial region of the Tokyo metropolitan complex. This region is encircled by such cities as Narashino, Matsudo, Sōka, and Koshigaya in the east, Shōwa, Kuki, Ageo, and Hazayama in the north, Yamato, Akishima, Hino, and Sagamihara in the west, and Atsugi, Hatano, and Ninomiya in the south.

The region delimited by Itakura has 13.4 percent of the total number of factories in the nation and 28.5 percent of the national total of values added. The structure of this region is changing, and it is difficult to clearly demarcate its geographical area, but it represents the most appropriately limited region showing the distribution of concentrated urban industrial activities.

The districts within this region having heavy concentration of factories and high production density include the ward section of Tokyo (excluding residential Nerima and Suginami Wards), Kawasaki City, the wards of Tsurumi, Kanagawa, Nishi, Naka, Minami, and Hodogaya of Yokohama City, and the northern cities of Kawaguchi, Warabi, and Toda. The combined number of factories and the combined total values added in these districts constitute 86 percent each of the totals for the Tokyo metropolitan complex, making the districts the core of the industrial region of the complex. Outside this core are areas of small-scale industrial concentration, such as Ōmiya, Urawa, Mitaka, Musashino, Chōfu, Hino, Machida, Sagamihara, and Atsugi. Thus, the urban industrial region extends some 30 kilometers eastward from the center of Tokyo, 40 kilometers towards the north, 50 kilometers towards the west, and 60 kilometers in the southwest direction. Industrial zones in the outskirts of this region represent the areas in which centrally-located industries have been relocated; these outskirt industrial zones have attained a high level of development since 1955.

The location and structural changes of factories differ from those of business offices and stores. For a factory, the central section of Tokyo is the place where the main office is located. Administrative and sales functions are performed there, with respect to capital utilization and general management, procurement of raw materials, and sales of finished products. The center of Tokyo is also a large consumer market for the large-scale integrative institutions and for the people that concentrate in the area; the city as a whole is a significant consumer market as well as an important source of labor supply. For these reasons, it would be beneficial to the operation of industrial plants to be located near the center of Tokyo. However, Tokyo's central area is the second lowest in the number of factories; only exclusively residential areas such as Nerima and Suginami Wards are lower. Because of the high land value and the limited land space, central Tokyo is not suitable for factory location, except for those factories dealing with a great volume of raw and finished materials that involve transportation problems.

In total number of factories, the wards of Chiyoda, Chūō, Minato, and Bunkyō, the most centrally located in Tokyo, rank 21st, 17th, 14th, and 12th, respectively, among the 23 wards of the city. The ward section of the city shows an increase in the total amount of goods shipped out in general, but the number of factories in the section is decreasing because of the rising land prices and the legal restrictions that are applied to industrial establishments in the area. Chiyoda Ward, especially, is losing factories rapidly.

Almost all industrial activities in central Tokyo are related to the production of daily consumer commodities and to the printing and publishing of commercial and special newspapers, books, and magazines--industries that reflect Tokyo's image as the center of communications activities. In 1962, Tokyo housed 53.8 percent of all the publishers and printers in the country; about 70 percent of the firms were concentrated in the central section, including the wards of Bunkyō, Chūō, and Chiyoda. Only 13 of all the publishers in Tokyo have 1,000 or more employees each, and 62 percent of the publishers have 10 or fewer employees each. Printing is done by 79 percent of the publishers, but only 2 percent of them have modern printing equipment. Many of these establishments are characterized by low standards of technical work.

In the eastern section of Tokyo are Sumida, Kōtō, and Arakawa Wards and also Taitō Ward, which has the character of a Tokyo subcenter. These wards have the greatest concentration of petty factories in the ward section of the city--32 percent--and their production makes up 20 percent of all production in the Tokyo metropolitan complex. Production of daily consumer commodities in this section of Tokyo constitutes 60 percent of the total production. In Sumida and Taitō Wards, the production of leather articles, hosiery, and small-scale metal and chemical industrial products--such as watches and clocks, injection needles, hardware for daily use, soap, toothpaste, cosmetics, drug bottles, and rubber shoes and boots--is more prevalent. Arakawa Ward produces leather works and sporting goods; Kōtō Ward's special industry relates to lumber and wood products. All of these industrial activities are very small in scale; each establishment employs 30 or fewer people. In the category of durable consumer goods, Arakawa and Taitō Wards have bicycle assembly and bicycle parts factories. Their production is more than a third of the national total in this field. Some factories are found in southern coastal areas, where such bulky products as construction lumber, bridge materials, and cranes are produced.

The hosiery industry, which produces such goods as gloves, socks, stockings, cardigans, sweaters, neckties, and cotton material for kimonos and dresses, is an important daily consumer goods industry for the Tokyo metropolitan complex. This industry is heavily concentrated in the two wards of Sumida and Kōtō, where 55 percent of all the hosiery industrial firms in the complex are located, and 2 percent of the total national production of hosiery (¥90 billion a year) is registered. Some hosiery industry is also found in Saitama and Chiba Prefectures. Concentration in the two wards noted above is owing to the close connections they maintain with the central wards of Taitō and Chūō where most transactions in hosiery products are made.

Tokyo's hosiery firms are generally small scale. Of the total of 2,101 factories, 37 percent employ two or three people, 86 percent have 19 or fewer employees, and only 10 percent have 100 or more employees. Except for those large-scale manufacturers having 3,300 or more employees each, the hosiery manufacturers in Tokyo are not able to produce on speculation, take orders individually, and decide on designs by themselves. Instead, they are subordinated to wholesalers. Some manufacturers produce and sell a large quantity of goods in direct collaboration with wholesalers, but many are small producers who subcontract for big manufacturers. Since the industry requires much needlework, there are professional cutters and needleworkers who employ a few hands each; under these professionals many individuals work at home under contract and at minimal wages. Relationships between parent producers and subcontractors usually grow out of the traditional master-apprentice relationship, but in matters of wages and time for delivery of goods the relationships often take on a control-subordination pattern.

The leather industry is prevalent in Taitō and Arakawa Wards. Because carcasses of cattle and hogs are used in this industry, special zones have been designated for purposes of health and sanitation; those wards constitute such zones. The production of leather goods in Tokyo makes up 25 percent of the total national production, the greatest proportion in the nation. Establishments in the industry are very small in size, however; 70 percent of the establishments employ only 5-19 people each. Most of the establishments are closely tied to wholesalers and related industrial enterprises (leather dyeing, fur finishing, and those dealing with oils and fats) and, as they produce, supply their products to wholesalers according to their own judgement.

Demands for leather products have been increasing recently, but factories in the ward section of Tokyo are faced with difficulties in physical expansion because of the high prices of land. Because the factories are located on low land, poor drainage is a sanitation problem and there is also a shortage of water for manufacturing. There are also transportation and shortage of labor problems. Under these conditions, relocation to peripheral areas has been discussed and recommended. In view of the anticipated disadvantages to individual related enterprises moving away from one another, however, it has been deemed necessary to relocate groups of related enterprises as units and to urge the rationalization of the collective production pattern.

As a result of the great increase in the demand for lumber that has accompanied the recent boom in housing construction and general industrial development, lumber piles at lumber yards in Kōtō and Sumida Wards and in Yamashita of Naka Ward in Yokohama have become large. Lumber consumption in Tokyo in 1950 was about two million cubic meters, but it reached six million in 1959, a threefold increase in ten years. Three-fourths of the lumber came from Tōhoku, Kinki, and Hokkaidō, and the rest was imported from overseas. Kōtō and Sumida Wards have 70 percent of the lumber wholesalers in Tokyo, 50 percent of the lumber mills, and 80 percent of the lumber mill productivity. Factories producing construction materials are found in various industrial districts, but the plywood industry is concentrated mostly in Adachi and Kōtō Wards. Its related industry--furniture manufacturing--is concentrated in Arakawa Ward, which has 20 percent of all the furniture manufacturers of Tokyo. Luxury furniture is produced mainly in Minato Ward; steel furniture is produced in Ōta Ward.

As for the durable consumer goods industry in this area, the district around Minamisenjū of Arakawa Ward, extending to Taitō Ward, has bicycle manufacturing. Tokyo, Osaka, and Nagoya are the three bicycle manufacturing centers of Japan; Tokyo alone has about one-third of all the bicycle manufacturers in the country and produces 40 percent of the national total. And in the district mentioned above 80 percent of all the manufacturers of Tokyo are concentrated. Because of the relatively simple techniques of bicycle manufacturing, wholesalers have exercised control of production, sales (in domestic and foreign markets), and financing in this field. These wholesalers, called manufacturing wholesalers, assign the production of 2,000 parts in 16 kinds of bicycles to subcontractors. They themselves assemble these parts into finished products. Mass production of bicycle parts on a large scale is being tried, but the manufacturing is still of small scale in general; each manufacturer employs 16 people on the average. Parts-producing factories congregate in clusters near the wholesalers for convenience of receiving orders and delivering products, and also for the better business operation that is ensured by geographical proximity. Thus, the manufacturing of bicycles represents a wholesaler-controlled, putting-out system industry. In the automobile industry, both foreign export and domestic demand seem to be at a peak at present.

The northern Tokyo wards of Toshima, Itabashi, and Kita and the adjoining cities of Kawaguchi, Warabi, and Toda of Saitama Prefecture make up another industrial zone. It is responsible for 8 percent of the total production of the Tokyo metropolitan complex, and its activities relate about equally to durable and daily consumer commodities.

The northern Tokyo wards, excluding the city of Kawaguchi which has developed as a center of the casting industry since the Edo period, represents a new industrial district that developed after 1935 as a result of the relocation of industries from the eastern and southern (Keihin) regions of the metropolitan complex. As far as durable consumer goods are concerned, Itabashi Ward is, like Ōta and Shinagawa, a center of the camera industry and related activities, as well as a center of binocular manufacturing (though on a smaller scale than the camera industry). In the production of daily consumer goods, relief printing, paper products manufacturing, and the food industry are prevalent; some domestic-type production of sundry goods is also found. Special steel and nonferrous metal industry exists, as does the industry classified as part of chemical and heavy industry that actually deals in such daily commodities as chemical drugs, ink, paints, and medicine. The city of Kawaguchi has changed from being a production center of small cast articles to one of big cast machinery and equipment since the demand has increased for such products owing to the recent development of machinery and iron and steel industry in Tokyo.

Camera manufacturing is a durable consumer goods category that has made great progress in recent years. A camera is made up of some 2,000 parts, and there are several assembly plants and many petty factories producing such parts. Of the 219 factories in Tokyo, 55 percent are parts-producing factories that employ 30 or fewer workers. In fact, 80 percent of these small-scale factories have five or fewer employees each. On the other hand, six big plants have 1,000 or more employees each and control 60 percent of the market for cameras. No assembly plant makes all the necessary parts of the camera for itself, but each makes and processes a few important parts in addition to handling the lens grinding operation. Of the parts of a camera, the lens and shutter are mass produced by large-scale manufacturers; the other parts are all manufactured by small producers.

Since cameras are not daily necessities of life, their production is easily influenced by the general economic conditions in society, and demands for preferred models fluctuate sharply from time to time. Thus, camera manufacturing is an unstable enterprise; many firms go bankrupt. Furthermore, there is the problem of the responsibility for cost reduction being shifted from big manufacturers to petty manufacturers. Many parts-producing factories have no direct individual connections with assembly plants, so that the relationships between assembly plants and subcontracting factories remain unsteady and fluctuating. The assembly plants and the subcontracting factories congregate in certain general areas that have become known as camera production centers.

In the binocular manufacturing industry, 95 percent of the products are intended for export, and 90 percent of the factories are located in Itabashi Ward. As in camera production, there are many parts to be manufactured, and these parts are generally produced by subcontracting factories which take orders from assembly plants. Products are exported overseas, but the excessive competition causes prices to be beaten down in the market and made to fall. The resulting burdens are imposed on parts-producing factories; they, in turn, shift them to the many part-time employees who work for them at low wages.

Functional and Structural Classification of Industrial Areas: South

Stated above is a general description of the structure of the northern industrial region of the Tokyo metropolitan complex. We shall now look at the largest industrial region of the complex, the Keihin industrial area located in the south, which has clusters of gigantic industrial establishments.

This region encompasses Minato, Shinagawa, Meguro, and Ōta Wards of Tokyo and extends 35 kilometers along the Tokyo Bay coast; the coast region includes such centers in Kanagawa Prefecture as Kawasaki, Tsurumi, Kanagawa, and Hodogaya. The region accounts for 30 percent of the total industrial production of the complex. Production of durable consumer goods such as transportation equipment, electrical appliances and equipment, cameras, and various gauging instruments makes up a high 83 percent of the region's total industrial production. Its daily consumer goods production accounts for only 16 percent. The scale of the various industries here is larger than in other parts of the complex, and these industries are also of different character.

The beginnings of the remarkable development of the durable consumer goods industry in this region were made in the early 1930's when military arsenals and ordnances found themselves unable to meet the demands for munitions that increased after the Manchurian Incident. They began placing orders with civilian firms in this region, especially for the production of optical instruments, electrical ammunitions, vehicles and tanks. The government, meanwhile, assured these firms of priorities in the procurement of necessary funds and materials. When mass production is particularly required the supply of materials must be adequate, and it was seen to that these firms were supplied. At this time, consolidation of the industrial system began, whereby assembly plants and parts-producing factories operated in concert. This system has matured and has made the region the most industrialized in Japan.

The wards of Minato, Shinagawa, and Meguro in Tokyo have a majority of the city's electrical industries, many of which produce mainly electric bulbs and other light electrical appliances. Ōta Ward has many factories specializing in the production of electrical parts for automobiles; it also has big automobile assembly plants, camera factories, gauging instruments manufacturers, elevator manufacturers, agricultural and printing equipment factories, and the mining industry. Small- and medium-scale factories are also located here; they produce parts for the assembly plants in Kawasaki and Yokohama that produce big electrical equipment and machinery.

In the durable consumer goods industry of Kawasaki and Yokohama, about 70 percent is related to the production of transportation equipment such as automobiles. These industrial centers also have large factories manufacturing television sets, transistor radios, and other communications equipment. In connection with these activities, they have close connections with Ōta Ward in Tokyo, which orders parts for these products. There is little other industry in these centers. Only a few firms manufacture parts for assembly plants operating in the centers.

No other industry in Japan has made as much progress as the automobile industry in the past ten years. The total number of automobiles produced in 1962 was 990,705, representing an increase of 25.7 times for the ten-year period. Japan ranked fifth in the world in this field. In 1966 Japan climbed to fourth place in world ranking.

At present, 56 percent of all the types of automobiles in the country are produced in the Tokyo metropolitan complex--66 percent are regular cars, 92 percent are buses, and 54 percent are minicars. Some 30,000 parts in 1,500 varieties are needed for the production of one automobile, and the assembly plants manufacture 20-30 percent of these parts for themselves. The rest are manufactured by subcontractors. One assembly plant usually has contracts with some 200 makers of parts, and each of these makers, in turn, has as many as 20 subcontractors. It is now technically possible in Japan for a large factory with the newest equipment and facilities to produce all of the necessary parts, but assembly plants do not find it beneficial to equip themselves with special facilities for producing small numbers of different parts. There is too wide a variety of materials and technical processes involved to make it feasible. Thus, manufacturing of automobile parts constitutes a separate industry.

Generally speaking, manufacturers of automobile parts fall into two main categories. Those who can use their facilities and equipment for the production of automobile parts and other goods enjoy a relatively independent status; they can operate well even in areas that are geographically remote from their parent plants. On the other hand, there are manufacturers who produce goods only for the automobile industry, and they find it imperative for economy of transportation to locate themselves near their parent plants. Some manufacturers in the second category have been able to expand their operations under conditions of expanding gross national automobile production, but the majority of these manufacturers operate on a very small scale. Their parent plants often control or exert influence over matters of capital accumulation, personnel, financing, and technical procedures.

Most of the big assembly plants are located in the southwestern, and recently in the western, sections of the Tokyo metropolitan complex: there are 3 plants in Yokohama, 2 in Kawasaki, and 1 each in Ōta, Mitaka, Hino, Hamura, Murayama, Kawaguchi, Ageo, and Fujisawa. There are 1,500 parts-manufacturing factories. Many of these factories produce quantities of all kinds of parts for automobiles and many other products, as well. They reflect the diversity of industry in these regions and form clusters of efficient production activities.

The electrical industry was given a hard blow by the closing down of the munitions factories at the end of the war. In the immediate postwar period there was manufacturing activity in the production of such things as electric bulbs, stoves, and toasters--just enough to sustain a minimal living for the manufacturers. Then, as demands for heavy electrical appliances increased following the development of power resources and the beginning of the "consumption boom" around 1955, production of durable household consumer goods--irons, fans, TV sets, washers, and refrigerators--came to constitute the greater part of the industry.

The electrical appliances industry in the Tokyo metropolitan complex represents about half of the electrical industry of the entire nation in terms of the output and the number of factories and employees. The same industry in the Kinki region accounts for 20 percent of the national total. Owing to demands from the military and other government agencies such as the Ministry of Communications and the Public Telephone and Telegraph Corporation during the war, the Keihin region developed a heavy electrical and communications industry. In recent years, the production of household electrical appliances has also advanced in this region.

As many as 80 percent of all the electrical appliances manufacturers of the Tokyo metropolitan complex are located in the wards of Shinagawa, Meguro, and Ōta and in the cities of Kawasaki and Yokohama. Especially along the banks of the Meguro and Shinagawa Rivers small-scale factories are concentrated; 90 percent of them are petty establishments with 30 or fewer employees each. Kawasaki and Yokohama, on the other hand, have big factories--assembly plants having contracts with smaller factories. Several thousand kinds of products are put out by giant corporations, ranging from transistor radios to big generators.

Because of constant change in models, it is profitable for a parent manufacturer to collect various parts from subcontractors and assemble them into finished products. For those products that are manufactured in small quantities, parent plants let subcontractors put out finished products. For those parts that cannot be mass produced, small- and medium-scale parts makers and small- and medium-scale assembly plants purchase necessary materials from one another in order to supplement their respective deficiencies, while they both take orders from various big parent plants. Subcontracting makers must therefore locate themselves near one another in clusters for efficient operation. They congregate in Shinagawa, Ōta, and Meguro, and the electrical industry of Kawasaki and Yokohama depends heavily on these subcontractors.

The recent liberalization of foreign trade has made it necessary to cut down on production costs. As labor wages have gone up, advanced technology has been introduced and parts have been standardized and mass produced. Furthermore, those enterprises specializing in the production of parts have expanded their business operations, and factories are being constructed in areas away from industrial concentration for the benefits of larger land space, cheaper labor and power supply, and convenient transportation. These phenomena, however, are limited to certain areas in the complex. Parts-manufacturing factories and their parent plants must be located near one another; despite the development of mass production of parts, there are still many parts for which demands are not very great that are still manufactured by petty factories. Thus, the development of giant assembly plants and factories which mass produce parts does not necessarily lessen the importance of subcontracting makers of parts.

Problems of the Industrial Regions

Under these circumstances, the concentration of factories and their increase in number and scale continues, but even now, residence and factory are not clearly separated. The result is the occurrence of such manifold problems as limited land space and water supply for industrial use, shortage of labor, traffic stagnation, spread of smog, ground sinking, river water pollution, stench, growth of slums, and a worsening social environment for educational programs. Social investment is too inadequate to make various enterprises function properly and to guarantee a healthful living for people; problems accumulate.

The national and prefectural governments are taking legal measures to control public nuisances, making investments to solve pressing problems and break bottlenecks in redevelopment programs, and planning for advance investments for long-range projects. But the present condition is such that factories keep concentrating and expanding in limited areas as long as such concentration and expansion promise managerial advantages for them. The great increase in land price, which entails greater funds for urban redevelopment, is making it harder for public investments to adequately solve problems. As a solution for these problems, it may be best, in principle, for the costs of redevelopment to be borne by the beneficiaries of anticipated improvements or by those who have caused such problems. It is a difficult task, however, to determine how much those beneficiaries must bear and, as we have pointed out earlier, how much should be regarded as social costs to be borne by the national and local governments.

Managerial necessity and the advantages of operating in urban centers make industries concentrate in these areas, but when this concentration is left to take its natural course and the disadvantages for industrial operations increase, factories may begin to change their locations and move out of such urban centers. In a negative sense, this voluntary dispersion of factories may serve to solve the problems that are described above. But it may also cause an increase in costs of production by private enterprises and bring about adverse effects on the national economy. By weakening Japan's position in competitive international trade, it may arrest national economic growth.

The problem of public nuisances caused by industrial activities in Tokyo is the result of the excessive concentration of industrial establishments in the city. To solve these problems without disrupting the national economy, the national government took two legal measures. One was the enactment, in 1956, of the Tokyo Metropolitan Complex Improvement Act, which sought to control the excessive expansion of the existing urban cores and to zone new urban cores into which industrial establishments might be relocated. The other measure was the 1961 Act Governing Financial Aids for the Promotion of Small- and Medium-Scale Enterprises, which authorized the prefectural governments to make interest-free loans to those enterprises capitalized at ¥10 million or less (and employing 300 or fewer people each) for purposes of land purchase, building construction, establishment of community facilities, and modernization of industrial facilities and equipment. This act reinforced attempts to create and develop industrial regions of small- and medium-scale enterprises.

As we have discussed earlier, easy access to market, sources of funds, related enterprises, and supply of raw materials and labor are the basic requisites of location for a factory. As long as this situation is not met, government measures such as the ones mentioned above cannot easily induce factories to move. As the Tokyo metropolitan complex has become more highly industrialized, factories have had to face the need for expansion and structural transformation, but with land space severely limited at their present sites they have been compelled to move elsewhere. Moreover, these factories have come to realize increasing disadvantages in continuing to operate at their present sites. They are confronted with the problems of increasing cost of production resulting from water shortage and traffic stagnation, labor shortage, rise in labor wages, and legal control and restrictions on new construction projects and measures against public nuisances. This condition has made more and more factories move out of their present sites to new locations.

Until some time ago, the influences of expanding industry in central Tokyo had been confined to the immediate neighboring prefectures of Saitama, Kanagawa, and Chiba. In the northern Kantō prefectures of Gunma, Tochigi, and Ibaragi, excepting the Maebashi-Kiryū area with its traditional silk industry and also the Hitachi area, industrial development was stagnant. The region extending from northern Saitama to central Ibaragi remained an industrially hollow zone, making a sharp contrast to the bustling southern Kantō industrial region centering in Tokyo.

In recent years, there has been developing in this northern region a number of "knock-down" system factories that import raw materials and export finished products from and to the Keihin region in the south. This kind of industrial activity is typical of underdeveloped areas where land and wages are cheap. We also find in the northern region the development of new industrial centers resulting from the relocation here of industries needing new sites for expansion and rationalization of mass production systems, and the relocation of industries that have splintered and become independent of their parent industries. Many industries are moving into this northern region in search of new land, water, and labor supply, and many of them still retain their main offices in Tokyo. These industries, then, are beginning to solidly link the Tokyo area with the industrializing northern region and will eventually contribute to the formation of a vast Kantō industrial complex.

Looking at regional differences in types and scales of industrial establishments we find that near Tokyo, which provides greater locational advantages for industrial activities, there are many relatively small-scale industries such as subcontracting plants for manufacturing of machinery and metal products and food industry establishments. In areas further away from Tokyo, where land is generally cheaper, there are many large-scale industries (chemical, steel, machinery and iron) which, together with the subcontracting firms located around them, represent core industries of the Tokyo region. With such big consumer centers as Tokyo and Yokohama in easy access, there are also many manufacturers of "instant" foodstuffs, canned goods, clothing, and other daily consumer products. Kitchen utensils, household appliances and furniture, and other durable consumer goods necessary for modern living are also produced.

Because of the difficulties involved in procuring land in and around Tokyo and the worsening public nuisances in the area, the national government has taken the initiative in the matter of industrial relocation by designating special zones and making advance investment in these zones. Municipal governments have been encouraging industrial relocation by providing their services for various industries in securing labor supply and industrial sites and in allowing temporary tax exemption for the improvement of drainage systems.

The availability of cheap land and the peasant labor force is an important incentive for industrial relocation. For inland-type industries, conveniences of transportation of raw materials and finished products are the prime consideration. It is estimated that the average transportation and housing expense per worker for an enterprise in Tokyo is several tens of thousand yen per year. If workers can be recruited in a newly developed area, the enterprise can save a great deal in transportation, housing, recreational, and other expenses.

As the economy advances, it becomes necessary to expand factories and introduce new and advanced technology, and new demands for labor appropriate for the changed condition arise. Especially when an industry faces keen competition at home and abroad, it needs to produce excellent goods; for this purpose it is necessary to have an integrated system of continuous factory operations. A number of factories under this system will become the core for further industrial development. For the production of new goods, the appropriate sectors of the industry could become independent and specialize in the production of new goods only. They would soon have their own factories constructed. These factories in turn would have their subcontracting factories working for them around the areas of their operation. This should be the new trend in industrial development. This type of development is, however, impossible in the existing factory areas of the metropolis, and now various industrial establishments, with bases of operation in Tokyo and Yokohama, are expanding their activities into areas 30-50 kilometers from those cities.

An integrated plant operation, where parts are produced and assembled into finished goods, is necessary for the manufacture of quality products. There are cases where such integrated-operation factories are established, and they induce the establishment and development of new industries around them. There are also cases where certain sectors of an industry develop into independent industries for the manufacture of new products, build and expand their own factories, and invite the establishment and development of new clusters of subcontracting plants. Thus, the Tokyo metropolitan complex is expanding its industrial organic structure from its previous 30-kilometer-radius core to a sphere of some 100 kilometers in radius.

High economic growth in Japan has further induced the development of large enterprises and stimulated the growth of heavy and chemical industry and technological renovations. With powerful industrial and financial systems as mainstays of the economy, the process of reorganization of production structures and their regional groupings has been accelerated. The development of heavy and chemical industry, accompanied by technological renovations, has altered conditions of location for factories. In contrast to the prewar activities of coal and pulp production, which were based on the availability of local raw materials, present-day industry depends on foreign imports to supply its need for raw materials and fuel. Its facilities and equipment are of gigantic scale, its roundabout-way production and mass production systems have expanded, and the use of substitutes for raw materials and finished products has increased. Operational relations between various sectors of an enterprise and between various enterprises have intensified. There is an increasing concentration along the coastline of steam power plants, oil refineries, petroleum chemical plants, steel plants, shipbuilding yards, sugar refineries, fodder producers, and many other big enterprises, all of which depend on imported raw materials. All of these developments have led to the formation of industrial kombinats [industrial estates] spreading over vast areas along sea coasts.

In the Tokyo metropolitan complex, kombinats are found in the Keiyō (Tokyo-Chiba) area, which extends from Funahashi to Kisarazu, in the southwestern area stretching from Kawasaki to Negishi, and in other areas beyond the central built-up area of the complex. In these regions raw materials, labor, capital, technical skills, power resources, and spacious land are readily available, and harbors and markets are located nearby. The national and local governments have been investing money and helping to develop the necessary foundations for industrial activities in those areas by reclaiming lands, laying out water, gas, and power supply lines and sewerage, and constructing roads, railroads, and harbor facilities.

In the Keiyō industrial area, there are the following kombinats: related to steel capital are the Goi-Anegasaki petroleum chemical kombinat of the Mitsui chain, the now-developing Kisarazu steel kombinat of the Yahata Steel Corporation and Chiba Iron Works of the Kawasaki Steel Corporation; related to oil capital is the Chiba Petroleum Chemical League of Maruzen Petroleum Corporation which covers the areas of Chiba, Goi, Ichihara, and Anegasaki, and, in the planning stage, the Ichihara kombinat of the Idemitsu Industry and Mitsubishi Chemicals and Tokyo Electric at Sodegaura. In the Keihin region, there are such kombinats as the Kawasaki-Tsurumi Plant of the Japan Steel Pipe Corporation and, in the planning stage, the Chidori (Kawasaki City) and Negishi (Yokohama City) petroleum kombinats of the Japan Petroleum Industry.

Kombinats carry no great weight in the Tokyo metropolitan complex as yet, but great efforts are now being made in the complex and in other new industrial centers of the country to invite the establishment of petroleum chemical kombinats. The development of such kombinats as a new direction of industrial progress in the country is looked upon with great hopes. On the other hand, however, there is the problem of local benefits. Administrative investments of the national and local governments are beneficial primarily to centrally located large enterprises and do not directly influence local labor wages and payments for raw materials; in most cases, the new industrial kombinats do not employ many local people, nor do they depend on the immediate neighborhoods for raw materials.

There has been little consideration of the public welfare in planning for the establishment of kombinats, and such nuisances as soot and harmful exhaust gas have been vexing local inhabitants. Areas where kombinats are to be established must have adequate conditions for industrial location, and for effective investment such kombinats must be large in scale. Investment must be made on a priority basis. Therefore, the number of areas where kombinats can be established is limited; differences between these areas and others will become greater, with more resources being poured into the former. In a democratic society, the problems of balancing economic development with the improvement of living conditions must be carefully studied and solved.

In community development, a particular community often lacks adequate industrial location conditions. It strives, however, to have chemical and heavy industrial kombinats established within its borders in order to catch up with industrially advanced communities in the quickest way possible. It is necessary to examine residential migration patterns and the roles of the various local industries of each community in the total national or metropolitan industrial structure and, through this examination, to consider the best ways to develop industry and simultaneously improve public welfare in the community.

Population decrease in a community does not necessarily lower living standards. An overpopulated community must encourage migration to areas where occupational opportunities are more readily available and higher wages can be obtained; within its own boundaries it should invite new technical skills and try to increase its productivity. In this way, living conditions of the community's residents can be bettered, and standards of living can be equal with those of more prosperous communities.

As for the kombinats, or industrial estates, which represent a new important feature in the industrialization process, a special characteristic must be noted. Each of the existing kombinats represents a joint venture of several capitalists of different lines of business who, for lack of capital and technical skills individually, cooperate in creating a kombinat. However, the discordant interests that are not uncommon among the participating individuals often cause problems in planning and the implementation of plans. In such a situation, the ones who suffer the consequences are the local public bodies that had invested money for the development of the kombinat. There is also a problem with delay and inefficiency by public investment where enterprises are being established in an unorderly fashion.

Needless to say, kombinats are essential for future international economic competition, but the present needs are for the amalgamation, consolidation, and cooperation of various corporations. Concentrated investments in the creation of a few large-scale kombinats, each of which may occupy a land space of 10-20 million tsubo and use 1 million tons of water [per day?] are also needed. A steel plant in such a large-scale operation would have to have at least 6 blast furnaces, each one capable of producing 3,000 tons per day; an oil refinery would need to produce 200,000-300,000 tons [daily?]; and a power plant would have to have a 1.5 million kilowatt capacity. These large-scale kombinats must replace the many existing small systems.

CHAPTER 7

STRUCTURAL CHANGE OF SUBURBAN AGRICULTURAL VILLAGES

In the preceding chapters we have described the structure and functions of the heart of Tokyo, the distribution of establishments dealing in consumer goods, the citizens and their living environments, and the locations and structures of industrial enterprises in the constantly changing Tokyo metropolitan complex. We have also discussed problems that arise in the complex and measures that must be taken to meet those problems.

The Tokyo metropolitan complex has agricultural districts within its boundaries, and the city of Tokyo and its satellite urban centers are linked with these agricultural districts in various ways. Housing units, factories, and shops and stores in the complex increase and expand as these agricultural communities undergo urbanization, and in this process of change there arise various problems. Therefore, we must now turn our attention to the structural change and urbanization process of those suburban agricultural communities as an aspect of the structural change of the complex as a whole. We shall proceed to a discussion of the problem of the geographical limits of the complex from the standpoint of its social and economic functions. In the present chapter we shall discuss the structural change of suburban agricultural villages.

The Changing Community Structure of Tokyo's Suburban Areas

The rapid urban expansion of recent years is the result of the concentration, numerical increase, and expansion in scale of commercial enterprises, financial institutions, factories, stores and shops, and cultural, social, and political institutions in cities. Expansion has been accelerated by the high level of economic growth in Japan, which in turn has led to the great concentration of population in the cities, where occupational opportunities and income are greater than in agricultural villages. Unlike industrial activities that involve constant interrelationships of removable materials and moving human beings and corporations, agricultural activities are closely bound to the immovable great outdoors, from which products that require large spaces of land and favorable climatic and soil conditions are obtained. Therefore, they are not concentrated in the way industrial activities are concentrated in cities, but are spread widely over large areas. However, agricultural activities may have to be performed in the future with greater consideration given to the maintenance of easy access to urban centers, as agricultural products and agricultural operation become more and more commercialized.

Looking at Japan's agriculture during the period of her economic growth, we find that the total agricultural population in 1955 was 37.1 percent of the total working population, but that the total agricultural income was only 18.8 percent of the total national income. This suggests a low farm living standard compared with that of other occupational groups. The difference between the farming and other groups became even greater in later years; in 1962 the farming population decreased to 27.6 percent of the total working population, and agricultural income further decreased to 9.6 percent of the national income. Farm living conditions became even worse.

During the period of economic growth, agricultural production increased from ¥942.2 billion in 1950 to ¥2,323.4 billion in 1962, and commercialization of agricultural products advanced greatly. The ratio of the commercialized products to all the agricultural products increased from 58 percent in 1950 to 76 percent in 1962. The rate of agricultural investment also increased, but the commercialization of products served to diminish the efficiency of such investment.

Income in agricultural households increased from ¥1,051.4 billion in 1950 to ¥3,020.3 billion in 1962, but the major part of this increase represented an increase in income from wages farmers received for working in occupations other than farming. The ratio of this income from wages to the total income of agricultural households increased from 23 percent in 1950 to 37 percent in 1962. The number of farmers engaging in secondary and tertiary industrial activities while remaining on their farms, so-called secondary part-time farmers (dainishu kengyō nōka), has been increasing. Their main income comes from occupations other than farming, and they commute to work. In this way, farmers manage to maintain a living.

Agricultural savings are increasing at a higher rate than the increase of agricultural income. However, a great part of agricultural investment is made up of government subsidy (24-25 percent), and most of the agricultural savings are invested not in agriculture but in heavy and chemical industries, so that the difference in productivity between agriculture and industry is still increasing. This also leads to a relative decline in agricultural income, and farmers are obliged to depend further on income from outside occupations in order to upgrade their living and defray their increasing household expenses. Especially in those farming areas located far from cities that lack convenient commuter transportation, the key labor force of young adults is being transformed from a seasonal labor force to a permanent one as various public works increase and require unskilled labor. Many of these people, however, cannot establish and maintain their own independent households because of the low wages they receive from such work. Thus, the ratio of the part-time farming households to the total number of farming households increased from 65.8 percent in 1960 (of which the secondary part-time farming households constituted 32.1 percent) to 76.1 percent in 1963 (the secondary part-time farming households constituted 42.2 percent).

In advanced Western countries, the decline in the agricultural population led to a decline in the number of agricultural households, an expansion of agricultural economic scale, mechanization of agriculture, and a rationalization of agricultural management. The problem in Japan's agriculture, on the other hand, lies in the development of part-time farming and the delay in the modernization of agricultural management.

Relative disadvantages for agricultural activities are inevitable in areas surrounding the cores of big cities, also, but the people in these areas have enjoyed better opportunities for side-work occupations and higher income from wages because of their physical proximity to cities. In Tokyo, the farming households numbered 55,633 in 1955, of which 38.7 percent were devoted entirely to farming while 61.3 percent were engaged in side work. By 1965, the number of farming households sharply decreased to 44,997; while the number of those entirely devoted to farming decreased in ratio to 22.6 percent, the ratio of those engaged in side work increased to 77.4 percent, with a greater proportion being those secondary part-time farming households whose side work was the principal source of their income.

With the index number for the total cultivated land area of Tokyo in 1950 set at 100, the index number for 1964 was 73, or a decrease of 27 percent. This indicates the progressing urbanization of the suburban areas. In the suburban agricultural villages of Tokyo, the trend is towards greater participation by farmers in other occupations and, finally, towards emigration from the farmlands. Comparing the numbers of farming households by levels of income from their products over the period from 1961 to 1964, we find that those with an annual income of ¥500,000 or less decreased in number, but that those making ¥500,000-¥700,000 increased by 38.9 percent; those making ¥750,000-¥1,000,000 and ¥1,000,000 and over increased by 84.3 percent and 122.1 percent, respectively. Many petty farmers, who make up the majority of the farming population, leave their farmlands, whereas a small number of farmers with large-scale farming operations remain. A greater portion of their products are commercialized, and they enjoy the advantage of being near urban consumer centers; thus they succeed in establishing commercial and enterprising agriculture.

Among the suburban farmers of Tokyo making the highest incomes from the sale of their different products in 1965, the number obtaining the greatest income from vegetables was the largest, indicating the farmers' preference of raising vegetables that can be shipped fresh and at low cost to nearby consumer centers. The next largest farm income category is the hog and chicken farmers; they can obtain leftovers and other necessary feed from nearby urban centers, and their pigpens and chicken farms are expanding at present. Easy access to high-income urban centers also makes it possible for flower raising in greenhouses and gravel beds to thrive as a characteristic suburban agricultural occupation.

The diversification of agricultural management and the shortage of labor in suburban farmlands have led to an extensive use of agricultural machinery. In 1965, 32.4 percent of all the cultivating work was done by power cultivators, and 44.5 percent of the grain threshing was done by power threshers. Use of other machines and tools, like sprayers of agricultural chemicals, milkers, trucks, and trimobiles, has also become very common.

In mountain farmlands, few farmers are engaged in other occupations, and those who are make only a small income from their side work. The people in these isolated mountain villages lack adequate information on occupational opportunities in urban and other areas, and they have little sense of the difference between agriculture and industrial activities. In agricultural villages near urban centers, differences between agricultural and other activities are clearly known; the people sense the disadvantages of agricultural pursuits and want to move into other occupations. Thus, the relative poverty of agricultural villages, coupled with the relative advantages of urban communities with the expanding and increasing enterprises that offer greater occupational opportunities, leads to the absorption of many young adults of the suburban farmlands by urban centers. In the process, the family structure in those farmlands undergoes transformation, and the working population becomes increasingly aged and feminized. In the absence of an adequate labor force, agriculture has become san-chan nōgyō, or "agriculture by three [kinds of people called by the suffix] chan"--jīchan (granddad), bāchan (grandma), and kāchan (mom).

The male-female ratio in the total industrial population of the nation was 72:28 in 1962, but the ratio in the total farming population of Tokyo in 1964 was 53.9 for males and 46.1 for females. The age composition of the farming population shows that 65.5 percent of the total are 40 years old or older, and only 1 percent are 20 or younger. When agriculture depends on this kind of people, in the absence of imaginative, energetic young male adults, it is difficult to expect any substantial improvement and modernization of agriculture.

Urban centers and suburban villages maintain demand-supply relations, where the increasing population of the former constantly demands products supplied by the latter, but relations between the two involve more than that. As we have described, the accessibility of villages to cities is a factor in the changes made in the kinds of products and agricultural management patterns in the villages. Urban expansion is accompanied by the inflow of urban residential and industrial elements into nearby villages, which results in their gradual urbanization.

As cities expand, people avoid living in crowded urban cores; homes and factories are built in suburban farming areas in increasing numbers. The ensuing competition for land leads to a further rise in land prices in those areas, which, in turn, greatly influences the structural change and development of new urban cores in the areas.

In the suburban villages where more and more farmlands are being diverted for purposes other than farming, farmowners take up side occupations but do not go so far as to release their lands and migrate. Despite the low income accrued from farming, these farmowners anticipate a rise in land prices and thus great profits from the eventual sale of their lands. There are government restrictions on the extent to which farmlands can be diverted for purposes other than farming--the restrictions imposed to honor the principles of self-sufficiency of food supply and of independent farming by individual farmers. The diversion of a farmland 5,000 tsubo or smaller in size needs authorization by the appropriate prefectural governor; that of larger lands needs the authorization of the Minister of Agriculture and Forestry. A tenant farmland carries, for the tenant, the guaranteed right to cultivate. Therefore, instead of renting his land, a landowner retains it as farmland and hires wage laborers until the time when the property can be sold for residential or industrial purposes.

The diversion of farmlands in the suburbs is increasing each year. In Tokyo, the total cultivated land was 34,150 hectares in area in 1955, but in ten years it decreased by 72.3 percent to 24,690 hectares, which indicates rapid urbanization. Under the land utilization plans for urban redevelopment that were incorporated into government acts such as the Tokyo Metropolitan Complex Improvement Act, farmlands in suburban areas are classified into three categories. Classification of specific pieces of land is determined by their usefulness for farming or other purposes in the process of urbanization, and the diversion of farmlands is authorized on a priority basis according to this classification. Class I farmlands have the highest agricultural productivity and adequate foundations for agricultural activities that have been built up through public investments; they had best remain as farmlands. Class II farmlands are located in industrial and semi-industrial zones, as was stipulated in the Construction Standards Act (Kenchiku kijun hō), and near railroad stations, harbors, municipal offices, and other pivotal urban sections. Class III farmlands are situated in areas of land zoning and improvement projects; residential areas occupy 40 percent or more of the total area, which is almost completely urbanized.

The diversion of farmlands for purposes other than farming is taking place mainly in large cities and their suburban villages. It occurs first within cities and their immediate surrounding areas. As more farmlands are diverted for residential and industrial purposes, land prices soar under heightened speculation, but buyers' funds for the purchase of lands are not unlimited. Therefore, diversion of farmlands does not necessarily occur in continuous outward directions from central sections of cities, but takes place in scattered areas where land prices are low enough for buyers; some farmlands are left intact here and there.

Large apartment zones have also been developed in this fashion by metro-politan and public housing corporations, spreading first to areas near central sections of cities and then gradually entering areas further removed from such centers and into remote areas. The fact that relatively high prices are paid for land for those apartment zones and for the construction of railroads and freeways tends to stimulate the subdivision of land near the zones and simultaneously causes land prices to rise in wide areas. Other contributing factors to land price rises are the subsequent development of new roads, gas and water supply lines, sewerage, new schools, and other community facilities. Under these conditions, many people attempting to have their own houses built with meager funds are pushed out to areas remote from urban centers where land prices are lower.

In the sale of paddy and dry fields to be used by independent farmers, the price of a paddy field is slightly less than that of a dry field in rural areas, but when these fields are sold for purposes other than farming, the difference becomes greater. As general land prices go up, the price of a dry field rises much higher than that of a paddy field, which is less suitable as residential or industrial land.

Whether it is a dry field or a paddy, the ownership of a piece of land in a suburb assures a great profit without any effort when land prices rise. This situation, in turn, causes the rising price of lands that are being speculated upon. Furthermore, in the suburban villages that are now being transformed into residential zones of cities, the rate of tax on farmlands has remained unchanged since 1962. At that time, farmland owners successfully argued that they would not be able to manage their lands if the tax rates were raised to the same levels as for the residential lands. As a result, taxes on farmlands are now as low as 1/30 to 1/50 of the taxes on residential lands, which have kept rising. This condition has given a further advantage to farmland owners, who retain their lands until they have a chance to sell them at high prices.

This rise in land prices obstructs the orderly process of planned urban development and renders urban functions and structures extremely inefficient and unsound. The great profits for landowners resulting from the land price boom represent the fruits of public investments and other social conditions rather than rewards for labor. As for the many individual families desiring to have their own homes, they cannot expect to see their dreams come true under the present condition. These people suffer the consequences of rising land prices, and each city is confronted with housing shortages. It has become a pressing issue to enact land price control measures.

The current situation calls for the formulation of a long-range land utilization plan and the establishment of zones for different purposes over a wide area. If these measures are strictly enforced, they may help stabilize land prices at reasonable levels. For instance, if the price of a piece of land rises beyond the prescribed limit, a tax might be levied against the rise after considering the value that the land had as farmland. New revenue accruing from such a tax might be appropriated for urban planning.

With the increase in land price following the inflow of factories, houses, and apartments into suburbs, hard-pressed petty farmers are obliged first to sell their lands and then to leave their villages. Middle-income farmers may also leave the villages, or they may devise new methods of farming and engage in the production of vegetables and other commercially disposable products. High-income farmers and those secondary part-time farmers who earn a great income from nonagricultural activities may retain their lands for a considerably longer period of time, in anticipation of further land speculation. Some of them may transform their large-scale operations into modern diversified commercial enterprises.

Vegetable gardening, which has developed as a necessitated adjustment in suburban villages, will eventually be faced with managerial problems resulting from limited land space, excess planting, and shortage of fertilizers. Such a condition, together with the attractively high income that can be earned from side work, will drive the farmers to release their lands to residential, commercial, and industrial interests, and thus lead to the dissolution of suburban agriculture. Unplanted lands are increasing year after year, and many of them are found in areas around the central sections of cities. In 1961, the unplanted lands in Tokyo constituted about 4 percent of the total cultivated land area, but the ratio went up to 12 percent in 1966. This situation may represent a pattern during the diversion of land uses and a preparatory step towards urbanization.

The Fact that land is made an object of speculation in suburban areas obstructs the implementation of land utilization plans and evidences a lack of concern for public good. And yet urbanization progresses at a rapid rate and on a large scale, even though schools, roads, water supply, and other facilities remain unimproved. For the local public bodies in these suburban villages that are faced with a sudden influx of people, it is a great financial burden to lay out the needed facilities, and the local financial situation is worsening.

An increase in urban population and its demands for land will, if effective control is not exercised, lead to an intensification of land speculation and a further rise in land prices. Land prices will eventually surpass the buying capacity of individuals. This will result in a large population remaining concentrated in cities, continuing to aggravate the already bad housing conditions. It will also arrest the progress of farmland diversion; however, urbanization of suburban villages makes agricultural activities become increasingly difficult, and suburban agriculture will gradually break down.

Many individuals desiring land have very limited funds, and they naturally seek less expensive land. Urbanization through the inflow of these people therefore occurs in areas where lands are subdivided into small units. These areas are not contiguous, and empty lands remain interspersed between central sections of cities and outward fringe areas. As a whole, urbanization takes place in an unorderly fashion over a wide area, and it progresses without the construction of necessary urban facilities for commuting and for other purposes.

The urbanization of suburban villages represents a negative aspect of the process of industrialization and housing development. It results from the decentralization, or dispersion, of homes, stores, and factories from the central sections of expanding cities in concentric, fan-shaped, or multinuclear patterns. Therefore, the urbanization of suburban villages takes place in a progressively larger area, in proportion to the decreasing distance from urban centers and their satellite cities that is made possible through the construction and improvement of railroads, freeways, and other transportation facilities.

The urbanization is manifested in the following changes: an increase in the nonagricultural population (secondary and tertiary industrial population); a rise in land price; the diversion of farmlands; an increase in population and housing density; a rise in the rate of population increase; a rise in the number of commuters for work and school, with improved transportation facilities; a subdivision of relatively large household units (including a number of domestic workers) into democratic nuclear household units of husband and wife and children; an increase in the proportion of the young male and female adult population; a decrease in the proportion of privately-owned houses and an increase in the proportion of rented houses and rooms or employer-provided housing units; a decrease in tatami space per person; an increase in the number of sales, clerical, professional, and technical employees in contrast to a decrease in the number of agriculture, forestry, and fishery workers, following the diversion of farmlands into residential lands; an increase in the number of technical production line workers and general laborers, which follow farmland diversion into industrial lands; and a rise in the educational standards of various occupational groups.

Changes in these aspects of community life bring about changes in the total community structure. The tightly-knit, relatively feudalistic neighborhood structure of a traditional village community, which was built around agricultural activities and based on stratified family and class structures, gradually becomes disorganized and gives way to new and relatively democratic neighborhood relationships. Heads of households who do not work in the neighborhood for their livelihood but commute to central sections or industrial zones of nearby cities become more common; they cooperate with one another in handling such community problems as education for the children, roads, water supply, and street cleaning. These new neighborhood relations revolve mainly around housewives, and similar changes take place in neighborhood associations. Unlike traditional neighborhood relationships, which had been relatively closed and isolated, these new community relationships become part of an urban socioeconomic system of a wide scope; they are also being organized into administrative structures of urban centers.

The inflow of urban elements into agricultural villages is not a smooth forward process, but is a succession (or continuous change) that gives rise to and then resolves conflicts of value systems and institutional patterns between traditional and new societies.

The preceding description of the changing community structure of suburban areas of the Tokyo metropolitan complex shows that demarcation between urban and nonurban areas depends upon the degree of qualitative and cumulative change in the given areas. For this reason, any area can be treated according to its degree of urbanization as specified by an established definition of the state of being urbanized. Distinction can be made, however, in a variety of ways, according to various indices to be employed. When it is necessary to set limits to an area for planning purposes, the question of the purpose of such delimitation becomes important. It may be said that the most appropriate way is to set limits for an area for each different purpose.

CHAPTER 8

PROBLEMS IN PLANNING FOR THE TOKYO METROPOLITAN COMPLEX

Using new methods of analysis in human ecology, we have discussed in the
preceding chapters the position of the Tokyo metropolitan complex in the
total Japanese society, the structures and functions of integrative institutions, and establishments for the distribution and sales of consumer goods,
housing and living conditions, the distribution and structural changes of
industrial enterprises, and structural changes in suburban agricultural
villages. We have also pointed out problems that are arising in the process
of change in the complex and have recommended some measures for the solution
of those problems. Thus far we have treated various problems in the complex
separately, but in the present chapter we shall discuss the current plans
for the complex as a whole and for individual local areas that either comprise
or are economically tied to metropolitan Tokyo; the related local areas constitute a unit of expanded regional planning. In discussing these plans we
shall also review the problems that necessitated them.

Current Plans for the Tokyo Metropolitan Complex

As we have pointed out, the metropolitan complexes centering in Tokyo, Osaka,
and Nagoya are rapidly absorbing a large population and a great number of industrial establishments. These complexes are beginning to form a megalopolis with
close organic structural connections between them. The Tokyo metropolitan complex is not only larger in scale than the Osaka-centered Kinki complex and the
Chūkyō complex with Nagoya as its nucleus, but is also the capital and center of
the nation. As such, it exercises integrative functions in the political, economic, social, and cultural fields of the entire national society; it is also
directly involved in international political, economic, and cultural relations.
Thus, the Tokyo metropolitan complex is basically different from the other
metropolitan complexes.

Tokyo, as the political center of the nation, has concentrated within its
boundary large-scale national institutions exercising legislative, executive,
and judicial functions. In the prewar political system, the fact that Tokyo
was the residence of the imperial household added great political and social
importance to the city. Tokyo's unique character is further enhanced by the
concentration of diplomatic and other representatives of the foreign nations
with which Japan maintains relations.

It is true of almost every city that its formation and development depends
largely on the economic functions of industry, finance, and commerce, but in
Japan, since the Meiji era, political activities have taken precedence over
economic activities. Although in the postwar period economic activities have
expanded and monopolization has progressed rapidly, concentration of political
power has intensified and stronger political leadership has provided for such
economic development, and the foundations for a democratic welfare state have
been strengthened. Under these conditions, business enterprises and people
have concentrated in Tokyo and its neighboring areas in great numbers; this

concentration has stimulated further inflow of business and population in this region. Big corporations have also come to Tokyo in order to maintain close connections with national government agencies.

Tokyo has strengthened its position of influence over the whole nation in the political field and in the economic sector as well. Furthermore, the concentration of mass communication media and cultural and educational institutions has ensued. Many people come to the Tokyo area to obtain jobs in these various institutions, and the urban prosperity of the area has spurred the concentration of the elite of society. Tokyo is a consumption center of comparatively high economic and cultural standards, providing opportunities for earning high income and for the pursuit of arts and sciences.

These trends in the Tokyo area will continue, and Tokyo will exercise even greater political, economic, and cultural functions. The expansion of these functions occurs at a very rapid rate, as can be observed in demographic, economic and other indices. The Tokyo metropolitan complex keeps growing in area and importance in relation to the whole national society.

In 1956, when the Tokyo Metropolitan Complex Improvement Act was promulgated, the area of a radius of 100 kilometers from Tokyo was delimited as the boundaries of the complex, but the increase of population and industrial establishments in this area has been far greater than was originally estimated. Spheres of various activities extended beyond the 100-kilometer limits, giving rise to a need for closer organic ties among various activities and establishments. Furthermore, the original boundary of the complex cut across some prefectures and divided them into halves; there also arose a need to establish nationwide key facilities. For these reasons, the original plan was reviewed and revised in 1966. In this revision the complex was expanded in area to include Tokyo and seven other prefectures, constituting an area of 3,654,332 square kilometers with a radius of 130 kilometers.

Demographic and economic statistics for the area newly defined as the Tokyo metropolitan complex are as follows. In 1950 the total national population was 83.19 million, of which the complex had 19.5 million, or 23 percent of the total, but in 1966 the national total was 99.05 million, of which the complex has 27.48 million, or 27 percent of the national total. The population of the complex increased by as many as 8.43 million over the eleven-year period. As for the output of finished goods, the national total in 1956 was ¥9,691.9 billion, of which ¥2,479.2 billion or 28.5 percent came from the complex. In 1964, the national total amounted to ¥27,682.8 billion while the total for the complex was ¥9,578.2 billion, or 34.6 percent of the national total.

Within the complex, the southern Kantō region, which has a radius of about 50 kilometers and includes the prefectures of Tokyo, Kanagawa, Saitama, and Chiba, has a greater concentration of population and industry and a longer history of urbanization than the other Kantō prefectures of Yamanashi, Gunma, Tochigi, and Ibaragi. In 1966 the population of the southern Kantō region was 3.6 times larger than that of the northern Kantō region, and the total output of finished products in 1964 was 8.3 times greater. Thus, the southern Kantō region has the advantages of concentrated population and industry, but at the same time it has been confronted with conditions of worsening public nuisances in recent years. Part of the population and industry in this expanding southern Kantō region is being dispersed into the northern region, and the two regions are becoming more and more organically related.

The expansion of the Tokyo metropolitan complex is basically the result of the increase in number and scale of integrative institutions that concentrate in this area. The institutions wish to avail themselves of the benefits that accrue from the concentration of various activities in the area, which result from the social and economic progress of the larger national society. The concentration of various institutions augment the benefits of concentration and invite more institutions to concentrate there. In turn, there is an increase in the number of employees of the institutions and a consequent increase in the number of businessmen catering to them. All these people live around the central section and subcenters of Tokyo and near industrial areas of the metropolis. Residence is distributed from the central section of the city to its fringes and beyond, and the pattern is determined by a multitude of factors. Functions of the various areas of the complex become specialized and their interrelationships are strengthened. In the process, administrative boundaries of various areas are crossed over, and a metropolitan complex of a vast geographical expanse is formed.

It is difficult to make a correct prediction of the population increase in the Tokyo metropolitan complex, but for its 50-kilometer region it has been estimated that the present population of 18.8 million will grow to 28 million by 1980, an increase of about 9 million. With this in mind, developmental planning for the complex must first consider how best to distribute and redistribute the increasing population and industry in order to prevent and solve problems in the population and socioeconomic structures of the complex, to increase efficiency in economic activities, and to promote general public welfare. The next step is to study the problem of alloting various functions to the component areas of the complex in such a way as to ensure the best organic interrelationships between the various areas. To guide citizens and industrial activities through such thoughtful steps is the basic task of those concerned with metropolitan planning.

The concentration of institutions and people in the Tokyo metropolitan complex does not create serious problems as long as balanced private and public investments are made and necessary facilities are provided to meet such concentration. If these conditions are not met, however, grave problems result, including those of traffic, housing, water supply, sewerage, street cleaning, rising land prices, smog, rising production costs, decreasing production efficiency, lack of green tracts of land, inadequate educational facilities, and worsening general social environment. Urban expansion occurs simultaneously with a decentralization or dispersion of institutions and people in search of better economic, social, and cultural opportunities; therefore, various localized problems may arise in wider areas as urban expansion continues.

On the basis of anticipated changes in the community structure of the complex, urban planning should aim to meet the physical and economic problems as they appear and to design short- and long-range measures for their prevention. The measures should also stimulate economic growth and promote social welfare, which are goals harmonious with the establishment of a democratic social system. Since reality is complex, it is still difficult to forecast future changes accurately despite the recent advances of the social sciences. It is thus necessary to make urban plans as flexible as possible, allowing for different approaches to the attainment of the stated goal.

We have touched on the circumstances of the revision of 1966 of the Tokyo Metropolitan Improvement Act of 1956. Under the revised basic plans, the heart and subcenters of Tokyo and other like areas in the ward section and in the cities of Mitaka, Musashino, Kawasaki, Yokohama, and Kawaguchi (selected by government ordinances) are designated as the Existing Urban Cores Area. The area encompassing all of these existing urban cores constitutes the nucleus of the Tokyo metropolitan complex; it extends 15 kilometers northeast of central Tokyo and 40 kilometers southwest. In this region, the evils of excessive concentration have become most prominent. Great control is required over the establishment of new factories, schools, and community facilities, and large investments are needed to lay out roads and sewerage and to restore and redevelop urban functions to normal standards.

The suburban belt that encircles this nuclear region of the complex, whose outer rim is approximately 50 kilometers from central Tokyo, is the area that includes many municipalities with the highest rates of population increase. The area has been designated the Suburban Improvement Zone to ensure an orderly development of urban cores, a retention of green tracts of land, and appropriate land use.

Beyond this suburban region, up to about 130 kilometers from the center of Tokyo, is the New Urban Cores Development Area, where proper relocation of population and industry from the Existing Urban Cores is planned to relieve the latter region of the over-concentration of population and industry. In this area, fourteen districts have been designated as industrial centers: Ōta-Ōizumi, Kumagaya-Fukaya, Maebashi-Takasaki, Mito-Katta, Utsunomiya, Koyama-Mamada, Tsuchiura-Ami, Furukawa-Sōwa, Sanada, Sano-Ashikaga, Ishioka, Kanuma, Tochigi, and Kōfu. The Tsukuba area has been designated as the center of research and educational activities. This area was formerly called the New Urban Cores Development Region (consisting of industrial satellite cities), but the addition of the research and educational activities in the planning of 1966 caused the designation to be changed to the New Urban Development Region.

Many discussions and recommendations have been advanced as to ways of solving problems in the extremely crowded Existing Urban Cores that constitute the nucleus of the Tokyo metropolitan complex. Such suggestions as a drastic reconstruction of the structure of the complex and a relocation of government offices to outside the complex have enlivened journalistic circles and attracted public attention, but the ideas all seem to be lofty ideals that have little possibility of being translated into actual plans.

The discussion of the complex may be said to have begun with the recommendation of Kanō Kyūrō in 1956 for the reclamation of Tokyo Bay. Reclamation of the Bay shoreline had been going on in the past for coastal industrial activities, but Kanō's scheme, although only a primary-stage plan, represented a plan for a wide metropolitan region including Tokyo. It called for the reclamation --for industrial, residential, and other purposes--of 252.5 million tsubo--an area 1.5 times the size of the 23-ward section of Tokyo.

In 1960, Tange Kenzō offered his Tokyo structural reform plan. This was prepared on the assumption that future cities would be built around tertiary industrial activities, which would become more important with the progress of the information revolution, and that such activities would concentrate in limited areas because of the necessity for convenient communication channels. He proposed to do away with the existing centripetal transportation system, which is confusing and reflective of a medieval closed society; in its place he wanted to construct a new and open transportation system along an "urban axis" running from the present Tsukiji and Tsukishima areas towards Tokyo Bay, to construct a "cycle transportation" system, to connect "cores and pillotis [pillars]," to connect roads and streets with homes, and, through these new networks of transportation routes, to create new government office districts, business districts, and residential areas. His plan envisioned a creation of a high-density and multi-function maritime metropolis with full use of open space.

In 1965, Shimizu Keihachirō proposed a plan to divide Tokyo into two cities by constructing a Keiyō [Tokyo-Chiba] central railroad line and highway. This plan was proposed to help balance the heavy westward urban development along the existing central railroad line of Tokyo by ensuring new eastward development. It aims to connect the heart of Tokyo with Kisarasu on the Bōsō Peninsula by means of a central railroad and highway route running over a wide steel bridge across Tokyo Bay; the route would extend as far as Kamogawa on the Pacific coast. With this central route as the axis, the vast, undeveloped peninsula region would be integrated with Tokyo, thus stimulating the development of business districts and the residential and school districts for which the area's mild climate is ideal.

There was also a plan proposed by Ishiwara Kenji, Isomura Eiichi, and Takayama Eika in 1964. Advanced as "A Statement of an Opinion as to the General Development of the Fuji Piedmont," this plan was based on estimates of future developments in transportation and communication facilities--especially an estimate of increased automobile traffic volume. It called for vast regional development programs, including the establishment in the area at the foot of Mt. Fuji of buildings for the Diet, government offices, technical research centers, international conferences, and schools; it also included the development of agricultural, dairy, forestry, and tourist facilities and activities. It was designed to transfer part of the existing functions and population of Tokyo to this new area.

In 1964, Okui Fukutarō made known his conception of a new urban center of government offices. He proposed to reclaim Lake Hamana--which lies near the center of the greatest population concentration and between the two most important economic regions of the country, Kantō and Kansai--and to create an artificial island on which to build a Diet building, various government office buildings, and international conference halls.

As we have previously discussed, the process of centralization, or the centripetal force, in the Tokyo metropolitan complex is the most basic factor determining the structural pattern of the complex as a whole. Great amounts of investment have accompanied that process, and in view of the fact that human and institutional interrelationships will become more intense and important for effective urban social and economic activities, we cannot readily accept the proposed solutions to problems in the complex that negate or belittle the influence of the centripetal force.

In fact, during the six years from 1958 to 1964, floor space in Tokyo's three central wards increased by 7 million square meters, and if we include

Tokyo's subcenters in our calculation, the total floor space increase was 10 million square meters. In the three central wards, the average annual increase is 1.2 million square meters. Because of the necessity of inter-institutional contact, office space in central Tokyo constantly increases. By 1985 it is estimated that the total need for office floor space will be about twice as much as is available at present, in order to accommodate the increasing employee population (which will increase from the present 1.35 million to 2.85 million in 1985). Judging from the pace of the current construction projects alone, it will not be long before a forest of high-rise buildings of 100 or more meters appears, accompanied by wider roads and streets and more extensive use of space aboveground and underground.

Thus, the functions of the heart of the city as the center of institutional and individual contacts will be further expanded and intensified. Economic growth and the advance of civil engineering will make possible a greater high-density use of the center of Tokyo, stimulating the development of taller buildings, multi-level road, highway, and railroad crossings, more parking lots, more underground facilities, clearly demarcated pedestrian walks, roadways, and stroll tracks. The vertical development of the center will make it possible to expand public squares and other open spaces.

Such development will cost a great deal of money. Part of the necessary funds will have to be contributed, as we have stated earlier, by the enterprising institutions in the central city. They should contribute in proportion to the benefits they expect to receive from the better locational conditions made possible by public investments and according to government tax regulations to be stipulated with respect to fixed assets. Needless to say, there are certain expenses that should be borne by national and local governments for reasons of general public welfare; the large, centrally located institutions should not be held responsible for the entire funds. It appears to be best to have the funds created in the way mentioned above because the future development of the center of the city would then benefit the contributors of the funds.

As was indicated by the increase in the number of government, business, and other offices in central Tokyo in the past, the number and size of integrative institutions will continue to increase. The horizontal and vertical expansion of the area will continue, and the functions characteristic of the central urban core will be performed not only in the three central wards of Chiyoda, Chūō, and Minato but in the Shibuya, Shinjuku, Nakano, Ikebukuro, Ueno, and Asakusa areas as well (mainly along traffic routes in those areas). Therefore, the present subcenters of Tokyo will become administrative and management centers as well as consumer centers, with favorable transportation, shopping, recreational, cultural, and other facilities. Each subcenter will undergo, as does the heart of Tokyo, a process of redevelopment through more intensive utilization of available land space. The single-core structural pattern, exhibited in Tokyo, will then give way to a multi-core structure.

In order to expedite intensive land utilization, the Act Concerning Urban Cores Renewal in Connection with Programs for Improvement of Public Facilities was promulgated in 1961. It broadly aimed to contribute to urban renewal and redevelopment. More specifically, it provided for "stipulations with respect to the execution of urban cores renewal projects and other related matters, with a view to aiding the maintenance and promotion of urban functions, facilitating rational utilization of land, and contributing to the promotion of public welfare."

The central bodies responsible for the execution of urban renewal projects are local governments, but in many cases public corporations become involved indirectly in these projects. Through these projects, roads and streets in the heart of the city and its surrounding areas will be widened greatly (formerly, an impossible task), and high-rise buildings will be constructed. The land and other property owners in these areas will be provided with floor space equivalent in value to the rights they relinquished for the execution of the renewal projects. Individuals and institutions who also rent floor space will be considered.

This Urban Cores Renewal Act of 1961 will be rescinded soon, however, because it has been realized that urban redevelopment should involve not only selected local areas or a few traffic routes but wider areas of several blocks each (i.e., a "superblock" formula). Facilities in these areas are improved and developed with due consideration given to their fireproofing, beautiful appearance, and other aspects. Like the Urban Improvement Act, Land Zoning Act, Residential Zones Improvement Act, and the Act Concerning the Fireproof Building Zones, the Urban Cores Renewal Act will be incorporated in part and in revised form into the Urban Redevelopment Act, an act passed to redevelop urban cores within cities; the Urban Planning Act, which is designed to prevent urban sprawl and to develop urban cores, will also be incorporated into the Urban Redevelopment Act.

The new approach aims to expedite redevelopment programs of the superblock formula under national and local governments; it also hopes to encourage participation of private capital in these programs, inasmuch as most of the building construction works in the city are done by private organizations. In the past, the most that could be done on the part of the government authorities was to give grants-in-aid for private redevelopment projects, and when private organizations encountered opposition in the execution of their projects, they could not do anything about it. They did not have the legal right of expropriation, nor were they able to touch any public facilities such as roads and streets.

The new urban cores development plans allow the formation of cooperatives of landowners and leaseholders (each consisting of at least five members)--if two-thirds of all the landowners and leaseholders in each of the plan-affected areas concur, and if those two-thirds occupy two-thirds of all the lands owned and leased. Through this measure and others, the plans aim to facilitate, wherever feasible, a more rational, sound, and intensive utilization of land and more efficient functions of the urban centers.

Under these various urban renewal laws, a number of certain types of businesses (i.e., insurance firms) are being relocated from the crowded business-management heart of the city to subcenters that were formerly mere retail business centers. In Shinjuku, the largest subcenter of Tokyo, the Public Construction Corporation has been established; they are planning the development of a business management center in an area as large as 960,000 square meters. Furthermore, metropolitan Tokyo has obtained a 130,000-square-meter land tract near the northern entrance of the Nakano Railroad Station on the Central Railroad Line and is planning to establish a business management center and a retail business center there. In the eastern section of Shinbashi, which lies on the rim of the heart of Tokyo, the metropolitan government has had two 9-story buildings constructed and roads and streets widened in an area of

40,000 square meters, completely changing the look of the area formerly characterized by shabby quarters of restaurants and bars.

For the Shibuya area, the Shibuya Redevelopment Promotion Association was organized in 1967 to work for redevelopment of the whole area, including the redevelopment of the Tōkyū business complex centering around the Shibuya Station. Plans are also being made for the establishment of the New Urban Development Center Company for the Seibu and Mitsubishi estates of Ikebukuro, where a 36-story high-rise building, a bus terminal, and parking lots are to be constructed. Similar major redevelopment plans are in the making for Ueno, Asakusa, and other areas as well.

Retail business functions in the heart of Tokyo and its subcenters will continue dispersing under continuing urban expansion and in accordance with the distribution and consumption patterns of the residents; gradually, railroad-station-side business sections and regional shopping centers will develop. Since residence is usually determined by ecological distance to places of work, it will be necessary to plan for the development of a compact metropolis where high-rise apartments are provided near places of work and where population density will be high and maximum investment efficiency guaranteed.

Many Public Housing Corporation apartments exist in the Tokyo metropolitan complex, and, as we have mentioned earlier, many of them were constructed on the outskirts when central-city land prices rose; this condition greatly inconveniences the commuting population. Recently, however, areas around the heart of Tokyo have been redeveloped, and apartment buildings were constructed there. Land utilization has become more intensive, efficiency of investment for urban reconstruction and the efficiency of urban functions has increased, and the living environment has been beautified and improved.

In order to ensure full exercise of urban functions in the cities of the Tokyo metropolitan complex through intensive land utilization, it is necessary to consolidate the connections, by means of automobile and other mass transportation networks, between various business management districts in the complex--for instance, between the heart of Tokyo and its subcenters--and also between these districts and industrial and residential districts. This will, in turn, necessitate the improvement of roads and streets, which are now in poor condition, especially in Tokyo. At present, low wooden buildings that serve both as residences and shops line the roads that connect the heart and subcenters of Tokyo with industrial and residential areas; behind these rows stand crowded many low, small wooden houses. In order to widen roads, acquire land, and solve housing problems under such conditions, we must depend on the Urban Cores Renewal Act and other laws mentioned above.

The application of these legal measures helped attain success in the cases of the Aoyama Route, a major Olympic Games route that is about two kilometers from central Tokyo, the Sangenjaya Route, which is about 10 kilometers from central Tokyo, and several other routes lined with shops and stores. In the case of the Aoyama Route, the Japan Public Housing Corporation in 1960 constructed, with the cooperation of the landowners concerned, a building with one story underground and eleven stories aboveground. In this building, space on the third floor and below was provided for shops and offices, while on the fourth floor and up, residential units were provided for 251 families. The people who had lived or owned land in the area occupied by this building were given the right to open shops and offices or to live in the residential units. In addition, three buildings, each with one underground story and ten stories aboveground, were constructed; residential units were provided for 164, 70, and 81 families, respectively. Thus, the appearance of the community was drastically changed and modernized. Plans are being made for similar buildings on both sides of the route. In the Sangenjaya area, the Metropolitan Fireproof Building Construction Corporation constructed four 5-story buildings in 1966, widened the street for better traffic, and beautified the community's environment.

Around the heart of Tokyo, problem-ridden areas are not the hillside residential districts such as Aoyama, Azabu, and Sangenjaya but are the districts of Kōtō, Sumida, Edogawa, Katsushika, and Arakawa (where factories and small homes exist side by side or single buildings are used both as factories and homes) and also Adachi, Shinagawa, and Ōta. Kōtō, especially, and the three neighboring wards are confronted with serious problems of ground sinking, traffic congestion, and public nuisances caused by industrial activities. Because of legal measures concerning industrial activities and establishments, factories are being relocated from these areas to the outskirts, and their number is decreasing. There still remain, as we have seen earlier, a large number of petty enterprises that have no ability to improve their locational conditions for themselves. Plans are also being made for the forestation of the former sites of big factories that have been relocated elsewhere.

The Public Housing Corporation has completed the following projects: in Kanemachi, Katsushika Ward, the construction in 1965 of four apartment buildings of 5, 11, 14, and 15 floors, respectively, in order to accommodate 1,417 families--they are complete with banking, shopping, and supermarket facilities near them; the construction in 1960 in Senjū, Adachi Ward, of one 7-story building and three 11-story buildings with accommodations for a total of 764 families; the construction in 1966 in Kameto, Kōtō Ward, of four 11-story buildings and one 8-story building with accommodations for 806 families.

These apartments are so-called urban core housing units. They are built in the sites vacated by factories and are relatively cheap in land value despite their nearness to the heart of Tokyo. Each site occupies an area of three hectares or larger, and each building takes up about 20 percent of the site, which is provided with lawns, flower gardens, and play yards. In Public Housing Corporation Apartment zones in other urban cores, it has been impossible to provide adequate space for each apartment building owing to the leasing of land from landowners or others with vested rights. In the new plans, this situation has been corrected. Construction plans are also being made for Ōshima, Kōtō Ward--three 14-story buildings and two 9-story and 8-story buildings during the years of 1966 and 1967 to accommodate 2,514 families.

The Public Housing Corporation maintains that their construction programs, like those described above, are designed to improve living conditions--the basic requirement in urban planning--and that they have significance as representatives of public housing units based on the community reconstruction formula of the government.

Because the construction of high-rise buildings of seven stories and taller involves the use of steel frames and the preparation of special facilities such as elevators, construction costs are high. The cost per 3.3 square meters is about ¥120,000, twice as much as the cost for medium-height buildings of five stories or lower. Rents are also higher in new buildings because of the cost-defraying formula of the Housing Corporation; a 2 DK unit rents from ¥20,000 up, compared with the same unit in other apartment zones for ¥7,000-10,000. A 3 LK unit unit in a new apartment rents for ¥30,000. Thus, as far as rents are concerned, the new apartments are not exactly meeting the housing demands of the masses. In future plans for high-rise apartment buildings near the heart of Tokyo, serious consideration must be given to drastic revisions in the formulas for determining rents.

Again in view of the fact that the areas of new apartment developments are those wards of Tokyo where private earnings are generally low and small-scale industrial and commercial enterprises coexist with small homes, consideration must be given to the possible bearing that the pouring of billions of yen of national funds into these areas for new residential construction might have on the organic structural relations of the areas with other parts of the metropolitan complex. It should also be determined if such building programs really have any significance in the promotion of public welfare in the planned community reconstruction. It appears that in the planning for the Tokyo metropolitan complex it has not been made clear what functions are envisioned for the complex in the future, what relation exists between construction plans of the Public Housing Corporation and the government plans for the complex, and what specific goals are considered for the benefit of the residents.

We have discussed the need for more intensive land use and open space in the heart of the city and its surrounding areas. There are views that recognize the great amount of money needed for redevelopment of the Existing Urban Cores area and favor relocating some functions away from the city, the transfer of the national capital to some other city, or the construction of residential districts in remote areas where land values are low. According to the Urban Development Bureau of the Ministry of Construction, per-house construction cost in the large-scale apartment zones in the Suburban Improvement Region is estimated at ¥3 million if costs of constructing accompanying facilities for railroad and vehicle traffic, water, electricity, gas supply, sewerage, and schools are disregarded, and ¥5 million if those additional costs are taken into consideration. On the other hand, per-house construction cost in the Existing Urban Cores is about ¥4 million if costs of constructing such new facilities as subways are not taken into account. Thus, the argument that it costs a great deal more to redevelop the Existing Urban Cores than to develop anew the Suburban Improvement Region is not founded on fact.

The Relationship between Current Plans and the Demands
of an Expanding Tokyo

The preceding discussion should not be construed as favoring as an ideal, a compact metropolitan area with high-level vertical development of every facility into open space. In line with the goal of purifying the character of pivotal sections of the Tokyo metropolitan complex as business districts or as apartment residential areas, and as clearly shown by the effective operation of the Act Governing Factories and Other Industrial Establishments, we are merely emphasizing the needs for structural modernization of factories, relocation of factories to peripheral and coastal industrial areas, relocation of central wholesale markets and stores to peripheral consumption centers, and relocation of public and private research institutions and schools to educational centers that have ideal environments and adequate facilities.

The Existing Urban Cores Region, which is now being redeveloped as a compact nucleus of the complex, must have improved roads and streets, transportation facilities, compulsory education facilities, and day nurseries; for these improvement projects the national government should, according to special financial measures, consider and give aid to local public bodies.

I believe the view that favors a compact metropolis and one favoring a dispersed structure, as advanced at the time of discussion in the Diet on the Tokyo Metropolitan Complex Improvement Act, are both unrealistic. A metropolis is basically structured by a centripetal force, and an institution needing centralization should be allowed to so locate itself as to ensure maximum efficiency of its functions. Those that can obtain positive benefits by operating in outer areas and those that feel more adverse effects than benefits in operating in central sections should be dispersed to outer areas.

In reality, the best and most effective approach may be to recognize special characteristics of the political, social, and economic structures of Tokyo as the national capital and plan for staged development and redevelopment without jeopardizing its urban functions at any moment.

The original basic plan, before revision, (following the example of the London urban plan) provided for a green belt of about 10 kilometers around the Existing Urban Cores. This would serve to prevent excessive sprawling of the areas and, at the same time, to preserve the physical environment in the form of parks or green tracts of land for recreational, urban beautification, and vegetable gardening purposes. But the opposition of local people and the lack of funds have rendered full implementation of the plan difficult; in the meantime, many homes were built in the areas without any planning, making it necessary to revise the original plan completely.

The Suburban Improvement Region that lies beyond the Existing Urban Cores Region and extends 50 kilometers from central Tokyo includes a number of municipalities with high rates of population increase. It is estimated that the present population of the 50-kilometer radius area, which stands at 18.8 million, will increase to 28 million by 1980. It is necessary to provide an environment that is conducive to the social and economic activities of some 2.5 million people who are expected to be working in the heart of Tokyo in 1980, and at the same time provide sound living conditions for the estimated 328 million residents of the areas surrounding the Existing Urban Cores area.

We have discussed at length the housing and social conditions of the Suburban Improvement Zone. In the southwestern area of this zone between 30 and 40 kilometers from central Tokyo, and in the northeastern area between 25 and 35 kilometers from the center of Tokyo, there are sections where homes are of low quality and roads and other facilities are meager. The situation is the result of the unplanned and rapid population increase caused by the migration of relatively low-income people from central Tokyo. There are also a number of structures that serve as both factories and homes, especially in the northeastern area. On the other hand, large open spaces still remain that can be converted into residential lots. Thus, this region has room for development and improvement through public and private investments.

From the standpoints of public welfare and investment efficiency, it is important that this region be made a pure residential region contiguous to the residential districts in and around the Existing Urban Cores; it can be done by preventing the new establishment of factories. The region must also have new high-density, compact urban cores within its boundaries. At the same time, it is necessary to construct extensions of the subways to directly connect the region with central Tokyo for the benefit of the increasing white-collar commuting population. The surface traffic congestion will be greatly lessened, as will the inconvenience of frequent transfer from one mode of transportation to another.

The phenomenal population increase in these peripheral areas of the metropolis makes it imperative to build new and adequate transportation, educational, and other urban facilities. This adds to the financial burdens of the local communities. To alleviate this situation, institutional reforms are necessary.

The government has divided this Suburban Improvement Zone into 22 districts that encompass 165 municipalities. For 12 of these districts, including 95 municipalities, a five-year residential road construction plan has been formulated; a similar plan for the remaining 10 districts is scheduled for formulation in 1967.

Within the 30-50 kilometer circular belt in the Suburban Improvement Region are large forested and scenic river-side areas that are conducive to the maintenance and improvement of general public health. In order to conserve this natural environment and other green tracts of land where public nuisances have been kept at the very minimum, the pertinent sections of the region were designated in 1966 as the Suburban Green Land Conservation Zones, and conservation plans have been formulated. In view of the failure of the green land conservation plans of previous years, the designation of the zones was carefully performed, and in the planning, cuneiform green tracts were provided at intervals along the radially extending railroad lines and roadways to avoid impact with the growth of the urban cores that develop along these traffic routes.

In 1967, ten new conservation zones--10,000 hectares in total area--were designated. It was stipulated that any new building construction, and the creation of any new residential sites and any other projects that might greatly alter the character of the land in the area was, in principle, subject to authorization by the prefectural governor. If governmental disapproval of the private agency's purchase of land is likely to hamper efficiency in land utilization, the prefectural governments are legitimately allowed to purchase the land in question with national financial aid as far as the land is included in the suburban green land conservation project. For this purpose, the national government set aside ¥200 million in the 1966 budget and ¥300 million in the 1967 budget.

Along with these natural environment conservation plans for the Suburban Improvement Region, plans are also being made for the construction of large-scale residential centers, with railroads, streets, water supply, sewers, and other facilities to be constructed with public and private funds.

In the beautiful green hill region between 25 and 35 kilometers from central Tokyo, which includes such municipalities as Hachiōji, Machida, Tama, and Inashiro (a total area of some 2,960 hectares), the Japan Public Housing

Corporation and the Metropolitan Housing Supply Corporation are planning to establish apartment zones. There they will build 72,000 housing units, schools, parks, hospitals, water supply and sewerage systems, and traffic routes to the heart and subcenters of Tokyo, in order to accommodate 300,000 people. The first phase of this program will take care of the construction of 34,000 housing units for 146,000 people in 40 percent of the total designated area by 1972. There are problems, however, in the way of full and smooth operation of this development program. They include the program's geographical coverage which does not agree well with the existing administrative boundaries of the municipalities involved, compensation for land use or acquisition, financial burdens on local governments, refuse disposal, and balance of development between these apartment zones and other zones of the municipalities whose water supply and sewerage facilities are still in poor condition.

We have already stated that in this Suburban Improvement Region the number of farmers engaged in side work or leaving the farmlands altogether has been increasing, but, on the other hand, many farmlands have relatively high productivity and a high degree of mechanization. Because of proximity to the big consumer market, this region is in a good position to supply vegetables and milk which must be kept fresh all the time. From this region, which covers part of Tokyo, Chiba, Saitama, and Kanagawa, are supplied 65 percent of the vegetables hauled into the central wholesale market and 95 percent of the milk for all of metropolitan Tokyo. With this in view, positive measures for further development and improvement of this region as a supply center of these products must be taken.

As we have pointed out earlier, the Urban Development Region has been designated to cover the area between 50 kilometers and 100-130 kilometers from central Tokyo beyond the Suburban Improvement Region, which represents the outer limits of the sphere of daily life and activity in the complex. It was intended that inland-type industrial establishments would be relocated in this region with a view to relieving the Existing Urban Cores of the pressure of concentrated population and industry. According to the 1962 survey of the Committee on the Tokyo Metropolitan Complex Improvement, 49 percent of the 3,321 factories having 30 or more employees each desired expansion or relocation elsewhere in the complex; and 40 percent of them had already obtained the necessary land for such expansion or relocation, while the remaining 60 percent were looking for land of some 2,118 square meters in area. Among those wanting to relocate, 34 percent desired new sites within the metropolis of Tokyo, and 13 percent wanted Kanagawa, Chiba, and Saitama. Between 1956 and 1963 there was an increase of about 1,600 factories in the complex as a whole, of which approximately 70 percent were located in the 40 to 50-kilometer limits from central Tokyo in such places as Sagamihara, Atsugi, Hachiōji, Oume, and Hamura. Only about half the increased number in the areas beyond the 50-kilometer limits found locations in the Urban Development Region.

Therefore, it was unwise to categorically designate as the Urban Development Area the region beyond the 50-kilometer limits from central Tokyo. The designation should have been based on the assumption that factories would move out of industrial concentration centers to outer areas only gradually. Generally, the closer the location to the Existing Urban Cores Region which offers the benefits of industrial concentration, the better a location is for a factory. In the Urban Development Region also, the closer a location is to the existing industrial concentration zones, the better the conditions are for the factory.

Therefore, the overall urban planning for new factory locations should proceed first to designate urban development zones in areas relatively close to the Existing Urban Cores (especially to the industrial zones in these cores). Such areas may include places where principal National Railroad lines meet loop roadways and highways as they radially extend from the Existing Urban Cores. New designations can then be made in progressively more remote areas near strategic traffic centers, until many of the factories that may have been established in these areas can finally be induced to relocate in what will be designated as the Urban Development Area.

Although not flawless in planning and execution, the Japan Public Housing Corporation and the local public bodies successfully executed the creation, in the Urban Development Region (which is basically an industrial region), of 4,800 hectares of industrial and residential zones. Of these, 1,130 hectares have been earmarked for industrial purposes, and plans have been formulated and put into operation for the construction of roads, waterways, compulsory education facilities, public squares and open spaces, domestic and industrial water supply and sewerage facilities, and street cleaning systems.

For the smooth and proper execution of the plan for land acquisition and industrial development in this region, industrial zones development projects have been treated as metropolitan planning projects for which the right of land expropriation was legally granted. Furthermore, as in the case of the Suburban Improvement Zone, this Urban Development Region is entitled to national financial aid according to special financial measures.

As part of the development program in this Urban Development Region, a measure was taken in 1963 to establish a research and educational center in the Tsukuba district, an area of 4,000 hectares, in which to relocate or establish government offices, public and private research centers, and colleges and universities. These institutions do not necessarily require locations in the Existing Urban Cores, or need new facilities or other improvements, but they can function best within a congregation of similar institutions and agencies. This was designed to help further relieve the pressure of concentrated population and industry in the metropolis, and since 1965 the Japan Public Housing Corporation has been acquiring or newly creating sites for the planned development, which is scheduled for completion in ten years.

One of the facilities near Tokyo that has become a serious problem in recent years is the airport of Haneda. With the ushering in of a new age of 500-passenger jumbo jets and supersonic transports, Haneda Airport has become obsolete; the construction of a new international airport is necessary.

The Airport Construction Corporation is currently planning for modern airport facilities at Narita. The total area of the new airport is about 1,000 hectares, and it will have 4,000-meter runways. The area itself is not very large, but emphasis has been placed on providing the best facilities possible. Narita is 50 kilometers directly from the heart of Tokyo, and with the completion of a freeway, the time needed to cover the distance will be 50 minutes-- a great reduction from the present two hours between Tokyo and Narita. A plan is also being made to construct an express railroad line, which would require only 30 minutes' travel time between the new airport and Tokyo. Other plans call for the construction of a modern airport apartment center at a place about 5 kilometers from the airport to accommodate 150,000 people, including about

50,000 airport employees, the creation of a buffer zone of sound-absorption forest around the airport (50-100 meters wide), and the improvement of jet engines to minimize annoying sounds for neighboring residents.

The flying time between Tokyo and Hong Kong will be an hour and a half, and between Tokyo and Honolulu, three hours. When the world is shrinking and international contact is becoming more intense and frequent, it goes without saying that the new airport development program must be fully executed, although opposition to this program is being aired; it can be completed while paying due attention to public welfare.

As for the harbors of the Tokyo metropolitan complex, which have a hinterland of gigantic industrial establishments and over twenty million people, the total tonnage of freight handled in 1964 reached 300 million tons (150,000 vessels were involved)--this figure far exceeds the 110 million tons handled at Europort. However, the harbor facilities are in very poor condition. Tokyo Harbor is now too small to handle the increasing demands for goods and the increasing size of vessels, and much of the freight is being handled for Tokyo by other harbors. In view of the continuous increase in the volume of freight, which is predicted to reach 400 million tons by 1975, and in the number of vessels, estimated to be about 300,000 in that year, the Ministry of Transportation formulated in 1967 an epoch-making development plan to be implemented during the period 1968-1975.

According to this plan, the harbors of Tokyo, Yokohama, Kawasaki, Chiba, Yokosuka, and Kisarazu on the Tokyo Bay coast will have individual roles assigned to them. Tokyo, Yokohama, and Kawasaki Harbors will handle regular foreign liners; domestic freight intended for metropolitan Tokyo will be handled at Tokyo Harbor, for Tōhoku at Chiba Harbor, and for Kanagawa at Yokosuka Harbor. The total number of berths in all the harbors will be increased to 135 for foreign trade purposes (51 berths at present) and 239 for domestic trade purposes (59 at present); a new 7,000-square-meter loading and unloading platform space will be added to the present 12,000 square meters.

A plan is also in the making to reclaim a total of 100 million square meters of land at the entrances of these harbors for road construction, forestation, or industrial purposes. The implementation of this plan will last for five years, beginning in 1968, and cost 1.2 trillion _yen_.

In the 130-kilometer radius Tokyo metropolitan complex, which comprises various regions with different characteristics that are structurally interrelated, perhaps the most important task is to improve the transportation and communication networks within and between the regions--Existing Urban Cores, Suburban Improvement Region, Urban Development Region--and the airport and harbor areas. This will ensure the full exercise of functions by each of these areas. Plans have been formulated for the improvement of the national and prefectural highways and roads, which center in the Existing Urban Cores Region and have been grouped as Radial Line System 16 and Loopline System 5; this improvement program is scheduled for completion in 1970. New plans must be created as soon as possible for the improvement of basic communication facilities as well.

The inner structure of the Tokyo metropolitan complex is extremely complicated, and future trends are hard to forecast. Therefore, it is difficult to formulate short- and long-range development plans that ensure the uncontradictory growth of an organically unified region. We must patiently continue our study to better grasp future trends of change and to set out goals with a sense of value commensurate with the new society to be established. On the basis of these trends and goals we should formulate development plans.

The legal, tax, and finance systems currently in force are too defective to meet the changing conditions of the complex, and many features in these systems have to be revised. It is also necessary to study ways to utilize private funds in executing development and redevelopment plans, since public investment for all such plans is usually limited to about a maximum of 20 percent of the annual national budget. Also, many more development projects, especially construction projects, are handled by private organizations than by government agencies.

There are some problems, such as housing, land use, transportation, water supply, and harbor facilities, that must be treated not as relating to individual administrative areas separately but as concerning a wider region that encompasses all the areas as a whole. There is a lack of unity between the national government, with its emphasis on vertical lines of coordination of administrative functions, and the local administrative bodies, which have limited geographical jurisdiction; this current administrative setup is inadequate for metropolitan redevelopment programs.

It is necessary now to organize a system in which the Tokyo metropolitan complex as a whole can be systematically studied. Plans are to be formulated and implemented according to the studies, and, at the same time, the wishes of the people of the individual local areas will be adequately reflected.

Some recommendations have been advanced. One is the establishment of a Tokyo Metropolitan Complex Agency, with a state minister as its head and the component prefectural authorities organized into one body; another is the amalgamation of the prefectures into one administrative unit. There have been a few suggestions for the establishment of various forms of cooperative administration between local public bodies, national government agencies, and public corporations. All these are important suggestions and warrant careful study.

PART II

DATA

CHAPTER 9

COMPILATION OF DATA ON THE TOKYO METROPOLITAN COMPLEX

In Part I we discussed the position of the Tokyo metropolitan complex in Japanese society and described its socioeconomic structure on the basis of human ecological analysis. Designed to help the reader understand the general characteristics of the structure and problems of the Tokyo metropolitan complex, the discussions and descriptions have been hypothetical in nature. However, to analyze the complexity of the problems of the area and to formulate plans for solving those problems, one must gather and systematically compile various data according to some basic principles. If the discussions and descriptions on the preceding pages have served a meaningful purpose by embodying the principles necessary for a compilation of the data, I will have been rewarded.

My purpose in publishing the present volume is to provide a wide circle of interested people with the systematically compiled statistical data needed to understand and analyze the Tokyo metropolitan complex. I have had to judge the most appropriate ways to select and compile the data. Most of the so-called community fact books that are available are based on national census reports and contain tabulated materials for each local community in a metropolitan region. Statistical materials in each fact book are arranged in alphabetical or some other order throughout the book. Each survey item is diagrammed for the metropolitan region as a whole, making it possible to see general trends of distributional patterns in the region. The community fact books of the past have seemed to have as their main purpose the clarification of the character- istics of individual local communities.

I have found much to learn in these community fact books, but in view of the current status of studies on urban communities and the nature of present urban problems, I have adopted a new method of compilation for basic data. The aim of this study is to make clear the community structure of the Tokyo metropol- itan complex as a whole; and the data in this book are presented within that certain frame of reference. This procedure may run the risk of narrowing the scope of usefulness of the data gathered, but I believe the method has allowed for the presentation of almost all the information that a community fact book presents. At the same time, it is not necessary to make any further tabulation from the materials presented to grasp many and varied meanings as to the struc- ture of the Tokyo metropolitan complex and its component local communities, since a compilation of data within a frame of reference indicates that some analytical operations have been completed. Furthermore, because of the univer- sality of our frame of reference, the materials presented for the Tokyo metro- politan complex can be used for comparison with other metropolitan regions in Japan and in foreign countries.

As for the selection of data for compilation, it is needless to say that as many and as varied data as possible have to be assembled and classified in a systematic manner to clarify facts about the Tokyo metropolitan complex. A great mass of data has been gathered and compiled, but we are presenting here only the materials taken from national census reports, which lend themselves to standardized compilation and to easy and accurate comparison with various indices.

Thus, the data has been compiled in the following manner:
1. The geographical boundary of the Tokyo metropolitan complex about which
    the data are presented encircles an area 50 kilometers in radius from
    the Tokyo Central (railroad) Station. This station is the point with
    the greatest accessibility in ecological distance, in which integrative
    institutions of the greatest scales are concentrated in the greatest
    degree. The purpose is to present data clearly so that structural dif-
    ferences in the component districts within the complex may be compared;
    therefore, the division of the area into such districts was an important
    operation. Japan has yet to have such unit areas as census tracts that
    Western nations have, so that the smallest units for national census
    purposes in Japan have to be <u>shi</u> (city), <u>ku</u> (ward), <u>machi</u> (town), or <u>mura</u>
    (village). For the purpose of this study, however, these units are too
    large and diverse in character for accurate comparisons of areas and
    populations. But at present, there are no materials available that are
    not based on these units. They are used for national census and other
    purposes and, in a way, the materials based on these units are useful for
    comparison; we have accordingly employed these units.

2. I have frequently pointed out that modern cities are in constant change,
    and that they should be studied not only for their structural patterns
    at one given moment of time but for their processes of change over time.
    It was necessary in this operation to base the study on the 1960 census
    report on the smallest units of survey (as mentioned above) and to
    include information on these units for the years 1955 and 1950 for com-
    parative purposes. Municipal boundary changes in 1950-1960 were frequent,
    owing to many mergers; because national census reports did not neces-
    sarily present accurate pictures of the actual conditions, it was diffi-
    cult to compile the data systematically. The materials have been
    tabulated according to the changes in municipal boundaries as shown in
    the table appended at the end of this volume and they have been compiled
    uniformly for the basic units that existed in 1960--this should facilitate
    analysis of changes.

3. The basic assumptions are that the nature and structure of urban society
    are most decidedly determined by the number, the scales, and the activi-
    ties of the integrative institutions functioning in a given metropolis--
    the institutions congregate in central and subcentral sections of the city,
    railroad-station-side areas, satellite centers, and other pivotal areas--
    and that the living patterns and residential distribution of urban resi-
    dents are closely connected with changes in these integrative institutions.
    The decisive influence on the structure of a big city, especially, is
    played by the condition of the central section and industrial zones of
    that city, and accessibility to these areas in terms of time-cost distance
    determines the distribution of residents and the locations of subcenters,
    station-side centers, neighborhood centers, and satellite cities. Inte-
    grative institutions have varying scales of operation and varying spheres
    of integrative activities, and they are distributed like satellites
    around the central section and industrial zones of the metropolis. View-
    ing urbanization as progressing according to time-cost distance from
    areas near the center of the metropolis to those further away from the
    center, the approach on the basis of the preceding assumptions is most
    useful and appropriate for the compilation of data. However, in reality,
    a number of distortions arise. For one thing, conditions of accessibility

differ from one area to another. A given area may be geographically
distant from the center of the metropolis but have a short ecological
distance, that is, a greater degree of accessibility. Such areas generally exist along railroad lines and freeways. Various patterns logically
assumed may differ in actuality, and it is necessary to take into account
such factors as the institutional structure, technological level, cultural level, and power structure of a society to explain concrete
societal phenomena. Be that as it may, data compiled on the basis of the
frame of reference mentioned above will render analysis of social phenomena in conjunction with other factors much more easily.

4. The compilation of data was built upon the assumptions mentioned above.
Geographical distances can be most simply denoted in meters or miles.
As for ecological distances, it is proper to assume at the outset that
the greater the geographical distance of a given area is to the center
of a city, the greater is the ecological distance as well. With the aid
of a map, one can also assume that the areas along railroad lines and
freeways have shorter ecological distances to the center of the city
than would those areas located away from such transportation routes. An
attempt has been made to compile the data on these assumptions in the
following manner, determining, in the process, a number of unit areas
within the metropolitan complex:
a) the 50-kilometer-radius circle with the Tokyo Central Station as its
   center has been divided into 10 circular belts (zones); see
   Chapter 9, Fig. 1.
b) the area is further divided into 10 fan-shaped sections (sectors),
   mainly in accordance with the railroad lines radially extending from
   the Tokyo Central Station.
c) the unit areas (districts) were thus determined by the lines delimiting the zones and sectors. Each district was designated after the
   name of the ku (ward), shi (city), machi (town), or mura (village)
   that is considered to be the most pivotal in the local area. In the
   case of a ku, population and other density is considered to be even
   throughout the whole area; accordingly, each ku constituted a unit
   district. In the case of other municipalities, a unit district was
   represented by the shi, machi, or mura that had the greatest concentration of population within the area. Each of these unit districts
   fall in a given zone and sector.

5. For each of the unit districts, figures were tabulated for various
indices, presenting totals, percentage distributions, arithmetic means,
medians, and, for an understanding of trends of change over time,
increases or decreases. The information is presented not only in
tables (Chapter 11) but also by maps (Chapter 10) for various
indices; the distribution patterns of phenomena at a given time and the
patterns of change over time can be easily observed.

Each unit district located in a given sector is identified by a roman numeral;
in a zone the unit district is identified by an arabic numeral. The simplest
assumption is that since urbanization progresses from central to outer sections,
changes will occur with certain regularity with respect to each index selected.
Therefore, figures for totals, percentage distributions, arithmetic means, and
medians have been tabulated for each of the indices with respect to each unit
district. Through this operation, patterns of change become clear. At the same time,

information is available for the years 1950, 1955, and 1960 for most of the indices, and thus the trends, extent, and speed of change over time can be observed. Lastly, national totals, national distributional patterns, and national arithmetic means and medians are provided so that comparisons can be made with the conditions in the Tokyo metropolitan complex. This will help clarify the relative importance of the complex in the national society at one point of time and the shift of such importance over time.

I hope the foregoing explanation has clarified the approach to the compilation of data. The data presented here can be used widely, not simply for the purposes mentioned above. The discussion and description in Part I pointed out that pursuing spatial structures and patterns of their change exclusively would produce merely a partial description of social phenomena. Integrative institutions of cities are not the only segments of national society; people and their daily life constitute important elements also. National society must be understood in its totality--political, economic, and cultural patterns. The Tokyo metropolitan complex possesses spatiality, and it cannot be understood properly without giving due attention to its spatial structure. In this sense, the data presented here and the method in which they were compiled have great significance. But it goes without saying that the data can be used jointly with other sources for clarification of many factual points.

CHAPTER 10

FIGURES

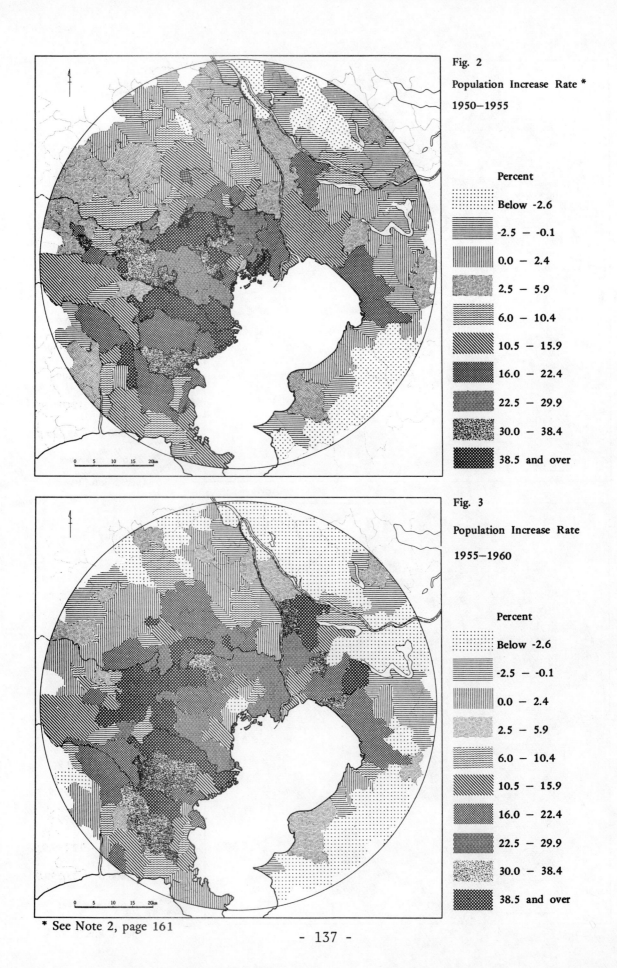

Fig. 2

Population Increase Rate *

1950—1955

Percent

Below -2.6

-2.5 — -0.1

0.0 — 2.4

2.5 — 5.9

6.0 — 10.4

10.5 — 15.9

16.0 — 22.4

22.5 — 29.9

30.0 — 38.4

38.5 and over

Fig. 3

Population Increase Rate

1955—1960

Percent

Below -2.6

-2.5 — -0.1

0.0 — 2.4

2.5 — 5.9

6.0 — 10.4

10.5 — 15.9

16.0 — 22.4

22.5 — 29.9

30.0 — 38.4

38.5 and over

* See Note 2, page 161

- 137 -

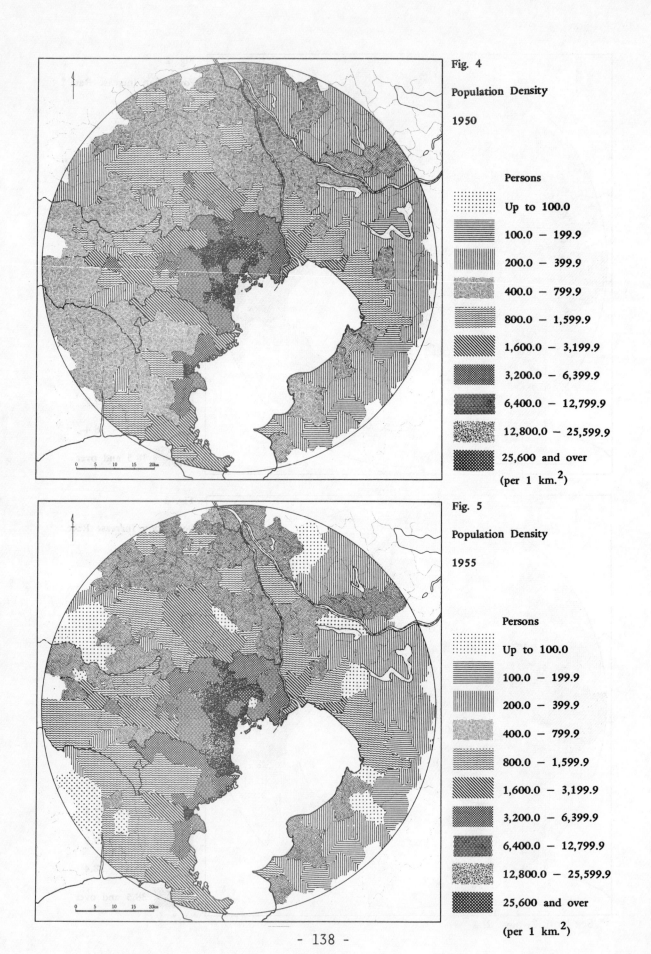

Fig. 4

Population Density

1950

Persons

Up to 100.0

100.0 — 199.9

200.0 — 399.9

400.0 — 799.9

800.0 — 1,599.9

1,600.0 — 3,199.9

3,200.0 — 6,399.9

6,400.0 — 12,799.9

12,800.0 — 25,599.9

25,600 and over

(per 1 km.^{2})

Fig. 5

Population Density

1955

Persons

Up to 100.0

100.0 — 199.9

200.0 — 399.9

400.0 — 799.9

800.0 — 1,599.9

1,600.0 — 3,199.9

3,200.0 — 6,399.9

6,400.0 — 12,799.9

12,800.0 — 25,599.9

25,600 and over

(per 1 km.^{2})

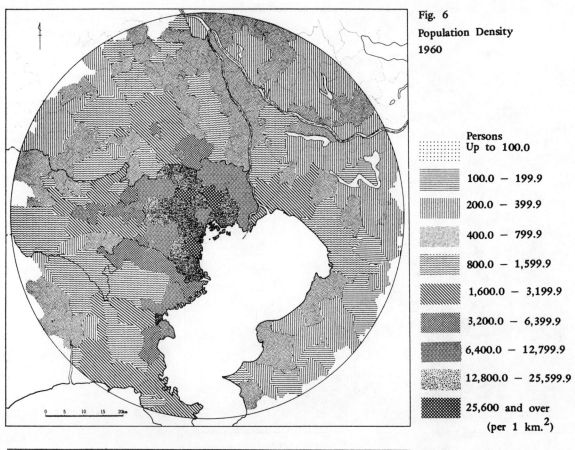

Fig. 6
Population Density
1960

Persons
Up to 100.0

100.0 — 199.9

200.0 — 399.9

400.0 — 799.9

800.0 — 1,599.9

1,600.0 — 3,199.9

3,200.0 — 6,399.9

6,400.0 — 12,799.9

12,800.0 — 25,599.9

25,600 and over
(per 1 km.^{2})

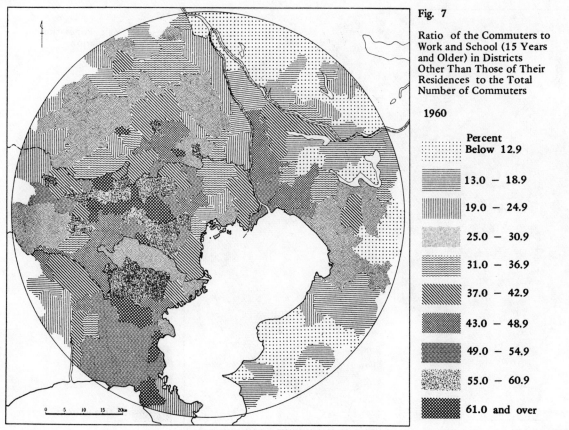

Fig. 7

Ratio of the Commuters to
Work and School (15 Years
and Older) in Districts
Other Than Those of Their
Residences to the Total
Number of Commuters

1960

Percent
Below 12.9

13.0 — 18.9

19.0 — 24.9

25.0 — 30.9

31.0 — 36.9

37.0 — 42.9

43.0 — 48.9

49.0 — 54.9

55.0 — 60.9

61.0 and over

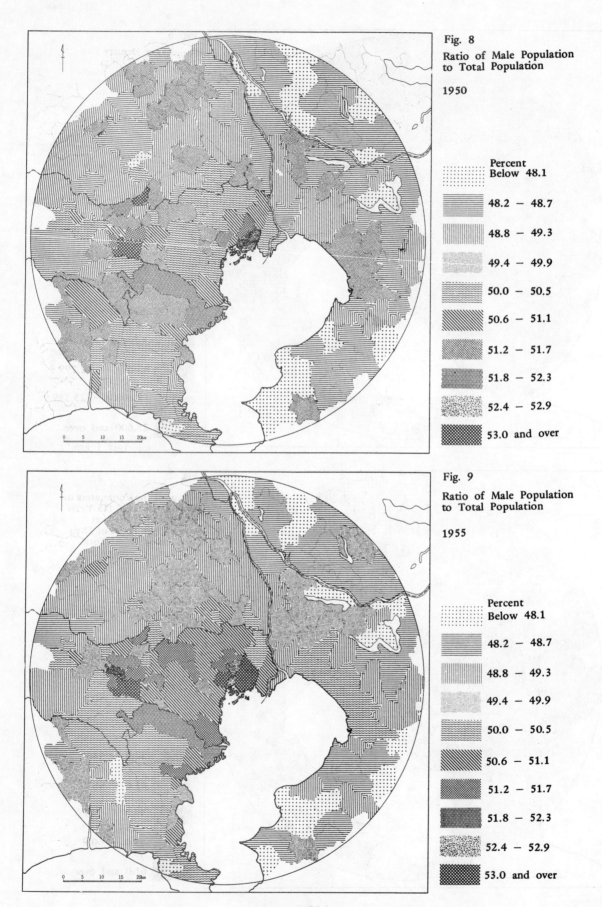

Fig. 8

Ratio of Male Population
to Total Population

1950

Percent
Below 48.1

48.2 — 48.7

48.8 — 49.3

49.4 — 49.9

50.0 — 50.5

50.6 — 51.1

51.2 — 51.7

51.8 — 52.3

52.4 — 52.9

53.0 and over

Fig. 9

Ratio of Male Population
to Total Population

1955

Percent
Below 48.1

48.2 — 48.7

48.8 — 49.3

49.4 — 49.9

50.0 — 50.5

50.6 — 51.1

51.2 — 51.7

51.8 — 52.3

52.4 — 52.9

53.0 and over

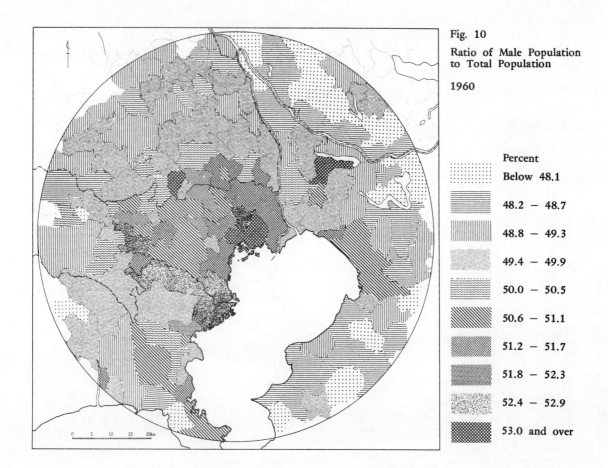

Fig. 10
Ratio of Male Population
to Total Population

1960

Percent
Below 48.1
48.2 — 48.7
48.8 — 49.3
49.4 — 49.9
50.0 — 50.5
50.6 — 51.1
51.2 — 51.7
51.8 — 52.3
52.4 — 52.9
53.0 and over

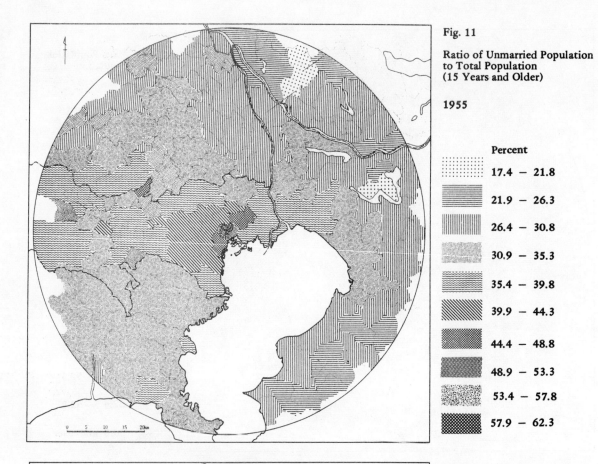

Fig. 11

Ratio of Unmarried Population
to Total Population
(15 Years and Older)

1955

Percent
17.4 — 21.8
21.9 — 26.3
26.4 — 30.8
30.9 — 35.3
35.4 — 39.8
39.9 — 44.3
44.4 — 48.8
48.9 — 53.3
53.4 — 57.8
57.9 — 62.3

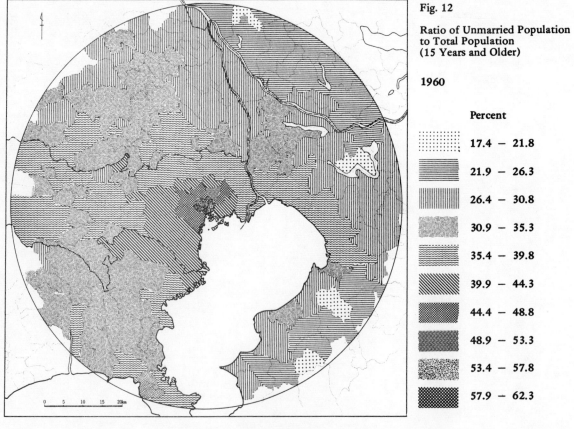

Fig. 12

Ratio of Unmarried Population
to Total Population
(15 Years and Older)

1960

Percent
17.4 — 21.8
21.9 — 26.3
26.4 — 30.8
30.9 — 35.3
35.4 — 39.8
39.9 — 44.3
44.4 — 48.8
48.9 — 53.3
53.4 — 57.8
57.9 — 62.3

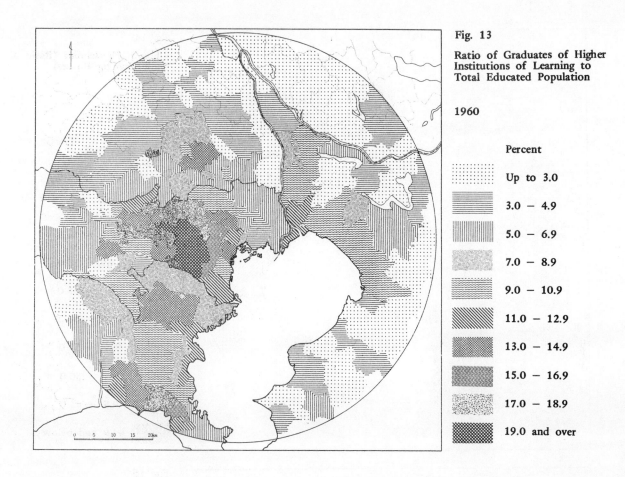

Fig. 13

Ratio of Graduates of Higher Institutions of Learning to Total Educated Population

1960

Percent

Up to 3.0

3.0 — 4.9

5.0 — 6.9

7.0 — 8.9

9.0 — 10.9

11.0 — 12.9

13.0 — 14.9

15.0 — 16.9

17.0 — 18.9

19.0 and over

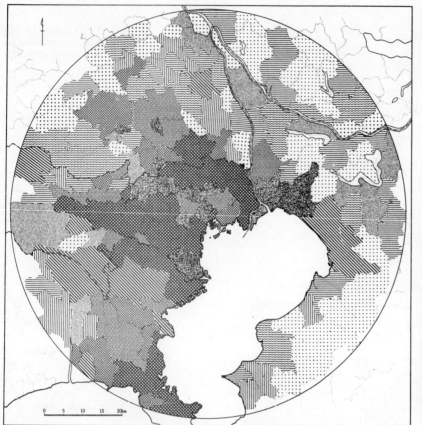

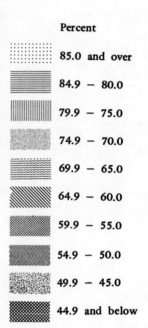

Fig. 14

Kinds of Households (Ratio of Those Owning Houses)

1950

Percent

	85.0 and over
	84.9 − 80.0
	79.9 − 75.0
	74.9 − 70.0
	69.9 − 65.0
	64.9 − 60.0
	59.9 − 55.0
	54.9 − 50.0
	49.9 − 45.0
	44.9 and below

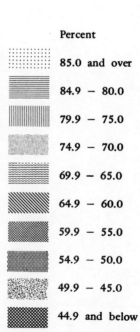

Fig. 15

Kinds of Households (Ratio of Those Owning Houses)

1955

Percent

	85.0 and over
	84.9 − 80.0
	79.9 − 75.0
	74.9 − 70.0
	69.9 − 65.0
	64.9 − 60.0
	59.9 − 55.0
	54.9 − 50.0
	49.9 − 45.0
	44.9 and below

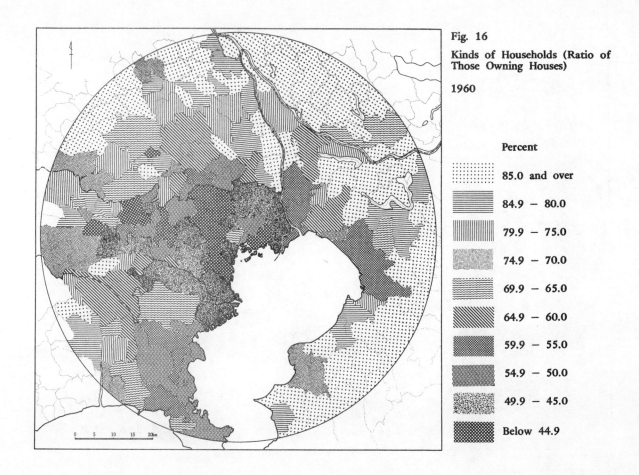

Fig. 16

Kinds of Households (Ratio of Those Owning Houses)

1960

Percent

	85.0 and over
	84.9 — 80.0
	79.9 — 75.0
	74.9 — 70.0
	69.9 — 65.0
	64.9 — 60.0
	59.9 — 55.0
	54.9 — 50.0
	49.9 — 45.0
	Below 44.9

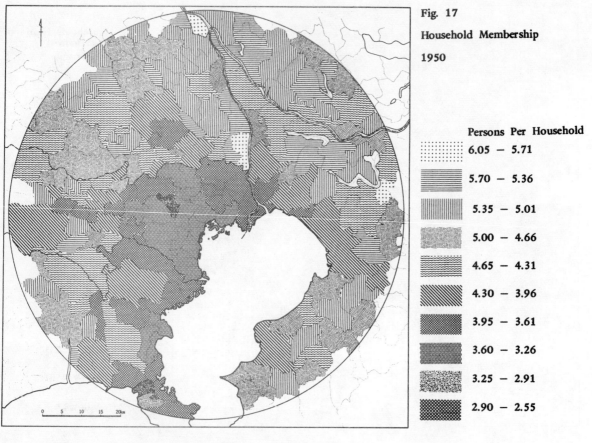

Fig. 17

Household Membership

1950

Persons Per Household

6.05 — 5.71

5.70 — 5.36

5.35 — 5.01

5.00 — 4.66

4.65 — 4.31

4.30 — 3.96

3.95 — 3.61

3.60 — 3.26

3.25 — 2.91

2.90 — 2.55

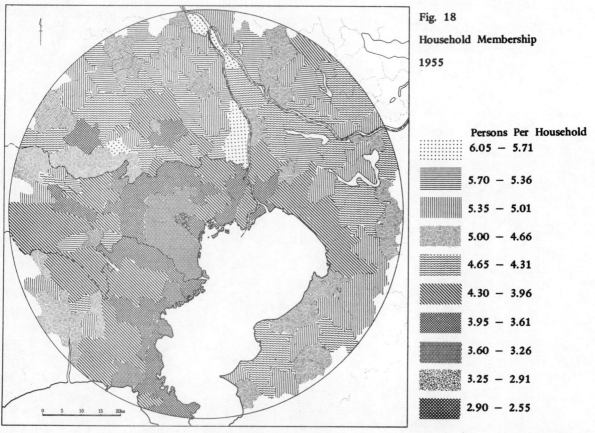

Fig. 18

Household Membership

1955

Persons Per Household

6.05 — 5.71

5.70 — 5.36

5.35 — 5.01

5.00 — 4.66

4.65 — 4.31

4.30 — 3.96

3.95 — 3.61

3.60 — 3.26

3.25 — 2.91

2.90 — 2.55

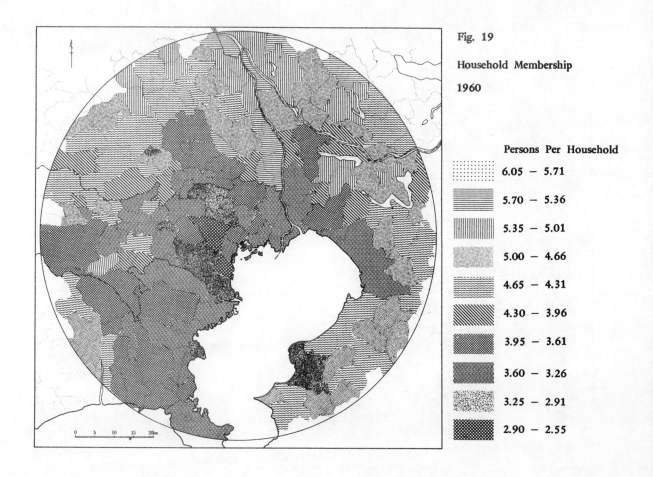

Fig. 19

Household Membership

1960

Persons Per Household

	6.05 — 5.71
	5.70 — 5.36
	5.35 — 5.01
	5.00 — 4.66
	4.65 — 4.31
	4.30 — 3.96
	3.95 — 3.61
	3.60 — 3.26
	3.25 — 2.91
	2.90 — 2.55

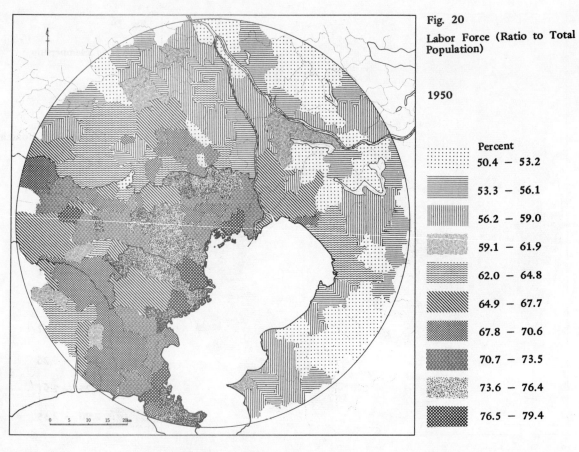

Fig. 20

Labor Force (Ratio to Total Population)

1950

	Percent
	50.4 — 53.2
	53.3 — 56.1
	56.2 — 59.0
	59.1 — 61.9
	62.0 — 64.8
	64.9 — 67.7
	67.8 — 70.6
	70.7 — 73.5
	73.6 — 76.4
	76.5 — 79.4

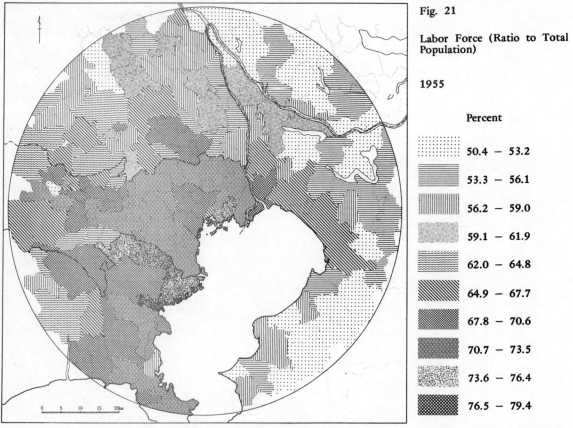

Fig. 21

Labor Force (Ratio to Total Population)

1955

	Percent
	50.4 — 53.2
	53.3 — 56.1
	56.2 — 59.0
	59.1 — 61.9
	62.0 — 64.8
	64.9 — 67.7
	67.8 — 70.6
	70.7 — 73.5
	73.6 — 76.4
	76.5 — 79.4

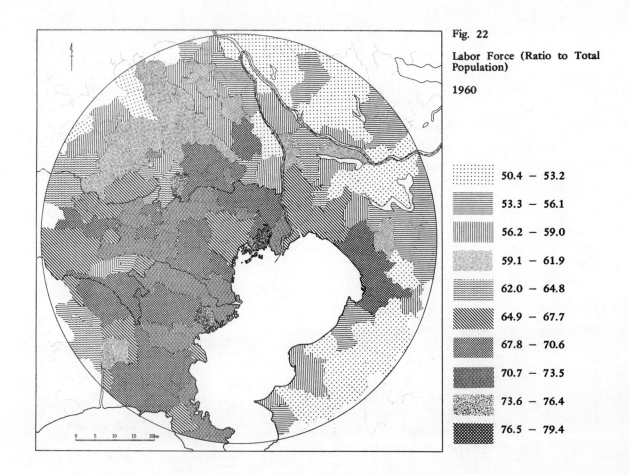

Fig. 22

Labor Force (Ratio to Total Population)

1960

	50.4 — 53.2
	53.3 — 56.1
	56.2 — 59.0
	59.1 — 61.9
	62.0 — 64.8
	64.9 — 67.7
	67.8 — 70.6
	70.7 — 73.5
	73.6 — 76.4
	76.5 — 79.4

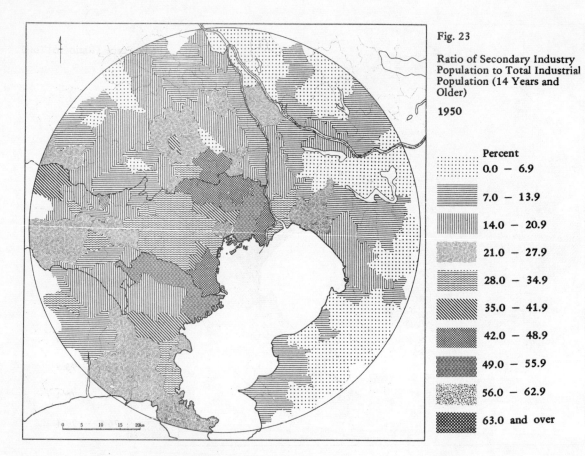

Fig. 23

Ratio of Secondary Industry
Population to Total Industrial
Population (14 Years and
Older)

1950

Percent
0.0 – 6.9
7.0 – 13.9
14.0 – 20.9
21.0 – 27.9
28.0 – 34.9
35.0 – 41.9
42.0 – 48.9
49.0 – 55.9
56.0 – 62.9
63.0 and over

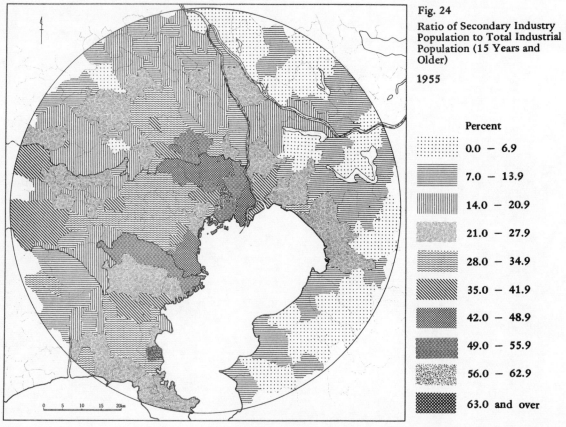

Fig. 24

Ratio of Secondary Industry
Population to Total Industrial
Population (15 Years and
Older)

1955

Percent
0.0 – 6.9
7.0 – 13.9
14.0 – 20.9
21.0 – 27.9
28.0 – 34.9
35.0 – 41.9
42.0 – 48.9
49.0 – 55.9
56.0 – 62.9
63.0 and over

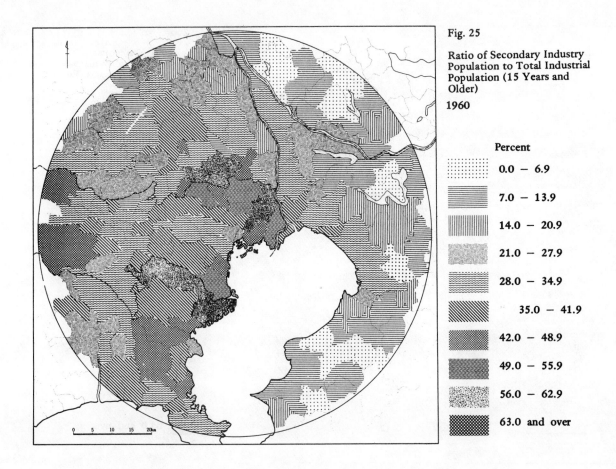

Fig. 25

Ratio of Secondary Industry
Population to Total Industrial
Population (15 Years and
Older)

1960

Percent

0.0 — 6.9

7.0 — 13.9

14.0 — 20.9

21.0 — 27.9

28.0 — 34.9

35.0 — 41.9

42.0 — 48.9

49.0 — 55.9

56.0 — 62.9

63.0 and over

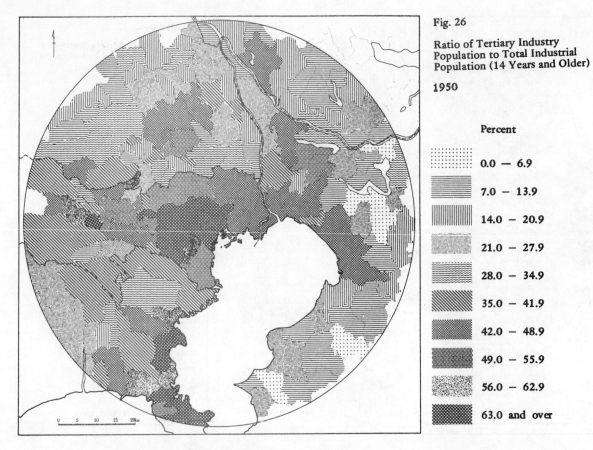

Fig. 26

Ratio of Tertiary Industry
Population to Total Industrial
Population (14 Years and Older)

1950

Percent

0.0 — 6.9

7.0 — 13.9

14.0 — 20.9

21.0 — 27.9

28.0 — 34.9

35.0 — 41.9

42.0 — 48.9

49.0 — 55.9

56.0 — 62.9

63.0 and over

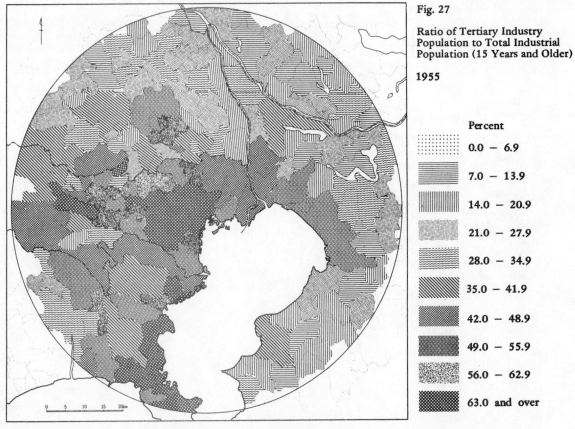

Fig. 27

Ratio of Tertiary Industry
Population to Total Industrial
Population (15 Years and Older)

1955

Percent

0.0 — 6.9

7.0 — 13.9

14.0 — 20.9

21.0 — 27.9

28.0 — 34.9

35.0 — 41.9

42.0 — 48.9

49.0 — 55.9

56.0 — 62.9

63.0 and over

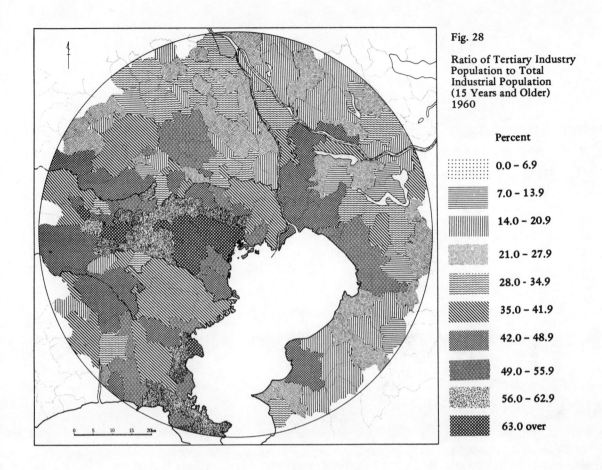

Fig. 28

Ratio of Tertiary Industry
Population to Total
Industrial Population
(15 Years and Older)
1960

Percent

	0.0 – 6.9
	7.0 – 13.9
	14.0 – 20.9
	21.0 – 27.9
	28.0 – 34.9
	35.0 – 41.9
	42.0 – 48.9
	49.0 – 55.9
	56.0 – 62.9
	63.0 over

CHAPTER 11

TABLES

TABLE 1. POPULATION

(Zone) (Sector)		District	Population			Increase or Decrease (△) in 1950-55		Increase or Decrease (△) in 1955-60		Population Density		
			1950	1955	1960	number	percent	number	percent	1950	1955	1960
1	I	Chiyoda-ku	110,348	122,745	116,944	12,397	11.2	△ 5,801	△ 4.7	9,578.8	10,654.9	10,151.4
		Minato-ku	216,120	254,592	267,024	38,472	17.8	12,432	4.9	11,368.8	13,392.5	14,046.5
		Chūō-ku	161,925	171,316	161,299	9,391	5.8	△ 10,017	△ 5.8	16,779.8	17,753.0	16,714.9
		Bunkyō-ku	190,746	236,971	259,383	46,225	24.2	22,412	9.5	16,673.6	20,714.2	22,673.3
		Taitō-ku	262,159	310,058	318,889	47,899	18.3	8,831	2.8	26,215.9	31,005.8	31,888.9
		Zone 1 Total	941,298	1,095,682	1,123,539	154,384	16.4	27,857	2.5	15,275.4	17,780.7	18,232.8
2	I	Shinagawa-ku	288,624	373,341	427,859	84,717	29.4	54,518	14.6	18,239.3	23,599.3	27,045.4
	II	Meguro-ku	204,382	253,941	293,763	49,559	24.2	39,822	15.7	14,183.3	17,622.6	20,386.1
		Shibuya-ku	181,244	243,410	282,687	62,166	34.3	39,277	16.1	11,995.0	16,109.2	18,708.6
	III	Shinjuku-ku	246,373	348,675	413,690	102,302	41.5	65,015	18.6	13,657.0	19,327.9	22,931.8
		Nakano-ku	213,461	289,165	351,360	75,704	35.5	62,552	21.7	13,570.3	18,383.0	22,336.9
	IV	Toshima-ku	217,148	300,557	363,193	83,409	38.4	62,636	20.8	16,690.3	23,102.0	27,916.4
	V	Kita-ku	267,386	351,532	418,603	84,146	31.5	67,071	19.1	13,002.9	17,106.2	20,370.0
	VI	Arakawa-ku	201,064	253,323	285,480	52,259	26.0	32,157	12.7	19,463.1	24,499.3	27,609.3
	VII	Sumida-ku	236,242	305,590	331,843	69,348	29.4	26,253	8.6	16,995.8	21,984.9	23,873.6
	VIII	Kōtō-ku	182,489	277,971	351,053	95,482	52.3	73,082	26.3	7,103.5	10,820.2	13,665.0
		Zone 2 Total	2,238,413	2,997,505	3,519,531	759,092	33.9	522,026	17.4	13,766.2	18,434.7	21,645.1
3	I	Ōta-ku	400,327	568,498	706,219	168,171	42.0	137,721	24.2	9,602.1	13,633.0	16,935.7
	II	Setagaya-ku	408,226	523,630	653,210	115,404	28.3	129,580	24.7	6,941.4	8,903.8	11,107.1
	III	Suginami-ku	326,610	405,665	487,210	79,055	24.2	81,188	20.0	9,737.9	12,095.0	14,526.2
	IV	Itabashi-ku	223,003	311,225	412,605	88,222	39.6	101,380	32.6	6,990.7	9,756.3	12,934.3
		Nerima-ku	125,197	185,814	305,628	60,617	48.4	119,814	64.5	2,663.2	3,952.6	6,501.3
	VI	Adachi-ku	268,304	332,181	408,768	63,877	23.8	76,587	23.1	5,038.6	6,238.1	7,676.4
	VII	Katsushika-ku	244,832	294,133	376,724	49,301	20.1	82,591	28.1	7,222.2	8,673.9	11,112.8
	VIII	Edogawa-ku	208,861	254,771	316,593	45,910	22.0	61,822	24.3	4,622.9	5,639.0	7,007.4
		Urayasu-machi	15,679	16,394	16,847	715	4.6	453	2.8	3,539.3	3,700.7	3,802.9
		Zone 3 Total	2,221,039	2,892,311	3,683,804	671,272	30.2	791,493	27.4	6,350.8	8,270.3	10,533.5
4	I	Kawasaki-shi	319,226	445,520	632,975	126,294	39.6	187,455	42.1	2,252.8	3,562.7	5,061.8
	II	Komae-machi	10,124	14,669	25,252	4,545	44.9	10,583	72.1	1,646.2	2,385.2	4,106.0
	III	Mitaka-shi	54,820	69,466	98,038	14,646	26.7	28,572	41.1	3,257.3	4,184.7	5,825.2
		Musashino-shi	73,149	94,948	120,337	21,799	29.8	25,389	26.7	6,631.8	8,799.6	10,910.0
		Chōfu-shi	34,865	45,362	68,621	10,497	30.1	23,259	51.3	1,599.3	2,064.7	3,147.8
		Hoya-machi	14,816	23,327	46,768	8,511	57.4	23,441	100.5	1,689.4	2,659.9	5,332.7
	IV	Yamato-machi	10,240	13,325	17,242	3,085	30.1	3,917	29.4	756.3	1,151.7	1,490.2
		Toda-machi	12,710	19,882	30,752	* 7,172	56.4	10,870	54.7	705.7	1,103.9	1,707.5
	V	Warabi-shi	29,846	35,184	50,952	5,338	17.9	15,768	44.8	5,863.7	6,912.4	10,010.2
		Kawaguchi-shi	111,558	134,091	170,066	* 22,533	20.2	35,975	26.8	2,315.4	2,783.1	3,529.8
		Hatogaya-machi	13,242	14,437	20,711	1,195	9.0	6,274	43.5	2,135.8	2,328.5	3,340.5
	VI	Sōka-shi	28,757	32,536	38,533	* 3,779	13.1	5,997	18.4	1,044.2	1,181.4	1,399.2
		Yashio-mura	12,837	12,589	13,307	549	4.3	718	5.7	708.8	695.1	734.8
		Misato-mura	16,771	17,313	17,738	542	3.2	425	2.5	551.3	569.1	583.1
		Matsudo-shi	59,670	68,509	86,372	* 8,839	14.8	17,863	26.1	975.2	1,119.6	1,441.5
	VII	Ichikawa-shi	114,192	136,739	157,301	* 22,547	19.7	20,562	15.0	2,220.8	1,129.6	3,059.1
		Zone 4 Total	916,823	1,177,897	1,594,965	261,074	28.5	417,068	35.4	1,961.6	2,520.2	3,412.6
5	I	Tsurumi-ku	170,868	201,028	230,377	30,160	17.7	29,349	14.6	6,397.2	7,526.3	8,625.1
	III	Koganei-shi	22,616	30,338	45,734	7,722	34.1	15,396	50.7	1,992.6	2,617.6	4,029.4

- 157 -

Table 1. Population

(Zone) (Sector)	District	Population 1950	Population 1955	Population 1960	Increase or Decrease (△) in 1950-55 number	percent	Increase or Decrease (△) in 1955-60 number	percent	Population Density 1950	1955	1960
III	Tanashi-machi	13,527	19,450	31,323	5,923	43.8	11,873	61.0	1,963.3	2,822.9	4,546.2
	Kurume-machi	8,415	10,319	19,637	1,904	22.6	9,318	90.3	648.3	795.0	1,512.9
IV	Niza-machi	11,059	11,700	14,401	641	5.8	2,701	23.1	483.1	511.1	629.1
	Kiyose-machi	11,610	14,544	17,863	2,934	25.3	3,319	22.8	1,139.4	1,427.3	1,753.0
	Adachi-machi	9,721	10,632	12,259	* 911	9.4	1,627	15.3	1,084.9	1,186.6	1,368.2
	Asaka-machi	14,685	16,356	24,182	* 1,671	11.4	7,826	47.8	825.9	919.9	1,360.1
V	Urawa-shi	124,419	144,519	168,757	* 20,100	16.2	24,238	16.8	2,110.2	2,451.1	2,862.2
	Misono-mura	9,527	9,444	9,306	* △83	△0.9	△138	△1.5	487.8	483.6	476.5
	Koshigaya-shi	42,253	46,250	49,585	* 3,997	9.5	3,335	7.2	712.1	773.9	829.7
VI	Yoshikawa-machi	16,015	16,354	16,300	339	2.1	△54	△0.3	516.6	527.5	525.8
	Nagareyama-machi	18,337	19,077	25,672	740	4.0	6,595	34.6	517.7	538.6	724.8
VII	Kamagaya-machi	8,981	10,168	13,496	1,187	13.2	3,328	32.7	437.5	491.9	657.4
VIII	Funahashi-shi	100,134	114,921	135,038	14,787	14.8	20,117	17.5	1,270.1	1,460.2	1,712.8
	Zone 5 Total	581,996	675,100	813,930	93,104	16.0	138,830	20.6	1,379.8	1,600.5	1,929.7
6 I	Nishi-ku	85,292	100,446	104,173	15,154	17.8	3,727	3.7	13,646.7	16,071.4	16,667.7
	Naka-ku	89,813	105,925	123,623	16,112	17.9	17,699	16.7	7,941.0	9,365.6	10,930.5
	Kanagawa-ku	107,068	142,797	172,068	35,729	33.4	29,271	20.5	4,615.0	6,155.0	7,416.7
II	Kōhoku-ku	93,421	111,095	147,688	17,674	18.9	36,593	32.9	763.2	907.6	1,206.5
	Inagi-machi	9,824	10,086	11,012	262	2.7	926	9.2	557.9	572.7	625.3
III	Tama-mura	7,394	7,600	9,746	206	2.8	2,146	28.2	395.2	406.2	520.9
	Fuchu-shi	45,342	58,937	82,098	13,595	30.0	23,161	39.3	1,513.4	1,963.3	2,740.3
	Kunitachi-machi	14,679	23,242	32,609	* 8,563	58.3	9,367	46.3	1,816.7	2,876.5	4,035.8
	Kokubunji-machi	19,125	25,638	39,098	* 6,513	34.1	13,460	52.5	1,694.0	2,270.9	3,463.1
	Kodaira-machi	21,659	29,175	52,923	7,516	34.7	23,748	81.4	1,038.8	1,399.3	2,538.3
	Higashimurayama-machi	17,993	24,102	42,946	6,109	34.0	18,844	78.2	1,085.2	1,453.7	2,590.2
IV	Tokorosawa-shi	52,188	56,249	65,903	4,061	7.8	9,654	17.2	726.4	783.0	917.4
	Miyoshi-mura	4,280	4,342	4,329	62	1.4	△13	△0.3	275.1	279.0	278.2
	Fujimi-mura	10,648	10,772	12,030	124	1.2	1,258	11.7	533.0	539.1	602.1
V	Yono-shi	29,072	35,162	40,840	6,090	20.9	5,678	16.1	3,502.7	4,221.1	4,920.5
	Ōmiya-shi	125,002	144,540	169,996	19,538	15.6	25,456	17.6	1,406.6	1,626.8	1,912.9
	Iwatsuki-shi	34,437	34,272	35,169	* △165	△0.5	897	2.6	692.1	688.7	706.8
VI	Matsubushi-mura	8,880	8,995	8,844	115	1.3	△151	△1.7	535.6	542.8	533.4
VII	Kashiwa-shi	38,473	45,028	63,745	* 6,555	17.0	18,717	41.6	522.0	611.0	864.9
	Shōnan-mura	10,686	10,765	11,849	225	2.1	1,084	10.1	251.6	253.4	278.9
	Shirai-mura	8,402	8,486	8,217	84	1.0	△269	△3.2	238.8	241.1	233.5
VIII	Narashino-shi	28,667	32,198	42,167	3,531	12.3	9,969	31.0	2,004.7	2,262.7	2,948.7
	Zone 6 Total	862,345	1,029,852	1,281,074	167,507	19.4	251,222	24.4	1,193.0	1,424.7	1,772.2
7 I	Isogo-ku	62,343	67,991	74,458	5,648	9.1	6,467	9.5	4,424.6	4,825.5	5,284.5
	Minami-ku	142,763	171,525	194,558	28,762	20.1	23,033	13.4	4,380.6	5,263.1	5,969.9
	Hodogaya-ku	74,156	96,822	143,804	22,666	30.6	46,982	48.5	1,438.8	1,878.6	2,790.1
II	Machida-shi	52,486	58,342	71,269	5,850	11.1	12,927	22.2	717.3	797.3	974.0
III	Yuki-mura	6,415	6,285	6,179	△130	△2.0	△106	△1.7	289.9	284.0	279.2
	Hino-machi	24,444	27,305	43,394	2,861	11.7	16,089	58.9	901.7	1,007.2	1,600.7
	Tachikawa-shi	51,651	63,644	67,949	11,993	23.2	4,305	6.8	5,876.1	7,240.5	7,730.3
	Sunakawa-machi	11,567	12,669	13,989	1,102	9.5	1,320	10.4	797.2	873.7	964.1
	Yamato-machi	12,366	12,975	14,239	609	4.9	1,264	9.7	913.3	958.3	1,051.6
IV	Ōi-mura	4,535	4,794	4,949	259	5.7	155	3.2	564.1	596.3	615.5
	Fukuoka-mura	7,461	7,820	16,652	359	4.8	8,832	112.9	1,386.8	1,453.5	3,095.2
V	Kasukabe-shi	31,125	32,517	34,280	1,392	4.5	1,763	5.4	820.4	853.0	903.5
	Shōwa-mura	14,725	14,781	14,815	56	0.4	34	0.2	563.7	563.3	567.2

Table 1. Population

(Zone)	(Sector)	District	Population 1950	Population 1955	Population 1960	Increase or Decrease (△) in 1950-55 number	percent	Increase or Decrease (△) in 1955-60 number	percent	Population Density 1950	1955	1960
	VI	Noda-shi	50,831	52,886	54,150	2,055	4.0	1,264	2.4	687.8	715.6	732.7
	VII	Abiko-machi	23,120	24,910	27,063	* 1,790	7.7	2,153	8.6	534.3	575.7	625.4
		Yachiyo-machi	14,792	15,301	21,709	* 509	3.4	6,408	41.9	289.7	299.7	425.2
	VIII	Chiba-shi	167,870	198,116	241,615	* 30,246	18.0	43,499	22.0	1,064.2	1,255.9	1,531.6
	IX	Goi-machi	17,958	20,975	21,560	* 3,017	16.8	585	2.8	503.2	587.7	604.1
		Sodegaura-machi	13,571	13,874	13,974	303	2.2	100	0.7	374.3	382.6	385.4
		Zone 7 Total	784,179	903,532	1,080,606	119,353	15.2	177,074	19.6	1,069.9	1,232.8	1,474.4
8	I	Kanazawa-ku	56,040	63,974	71,446	7,934	14.2	7,472	11.7	2,453.6	2,801.0	3,128.1
		Totsuka-ku	69,425	82,084	113,514	12,659	18.2	31,430	38.3	733.4	867.5	1,199.2
	II	Yamato-shi	17,586	30,375	40,975	* 12,789	72.7	10,600	34.9	614.9	1,062.1	1,432.7
		Sagamihara-shi	68,896	83,841	101,655	14,943	21.7	17,814	21.2	759.0	921.6	1,119.9
		Zama-machi	11,804	13,197	15,402	1,387	11.7	2,205	16.7	658.0	743.9	858.5
	III	Hachiōji-shi	125,055	141,846	158,443	16,791	13.4	16,597	11.7	753.1	854.2	954.1
		Akishima-shi	31,692	38,519	44,805	6,827	21.5	6,286	16.3	1,756.8	2,135.2	2,483.6
		Fussa-machi	14,669	19,096	21,998	4,427	30.3	2,902	15.2	1,417.3	1,845.0	2,125.4
		Mizuho-machi	9,210	11,737	12,092	* 2,527	27.4	355	3.0	563.6	718.3	740.0
		Murayama-machi	10,989	11,799	12,065	810	7.4	266	2.3	710.8	763.2	780.4
		Musashi-machi	26,068	29,007	30,604	* 2,939	11.3	1,597	5.5	648.3	721.4	761.1
	IV	Sayama-shi	30,583	31,341	32,785	758	2.5	1,444	4.6	616.0	631.1	660.3
		Kawagoe-shi	100,407	104,612	107,523	4,205	4.2	2,911	2.8	913.3	951.3	978.0
		Seibu-machi	8,627	5,691	6,299	*△2,936	△ 34.0	608	10.7	811.6	1,107.2	1,225.5
	V	Ageo-shi	32,673	35,395	38,889	* 2,722	8.3	3,494	9.9	716.0	775.2	852.3
		Ina-mura	7,327	7,036	6,755	△ 291	△ 4.0	△ 281	△ 4.0	490.1	470.6	451.8
		Hasuda-machi	18,574	20,016	20,743	* 1,442	7.8	727	3.6	680.6	733.5	760.1
		Shiraoka-machi	15,275	15,655	16,026	380	2.5	371	2.4	623.0	638.5	653.6
		Miyashiro-machi	10,463	10,755	11,152	295	2.8	397	3.7	643.5	666.4	685.9
		Sugito-machi	17,805	17,772	17,450	* △ 33	△ 0.2	△ 322	△ 1.8	557.1	625.0	546.0
	VI	Sekiyado-machi	14,463	13,795	12,759	△ 668	△ 4.6	△ 1,036	△ 7.5	484.2	464.2	427.2
		Moriya-machi	12,160	12,095	11,449	△ 65	△ 0.5	△ 646	△ 5.3	342.4	340.6	322.4
	VII	Toride-machi	19,630	21,233	22,582	1,603	8.2	1,349	6.4	532.1	575.6	612.1
		Inzai-machi	17,659	17,898	17,315	239	1.4	△ 583	△ 3.3	333.0	337.0	326.5
		Inba-mura	8,526	8,340	7,912	△ 186	△ 2.2	428	5.1	183.0	203.0	169.9
	VIII	Yotsukaidō-machi	17,888	18,014	16,623	* 126	0.7	781	4.9	495.8	499.3	460.7
	IX	Ichihara-machi	14,547	13,059	14,239	*△1,488	△ 10.2	1,180	9.0	514.0	461.4	503.1
		Anegasaki-machi	11,199	11,323	11,307	124	1.1	△ 16	△ 0.1	408.9	413.4	412.8
		Hirakawa-machi	11,651	11,637	11,018	△ 14	△ 0.1	△ 619	△ 5.3	249.8	249.5	236.2
		Miwa-machi	11,760	9,809	9,404	*△1,951	△ 16.6	△ 405	△ 4.1	296.9	247.6	237.4
	X	Kisarazu-shi	50,153	51,741	52,689	1,588	3.2	948	1.8	548.8	566.2	576.6
		Zone 8 Total	877,546	960,520	1,066,918	82,974	9.5	106,398	11.1	666.2	729.2	810.0
9	I	Kamakura-shi	85,391	91,328	98,617	5,937	7.0	7,289	8.0	2,164.0	2,314.4	2,499.2
	II	Ayase-machi	8,181	8,221	8,304	40	0.5	83	1.0	367.9	369.4	373.4
		Ebina-machi	15,549	16,535	17,938	986	6.3	1,403	8.5	617.0	658.2	711.8
		Shiroyama-machi	4,983	4,932	5,280	△ 51	△ 1.0	348	7.1	255.9	253.6	271.2
	III	Akita-machi	13,411	13,835	14,433	424	3.2	598	4.3	616.9	636.4	663.9
		Hamura-machi	8,373	10,104	11,003	1,731	20.7	899	8.9	869.5	1,049.2	1,142.6
	IV	Hannō-shi	41,935	43,436	44,153	* 1,501	3.6	717	1.7	312.8	324.0	329.4
		Tsurugashima-mura	6,826	6,976	7,008	150	2.2	32	0.5	384.1	381.6	394.4
		Hidaka-machi	16,108	16,776	16,683	668	4.1	△ 93	△ 0.6	340.3	354.4	352.4
		Kawashima-mura	18,014	17,597	16,443	△ 417	△ 2.3	△ 1,154	△ 6.6	427.6	417.7	390.3
	V	Kitamoto-machi	13,457	14,263	15,483	806	6.0	1,220	8.6	685.5	726.6	788.7

Table 1. Population

(Zone) (Sector)	District	Population 1950	1955	1960	Increase or Decrease (△) in 1950-55 number	percent	Increase or Decrease (△) in 1955-60 number	percent	Population Density 1950	1955	1960
V	Higawa-machi	19,495	19,790	21,309	* 295	1.5	1,519	7.7	772.7	784.4	844.6
	Shobu-machi	17,119	16,718	16,054	△ 401	△ 2.3	△ 664	△ 4.6	627.4	613.5	588.3
	Kuki-machi	21,069	22,082	23,114	1,013	4.8	1,032	4.7	841.7	880.5	923.5
	Satte-machi	24,574	23,985	23,378	*△ 589	△ 2.4	△ 607	△ 2.5	684.1	667.7	650.8
VI	Iwai-machi	35,922	35,154	33,366	△ 768	△ 2.1	△ 1,788	△ 5.1	391.3	385.1	363.5
	Mitsukaidō-shi	35,126	39,971	37,577	△ 1,342	△ 3.8	△ 2,394	△ 6.0	443.1	504.2	474.0
	Yawahara-mura	12,120	11,564	10,746	△ 556	△ 4.6	△ 818	△ 7.1	351.6	335.5	311.7
	Ina-mura	13,106	12,568	12,010	△ 538	△ 4.1	△ 558	△ 4.4	280.6	275.8	257.2
VII	Fujishiro-machi	13,069	12,941	12,606	△ 128	△ 1.0	△ 335	△ 2.6	407.1	463.1	392.7
	Ryūgasaki-shi	34,528	34,337	33,581	△ 191	△ 0.6	△ 756	△ 2.2	461.0	458.4	448.3
	Tone-mura	9,796	9,746	9,279	△ 50	△ 0.5	△ 467	△ 4.8	391.5	389.4	370.9
	Motono-mura	5,586	5,470	5,213	△ 116	△ 2.1	△ 257	△ 4.7	244.7	239.6	228.3
VIII	Sakura-shi	35,298	37,496	36,869	* 2,198	6.2	△ 627	△ 1.7	344.8	311.2	360.2
	Izumi-machi	9,919	9,745	9,333	△ 174	△ 1.8	△ 412	△ 4.2	200.9	197.4	189.0
IX	Shitsu-mura	9,975	9,703	9,292	△ 272	△ 2.7	△ 411	△ 4.2	180.4	175.2	168.1
	Nansō-machi	19,493	18,753	17,552	△ 740	△ 3.8	△ 1,201	△ 6.4	246.9	237.6	222.3
	Fukuta-machi	7,912	7,654	7,276	△ 254	△ 3.2	△ 382	△ 5.0	190.9	184.8	175.5
X	Kimitsu-machi	14,064	13,747	12,910	△ 317	△ 2.3	△ 837	△ 6.1	314.8	307.7	288.9
	Futtsu-machi	16,864	16,854	16,567	△ 10	△ 0.1	△ 287	△ 1.7	844.0	843.5	829.2
	Ōsawa-machi	14,998	14,526	14,059	△ 472	△ 3.1	△ 467	△ 3.2	447.6	433.5	419.5
	Zone 9 Total	602,261	616,811	617,436	14,550	2.4	△ 625	△ 0.1	447.7	458.5	458.9
10 I	Yokosuka-shi	250,533	279,132	287,309	28,599	11.4	8,177	2.9	2,607.3	2,904.9	2,990.0
	Zushi-shi	35,908	38,091	39,571	2,183	6.1	1,480	3.9	2,033.3	2,156.9	2,240.7
	Hayama-machi	15,484	15,229	15,762	△ 255	△ 1.6	533	3.5	914.0	899.0	930.5
	Chigasaki-shi	50,112	56,895	68,054	6,783	13.5	11,159	19.6	1,401.3	1,591.0	1,903.1
	Fujisawa-shi	99,640	109,101	124,601	12,221	12.6	15,500	14.2	1,432.2	1,566.4	1,791.0
II	Aikawa-machi	14,490	14,767	14,321	△ 346	△ 2.3	△ 580	△ 4.0	432.7	419.6	402.6
	Atsugi-shi	43,191	44,551	46,239	1,360	3.1	1,688	3.8	465.2	479.7	498.1
	Samukawa-machi	11,206	11,183	11,564	△ 23	△ 0.2	381	3.4	847.7	845.9	874.7
III	Ōme-shi	53,166	55,218	56,896	2,052	3.9	1,678	3.0	511.2	532.7	547.0
IV	Sakado-machi	23,682	23,962	23,569	280	1.2	△ 393	△ 1.0	576.1	591.2	573.3
	Yoshimi-mura	15,999	15,647	14,915	△ 352	△ 2.2	△ 732	△ 4.7	428.1	403.6	384.7
	Moroyama-mura	10,823	11,251	11,173	428	4.0	△ 78	△ 0.7	320.8	333.5	331.1
V	Kōnosu-shi	30,888	31,434	31,868	548	1.8	434	1.4	868.6	885.2	896.2
	Kisai-machi	16,765	16,352	15,466	△ 413	△ 2.5	△ 886	△ 5.4	593.9	584.4	547.9
	Washimiya-machi	8,703	8,670	8,351	△ 33	△ 0.4	△ 319	△ 3.7	633.9	631.5	608.2
	Kurihashi-machi	12,223	12,527	12,890	304	2.5	363	2.9	777.1	796.4	819.5
	Goka-mura	9,985	9,734	9,157	△ 251	△ 2.5	△ 577	△ 5.9	428.2	417.4	392.7
VI	Sakai-machi	24,333	23,516	22,587	△ 817	△ 3.4	△ 929	△ 4.0	529.7	509.7	491.7
	Sashima-machi	15,476	15,636	14,810	△ 309	△ 2.0	△ 826	△ 5.3	487.4	492.5	466.5
	Yatabe-machi	22,455	22,048	20,570	△ 407	△ 1.8	△ 1,478	△ 6.7	282.4	277.3	258.7
VII	Kukizaki-mura	6,569	6,495	6,338	△ 74	△ 1.1	△ 157	△ 2.4	239.1	236.4	230.7
	Ushiku-machi	15,176	15,627	16,131	* 451	3.0	385	2.4	256.5	264.1	272.7
	Kawachi-mura	14,205	13,884	13,065	△ 335	△ 3.7	△ 819	△ 5.9	321.4	314.1	295.6
	Sakae-machi	10,162	10,136	9,732	*△ 26	△ 0.3	△ 497	△ 4.9	295.7	314.1	283.2
	Narita-shi	44,312	44,969	43,149	657	1.5	△ 1,820	△ 4.0	339.5	344.6	330.6
VIII	Shisui-machi	6,279	6,207	6,093	△ 72	△ 1.1	△ 114	△ 1.8	326.5	322.8	316.8
	Yachimata-machi	24,867	25,807	25,387	* 940	3.8	△ 420	△ 1.6	329.4	341.9	336.3
	Toke-machi	6,674	6,734	6,811	60	0.9	77	1.1	227.2	229.8	231.8
IX	Nagara-machi	9,812	9,364	8,817	△ 448	△ 4.6	△ 547	△ 5.8	208.6	199.1	187.4
	Obitsu-mura	7,782	7,489	6,988	△ 293	△ 3.8	△ 501	△ 6.7	240.6	231.5	216.0

Table 1. Population

(Zone) (Sector)	District	Population			Increase or Decrease (△) in 1950-55		Increase or Decrease (△) in 1955-60		Population Density		
		1950	1955	1960	number	percent	number	percent	1950	1955	1960
X	Koito-machi	6,773	6,504	6,056	△ 269	△ 4.0	△ 448	△ 6.9	159.3	156.6	145.8
	Zone 10 Total	917,950	967,709	997,660	49,759	5.4	29,951	3.1	648.9	684.1	705.3
	Total for 50 km Region	10,943,350	13,316,919	15,780,463	2,373,569	21.7	2,463,544	18.5	1,564.3	1,903.5	2,255.7
	National Total	83,199,637	89,275,529	93,418,501	6,075,892	7.3	4,142,972	4.6	226	242	253

Note 1. The asterisk (*) indicates that the 1955-60 figure does not reflect the population changes resulting from boundary changes that took place between 1955 and 1960.

Note 2. In Fig. 2 the rate of increase given for 1950-55 was computed prior to any boundary changes.

TABLE 2. COMMUTERS TO WORK AND SCHOOL, 15 YEARS AND OLDER, BY DISTRICT OF RESIDENCE

1960

(Zone) (Sector)	District	No. of Commuters	Percent	(Zone) (Sector)	District	No. of Commuters	Percent
1 I	Chiyoda-ku				Total No. of Commuters Residing in District	199,441	100.0
	Total No. of Commuters Residing in District	79,219	100.0		Commuters within District	154,853	77.6
	Commuters within District	64,685	81.7		Commuters Going Out of District	44,588	22.4 (100.0)
	Commuters Going Out of District	14,534	18.3 (100.0)		Chiyoda-ku	9,023	20.2
	Chūō-ku	3,615	24.9		Chūō-ku	8,741	19.6
	Minato-ku	1,831	12.6		Bunkyō-ku	3,896	8.7
	Bunkyō-ku	1,608	11.1		Minato-ku	3,277	7.3
	Shinjuku-ku	1,508	10.4		Sumida-ku	2,526	5.7
	Taitō-ku	900	6.2		Arakawa-ku	2,521	5.7
	Others	5,072	34.8		Others	14,604	32.8
	Minato-ku			2 I	Shinagawa-ku		
	Total No. of Commuters Residing in District	158,723	100.0		Total No. of Commuters Residing in District	245,389	100.0
	Commuters within District	108,341	68.3		Commuters within District	146,393	59.7
	Commuters Going Out of District	50,382	31.7 (100.0)		Commuters Going Out of District	98,996	40.3 (100.0)
	Chiyoda-ku	12,845	25.5		Minato-ku	18,028	18.2
	Chūō-ku	12,720	25.2		Chūō-ku	15,507	15.7
	Shinagawa-ku	3,419	6.8		Chiyoda-ku	15,265	15.4
	Shibuya-ku	3,174	6.3		Ōta-ku	14,048	14.2
	Others	18,224	36.2		Meguro-ku	6,237	6.3
	Chūō-ku				Others	29,911	30.2
	Total No. of Commuters Residing in District	107,799	100.0	II	Meguro-ku		
	Commuters within District	90,792	84.2		Total No. of Commuters Residing in District	164,834	100.0
	Commuters Going Out of District	17,007	15.8 (100.0)		Commuters within District	74,815	45.4
	Chiyoda-ku	4,862	28.6		Commuters Going Out of District	90,019	54.6 (100.0)
	Minato-ku	2,309	13.6		Chiyoda-ku	14,878	16.5
	Kōtō-ku	2,006	11.8		Chūō-ku	12,349	13.7
	Taitō-ku	1,107	6.5		Minato-ku	12,037	13.4
	Bunkyō-ku	1,018	6.0		Shinagawa-ku	9,948	11.1
	Shinjuku-ku	909	5.3		Shibuya-ku	7,529	8.4
	Others	4,796	28.2		Setagaya-ku	6,688	7.4
	Bunkyō-ku				Ōta-ku	5,220	5.8
	Total No. of Commuters Residing in District	152,921	100.0		Others	21,370	23.7
	Commuters within District	85,559	55.9		Shibuya-ku		
	Commuters Going Out of District	67,362	44.1 (100.0)		Total No. of Commuters Residing in District	162,385	100.0
	Chiyoda-ku	19,976	29.6		Commuters within District	76,411	47.1
	Chūō-ku	11,757	17.5		Commuters Going Out of District	85,974	52.9 (100.0)
	Shinjuku-ku	5,314	7.9		Chiyoda-ku	18,173	21.2
	Taitō-ku	5,092	7.6		Chūō-ku	14,112	16.4
	Minato-ku	4,671	6.9		Minato-ku	10,760	12.5
	Toshima-ku	3,497	5.2		Shinjuku-ku	9,383	10.9
	Others	17,055	25.3		Setagaya-ku	5,440	6.3
	Taitō-ku				Others	28,106	32.7

Table 2. Commuters to Work and School, 15 Years and Older, by District of Residence

(Zone)	(Sector)	District	No. of Commuters	Percent
2	III	Shinjuku-ku		
		Total No. of Commuters Residing in District	243,586	100.0
		Commuters within District	134,639	55.3
		Commuters Going Out of District	108,947	44.7 (100.0)
		Chiyoda-ku	29,324	26.9
		Chūō-ku	19,163	17.6
		Minato-ku	9,618	8.8
		Bunkyō-ku	6,609	6.1
		Shibuya-ku	5,795	5.3
		Others	38,438	35.3
		Nakano-ku		
		Total No. of Commuters Residing in District	285,713	100.0
		Commuters within District	145,169	50.8
		Commuters Going Out of District	140,544	49.2 (100.0)
		Chiyoda-ku	31,404	22.4
		Shinjuku-ku	20,974	14.9
		Chūō-ku	19,664	14.0
		Minato-ku	10,326	7.3
		Suginami-ku	8,461	6.0
		Shibuya-ku	8,236	5.9
		Others	41,479	29.5
	IV	Toshima-ku		
		Total No. of Commuters Residing in District	205,948	100.0
		Commuters within District	99,309	48.2
		Commuters Going Out of District	106,639	51.8 (100.0)
		Chiyoda-ku	20,916	19.6
		Chūō-ku	15,725	14.7
		Bunkyō-ku	11,174	10.5
		Shinjuku-ku	10,030	9.4
		Itabashi-ku	7,069	6.6
		Minato-ku	6,826	6.4
		Others	33,899	32.8
	V	Kita-ku		
		Total No. of Commuters Residing in District	224,596	100.0
		Commuters within District	110,780	49.3
		Commuters Going Out of District	113,816	50.7 (100.0)
		Chiyoda-ku	20,484	18.0
		Chūō-ku	16,531	14.5
		Taitō-ku	8,793	7.7
		Itabashi-ku	8,330	7.3
		Bunkyō-ku	8,079	7.1
		Minato-ku	7,684	6.8
		Toshima-ku	7,513	6.6
		Arakawa-ku	5,720	5.0
		Others	30,682	27.0
	VI	Arakawa-ku		
		Total No. of Commuters Residing in District	156,966	100.0

(Zone)	(Sector)	District	No. of Commuters	Percent
		Commuters within District	105,243	67.0
		Commuters Going Out of District	51,723	33.0 (100.0)
		Taitō-ku	9,021	17.4
		Chiyoda-ku	7,217	14.0
		Chūō-ku	6,794	13.1
		Adachi-ku	4,067	7.9
		Kita-ku	3,933	7.6
		Minato-ku	3,244	6.3
		Bunkyō-ku	3,144	6.1
		Others	14,303	27.6
	VII	Sumida-ku		
		Total No. of Commuters Residing in District	195,305	100.0
		Commuters within District	153,982	78.8
		Commuters Going Out of District	41,323	21.2 (100.0)
		Chiyoda-ku	6,425	15.4
		Chūō-ku	6,177	14.8
		Taitō-ku	5,833	14.1
		Kōtō-ku	4,953	12.0
		Katsushika-ku	2,997	7.6
		Bunkyō-ku	2,144	5.2
		Others	12,794	30.9
	VIII	Kōtō-ku		
		Total No. of Commuters Residing in District	193,351	100.0
		Commuters within District	142,983	73.9
		Commuters Going Out of District	50,368	26.1 (100.0)
		Chūō-ku	13,786	27.4
		Chiyoda-ku	7,965	15.8
		Sumida-ku	7,742	15.3
		Edogawa-ku	3,702	7.3
		Minato-ku	3,135	6.2
		Taitō-ku	2,636	5.2
		Others	10,402	22.8
3	I	Ōta-ku		
		Total No. of Commuters Residing in District	386,096	100.0
		Commuters within District	239,978	62.2
		Commuters Going Out of District	146,118	37.8 (100.0)
		Chiyoda-ku	23,366	16.0
		Shinagawa-ku	22,259	15.2
		Chūō-ku	20,668	14.1
		Minato-ku	20,550	14.1
		Kawasaki-shi	14,033	9.6
		Others	45,242	31.0
	II	Setagaya-ku		
		Total No. of Commuters Residing in District	351,488	100.0
		Commuters within District	154,071	43.8
		Commuters Going Out of District	197,397	56.2 (100.0)

Table 2. Commuters to Work and School, 15 Years and Older, by District of Residence

(Zone)	(Sector)	District	No. of Commuters	Percent	(Zone)	(Sector)	District	No. of Commuters	Percent
		Chiyoda-ku	40,677	20.6			Sumida-ku	5,343	7.5
		Chūō-ku	29,119	14.8			Kita-ku	4,001	5.6
		Minato-ku	21,125	10.7			Katsushika-ku	3,996	5.6
		Shibuya-ku	18,556	9.4			Minato-ku	3,714	5.2
		Shinjuku-ku	13,749	7.0			Others	25,640	36.4
		Meguro-ku	11,701	5.9		VII	Katsushika-ku		
		Others	62,470	31.6			Total No. of Commuters Residing in District	193,774	100.0
3	III	Suginami-ku					Commuters within District	118,421	61.1
		Total No. of Commuters Residing in District	393,806	100.0			Commuters Going Out of District	75,353	38.9 (100.0)
		Commuters within District	97,343	24.7			Sumida-ku	13,162	17.5
		Commuters Going Out of District	296,463	75.3 (100.0)			Chiyoda-ku	10,106	13.4
		Chiyoda-ku	75,994	25.6			Chūō-ku	8,921	11.8
		Chūō-ku	47,603	16.1			Taitō-ku	6,837	9.1
		Shinjuku-ku	30,481	10.3			Kōtō-ku	5,687	7.5
		Minato-ku	23,036	7.8			Adachi-ku	4,679	6.2
		Others	119,349	40.8			Edogawa-ku	4,589	6.1
	IV	Itabashi-ku					Others	21,372	28.4
		Total No. of Commuters Residing in District	213,559	100.0		VIII	Edogawa-ku		
		Commuters within District	123,146	57.7			Total No. of Commuters Residing in District	163,467	100.0
		Commuters Going Out of District	90,413	42.3 (100.0)			Commuters within District	95,100	58.2
		Chiyoda-ku	16,247	18.0			Commuters Going Out of District	68,367	41.8 (100.0)
		Toshima-ku	11,940	13.2			Kōtō-ku	15,922	23.3
		Chūō-ku	10,701	11.8			Chiyoda-ku	9,474	13.9
		Bunkyō-ku	8,519	9.4			Sumida-ku	9,371	13.7
		Kita-ku	6,428	7.1			Chūō-ku	8,825	12.9
		Shinjuku-ku	6,018	6.7			Katsushika-ku	3,929	5.7
		Minato-ku	4,997	5.5			Taitō-ku	3,796	5.6
		Others	25,563	28.3			Others	17,055	24.9
		Nerima-ku					Urayasu-machi		
		Total No. of Commuters Residing in District	151,648	100.0			Total No. of Commuters Residing in District	7,800	100.0
		Commuters within District	60,209	39.7			Commuters within District	5,434	69.7
		Commuters Going Out of District	91,439	60.3 (100.0)			Commuters Going Out of District	2,366	30.3 (100.0)
		Chiyoda-ku	17,022	18.6			Edogawa-ku	938	39.7
		Chūō-ku	11,476	12.6			Kōtō-ku	471	19.9
		Toshima-ku	9,210	10.1			Chūō-ku	334	14.1
		Shinjuku-ku	7,877	8.6			Ichikawa-shi	138	5.8
		Itabashi-ku	6,356	7.0			Others	485	20.5
		Bunkyō-ku	5,822	6.4	4	I	Kawasaki-shi		
		Minato-ku	5,103	5.6			Total No. of Commuters Residing in District	326,188	100.0
		Others	28,573	31.1			Commuters within District	231,108	70.9
	VI	Adachi-ku					Commuters Going Out of District	95,080	29.1 (100.0)
		Total No. of Commuters Residing in District	204,843	100.0			Ōta-ku	18,599	19.6
		Commuters within District	134,014	65.4			Tsurumi-ku	10,964	11.5
		Commuters Going Out of District	70,829	34.6 (100.0)			Chiyoda-ku	10,426	11.0
		Taitō-ku	10,137	14.3			Shinagawa-ku	7,324	7.7
		Chiyoda-ku	9,428	13.3			Minato-ku	7,192	7.6
		Chūō-ku	8,570	12.1					

Table 2. Commuters to Work and School, 15 Years and Older, by District of Residence

(Zone) (Sector)	District	No. of Commuters	Percent	(Zone) (Sector)	District	No. of Commuters	Percent
	Chūō-ku	7,071	7.4		Mitaka-shi	854	5.1
	Setagaya-ku	4,908	5.2		Others	5,795	34.7
4 II	Others	28,596	30.0		Hoya-machi		
	Komae-machi				Total No. of Commuters Residing in District	21,954	100.0
	Total No. of Commuters Residing in District	12,323	100.0		Commuters within District	6,068	27.6
	Commuters within District	4,355	35.3		Commuters Going Out of District	15,886	72.4 (100.0)
	Commuters Going Out of District	7,968	64.7 (100.0)		Chiyoda-ku	2,474	15.6
	Setagaya-ku	1,673	21.0		Chūō-ku	1,633	10.3
	Chiyoda-ku	1,124	14.1		Shinjuku-ku	1,592	10.0
	Chūō-ku	791	9.9		Nerima-ku	1,125	7.1
	Shinjuku-ku	666	8.4		Musashino-shi	874	5.5
	Minato-ku	557	7.0		Minato-ku	824	5.2
	Shibuya-ku	534	6.7		Toshima-ku	804	5.1
	Kawasaki-shi	451	5.7		Others	6,560	42.2
	Others	2,172	27.2	IV	Yamato-machi		
III	Mitaka-shi				Total No. of Commuters Residing in District	8,278	100.0
	Total No. of Commuters Residing in District	49,787	100.0		Commuters within District	4,029	48.7
	Commuters within District	20,570	41.3		Commuters Going Out of District	4,249	51.3 (100.0)
	Commuters Going Out of District	29,217	58.7 (100.0)		Itabashi-ku	1,145	26.9
	Chiyoda-ku	5,268	18.0		Toshima-ku	407	9.6
	Chūō-ku	3,532	12.1		Asaka-machi	336	7.9
	Musashino-shi	2,752	9.4		Chiyoda-ku	332	7.8
	Suginami-ku	2,280	7.8		Chūō-ku	286	6.7
	Shinjuku-ku	2,113	7.2		Nerima-ku	260	6.1
	Minato-ku	1,678	5.7		Others	1,483	35.0
	Others	11,594	39.8		Toda-machi		
	Musashino-shi				Total No. of Commuters Residing in District	15,698	100.0
	Total No. of Commuters Residing in District	64,644	100.0		Commuters within District	8,472	54.0
	Commuters within District	22,865	35.4		Commuters Going Out of District	7,226	46.0 (100.0)
	Commuters Going Out of District	41,779	64.6 (100.0)		Itabashi-ku	2,129	29.5
	Chiyoda-ku	9,662	23.1		Kawaguchi-shi	1,028	14.2
	Chūō-ku	5,745	13.8		Kita-ku	634	8.8
	Suginami-ku	3,309	7.9		Chūō-ku	494	6.8
	Shinjuku-ku	3,092	7.4		Chiyoda-ku	483	6.7
	Minato-ku	2,476	5.9		Others	2,458	34.0
	Mitaka-shi	2,456	5.9	V	Warabi-shi		
	Others	15,039	36.0		Total No. of Commuters Residing in District	25,275	100.0
	Chōfu-shi				Commuters within District	9,640	38.1
	Total No. of Commuters Residing in District	32,873	100.0		Commuters Going Out of District	15,635	61.9 (100.0)
	Commuters within District	16,157	49.1		Kawaguchi-shi	2,301	14.7
	Commuters Going Out of District	16,716	50.9 (100.0)		Chiyoda-ku	2,085	13.3
	Chiyoda-ku	2,594	15.5		Chūō-ku	1,679	10.7
	Setagaya-ku	2,014	12.0		Kita-ku	1,520	9.7
	Shinjuku-ku	1,684	10.1		Minato-ku	978	6.3
	Chūō-ku	1,501	9.0		Taitō-ku	880	5.6
	Shibuya-ku	1,243	7.4		Urawa-shi	815	5.2
	Minato-ku	1,031	6.2		Others	5,377	34.5

Table 2. Commuters to Work and School, 15 Years and Older, by District of Residence

(Zone) (Sector)	District	No. of Commuters	Percent
4 V	Kawaguchi-shi		
	Total No. of Commuters Residing in District	85,915	100.0
	Commuters within District	60,653	71.9
	Commuters Going Out of District	25,262	28.1 (100.0)
	Kita-ku	3,862	15.2
	Chiyoda-ku	3,431	13.6
	Chūo-ku	2,862	11.3
	Taitō-ku	1,652	6.5
	Minato-ku	1,547	6.1
	Others	11,908	47.3
	Hatogaya-machi		
	Total No. of Commuters Residing in District	9,649	100.0
	Commuters within District	4,162	43.1
	Commuters Going Out of District	5,487	56.9 (100.0)
	Kawaguchi-shi	2,043	37.2
	Kita-ku	567	10.3
	Chiyoda-ku	561	10.2
	Chūo-ku	404	7.4
	Others	1,912	34.9
VI	Sōka-shi		
	Total No. of Commuters Residing in District	19,899	100.0
	Commuters within District	13,634	68.5
	Commuters Going Out of District	6,265	31.5 (100.0)
	Adachi-ku	1,367	21.8
	Taitō-ku	670	10.7
	Chiyoda-ku	570	9.1
	Chūo-ku	497	7.9
	Sumida-ku	462	7.4
	Others	2,699	43.1
	Yashio-mura		
	Total No. of Commuters Residing in District	6,960	100.0
	Commuters within District	5,303	76.2
	Commuters Going Out of District	1,657	23.8 (100.0)
	Adachi-ku	540	32.6
	Kusaka-shi	258	15.6
	Katsushika-ku	219	13.2
	Sumida-ku	90	5.4
	Others	550	33.2
	Misato-mura		
	Total No. of Commuters Residing in District	9,540	100.0
	Commuters within District	7,208	75.6
	Commuters Going Out of District	2,332	24.4 (100.0)
	Katsushika-ku	707	30.3
	Adachi-ku	352	15.1
	Kusaka-shi	160	6.9
	Sumida-ku	152	6.5

(Zone) (Sector)	District	No. of Commuters	Percent
	Others	961	41.2
	Matsudo-shi		
	Total No. of Commuters Residing in District	43,327	100.0
	Commuters within District	23,292	53.8
	Commuters Going Out of District	20,035	46.2 (100.0)
	Chiyoda-ku	3,126	15.6
	Chūo-ku	2,295	11.5
	Katsushika-ku	1,976	9.9
	Taitō-ku	1,757	8.8
	Adachi-ku	1,335	6.7
	Minato-ku	1,058	5.3
	Others	8,488	42.2
VII	Ichikawa-shi		
	Total No. of Commuters Residing in District	81,000	100.0
	Commuters within District	40,786	50.4
	Commuters Going Out of District	40,214	49.6 (100.0)
	Chiyoda-ku	6,587	16.4
	Chūo-ku	6,366	15.8
	Kōto-ku	4,081	10.1
	Edogawa-ku	3,821	9.5
	Sumida-ku	3,334	8.3
	Taitō-ku	2,299	5.7
	Others	13,726	34.1
5 I	Tsurumi-ku		
	Total No. of Commuters Residing in District	118,381	100.0
	Commuters within District	70,558	59.6
	Commuters Going Out of District	47,823	40.4 (100.0)
	Kawasaki-shi	17,087	35.7
	Ōta-ku	5,536	11.6
	Chiyoda-ku	3,637	7.6
	Kanagawa-ku	3,404	7.1
	Minato-ku	2,761	5.8
	Chūo-ku	2,697	5.6
	Others	12,701	26.6
III	Koganei-shi		
	Total No. of Commuters Residing in District	23,164	100.0
	Commuters within District	7,391	31.9
	Commuters Going Out of District	15,773	68.1 (100.0)
	Chiyoda-ku	2,791	17.7
	Chūo-ku	1,509	9.6
	Musashino-shi	1,348	8.5
	Suginami-ku	1,041	6.6
	Shinjuku-ku	971	6.2
	Minato-ku	835	5.3
	Mitaka-ku	789	5.0
	Others	6,489	41.1

Table 2. Commuters to Work and School, 15 Years and Older, by District of Residence

(Zone)	(Sector)	District	No. of Commuters	Percent	(Zone)	(Sector)	District	No. of Commuters	Percent
5	III	Tanashi-machi					Total No. of Commuters Residing in District	6,140	100.0
		Total No. of Commuters Residing in District	15,180	100.0			Commuters within District	3,313	54.0
		Commuters within District	5,944	39.2			Commuters Going Out of District	2,827	46.0 (100.0)
		Commuters Going Out of District	9,236	60.8 (100.0)			Itabashi-ku	605	21.4
		Chiyoda-ku	1,188	12.9			Toshima-ku	247	8.7
		Shinjuku-ku	1,042	11.3			Chiyoda-ku	229	8.1
		Chūō-ku	735	8.0			Shinza-machi	221	7.8
		Nerima-ku	537	5.8			Asaka-machi	174	6.2
		Musashino-shi	527	5.7			Chūō-ku	164	5.8
		Suginami-ku	504	5.5			Others	1,187	42.0
		Hoya-machi	466	5.0			Asaka-machi		
		Toshima-ku	463	5.0			Total No. of Commuters Residing in District	12,534	100.0
		Others	3,774	40.8			Commuters within District	7,637	60.9
		Kurume-machi					Commuters Going Out of District	4,897	39.1 (100.0)
		Total No. of Commuters Residing in District	9,322	100.0			Itabashi-ku	1,133	23.1
		Commuters within District	3,672	39.4			Toshima-ku	511	10.4
		Commuters Going Out of District	5,650	60.6 (100.0)			Chiyoda-ku	472	9.6
		Chiyoda-ku	991	17.5			Chūō-ku	386	7.9
		Chūō-ku	615	10.9			Yamato-machi	382	7.8
		Nerima-ku	455	8.1			Others	2,013	41.2
		Toshima-ku	419	7.4		V	Urawa-shi		
		Shinjuku-ku	344	6.1			Total No. of Commuters Residing in District	85,019	100.0
		Minato-ku	292	5.2			Commuters within District	44,125	51.9
		Others	2,534	44.8			Commuters Going Out of District	40,894	48.1 (100.0)
	IV	Niza-machi					Chiyoda-ku	7,746	18.9
		Total No. of Commuters Residing in District	7,261	100.0			Chūō-ku	6,040	14.8
		Commuters within District	4,553	62.7			Kita-ku	2,992	7.3
		Commuters Going Out of District	2,708	37.3 (100.0)			Kawaguchi-shi	2,905	7.1
		Asaka-machi	346	12.8			Minato-ku	2,419	5.9
		Itabashi-ku	299	11.0			Taitō-ku	2,360	5.8
		Nerima-ku	265	9.8			Others	16,432	40.2
		Chiyoda-ku	214	7.9			Misono-mura		
		Toshima-ku	197	7.3			Total No. of Commuters Residing in District	5,058	100.0
		Chūō-ku	164	6.1			Commuters within District	4,015	79.4
		Others	1,223	45.1			Commuters Going Out of District	1,043	20.6 (100.0)
		Kiyose-machi					Kawaguchi-shi	267	25.6
		Total No. of Commuters Residing in District	8,192	100.0			Urawa-shi	260	24.9
		Commuters within District	4,705	57.4			Ōmiya-shi	67	6.4
		Commuters Going Out of District	3,487	42.6 (100.0)			Koshigaya-shi	67	6.4
		Chiyoda-ku	418	12.0			Others	382	36.7
		Nerima-ku	373	10.7			Koshigaya-shi		
		Toshima-ku	370	10.6			Total No. of Commuters Residing in District	25,045	100.0
		Chūō-ku	222	6.4			Commuters within District	18,704	74.7
		Shinjuku-ku	205	5.9			Commuters Going Out of District	6,341	25.3 (100.0)
		Others	1,899	54.4			Adachi-ku	1,249	19.7
		Adachi-machi					Sumida-ku	766	12.1

Table 2. Commuters to Work and School, 15 Years and Older, by District of Residence

(Zone)	(Sector)	District	No. of Commuters	Percent	(Zone)	(Sector)	District	No. of Commuters	Percent
		Kusaka-shi	662	10.4			Kōtō-ku	3,090	10.4
		Taitō-ku	555	8.8			Ichikawa-shi	2,741	9.2
		Chiyoda-ku	433	6.8			Sumida-ku	2,024	6.8
		Chūō-ku	361	5.7			Edogawa-ku	1,839	6.2
		Others	2,315	36.5			Chiba-shi	1,739	5.8
5	VI	Yoshikawa-machi					Katsushika-ku	1,565	5.3
		Total No. of Commuters Residing in District	9,146	100.0			Others	9,543	31.9
		Commuters within District	7,476	81.7	6	I	Nishi-ku		
		Commuters Going Out of District	1,670	18.3 (100.0)			Total No. of Commuters Residing in District	52,444	100.0
		Koshigaya-shi	279	16.7					
		Adachi-ku	208	12.5			Commuters within District	24,592	46.9
		Noda-shi	183	11.0			Commuters Going Out of District	27,852	53.1 (100.0)
		Sōka-shi	136	8.1			Naka-ku	6,933	24.9
		Katsushika-ku	128	7.7			Kanagawa-ku	3,291	11.8
		Sumida-ku	91	5.4			Kawasaki-shi	2,630	9.4
		Others	645	38.6			Tsurumi-ku	2,181	7.8
		Nagareyama-machi					Minami-ku	1,801	6.5
		Total No. of Commuters Residing in District	12,982	100.0			Hodogaya-ku	1,731	6.2
		Commuters within District	7,290	56.2			Chiyoda-ku	1,414	5.1
		Commuters Going Out of District	5,692	43.8 (100.0)			Others	7,871	28.3
		Chiyoda-ku	743	13.1			Naka-ku		
		Kashiwa-shi	552	9.7			Total No. of Commuters Residing in District	65,286	100.0
		Chūō-ku	531	9.3			Commuters within District	45,322	69.4
		Katsushika-ku	476	8.4			Commuters Going Out of District	19,964	30.6 (100.0)
		Matsudo-shi	438	7.7			Kanagawa-ku	2,277	11.4
		Adachi-ku	406	7.1			Nishi-ku	2,201	11.0
		Taitō-ku	352	6.2			Minami-ku	1,880	9.4
		Noda-shi	321	5.6			Chiyoda-ku	1,839	9.2
		Others	1,873	32.9			Kawasaki-shi	1,728	8.7
	VII	Kamagaya-machi					Chūō-ku	1,473	7.4
		Total No. of Commuters Residing in District	6,689	100.0			Tsurumi-ku	1,453	7.3
							Minato-ku	1,042	5.2
		Commuters within District	4,288	64.1			Others	6,071	30.4
		Commuters Going Out of District	2,401	35.9 (100.0)			Kanagawa-ku		
		Funahashi-shi	386	16.1			Total No. of Commuters Residing in District	86,345	100.0
		Chiyoda-ku	306	12.7					
		Kōtō-ku	261	10.9			Commuters within District	41,786	48.4
		Ichikawa-shi	202	8.4			Commuters Going Out of District	44,559	51.6 (100.0)
		Chūō-ku	179	7.5			Kawasaki-shi	6,487	14.6
		Matsudo-shi	152	6.3			Tsurumi-ku	6,476	14.5
		Sumida-ku	121	5.0			Naka-ku	6,374	14.3
		Others	794	33.1			Nishi-ku	3,901	8.8
	VIII	Funahashi-shi					Chiyoda-ku	2,926	6.6
		Total No. of Commuters Residing in District	69,069	100.0			Ōta-ku	2,512	5.6
							Chūō-ku	2,509	5.6
		Commuters within District	39,338	57.0			Others	13,374	30.0
		Commuters Going Out of District	29,731	43.0 (100.0)		II	Kōhoku-ku		
		Chiyoda-ku	3,972	13.4			Total No. of Commuters Residing in District	74,046	100.0
		Chūō-ku	3,718	12.5					

Table 2. Commuters to Work and School, 15 Years and Older, by District of Residence

(Zone) (Sector)	District	No. of Commuters	Percent	(Zone) (Sector)	District	No. of Commuters	Percent
	Commuters within District	31,526	42.6		Chūō-ku	936	8.3
	Commuters Going Out of District	42,520	57.4 (100.0)		Others	7,423	65.9
	Kawasaki-shi	7,402	17.4		Kokubunji-machi		
	Kanagawa-ku	5,480	12.9		Total No. of Commuters Residing in District	19,812	100.0
	Naka-ku	4,017	9.4		Commuters within District	6,951	35.1
	Tsurumi-ku	3,595	8.5		Commuters Going Out of District	12,861	64.9 (100.0)
	Chiyoda-ku	2,859	6.7		Chiyoda-ku	1,975	15.4
	Ōta-ku	2,594	6.1		Chūō-ku	995	7.7
	Chūō-ku	2,185	5.1		Fuchū-shi	943	7.3
	Nishi-ku	2,168	5.1		Shinjuku-ku	841	6.5
	Others	12,220	28.7		Suginami-ku	737	5.7
6 II Inagi-machi					Minato-ku	727	5.7
	Total No. of Commuters Residing in District	5,465	100.0		Others	6,643	51.7
	Commuters within District	2,791	51.1		Kodaira-machi		
	Commuters Going Out of District	2,674	48.9 (100.0)		Total No. of Commuters Residing in District	24,774	100.0
	Kawasaki-shi	645	24.1		Commuters within District	10,811	43.6
	Fuchū-shi	424	15.9		Commuters Going Out of District	13,963	56.4 (100.0)
	Chōfu-shi	244	9.1		Chiyoda-ku	1,920	13.8
	Setagaya-ku	174	6.5		Shinjuku-ku	1,266	9.1
	Others	1,187	44.4		Chūō-ku	856	6.1
III Tama-mura					Suginami-ku	806	5.8
	Total No. of Commuters Residing in District	4,576	100.0		Tachikawa-shi	734	5.3
	Commuters within District	2,404	52.5		Minato-ku	723	5.2
	Commuters Going Out of District	2,172	47.5 (100.0)		Others	7,658	54.7
	Fuchū-shi	487	22.4		Higashimurayama-machi		
	Chōfu-shi	225	10.4		Total No. of Commuters Residing in District	18,536	100.0
	Setagaya-ku	136	6.3		Commuters within District	6,622	35.7
	Shinjuku-ku	134	6.2		Commuters Going Out of District	11,914	64.3 (100.0)
	Chiyoda-ku	129	5.9		Chiyoda-ku	1,425	12.0
	Others	1,061	48.8		Shinjuku-ku	1,040	8.7
	Fuchū-shi				Chūō-ku	773	6.5
	Total No. of Commuters Residing in District	37,213	100.0		Others	8,676	72.8
	Commuters within District	19,305	51.9	IV Tokorosawa-shi			
	Commuters Going Out of District	17,908	48.1 (100.0)		Total No. of Commuters Residing in District	32,404	100.0
	Chiyoda-ku	2,172	12.1		Commuters within District	20,762	64.1
	Chōfu-shi	1,503	8.4		Commuters Going Out of District	11,642	35.9 (100.0)
	Shinjuku-ku	1,307	7.3		Chiyoda-ku	979	8.4
	Chūō-ku	1,293	7.2		Toshima-ku	971	8.3
	Tachikawa-shi	1,057	5.9		Nerima-ku	907	7.8
	Setagaya-ku	992	5.5		Shinjuku-ku	781	6.7
	Others	9,584	53.6		Tanashi-machi	759	6.5
	Kunitachi-machi				Musashino-shi	678	5.8
	Total No. of Commuters Residing in District	16,141	100.0		Chūō-ku	595	5.1
	Commuters within District	5,878	36.4		Others	5,972	51.4
	Commuters Going Out of District	11,263	63.6 (100.0)		Miyoshi-mura		
	Chiyoda-ku	1,471	13.1		Total No. of Commuters Residing in District	2,482	100.0
	Tachikawa-shi	1,433	12.7				

Table 2. Commuters to Work and School, 15 Years and Older, by District of Residence

(Zone) (Sector)	District	No. of Commuters	Percent	(Zone) (Sector)	District	No. of Commuters	Percent
	Commuters within District	1,991	80.2		Urawa-shi	496	10.8
	Commuters Going Out of District	491	19.8 (100.0)		Kasukabe-shi	428	9.3
	Itabashi-ku	81	16.5		Kawaguchi-shi	358	7.8
	Tokorosawa-shi	65	13.2		Chiyoda-ku	287	6.2
	Kawagoe-shi	53	10.8		Yono-shi	235	5.1
	Niza-machi	39	7.9		Others	1,951	42.4
	Toshima-ku	33	6.7	VI	Matsubushi-mura		
	Ōi-mura	32	6.5				
	Nerima-ku	30	6.1		Total No. of Commuters Residing in District	5,005	100.0
	Others	158	32.3		Commuters within District	3,891	77.7
6 IV	Fujimi-mura				Commuters Going Out of District	2,114	22.3 (100.0)
	Total No. of Commuters Residing in District	6,437	100.0		Noda-shi	295	14.0
	Commuters within District	4,221	65.6		Koshigaya-shi	218	10.3
	Commuters Going Out of District	2,216	34.4 (100.0)		Adachi-ku	125	5.9
	Itabashi-ku	541	24.4		Others	1,476	69.8
	Toshima-ku	196	8.8	VII	Kashiwa-shi		
	Chiyoda-ku	192	8.7				
	Adachi-machi	151	6.8		Total No. of Commuters Residing in District	31,301	100.0
	Kawagoe-shi	146	6.6		Commuters within District	17,952	57.4
	Others	990	44.7		Commuters Going Out of District	13,349	42.6 (100.0)
V	Yono-shi				Chiyoda-ku	2,508	18.8
					Chūō-ku	1,429	10.7
	Total No. of Commuters Residing in District	20,080	100.0		Taitō-ku	1,040	7.8
	Commuters within District	8,727	43.5		Adachi-ku	942	7.1
	Commuters Going Out of District	11,353	56.5 (100.0)		Katsushika-ku	829	6.2
	Urawa-shi	2,438	21.5		Minato-ku	826	6.2
	Chiyoda-ku	1,525	13.4		Matsuda-shi	816	6.1
	Ōmiya-shi	1,137	10.0		Others	4,959	37.1
	Chūō-ku	1,051	9.3		Shonan-mura		
	Kita-ku	747	6.6				
	Kawaguchi-shi	637	5.6		Total No. of Commuters Residing in District	7,174	100.0
	Others	3,818	33.6		Commuters within District	6,204	86.5
	Ōmiya-shi				Commuters Going Out of District	970	13.5 (100.0)
	Total No. of Commuters Residing in District	85,001	100.0		Kashiwa-shi	242	24.9
	Commuters within District	49,226	57.9		Matsudo-shi	112	11.5
	Commuters Going Out of District	35,775	42.1 (100.0)		Katsushika-ku	76	7.8
	Chiyoda-ku	4,750	13.4		Funahashi-shi	61	6.3
	Urawa-shi	4,556	12.6		Chiyoda-ku	54	5.6
	Chūō-ku	3,339	9.3		Others	425	43.8
	Kita-ku	2,949	8.2		Shirai-mura		
	Yono-shi	2,843	7.9				
	Kawaguchi-shi	2,416	6.8		Total No. of Commuters Residing in District	4,812	100.0
	Others	14,822	41.7		Commuters within District	4,306	89.5
	Iwatsuki-shi				Commuters Going Out of District	506	10.5 (100.0)
	Total No. of Commuters Residing in District	18,379	100.0		Funahashi-shi	121	23.9
					Inzai-machi	77	15.2
	Commuters within District	13,777	75.0		Ichikawa-shi	53	10.5
	Commuters Going Out of District	4,602	25.0 (100.0)		Kashiwa-shi	32	6.3
	Ōmiya-shi	847	18.4		Matsudo-shi	30	5.9
					Others	193	38.2
				VIII	Narashino-shi		

Table 2. Commuters to Work and School, 15 Years and Older, by District of Residence

(Zone) (Sector)	District	No. of Commuters	Percent	(Zone) (Sector)	District	No. of Commuters	Percent
	Total No. of Commuters Residing in District	21,186	100.0		Total No. of Commuters Residing in District	34,531	100.0
	Commuters within District	9,702	45.8		Commuters within District	18,017	52.2
	Commuters Going Out of District	11,484	54.2 (100.0)		Commuters Going Out of District	16,514	47.8 (100.0)
	Funahashi-shi	1,724	15.0		Sagamihara-shi	1,791	10.8
	Chiyoda-ku	1,489	13.0		Kawasaki-shi	1,739	10.5
	Chiba-shi	1,304	11.4		Chiyoda-ku	1,343	8.1
	Chūō-ku	949	8.3		Setagaya-ku	1,249	7.6
	Kōtō-ku	933	8.1		Hachiōji-shi	1,025	6.2
	Ichikawa-shi	780	6.8		Shinjuku-ku	853	5.2
	Katsushika-ku	635	5.5		Others	8,514	51.6
	Sumida-ku	616	5.4	III	Yuki-mura		
	Others	3,054	26.5		Total No. of Commuters Residing in District	3,423	100.0
7 I	Isogo-ku				Commuters within District	2,263	66.1
	Total No. of Commuters Residing in District	36,126	100.0		Commuters Going Out of District	1,160	33.9 (100.0)
	Commuters within District	13,716	38.0		Hachiōji-shi	302	26.0
	Commuters Going Out of District	22,410	62.0 (100.0)		Fuchū-shi	195	16.8
	Naka-ku	6,593	29.3		Hino-machi	133	11.5
	Minami-ku	2,367	10.6		Tama-mura	77	6.6
	Nishi-ku	1,652	7.4		Chōfu-shi	73	6.3
	Kanagawa-ku	1,539	6.9		Sagamihara-shi	67	5.8
	Kawasaki-shi	1,458	6.5		Others	313	27.0
	Kanazawa-ku	1,436	6.4		Hino-machi		
	Tsurumi-ku	1,139	5.1		Total No. of Commuters Residing in District	20,710	100.0
	Others	6,226	27.8		Commuters within District	8,901	43.0
	Minami-ku				Commuters Going Out of District	11,809	57.0 (100.0)
	Total No. of Commuters Residing in District	94,827	100.0		Chiyoda-ku	1,556	13.2
	Commuters within District	45,611	48.1		Hachiōji-shi	1,290	10.9
	Commuters Going Out of District	49,216	51.9 (100.0)		Tachikawa-shi	1,161	9.8
	Naka-ku	16,000	32.5		Chūō-ku	1,090	9.2
	Kanagawa-ku	4,473	9.1		Shinjuku-ku	734	6.2
	Nishi-ku	4,339	8.8		Others	5,978	50.6
	Kawasaki-shi	3,936	8.0		Tachikawa-shi		
	Tsurumi-ku	3,212	6.5		Total No. of Commuters Residing in District	34,984	100.0
	Others	17,256	35.1		Commuters within District	20,398	58.3
	Hodogaya-ku				Commuters Going Out of District	14,586	41.7 (100.0)
	Total No. of Commuters Residing in District	66,905	100.0		Chiyoda-ku	1,413	9.7
	Commuters within District	25,983	38.8		Fuchū-shi	853	5.8
	Commuters Going Out of District	40,922	61.2 (100.0)		Shinjuku-ku	826	5.7
	Naka-ku	6,213	15.2		Suginami-ku	806	5.5
	Nishi-ku	5,528	13.5		Chūō-ku	801	5.5
	Kawasaki-shi	4,877	11.9		Hachiōji-shi	790	5.4
	Kanagawa-ku	3,928	9.6		Mitaka-shi	760	5.2
	Tsurumi-ku	3,683	9.0		Others	8,337	57.2
	Chiyoda-ku	2,615	6.4		Sunakawa-machi		
	Others	14,078	34.4		Total No. of Commuters Residing in District	6,553	100.0
II	Machida-shi				Commuters within District	2,902	44.3

Table 2. Commuters to Work and School, 15 Years and Older, by District of Residence

(Zone) (Sector)	District	No. of Commuters	Percent	(Zone) (Sector)	District	No. of Commuters	Percent
	Commuters Going Out of District	3,651	55.7 (100.0)		Total No. of Commuters Residing in District	7,420	100.0
	Tachikawa-shi	1,331	36.5		Commuters within District	5,715	77.0
	Akishima-shi	253	6.9		Commuters Going Out of District	1,705	23.0 (100.0)
	Others	2,067	56.6		Kasukabe-shi	252	14.8
7 III	Yamato-machi				Adachi-ku	191	11.2
	Total No. of Commuters Residing in District	6,790	100.0		Noda-shi	169	9.9
	Commuters within District	3,234	47.6		Sumida-ku	163	9.6
	Commuters Going Out of District	3,556	52.4 (100.0)		Others	930	54.5
	Tachikawa-shi	666	18.7	VI	Noda-shi		
	Kodaira-machi	216	6.1		Total No. of Commuters Residing in District	28,749	100.0
	Mitaka-shi	211	5.9		Commuters within District	23,800	82.8
	Fuchū-shi	198	5.6		Commuters Going Out of District	4,949	17.2 (100.0)
	Musashino-shi	190	5.3		Adachi-ku	405	8.2
	Others	2,075	58.4		Chūō-ku	350	7.1
IV	Ōi-mura				Kashiwa-shi	336	6.8
	Total No. of Commuters Residing in District	2,770	100.0		Chiyoda-ku	322	6.5
	Commuters within District	2,100	75.8		Sumida-ku	295	6.0
	Commuters Going Out of District	670	24.2 (100.0)		Katsushika-ku	289	5.8
	Itabashi-ku	170	25.4		Matsudo-shi	279	5.6
	Kawagoe-shi	100	14.9		Others	2,673	54.0
	Toshima-ku	49	7.3	VII	Abiko-machi		
	Yamato-machi	37	5.5		Total No. of Commuters Residing in District	13,885	100.0
	Fukuoka-mura	35	5.2		Commuters within District	8,674	62.5
	Others	279	41.7		Commuters Going Out of District	5,211	37.5 (100.0)
	Fukuoka-mura				Chiyoda-ku	681	13.1
	Total No. of Commuters Residing in District	7,936	100.0		Chūō-ku	506	9.7
	Commuters within District	2,524	31.8		Taitō-ku	458	8.8
	Commuters Going Out of District	5,412	68.2 (100.0)		Kashiwa-shi	362	6.9
	Chiyoda-ku	971	17.9		Katsushika-ku	339	6.5
	Itabashi-ku	740	13.7		Adachi-ku	321	6.2
	Chūō-ku	667	12.3		Arakawa-ku	291	5.6
	Toshima-ku	416	7.7		Matsudo-shi	280	5.4
	Kawagoe-shi	326	6.0		Others	1,973	37.8
	Minato-ku	280	5.2		Yachiyo-machi		
	Others	2,012	37.2		Total No. of Commuters Residing in District	11,305	100.0
V	Kasukabe-shi				Commuters within District	7,397	65.4
	Total No. of Commuters Residing in District	17,432	100.0		Commuters Going Out of District	3,908	34.6 (100.0)
	Commuters Going Out of District	12,322	70.7		Funahashi-shi	523	13.4
	Commuters within District	5,110	29.3 (100.0)		Chiba-shi	495	12.7
	Adachi-ku	723	14.1		Chiyoda-ku	445	11.4
	Sumida-ku	643	12.6		Chūō-ku	307	7.9
	Taitō-ku	388	7.6		Narashino-shi	285	7.3
	Chiyoda-ku	310	6.1		Ichikawa-shi	254	6.5
	Sōka-shi	306	6.0		Katsushika-ku	225	5.8
	Chūō-ku	291	5.7		Kōtō-ku	198	5.1
	Others	2,449	47.9		Others	1,176	29.9
	Shōwa-mura			VIII	Chiba-shi		

- 172 -

Table 2. Commuters to Work and School, 15 Years and Older, by District of Residence

(Zone)	(Sector)	District	No. of Commuters	Percent	(Zone)	(Sector)	District	No. of Commuters	Percent
		Total No. of Commuters Residing in District	122,868	100.0			Tsurumi-ku	2,188	7.7
		Commuters within District	91,288	74.3			Chiyoda-ku	2,058	7.2
		Commuters Going Out of District	31,580	25.7 (100.0)			Kamakura-shi	1,899	6.6
		Chiyoda-ku	4,709	14.9			Hodogaya-ku	1,531	5.4
		Chūō-ku	3,520	11.1			Chūō-ku	1,510	5.3
		Kōtō-ku	2,939	9.3			Others	9,272	32.3
		Ichikawa-shi	2,269	7.2	II		Yamato-shi		
		Funahashi-shi	2,248	7.1			Total No. of Commuters Residing in District	18,840	100.0
		Sumida-ku	1,828	5.8			Commuters within District	9,433	50.1
		Edogawa-ku	1,731	5.5			Commuters Going Out of District	9,407	49.9 (100.0)
		Others	12,336	39.1			Fujisawa-shi	870	9.2
7	IX	Goi-machi					Hodogaya-ku	685	7.3
		Total No. of Commuters Residing in District	11,836	100.0			Kawasaki-shi	614	6.5
		Commuters within District	9,726	82.2			Ayase-machi	579	6.2
		Commuters Going Out of District	2,110	17.8 (100.0)			Naka-ku	561	6.0
		Chiba-shi	1,142	54.1			Nishi-ku	525	5.6
		Kisarazu-shi	140	6.6			Chiyoda-ku	513	5.5
		Others	828	39.3			Others	5,060	53.7
		Sodegaura-machi					Sagamihara-shi		
		Total No. of Commuters Residing in District	7,864	100.0			Total No. of Commuters Residing in District	47,860	100.0
		Commuters within District	6,912	87.9			Commuters within District	29,001	60.6
		Commuters Going Out of District	952	12.1 (100.0)			Commuters Going Out of District	18,859	39.4 (100.0)
		Kisarazu-shi	359	37.7			Kawasaki-shi	2,013	10.7
		Chiba-shi	293	30.8			Chiyoda-ku	1,224	6.5
		Others	300	31.5			Zama-machi	1,164	6.2
8	I	Kanazawa-ku					Machida-shi	1,044	5.5
		Total No. of Commuters Residing in District	34,150	100.0			Tsurumi-ku	1,003	5.3
		Commuters within District	15,435	45.2			Kanagawa-ku	980	5.2
		Commuters Going Out of District	18,715	54.8 (100.0)			Hachiōji-shi	962	5.1
		Yokosuka-shi	3,158	17.0			Others	10,469	55.5
		Naka-ku	2,752	14.7			Zama-machi		
		Kawasaki-shi	1,582	8.5			Total No. of Commuters Residing in District	7,628	100.0
		Minami-ku	1,344	7.2			Commuters within District	4,333	56.8
		Kanagawa-ku	1,321	7.1			Commuters Going Out of District	3,295	43.2 (100.0)
		Tsurumi-ku	1,198	6.4			Atsugi-shi	384	11.7
		Nishi-ku	1,090	5.8			Sagamihara-shi	381	11.6
		Others	6,220	33.3			Yamato-shi	237	7.2
		Totsuka-ku					Kawasaki-shi	210	6.4
		Total No. of Commuters Residing in District	55,108	100.0			Chiyoda-ku	169	5.1
		Commuters within District	26,523	48.1			Others	1,914	58.0
		Commuters Going Out of District	28,585	51.9 (100.0)	III		Hachiōji-shi		
		Naka-ku	2,819	9.9			Total No. of Commuters Residing in District	77,945	100.0
		Kawasaki-shi	2,701	9.4			Commuters within District	55,899	71.7
		Kanagawa-ku	2,332	8.2			Commuters Going Out of District	22,046	28.3 (100.0)
		Nishi-ku	2,280	8.0			Hino-machi	3,621	16.4
							Tachikawa-shi	2,492	11.3
							Chiyoda-ku	1,608	7.3

Table 2. Commuters to Work and School, 15 Years and Older, by District of Residence

(Zone) (Sector)	District	No. of Commuters	Percent	(Zone) (Sector)	District	No. of Commuters	Percent
	Fuchū-shi	1,372	6.2		Hannō-shi	328	8.3
	Others	12,953	58.8		Nerima-ku	233	5.9
8 III	Akishima-shi				Others	2,202	56.0
	Total No. of Commuters Residing in District	20,039	100.0	IV	Sayama-shi		
	Commuters within District	9,167	45.7		Total No. of Commuters Residing in District	17,241	100.0
	Commuters Going Out of District	10,872	54.3 (100.0)		Commuters within District	12,022	69.7
	Tachikawa-shi	3,019	27.8		Commuters Going Out of District	5,219	30.0 (100.0)
	Chiyoda-ku	774	7.1		Musashi-machi	1,109	21.2
	Fussa-machi	662	6.1		Tokorosawa-shi	934	17.9
	Others	6,417	59.0		Kawagoe-shi	653	12.6
	Fussa-machi				Tanashi-machi	279	5.3
	Total No. of Commuters Residing in District	10,546	100.0		Nerima-ku	265	5.1
	Commuters within District	6,581	62.4		Others	1,979	37.9
	Commuters Going Out of District	3,965	37.6 (100.0)		Kawagoe-shi		
	Tachikawa-shi	696	17.5		Total No. of Commuters Residing in District	55,863	100.0
	Akishima-shi	499	12.6		Commuters within District	41,753	74.7
	Ōme-shi	308	7.8		Commuters Going Out of District	14,110	25.3 (100.0)
	Hachiōji-shi	243	6.1		Itabashi-ku	2,270	16.1
	Chiyoda-ku	223	5.6		Toshima-ku	1,136	8.1
	Others	1,996	50.4		Chiyoda-ku	914	6.5
	Mizuho-machi				Tokorosawa-shi	819	5.8
	Total No. of Commuters Residing in District	5,799	100.0		Others	8,971	63.5
	Commuters within District	3,552	61.3		Seibu-machi		
	Commuters Going Out of District	2,247	38.7 (100.0)		Total No. of Commuters Residing in District	3,582	100.0
	Fussa-machi	460	20.5		Commuters within District	2,413	67.4
	Tachikawa-shi	276	12.3		Commuters Going Out of District	1,169	32.6 (100.0)
	Ōme-shi	250	11.1		Musashi-machi	269	23.0
	Hachiōji-shi	196	8.6		Hannō-shi	266	22.8
	Akishima-shi	194	8.6		Tokorosawa-shi	107	9.2
	Others	871	38.9		Sayama-shi	100	8.6
	Murayama-machi				Nerima-ku	76	6.5
	Total No. of Commuters Residing in District	5,568	100.0		Toshima-ku	75	6.4
	Commuters within District	3,357	60.3		Others	276	23.5
	Commuters Going Out of District	2,211	39.7 (100.0)	V	Ageo-shi		
	Tachikawa-shi	627	28.4		Total No. of Commuters Residing in District	20,665	100.0
	Akishima-shi	200	9.0		Commuters within District	14,469	70.0
	Yamato-machi	164	7.4		Commuters Going Out of District	6,196	30.0 (100.0)
	Fussa-machi	119	5.4		Ōmiya-shi	1,250	20.2
	Fuchū-shi	113	5.1		Urawa-shi	589	9.5
	Others	988	44.7		Chūō-ku	556	9.0
	Musashi-machi				Kita-ku	498	8.0
	Total No. of Commuters Residing in District	15,263	100.0		Kawaguchi-shi	351	5.7
	Commuters within District	11,330	74.2		Others	2,952	47.6
	Commuters Going Out of District	3,933	25.8 (100.0)		Ina-mura		
	Tokorosawa-shi	712	18.1		Total No. of Commuters Residing in District	3,999	100.0
	Sayama-shi	458	11.7		Commuters within District	2,759	69.0

Table 2. Commuters to Work and School, 15 Years and Older, by District of Residence

(Zone) (Sector)	District	No. of Com-muters	Per-cent	(Zone) (Sector)	District	No. of Com-muters	Per-cent
	Commuters Going Out of District	1,240	31.0 (100.0)		Kasukabe-shi	260	11.5
	Ageo-shi	270	21.8		Sumida-ku	251	11.1
	Ōmiya-shi	164	13.2		Taitō-ku	163	7.2
	Urawa-shi	91	7.3		Satte-machi	147	6.5
	Chiyoda-ku	81	6.5		Miyashiro-machi	114	5.0
	Kita-ku	69	5.6		Others	1,039	45.8
	Others	565	45.6	VI	Sekiyado-machi		
8 V	Hasuda-machi				Total No. of Commuters Residing in District	6,769	100.0
	Total No. of Commuters Residing in District	10,803	100.0		Commuters within District	6,004	88.7
	Commuters within District	6,818	63.1		Commuters Going Out of District	765	11.3 (100.0)
	Commuters Going Out of District	3,985	36.9 (100.0)		Noda-shi	362	47.3
	Ōmiya-shi	527	13.2		Sakai-machi	65	8.5
	Kita-ku	357	9.0		Shōwa-mura	54	7.1
	Urawa-shi	346	8.7		Others	284	37.1
	Chiyoda-ku	346	8.7		Moriya-machi		
	Kawaguchi-shi	267	6.7		Total No. of Commuters Residing in District	6,451	100.0
	Taitō-ku	238	6.0		Commuters within District	5,270	81.7
	Yono-shi	206	5.2		Commuters Going Out of District	1,181	18.3 (100.0)
	Others	1,698	42.5		Mitsukaidō-shi	207	17.5
	Shiraoka-machi				Toride-machi	153	13.0
	Total No. of Commuters Residing in District	8,403	100.0		Chiyoda-ku	81	6.9
	Commuters within District	5,424	64.5		Adachi-ku	71	6.0
	Commuters Going Out of District	2,979	35.5 (100.0)		Arakawa-ku	64	5.4
	Kita-ku	345	11.6		Others	605	51.2
	Chiyoda-ku	281	9.4	VII	Toride-machi		
	Ōmiya-shi	255	8.6		Total No. of Commuters Residing in District	12,051	100.0
	Urawa-shi	234	7.9		Commuters within District	7,955	66.0
	Kawaguchi-shi	167	5.6		Commuters Going Out of District	4,096	34.0 (100.0)
	Taitō-ku	160	5.4		Chiyoda-ku	633	15.5
	Kuki-machi	152	5.1		Taitō-ku	398	9.7
	Others	1,385	46.4		Chūō-ku	393	9.6
	Miyashiro-machi				Minato-ku	251	6.1
	Total No. of Commuters Residing in District	5,783	100.0		Adachi-ku	241	5.9
	Commuters within District	3,741	64.7		Arakawa-ku	230	5.6
	Commuters Going Out of District	2,042	35.3 (100.0)		Katsushika-ku	221	5.4
	Sumida-ku	300	14.7		Others	1,729	42.2
	Adachi-ku	276	13.5		Inzai-machi		
	Kasukabe-shi	178	8.7		Total No. of Commuters Residing in District	9,528	100.0
	Sugito-machi	119	5.8		Commuters within District	8,252	86.6
	Chiyoda-ku	112	5.5		Commuters Going Out of District	1,276	13.4 (100.0)
	Taitō-ku	103	5.0		Chiyoda-ku	130	10.2
	Others	954	46.8		Kashiwa-shi	103	8.1
	Sugito-machi				Narita-shi	95	7.4
	Total No. of Commuters Residing in District	9,349	100.0		Matsudo-shi	88	6.9
	Commuters within District	7,083	75.8		Chūō-ku	82	6.5
	Commuters Going Out of District	2,266	24.2 (100.0)		Taitō-ku	76	6.0
	Adachi-ku	292	12.9		Others	701	54.9

Table 2. Commuters to Work and School, 15 Years and Older by District of Residence

(Zone) (Sector)	District	No. of Commuters	Percent	(Zone) (Sector)	District	No. of Commuters	Percent
8 VII	**Inba-mura**				Commuters within District	4,554	85.3
	Total No. of Commuters	4,892	100.0		Commuters Going Out of District	784	14.7 (100.0)
	Residing in District				Chiba-shi	319	40.6
	Commuters within District	4,516	92.3		Goi-machi	141	18.0
	Commuters Going Out of District	376	7.7 (100.0)		Nansō-machi	127	16.2
	Inzai-machi	86	22.9		Ichihara-machi	46	5.9
	Sakura-shi	78	20.7		Others	151	19.3
	Chiba-shi	42	11.2	X	**Kisarazu-shi**		
	Narita-shi	26	6.9		Total No. of Commuters	28,981	100.0
	Funahashi-shi	23	6.1		Residing in District		
	Narashino-shi	19	5.1		Commuters within District	26,293	90.7
	Others	102	27.1		Commuters Going Out of District	2,688	9.3 (100.0)
VIII	**Yotsukaidō-machi**				Chiba-shi	1,222	45.5
	Total No. of Commuters	8,452	100.0		Goi-machi	146	5.4
	Residing in District				Others	1,320	49.1
	Commuters within District	5,130	60.7	9 I	**Kamakura-shi**		
	Commuters Going Out of District	3,322	39.3 (100.0)		Total No. of Commuters	48,392	100.0
	Chiba-shi	1,586	47.7		Residing in District		
	Kōtō-ku	231	7.0		Commuters within District	22,813	47.1
	Sakura-shi	208	6.3		Commuters Going Out of District	25,579	52.9 (100.0)
	Others	1,297	39.0		Chiyoda-ku	3,391	13.3
IX	**Ichihara-machi**				Chūō-ku	2,869	11.2
	Total No. of Commuters	7,832	100.0		Fujisawa-shi	2,398	9.4
	Residing in District				Totsuka-ku	2,081	8.1
	Commuters within District	5,493	70.1		Minato-ku	1,637	6.4
	Commuters Going Out of District	2,339	29.9 (100.0)		Naka-ku	1,614	6.3
	Chiba-shi	1,333	56.9		Yokosuka-shi	1,524	6.0
	Goi-machi	307	13.1		Kawasaki-shi	1,325	5.2
	Others	699	30.0		Others	8,740	34.1
	Anegasaki-machi			II	**Ayase-machi**		
	Total No. of Commuters	6,265	100.0		Total No. of Commuters	4,276	100.0
	Residing in District				Residing in District		
	Commuters within District	4,910	78.4		Commuters within District	2,917	68.2
	Commuters Going Out of District	1,355	21.6 (100.0)		Commuters Going Out of District	1,359	31.8 (100.0)
	Chiba-shi	627	46.3		Fujisawa-shi	175	12.9
	Kisarazu-shi	135	10.0		Yamato-shi	162	11.9
	Goi-machi	130	9.6		Atsugi-shi	150	11.0
	Others	423	34.1		Totsuka-ku	99	7.3
	Hirakawa-machi				Ebina-machi	84	6.2
	Total No. of Commuters	6,303	100.0		Nishi-ku	79	5.8
	Residing in District				Others	610	44.9
	Commuters within District	5,590	88.7		**Ebina-machi**		
	Commuters Going Out of District	713	11.3 (100.0)		Total No. of Commuters	9,326	100.0
	Kisarazu-shi	329	46.1		Residing in District		
	Chiba-shi	123	17.3		Commuters within District	5,871	63.0
	Obitsu-mura	71	10.0		Commuters Going Out of District	3,455	37.0 (100.0)
	Kazusa-machi	50	7.0		Atsugi-shi	684	19.8
	Others	140	19.6		Yamato-shi	217	6.3
	Miwa-machi				Kawasaki-shi	203	5.9
	Total No. of Commuters	5,338	100.0		Hodogaya-ku	200	5.8
	Residing in District						

(Zone) (Sector)	District	No. of Commuters	Percent	(Zone) (Sector)	District	No. of Commuters	Percent
	Others	2,151	62.2		Others	537	43.3
9 II	Shiroyama-machi				Hidaka-machi		
	Total No. of Commuters	2,540	100.0		Total No. of Commuters	9,215	100.0
	Residing in District				Residing in District		
	Commuters within District	1,434	56.5		Commuters within District	6,871	74.6
	Commuters Going Out of District	1,106	43.5 (100.0)		Commuters Going Out of District	2,344	25.4 (100.0)
	Sagamihara-shi	393	35.5		Hanno-shi	695	29.7
	Hachiōji-shi	136	12.3		Kawagoe-shi	442	18.9
	Tsukui-machi	99	9.0		Tokorozawa-shi	169	7.2
	Others	478	43.2		Musashi-machi	153	6.5
III	Akita-machi				Sayama-shi	129	5.5
					Others	756	32.2
	Total No. of Commuters	6,909	100.0				
	Residing in District				Kawashima-mura		
	Commuters within District	3,477	50.3		Total No. of Commuters	9,412	100.0
	Commuters Going Out of District	3,432	49.7 (100.0)		Residing in District		
	Fussa-machi	737	21.5		Commuters within District	7,681	81.6
	Tachikawa-shi	434	12.6		Commuters Going Out of District	1,731	18.4 (100.0)
	Akishima-shi	369	10.8		Kawagoe-shi	805	46.5
	Ōme-shi	317	9.2		Higashimatsuyama-shi	222	12.8
	Hachiōji-shi	199	5.8		Others	704	40.7
	Others	1,376	40.1	V	Kitamoto-machi		
					Total No. of Commuters	7,854	100.0
	Hamura-machi				Residing in District		
	Total No. of Commuters	5,226	100.0		Commuters within District	4,583	58.4
	Residing in District				Commuters Going Out of District	3,271	41.6 (100.0)
	Commuters within District	2,188	41.9		Higawa-machi	297	9.1
	Commuters Going Out of District	3,038	58.1 (100.0)		Kōnosu-shi	291	9.0
	Fussa-machi	556	18.3		Chiyoda-ku	281	8.6
	Ōme-shi	524	17.2		Kita-ku	256	7.8
	Tachikawa-shi	341	11.2		Ōmiya-shi	245	7.5
	Akishima-shi	206	6.8		Urawa-shi	227	6.9
	Others	1,411	46.5		Chūō-ku	184	5.6
IV	Hannō-shi				Ageo-shi	173	5.3
	Total No. of Commuters	21,735	100.0		Kawaguchi-shi	166	5.1
	Residing in District				Others	1,151	35.1
	Commuters within District	16,571	76.2				
	Commuters Going Out of District	5,164	23.8 (100.0)		Higawa-machi		
	Musashi-machi	960	18.6		Total No. of Commuters	11,168	100.0
	Tokorozawa-shi	719	13.9		Residing in District		
	Toshima-ku	413	8.0		Commuters within District	7,228	64.7
	Ōme-shi	291	5.6		Commuters Going Out of District	3,940	35.3 (100.0)
	Nerima-ku	260	5.0		Ageo-shi	472	12.0
	Others	2,521	48.9		Ōmiya-shi	465	11.8
					Chiyoda-ku	352	8.9
	Tsurugashima-mura				Urawa-shi	313	7.9
	Total No. of Commuters	4,116	100.0		Kita-ku	269	6.8
	Residing in District				Chūō-ku	210	5.3
	Commuters within District	2,876	69.9		Kawaguchi-shi	206	5.2
	Commuters Going Out of District	1,240	30.1 (100.0)		Others	1,653	42.1
	Kawagoe-shi	344	27.7		Shōbu-machi		
	Itabashi-ku	170	13.7		Total No. of Commuters	8,367	100.0
	Sakado-machi	109	8.8		Residing in District		
	Higashimatsuyama-shi	80	6.5				

Table 2. Commuters to Work and School, 15 Years and Older, by District of Residence

(Zone) (Sector)	District	No. of Commuters	Percent
	Commuters within District	6,793	81.2
	Commuters Going Out of District	1,574	18.8 (100.0)
	Kuki-machi	137	8.7
	Urawa-shi	134	8.5
	Ōmiya-shi	128	8.1
	Higawa-machi	112	7.1
	Chiyoda-ku	112	7.1
	Ageo-shi	91	5.8
	Kita-ku	90	5.7
	Others	770	49.0
9 V	Kuki-machi		
	Total No. of Commuters Residing in District	11,613	100.0
	Commuters within District	7,686	66.2
	Commuters Going Out of District	3,927	33.8 (100.0)
	Kita-ku	332	8.5
	Ōmiya-shi	320	8.1
	Chiyoda-ku	314	8.0
	Taitō-ku	270	6.9
	Urawa-shi	266	6.8
	Kawaguchi-shi	230	5.9
	Chūo-ku	197	5.0
	Others	1,998	50.8
	Satte-machi		
	Total No. of Commuters Residing in District	12,253	100.0
	Commuters within District	9,717	66.2
	Commuters Going Out of District	2,536	33.8 (100.0)
	Sumida-ku	340	13.4
	Adachi-ku	310	12.2
	Taitō-ku	197	7.8
	Chiyoda-ku	160	6.3
	Kasukabe-shi	159	6.3
	Sugita-machi	157	6.2
	Chūo-ku	153	6.0
	Others	1,060	41.8
VI	Iwai-machi		
	Total No. of Commuters Residing in District	18,938	100.0
	Commuters within District	18,117	95.7
	Commuters Going Out of District	821	4.3 (100.0)
	Mitsukaidō-shi	277	33.7
	Noda-shi	267	32.5
	Sakai-machi	90	11.0
	Others	187	22.8
	Mitsukaidō-shi		
	Total No. of Commuters Residing in District	20,656	100.0
	Commuters within District	19,376	93.8
	Commuters Going Out of District	1,280	6.2 (100.0)
	Chiyoda-ku	105	8.2

(Zone) (Sector)	District	No. of Commuters	Percent
	Chūo-ku	81	6.3
	Iwai-machi	80	6.3
	Toyosato-machi	75	5.9
	Ishige-machi	67	5.2
	Adachi-ku	65	5.1
	Others	807	63.0
	Yawahara-mura		
	Total No. of Commuters Residing in District	6,168	100.0
	Commuters within District	5,156	83.6
	Commuters Going Out of District	1,012	16.4 (100.0)
	Mitsukaidō-shi	409	40.4
	Yatabe-machi	114	11.3
	Ina-mura	86	8.5
	Others	403	39.8
	Ina-mura		
	Total No. of Commuters Residing in District	7,360	100.0
	Commuters within District	6,518	88.6
	Commuters Going Out of District	842	11.4 (100.0)
	Toride-machi	215	25.5
	Mitsukaidō-shi	100	11.9
	Yatabe-machi	73	8.7
	Others	454	53.9
VII	Fujishiro-machi		
	Total No. of Commuters Residing in District	7,446	100.0
	Commuters within District	5,643	75.8
	Commuters Going Out of District	1,803	24.2 (100.0)
	Toride-machi	411	22.8
	Chiyoda-ku	177	9.8
	Ryūgasaki-shi	148	8.2
	Chūo-ku	134	7.4
	Taitō-ku	108	6.0
	Arakawa-ku	99	5.5
	Others	726	40.3
	Ryūgasaki-shi		
	Total No. of Commuters Residing in District	18,464	100.0
	Commuters within District	16,100	87.2
	Commuters Going Out of District	2,364	12.8 (100.0)
	Chiyoda-ku	286	12.1
	Toride-machi	189	8.0
	Taitō-ku	177	7.5
	Chūo-ku	168	7.1
	Tsuchiura-shi	150	6.3
	Arakawa-ku	144	6.1
	Others	1,250	52.9
	Tone-mura		
	Total No. of Commuters Residing in District	5,324	100.0

Table 2. Commuters to Work and School, 15 Years and Older, by District of Residence

(Zone)(Sector)	District	No. of Commuters	Percent	(Zone)(Sector)	District	No. of Commuters	Percent
	Commuters within District	4,334	81.4		Total No. of Commuters Residing in District	9,911	100.0
	Commuters Going Out of District	990	18.6 (100.0)		Commuters within District	9,238	93.2
	Ryūgasaki-shi	208	20.9		Commuters Going Out of District	673	6.8 (100.0)
	Inzai-machi	84	8.5		Chiba-shi	243	36.1
	Chiyoda-ku	77	7.8		Goi-machi	96	14.3
	Toride-machi	74	7.5		Mobara-shi	91	13.5
	Chūō-ku	53	5.4		Mitsuwa-machi	35	5.2
	Taitō-ku	53	5.4		Others	208	30.9
	Adachi-ku	51	5.2		Fukuta-machi		
	Others	390	39.3		Total No. of Commuters Residing in District	4,117	100.0
9 VII	Motono-mura				Commuters within District	3,521	85.5
	Total No. of Commuters Residing in District	3,147	100.0		Commuters Going Out of District	596	14.5 (100.0)
	Commuters within District	2,733	86.8		Kisarazu-shi	284	47.7
	Commuters Going Out of District	414	13.2 (100.0)		Chiba-shi	102	17.1
	Inzai-machi	97	23.4		Obitsu-mura	56	9.4
	Narita-shi	42	10.2		Hirakawa-machi	48	8.1
	Sakae-machi	23	5.6		Kazusa-machi	40	6.7
	Chiyoda-ku	22	5.3		Others	66	11.0
	Others	230	55.5	X	Kimitsu-machi		
VIII	Sakura-shi				Total No. of Commuters Residing in District	7,444	100.0
	Total No. of Commuters Residing in District	20,135	100.0		Commuters within District	6,078	81.6
	Commuters within District	14,877	73.9		Commuters Going Out of District	1,366	18.4 (100.0)
	Commuters Going Out of District	5,258	26.1 (100.0)		Kisarazu-shi	638	46.7
	Chiba-shi	1,204	22.9		Chiba-shi	206	15.1
	Funahashi-shi	512	9.7		Koito-machi	105	7.7
	Katsushika-ku	363	6.9		Futtsu-machi	87	6.4
	Narashino-shi	350	6.7		Osawa-machi	73	5.3
	Chiyoda-ku	347	6.6		Others	257	18.8
	Ichikawa-shi	339	6.4		Futtsu-machi		
	Others	2,143	40.8		Total No. of Commuters Residing in District	9,009	100.0
	Izumi-machi				Commuters within District	8,112	90.0
	Total No. of Commuters Residing in District	5,419	100.0		Commuters Going Out of District	897	10.0 (100.0)
	Commuters within District	4,746	87.6		Kisarazu-shi	391	43.5
	Commuters Going Out of District	673	12.4 (100.0)		Chiba-shi	154	17.2
	Chiba-shi	467	69.4		Osawa-machi	103	11.5
	Tōgane-shi	44	6.5		Amaha-machi	61	6.8
	Others	162	24.1		Kimitsu-machi	52	5.8
IX	Shitsu-mura				Others	136	15.2
	Total No. of Commuters Residing in District	5,344	100.0		Ōsawa-machi		
	Commuters within District	4,438	83.0		Total No. of Commuters Residing in District	7,528	100.0
	Commuters Going Out of District	906	17.0 (100.0)		Commuters within District	6,234	82.8
	Chiba-shi	577	63.6		Commuters Going Out of District	1,294	17.2 (100.0)
	Shigehara-shi	89	9.9		Kisarazu-shi	438	33.9
	Ichihara-machi	51	5.6		Chiba-shi	210	16.2
	Others	189	20.9		Amaha-machi	167	12.9
	Nansō-machi				Futtsu-machi	100	7.7

Table 2. Commuters to Work and School, 15 Years and Older, by District of Residence

(Zone) (Sector)	District	No. of Commuters	Percent	(Zone) (Sector)	District	No. of Commuters	Percent
	Others	379	293		Chūō-ku	1,143	7.2
					Naka-ku	945	5.9
10 I	Yokosuka-shi				Minato-ku	815	5.1
	Total No. of Commuters Residing in District	139,937	100.0		Kawasaki-shi	798	5.0
					Others	6,746	42.5
	Commuters within District	105,446	75.4		Fujisawa-shi		
	Commuters Going Out of District	34,491	24.6 (100.0)		Total No. of Commuters Residing in District	59,994	100.0
	Naka-ku	3,670	10.6				
	Kanazawa-ku	3,476	10.1		Commuters within District	34,786	58.0
	Kawasaki-shi	3,216	9.3		Commuters Going Out of District	25,208	42.0 (100.0)
	Tsurumi-ku	2,040	5.9		Chiyoda-ku	3,159	12.5
	Chiyoda-ku	1,933	5.6		Chūō-ku	2,434	9.7
	Kanagawa-ku	1,920	5.6		Kamakura-shi	1,956	7.8
	Zushi-shi	1,837	5.3		Naka-ku	1,703	6.8
	Totsuka-ku	1,811	5.3		Minato-ku	1,545	6.1
	Nishi-ku	1,783	5.2		Kawasaki-shi	1,457	5.8
	Kamakura-shi	1,771	5.1		Totsuka-ku	1,279	5.1
	Others	11,034	32.0		Others	11,675	46.2
	Zushi-shi			II	Aikawa-machi		
	Total No. of Commuters Residing in District	18,880	100.0		Total No. of Commuters Residing in District	7,521	100.0
	Commuters within District	6,258	33.1		Commuters within District	6,293	83.7
	Commuters Going Out of District	12,622	66.9 (100.0)		Commuters Going Out of District	1,228	16.3 (100.0)
	Yokosuka-shi	2,601	20.6		Atsugi-shi	476	38.7
	Chiyoda-ku	1,100	8.7		Sagamihara-shi	301	24.5
	Kamakura-shi	1,045	8.3		Zama-machi	72	5.9
	Chūō-ku	908	7.2		Others	379	30.9
	Naka-ku	745	5.9		Atsugi-shi		
	Kawasaki-shi	662	5.2		Total No. of Commuters Residing in District	23,688	100.0
	Others	5,561	44.1				
	Hayama-machi				Commuters within District	17,811	75.2
	Total No. of Commuters Residing in District	7,557	100.0		Commuters Going Out of District	5,877	24.8 (100.0)
	Commuters within District	2,870	38.0		Sagamihara-shi	452	7.7
	Commuters Going Out of District	4,687	62.0 (100.0)		Kawasaki-shi	411	7.0
	Yokosuka-shi	1,089	23.2		Ebina-machi	383	6.5
	Zushi-shi	447	9.5		Hiratsuka-shi	360	6.1
	Chūō-ku	357	7.6		Yamato-shi	298	5.1
	Chiyoda-ku	347	7.4		Others	3,973	67.6
	Kamakura-shi	267	5.7		Samukawa-machi		
	Naka-ku	258	5.5		Total No. of Commuters Residing in District	5,953	100.0
	Totsuka-ku	240	5.1		Commuters within District	3,882	65.2
	Others	1,682	36.0		Commuters Going Out of District	2,071	34.8 (100.0)
	Chigasaki-shi				Chigasaki-shi	452	21.8
	Total No. of Commuters Residing in District	31,986	100.0		Fujisawa-shi	361	17.4
	Commuters within District	16,087	50.3		Hiratsuka-shi	269	13.0
	Commuters Going Out of District	15,899	49.7 (100.0)		Others	989	47.8
	Fujisawa-shi	2,778	17.5	III	Ome-shi		
	Chiyoda-ku	1,422	8.9		Total No. of Commuters Residing in District	29,020	100.0
	Hiratsuka-shi	1,252	7.9		Commuters within District	22,959	79.1

Table 2. Commuters to Work and School, 15 Years and Older, by District of Residence

(Zone) (Sector)	District	No. of Commuters	Percent	(Zone) (Sector)	District	No. of Commuters	Percent
	Commuters Going Out of District	6,061	20.9 (100.0)		Total No. of Commuters Residing in District	8,434	100.0
	Tachikawa-shi	1,015	16.7		Commuters within District	7,053	83.6
	Fussa-machi	801	13.2		Commuters Going Out of District	1,381	16.4 (100.0)
	Akishima-shi	400	6.6		Kazo-shi	435	31.4
	Hachiōji-shi	318	5.2		Shobu-machi	84	6.1
	Others	3,527	58.3		Others	862	62.4
10 IV	Sakado-machi				Washimiya-machi		
	Total No. of Commuters Residing in District	12,747	100.0		Total No. of Commuters Residing in District	4,466	100.0
	Commuters within District	9,316	73.1		Commuters within District	3,290	73.7
	Commuters Going Out of District	3,431	26.9 (100.0)		Commuters Going Out of District	1,176	26.3 (100.0)
	Kawagoe-shi	988	28.8		Kuki-machi	155	13.2
	Itabashi-ku	502	14.6		Ōmiya-shi	72	6.1
	Higashimatsuyama-shi	310	9.0		Sumida-ku	65	5.5
	Toshima-ku	203	5.9		Chiyoda-ku	61	5.2
	Others	1,428	41.7		Urawa-shi	60	5.1
	Yoshimi-mura				Others	763	64.9
	Total No. of Commuters Residing in District	8,388	100.0		Kurihashi-machi		
	Commuters within District	6,790	80.9		Total No. of Commuters Residing in District	6,470	100.0
	Commuters Going Out of District	1,598	19.1 (100.0)		Commuters within District	4,326	66.9
	Higashimatsuyama-shi	613	38.4		Commuters Going Out of District	2,144	33.1 (100.0)
	Kōnosu-shi	99	6.2		Kita-ku	179	8.3
	Others	886	55.4		Chiyoda-ku	176	8.2
	Moroyama-mura				Taitō-ku	157	7.3
	Total No. of Commuters Residing in District	5,943	100.0		Ōmiya-shi	145	6.8
	Commuters within District	4,600	77.4		Urawa-shi	117	5.5
	Commuters Going Out of District	1,343	22.6 (100.0)		Others	1,370	63.9
	Kawagoe-shi	216	16.1		Goka-mura		
	Hannō-shi	155	11.5		Total No. of Commuters Residing in District	4,874	100.0
	Sakado-machi	104	7.7		Commuters within District	4,336	89.0
	Itabashi-ku	84	6.3		Commuters Going Out of District	538	11.0 (100.0)
	Higashimatsuyama-shi	74	5.5		Satte-machi	110	20.4
	Ogose-machi	74	5.5		Sugito-machi	35	6.5
	Others	636	47.4		Sakai-machi	34	6.3
V	Kōnosu-shi				Sumida-ku	29	5.4
	Total No. of Commuters Residing in District	16,558	100.0		Koga-shi	27	5.0
	Commuters within District	11,733	70.9		Others	303	56.6
	Commuters Going Out of District	4,825	29.2 (100.0)	VI	Sakai-machi		
	Chiyoda-ku	454	9.4		Total No. of Commuters Residing in District	12,194	100.0
	Kita-ku	444	9.2		Commuters within District	11,916	97.7
	Ōmiya-shi	413	8.6		Commuters Going Out of District	278	2.3 (100.0)
	Kawaguchi-shi	327	6.8		Koga-shi	50	18.0
	Urawa-shi	307	6.4		Iwai-machi	33	11.9
	Chūō-ku	289	6.0		Shōwa-mura	18	6.5
	Taitō-ku	251	5.2		Mitsuwa-mura	16	5.8
	Others	2,340	48.4		Sashima-machi	16	5.8
	Kisai-machi				Sekiyado-machi	15	5.4

(Zone)	(Sector)	District	No. of Commuters	Percent	(Zone)	(Sector)	District	No. of Commuters	Percent
		Adachi-ku	15	5.4			Others	235	38.0
		Others	115	41.2			Sakae-machi		
10	VI	Sashima-machi					Total No. of Commuters Residing in District	5,593	100.0
		Total No. of Commuters Residing in District	8,192	100.0			Commuters within District	4,695	83.9
		Commuters within District	7,853	95.9			Commuters Going Out of District	898	16.1 (100.0)
		Commuters Going Out of District	339	4.1 (100.0)			Narita-shi	216	24.1
		Sakai-machi	134	39.5			Inzai-machi	136	15.1
		Iwai-machi	107	31.6			Chiyoda-ku	68	7.6
		Mitsukaidō-shi	24	7.1			Sakura-shi	64	7.1
		Ishige-machi	19	5.6			Chiba-shi	54	6.0
		Others	55	16.2			Others	360	40.1
		Yatabe-machi					Narita-shi		
		Total No. of Commuters Residing in District	12,387	100.0			Total No. of Commuters Residing in District	23,292	100.0
		Commuters within District	11,492	92.8			Commuters within District	19,836	85.2
		Commuters Going Out of District	895	7.2 (100.0)			Commuters Going Out of District	3,456	14.8 (100.0)
		Tsuchiura-shi	288	32.2			Chiba-shi	635	18.4
		Mitsukaidō-shi	227	25.4			Sakura-shi	388	11.2
		Ina-mura	89	9.9			Funahashi-shi	274	7.9
		Others	291	32.5			Chiyoda-ku	212	6.1
	VII	Kukizaki-mura					Narashino-shi	178	5.2
		Total No. of Commuters Residing in District	3,735	100.0			Others	1,769	51.2
		Commuters within District	3,250	87.0		VIII	Shisui-machi		
		Commuters Going Out of District	485	13.0 (100.0)			Total No. of Commuters Residing in District	3,386	100.0
		Ryūgasaki-shi	64	13.2			Commuters within District	2,259	66.7
		Ushiku-machi	62	12.8			Commuters Going Out of District	1,127	33.3 (100.0)
		Yatabe-machi	57	11.8			Sakura-shi	200	17.7
		Toride-machi	56	11.5			Chiba-shi	150	13.3
		Tsuchiura-shi	44	9.1			Narita-shi	115	10.2
		Chiyoda-ku	27	5.6			Funahashi-shi	105	9.3
		Others	175	36.0			Katsushika-ku	86	7.6
		Ushiku-machi					Narashino-shi	79	7.0
		Total No. of Commuters Residing in District	8,706	100.0			Sumida-ku	59	5.2
		Commuters within District	7,044	80.9			Ichikawa-shi	58	5.1
		Commuters Going Out of District	1,662	19.1 (100.0)			Others	275	24.3
		Ryūgasaki-shi	377	22.7			Yachimata-machi		
		Tsuchiura-shi	157	9.4			Total No. of Commuters Residing in District	13,738	100.0
		Chiyoda-ku	145	8.7			Commuters within District	12,413	90.4
		Toride-machi	111	6.7			Commuters Going Out of District	1,325	9.6 (100.0)
		Others	872	52.5			Chiba-shi	553	41.8
		Kawachi-mura					Sakura-shi	175	13.2
		Total No. of Commuters Residing in District	7,648	100.0			Tōgane-shi	110	8.3
		Commuters within District	7,029	91.9			Others	487	36.7
		Commuters Going Out of District	619	8.1 (100.0)			Toke-machi		
		Ryūgasaki-shi	290	46.8			Total No. of Commuters Residing in District	3,573	100.0
		Sawara-shi	48	7.8			Commuters within District	2,577	72.1
		Narita-shi	46	7.4			Commuters Going Out of District	996	27.9 (100.0)

Table 2. Commuters to Work and School, 15 Years and Older, by District of Residence

(Zone) (Sector)	District	No. of Commuters	Percent	(Zone) (Sector)	District	No. of Commuters	Percent
	Chiba-shi	431	43.3		Commuters within District	3,458	87.6
	Mobara-shi	83	8.3		Commuters Going Out of District	490	12.4 (100.0)
	Ōamishirasato-machi	75	7.5		Kisarazu-shi	263	53.7
	Tōgane-shi	70	7.0		Kazusa-machi	76	15.5
	Others	337	33.9		Chiba-shi	67	13.7
10 IX	Nagara-machi				Others	84	17.1
	Total No. of Commuters Residing in District	5,174	100.0	X	Koito-machi		
	Commuters within District	4,323	83.6		Total No. of Commuters Residing in District	3,669	100.0
	Commuters Going Out of District	851	16.4 (100.0)		Commuters within District	3,396	92.6
	Mobara-shi	600	70.5		Commuters Going Out of District	273	7.4 (100.0)
	Chiba-shi	81	9.5		Kisarazu-shi	159	58.2
	Others	170	20.0		Kimitsu-machi	25	9.2
	Obitsu-mura				Seiwa-mura	23	8.4
	Total No. of Commuters Residing in District	3,948	100.0		Chiba-shi	16	5.9
					Others	50	18.3

Note: The names of the districts (ku, shi, machi, and mura) to which commuters go from the districts of their residence are given only when the number commuting to those districts exceed 5 percent of the total commuting population of a given district of residence.

1950

TABLE 3. POPULATION BY AGE (5-YEAR BRACKET) AND SEX

(Zone)	(Sector)	District	Total	M	F	Age 0-4 M	Age 0-4 F	Age 5-9 M	Age 5-9 F	Age 10-14 M	Age 10-14 F	Age 15-19 M	Age 15-19 F	Age 20-24 M	Age 20-24 F	Age 25-29 M	Age 25-29 F	Age 30-34 M	Age 30-34 F	Age 35-39 M	Age 35-39 F	Age 40-44 M	Age 40-44 F	Age 45-49 M	Age 45-49 F	Age 50-54 M	Age 50-54 F	Age 55-59 M	Age 55-59 F	Age 60-64 M	Age 60-64 F	Age 65-69 M	Age 65-69 F	Age 70-74 M	Age 70-74 F	75 & over M	75 & over F	Unknown M	Unknown F
1	I	Chiyoda-ku	(110,348) 100.0	52.2	47.8	5.2	5.0	4.5	4.3	3.6	3.5	7.4	5.7	8.6	6.0	4.8	4.9	3.3	3.8	3.3	3.3	3.0	2.9	2.7	2.3	2.1	1.9	1.6	1.4	1.2	1.1	0.7	0.8	0.3	0.5	0.2	0.4	—	—
		Minato-ku	(216,120) 100.0	50.2	49.8	5.2	5.5	4.9	4.8	3.9	3.9	5.5	5.0	6.5	5.5	4.5	5.1	3.5	4.1	3.5	3.7	3.0	3.0	2.8	2.5	2.4	2.0	1.7	1.6	1.2	1.2	0.7	0.9	0.4	0.6	0.2	0.4	—	—
		Chuo-ku	(161,925) 100.0	50.7	49.3	5.1	5.0	4.4	4.4	3.7	3.7	7.3	5.5	7.0	5.8	4.4	4.9	3.2	3.9	3.2	3.6	3.0	3.1	2.9	2.7	2.4	2.1	1.6	1.6	1.2	1.2	0.7	0.8	0.4	0.6	0.2	0.4	—	—
		Bunkyo-ku	(190,746) 100.0	50.5	49.5	5.7	5.4	4.9	4.7	3.9	3.8	5.8	5.0	6.7	5.5	4.5	4.8	3.4	4.0	3.3	3.5	3.0	3.0	2.7	2.6	2.3	2.1	1.7	1.7	1.3	1.3	0.8	1.0	0.4	0.6	0.2	0.4	—	—
		Taito-ku	(262,159) 100.0	51.0	49.0	5.7	5.5	4.9	4.6	4.0	3.9	7.0	5.7	5.9	5.6	4.3	4.8	3.4	3.9	3.4	3.5	3.1	2.9	2.8	2.3	2.3	1.9	1.4	1.4	1.2	1.2	0.7	0.8	0.4	0.5	0.2	0.4	—	—
		Zone 1 Total	(941,298) 100.0	50.8	49.2	5.5	5.3	4.7	4.6	3.9	3.8	6.5	5.4	6.7	5.7	4.5	4.9	3.3	3.9	3.4	3.5	3.0	3.0	2.8	2.5	2.2	2.0	1.6	1.5	1.2	1.1	0.7	0.9	0.4	0.6	0.2	0.4	—	—
2	I	Shinagawa-ku	(288,545) 100.0	50.4	49.6	6.3	6.0	5.1	5.1	4.1	4.1	5.3	4.8	6.0	5.3	4.6	5.0	3.7	4.0	3.4	3.4	2.9	2.9	2.7	2.6	2.3	2.1	1.7	1.5	1.2	1.1	0.6	0.8	0.3	0.5	0.2	0.4	—	—
	II	Meguro-ku	(204,382) 100.0	50.5	49.5	5.8	5.6	5.2	5.2	4.2	4.0	5.4	4.8	6.3	5.3	4.4	4.9	3.6	4.0	3.4	3.6	3.1	3.0	2.8	2.6	2.3	2.1	1.6	1.5	1.2	1.1	0.6	0.8	0.4	0.6	0.2	0.4	—	—
	III	Shibuya-ku	(181,244) 100.0	49.6	50.4	5.8	5.6	4.9	4.8	3.8	3.8	5.2	5.0	6.4	5.9	4.6	5.3	3.5	4.2	3.4	3.5	2.9	2.9	2.6	2.5	2.2	2.1	1.7	1.7	1.2	1.3	0.8	0.9	0.4	0.5	0.2	0.4	—	—
	IV	Shinjuku-ku	(246,373) 100.0	49.9	50.1	6.0	5.7	4.9	4.8	3.8	3.8	5.2	5.0	6.5	6.0	4.6	5.3	3.6	4.2	3.6	3.5	3.0	2.9	2.6	2.4	2.1	2.0	1.6	1.5	1.2	1.2	0.7	0.9	0.3	0.5	0.2	0.4	—	—
	V	Nakano-ku	(213,461) 100.0	50.3	49.7	5.9	5.7	5.2	5.0	4.1	4.0	5.0	4.7	6.4	5.3	4.7	5.1	3.7	4.0	3.4	3.6	3.0	3.0	2.6	2.3	2.1	2.1	1.6	1.6	1.1	1.2	0.7	0.8	0.4	0.6	0.2	0.4	—	—
		Toshima-ku	(217,141) 100.0	50.4	49.6	6.0	5.8	5.3	5.1	4.1	4.0	5.3	4.9	6.0	5.3	4.4	5.1	3.8	4.0	3.6	3.6	3.0	2.9	2.7	2.3	2.0	2.0	1.7	1.5	1.2	1.1	0.6	0.8	0.3	0.5	0.2	0.4	—	—
		Kita-ku	(267,209) 100.0	50.5	49.5	6.5	6.1	5.4	5.3	4.4	4.3	5.4	4.9	5.8	5.0	4.2	4.7	3.5	3.9	3.4	3.4	2.9	2.9	2.7	2.4	2.1	2.0	1.7	1.5	1.2	1.1	0.6	0.8	0.3	0.5	0.2	0.4	—	—
	VI	Arakawa-ku	(201,248) 100.0	50.9	49.1	6.6	6.4	5.5	5.4	4.5	4.4	6.1	5.6	5.5	5.0	4.1	4.5	3.3	3.6	3.2	3.2	2.9	2.7	2.4	2.1	1.8	1.6	1.4	1.3	1.1	1.1	0.6	0.7	0.3	0.4	0.2	0.3	—	—
	VII	Sumida-ku	(236,242) 100.0	51.3	48.7	6.4	6.1	5.5	5.2	4.4	4.3	6.8	5.6	5.8	5.2	4.3	4.5	3.4	3.7	3.3	3.3	2.9	2.7	2.4	2.2	1.9	1.6	1.5	1.1	1.0	1.0	0.5	0.7	0.3	0.4	0.2	0.3	—	—
	VIII	Koto-ku	(182,489) 100.0	52.8	47.2	7.2	6.9	5.5	5.4	4.2	4.1	5.6	4.4	6.1	4.7	4.8	4.8	3.9	4.1	3.9	3.3	3.3	2.6	2.8	2.1	1.6	1.5	1.1	0.8	0.5	0.6	0.2	0.4	—	—
		Zone 2 Total	(2,238,334) 100.0	50.6	49.4	6.3	6.0	5.2	5.1	4.2	4.1	5.5	5.0	6.1	5.3	4.5	4.9	3.6	4.0	3.5	3.4	3.0	2.9	2.7	2.5	2.1	2.0	1.6	1.5	1.2	1.1	0.6	0.8	0.3	0.5	0.2	0.4	—	—
3	I	Ota-ku	(400,406) 100.0	50.7	49.3	6.5	6.2	5.7	5.4	4.2	4.2	5.1	4.5	5.9	4.9	4.5	4.9	3.7	4.1	3.6	3.6	3.1	2.9	2.6	2.5	2.1	1.9	1.5	1.3	1.1	1.1	0.6	0.8	0.3	0.4	0.2	0.4	—	—
	II	Setagaya-ku	(408,226) 100.0	50.0	50.0	6.1	5.8	5.4	5.2	4.3	4.2	5.1	4.8	6.1	5.2	4.3	4.8	3.4	3.9	3.4	3.6	2.9	3.0	2.7	2.6	2.1	2.0	1.6	1.6	1.2	1.3	0.7	0.9	0.4	0.5	0.3	0.5	—	—
	III	Suginami-ku	(326,610) 100.0	50.2	49.8	5.9	5.8	5.2	4.9	4.1	4.0	5.2	4.7	6.3	5.4	4.5	4.8	3.6	3.9	3.5	3.5	2.9	2.9	2.6	2.6	2.2	2.1	1.7	1.6	1.3	1.3	0.8	1.0	0.4	0.5	0.2	0.5	—	—
	IV	Itabashi-ku	(223,003) 100.0	50.4	49.6	7.1	6.8	6.0	5.8	4.4	4.2	4.9	4.6	5.3	4.8	4.1	4.7	3.6	4.2	3.7	3.6	3.0	2.7	2.6	2.3	1.9	1.8	1.4	1.4	1.0	1.0	0.6	0.8	0.3	0.4	0.2	0.4	—	—
		Nerima-ku	(125,197) 100.0	49.7	50.3	6.3	5.9	5.7	5.5	4.5	4.5	5.3	5.1	5.9	5.5	3.9	4.7	3.2	3.8	3.2	3.4	2.9	2.8	2.6	2.4	2.0	1.9	1.5	1.4	1.1	1.1	0.7	0.9	0.4	0.5	0.2	0.4	—	—
	VI	Adachi-ku	(268,304) 100.0	50.3	49.7	7.2	6.8	6.0	5.9	4.8	4.8	5.3	5.1	4.8	4.4	3.7	4.4	3.2	3.8	3.3	3.4	3.0	2.8	2.3	1.9	1.7	1.7	1.3	1.2	0.7	0.8	0.3	0.4	0.2	0.4	—	—
	VII	Katsushika-ku	(244,832) 100.0	50.6	49.4	7.0	6.7	6.0	5.8	4.6	4.5	5.1	4.8	5.3	4.6	4.1	4.3	3.3	3.9	3.4	3.5	3.0	2.8	2.3	1.9	1.7	1.7	1.3	1.2	0.7	0.8	0.3	0.4	0.2	0.4	—	—
	VIII	Edogawa-ku	(208,861) 100.0	50.3	49.7	6.9	6.7	6.1	5.9	4.8	4.7	5.2	4.8	5.2	4.5	3.7	4.3	3.2	3.9	3.3	3.5	2.9	2.9	2.2	1.9	1.7	1.7	1.2	1.2	0.7	0.8	0.4	0.6	0.2	0.3	—	—
		Urayasu-machi	(15,679) 100.0	49.9	50.1	7.3	7.3	5.8	5.9	5.4	5.1	4.8	4.3	4.5	3.9	3.1	3.8	2.7	3.4	3.4	3.5	2.9	2.7	2.1	2.3	1.7	1.8	1.2	1.1	1.1	1.1	0.6	0.9	0.4	0.6	0.2	0.4	—	—
		Zone 3 Total	(2,221,118) 100.0	50.3	49.7	6.6	6.3	5.7	5.5	4.4	4.3	5.1	4.7	5.6	4.9	4.2	4.6	3.5	4.0	3.4	3.5	3.0	2.9	2.5	2.3	1.9	1.9	1.6	1.5	1.2	1.1	0.7	0.9	0.4	0.6	0.2	0.4	—	—
4	I	Kawasaki-shi	(319,226) 100.0	52.0	48.0	7.4	7.1	6.0	5.7	4.4	4.3	4.9	4.3	6.2	4.5	4.6	4.7	3.3	4.2	4.1	3.4	3.0	2.5	2.4	2.0	1.8	1.5	1.3	1.2	0.9	1.0	0.5	0.7	0.3	0.5	0.2	0.4	—	—
	II	Komae-machi	(10,124) 100.0	49.6	50.4	7.0	6.8	5.8	5.9	4.6	5.0	4.7	5.5	5.6	4.4	4.1	4.2	3.3	3.5	3.2	3.5	2.8	2.5	2.3	2.3	1.8	1.7	1.4	1.6	1.2	1.2	0.9	1.0	0.6	0.7	0.3	0.7	—	—

Table 3. Population by Age (5-Year Bracket) and Sex

(Zone)	(Sector)	District	Total	M	F	Age 0-4		Age 5-9		Age 10-14		Age 15-19		Age 20-24		Age 25-29		Age 30-34		Age 35-39		Age 40-44		Age 45-49		Age 50-54		Age 55-59		Age 60-64		Age 65-69		Age 70-74		Age 75 & over		Un-known	
			Total	M	F	M	F	M	F	M	F	M	F	M	F	M	F	M	F	M	F	M	F	M	F	M	F	M	F	M	F	M	F	M	F	M	F	M	F
	III	Mitaka-shi	(54,820) 100.0	50.9	49.1	7.6	7.1	6.3	6.0	4.3	4.1	4.5	3.9	5.6	4.4	4.3	5.1	4.0	4.6	4.0	3.7	3.1	2.6	2.4	1.8	1.6	1.5	1.1	1.3	0.9	1.1	0.6	0.9	0.4	0.6	0.2	0.4	—	—
		Musashino-shi	(73,149) 100.0	50.6	49.4	6.2	5.9	5.5	5.3	4.3	4.2	5.0	4.5	6.4	5.2	4.4	4.9	3.7	4.1	3.7	3.6	3.0	2.9	2.7	2.5	1.9	1.8	1.4	1.4	1.1	1.2	0.7	0.9	0.4	0.5	0.2	0.5	—	—
		Chōfu-shi	(34,865) 100.0	49.6	50.4	6.9	6.9	6.2	6.1	4.9	4.8	5.0	4.8	5.2	4.7	3.7	4.6	3.6	3.9	3.2	3.3	2.7	2.6	2.3	2.3	1.9	1.8	1.3	1.4	1.2	1.2	0.7	0.9	0.5	0.7	0.3	0.6	—	—
		Hoya-machi	(14,816) 100.0	50.5	49.5	7.2	6.9	6.1	6.0	4.5	4.7	5.3	4.2	5.9	4.5	3.6	4.6	3.6	3.8	3.5	3.5	2.8	2.5	2.3	2.2	1.9	1.6	1.3	1.4	1.0	1.2	0.7	1.0	0.5	0.8	0.3	0.6	—	—
	IV	Yamato-machi	(10,240) 100.0	48.4	51.6	6.8	6.7	5.7	5.9	4.6	4.6	4.4	5.4	5.2	5.4	3.8	4.9	3.6	4.1	3.3	3.4	2.5	2.2	2.3	2.0	2.0	1.7	1.4	1.5	1.2	1.4	0.8	1.1	0.5	0.8	0.3	0.6	—	—
		Toda-machi	(18,223) 100.0	49.0	51.0	7.5	7.3	6.4	6.5	5.2	5.3	4.5	4.7	4.1	4.4	3.5	3.9	2.9	3.7	3.4	3.4	2.9	2.7	2.3	2.0	2.0	1.7	1.5	1.5	1.1	1.4	0.9	1.1	0.5	0.8	0.3	0.6	—	—
	V	Warabi-shi	(29,846) 100.0	48.8	51.2	7.9	7.7	6.7	6.6	4.6	4.8	4.3	4.9	4.1	4.1	3.2	2.4	3.6	4.6	3.8	3.9	3.2	2.6	2.4	2.0	1.7	1.5	1.3	1.2	1.0	1.1	0.5	0.8	0.3	0.6	0.2	0.4	—	—
		Kawaguchi-shi	(129,246) 100.0	50.1	49.9	7.7	7.2	6.2	6.2	5.0	4.9	5.0	4.8	4.8	4.3	3.8	4.2	3.3	3.8	3.3	3.5	2.9	2.6	2.4	2.1	2.0	1.8	1.4	1.4	1.1	1.1	0.6	0.9	0.4	0.6	0.2	0.5	—	—
		Hatogaya-machi																																					
	VI	Sōka-shi	(28,757) 100.0	49.4	50.6	7.6	7.1	6.1	6.0	5.2	5.2	5.1	4.9	4.2	4.3	3.2	4.0	2.9	3.7	2.9	3.3	2.9	2.7	2.5	2.3	2.1	1.9	1.6	1.6	1.3	1.3	0.9	1.0	0.6	0.7	0.3	0.6	—	—
		Yashio-mura	(12,837) 100.0	49.5	50.5	7.9	6.7	6.1	5.7	5.6	5.8	5.2	5.6	4.8	4.6	3.0	3.2	1.9	2.9	2.5	3.0	2.7	2.5	2.4	2.2	2.1	1.9	1.7	1.5	1.3	1.6	1.1	1.3	0.7	1.2	0.5	0.8	—	—
		Misato-mura	(16,771) 100.0	48.6	51.4	7.4	7.3	5.9	5.8	5.3	5.9	5.2	5.6	4.6	4.3	3.0	3.4	2.3	2.8	2.4	2.9	2.6	2.7	2.4	2.2	2.0	1.9	1.8	1.8	1.5	1.7	1.0	1.2	0.7	1.0	0.5	0.9	—	—
	VII	Matsudo-shi	(52,531) 100.0	49.1	50.9	7.0	7.0	5.9	6.0	5.1	4.9	4.8	5.0	4.9	4.5	3.5	4.2	3.0	3.8	3.3	3.4	2.8	2.8	2.5	2.3	2.0	1.8	1.5	1.5	1.2	1.3	0.8	1.0	0.5	0.8	0.3	0.6	—	—
		Ichikawa-shi	(120,595) 100.0	48.6	51.4	6.3	6.1	5.7	5.5	4.7	4.6	5.1	5.7	4.8	5.0	3.6	4.4	3.2	3.9	3.2	3.6	2.9	2.9	2.6	2.5	2.1	1.9	1.6	1.6	1.2	1.2	0.8	1.0	0.4	0.7	0.3	0.6	—	—
		Zone 4 Total	(926,046) 100.0	50.4	49.6	7.1	6.9	6.0	5.8	4.6	4.6	4.9	4.7	5.4	4.6	4.0	4.5	3.5	4.0	3.6	3.5	2.9	2.6	2.4	2.2	1.9	1.7	1.4	1.4	1.1	1.2	0.7	0.9	0.4	0.6	0.2	0.5	—	—
5	I	Tsurumi-ku	(170,888) 100.0	52.2	47.8	7.3	6.8	5.7	5.5	4.2	4.1	4.8	4.2	6.6	4.7	4.8	4.8	4.0	4.1	4.0	3.4	3.1	2.7	2.6	2.2	1.9	1.7	1.4	1.2	0.9	0.9	0.5	0.7	0.3	0.5	0.1	0.3	—	—
	III	Koganei-shi	(22,604) 100.0	51.3	49.7	6.5	6.2	6.1	5.7	5.3	4.7	5.5	4.9	6.5	4.8	3.9	4.4	3.1	3.9	3.5	3.6	2.9	2.5	2.4	2.1	1.7	1.6	1.2	1.5	1.1	1.2	0.8	0.9	0.5	0.7	0.3	0.6	—	—
		Tanashi-machi	(13,527) 100.0	49.9	50.1	7.9	7.7	6.8	6.6	4.5	4.7	4.4	4.7	4.7	4.5	3.4	4.7	3.9	4.4	4.3	3.8	3.1	2.3	2.3	1.7	1.5	1.2	1.1	1.0	0.7	0.9	0.4	0.5	0.2	0.3	—	—	—	—
	IV	Kurume-machi	(8,415) 100.0	48.8	51.2	7.1	6.8	6.8	6.1	5.9	5.8	5.0	5.9	4.6	4.5	3.3	4.1	2.4	3.7	3.1	2.7	2.6	2.3	2.1	1.8	1.6	1.5	1.2	1.3	1.1	1.1	0.7	1.1	0.5	0.7	0.2	0.3	—	—
		Nīza-machi	(10,959) 100.0	49.3	50.7	7.0	6.8	6.1	6.1	4.7	5.1	5.1	5.2	4.8	4.7	3.5	4.1	2.9	3.4	2.8	3.0	2.4	2.3	2.1	1.8	1.9	1.6	1.5	1.8	1.2	1.6	0.8	1.1	0.5	0.7	0.5	0.7	—	—
	V	Kiyose-machi	(11,610) 100.0	53.3	46.7	4.7	4.4	4.5	3.9	3.7	3.4	3.9	4.0	8.3	7.3	7.7	6.6	6.1	4.3	4.2	3.2	2.2	2.2	2.1	1.7	1.3	1.4	1.2	1.4	0.6	0.7	0.4	0.7	0.3	0.4	—	—	—	—
		Adachi-machi	(9,721) 100.0	49.3	50.7	7.2	6.7	6.7	6.4	4.9	4.9	5.0	4.8	4.4	4.3	3.1	3.5	3.1	3.5	3.1	3.1	2.8	2.6	2.3	2.4	1.8	1.8	1.3	1.6	1.0	1.2	0.5	0.9	0.5	0.9	0.4	0.9	—	—
		Asaka-machi	(14,685) 100.0	49.0	51.0	6.4	6.2	5.9	5.7	4.8	4.8	5.1	4.8	4.5	4.7	3.3	4.4	3.4	4.2	3.4	3.2	3.0	2.9	2.5	2.4	2.1	1.9	1.6	1.5	1.5	1.3	0.8	1.0	0.5	0.7	0.3	0.6	—	—
	V	Urawa-shi	(124,419) 100.0	49.6	50.4	6.9	6.8	6.1	6.1	4.9	4.9	4.5	4.8	4.9	4.7	3.7	4.4	3.2	3.8	3.3	3.6	3.0	2.7	2.6	2.5	2.1	1.9	1.6	1.6	1.5	1.4	1.0	1.4	0.6	0.9	0.4	0.7	—	—
		Misono-mura	(9,356) 100.0	49.0	51.0	7.7	7.2	5.6	5.9	5.3	5.4	5.5	5.4	4.5	4.2	2.9	3.4	2.5	3.0	2.8	2.5	2.7	2.7	2.6	2.3	2.2	2.0	1.7	1.8	1.4	1.5	1.0	1.1	0.6	1.1	0.4	0.7	—	—
	VI	Koshigaya-shi	(42,253) 100.0	49.0	51.0	7.5	7.6	6.0	5.9	5.7	5.7	4.8	5.1	4.5	4.2	3.0	3.6	2.3	3.2	2.4	2.8	2.5	2.6	2.6	2.3	2.0	1.9	1.8	1.6	1.4	1.6	1.0	1.3	0.6	1.1	0.4	0.7	—	—
		Yoshikawa-machi	(16,015) 100.0	48.5	51.5	7.1	6.9	5.9	6.0	5.1	5.7	5.1	5.2	4.1	4.0	2.7	3.2	2.6	3.1	2.6	3.1	2.8	2.6	2.4	2.3	2.1	2.0	1.7	1.6	1.5	1.3	1.0	1.2	0.6	0.9	0.4	0.9	—	—
	VII	Nagareyama-machi	(18,337) 100.0	49.2	50.8	7.3	7.7	6.2	6.0	5.1	5.3	5.3	5.1	4.5	4.3	3.3	3.9	2.8	3.5	2.4	2.9	2.3	2.4	2.4	2.0	2.1	1.9	1.5	1.5	1.5	1.5	0.8	1.1	0.7	0.8	0.4	0.5	—	—
	VIII	Kamagaya-machi	(8,981) 100.0	49.2	50.8	6.7	6.5	6.2	6.1	5.7	5.6	5.0	5.0	4.8	4.7	3.5	4.3	3.1	3.9	3.3	3.5	2.9	2.7	2.5	2.3	1.9	1.8	1.5	1.5	1.2	1.4	0.8	1.1	0.5	0.8	0.4	0.6	—	—
		Funahashi-shi	(100,344) 100.0	50.3	49.7	7.7	7.7	6.5	6.1	5.0	4.8	5.0	5.0	4.8	4.7	3.5	4.3	3.1	3.5	3.3	3.4	2.9	2.7	2.5	2.5	2.0	1.9	1.5	1.5	1.2	1.4	0.7	0.9	0.5	0.7	0.3	0.6	—	—
		Zone 5 Total	(582,094) 100.0	50.3	49.7	7.7	6.6	5.9	5.7	4.7	4.7	4.9	4.7	5.4	4.6	4.0	4.4	3.4	3.9	3.4	3.4	2.9	2.7	2.5	2.2	1.9	1.7	1.4	1.4	1.1	1.2	0.7	0.9	0.5	0.7	0.2	0.5	—	—
6	I	Nishi-ku	(85,292) 100.0	50.8	49.2	6.3	5.9	5.2	5.0	4.4	4.3	5.2	4.8	6.0	5.1	4.2	4.6	3.5	3.9	3.5	3.3	2.8	2.8	2.7	2.4	2.4	2.1	1.9	1.7	1.4	1.3	0.7	0.9	0.4	0.6	0.2	0.4	—	—
		Naka-ku	(89,813) 100.0	49.7	50.3	5.9	5.5	4.8	4.5	4.0	4.0	5.5	5.3	6.3	6.3	4.4	5.3	3.2	3.7	3.1	3.4	2.9	2.9	2.8	2.6	2.2	2.2	1.9	1.6	1.3	1.3	0.8	0.9	0.4	0.6	0.2	0.5	—	—

Table 3. Population by Age (5-Year Bracket) and Sex

(Zone)	(Sector)	District	Total	Total M	Total F	0-4 M	0-4 F	5-9 M	5-9 F	10-14 M	10-14 F	15-19 M	15-19 F	20-24 M	20-24 F	25-29 M	25-29 F	30-34 M	30-34 F	35-39 M	35-39 F	40-44 M	40-44 F	45-49 M	45-49 F	50-54 M	50-54 F	55-59 M	55-59 F	60-64 M	60-64 F	65-69 M	65-69 F	70-74 M	70-74 F	75 & over M	75 & over F	Unknown M	Unknown F
	I	Kanagawa-ku	(107,068) 100.0	50.7	49.3	6.6	6.4	5.5	5.4	4.5	4.3	5.3	4.7	5.8	4.8	4.3	4.5	3.3	3.7	3.3	3.5	3.0	2.8	2.6	2.5	2.2	2.1	1.8	1.5	1.2	1.2	0.7	0.9	0.4	0.6	0.2	0.4	—	—
	II	Kōhoku-ku	(93,421) 100.0	49.6	50.4	6.7	6.4	5.8	5.9	5.2	5.1	5.1	4.9	4.9	4.5	3.6	4.1	3.0	3.6	3.1	3.4	2.7	2.7	2.6	2.3	2.0	1.9	1.6	1.6	1.3	1.4	0.9	1.1	0.6	0.9	0.5	0.7	—	—
	III	Inagi-machi	(9,824) 100.0	50.5	49.5	7.2	7.1	6.9	6.0	5.1	4.8	4.8	4.0	4.2	3.8	3.5	4.5	3.4	3.9	3.4	3.2	2.9	2.7	2.3	1.9	1.9	1.7	1.5	1.5	1.2	1.4	1.0	1.3	0.8	0.8	0.4	0.9	—	—
		Tama-mura	(7,799) 100.0	50.1	49.9	6.4	6.2	5.9	5.4	4.9	5.2	5.3	4.8	5.1	4.7	3.5	3.9	2.8	3.7	3.1	3.4	2.7	2.8	2.7	2.4	2.3	2.1	1.8	1.4	1.3	1.2	0.9	1.2	0.8	0.8	0.6	0.7	—	—
		Fuchu-shi	(45,295) 100.0	54.2	45.8	6.6	6.3	5.5	5.5	4.4	4.1	4.4	4.1	7.0	4.9	5.6	3.9	4.3	3.7	4.2	3.2	3.4	2.4	2.7	1.8	2.0	1.5	1.4	1.2	1.1	1.1	0.8	0.9	0.5	0.6	0.3	0.5	—	—
		Kunitachi-machi	(14,333) 100.0	51.7	48.3	7.1	6.8	6.0	5.4	4.3	4.0	4.9	4.5	7.2	4.5	4.0	4.8	3.7	4.3	4.0	3.1	2.7	2.6	2.5	2.1	1.7	1.7	1.2	1.2	1.0	1.3	0.7	0.9	0.4	0.6	0.3	0.5	—	—
		Kokubunji-machi	(19,125) 100.0	51.0	49.0	6.5	6.6	6.4	5.8	5.4	4.9	5.6	4.5	5.6	4.4	3.8	4.0	3.3	4.0	3.4	3.4	3.2	3.0	2.5	2.1	1.7	1.7	1.3	1.5	1.0	1.1	0.6	0.8	0.4	0.6	0.3	0.6	—	—
		Kodaira-machi	(21,659) 100.0	50.5	49.5	6.8	6.7	5.7	5.6	4.3	4.1	5.3	5.2	5.3	5.5	4.4	4.7	4.3	4.0	3.6	3.6	2.6	2.5	2.2	1.8	1.7	1.6	1.4	1.4	1.2	1.2	0.8	1.0	0.5	0.7	0.4	0.5	—	—
IV		Higashimurayama-machi	(17,993) 100.0	52.1	47.9	6.5	5.9	6.0	5.8	5.4	5.2	5.1	4.3	5.3	4.7	4.7	4.6	4.2	3.5	3.1	3.3	3.1	2.4	2.4	2.3	2.0	1.8	1.6	1.5	1.1	1.3	0.9	1.0	0.6	1.0	0.3	0.7	—	—
		Tokorosawa-shi	(52,188) 100.0	49.2	50.8	7.1	6.9	6.0	5.5	5.4	5.1	4.9	4.9	4.5	4.7	3.4	4.2	3.0	3.5	2.9	2.8	2.4	2.5	2.3	2.2	1.9	1.9	1.8	1.5	1.4	1.4	1.1	1.2	0.6	1.0	0.5	0.8	—	—
		Miyoshi-mura	(4,280) 100.0	50.0	50.0	7.1	6.0	5.7	5.5	5.4	5.1	6.2	5.3	5.2	5.1	3.2	3.9	2.4	3.0	2.5	2.9	2.4	2.2	2.3	2.2	2.1	1.9	2.0	1.5	1.6	1.8	1.1	1.7	1.0	1.0	0.5	1.0	—	—
		Fujimi-mura	(10,648) 100.0	48.9	51.1	6.7	6.6	5.4	5.5	5.4	5.4	5.3	5.3	4.7	5.2	3.6	3.8	2.7	3.2	2.4	2.7	2.2	2.4	2.4	2.3	2.1	2.0	1.9	1.5	1.6	1.6	1.1	1.3	0.8	1.1	0.4	0.9	—	—
V		Yono-shi	(29,072) 100.0	49.4	50.6	7.6	7.2	6.3	6.4	4.7	4.8	4.2	4.6	4.5	4.4	3.7	4.5	3.4	4.3	3.4	3.6	2.2	2.4	2.5	2.1	1.8	1.6	1.4	1.2	1.0	1.2	0.8	0.8	0.4	0.6	0.3	0.5	—	—
		Ōmiya-shi	(118,090) 100.0	49.3	50.7	7.7	7.2	6.1	6.0	5.0	4.8	4.8	5.0	4.7	4.7	3.5	4.3	3.3	3.9	3.6	3.2	2.8	2.7	2.4	2.3	1.9	1.8	1.5	1.4	1.2	1.3	0.8	1.0	0.5	0.7	0.3	0.5	—	—
		Iwatsuki-shi	(34,437) 100.0	48.9	51.1	7.4	7.2	5.9	5.8	5.4	5.3	4.9	5.2	4.4	4.2	3.0	3.4	2.8	3.3	3.2	2.5	2.5	2.6	2.4	2.3	2.2	1.9	1.7	1.8	1.4	1.6	1.0	1.3	0.7	0.8	0.5	0.8	—	—
VI		Matsubushi-mura	(8,880) 100.0	48.7	51.3	7.4	7.2	5.8	5.7	5.7	6.2	5.0	5.2	4.4	4.1	2.7	3.4	2.2	2.7	2.5	3.1	2.7	2.8	2.4	2.3	2.0	1.8	1.9	1.7	1.6	1.9	1.2	1.5	0.8	0.9	0.4	0.8	—	—
VII		Kashiwa-shi	(47,635) 100.0	49.4	50.6	7.6	7.4	6.1	6.0	5.1	5.1	5.0	4.8	4.5	4.4	3.5	4.1	3.1	3.6	3.4	3.1	2.7	2.5	2.3	2.1	2.0	1.8	1.6	1.6	1.3	1.3	0.8	1.1	0.5	0.8	0.3	0.6	—	—
		Shōnan-mura	(10,866) 100.0	48.6	51.4	7.1	6.5	5.2	5.7	5.3	5.5	5.1	5.0	4.7	4.9	3.3	3.9	2.6	3.1	2.5	2.6	2.6	2.5	2.6	2.2	2.0	2.2	1.6	1.5	1.3	1.7	1.1	1.3	1.0	1.0	0.6	1.0	—	—
		Shirai-mura	(6,373) 100.0	49.6	50.4	6.5	6.5	6.6	5.4	5.4	5.5	5.1	5.1	4.5	4.5	3.0	3.6	2.7	3.2	2.6	3.1	2.5	2.2	2.5	2.7	2.6	2.0	1.9	1.9	1.7	1.5	1.1	1.1	1.0	1.1	0.5	1.0	—	—
VIII		Narashino-shi	(23,660) 100.0	49.3	50.7	6.8	6.7	5.8	6.1	4.8	4.8	4.6	4.9	5.5	4.8	3.8	4.5	3.5	3.9	3.3	3.6	2.9	2.9	2.6	2.0	1.7	1.5	1.2	1.4	1.1	1.3	0.8	0.9	0.5	0.6	0.4	0.6	—	—
		Zone 6 Total	(857,751) 100.0	50.2	49.8	6.8	6.5	5.7	5.6	4.8	4.7	5.1	5.1	5.4	4.8	3.9	4.4	3.3	3.7	3.3	3.4	2.8	2.7	2.5	2.3	2.1	1.9	1.6	1.5	1.3	1.3	0.8	1.0	0.5	0.7	0.3	0.6	—	—
7	I	Isogo-ku	(62,343) 100.0	49.3	50.7	6.3	6.0	5.6	5.3	4.5	4.3	4.8	4.9	5.5	5.1	3.9	4.6	3.1	4.0	3.3	3.4	2.8	2.8	2.7	2.6	2.2	2.1	1.7	1.7	1.3	1.4	0.8	1.0	0.5	0.5	0.3	0.5	—	—
		Minami-ku	(142,763) 100.0	50.2	49.8	6.2	6.0	5.2	5.1	4.3	4.3	5.0	5.1	5.9	5.3	4.5	4.6	3.5	3.6	3.3	3.4	2.8	2.7	2.7	2.6	2.3	2.2	1.8	1.6	1.3	1.3	0.7	0.9	0.4	0.6	0.3	0.5	—	—
II		Hodogaya-ku	(74,156) 100.0	50.0	50.0	6.6	6.3	5.7	5.6	5.0	5.0	5.3	5.0	5.2	4.7	4.0	4.3	3.2	3.5	3.1	3.3	2.7	2.8	2.6	2.4	2.1	2.0	1.6	1.6	1.3	1.3	0.8	1.0	0.5	0.7	0.3	0.5	—	—
III		Machida-shi	(52,481) 100.0	49.8	50.2	7.1	6.7	6.1	6.1	5.2	5.3	5.2	5.0	4.9	4.5	3.5	4.0	3.2	3.6	3.0	3.3	2.6	2.7	2.5	2.1	2.0	1.8	1.5	1.5	1.3	1.3	0.9	1.0	0.6	0.6	0.4	0.6	—	—
		Yuki-mura	(6,415) 100.0	49.1	50.9	6.6	6.1	6.2	5.3	5.6	5.2	5.0	4.9	4.8	4.5	2.5	3.9	2.6	3.2	2.6	3.3	2.4	2.4	2.3	2.1	1.9	1.9	1.6	1.9	1.8	2.0	1.3	1.4	1.0	1.2	0.7	1.0	—	—
		Hino-machi	(24,444) 100.0	49.9	50.1	7.6	7.0	6.4	6.1	4.6	4.4	4.8	4.4	4.4	4.3	3.6	4.4	3.3	4.0	3.5	3.6	3.0	2.7	2.4	2.1	1.8	1.7	1.4	1.4	1.1	1.0	0.8	0.8	0.5	0.5	0.3	0.3	—	—
		Tachikawa-shi	(51,651) 100.0	49.3	50.7	7.1	6.7	6.0	6.0	4.6	4.4	5.0	5.0	5.2	5.5	3.8	4.9	3.5	4.3	3.6	3.5	3.1	2.8	2.5	2.3	1.8	1.6	1.2	1.2	0.9	1.0	0.5	0.7	0.3	0.5	0.2	0.3	—	—
		Sunakawa-machi	(11,567) 100.0	50.8	49.2	7.6	7.3	7.0	6.4	5.2	4.9	5.0	4.7	4.7	4.0	3.6	4.3	3.1	3.6	3.6	3.3	2.9	2.3	2.3	1.9	1.6	1.5	1.3	1.1	1.2	1.3	0.8	1.1	0.6	0.9	0.4	0.7	—	—
		Yamato-machi	(12,366) 100.0	49.5	50.5	7.8	8.0	6.9	6.7	5.0	5.0	4.6	4.2	4.2	3.8	3.1	3.8	3.3	4.1	3.5	3.6	2.5	2.4	2.0	1.9	1.7	1.7	1.4	1.3	1.2	1.2	0.7	1.0	0.6	0.9	0.3	0.7	—	—
IV		Ōi-mura	(4,535) 100.0	48.7	51.3	6.4	7.2	6.8	6.8	5.1	5.0	4.6	4.8	4.4	4.9	3.6	4.0	3.1	4.0	3.6	3.5	2.5	2.4	2.0	2.1	2.1	1.6	1.6	1.8	1.6	1.8	1.2	1.4	0.7	1.1	0.5	0.9	—	—
		Fukuoka-mura	(7,461) 100.0	49.4	50.6	8.5	7.9	6.8	6.8	5.1	5.3	3.9	4.1	3.7	4.0	3.0	4.1	3.8	4.7	3.6	3.5	3.0	2.5	2.2	1.7	1.5	1.5	1.4	1.1	1.1	1.6	0.9	0.8	0.6	0.6	0.3	0.4	—	—
V		Kasukabe-shi	(14,922) 100.0	48.7	51.3	7.8	6.9	6.3	6.2	5.2	5.5	5.0	4.7	4.2	4.4	3.0	3.9	2.6	3.4	3.1	3.3	2.8	2.8	2.6	2.6	2.0	1.8	1.0	1.7	1.4	1.4	0.8	1.2	0.6	0.9	0.3	0.8	—	—
		Shōwa-mura	(14,725) 100.0	49.3	50.7	8.1	7.7	6.2	5.9	5.3	5.4	4.8	4.5	4.1	4.0	2.7	3.6	2.9	3.4	2.9	3.3	2.6	2.6	2.2	2.3	2.0	1.8	1.8	1.8	1.6	1.6	1.0	1.4	0.7	1.0	0.4	0.7	—	—

- 186 -

Table 3. Population By Age (5-Year Bracket) and Sex

(Zone)	(Sector)	District	Total	M	F	0-4 M	0-4 F	5-9 M	5-9 F	10-14 M	10-14 F	15-19 M	15-19 F	20-24 M	20-24 F	25-29 M	25-29 F	30-34 M	30-34 F	35-39 M	35-39 F	40-44 M	40-44 F	45-49 M	45-49 F	50-54 M	50-54 F	55-59 M	55-59 F	60-64 M	60-64 F	65-69 M	65-69 F	70-74 M	70-74 F	75 & over M	75 & over F	Unknown M	Unknown F
7	VI	Noda-shi	(51,039)100.0	48.7	51.3	6.9	6.6	5.8	5.5	5.3	5.6	4.9	5.1	4.2	4.7	3.1	3.8	2.8	3.1	2.8	3.3	2.7	2.9	2.6	2.4	2.0	2.0	1.7	1.8	1.4	1.5	1.0	1.2	0.7	1.0	0.8	0.8	—	—
	VII	Abiko-machi	(21,097)100.0	48.2	51.8	6.6	6.7	6.3	6.0	5.1	5.3	4.8	5.3	4.3	4.5	3.1	3.9	3.0	3.7	2.9	3.4	2.9	3.0	2.7	2.3	2.0	1.7	1.3	1.5	1.3	1.3	0.8	1.2	0.6	0.9	0.3	0.9	—	—
		Yachiyo-machi	(15,009)100.0	49.1	50.9	6.7	6.1	5.7	5.8	5.1	5.4	5.1	5.2	4.8	4.3	3.2	4.0	2.9	3.4	2.9	3.5	2.3	2.2	2.4	2.1	2.3	1.8	1.7	1.9	1.8	1.5	1.0	1.1	0.8	1.1	0.5	0.9	—	—
	VIII	Chiba-shi	(172,874)100.0	49.8	50.2	6.7	6.0	5.9	5.7	4.9	4.8	5.0	4.9	5.2	4.6	3.8	3.7	3.4	3.9	2.8	3.4	2.9	2.7	2.5	2.3	2.2	1.8	1.5	1.4	1.2	1.4	0.8	1.0	0.5	0.8	0.4	0.7	—	—
	IX	Goi-machi	(20,214)100.0	49.2	50.8	6.3	6.0	5.9	5.8	5.4	5.4	5.1	5.1	4.4	4.4	3.2	3.7	2.8	3.3	2.8	3.3	2.6	2.5	2.7	2.7	2.4	2.4	1.6	1.6	1.5	1.4	1.0	1.3	0.9	1.0	0.6	1.0	—	—
		Sodegaura-machi	(14,324)100.0	48.4	51.6	6.4	6.3	6.1	6.2	5.3	5.5	5.3	5.1	4.5	4.5	2.8	3.8	2.6	3.2	2.7	3.6	2.1	2.8	2.3	2.6	2.0	2.0	1.8	1.6	1.4	1.7	0.9	1.2	0.8	1.0	0.7	1.4	—	—
		Zone 7 Total	(774,386)100.0	49.6	50.4	6.7	6.4	5.8	5.7	4.8	4.8	5.0	4.9	5.1	4.8	3.8	4.3	3.2	3.7	2.7	3.4	2.8	2.8	2.5	2.5	2.1	1.9	1.6	1.5	1.3	1.4	0.8	1.0	0.5	0.8	0.4	0.6	—	—
8	I	Kanazawa-ku	(56,040)100.0	50.3	49.7	8.1	6.9	6.5	6.6	4.5	4.4	4.2	4.0	4.2	4.2	3.8	4.6	3.9	4.4	4.1	3.7	3.1	2.6	2.5	2.0	1.7	1.5	1.2	1.3	0.9	1.2	0.7	0.9	0.4	0.7	0.2	0.2	—	—
	II	Totsuka-ku	(69,425)100.0	50.1	49.9	7.1	6.9	6.2	5.9	5.2	5.1	5.1	4.7	5.0	4.5	3.6	4.0	3.3	3.3	2.8	3.4	2.8	2.7	2.4	2.1	1.8	1.7	1.4	1.3	1.2	1.1	0.8	1.1	0.6	0.8	0.4	0.8	—	—
		Yamato-shi	(17,586)100.0	50.0	50.0	8.6	8.0	6.3	6.0	4.9	4.5	4.1	4.4	4.5	4.6	4.0	4.8	3.9	4.1	3.6	3.5	2.8	2.2	2.1	1.9	1.6	1.6	1.1	1.3	1.2	1.0	0.6	0.9	0.4	0.7	0.3	0.4	—	—
		Sagamihara-shi	(68,898)100.0	50.6	49.4	7.3	7.2	6.0	5.9	5.1	4.8	4.9	4.6	5.2	4.8	4.1	4.4	3.6	3.4	3.4	3.2	2.7	2.3	2.2	2.0	1.9	1.6	1.4	1.3	1.3	1.2	0.7	0.9	0.5	0.7	0.4	0.6	—	—
		Zama-machi	(11,804)100.0	49.8	50.2	7.1	6.9	6.0	6.0	5.6	5.3	5.4	4.6	4.5	5.1	3.7	4.3	3.0	3.7	2.9	3.0	2.5	2.8	2.4	2.2	2.0	1.9	1.6	1.4	1.3	1.2	0.8	0.9	0.6	0.9	0.4	0.7	—	—
	III	Hachiōji-shi	(125,055)100.0	48.7	51.3	6.6	6.2	5.9	5.7	4.3	4.4	5.3	5.6	6.7	6.7	3.5	5.0	2.9	4.5	3.3	3.3	2.8	2.4	2.2	2.4	1.6	2.0	1.6	1.5	0.8	1.3	0.5	1.0	0.4	0.8	0.3	0.6	—	—
		Akishima-shi	(31,055)100.0	50.4	49.6	8.3	7.8	6.6	6.3	4.5	4.3	4.4	4.2	4.9	4.6	3.9	5.0	4.1	3.6	3.4	3.4	3.0	2.4	2.2	1.7	2.0	1.4	1.1	1.1	0.9	1.0	0.5	0.8	0.4	0.6	0.3	0.4	—	—
		Fussa-machi	(14,669)100.0	50.6	49.4	6.7	6.7	5.8	5.3	5.4	5.5	5.0	5.1	6.7	6.7	4.8	3.7	3.6	3.4	3.1	3.1	2.8	2.2	2.2	1.9	1.6	1.5	1.4	1.3	1.5	1.1	1.0	0.7	0.6	0.7	0.4	0.4	—	—
		Mizuho-machi	(9,210)100.0	49.3	50.7	7.2	7.2	6.4	6.0	5.6	5.4	5.2	4.7	4.3	4.4	3.2	4.0	2.8	3.1	3.3	3.2	2.5	2.5	2.4	2.0	2.1	1.8	1.3	1.5	1.3	1.5	1.2	1.0	0.9	0.9	0.4	0.8	—	—
		Murayama-machi	(10,989)100.0	49.3	50.7	6.6	6.6	6.4	6.0	5.0	4.8	4.9	5.0	4.7	4.6	3.6	4.7	2.7	3.5	3.0	3.3	2.5	2.3	2.0	2.0	2.0	1.7	1.6	1.6	1.4	1.3	1.1	1.2	0.8	1.1	0.4	1.2	—	—
		Musashi-machi	(25,844)100.0	48.4	51.6	6.7	6.9	5.4	5.0	5.0	4.8	4.7	5.0	4.7	5.8	3.8	4.7	3.0	3.3	2.8	3.2	2.6	2.2	2.2	2.0	2.1	2.1	1.8	1.6	1.6	1.6	1.2	1.3	0.7	1.1	0.5	0.5	—	—
	IV	Sayama-shi	(30,483)100.0	49.3	50.7	7.0	6.6	5.9	5.5	5.3	5.1	5.0	5.2	4.8	4.8	3.5	4.2	2.9	3.6	2.7	3.2	2.4	2.4	2.4	2.1	1.9	1.9	1.9	1.9	1.6	1.4	1.2	1.4	0.6	1.0	0.5	0.9	—	—
		Kawagoe-shi	(100,407)100.0	49.0	51.0	7.0	6.8	5.9	5.7	5.2	5.3	5.3	5.2	4.4	4.6	3.2	3.9	3.0	3.3	2.9	3.5	2.4	2.5	2.5	2.3	2.0	1.9	1.7	1.7	1.4	1.6	0.9	1.3	1.0	0.9	0.4	0.7	—	—
		Seibu-machi	(3,472)100.0	50.1	49.9	6.6	7.0	6.7	5.6	6.1	5.2	4.7	4.5	4.5	4.5	3.0	3.6	2.9	3.6	3.1	3.4	2.6	1.8	1.7	2.3	2.3	1.8	1.6	1.8	2.0	1.6	1.6	1.6	0.7	1.0	0.3	0.8	—	—
	V	Ageo-shi	(32,673)100.0	49.7	50.3	7.3	7.0	6.3	6.0	5.5	4.7	5.0	4.9	5.0	4.5	3.4	3.5	2.4	2.6	2.9	2.9	2.4	2.5	2.3	2.1	1.9	1.7	1.6	1.6	1.4	1.5	1.0	0.9	1.0	0.9	0.5	0.7	—	—
		Ina-mura	(7,327)100.0	49.5	50.5	6.5	6.2	6.4	5.9	5.6	5.7	5.5	5.5	4.5	4.2	3.9	3.7	3.0	3.4	2.0	3.2	2.2	2.4	2.2	2.2	2.4	1.9	1.9	1.6	1.5	1.5	1.1	1.4	0.7	1.3	0.6	1.1	—	—
		Hasuda-machi	(18,574)100.0	49.5	50.5	6.4	6.7	6.0	5.6	5.5	5.2	4.9	5.2	4.9	4.6	3.1	3.5	2.8	3.3	2.9	3.2	2.6	2.5	2.2	2.1	1.9	1.8	1.6	1.6	1.5	1.5	1.0	1.1	0.7	0.9	0.5	0.8	—	—
		Shiraoka-machi	(15,993)100.0	49.4	50.6	6.7	7.5	6.2	5.8	5.8	5.3	5.2	5.0	5.0	4.4	3.1	3.4	2.3	2.2	2.7	3.2	2.5	2.7	2.3	2.0	2.0	1.9	1.8	1.6	1.5	1.5	1.1	1.2	0.7	1.1	0.5	0.9	—	—
		Miyashiro-machi	(10,463)100.0	49.3	50.7	7.6	7.6	5.9	5.8	5.5	5.7	4.9	5.4	4.6	4.6	2.9	3.6	2.4	3.1	3.0	3.2	2.5	2.7	2.3	2.4	2.0	2.0	1.6	1.7	1.6	1.9	1.2	1.1	0.7	1.1	0.5	0.7	—	—
		Sugito-machi	(18,482)100.0	48.7	51.3	7.4	7.1	5.8	5.9	5.7	5.6	4.9	5.1	4.2	3.9	2.9	3.6	2.6	2.9	2.5	2.8	3.0	2.8	2.2	2.1	1.7	1.7	1.5	1.8	1.1	1.3	0.7	1.4	0.5	1.0	—	—	—	—
	VI	Sekiyado-machi	(14,463)100.0	47.8	52.2	7.1	7.3	5.7	6.1	6.1	5.9	4.9	5.9	3.9	4.3	2.7	4.0	2.6	3.2	2.5	2.9	1.9	2.4	2.2	2.2	1.8	1.9	2.0	1.6	1.6	1.7	1.2	1.4	0.9	1.0	0.6	1.0	—	—
		Moriya-machi	(10,214)100.0	47.6	52.4	7.6	6.9	5.7	6.2	5.6	5.4	4.8	5.1	4.2	4.6	3.0	3.9	2.4	3.5	2.9	3.0	2.5	2.3	2.4	2.5	2.1	2.1	1.7	1.6	1.6	1.5	0.9	1.0	0.8	1.0	0.6	1.1	—	—
	VII	Toride-machi	(19,820)100.0	48.4	51.6	6.6	6.2	6.1	5.9	5.3	5.1	4.9	5.1	3.9	4.4	3.0	3.7	2.7	3.6	3.0	3.0	3.0	3.0	2.5	2.5	2.2	1.8	1.7	1.7	1.3	1.6	0.8	1.3	0.8	1.0	0.6	1.0	—	—
		Inzai-machi	(19,688)100.0	49.1	50.9	6.6	6.6	6.0	5.8	5.2	5.1	5.4	4.9	4.2	4.2	3.0	4.2	2.6	3.4	2.7	3.1	2.5	2.6	2.6	2.5	2.2	1.8	1.8	1.7	1.5	1.5	1.0	1.4	0.9	1.1	0.6	1.0	—	—
	VIII	Inba-mura	(8,526)100.0	47.9	52.1	6.8	6.6	6.1	4.8	4.2	4.9	4.5	4.4	4.1	4.3	3.1	3.9	3.0	3.7	2.8	3.4	2.7	2.5	2.8	2.9	2.9	2.9	1.9	1.9	2.1	2.1	1.3	1.7	1.3	1.7	0.9	1.6	—	—
		Yotsukaidō-machi	(18,252)100.0	49.5	50.5	5.6	6.5	5.7	5.6	5.2	5.2	5.0	4.9	5.2	4.6	3.5	3.9	2.9	3.3	2.8	2.9	2.7	2.6	2.5	2.5	2.0	1.8	2.0	1.3	1.4	1.4	0.9	1.2	0.6	1.1	0.5	0.8	—	—
	IX	Ichihara-machi	(14,547)100.0	48.4	51.6	6.4	6.2	6.1	6.0	5.8	5.5	5.1	5.3	4.1	4.2	2.7	3.9	2.4	3.3	2.9	3.1	2.7	2.8	2.6	2.4	2.3	2.1	1.6	1.9	1.4	1.4	1.0	1.4	0.8	1.2	0.6	0.9	—	—

Table 3. Population By Age (5-Year Bracket) and Sex

(Zone)	(Sector)	District	Total	M	F	0-4 M	0-4 F	5-9 M	5-9 F	10-14 M	10-14 F	15-19 M	15-19 F	20-24 M	20-24 F	25-29 M	25-29 F	30-34 M	30-34 F	35-39 M	35-39 F	40-44 M	40-44 F	45-49 M	45-49 F	50-54 M	50-54 F	55-59 M	55-59 F	60-64 M	60-64 F	65-69 M	65-69 F	70-74 M	70-74 F	75& over M	75& over F	Unknown M	Unknown F
	IX	Anegasaki-machi	(8,943) 100.0	47.5	52.5	6.5	6.7	6.2	6.3	5.3	5.3	4.8	4.8	3.9	4.2	3.0	3.8	2.4	3.5	2.5	3.3	2.6	3.0	2.9	2.6	2.1	2.1	1.5	1.7	1.3	1.5	1.0	1.3	0.9	1.3	0.6	1.1	—	—
		Hirakawa-machi	(13,364) 100.0	48.4	51.6	6.4	6.9	5.7	5.8	5.5	5.2	5.2	4.9	4.0	4.3	3.1	3.4	2.6	3.1	2.6	3.3	2.4	2.5	2.3	2.3	2.1	2.2	2.0	1.7	1.4	1.9	1.2	1.5	1.0	1.4	0.9	1.2	—	—
		Miwa-machi	(11,760) 100.0	48.5	51.5	6.0	6.2	6.0	5.7	5.7	5.4	5.3	5.4	4.1	4.7	2.6	3.4	2.4	3.3	2.9	2.9	2.4	2.8	2.6	2.4	2.4	2.2	1.9	1.7	1.6	1.8	1.2	1.4	0.9	1.1	0.5	1.1	—	—
	X	Kisarazu-shi	(50,153) 100.0	48.1	51.9	6.9	6.5	5.9	5.9	5.1	5.0	4.7	4.8	3.8	4.7	3.0	4.1	2.8	3.8	3.0	3.4	2.7	2.6	2.5	2.5	2.3	2.1	1.6	1.7	1.5	1.6	1.0	1.3	0.7	0.9	0.6	1.0	—	—
		Zone 8 Total	(868,816) 100.0	49.0	51.0	7.1	6.8	6.0	5.9	5.2	5.0	5.0	5.0	4.6	4.7	3.5	4.2	3.1	3.6	3.1	3.3	2.7	2.6	2.4	2.2	2.0	1.9	1.6	1.6	1.3	1.4	0.9	1.2	0.6	0.9	0.4	0.8	—	—
9	I	Kamakura-shi	(85,391) 100.0	48.5	51.5	7.1	5.7	5.5	5.6	4.6	4.4	4.6	4.9	4.1	4.9	3.6	4.6	3.1	3.9	3.4	3.8	3.1	3.0	2.8	2.8	2.1	2.1	1.6	1.7	1.3	1.4	0.8	1.1	0.5	0.8	0.4	0.7	—	—
	II	Ayase-machi	(8,181) 100.0	49.7	50.3	7.2	6.9	5.9	5.7	5.8	5.6	5.2	5.2	4.6	5.0	3.3	3.3	2.6	3.3	2.4	2.7	2.3	2.4	2.5	2.1	1.9	1.6	2.0	1.8	1.4	1.6	1.0	1.1	0.7	1.0	0.5	1.0	—	—
		Ebina-machi	(15,555) 100.0	50.1	49.9	7.2	6.7	6.4	5.8	5.7	5.4	5.4	5.1	4.9	4.4	3.1	3.7	2.7	3.4	2.9	3.1	2.5	2.4	2.2	2.4	2.0	1.8	1.7	1.5	1.6	1.4	0.9	1.0	0.7	1.0	0.5	0.8	—	—
	III	Shiroyama-machi	(5,519) 100.0	49.5	50.5	6.4	6.4	5.7	5.5	5.8	6.2	5.1	4.7	5.1	4.5	3.1	3.3	2.7	3.1	2.3	2.8	2.0	2.4	2.4	2.3	2.3	2.4	1.9	1.9	1.8	1.5	1.1	1.4	1.1	1.1	0.9	1.0	—	—
		Akita-machi	(13,411) 100.0	50.3	49.7	6.7	5.9	6.0	5.8	5.6	5.3	5.2	4.6	4.7	4.4	3.4	3.9	2.6	3.4	2.5	2.9	2.4	2.3	2.4	2.2	2.3	2.2	2.0	1.9	1.6	1.5	1.1	1.5	1.0	1.0	0.8	1.0	—	—
	IV	Hamura-machi	(8,373) 100.0	50.2	49.8	6.8	6.5	5.9	6.0	6.3	5.3	5.0	5.0	5.3	4.6	3.4	3.8	2.7	3.2	2.9	3.0	2.4	2.4	2.3	2.2	1.8	1.9	1.9	1.6	1.2	1.4	0.9	1.1	0.8	0.9	0.6	0.7	—	—
		Hannō-shi	(47,090) 100.0	49.0	51.0	6.6	6.0	6.2	5.7	5.5	5.2	4.6	5.1	4.3	4.4	3.3	4.0	2.8	3.6	2.7	3.3	2.5	2.4	2.3	2.4	2.0	2.0	1.8	1.8	1.7	1.7	1.1	1.4	0.8	1.1	0.6	0.8	—	—
	V	Tsurugashima-mura	(6,826) 100.0	50.6	49.4	6.6	6.6	6.8	5.7	6.2	5.8	5.7	4.5	4.3	4.2	3.5	3.5	2.3	2.9	2.6	3.0	2.4	2.5	2.3	2.3	2.3	2.1	1.7	1.4	1.4	1.7	1.3	1.3	0.8	1.0	0.7	1.0	—	—
		Hidaka-machi	(16,108) 100.0	48.8	51.2	6.3	6.6	5.9	5.9	5.8	5.4	4.8	4.6	4.2	4.4	3.1	3.8	2.6	3.5	2.7	3.0	2.3	2.3	2.4	2.3	1.8	1.8	1.8	1.8	1.4	1.8	1.1	1.6	0.8	1.2	0.7	0.9	—	—
		Kawashima-mura	(18,014) 100.0	48.3	51.7	6.9	6.8	6.4	5.5	6.0	5.9	5.3	5.8	4.3	4.7	2.8	3.4	2.4	2.8	2.7	3.0	2.3	2.4	2.3	2.3	2.0	2.0	1.8	1.8	1.4	1.7	1.2	1.4	0.8	1.2	0.5	0.8	—	—
		Kitamoto-machi	(13,457) 100.0	49.5	50.5	7.6	7.7	6.7	6.3	5.4	5.2	4.8	4.9	4.5	4.2	3.0	3.7	3.2	3.5	3.0	3.2	2.5	2.6	2.2	1.9	1.9	1.6	1.3	1.4	1.1	1.4	1.0	1.1	0.6	0.8	0.5	0.6	—	—
	VI	Higawa-machi	(19,495) 100.0	49.0	51.0	7.2	7.3	6.3	6.2	5.5	5.5	4.9	5.1	4.5	4.2	3.2	3.9	2.9	3.6	3.1	3.1	2.5	2.4	2.3	2.2	2.1	1.8	1.5	1.5	1.2	1.4	1.0	1.3	0.6	0.9	0.3	0.9	—	—
		Shobu-machi	(19,404) 100.0	49.3	50.7	7.4	6.6	6.3	5.5	5.6	5.6	5.3	5.2	4.4	4.3	3.0	3.5	2.4	2.8	2.5	2.9	2.4	2.4	2.4	2.1	2.0	2.2	1.9	1.8	1.7	1.8	1.3	1.4	0.8	1.2	0.6	1.0	—	—
		Kuki-machi	(21,069) 100.0	49.6	50.4	7.8	6.7	5.8	5.8	5.5	5.2	5.1	4.8	4.4	4.5	3.4	3.7	2.8	3.3	2.7	3.1	2.9	2.5	2.5	2.5	2.0	1.9	1.7	1.4	1.4	1.6	1.1	1.2	0.6	1.0	0.4	0.7	—	—
	VII	Satte-machi	(22,945) 100.0	48.6	51.4	7.4	7.0	6.1	5.7	5.5	5.5	5.0	5.8	4.2	4.3	2.9	3.6	2.3	3.0	2.5	3.0	2.6	2.5	2.5	2.4	2.0	1.9	1.7	1.7	1.5	1.7	1.1	1.3	0.8	1.0	0.5	0.9	—	—
		Iwai-machi	(35,922) 100.0	48.7	51.3	7.2	6.9	6.0	6.0	5.9	5.7	4.8	5.5	4.3	4.3	3.1	3.9	2.2	2.9	2.7	3.2	2.4	2.5	2.4	2.3	2.2	2.0	1.9	1.9	1.5	1.6	1.2	1.2	0.8	1.0	0.6	1.1	—	—
		Mitsukaidō-shi	(48,277) 100.0	48.1	51.9	6.6	6.5	5.7	5.8	5.4	5.6	4.8	5.3	4.1	4.6	3.2	3.9	2.3	2.6	2.7	3.2	2.7	2.7	2.3	2.3	1.9	2.0	1.9	2.0	1.6	1.8	1.2	1.2	0.9	1.2	0.7	1.0	—	—
	VIII	Yawahara-mura	(8,640) 100.0	48.5	51.5	6.2	6.1	6.0	5.8	5.5	5.5	5.2	4.8	4.0	4.3	3.0	3.8	2.8	3.0	2.6	3.4	2.6	2.4	2.4	2.4	2.1	2.2	1.9	2.3	1.5	1.6	1.1	1.4	0.9	1.3	0.7	1.2	—	—
		Ina-mura	(11,741) 100.0	48.6	51.4	6.7	6.2	5.2	5.2	5.6	5.1	5.0	5.3	4.1	4.5	3.1	3.6	2.5	3.2	2.7	3.0	2.8	2.9	2.3	2.1	1.8	2.6	2.2	2.1	1.8	2.0	0.9	0.9	0.8	1.3	0.7	1.3	—	—
		Fujishiro-machi	(14,783) 100.0	48.3	51.7	6.1	6.1	5.4	5.3	5.2	5.4	4.7	5.1	4.7	4.2	2.9	3.7	2.6	3.0	3.1	3.7	2.8	2.8	2.4	2.3	2.2	2.5	2.0	2.0	1.7	1.5	1.0	1.4	0.8	1.2	0.7	1.3	—	—
	IX	Ryūgasaki-shi	(34,179) 100.0	48.3	51.7	6.7	6.7	6.2	6.0	5.0	5.3	4.7	4.8	4.1	4.0	3.0	3.9	2.8	3.8	3.3	3.6	2.8	2.8	2.4	2.3	2.1	2.0	1.7	1.7	1.4	1.6	0.9	1.1	0.7	1.1	0.5	0.9	—	—
		Tone-mura	(9,796) 100.0	48.1	51.9	6.3	6.5	5.9	5.5	5.3	5.2	4.7	5.1	4.4	4.5	3.0	3.8	2.3	2.6	2.6	2.9	2.8	2.8	2.5	2.5	2.5	2.6	1.8	1.9	1.9	1.7	1.1	1.3	0.8	1.2	0.6	1.4	—	—
		Motono-mura	(5,586) 100.0	49.2	50.8	6.5	6.0	5.8	5.5	5.6	5.3	5.0	5.0	4.2	4.0	2.5	3.9	2.7	3.9	3.1	2.9	2.8	2.4	2.6	2.4	2.7	2.7	2.0	1.8	1.3	1.9	1.1	1.5	1.0	1.1	0.6	0.9	—	—
	X	Sakura-shi	(34,510) 100.0	48.2	51.8	6.3	6.3	5.8	5.6	5.2	5.5	4.7	5.1	4.4	4.5	3.4	3.9	2.9	3.4	2.8	3.4	2.5	2.6	2.6	2.4	2.2	2.1	1.8	1.8	1.4	1.9	1.0	1.2	0.7	1.0	0.6	0.9	—	—
		Izumi-machi	(9,919) 100.0	48.2	51.8	6.7	6.6	5.7	5.4	4.9	5.4	4.9	5.0	4.2	4.6	3.1	3.5	2.7	3.4	2.5	2.9	2.4	3.0	2.7	2.4	2.4	2.2	2.0	2.0	1.6	1.9	1.2	1.3	1.0	1.3	0.6	1.1	—	—
		Shitsu-mura	(9,975) 100.0	48.9	51.1	6.3	6.2	6.1	5.8	5.6	5.5	5.0	4.9	4.2	4.0	3.2	3.5	2.4	2.7	2.4	2.9	2.4	3.0	2.9	2.3	2.4	2.3	1.8	1.8	1.6	1.7	1.4	1.5	0.9	1.4	0.7	1.1	—	—
		Nansō-machi	(19,493) 100.0	48.7	51.3	6.2	5.8	6.3	5.8	5.6	5.6	5.1	5.4	3.9	4.0	2.8	3.5	2.5	3.3	2.5	3.1	2.4	3.0	2.6	2.5	2.4	2.4	1.6	1.6	1.6	1.8	1.2	1.5	1.0	1.4	0.6	1.2	—	—
		Fukuta-machi	(5,446) 100.0	48.5	51.5	6.8	7.0	5.9	6.0	4.9	5.0	5.0	4.2	3.6	4.4	2.8	3.6	2.6	3.8	3.0	3.0	2.5	2.8	2.6	2.1	2.4	2.4	1.6	1.7	1.8	2.0	1.1	1.3	1.0	1.1	0.9	1.0	—	—
		Kimitsu-machi	(14,064) 100.0	48.0	52.0	6.5	6.3	5.9	5.9	5.1	5.1	4.8	5.1	4.1	4.3	2.6	3.6	2.5	3.3	2.5	3.3	2.8	2.9	2.7	2.6	2.4	2.2	1.6	1.9	1.6	1.7	1.1	1.3	0.9	1.2	0.9	1.3	—	—

Table 3. Population by Age (5-Year Bracket) and Sex

(Zone) (Sector)	District	Total Total	Total M	Total F	0-4 M	0-4 F	5-9 M	5-9 F	10-14 M	10-14 F	15-19 M	15-19 F	20-24 M	20-24 F	25-29 M	25-29 F	30-34 M	30-34 F	35-39 M	35-39 F	40-44 M	40-44 F	45-49 M	45-49 F	50-54 M	50-54 F	55-59 M	55-59 F	60-64 M	60-64 F	65-69 M	65-69 F	70-74 M	70-74 F	75 & over M	75 & over F	Unknown M	Unknown F
X	Futtsu-machi	(16,864) 100.0	48.1	51.9	6.8	6.5	6.0	5.9	5.7	5.8	5.0	5.0	3.9	4.5	2.7	3.5	2.4	3.3	2.5	3.0	2.6	2.9	2.7	2.5	2.3	2.2	1.5	1.6	1.6	1.7	0.9	1.2	0.8	1.1	0.7	1.2	—	—
	Ōsawa-machi	(14,998) 100.0	47.8	52.2	6.8	6.7	6.0	6.0	5.2	5.6	5.1	4.7	3.8	3.9	2.7	3.7	2.4	3.3	2.8	3.3	2.5	2.9	2.0	2.5	2.4	2.2	1.7	1.8	1.5	2.0	1.2	1.4	1.0	1.3	0.7	1.3	—	—
	Zone 9 Total	(615,031) 100.0	48.7	51.3	6.7	6.4	5.9	5.7	5.4	5.3	4.9	5.0	4.3	4.4	3.1	3.8	2.7	3.4	2.8	3.2	2.6	2.7	2.5	2.4	2.2	2.1	1.8	1.8	1.5	1.7	1.1	1.3	0.8	1.1	0.6	1.0	—	—
10 I	Yokosuka-shi	(250,553) 100.0	50.2	49.8	7.8	7.3	5.8	5.6	4.5	4.4	4.8	4.4	5.7	4.6	4.1	4.6	3.7	3.9	3.6	3.5	2.8	2.7	2.3	2.3	2.0	1.9	1.5	1.5	1.2	1.3	0.8	1.0	0.5	0.7	0.3	0.5	—	—
	Zushi-shi	(35,908) 100.0	48.5	51.5	6.4	6.4	5.7	5.9	4.6	4.5	4.6	4.8	4.7	5.0	3.7	4.9	3.4	3.3	3.5	3.8	3.0	3.2	2.5	2.6	2.0	2.1	1.6	1.6	1.2	1.4	0.8	1.0	0.4	0.7	0.3	0.5	—	—
	Hayama-machi	(15,484) 100.0	47.6	52.4	6.4	6.1	5.7	5.8	4.9	4.6	4.2	4.4	4.2	4.6	3.4	4.3	2.7	3.8	3.3	3.5	2.9	3.2	2.6	2.6	1.9	2.1	1.7	2.1	1.6	1.9	1.0	1.4	0.6	1.1	0.5	1.1	—	—
	Chigasaki-shi	(52,092) 100.0	49.3	50.7	6.8	6.5	6.3	5.7	5.2	5.1	4.9	4.7	4.5	4.4	3.4	4.2	3.0	3.8	3.3	3.6	2.7	2.8	2.5	2.3	1.9	1.9	1.5	1.6	1.2	1.4	1.0	1.2	0.7	0.9	0.5	0.7	—	—
	Fujisawa-shi	(99,640) 100.0	49.2	50.8	6.7	6.5	6.1	5.7	5.1	4.9	5.0	5.0	4.8	4.7	3.4	4.2	3.0	3.6	3.1	3.6	2.8	2.9	2.6	2.4	2.0	1.8	1.5	1.5	1.2	1.4	0.9	1.1	0.6	0.8	0.4	0.7	—	—
	Aikawa-machi	(14,767) 100.0	48.4	51.6	6.8	6.1	5.9	5.7	5.4	5.8	5.0	5.7	4.4	5.4	3.1	3.9	2.6	3.2	2.5	2.9	2.5	2.5	2.6	2.3	2.2	2.0	1.8	1.7	1.6	1.5	0.9	1.1	0.7	0.9	0.6	0.9	—	—
II	Atsugi-shi	(43,191) 100.0	49.4	50.6	6.7	6.4	5.9	5.7	5.7	5.5	5.3	5.2	4.6	4.6	3.4	3.6	2.6	3.1	2.5	3.1	2.4	2.6	2.6	2.3	2.2	2.0	1.6	1.7	1.6	1.5	1.0	1.2	0.5	0.9	0.6	0.8	—	—
	Samukawa-machi	(11,166) 100.0	50.6	49.4	7.5	6.7	6.7	6.0	5.7	5.1	4.7	4.8	4.6	3.9	3.2	3.7	2.8	3.5	3.1	3.4	2.7	2.7	2.6	2.2	1.7	1.8	1.6	1.5	1.2	1.3	0.8	1.1	0.8	0.9	0.4	0.9	—	—
III	Ōme-shi	(53,166) 100.0	48.9	51.1	6.4	6.4	6.1	5.8	5.7	5.4	5.2	5.7	4.5	4.9	3.3	4.0	2.8	3.3	2.7	3.1	2.5	2.6	2.5	2.2	2.1	2.0	1.8	1.6	1.3	1.5	1.0	1.2	0.7	0.8	0.5	0.8	—	—
IV	Sakado-machi	(23,682) 100.0	48.9	51.1	6.8	6.9	6.0	5.7	5.9	5.4	4.8	5.1	4.1	4.5	3.3	3.7	2.5	3.1	2.4	2.8	2.4	2.7	2.3	2.3	2.1	2.1	2.0	1.8	1.7	1.7	1.1	1.5	0.8	1.1	0.6	0.8	—	—
	Yoshimi-mura	(15,999) 100.0	49.0	51.0	7.2	7.2	6.3	6.0	6.3	5.7	5.4	5.2	4.5	4.3	3.0	3.4	2.4	3.1	2.4	2.8	2.5	2.5	2.4	2.4	2.1	2.1	1.8	1.8	1.4	1.4	1.3	1.3	0.7	0.7	0.5	0.8	—	—
	Moroyama-mura	(10,823) 100.0	49.0	51.0	6.4	6.6	5.9	5.4	5.5	5.4	4.9	4.7	4.4	4.3	3.4	4.4	2.8	3.2	2.4	3.0	2.4	2.5	2.3	2.3	2.0	1.9	1.9	1.9	1.6	1.6	1.1	1.6	1.1	1.1	0.6	1.1	—	—
V	Kōnosu-shi	(30,888) 100.0	49.4	50.6	7.3	6.8	6.6	6.0	6.1	5.6	5.2	5.1	4.4	4.5	3.3	3.9	2.9	3.4	2.7	3.1	2.6	2.6	2.3	2.1	1.8	1.7	1.4	1.5	1.3	1.3	0.9	1.3	0.7	0.9	0.4	0.7	—	—
	Kisai-machi	(16,765) 100.0	48.7	51.3	6.8	7.0	5.3	6.0	6.6	5.3	5.2	5.3	4.4	4.3	2.6	3.6	2.5	3.0	2.5	2.8	2.4	2.4	2.4	2.1	2.1	2.0	1.7	1.8	1.7	1.7	1.2	1.4	0.8	1.1	0.6	1.1	—	—
	Washimiya-machi	(9,487) 100.0	48.5	51.5	7.1	7.5	5.3	6.0	6.1	6.6	4.7	5.3	4.5	3.9	3.4	3.6	2.6	2.8	2.4	3.0	2.4	2.4	2.5	2.0	2.1	2.0	1.7	1.7	1.5	1.6	1.0	1.5	0.7	1.1	0.5	0.8	—	—
	Kurihashi-machi	(12,223) 100.0	48.4	51.6	7.7	7.3	6.0	6.0	5.6	5.3	5.2	5.1	4.2	4.4	2.9	3.4	2.8	3.6	2.9	3.5	2.3	2.2	2.4	2.2	2.0	2.0	1.5	1.6	1.4	1.6	1.0	1.3	0.8	0.9	0.5	0.8	—	—
	Goka-mura	(9,985) 100.0	48.6	51.4	7.9	7.1	6.0	5.6	6.0	6.1	5.8	5.4	4.4	3.9	2.7	3.4	2.2	2.7	2.4	2.9	2.0	2.4	2.4	2.2	2.3	1.9	1.8	1.6	1.5	1.6	1.2	1.3	0.9	1.2	0.8	1.0	—	—
VI	Sakai-machi	(24,333) 100.0	48.4	51.6	7.5	7.1	6.1	5.9	5.8	5.8	4.8	5.4	3.9	4.3	3.0	3.8	2.3	3.1	2.4	2.9	2.4	2.6	2.4	2.1	2.0	2.0	1.7	1.8	1.4	1.4	1.1	1.2	0.8	1.0	0.7	0.9	—	—
	Sashima-machi	(15,785) 100.0	48.5	51.5	7.6	7.6	6.2	5.9	5.9	5.9	4.8	5.3	4.2	4.2	2.8	3.5	2.3	2.9	2.4	2.8	2.3	2.3	1.9	2.1	1.9	1.8	1.9	1.8	1.4	1.4	1.1	1.5	0.7	1.1	0.6	1.1	—	—
	Yatabe-machi	(18,971) 100.0	48.7	51.3	5.8	5.8	5.9	5.4	5.1	5.2	5.0	5.0	4.2	4.6	3.4	3.9	2.7	3.4	3.1	3.2	2.6	2.6	2.1	2.4	2.0	2.0	2.0	1.9	1.6	1.8	1.2	1.5	1.1	1.1	0.6	1.1	—	—
VII	Kukizaki-mura	(6,569) 100.0	49.2	50.8	5.9	5.8	5.9	6.0	5.4	5.5	5.7	5.1	4.5	4.5	3.1	3.6	2.3	3.1	2.7	2.9	2.6	2.8	2.8	2.4	2.2	1.8	1.8	2.0	1.6	1.7	1.2	1.5	0.7	1.2	0.7	1.2	—	—
	Ushiku-machi	(15,176) 100.0	49.7	50.3	6.3	6.3	5.7	5.5	5.2	5.2	5.8	5.1	4.7	4.5	3.5	3.9	2.9	3.5	3.1	3.4	2.5	2.5	2.3	1.9	1.7	1.8	1.8	1.8	1.6	1.7	1.1	1.2	0.8	1.0	0.7	1.0	—	—
	Kawachi-mura	(9,161) 100.0	48.4	51.6	6.8	6.3	5.9	5.9	5.7	6.0	5.1	5.3	4.0	4.1	2.6	3.2	2.1	3.2	2.8	3.1	2.4	2.5	2.6	2.7	2.3	2.4	1.9	1.8	1.6	1.6	1.1	1.2	0.9	1.0	0.5	1.0	—	—
	Sakae-machi	(14,794) 100.0	48.2	51.8	6.6	6.2	5.9	6.0	5.5	5.3	4.8	5.0	4.2	4.4	2.7	3.6	2.4	3.6	2.9	3.3	2.7	2.8	2.4	2.5	2.3	2.4	1.7	1.8	1.6	1.8	1.0	1.2	0.8	1.2	0.6	1.1	—	—
VIII	Narita-shi	(44,724) 100.0	48.3	51.7	6.4	6.1	5.6	5.3	5.2	5.3	5.1	5.0	4.4	4.5	3.1	3.9	2.9	2.4	2.7	3.4	2.6	2.8	2.4	2.6	2.0	2.2	1.9	1.9	1.6	1.8	1.0	1.1	0.7	1.1	0.5	1.0	—	—
	Shisui-machi	(6,279) 100.0	48.3	51.7	6.5	6.6	5.9	6.0	4.9	5.3	4.8	5.0	3.9	4.7	3.2	3.6	2.8	3.3	2.8	3.2	2.7	2.7	2.9	2.8	2.3	2.2	1.6	1.8	1.6	1.8	0.9	1.1	0.7	1.1	0.7	1.1	—	—
	Yachimata-machi	(29,469) 100.0	49.3	50.7	7.0	6.7	5.9	5.8	5.3	5.6	5.4	5.2	4.5	4.4	3.3	3.5	2.7	3.4	2.8	2.9	2.8	2.9	2.4	2.3	2.2	2.2	1.6	1.4	1.4	1.5	0.9	1.1	0.8	1.1	0.6	0.9	—	—
IX	Toke-machi	(6,674) 100.0	48.2	51.8	7.0	6.7	6.0	6.0	5.2	5.6	4.7	5.2	3.8	4.2	3.3	3.5	2.7	3.5	2.5	2.8	2.2	2.5	2.2	2.5	2.2	2.3	1.8	1.4	1.5	1.7	0.9	1.3	1.1	1.1	0.6	1.3	—	—
	Nagara-machi	(10,182) 100.0	48.1	51.9	6.5	6.4	5.7	5.3	5.5	5.3	4.9	4.9	3.9	4.1	2.7	3.4	2.6	3.3	2.5	2.8	2.2	2.5	2.6	2.7	2.6	2.3	1.8	2.1	1.6	2.0	1.2	1.4	1.1	1.7	0.6	1.2	—	—
	Obitsu-mura	(7,782) 100.0	48.2	51.8	6.5	6.9	5.9	5.9	5.4	5.2	4.8	5.0	3.8	4.2	3.0	3.4	2.2	3.1	3.0	3.3	2.4	2.8	2.3	2.3	2.2	2.6	1.7	2.0	2.0	2.0	1.1	1.4	0.8	1.3	0.5	1.1	—	—
X	Koito-machi	(6,773) 100.0	49.5	51.5	6.9	6.5	6.0	5.2	5.1	5.1	5.4	4.8	4.3	4.7	3.1	3.5	2.1	2.9	2.3	3.0	2.6	2.8	2.3	2.5	2.6	2.6	2.2	2.2	1.9	1.9	1.2	1.3	0.7	1.4	0.7	1.4	—	—

- 189 -

Table 3. Population By Age (5-Year Bracket) and Sex

(Zone)	(Sector)	District	Total	Total %	M	F	0-4 M	0-4 F	5-9 M	5-9 F	10-14 M	10-14 F	15-19 M	15-19 F	20-24 M	20-24 F	25-29 M	25-29 F	30-34 M	30-34 F	35-39 M	35-39 F	40-44 M	40-44 F	45-49 M	45-49 F	50-54 M	50-54 F	55-59 M	55-59 F	60-64 M	60-64 F	65-69 M	65-69 F	70-74 M	70-74 F	75 & over M	75 & over F	Unknown M	Unknown F
		Zone 10 Total	(922,471)	100.0	49.3	50.7	6.8	6.6	5.9	5.7	5.2	5.0	4.9	4.9	4.8	4.5	3.5	4.1	3.0	3.5	3.0	3.3	2.6	2.7	2.5	2.3	2.0	2.0	1.6	1.6	1.4	1.5	0.9	1.2	0.7	0.9	0.5	0.8	—	—
		Total for 50 km. Region	(10,947,345)	100.0	50.1	49.9	6.6	6.3	5.6	5.6	4.6	4.5	5.2	4.9	5.5	4.9	4.0	4.5	3.3	3.8	3.3	3.4	2.9	2.8	2.6	2.4	2.1	1.9	1.6	1.5	1.2	1.3	0.8	0.9	0.5	0.7	0.3	0.8	—	—
		National Total	(83,199,637)	100.0	49.0	51.0	6.8	6.5	5.7	5.7	5.3	5.2	5.2	5.1	4.6	4.7	3.4	4.0	2.8	3.4	2.9	3.2	2.6	2.8	2.4	2.4	2.1	2.0	1.7	1.7	1.3	1.4	1.0	1.2	0.7	0.9	0.5	0.8	—	—

1955

(Zone)	(Sector)	District	Total	Total %	M	F	0-4 M	0-4 F	5-9 M	5-9 F	10-14 M	10-14 F	15-19 M	15-19 F	20-24 M	20-24 F	25-29 M	25-29 F	30-34 M	30-34 F	35-39 M	35-39 F	40-44 M	40-44 F	45-49 M	45-49 F	50-54 M	50-54 F	55-59 M	55-59 F	60-64 M	60-64 F	65-69 M	65-69 F	70-74 M	70-74 F	75 & over M	75 & over F	Unknown M	Unknown F
1	I	Chiyoda-ku	(122,745)	100.0	54.4	45.6	2.8	2.6	4.0	3.9	3.8	3.6	10.3	5.9	11.4	6.6	5.4	5.4	3.7	2.9	2.4	3.0	2.5	2.9	2.5	2.4	2.1	2.0	1.6	1.5	1.2	1.1	0.8	0.8	0.4	0.5	0.3	0.5	—	—
1	II	Minato-ku	(254,592)	100.0	50.7	49.3	3.4	3.6	4.8	4.5	4.4	4.2	6.9	5.2	7.6	6.9	5.1	4.9	3.3	3.3	2.8	3.5	2.9	3.2	2.5	2.5	2.3	2.2	1.7	1.7	1.3	1.3	0.9	1.0	0.5	0.6	0.3	0.6	—	—
1	III	Chūō-ku	(171,316)	100.0	52.4	47.1	2.8	2.6	4.0	3.9	3.8	3.8	9.9	5.9	11.1	6.6	5.3	4.6	2.7	3.8	2.1	3.1	2.3	3.1	2.3	2.6	2.2	2.2	1.8	1.7	1.2	1.2	0.8	0.9	0.4	0.6	0.2	0.5	—	—
1	IV	Bunkyō-ku	(236,971)	100.0	51.2	48.8	3.5	3.4	4.8	4.5	4.3	4.3	6.9	5.1	8.4	5.8	5.3	5.0	3.3	3.4	2.7	3.1	2.5	3.1	2.5	2.5	2.1	2.2	1.7	1.7	1.3	1.2	0.9	1.0	0.5	0.7	0.3	0.6	—	—
1	V	Taitō-ku	(310,058)	100.0	52.4	47.6	3.5	3.3	4.4	4.4	4.1	4.1	9.0	5.9	8.6	6.3	5.0	4.8	3.2	3.8	2.6	3.2	2.5	2.9	2.5	2.4	2.3	2.0	1.8	1.5	1.2	1.1	0.8	0.8	0.4	0.6	0.3	0.5	—	—
1		Zone 1 Total	(1,095,682)	100.0	52.0	48.0	3.3	3.1	4.4	4.3	4.2	4.1	8.3	5.6	9.0	6.2	5.2	4.8	3.1	3.1	2.6	3.3	2.7	3.0	2.4	2.5	2.2	2.2	1.7	1.6	1.2	1.2	0.8	0.9	0.4	0.6	0.3	0.5	—	—
2	I	Shinagawa-ku	(373,341)	100.0	50.9	49.1	4.0	3.9	5.2	5.0	4.4	4.4	5.9	4.9	7.2	6.6	5.4	4.6	3.9	4.3	3.0	3.4	2.8	2.9	2.4	2.4	2.1	2.1	1.7	1.7	1.2	1.1	0.8	0.8	0.4	0.5	0.2	0.5	—	—
2	II	Meguro-ku	(253,941)	100.0	51.0	49.0	3.6	3.4	5.1	4.9	4.6	4.5	6.1	5.0	7.4	5.6	5.3	5.1	3.7	4.2	2.8	3.4	2.9	3.2	2.5	2.6	2.3	2.2	1.7	1.7	1.3	1.3	0.9	1.0	0.5	0.6	0.3	0.6	—	—
2	III	Shibuya-ku	(243,410)	100.0	49.8	50.2	3.7	3.5	4.8	4.6	4.3	4.1	5.8	5.5	7.7	6.6	5.6	4.6	3.7	4.5	2.9	3.5	2.3	2.9	2.3	2.6	2.0	2.0	1.8	1.7	1.2	1.2	0.8	1.0	0.4	0.6	0.2	0.5	—	—
2	IV	Shinjuku-ku	(348,675)	100.0	50.6	49.4	3.7	3.5	4.8	4.6	4.2	4.0	6.1	5.0	7.9	6.4	5.8	5.3	3.8	4.6	3.0	3.5	2.9	2.9	2.5	2.5	2.0	2.0	1.6	1.5	1.2	1.2	0.8	0.9	0.5	0.6	0.3	0.5	—	—
2	V	Nakano-ku	(289,165)	100.0	51.3	48.7	3.8	3.6	5.0	4.7	4.4	4.3	5.8	4.5	8.2	5.5	5.6	5.4	3.9	4.4	3.0	3.4	2.8	3.0	2.4	2.5	2.1	2.1	1.7	1.6	1.2	1.1	0.7	0.9	0.4	0.5	0.2	0.5	—	—
2	VI	Toshima-ku	(300,557)	100.0	50.8	49.2	4.0	3.8	5.1	4.8	4.5	4.4	6.0	4.9	7.5	6.1	5.5	5.5	3.8	4.4	2.9	3.4	2.8	2.9	2.4	2.4	2.2	2.1	1.7	1.6	1.2	1.2	0.8	0.8	0.4	0.5	0.2	0.5	—	—
2	VII	Kita-ku	(351,532)	100.0	50.7	49.3	4.3	4.2	5.5	5.3	4.8	4.7	5.5	4.7	6.7	5.4	5.3	4.7	3.8	4.2	3.0	3.4	2.8	2.8	2.4	2.4	2.1	2.1	1.7	1.6	1.2	1.2	0.7	0.8	0.4	0.5	0.2	0.5	—	—
2	VIII	Arakawa-ku	(253,323)	100.0	51.7	48.3	4.6	4.4	5.6	5.3	4.9	4.9	7.2	5.2	6.3	5.5	5.0	4.6	3.5	3.8	2.8	3.1	2.7	2.8	2.3	2.3	2.0	1.9	1.8	1.6	1.2	1.2	0.8	0.8	0.4	0.5	0.2	0.4	—	—
2		Sumida-ku	(305,590)	100.0	53.0	47.0	4.5	4.2	5.3	4.9	4.6	4.4	9.0	6.6	7.9	5.8	4.9	4.6	3.3	3.7	2.6	3.1	2.8	2.7	2.6	2.3	2.0	1.9	1.7	1.4	1.1	1.0	0.7	0.7	0.3	0.4	0.2	0.4	—	—
2		Kōtō-ku	(279,971)	100.0	53.7	46.3	5.1	4.8	5.8	5.4	4.6	4.3	6.6	5.0	7.6	5.3	5.7	4.9	3.9	4.0	3.1	3.3	3.1	2.8	2.6	2.0	2.0	1.6	1.5	1.2	1.0	0.8	0.6	0.6	0.3	0.4	0.2	0.3	—	—
2		Zone 2 Total	(2,997,505)	100.0	51.4	48.6	4.1	3.9	5.2	5.0	4.5	4.4	6.4	5.0	7.5	5.8	5.4	5.2	3.7	4.2	3.0	3.3	2.8	2.9	2.4	2.4	2.1	2.0	1.7	1.6	1.2	1.1	0.7	0.8	0.4	0.5	0.2	0.5	—	—
3	I	Ōta-ku	(568,498)	100.0	51.6	48.4	4.5	4.3	5.6	5.2	4.8	4.5	5.8	4.5	6.7	5.1	5.4	5.1	4.0	4.4	3.2	3.5	3.0	3.0	2.4	2.4	2.1	2.0	1.6	1.4	1.1	1.0	0.7	0.8	0.4	0.5	0.3	0.5	—	—
3	II	Setagaya-ku	(523,630)	100.0	50.7	49.3	3.7	3.6	5.2	5.0	4.8	4.6	5.8	4.9	7.5	5.4	5.1	5.1	3.7	4.2	2.9	3.4	2.9	3.0	2.4	2.6	2.2	2.2	1.7	1.7	1.2	1.3	0.8	1.0	0.5	0.7	0.3	0.6	—	—
3	III	Suginami-ku	(405,665)	100.0	50.8	49.2	3.6	3.4	5.1	4.9	4.7	4.5	5.6	5.6	7.8	5.4	5.2	5.2	3.8	4.2	2.9	3.4	2.9	3.1	2.4	2.6	2.2	2.2	1.7	1.7	1.2	1.3	0.9	1.0	0.5	0.7	0.3	0.7	—	—
3	IV	Itabashi-ku	(311,225)	100.0	51.1	48.9	4.8	4.5	6.0	5.8	5.1	4.9	5.5	4.5	6.4	5.0	5.1	4.4	3.8	4.3	3.1	3.5	3.0	2.9	2.4	2.2	2.0	1.9	1.5	1.4	1.1	1.1	0.7	0.8	0.4	0.4	0.2	0.5	—	—
3	V	Nerima-ku	(186,814)	100.0	51.3	48.7	4.5	4.3	5.7	5.2	4.9	4.7	5.3	5.3	7.5	5.2	5.3	4.4	3.8	4.3	3.0	3.3	2.8	2.9	2.4	2.3	2.0	2.0	1.5	1.6	1.1	1.2	0.8	0.9	0.5	0.5	0.3	0.6	—	—
3	VI	Adachi-ku	(332,181)	100.0	51.1	48.9	4.4	4.6	6.3	6.0	5.3	5.3	5.7	4.7	5.6	4.7	4.6	4.4	3.4	3.8	2.9	3.3	2.8	3.0	2.5	2.4	2.3	2.0	1.8	1.5	1.2	1.1	0.8	0.8	0.5	0.7	0.3	0.6	—	—
3	VII	Katsushika-ku	(294,133)	100.0	50.3	49.7	4.4	4.6	6.1	6.0	5.3	5.4	5.6	5.4	5.8	4.9	4.8	4.6	3.5	3.9	2.9	3.4	2.8	3.0	2.5	2.4	2.2	2.0	1.7	1.5	1.2	1.2	0.8	0.9	0.4	0.6	0.3	0.5	—	—
3	VIII	Edogawa-ku	(254,771)	100.0	50.7	49.3	4.8	4.6	6.1	5.9	5.3	5.1	5.7	5.1	5.8	4.9	4.9	4.5	3.4	3.9	2.8	3.4	2.8	3.0	2.5	2.5	2.2	2.0	1.7	1.5	1.2	1.1	0.8	0.9	0.4	0.5	0.3	0.5	—	—
3		Urayasu-machi	(16,394)	100.0	50.6	49.4	6.0	5.6	6.9	6.6	5.4	5.4	4.6	4.6	4.3	4.0	4.9	3.6	2.6	3.5	2.4	3.2	2.8	3.1	2.7	2.6	2.1	2.0	1.8	1.7	1.4	1.6	1.3	1.3	0.8	0.8	0.6	0.9	—	—

Table 3. Population By Age (5-Year Bracket) and Sex

(Zone)	(Sector)	District	Total			Age 0-4		Age 5-9		Age 10-14		Age 15-19		Age 20-24		Age 25-29		Age 30-34		Age 35-39		Age 40-44		Age 45-49		Age 50-54		Age 55-59		Age 60-64		Age 65-69		Age 70-74		Age 75 & over		Unknown	
			Total	M	F	M	F	M	F	M	F	M	F	M	F	M	F	M	F	M	F	M	F	M	F	M	F	M	F	M	F	M	F	M	F	M	F	M	F
4		Zone 3 Total	(2,892,311) 100.0	50.9	49.1	4.4	4.2	5.7	5.4	5.0	4.8	5.7	4.7	6.7	5.1	5.1	4.9	3.7	4.2	3.0	3.4	2.9	3.0	2.4	2.4	2.1	2.0	1.7	1.6	1.2	1.2	0.8	0.9	0.4	0.6	0.3	0.6	—	—
	I	Kawasaki-shi	(445,520) 100.0	52.1	47.9	5.3	5.1	6.4	6.0	5.0	4.8	5.0	4.3	6.3	5.9	5.7	5.0	4.1	4.3	3.4	3.6	3.3	2.8	2.4	2.0	1.9	1.6	1.3	1.2	0.9	0.9	0.6	0.7	0.3	0.5	0.2	0.4	—	—
	II	Komae-machi	(14,669) 100.0	49.8	50.2	5.2	4.7	5.6	5.6	4.8	5.0	4.7	5.2	5.9	4.9	5.0	5.3	3.9	4.3	3.0	3.2	2.9	3.0	2.4	2.2	1.9	2.0	1.5	1.4	1.3	1.0	0.9	0.8	0.6	0.6	0.4	0.8	—	—
	III	Mitaka-shi	(69,466) 100.0	51.8	48.2	4.5	4.3	6.3	5.9	5.3	5.1	5.3	4.2	6.7	4.5	5.1	4.7	3.8	4.3	3.3	3.8	3.4	3.2	2.5	2.4	2.0	1.4	1.4	1.3	1.0	0.9	0.6	0.8	0.4	0.6	0.3	0.5	—	—
		Musashino-shi	(94,948) 100.0	51.0	49.0	3.9	3.6	5.4	5.0	4.7	4.6	5.6	4.8	7.5	4.7	5.4	5.2	3.9	4.3	3.0	3.4	3.0	3.1	2.5	2.5	2.1	1.5	1.5	1.5	1.0	1.2	0.8	0.9	0.4	0.5	0.3	0.5	—	—
		Chōfu-shi	(45,362) 100.0	50.8	49.2	4.7	4.6	6.3	6.0	5.1	5.0	5.0	4.5	4.7	4.7	4.6	4.8	3.7	4.3	3.1	3.4	2.9	2.8	2.3	2.2	2.0	1.5	1.5	1.5	1.0	1.2	0.8	0.8	0.4	0.7	0.4	0.6	—	—
	IV	Hoya-machi	(23,327) 100.0	50.6	49.4	5.4	4.8	6.9	5.8	5.1	5.1	4.6	4.4	5.8	4.4	4.6	4.8	3.8	4.6	3.5	3.7	3.1	2.8	2.3	2.1	1.8	1.7	1.3	1.4	1.1	1.1	0.7	1.1	0.4	0.4	0.3	0.6	—	—
		Yamato-machi	(13,325) 100.0	49.2	50.8	5.4	4.8	5.9	5.8	4.8	5.1	4.4	4.4	5.4	5.9	5.1	5.3	3.7	4.2	3.1	3.5	2.8	2.9	2.2	1.9	1.9	1.7	1.4	1.4	1.0	1.1	0.8	0.9	0.5	0.8	0.3	0.6	—	—
		Toda-machi	(21,357) 100.0	49.4	50.6	5.4	5.2	6.6	6.5	5.7	5.9	5.2	5.5	4.4	4.2	4.3	4.3	3.3	3.6	2.8	3.4	2.9	3.2	2.5	2.3	1.9	1.8	1.7	1.4	1.0	1.1	0.9	1.1	0.5	0.8	0.3	0.7	—	—
	V	Warabi-shi	(35,184) 100.0	49.1	50.9	4.5	4.7	6.5	6.2	6.0	5.4	5.8	5.0	4.8	4.6	4.4	4.2	3.4	3.4	3.1	3.8	3.2	3.4	2.7	2.3	2.0	1.8	1.5	1.4	1.1	1.0	0.7	0.8	0.3	0.4	0.2	0.5	—	—
		Kawaguchi-shi	(135,121) 100.0	50.8	49.2	5.2	5.1	6.5	6.2	5.4	5.4	5.7	5.0	5.2	4.6	4.4	4.2	4.7	3.8	2.9	3.3	2.8	3.3	2.4	2.3	1.9	1.8	1.5	1.5	1.2	1.3	0.6	0.8	0.4	0.4	0.2	0.5	—	—
		Hatogaya-machi	(14,437) 100.0	50.2	49.8	5.4	5.1	6.9	6.8	6.1	5.8	5.8	4.7	4.7	4.1	4.0	3.8	3.1	3.3	2.7	3.6	2.8	3.3	2.8	2.4	2.2	1.8	1.7	1.6	1.3	1.2	1.0	1.0	0.5	0.7	0.3	0.6	—	—
	VI	Sōka-shi	(31,875) 100.0	49.9	50.1	5.9	5.4	6.8	6.4	5.5	5.5	5.0	5.2	4.8	4.5	4.1	3.9	2.9	3.4	2.6	3.4	2.7	3.0	2.5	2.4	2.2	1.9	1.8	1.6	1.3	1.3	1.0	1.0	0.5	0.7	0.4	0.7	—	—
		Yashio-mura	(13,386) 100.0	50.2	49.8	6.5	6.3	7.2	6.4	5.7	6.4	5.2	5.2	4.6	4.6	4.0	3.8	2.6	2.6	1.8	2.8	2.4	2.7	2.4	2.2	2.2	2.6	1.8	1.8	1.5	1.6	0.9	1.3	0.6	1.1	0.6	0.3	—	—
		Misato-mura	(17,313) 100.0	49.1	50.9	6.1	5.7	7.0	6.8	5.4	5.5	4.9	5.3	4.7	4.7	3.9	3.2	2.7	3.2	2.1	2.5	2.3	2.8	2.3	2.4	2.2	2.1	1.8	1.7	1.4	1.6	1.1	1.4	0.7	1.0	0.5	1.0	—	—
	VII	Matsudo-shi	(68,363) 100.0	49.8	50.2	5.0	4.8	6.4	6.1	5.2	5.4	4.8	4.7	5.5	5.4	4.6	4.3	3.4	3.9	2.7	3.3	2.9	3.0	2.4	2.4	2.2	2.0	1.7	1.6	1.2	1.3	0.9	1.1	0.5	0.8	0.4	0.7	—	—
		Ichikawa-shi	(136,739) 100.0	49.1	50.9	4.3	4.2	5.7	5.5	5.2	5.0	5.3	5.5	5.7	5.4	4.5	4.5	3.3	3.9	2.8	3.4	2.9	3.1	2.5	2.6	2.2	2.2	1.7	1.7	1.3	1.3	0.8	1.1	0.5	0.8	0.4	0.7	—	—
		Zone 4 Total	(1,180,392) 100.0	50.9	49.1	5.0	4.8	6.3	5.9	5.2	5.0	5.1	4.7	6.0	4.8	5.1	4.7	3.7	4.1	3.1	3.5	3.0	3.0	2.4	2.2	2.0	1.8	1.5	1.4	1.0	1.1	0.7	0.9	0.4	0.6	0.3	0.6	—	—
	I	Tsurumi-ku	(201,028) 100.0	51.9	48.1	4.9	4.8	6.2	5.8	5.0	5.0	4.3	4.3	6.4	4.8	5.9	4.9	3.9	4.2	3.2	3.5	3.2	2.9	2.5	2.2	2.1	1.8	1.5	1.4	1.0	1.0	0.6	0.7	0.3	0.5	0.2	0.4	—	—
	III	Koganei-shi	(30,338) 100.0	51.5	48.5	4.5	4.0	5.6	5.3	5.4	5.4	4.6	5.4	7.3	5.1	5.4	5.2	3.7	4.1	2.9	3.3	3.0	2.8	2.4	2.4	2.0	1.9	1.5	1.4	0.9	1.2	0.8	0.9	0.4	0.6	0.3	0.6	—	—
		Tanashi-machi	(19,450) 100.0	50.0	50.0	5.0	4.9	6.8	6.4	5.7	5.4	4.6	4.7	4.9	4.9	4.6	4.8	3.6	4.7	3.5	3.7	3.6	3.1	2.6	2.1	1.8	1.5	1.2	1.1	0.9	0.9	0.6	0.9	0.4	0.5	0.4	0.4	—	—
		Kurume-machi	(10,319) 100.0	49.8	50.2	5.8	5.8	7.0	6.3	6.6	6.2	5.5	5.5	4.2	3.9	3.9	4.2	3.3	3.9	2.5	3.2	2.7	2.4	2.1	1.9	1.9	1.6	1.3	1.4	1.2	1.4	0.9	0.9	0.5	0.8	0.5	0.9	—	—
	IV	Nīza-machi	(11,700) 100.0	50.1	49.9	6.0	5.8	6.5	6.2	5.7	5.1	4.7	4.5	4.4	4.4	4.4	7.1	3.2	3.8	2.5	3.0	2.5	2.8	2.1	1.9	2.2	2.0	1.6	1.7	1.4	1.5	1.1	1.3	0.8	0.8	0.7	0.8	—	—
		Kiyose-machi	(14,544) 100.0	51.6	49.4	4.1	3.9	4.7	4.6	4.0	3.6	3.5	4.0	5.1	5.9	7.3	4.4	6.3	5.5	4.9	3.9	3.5	3.0	2.8	2.0	1.7	1.6	1.3	1.4	0.9	1.0	0.8	1.0	0.5	0.5	0.5	0.9	—	—
		Adachi-machi	(10,523) 100.0	49.2	50.8	5.4	5.2	6.5	6.2	5.8	6.2	4.5	4.8	4.5	4.6	4.0	4.2	3.2	4.0	2.7	3.2	2.7	2.9	2.5	2.4	2.1	1.7	1.7	1.7	1.5	1.4	1.0	1.3	0.5	0.9	0.4	0.6	—	—
	V	Asaka-machi	(16,465) 100.0	49.8	50.2	5.6	5.3	7.3	6.8	6.3	6.3	4.8	4.4	4.5	4.6	4.4	4.6	3.5	3.9	3.1	3.2	3.0	2.8	2.3	2.2	1.9	1.7	1.6	1.6	1.2	1.3	0.8	0.9	0.4	0.7	0.4	0.6	—	—
		Urawa-shi	(143,044) 100.0	49.9	50.1	4.5	4.2	5.9	5.5	5.5	5.4	5.0	4.9	5.4	4.8	4.6	4.7	3.5	4.0	2.9	3.3	3.0	2.8	2.4	2.5	2.3	1.8	1.8	1.6	1.3	1.3	0.9	1.1	0.5	0.7	0.4	0.7	—	—
	VI	Misono-mura	(9,527) 100.0	49.5	50.5	5.9	5.8	6.7	6.5	6.6	6.3	5.4	5.4	4.0	4.2	3.6	3.6	2.8	3.2	2.3	2.7	1.6	2.0	2.4	2.5	2.4	2.2	2.0	1.7	1.3	1.4	1.1	1.4	0.6	1.1	0.3	0.6	—	—
		Koshigaya-shi	(45,001) 100.0	49.2	50.8	6.4	5.9	6.9	6.5	5.7	5.5	4.9	5.3	4.5	4.2	4.2	3.8	2.8	3.3	2.4	2.7	2.5	2.9	2.5	2.5	2.5	2.1	1.9	1.7	1.5	1.5	1.3	1.4	0.7	1.0	0.4	0.7	—	—
	VII	Yoshikawa-machi	(16,354) 100.0	49.2	50.8	6.1	6.0	7.2	6.9	5.6	5.5	5.3	5.3	4.3	4.2	3.6	3.3	2.4	2.9	2.1	2.5	2.3	2.8	2.3	2.6	2.5	2.1	1.8	1.8	1.6	1.5	1.1	1.3	1.0	1.1	0.5	1.1	—	—
	VIII	Nagareyama-machi	(19,077) 100.0	49.1	50.9	5.5	5.5	6.6	6.5	5.5	5.5	4.6	4.8	4.6	4.7	3.8	4.0	2.8	3.4	2.5	3.0	2.5	3.2	2.4	2.4	2.3	2.0	1.8	1.8	1.4	1.5	1.1	1.3	0.7	1.0	0.5	1.1	—	—
		Kamagaya-machi	(10,168) 100.0	49.9	50.1	6.0	6.1	6.6	6.6	5.5	5.3	4.8	4.9	5.3	4.4	4.4	4.0	3.0	3.7	2.7	3.0	2.3	2.5	2.2	2.2	2.1	1.6	1.7	1.6	1.3	1.3	1.1	1.1	0.5	0.6	0.6	0.9	—	—
		Funahashi-shi	(114,921) 100.0	50.4	49.6	4.8	4.6	6.1	5.9	5.4	5.2	5.1	4.8	6.2	4.7	4.7	4.3	3.0	3.5	2.8	3.5	2.9	3.1	2.5	2.3	2.0	1.5	1.6	1.5	1.2	1.2	0.9	1.1	0.5	0.8	0.4	0.7	—	—

- 191 -

Table 3. Population By Age (5-Year Bracket) and Sex

Zone	Sector	District	Total (count)	Total	M	F	0-4 M	0-4 F	5-9 M	5-9 F	10-14 M	10-14 F	15-19 M	15-19 F	20-24 M	20-24 F	25-29 M	25-29 F	30-34 M	30-34 F	35-39 M	35-39 F	40-44 M	40-44 F	45-49 M	45-49 F	50-54 M	50-54 F	55-59 M	55-59 F	60-64 M	60-64 F	65-69 M	65-69 F	70-74 M	70-74 F	75 & over M	75 & over F	Unknown M	Unknown F
6		Zone 5 Total	(672,459)	100.0	50.6	49.4	5.0	4.8	6.2	5.9	5.3	5.1	4.9	4.7	5.7	4.7	5.0	4.6	3.5	4.0	2.9	3.4	3.0	3.0	2.5	2.4	2.1	1.9	1.6	1.5	1.2	1.2	0.8	1.0	0.5	0.7	0.3	0.7	—	—
	I	Nishi-ku	(100,446)	100.0	50.7	49.3	4.5	4.2	5.6	5.3	4.8	4.6	4.9	4.6	5.8	5.1	5.6	4.9	3.8	4.3	3.0	3.5	3.0	2.9	2.4	2.5	2.2	2.1	1.9	1.7	1.4	1.3	1.0	1.0	0.5	0.7	0.3	0.6	—	—
		Naka-ku	(105,925)	100.0	49.9	50.1	4.0	3.9	5.0	4.8	4.4	4.2	5.2	4.8	6.5	6.0	5.7	5.5	3.8	4.4	2.8	3.3	2.8	3.0	2.5	2.5	2.3	2.3	1.8	1.8	1.4	1.3	0.9	1.0	0.5	0.7	0.3	0.6	—	—
		Kanagawa-ku	(142,797)	100.0	51.3	48.7	4.8	4.6	5.8	5.7	4.9	4.7	5.0	4.3	6.4	4.7	5.5	5.0	3.9	4.1	3.1	3.4	2.9	3.0	2.5	2.3	2.0	2.0	1.7	1.7	1.3	1.2	0.8	0.9	0.4	0.6	0.3	0.5	—	—
	II	Kōhoku-ku	(111,095)	100.0	50.2	49.8	4.9	4.8	6.1	5.9	5.3	5.1	5.0	4.6	5.4	4.5	4.6	4.5	3.4	3.9	2.9	3.3	3.1	3.2	2.3	2.4	2.2	2.0	1.7	1.7	1.3	1.3	0.9	1.1	0.6	0.8	0.5	0.9	—	—
		Inagi-machi	(10,086)	100.0	50.3	49.7	5.5	4.9	6.6	6.6	6.4	5.7	4.6	4.3	4.2	3.8	3.9	3.5	3.2	4.1	3.1	3.7	3.1	3.2	2.5	2.4	2.1	1.6	1.5	1.9	1.2	1.3	1.0	1.2	0.7	1.0	0.7	0.9	—	—
	III	Tama-mura	(7,600)	100.0	50.4	49.6	4.3	4.7	5.9	5.8	5.5	5.1	4.7	4.5	5.6	4.7	4.5	4.4	3.4	3.6	2.6	3.4	2.9	3.1	2.5	2.4	2.5	2.0	2.1	1.9	1.6	1.3	0.9	0.9	0.6	0.6	0.8	0.8	—	—
		Fuchu-shi	(58,937)	100.0	53.5	46.5	5.1	4.8	6.0	5.9	4.8	4.8	4.4	4.0	5.8	4.3	6.3	4.6	4.8	4.2	3.9	3.4	3.5	2.7	2.8	2.0	2.1	1.6	1.5	1.2	1.1	0.9	0.7	0.9	0.4	0.6	0.3	0.6	—	—
		Kunitachi-machi	(23,125)	100.0	51.4	48.6	4.9	4.8	5.8	5.8	5.0	4.5	5.3	4.2	7.1	5.1	5.6	5.2	3.7	4.7	3.3	3.3	3.3	2.6	2.6	2.1	1.8	1.7	1.3	1.3	0.8	1.0	0.7	0.7	0.4	0.6	0.3	0.6	—	—
		Kokubunji-machi	(25,755)	100.0	52.2	47.8	4.4	4.1	5.8	5.3	5.3	4.9	5.5	4.6	7.6	4.4	6.0	4.9	3.8	3.9	3.0	3.4	2.9	2.9	2.3	2.3	1.9	1.8	1.4	1.4	1.0	1.2	0.8	0.8	0.4	0.6	0.3	0.6	—	—
		Kodaira-machi	(29,175)	100.0	52.0	48.0	5.1	4.6	6.2	5.6	5.4	4.8	4.8	4.6	6.0	5.2	5.2	4.5	4.4	4.5	4.0	3.3	3.0	2.5	2.1	2.3	1.8	1.5	1.3	1.4	1.0	1.3	0.8	1.1	0.5	0.8	0.4	0.6	—	—
		Higashimurayama-machi	(24,102)	100.0	51.0	49.0	5.4	5.3	5.9	5.7	5.5	4.7	4.5	4.1	4.2	4.5	4.9	5.0	4.4	4.3	3.7	3.3	2.6	2.8	2.6	2.6	2.0	1.8	1.7	1.4	1.2	1.3	0.8	0.8	0.6	0.8	0.4	1.0	—	—
	IV	Tokorosawa-shi	(56,249)	100.0	49.1	50.9	5.7	5.6	6.3	6.2	5.4	5.4	5.1	4.9	4.5	4.8	4.0	4.3	3.1	3.8	2.7	2.7	2.6	2.8	2.3	2.3	1.9	1.9	1.7	1.7	1.4	1.4	1.1	1.2	0.7	0.9	0.5	1.0	—	—
		Miyoshi-mura	(4,342)	100.0	49.8	50.2	5.8	5.7	6.7	5.7	5.2	5.2	5.3	5.1	5.0	4.7	4.4	4.4	2.9	3.1	2.2	3.0	2.3	2.6	2.0	1.8	2.2	2.1	1.7	1.8	1.6	1.5	1.3	1.4	0.8	1.3	0.6	1.2	—	—
		Fujimi-mura	(10,772)	100.0	49.7	50.3	6.0	5.5	6.4	6.2	5.2	5.3	4.8	4.9	4.5	4.6	4.0	3.7	3.1	3.4	2.6	3.0	2.4	2.6	2.0	2.4	2.2	2.1	1.8	1.7	1.7	1.6	1.2	1.3	0.8	1.0	0.6	1.1	—	—
	V	Yono-shi	(35,162)	100.0	49.7	50.3	5.1	4.8	6.5	6.2	5.3	5.4	4.7	4.9	4.6	4.7	4.7	4.6	3.6	4.3	3.0	3.5	3.2	3.1	2.7	2.4	2.1	1.8	1.5	1.4	1.1	1.1	0.8	0.8	0.4	0.5	0.3	0.6	—	—
		Ōmiya-shi	(144,540)	100.0	49.5	50.5	5.1	4.8	6.2	6.1	5.5	5.2	4.8	4.7	4.7	4.9	4.6	4.6	3.4	4.0	3.0	3.5	3.0	3.1	2.4	2.3	2.2	1.9	1.7	1.7	1.4	1.2	0.9	1.0	0.5	0.7	0.4	0.7	—	—
	VI	Iwatsuki-shi	(34,977)	100.0	49.1	50.9	5.6	5.4	6.9	6.6	5.7	5.5	4.8	4.7	4.3	4.6	3.9	3.7	2.7	3.4	2.6	3.0	2.5	3.0	2.3	2.2	2.2	2.1	1.9	1.8	1.4	1.5	1.1	1.4	0.6	0.9	0.5	0.9	—	—
	VII	Matsubushi-mura	(8,995)	100.0	49.1	50.9	6.1	6.1	6.8	6.5	5.5	5.4	4.8	5.3	4.0	3.3	4.0	3.3	2.3	3.1	2.2	2.7	2.4	3.0	2.6	2.5	2.2	2.1	1.7	1.7	1.6	1.5	1.3	1.3	0.8	1.1	0.6	1.0	—	—
		Kashiwa-shi	(45,020)	100.0	49.8	50.2	5.7	5.5	6.6	6.5	5.5	5.3	5.0	4.9	4.5	4.5	4.3	4.5	3.5	3.8	3.0	3.2	2.7	3.2	2.4	2.4	1.7	1.7	1.6	1.6	1.3	1.2	0.9	1.0	0.5	0.8	0.4	0.7	—	—
		Shōnan-mura	(10,911)	100.0	49.4	50.6	6.1	5.8	6.4	6.0	4.9	5.2	4.6	5.0	4.8	4.8	4.2	4.0	2.9	3.6	2.4	2.9	2.4	2.6	2.3	2.2	2.5	2.0	1.9	2.0	1.7	1.8	1.1	1.5	0.8	1.1	0.8	1.1	—	—
		Shirai-mura	(8,486)	100.0	49.5	50.5	5.9	5.7	6.1	6.1	5.2	5.2	4.7	4.8	4.4	4.4	3.6	3.6	2.9	3.1	2.5	3.1	2.4	2.8	2.1	2.2	2.2	2.2	2.1	1.8	1.8	1.8	1.3	1.3	0.7	0.9	0.6	1.2	—	—
	VIII	Narashino-shi	(32,198)	100.0	50.5	49.5	4.6	4.9	5.9	5.7	5.3	5.5	5.5	4.8	6.5	6.1	4.3	4.2	3.2	3.9	3.0	3.4	3.1	3.1	2.4	2.5	2.2	1.8	1.5	1.3	1.0	1.1	0.8	0.9	0.5	0.7	0.4	0.7	—	—
		Zone 6 Total	(1,030,695)	100.0	50.5	49.5	5.0	4.7	6.0	5.8	5.1	5.0	4.9	4.6	5.5	4.8	5.0	4.7	3.6	4.1	3.0	3.3	3.1	2.9	2.4	2.4	2.2	1.8	1.7	1.6	1.3	1.2	0.9	1.0	0.5	0.7	0.4	0.7	—	—
7	I	Isogo-ku	(67,991)	100.0	49.4	50.6	4.3	4.0	5.8	5.5	5.0	4.5	4.7	4.6	5.3	5.1	5.1	4.9	3.5	4.1	2.8	3.4	2.8	3.1	2.5	2.5	2.4	2.2	1.8	1.8	1.4	1.4	0.9	1.1	0.5	0.8	0.4	0.7	—	—
		Minami-ku	(171,525)	100.0	50.8	49.2	4.6	4.3	5.5	5.2	4.6	4.5	4.8	4.4	5.6	5.3	5.6	5.1	4.0	4.1	3.0	3.4	2.9	2.9	2.5	2.4	2.2	2.2	1.9	1.8	1.4	1.3	0.9	0.9	0.5	0.6	0.3	0.6	—	—
		Hodogaya-ku	(96,822)	100.0	50.4	49.6	5.2	4.8	6.0	5.7	5.0	5.0	4.8	4.4	5.4	4.9	5.2	5.0	3.9	4.1	3.0	3.2	2.8	2.8	2.3	2.3	2.1	2.0	1.7	1.6	1.2	1.3	0.9	1.0	0.5	0.7	0.4	0.7	—	—
		Machida-shi	(58,342)	100.0	49.9	50.1	5.3	5.1	6.2	5.6	5.5	5.5	5.1	5.0	5.1	4.6	4.4	4.2	3.2	3.7	2.7	3.3	3.0	3.0	2.4	2.4	2.1	1.8	1.7	1.6	1.3	1.3	1.0	1.0	0.5	0.7	0.5	0.8	—	—
	II	Yuki-mura	(6,285)	100.0	50.3	49.7	5.5	5.4	6.6	6.1	6.2	5.2	5.1	4.6	4.6	4.5	3.8	3.0	2.2	3.3	2.4	3.0	2.5	3.1	2.4	2.3	2.3	2.0	1.7	1.7	1.5	1.7	1.5	1.4	1.1	1.1	0.9	1.3	—	—
		Hino-machi	(27,305)	100.0	50.2	49.8	5.1	4.8	6.8	6.3	5.9	5.5	4.9	4.5	4.8	4.6	4.4	4.3	3.4	4.1	3.0	3.5	2.8	3.2	2.5	2.3	2.1	1.8	1.6	1.4	1.0	1.0	0.8	0.9	0.5	0.7	0.3	0.7	—	—
		Tachikawa-shi	(63,644)	100.0	50.3	49.7	4.8	4.3	5.9	5.4	5.0	4.9	5.0	4.7	6.8	6.1	5.8	5.7	3.4	4.2	2.9	3.4	2.8	3.4	2.4	2.3	2.0	1.8	1.5	1.3	0.9	1.0	0.6	0.7	0.3	0.5	0.2	0.5	—	—
	III	Sunakawa-machi	(12,669)	100.0	49.9	50.1	5.5	5.7	7.3	6.5	6.2	6.8	4.8	4.5	4.2	4.2	4.2	4.0	3.3	3.6	2.8	3.4	2.9	2.9	2.5	2.3	2.0	1.6	1.3	1.4	1.0	0.9	0.8	1.1	0.5	0.8	0.5	0.9	—	—
		Yamato-machi	(12,975)	100.0	50.0	50.0	5.7	5.4	7.0	7.2	6.2	5.9	4.4	4.6	4.6	3.8	3.8	3.9	3.2	3.4	2.9	3.5	3.1	3.2	2.7	2.7	2.2	1.7	1.6	1.4	1.1	1.1	0.9	1.0	0.5	0.8	0.5	0.9	—	—

Table 3. Population by Age (5-Year Bracket) and Sex

(Zone)	(Sector)	District	Total	M	F	Age 0-4 M	F	Age 5-9 M	F	Age 10-14 M	F	Age 15-19 M	F	Age 20-24 M	F	Age 25-29 M	F	Age 30-34 M	F	Age 35-39 M	F	Age 40-44 M	F	Age 45-49 M	F	Age 50-54 M	F	Age 55-59 M	F	Age 60-64 M	F	Age 65-69 M	F	Age 70-74 M	F	75 & over M	F	Unknown M	F
7	IV	Ōi-mura	4,794 100.0	50.2	49.8	5.3	5.6	6.2	6.5	5.7	5.4	4.5	4.6	5.4	3.9	5.1	4.0	3.2	3.6	2.9	3.0	2.6	2.7	2.2	2.0	1.8	1.8	1.6	1.7	1.3	1.4	1.3	1.3	0.6	1.0	0.5	1.3	—	—
		Fukuoka-mura	7,820 100.0	49.9	50.1	5.8	5.5	6.1	6.8	6.1	5.9	4.5	5.0	3.7	4.2	3.9	4.2	3.3	3.5	3.1	3.8	3.2	3.2	2.6	2.2	2.1	1.5	1.4	1.3	1.0	0.9	0.8	1.0	0.6	0.5	0.4	0.6	—	—
	V	Kasukabe-shi	32,517 100.0	49.4	50.6	6.1	5.5	6.9	6.4	5.5	5.6	4.7	4.6	4.5	4.5	4.0	3.8	2.8	3.5	2.4	3.0	2.6	3.1	2.4	2.5	2.2	2.1	1.8	1.6	1.3	1.5	1.2	1.2	0.6	0.8	0.4	0.9	—	—
		Shōwa-mura	14,781 100.0	49.0	51.0	6.0	6.3	7.3	7.0	5.9	5.7	4.2	4.7	4.1	4.1	3.8	3.5	2.6	3.3	2.6	3.0	2.6	2.9	2.3	2.3	1.9	1.8	1.8	1.6	1.5	1.5	1.2	1.3	0.7	1.0	0.5	1.0	—	—
	VI	Noda-shi	52,886 100.0	48.5	51.5	5.3	5.3	6.5	6.0	5.4	5.3	4.5	5.1	4.5	4.6	4.1	4.2	2.9	3.6	2.6	3.0	2.6	3.1	2.3	2.8	2.3	2.2	1.8	1.8	1.4	1.5	1.1	1.3	0.6	0.9	0.6	0.9	—	—
	VII	Abiko-machi	24,918 100.0	48.6	51.4	5.1	5.2	6.2	6.5	5.6	5.4	4.9	5.3	4.6	4.6	4.1	3.9	2.9	3.7	2.9	3.3	2.6	3.1	2.6	2.7	2.3	2.0	1.7	1.6	1.1	1.5	1.1	1.2	0.6	0.8	0.4	0.8	—	—
		Yachiyo-machi	15,315 100.0	48.9	51.1	5.5	5.2	6.3	5.8	5.5	5.5	4.6	5.0	4.3	4.7	4.2	3.6	2.8	3.6	2.6	3.2	2.7	3.1	2.2	2.2	2.1	2.0	2.0	1.9	1.5	1.7	1.4	1.6	0.6	0.8	0.6	1.2	—	—
	VIII	Chiba-shi	197,962 100.0	50.1	49.9	4.8	4.6	6.0	5.8	5.3	5.1	4.7	4.7	5.6	4.9	5.0	4.5	3.6	4.0	3.0	3.4	2.9	3.0	2.5	2.4	2.1	2.0	1.6	1.6	1.1	1.2	0.9	1.1	0.5	0.8	0.6	0.8	—	—
	IX	Goi-machi	17,955 100.0	48.4	51.6	4.8	4.7	6.0	5.7	5.3	5.5	4.6	5.1	4.5	4.8	3.7	4.1	3.0	3.5	2.5	3.2	2.5	3.1	2.3	2.4	2.1	2.3	1.9	1.8	1.4	1.4	1.1	1.1	0.7	1.0	0.8	1.2	—	—
		Sodegaura-machi	13,874 100.0	48.8	51.2	5.0	4.9	6.3	6.1	6.1	6.2	5.2	5.1	4.5	4.3	3.8	3.8	2.6	3.6	2.5	2.8	2.5	3.2	2.4	2.0	2.2	2.3	1.9	1.8	1.2	1.5	1.1	1.0	0.7	1.0	0.7	1.3	—	—
		Zone 7 Total	900,380 100.0	49.9	50.1	4.9	4.7	6.0	5.8	5.2	5.1	4.8	4.7	5.4	5.0	4.9	4.6	3.5	3.9	2.9	3.3	2.8	3.0	2.4	2.4	2.2	2.0	1.7	1.7	1.2	1.3	0.9	1.1	0.5	0.7	0.4	0.8	—	—
8	I	Kanazawa-ku	63,974 100.0	51.0	49.0	5.1	4.6	6.9	6.5	5.8	5.4	4.5	4.1	5.3	4.0	4.6	4.5	3.6	4.3	3.4	3.8	3.5	3.2	2.6	2.3	2.1	1.7	1.4	1.3	0.9	1.1	0.6	0.9	0.4	0.7	0.3	0.6	—	—
		Totsuka-ku	82,064 100.0	50.4	49.6	5.3	5.0	6.7	6.4	5.5	5.2	4.6	4.5	5.1	4.4	4.8	4.6	3.5	4.0	3.1	3.4	3.0	3.0	2.4	2.2	2.0	1.8	1.5	1.5	1.1	1.1	0.8	1.0	0.5	0.7	0.5	0.8	—	—
	II	Yamato-shi	24,981 100.0	48.1	51.9	5.9	5.5	7.0	6.9	5.1	5.1	4.2	4.1	3.8	5.8	4.5	5.6	3.7	4.5	3.3	3.7	2.6	3.0	2.2	1.9	1.8	1.6	1.8	1.3	0.8	1.0	0.7	0.7	0.4	0.6	0.3	0.6	—	—
		Sagamihara-shi	83,841 100.0	50.3	49.7	6.0	5.4	6.4	6.3	5.2	5.2	4.8	4.4	4.9	4.8	4.9	4.9	3.7	4.1	3.1	3.4	2.8	2.8	2.3	2.3	1.8	1.7	1.3	1.3	0.8	0.9	0.6	0.8	0.4	0.7	0.4	0.7	—	—
		Zama-machi	13,197 100.0	48.8	51.2	5.3	5.5	6.5	6.1	5.4	5.3	4.8	4.9	4.8	5.4	4.3	5.0	3.3	4.0	2.6	3.0	2.5	2.8	2.5	2.4	2.0	1.9	1.6	1.5	1.3	1.2	1.0	1.0	0.5	0.6	0.5	0.8	—	—
	III	Hachiōji-shi	141,846 100.0	49.2	50.8	5.0	5.1	5.7	5.7	5.2	5.2	4.8	5.0	4.9	5.1	5.0	3.8	3.4	3.9	2.7	3.2	2.6	2.9	2.4	1.9	2.2	1.4	1.6	1.8	1.3	1.3	1.0	1.1	0.6	0.9	0.5	0.8	—	—
		Akishima-shi	38,519 100.0	49.4	50.6	5.6	5.6	7.0	6.7	5.5	5.5	4.2	4.1	4.4	4.7	4.5	5.3	3.7	4.7	3.5	3.9	2.8	2.8	2.4	1.8	1.7	1.4	1.3	1.2	0.9	0.9	0.6	0.8	0.4	0.6	0.4	0.6	—	—
		Fussa-machi	19,096 100.0	50.8	49.2	5.9	5.2	6.0	5.5	4.8	4.7	4.6	4.6	5.9	6.0	6.1	5.9	4.4	4.3	2.9	3.4	2.6	2.6	2.4	1.8	1.7	1.7	1.1	1.3	0.9	0.9	0.6	0.7	0.3	0.5	0.3	0.6	—	—
		Mizuho-machi	9,607 100.0	49.0	51.0	5.7	5.8	6.4	6.0	5.7	5.8	5.1	5.3	4.7	4.5	3.9	3.8	3.2	3.6	2.5	3.1	2.8	3.0	2.2	2.3	2.2	1.8	1.6	1.6	1.3	1.4	1.2	1.2	0.6	0.9	0.6	1.1	—	—
		Murayama-machi	11,799 100.0	49.5	50.5	5.8	4.9	5.8	6.3	5.8	5.6	4.7	5.3	5.0	5.1	4.5	4.2	3.2	3.8	2.7	2.7	2.4	2.7	2.3	2.1	1.7	1.8	1.7	1.5	1.3	1.4	1.0	1.3	0.7	0.9	0.6	1.2	—	—
		Musashi-machi	27,673 100.0	48.6	51.4	5.7	5.5	6.2	6.3	5.6	5.6	4.9	4.8	4.7	4.7	4.0	4.0	3.1	3.9	2.7	3.0	2.4	3.0	2.2	2.0	1.7	1.8	1.5	1.8	1.6	1.5	1.3	1.3	0.7	1.0	0.6	1.1	—	—
	IV	Sayama-shi	31,341 100.0	49.2	50.8	5.4	5.2	6.3	5.9	5.5	5.5	4.8	5.2	4.4	4.8	4.1	3.2	3.0	3.7	2.3	3.0	2.6	2.9	2.2	2.3	2.2	2.0	1.7	1.7	1.6	1.6	1.1	1.3	0.7	1.0	0.5	0.9	—	—
		Kawagoe-shi	104,612 100.0	46.8	53.2	5.2	5.0	6.6	6.2	5.6	5.6	4.9	4.8	4.0	6.2	4.0	4.0	2.8	3.3	2.7	3.3	2.4	3.0	2.4	2.3	2.2	2.0	1.7	1.8	1.4	1.5	1.1	1.4	0.6	0.9	0.5	0.9	—	—
		Seibu-machi	9,155 100.0	49.3	50.7	5.5	4.9	5.9	5.6	5.6	5.4	4.7	4.9	4.6	4.7	4.0	3.9	2.9	3.7	2.6	3.1	2.4	2.6	2.1	2.3	1.8	1.8	1.8	1.5	1.3	1.4	1.0	1.0	0.7	1.0	0.5	0.8	—	—
	V	Ageo-shi	35,480 100.0	49.3	50.7	5.3	5.2	6.7	6.3	5.8	5.8	4.9	5.2	5.0	4.8	4.2	4.0	2.9	3.7	2.8	3.2	2.8	2.9	2.2	2.3	2.0	1.8	1.6	1.7	1.7	1.7	1.1	1.3	0.7	1.0	0.5	0.8	—	—
		Ina-mura	7,036 100.0	49.9	50.1	5.7	4.9	6.3	6.0	6.0	5.7	4.9	5.2	4.7	4.9	4.3	4.2	3.3	3.4	2.6	3.1	2.4	2.6	2.4	2.2	2.1	2.3	2.1	1.8	1.7	1.7	1.1	1.1	0.8	1.1	0.7	1.4	—	—
		Hasuda-machi	19,311 100.0	49.5	50.5	5.4	4.9	6.6	6.2	5.5	5.6	5.0	4.8	4.4	4.5	4.0	3.6	2.8	3.3	2.5	3.0	2.4	2.9	2.4	2.3	2.0	1.9	1.8	1.6	1.6	1.6	1.1	1.3	0.7	0.8	0.9	1.0	—	—
		Shiraoka-machi	15,655 100.0	49.8	50.2	5.9	5.3	6.6	6.5	5.9	5.6	4.8	5.0	4.4	4.5	4.0	3.6	2.8	3.3	2.3	3.0	2.6	2.9	2.4	2.3	2.2	1.9	1.8	1.5	1.4	1.4	1.3	1.3	0.7	0.9	0.5	1.2	—	—
		Miyashiro-machi	10,755 100.0	49.3	50.7	6.2	5.8	6.9	6.8	5.3	5.3	4.5	5.1	4.4	4.4	4.3	4.0	2.7	3.2	2.3	2.8	2.6	2.9	2.4	2.3	2.1	2.2	1.8	1.4	1.4	1.4	1.2	1.4	0.8	1.0	0.6	0.9	—	—
		Sugito-machi	17,297 100.0	49.2	50.8	5.8	5.7	6.8	6.2	5.4	5.4	5.4	5.4	4.2	4.1	3.7	3.6	2.6	3.3	2.6	2.7	2.5	2.6	1.9	2.8	2.0	2.1	2.0	1.7	1.8	1.8	1.2	1.4	1.3	1.0	0.5	1.1	—	—
	VI	Sekiyado-machi	13,795 100.0	47.8	52.2	6.3	6.1	7.0	6.8	5.5	5.8	4.2	5.1	3.4	4.0	3.4	3.4	2.6	3.5	2.6	2.7	2.5	2.6	2.3	2.2	2.1	2.1	2.1	1.7	1.8	1.8	1.4	1.5	0.8	1.1	0.8	1.2	—	—
		Moriya-machi	12,095 100.0	48.6	51.4	5.8	5.5	6.9	6.5	5.6	5.6	4.3	4.4	3.6	4.0	3.7	3.8	2.8	3.7	2.3	2.8	2.6	3.0	2.5	2.8	2.3	2.2	1.9	1.9	1.4	1.5	1.3	1.3	0.7	1.3	0.8	1.2	—	—
	VII	Toride-machi	21,233 100.0	48.8	51.2	4.9	4.8	6.2	6.0	5.6	5.6	4.7	4.9	4.6	4.6	3.9	4.0	2.9	3.7	2.6	3.2	2.8	3.3	2.8	2.7	2.3	2.2	1.9	1.7	1.4	1.4	1.0	1.3	0.6	1.0	0.6	1.0	—	—

Table 3. Population By Age (5-Year Bracket) and Sex

(Zone)	(Sector)	District	Total	M	F	0-4 M	0-4 F	5-9 M	5-9 F	10-14 M	10-14 F	15-19 M	15-19 F	20-24 M	20-24 F	25-29 M	25-29 F	30-34 M	30-34 F	35-39 M	35-39 F	40-44 M	40-44 F	45-49 M	45-49 F	50-54 M	50-54 F	55-59 M	55-59 F	60-64 M	60-64 F	65-69 M	65-69 F	70-74 M	70-74 F	75 & over M	75 & over F	Unknown M	Unknown F
	VII	Inzai-machi	(17,898)100.0	49.4	50.6	5.5	5.0	6.4	6.0	5.7	5.5	4.7	4.5	4.4	4.5	3.7	3.6	2.9	3.4	2.6	3.2	2.8	3.0	2.4	2.5	2.4	2.4	1.9	1.9	1.4	1.5	1.2	1.4	0.7	1.0	0.7	1.2	—	—
		Inba-mura	(8,340)100.0	48.0	52.0	4.7	4.6	5.2	5.9	4.6	4.7	3.8	4.3	4.2	3.8	3.8	3.8	3.0	3.9	2.8	3.0	2.6	2.9	2.6	2.4	2.6	2.9	2.8	2.7	1.6	1.9	1.6	1.8	1.0	1.4	1.1	2.0	—	—
	VIII	Yotsukaidō-machi	(18,014)100.0	49.0	51.0	5.5	4.9	6.3	6.0	5.3	5.4	4.7	5.1	4.3	4.8	4.4	4.0	3.0	3.6	2.7	3.3	2.7	3.0	2.4	2.4	2.3	2.2	1.8	1.9	1.4	1.3	1.1	1.2	0.6	0.9	0.5	1.0	—	—
	IX	Ichihara-machi	(14,450)100.0	49.1	50.9	5.2	4.9	6.3	5.7	5.7	5.7	5.1	4.9	4.3	4.1	3.8	3.9	2.7	3.5	2.6	3.0	2.7	2.9	2.5	2.6	2.4	2.2	1.9	2.0	1.4	1.7	1.0	1.3	0.7	1.2	0.8	1.3	—	—
		Anegasaki-machi	(11,323)100.0	48.4	51.6	5.2	4.9	6.1	6.4	5.8	5.7	4.6	4.8	4.2	4.0	3.7	3.8	2.9	3.5	2.5	3.1	2.4	3.1	2.3	2.6	2.6	2.4	1.9	1.9	1.4	1.4	1.2	1.3	0.8	1.1	0.8	1.4	—	—
		Hirakawa-machi	(11,637)100.0	47.8	52.2	5.6	5.3	6.0	6.4	5.2	5.6	4.4	4.6	4.0	4.3	3.5	3.9	2.9	3.4	2.4	2.7	2.3	3.1	2.4	2.2	2.2	2.3	2.1	2.3	1.7	1.4	1.3	1.8	0.8	1.2	1.0	1.7	—	—
		Miwa-machi	(11,438)100.0	48.5	51.5	5.3	5.4	5.9	6.2	6.1	5.8	4.5	4.5	3.9	4.4	3.5	3.8	2.6	3.0	2.4	3.3	2.6	2.8	2.4	2.5	2.4	2.3	2.2	2.0	1.6	1.7	1.4	1.6	0.9	1.1	1.0	1.5	—	—
	X	Kisarazu-shi	(51,741)100.0	48.0	52.0	4.9	4.8	6.5	6.1	5.6	5.5	4.4	4.9	4.0	4.6	3.8	4.3	2.8	3.8	2.6	3.2	2.7	3.1	2.4	2.7	2.3	2.3	2.0	1.8	1.4	1.5	1.2	1.3	0.7	1.0	0.7	1.1	—	—
		Zone 8 Total	(959,223)100.0	49.4	50.6	5.4	5.1	6.4	6.1	5.5	5.3	4.7	4.8	4.7	4.7	3.4	4.3	3.2	3.8	2.8	3.2	2.8	2.9	2.4	2.3	2.1	1.9	1.7	1.6	1.3	1.3	1.0	1.1	0.6	0.8	0.5	0.9	—	—
9	I	Kamakura-shi	(91,328)100.0	48.6	51.4	3.8	3.6	5.8	5.2	5.3	5.1	4.9	5.1	4.9	5.0	4.4	4.7	3.3	4.1	2.8	3.5	3.0	3.4	2.7	2.9	2.4	2.4	2.0	2.0	1.3	1.4	1.0	1.2	0.6	0.9	0.5	0.9	—	—
	II	Ayase-machi	(8,221)100.0	50.0	50.0	5.4	5.4	6.8	6.3	5.5	5.5	5.2	5.0	5.3	4.5	3.9	3.8	2.8	3.3	2.8	3.0	2.0	2.5	2.3	2.3	2.3	2.1	1.8	1.4	1.4	1.5	1.2	1.4	0.7	0.9	0.7	1.3	—	—
		Ebina-machi	(16,535)100.0	50.1	49.9	5.3	5.3	6.5	6.1	6.2	5.4	5.3	5.6	4.9	4.5	4.3	3.9	2.8	3.3	2.4	3.0	2.5	2.8	2.2	2.1	2.1	2.1	1.8	1.7	1.5	1.2	1.0	1.1	0.7	0.8	0.6	1.0	—	—
		Shiroyama-machi	(4,932)100.0	49.5	50.5	5.3	5.0	6.2	6.2	5.5	5.2	4.5	4.9	4.7	4.6	4.6	4.2	2.8	3.1	2.6	3.0	2.4	2.7	1.9	2.4	2.3	2.0	2.1	2.2	1.5	1.6	1.5	1.1	0.7	1.1	1.1	1.2	—	—
	III	Akita-machi	(13,885)100.0	50.4	49.6	5.3	4.8	6.4	5.7	5.6	5.5	5.1	4.4	4.6	4.6	4.0	3.9	3.1	3.5	2.5	3.1	2.7	2.7	2.1	2.1	2.1	2.0	2.1	2.0	1.8	1.5	1.5	1.4	0.8	1.1	1.1	1.3	—	—
		Hamura-machi	(10,104)100.0	50.0	50.0	5.4	5.0	6.0	5.8	5.0	5.3	5.6	4.6	5.3	5.5	5.2	5.0	3.3	3.6	2.4	3.1	2.6	2.5	2.1	1.9	1.9	1.8	1.5	1.6	1.5	1.5	0.9	1.0	0.6	0.7	0.6	0.9	—	—
	IV	Hannō-shi	(43,436)100.0	48.9	51.1	5.3	5.0	6.0	5.9	5.7	5.4	4.5	4.5	4.0	4.5	4.1	4.0	3.1	3.9	2.7	3.0	2.5	2.9	2.2	2.3	2.3	2.2	2.0	1.9	1.6	1.6	1.3	1.4	0.8	1.1	0.8	1.2	—	—
		Tsurugashima-mura	(6,976)100.0	50.7	49.3	5.4	5.1	6.1	6.2	6.4	5.3	5.1	5.1	4.3	4.2	4.0	3.4	2.8	3.3	2.2	2.7	2.6	3.2	2.5	2.2	2.1	2.3	2.1	1.7	1.4	1.3	1.1	1.3	0.9	1.1	0.8	1.1	—	—
		Hidaka-machi	(16,776)100.0	50.3	49.7	5.9	5.3	6.5	6.3	5.4	5.6	4.5	3.9	4.0	4.1	4.2	4.0	3.1	3.5	2.6	3.2	2.7	2.7	2.3	2.3	2.2	2.1	2.0	2.0	1.6	1.6	1.1	1.4	0.9	1.2	0.8	1.2	—	—
		Kawashima-mura	(17,597)100.0	48.2	51.8	5.7	5.6	6.6	6.5	5.4	5.4	5.1	4.9	4.2	4.8	3.5	3.4	2.6	3.1	2.3	2.8	2.6	3.0	2.3	2.4	2.2	2.2	1.8	2.0	1.5	1.7	1.1	1.4	0.7	1.2	0.6	1.2	—	—
	V	Kitamoto-machi	(14,263)100.0	50.1	49.9	6.2	5.8	7.2	7.1	6.1	5.8	4.4	4.3	4.0	4.4	4.4	4.0	2.9	3.5	3.0	3.3	2.7	2.8	2.4	2.4	1.9	1.7	1.6	1.5	1.2	1.1	0.8	0.8	0.6	0.9	0.5	0.8	—	—
		Higawa-machi	(19,705)100.0	49.0	51.0	5.3	5.3	6.7	6.9	6.0	5.9	4.7	4.6	4.4	4.6	4.1	3.9	2.9	3.5	2.6	3.0	2.9	2.9	2.3	2.2	2.1	2.0	1.8	1.5	1.2	1.4	0.9	1.2	0.7	1.0	0.4	0.9	—	—
		Shobu-machi	(16,718)100.0	49.5	50.5	5.8	5.3	7.0	6.2	5.4	5.2	4.6	5.3	4.5	4.3	3.6	3.5	2.6	3.3	2.2	2.6	2.3	2.8	2.2	2.4	2.2	2.1	1.8	2.0	1.7	1.8	1.4	1.4	0.9	1.2	0.8	1.1	—	—
		Kuki-machi	(22,082)100.0	49.5	50.5	5.9	5.8	7.1	6.5	5.3	5.3	4.7	4.8	4.3	4.6	4.1	4.2	3.2	3.5	2.3	3.1	2.4	2.4	2.2	2.3	2.2	2.3	1.8	1.8	1.4	1.4	1.2	1.4	0.7	0.8	0.5	0.8	—	—
		Satte-machi	(24,460)100.0	48.5	51.5	5.4	5.3	6.9	6.5	5.8	5.4	4.5	5.4	3.4	4.6	3.8	3.6	2.7	3.2	2.1	2.8	2.4	3.0	2.3	2.4	2.2	2.3	2.0	1.9	1.7	1.4	1.2	1.4	0.8	1.0	0.6	1.1	—	—
	VI	Iwai-machi	(35,154)100.0	48.6	51.4	6.0	5.7	6.8	6.5	5.7	5.6	4.3	4.8	3.8	4.1	3.8	4.2	2.9	3.4	2.4	3.1	2.8	2.8	2.3	2.5	2.4	2.1	2.0	2.0	1.7	1.7	1.3	1.3	0.8	0.9	0.8	1.5	—	—
		Mitsukaidō-shi	(39,971)100.0	48.0	52.0	5.0	5.2	6.5	6.4	5.7	5.6	4.3	4.9	3.8	4.2	3.6	3.6	2.9	3.6	2.5	3.0	2.7	3.1	2.6	2.4	2.3	2.2	2.1	2.1	1.7	1.8	1.2	1.5	0.8	1.0	0.7	1.3	—	—
		Yawahara-mura	(11,564)100.0	48.4	51.6	4.9	4.5	6.1	6.2	5.8	5.6	4.4	4.8	3.8	3.9	3.6	3.6	2.8	3.6	2.5	3.0	3.3	3.3	2.5	2.6	2.3	2.3	2.0	2.0	1.8	2.2	1.4	1.6	0.8	0.8	0.8	1.5	—	—
		Ina-mura	(12,568)100.0	48.3	51.7	4.6	5.0	6.5	6.0	4.9	5.2	4.7	4.3	4.2	4.6	3.7	3.6	2.8	3.4	2.3	2.8	2.8	3.5	2.8	2.6	2.2	2.1	2.1	2.6	1.9	2.1	1.5	1.7	0.7	1.0	0.8	1.4	—	—
	VII	Fujishiro-machi	(12,941)100.0	48.3	51.7	4.9	4.8	5.9	5.9	5.4	5.9	4.4	5.1	4.1	4.3	4.2	3.7	2.7	3.4	2.4	2.8	2.9	3.5	2.4	2.8	2.2	2.1	2.1	2.3	1.8	1.8	1.1	1.5	0.6	1.0	0.8	1.2	—	—
		Ryūgasaki-shi	(34,337)100.0	48.4	51.6	4.8	4.9	6.3	6.1	5.9	5.8	4.4	4.8	4.1	4.3	3.8	3.7	2.6	3.5	2.6	3.4	3.1	3.4	2.5	3.4	2.1	2.4	2.0	1.9	1.5	1.5	1.1	1.4	0.6	0.7	0.7	1.1	—	—
		Tone-mura	(9,746)100.0	48.4	51.6	5.5	5.4	6.0	6.2	5.4	5.4	4.4	5.2	4.3	4.5	3.7	4.0	2.9	3.3	2.3	3.2	2.6	3.1	2.5	2.7	2.1	2.4	2.4	2.3	1.7	1.7	1.5	1.2	0.6	1.1	0.7	1.4	—	—
		Motono-mura	(5,470)100.0	49.2	50.8	5.0	4.4	6.4	6.0	6.0	6.0	4.8	5.4	4.2	4.6	3.2	4.0	2.4	3.7	2.6	3.8	3.0	3.1	2.6	2.5	2.6	2.3	1.9	1.8	1.7	1.7	1.5	1.7	0.6	1.1	0.9	1.2	—	—
	VIII	Sakura-shi	(35,464)100.0	48.8	51.2	5.1	4.8	5.9	6.0	5.4	5.4	4.7	4.6	4.2	4.2	4.0	4.0	3.2	3.8	2.7	3.1	2.5	3.1	2.4	2.6	2.4	2.2	2.2	1.8	1.5	1.6	1.2	1.6	0.7	1.1	0.6	1.3	—	—
		Izumi-machi	(9,745)100.0	48.8	51.2	5.4	5.2	6.5	6.2	5.7	5.2	4.0	4.3	3.9	4.0	3.6	4.0	2.9	3.4	2.7	3.2	2.4	3.2	2.2	2.4	2.4	2.2	2.2	2.1	1.9	1.9	1.4	1.7	0.8	1.1	0.8	1.5	—	—

Table 3. Population by Age (5-Year Bracket) and Sex

(Zone)	(Sector)	District	Total	M	F	0–4 M	0–4 F	5–9 M	5–9 F	10–14 M	10–14 F	15–19 M	15–19 F	20–24 M	20–24 F	25–29 M	25–29 F	30–34 M	30–34 F	35–39 M	35–39 F	40–44 M	40–44 F	45–49 M	45–49 F	50–54 M	50–54 F	55–59 M	55–59 F	60–64 M	60–64 F	65–69 M	65–69 F	70–74 M	70–74 F	75 & Over M	75 & Over F	Unknown M	Unknown F
	IX	Shitsu-mura	(9,703)100.0	48.7	51.3	5.4	5.3	6.3	6.0	6.0	5.6	4.6	5.2	4.1	4.1	3.6	3.9	2.9	3.1	2.3	3.1	2.2	2.9	2.4	2.3	2.1	2.3	2.3	2.3	1.7	1.6	1.0	1.2	0.7	1.1	1.1	1.6	—	—
		Nansō-machi	(18,753)100.0	48.9	51.1	5.4	5.0	6.1	5.6	6.0	5.7	4.2	4.4	3.8	4.0	3.6	3.6	2.8	3.4	2.5	3.1	2.5	2.8	2.3	2.8	2.6	2.5	2.3	2.3	1.7	1.6	1.3	1.4	0.9	1.3	0.9	1.6	—	—
		Fukuta-machi	(7,658)100.0	48.7	51.3	5.8	5.8	6.4	6.6	5.7	5.6	3.8	3.9	3.6	3.6	3.3	3.7	2.7	3.3	2.6	3.1	2.8	3.0	2.3	2.7	2.4	1.9	2.2	2.1	1.6	1.6	1.4	1.8	0.9	1.3	1.2	1.3	—	—
	X	Kimitsu-machi	(13,747)100.0	48.2	51.8	4.9	4.6	6.2	6.0	5.6	5.6	4.5	4.6	3.8	4.3	3.7	4.1	2.7	3.4	2.3	3.0	2.4	3.2	2.6	2.7	2.6	2.4	2.2	2.1	1.6	1.7	1.4	1.4	0.7	1.1	0.9	1.5	—	—
		Futtsu-machi	(16,854)100.0	48.2	51.8	5.0	5.2	6.5	6.2	5.7	5.7	4.9	5.1	4.3	4.3	3.6	4.1	2.5	3.2	2.3	3.0	2.3	2.9	2.5	2.7	2.5	2.4	2.0	2.1	1.4	1.4	1.3	1.4	0.6	0.9	0.8	1.2	—	—
		Ōsawa-machi	(14,526)100.0	47.8	52.2	5.0	5.0	6.6	6.5	5.6	5.3	4.3	4.5	3.9	4.1	3.4	2.4	2.7	3.4	2.3	3.0	2.6	3.1	2.4	2.8	2.3	2.5	2.2	2.1	1.5	1.7	1.3	1.8	0.9	1.3	0.8	1.7	—	—
		Zone 9 Total	(615,169)100.0	48.8	51.2	5.1	4.9	6.3	6.1	5.6	5.4	4.6	4.8	4.3	4.5	4.0	3.9	2.9	3.6	2.5	3.1	2.6	3.0	2.4	2.5	2.3	2.2	2.0	1.9	1.5	1.5	1.2	1.4	0.7	1.0	0.7	1.2	—	—
10	I	Yokosuka-shi	(279,132)100.0	50.3	49.7	4.6	4.4	6.3	6.0	5.1	5.0	5.0	4.3	5.9	5.1	4.9	4.7	3.6	4.1	3.1	3.4	3.0	3.0	2.4	2.4	2.0	2.0	1.6	1.6	1.2	1.2	0.8	1.0	0.5	0.7	0.4	0.7	—	—
		Zushi-shi	(38,091)100.0	48.6	51.4	4.2	3.8	6.1	5.9	5.5	5.5	4.7	4.6	4.6	4.8	4.3	4.7	3.4	4.2	3.0	3.6	3.1	3.3	2.6	2.8	2.6	2.4	1.8	1.8	1.4	1.4	1.0	1.1	0.5	0.8	0.3	0.7	—	—
		Hayama-machi	(15,229)100.0	47.9	52.1	4.3	3.7	5.9	5.9	5.4	5.4	4.7	4.5	4.1	4.4	3.9	4.3	3.0	3.9	2.5	2.9	3.0	3.4	2.5	3.1	2.4	2.3	1.7	2.0	1.5	1.9	1.3	1.6	0.8	1.1	0.8	1.3	—	—
		Chigasaki-shi	(56,895)100.0	49.4	50.6	4.7	4.4	6.3	6.2	5.5	5.2	4.7	4.6	4.5	4.6	4.3	4.3	3.3	3.9	3.0	3.0	2.9	3.1	2.5	2.6	2.3	2.1	1.7	1.7	1.3	1.3	0.9	1.1	0.7	0.9	0.6	0.9	—	—
		Fujisawa-shi	(114,495)100.0	49.1	50.9	4.7	4.4	6.0	5.8	5.6	5.2	4.9	5.1	4.9	4.7	4.3	4.5	3.3	3.9	2.8	3.4	2.8	3.3	2.6	2.6	2.3	2.3	1.6	1.7	1.3	1.4	0.9	1.1	0.6	0.9	0.5	0.9	—	—
	II	Aikawa-machi	(14,321)100.0	48.3	51.7	5.1	5.1	6.5	5.9	5.7	5.6	4.5	5.6	4.5	5.4	3.9	3.8	2.8	3.4	2.5	2.8	2.4	2.8	2.1	2.4	2.2	2.1	2.1	2.0	1.6	1.5	1.3	1.3	0.6	0.8	0.7	1.1	—	—
		Atsugi-shi	(44,551)100.0	49.7	50.3	5.5	5.4	6.0	5.9	5.0	5.6	5.0	5.0	4.8	4.5	4.2	3.9	3.0	3.4	2.5	3.4	2.4	2.8	2.2	2.3	2.4	2.2	1.8	1.8	1.4	1.3	1.0	1.2	0.7	1.0	0.7	1.1	—	—
		Samukawa-machi	(11,183)100.0	50.5	49.5	5.5	5.1	7.0	6.4	6.1	5.7	4.8	4.4	4.4	4.3	4.4	3.9	2.9	3.2	2.9	3.2	2.6	3.0	2.2	2.5	2.2	2.0	1.5	1.5	1.4	1.3	1.0	1.2	0.7	0.8	0.7	1.0	—	—
	III	Ōme-shi	(55,218)100.0	48.3	51.7	4.8	4.5	5.8	5.8	5.5	5.5	5.2	6.1	4.6	5.4	4.0	4.3	2.9	3.5	2.5	3.0	2.4	2.9	2.3	2.4	2.2	2.2	1.9	1.7	1.4	1.4	1.1	1.2	0.7	0.8	0.7	1.0	—	—
	IV	Sakado-machi	(23,962)100.0	49.1	50.9	5.6	5.5	6.3	6.3	4.9	4.9	4.9	4.6	4.3	4.2	3.7	3.5	2.7	3.4	2.4	3.4	2.6	3.0	2.5	2.5	2.2	2.3	2.0	2.0	1.5	1.5	1.2	1.4	0.8	0.8	0.7	1.2	—	—
		Yoshimi-mura	(15,647)100.0	49.4	50.6	6.0	5.8	6.7	6.7	5.5	5.1	5.1	4.6	4.2	4.3	3.7	3.5	2.8	3.3	2.3	3.3	2.2	2.7	2.4	2.4	2.4	2.3	1.9	1.9	1.5	1.5	1.2	1.3	0.8	0.8	0.6	1.0	—	—
		Moroyama-mura	(11,251)100.0	49.5	50.5	5.4	5.0	5.9	6.3	5.7	5.0	4.4	4.7	4.2	4.2	4.3	4.2	3.2	3.9	2.8	3.3	2.7	2.7	2.5	2.5	2.3	2.3	1.7	1.7	1.7	1.7	1.2	1.5	0.8	0.8	0.8	1.1	—	—
	V	Kōnosu-shi	(31,434)100.0	49.5	50.5	5.7	5.0	6.7	6.6	5.7	5.5	4.8	5.3	4.5	4.5	4.0	3.9	2.9	3.6	2.6	3.2	2.4	2.7	2.2	2.4	2.1	1.9	1.9	1.5	1.3	1.4	1.0	1.2	0.6	1.0	0.5	0.5	—	—
		Kisai-machi	(16,352)100.0	48.7	51.3	5.8	5.6	6.3	6.6	5.7	5.8	4.7	4.7	4.1	4.5	3.8	3.5	2.4	3.2	2.4	2.7	2.6	2.8	2.2	2.4	2.4	2.3	2.0	2.0	1.7	1.6	1.4	1.6	0.9	1.1	0.7	1.2	—	—
		Washimiya-machi	(8,670)100.0	48.9	51.1	5.5	5.7	6.7	6.7	4.9	5.7	4.8	5.0	5.0	4.2	3.9	3.7	3.0	3.1	2.4	2.4	2.6	2.7	2.4	2.4	2.2	2.3	2.0	1.9	1.5	1.3	1.3	1.3	0.8	0.9	0.5	1.1	—	—
		Kurihashi-machi	(12,527)100.0	48.6	51.4	6.4	5.8	6.2	7.1	5.6	5.6	4.5	4.5	3.9	4.4	4.0	3.9	2.9	3.5	2.2	2.4	2.6	3.1	2.2	2.4	1.9	2.0	1.8	1.8	1.4	1.4	1.1	1.2	0.7	1.1	0.6	0.9	—	—
		Goka-mura	(9,734)100.0	48.7	51.3	6.5	6.3	7.6	6.6	5.9	5.7	3.9	5.2	3.8	4.4	3.6	3.4	2.5	3.4	2.6	2.6	2.1	2.8	1.9	2.3	2.3	2.1	2.2	1.8	1.4	1.5	1.2	1.3	0.8	1.0	0.8	1.3	—	—
	VI	Sakai-machi	(23,516)100.0	48.0	52.0	6.0	6.2	7.1	6.6	5.7	5.7	4.0	4.9	3.5	4.2	3.6	3.6	2.5	3.3	2.3	2.9	2.3	2.7	2.2	2.5	2.0	2.0	2.0	1.8	1.6	1.7	1.1	1.4	0.9	0.9	0.7	1.1	—	—
		Sashima-machi	(15,476)100.0	48.3	51.7	6.9	6.4	7.0	7.2	5.9	5.7	4.2	4.6	3.4	4.1	3.8	3.8	2.5	3.3	2.2	2.8	2.2	2.9	2.2	2.3	1.8	1.9	1.9	1.7	1.6	1.6	1.4	1.4	0.9	1.0	0.7	1.1	—	—
		Yatabe-machi	(22,048)100.0	49.2	50.8	5.0	4.8	6.2	5.4	5.4	5.1	4.2	4.2	4.1	4.2	3.8	4.0	3.4	4.0	2.6	2.9	2.8	3.1	2.5	2.6	2.3	2.2	2.0	2.0	1.9	1.8	1.4	1.6	0.8	0.8	0.8	1.5	—	—
	VII	Kukizaki-mura	(6,495)100.0	49.5	50.5	5.4	4.9	5.8	5.6	4.4	5.0	4.2	4.8	4.5	4.3	4.1	4.1	2.8	3.5	2.4	2.9	2.7	2.8	2.3	2.5	2.6	2.4	1.6	1.7	1.6	1.6	1.6	1.5	0.9	1.0	0.7	1.5	—	—
		Ushiku-machi	(15,627)100.0	49.9	50.1	5.2	5.2	6.0	5.7	5.2	4.9	5.8	5.6	4.3	4.1	3.5	3.5	3.2	3.6	2.5	3.2	2.8	3.1	2.5	2.3	1.9	2.3	1.9	2.1	1.4	1.6	1.2	1.5	0.7	0.9	0.8	1.1	—	—
		Kawachi-mura	(8,825)100.0	48.4	51.4	4.9	4.9	6.7	6.0	5.0	5.6	5.0	5.4	4.1	4.2	3.5	3.5	2.5	3.1	2.1	3.1	2.7	3.0	2.1	2.5	2.2	2.3	2.2	2.0	1.7	1.8	1.5	1.8	0.7	1.2	0.6	1.2	—	—
		Sakae-machi	(15,287)100.0	48.0	52.0	4.9	5.4	6.5	6.1	5.7	5.5	4.8	5.1	4.2	4.7	3.8	3.7	2.6	3.3	2.2	3.3	2.5	3.2	2.4	2.6	2.3	2.4	1.9	2.1	1.6	1.7	1.3	1.5	0.6	1.2	0.6	1.2	—	—
		Narita-shi	(44,969)100.0	48.3	51.7	5.1	5.0	6.0	5.8	5.2	5.3	4.7	4.7	4.2	4.6	3.9	4.2	3.0	3.6	2.8	3.6	2.5	2.9	2.4	2.6	2.3	2.4	1.9	2.0	1.6	1.6	1.3	1.5	0.7	0.9	0.6	1.2	—	—
	VIII	Shisui-machi	(6,207)100.0	48.4	51.6	4.8	5.3	6.3	6.3	4.6	4.7	4.1	4.1	4.2	4.4	3.8	4.2	2.8	3.7	2.7	3.3	2.5	3.0	2.5	2.5	2.6	2.5	1.9	2.1	1.3	1.5	1.4	1.5	0.7	1.3	0.7	1.3	—	—
		Yachimata-machi	(25,754)100.0	49.2	50.8	5.3	5.5	6.8	6.3	5.8	5.4	5.3	5.0	4.2	4.1	3.9	4.2	3.1	3.8	2.6	3.1	2.4	2.7	2.1	2.7	2.2	2.1	1.9	2.1	1.3	1.4	1.1	1.2	0.8	0.8	0.6	1.1	—	—

Table 3. Population By Age (5-Year Bracket) and Sex

Zone	Sector	District	Total	M	F	0-4 M	0-4 F	5-9 M	5-9 F	10-14 M	10-14 F	15-19 M	15-19 F	20-24 M	20-24 F	25-29 M	25-29 F	30-34 M	30-34 F	35-39 M	35-39 F	40-44 M	40-44 F	45-49 M	45-49 F	50-54 M	50-54 F	55-59 M	55-59 F	60-64 M	60-64 F	65-69 M	65-69 F	70-74 M	70-74 F	75& over M	75& over F	Unk. M	Unk. F
	VIII	Toke-machi	(6,734) 100.0	47.9	52.1	5.4	5.4	6.6	6.4	5.7	5.8	4.1	5.9	3.9	4.1	3.3	3.5	3.0	3.6	2.5	3.0	2.6	2.9	2.7	2.3	2.1	2.2	1.9	2.1	1.5	1.3	1.3	1.1	0.6	1.1	0.7	1.3	—	—
	IX	Nagara-machi	(9,364) 100.0	48.0	52.0	5.8	6.1	6.1	6.2	5.8	5.6	4.1	3.7	3.4	4.0	3.5	3.3	2.7	3.3	2.4	3.2	2.6	2.7	2.1	2.4	2.3	2.6	2.4	2.3	1.6	2.0	1.5	1.5	0.8	1.3	0.9	1.8	—	—
	X	Obitsu-mura	(7,489) 100.0	48.3	51.7	5.2	5.4	6.2	6.6	5.8	5.8	4.2	4.0	3.5	3.8	3.7	3.8	2.8	3.2	2.2	3.0	2.9	3.1	2.2	2.7	2.5	2.2	2.6	2.3	1.5	1.6	1.3	1.5	0.9	1.2	0.8	1.5	—	—
		Koito-machi	(6,504) 100.0	49.4	50.6	5.2	5.0	6.7	5.9	5.8	5.1	4.2	4.0	3.8	3.8	3.9	4.2	3.0	3.2	2.0	2.8	2.3	2.9	2.5	2.4	2.2	2.4	2.5	2.4	2.1	1.9	1.6	1.8	0.7	1.0	0.9	1.8	—	—
		Zone 10 Total	(972,998) 100.0	49.3	50.7	5.0	4.8	6.3	6.1	5.6	5.4	4.8	4.7	4.8	4.7	4.3	4.3	3.2	3.8	2.7	3.2	2.7	3.0	2.4	2.5	2.2	2.1	1.8	1.8	1.4	1.4	1.1	1.2	0.6	0.9	0.6	0.9	—	—
		Total for 50 km. Region	(13,316,804) 100.0	50.7	49.3	4.6	4.3	5.7	5.6	5.0	4.8	5.7	4.8	6.5	5.2	5.0	4.8	3.5	4.0	2.9	3.3	2.8	3.0	2.4	2.4	2.1	2.0	1.7	1.6	1.2	1.2	0.8	1.0	0.5	0.7	0.3	0.6	—	—
		National Total	(89,275,529) 100.0	49.1	50.9	5.3	5.2	6.2	6.0	5.4	5.2	4.9	4.8	4.7	4.7	4.2	4.3	3.1	3.7	2.6	3.1	2.6	2.9	2.4	2.5	2.2	2.2	1.8	1.8	1.4	1.4	1.0	1.2	0.7	0.9	0.6	1.0	—	—
1960																																						
1	I	Chiyoda-ku	(116,944) 100.0	54.8	45.2	2.1	2.0	2.5	2.3	3.5	3.8	11.2	5.8	12.6	6.8	6.3	4.2	3.0	3.5	2.1	3.2	2.0	2.7	2.1	2.7	2.2	2.2	1.8	1.8	1.3	1.3	0.9	0.9	0.5	0.6	0.4	0.6	—	—
		Minato-ku	(267,024) 100.0	51.2	48.8	2.8	2.6	3.0	2.8	4.3	4.1	8.4	6.3	8.4	6.2	5.7	5.1	3.6	4.3	2.7	3.7	2.3	3.2	2.5	2.8	2.3	2.3	1.9	1.9	1.4	1.4	0.9	1.0	0.6	0.7	0.4	0.4	—	—
		Chūō-ku	(161,299) 100.0	54.0	46.0	2.3	2.3	2.4	2.3	3.8	3.6	10.6	6.6	12.1	6.3	6.6	4.4	3.1	3.5	2.1	3.1	1.8	2.8	2.1	2.7	2.0	2.4	1.9	1.7	1.5	1.5	1.0	1.0	0.5	0.7	0.3	0.7	—	—
		Bunkyō-ku	(259,383) 100.0	51.6	48.4	3.0	2.8	2.9	2.8	4.3	4.0	7.8	6.2	9.3	6.5	6.4	5.2	3.9	4.1	2.6	3.5	2.2	2.9	2.3	2.6	2.0	2.1	1.7	1.8	1.3	1.4	0.9	0.9	0.6	0.7	0.4	0.7	—	—
		Taitō-ku	(318,889) 100.0	52.8	47.2	2.9	2.7	2.9	2.8	3.9	3.9	9.3	6.7	9.4	6.8	6.4	4.9	3.7	3.7	2.7	3.2	2.2	2.7	2.3	2.6	2.1	2.1	1.7	1.7	1.4	1.3	0.9	0.9	0.6	0.6	0.4	0.6	—	—
		Zone 1 Total	(1,123,539) 100.0	52.5	47.5	2.7	2.6	2.8	2.6	4.1	3.9	9.3	6.5	9.9	6.5	6.3	4.8	3.6	3.9	3.4	2.5	2.2	2.9	2.3	2.7	2.1	2.2	1.7	1.8	1.4	1.4	0.9	1.0	0.5	0.7	0.4	0.6	—	—
2	I	Shinagawa-ku	(427,859) 100.0	51.5	48.5	3.3	3.2	3.2	3.0	4.3	4.2	7.7	5.9	8.1	6.5	6.4	5.6	4.4	4.4	2.9	3.5	2.4	2.8	2.3	2.4	1.9	2.0	1.7	1.8	1.3	1.3	0.8	0.9	0.5	0.6	0.3	0.5	—	—
	II	Meguro-ku	(293,763) 100.0	51.4	48.6	2.8	3.0	3.0	2.9	4.5	4.3	7.5	5.8	8.3	6.1	6.1	5.3	4.1	4.3	3.0	3.6	2.5	3.0	2.5	2.6	2.1	2.2	1.8	1.9	1.4	1.4	0.9	1.0	0.6	0.7	0.4	0.6	—	—
	III	Shibuya-ku	(282,687) 100.0	49.8	50.2	2.3	2.9	2.4	2.8	3.8	3.9	6.7	6.4	8.6	7.3	6.4	6.0	4.2	4.6	2.9	3.7	2.3	2.9	2.3	2.5	2.0	2.4	1.6	1.7	1.2	1.5	0.8	1.0	0.5	0.7	0.4	0.7	—	—
		Shinjuku-ku	(413,690) 100.0	51.2	48.8	3.0	2.8	2.8	2.8	4.0	3.8	7.2	5.9	9.4	7.4	6.8	6.1	4.2	4.6	2.9	3.3	2.3	2.8	2.3	2.4	1.9	2.0	1.6	1.6	1.2	1.2	0.8	0.9	0.6	0.6	0.4	0.7	—	—
	IV	Nakano-ku	(351,360) 100.0	51.9	48.1	3.4	3.2	3.0	2.9	4.3	4.1	6.6	5.3	9.1	6.2	6.7	5.7	4.5	4.5	3.0	3.6	2.4	2.8	2.3	2.5	2.0	2.1	1.7	1.7	1.3	1.3	0.8	0.8	0.5	0.6	0.3	0.6	—	—
	V	Toshima-ku	(363,193) 100.0	50.9	49.1	3.3	3.1	3.0	2.9	4.1	4.0	6.8	5.5	8.5	7.2	7.0	6.3	4.5	4.5	2.9	3.5	2.3	2.8	2.2	2.4	1.9	2.0	1.6	1.7	1.2	1.3	0.8	0.8	0.5	0.6	0.3	0.5	—	—
	VI	Kita-ku	(418,603) 100.0	50.7	49.3	3.7	3.6	3.5	3.4	4.7	4.5	6.3	5.5	7.1	6.2	6.5	5.9	4.5	4.5	3.0	3.5	2.4	2.8	2.3	2.4	2.0	2.0	1.6	1.6	1.3	1.3	0.8	0.8	0.5	0.5	0.3	0.5	—	—
		Arakawa-ku	(285,480) 100.0	52.8	47.2	3.7	3.6	3.8	3.6	4.7	4.5	7.9	6.1	7.4	5.7	6.3	5.0	4.3	3.9	3.0	3.2	2.4	2.7	2.3	2.3	2.0	1.9	1.8	1.6	1.4	1.2	0.8	0.8	0.4	0.5	0.2	0.5	—	—
	VII	Sumida-ku	(331,843) 100.0	53.3	46.7	3.5	3.3	3.7	3.4	4.6	4.3	9.8	7.0	8.6	5.9	6.0	4.7	3.7	3.6	2.7	3.1	2.2	2.6	2.2	2.3	1.9	1.9	1.7	1.6	1.3	1.2	0.6	0.8	0.3	0.4	0.2	0.4	—	—
	VIII	Kōtō-ku	(351,053) 100.0	54.8	45.2	4.2	4.0	4.1	3.9	4.6	4.5	8.1	5.4	8.6	5.3	6.6	5.1	4.6	4.0	3.2	3.3	2.5	2.7	2.4	2.2	2.0	2.0	1.5	1.5	1.0	0.9	0.6	0.6	0.3	0.3	0.2	0.4	—	—
		Zone 2 Total	(3,519,531) 100.0	51.9	48.1	3.4	3.3	3.3	3.2	4.4	4.2	7.5	5.9	8.4	6.3	6.5	5.6	4.3	4.3	3.0	3.5	2.4	2.8	2.3	2.4	2.0	2.0	1.6	1.6	1.2	1.2	0.8	0.8	0.5	0.5	0.3	0.5	—	—
3	I	Ōta-ku	(706,219) 100.0	52.7	47.3	3.7	3.5	3.6	3.4	4.6	4.4	8.2	5.5	7.9	5.5	6.1	5.3	4.4	4.3	3.2	3.6	2.5	2.8	2.4	2.4	1.9	1.9	1.6	1.6	1.2	1.1	0.7	0.8	0.4	0.6	0.3	0.6	—	—
	II	Setagaya-ku	(653,210) 100.0	51.0	49.0	3.5	3.3	3.2	3.1	4.6	4.3	6.8	5.7	7.9	5.8	5.6	5.3	4.4	4.5	3.1	3.7	2.5	2.9	2.4	2.6	2.0	2.2	1.8	1.8	1.3	1.4	0.9	1.0	0.6	0.7	0.4	0.7	—	—
	III	Suginami-ku	(487,210) 100.0	51.0	49.0	3.3	3.1	3.1	2.9	4.6	4.4	6.6	5.6	8.2	6.0	6.0	5.3	4.2	4.4	3.0	3.6	2.5	2.9	2.4	2.7	2.1	2.2	1.8	1.9	1.3	1.4	0.9	1.0	0.6	0.8	0.4	0.8	—	—
	IV	Itabashi-ku	(412,605) 100.0	51.9	48.1	4.1	4.0	3.9	3.7	4.9	4.6	7.2	5.5	7.1	5.4	5.8	5.4	4.7	4.4	3.2	3.5	2.5	2.8	2.4	2.4	1.9	1.8	1.6	1.5	1.1	1.1	0.8	0.8	0.4	0.6	0.3	0.6	—	—
		Nerima-ku	(305,628) 100.0	51.1	48.9	4.6	4.3	4.0	3.7	4.8	4.5	5.8	4.9	6.6	5.1	5.7	5.7	5.1	5.0	3.6	3.7	2.6	2.8	2.3	2.4	1.9	1.9	1.5	1.6	1.1	1.2	0.7	0.9	0.5	0.6	0.3	0.6	—	—

- 196 -

Table 3. Population by Age (5-Year Bracket) and Sex

(Zone) (Sector)	District	Total (No.)	Total %	Total M	Total F	0–4 M	0–4 F	5–9 M	5–9 F	10–14 M	10–14 F	15–19 M	15–19 F	20–24 M	20–24 F	25–29 M	25–29 F	30–34 M	30–34 F	35–39 M	35–39 F	40–44 M	40–44 F	45–49 M	45–49 F	50–54 M	50–54 F	55–59 M	55–59 F	60–64 M	60–64 F	65–69 M	65–69 F	70–74 M	70–74 F	75 & Over M	75 & Over F	Unk M	Unk F
VI	Adachi-ku	(408,768)	100.0	51.4	48.6	4.4	4.1	4.5	4.3	5.4	5.2	6.8	5.6	6.0	5.0	5.4	4.9	4.3	4.0	3.3	3.4	3.0	2.4	2.4	2.5	2.1	2.0	1.8	1.6	1.3	1.2	0.8	0.8	0.5	0.6	0.3	0.6	—	—
VII	Katsushika-ku	(376,724)	100.0	51.3	48.7	4.2	4.0	4.1	3.9	5.2	5.0	7.1	5.7	6.2	5.3	5.6	5.2	4.6	4.2	3.4	3.5	3.1	2.4	2.3	2.3	2.0	2.0	1.7	1.6	1.2	1.2	0.8	0.8	0.5	0.6	0.3	0.5	—	—
VIII	Edogawa-ku	(316,593)	100.0	51.6	48.4	4.1	4.0	4.1	3.9	5.1	5.0	7.1	5.4	6.7	5.4	5.7	5.2	4.4	4.0	3.3	3.7	3.0	2.4	2.4	2.6	2.0	2.0	1.8	1.6	1.3	1.2	0.8	0.8	0.5	0.6	0.3	0.6	—	—
	Urayasu-machi	(16,847)	100.0	49.7	50.3	4.0	3.8	5.8	5.5	6.6	6.5	4.8	5.0	4.4	4.0	4.2	3.7	3.8	3.4	2.5	3.4	2.5	3.0	2.6	2.6	2.5	2.3	1.9	1.8	1.1	1.6	1.1	1.0	1.0	1.0	0.6	1.0	—	—
	Zone 3 Total	(3,683,804)	100.0	51.5	48.5	3.9	3.7	3.7	3.5	4.9	4.6	7.0	5.5	7.2	5.5	5.8	5.3	4.5	4.4	3.2	3.2	3.5	2.5	2.4	2.5	2.0	2.0	1.7	1.7	1.2	1.2	0.8	0.9	0.5	0.6	0.3	0.6	—	—
4 I	Kawasaki-shi	(632,975)	100.0	52.8	47.2	4.6	4.3	4.2	4.1	4.9	4.7	6.6	5.2	7.2	5.4	6.2	5.4	5.5	4.5	3.5	3.5	2.7	2.8	2.5	2.2	1.8	2.2	1.4	1.6	0.9	1.3	0.6	0.8	0.3	0.5	0.2	0.5	—	—
II	Komae-machi	(25,252)	100.0	51.0	49.0	5.0	4.6	4.0	3.7	4.3	4.3	6.1	5.2	6.0	5.9	5.5	5.3	5.3	5.1	3.8	3.5	2.5	2.7	2.2	2.3	1.9	2.3	1.6	1.7	1.1	1.2	0.8	0.9	0.5	0.6	0.4	0.7	—	—
III	Mitaka-shi	(98,038)	100.0	51.7	48.3	4.1	3.8	3.8	3.5	5.1	4.7	6.4	5.3	6.8	5.4	5.8	5.4	5.0	4.5	3.4	3.7	2.7	3.1	2.4	2.6	2.0	2.6	1.6	1.4	1.0	1.0	0.7	0.8	0.4	0.6	0.3	0.7	—	—
	Musashino-shi	(120,337)	100.0	51.8	48.2	3.7	3.5	3.3	3.0	4.6	4.2	6.4	5.2	7.7	5.6	6.1	5.4	5.0	4.6	3.2	3.6	2.7	3.1	2.4	2.6	2.0	2.1	1.7	1.4	1.0	1.0	0.7	0.8	0.5	0.7	0.4	0.7	—	—
	Chōfu-shi	(68,621)	100.0	50.6	49.4	4.6	4.4	4.1	4.0	5.2	4.9	5.8	5.1	5.9	5.4	5.3	5.1	4.4	4.8	3.5	3.7	2.6	2.8	2.3	2.5	1.7	1.9	1.6	1.6	1.0	1.2	0.6	0.9	0.5	0.7	0.4	0.7	—	—
	Hoya-machi	(46,768)	100.0	50.4	49.6	5.7	5.2	4.2	4.1	4.7	4.7	5.0	4.1	4.1	4.1	5.5	6.7	3.9	5.5	3.9	3.7	2.6	2.6	2.2	2.0	1.8	1.7	1.6	1.4	0.9	1.1	0.6	0.8	0.4	0.5	0.2	0.7	—	—
IV	Yamato-machi	(17,242)	100.0	46.7	53.3	5.1	5.0	5.0	4.5	5.1	5.1	5.5	5.3	5.5	5.5	6.4	5.5	3.3	4.4	3.0	3.6	2.7	2.9	2.4	2.0	1.8	1.7	1.6	1.4	0.8	1.0	0.8	0.8	0.4	0.7	0.2	0.6	—	—
	Toda-machi	(30,752)	100.0	51.8	48.2	5.1	5.0	4.5	4.4	5.2	5.0	6.9	5.3	4.9	5.9	5.1	4.9	4.5	4.0	3.3	3.1	2.4	2.6	2.3	2.3	1.9	1.8	1.6	1.3	1.0	1.1	0.6	0.8	0.4	0.6	0.3	0.6	—	—
V	Warabi-shi	(50,952)	100.0	49.8	50.2	4.8	4.4	3.9	4.0	5.4	5.2	6.9	6.2	5.8	5.3	5.4	5.4	4.2	4.2	3.1	3.4	2.5	3.0	2.5	2.7	2.0	2.0	1.6	1.5	1.1	1.1	0.7	0.7	0.5	0.5	0.2	0.6	—	—
	Kawaguchi-shi	(170,066)	100.0	51.7	48.3	4.5	4.2	4.6	4.4	5.5	5.3	7.2	5.7	7.2	6.0	5.2	4.8	4.0	4.0	3.1	3.3	2.4	2.8	2.3	2.5	2.0	1.9	1.6	1.5	1.2	1.2	0.8	0.8	0.4	0.6	0.3	0.6	—	—
	Hatogaya-machi	(20,711)	100.0	50.9	49.1	5.2	4.8	4.8	4.4	5.8	5.4	5.5	4.7	4.7	4.7	5.3	5.7	2.7	4.4	3.1	3.1	2.4	2.7	2.3	2.5	1.7	2.1	1.4	1.4	0.9	1.0	0.8	0.9	0.6	0.7	0.3	0.6	—	—
VI	Sōka-shi	(38,533)	100.0	50.5	49.5	4.7	4.7	5.3	4.8	5.9	5.7	5.7	5.1	5.4	5.1	4.9	4.5	2.5	3.8	2.7	2.7	2.3	2.8	2.3	2.5	2.1	2.0	1.8	1.7	1.2	1.7	0.9	1.0	0.6	0.7	0.7	0.7	—	—
	Yashio-mura	(13,307)	100.0	51.3	48.7	5.3	4.6	6.3	5.7	6.9	6.9	5.7	4.8	5.4	5.1	4.7	3.4	2.5	3.3	2.9	2.5	1.8	2.6	2.3	3.6	2.2	2.0	1.9	1.8	1.4	1.4	1.1	1.0	0.7	0.9	0.7	1.2	—	—
	Misato-mura	(17,738)	100.0	49.5	50.5	4.5	4.7	5.6	5.6	6.6	6.7	6.6	4.9	5.2	4.6	4.6	3.7	2.9	3.1	3.1	3.1	2.0	2.4	2.2	3.1	2.1	2.0	1.7	1.7	1.5	1.5	1.2	1.4	0.8	1.0	0.5	1.1	—	—
	Matsudo-shi	(86,372)	100.0	50.3	49.7	4.6	4.3	4.2	4.3	5.6	5.3	6.7	5.2	6.0	6.0	5.2	5.1	3.4	4.2	2.9	3.4	2.4	2.8	2.5	2.8	2.2	2.2	1.8	1.7	1.3	1.3	0.9	1.0	0.4	0.7	0.4	0.8	—	—
VII	Ichikawa-shi	(157,301)	100.0	49.7	50.3	3.8	3.6	3.9	3.8	5.1	4.8	5.3	4.8	5.8	5.8	4.9	4.9	2.9	4.1	3.3	3.5	2.8	2.8	2.5	2.6	2.2	2.1	1.8	1.5	1.4	1.4	1.0	1.0	0.4	0.8	0.4	0.8	—	—
	Zone 4 Total	(1,594,965)	100.0	51.6	48.4	4.5	4.2	4.2	4.0	5.1	4.9	6.3	5.3	6.3	5.3	5.7	5.3	3.3	4.4	3.2	3.3	2.6	2.8	2.4	2.4	1.9	2.1	1.6	1.5	1.1	1.1	0.8	0.8	0.4	0.6	0.3	0.6	—	—
5 I	Tsurumi-ku	(230,377)	100.0	52.6	47.4	4.1	4.0	4.0	3.9	5.1	4.9	6.7	5.2	7.3	5.0	6.2	5.1	4.2	4.2	3.2	3.5	2.6	2.9	2.6	2.4	2.0	2.0	1.6	1.6	1.1	1.1	0.7	0.9	0.4	0.5	0.2	0.5	—	—
III	Koganei-shi	(45,734)	100.0	51.0	49.0	4.3	4.1	3.7	3.4	4.8	4.4	5.8	5.1	5.7	5.3	5.6	5.8	4.8	4.8	3.6	3.6	2.4	2.7	2.3	2.6	2.0	2.2	1.8	1.6	1.1	1.1	0.7	0.9	0.7	0.7	0.4	0.7	—	—
	Tanashi-machi	(31,323)	100.0	49.9	50.1	4.9	4.5	4.4	4.2	5.3	5.1	5.4	5.4	5.4	5.4	5.5	5.5	3.6	4.9	3.9	3.9	2.9	3.0	2.7	2.5	1.8	1.8	1.4	1.4	0.9	1.0	0.6	0.8	0.3	0.5	0.3	0.5	—	—
	Kurume-machi	(19,637)	100.0	50.5	49.5	5.9	5.4	4.9	4.4	5.6	5.0	4.9	4.6	4.6	4.2	4.9	6.4	3.8	5.2	3.5	3.5	2.3	2.6	2.1	1.8	1.5	1.5	1.3	1.3	0.9	1.2	0.7	0.9	0.6	0.6	0.3	0.8	—	—
IV	Niza-machi	(14,401)	100.0	50.5	49.5	5.2	4.9	5.1	5.2	5.8	5.5	5.6	5.5	4.4	4.6	4.7	4.6	3.1	4.5	3.5	3.5	2.4	2.7	2.2	2.4	1.9	1.9	1.8	1.8	1.2	1.2	0.7	0.7	0.6	0.7	0.6	0.7	—	—
	Kiyose-machi	(17,863)	100.0	50.5	49.5	3.8	3.9	3.7	3.7	4.2	4.1	4.2	4.4	4.8	4.8	5.6	5.8	4.5	5.5	4.3	4.3	3.5	3.2	2.6	2.4	2.2	1.6	1.7	1.5	1.3	1.1	0.9	1.1	0.8	0.8	0.4	0.7	—	—
	Adachi-machi	(12,259)	100.0	49.5	50.5	4.4	4.8	4.9	4.9	5.9	5.3	5.6	5.3	5.6	4.3	4.6	4.8	3.0	4.1	2.4	3.6	2.4	2.9	2.5	2.6	1.8	2.1	1.8	1.9	1.4	1.4	1.1	1.0	0.9	0.9	0.4	0.8	—	—
	Asaka-machi	(24,182)	100.0	54.3	45.7	4.8	4.5	4.2	4.2	5.4	5.2	6.5	5.1	7.9	4.3	6.8	4.3	4.1	4.3	3.2	3.1	2.5	2.9	2.2	2.3	1.4	1.6	1.4	1.3	1.0	1.4	0.7	1.0	0.6	0.9	0.3	0.6	—	—
V	Urawa-shi	(168,757)	100.0	50.0	50.0	4.1	3.8	4.1	4.0	5.5	4.9	5.6	5.5	4.4	4.8	5.0	4.8	3.6	4.4	3.6	3.6	2.6	2.7	2.7	2.8	2.3	2.3	1.9	1.9	1.4	1.4	0.9	1.1	0.6	0.8	0.4	0.8	—	—
	Misono-mura	(9,306)	100.0	49.9	50.1	4.4	4.5	5.8	5.5	7.6	6.3	5.1	4.9	4.3	3.0	3.7	3.0	2.6	3.4	2.6	2.6	2.1	2.3	2.2	2.8	2.3	2.4	2.3	2.1	1.8	1.6	1.1	1.1	0.9	1.1	0.5	1.3	—	—
	Koshigaya-shi	(49,585)	100.0	49.4	50.6	4.9	5.0	5.9	5.5	6.5	6.2	5.1	5.2	4.3	3.9	4.2	3.5	2.6	3.5	3.1	3.1	2.7	2.7	2.6	2.6	2.2	2.2	1.9	1.8	1.5	1.5	1.0	1.2	0.6	0.9	0.5	0.9	—	—

Table 3. Population by Age (5-Year Bracket) and Sex

(Zone)	(Sector)	District	Total	M	F	0-4 M	0-4 F	5-9 M	5-9 F	10-14 M	10-14 F	15-19 M	15-19 F	20-24 M	20-24 F	25-29 M	25-29 F	30-34 M	30-34 F	35-39 M	35-39 F	40-44 M	40-44 F	45-49 M	45-49 F	50-54 M	50-54 F	55-59 M	55-59 F	60-64 M	60-64 F	65-69 M	65-69 F	70-74 M	70-74 F	75 & Over M	75 & Over F	Unk M	Unk F
	VI	Yoshikawa-machi	(16,300) 100.0	49.7	50.3	5.0	4.3	6.1	5.8	6.8	6.7	4.9	4.9	4.5	4.0	3.7	3.4	3.3	3.1	2.5	2.9	2.1	2.8	2.2	2.7	2.2	2.1	2.0	1.6	1.3	1.3	1.3	1.3	0.8	1.3	0.6	1.3	—	—
	VII	Nagareyama-machi	(25,672) 100.0	49.3	50.7	4.9	4.8	5.1	4.9	5.8	5.7	4.8	4.8	4.4	4.1	4.4	4.9	4.4	4.3	3.3	3.4	2.4	2.8	2.2	2.4	2.1	2.2	1.8	1.3	1.0	1.2	1.0	1.2	0.7	1.2	0.4	1.0	—	—
	VIII	Kamagaya-machi	(13,496) 100.0	51.1	48.9	5.3	4.7	5.6	5.6	5.7	5.5	4.3	4.3	5.2	4.3	5.2	4.6	4.5	4.3	3.2	3.3	2.4	2.7	2.1	2.8	1.8	2.1	1.7	1.5	1.0	0.9	0.9	0.9	0.7	0.9	0.4	0.8	—	—
		Funahashi-shi	(135,038) 100.0	50.5	49.5	4.1	3.4	4.4	4.2	5.2	5.2	6.0	5.2	6.1	5.1	6.1	4.8	4.6	4.0	2.9	3.5	2.5	3.3	2.1	2.8	2.1	2.5	1.9	1.3	0.9	0.9	0.9	0.9	0.6	0.9	0.4	0.8	—	—
		Zone 5 Total	(813,930) 100.0	51.0	49.0	4.4	4.2	4.4	4.2	5.4	5.1	5.8	5.2	5.9	4.8	5.4	4.9	4.6	4.3	3.1	3.5	2.5	2.9	2.5	2.6	2.1	2.5	1.8	1.2	0.9	0.9	0.9	0.9	0.5	0.9	0.4	0.7	—	—
6	I	Nishi-ku	(104,173) 100.0	50.7	49.3	3.7	3.6	4.5	3.7	5.1	4.8	5.5	5.1	5.7	4.9	5.3	5.0	4.9	4.5	3.3	3.8	2.7	3.1	2.7	3.1	2.7	2.7	1.9	1.5	1.0	1.1	1.0	1.1	0.6	1.1	0.4	0.7	—	—
		Naka-ku	(123,624) 100.0	49.7	50.3	3.9	3.6	3.6	3.5	4.5	4.3	5.3	4.3	5.6	5.5	5.8	6.2	5.2	5.4	3.5	3.9	2.5	2.8	2.4	2.8	2.4	2.4	1.9	1.4	1.0	1.1	1.0	1.1	0.6	1.1	0.4	0.7	—	—
	II	Kanagawa-ku	(172,068) 100.0	51.8	48.2	4.2	3.9	4.2	3.9	5.1	5.0	5.7	4.7	6.7	4.7	5.6	5.2	4.9	4.6	3.4	3.6	2.6	2.9	2.6	2.9	2.5	2.5	1.7	1.3	0.9	0.9	0.9	0.9	0.5	0.9	0.3	0.6	—	—
		Kōhoku-ku	(147,688) 100.0	50.8	49.2	4.4	4.1	4.4	4.3	5.3	5.2	6.0	5.2	5.9	4.5	4.8	4.9	4.7	4.5	3.4	3.7	2.6	2.9	2.6	2.9	2.6	2.6	1.8	1.3	0.9	1.0	0.9	1.0	0.6	1.0	0.5	0.8	—	—
		Inagi-machi	(11,012) 100.0	51.3	48.7	4.3	4.1	5.2	4.8	6.2	5.8	5.1	5.7	4.7	4.3	4.7	3.8	3.9	4.3	3.0	3.7	2.8	3.2	2.7	3.2	2.9	2.9	1.8	1.2	0.9	0.9	0.9	1.1	0.7	1.2	0.6	1.0	—	—
	III	Tama-mura	(9,746) 100.0	49.8	50.2	3.9	3.7	3.9	4.1	4.8	4.8	5.7	4.7	4.6	4.9	5.8	4.7	4.7	4.3	3.4	3.4	2.3	2.9	2.3	2.9	2.6	2.7	2.0	1.6	1.2	1.2	1.2	1.2	0.8	1.1	0.7	1.1	—	—
		Fuchu-shi	(82,098) 100.0	52.5	47.5	4.3	4.3	4.5	4.2	5.2	5.0	5.1	4.7	6.0	4.4	6.2	5.0	5.7	4.8	4.0	3.8	2.9	2.9	2.2	2.9	2.2	2.3	1.5	1.1	0.7	0.8	0.7	0.8	0.4	0.8	0.3	0.6	—	—
		Kunitachi-machi	(32,609) 100.0	50.2	49.8	4.2	4.2	4.2	4.1	5.1	5.0	5.6	5.2	6.4	4.9	5.3	5.7	4.9	4.9	3.4	4.0	2.6	2.7	2.3	2.7	2.6	2.2	1.6	1.1	0.7	0.9	0.7	0.9	0.4	0.9	0.3	0.6	—	—
		Kokubunji-machi	(39,098) 100.0	52.6	47.4	4.5	4.1	4.2	4.2	4.8	4.4	6.2	4.7	7.2	5.0	5.8	5.3	5.8	4.8	3.6	3.5	2.7	2.9	2.3	2.4	2.6	2.0	1.6	1.0	0.7	1.0	0.7	1.0	0.5	1.0	0.3	0.7	—	—
		Kodaira-machi	(52,923) 100.0	52.2	47.8	4.9	4.6	4.8	4.3	5.3	4.5	5.4	4.9	5.5	4.8	5.3	5.4	5.6	4.9	4.3	3.8	3.0	2.7	2.4	2.7	2.3	2.0	1.5	1.0	0.7	0.9	0.7	0.9	0.4	0.9	0.4	0.6	—	—
		Higashimurayama-machi	(42,946) 100.0	50.9	49.1	5.5	5.0	5.0	4.6	5.2	4.5	5.0	4.8	3.8	4.2	4.9	5.9	6.3	5.3	4.3	3.7	3.0	2.7	2.4	2.7	2.3	1.9	1.4	1.2	0.8	1.1	0.8	1.1	0.5	0.9	0.5	0.9	—	—
	IV	Tokorosawa-shi	(65,903) 100.0	49.6	50.4	4.7	4.8	5.1	5.1	5.7	5.5	4.9	5.0	4.5	4.6	4.8	4.8	4.6	4.2	3.1	3.5	2.5	2.8	2.2	2.8	2.4	2.4	1.7	1.3	1.0	1.1	1.0	1.1	0.7	1.1	0.6	1.0	—	—
		Miyoshi-mura	(4,329) 100.0	50.2	49.8	5.3	5.2	5.7	5.4	6.6	6.5	4.7	4.9	4.2	4.5	4.1	3.1	3.8	3.9	2.8	2.9	2.2	2.6	2.3	2.6	2.2	2.2	2.2	1.9	1.0	1.1	1.0	1.1	0.8	1.1	0.7	0.8	—	—
		Fujimi-mura	(12,030) 100.0	49.5	50.5	4.8	5.0	5.5	5.2	5.9	5.8	4.7	4.7	4.2	4.4	4.3	4.3	4.1	3.9	3.2	3.3	2.4	2.8	2.3	2.4	2.3	2.3	2.0	1.6	1.2	1.3	1.2	1.3	0.8	1.3	0.6	1.0	—	—
	V	Yono-shi	(40,840) 100.0	50.1	49.9	4.4	3.8	4.5	4.2	5.8	5.4	5.6	5.4	4.9	4.9	4.8	5.0	4.6	5.0	3.4	3.7	3.2	3.2	2.7	3.2	2.7	2.7	1.7	1.3	0.8	0.9	0.8	0.9	0.6	0.8	0.4	0.6	—	—
		Ōmiya-shi	(169,996) 100.0	49.6	50.4	4.4	4.2	4.7	4.4	5.7	5.6	5.4	5.4	4.7	4.7	4.6	4.9	4.6	4.9	3.2	3.6	2.7	3.0	2.6	3.0	2.5	2.6	1.7	1.6	0.9	0.9	0.9	0.9	0.6	0.9	0.6	0.7	—	—
	VI	Iwatsuki-shi	(35,169) 100.0	49.5	50.5	4.7	4.1	5.5	5.3	5.5	6.3	5.1	5.1	4.4	4.1	3.8	3.9	3.4	3.3	2.5	3.0	2.3	2.7	2.5	2.7	2.3	2.3	2.1	1.6	1.2	1.3	1.2	1.3	0.8	1.3	0.6	1.0	—	—
	VII	Matsubushi-mura	(8,844) 100.0	48.9	51.1	4.2	4.6	6.0	6.0	6.9	6.4	4.9	4.8	4.2	4.2	4.5	3.5	5.0	4.6	3.4	3.4	3.4	2.5	2.2	2.5	2.2	2.3	2.0	1.6	1.3	1.4	1.3	1.4	0.6	1.2	0.6	1.1	—	—
		Kashiwa-shi	(63,745) 100.0	49.9	50.1	5.2	5.0	5.1	5.5	5.7	5.2	5.4	5.1	4.3	4.5	5.7	5.0	3.9	3.4	2.9	3.4	2.3	2.7	2.0	2.7	2.0	2.2	1.6	1.4	0.8	1.0	0.8	1.0	0.5	1.0	0.4	0.7	—	—
		Shōnan-mura	(11,849) 100.0	53.0	47.0	4.3	4.0	5.7	5.3	6.0	5.5	4.7	4.7	7.6	3.6	3.8	3.5	3.5	3.5	2.8	3.1	2.8	3.0	2.5	3.0	2.5	2.0	2.2	1.6	1.0	1.0	1.0	1.0	0.7	1.1	0.6	1.2	—	—
		Shirai-mura	(8,217) 100.0	49.5	50.5	4.4	4.4	5.9	5.3	6.0	6.3	4.8	4.6	4.1	3.9	4.1	3.6	4.6	4.3	3.3	3.6	2.8	2.8	2.4	2.8	2.4	2.5	2.0	1.6	1.5	1.6	1.5	1.6	0.7	1.2	0.7	1.3	—	—
	VIII	Narashino-shi	(42,167) 100.0	51.3	48.7	4.4	4.2	4.3	4.4	5.4	5.3	6.4	5.3	7.1	4.4	4.7	4.9	7.1	4.4	3.4	3.7	2.6	2.8	2.5	2.8	2.4	2.4	1.2	1.1	0.8	1.1	0.8	1.1	0.5	0.8	0.4	0.7	—	—
		Zone 6 Total	(1,281,074) 100.0	50.7	49.3	4.4	4.2	4.5	4.3	5.4	5.1	5.5	4.9	5.5	4.7	5.1	5.1	4.9	4.5	3.4	3.7	2.6	2.9	2.5	2.9	2.5	2.5	1.7	1.3	0.9	1.0	0.9	1.0	0.6	1.0	0.4	0.7	—	—
7	I	Isogo-ku	(74,458) 100.0	49.5	50.5	3.8	3.8	3.9	3.8	5.4	5.0	5.5	5.0	4.6	4.6	4.9	5.1	4.7	4.6	3.3	3.7	2.6	3.1	2.6	3.1	2.5	2.5	2.0	1.6	1.0	1.1	1.0	1.1	0.7	1.0	0.5	0.8	—	—
		Minami-ku	(194,558) 100.0	50.4	49.6	4.0	3.8	4.1	4.0	5.0	4.9	5.1	5.0	5.4	4.3	5.5	5.7	5.0	4.6	3.6	3.7	2.7	3.0	2.5	2.7	2.5	2.5	1.9	1.5	1.0	1.1	1.0	1.1	0.6	1.0	0.4	0.6	—	—
	II	Hodogaya-ku	(143,804) 100.0	50.2	49.8	4.9	4.8	4.6	4.3	5.2	4.9	4.8	4.5	4.6	4.6	5.2	5.9	5.5	5.1	3.8	3.6	2.6	2.7	2.3	2.7	2.3	2.3	1.6	1.3	1.1	0.9	1.1	0.9	0.5	1.1	0.4	0.7	—	—
		Machida-shi	(71,269) 100.0	49.9	50.1	4.6	4.2	5.0	4.7	5.8	5.7	5.5	5.6	4.8	4.7	4.5	4.6	4.3	4.2	3.5	3.5	2.5	2.9	2.7	2.9	2.6	2.5	1.8	1.4	0.9	1.1	0.9	1.1	0.7	1.1	0.5	0.9	—	—
	III	Yuki-mura	(6,179) 100.0	50.5	49.5	4.1	4.1	5.5	6.2	6.3	6.2	5.6	4.7	4.7	4.2	3.6	2.8	3.1	2.8	2.5	3.2	2.5	2.9	2.4	3.0	2.4	2.3	2.3	1.9	1.6	1.6	1.6	1.6	1.4	1.6	1.3	1.5	—	—

Table 3. Population by Age (5-Year Bracket) and Sex

Zone	Sector	District	Total	Total M	Total F	0–4 M	0–4 F	5–9 M	5–9 F	10–14 M	10–14 F	15–19 M	15–19 F	20–24 M	20–24 F	25–29 M	25–29 F	30–34 M	30–34 F	35–39 M	35–39 F	40–44 M	40–44 F	45–49 M	45–49 F	50–54 M	50–54 F	55–59 M	55–59 F	60–64 M	60–64 F	65–69 M	65–69 F	70–74 M	70–74 F	75 & Over M	75 & Over F	Unknown M	Unknown F
7	III	Hino-machi	(43,394)	50.1	49.9	5.0	4.9	4.2	4.0	5.0	4.9	4.9	4.7	4.6	4.8	5.8	6.1	4.9	6.5	3.5	3.4	2.6	2.4	2.6	2.3	1.9	1.9	1.5	1.5	1.1	1.2	0.7	0.9	0.5	0.6	0.3	0.6	—	—
		Tachikawa-shi	(67,949)	49.5	50.5	3.8	3.6	3.9	3.7	5.3	5.3	5.8	5.6	5.6	5.7	5.5	5.7	4.4	4.8	2.9	3.7	2.6	2.5	2.6	2.7	2.1	2.1	1.7	1.7	1.2	1.2	1.3	0.8	0.4	0.6	0.3	0.6	—	—
		Sunakawa-machi	(13,989)	49.5	50.5	4.7	4.4	4.9	5.2	6.3	5.9	5.6	5.3	4.5	4.4	4.2	4.8	4.3	4.1	3.0	3.3	2.6	3.1	2.6	2.5	2.2	2.1	1.8	1.5	1.1	1.1	0.7	0.8	0.6	0.9	0.5	1.0	—	—
		Yamato-machi	(14,239)	50.1	49.9	4.3	4.5	5.2	5.0	6.4	6.6	5.6	5.4	4.4	4.1	4.2	4.1	3.6	3.7	3.0	3.2	2.7	2.7	2.8	2.8	2.7	1.9	1.9	1.8	1.3	1.2	0.9	0.8	0.7	0.7	0.4	0.9	—	—
	IV	Ōi-mura	(4,949)	50.9	49.1	4.1	4.6	4.9	5.3	5.9	5.8	5.9	4.8	4.2	4.4	4.8	3.2	3.8	3.6	2.9	2.9	2.7	2.7	2.4	2.5	1.9	1.9	1.7	1.7	1.4	1.5	0.9	1.1	1.0	1.2	0.8	1.4	—	—
		Fukuoka-mura	(16,652)	50.4	49.6	6.4	6.1	4.0	3.7	4.5	4.2	4.1	3.5	5.8	5.6	7.5	8.7	7.6	5.0	3.6	2.9	2.5	2.5	2.0	2.0	1.5	1.4	1.2	1.3	0.8	1.1	0.6	0.6	0.3	0.5	0.3	0.5	—	—
	V	Kasukabe-shi	(34,280)	49.3	50.6	4.6	4.6	5.6	5.2	6.5	6.2	4.9	5.1	4.3	4.3	4.3	4.1	3.8	3.6	2.6	3.2	2.8	2.3	2.5	2.9	2.2	2.2	2.0	2.0	1.5	1.4	1.0	1.2	0.7	0.9	0.5	1.0	—	—
		Shōwa-mura	(14,815)	49.4	50.6	5.1	4.4	6.0	6.2	7.5	6.7	4.4	5.1	3.7	3.7	3.6	3.4	3.5	3.3	2.2	3.5	2.4	2.9	2.4	2.8	2.3	2.2	1.8	1.7	1.6	1.6	1.3	1.2	0.9	1.0	0.6	1.2	—	—
	VI	Noda-shi	(54,150)	48.6	51.4	4.3	4.1	5.0	5.0	6.2	6.0	4.7	5.0	4.1	4.7	4.4	4.2	3.9	3.8	2.7	3.0	2.5	2.8	2.4	2.8	2.3	2.4	2.1	2.0	1.6	1.6	1.1	1.3	0.8	1.0	0.6	1.1	—	—
	VII	Abiko-machi	(27,063)	49.0	51.0	4.6	4.1	4.9	5.0	5.8	5.9	5.2	5.1	4.4	4.5	4.4	4.4	4.0	3.7	2.7	3.5	2.6	2.7	2.5	2.9	2.3	2.5	1.8	1.7	1.5	1.4	0.9	1.1	0.7	0.9	0.5	1.0	—	—
		Yachiyo-machi	(21,709)	49.3	50.7	5.0	5.0	5.4	4.8	5.6	5.3	4.4	4.6	3.7	4.1	4.0	4.8	4.8	5.0	3.5	3.6	2.7	2.9	2.4	2.5	2.0	1.9	1.8	1.7	1.6	1.3	1.1	1.3	0.7	0.8	0.5	1.0	—	—
	VIII	Chiba-shi	(241,615)	51.0	49.0	4.3	4.0	4.3	4.1	5.1	5.4	5.6	5.2	6.2	4.3	5.8	5.0	4.8	4.5	3.0	3.4	2.5	2.5	2.4	2.4	2.2	2.0	1.7	1.6	1.2	1.3	0.8	0.9	0.6	0.8	0.4	0.8	—	—
	IX	Goi-machi	(21,560)	48.7	51.3	4.2	4.1	5.0	4.9	5.9	5.8	4.9	5.5	4.4	4.4	4.3	3.5	3.7	4.0	2.5	2.9	2.4	2.5	2.4	2.8	2.2	2.3	2.0	2.2	1.9	2.0	1.3	1.3	0.8	0.9	0.7	1.4	—	—
		Sodegaura-machi	(13,974)	49.2	50.8	3.8	3.6	4.9	4.8	7.0	6.2	6.0	5.7	5.5	4.4	4.0	3.5	2.5	3.6	2.5	3.4	3.1	3.1	2.4	2.8	2.3	2.2	2.0	2.2	1.7	2.0	1.1	1.2	0.9	1.2	0.8	1.3	—	—
		Zone 7 Total	(1,080,606)	50.1	49.9	4.4	4.2	4.2	4.0	5.4	5.2	5.2	5.0	5.1	4.8	5.2	5.2	4.8	4.4	3.3	3.5	2.2	2.6	2.5	2.6	2.1	2.1	1.8	1.7	1.3	1.4	0.9	1.0	0.6	0.8	0.4	0.8	—	—
8	I	Kanazawa-ku	(71,446)	51.2	48.8	3.7	3.6	4.7	4.3	6.2	6.0	5.3	5.5	4.2	4.4	4.3	4.6	4.3	4.2	3.7	3.4	3.0	3.4	3.0	2.8	2.3	2.1	1.7	1.5	1.1	1.1	0.9	0.9	0.5	0.7	0.4	0.7	—	—
		Totsuka-ku	(113,514)	50.7	49.3	4.8	4.7	4.7	4.5	5.5	5.2	5.2	4.6	4.9	4.5	5.2	5.5	5.4	5.7	3.6	3.5	2.4	2.7	2.4	2.4	1.9	1.9	1.6	1.5	1.1	1.2	0.8	0.9	0.5	0.7	0.4	0.8	—	—
	II	Yamato-shi	(40,975)	49.2	50.8	5.2	4.8	5.2	4.8	5.8	5.5	5.0	4.8	4.1	4.6	4.7	5.2	3.5	3.9	3.0	3.6	2.8	2.8	2.5	2.5	1.9	1.7	1.5	1.4	1.2	1.2	0.9	0.9	0.5	0.6	0.4	0.7	—	—
		Sagamihara-shi	(101,655)	49.9	50.1	5.2	4.8	5.2	4.8	5.6	5.4	5.1	5.2	4.6	4.7	4.7	5.0	5.1	4.7	3.4	3.6	2.3	2.9	2.3	2.7	1.8	1.7	1.5	1.5	1.2	1.2	0.8	0.8	0.5	0.7	0.4	0.7	—	—
		Zama-machi	(15,402)	49.8	50.2	5.0	4.6	4.9	5.3	5.9	5.4	5.1	5.0	4.6	4.8	4.8	3.2	3.2	3.5	2.9	3.5	2.2	2.2	2.2	2.4	1.6	1.7	1.3	1.4	1.1	1.0	0.6	0.7	0.6	0.8	0.4	0.8	—	—
	III	Hachiōji-shi	(158,443)	49.2	50.8	4.1	3.9	4.7	4.6	5.4	5.2	5.7	5.8	4.8	4.8	4.6	4.7	4.5	4.1	3.1	3.6	2.3	2.7	2.5	2.8	2.2	2.2	1.8	1.8	1.3	1.4	1.0	1.1	0.7	0.8	0.5	0.9	—	—
		Akishima-shi	(44,805)	49.3	50.7	4.5	4.2	5.0	5.1	6.3	5.8	5.0	5.0	4.0	4.3	4.5	4.9	4.8	4.1	3.3	4.1	2.9	2.5	2.3	2.7	2.2	1.7	1.4	1.3	0.8	0.8	0.7	0.8	0.4	0.7	0.4	0.7	—	—
		Fussa-machi	(21,998)	47.8	52.2	4.7	4.5	4.8	4.6	5.3	5.3	5.8	6.2	5.3	5.1	4.7	6.9	3.5	4.0	3.5	4.0	2.3	2.3	2.3	2.5	1.6	1.4	1.4	1.4	1.0	1.1	0.7	0.8	0.4	0.5	0.3	0.6	—	—
		Mizuho-machi	(12,092)	49.4	50.6	4.7	4.3	5.6	5.6	6.1	5.9	4.9	5.5	4.8	4.5	4.1	4.1	3.2	3.5	2.8	2.8	2.5	2.3	2.5	2.6	2.1	2.1	1.6	1.6	1.1	1.0	0.8	0.8	0.4	0.5	0.3	0.6	—	—
		Murayama-machi	(12,065)	49.6	50.4	4.3	4.0	5.5	4.8	5.6	5.6	5.9	5.9	5.5	5.2	4.1	4.1	3.8	3.2	2.9	3.4	2.7	2.6	2.7	2.7	2.0	2.1	1.6	1.5	1.1	1.2	0.8	1.0	0.7	0.9	0.7	1.2	—	—
		Musashi-machi	(30,604)	48.7	51.3	4.6	5.2	5.4	5.1	5.6	5.9	4.8	4.9	4.2	4.5	4.2	4.7	3.7	4.2	3.0	3.7	2.4	2.6	2.5	2.7	1.8	2.0	1.6	1.6	1.2	1.2	0.8	0.8	0.7	0.7	0.7	1.2	—	—
	IV	Sayama-shi	(32,785)	49.9	50.1	4.6	5.1	5.1	5.0	5.8	5.6	4.7	5.1	4.3	4.4	4.0	4.2	2.9	3.3	2.9	3.4	2.3	2.5	2.0	2.0	1.6	1.4	1.4	1.4	0.9	1.1	0.7	0.9	0.5	0.8	0.5	1.0	—	—
		Kawagoe-shi	(107,523)	49.3	50.7	4.1	3.9	4.8	5.0	6.3	5.9	5.5	5.6	5.2	5.9	4.7	5.2	3.8	3.7	2.9	3.4	2.9	2.2	2.2	2.2	2.0	1.8	1.5	1.5	1.1	1.3	0.9	0.9	0.7	0.8	0.5	0.9	—	—
		Seibu-machi	(6,299)	43.7	56.3	3.7	3.9	4.8	4.8	5.5	4.7	4.7	4.6	3.5	4.3	8.2	12.9	2.6	3.0	2.6	3.0	1.9	2.8	2.2	2.2	1.6	1.8	1.3	1.2	0.9	0.9	0.9	0.9	0.5	0.8	0.5	0.9	—	—
	V	Ageo-shi	(38,889)	49.3	50.7	4.3	4.2	5.1	4.8	6.2	5.9	5.1	5.5	4.7	4.8	4.2	4.3	3.8	3.7	2.8	3.4	2.5	3.0	2.5	3.0	1.8	2.0	1.4	1.6	1.0	1.1	0.7	0.9	0.5	0.9	0.5	1.0	—	—
		Ina-mura	(6,735)	50.0	50.0	4.2	4.3	5.6	5.0	6.2	6.3	6.1	5.7	4.4	4.3	3.6	3.6	3.5	3.0	2.7	3.1	2.4	2.6	2.1	2.6	2.0	1.8	1.8	1.6	1.4	1.6	1.0	1.1	0.8	1.1	0.8	1.5	—	—
		Hasuda-machi	(20,743)	49.7	50.3	4.1	4.1	5.3	4.7	5.9	5.9	5.3	5.0	4.6	4.7	4.5	4.2	3.0	3.3	3.0	3.3	2.5	2.8	2.5	2.8	2.1	1.7	1.6	1.6	1.1	1.4	0.8	1.0	0.7	0.8	0.7	1.0	—	—
		Shiraoka-machi	(16,026)	50.1	49.9	4.5	4.3	5.6	5.2	6.6	6.2	5.0	5.0	4.5	4.1	3.9	3.9	2.7	3.1	2.7	3.1	2.4	2.9	2.3	2.8	2.3	2.2	1.9	1.7	1.2	1.4	0.9	1.0	0.9	1.0	0.7	1.2	—	—
		Miyashiro-machi	(11,152)	49.5	50.5	4.5	4.6	5.9	5.7	6.6	5.8	4.8	4.9	4.3	4.3	4.1	4.1	2.7	3.0	2.7	3.0	2.4	2.6	2.4	2.7	2.2	2.2	1.9	1.9	1.1	1.1	0.9	1.1	0.9	1.1	0.6	1.0	—	—

- 199 -

Table 3. Population by Age (5-Year Bracket) and Sex

(Zone)	(Sector)	District	Total			Age 0-4		Age 5-9		Age 10-14		Age 15-19		Age 20-24		Age 25-29		Age 30-34		Age 35-39		Age 40-44		Age 45-49		Age 50-54		Age 55-59		Age 60-64		Age 65-69		Age 70-74		Age 75 & Over		Unknown	
			Total	M	F	M	F	M	F	M	F	M	F	M	F	M	F	M	F	M	F	M	F	M	F	M	F	M	F	M	F	M	F	M	F	M	F	M	F
8	V	Sugito-machi	(17,450)	100.0	49.4	50.6	4.5	4.2	6.0	5.7	6.9	6.5	4.7	4.3	4.2	4.3	3.7	4.3	3.3	3.4	2.6	3.2	2.3	2.3	2.1	2.8	2.6	2.6	2.0	1.9	1.8	1.7	1.1	1.3	0.8	1.1	0.7	1.2	—	—
	VI	Sekiyado-machi	(12,759)	100.0	47.9	52.1	4.6	4.4	6.5	6.3	7.2	7.4	3.2	4.5	3.2	3.3	3.0	3.3	3.3	3.7	2.8	3.7	2.5	2.8	2.5	2.5	1.8	2.6	2.1	2.1	1.6	1.9	1.6	1.8	1.0	1.2	0.8	1.4	—	—
	VII	Moriya-machi	(11,449)	100.0	48.7	51.3	4.2	4.1	5.9	5.8	7.3	6.2	3.9	4.6	3.3	3.5	3.5	3.7	3.5	3.9	2.7	3.8	2.3	2.9	2.7	3.1	2.5	2.3	2.2	1.9	1.9	1.3	1.3	1.4	0.9	1.2	0.8	1.5	—	—
		Toride-machi	(22,582)	100.0	48.6	51.4	4.0	4.1	4.8	4.7	5.9	5.6	5.0	5.2	4.2	4.6	3.7	3.7	2.8	2.8	2.4	3.1	2.4	2.4	2.6	3.1	2.6	2.6	2.1	1.6	1.6	1.1	1.1	1.2	0.7	1.0	0.6	1.3	—	—
		Inzai-machi	(17,315)	100.0	49.3	50.7	3.7	3.8	5.6	5.1	6.5	6.0	5.0	4.8	3.5	3.7	3.7	3.5	2.8	3.4	2.4	3.2	2.4	2.4	2.2	3.0	2.6	2.5	2.2	1.7	1.7	1.2	1.2	1.3	0.7	1.3	0.7	1.3	—	—
		Inba-mura	(7,912)	100.0	47.6	52.4	3.7	3.6	4.8	4.9	5.5	6.0	3.4	3.7	2.7	2.8	4.0	3.5	2.9	4.0	2.9	3.8	3.0	3.1	2.6	2.9	2.5	2.4	2.5	2.6	1.8	1.2	1.2	1.6	1.0	2.2	—	—
	VIII	Yotsukaidō-machi	(16,623)	100.0	48.5	51.5	4.7	4.7	5.4	4.9	6.0	5.9	4.5	5.2	3.7	4.7	3.8	4.7	3.1	3.5	2.5	3.0	2.3	2.5	2.2	2.9	2.6	2.5	2.1	1.4	1.4	1.0	1.1	1.0	0.7	0.6	0.6	1.1	—	—
	IX	Ichihara-machi	(14,239)	100.0	49.8	50.2	4.3	4.5	5.2	4.9	6.2	5.4	4.6	5.2	4.8	4.9	4.4	4.0	2.8	2.7	2.4	2.6	2.6	2.3	2.3	2.3	2.3	2.1	1.5	1.1	1.1	0.7	1.1	1.1	0.5	0.6	0.6	1.2	—	—
		Anegasaki-machi	(11,307)	100.0	48.3	51.7	4.1	4.2	5.1	4.8	6.1	6.2	4.7	4.8	3.9	4.3	3.7	3.8	2.9	3.3	2.4	3.2	2.5	2.4	2.3	2.5	2.4	2.2	1.7	1.5	1.1	1.1	1.1	1.3	0.8	0.8	0.8	1.5	—	—
		Hirakawa-machi	(9,404)	100.0	48.6	51.4	4.5	4.1	5.6	5.5	6.0	6.2	4.1	4.3	3.3	3.5	3.3	3.6	2.5	3.1	2.5	3.4	2.5	2.8	2.5	2.6	2.4	2.1	1.5	1.3	1.3	1.0	1.3	1.5	0.9	0.9	0.9	1.6	—	—
		Miwa-machi	(11,018)	100.0	48.1	51.9	4.3	4.2	5.7	5.4	6.2	6.8	3.8	3.8	3.1	3.3	3.7	3.2	2.8	3.4	2.5	3.9	2.5	2.4	2.5	3.1	2.2	2.2	2.0	1.5	1.6	1.3	1.0	1.0	1.0	1.8	—	—
	X	Kisarazu-shi	(52,689)	100.0	48.7	51.3	4.0	3.9	4.7	4.6	6.0	5.8	4.5	5.0	4.6	4.6	4.3	4.2	2.9	2.5	2.9	3.6	2.6	2.6	2.5	2.9	2.5	2.1	2.1	1.1	1.1	0.9	0.9	1.1	0.7	0.7	0.7	1.2	—	—
		Zone 8 Total	(1,067,918)	100.0	49.5	50.5	4.4	4.2	5.0	4.8	5.9	5.7	5.7	5.2	4.6	4.5	4.4	4.5	3.1	2.6	2.9	3.6	2.6	2.5	2.5	2.7	2.1	1.8	1.7	1.4	1.4	1.1	1.0	1.1	0.7	0.5	0.5	1.0	—	—
9	I	Kamakura-shi	(98,617)	100.0	48.5	51.5	3.4	3.1	3.6	3.4	5.3	5.0	5.5	5.6	4.5	5.0	4.7	4.5	4.0	3.0	2.6	3.8	2.8	3.1	2.8	3.1	2.4	2.2	2.3	1.8	1.8	1.3	1.1	1.3	0.8	1.0	0.6	1.1	—	—
	II	Ayase-machi	(8,304)	100.0	49.2	50.8	4.0	4.0	5.3	5.3	6.7	6.5	5.2	5.4	4.1	4.6	4.1	3.8	2.4	2.4	2.7	3.4	2.7	2.7	2.4	2.4	2.1	1.9	1.5	1.4	1.2	1.2	1.0	1.1	0.8	1.3	—	—
		Ebina-machi	(17,938)	100.0	48.9	51.1	4.2	3.8	5.0	5.1	6.1	5.9	5.5	7.5	4.8	5.0	4.4	3.9	2.6	2.6	2.3	3.1	2.3	2.1	2.3	2.5	1.8	1.5	1.5	1.2	1.0	0.8	0.7	0.7	0.7	1.0	—	—
		Shiroyama-machi	(5,280)	100.0	49.5	50.5	4.7	4.8	5.6	5.2	5.7	6.0	4.4	4.4	3.8	4.3	4.7	4.2	3.0	2.9	2.4	3.7	2.4	2.3	2.2	2.3	1.8	1.8	1.5	1.2	1.2	1.0	0.9	1.3	0.9	1.3	—	—
	III	Akita-machi	(14,433)	100.0	50.3	49.7	4.3	4.2	5.1	4.6	5.7	6.0	5.2	5.2	4.7	4.9	4.1	3.8	2.9	2.3	2.6	3.7	2.6	2.6	2.4	2.6	2.1	1.8	1.5	1.5	1.1	1.2	0.6	0.9	0.6	1.5	—	—
		Hamura-machi	(11,003)	100.0	49.8	50.2	4.9	4.4	5.4	4.8	5.9	5.7	4.8	5.2	4.7	4.5	4.4	4.4	3.1	2.2	2.8	4.4	2.6	2.5	2.3	2.2	1.9	1.6	1.6	1.4	1.2	1.3	0.6	0.9	0.5	0.6	—	—
	IV	Hannō-shi	(44,153)	100.0	48.9	51.1	4.4	4.1	5.1	5.1	6.0	6.0	4.8	5.7	4.0	4.9	3.9	4.2	3.0	2.6	2.6	3.7	2.6	2.4	2.4	2.8	2.0	1.7	1.7	1.4	1.4	1.1	0.8	1.1	0.8	1.4	—	—
		Tsurugashima-mura	(7,008)	100.0	49.9	50.1	3.6	4.1	5.0	5.2	6.0	6.1	c.4	5.3	4.7	5.3	3.9	3.5	2.7	2.5	2.5	3.3	2.5	2.5	2.0	2.7	2.1	1.6	1.6	1.3	1.3	1.1	0.8	1.1	0.8	1.4	—	—
		Hidaka-machi	(16,683)	100.0	49.9	50.1	4.4	4.1	5.9	5.6	5.8	6.1	4.5	4.5	4.5	4.4	3.8	3.6	3.0	2.9	2.5	3.5	2.5	2.6	2.1	2.6	2.1	1.7	1.4	1.4	1.3	1.3	0.9	1.3	0.9	1.5	—	—
		Kawashima-mura	(16,443)	100.0	48.7	51.3	4.3	4.1	5.8	5.7	6.9	6.8	4.2	4.5	4.1	4.2	3.4	3.2	2.7	2.5	2.4	3.3	2.5	2.4	2.3	2.7	1.8	1.5	1.5	1.3	1.2	1.2	0.8	1.2	0.7	1.5	—	—
	V	Kitamoto-machi	(15,483)	100.0	50.3	49.7	5.0	4.4	5.8	4.8	6.6	6.9	5.3	5.0	4.4	5.4	4.5	4.3	3.8	2.9	2.7	3.8	2.6	2.7	2.5	2.6	1.7	1.4	1.5	0.9	0.9	0.6	0.6	0.9	0.6	0.9	—	—
		Higawa-machi	(21,309)	100.0	49.5	50.5	4.6	4.4	5.1	5.0	6.2	6.3	5.6	5.4	4.4	4.7	4.5	4.2	2.8	2.4	2.4	3.3	2.6	2.3	2.2	2.7	1.9	1.6	1.6	1.3	1.4	1.1	0.9	1.1	0.6	1.0	—	—
		Shobu-machi	(16,054)	100.0	49.4	50.6	4.4	4.2	5.8	5.3	7.1	6.3	4.3	4.7	4.1	4.3	3.3	3.4	2.6	2.2	2.5	3.4	2.5	2.5	2.3	2.8	2.0	1.9	1.6	1.6	1.1	1.2	0.8	0.9	0.5	1.4	—	—
		Kuki-machi	(23,114)	100.0	49.9	50.1	4.9	4.5	5.7	5.4	6.9	6.0	4.7	4.8	4.0	4.1	4.0	3.8	2.9	2.4	2.6	3.9	2.6	2.6	2.4	2.6	2.0	1.9	1.5	1.5	1.1	1.2	0.9	0.9	0.5	1.2	—	—
		Satte-machi	(23,378)	100.0	48.7	51.3	4.2	4.0	5.5	5.3	7.0	6.5	-.7	5.3	4.6	5.3	3.2	3.4	2.9	2.0	2.4	3.8	2.4	2.4	2.3	3.0	2.1	2.2	1.7	1.7	1.2	0.8	0.8	0.9	0.7	1.2	—	—
	VI	Iwai-machi	(33,366)	100.0	48.5	51.5	4.9	4.5	6.0	5.8	6.9	6.7	3.6	4.6	3.0	3.4	3.5	3.2	3.0	2.6	2.6	3.9	2.6	2.3	2.3	2.4	2.1	1.8	1.5	1.5	1.4	1.4	1.0	1.5	0.8	1.2	—	—
		Mitsukaidō-shi	(37,577)	100.0	47.7	52.3	4.2	4.0	5.2	5.3	6.5	6.5	3.8	5.3	3.8	4.4	3.5	3.6	2.8	2.2	2.6	4.1	2.6	2.6	2.5	3.1	2.0	1.8	1.8	1.4	1.4	1.7	1.0	1.7	0.7	1.6	—	—
		Yawahara-mura	(10,746)	100.0	47.9	52.1	3.8	3.7	5.0	4.8	6.5	6.6	4.2	4.4	3.2	3.7	3.5	3.5	2.8	2.9	2.6	4.3	2.6	2.4	2.4	3.4	2.5	1.9	1.9	1.5	1.5	2.2	0.7	1.6	0.7	1.6	—	—
		Ina-mura	(12,010)	100.0	47.9	52.1	3.8	3.6	4.9	4.9	6.4	6.1	3.8	4.9	3.8	4.3	3.6	3.7	2.7	2.5	2.6	3.7	2.6	2.7	2.7	2.8	1.9	1.9	1.9	1.5	1.5	1.2	1.2	1.5	0.7	1.3	—	—
	VII	Fujishiro-machi	(12,606)	100.0	48.2	51.8	3.7	3.7	4.9	4.9	5.9	6.0	4.7	4.5	3.9	4.7	4.1	3.8	2.6	2.4	2.5	4.1	2.5	2.6	2.7	3.4	2.0	2.0	1.9	1.4	1.6	0.8	0.8	1.2	0.7	1.3	—	—
		Ryūgasaki-shi	(33,581)	100.0	48.0	52.0	3.9	3.8	4.9	4.9	6.1	6.1	4.8	5.2	3.6	4.3	4.0	3.6	2.6	2.5	2.6	3.6	2.6	2.5	2.5	3.3	2.0	2.0	1.9	1.8	1.3	1.1	0.8	1.3	0.6	1.3	—	—

Table 3.　Population by Age (5-Year Bracket) and Sex

(Zone)	(Sector)	District	Total				Age 0–4		Age 5–9		Age 10–14		Age 15–19		Age 20–24		Age 25–29		Age 30–34		Age 35–39		Age 40–44		Age 45–49		Age 50–54		Age 55–59		Age 60–64		Age 65–69		Age 70–74		75 & Over		Un-known	
			Total		M	F	M	F	M	F	M	F	M	F	M	F	M	F	M	F	M	F	M	F	M	F	M	F	M	F	M	F	M	F	M	F	M	F	M	F
	VII	Tone-mura	(9,279)	100.0	48.3	51.7	4.4	4.1	5.4	5.4	6.3	6.3	4.1	4.2	3.6	3.8	3.6	3.5	2.8	3.5	3.2	3.2	2.2	2.2	2.2	3.1	2.5	2.2	2.0	2.3	2.3	2.2	1.5	1.7	1.2	1.3	0.7	1.5	—	—
	VIII	Motono-mura	(5,213)	100.0	48.6	51.4	3.6	3.8	4.8	4.5	6.5	6.2	4.7	4.8	4.0	4.2	3.6	3.4	3.1	3.1	3.7	3.4	2.7	2.9	2.9	2.6	2.3	2.5	2.6	2.4	1.7	1.9	1.5	1.3	0.9	1.4	0.8	1.5	—	—
		Sakura-shi	(36,869)	100.0	48.5	51.5	4.0	4.0	5.5	5.0	5.9	5.7	4.9	5.1	3.7	4.1	3.7	3.9	3.0	2.9	3.6	3.0	2.6	3.0	2.4	2.8	2.2	2.5	2.2	2.5	1.7	1.7	1.3	1.4	0.9	1.3	0.7	1.3	—	—
	IX	Izumi-machi	(9,333)	100.0	48.5	51.5	3.8	3.7	5.5	5.3	6.4	6.2	4.4	4.4	3.2	3.5	3.6	3.5	2.9	3.3	3.6	2.9	2.6	3.4	2.3	2.8	2.2	2.3	2.4	2.3	2.1	2.0	1.7	1.7	1.1	1.5	0.8	1.7	—	—
		Shitsu-mura	(9,292)	100.0	49.2	50.8	4.5	4.5	5.7	5.6	6.2	6.0	3.8	3.9	3.4	3.7	3.5	3.6	3.1	3.1	3.3	3.1	2.4	3.0	2.2	2.9	2.4	2.3	2.2	2.2	2.0	2.0	1.5	1.4	1.2	1.2	1.1	1.7	—	—
		Nanso-machi	(17,552)	100.0	48.5	51.5	4.3	4.3	5.4	5.2	6.2	6.0	3.8	3.6	2.8	3.4	3.5	3.3	2.8	2.7	3.6	2.8	2.6	3.1	2.6	3.1	2.3	2.7	2.7	2.7	2.3	1.7	1.5	1.5	1.0	1.3	1.1	1.9	—	—
		Fukuta-machi	(7,276)	100.0	48.4	51.6	5.0	4.4	5.8	6.3	6.8	6.8	3.5	3.6	2.3	2.8	3.3	3.8	2.7	2.6	3.3	2.7	2.6	3.1	2.7	3.0	2.3	2.6	2.6	1.8	2.0	2.1	1.4	1.5	1.0	1.6	1.1	1.6	—	—
	X	Kimitsu-machi	(12,910)	100.0	48.1	51.9	4.0	3.6	5.2	4.6	6.3	6.3	4.0	4.6	3.2	3.8	3.6	3.8	2.6	2.6	3.4	2.6	2.3	3.1	2.5	3.1	2.5	2.7	2.4	2.4	2.2	2.2	1.4	1.6	1.1	1.2	0.9	1.5	—	—
		Futtsu-machi	(16,567)	100.0	48.2	51.8	4.3	4.3	4.9	5.3	6.4	6.2	4.4	4.8	4.1	4.2	3.7	3.7	2.5	2.5	3.1	2.5	2.3	3.0	2.3	2.8	2.5	2.6	2.3	2.3	1.9	1.9	1.1	1.3	1.0	1.2	0.7	1.1	—	—
		Ōsawa-machi	(14,059)	100.0	47.7	52.3	4.0	4.3	5.1	5.1	6.4	6.5	4.3	4.4	3.3	4.0	3.6	3.5	2.7	2.7	3.3	2.7	2.7	3.1	2.5	3.1	2.5	2.7	2.2	2.5	2.0	1.9	1.4	1.5	1.0	1.5	0.8	1.7	—	—
		Zone 9 Total	(617,436)	100.0	48.7	51.3	4.1	3.9	5.1	4.9	6.2	6.0	4.7	5.0	3.9	4.2	3.8	3.7	2.9	2.9	3.1	2.9	2.5	3.0	2.5	2.9	2.3	2.4	2.1	2.1	1.8	1.8	1.3	1.4	0.9	1.1	0.7	1.3	—	—
10	I	Yokosuka-shi	(287,309)	100.0	50.8	49.2	3.6	3.4	4.3	4.1	5.8	5.8	6.0	5.0	5.9	4.4	4.3	4.2	3.1	3.1	3.7	3.1	2.7	2.7	2.7	2.7	2.1	2.1	1.7	1.8	1.3	1.4	0.9	1.0	0.6	0.8	0.5	0.8	—	—
		Zushi-shi	(39,571)	100.0	48.1	51.9	3.2	3.4	3.9	3.6	5.5	5.3	5.4	5.5	4.5	4.8	4.1	4.7	3.1	3.1	3.8	3.4	2.9	3.1	2.8	2.7	2.3	2.1	2.2	2.2	1.6	1.6	1.0	1.3	0.8	1.0	0.7	1.0	—	—
		Hayama-machi	(15,762)	100.0	47.4	52.6	3.1	3.1	4.1	3.7	5.8	5.7	5.3	5.6	4.3	4.4	4.0	4.4	3.1	2.9	3.8	3.1	2.7	2.5	2.7	3.1	2.4	2.3	2.3	2.4	1.6	1.6	1.0	1.3	0.8	1.0	0.9	1.5	—	—
		Chigasaki-shi	(68,054)	100.0	49.4	50.6	4.1	4.1	4.6	4.4	5.8	5.5	5.2	5.0	4.4	4.4	3.5	4.0	2.9	3.3	3.7	2.9	2.5	2.7	2.9	3.3	2.1	2.3	2.1	1.9	1.4	1.5	1.0	1.1	0.6	0.8	0.6	1.0	—	—
		Fujisawa-shi	(124,601)	100.0	49.0	51.0	3.9	3.7	4.3	4.1	5.7	5.4	5.5	5.7	4.7	4.8	4.2	4.4	3.1	3.2	3.7	3.1	2.6	2.6	2.6	3.0	2.2	2.4	2.1	1.9	1.4	1.5	1.0	1.2	0.7	0.9	0.6	1.1	—	—
	II	Aikawa-machi	(13,741)	100.0	48.1	51.9	4.3	4.0	5.2	5.1	6.5	5.8	4.3	5.9	3.5	5.1	3.6	3.8	2.8	3.2	3.7	2.8	2.4	2.4	2.2	2.8	2.1	2.3	2.2	2.3	1.9	1.9	1.4	1.5	1.1	1.0	0.7	1.2	—	—
		Atsugi-shi	(46,239)	100.0	49.9	50.1	4.3	4.0	5.3	5.1	5.9	5.7	5.2	5.2	4.8	4.5	3.9	4.0	3.0	3.2	3.3	3.0	2.4	2.9	2.2	2.6	2.3	2.2	2.1	1.9	1.5	1.6	1.2	1.2	0.9	1.0	0.8	1.2	—	—
		Samukawa-machi	(11,564)	100.0	51.7	48.3	3.9	3.7	5.1	4.7	6.5	6.0	6.8	5.2	5.6	4.0	3.7	3.7	2.7	3.0	3.3	2.7	2.7	2.9	2.4	2.8	2.2	2.2	1.9	1.8	1.3	1.3	1.0	1.0	0.7	1.0	0.8	1.1	—	—
	III	Ōme-shi	(56,896)	100.0	48.4	51.6	4.1	3.7	4.5	4.4	5.9	5.7	5.5	6.4	4.5	5.4	3.8	4.5	2.8	3.4	3.0	2.8	2.4	2.8	2.3	2.7	2.1	2.3	2.0	1.9	1.6	1.5	1.2	1.1	1.0	1.0	0.7	1.2	—	—
	IV	Sakado-machi	(23,569)	100.0	49.0	51.0	4.3	4.0	5.6	5.4	6.4	5.9	4.5	4.9	4.1	4.2	3.6	3.6	2.7	2.9	3.4	2.7	2.3	2.9	2.5	2.9	2.4	2.3	2.3	2.3	1.7	1.8	1.2	1.4	1.0	1.1	0.7	1.4	—	—
		Yoshimi-mura	(14,915)	100.0	49.5	50.5	4.3	4.3	6.3	5.9	7.2	6.9	4.3	4.2	4.4	3.7	3.4	3.2	2.7	3.4	3.4	2.7	2.3	2.7	2.2	2.7	2.3	2.3	2.3	2.3	1.7	1.7	1.3	1.4	0.8	1.1	0.6	1.3	—	—
		Moroyama-mura	(11,173)	100.0	49.5	50.5	4.1	3.6	5.4	5.0	6.0	6.3	4.5	4.8	3.8	4.1	3.8	4.1	3.2	3.0	3.2	2.7	2.7	3.0	2.7	3.0	2.3	2.0	1.7	1.7	1.5	1.3	1.1	0.9	0.7	0.9	0.9	1.5	—	—
	V	Kōnosu-shi	(31,868)	100.0	49.4	50.6	4.3	4.1	5.6	4.9	6.5	6.2	5.3	5.3	4.0	4.4	3.9	4.0	3.5	3.8	3.8	3.2	2.5	2.5	2.2	3.0	2.2	2.2	1.8	1.8	1.4	1.4	1.0	1.0	0.5	0.6	0.5	1.0	—	—
		Kisai-machi	(15,466)	100.0	48.9	51.1	4.6	4.3	5.9	5.6	6.6	6.7	4.5	4.5	3.6	3.5	3.5	3.4	3.4	3.4	3.5	2.6	2.6	2.4	2.4	2.7	2.4	2.7	1.8	1.8	1.4	1.4	1.0	0.9	0.7	0.7	0.7	1.4	—	—
		Washimiya-machi	(8,351)	100.0	48.7	51.3	4.0	3.8	5.8	5.8	6.7	5.8	4.2	5.1	4.3	4.4	3.4	4.2	3.0	3.7	3.2	3.0	2.6	2.4	2.2	2.8	2.1	2.1	1.8	1.8	1.1	1.4	0.9	1.0	0.6	0.8	0.6	1.3	—	—
		Kurihashi-machi	(12,890)	100.0	48.9	51.1	4.8	4.3	6.0	5.6	6.7	6.2	4.6	5.1	3.8	4.3	3.7	3.8	2.7	3.2	3.3	2.7	2.3	2.4	2.1	3.0	2.5	2.2	1.8	1.7	1.1	1.1	0.7	0.9	0.6	0.6	0.9	1.5	—	—
		Goka-mura	(9,157)	100.0	48.9	51.1	4.7	4.7	6.8	6.4	8.0	6.7	3.9	4.6	3.2	3.7	3.2	2.9	2.8	3.5	2.9	2.5	2.5	2.4	2.2	2.9	2.2	2.4	2.0	2.0	1.4	1.5	0.9	1.1	0.9	1.5	0.9	1.5	—	—
	VI	Sakai-machi	(22,587)	100.0	47.6	52.4	5.1	5.1	6.1	6.3	7.0	6.6	3.4	4.6	2.7	3.7	3.4	3.3	3.0	3.2	3.6	3.5	2.8	2.5	2.3	2.6	2.2	2.1	1.8	1.8	1.4	1.5	0.8	1.2	0.9	0.9	0.9	1.2	—	—
		Sashima-machi	(14,810)	100.0	48.7	51.3	5.3	4.8	7.2	6.6	7.4	7.3	3.4	4.3	2.6	2.8	3.0	3.0	2.7	3.1	3.7	3.8	2.6	2.1	2.2	2.8	2.3	2.0	1.6	1.7	1.5	1.6	0.8	1.2	0.9	1.0	0.8	1.2	—	—
		Yatabe-machi	(20,570)	100.0	48.9	51.1	3.8	3.6	5.2	5.1	6.2	5.6	3.9	4.3	3.8	3.4	3.6	3.2	2.8	3.4	3.8	2.8	2.7	2.5	2.6	3.0	2.4	2.3	1.9	2.0	1.2	1.4	1.2	1.4	0.9	1.6	0.8	1.4	—	—
	VII	Kukizaki-mura	(6,338)	100.0	49.5	50.5	4.5	3.8	5.4	5.0	5.7	5.7	4.2	3.9	4.0	4.0	3.7	3.9	2.8	3.8	3.5	3.2	2.5	2.4	2.5	2.3	2.3	2.3	1.8	1.8	1.7	1.5	1.3	1.2	0.7	0.7	0.7	1.8	—	—
		Ushiku-machi	(16,131)	100.0	49.7	50.3	4.3	4.3	5.3	5.3	5.9	5.6	5.4	3.9	3.6	3.8	4.2	3.6	3.2	4.2	3.5	2.4	2.4	2.1	2.1	3.1	2.1	2.3	1.7	1.5	0.9	1.4	0.9	1.1	0.8	1.1	—	—	—	—
		Kawachi-mura	(13,065)	100.0	48.5	51.5	4.2	4.0	5.5	5.3	6.9	6.4	4.0	4.1	3.5	3.9	3.7	3.5	2.6	3.5	2.1	2.1	2.4	2.3	3.2	3.1	2.3	2.7	2.4	2.3	1.8	2.1	1.4	1.5	1.0	1.3	0.7	1.3	—	—

- 201 -

Table 3. Population by Age (5-Year Bracket) and Sex

(Zone)	(Sector)	District	Total			Age 0–4		Age 5–9		Age 10–14		Age 15–19		Age 20–24		Age 25–29		Age 30–34		Age 35–39		Age 40–44		Age 45–49		Age 50–54		Age 55–59		Age 60–64		Age 65–69		Age 70–74		75 & Over		Un-known	
			Total	M	F	M	F	M	F	M	F	M	F	M	F	M	F	M	F	M	F	M	F	M	F	M	F	M	F	M	F	M	F	M	F	M	F	M	F
	VII	Sakae-machi	(9,732) 100.0	48.0	52.0	4.1	3.4	4.9	5.0	6.1	5.9	4.7	4.9	3.8	4.3	3.8	3.7	3.5	3.6	2.8	3.2	2.4	3.4	2.7	3.2	2.3	2.6	2.1	2.3	1.9	2.3	1.4	1.4	0.8	1.4	0.7	1.4	—	—
		Narita-shi	(43,149) 100.0	47.9	52.1	3.9	3.8	5.2	5.1	6.1	5.9	4.4	4.9	3.5	4.2	3.8	4.1	3.7	3.9	2.9	3.6	2.6	3.1	2.5	3.0	2.2	2.5	2.2	2.3	1.8	1.7	1.3	1.5	1.0	1.3	0.7	1.2	—	—
	VIII	Shisui-machi	(6,093) 100.0	48.2	51.8	3.9	3.9	4.8	5.4	6.2	6.3	4.9	5.2	3.9	3.9	3.6	3.9	3.6	3.4	2.7	3.4	2.6	3.2	2.4	3.0	2.5	2.4	2.4	2.4	1.8	1.9	1.1	1.3	0.7	1.1	0.7	1.1	—	—
		Yachimata-machi	(25,387) 100.0	49.1	50.9	4.3	4.1	5.4	5.5	6.8	6.1	4.9	4.6	3.7	4.0	3.7	3.8	3.9	3.6	2.6	2.6	2.4	3.0	2.4	3.0	2.0	2.1	1.7	1.8	1.7	1.8	1.1	1.3	0.8	1.1	0.7	1.2	—	—
		Toke-machi	(6,811) 100.0	48.1	51.9	4.2	4.4	5.2	5.7	6.6	6.3	4.2	4.2	3.6	3.8	3.6	3.7	3.6	3.6	3.0	3.2	2.5	2.9	2.5	2.9	2.5	2.2	2.0	2.0	1.7	2.0	1.1	1.0	1.0	0.9	0.8	1.5	—	—
	IX	Nagara-machi	(8,817) 100.0	48.2	51.8	4.4	4.0	6.0	6.0	6.5	6.4	3.9	4.3	3.0	2.9	3.1	3.5	3.4	3.2	2.8	3.5	2.5	2.7	2.5	2.7	2.5	2.8	2.4	2.7	2.4	2.4	1.3	1.8	1.2	1.3	1.1	2.0	—	—
		Obitsu-mura	(6,988) 100.0	47.9	52.1	4.7	4.1	5.3	5.6	6.5	7.1	3.4	3.8	3.0	3.2	3.1	3.5	3.7	3.6	2.7	3.2	3.0	2.8	2.3	2.8	2.2	2.5	2.5	2.3	2.4	2.1	1.3	1.5	1.1	1.4	0.7	1.7	—	—
	X	Koito-machi	(6,056) 100.0	49.6	50.4	4.1	3.7	5.2	5.6	7.1	6.2	4.6	5.1	3.1	3.3	3.2	3.3	3.8	3.9	2.9	3.4	2.9	3.6	2.3	2.9	2.0	2.3	2.2	2.4	2.4	2.4	1.9	1.7	1.3	1.6	0.9	1.6	—	—
		Zone 10 Total	(997,660) 100.0	49.4	50.6	4.0	3.8	4.8	4.6	6.1	5.8	5.3	5.1	4.6	4.4	4.6	4.4	4.0	3.6	3.0	3.6	2.6	3.0	2.4	2.6	2.0	2.3	2.0	2.2	1.5	1.6	1.1	1.6	0.8	1.0	0.6	1.1	—	—
		Total for 50 km. Region	(15,780,463) 100.0	51.1	48.9	3.9	3.7	4.0	3.8	5.0	4.8	6.6	5.5	6.8	5.4	5.6	5.1	4.3	3.5	3.1	3.5	2.5	2.6	2.0	2.0	1.7	2.0	1.7	1.3	1.3	1.3	0.9	0.9	0.5	0.7	0.4	0.7	—	—
		National Total	(93,418,501) 100.0	49.1	50.9	4.3	4.1	5.0	4.8	6.1	5.9	5.1	5.0	4.4	4.5	4.4	4.4	4.0	3.5	3.0	3.5	2.4	2.7	2.2	2.3	1.9	2.3	1.9	2.0	1.5	2.0	1.1	1.2	0.7	0.9	0.6	1.1	—	—

TABLE 4. MARITAL STATUS (15 YEARS AND OLDER)

1955

(Zone) Sector	District	Total (no.)	Total	M	F	Total	Not Married	Married	Widowed	Separated	Total	NM M	NM F	Married M	Married F	Widowed M	Widowed F	Separated M	Separated F
1 I	Chiyoda-ku	(97,277)	100.0	55.2	44.8	100.0	54.0	37.9	6.4	1.7	100.0	34.3	19.7	19.3	18.6	1.1	5.3	0.5	1.2
	Minato-ku	(191,559)	100.0	50.6	49.4	100.0	44.7	45.6	7.7	2.0	100.0	25.8	18.9	23.0	22.6	1.2	6.5	0.6	1.4
	Chūō-ku	(135,500)	100.0	53.5	46.5	100.0	52.4	38.4	7.3	1.9	100.0	32.5	19.9	19.6	18.8	1.0	6.3	0.4	1.5
	Bunkyō-ku	(91,206)	100.0	51.2	48.8	100.0	44.2	46.7	7.5	1.6	100.0	26.2	18.0	23.4	23.3	1.2	6.3	0.4	1.2
	Taitō-ku	(124,882)	100.0	52.9	47.1	100.0	47.5	43.3	7.1	2.1	100.0	28.8	18.7	21.9	21.4	1.5	5.6	0.7	1.4
	Zone 1 Total	(838,726)	100.0	52.4	47.6	100.0	47.7	43.1	7.3	1.9	100.0	28.8	18.9	21.8	21.3	1.3	6.0	0.5	1.4
2 I	Shinagawa-ku	(273,015)	100.0	51.0	49.0	100.0	40.2	50.8	7.2	1.8	100.0	23.9	16.3	25.4	25.4	1.2	6.0	0.5	1.3
II	Meguro-ku	(187,469)	100.0	51.0	49.0	100.0	41.0	50.2	7.3	1.5	100.0	24.4	16.6	25.1	25.1	1.1	6.2	0.4	1.1
III	Shibuya-ku	(182,763)	100.0	49.3	50.7	100.0	43.4	47.7	7.1	1.8	100.0	24.1	19.3	23.8	23.9	1.0	6.1	0.4	1.4
III	Shinjuku-ku	(261,924)	100.0	50.5	49.5	100.0	43.2	47.8	7.1	1.9	100.0	25.0	18.2	23.9	23.9	1.1	6.0	0.5	1.4
IV	Nakano-ku	(214,119)	100.0	51.5	48.5	100.0	40.6	50.8	7.0	1.6	100.0	24.7	15.9	25.4	25.4	1.0	6.0	0.4	1.2
V	Toshima-ku	(220,963)	100.0	50.6	49.4	100.0	40.7	50.6	7.0	1.7	100.0	23.8	16.9	25.3	25.3	1.1	5.9	0.4	1.3
	Kita-ku	(250,140)	100.0	50.7	49.3	100.0	37.9	53.5	7.1	1.5	100.0	22.4	15.5	26.7	26.8	1.2	5.9	0.4	1.1
VI	Arakawa-ku	(178,817)	100.0	52.7	47.3	100.0	40.6	51.1	6.7	1.6	100.0	25.0	15.6	25.7	25.4	1.4	5.3	0.6	1.0
VII	Sumida-ku	(220,267)	100.0	53.7	46.3	100.0	44.7	47.7	6.3	1.3	100.0	28.1	16.6	24.0	23.7	1.2	5.1	0.4	0.9
VIII	Kōtō-ku	(193,491)	100.0	54.6	45.4	100.0	39.8	53.0	5.9	1.3	100.0	25.8	14.0	26.9	26.1	1.4	4.5	0.5	0.8
	Zone 2 Total	(2,182,968)	100.0	51.5	48.5	100.0	41.2	50.3	6.9	1.6	100.0	24.6	16.6	25.2	25.1	1.2	5.7	0.5	1.1
3 I	Ōta-ku	(403,577)	100.0	51.5	48.5	100.0	38.0	53.8	6.8	1.4	100.0	23.1	14.9	26.9	26.9	1.1	5.7	0.4	1.0
II	Setagaya-ku	(383,222)	100.0	50.6	49.4	100.0	40.4	50.8	7.4	1.4	100.0	23.9	16.5	25.3	25.5	1.0	6.4	0.4	1.0
III	Suginami-ku	(299,173)	100.0	50.6	49.4	100.0	40.5	50.6	7.6	1.3	100.0	24.0	16.5	25.2	25.4	1.1	6.5	0.3	1.0
IV	Itabashi-ku	(214,605)	100.0	51.2	48.8	100.0	36.7	54.5	7.3	1.5	100.0	22.0	14.7	27.3	27.2	1.4	5.9	0.5	1.0
	Nerima-ku	(131,139)	100.0	51.4	48.6	100.0	38.9	52.4	7.4	1.3	100.0	23.8	15.1	26.1	26.3	1.2	6.2	0.3	1.0
VI	Adachi-ku	(223,100)	100.0	51.0	49.0	100.0	35.1	55.6	7.8	1.5	100.0	21.0	14.1	27.8	27.8	1.7	6.1	0.5	1.0
VII	Katsushika-ku	(200,320)	100.0	50.8	49.2	100.0	36.1	54.7	7.7	1.5	100.0	21.3	14.8	27.4	27.3	1.6	6.1	0.5	1.0
VIII	Edogawa-ku	(174,007)	100.0	50.6	49.4	100.0	36.2	54.9	7.6	1.3	100.0	21.2	15.0	27.5	27.4	1.5	6.1	0.4	0.9
	Urayasu-machi	(10,475)	100.0	48.8	51.2	100.0	31.0	57.4	10.3	1.3	100.0	17.2	13.8	28.6	28.8	2.6	7.7	0.4	0.9
	Zone 3 Total	(2,039,618)	100.0	50.9	49.1	100.0	38.0	53.2	7.4	1.4	100.0	22.6	15.4	26.6	26.6	1.3	6.1	0.5	1.0
4 I	Kawasaki-shi	(300,723)	100.0	52.5	47.5	100.0	35.1	57.2	6.4	1.3	100.0	22.0	13.1	28.8	28.4	1.2	5.2	0.5	0.8
II	Komae-machi	(10,139)	100.0	49.5	50.5	100.0	37.1	54.4	7.4	1.1	100.0	20.4	16.7	27.4	27.0	1.4	6.0	0.3	0.8

Table 4. Marital Status (15 Years and Older)

(Zone)	(Sector)	District	Total			Total	Not Married	Married	Widowed	Separated	Total	Not Married		Married		Widowed		Separated	
			Total	M	F							M	F	M	F	M	F	M	F
III		Mitaka-shi	(47,653) 100.0	52.1	47.9	100.0	37.7	53.9	7.1	1.3	100.0	23.6	14.1	27.0	26.9	1.1	6.0	0.4	0.9
		Musashino-shi	(69,137) 100.0	50.8	49.2	100.0	40.1	51.6	7.0	1.3	100.0	23.8	16.3	25.7	25.9	1.0	6.0	0.3	1.0
		Chōfu-shi	(30,909) 100.0	50.8	49.2	100.0	36.6	54.0	8.0	1.4	100.0	21.8	14.8	27.1	26.9	1.5	6.5	0.4	1.0
		Hoya-machi	(15,515) 100.0	50.1	49.9	100.0	34.1	56.9	7.9	1.1	100.0	20.2	13.9	28.3	28.6	1.3	6.6	0.3	0.8
IV		Yamato-machi	(8,935) 100.0	48.5	51.5	100.0	35.7	55.2	7.7	1.4	100.0	19.0	16.7	27.6	27.6	1.5	6.2	0.4	1.0
		Toda-machi	(13,829) 100.0	48.8	51.2	100.0	33.1	57.4	8.5	1.0	100.0	17.9	15.2	28.7	28.7	1.9	6.6	0.3	0.7
V		Warabi-shi	(23,207) 100.0	48.6	51.4	100.0	33.9	57.1	7.5	1.5	100.0	18.5	15.4	28.4	28.7	1.3	6.2	0.4	1.1
		Kawaguchi-shi	(88,874) 100.0	50.7	49.3	100.0	35.0	56.2	7.6	1.2	100.0	20.6	14.4	28.1	28.1	1.6	6.0	0.4	0.8
		Hatogaya-machi	(9,243) 100.0	49.6	50.4	100.0	31.6	58.8	8.6	1.0	100.0	17.9	13.7	29.4	29.4	2.0	6.6	0.3	0.7
VI		Sōka-shi	(20,565) 100.0	49.3	50.7	100.0	30.4	59.6	8.8	1.2	100.0	17.1	13.3	29.7	29.9	2.1	6.7	0.4	0.8
		Yashio-mura	(8,451) 100.0	48.7	51.3	100.0	29.7	59.5	9.8	1.0	100.0	16.2	13.5	29.7	29.8	2.4	7.4	0.4	0.6
		Misato-mura	(10,992) 100.0	48.3	51.7	100.0	29.8	59.3	10.1	0.8	100.0	16.0	13.8	29.6	29.7	2.4	7.7	0.3	0.5
		Matsudo-shi	(45,788) 100.0	49.6	50.4	100.0	33.1	57.4	8.2	1.3	100.0	18.9	14.2	28.7	28.7	1.6	6.6	0.4	0.9
VII		Ichikawa-shi	(95,923) 100.0	48.3	51.7	100.0	37.6	52.8	8.3	1.3	100.0	20.3	17.3	26.3	26.5	1.4	6.9	0.3	1.0
		Zone 4 Total	(799,883) 100.0	50.9	49.1	100.0	35.4	55.9	7.4	1.3	100.0	21.1	14.3	28.0	27.9	1.4	6.0	0.4	0.9
5	I	Tsurumi-ku	(137,766) 100.0	52.4	47.6	100.0	35.6	56.6	6.6	1.2	100.0	22.3	13.3	28.5	28.1	1.2	5.4	0.4	0.8
	III	Koganei-shi	(21,388) 100.0	51.4	48.6	100.0	39.3	52.7	7.0	1.0	100.0	23.8	15.5	26.3	26.4	1.0	6.0	0.3	0.7
		Tanashi-machi	(12,793) 100.0	49.3	50.7	100.0	34.1	57.9	6.9	1.1	100.0	18.8	15.3	28.9	29.0	1.2	5.7	0.4	0.7
		Kurume-machi	(6,460) 100.0	48.6	51.4	100.0	35.2	56.3	7.9	0.6	100.0	18.6	16.6	28.0	28.3	1.8	6.1	0.2	0.4
IV		Niza-machi	(7,570) 100.0	49.4	50.6	100.0	33.3	57.3	8.5	0.9	100.0	18.4	14.9	28.5	28.8	2.2	6.3	0.3	0.6
		Kiyose-machi	(10,965) 100.0	51.5	48.5	100.0	46.5	43.9	7.4	2.2	100.0	24.3	22.2	25.1	18.8	1.4	6.0	0.7	1.5
V		Adachi-machi	(6,911) 100.0	47.9	52.1	100.0	32.9	56.7	9.4	1.0	100.0	17.3	15.6	28.2	28.5	2.1	7.3	0.3	0.7
		Asaka-machi	(10,581) 100.0	49.1	50.9	100.0	32.4	58.9	7.7	1.0	100.0	17.7	14.7	29.4	29.5	1.7	6.0	0.3	0.7
VI		Urawa-shi	(99,068) 100.0	49.2	50.8	100.0	34.7	56.0	8.1	1.2	100.0	19.5	15.2	28.0	28.0	1.4	6.7	0.3	0.9
		Misono-mura	(6,082) 100.0	48.3	51.7	100.0	28.9	59.6	10.7	0.8	100.0	15.6	13.3	29.7	29.9	2.7	8.0	0.3	0.5
VII		Koshigaya-shi	(28,608) 100.0	48.4	51.6	100.0	27.6	61.4	10.1	0.9	100.0	15.0	12.6	30.5	30.9	2.6	7.5	0.3	0.6
		Yoshikawa-machi	(10,268) 100.0	48.2	51.8	100.0	28.4	60.4	10.3	0.9	100.0	15.3	13.1	30.1	30.3	2.5	7.8	0.3	0.6
VIII		Nagareyama-machi	(12,398) 100.0	48.3	51.7	100.0	30.2	59.0	9.9	0.9	100.0	16.4	13.8	29.4	29.6	2.2	7.7	0.3	0.6
		Kamagaya-machi	(6,482) 100.0	49.7	50.3	100.0	32.0	58.9	8.3	0.8	100.0	18.0	14.0	29.3	29.6	2.1	6.2	0.3	0.5
		Funahashi-shi	(78,170) 100.0	50.1	49.9	100.0	35.8	54.4	8.3	1.5	100.0	20.9	14.9	27.2	27.2	1.6	6.7	0.4	1.1
		Zone 5 Total	(455,510) 100.0	50.4	49.6	100.0	34.8	56.2	7.8	1.2	100.0	20.3	14.5	28.2	28.0	1.5	6.3	0.4	0.8
6	I	Nishi-ku	(71,448) 100.0	50.5	49.5	100.0	35.5	54.2	8.5	1.8	100.0	20.9	14.6	27.2	27.0	1.8	6.7	0.6	1.2
		Naka-ku	(78,105) 100.0	49.4	50.6	100.0	39.6	49.9	8.2	2.3	100.0	22.0	17.6	25.2	24.7	1.5	6.7	0.7	1.6

Table 4. Marital Status (15 Years and Older)

(Zone)(Sector)	District	Total			Total	Not Married	Married	Widowed	Separated	Total	Not Married		Married		Widowed		Separated	
		Total	M	F							M	F	M	F	M	F	M	F
I	Kanagawa-ku	(99,285) 100.0	51.5	48.5	100.0	35.1	55.7	7.7	1.5	100.0	21.6	13.5	27.9	27.8	1.5	6.2	0.5	1.0
II	Kōhoku-ku	(74,979) 100.0	49.9	50.1	100.0	33.7	56.9	8.4	1.0	100.0	19.6	14.1	28.3	28.6	1.7	6.7	0.3	0.7
III	Inagi-machi	(3,747) 100.0	49.4	50.6	100.0	31.6	57.7	9.5	1.2	100.0	17.9	13.7	28.8	28.9	2.1	7.4	0.6	0.6
	Tama-mura	(2,625) 100.0	50.4	49.6	100.0	39.3	50.2	8.7	1.8	100.0	21.8	17.5	25.5	24.7	2.4	6.3	0.7	1.1
	Fuchu-shi	(21,989) 100.0	54.8	45.2	100.0	35.3	54.3	7.4	3.0	100.0	21.9	13.4	28.7	25.6	2.1	5.3	2.1	0.9
	Kunitachi-machi	(8,633) 100.0	51.6	48.4	100.0	38.1	54.0	6.7	1.2	100.0	23.3	14.8	26.9	27.1	1.1	5.6	0.3	0.9
	Kokubunji-machi	(9,502) 100.0	53.3	46.7	100.0	39.3	52.8	7.0	0.9	100.0	24.8	14.5	26.9	25.9	1.3	5.7	0.3	0.6
	Kodaira-machi	(10,375) 100.0	51.7	48.3	100.0	39.8	52.2	6.8	1.2	100.0	23.1	16.7	26.9	25.3	1.3	5.5	0.4	0.8
	Higashimurayama-machi	(8,878) 100.0	50.7	49.3	100.0	34.4	54.5	9.1	2.0	100.0	19.5	14.9	28.0	26.5	2.3	6.8	0.9	1.1
IV	Tokorosawa-shi	(20,231) 100.0	48.1	51.9	100.0	35.4	54.8	8.9	0.9	100.0	18.5	16.9	27.3	27.5	2.1	6.8	0.2	0.7
	Miyoshi-mura	(1,539) 100.0	48.8	51.2	100.0	36.4	54.0	9.2	0.4	100.0	19.5	16.9	27.0	27.0	2.1	7.1	0.2	0.2
	Fujimi-mura	(4,008) 100.0	49.1	50.9	100.0	32.9	56.9	9.6	0.6	100.0	17.8	15.1	28.4	28.5	2.7	6.9	0.2	0.4
V	Yono-shi	(13,716) 100.0	49.2	50.8	100.0	32.9	58.6	7.4	1.1	100.0	18.2	14.7	29.2	29.4	1.5	5.9	0.3	0.8
	Ōmiya-shi	(56,077) 100.0	48.7	51.3	100.0	32.9	58.0	8.1	1.0	100.0	17.8	15.1	28.9	29.1	1.7	6.4	0.3	0.7
	Iwatsuki-shi	(13,368) 100.0	48.2	51.8	100.0	29.7	59.4	10.1	0.8	100.0	15.9	13.8	29.6	29.8	2.5	7.6	0.2	0.6
VI	Matsubushi-mura	(3,498) 100.0	48.1	51.9	100.0	27.1	61.1	11.0	0.8	100.0	14.4	12.7	30.4	30.7	3.0	8.0	0.3	0.5
VII	Kashiwa-shi	(17,360) 100.0	49.1	50.9	100.0	31.4	59.4	8.2	1.0	100.0	17.2	14.2	29.7	29.7	1.9	6.3	0.3	0.7
	Shōnan-mura	(4,425) 100.0	48.7	51.3	100.0	27.5	62.0	9.6	0.9	100.0	15.0	12.5	30.8	31.2	2.6	7.0	0.3	0.6
	Shirai-mura	(3,338) 100.0	48.3	51.7	100.0	28.7	60.5	9.9	0.9	100.0	15.0	13.7	30.2	30.3	2.7	7.2	0.4	0.5
VIII	Narashino-shi	(11,903) 100.0	50.9	49.1	100.0	36.0	55.2	7.7	1.1	100.0	21.5	14.5	27.6	27.6	1.5	6.2	0.3	0.8
	Zone 6 Total	(390,828) 100.0	50.2	49.8	100.0	35.0	55.5	8.1	1.4	100.0	20.1	14.9	27.9	27.6	1.7	6.4	0.5	0.9
7 I	Isogo-ku	(47,841) 100.0	48.6	51.4	100.0	34.4	55.1	8.9	1.6	100.0	19.2	15.2	27.4	27.7	1.5	7.4	0.5	1.1
	Minami-ku	(121,884) 100.0	50.1	49.9	100.0	35.3	53.8	8.7	2.2	100.0	20.3	15.0	27.1	26.7	1.8	6.9	0.9	1.3
	Hodogaya-ku	(66,040) 100.0	50.1	49.9	100.0	33.5	57.1	8.1	1.3	100.0	19.5	14.0	28.5	28.6	1.6	6.5	0.5	0.8
II	Machida-shi	(38,575) 100.0	49.7	50.3	100.0	34.6	56.9	7.6	0.9	100.0	19.2	15.4	28.5	28.4	1.7	5.9	0.3	0.6
	Yuki-mura	(4,104) 100.0	49.2	50.8	100.0	34.0	55.8	9.3	0.9	100.0	18.4	15.6	27.7	28.1	2.7	6.6	0.4	0.5
III	Hino-machi	(17,866) 100.0	49.6	50.4	100.0	34.1	57.4	7.8	0.7	100.0	19.1	15.0	28.7	28.7	1.6	6.2	0.2	0.5
	Tachikawa-shi	(44,595) 100.0	49.9	50.1	100.0	40.0	51.3	7.0	1.7	100.0	22.7	17.3	25.7	25.6	1.1	5.9	0.4	1.3
	Sunakawa-machi	(7,972) 100.0	49.3	50.7	100.0	33.6	57.2	8.2	1.0	100.0	18.6	15.0	28.5	28.7	1.8	6.4	0.4	0.6
	Yamato-machi	(8,095) 100.0	49.8	50.2	100.0	34.0	56.5	8.6	0.9	100.0	18.6	15.4	28.3	28.2	2.4	6.2	0.5	0.4
IV	Ōi-mura	(3,134) 100.0	50.5	49.5	100.0	35.3	54.6	9.5	0.6	100.0	20.6	14.7	27.3	27.3	2.3	7.2	0.3	0.3
	Fukuoka-mura	(4,872) 100.0	48.8	51.2	100.0	29.2	63.0	7.0	0.8	100.0	15.2	14.0	31.3	31.7	1.9	5.1	0.4	0.3
V	Kasukabe-shi	(20,837) 100.0	48.4	51.6	100.0	29.0	59.8	10.3	0.9	100.0	15.8	13.2	29.8	30.0	2.5	7.8	0.3	0.6
	Shōwa-mura	(9,143) 100.0	48.4	51.6	100.0	26.8	61.6	10.4	1.2	100.0	14.3	12.5	30.9	30.7	2.7	7.7	0.5	0.7

Table 4. Marital Status (15 Years and Older)

(Zone)	(Sector)	District	Total (Total)	Total (M)	Total (F)	Total	Not Married	Married	Widowed	Separated	Total	Not Married (M)	Not Married (F)	Married (M)	Married (F)	Widowed (M)	Widowed (F)	Separated (M)	Separated (F)
	VI	Noda-shi	(35,073)	47.6	52.4	100.0	29.4	59.7	9.7	1.2	100.0	15.1	14.3	29.8	29.9	2.3	7.4	0.4	0.8
	VII	Abiko-machi	(16,491)	48.0	52.0	100.0	30.8	58.9	9.0	1.3	100.0	16.5	14.3	29.2	29.7	1.9	7.1	0.4	0.9
	VIII	Yachiyo-machi	(10,130)	47.9	52.1	100.0	31.1	57.1	10.5	1.3	100.0	16.3	14.8	28.4	28.7	2.8	7.7	0.4	0.9
	VIII	Chiba-shi	(135,724)	49.8	50.2	100.0	35.2	54.9	8.4	1.5	100.0	20.0	15.2	27.7	27.2	1.6	6.8	0.5	1.0
	IX	Goi-machi	(12,190)	47.6	52.4	100.0	30.4	58.3	10.2	1.1	100.0	15.4	15.0	29.1	29.2	2.7	7.5	0.4	0.7
		Sodegaura-machi	(9,068)	47.9	52.1	100.0	29.9	58.5	10.5	1.1	100.0	16.1	13.8	29.1	29.4	2.3	8.2	0.4	0.7
		Zone 7 Total	(613,634)	49.4	50.6	100.0	34.2	55.8	8.6	1.4	100.0	19.1	15.1	28.0	27.8	1.8	6.8	0.5	0.9
8	I	Kanazawa-ku	(42,004)	50.5	49.5	100.0	32.2	58.4	8.0	1.4	100.0	19.3	12.9	29.3	29.1	1.4	6.6	0.5	0.9
		Totsuka-ku	(54,159)	49.9	50.1	100.0	33.1	57.9	8.1	0.9	100.0	18.9	14.2	29.0	28.9	1.7	6.4	0.3	0.6
	II	Yamato-shi	(16,046)	46.5	53.5	100.0	31.9	59.9	7.0	1.2	100.0	15.3	16.6	29.8	30.1	1.1	5.9	0.3	0.9
		Sagamihara-shi	(54,831)	50.0	50.0	100.0	33.1	58.9	7.0	1.0	100.0	18.6	14.5	29.5	29.4	1.6	5.4	0.3	0.7
		Zama-machi	(8,738)	47.8	52.2	100.0	34.9	56.8	7.3	1.0	100.0	17.7	17.2	28.3	28.5	1.6	5.7	0.2	0.8
	III	Hachiōji-shi	(96,219)	48.3	51.7	100.0	36.7	54.1	8.1	1.1	100.0	19.2	17.5	27.0	27.1	1.8	6.3	0.3	0.8
		Akishima-shi	(24,681)	48.6	51.4	100.0	32.9	57.7	7.9	1.5	100.0	17.4	15.5	28.8	28.9	1.8	6.1	0.6	0.9
		Fussa-machi	(12,984)	50.5	49.5	100.0	36.6	56.1	6.1	1.2	100.0	20.1	16.5	28.7	27.4	1.3	4.8	0.4	0.8
		Mizuho-machi	(6,140)	48.8	51.2	100.0	36.4	55.1	7.8	0.7	100.0	19.0	17.4	27.5	27.6	2.0	5.8	0.3	0.4
		Murayama-machi	(7,809)	48.4	51.6	100.0	39.6	50.4	9.0	1.0	100.0	20.2	19.4	25.5	24.9	2.3	6.7	0.4	0.6
		Musashi-machi	(18,408)	48.0	52.0	100.0	36.9	53.4	8.9	0.8	100.0	18.8	18.1	26.8	26.6	2.2	6.7	0.2	0.6
	IV	Sayama-shi	(20,917)	48.0	52.0	100.0	34.6	55.4	9.3	0.7	100.0	17.8	16.8	27.6	27.8	2.4	6.9	0.2	0.5
		Kawagoe-shi	(69,213)	48.4	51.6	100.0	33.0	56.6	9.5	0.9	100.0	17.7	15.3	28.3	28.3	2.1	7.4	0.3	0.6
		Seibu-machi	(6,187)	44.1	55.9	100.0	40.9	50.2	8.2	0.7	100.0	16.8	24.1	25.0	25.2	2.1	6.1	0.2	0.5
	V	Ageo-shi	(23,146)	48.2	51.8	100.0	32.5	57.7	9.1	0.7	100.0	17.0	15.5	28.8	28.9	2.2	6.9	0.2	0.5
		Ina-mura	(4,612)	48.8	51.2	100.0	32.4	56.1	10.9	0.6	100.0	17.8	14.6	28.0	28.1	2.7	8.2	0.3	0.3
		Hasuda-machi	(12,822)	48.8	51.2	100.0	33.0	56.4	9.6	1.0	100.0	17.7	15.3	28.4	28.0	2.4	7.2	0.3	0.7
		Shiraoka-machi	(10,060)	48.9	51.1	100.0	30.1	59.3	9.9	0.7	100.0	16.5	13.6	29.6	29.7	2.6	7.3	0.2	0.5
		Miyashiro-machi	(6,906)	48.3	51.7	100.0	29.5	60.4	9.4	0.7	100.0	15.6	13.9	30.1	30.3	2.4	7.0	0.2	0.5
		Sugito-machi	(11,060)	48.2	51.8	100.0	28.2	60.1	11.0	0.7	100.0	15.4	12.8	29.9	30.2	2.7	8.3	0.2	0.5
	VI	Sekiyado-machi	(8,602)	46.7	53.3	100.0	25.0	63.3	11.0	0.7	100.0	12.3	12.7	31.4	31.9	2.8	8.2	0.2	0.5
	VII	Moriya-machi	(7,745)	47.3	52.7	100.0	26.9	61.3	10.7	1.1	100.0	13.8	13.1	30.4	30.9	2.8	7.9	0.3	0.8
		Toride-machi	(14,222)	47.8	52.2	100.0	30.6	58.3	9.9	1.2	100.0	16.1	14.5	28.9	29.4	2.4	7.5	0.4	0.8
		Inzai-machi	(11,802)	48.3	51.7	100.0	27.8	60.1	10.9	1.2	100.0	15.1	12.7	30.0	30.1	2.8	8.1	0.4	0.8
		Inba-mura	(5,862)	47.5	52.5	100.0	21.8	64.7	12.3	1.2	100.0	11.6	10.2	32.2	32.5	3.3	9.0	0.4	0.8
	VII	Yotsukaidō-machi	(11,994)	47.8	52.2	100.0	31.6	57.8	9.2	1.4	100.0	16.4	15.2	28.4	28.9	2.0	7.2	0.5	0.9
	IX	Ichihara-machi	(9,560)	47.9	52.1	100.0	31.5	57.1	10.6	0.8	100.0	17.0	14.5	28.4	28.7	2.2	8.4	0.3	0.5

Table 4. Marital Status (15 Years and Older)

(Zone)	(Sector)	District	Total	Total M	Total F	Total	Not Married	Married	Widowed	Separated	Total	Not Married M	Not Married F	Married M	Married F	Widowed M	Widowed F	Separated M	Separated F
	IX	Anegasaki-machi	(7,470) 100.0	47.4	52.6	100.0	28.9	59.4	10.7	1.0	100.0	15.2	13.7	29.4	30.0	2.5	8.2	0.3	0.7
		Hirakawa-machi	(7,658) 100.0	47.1	52.9	100.0	26.1	61.4	11.3	1.2	100.0	13.6	12.5	30.5	30.9	2.6	8.7	0.4	0.8
		Miwa-machi	(7,511) 100.0	47.7	52.3	100.0	27.4	60.6	11.1	0.9	100.0	14.4	13.0	30.0	30.6	3.0	8.1	0.3	0.6
	X	Kisarazu-shi	(34,593) 100.0	46.5	53.5	100.0	28.7	59.8	10.3	1.2	100.0	14.2	14.5	29.7	30.1	2.3	8.0	0.3	0.9
		Zone 8 Total	(633,961) 100.0	48.5	51.5	100.0	32.9	57.3	8.8	1.0	100.0	17.6	15.3	28.6	28.7	2.0	6.8	0.3	0.7
9	I	Kamakura-shi	(65,078) 100.0	47.5	52.5	100.0	35.5	53.8	9.0	1.7	100.0	18.9	16.6	26.7	27.1	1.4	7.6	0.5	1.2
	II	Ayase-machi	(5,326) 100.0	49.6	50.4	100.0	34.1	56.0	9.0	0.9	100.0	19.2	14.9	27.9	28.1	2.2	6.8	0.3	0.6
		Ebina-machi	(10,777) 100.0	49.2	50.8	100.0	34.1	56.5	8.5	0.9	100.0	18.5	15.6	28.2	28.3	2.2	6.3	0.3	0.6
		Shiroyama-machi	(3,288) 100.0	48.9	51.1	100.0	32.9	56.2	10.4	0.5	100.0	17.5	15.4	28.0	28.2	3.2	7.2	0.2	0.3
	III	Akita-machi	(9,253) 100.0	49.6	50.4	100.0	34.9	54.7	9.8	0.6	100.0	19.0	15.9	27.3	27.4	3.1	6.7	0.2	0.4
		Hamura-machi	(6,823) 100.0	49.7	50.3	100.0	39.7	52.1	7.6	0.6	100.0	21.6	18.1	26.1	26.0	1.8	5.8	0.2	0.4
	IV	Hannō-shi	(28,895) 100.0	47.8	52.2	100.0	31.6	57.9	9.6	0.9	100.0	16.4	15.2	28.8	29.1	2.3	7.3	0.3	0.6
		Tsurugashima-mura	(4,576) 100.0	50.1	49.9	100.0	33.0	57.6	8.7	0.7	100.0	18.8	14.2	28.8	28.8	2.3	6.4	0.2	0.5
		Hidaka-machi	(10,936) 100.0	49.3	50.7	100.0	29.9	59.5	9.8	0.8	100.0	16.4	13.5	29.9	29.6	2.7	7.1	0.3	0.5
		Kawashima-mura	(11,398) 100.0	47.1	52.9	100.0	30.5	57.4	11.5	0.6	100.0	15.5	15.0	28.6	28.8	2.8	8.7	0.2	0.4
	V	Kitamoto-machi	(8,885) 100.0	49.0	51.0	100.0	28.9	61.0	9.4	0.7	100.0	15.9	13.0	30.4	30.6	2.5	6.9	0.2	0.5
		Higawa-machi	(12,636) 100.0	48.6	51.4	100.0	31.1	59.3	8.9	0.7	100.0	16.9	14.2	29.5	29.8	1.9	7.0	0.3	0.4
		Shobu-machi	(10,897) 100.0	48.0	52.0	100.0	29.7	58.3	11.2	0.8	100.0	15.5	14.2	29.0	29.3	3.2	8.0	0.3	0.5
		Kuki-machi	(14,180) 100.0	48.5	51.5	100.0	29.8	60.1	9.3	0.8	100.0	16.0	13.8	29.9	30.2	2.3	7.0	0.3	0.5
		Satte-machi	(15,829) 100.0	47.1	52.9	100.0	31.2	56.9	10.9	1.0	100.0	15.7	15.5	28.3	28.6	2.7	8.2	0.4	0.6
	VI	Iwai-machi	(22,280) 100.0	47.4	52.6	100.0	25.9	62.8	10.6	0.7	100.0	12.8	13.1	31.1	31.7	3.2	7.4	0.3	0.4
		Mitsukaidō-shi	(26,402) 100.0	46.8	53.2	100.0	27.2	60.7	11.1	1.0	100.0	13.6	13.6	30.1	30.6	2.8	8.3	0.3	0.7
		Yawahara-mura	(7,730) 100.0	47.1	52.9	100.0	26.6	60.9	11.6	0.9	100.0	13.6	13.0	30.2	30.7	3.1	8.5	0.2	0.7
		Ina-mura	(8,559) 100.0	47.5	52.5	100.0	26.6	60.3	11.9	1.2	100.0	14.0	12.6	30.1	30.2	3.0	8.9	0.4	0.8
	VII	Fujishiro-machi	(8,783) 100.0	47.3	52.7	100.0	27.2	60.4	11.4	1.3	100.0	14.1	13.1	30.0	30.4	2.8	8.6	0.4	0.6
		Ryūgasaki-shi	(22,716) 100.0	47.4	52.6	100.0	27.2	61.2	10.3	1.3	100.0	14.2	13.0	30.4	30.8	2.4	7.9	0.4	0.9
		Tone-mura	(6,458) 100.0	47.4	52.6	100.0	26.1	61.6	10.9	1.4	100.0	13.8	12.3	30.7	30.9	2.5	8.4	0.4	1.0
		Motono-mura	(3,659) 100.0	47.7	52.3	100.0	25.5	62.3	11.0	1.2	100.0	13.0	12.5	31.0	31.3	3.2	7.8	0.5	1.0
	VIII	Sakura-shi	(23,924) 100.0	47.5	52.5	100.0	29.8	57.8	11.0	1.4	100.0	15.9	13.9	28.8	29.0	2.4	8.6	0.4	1.0
		Izumi-machi	(6,459) 100.0	47.4	52.6	100.0	27.8	61.1	10.1	1.0	100.0	14.3	13.5	30.4	30.7	2.3	7.8	0.4	0.6
	IX	Shitsu-mura	(6,408) 100.0	47.7	52.3	100.0	29.7	58.3	11.1	0.9	100.0	15.4	14.3	29.0	29.3	3.1	8.0	0.2	0.7
		Nansō-machi	(12,450) 100.0	47.5	52.5	100.0	26.8	60.1	12.0	1.1	100.0	14.3	12.5	29.8	30.3	3.0	9.0	0.4	0.7
		Fukuta-machi	(4,894) 100.0	50.2	49.8	100.0	23.6	64.4	10.7	1.3	100.0	12.8	10.8	32.0	32.4	2.8	7.9	0.6	0.7
	X	Kimitsu-machi	(9,216) 100.0	46.9	53.1	100.0	26.2	62.1	10.7	1.0	100.0	13.4	12.8	30.7	31.4	2.5	8.2	0.3	0.7

- 207 -

Table 4. Marital Status (15 Years and Older)

(Zone)	(Sector)	District	Total			Total	Not Married	Married	Widowed	Separated	Total	Not Married		Married		Widowed		Separated	
			Total	M	F							M	F	M	F	M	F	M	F
	X	Futtsu-machi	(11,078) 100.0	47.3	52.7	100.0	29.8	58.3	10.9	1.0	100.0	15.5	14.3	28.9	29.4	2.6	8.3	0.3	0.7
		Ōsawa-machi	(9,609) 100.0	46.5	53.5	100.0	27.8	58.6	12.3	1.3	100.0	14.5	13.3	28.8	29.8	2.7	9.6	0.5	0.8
		Zone 9 Total	(409,402) 100.0	47.8	52.2	100.0	30.4	58.4	10.2	1.0	100.0	16.1	14.3	29.0	29.4	2.4	7.8	0.3	0.7
10	I	Yokosuka-shi	(191,099) 100.0	50.1	49.9	100.0	35.1	54.9	8.6	1.4	100.0	20.5	14.6	27.6	27.3	1.5	7.1	0.5	0.9
		Zushi-shi	(26,556) 100.0	47.8	52.2	100.0	33.5	56.1	9.0	1.4	100.0	18.2	15.3	27.8	28.3	1.4	7.6	0.4	1.0
		Hayama-machi	(10,556) 100.0	46.5	53.5	100.0	32.0	56.0	10.7	1.3	100.0	16.8	15.2	27.7	28.3	1.6	9.1	0.4	0.9
		Chigasaki-shi	(38,157) 100.0	48.4	51.6	100.0	31.9	58.5	8.7	0.9	100.0	17.4	14.5	29.1	29.4	1.6	7.1	0.3	0.6
		Fujisawa-shi	(74,583) 100.0	48.0	52.0	100.0	33.8	56.1	8.7	1.4	100.0	18.2	15.6	27.9	28.2	1.5	7.2	0.4	1.0
	II	Aikawa-machi	(9,483) 100.0	46.9	53.1	100.0	34.3	55.2	9.7	0.8	100.0	16.5	17.8	27.7	27.5	2.4	7.3	0.3	0.5
		Atsugi-shi	(29,309) 100.0	45.9	54.1	100.0	33.4	56.6	9.2	0.8	100.0	15.1	18.3	28.2	28.4	2.3	6.9	0.3	0.5
		Samukawa-machi	(7,148) 100.0	49.5	50.5	100.0	30.6	59.7	9.0	0.7	100.0	17.2	13.4	29.8	29.9	2.2	6.8	0.3	0.4
	III	Ōme-shi	(37,293) 100.0	47.1	52.9	100.0	38.7	52.0	8.5	0.8	100.0	18.9	19.8	25.9	26.1	2.1	6.4	0.2	0.6
	IV	Sakado-machi	(15,561) 100.0	48.4	51.6	100.0	30.1	59.3	9.9	0.7	100.0	16.3	13.8	29.5	29.8	2.4	7.5	0.2	0.5
		Yoshimi-mura	(9,956) 100.0	48.6	51.4	100.0	29.0	58.7	11.5	0.8	100.0	15.9	13.1	29.1	29.6	3.3	8.2	0.3	0.5
		Moroyama-mura	(7,505) 100.0	48.6	51.4	100.0	33.3	55.6	9.9	1.2	100.0	17.9	15.4	27.9	27.7	2.4	7.5	0.4	0.8
	V	Kōnosu-shi	(20,287) 100.0	48.0	52.0	100.0	31.9	57.8	9.3	1.0	100.0	16.7	15.2	28.8	29.0	2.2	7.1	0.3	0.7
		Kisai-machi	(10,506) 100.0	48.0	52.0	100.0	28.2	60.1	10.9	0.8	100.0	14.9	13.3	30.0	30.1	2.9	8.0	0.2	0.6
		Washimiya-machi	(5,631) 100.0	49.0	51.0	100.0	30.8	58.1	10.3	0.8	100.0	17.2	13.6	29.0	29.1	2.5	7.8	0.3	0.5
		Kurihashi-machi	(7,947) 100.0	47.2	52.8	100.0	28.2	60.3	10.6	0.9	100.0	14.8	13.4	30.0	30.3	2.2	8.4	0.2	0.7
		Goka-mura	(5,996) 100.0	46.6	53.4	100.0	27.8	60.8	10.5	0.9	100.0	13.0	14.8	30.3	30.5	2.9	7.6	0.4	0.5
	VI	Sakai-machi	(14,784) 100.0	46.6	53.4	100.0	26.1	62.6	10.6	0.7	100.0	12.5	13.6	31.1	31.5	2.8	7.8	0.2	0.5
		Sashima-machi	(9,415) 100.0	47.2	52.8	100.0	25.6	62.6	10.9	0.9	100.0	12.7	12.9	30.9	31.7	3.3	7.6	0.3	0.6
		Yatabe-machi	(15,031) 100.0	48.0	52.0	100.0	26.2	62.8	10.1	0.9	100.0	13.7	12.5	31.3	31.5	2.7	7.4	0.3	0.6
	VII	Kukizaki-mura	(4,397) 100.0	48.3	51.7	100.0	26.6	63.3	9.2	0.9	100.0	14.0	12.6	31.5	31.8	2.5	6.7	0.3	0.6
		Ushiku-machi	(10,549) 100.0	49.6	50.4	100.0	28.5	60.6	9.8	1.1	100.0	16.4	12.1	30.2	30.4	2.6	7.2	0.4	0.7
		Kawachi-mura	(9,220) 100.0	47.0	53.0	100.0	26.1	61.8	11.0	1.1	100.0	13.3	12.8	30.7	31.1	2.6	8.4	0.4	0.7
		Sakae-machi	(6,857) 100.0	46.6	53.4	100.0	27.9	59.0	11.7	1.4	100.0	14.3	13.6	29.2	29.8	2.8	8.9	0.3	1.1
		Narita-shi	(30,291) 100.0	47.1	52.9	100.0	29.0	58.8	10.6	1.6	100.0	15.1	13.9	29.3	29.5	2.3	8.3	0.4	1.2
	VIII	Shisui-machi	(4,100) 100.0	48.3	51.7	100.0	29.1	58.9	10.4	1.6	100.0	15.7	13.4	29.4	29.5	2.6	7.8	0.6	1.0
		Yachimata-machi	(16,801) 100.0	48.2	51.8	100.0	30.9	59.0	9.1	1.0	100.0	16.6	14.3	29.3	29.7	2.0	7.1	0.3	0.7
		Toke-machi	(4,363) 100.0	46.8	53.2	100.0	30.3	58.5	10.1	1.1	100.0	14.9	15.4	29.0	29.5	2.5	7.6	0.4	0.7
	IX	Nagara-machi	(6,054) 100.0	47.2	52.8	100.0	24.4	62.1	12.7	0.8	100.0	13.4	11.0	30.7	31.4	2.8	9.9	0.3	0.5
		Obitsu-mura	(4,861) 100.0	47.9	52.1	100.0	23.3	64.0	11.7	1.1	100.0	12.8	10.5	31.7	32.3	3.1	8.6	0.3	0.7
	X	Koito-machi	(4,319) 100.0	48.0	52.0	100.0	25.4	61.5	12.0	1.1	100.0	14.1	11.3	30.6	30.9	2.9	9.1	0.4	0.7

Table 4. Marital Status (15 Years and Older)

(Zone)	(Sector)	District	Total			Total	Not Married	Married	Widowed	Separated	Total	Not Married		Married		Widowed		Separated	
			Total	M	F							M	F	M	F	M	F	M	F
		Zone 10 Total	(648,615) 100.0	48.4	51.6	100.0	32.3	57.1	9.4	1.2	100.0	17.5	14.8	28.5	28.6	2.0	7.4	0.4	0.8
		Total for 50km.Region	(9,327,110) 100.0	50.5	49.5	100.0	37.7	53.1	7.8	1.4	100.0	22.0	15.7	26.6	26.5	1.5	6.3	0.4	1.0
		National Total	(59,474,007) 100.0	48.2	51.8	100.0	31.0	57.7	9.8	1.5	100.0	17.0	14.0	28.8	28.9	1.9	7.9	0.5	1.0
		1960																	
1	I	Chiyoda-ku	(98,108) 100.0	55.4	44.6	100.0	57.5	35.0	5.8	1.7	100.0	36.4	21.1	17.7	17.3	0.9	4.9	0.4	1.3
		Minato-ku	(214,886) 100.0	51.1	48.9	100.0	48.2	42.8	6.9	2.1	100.0	28.1	20.1	21.5	21.3	1.0	5.9	0.5	1.6
		Chūō-ku	(134,525) 100.0	54.6	45.4	100.0	55.7	35.9	6.6	1.8	100.0	35.2	20.5	18.2	17.7	0.9	5.7	0.3	1.5
		Bunkyō-ku	(208,037) 100.0	51.6	48.4	100.0	46.9	44.8	6.6	1.7	100.0	27.8	19.1	22.4	22.4	1.0	5.6	0.4	1.3
		Taitō-ku	(257,971) 100.0	53.3	46.7	100.0	49.1	42.2	6.3	2.4	100.0	29.9	19.2	21.2	21.0	1.3	5.0	0.9	1.5
		Zone 1 Total	(913,527) 100.0	52.8	47.2	100.0	50.5	41.2	6.4	1.9	100.0	30.7	19.8	20.7	20.5	1.0	5.4	0.4	1.5
2	I	Shinagawa-ku	(337,220) 100.0	51.7	48.3	100.0	43.8	48.1	6.2	1.9	100.0	26.1	17.7	24.1	24.0	1.0	5.2	0.5	1.4
	II	Meguro-ku	(232,624) 100.0	51.5	48.5	100.0	44.3	47.9	6.2	1.6	100.0	26.3	18.0	23.9	24.0	0.9	5.3	0.4	1.2
	III	Shibuya-ku	(227,227) 100.0	49.5	50.5	100.0	46.2	45.6	6.2	2.0	100.0	25.4	20.8	22.8	22.8	0.9	5.3	0.4	1.6
	III	Shinjuku-ku	(334,028) 100.0	51.2	48.8	100.0	46.7	45.2	6.0	2.1	100.0	27.1	19.6	22.7	22.5	0.9	5.1	0.5	1.6
	IV	Nakano-ku	(277,753) 100.0	52.1	47.9	100.0	43.0	49.3	6.0	1.7	100.0	26.2	16.8	24.7	24.6	0.8	5.2	0.4	1.3
	V	Toshima-ku	(288,959) 100.0	50.8	49.2	100.0	43.3	48.6	6.0	2.1	100.0	25.1	18.2	24.3	24.3	0.9	5.1	0.5	1.6
	VI	Kita-ku	(320,622) 100.0	50.7	49.3	100.0	39.7	52.4	6.2	1.7	100.0	23.1	16.6	26.2	26.2	1.0	5.2	0.4	1.3
	VII	Arakawa-ku	(216,571) 100.0	53.4	46.6	100.0	42.5	49.6	6.1	1.8	100.0	26.5	16.0	24.9	24.7	1.3	4.8	0.7	1.1
	VIII	Sumida-ku	(256,266) 100.0	53.8	46.2	100.0	47.6	45.4	5.6	1.4	100.0	29.6	18.0	22.8	22.6	1.0	4.6	0.4	1.0
		Kōtō-ku	(262,278) 100.0	56.0	44.0	100.0	43.0	50.6	5.0	1.4	100.0	28.7	14.3	25.6	25.0	1.1	3.9	0.6	0.8
		Zone 2 Total	(2,753,548) 100.0	52.0	48.0	100.0	43.9	48.3	6.0	1.8	100.0	26.3	17.6	24.2	24.1	1.0	5.0	0.5	1.3
3	I	Ōta-ku	(541,810) 100.0	53.2	46.8	100.0	42.2	50.6	5.7	1.5	100.0	26.6	15.6	25.3	25.3	0.9	4.8	0.4	1.1
	II	Setagaya-ku	(508,371) 100.0	50.9	49.1	100.0	41.8	50.4	6.4	1.4	100.0	24.7	17.1	25.1	25.3	0.8	5.6	0.3	1.1
	III	Suginami-ku	(383,096) 100.0	50.8	49.2	100.0	42.4	49.6	6.6	1.4	100.0	24.9	17.5	24.7	24.9	0.9	5.7	0.3	1.1
	IV	Itabashi-ku	(307,278) 100.0	52.2	47.8	100.0	39.6	52.8	6.1	1.5	100.0	24.3	15.3	26.4	26.4	1.1	5.0	0.4	1.1
		Nerima-ku	(226,540) 100.0	50.9	49.1	100.0	37.3	55.2	6.3	1.2	100.0	22.1	15.2	27.5	27.7	1.0	5.3	0.3	0.9
	VI	Adachi-ku	(294,341) 100.0	51.4	48.6	100.0	37.2	54.5	6.8	1.5	100.0	22.3	14.9	27.3	27.2	1.3	5.5	0.5	1.0
	VII	Katsushika-ku	(277,158) 100.0	51.3	48.7	100.0	38.6	53.4	6.5	1.5	100.0	22.9	15.7	26.7	26.7	1.2	5.3	0.5	1.0
	VIII	Edogawa-ku	(233,673) 100.0	51.8	48.2	100.0	38.8	53.3	6.5	1.4	100.0	23.5	15.3	26.7	26.6	1.2	5.3	0.4	1.0
		Urayasu-machi	(11,423) 100.0	49.1	50.9	100.0	32.1	57.0	9.5	1.4	100.0	17.8	14.3	28.5	28.5	2.3	7.2	0.5	0.9

Table 4. Marital Status (15 Years and Older)

(Zone) (Sector)	District	Total				Not Married	Married	Widowed	Separated	Total	Not Married		Married		Widowed		Separated	
		Total	M	F	Total						M	F	M	F	M	F	M	F
	Zone 3 Total	(2,783,690)	51.6	48.4	100.0	40.3	52.0	6.3	1.4	100.0	24.2	16.1	26.0	26.0	1.0	5.3	0.4	1.0
4 I	Kawasaki-shi	(463,162)	53.5	46.5	100.0	38.2	55.1	5.4	1.3	100.0	24.2	14.0	27.8	27.3	1.0	4.4	0.5	0.8
II	Komae-machi	(18,618)	50.7	49.3	100.0	36.5	56.1	6.2	1.2	100.0	21.3	15.2	28.1	28.0	1.0	5.2	0.3	0.9
III	Mitaka-shi	(73,197)	51.6	48.4	100.0	38.5	54.0	6.1	1.4	100.0	23.3	15.2	27.0	27.0	0.9	5.2	0.4	1.0
	Musashino-shi	(93,385)	51.2	48.8	100.0	40.5	52.2	6.1	1.2	100.0	24.1	16.4	26.0	26.2	0.8	5.3	0.3	0.9
	Chōfu-shi	(49,928)	50.4	49.6	100.0	36.5	55.4	6.7	1.4	100.0	21.3	15.2	27.7	27.7	1.0	5.7	0.4	1.0
IV	Hoya-machi	(33,448)	50.1	49.9	100.0	31.1	61.3	6.5	1.1	100.0	18.3	12.8	30.5	30.8	1.0	5.5	0.3	0.8
	Yamato-machi	(12,114)	49.2	50.8	100.0	34.6	57.5	6.7	1.2	100.0	18.8	15.8	28.7	28.8	1.3	5.4	0.4	0.8
	Toda-machi	(21,753)	52.2	47.8	100.0	35.9	57.0	6.1	1.0	100.0	22.0	13.9	28.6	28.4	1.3	4.8	0.3	0.7
V	Warabi-shi	(36,885)	49.3	50.7	100.0	35.5	57.1	6.1	1.3	100.0	19.4	16.1	28.5	28.6	1.0	5.1	0.4	0.9
	Kawaguchi-shi	(121,459)	51.9	48.1	100.0	37.4	54.9	6.5	1.2	100.0	22.8	14.6	27.5	27.4	1.2	5.3	0.4	0.8
	Hatogaya-machi	(14,411)	50.6	49.4	100.0	31.1	61.2	6.8	0.9	100.0	18.3	12.8	30.6	30.6	1.4	5.4	0.3	0.6
VI	Sōka-shi	(26,417)	50.3	49.7	100.0	32.8	58.6	7.6	1.0	100.0	19.1	13.7	29.3	29.3	1.6	6.0	0.3	0.7
	Yashio-mura	(8,720)	50.3	49.7	100.0	31.1	59.5	8.5	0.9	100.0	18.1	13.0	29.9	29.6	2.1	6.4	0.2	0.7
	Misato-mura	(11,715)	49.4	50.6	100.0	30.4	59.7	9.3	0.6	100.0	17.2	13.2	29.8	29.9	2.2	7.1	0.2	0.4
	Matsudo-shi	(61,689)	50.0	50.0	100.0	33.3	58.7	6.9	1.1	100.0	19.0	14.3	29.4	29.3	1.3	5.6	0.3	0.8
VII	Ichikawa-shi	(117,331)	49.2	50.8	100.0	38.2	53.3	7.2	1.3	100.0	21.1	17.1	26.6	26.7	1.2	6.0	0.3	1.0
	Zone 4 Total	(1,166,214)	51.8	48.2	100.0	37.2	55.3	6.2	1.3	100.0	22.6	14.6	27.7	27.6	1.1	5.1	0.4	0.9
5 I	Tsurumi-ku	(170,348)	53.1	46.9	100.0	38.7	54.4	5.7	1.2	100.0	24.4	14.3	27.4	27.0	0.9	4.8	0.4	0.8
III	Koganei-shi	(34,344)	50.8	49.2	100.0	37.9	55.1	5.8	1.2	100.0	22.3	15.6	27.4	27.7	0.8	5.0	0.3	0.9
	Tanashi-machi	(22,445)	49.2	50.8	100.0	33.9	58.5	6.3	1.3	100.0	18.5	15.4	29.2	29.3	1.0	5.3	0.5	0.8
	Kurume-machi	(13,551)	49.6	50.4	100.0	31.0	62.2	6.0	0.8	100.0	17.3	13.7	31.1	31.1	1.0	5.0	0.2	0.6
IV	Niza-machi	(9,826)	50.3	49.7	100.0	32.9	58.6	7.6	0.9	100.0	19.1	13.8	29.2	29.4	1.7	5.9	0.3	0.6
	Kiyose-machi	(13,631)	50.4	49.6	100.0	40.7	48.8	7.7	2.8	100.0	21.0	19.7	26.5	22.3	1.8	5.9	1.1	1.7
	Adachi-machi	(8,541)	49.0	51.0	100.0	33.4	57.5	8.0	1.1	100.0	18.3	15.1	28.7	28.8	1.6	6.4	0.4	0.7
	Asaka-machi	(17,344)	55.4	44.6	100.0	38.2	55.1	5.9	0.8	100.0	26.0	12.2	28.0	27.1	1.1	4.8	0.3	0.5
V	Urawa-shi	(124,391)	49.4	50.6	100.0	35.8	56.0	7.0	1.2	100.0	19.9	15.9	28.1	27.9	1.1	5.9	0.3	0.9
	Misono-mura	(6,137)	48.6	51.4	100.0	30.4	59.2	9.6	0.8	100.0	16.6	13.8	29.5	29.7	2.2	7.4	0.3	0.5
	Koshigaya-shi	(32,765)	48.8	51.2	100.0	29.4	60.7	9.0	0.9	100.0	16.0	13.4	30.3	30.4	2.2	6.8	0.3	0.6
VI	Yoshikawa-machi	(10,604)	48.7	51.3	100.0	28.5	60.7	10.0	0.7	100.0	15.7	12.8	30.3	30.4	2.4	7.6	0.3	0.5
	Nagareyama-machi	(17,671)	48.8	51.2	100.0	29.3	61.8	8.2	0.7	100.0	16.2	13.1	30.8	31.0	1.6	6.6	0.2	0.5
VII	Kamagaya-machi	(9,068)	51.3	48.7	100.0	30.8	61.3	6.9	1.0	100.0	18.8	12.0	30.5	30.8	1.7	5.2	0.3	0.7
VIII	Funahashi-shi	(98,199)	50.3	49.7	100.0	36.5	54.9	7.2	1.4	100.0	21.2	15.3	27.4	27.5	1.3	5.9	0.4	1.0

Table 4. Marital Status (15 Years and Older)

(Zone) (Sector)	District	Total	Total	M	F	Total	Not Married	Married	Widowed	Separated	Total	Not Married M	Not Married F	Married M	Married F	Widowed M	Widowed F	Separated M	Separated F
	Zone 5 Total	(588,865)	100.0	50.9	49.1	100.0	36.0	56.0	6.8	1.2	100.0	21.2	14.8	28.1	27.9	1.2	5.6	0.4	0.8
6 I	Nishi-ku	(78,139)	100.0	50.4	49.6	100.0	35.6	54.4	8.0	2.0	100.0	20.9	14.7	27.3	27.1	1.5	6.5	0.7	1.3
	Naka-ku	(94,593)	100.0	49.2	50.8	100.0	37.7	52.6	7.4	2.3	100.0	20.9	16.8	26.4	26.2	1.2	6.2	0.7	1.6
	Kanagawa-ku	(127,171)	100.0	52.0	48.0	100.0	36.3	55.4	6.8	1.5	100.0	22.5	13.8	27.7	27.7	1.3	5.5	0.5	1.0
	Kōhoku-ku	(106,437)	100.0	50.7	49.3	100.0	34.5	57.4	7.0	1.1	100.0	20.6	13.9	28.5	28.9	1.3	5.7	0.3	0.8
II	Inagi-machi	(7,665)	100.0	51.2	48.8	100.0	34.5	56.0	8.7	1.5	100.0	20.4	14.1	28.2	27.8	1.8	6.2	0.8	0.7
	Tama-mura	(7,284)	100.0	49.7	50.3	100.0	40.0	48.5	8.7	2.8	100.0	21.7	18.3	24.5	24.0	2.1	6.6	1.4	1.4
III	Fuchu-shi	(59,515)	100.0	53.1	46.9	100.0	35.5	56.5	6.0	2.0	100.0	21.6	13.9	29.3	27.2	1.1	4.9	1.1	0.9
	Kunitachi-machi	(23,807)	100.0	50.1	49.9	100.0	37.2	55.6	5.9	1.3	100.0	21.4	15.8	27.6	28.0	0.8	5.1	0.3	1.0
	Kokubunji-machi	(29,133)	100.0	52.8	47.2	100.0	37.9	55.0	6.0	1.1	100.0	23.6	14.3	28.0	27.0	0.9	5.1	0.3	0.8
	Kodaira-machi	(37,855)	100.0	52.0	48.0	100.0	36.5	55.9	5.9	1.7	100.0	21.7	14.8	28.5	27.4	1.1	4.8	0.7	1.0
	Higashimurayama-machi	(30,108)	100.0	50.3	49.7	100.0	30.7	60.0	7.7	1.6	100.0	17.4	13.3	30.5	29.5	1.7	6.0	0.7	0.9
IV	Tokorosawa-shi	(45,547)	100.0	49.2	50.8	100.0	33.4	58.1	7.7	0.8	100.0	18.2	15.2	29.1	29.0	1.7	6.0	0.2	0.6
	Miyoshi-mura	(2,868)	100.0	49.3	50.7	100.0	34.1	56.5	9.0	0.4	100.0	18.9	15.2	28.2	28.3	2.1	6.9	0.1	0.3
	Fujimi-mura	(8,142)	100.0	48.9	51.1	100.0	31.0	59.7	8.7	0.6	100.0	16.6	14.4	29.8	29.9	2.3	6.4	0.2	0.4
V	Yono-shi	(29,358)	100.0	49.3	50.7	100.0	35.0	57.4	6.5	1.1	100.0	19.2	15.8	28.6	28.8	1.2	5.3	0.3	0.8
	Ōmiya-shi	(120,999)	100.0	49.0	51.0	100.0	33.6	58.3	7.0	1.1	100.0	18.3	15.3	29.1	29.2	1.3	5.7	0.3	0.8
VI	Iwatsuki-shi	(23,780)	100.0	48.6	51.4	100.0	29.8	60.0	9.3	0.9	100.0	16.2	13.6	29.9	30.1	2.2	7.1	0.3	0.6
	Matsubushi-mura	(5,826)	100.0	48.2	51.8	100.0	27.8	60.4	11.0	0.8	100.0	15.0	12.8	30.1	30.3	2.8	8.2	0.3	0.5
VII	Kashiwa-shi	(43,879)	100.0	49.2	50.8	100.0	31.2	60.9	6.8	1.1	100.0	17.1	14.1	30.4	30.5	1.4	5.4	0.3	0.8
	Shōnan-mura	(8,170)	100.0	53.7	46.3	100.0	32.3	58.8	8.0	0.9	100.0	21.4	10.9	30.0	28.8	2.0	6.0	0.4	0.6
	Shirai-mura	(5,516)	100.0	49.2	50.8	100.0	27.7	61.4	9.9	1.0	100.0	15.6	12.1	30.7	30.7	2.5	7.4	0.4	0.6
VIII	Narashino-shi	(30,376)	100.0	51.7	48.3	100.0	36.6	55.7	6.6	1.1	100.0	22.3	14.3	28.0	27.7	1.1	5.5	0.3	0.8
	Zone 6 Total	(926,168)	100.0	50.5	49.5	100.0	34.9	56.5	7.2	1.4	100.0	20.2	14.7	28.4	28.1	1.4	5.8	0.5	0.9
7 I	Isogo-ku	(55,314)	100.0	48.9	51.1	100.0	34.1	56.1	8.1	1.7	100.0	19.1	15.0	28.0	28.1	1.3	6.8	0.5	1.2
	Minami-ku	(144,398)	100.0	50.2	49.8	100.0	34.4	55.5	7.8	2.3	100.0	19.9	14.5	27.9	27.6	1.5	6.3	0.9	1.4
	Hodogaya-ku	(102,794)	100.0	50.0	50.0	100.0	31.5	60.4	6.9	1.2	100.0	18.1	13.4	30.2	30.2	1.3	5.6	0.4	0.8
II	Machida-shi	(49,877)	100.0	49.2	50.8	100.0	34.4	57.7	6.9	1.0	100.0	18.7	15.7	28.8	28.9	1.4	5.5	0.3	0.7
	Yuki-mura	(4,235)	100.0	50.5	49.5	100.0	34.3	55.2	9.7	0.8	100.0	19.5	14.8	27.5	27.7	3.1	6.6	0.4	0.4
III	Hino-machi	(31,135)	100.0	49.7	50.3	100.0	32.3	60.4	6.3	1.0	100.0	18.1	14.2	30.2	30.2	1.1	5.2	0.3	0.7
	Tachikawa-shi	(50,670)	100.0	48.7	51.3	100.0	39.5	52.0	6.6	1.9	100.0	21.3	18.2	26.0	26.0	1.0	5.6	0.4	1.5
	Sunakawa-machi	(9,571)	100.0	49.0	51.0	100.0	34.9	57.0	7.2	0.9	100.0	18.9	16.0	28.5	28.5	1.3	5.9	0.3	0.6
	Yamato-machi	(9,654)	100.0	50.1	49.9	100.0	36.3	55.5	7.4	0.8	100.0	19.9	16.4	27.8	27.7	1.9	5.5	0.5	0.3

Table 4. Marital Status (15 Years and Older)

(Zone)	(Sector)	District	Total	M	F	Total	Not Married	Married	Widowed	Separated	Total	Not Married M	Not Married F	Married M	Married F	Widowed M	Widowed F	Separated M	Separated F
7	IV	Ōi-mura	(3,426) 100.0	52.0	48.0	100.0	36.2	54.4	8.8	0.6	100.0	22.4	13.8	27.3	27.1	2.1	6.7	0.2	0.4
		Fukuoka-mura	(11,824) 100.0	49.8	50.2	100.0	25.7	68.3	5.4	0.6	100.0	14.4	11.3	34.2	34.1	1.0	4.4	0.2	0.4
	V	Kasukabe-shi	(23,059) 100.0	48.4	51.6	100.0	30.1	59.6	9.3	1.0	100.0	16.2	13.9	29.7	29.9	2.2	7.1	0.3	0.7
		Shōwa-mura	(9,495) 100.0	48.4	51.6	100.0	28.0	60.4	10.1	1.5	100.0	14.9	13.1	30.4	30.0	2.5	7.6	0.6	0.9
	VI	Noda-shi	(37,619) 100.0	47.7	52.3	100.0	29.7	60.0	9.2	1.1	100.0	15.4	14.3	29.9	30.1	2.1	7.1	0.3	0.8
	VII	Abiko-machi	(18,817) 100.0	48.2	51.8	100.0	30.7	59.7	8.3	1.3	100.0	16.6	14.1	29.8	29.9	1.5	6.8	0.3	1.0
		Yachiyo-machi	(14,988) 100.0	48.3	51.7	100.0	28.6	61.4	8.9	1.1	100.0	15.2	13.4	30.7	30.7	2.1	6.8	0.3	0.8
	VIII	Chiba-shi	(176,147) 100.0	51.1	48.9	100.0.	35.9	55.5	7.1	1.5	100.0	21.3	13.4	28.0	27.5	1.3	5.8	0.5	1.0
	IX	Goi-machi	(15,112) 100.0	47.9	52.1	100.0	28.2	61.0	9.7	1.1	100.0	14.8	13.4	30.4	30.6	2.3	7.4	0.4	0.7
		Sodegaura-machi	(9,739) 100.0	48.1	51.9	100.0	31.8	57.4	9.6	1.2	100.0	17.1	14.7	28.6	28.8	2.0	7.6	0.4	0.8
		Zone 7 Total	(777,874) 100.0	49.7	50.3	100.0	33.6	57.3	7.6	1.5	100.0	19.0	14.6	28.7	28.6	1.5	6.1	0.5	1.0
8	I	Kanazawa-ku	(51,140) 100.0	51.0	49.0	100.0	34.8	56.9	7.0	1.3	100.0	20.9	13.9	28.5	28.4	1.2	5.8	0.4	0.9
		Totsuka-ku	(80,225) 100.0	50.5	49.5	100.0	32.2	60.1	6.7	1.0	100.0	18.9	13.3	30.1	30.0	1.2	5.5	0.3	0.7
	II	Yamato-shi	(28,235) 100.0	47.7	52.3	100.0	32.4	59.8	6.4	1.4	100.0	16.5	15.9	29.8	30.0	1.0	5.4	0.4	1.0
		Sagamihara-shi	(70,330) 100.0	49.3	50.7	100.0	32.4	60.4	6.2	1.0	100.0	17.5	14.9	30.2	30.2	1.3	4.9	0.3	0.7
		Zama-machi	(10,663) 100.0	48.9	51.1	100.0	33.0	59.2	6.8	1.0	100.0	17.9	15.1	29.5	29.7	1.3	5.5	0.2	0.8
	III	Hachiōji-shi	(113,971) 100.0	48.5	51.5	100.0	36.9	54.1	7.6	1.4	100.0	19.3	17.6	27.1	27.0	1.7	5.9	0.4	1.0
		Akishima-shi	(30,984) 100.0	48.5	51.5	100.0	34.2	56.6	7.4	1.8	100.0	17.8	16.4	28.3	28.3	1.8	5.6	0.6	1.2
		Fussa-machi	(15,653) 100.0	46.4	53.6	100.0	36.9	55.3	5.9	1.9	100.0	17.3	19.6	27.6	27.7	1.2	4.7	0.3	1.6
		Mizuho-machi	(8,168) 100.0	48.8	51.2	100.0	35.4	56.4	7.6	0.6	100.0	18.3	17.1	28.2	28.2	2.1	5.5	0.2	0.4
		Murayama-machi	(8,424) 100.0	48.8	51.2	100.0	38.5	51.2	8.8	1.5	100.0	20.0	18.5	25.9	25.3	2.3	6.5	0.6	0.9
		Musashi-machi	(21,142) 100.0	47.8	52.2	100.0	35.7	55.1	8.2	1.0	100.0	18.1	17.6	27.5	27.6	2.0	6.2	0.2	0.8
	IV	Sayama-shi	(22,936) 100.0	49.0	51.0	100.0	35.4	55.4	8.5	0.7	100.0	19.1	16.3	27.7	27.7	2.0	6.5	0.2	0.5
		Kawagoe-shi	(75,192) 100.0	48.5	51.5	100.0	33.8	56.5	8.7	1.0	100.0	18.2	15.6	28.2	28.3	1.8	6.9	0.3	0.7
		Seibu-machi	(4,609) 100.0	40.1	59.9	100.0	46.2	46.5	6.5	0.8	100.0	15.3	30.9	23.2	23.3	1.3	5.2	0.3	0.5
	V	Ageo-shi	(27,040) 100.0	48.3	51.7	100.0	34.3	56.8	8.1	0.8	100.0	17.8	16.5	28.4	28.4	1.8	6.3	0.3	0.5
		Ina-mura	(4,628) 100.0	49.4	50.6	100.0	33.2	56.3	10.0	0.5	100.0	18.7	14.5	28.1	28.2	2.4	7.6	0.2	0.3
		Hasuda-machi	(14,437) 100.0	49.2	50.8	100.0	33.2	57.5	8.5	0.8	100.0	17.8	15.4	29.0	28.5	2.1	6.4	0.3	0.5
		Shiraoka-machi	(10,819) 100.0	49.5	50.5	100.0	30.9	59.4	9.1	0.6	100.0	17.4	13.5	29.7	29.7	2.2	6.9	0.2	0.4
		Miyashiro-machi	(7,454) 100.0	48.6	51.4	100.0	29.8	60.3	9.1	0.8	100.0	16.2	13.6	30.1	30.2	2.1	7.0	0.2	0.6
		Sugito-machi	(11,590) 100.0	48.2	51.8	100.0	28.3	60.6	10.2	0.9	100.0	15.4	12.9	30.2	30.4	2.3	7.9	0.3	0.6
	VI	Sekiyado-machi	(8,103) 100.0	46.6	53.4	100.0	22.2	65.5	11.8	0.5	100.0	10.9	11.3	32.6	32.9	2.9	8.9	0.2	0.3
		Moriya-machi	(7,621) 100.0	47.2	52.8	100.0	26.0	63.0	9.9	1.1	100.0	13.2	12.8	31.2	31.8	2.5	7.4	0.3	0.8
	VII	Toride-machi	(15,990) 100.0	47.8	52.2	100.0	30.7	58.7	9.2	1.4	100.0	16.2	14.5	29.2	29.5	2.0	7.2	0.4	1.0

- 212 -

Table 4. Marital Status (15 Years and Older)

(Zone) (Sector)	District	Total	M	F	Total	Not Married	Married	Widowed	Separated	Total	Not Married M	Not Married F	Married M	Married F	Widowed M	Widowed F	Separated M	Separated F
VII	Inzai-machi	(11,983) 100.0	48.4	51.6	100.0	28.7	59.9	10.2	1.2	100.0	16.1	12.6	29.7	30.2	2.3	7.9	0.3	0.9
	Inba-mura	(5,674) 100.0	47.0	53.0	100.0	19.9	67.3	11.7	1.1	100.0	10.3	9.6	33.5	33.8	2.9	8.8	0.3	0.8
VIII	Yotsukaidō-machi	(11,398) 100.0	47.4	52.6	100.0	29.9	60.5	8.5	1.1	100.0	15.2	14.7	30.0	30.5	1.8	6.7	0.4	0.7
IX	Ichihara-machi	(9,929) 100.0	49.1	50.9	100.0	31.0	58.6	9.4	0.9	100.0	17.3	13.7	29.7	28.9	1.7	7.7	0.4	0.6
	Anegasaki-machi	(7,844) 100.0	47.5	52.5	100.0	28.8	60.6	9.7	1.0	100.0	15.0	13.8	30.2	30.4	2.1	7.6	0.2	0.7
	Hirakawa-machi	(7,417) 100.0	47.2	52.8	100.0	23.0	65.0	11.0	1.0	100.0	12.0	11.0	32.4	32.6	2.5	8.5	0.3	0.7
	Miwa-machi	(6,385) 100.0	47.8	52.2	100.0	24.7	63.4	10.9	1.0	100.0	13.0	11.7	31.5	31.9	3.0	7.9	0.3	0.7
X	Kisarazu-shi	(37,333) 100.0	47.8	52.2	100.0	28.9	60.7	9.2	1.2	100.0	15.3	13.6	30.3	30.4	1.9	7.3	0.3	0.9
	Zone 8 Total	(747,317) 100.0	48.7	51.3	100.0	33.2	57.8	7.9	1.1	100.0	17.8	15.4	28.9	28.9	1.7	6.2	0.3	0.8
9 I	Kamakura-shi	(74,935) 100.0	47.6	52.4	100.0	36.0	54.0	8.4	1.6	100.0	19.0	17.0	26.9	27.1	1.3	7.1	0.4	1.2
II	Ayase-machi	(5,674) 100.0	48.6	51.4	100.0	34.3	56.0	8.7	1.0	100.0	18.4	15.9	28.0	28.0	1.9	6.8	0.3	0.7
	Ebina-machi	(12,546) 100.0	48.0	52.0	100.0	37.0	54.8	7.5	0.7	100.0	18.6	18.4	27.3	27.5	1.9	5.6	0.2	0.5
	Shiroyama-machi	(3,584) 100.0	49.3	50.7	100.0	30.4	59.4	9.3	0.9	100.0	16.7	13.7	29.7	29.7	2.5	6.8	0.4	0.5
III	Akita-machi	(10,137) 100.0	49.7	50.3	100.0	34.5	55.5	9.0	1.0	100.0	18.8	15.7	27.8	27.7	2.8	6.2	0.3	0.7
	Hamura-machi	(7,635) 100.0	48.9	51.1	100.0	34.7	57.8	7.0	0.5	100.0	18.1	16.6	29.1	28.7	1.6	5.4	0.1	0.4
IV	Hannō-shi	(30,756) 100.0	47.9	52.1	100.0	31.8	58.3	9.0	0.9	100.0	16.5	15.3	29.1	29.2	2.0	7.0	0.3	0.6
	Tsurugashima-mura	(4,898) 100.0	50.4	49.6	100.0	33.8	57.4	8.3	0.5	100.0	19.3	14.5	28.8	28.6	2.1	6.2	0.2	0.3
	Hidaka-machi	(11,314) 100.0	49.6	50.4	100.0	29.4	60.3	9.6	0.7	100.0	16.5	12.9	30.3	30.0	2.6	7.0	0.2	0.5
	Kawashima-mura	(10,902) 100.0	48.6	51.4	100.0	28.2	60.0	11.1	0.7	100.0	14.8	13.4	29.9	30.1	2.7	8.4	0.2	0.5
V	Kitamoto-machi	(10,294) 100.0	49.4	50.6	100.0	29.9	61.7	7.9	0.5	100.0	16.5	13.4	30.8	30.9	2.0	5.9	0.1	0.4
	Higawa-machi	(14,597) 100.0	49.1	50.9	100.0	32.2	59.1	7.9	0.8	100.0	17.9	14.3	29.4	29.7	1.5	6.4	0.3	0.5
	Shobu-machi	(10,730) 100.0	48.0	52.0	100.0	28.2	60.2	11.0	0.6	100.0	14.9	13.3	30.0	30.2	2.9	8.1	0.2	0.4
	Kuki-machi	(15,445) 100.0	48.7	51.3	100.0	30.1	60.3	8.8	0.8	100.0	16.3	13.8	30.1	30.2	2.1	6.7	0.2	0.6
	Satte-machi	(15,738) 100.0	47.6	52.4	100.0	30.2	58.1	10.6	1.1	100.0	15.9	14.3	29.0	29.1	2.4	8.2	0.3	0.8
VI	Iwai-machi	(21,670) 100.0	47.3	52.7	100.0	23.1	65.5	10.7	0.7	100.0	11.3	11.8	32.6	32.9	3.1	7.6	0.3	0.4
	Mitsukaidō-shi	(25,607) 100.0	46.5	53.5	100.0	24.3	63.6	11.1	1.0	100.0	12.0	12.3	31.6	32.0	2.7	8.4	0.2	0.8
	Yawahara-mura	(7,474) 100.0	46.9	53.1	100.0	24.0	63.6	11.4	1.0	100.0	12.2	11.8	31.6	32.0	2.8	8.6	0.3	0.7
	Ina-mura	(8,422) 100.0	46.7	53.3	100.0	24.8	62.3	11.7	1.2	100.0	12.5	12.3	31.0	31.3	2.9	8.8	0.3	0.9
VII	Fujishiro-machi	(8,939) 100.0	47.5	52.5	100.0	26.7	61.6	10.7	1.0	100.0	14.1	12.6	30.6	31.0	2.5	8.2	0.3	0.7
	Ryūgasaki-shi	(23,591) 100.0	47.0	53.0	100.0	27.6	61.2	9.8	1.4	100.0	14.0	13.6	30.5	30.7	2.1	7.7	0.4	1.0
	Tone-mura	(6,326) 100.0	47.1	52.9	100.0	24.8	63.3	10.7	1.2	100.0	13.0	11.8	31.4	31.9	2.4	8.3	0.3	0.9
	Motono-mura	(3,689) 100.0	47.8	52.2	100.0	26.0	62.1	10.6	1.3	100.0	13.6	12.4	31.0	31.1	2.7	7.9	0.5	0.9
VIII	Sakura-shi	(25,895) 100.0	47.6	52.4	100.0	29.5	59.1	10.2	1.2	100.0	15.5	14.0	29.5	29.6	2.3	7.9	0.3	0.8
	Izumi-machi	(6,420) 100.0	47.5	52.5	100.0	26.4	62.9	9.5	1.2	100.0	13.8	12.6	31.3	31.6	2.0	7.5	0.4	0.8

Table 4. Marital Status (15 Years and Older)

Sector	District	Total	M	F	Total	Not Married	Married	Widowed	Separated	Total	Not Married M	Not Married F	Married M	Married F	Widowed M	Widowed F	Separated M	Separated F
IX	Shitsu-mura	(6,263) 100.0	48.5	51.5	100.0	26.2	62.7	10.5	0.6	100.0	14.3	11.9	31.2	31.5	2.8	7.7	0.2	0.4
	Nanso-machi	(12,085) 100.0	47.2	52.8	100.0	23.8	63.1	12.0	1.1	100.0	12.4	11.4	31.5	31.6	2.9	9.1	0.4	0.7
	Fukuta-machi	(4,717) 100.0	47.3	52.7	100.0	20.6	67.8	10.6	1.0	100.0	10.9	9.7	33.6	34.2	2.4	8.2	0.4	0.6
X	Kimitsu-machi	(9,059) 100.0	46.6	53.4	100.0	24.6	63.8	10.4	1.2	100.0	12.3	12.3	31.6	32.2	2.4	8.0	0.3	0.9
	Futtsu-machi	(11,345) 100.0	47.5	52.5	100.0	28.0	61.0	10.2	0.8	100.0	14.6	13.4	30.4	30.6	2.3	7.9	0.2	0.6
	Ōsawa-machi	(9,698) 100.0	46.8	53.2	100.0	27.2	60.0	11.5	1.3	100.0	14.1	13.1	29.8	30.2	2.5	9.0	0.4	0.9
	Zone 9 Total	(430,385) 100.0	47.8	52.2	100.0	29.7	59.5	9.7	1.1	100.0	15.6	14.1	29.7	29.8	2.2	7.5	0.3	0.8
10 I	Yokosuka-shi	(210,122) 100.0	50.8	49.2	100.0	36.3	54.5	7.7	1.5	100.0	21.8	14.5	27.4	27.1	1.2	6.5	0.4	1.1
	Zushi-shi	(29,626) 100.0	47.3	52.7	100.0	34.6	55.8	8.1	1.5	100.0	18.2	16.4	27.6	28.2	1.1	7.0	0.4	1.1
	Hayama-machi	(11,746) 100.0	46.2	53.8	100.0	33.9	54.8	9.9	1.4	100.0	17.3	16.6	27.1	27.7	1.3	8.6	0.5	0.9
	Chigasaki-shi	(48,558) 100.0	48.8	51.2	100.0	32.1	59.3	7.5	1.1	100.0	17.6	14.5	29.6	29.7	1.3	6.2	0.3	0.8
	Fujisawa-shi	(90,986) 100.0	48.1	51.9	100.0	34.5	56.4	7.8	1.3	100.0	18.4	16.1	28.1	28.3	1.3	6.5	0.3	1.0
II	Aikawa-machi	(9,518) 100.0	46.5	53.5	100.0	32.4	57.8	9.0	0.8	100.0	15.2	17.2	28.9	28.9	2.2	6.8	0.2	0.6
	Atsugi-shi	(32,144) 100.0	49.3	50.7	100.0	33.4	57.3	8.6	0.7	100.0	18.4	15.0	28.6	28.7	2.1	6.5	0.2	0.5
	Samukawa-machi	(8,053) 100.0	51.8	48.2	100.0	35.7	55.5	7.9	0.9	100.0	21.8	13.9	27.8	27.7	1.9	6.0	0.3	0.6
III	Ōme-shi	(40,752) 100.0	47.3	52.7	100.0	38.5	52.6	7.9	1.0	100.0	18.9	19.6	26.2	26.4	1.9	6.0	0.3	0.7
IV	Sakado-machi	(16,014) 100.0	48.1	51.9	100.0	30.1	59.6	9.6	0.7	100.0	16.0	14.1	29.7	29.9	2.2	7.4	0.2	0.5
	Yoshimi-mura	(9,730) 100.0	48.8	51.2	100.0	28.1	59.8	11.3	0.8	100.0	15.7	12.4	29.8	30.0	3.0	8.3	0.3	0.5
	Moroyama-mura	(7,773) 100.0	48.9	51.1	100.0	33.7	54.9	9.4	2.0	100.0	18.0	15.7	27.6	27.3	2.3	7.1	1.0	1.0
V	Kōnosu-shi	(21,746) 100.0	48.3	51.7	100.0	31.4	58.9	8.8	0.9	100.0	16.8	14.6	29.4	29.5	1.9	6.9	0.2	0.7
	Kisai-machi	(10,227) 100.0	47.9	52.1	100.0	26.7	61.5	11.1	0.7	100.0	14.2	12.5	30.7	30.8	2.8	8.3	0.2	0.5
	Washimiya-machi	(5,618) 100.0	48.0	52.0	100.0	29.4	59.8	10.0	0.8	100.0	15.7	13.7	29.8	30.0	2.3	7.7	0.2	0.6
	Kurihashi-machi	(8,583) 100.0	47.3	52.7	100.0	29.0	60.8	9.4	0.8	100.0	15.0	14.0	30.3	30.5	1.9	7.5	0.1	0.7
	Goka-mura	(5,733) 100.0	47.1	52.9	100.0	26.5	62.3	10.5	0.7	100.0	13.2	13.3	31.0	31.3	2.6	7.9	0.3	0.4
VI	Sakai-machi	(14,452) 100.0	46.0	54.0	100.0	23.0	65.8	10.3	0.9	100.0	10.4	12.6	32.7	33.1	2.6	7.7	0.3	0.6
	Sashima-machi	(9,100) 100.0	46.9	53.1	100.0	21.6	66.6	10.6	1.2	100.0	10.6	11.0	33.1	33.5	2.8	7.8	0.4	0.8
	Yatabe-machi	(14,482) 100.0	47.8	52.2	100.0	22.6	66.1	10.2	1.1	100.0	11.9	10.7	32.9	33.2	2.6	7.6	0.4	0.7
VII	Kukizaki-mura	(4,432) 100.0	48.4	51.6	100.0	25.3	64.4	9.2	1.1	100.0	13.6	11.7	32.0	32.4	2.4	6.8	0.4	0.7
	Ushiku-machi	(11,164) 100.0	49.4	50.6	100.0	26.0	63.3	9.5	1.2	100.0	15.0	11.0	31.6	31.7	2.4	7.1	0.4	0.8
	Kawachi-mura	(8,846) 100.0	47.0	53.0	100.0	22.3	66.0	10.5	1.2	100.0	11.5	10.8	32.8	33.2	2.3	8.2	0.4	0.8
	Sakae-machi	(6,882) 100.0	46.6	53.4	100.0	26.1	61.5	11.1	1.3	100.0	13.3	12.8	30.7	30.8	2.3	8.8	0.3	1.0
VIII	Narita-shi	(30,127) 100.0	46.6	53.4	100.0	27.5	60.8	10.2	1.5	100.0	13.7	13.8	30.3	30.5	2.2	8.0	0.4	1.1
	Shisui-machi	(4,236) 100.0	47.9	52.1	100.0	29.7	59.5	9.4	1.4	100.0	15.6	14.1	29.6	29.9	2.2	7.2	0.5	0.9
	Yachimata-machi	(17,164) 100.0	48.1	51.9	100.0	28.6	61.4	8.9	1.1	100.0	15.3	13.3	30.6	30.8	1.9	7.0	0.3	0.8

Table 4. Marital Status (15 Years and Older)

(Zone) (Sector) District	Total				Not Married	Married	Widowed	Separated	Total	Not Married		Married		Widowed		Separated	
	Total	M	F	Total						M	F	M	F	M	F	M	F
VIII Toke-machi	(4,612) 100.0	47.3	52.7	100.0	28.8	60.7	9.3	1.2	100.0	14.5	14.3	30.1	30.6	2.1	7.2	0.6	0.6
IX Nagara-machi	(5,889) 100.0	46.8	53.2	100.0	22.3	64.2	12.7	0.8	100.0	11.8	10.5	31.9	32.3	2.8	9.9	0.3	0.5
Obitsu-mura	(4,663) 100.0	47.0	53.0	100.0	20.6	66.7	11.6	1.1	100.0	10.7	9.9	33.2	33.5	2.8	8.8	0.3	0.8
X Koito-machi	(4,163) 100.0	48.3	51.7	100.0	22.3	65.3	11.4	1.0	100.0	12.6	9.7	32.4	32.9	3.0	8.4	0.3	0.7
Zone 10 Total	(707,141) 100.0	48.7	51.3	100.0	32.6	57.5	8.6	1.3	100.0	17.9	14.7	28.7	28.8	1.7	6.9	0.4	0.9
Total for 50 km. Region	(11,792,729) 100.0	51.1	48.9	100.0	39.3	52.5	6.7	1.5	100.0	23.2	16.1	26.3	26.2	1.2	5.5	0.4	1.1
National Total	(65,338,448) 100.0	48.3	51.7	100.0	30.7	58.8	9.0	1.5	100.0	16.8	13.9	29.4	29.4	1.7	7.3	0.4	1.1

Note: Those whose marital status are unknown are excluded in the figures of this table.

Zone	Sector	District	Total	M	F	Total	Graduates Elementary	Graduates Intermediate	Graduates Higher	Still in School	Not in School	Unknown	Total	Grad. Elem. M	Grad. Elem. F	Grad. Inter. M	Grad. Inter. F	Grad. Higher M	Grad. Higher F	Still in School M	Still in School F	Not in School M	Not in School F	Unknown M	Unknown F
1	I	Chiyoda-ku	(98,110)	55.4	44.6	100.0	42.1	35.2	11.5	10.9	0.3	0.0	100.0	22.2	19.9	17.5	17.7	8.6	2.9	7.0	3.9	0.1	0.2	0.0	0.0
		Minato-ku	(214,959)	51.1	48.9	100.0	42.1	33.1	14.1	10.3	0.4	0.0	100.0	21.0	21.1	13.2	19.9	10.5	3.6	6.3	4.0	0.1	0.3	0.0	0.0
		Chūō-ku	(134,540)	54.6	45.4	100.0	50.7	33.4	7.7	7.7	0.5	0.0	100.0	25.9	24.8	17.9	15.5	6.1	1.6	4.6	3.1	0.1	0.4	0.0	0.0
		Bunkyō-ku	(208,128)	51.6	48.4	100.0	40.7	32.0	14.1	12.8	0.4	0.0	100.0	19.2	21.5	13.1	18.9	10.7	3.4	8.5	4.3	0.1	0.3	0.0	0.0
		Taitō-ku	(258,009)	53.2	46.8	100.0	56.1	29.0	6.8	7.5	0.6	0.0	100.0	28.9	27.2	14.2	14.8	5.4	1.4	4.5	3.0	0.2	0.4	0.0	0.0
		Zone 1 Total	(913,776)	52.6	47.4	100.0	47.0	32.0	10.7	9.8	0.5	0.0	100.0	23.6	23.4	14.6	17.4	8.2	2.5	6.1	3.7	0.1	0.4	0.0	0.0
2	I	Shinagawa-ku	(337,284)	51.6	48.4	100.0	47.7	32.4	10.7	8.7	0.5	0.0	100.0	23.3	24.4	14.2	18.2	8.6	2.1	5.4	3.3	0.1	0.4	0.0	0.0
	II	Meguro-ku	(232,687)	51.4	48.6	100.0	35.7	34.2	17.2	12.5	0.4	0.0	100.0	16.8	18.9	12.8	21.4	13.4	3.8	8.3	4.2	0.1	0.3	0.0	0.0
		Shibuya-ku	(227,267)	49.5	50.5	100.0	35.0	35.1	16.8	12.7	0.4	0.0	100.0	15.9	19.1	12.7	22.4	12.7	4.1	8.1	4.6	0.1	0.3	0.0	0.0
	III	Shinjuku-ku	(334,082)	51.1	48.9	100.0	37.1	35.1	15.3	12.1	0.4	0.0	100.0	17.1	20.0	14.0	21.1	11.8	3.5	8.1	4.0	0.1	0.3	0.0	0.0
		Nakano-ku	(277,844)	51.9	48.1	100.0	32.2	35.9	17.8	13.7	0.4	0.0	100.0	14.8	17.4	13.8	22.1	13.8	4.0	9.4	4.3	0.1	0.3	0.0	0.0
	IV	Toshima-ku	(289,004)	50.8	49.2	100.0	40.6	34.4	13.3	11.3	0.4	0.0	100.0	18.8	21.8	14.2	20.2	10.5	2.8	7.2	4.1	0.1	0.3	0.0	0.0
	V	Kita-ku	(320,725)	50.6	49.4	100.0	48.9	32.2	9.8	8.6	0.5	0.0	100.0	22.6	26.3	14.6	17.5	8.0	1.8	5.3	3.3	0.1	0.4	0.0	0.0
	VI	Arakawa-ku	(216,840)	53.4	46.6	100.0	63.8	23.6	4.9	6.8	0.9	0.0	100.0	33.0	30.8	12.0	11.6	4.1	0.8	4.1	2.7	0.2	0.7	0.0	0.0
	VII	Sumida-ku	(256,288)	53.8	46.2	100.0	64.6	23.4	4.7	6.6	0.7	0.0	100.0	34.2	30.4	11.8	11.6	3.8	0.9	3.9	2.7	0.1	0.6	0.0	0.0
	VIII	Kōtō-ku	(262,311)	56.0	44.0	100.0	62.9	25.1	4.9	6.5	0.6	0.0	100.0	34.1	28.8	13.5	11.6	4.1	0.8	4.1	2.4	0.2	0.4	0.0	0.0
		Zone 2 Total	(2,754,332)	52.0	48.0	100.0	46.5	31.4	11.6	10.0	0.5	0.0	100.0	22.8	23.7	13.5	17.9	9.2	2.4	6.4	3.6	0.1	0.4	0.0	0.0
3	I	Ōta-ku	(541,951)	52.9	47.1	100.0	46.2	31.8	12.3	9.2	0.5	0.0	100.0	23.4	22.8	13.9	17.9	9.8	2.5	5.7	3.5	0.1	0.4	0.0	0.0
	II	Setagaya-ku	(508,753)	50.7	49.3	100.0	30.6	34.1	19.9	14.9	0.4	0.1	100.0	13.6	17.0	11.9	22.2	15.3	4.6	9.8	5.1	0.1	0.3	0.0	0.1
	III	Suginami-ku	(383,139)	50.8	49.2	100.0	27.6	35.5	21.5	15.0	0.4	0.0	100.0	12.1	15.5	12.2	23.3	16.5	5.0	9.9	5.1	0.1	0.3	0.0	0.0
	IV	Itabashi-ku	(307,965)	52.0	48.0	100.0	49.2	30.7	9.7	9.5	0.7	0.2	100.0	23.9	25.3	14.1	16.6	7.8	1.9	5.9	3.6	0.2	0.5	0.1	0.1
		Nerima-ku	(226,606)	50.8	49.2	100.0	36.9	33.7	17.0	11.9	0.5	0.0	100.0	16.7	20.2	13.0	20.7	13.2	3.8	7.8	4.1	0.1	0.4	0.0	0.0
	VI	Adachi-ku	(294,483)	51.3	48.7	100.0	65.3	22.1	5.0	6.5	1.1	0.0	100.0	31.8	33.5	11.2	10.9	4.2	0.8	3.9	2.6	0.2	0.9	0.0	0.0
	VII	Katsushika-ku	(277,285)	51.1	48.9	100.0	60.4	24.9	6.6	7.2	0.9	0.0	100.0	29.1	31.3	12.1	12.8	5.4	1.2	4.3	2.9	0.2	0.7	0.0	0.0
	VIII	Edogawa-ku	(233,706)	51.7	48.3	100.0	60.3	25.0	6.3	7.6	0.8	0.0	100.0	29.4	30.9	12.3	12.7	5.1	1.2	4.7	2.9	0.2	0.6	0.0	0.0
		Urayasu-machi	(11,423)	49.2	50.8	100.0	84.7	7.2	1.4	3.5	3.2	—	100.0	40.7	44.0	4.0	3.2	1.1	0.3	2.1	1.4	1.2	2.0	—	—
		Zone 3 Total	(2,785,311)	51.5	48.5	100.0	45.2	30.4	13.2	10.6	0.6	0.0	100.0	21.6	23.6	12.7	17.7	10.3	2.9	6.8	3.8	0.1	0.5	0.0	0.0

Table 5. Educational Backgrounds, School Enrollment, and Graduates, 15 Years and Older, by Sex

Zone	Sector	District	Total	Total M	Total F	Total %	Grad. Elementary	Grad. Intermediate	Grad. Higher	Still in School	Not in School	Unknown	Total %	Elem. M	Elem. F	Inter. M	Inter. F	Higher M	Higher F	Still M	Still F	Not-Sch. M	Not-Sch. F	Unk. M	Unk. F
4	I	Kawasaki-shi	(463,209) 100.0	53.2	46.8	100.0	55.7	28.2	8.1	7.4	0.6	0.0	100.0	28.0	27.7	13.9	14.3	6.6	1.5	4.6	2.8	0.1	0.5	0.0	0.0
	II	Komae-machi	(18,620) 100.0	50.5	49.5	100.0	37.7	32.8	17.5	11.4	0.6	0.0	100.0	16.9	20.8	12.3	20.5	13.5	4.0	7.7	3.7	0.1	0.5	0.0	0.0
	III	Mitaka-shi	(73,441) 100.0	51.5	48.5	100.0	36.0	33.4	17.3	12.7	0.6	0.0	100.0	16.3	19.7	13.2	20.2	13.4	3.9	8.4	4.3	0.2	0.4	0.0	0.0
		Musashino-shi	(93,394) 100.0	51.2	48.8	100.0	27.0	35.2	22.7	14.7	0.4	0.0	100.0	11.8	15.2	12.3	22.9	17.3	5.4	9.7	5.0	0.1	0.3	0.0	0.0
		Chōfu-shi	(49,937) 100.0	50.4	49.6	100.0	44.1	31.6	13.2	10.3	0.8	0.0	100.0	19.8	24.3	13.4	18.2	10.3	2.9	6.7	3.6	0.2	0.6	0.0	0.0
		Hoya-machi	(33,451) 100.0	50.1	49.9	100.0	36.7	34.4	18.6	9.7	0.6	—	100.0	16.5	20.2	12.6	21.8	14.5	4.1	6.4	3.3	0.1	0.5	—	—
	IV	Yamato-machi	(12,117) 100.0	49.2	50.8	100.0	59.2	24.7	7.5	7.6	1.0	—	100.0	27.7	31.5	11.9	12.8	5.5	2.0	4.0	3.6	0.1	0.9	—	—
		Toda-machi	(21,741) 100.0	52.1	47.9	100.0	66.1	20.9	6.1	5.3	1.6	0.0	100.0	32.7	33.4	10.9	10.0	5.0	1.1	3.2	2.1	0.3	1.3	0.0	0.0
	V	Warabi-shi	(36,889) 100.0	49.3	50.7	100.0	55.4	28.2	7.5	8.0	0.9	—	100.0	25.0	30.4	13.3	14.9	6.2	1.3	4.6	3.4	0.2	0.7	—	!
		Kawaguchi-shi	(121,479) 100.0	51.8	48.2	100.0	66.0	21.3	5.2	6.2	1.3	0.0	100.0	33.3	32.7	10.4	10.9	4.2	1.0	3.6	2.6	0.3	1.0	0.0	0.0
		Hatogaya-machi	(14,415) 100.0	50.6	49.4	100.0	61.3	22.5	9.0	6.1	1.1	0.0	100.0	29.7	31.6	10.0	12.5	7.1	1.9	3.6	2.5	0.2	0.9	0.0	0.0
	VI	Sōka-shi	(26,418) 100.0	50.3	49.7	100.0	69.9	17.1	5.2	5.9	1.9	0.0	100.0	33.6	36.3	8.8	8.3	4.1	1.1	3.4	2.5	0.4	1.5	0.0	0.0
		Yashio-mura	(8,721) 100.0	50.3	49.7	100.0	84.2	8.1	1.8	3.1	2.8	—	100.0	41.5	42.7	4.9	3.2	1.5	0.3	1.9	1.2	0.5	2.3	—	—
		Misato-mura	(11,716) 100.0	49.4	50.6	100.0	81.4	8.6	1.6	4.2	4.2	0.0	100.0	39.2	42.2	5.5	3.1	1.6	0.3	2.5	1.7	0.9	3.3	0.0	0.0
		Matsudo-shi	(61,696) 100.0	50.0	50.0	100.0	55.9	25.2	9.5	8.2	1.2	0.0	100.0	25.6	30.3	11.4	13.8	7.6	1.9	5.2	3.0	0.2	1.0	0.0	0.0
	VII	Ichikawa-shi	(117,382) 100.0	49.3	50.7	100.0	47.0	29.3	12.3	10.5	0.9	0.0	100.0	20.6	26.4	12.2	17.1	9.7	2.6	6.6	3.9	0.2	0.7	0.0	0.0
		Zone 4 Total	(1,164,626) 100.0	51.6	48.4	100.0	52.0	27.9	10.5	8.7	0.9	0.0	100.0	25.1	26.9	12.6	15.3	8.3	2.2	5.5	3.2	0.1	0.8	0.0	0.0
5	I	Tsurumi-ku	(170,370) 100.0	52.4	47.6	100.0	55.2	28.2	8.3	7.7	0.6	0.0	100.0	27.3	27.9	13.6	14.6	6.8	1.5	4.0	3.7	0.1	0.5	0.0	0.0
	III	Koganei-shi	(34,446) 100.0	50.7	49.3	100.0	33.4	33.9	18.1	13.8	0.5	0.3	100.0	14.2	19.2	12.8	21.1	14.0	4.1	9.5	4.3	0.1	0.4	0.1	0.2
		Tanashi-machi	(22,446) 100.0	49.0	51.0	100.0	43.7	31.8	13.4	10.5	0.6	0.0	100.0	19.5	24.2	12.9	18.9	10.7	2.7	5.8	4.7	0.1	0.5	0.0	0.0
		Kurume-machi	(13,553) 100.0	49.5	50.5	100.0	43.6	27.7	18.1	9.8	0.8	—	100.0	19.8	23.8	10.1	17.6	13.6	4.5	5.9	3.9	0.1	0.7	—	—
	IV	Niiza-machi	(9,826) 100.0	50.2	49.8	100.0	68.6	18.2	5.8	6.3	1.1	—	100.0	32.6	36.0	8.3	9.9	4.8	1.0	4.3	2.0	0.2	0.9	—	—
		Kiyose-machi	(13,645) 100.0	50.2	49.8	100.0	48.4	32.0	11.5	7.2	0.9	—	100.0	23.2	25.2	14.2	17.8	8.7	2.8	4.0	3.2	0.1	0.8	—	—
		Adachi-machi	(8,541) 100.0	49.1	50.9	100.0	65.1	19.9	6.4	7.4	1.2	0.0	100.0	30.7	34.4	8.7	11.2	5.2	1.2	4.3	3.1	0.2	1.0	0.0	0.0
		Asaka-machi	(17,347) 100.0	55.3	44.7	100.0	59.6	26.2	7.8	5.5	0.9	0.0	100.0	30.9	28.7	14.6	11.6	6.3	1.5	3.3	2.2	0.2	0.7	0.0	0.0
	V	Urawa-shi	(124,403) 100.0	49.3	50.7	100.0	42.4	32.0	14.2	10.4	1.0	0.0	100.0	18.9	23.5	12.8	19.2	11.2	3.0	6.2	4.2	0.2	0.8	0.0	0.0
		Misono-mura	(6,137) 100.0	48.4	51.6	100.0	79.9	10.1	1.8	5.4	2.8	—	100.0	37.0	42.9	6.4	3.7	1.3	0.5	3.2	2.2	0.5	2.3	—	—
	VI	Koshigaya-shi	(32,768) 100.0	48.7	51.3	100.0	76.1	12.9	3.2	5.2	2.6	—	100.0	35.9	40.2	7.0	5.9	2.5	0.7	2.9	2.3	0.4	2.2	—	—
		Yoshikawa-machi	(10,607) 100.0	48.5	51.5	100.0	80.8	9.3	1.7	4.4	3.8	0.0	100.0	38.1	42.7	5.9	3.4	1.2	0.5	2.7	1.7	0.6	3.2	0.0	0.0
	VII	Nagareyama-machi	(17,677) 100.0	48.7	51.3	100.0	62.5	20.8	8.8	6.5	1.4	0.0	100.0	28.0	34.5	9.3	11.5	7.1	1.7	4.1	2.4	0.2	1.2	0.0	0.0
		Kamagaya-machi	(9,071) 100.0	51.1	48.9	100.0	66.9	19.7	6.3	5.0	2.1	0.0	100.0	32.3	34.6	10.3	9.4	5.1	1.2	3.1	1.9	0.3	1.8	0.0	0.0
	VIII	Funahashi-shi	(98,204) 100.0	50.2	49.8	100.0	55.8	25.5	8.7	8.8	1.2	0.0	100.0	25.8	30.0	11.7	13.8	6.9	1.8	5.5	3.3	0.3	0.9	0.0	0.0

Table 5. Educational Backgrounds, School Enrollment, and Graduates, 15 Years and Older, by Sex

(Zone)	(Sector)	District	Total	Total	M	F	Total	Elementary	Intermediate	Higher	Still in School	Not in School	Unknown	Total	Elem. M	Elem. F	Inter. M	Inter. F	Higher M	Higher F	Still in School M	Still in School F	Not in School M	Not in School F	Unknown M	Unknown F
6		Zone 5 Total	(589,041)	100.0	50.6	49.4	100.0	53.2	27.0	10.1	8.6	1.1	0.0	100.0	25.1	28.1	12.1	14.9	8.0	2.1	5.2	3.4	0.2	0.9	0.0	0.0
	I	Nishi-ku	(78,147)	100.0	50.1	49.9	100.0	54.9	28.8	8.1	7.4	0.8	0.0	100.0	26.0	28.9	12.8	16.0	6.6	1.5	4.5	2.9	0.2	0.6	0.0	0.0
		Naka-ku	(94,603)	100.0	48.8	51.2	100.0	49.4	31.4	11.2	7.1	0.9	0.0	100.0	23.0	26.4	12.8	18.6	8.7	2.5	4.1	3.0	0.2	0.7	0.0	0.0
	II	Kanagawa-ku	(127,196)	100.0	51.9	48.1	100.0	49.5	29.3	11.0	9.5	0.7	0.0	100.0	23.8	25.7	12.5	16.8	9.0	2.0	6.4	3.1	0.2	0.5	0.0	0.0
		Kōhoku-ku	(106,448)	100.0	50.6	49.4	100.0	49.0	27.0	13.1	10.1	0.8	0.0	100.0	22.7	26.3	10.6	16.4	10.5	2.6	6.6	3.5	0.2	0.6	0.0	0.0
	III	Inagi-machi	(7,666)	100.0	50.9	49.1	100.0	66.2	20.3	4.9	7.5	1.1	—	100.0	31.9	34.3	10.6	9.7	3.9	1.0	4.3	3.2	0.2	0.9	—	—
		Tama-mura	(7,284)	100.0	49.6	50.4	100.0	63.3	21.4	7.0	6.0	2.3	—	100.0	30.2	33.1	9.6	11.8	5.4	1.6	3.6	2.4	0.8	1.5	—	—
		Fuchu-shi	(59,561)	100.0	52.8	47.2	100.0	50.6	29.1	10.7	8.3	1.3	0.0	100.0	25.8	24.8	12.8	16.3	8.5	2.2	5.0	3.3	0.7	0.6	0.0	0.0
		Kunitachi-machi	(23,808)	100.0	50.1	49.9	100.0	35.1	33.1	17.3	13.9	0.6	0.0	100.0	15.3	19.8	12.8	20.6	13.5	3.8	8.7	5.2	0.1	0.6	0.0	0.0
		Kokubunji-machi	(29,133)	100.0	52.9	47.1	100.0	36.9	34.1	16.1	12.3	0.6	0.0	100.0	16.8	20.1	14.6	19.5	12.8	3.3	8.6	3.7	0.1	0.5	0.0	0.0
		Kodaira-machi	(37,859)	100.0	51.9	48.1	100.0	40.5	32.5	14.1	12.0	0.9	0.0	100.0	19.1	21.4	14.1	18.4	11.4	2.7	7.0	5.0	0.3	0.6	0.0	0.0
	IV	Higashimurayama-machi	(30,138)	100.0	50.2	49.8	100.0	50.7	29.2	12.3	6.1	1.7	0.0	100.0	24.1	26.6	12.1	17.1	9.8	2.5	3.8	2.3	0.4	1.3	0.0	0.0
		Tokorosawa-shi	(45,551)	100.0	49.1	50.9	100.0	65.1	20.6	6.9	6.3	1.1	0.0	100.0	30.4	34.7	9.2	11.4	5.5	1.4	3.8	2.5	0.2	0.9	0.0	0.0
		Miyoshi-mura	(2,868)	100.0	49.2	50.8	100.0	82.4	9.8	1.3	4.4	2.1	—	100.0	39.7	42.7	5.5	4.3	1.2	0.1	2.5	1.9	0.3	1.8	—	—
		Fujimi-mura	(8,142)	100.0	48.4	51.6	100.0	76.3	12.4	5.1	4.4	1.8	0.0	100.0	36.6	39.7	5.2	7.2	4.0	1.1	2.5	1.9	0.1	1.7	0.0	0.0
	V	Yono-shi	(29,366)	100.0	49.2	50.8	100.0	49.3	29.6	10.7	9.5	0.9	0.0	100.0	22.2	27.1	13.0	16.6	8.5	2.2	5.3	4.2	0.2	0.7	0.0	0.0
		Ōmiya-shi	(121,006)	100.0	48.9	51.1	100.0	54.6	27.7	7.9	8.4	1.4	0.0	100.0	24.4	30.2	13.1	14.6	6.4	3.5	4.8	3.6	0.6	1.2	0.0	0.0
		Iwatsuki-shi	(23,783)	100.0	48.7	51.3	100.0	71.9	15.4	3.3	6.2	3.2	0.0	100.0	33.9	38.0	8.2	7.2	2.6	0.7	3.4	2.8	0.6	2.6	0.0	0.0
	VI	Matsubushi-mura	(5,826)	100.0	47.9	52.1	100.0	83.2	7.6	1.6	3.7	3.9	—	100.0	39.3	43.9	4.5	3.1	1.3	0.3	2.4	1.3	0.4	3.5	—	—
	VII	Kashiwa-shi	(43,881)	100.0	48.9	51.1	100.0	56.4	24.8	9.6	8.0	1.2	—	100.0	25.3	31.1	11.1	13.7	7.6	2.0	4.7	3.3	0.2	1.0	—	—
		Shōnan-mura	(8,171)	100.0	53.6	46.4	100.0	75.3	17.1	2.3	3.7	1.6	—	100.0	36.0	39.3	13.2	3.9	2.0	0.3	2.2	1.5	0.2	1.4	—	—
		Shirai-mura	(5,516)	100.0	49.1	50.9	100.0	80.0	12.3	1.5	4.5	1.7	—	100.0	37.2	42.8	7.6	4.7	1.2	0.3	2.8	1.7	0.3	1.4	—	—
	VIII	Narashino-shi	(30,378)	100.0	51.5	48.5	100.0	47.7	27.8	9.6	13.9	1.0	0.0	100.0	21.3	26.4	12.1	15.7	7.7	1.9	10.3	3.6	0.1	0.9	0.0	0.0
		Zone 6 Total	(926,331)	100.0	50.1	49.9	100.0	52.4	27.6	10.2	8.7	1.1	0.0	100.0	24.3	28.1	12.0	15.6	8.1	2.1	5.4	3.3	0.3	0.8	0.0	0.0
7	I	Isogo-ku	(55,317)	100.0	51.5	48.5	100.0	49.8	30.5	10.2	8.7	0.8	0.0	100.0	22.6	27.2	12.6	17.9	8.1	2.1	8.1	0.6	0.1	0.7	—	0.0
		Minami-ku	(144,440)	100.0	50.1	49.9	100.0	56.4	28.0	7.4	7.2	1.0	0.0	100.0	26.6	29.8	12.8	15.2	6.0	1.4	4.4	2.8	0.3	0.7	0.0	0.0
		Hodogaya-ku	(102,808)	100.0	49.9	50.1	100.0	51.5	29.6	10.8	7.2	0.9	0.0	100.0	24.3	27.2	12.5	17.1	8.6	2.2	4.3	2.9	0.2	0.7	0.0	0.0
	II	Machida-shi	(49,973)	100.0	49.1	50.9	100.0	55.6	24.4	9.3	9.6	1.1	0.0	100.0	25.6	30.0	10.5	13.9	7.2	2.1	5.6	4.0	0.2	0.9	0.0	0.0
		Yuki-mura	(4,236)	100.0	50.5	49.5	100.0	79.6	10.6	1.9	6.0	1.9	0.0	100.0	38.2	41.4	6.2	4.4	1.6	0.3	4.0	2.0	0.5	1.4	—	0.0
	III	Hino-machi	(31,140)	100.0	49.8	50.2	100.0	46.0	30.8	14.3	8.1	0.8	—	100.0	20.4	25.6	12.8	18.0	11.5	2.8	4.8	3.3	0.3	0.5	—	—
		Tachikawa-shi	(50,682)	100.0	48.6	51.4	100.0	50.3	30.6	9.5	9.0	0.6	0.0	100.0	21.9	28.4	13.8	16.8	7.5	2.0	5.3	3.7	0.1	0.5	0.0	0.0

Table 5. Educational Backgrounds, School Enrollment, and Graduates, 15 Years and Older, by Sex

(Zone)	(Sector)	District	Total	M	F	Total	Graduates Elementary	Graduates Intermediate	Graduates Higher	Still in School	Not in School	Unknown	Elem. M	Elem. F	Inter. M	Inter. F	Higher M	Higher F	Still M	Still F	Not M	Not F	Unk. M	Unk. F
	III	Sunakawa-machi	(9,571) 100.0	48.8	51.2	100.0	68.4	18.8	3.9	7.3	1.6	—	31.1	37.3	9.7	9.1	3.1	0.8	4.5	2.8	0.4	1.2	—	—
	IV	Yamato-machi	(9,657) 100.0	50.1	49.9	100.0	67.8	17.7	4.6	8.2	1.7	0.0	32.2	35.6	8.7	9.0	3.8	0.8	5.0	3.2	0.4	1.3	0.0	0.0
		Ōi-mura	(3,427) 100.0	51.8	48.2	100.0	77.3	14.4	1.8	5.0	1.5	0.0	38.7	38.6	8.7	5.7	1.6	0.2	2.6	2.4	0.2	1.3	0.0	0.0
	V	Fukuoka-mura	(11,825) 100.0	49.7	50.3	100.0	44.4	31.2	18.2	5.6	0.6	0.0	21.0	23.4	10.9	20.3	14.4	3.8	3.3	2.3	0.1	0.5	0.0	0.0
		Kasukabe-shi	(23,063) 100.0	48.3	51.7	100.0	71.0	16.5	3.8	6.4	2.3	0.0	33.3	37.7	8.2	8.3	3.0	0.8	3.5	2.9	0.3	2.0	0.0	0.0
	VI	Shōwa-mura	(9,495) 100.0	48.2	51.8	100.0	77.7	11.8	2.2	4.9	3.4	0.0	36.5	41.2	6.8	5.0	1.7	0.5	2.7	2.2	0.5	2.9	0.0	0.0
		Noda-shi	(37,622) 100.0	47.6	52.4	100.0	74.7	14.1	3.5	5.2	2.5	0.0	34.2	40.5	7.4	6.7	2.7	1.7	2.9	2.3	0.4	2.1	0.0	0.0
	VII	Abiko-machi	(18,825) 100.0	48.3	51.7	100.0	62.8	22.2	6.4	7.1	1.5	0.0	28.0	34.8	10.8	11.4	5.2	1.2	4.1	3.0	0.2	1.3	0.0	0.0
		Yachiyo-machi	(14,996) 100.0	48.2	51.8	100.0	58.4	24.5	8.6	6.3	2.0	0.2	26.2	32.2	11.6	12.9	6.7	1.9	3.4	2.9	0.3	1.7	0.0	0.2
	VIII	Chiba-shi	(176,168) 100.0	51.0	49.0	100.0	52.9	28.2	9.2	8.5	1.2	0.0	25.7	27.2	13.0	15.2	7.1	2.1	5.0	3.5	0.2	1.0	0.0	0.0
	IX	Goi-machi	(15,113) 100.0	47.8	52.2	100.0	73.3	15.1	2.8	6.1	2.7	0.0	34.3	39.0	7.9	7.2	2.0	0.8	3.1	3.0	0.5	2.2	0.0	0.0
		Sodegaura-machi	(9,740) 100.0	47.7	52.3	100.0	71.3	12.8	2.7	8.4	4.8	0.0	32.1	39.2	7.5	5.3	1.8	0.9	4.4	4.0	1.9	2.9	0.0	0.0
		Zone 7 Total	(778,098) 100.0	49.5	50.4	100.0	56.2	26.3	8.5	7.7	1.3	0.0	26.2	30.0	11.8	14.5	6.7	1.8	4.5	3.2	0.3	1.0	0.0	0.0
8	I	Kanazawa-ku	(51,140) 100.0	50.9	49.1	100.0	50.4	28.3	9.2	11.3	0.8	—	23.7	26.7	12.2	16.1	7.4	1.8	7.4	3.9	0.2	0.6	—	—
		Totsuka-ku	(80,233) 100.0	50.2	49.8	100.0	52.6	28.9	10.5	7.2	0.8	0.0	24.6	28.0	12.8	16.1	8.4	2.1	4.2	3.0	0.2	0.6	0.0	0.0
	II	Yamato-shi	(28,235) 100.0	47.7	52.3	100.0	57.1	26.5	8.4	7.2	0.8	0.0	25.8	31.3	11.1	15.4	6.6	1.8	4.1	3.1	0.1	0.7	0.0	0.0
		Zama-machi	(70,349) 100.0	49.1	50.9	100.0	57.9	24.9	8.1	8.2	0.9	0.0	26.7	31.2	11.4	13.5	5.4	1.7	4.4	3.8	0.2	0.7	0.0	0.0
		Sagamihara-shi	(10,664) 100.0	48.8	51.2	100.0	60.9	24.1	6.9	7.0	1.1	—	28.0	39.9	11.1	13.0	5.3	1.6	4.2	2.8	0.2	0.9	—	—
	III	Hachiōji-shi	(114,115) 100.0	48.5	51.5	100.0	63.5	21.7	5.9	7.6	1.3	0.0	28.5	35.0	10.6	11.1	4.6	1.3	4.4	3.2	0.4	0.9	0.0	0.0
		Akishima-shi	(30,991) 100.0	48.2	51.8	100.0	59.0	24.7	6.7	8.4	1.2	0.0	26.5	32.5	11.1	13.6	5.4	1.3	4.9	3.5	0.3	0.9	0.0	0.0
		Fussa-machi	(15,656) 100.0	46.4	53.6	100.0	61.9	24.5	5.7	7.2	0.7	0.0	27.3	34.6	10.3	14.2	4.4	1.3	4.2	3.0	0.2	0.5	0.0	0.0
		Mizuho-machi	(8,168) 100.0	48.6	51.4	100.0	78.8	11.0	2.4	6.4	1.4	—	36.6	42.2	6.2	4.8	1.7	0.7	3.9	2.5	0.2	1.2	—	—
		Murayama-machi	(8,424) 100.0	48.5	51.5	100.0	77.4	11.9	2.4	6.2	2.1	—	36.3	41.1	6.2	5.7	1.9	0.5	3.6	2.6	0.5	1.6	—	—
		Musashi-machi	(21,142) 100.0	47.8	52.2	100.0	75.3	15.3	3.1	5.2	1.1	0.0	34.5	40.8	7.6	7.7	2.4	0.7	3.1	2.1	0.2	0.9	0.0	0.0
	IV	Sayama-shi	(22,937) 100.0	48.9	51.1	100.0	72.4	17.5	3.1	5.7	1.3	—	33.9	38.5	8.8	8.7	2.5	0.6	3.4	2.3	0.3	1.0	0.0	0.0
		Kawagoe-shi	(75,200) 100.0	48.1	51.9	100.0	68.7	18.0	4.5	7.0	1.8	0.0	32.3	36.4	8.1	10.8	3.5	1.0	3.9	3.1	0.3	1.5	0.0	0.0
		Seibu-machi	(4,611) 100.0	40.0	60.0	100.0	79.9	11.4	2.1	5.3	1.3	—	28.7	51.2	6.6	4.8	1.4	0.7	3.0	2.3	0.3	1.0	0.0	0.0
	V	Ageo-shi	(27,042) 100.0	48.2	51.8	100.0	70.5	17.7	3.8	6.2	1.8	0.0	31.6	38.9	9.6	8.1	3.1	0.7	3.6	2.6	0.3	1.5	0.0	0.0
		Ina-mura	(4,628) 100.0	49.4	50.6	100.0	73.5	13.6	2.4	5.8	4.7	0.0	34.7	38.8	8.3	5.3	2.1	0.3	3.6	2.2	0.7	4.0	0.0	0.0
		Hasuda-machi	(14,437) 100.0	49.0	51.0	100.0	66.9	19.2	3.5	6.9	3.5	—	31.5	35.4	10.2	9.0	2.9	0.6	3.9	3.0	0.5	3.0	—	—
		Shiraoka-machi	(10,820) 100.0	49.6	50.4	100.0	71.5	16.3	2.3	6.6	3.3	0.0	33.3	38.2	9.8	6.5	2.0	0.3	4.0	2.6	0.5	2.8	0.0	0.0
		Miyashiro-machi	(7,454) 100.0	48.5	51.5	100.0	70.9	16.8	2.9	6.6	2.8	—	32.8	38.1	8.9	7.9	2.3	0.6	4.0	2.6	0.5	2.3	—	—

- 219 -

Table 5. Educational Backgrounds, School Enrollment, and Graduates, 15 Years and Older, by Sex

(Zone) / (Sector)	District	Total	Total %	M	F	Grad. Elementary	Grad. Intermediate	Grad. Higher	Still in School	Not in School	Unknown	Total %	Elem. M	Elem. F	Inter. M	Inter. F	Higher M	Higher F	Still M	Still F	Not in Sch. M	Not in Sch. F	Unk. M	Unk. F
V	Sugito-machi	(11,590) 100.0	100.0	48.3	51.7	73.4	14.8	2.5	6.0	3.3	—	100.0	34.2	39.2	8.0	6.8	2.1	0.4	3.5	2.5	0.5	2.8	—	—
VI	Sekiyado-machi	(8,105) 100.0	100.0	46.5	53.5	85.9	5.8	1.2	3.4	3.7	—	100.0	39.7	46.2	3.4	2.4	0.9	0.3	2.0	1.4	0.5	3.2	—	—
	Moriya-machi	(7,621) 100.0	100.0	47.1	52.9	74.2	14.6	2.5	5.6	3.1	—	100.0	33.2	41.0	8.5	6.1	1.9	0.6	3.1	2.5	0.4	2.7	—	—
VII	Toride-machi	(15,991) 100.0	100.0	47.8	52.2	59.2	24.8	1.0	8.4	1.6	0.0	100.0	25.5	33.7	12.5	12.3	4.6	1.4	5.0	3.4	0.2	1.4	0.0	—
	Inzai-machi	(11,984) 100.0	100.0	48.5	51.5	70.3	17.5	3.3	7.0	1.9	0.0	100.0	33.2	37.1	9.1	8.4	2.3	1.0	3.7	3.3	0.2	1.7	—	0.0
	Inba-mura	(5,676) 100.0	100.0	46.9	53.1	77.8	13.5	1.5	4.1	3.1	0.0	100.0	35.6	42.2	7.7	5.8	1.1	0.4	2.1	2.0	0.4	2.7	—	—
VIII	Yotsukaidō-machi	(11,399) 100.0	100.0	47.4	52.6	58.3	24.7	3.5	9.5	1.7	0.0	100.0	26.2	32.1	11.9	12.8	4.4	1.4	4.6	4.9	0.3	1.4	0.0	0.0
IX	Ichihara-machi	(9,930) 100.0	100.0	48.8	51.2	69.4	17.5	3.5	6.9	2.7	—	100.0	32.9	36.5	9.3	8.2	2.6	0.9	3.5	3.4	0.5	2.2	—	—
	Anegasaki-machi	(7,844) 100.0	100.0	47.4	52.6	73.9	14.9	3.5	5.9	1.8	0.0	100.0	33.7	40.2	7.4	7.5	2.6	0.9	3.4	2.5	0.3	1.5	—	0.0
	Hirakawa-machi	(7,420) 100.0	100.0	47.0	53.0	76.0	14.5	1.5	5.0	3.0	0.0	100.0	33.0	43.0	9.4	5.1	1.1	0.4	2.9	2.1	0.6	2.4	—	—
	Miwa-machi	(6,386) 100.0	100.0	47.6	52.4	76.1	13.4	2.4	4.9	3.2	0.0	100.0	35.3	40.8	7.3	6.1	1.7	0.7	2.7	2.2	0.6	2.6	—	—
X	Kisarazu-shi	(37,336) 100.0	100.0	47.6	52.4	68.6	19.6	3.7	6.3	1.8	0.0	100.0	30.0	38.6	11.1	8.5	2.8	0.9	3.3	3.0	0.4	1.4	0.0	0.0
	Zone 8 Total	(747,528) 100.0	100.0	48.4	51.6	63.8	21.5	5.9	7.3	1.5	0.0	100.0	29.1	34.7	10.2	11.3	4.6	1.3	4.2	3.1	0.3	1.2	0.0	0.0
9 I	Kamakura-shi	(74,957) 000.0	100.0	47.4	52.6	39.3	31.7	17.4	10.8	0.8	0.0	100.0	17.1	22.2	10.5	21.2	13.3	4.1	6.3	4.5	0.2	0.6	0.0	0.0
II	Ayase-machi	(5,675) 000.0	100.0	48.6	51.4	74.8	14.4	2.8	6.0	2.0	0.0	100.0	36.1	38.7	7.1	7.3	2.0	0.8	3.1	2.9	0.3	1.7	0.0	0.0
	Ebina-machi	(12,548) 000.0	100.0	47.9	52.1	69.3	18.6	4.1	6.6	1.4	0.0	100.0	31.3	38.0	9.1	9.5	3.3	0.8	3.9	2.7	0.3	1.1	0.0	0.0
	Shiroyama-machi	(3,584) 000.0	100.0	49.2	50.8	72.0	16.9	3.6	6.7	0.8	—	100.0	33.6	38.4	8.8	8.1	2.9	0.7	3.7	3.0	0.2	0.6	0.0	0.0
III	Akita-machi	(10,141) 000.0	100.0	49.5	50.5	74.5	13.5	3.1	7.2	1.7	0.0	100.0	35.5	39.0	7.1	6.4	2.3	0.8	4.2	3.0	0.4	1.3	0.0	0.0
	Hamura-machi	(7,635) 000.0	100.0	48.5	51.5	66.4	18.7	5.4	8.5	1.0	0.0	100.0	30.3	36.1	9.3	9.4	3.9	1.5	4.7	3.8	0.3	0.7	0.0	0.0
	Hannō-shi	(30,758) 000.0	100.0	47.8	52.2	73.0	16.1	3.6	6.1	1.2	—	100.0	33.6	39.4	7.8	8.3	2.7	1.9	3.5	2.6	0.2	1.0	0.0	0.0
	Tsurugashima-mura	(4,898) 000.0	100.0	50.4	49.6	73.0	15.8	2.5	6.5	2.2	0.0	100.0	36.9	36.1	7.3	8.5	1.9	0.6	3.8	2.7	0.5	1.7	0.0	0.0
IV	Hidaka-machi	(11,315) 000.0	100.0	49.5	50.5	76.6	13.9	2.2	5.5	1.8	0.0	100.0	37.3	39.3	7.0	6.9	1.8	0.4	3.1	2.4	0.3	1.5	0.0	0.0
	Kawashima-mura	(10,906) 000.0	100.0	47.6	52.4	75.4	12.8	1.4	5.6	4.8	0.0	100.0	36.6	38.8	6.2	6.6	1.2	0.2	2.9	2.7	0.7	4.1	0.0	0.0
V	Kitamoto-machi	(10,295) 000.0	100.0	49.4	50.6	69.9	17.6	3.5	7.0	2.0	0.0	100.0	32.3	37.6	10.0	7.6	2.7	0.8	4.1	2.9	0.3	1.7	0.0	0.0
	Higawa-machi	(14,604) 000.0	100.0	49.1	50.9	67.2	18.7	4.1	8.0	2.0	0.0	100.0	31.0	36.2	9.9	8.8	3.3	0.8	4.6	3.4	0.3	1.7	0.0	0.0
	Shobu-machi	(10,731) 000.0	100.0	48.0	52.0	75.4	11.8	2.2	6.1	4.5	0.0	100.0	35.6	39.8	6.5	5.3	1.6	0.6	3.4	2.7	0.9	3.6	0.0	0.0
	Kuki-machi	(15,445) 000.0	100.0	45.5	54.5	69.0	17.6	4.1	6.6	2.7	0.0	100.0	32.0	37.0	9.2	8.4	3.1	1.0	3.8	2.8	0.5	2.2	0.0	0.0
	Satte-machi	(15,739) 000.0	100.0	47.5	52.5	73.2	14.2	2.7	6.0	3.9	0.0	100.0	33.7	39.5	7.5	6.7	2.1	0.6	3.5	2.5	0.7	3.2	0.0	0.0
VI	Iwai-machi	(21,672) 000.0	100.0	47.3	52.7	80.8	9.5	1.6	4.5	3.6	—	100.0	37.6	43.2	5.4	4.1	1.3	0.3	2.5	2.0	0.5	3.1	—	—
	Mitsukaidō shi	(25,609) 000.0	100.0	46.5	53.5	74.3	14.5	2.6	5.4	3.2	0.0	100.0	33.6	40.7	7.6	6.9	1.9	0.7	2.9	2.5	0.5	2.7	0.0	0.0
	Yawahara-mura	(7,474) 000.0	100.0	46.6	53.4	71.5	17.5	1.7	6.7	2.6	—	100.0	31.3	40.2	9.9	7.6	1.4	0.3	3.7	3.0	0.3	2.3	—	—
	Ina-mura	(8,422) 000.0	100.0	46.4	53.6	71.1	18.8	1.7	5.6	2.8	0.0	100.0	30.6	40.5	11.0	7.8	1.3	0.4	3.0	2.6	0.5	2.3	—	0.0

Table 5. Educational Backgrounds, School Enrollment, and Graduates, 15 Years and Older, by Sex

(Zone)	(Sector)	District	Total (count)	Total	M	F	Elementary	Intermediate	Higher	Still in School	Not in School	Unknown	Total	Elem. M	Elem. F	Inter. M	Inter. F	Higher M	Higher F	Still M	Still F	NotIn M	NotIn F	Unk. M	Unk. F
	VII	Fujishiro-machi	(8,940)	100.0	47.2	52.8	63.1	24.3	2.9	7.6	2.1	—	100.0	26.3	36.8	13.8	10.5	2.3	0.6	4.5	3.1	0.3	1.8	—	—
		Ryugasaki-shi	(23,592)	100.0	46.9	53.1	66.7	20.3	3.9	7.2	1.9	—	100.0	30.0	36.7	9.7	10.6	3.0	0.9	3.9	3.3	0.3	1.6	—	—
		Tone-mura	(6,326)	100.0	46.9	53.1	73.0	16.9	2.7	5.5	1.9	0.0	100.0	32.7	40.3	9.2	7.7	1.9	0.8	2.8	2.7	0.3	1.6	0.0	0.0
		Motono-mura	(3,689)	100.0	47.8	52.2	73.7	17.0	1.3	5.8	2.2	—	100.0	33.9	39.8	9.6	7.4	0.9	0.4	3.0	2.8	0.4	1.8	—	—
	VIII	Sakura-shi	(25,898)	100.0	47.7	52.3	60.7	24.1	5.0	8.2	2.0	—	100.0	28.0	32.7	11.3	12.8	3.7	1.3	4.4	3.8	0.3	1.7	0.0	0.0
		Izumi-machi	(6,421)	100.0	47.2	52.8	75.3	13.4	1.9	5.1	4.3	—	100.0	35.4	39.9	7.0	6.4	1.3	0.6	2.8	2.3	0.7	3.6	—	—
	IX	Shitsu-mura	(6,263)	100.0	48.5	51.5	75.1	13.6	2.6	4.7	4.0	—	100.0	34.9	40.2	8.2	5.4	1.9	0.7	2.7	2.0	0.8	3.2	—	—
		Nanso-machi	(12,088)	100.0	47.3	52.7	73.6	13.5	3.3	5.8	3.8	0.0	100.0	34.4	39.2	6.9	6.6	2.2	1.1	3.2	2.6	0.6	3.2	0.0	0.0
	X	Fukuta-machi	(4,717)	100.0	47.1	52.9	76.0	13.6	2.4	5.4	2.6	—	100.0	33.3	42.7	8.3	5.3	1.8	0.6	3.1	2.3	0.6	2.0	—	—
		Kimitsu-machi	(9,059)	100.0	46.5	53.5	70.9	17.3	2.9	6.5	2.4	—	100.0	30.1	40.8	10.4	6.9	2.2	0.7	3.4	3.1	0.4	2.0	—	—
		Futtsu-machi	(11,345)	100.0	47.4	52.6	82.7	9.2	1.9	4.0	2.2	—	100.0	38.6	44.1	4.7	4.5	1.4	0.5	2.1	1.9	0.6	1.6	—	—
		Osawa-machi	(9,701)	100.0	46.6	53.4	71.7	16.5	3.3	6.1	2.4	—	100.0	31.5	40.2	9.1	7.4	2.3	1.0	3.3	2.8	0.4	2.0	0.0	0.0
		Zone 9 Total	(430,447)	100.0	47.8	52.2	66.1	19.0	5.6	7.1	2.2	0.0	100.0	30.3	35.8	8.8	10.2	4.3	1.3	4.0	3.1	0.4	1.8	0.0	0.0
10	I	Yokosuka-shi	(210,136)	100.0	50.6	49.4	56.6	27.5	6.4	8.7	0.8	0.0	100.0	27.0	29.6	13.0	14.5	5.0	1.4	5.4	3.3	0.2	0.6	0.0	0.0
		Zushi-shi	(29,630)	100.0	47.0	53.0	42.1	31.5	15.0	10.5	0.9	0.0	100.0	18.4	23.7	10.7	20.8	11.6	3.4	6.1	4.4	0.2	0.7	0.0	0.0
		Hayama-machi	(11,749)	100.0	46.2	53.8	48.6	26.9	12.8	10.3	1.4	0.0	100.0	21.1	27.5	8.9	18.0	9.7	3.1	6.2	4.1	0.3	1.1	0.0	0.0
		Chigasaki-shi	(48,560)	100.0	48.9	51.1	50.7	27.9	11.6	8.7	1.1	0.0	100.0	22.9	27.8	11.2	16.7	9.2	2.4	5.2	3.5	0.2	0.9	0.0	0.0
		Fujisawa-shi	(90,992)	100.0	47.7	52.3	46.9	29.0	13.6	9.6	0.9	0.0	100.0	20.7	26.2	10.8	18.2	10.4	3.2	5.6	4.0	0.2	0.7	0.0	0.0
	II	Aikawa-machi	(9,518)	100.0	44.6	55.4	81.7	10.6	1.8	4.7	1.2	—	100.0	36.4	45.3	5.8	4.8	1.2	0.6	1.0	3.7	0.2	1.0	—	—
		Atsugi-shi	(32,145)	100.0	49.5	50.5	67.5	19.0	5.0	7.2	1.3	0.0	100.0	32.1	35.4	9.1	9.9	3.9	1.1	4.1	3.1	0.3	1.0	0.0	0.0
		Samukawa-machi	(8,058)	100.0	51.8	48.2	65.9	20.7	4.4	7.4	1.6	0.0	100.0	32.5	33.4	11.0	9.7	3.6	0.8	4.4	3.0	0.3	1.3	0.0	0.0
	III	Ome-shi	(40,758)	100.0	47.2	52.8	71.8	15.4	4.1	7.4	1.3	0.0	100.0	32.0	39.8	7.5	7.9	3.2	0.9	4.2	3.2	0.3	1.0	0.0	0.0
	IV	Sakado-machi	(16,014)	100.0	48.0	52.0	72.6	16.3	2.7	6.5	1.9	0.0	100.0	34.7	37.9	7.5	8.8	2.1	0.6	3.5	3.0	0.2	1.7	0.0	0.0
		Yoshimi-mura	(9,730)	100.0	48.4	51.6	76.7	11.5	1.7	5.4	4.7	—	100.0	36.6	40.1	6.5	5.1	1.4	0.3	3.1	2.3	0.9	3.8	—	—
		Moroyama-mura	(7,773)	100.0	48.6	51.4	73.2	15.0	2.8	5.9	3.1	—	100.0	34.9	38.3	6.9	8.1	2.0	0.8	3.5	2.4	1.3	1.8	—	—
	V	Konosu-shi	(21,741)	100.0	48.4	51.6	68.7	17.7	4.0	7.4	2.2	0.0	100.0	30.9	37.8	9.5	8.1	3.2	0.8	4.4	3.0	0.4	1.8	0.0	0.0
		Kisai-machi	(10,228)	100.0	48.0	52.0	76.0	10.9	1.9	6.9	4.3	—	100.0	36.8	39.2	5.5	5.4	1.4	0.5	3.6	3.3	0.7	3.6	—	—
		Washimiya-machi	(5,620)	100.0	47.7	52.3	75.0	13.8	2.2	5.4	3.6	0.0	100.0	34.9	40.1	7.6	6.2	1.8	0.4	2.9	2.5	0.5	3.1	0.0	0.0
		Kurihashi-machi	(8,586)	100.0	47.1	52.9	69.6	16.1	3.1	6.7	4.5	—	100.0	32.0	37.6	7.9	8.2	2.5	0.6	3.8	2.9	0.9	3.6	—	—
		Goka-mura	(5,734)	100.0	47.3	52.7	80.1	8.0	1.3	4.2	6.4	—	100.0	37.6	42.5	4.8	3.2	1.0	0.3	2.6	1.6	1.3	5.1	—	—
	VI	Sakai-machi	(14,454)	100.0	45.9	54.1	81.2	9.1	1.8	4.4	3.5	0.0	100.0	36.9	44.3	4.8	4.3	1.3	0.5	2.4	2.0	0.5	3.0	0.0	0.0
		Sashima-machi	(9,102)	100.0	46.5	53.5	84.9	5.9	1.4	3.3	4.5	—	100.0	39.9	45.0	3.2	2.7	1.0	0.4	1.7	1.6	0.7	3.8	—	—

Table 5. Educational Backgrounds, School Enrollment, and Graduates, 15 Years and Older, by Sex

Zone (Sector)	District	Total	M	F	Total	Graduates Elementary	Graduates Intermediate	Graduates Higher	Still in School	Not in School	Unknown	Total	Grad. Elem. M	Grad. Elem. F	Grad. Inter. M	Grad. Inter. F	Grad. Higher M	Grad. Higher F	Still in School M	Still in School F	Not in School M	Not in School F	Unknown M	Unknown F
VI	Yatabe-machi	(14,483) 100.0	47.8	52.2	100.0	73.4	16.2	2.0	5.3	3.1	0.0	100.0	34.6	38.8	8.5	7.7	1.5	0.5	2.8	2.5	0.4	2.7	—	0.0
VII	Kukizaki-mura	(4,432) 100.0	48.2	51.8	100.0	74.3	15.6	1.1	5.2	3.8	—	100.0	34.9	39.4	9.1	6.5	0.9	0.2	2.8	2.4	0.5	3.3	—	—
	Ushiku-machi	(11,164) 100.0	49.3	50.7	100.0	71.4	17.3	3.4	5.6	2.3	—	100.0	34.1	37.3	9.1	8.2	2.7	0.7	3.1	2.5	0.3	2.0	—	—
	Kawachi-mura	(8,846) 100.0	47.0	53.0	100.0	79.0	12.5	1.4	5.1	2.0	—	100.0	35.9	43.1	7.1	5.4	1.1	0.3	2.6	2.5	0.3	1.7	—	—
	Sakae-machi	(6,882) 100.0	46.4	53.6	100.0	67.4	21.4	2.5	7.2	1.5	0.0	100.0	29.7	37.7	10.9	10.5	1.8	0.7	3.7	3.5	0.3	1.2	0.0	—
	Narita-shi	(30,128) 100.0	46.4	53.6	100.0	62.6	24.3	4.1	7.0	2.0	0.0	100.0	26.9	35.7	12.5	11.8	3.0	1.1	3.7	3.3	0.3	1.7	0.0	—
VIII	Shisui-machi	(4,236) 100.0	47.9	52.1	100.0	65.7	21.9	3.1	7.5	1.8	—	100.0	29.9	35.8	11.0	10.9	2.5	0.6	4.2	3.3	0.3	1.5	—	—
	Yachimata-machi	(17,169) 100.0	48.1	51.9	100.0	72.2	16.5	2.7	6.3	2.3	0.0	100.0	33.5	38.7	11.0	7.7	1.9	0.8	3.5	2.8	0.4	1.9	0.0	0.0
	Toke-machi	(4,612) 100.0	47.1	52.9	100.0	66.3	21.6	2.9	6.8	2.4	0.0	100.0	29.9	36.4	11.6	10.0	2.0	0.9	3.2	3.6	0.4	2.0	0.0	—
IX	Nagara-machi	(5,892) 100.0	46.9	53.1	100.0	65.7	21.1	2.6	6.5	4.1	0.0	100.0	29.6	36.1	11.4	9.7	1.7	0.9	3.3	3.2	0.3	3.5	0.0	0.0
	Obitsu-mura	(4,664) 100.0	46.9	53.1	100.0	75.5	15.5	1.9	5.0	2.2	—	100.0	32.8	42.7	9.8	5.7	1.4	0.5	2.6	2.4	0.4	1.9	—	—
X	Koito-machi	(4,164) 100.0	48.3	51.7	100.0	69.2	19.9	2.0	6.4	2.5	—	100.0	30.3	38.9	12.6	7.3	1.4	0.6	3.6	2.8	0.4	2.1	—	—
	Zone 10 Total	(707,207) 100.0	48.6	51.4	100.0	60.9	22.9	6.7	7.9	1.6	0.0	100.0	28.1	32.8	10.4	12.5	5.2	1.5	4.6	3.3	0.3	1.3	0.0	0.0
	Total for 50 km. Region	(11,796,697) 100.0	51.0	49.0	100.0	51.0	28.4	10.5	9.3	0.8	0.0	100.0	24.3	26.7	12.4	16.0	8.3	2.2	5.8	3.5	0.2	0.6	0.0	0.0
	National Total	(65,351,895) 100.0	48.3	51.7	100.0	63.1	22.2	5.2	7.3	2.2	0.0	100.0	29.6	33.5	10.0	12.2	4.1	1.1	4.2	3.1	0.5	1.7	0.0	0.0

Note: The designations "Elementary," "Intermediate," and "Higher" for educational backgrounds of "Graduates" denote the following, (according to national census standards):

"Elementary":   primary school, prewar higher primary school, postwar junior high school, and youth school.

"Intermediate":   prewar middle school, and youth school.

"Higher":   junior college, prewar higher technical school, and university.

TABLE 6. NUMBER OF HOUSEHOLDS BY TYPE OF DWELLING

1950

(Zone) (Sector)	District	Total	Ordinary Dwellings					Non-Dwellings	Unknown
			Own Houses	Rented Houses	Employee Houses	Rented Rooms	Unknown		
1 I	Chiyoda-ku	(22,931)100.0	47.2	19.1	12.8	16.0	0.1	4.8	—
	Minato-ku	(50,204)100.0	43.4	24.0	9.6	17.7	0.1	5.2	—
	Chūō-ku	(35,899)100.0	38.4	27.6	10.5	19.6	0.1	3.8	—
	Bunkyō-ku	(44,329)100.0	47.4	23.6	5.6	20.4	0.2	2.8	—
	Taitō-ku	(55,766)100.0	52.8	23.9	3.2	17.3	0.1	2.7	—
	Zone 1 Total	(209,129)100.0	46.2	24.0	7.6	18.4	0.1	3.7	—
2 I	Shinagawa-ku	(68,257)100.0	44.1	26.2	6.6	18.9	—	4.2	—
II	Meguro-ku	(47,668)100.0	44.1	27.0	6.3	19.7	—	2.9	—
	Shibuya-ku	(42,899)100.0	47.0	23.4	6.2	18.4	—	5.0	
III	Shinjuku-ku	(57,944)100.0	52.8	21.2	5.6	15.5	0.1	4.8	—
	Nakano-ku	(52,169)100.0	45.0	24.3	5.2	23.0	—	2.5	—
IV	Toshima-ku	(51,428)100.0	49.2	25.9	4.1	18.7	—	2.1	—
V	Kita-ku	(61,356)100.0	42.7	33.8	5.2	17.0	—	1.3	—
VI	Arakawa-ku	(44,260)100.0	47.0	31.3	5.7	13.7	—	2.3	—
VII	Sumida-ku	(50,259)100.0	51.2	29.4	6.1	10.9	—	2.4	—
VIII	Kōtō-ku	(48,091)100.0	59.7	18.5	10.5	7.3	—	4.0	—
	Zone 2 Total	(524,331)100.0	47.9	26.3	6.1	16.5		3.2	—
3 I	Ōta-ku	(93,603)100.0	46.3	24.5	7.6	19.2	—	2.4	—
II	Setagaya-ku	(95,897)100.0	41.5	28.8	9.4	18.5	—	1.8	—
III	Suginami-ku	(77,065)100.0	41.3	26.4	6.5	23.0	—	2.8	—
IV	Itabashi-ku	(50,686)100.0	35.9	38.6	6.5	17.2	—	1.8	—
	Nerima-ku	(26,943)100.0	46.8	28.5	4.9	17.2	—	2.6	—
VI	Adachi-ku	(58,839)100.0	38.9	42.6	5.0	12.3	—	1.2	—
VII	Katsushika-ku	(53,678)100.0	36.1	41.7	6.6	14.4	—	1.2	—
VIII	Edogawa-ku	(45,603)100.0	41.2	37.6	6.1	13.7	—	1.4	—
	Urayasu-machi	(3,052)100.0	53.8	34.7	1.3	6.6	—	3.6	—
	Zone 3 Total	(505,363)100.0	41.3	32.4	7.0	17.5	—	1.8	
4 I	Kawasaki-shi	(67,386)100.0	43.0	23.0	10.9	11.7	—	11.4	—
II	Komae-machi	(2,097)100.0	51.9	22.9	10.1	11.6	—	3.5	—
III	Mitaka-shi	(12,533)100.0	34.5	33.8	10.2	19.3	—	2.2	—
	Musashino-shi	(17,090)100.0	35.5	33.3	9.6	20.3	—	1.3	—
	Chōfu-shi	(7,506)100.0	36.7	37.6	10.2	13.4	—	2.1	—
	Hoya-machi	(3,109)100.0	45.2	34.9	5.2	12.6	—	2.1	—
IV	Yamato-machi	(2,025)100.0	48.5	38.9	2.2	6.5	—	3.9	—
	Toda-machi	(3,523)100.0	56.4	27.1	7.6	6.4	—	2.5	—
V	Warabi-shi	(6,390)100.0	32.2	48.1	6.0	13.4	—	0.3	—
	Kawaguchi-shi	(25,741)100.0	39.6	41.2	5.7	11.3	—	2.2	—
	Hatogaya-machi	—	—	—	—	—		—	—
VI	Sōka-shi	(5,514)100.0	55.4	28.4	8.0	6.5	—	1.7	—
	Yashio-mura	(2,070)100.0	78.9	8.5	7.0	4.0	—	1.6	—
	Misato-mura	(2,652)100.0	85.3	6.1	2.7	3.3	—	2.6	—
	Matsudo-shi	(10,475)100.0	55.1	29.0	4.2	9.1	—	2.6	—
VII	Ichikawa-shi	(25,340)100.0	47.8	32.2	5.5	12.9	—	1.6	—
	Zone 4 Total	(194,176)100.0	43.7	30.1	8.3	12.6		5.2	—
5 I	Tsurumi-ku	(36,861)100.0	36.4	27.6	16.8	15.3		3.9	—

Table 6. Number of Households by Type of Dwelling

(Zone)	(Sector)	District	Total	Ordinary Dwellings					Non-Dwellings	Unknown
				Own Houses	Rented Houses	Employee Houses	Rented Rooms	Unknown		
	III	Koganei-shi	(4,672) 100.0	42.9	30.2	8.5	16.8	–	1.6	–
		Tanashi-machi	(2,989) 100.0	39.6	30.1	1.8	16.8	–	11.7	–
		Kurume-machi	(1,440) 100.0	69.5	17.7	3.9	5.2	–	3.7	–
	IV	Nīza-machi	(2,046) 100.9	71.6	14.6	6.6	5.4	–	1.8	–
		Kiyose-machi	(1,498) 100.0	52.9	15.8	13.0	15.4	–	2.9	–
		Adachi-machi	(1,911) 100.0	56.7	30.3	2.4	7.1	–	3.5	–
		Asaka-machi	(2,884) 100.0	59.0	27.8	5.4	6.4	–	1.4	–
	V	Urawa-shi	(26,223) 100.0	50.4	30.0	5.9	12.0	–	1.7	–
		Misono-mura	(1,523) 100.0	85.9	6.0	2.4	4.6	–	1.1	–
		Koshigaya-shi	(7,498) 100.0	76.0	13.2	3.2	4.6	–	3.0	–
	VI	Yoshikawa-machi	(2,719) 100.0	82.6	10.2	1.5	3.7	–	2.0	–
		Nagareyama-machi	(3,269) 100.0	80.4	9.9	2.7	4.7	–	2.3	–
	VII	Kamagaya-machi	(1,609) 100.0	81.0	7.6	2.6	4.0	–	4.8	–
	VIII	Funahashi-shi	(20,483) 100.0	48.5	31.7	7.2	10.7	–	1.9	–
		Zone 5 Total	(117,625) 100.0	50.1	26.3	9.1	11.6	–	2.9	–
6	I	Nishi-ku	(19,551) 100.0	60.3	16.4	7.5	11.1	–	4.7	–
		Naka-ku	(20,608) 100.0	61.8	16.7	4.6	12.3	–	4.6	–
		Kanagawa-ku	(23,686) 100.0	54.7	21.3	6.7	12.4	–	4.9	–
	II	Kōhoku-ku	(18,315) 100.0	61.9	19.1	5.0	11.4	–	2.6	–
		Inagi-machi	(1,931) 100.0	51.4	19.8	2.1	5.3	–	21.4	–
	III	Tama-mura	(1,328) 100.0	72.1	13.8	4.3	5.6	–	4.2	–
		Fuchu-shi	(8,430) 100.0	43.2	29.6	15.0	9.9	–	2.3	–
		Kunitachi-machi	(3,075) 100.0	44.4	31.4	7.4	12.2	–	4.6	–
		Kokubunji-machi	(3,787) 100.0	44.5	26.9	16.1	10.9	–	1.6	–
		Kodaira-machi	(4,172) 100.0	53.5	26.1	12.3	6.5	–	1.6	–
		Higashimurayama-machi	(2,987) 100.0	59.8	19.8	12.7	5.8	–	1.9	–
	IV	Tokorosawa-shi	(9,755) 100.0	66.3	24.0	1.2	6.5	–	2.0	–
		Miyoshi-mura	(678) 100.0	87.4	6.4	1.4	3.5	–	1.3	–
		Fujimi-mura	(1,832) 100.0	84.7	5.1	0.7	3.7	–	5.7	–
	V	Yono-shi	(6,170) 100.0	45.5	32.2	10.4	10.5	–	1.4	–
		Ōmiya-shi	(23,901) 100.0	53.0	29.2	5.6	9.7	–	2.5	–
		Iwatsuki-shi	(6,025) 100.0	69.4	22.1	1.9	5.3	–	1.3	–
	VI	Matsubushi-mura	(1,460) 100.0	88.7	5.0	1.1	3.6	–	1.6	–
	VII	Kashiwa-shi	(8,834) 100.0	67.6	16.5	8.9	5.3	–	1.7	–
		Shōnan-mura	(1,755) 100.0	90.4	3.3	1.7	2.7	–	1.9	–
		Shirai-mura	(1,072) 100.0	89.4	4.6	1.6	1.5	–	2.9	–
	VIII	Narashino-shi	(4,856) 100.0	47.7	29.9	5.8	15.7	–	0.9	–
		Zone 6 Total	(174,208) 100.0	58.3	21.7	6.6	10.0	–	3.4	–
7	I	Isogo-ku	(14,295) 100.0	38.7	39.5	3.8	16.7	–	1.3	–
		Minami-ku	(31,605) 100.0	57.8	24.2	3.0	11.9	–	3.1	–
		Hodogaya-ku	(15,537) 100.0	56.2	25.6	5.4	10.0	–	2.8	–
	II	Machida-shi	(10,123) 100.0	61.0	26.0	2.1	7.8	–	3.1	–
	III	Yuki-mura	(1,077) 100.0	87.9	7.5	0.2	3.1	–	1.3	–
		Hino-machi	(5,014) 100.0	60.9	17.8	10.1	8.9	–	2.3	–
		Tachikawa-shi	(11,439) 100.0	37.9	37.1	3.4	17.8	–	2.8	–
		Sunakawa-machi	(2,135) 100.0	51.9	39.0	3.4	3.3	–	2.4	–
		Yamato-machi	(2,301) 100.0	82.4	9.1	2.0	5.3	–	1.2	–
	IV	Ōi-mura	(793) 100.0	74.5	17.2	0.7	5.9	–	1.7	–
		Fukuoka-mura	(1,483) 100.0	48.2	43.4	3.1	5.1	–	0.2	–
	V	Kasukabe-shi	(2,915) 100.0	63.2	22.2	3.6	10.9	–	0.1	–

Table 6. Number of Households by Type of Dwelling

(Zone) (Sector)	District	Total	Ordinary Dwellings					Non-Dwellings	Unknown
			Own Houses	Rented Houses	Employee Houses	Rented Rooms	Unknown		
V	Shōwa-mura	(2,585) 100.0	66.2	28.5	1.7	2.8	–	0.8	–
VI	Noda-shi	(9,520) 100.0	74.1	16.5	2.7	4.8	–	1.9	–
VII	Abiko-machi	(4,019) 100.0	71.4	14.9	5.7	5.9	–	2.1	–
	Yachiyo-machi	(2,613) 100.0	85.8	6.1	2.6	3.4	–	2.1	–
VIII	Chiba-shi	(35,051) 100.0	60.2	22.1	5.3	8.0	–	4.4	–
IX	Goi-machi	(3,606) 100.0	81.8	9.9	1.7	4.4	–	2.2	–
	Sodegaura-machi	(2,563) 100.0	87.2	7.3	1.9	1.9	–	1.7	–
	Zone 7 Total	(158,674) 100.0	58.7	24.6	4.1	9.8	–	2.9	–
8 I	Kanazawa-ku	(12,585) 100.0	32.4	51.5	2.8	11.8	–	1.5	
	Totsuka-ku	(13,218) 100.0	51.3	25.3	9.6	9.3	–	4.5	–
II	Yamato-shi	(3,651) 100.0	54.0	33.6	2.3	7.2	–	2.9	–
	Sagamihara-shi	(13,135) 100.0	60.3	19.4	6.9	7.6	–	5.8	–
	Zama-machi	(2,221) 100.0	72.4	13.1	3.7	8.6	–	2.2	–
III	Hachiōji-shi	(24,489) 100.0	71.4	16.1	3.5	6.5	–	2.5	–
	Akishima-shi	(6,971) 100.0	35.7	47.3	3.1	12.4	–	1.5	–
	Fussa-machi	(2,823) 100.0	52.5	23.8	8.4	11.9	–	3.4	–
	Mizuho-machi	(1,615) 100.0	77.3	14.9	1.8	5.5	–	0.5	–
	Murayama-machi	(1,864) 100.0	80.4	13.5	0.8	4.6	–	0.7	–
	Musashi-machi	(4,641) 100.0	70.4	22.0	2.4	5.0	–	0.2	–
IV	Sayama-shi	(5,625) 100.0	70.0	20.1	1.5	5.9	–	2.5	–
	Kawagoe-shi	(18,712) 100.0	57.6	30.8	3.2	7.1	–	1.3	–
	Seibu-machi	(609) 100.0	75.9	11.9	2.3	8.5	–	1.4	–
V	Ageo-shi	(5,822) 100.0	68.9	19.4	5.2	4.9	–	1.6	–
	Ina-mura	(1,176) 100.0	83.6	7.3	5.4	2.9	–	0.8	–
	Hasuda-machi	(3,076) 100.0	75.4	13.3	2.6	5.3	–	3.4	–
	Shiraoka-machi	(2,724) 100.0	80.6	11.3	1.1	4.9	–	1.5	–
	Miyashiro-machi	(1,828) 100.0	76.4	11.5	4.1	5.0	–	3.0	–
	Sugito-machi	(3,035) 100.0	81.4	11.5	1.6	3.9	–	1.6	–
VI	Sekiyado-machi	(2,315) 100.0	86.8	6.0	0.9	2.9	–	3.4	–
	Moriya-machi	(1,803) 100.0	83.4	9.7	2.7	2.5	–	1.7	–
VII	Toride-machi	(3,831) 100.0	66.6	23.3	1.5	6.0	–	2.6	–
	Inzai-machi	(3,457) 100.0	83.1	9.2	1.8	2.8	–	3.1	–
	Inba-mura	(1,534) 100.0	91.5	3.1	1.2	0.8	–	3.4	–
VIII	Yotsukaidō-machi	(3,532) 100.0	68.8	11.6	1.3	6.5	–	11.8	–
IX	Ichihara-machi	(2,659) 100.0	81.1	11.5	2.1	3.6	–	1.7	–
	Anegasaki-machi	(1,733) 100.0	76.7	13.2	1.3	6.4	–	2.4	–
	Hirakawa-machi	(2,437) 100.0	88.9	6.1	1.6	1.6	–	1.8	–
	Miwa-machi	(2,045) 100.0	90.1	5.7	1.0	1.4	–	1.8	–
X	Kisarazu-shi	(9,970) 100.0	65.9	24.3	2.2	4.7	–	2.9	–
	Zone 8 Total	(164,350) 100.0	63.3	23.1	3.7	6.9	–	2.9	–
9 I	Kamakura-shi	(19,137) 100.0	44.9	30.9	4.3	17.5	–	2.4	–
II	Ayase-machi	(1,404) 100.0	77.4	15.8	1.0	4.0	–	1.8	–
	Ebina-machi	(2,819) 100.0	75.0	11.5	5.9	6.7	–	0.9	–
	Shiroyama-machi	(1,004) 100.0	79.2	10.7	4.8	4.2	–	1.1	–
III	Akita-machi	(2,357) 100.0	82.6	9.9	0.8	5.5	–	1.2	–
	Hamura-machi	(1,489) 100.0	69.0	13.2	3.0	10.7	–	4.1	–
IV	Hannō-shi	(8,939) 100.0	68.5	21.4	3.0	5.9	–	1.2	–
	Tsurugashima-mura	(1,180) 100.0	87.7	6.0	2.4	2.5	–	1.4	–
	Hidaka-machi	(2,918) 100.0	86.3	7.6	1.4	3.3	–	1.4	–
	Kawashima-mura	(2,913) 100.0	91.8	4.1	1.3	1.1	–	1.7	–

Table 6. Number of Households by Type of Dwelling

(Zone)	(Sector)	District	Total	Ordinary Dwellings					Non-Dwellings	Unknown
				Own Houses	Rented Houses	Employee Houses	Rented Rooms	Unknown		
V		Kitamoto-machi	(2,399) 100.0	79.4	8.7	4.2	5.4	−	2.3	−
		Higawa-machi	(3,510) 100.0	57.8	28.2	6.5	6.3	−	1.2	−
		Shobu-machi	(3,238) 100.0	85.8	8.3	1.3	3.0	−	1.6	−
		Kuki-machi	(3,751) 100.0	77.1	12.7	3.1	6.4	−	1.2	−
		Satte-machi	(3,917) 100.0	73.3	17.9	2.9	3.8	−	2.1	−
VI		Iwai-machi	(5,951) 100.0	91.1	4.6	0.6	1.6	−	2.1	−
		Mitsukaidō-shi	(8,597) 100.0	82.8	10.7	1.5	3.4	−	1.6	−
		Yawahara-mura	(1,499) 100.0	89.9	4.8	0.7	2.6	−	2.0	−
		Ina-mura	(1,940) 100.0	91.6	4.3	0.7	2.4	−	1.0	−
VII		Fujishiro-machi	(2,605) 100.0	86.5	7.8	1.2	2.7	−	1.8	−
		Ryūgasaki-shi	(6,642) 100.0	68.9	23.5	1.0	4.7	−	1.9	−
		Tone-mura	(2,754) 100.0	87.8	6.3	1.0	2.6	−	2.3	−
		Motono-mura	(994) 100.0	90.4	4.2	0.8	1.1	−	3.5	−
VIII		Sakura-shi	(6,587) 100.0	74.3	13.8	2.6	5.1	−	4.2	−
		Izumi-machi	(1,677) 100.0	95.4	2.2	1.4	0.4	−	0.6	−
IX		Shitsu-mura	(1,712) 100.0	92.3	3.4	1.2	1.5	−	1.6	−
		Nansō-machi	(3,647) 100.0	86.4	8.0	1.1	2.6	−	1.9	−
		Fukuta-machi	(1,808) 100.0	87.3	7.4	1.2	1.6	−	2.5	−
X		Kimitsu-machi	(2,609) 100.0	79.4	14.4	1.4	2.4	−	2.4	−
		Futtsu-machi	(2,990) 100.0	82.2	11.2	1.1	3.8	−	1.7	−
		Ōsawa-machi	(2,849) 100.0	80.0	10.9	2.2	4.5	−	2.4	−
		Zone 9 Total	(114,878) 100.0	73.7	15.5	2.5	6.3	−	2.1	−
10	I	Yokosuka-shi	(53,812) 100.0	42.9	38.0	4.2	12.5	−	2.4	−
		Zushi-shi	(8,073) 100.0	41.4	31.1	3.0	14.4	−	10.1	−
		Hayama-machi	(3,231) 100.0	56.5	24.3	4.1	12.7	−	2.4	−
		Chigasaki-shi	(10,509) 100.0	61.0	24.1	3.3	10.5	−	1.1	−
		Fujisawa-shi	(20,098) 100.0	55.4	26.4	6.3	10.5	−	1.4	−
	II	Aikawa-machi	(2,545) 100.0	85.0	10.0	1.8	2.5	−	0.7	−
		Atsugi-shi	(7,741) 100.0	79.8	11.0	2.3	5.0	−	1.9	−
		Samukawa-machi	(2,069) 100.0	59.0	18.7	5.4	3.7	−	13.2	−
	III	Ōme-shi	(9,694) 100.0	64.6	22.3	3.0	8.5	−	1.6	−
	IV	Sakado-machi	(4,202) 100.0	84.0	9.0	2.0	3.9	−	1.1	−
		Yoshimi-mura	(2,655) 100.0	90.8	3.8	0.9	1.4	−	3.1	−
		Moroyama-mura	(1,853) 100.0	95.4	7.4	2.1	4.3	−	0.8	−
	V	Kōnosu-shi	(5,499) 100.0	65.4	21.2	4.6	6.4	−	2.4	−
		Kisai-machi	(2,826) 100.0	87.5	8.0	1.5	2.6	−	0.4	−
		Washimiya-machi	(1,596) 100.0	85.4	7.1	1.1	4.3	−	2.1	−
		Kurihashi-machi	(2,288) 100.0	71.9	20.0	2.4	3.8	−	1.9	−
		Goka-mura	(1,523) 100.0	91.5	2.2	0.9	0.7	−	4.7	−
	VI	Sakai-machi	(4,112) 100.0	82.3	9.8	1.4	3.3	−	3.2	−
		Sashima-machi	(2,550) 100.0	92.8	4.0	0.5	1.2	−	1.5	−
		Yatabe-machi	(3,450) 100.0	85.4	8.0	2.0	3.5	−	1.1	−
	VII	Kukizaki-mura	(1,088) 100.0	93.3	2.6	0.4	0.7	−	3.0	−
		Ushiku-machi	(2,829) 100.0	83.5	7.9	2.4	5.0	−	1.2	−
		Kawachi-mura	(1,542) 100.0	91.3	4.4	0.4	2.0	−	1.8	−
		Sakae-machi	(2,690) 100.0	85.3	8.9	1.1	3.0	−	1.7	−
		Narita-shi	(8,696) 100.0	74.5	14.9	3.0	4.6	−	3.0	−
	VIII	Shisui-machi	(1,167) 100.0	82.5	8.4	2.5	3.8	−	2.8	−
		Yachimata-machi	(5,370) 100.0	81.6	9.9	2.0	3.1	−	3.4	−
		Toke-machi	(1,240) 100.0	87.3	7.1	1.7	2.6	−	1.3	−
	IX	Nagara-machi	(1,844) 100.0	89.5	5.0	1.4	1.5	−	2.6	−

Table 6. Number of Households by Type of Dwelling

(Zone)(Sector)	District	Total	Ordinary Dwellings					Non-Dwellings	Unknown
			Own Houses	Rented Houses	Employee Houses	Rented Rooms	Unknown		
IX	Obitsu-mura	(1,403) 100.0	88.7	6.5	0.5	2.2	–	2.1	–
X	Koito-machi	(1,175) 100.0	89.9	5.4	1.7	1.3	–	1.7	–
	Zone 10 Total	(178,173) 100.0	62.4	23.2	3.4	8.4	–	2.6	–
	Total for 50 km. Region	(2,340,907) 100.0	51.0	26.3	6.1	13.6	–	3.0	–
	National Total	(16,425,390) 100.0	62.1	20.7	6.2	8.5	–	2.5	–

1955

(Zone)(Sector)	District	Total	Ordinary Households	Quasi Households	Ordinary Households							
					Total	Own Houses	Rented Houses	Employee Houses	Rented Rooms	Unknown	Boarding Houses	Others
1 I	Chiyoda-ku	(23,420) 100.0	87.9	12.1	(20,593) 100.0	57.3	19.0	13.1	8.3	–	–	2.3
	Minato-ku	(36,567) 100.0	91.2	8.8	(51,577) 100.0	52.6	23.8	10.5	11.2	–	–	1.9
	Chūō-ku	(30,472) 100.0	87.7	12.3	(30,239) 100.0	53.6	23.8	8.6	10.6	–	0.1	3.3
	Bunkyō-ku	(53,310) 100.0	90.0	10.0	(48,487) 100.0	55.6	23.6	6.1	13.4	–	0.5	0.8
	Taitō-ku	(61,540) 100.0	92.3	7.7	(56,811) 100.0	58.4	23.6	2.6	13.1	–	–	2.3
	Zone 1 Total	(229,309) 100.0	90.6	9.4	(207,707) 100.0	55.1	23.7	7.3	11.9	–	0.3	1.7
2 I	Shinagawa-ku	(88,334) 100.0	92.3	7.7	(81,572) 100.0	50.3	28.1	6.9	13.7	–	0.4	0.6
II	Meguro-ku	(60,463) 100.0	92.6	7.4	(55,605) 100.0	51.7	26.5	8.3	12.8	–	0.3	0.4
	Shibuya-ku	(58,604) 100.0	89.3	10.7	(52,338) 100.0	53.6	23.2	8.6	13.8	–	0.4	0.4
III	Shinjuku-ku	(82,497) 100.0	89.6	10.4	(73,937) 100.0	54.6	23.9	6.9	13.4	–	0.2	1.0
	Nakano-ku	(71,536) 100.0	90.5	9.5	(64,755) 100.0	51.2	28.3	7.0	13.0	–	0.2	0.3
IV	Toshima-ku	(72,716) 100.0	90.5	9.5	(65,804) 100.0	52.0	27.0	4.8	15.6	–	0.2	0.4
V	Kita-ku	(82,273) 100.0	93.0	7.0	(76,520) 100.0	50.4	30.1	5.2	13.9	–	0.1	0.3
VI	Arakawa-ku	(53,374) 100.0	95.0	5.0	(50,730) 100.0	53.6	29.7	4.4	11.3	–	0.4	0.6
VII	Sumida-ku	(60,625) 100.0	94.9	5.1	(57,507) 100.0	56.5	28.2	4.6	9.2	–	0.3	1.2
VIII	Kōtō-ku	(59,254) 100.0	93.7	6.3	(55,537) 100.0	57.4	19.8	10.1	10.0	–	0.3	2.4
	Zone 2 Total	(689,676) 100.0	92.0	8.0	(634,305) 100.0	53.0	26.6	6.6	12.8	–	0.3	0.7
3 I	Ōta-ku	(133,365) 100.0	92.7	7.3	(123,708) 100.0	55.0	24.2	7.5	12.7	–	0.2	0.4
II	Setagaya-ku	(123,886) 100.0	91.4	8.6	(113,187) 100.0	53.3	26.4	7.6	12.2	–	0.2	0.3
III	Suginami-ku	(97,759) 100.0	90.8	9.2	(88,720) 100.0	52.7	24.1	9.8	12.8	–	0.1	0.5
IV	Itabashi-ku	(71,180) 100.0	93.4	6.6	(66,513) 100.0	48.4	31.6	5.5	13.6	–	0.2	0.7
	Nerima-ku	(41,290) 100.0	93.2	6.8	(38,464) 100.0	58.8	25.3	4.5	11.1	–	0.1	0.2
VI	Adachi-ku	(71,309) 100.0	96.5	3.5	(68,822) 100.0	49.2	37.3	4.2	8.8	–	0.1	0.4
VII	Katsushika-ku	(63,418) 100.0	96.4	3.6	(61,153) 100.0	49.4	35.8	5.8	8.5	–	0.1	0.4
VIII	Edogawa-ku	(55,047) 100.0	95.8	4.2	(52,733) 100.0	52.0	31.6	5.5	10.2	–	0.1	0.6
	Urayasu-machi	(3,174) 100.0	98.1	1.9	(3,115) 100.0	61.1	33.4	1.5	3.7	–	–	0.3
	Zone 3 Total	(660,428) 100.0	93.3	6.7	(616,415) 100.0	52.5	28.8	6.7	11.5	–	0.1	0.4
4 I	Kawasaki-shi	(98,755) 100.0	93.7	6.3	(92,540) 100.0	52.9	24.6	10.0	9.6	–	0.2	2.7
II	Komae-machi	(3,205) 100.0	92.6	7.4	(2,969) 100.0	64.7	22.5	3.6	7.9	–	1.2	0.1
III	Mitaka-shi	(15,863) 100.0	92.0	8.0	(14,595) 100.0	49.9	28.1	10.1	11.3	–	0.3	0.3
	Musashino-shi	(22,420) 100.0	90.9	9.1	(20,390) 100.0	47.1	29.0	9.5	13.5	–	0.2	0.7
	Chōfu-shi	(9,650) 100.0	95.8	4.2	(9,247) 100.0	49.7	31.0	10.0	7.3	–	0.7	1.3
	Hoya-machi	(5,190) 100.0	95.4	4.6	(4,950) 100.0	50.3	38.5	3.1	6.8	–	0.4	0.9
IV	Yamato-machi	(2,753) 100.0	95.4	4.6	(2,625) 100.0	54.1	32.0	5.7	7.0	–	–	1.2
	Toda-machi	(4,221) 100.0	97.7	2.3	(4,112) 100.0	65.5	25.7	4.9	3.8	–	–	0.1
V	Warabi-shi	(7,620) 100.0	96.5	3.5	(7,313) 100.0	51.9	36.3	4.5	6.5	–	–	0.8
	Kawaguchi-shi	(27,622) 100.0	96.4	3.6	(26,667) 100.0	49.6	37.0	5.0	7.6	–	–	0.8

Table 6. Number of Households by Type of Dwelling

(Zone) (Sector)	District	Total	Ordinary Households	Quasi Households	Ordinary Households							
					Total	Own Houses	Rented Houses	Employee Houses	Rented Rooms	Unknown	Boarding Houses	Others
V	Hatogaya-machi	(2,909) 100.0	98.0	2.0	(2,852) 100.0	53.6	38.3	2.7	5.4	–	–	–
VI	Sōka-shi	(6,025) 100.0	98.2	1.8	(5,918) 100.0	63.5	24.8	6.7	3.7	–	–	1.3
	Yashio-mura	(2,107) 100.0	99.1	0.9	(2,087) 100.0	82.1	8.6	6.0	2.3	–	–	1.0
	Misato-mura	(2,690) 100.0	99.1	0.9	(2,667) 100.0	89.4	6.5	1.6	1.6	–	–	0.9
	Matsudo-shi	(13,875) 100.0	96.4	3.6	(13,376) 100.0	63.4	24.5	3.4	7.2	–	0.1	1.4
VII	Ichikawa-shi	(28,926) 100.0	95.3	4.7	(27,564) 100.0	58.2	27.9	6.1	7.4	–	0.1	0.3
	Zone 4 Total	(253,831) 100.0	96.5	3.5	(239,872) 100.0	53.9	27.8	7.8	8.8	–	0.2	1.5
5 I	Tsurumi-ku	(45,118) 100.0	93.6	6.4	(42,208) 100.0	48.2	22.4	15.7	11.2	–	1.7	0.8
III	Koganei-shi	(6,887) 100.0	91.4	8.6	(6,297) 100.0	55.4	25.3	8.1	10.6	–	0.1	0.5
	Tanashi-machi	(4,263) 100.0	94.6	5.4	(4,032) 100.0	54.2	31.1	5.6	9.0	–	0.1	–
	Kurume-machi	(1,886) 100.0	97.6	2.4	(1,841) 100.0	66.4	28.5	3.2	1.5	–	0.1	0.3
IV	Niza-machi	(2,164) 100.0	98.4	1.6	(2,130) 100.0	77.5	15.2	5.0	1.7	–	–	0.6
	Kiyose-machi	(2,178) 100.0	92.8	7.2	(2,022) 100.0	53.9	32.1	10.8	3.2	–	–	–
	Adachi-machi	(2,091) 100.0	98.5	1.5	(2,059) 100.0	66.1	26.8	1.7	5.1	–	–	0.3
	Asaka-machi	(3,345) 100.0	97.3	2.7	(3,256) 100.0	67.9	23.3	3.6	4.6	–	–	0.6
V	Urawa-shi	(30,842) 100.0	96.7	3.3	(29,826) 100.0	59.8	25.6	6.6	7.5	–	–	0.5
	Misono-mura	(1,538) 100.0	98.4	1.6	(1,521) 100.0	90.5	4.4	3.2	1.6	–	–	0.3
	Koshigaya-shi	(7,906) 100.0	98.8	1.2	(7,809) 100.0	81.3	12.9	2.2	3.0	–	–	0.6
VI	Yoshikawa-machi	(2,564) 100.0	99.2	0.8	(2,543) 100.0	89.0	8.2	0.6	1.1	–	–	1.1
	Nagareyama-machi	(3,393) 100.0	99.0	1.0	(3,359) 100.0	83.8	10.6	1.9	2.8	–	–	0.9
VII	Kamagaya-machi	(1,841) 100.0	97.8	2.2	(1,800) 100.0	85.2	9.0	2.0	3.7	–	–	0.1
VIII	Funahashi-shi	(23,409) 100.0	96.2	3.8	(22,514) 100.0	61.0	26.0	5.5	7.2	–	–	0.3
	Zone 5 Total	(139,425) 100.0	95.5	4.5	(133,217) 100.0	59.8	22.7	8.6	7.8	–	0.6	0.5
6 I	Nishi-ku	(23,442) 100.0	94.1	5.9	(22,070) 100.0	62.7	19.4	5.6	10.1	–	0.7	1.5
	Naka-ku	(24,692) 100.0	91.4	8.6	(22,577) 100.0	65.7	19.9	4.2	7.0	–	0.2	3.0
	Kanagawa-ku	(32,754) 100.0	93.1	6.9	(30,489) 100.0	61.3	20.9	6.7	9.8	–	–	1.3
II	Kōhoku-ku	(22,840) 100.0	96.2	3.8	(21,967) 100.0	71.5	16.9	4.0	6.5	–	0.1	1.0
	Inagi-machi	(1,982) 100.0	98.3	1.7	(1,948) 100.0	59.1	36.1	1.4	3.1	–	–	0.3
III	Tama-mura	(1,305) 100.0	97.6	2.4	(1,274) 100.0	82.8	10.7	4.3	1.5	–	–	0.7
	Fuchu-shi	(11,708) 100.0	95.4	4.6	(11,169) 100.0	46.7	35.5	11.2	5.5	–	0.2	0.9
	Kunitachi-machi	(5,302) 100.0	92.3	7.7	(4,894) 100.0	57.0	26.9	7.5	8.2	–	0.3	0.1
	Kokubunji-machi	(5,350) 100.0	94.0	6.0	(5,028) 100.0	55.0	23.3	13.5	7.3	–	0.5	0.4
	Kodaira-machi	(5,542) 100.0	95.4	4.6	(5,286) 100.0	58.4	26.6	9.7	4.4	–	0.1	0.8
	Higashimurayama-machi	(4,386) 100.0	96.9	3.1	(4,251) 100.0	58.4	27.1	9.9	2.9	–	0.1	1.6
IV	Tokorosawa-shi	(10,632) 100.0	97.9	2.1	(10,408) 100.0	73.1	21.6	1.5	3.0	–	–	0.8
	Miyoshi-mura	(684) 100.0	100.0	–	(684) 100.0	93.0	5.3	1.0	0.6	–	–	0.1
	Fujimi-mura	(1,854) 100.0	99.5	0.5	(1,845) 100.0	92.1	6.4	0.8	0.2	–	–	0.5
V	Yono-shi	(7,545) 100.0	96.9	3.1	(7,313) 100.0	59.4	24.3	8.6	6.5	–	–	1.2
	Ōmiya-shi	(29,581) 100.0	97.7	2.3	(28,908) 100.0	65.6	24.7	4.1	5.1	–	–	0.5
	Iwatsuki-shi	(6,082) 100.0	99.4	0.6	(6,043) 100.0	76.8	17.8	2.5	2.6	–	–	0.3
VI	Matsubushi-mura	(1,461) 100.0	99.1	0.9	(1,448) 100.0	93.5	4.6	0.6	1.0	–	–	0.3
VII	Kashiwa-shi	(8,586) 100.0	97.5	2.5	(8,370) 100.0	73.3	13.5	8.0	4.8	–	0.1	0.3
	Shōnan-mura	(1,804) 100.0	98.2	1.8	(1,771) 100.0	94.2	3.5	1.5	0.7	–	–	0.1
	Shirai-mura	(1,411) 100.0	98.9	1.1	(1,395) 100.0	94.8	2.7	1.0	1.1	–	–	0.4
VIII	Narashino-shi	(6,709) 100.0	95.2	4.8	(6,387) 100.0	55.2	27.2	10.4	7.1	–	–	0.1
	Zone 6 Total	(215,652) 100.0	95.3	4.7	(205,525) 100.0	65.0	21.5	5.8	6.5	–	0.1	1.1
7 I	Isogo-ku	(15,881) 100.0	95.2	4.8	(15,113) 100.0	51.1	32.6	5.1	10.4	–	0.5	0.3
	Minami-ku	(39,295) 100.0	94.7	5.3	(37,202) 100.0	61.6	24.1	2.9	10.6	–	0.1	0.7
	Hodogaya-ku	(21,107) 100.0	96.8	3.2	(20,422) 100.0	63.4	24.7	4.0	7.2	–	0.2	0.5

Table 6. Number of Households by Type of Dwelling

(Zone) (Sector)	District	Total	Ordinary Households	Quasi Households	Ordinary Households							
					Total	Own Houses	Rented Houses	Employee Houses	Rented Rooms	Unknown	Boarding Houses	Others
II	Machida-shi	(11,671) 100.0	96.2	3.8	(11,233) 100.0	66.4	24.4	3.5	5.2	—	0.1	0.4
III	Yuki-mura	(1,283) 100.0	99.3	0.7	(1,052) 100.0	93.5	4.0	1.3	0.9	—	—	0.3
	Hino-machi	(5,640) 100.0	95.5	4.5	(5,443) 100.0	67.4	16.3	9.6	6.5	—	0.1	0.1
	Tachikawa-shi	(14,236) 100.0	91.8	8.2	(13,075) 100.0	50.4	32.7	4.1	11.5	—	0.4	0.9
	Sunakawa-machi	(2,435) 100.0	98.7	1.3	(2,404) 100.0	69.1	22.0	5.0	3.8	—	—	0.1
	Yamato-machi	(2,376) 100.0	98.8	1.2	(2,347) 100.0	84.3	9.9	1.4	2.8	—	1.5	0.1
IV	Ōi-mura	(814) 100.0	98.6	1.4	(803) 100.0	82.4	12.5	1.1	3.4	—	—	0.6
	Fukuoka-mura	(1,535) 100.0	99.1	0.9	(1,521) 100.0	73.1	18.3	4.0	4.1	—	0.1	0.4
V	Kasukabe-shi	(5,869) 100.0	98.9	1.1	(5,805) 100.0	79.1	15.1	2.0	3.2	—	—	0.6
	Shōwa-mura	(2,443) 100.0	99.3	0.7	(2,427) 100.0	81.5	15.5	1.3	0.8	—	—	0.9
VI	Noda-shi	(9,984) 100.0	98.8	1.2	(9,864) 100.0	78.1	16.6	2.4	2.3	—	—	0.6
VII	Abiko-machi	(4,833) 100.0	98.3	1.7	(4,751) 100.0	77.6	12.9	5.6	3.1	—	0.1	0.7
	Yachiyo-machi	(2,709) 100.0	98.9	1.1	(2,679) 100.0	89.4	6.8	1.3	2.1	—	—	0.4
VIII	Chiba-shi	(40,868) 100.0	96.1	3.9	(39,269) 100.0	66.5	18.9	6.9	6.7	—	0.1	0.9
IX	Goi-machi	(3,279) 100.0	98.8	1.2	(3,241) 100.0	85.1	10.0	1.1	2.8	—	—	1.0
	Sodegaura-machi	(2,494) 100.0	98.8	1.2	(2,464) 100.0	89.8	6.4	1.8	1.4	—	—	0.6
	Zone 7 Total	(194,195) 100.0	96.1	3.9	(181,115) 100.0	65.8	21.9	4.3	7.2	—	0.2	0.6
8 I	Kanazawa-ku	(14,266) 100.0	94.0	6.0	(13,403) 100.0	49.5	35.5	4.9	8.4	—	0.2	1.5
	Totsuka-ku	(16,438) 100.0	97.5	2.5	(16,029) 100.0	59.6	28.0	6.6	5.7	—	—	0.1
II	Yamato-shi	(5,729) 100.0	94.7	5.3	(5,369) 100.0	69.2	23.1	2.1	5.3	—	—	0.3
	Sagamihara-shi	(17,426) 100.0	95.1	4.9	(16,565) 100.0	64.6	23.0	5.5	5.3	—	0.4	1.2
	Zama-machi	(2,638) 100.0	95.0	5.0	(2,507) 100.0	71.9	18.5	4.5	4.3	—	0.1	0.7
III	Hachiōji-shi	(28,096) 100.0	97.9	2.1	(27,520) 100.0	76.7	16.4	3.1	3.6	—	—	0.2
	Akishima-shi	(8,544) 100.0	94.7	5.3	(8,091) 100.0	45.1	43.0	2.0	6.4	—	—	3.5
	Fussa-machi	(4,137) 100.0	91.7	8.3	(3,792) 100.0	56.5	28.6	3.3	10.9	—	0.4	0.3
	Mizuho-machi	(1,720) 100.0	99.1	0.9	(1,704) 100.0	83.1	12.3	2.1	2.5	—	—	—
	Murayama-machi	(1,897) 100.0	98.5	1.5	(1,868) 100.0	84.8	11.1	1.6	2.1	—	0.1	0.3
	Musashi-machi	(5,156) 100.0	96.5	3.5	(4,976) 100.0	74.8	20.5	1.4	2.6	—	—	0.7
IV	Sayama-shi	(5,792) 100.0	97.7	2.3	(5,660) 100.0	76.6	18.4	1.4	2.8	—	—	0.8
	Kawagoe-shi	(19,829) 100.0	98.2	1.8	(19,474) 100.0	64.9	28.6	2.5	3.0	—	—	1.0
	Seibu-machi	(1,600) 100.0	97.8	2.2	(1,564) 100.0	80.6	14.5	1.4	3.5	—	—	—
V	Ageo-shi	(6,382) 100.0	99.1	0.9	(6,328) 100.0	75.7	18.1	4.3	1.5	—	—	0.4
	Ina-mura	(1,143) 100.0	99.3	0.7	(1,135) 100.0	87.6	5.0	5.7	1.1	—	—	0.6
	Hasuda-machi	(3,265) 100.0	98.5	1.5	(3,217) 100.0	82.3	11.9	3.2	2.3	—	—	0.3
	Shiraoka-machi	(2,701) 100.0	99.7	0.3	(2,692) 100.0	87.2	9.2	1.5	1.8	—	—	0.3
	Miyashiro-machi	(1,856) 100.0	99.4	0.6	(1,844) 100.0	82.0	11.6	1.7	3.0	—	—	1.7
	Sugito-machi	(2,908) 100.0	99.6	0.4	(2,895) 100.0	85.4	10.5	1.3	2.0	—	—	0.8
VI	Sekiyado-machi	(2,231) 100.0	99.1	0.9	(2,211) 100.0	92.5	4.5	1.2	1.2	—	—	0.6
	Moriya-machi	(2,169) 100.0	99.2	0.8	(2,151) 100.0	91.1	5.3	1.8	1.6	—	—	0.2
VII	Toride-machi	(4,190) 100.0	97.5	2.5	(4,086) 100.0	70.7	23.3	1.7	3.7	—	0.2	0.4
	Inzai-machi	(3,239) 100.0	98.8	1.2	(3,201) 100.0	84.4	10.4	2.4	2.1	—	—	0.7
	Inba-mura	(1,498) 100.0	99.3	0.7	(1,488) 100.0	96.2	2.5	0.2	0.5	—	—	0.6
VIII	Yotsukaidō-machi	(3,519) 100.0	97.2	0.8	(3,422) 100.0	76.4	11.5	0.9	4.4	—	—	6.8
IX	Ichihara-machi	(2,669) 100.0	99.3	0.7	(2,649) 100.0	84.6	9.7	2.2	2.8	—	—	0.5
	Anegasaki-machi	(2,130) 100.0	98.9	1.1	(2,106) 100.0	84.5	10.6	0.9	3.5	—	—	0.5
	Hirakawa-machi	(2,014) 100.0	99.4	0.6	(2,002) 100.0	93.8	4.3	0.9	0.6	—	—	0.4
	Miwa-machi	(1,996) 100.0	99.6	0.4	(1,988) 100.0	93.9	3.9	1.3	0.6	—	—	0.3
X	Kisarazu-shi	(10,435) 100.0	96.9	3.1	(10,110) 100.0	73.3	21.4	2.0	2.5	—	—	0.8
	Zone 8 Total	(187,613) 100.0	97.0	3.0	(182,047) 100.0	70.2	21.5	3.2	4.1	—	0.1	0.9
9 I	Kamakura-shi	(20,445) 100.0	95.5	4.5	(19,536) 100.0	57.1	26.0	5.7	10.3	—	0.1	0.8

Table 6. Number of Households by Type of Dwelling

(Zone)	(Sector)	District	Total	Ordinary Households	Quasi Households	Ordinary Households							
						Total	Own Houses	Rented Houses	Employee Houses	Rented Rooms	Unknown	Boarding Houses	Others
	II	Ayase-machi	(1,419) 100.0	98.0	2.0	(1,390) 100.0	81.6	13.5	1.6	2.1	—	—	1.2
		Ebina-machi	(3,015) 100.0	98.2	1.8	(2,960) 100.0	78.6	12.4	3.5	2.9	—	0.7	1.9
		Shiroyama-machi	(896) 100.0	98.5	1.5	(883) 100.0	84.8	8.9	5.0	1.2	—	—	0.1
	III	Akita-machi	(2,516) 100.0	97.8	2.2	(2,460) 100.0	84.5	10.3	1.2	3.8	—	—	0.2
		Hamura-machi	(1,887) 100.0	97.4	2.6	(1,838) 100.0	70.2	21.5	2.7	5.1	—	—	0.5
	IV	Hannō-shi	(8,515) 100.0	97.9	2.1	(8,340) 100.0	73.4	20.6	2.3	3.2	—	—	0.5
		Tsurugashima-mura	(1,205) 100.0	99.3	0.7	(1,196) 100.0	91.4	4.3	1.3	2.4	—	—	0.6
		Hidaka-machi	(3,007) 100.0	98.9	1.1	(2,974) 100.0	88.0	6.7	3.5	1.4	—	—	0.4
		Kawashima-mura	(2,884) 100.0	99.6	0.4	(2,872) 100.0	95.0	3.6	0.7	0.6	—	—	0.1
	V	Kitamoto-machi	(2,593) 100.0	99.4	0.6	(2,577) 100.0	84.8	9.0	3.1	2.1	—	—	1.0
		Higawa-machi	(3,584) 100.0	99.2	0.8	(3,556) 100.0	65.9	20.4	10.8	2.6	—	—	0.3
		Shobu-machi	(2,812) 100.0	99.4	0.6	(2,794) 100.0	90.8	7.5	0.4	0.8	—	—	0.5
		Kuki-machi	(4,023) 100.0	99.2	0.8	(3,991) 100.0	83.0	11.5	2.1	2.2	—	—	1.2
		Satte-machi	(4,135) 100.0	99.1	0.9	(4,096) 100.0	80.6	15.3	1.5	1.8	—	—	0.8
	VI	Iwai-machi	(5,857) 100.0	99.6	0.4	(5,832) 100.0	95.2	3.5	0.7	0.5	—	—	0.1
		Mitsukaidō-shi	(7,297) 100.0	98.9	1.1	(7,220) 100.0	86.2	9.9	1.7	1.9	—	—	0.3
		Yawahara-mura	(2,013) 100.0	99.6	0.4	(2,004) 100.0	94.1	3.9	0.8	0.8	—	—	0.4
		Ina-mura	(2,138) 100.0	9 .6	0.4	(2,130) 100.0	94.9	3.1	1.3	0.5	—	—	0.2
	VII	Fujishiro-machi	(2,309) 100.0	98.6	1.4	(2,276) 100.0	89.2	8.1	1.2	1.1	—	—	0.4
		Ryūgasaki-shi	(6,631) 100.0	98.8	1.2	(6,554) 100.0	81.6	14.3	1.4	2.3	—	—	0.4
		Tone-mura	(1,750) 100.0	99.1	0.9	(1,734) 100.0	90.2	5.8	2.4	1.3	—	—	0.3
		Motono-mura	(975) 100.0	99.8	0.2	(973) 100.0	94.7	2.7	2.1	0.4	—	—	0.1
	VIII	Sakura-shi	(6,759) 100.0	98.6	1.4	(6,663) 100.0	78.7	15.4	2.3	2.8	—	0.1	0.7
		Izumi-machi	(1,703) 100.0	99.6	0.4	(1,697) 100.0	96.2	1.9	0.8	0.5	—	—	0.6
	IX	Shitsu-mura	(1,678) 100.0	99.4	0.6	(1,668) 100.0	95.7	1.9	1.4	0.6	—	—	0.4
		Nansō-machi	(3,566) 100.0	99.0	1.0	(3,523) 100.0	91.9	6.5	0.6	0.6	—	—	0.4
		Fukuta-machi	(1,418) 100.0	99.6	0.4	(1,413) 100.0	92.6	4.7	0.9	1.0	—	—	0.8
	X	Kimitsu-machi	(2,576) 100.0	99.5	0.5	(2,564) 100.0	88.4	8.7	1.5	0.9	—	—	0.5
		Futtsu-machi	(3,005) 100.0	99.4	0.6	(2,988) 100.0	87.4	9.5	0.8	1.7	—	—	0 6
		Ōsawa-machi	(2,777) 100.0	98.8	1.2	(2,744) 100.0	85.2	10.4	1.8	2.2	—	—	0.4
		Zone 9 Total	(115,398) 100.0	98.3	1.7	(113,446) 100.0	80.0	13.4	2.7	3.3	—	—	0.6
10	I	Yokosuka-shi	(60,890) 100.0	93.9	6.1	(57,154) 100.0	52.4	34.9	3.3	8.8	—	—	0.6
		Zushi-shi	(8,761) 100.0	94.9	5.1	(8,314) 100.0	52.1	26.3	3.4	9.6	—	—	8.6
		Hayama-machi	(3,259) 100.0	96.6	3.4	(3,148) 100.0	66.2	23.1	3.3	6.7	—	—	0.7
		Chigasaki-shi	(11,850) 100.0	98.1	1.9	(11,625) 100.0	70.0	19.5	3.9	6.4	—	—	0.2
		Fujisawa-shi	(22,696) 100.0	97.0	3.0	(22,016) 100.0	65.3	20.7	5.9	7.1	—	—	1.0
	II	Aikawa-machi	(2,554) 100.0	99.2	0.8	(2,533) 100.0	90.8	6.0	1.0	1.1	—	—	1.1
		Atsugi-shi	(8,127) 100.0	98.6	1.4	(8,010) 100.0	82.8	11.5	2.3	2.4	—	—	1.0
		Samukawa-machi	(2,086) 100.0	98.3	1.7	(2,050) 100.0	67.7	14.4	5.8	2.4	—	—	9.7
	III	Ōme-shi	(10,141) 100.0	97.8	2.2	(9,922) 100.0	74.0	19.2	2.5	3.9	—	0.1	0.3
	IV	Sakado-machi	(4,273) 100.0	99.1	0.9	(4,235) 100.0	87.9	8.3	1.4	1.5	—	—	0.9
		Yoshimi-mura	(2,605) 100.0	99.5	0.5	(2,593) 100.0	94.3	4.0	0.8	0.5	—	—	0.4
		Moroyama-mura	(1,890) 100.0	98.9	1.1	(1,870) 100.0	89.1	6.2	2.1	2.0	—	—	0.6
	V	Kōnosu-shi	(5,681) 100.0	98.8	1.2	(5,614) 100.0	70.6	22.1	3.3	3.0	—	—	1.0
		Kisai-machi	(2,735) 100.0	99.3	0.7	(2,716) 100.0	91.0	7.0	1.0	0.6	—	—	0.4
		Washimiya-machi	(1,468) 100.0	99.5	0.5	(1,460) 100.0	90.5	6.6	1.2	1.5	—	—	0.2
		Kurihashi-machi	(2,336) 100.0	99.1	0.9	(2,314) 100.0	83.8	9.9	1.1	3.3	—	—	1.9
		Goka-mura	(1,505) 100.0	99.5	0.5	(1,498) 100.0	94.6	2.5	1.1	0.6	—	—	1.2
	VI	Sakai-machi	(4,039) 100.0	98.8	1.2	(3,990) 100.0	87.1	9.2	1.8	1.7	—	—	0.2
		Sashima-machi	(2,501) 100.0	99.7	0.3	(2,494) 100.0	96.1	2.5	0.4	0.6	—	—	0.4
		Yatabe-machi	(3,985) 100.0	99.7	0.3	(3,972) 100.0	92.0	5.3	1.7	1.0	—	—	—

Table 6. Number of Households by Type of Dwelling

(Zone)(Sector)	District	Total	Ordinary Households	Quasi Households	Ordinary Households							
					Total	Own Houses	Rented Houses	Employee Houses	Rented Rooms	Unknown	Boarding Houses	Others
VII	Kukizaki-mura	(1,084) 100.0	99.7	0.3	(1,081) 100.0	96.8	2.6	0.2	0.3	−	−	0.1
	Ushiku-machi	(2,915) 100.0	99.2	0.8	(2,891) 100.0	90.2	7.3	1.2	1.3	−	−	−
	Kawachi-mura	(2,394) 100.0	99.5	0.5	(2,382) 100.0	94.9	3.9	0.5	0.6	−	−	0.1
	Sakae-machi	(1,870) 100.0	99.4	0.6	(1,858) 100.0	87.5	8.9	1.5	1.9	−	−	0.2
	Narita-shi	(8,648) 100.0	98.5	1.5	(8,514) 100.0	80.8	12.7	2.7	2.7	−	0.1	1.0
VIII	Shisui-machi	(1,140) 100.0	99.2	0.8	(1,131) 100.0	88.9	7.6	0.9	2.2	−	−	0.4
	Yachimata-machi	(4,726) 100.0	99.3	0.7	(4,692) 100.0	85.3	10.6	2.0	1.6	−	−	0.5
	Toke-machi	(1,256) 100.0	98.8	1.2	(1,241) 100.0	91.6	5.3	1.8	1.2	−	−	0.1
IX	Nagara-machi	(1,696) 100.0	99.7	0.3	(1,691) 100.0	94.7	3.7	0.8	0.7	−	−	0.1
	Obitsu-mura	(1,373) 100.0	98.9	1.1	(1,358) 100.0	94.0	4.3	0.6	0.7	−	−	0.4
X	Koito-machi	(1,160) 100.0	99.5	0.5	(1,154) 100.0	94.0	4.2	1.3	0.5	−	−	−
	Zone 10 Total	(191,644) 100.0	96.8	3.2	(185,521) 100.0	69.8	20.7	3.0	5.4	−	−	1.1
	Total for 50 km. Region	(2,871,521)100.0	94.0	6.0	(2,699,170)100.0	58.7	24.8	6.0	9.5		−	1.0
	National Total	(17,959,923)100.0	96.8	3.2	17,383,321)100.0	67.4	20.2	6.2	5.4	−	0.1	0.7

1960

(Zone)(Sector)	District	Total	Ordinary Households	Quasi Households	Ordinary Households						
					Total	Own Houses	Rented Houses	Employee Houses	Rented Rooms	Boarding Houses	Others
1 I	Chiyoda-ku	(21,409) 100.0	93.0	7.0	(19,907) 100.0	57.8	21.2	14.9	5.5	0.1	0.5
	Minato-ku	(60,887) 100.0	96.6	3.4	(57,928) 100.0	47.4	32.5	12.2	7.3	0.2	0.4
	Chūō-ku	(29,248) 100.0	95.0	5.0	(28,243) 100.0	51.5	29.5	10.7	7.4	0.1	0.8
	Bunkyō-ku	(65,991) 100.0	91.2	8.8	(60,202) 100.0	46.8	38.3	6.2	8.4	0.2	0.1
	Taitō-ku	(67,410) 100.0	95.5	4.5	(64,388) 100.0	50.3	36.6	3.3	8.3	−	1.5
	Zone 1 Total	(244,945) 100.0	94.2	5.8	(230,668) 100.0	49.3	34.0	8.2	7.7	0.1	0.7
2 I	Shinagawa-ku	(111,215) 100.0	95.3	4.7	(105,988) 100.0	39.8	47.5	6.6	5.8	0.1	0.2
II	Meguro-ku	(77,977) 100.0	91.6	8.4	(71,388) 100.0	42.8	40.2	9.4	7.4	0.1	0.1
	Shibuya-ku	(79,321) 100.0	88.8	11.2	(70,407) 100.0	42.0	40.4	8.7	8.7	0.1	0.1
III	Shinjuku-ku	(115,035) 100.0	91.8	8.2	(105,549) 100.0	39.2	48.4	6.3	5.9	0.1	0.1
	Nakano-ku	(102,015) 100.0	89.9	10.1	(91,739) 100.0	40.2	45.7	6.6	7.3	0.2	−
IV	Toshima-ku	(103,292) 100.0	94.4	5.6	(97,504) 100.0	36.8	51.7	4.6	6.3	0.3	0.2
V	Kita-ku	(11,640) 100.0	95.2	4.8	(106,298) 100.0	39.1	50.5	5.0	5.3	−	0.1
VI	Arakawa-ku	(64,119) 100.0	97.2	2.8	(62,300) 100.0	45.4	43.4	4.3	5.8	−	1.1
VII	Sumida-ku	(66,738) 100.0	97.6	2.4	(65,166) 100.0	50.6	38.5	5.4	4.9	−	0.6
VIII	Kōtō-ku	(78,061) 100.0	95.8	4.2	(74,779) 100.0	44.9	35.6	10.1	8.1	−	1.3
	Zone 2 Total	(909,413) 100.0	93.6	6.4	(851,118) 100.0	41.5	45.0	6.6	6.5	0.1	0.3
3 I	Ōta-ku	(177,703) 100.0	94.4	5.6	(167,718) 100.0	45.4	40.9	7.7	5.8	0.1	0.1
II	Setagaya-ku	(176,241) 100.0	90.0	10.0	(158,547) 100.0	46.2	38.8	8.4	6.4	0.1	0.1
III	Suginami-ku	(135,828) 100.0	87.2	12.8	(118,494) 100.0	46.3	35.2	10.1	8.3	0.1	−
IV	Itabashi-ku	(102,381) 100.0	95.7	4.3	(98,020) 100.0	43.6	46.1	5.1	5.2	−	−
	Nerima-ku	(76,051) 100.0	95.5	4.5	(72,597) 100.0	52.6	37.4	4.6	5.1	0.2	0.1
VI	Adachi-ku	(91,644) 100.0	98.1	1.9	(89,901) 100.0	46.7	44.1	4.0	4.7	−	0.5
VII	Katsushika-ku	(86,833) 100.0	97.6	2.4	(84,765) 100.0	45.8	44.8	4.5	4.7	0.1	0.1
VIII	Edogawa-ku	(74,352) 100.0	96.5	3.5	(71,771) 100.0	47.8	42.7	4.8	4.6	−	0.1
	Urayasu-machi	(3,409) 100.0	99.2	0.8	(3,383) 100.0	62.7	32.7	2.5	2.0	−	0.1
	Zone 3 Total	(924,442) 100.0	93.6	6.4	(865,196) 100.0	47.6	40.9	5.5	5.8	0.1	0.1
4 I	Kawasaki-shi	(152,799) 100.0	94.7	5.3	(144,742) 100.0	45.6	39.2	9.7	5.1	0.1	0.3
II	Komae-machi	(6,428) 100.0	90.1	9.9	(5,792) 100.0	64.5	21.4	6.3	7.6	0.1	0.1

Table 6. Number of Households by Type of Dwelling

(Zone) (Sector)	District	Total	Ordinary Households	Quasi Households	Ordinary Households						
					Total	Own Houses	Rented Houses	Employee Houses	Rented Rooms	Boarding Houses	Others
III	Mitaka-shi	(24,925) 100.0	91.1	8.9	(22,709) 100.0	44.8	37.9	7.9	9.1	0.1	0.2
	Musashino-shi	(32,712) 100.0	89.5	10.5	(29,274) 100.0	39.2	41.6	9.7	9.3	0.2	–
	Chōfu-shi	(16,105) 100.0	95.8	4.2	(15,424) 100.0	54.7	33.5	5.2	6.4	0.1	0.1
	Hoya-machi	(11,696) 100.0	96.5	3.5	(11,286) 100.0	43.7	48.9	2.8	4.6	–	–
IV	Yamato-machi	(3,840) 100.0	97.9	2.1	(3,758) 100.0	52.3	38.2	4.8	4.7	–	–
	Toda-machi	(6,699) 100.0	98.8	1.2	(6,616) 100.0	58.1	34.7	4.6	2.5	–	0.1
V	Warabi-shi	(11,988) 100.0	97.9	2.1	(11,734) 100.0	55.8	34.8	4.8	4.5	–	0.1
	Kawaguchi-shi	(37,068) 100.0	97.5	2.5	(36,141) 100.0	53.7	36.2	5.3	4.7	–	0.1
	Hatogaya-machi	(4,622) 100.0	99.4	0.6	(4,595) 100.0	53.9	40.9	2.8	2.4	–	–
VI	Sōka-shi	(7,700) 100.0	99.0	1.0	(7,623) 100.0	62.4	27.5	7.6	2.4	–	0.1
	Yashio-mura	(2,198) 100.0	99.5	0.5	(2,188) 100.0	83.2	9.6	5.8	1.4	–	–
	Misato-mura	(2,918) 100.0	99.7	0.3	(2,909) 100.0	88.7	6.1	3.1	2.0	–	0.1
	Matsudo-shi	(19,393) 100.0	97.6	2.4	(18,925) 100.0	58.7	33.3	3.3	4.5	–	0.2
VII	Ichikawa-shi	(36,838) 100.0	95.4	4.6	(35,107) 100.0	56.3	31.4	7.3	5.0	–	–
	Zone 4 Total	(377,929) 100.0	94.9	5.1	(358,823) 100.0	49.8	36.8	7.6	5.5	0.1	0.2
5 I	Tsurumi-ku	(54,886) 100.0	95.3	4.7	(52,309) 100.0	45.7	33.6	13.5	6.9	0.1	0.2
III	Koganei-shi	(11,774) 100.0	90.0	10.0	(10,597) 100.0	54.2	32.7	5.6	7.1	0.1	0.3
	Tanashi-machi	(7,544) 100.0	95.0	5.0	(7,168) 100.0	51.3	39.2	3.0	5.8	–	0.7
	Kurume-machi	(4,531) 100.0	97.9	2.1	(4,438) 100.0	49.3	44.9	2.7	3.1	–	–
IV	Niza-machi	(2,907) 100.0	99.3	0.7	(2,888) 100.0	77.7	13.5	6.8	2.0	–	–
	Kiyose-machi	(3,277) 100.0	97.1	2.9	(3,179) 100.0	52.6	34.0	8.1	5.3	–	–
	Adachi-machi	(2,582) 100.0	99.2	0.8	(2,562) 100.0	70.3	25.0	1.9	2.8	–	–
	Asaka-machi	(5,136) 100.0	97.9	2.1	(5,028) 100.0	60.5	33.9	3.3	2.2	–	0.1
V	Urawa-shi	(38,758) 100.0	96.7	3.3	(37,485) 100.0	61.2	26.3	6.8	5.4	0.1	0.2
	Misono-mura	(1,525) 100.0	99.7	0.3	(1,521) 100.0	91.4	4.1	3.4	1.1	–	–
	Koshigaya-shi	(9,036) 100.0	99.4	0.6	(8,983) 100.0	82.0	13.3	2.6	2.0	–	0.1
VI	Yoshikawa-machi	(2,661) 100.0	99.4	0.6	(2,645) 100.0	89.7	7.4	1.2	1.6	–	0.1
	Nagareyama-machi	(5,259) 100.0	99.4	0.6	(5,229) 100.0	85.8	10.2	2.8	1.1	–	0.1
VII	Kamagaya-machi	(2,748) 100.0	99.5	0.5	(2,733) 100.0	75.7	14.7	6.5	3.1	–	–
VIII	Funahashi-shi	(30,396) 100.0	97.2	2.8	(29,533) 100.0	60.3	31.3	5.0	3.3	–	0.1
	Zone 5 Total	(183,020) 100.0	96.3	3.7	(176,298) 100.0	58.2	29.0	7.6	5.0	0.1	0.1
6 I	Nishi-ku	(25,907) 100.0	94.4	5.6	(24,448) 100.0	56.5	27.4	6.3	9.4	–	0.4
	Naka-ku	(30,761) 100.0	95.7	4.3	(29,451) 100.0	52.8	33.2	4.8	7.5	–	1.7
	Kanagawa-ku	(43,962) 100.0	90.5	9.5	(39,787) 100.0	54.2	29.1	7.0	9.4	0.1	0.2
II	Kōhoku-ku	(33,613) 100.0	96.9	3.1	(32,556) 100.0	65.5	25.3	5.0	3.9	0.2	0.1
	Inagi-machi	(2,291) 100.0	99.0	1.0	(2,269) 100.0	61.5	32.8	1.4	3.8	–	0.5
III	Tama-mura	(1,771) 100.0	96.7	3.3	(1,713) 100.0	77.9	14.6	4.7	2.8	–	–
	Fuchu-shi	(18,459) 100.0	95.5	4.5	(17,629) 100.0	46.5	42.5	7.0	3.9	0.1	–
	Kunitachi-machi	(8,354) 100.0	91.1	8.9	(7,613) 100.0	51.9	35.7	5.8	6.4	0.2	–
	Kokubunji-machi	(9,835) 100.0	87.1	12.9	(8,568) 100.0	55.4	26.6	9.6	8.0	–	0.4
	Kodaira-machi	(11,455) 100.0	97.2	2.8	(11,132) 100.0	42.2	44.6	10.0	3.1	–	0.1
	Higashimurayama-machi	(9,175) 100.0	99.0	1.0	(9,079) 100.0	41.5	48.9	7.8	1.6	–	0.2
IV	Tokorosawa-shi	(13,517) 100.0	98.7	1.3	(13,348) 100.0	65.7	30.7	1.3	2.1	–	0.2
	Miyoshi-mura	(718) 100.0	100.0	–	(718) 100.0	95.0	3.9	0.3	0.8	–	–
	Fujimi-mura	(2,264) 100.0	99.8	0.2	(2,260) 100.0	82.8	15.3	0.7	1.2	–	–
V	Yono-shi	(9,349) 100.0	97.2	2.8	(9,083) 100.0	60.7	24.2	9.8	5.3	–	–
	Ōmiya-shi	(37,087) 100.0	98.4	1.6	(36,481) 100.0	64.7	25.4	5.7	4.2	–	–
	Iwatsuki-shi	(6,512) 100.0	99.6	0.4	(6,489) 100.0	78.0	17.7	2.4	1.9	–	–
VI	Matsubushi-mura	(1,494) 100.0	100.0	–	(1,494) 100.0	93.9	4.6	0.5	0.9	–	0.1
VII	Kashiwa-shi	(13,490) 100.0	99.0	1.0	(13,350) 100.0	66.7	25.8	7.3	0.2	–	–

Table 6. Number of Households by Type of Dwelling

(Zone) (Sector)	District	Total	Ordinary Households	Quasi Households	Ordinary Households Total	Own Houses	Rented Houses	Employee Houses	Rented Rooms	Boarding Houses	Others
VII	Shōnan-mura	(1,911) 100.0	99.7	0.3	(1,906) 100.0	90.9	5.1	3.3	0.6	–	0.1
	Shirai-mura	(1,414) 100.0	100.0	–	(1,412) 100.0	96.9	1.8	1.0	0.2	–	0.1
VIII	Narashino-shi	(10,013) 100.0	93.5	6.5	(9,364) 100.0	52.2	32.7	9.3	5.6	0.1	0.1
	Zone 6 Total	(293,352) 100.0	95.6	4.4	(280,150) 100.0	59.3	29.0	6.0	5.3	0.1	0.3
7 I	Isogo-ku	(18,135) 100.0	96.3	3.7	(17,465) 100.0	52.8	36.2	3.7	7.1	–	0.2
	Minami-ku	(48,412) 100.0	95.3	4.7	(46,118) 100.0	55.5	32.6	2.9	8.5	–	0.5
	Hodogaya-ku	(34,410) 100.0	97.2	2.8	(33,458) 100.0	58.7	32.0	4.7	4.6	–	–
II	Machida-shi	(15,600) 100.0	96.2	3.8	(15,009) 100.0	62.6	31.3	2.2	3.9	–	–
III	Yuki-mura	(1,061) 100.0	99.7	0.3	(1,058) 100.0	95.0	2.7	1.2	1.0	–	0.1
	Hino-machi	(10,377) 100.0	98.0	2.0	(10,167) 100.0	46.9	45.9	4.1	3.1	–	–
	Tachikawa-shi	(16,785) 100.0	91.7	8.3	(15,400) 100.0	47.5	38.5	3.5	10.2	0.2	0.1
	Sunakawa-machi	(2,992) 100.0	88.0	2.0	(2,933) 100.0	65.9	27.7	3.2	3.2	–	–
	Yamato-machi	(2,777) 100.0	99.3	0.7	(2,757) 100.0	80.0	15.3	2.9	1.8	–	–
IV	Ōi-mura	(879) 100.0	99.4	0.6	(874) 100.0	82.0	13.3	2.6	1.1	–	1.0
	Fukuoka-mura	(4,256) 100.0	99.7	0.3	(4,242) 100.0	32.1	63.7	2.2	1.5	–	0.5
V	Kasukabe-shi	(6,487) 100.0	99.5	0.5	(6,452) 100.0	78.3	17.9	1.7	2.1	–	–
	Shōwa-mura	(2,482) 100.0	99.8	0.2	(2,477) 100.0	83.9	12.7	2.5	0.7	–	0.2
VI	Noda-shi	(10,755) 100.0	99.3	0.7	(10,685) 100.0	79.0	16.1	2.8	2.1	–	–
VII	Abiko-machi	(5,566) 100.0	98.9	1.1	(5,505) 100.0	78.1	15.2	4.2	2.4	–	0.1
	Yachiyo-machi	(4,505) 100.0	99.3	0.7	(4,474) 100.0	86.7	8.6	2.8	1.7	–	0.2
VIII	Chiba-shi	(54,240) 100.0	97.3	2.7	(52,779) 100.0	59.5	27.8	8.2	4.4	–	0.1
IX	Goi-machi	(4,139) 100.0	99.1	0.9	(4,101) 100.0	81.5	11.0	4.7	2.7	–	0.1
	Sodegaura-machi	(2,533) 100.0	99.8	0.2	(2,527) 100.0	90.6	5.6	2.8	0.9	–	0.1
	Zone 7 Total	(246,391) 100.0	96.8	3.2	(238,481) 100.0	60.6	29.8	4.4	5.2	–	–
8 I	Kanazawa-ku	(17,139) 100.0	92.4	7.6	(15,816) 100.0	54.3	32.9	5.7	7.0	–	0.1
	Totsuka-ku	(25,415) 100.0	98.0	2.0	(24,913) 100.0	54.9	37.1	5.0	2.9	–	0.1
II	Yamato-shi	(9,889) 100.0	97.7	2.3	(9,666) 100.0	64.3	30.5	2.4	2.7	–	0.1
	Sagamihara-shi	(22,645) 100.0	98.0	2.0	(22,187) 100.0	60.7	32.9	3.5	2.8	–	0.1
	Zama-machi	(3,298) 100.0	98.7	1.3	(3,255) 100.0	67.9	27.1	2.3	2.5	0.2	–
III	Hachiōji-shi	(32,948) 100.0	98.3	1.7	(32,380) 100.0	73.6	20.3	2.7	3.4	–	–
	Akishima-shi	(10,335) 100.0	96.8	3.2	(10,006) 100.0	46.5	45.8	2.5	4.8	–	0.4
	Fussa-machi	(5,500) 100.0	91.5	8.5	(5,033) 100.0	54.3	34.2	3.0	8.4	0.1	–
	Mizuho-machi	(2,238) 100.0	99.2	0.8	(2,220) 100.0	84.5	12.9	0.8	1.8	–	–
	Murayama-machi	(2,021) 100.0	99.5	0.5	(2,010) 100.0	83.5	12.6	2.2	1.7	–	–
	Musashi-machi	(6,009) 100.0	98.8	1.2	(5,938) 100.0	72.8	22.4	2.8	2.0	–	–
IV	Sayama-shi	(6,271) 100.0	99.2	0.8	(6,218) 100.0	76.0	20.0	2.1	1.9	–	–
	Kawagoe-shi	(21,373) 100.0	98.8	1.2	(21,117) 100.0	67.3	26.0	3.5	3.1	–	0.1
	Seibu-machi	(1,097) 100.0	99.8	0.2	(1,095) 100.0	78.2	16.7	1.6	3.5	–	–
V	Ageo-shi	(7,484) 100.0	99.1	0.9	(7,416) 100.0	76.9	15.5	6.0	1.5	–	0.1
	Ina-mura	(1,112) 100.0	100.0	–	(1,112) 100.0	89.3	3.7	6.6	0.4	–	–
	Hasuda-machi	(3,758) 100.0	99.3	0.7	(3,752) 100.0	83.4	11.7	2.9	2.0	–	–
	Shiraoka-machi	(2,924) 100.0	99.8	0.2	(2,919) 100.0	88.4	8.4	2.1	1.1	–	–
	Miyashiro-machi	(2,029) 100.0	99.5	0.5	(2,019) 100.0	83.4	12.4	2.2	2.0	–	–
	Sugito-machi	(3,054) 100.0	99.4	0.6	(3,036) 100.0	86.5	10.2	1.5	1.7	–	0.1
VI	Sekiyado-machi	(2,179) 100.0	99.4	0.6	(2,167) 100.0	93.9	4.3	1.3	0.4	–	0.1
	Moriya-machi	(2,181) 100.0	99.6	0.4	(2,173) 100.0	94.1	4.1	1.1	0.7	–	–
VII	Toride-machi	(4,772) 100.0	97.9	2.1	(4,674) 100.0	69.3	25.1	2.1	3.5	–	–
	Inzai-machi	(3,219) 100.0	99.5	0.5	(3,203) 100.0	86.6	9.1	2.2	2.0	-	0.1
	Inba-mura	(1,496) 100.0	99.9	0.1	(1,494) 100.0	96.7	2.0	0.9	0.3	0.1	–
VIII	Yotsukaidō-machi	(3,498) 100.0	98.6	1.4	(3,449) 100.0	68.9	24.0	1.7	5.3	–	0.1

Table 6. Number of Households by Type of Dwelling

(Zone) (Sector)	District	Total	Ordinary Households	Quasi Households	Ordinary Households						
					Total	Own Houses	Rented Houses	Employee Houses	Rented Rooms	Boarding Houses	Others
IX	Ichihara-machi	(2,767) 100.0	99.1	0.9	(2,743) 100.0	78.6	12.3	6.9	2.2	—	—
	Anegasaki-machi	(2,224) 100.0	99.6	0.4	(2,214) 100.0	83.8	11.1	1.1	3.5	—	0.5
	Hirakawa-machi	(2,003) 100.0	99.9	0.1	(2,000) 100.0	95.4	3.2	1.2	0.2	—	—
	Miwa-machi	(1,781) 100.0	99.9	0.1	(1,779) 100.0	92.4	6.2	1.1	0.3	—	—
X	Kisarazu-shi	(11,175) 100.0	97.8	2.2	(10,928) 100.0	74.0	20.3	3.1	2.6	—	—
	Zone 8 Total	(223,834) 100.0	97.8	2.2	(218,932) 100.0	68.2	25.2	3.3	3.2	—	0.1
9 I	Kamakura-shi	(23,489) 100.0	96.4	3.6	(22,641) 100.0	59.7	26.6	6.2	7.3	0.1	0.1
II	Ayase-machi	(1,551) 100.0	99.4	0.6	(1,541) 100.0	79.9	18.0	0.9	0.9	0.1	0.2
	Ebina-machi	(3,393) 100.0	99.0	1.0	(3,358) 100.0	77.2	15.7	4.7	2.3	—	0.1
	Shiroyama-machi	(1,043) 100.0	98.8	1.2	(1,031) 100.0	76.6	17.0	4.5	1.9	—	—
III	Akita-machi	(2,718) 100.0	99.4	0.6	(2,703) 100.0	84.1	12.4	0.9	2.6	—	—
	Hamura-machi	(2,264) 100.0	98.6	1.4	(2,232) 100.0	69.3	22.6	2.3	5.8	—	—
IV	Hanno-shi	(9,010) 100.0	98.7	1.3	(8,891) 100.0	73.9	21.3	2.4	2.3	—	0.1
	Tsurugashima-mura	(1,286) 100.0	99.5	0.5	(1,280) 100.0	89.0	7.6	2.3	1.1	—	—
	Hidaka-machi	(3,180) 100.0	99.7	0.3	(3,169) 100.0	87.7	6.6	4.3	1.1	0.2	0.1
	Kawashima-mura	(2,825) 100.0	99.8	0.2	(2,819) 100.0	95.7	2.8	1.2	0.3	—	—
V	Kitamoto-machi	(2,992) 100.0	99.8	0.2	(2,985) 100.0	82.9	9.9	5.4	1.8	—	—
	Higawa-machi	(4,134) 100.0	99.5	0.5	(4,112) 100.0	76.8	18.6	3.0	1.6	—	—
	Shobu-machi	(2,836) 100.0	99.3	0.7	(2,817) 100.0	90.9	6.5	1.3	1.3	—	—
	Kuki-machi	(4,408) 100.0	99.6	0.4	(4,389) 100.0	85.0	10.3	2.6	2.1	—	—
	Satte-machi	(4,168) 100.0	99.4	0.6	(4,145) 100.0	83.1	13.5	1.9	1.4	—	0.1
VI	Iwai-machi	(5,881) 100.0	99.7	0.3	(5,866) 100.0	95.6	3.2	0.7	0.5	—	—
	Mitsukaido-shi	(7,384) 100.0	99.0	1.0	(7,310) 100.0	87.8	8.4	2.2	1.6	—	—
	Yawahara-mura	(1,990) 100.0	99.6	0.4	(1,983) 100.0	95.1	3.5	0.8	0.4	—	0.2
	Ina-mura	(2,154) 100.0	99.8	0.2	(2,150) 100.0	95.7	2.7	1.2	0.3	0.1	—
VII	Fujishiro-machi	(2,354) 100.0	99.7	0.3	(2,348) 100.0	88.8	8.7	1.1	1.1	—	0.3
	Ryugasaki-shi	(6,867) 100.0	98.3	1.7	(6,798) 100.0	69.4	26.1	1.7	2.8	—	—
	Tone-mura	(1,721) 100.0	99.8	0.2	(1,717) 100.0	92.5	4.4	2.3	0.7	—	0.1
	Motono-mura	(960) 100.0	100.0	—	(960) 100.0	96.6	1.7	1.0	0.7	—	—
VIII	Sakura-shi	(7,411) 100.0	99.1	0.9	(7,348) 100.0	80.5	14.7	2.6	2.2	—	—
	Izumi-machi	(1,719) 100.0	99.9	0.1	(1,718) 100.0	96.3	2.1	1.0	0.5	—	0.1
IX	Shitsu-mura	(1,712) 100.0	99.9	0.1	(1,711) 100.0	93.8	4.0	1.9	0.2	—	0.1
	Nanso-machi	(3,507) 100.0	99.9	0.1	(3,504) 100.0	92.1	6.4	1.0	0.5	—	—
	Fukuta-machi	(1,421) 100.0	99.9	0.1	(1,420) 100.0	93.6	4.9	0.9	0.6	—	—
X	Kimitsu-machi	(2,556) 100.0	99.8	0.2	(2,551) 100.0	90.9	6.5	1.8	0.8	—	—
	Futtsu-machi	(3,096) 100.0	99.7	0.3	(3,086) 100.0	89.2	8.3	1.9	0.6	—	—
	Osawa-machi	(2,767) 100.0	99.4	0.6	(2,750) 100.0	84.8	11.5	2.0	1.7	—	—
	Zone 9 Total	(122,797) 100.0	98.8	1.2	(121,333) 100.0	80.3	14.0	3.0	2.7	—	—
10 I	Yokosuka-shi	(65,834) 100.0	95.5	4.5	(62,871) 100.0	52.9	36.1	3.8	7.1	—	0.1
	Zushi-shi	(9,717) 100.0	95.6	4.4	(9,286) 100.0	55.2	32.6	4.0	8.1	—	0.1
	Hayama-machi	(3,525) 100.0	98.8	1.2	(3,483) 100.0	68.3	22.7	4.9	4.1	—	—
	Chigasaki-shi	(15,227) 100.0	98.5	1.5	(15,005) 100.0	71.5	20.7	4.4	3.3	—	0.1
	Fujisawa-shi	(27,720) 100.0	98.2	1.8	(27,233) 100.0	65.7	24.1	5.9	4.2	—	0.1
II	Aikawa-machi	(2,626) 100.0	99.8	0.2	(2,620) 100.0	88.4	7.6	2.9	1.1	—	—
	Atsugi-shi	(8,948) 100.0	99.3	0.7	(8,884) 100.0	80.7	15.1	2.4	1.7	—	0.1
	Samukawa-machi	(2,194) 100.0	99.1	0.9	(2,175) 100.0	70.4	16.3	11.5	1.6	—	0.2
III	Ome-shi	(11,104) 100.0	98.5	1.5	(10,936) 100.0	75.2	17.4	3.8	3.6	—	—
IV	Sakado-machi	(4,467) 100.0	99.7	0.3	(4,454) 100.0	88.4	7.7	1.7	2.1	—	0.1
	Yoshimi-mura	(2,552) 100.0	100.0	—	(2,551) 100.0	96.6	2.4	0.9	0.1	—	—
	Moroyama-mura	(1,919) 100.0	99.8	0.2	(1,916) 100.0	90.1	7.2	1.2	1.4	0.1	—

Table 6. Number of Households by Type of Dwelling

(Zone)(Sector)	District	Total	Ordinary Households	Quasi Households	Ordinary Households						
					Total	Own Houses	Rented Houses	Employee Houses	Rooms Rented	Boarding Houses	Others
V	Kōnosu-shi	(6,145) 100.0	99.6	0.4	(6,118) 100.0	73.6	21.8	2.4	2.1	–	0.1
	Kisai-machi	(2,731) 100.0	99.8	0.2	(2,724) 100.0	92.3	5.6	1.5	0.6	–	–
	Washimiya-machi	(1,498) 100.0	99.8	0.2	(1,495) 100.0	91.7	5.6	1.3	1.4	–	–
	Kurihashi-machi	(2,502) 100.0	99.6	0.4	(2,492) 100.0	83.3	13.6	1.3	1.8	–	–
	Goka-mura	(1,506) 100.0	99.7	0.3	(1,501) 100.0	95.5	2.6	1.5	0.4	–	–
VI	Sakai-machi	(4,040) 100.0	99.6	0.4	(4,024) 100.0	88.0	10.1	1.3	0.5	–	0.1
	Sashima-machi	(2,510) 100.0	99.7	0.3	(2,503) 100.0	96.9	2.2	0.6	0.3	–	–
	Yatabe-machi	(3,993) 100.0	99.3	0.7	(3,967) 100.0	92.5	5.0	1.6	0.9	–	–
VII	Kukizaki-mura	(1,104) 100.0	100.0	–	(1,104) 100.0	96.4	2.4	0.9	0.3	–	–
	Ushiku-machi	(3,201) 100.0	99.7	0.3	(3,192) 100.0	85.0	12.1	1.9	1.0	–	–
	Kawachi-mura	(2,408) 100.0	99.8	0.2	(2,402) 100.0	95.6	3.2	0.9	0.3	–	–
	Sakae-machi	(1,833) 100.0	99.7	0.3	(1,827) 100.0	92.0	6.2	1.3	0.4	–	0.1
	Narita-shi	(8,813) 100.0	98.9	1.1	(8,720) 100.0	81.6	12.9	3.1	2.2	–	0.2
VIII	Shisui-machi	(1,176) 100.0	99.5	0.5	(1,170) 100.0	90.9	6.0	1.7	1.4	–	–
	Yachimata-machi	(4,981) 100.0	99.7	0.3	(4,964) 100.0	85.0	11.2	2.6	1.2	–	–
	Toke-machi	(1,371) 100.0	99.5	0.5	(1,364) 100.0	85.3	12.1	1.7	0.9	–	–
IX	Nagara-machi	(1,676) 100.0	99.9	0.1	(1,674) 100.0	95.1	3.2	1.3	0.4	–	–
	Obitsu-mura	(1,323) 100.0	99.8	0.2	(1,321) 100.0	94.1	4.2	0.8	0.9	–	–
X	Koito-machi	(1,151) 100.0	99.7	0.3	(1,147) 100.0	94.5	3.4	1.7	0.4	–	–
	Zone 10 Total	(209,795) 100.0	97.8	2.2	(205,123) 100.0	70.5	22.3	3.1	4.1	–	–
	Total for 50 km. Region	(3,735,918) 100.0	94.9	5.1	(3,546,122) 100.0	52.4	35.8	6.2	5.6	–	–
	National Total	(20,256,819) 100.0	97.1	2.9	(19,678,263) 100.0	64.4	24.8	6.6	4.0	–	0.2

TABLE 7. TATAMI SPACE PER PERSON BY TYPE OF DWELLING

1950

(Zone) (Sector)	District	Ordinary Dwellings					
		Total	Own Houses	Rented Houses	Employee Houses	Rented Rooms	Unknown
1 I	Chiyoda-ku	2.8	3.0	2.6	2.7	2.3	2.5
	Minato-ku	2.9	3.1	2.8	2.8	2.5	2.4
	Chūō-ku	2.7	3.1	2.5	2.7	2.2	2.2
	Bunkyō-ku	2.8	3.0	2.8	2.8	2.4	2.4
	Taitō-ku	2.5	2.7	2.4	2.8	2.1	2.4
	Zone 1 Total	2.7	2.9	2.6	2.8	2.3	2.4
2 I	Shinagawa-ku	2.6	2.8	2.4	2.5	2.1	2.3
II	Meguro-ku	3.2	3.6	2.8	3.0	2.4	2.0
	Shibuya-ku	2.9	3.1	2.8	3.0	2.3	5.0
III	Shinjuku-ku	2.7	2.8	2.7	2.9	2.2	2.1
	Nakano-ku	3.1	3.4	2.8	3.0	2.4	0.8
IV	Toshima-ku	2.7	2.9	2.5	2.9	2.3	0.6
V	Kita-ku	3.7	5.2	2.3	2.5	2.0	1.9
VI	Arakawa-ku	2.1	2.3	1.9	2.3	1.8	0.3
VII	Sumida-ku	2.2	2.4	2.0	2.2	1.7	1.7
VIII	Kōtō-ku	2.1	2.2	2.0	2.2	1.8	1.2
	Zone 2 Total	2.7	3.1	2.4	2.6	2.1	1.8
3 I	Ōta-ku	2.8	3.1	2.5	2.6	2.2	1.0
II	Setagaya-ku	3.3	4.0	2.8	2.7	2.2	2.0
III	Suginami-ku	3.4	4.0	2.9	3.3	2.3	0.6
IV	Itabashi-ku	2.5	2.9	2.2	2.4	1.9	0.6
	Nerima-ku	3.1	3.5	2.5	2.9	2.3	—
VI	Adachi-ku	2.3	2.6	2.0	2.3	1.8	1.4
VII	Katsushika-ku	2.4	2.8	2.2	2.5	1.8	1.1
VIII	Edogawa-ku	2.5	2.9	2.2	2.4	1.9	0.8
	Urayasu-machi	2.2	2.5	1.7	3.3	1.7	—
	Zone 3 Total	2.8	3.3	2.4	2.7	2.1	1.2
4 I	Kawasaki-shi	2.5	2.7	2.3	2.3	1.9	4.0
II	Komae-machi	3.1	3.4	2.6	3.1	2.4	—
III	Mitaka-shi	2.9	3.5	2.5	2.6	2.2	—
	Musashino-shi	3.4	4.2	2.8	3.1	2.6	1.9
	Chōfu-shi	2.8	3.3	2.6	3.0	2.2	—
	Hoya-machi	3.0	3.4	2.6	2.6	2.2	—
IV	Yamato-machi	3.0	3.4	2.5	3.2	2.5	—
	Toda-machi	2.8	3.2	2.1	2.4	2.2	1.3
V	Warabi-shi	2.5	2.9	2.3	2.6	2.0	0.6
	Kawaguchi-shi	2.6	3.0	2.1	2.8	2.0	—
	Hatogaya-machi	—	—	—	—	—	—
VI	Sōka-shi	2.8	3.1	2.3	2.7	2.1	—
	Yashio-mura	2.9	3.1	2.0	3.0	1.8	—
	Misato-mura	2.9	2.9	2.1	3.8	1.9	—
	Matsudo-shi	2.9	3.1	2.5	2.8	2.1	—
VII	Ichikawa-shi	3.1	3.5	2.7	3.1	2.2	—

Table 7. Tatami Space Per Person by Type of Dwelling

(Zone) (Sector)	District	Ordinary Dwellings					
		Total	Own Houses	Rented Houses	Employee Houses	Rented Rooms	Unknown
	Zone 4 Total	2.7	3.1	2.4	2.6	2.1	1.1
5 I	Tsurumi-ku	2.6	2.9	2.4	2.4	2.0	—
III	Koganei-shi	3.1	3.6	2.6	2.9	2.4	—
	Tanashi-machi	2.7	3.0	2.5	2.4	2.4	—
	Kurume-machi	3.3	3.3	3.0	2.9	3.0	—
IV	Niza-machi	2.9	3.0	2.3	3.3	2.3	5.0
	Kiyose-machi	3.2	3.4	2.7	3.8	2.0	—
	Adachi-machi	2.9	3.2	2.5	3.2	2.4	—
	Asaka-machi	3.0	3.2	2.4	3.0	2.6	—
V	Urawa-shi	3.2	3.5	2.8	3.2	2.3	2.4
	Misono-mura	3.0	3.1	2.3	4.2	2.0	—
	Koshigaya-shi	2.5	2.6	2.3	2.7	1.8	—
VI	Yoshikawa-machi	3.0	3.1	2.4	3.6	2.1	—
	Nagareyama-machi	2.9	3.0	2.4	3.4	2.3	—
VII	Kamagaya-machi	2.9	3.0	2.3	3.1	2.1	—
VIII	Funahashi-shi	2.9	3.3	2.5	2.7	2.2	—
	Zone 5 Total	2.9	3.2	2.6	2.6	2.2	2.2
6 I	Nishi-ku	2.3	2.3	2.3	2.6	2.0	—
	Naka-ku	2.6	2.5	2.6	3.2	2.5	—
	Kanagawa-ku	2.5	2.6	2.4	2.4	2.0	—
II	Kōhoku-ku	3.2	3.5	2.5	2.8	2.3	—
	Inagi-machi	3.1	3.3	2.4	3.3	2.4	—
III	Tama-mura	3.3	3.5	2.4	3.6	2.3	—
	Fuchu-shi	2.9	3.3	2.6	2.8	2.4	—
	Kunitachi-machi	2.9	3.2	2.5	3.0	2.4	—
	Kokubunji-machi	3.0	3.4	2.7	2.6	2.3	—
	Kodaira-machi	3.0	3.2	2.5	3.3	2.1	—
	Higashimurayama-machi	2.9	3.2	2.4	2,4	2.5	—
IV	Tokorosawa-shi	3.4	3.6	2.8	3.3	2.5	—
	Miyoshi-mura	3.5	3.6	2.4	4.0	2.0	—
	Fujimi-mura	3.1	3.2	2.1	3.9	2.0	—
V	Yono-shi	2.9	3.3	2.5	2.8	2.2	—
	Ōmiya-shi	2.9	3.3	2.5	2.8	2.2	—
	Iwatsuki-shi	2.9	3.1	2.4	3.6	2.1	—
VI	Matsubushi-mura	3.2	3.2	2.5	3.8	1.9	—
VII	Kashiwa-shi	3.0	3.1	2.4	3.0	2.2	—
	Shōnan-mura	3.7	3.8	2.9	6.1	2.5	—
	Shirai-mura	3.6	3.6	2.6	4.6	2.7	—
VIII	Narashino-shi	2.9	3.3	2.6	2.4	2.1	—
	Zone 6 Total	2.8	3.1	2.5	2.8	2.2	—
7 I	Isogo-ku	2.9	3.5	2.5	2.7	2.3	—
	Minami-ku	2.5	2.6	2.3	2.7	2.0	—
	Hodogaya-ku	2.6	2.8	2.3	2.7	2.0	—
II	Machida-shi	3.2	3.5	2.6	3.2	2.4	3.3
III	Yuki-mura	3.9	3.9	2.8	2.6	2.4	—
	Hino-machi	3.0	3.3	2.5	2.7	2.4	4.0
	Tachikawa-shi	2.9	3.3	2.6	2.6	2.3	1.1
	Sunakawa-machi	3.0	3.6	2.1	2.8	2.6	—
	Yamato-machi	3.2	3.4	2.3	2.9	2.1	—

Table 7. Tatami Space Per Person by Type of Dwelling

(Zone) (Sector)	District	Ordinary Dwellings					
		Total	Own Houses	Rented Houses	Employee Houses	Rented Rooms	Unknown
IV	Ōi-mura	3.2	3.4	2.5	3.3	2.3	—
	Fukuoka-mura	2.9	3.3	2.3	3.6	2.3	—
V	Kasukabe-shi	2.9	3.0	1.9	3.0	3.0	2.5
	Shōwa-mura	3.1	3.3	2.5	4.8	2.1	—
VI	Noda-shi	3.1	3.3	2.5	3.4	2.2	—
VII	Abiko-machi	3.1	3.3	2.6	3.0	2.5	—
	Yachiyo-machi	3.8	4.0	2.7	3.0	2.6	—
VIII	Chiba-shi	3.0	3.2	2.7	3.3	2.4	—
IX	Goi-machi	3.3	3.4	2.6	3.5	2.1	—
	Sodegaura-machi	3.4	3.5	2.9	3.9	2.6	—
	Zone 7 Total	2.9	3.2	2.5	3.0	2.2	2.1
8 I	Kanazawa-ku	2.9	3.3	2.6	3.0	2.5	—
	Totsuka-ku	3.1	3.5	2.6	2.7	2.3	—
II	Yamato-shi	3.0	3.4	2.3	2.7	2.5	—
	Sagamihara-shi	3.1	3.4	2.5	2.7	2.3	2.0
	Zama-machi	3.5	3.8	2.5	2.6	2.4	—
III	Hachiōji-shi	2.7	2.9	2.4	3.1	2.2	—
	Akishima-shi	2.9	3.3	2.8	3.0	2.8	—
	Fussa-machi	3.1	3.4	2.6	3.0	2.6	—
	Mizuho-machi	3.3	3.4	2.3	3.0	2.9	—
	Murayama-machi	3.3	3.5	2.4	2.5	2.4	—
	Musashi-machi	3.5	3.8	2.6	3.0	2.7	—
IV	Sayama-shi	3.4	3.7	2.5	4.2	2.3	4.0
	Kawagoe-shi	3.2	3.6	2.6	3.3	2.3	—
	Seibu-machi	3.3	3.5	2.4	4.6	1.9	—
V	Ageo-shi	3.1	3.3	2.4	3.0	2.3	—
	Ina-mura	3.2	3.3	2.3	3.8	1.7	—
	Hasuda-machi	3.1	3.3	2.4	3.7	2.2	—
	Shiraoka-machi	3.0	3.1	2.1	5.1	2.3	—
	Miyashiro-machi	3.0	3.1	2.7	2.8	2.1	—
	Sugito-machi	3.1	3.2	2.5	3.0	1.9	—
VI	Sekiyado-machi	3.0	3.1	2.7	4.9	2.4	—
	Moriya-machi	3.2	3.4	2.5	3.2	2.3	—
VII	Toride-machi	3.3	3.6	2.6	3.4	2.5	—
	Inzai-machi	3.6	3.8	2.6	3.3	2.3	—
	Inba-mura	4.7	4.9	3.0	4.9	2.8	—
VIII	Yotsukaidō-machi	3.4	3.9	3.2	3.8	2.9	—
IX	Ichihara-machi	3.4	3.5	2.3	4.4	2.6	—
	Anegasaki-machi	3.4	3.6	2.8	3.9	2.2	—
	Hirakawa-machi	5.4	5.8	3.3	3.6	2.8	—
	Miwa-machi	3.5	3.5	2.9	4.2	2.1	—
X	Kisarazu-shi	3.3	3.6	2.8	3.1	2.7	—
	Zone 8 Total	3.1	3.4	2.6	3.0	2.4	0.6
9 I	Kamakura-shi	3.8	4.3	3.3	3.4	3.0	—
II	Ayase-machi	3.5	3.7	2.6	3.6	2.6	—
	Ebina-machi	3.6	3.8	2.4	2.9	2.5	—
	Shiroyama-machi	3.5	3.6	2.4	3.4	3.3	—
III	Akita-machi	3.4	3.6	2.6	3.6	2.8	—
	Hamura-machi	3.1	3.2	2.5	2.1	2.7	—
IV	Hannō-shi	3.7	4.0	2.9	3.7	2.6	—

Table 7. Tatami Space Per Person by Type of Dwelling

(Zone) (Sector)	District	Ordinary Dwellings					
		Total	Own Houses	Rented Houses	Employee Houses	Rented Rooms	Unknown
IV	Tsurugashima-mura	3.6	3.6	2.5	3.7	2.2	—
	Hidaka-machi	3.9	4.0	2.7	3.7	2.6	—
	Kawashima-mura	3.4	3.6	3.2	4.4	2.6	—
V	Kitamoto-machi	3.1	3.2	2.4	3.0	2.3	—
	Higawa-machi	3.1	3.4	2.4	2.8	2.3	—
	Shobu-machi	3.3	3.4	2.6	3.6	2.1	—
	Kuki-machi	3.1	8.2	2.5	3.0	2.2	—
	Satte-machi	3.0	3.1	2.1	2.9	2.0	—
VI	Iwai-machi	3.2	3.2	2.6	4.4	2.2	—
	Mitsukaidō-shi	3.7	3.9	2.7	3.4	2.4	—
	Yawahara-mura	3.8	3.9	2.5	6.6	2.9	—
	Ina-mura	3.8	3.8	2.8	5.0	2.4	—
VII	Fujishiro-machi	3.9	4.0	2.6	5.1	5.6	—
	Ryūgasaki-shi	3.5	3.8	2.8	3.6	2.4	—
	Tone-mura	3.5	3.6	2.8	3.5	2.3	—
	Motono-mura	3.5	3.6	2.3	3.1	2.4	—
VIII	Sakura-shi	3.7	4.0	3.1	3.8	2.6	—
	Izumi-machi	3.6	3.6	2.8	4.8	2.5	—
IX	Shitsu-mura	3.7	3.7	2.7	6.4	3.3	—
	Nansō-machi	3.7	3.8	2.9	4.6	2.7	—
	Fukuta-machi	3.6	3.7	3.0	4.6	2.5	—
X	Kimitsu-machi	4.0	4.2	3.1	3.9	2.5	—
	Futtsu-machi	3.3	3.4	2.4	3.5	2.6	—
	Ōsawa-machi	4.2	4.4	3.3	4.1	2.7	—
	Zone 9 Total	3.5	3.7	2.9	3.4	2.7	—
10 I	Yokosuka-shi	3.0	3.5	2.6	3.0	2.5	—
	Zushi-shi	3.6	4.0	3.2	3.3	2.9	—
	Hayama-machi	4.2	4.4	4.0	4.3	3.1	—
	Chigasaki-shi	3.2	3.5	2.7	3.0	2.5	—
	Fujisawa-shi	3.4	3.8	3.0	3.0	2.7	—
II	Aikawa-machi	3.7	3.8	2.8	3.9	2.5	—
	Atsugi-shi	3.4	3.6	2.6	3.6	2.2	—
	Samukawa-machi	3.7	3.9	3.0	3.7	2.5	—
III	Ōme-shi	3.4	3.7	2.7	3.2	2.4	—
IV	Sakado-machi	3.7	3.9	2.5	3.2	2.3	—
	Yoshimi-mura	3.6	3.7	2.4	3.4	2.1	—
	Moroyama-mura	3.8	4.0	2.9	3.5	2.1	—
V	Kōnosu-shi	3.1	3.3	2.5	3.2	2.4	—
	Kisai-machi	3.6	3.7	2.6	5.9	1.8	—
	Washimiya-machi	3.1	3.2	2.6	3.9	2.3	—
	Kurihashi-machi	3.0	3.2	2.2	3.1	2.6	—
	Goka-mura	3.1	3.1	2.6	3.6	1.8	—
VI	Sakai-machi	3.2	3.3	2.8	3.4	2.4	—
	Sashima-machi	3.2	3.2	2.4	4.0	2.1	—
	Yatabe-machi	3.9	3.6	2.8	3.9	3.2	—
VII	Kukizaki-mura	3.5	3.5	2.2	4.1	1.8	—
	Ushiku-machi	3.7	3.9	2.6	3.1	1.9	—
	Kawachi-mura	3.6	3.6	3.1	3.0	2.1	—
	Sakae-machi	3.5	3.7	2.8	3.7	2.2	—
	Narita-shi	3.6	3.9	2.8	3.5	2.4	—
VIII	Shisui-machi	3.7	3.8	2.8	3.8	2.4	—

Table 7. <u>Tatami</u> Space Per Person by Type of Dwelling

(Zone)	(Sector)	District	Ordinary Dwellings					
			Total	Own Houses	Rented Houses	Employee Houses	Rented Rooms	Unknown
VIII		Yachimata-machi	3.3	3.5	2.6	3.6	2.3	—
		Toke-machi	3.6	3.7	2.8	5.0	2.6	—
IX		Nagara-machi	4.4	4.5	3.5	4.4	2.7	—
		Obitsu-mura	3.9	4.0	2.8	3.5	2.9	—
X		Koito-machi	4.0	4.1	2.6	5.1	2.3	—
		Zone 10 Total	3.4	3.7	2.8	3.2	2.5	1.3
		Total for 50 km. Region	2.9	3.3	2.5	2.7	2.2	2.3
		National Total	3.7	4.0	2.9	3.1	2.6	2.2

1955

(Zone)	(Sector)	District	Ordinary House-holds	Quasi House-holds	Ordinary Households						
					Own Houses	Rented Houses	Employee Houses	Rented Rooms	Un-known	Boarding Houses	Others
1	I	Chiyoda-ku	—	—	3.23	2.76	3.02	2.10	—	—	—
		Minato-ku	—	—	3.40	2.83	3.07	2.11	—	—	—
		Chūō-ku	—	—	3.10	2.51	2.79	1.96	—	—	—
		Bunkyō-ku	—	—	3.31	2.76	3.15	2.05	—	—	—
		Taitō-ku	—	—	2.93	2.36	2.96	1.79	—	—	—
		Zone 1 Total	—	—	3.17	2.62	3.02	1.98	—	—	—
2	I	Shinagawa-ku	—	—	3.07	2.35	2.71	1.86	—	—	—
	II	Meguro-ku	—	—	3.78	2.68	3.33	2.11	—	—	—
		Shibuya-ku	—	—	3.49	2.79	3.36	2.03	—	—	—
	III	Shinjuku-ku	—	—	3.19	2.67	3.15	1.98	—	—	—
		Nakano-ku	—	—	3.54	2.69	3.36	2.06	—	—	—
	IV	Toshima-ku	—	—	3.19	2.38	3.10	1.83	—	—	—
	V	Kita-ku	—	—	2.93	2.25	2.64	1.73	—	—	—
	VI	Arakawa-ku	—	—	2.53	1.94	2.47	1.55	—	—	—
	VII	Sumida-ku	—	—	2.62	2.03	2.33	1.65	—	—	—
	VIII	Kōtō-ku	—	—	2.45	1.99	2.26	1.60	—	—	—
		Zone 2 Total	—	—	3.05	2.36	2.89	1.86	—	—	—
3	I	Ōta-ku	—	—	3.21	2.36	2.86	1.91	—	—	—
	II	Setagaya-ku	—	—	4.04	2.74	3.51	2.27	—	—	—
	III	Suginami-ku	—	—	4.06	2.84	3.69	2.24	—	—	—
	IV	Itabashi-ku	—	—	2.95	2.24	2.51	1.66	—	—	—
		Nerima-ku	—	—	3.52	2.51	3.20	1.92	—	—	—
	VI	Adachi-ku	—	—	2.60	1.97	2.35	1.55	—	—	—
	VII	Katsushika-ku	—	—	2.80	2.11	2.49	1.67	—	—	—
	VIII	Edogawa-ku	—	—	2.90	2.16	2.34	1.64	—	—	—
		Urayasu-machi	—	—	2.48	1.65	2.54	1.73	—	—	—
		Zone 3 Total	—	—	3.26	2.36	3.05	1.92	—	—	—
4	I	Kawasaki-shi	—	—	2.87	2.24	2.41	1.72	—	—	—
	II	Komae-machi	—	—	3.45	2.62	3.23	2.03	—	—	—
	III	Mitaka-shi	—	—	3.44	2.51	3.10	1.94	—	—	—
		Musashino-shi	—	—	4.19	2.93	3.46	2.22	—	—	—
		Chōfu-shi	—	—	3.24	2.77	2.85	2.02	—	—	—
		Hoya-machi	—	—	3.30	2.53	3.16	1.85	—	—	—

Table 7. Tatami Space Per Person by Type of Dwelling

(Zone) (Sector)	District	Ordinary House-holds	Quasi House-holds	Ordinary Households						
				Own Houses	Rented Houses	Employee Houses	Rented Rooms	Un-known	Boarding Houses	Others
IV	Yamato-machi	–	–	3.11	2.35	3.17	1.73	–	–	–
	Toda-machi	–	–	3.08	2.11	2.40	0.79	–	–	–
V	Warabi-shi	–	–	2.87	2.28	2.74	1.67	–	–	–
	Kawaguchi-shi	–	–	3.00	2.09	2.64	1.77	–	–	–
	Hatogaya-machi	–	–	3.13	2.28	3.85	1.93	–	–	–
VI	Sōka-shi	–	–	3.11	2.14	2.65	1.87	–	–	–
	Yashio-mura	–	–	3.01	2.13	2.87	2.10	–	–	–
	Misato-mura	–	–	2.95	2.00	3.76	1.67	–	–	–
	Matsudo-shi	–	–	3.15	2.51	3.05	1.93	–	–	–
VII	Ichikawa-shi	–	–	5.52	2.55	5.38	2.74	–	–	–
	Zone 4 Total	–	–	3.33	2.46	2.92	1.92	–	–	–
5 I	Tsurumi-ku	–	–	3.04	2.36	2.54	1.80	–	–	–
III	Koganei-shi	–	–	3.60	2.67	3.11	2.08	–	–	–
	Tanashi-machi	–	–	2.98	2.68	2.53	1.91	–	–	–
	Kurume-machi	–	–	3.72	2.91	3.91	2.75	–	–	–
IV	Niza-machi	–	–	3.32	2.33	3.36	3.20	–	–	–
	Kiyose-machi	–	–	3.44	2.58	3.75	2.29	–	–	–
	Adachi-machi	–	–	3.26	2.53	3.66	2.09	–	–	–
	Asaka-machi	–	–	3.14	2.38	2.96	1.97	–	–	–
V	Urawa-shi	–	–	3.63	2.78	3.35	2.09	–	–	–
	Misono-mura	–	–	3.14	2.32	4.81	1.85	–	–	–
	Koshigaya-shi	–	–	2.60	2.26	2.95	1.81	–	–	–
VI	Yoshikawa-machi	–	–	3.05	2.42	4.66	2.07	–	–	–
	Nagareyama-machi	–	–	3.17	2.40	3.49	1.95	–	–	–
VII	Kamagaya-machi	–	–	3.01	2.28	2.95	1.87	–	–	–
VIII	Funahashi-shi	–	–	3.27	2.56	2.95	2.03	–	–	–
	Zone 5 Total	–	–	3.22	2.55	2.81	1.93	–	–	–
6 I	Nishi-ku	–	–	2.65	2.32	3.08	1.71	–	–	–
	Naka-ku	–	–	2.90	2.80	3.99	1.92	–	–	–
	Kanagawa-ku	–	–	2.87	2.37	2.73	1.79	–	–	–
II	Kōhoku-ku	–	–	3.62	2.58	3.26	2.10	–	–	–
	Inagi-machi	–	–	3.53	2.08	3.23	2.14	–	–	–
III	Tama-mura	–	–	3.83	2.64	3.30	1.56	–	–	–
	Fuchu-shi	–	–	3.27	2.66	2.89	1.98	–	–	–
	Kunitachi-machi	–	–	3.43	2.60	3.07	2.24	–	–	–
	Kokubunji-machi	–	–	3.46	2.67	2.71	2.05	–	–	–
	Kodaira-machi	–	–	3.45	2.60	3.58	1.99	–	–	–
	Higashimurayama-machi	–	–	3.37	2.74	3.28	2.10	–	–	–
IV	Tokorosawa-shi	–	–	3.64	2.78	3.46	2.30	–	–	–
	Miyoshi-mura	–	–	3.45	2.46	4.65	1.71	–	–	–
	Fujimi-mura	–	–	3.38	2.32	2.85	2.24	–	–	–
V	Yono-shi	–	–	3.25	2.51	3.02	1.93	–	–	–
	Ōmiya-shi	–	–	3.25	2.52	2.96	1.99	–	–	–
	Iwatsuki-shi	–	–	3.16	2.39	3.57	2.04	–	–	–
VI	Matsubushi-mura	–	–	3.27	2.78	4.31	2.11	–	–	–
VII	Kashiwa-shi	–	–	3.21	2.43	3.02	1.93	–	–	–
	Shōnan-mura	–	–	3.84	2.78	4.56	2.69	–	–	–
	Shirai-mura	–	–	3.89	2.95	4.98	1.77	–	–	–
VIII	Narashino-shi	–	–	3.36	2.49	2.92	2.00	–	–	–

Table 7. <u>Tatami</u> Space Per Person by Type of Dwelling

(Zone) (Sector)	District	Ordinary House-holds	Quasi House-holds	Ordinary Households						
				Own Houses	Rented Houses	Employee Houses	Rented Rooms	Un-known	Boarding Houses	Others
	Zone 6 Total	—	—	3.22	2.54	3.07	1.92	—	—	—
7 I	Isogo-ku	—	—	3.49	2.59	2.64	1.99	—	—	—
	Minami-ku	—	—	2.79	2.28	2.70	1.73	—	—	—
	Hodogaya-ku	—	—	3.03	2.42	2.82	1.84	—	—	—
II	Machida-shi	—	—	3.53	2.64	3.25	2.01	—	—	—
III	Yuki-mura	—	—	4.05	2.68	3.15	2.90	—	—	—
	Hino-machi	—	—	3.30	2.66	2.88	2.09	—	—	—
	Tachikawa-shi	—	—	3.28	2.73	2.68	2.02	—	—	—
	Sunakawa-machi	—	—	3.27	2.32	2.12	1.97	—	—	—
	Yamato-machi	—	—	3.26	2.48	3.25	1.88	—	—	—
IV	Ōi-mura	—	—	3.30	2.36	3.06	2.02	—	—	—
	Fukuoka-mura	—	—	3.08	2.42	3.64	2.23	—	—	—
V	Kasukabe-shi	—	—	3.08	2.46	3.42	2.08	—	—	—
	Shōwa-mura	—	—	3.13	2.58	3.93	1.82	—	—	—
VI	Noda-shi	—	—	3.41	2.59	3.68	1.90	—	—	—
VII	Abiko-machi	—	—	3.54	2.67	2.99	1.87	—	—	—
	Yachiyo-machi	—	—	4.06	2.61	3.53	2.25	—	—	—
VIII	Chiba-shi	—	—	3.29	2.66	3.32	2.07	—	—	—
IX	Goi-machi	—	—	3.55	2.52	4.03	1.93	—	—	—
	Sodegaura-machi	—	—	3.79	3.86	4.13	2.80	—	—	—
	Zone 7 Total	—	—	3.25	2.53	3.03	1.92	—	—	—
8 I	Kanazawa-ku	—	—	3.23	2.53	3.09	2.03	—	—	—
	Totsuka-ku	—	—	3.54	2.51	2.95	2.06	—	—	—
II	Yamato-shi	—	—	3.32	2.88	3.13	2.14	—	—	—
	Sagamihara-shi	—	—	3.45	2.56	2.80	2.06	—	—	—
	Zama-machi	—	—	3.86	2.86	2.29	2.00	—	—	—
III	Hachiōji-shi	—	—	3.05	2.44	3.17	1.89	—	—	—
	Akishima-shi	—	—	3.15	2.67	2.97	2.13	—	—	—
	Fussa-machi	—	—	3.41	2.76	3.02	2.25	—	—	—
	Mizuho-machi	—	—	3.22	2.81	3.64	2.05	—	—	—
	Murayama-machi	—	—	3.48	2.38	2.61	2.34	—	—	—
	Musashi-machi	—	—	3.82	2.82	3.41	2.58	—	—	—
IV	Sayama-shi	—	—	3.69	2.61	3.34	2.23	—	—	—
	Kawagoe-shi	—	—	3.68	2.63	3.31	2.16	—	—	—
	Seibu-machi	—	—	3.85	2.62	3.85	2.45	—	—	—
V	Ageo-shi	—	—	3.53	2.57	3.22	1.99	—	—	—
	Ina-mura	—	—	3.85	2.33	4.54	1.62	—	—	—
	Hasuda-machi	—	—	3.37	2.34	3.86	1.91	—	—	—
	Shiraoka-machi	—	—	3.24	2.28	3.79	1.97	—	—	—
	Miyashiro-machi	—	—	3.13	2.51	3.20	1.95	—	—	—
	Sugito-machi	—	—	3.22	2.46	3.61	2.00	—	—	—
VI	Sekiyado-machi	—	—	3.14	2.85	3.70	2.45	—	—	—
	Moriya-machi	—	—	3.54	2.41	4.13	1.94	—	—	—
VII	Toride-machi	—	—	3.65	2.73	3.17	2.05	—	—	—
	Inzai-machi	—	—	3.87	2.93	3.54	2.20	—	—	—
	Inba-mura	—	—	5.02	2.79	4.00	2.85	—	—	—
VIII	Yotsukaidō-machi	—	—	3.95	3.23	3.42	2.44	—	—	—
IX	Ichihara-machi	—	—	3.35	2.55	3.45	2.29	—	—	—
	Anegasaki-machi	—	—	3.63	2.98	3.47	2.16	—	—	—
	Hirakawa-machi	—	—	4.11	3.32	3.02	2.33	—	—	—

Table 7. Tatami Space Per Person by Type of Dwelling

(Zone) (Sector)	District	Ordinary House-holds	Quasi House-holds	Ordinary Households						
				Own Houses	Rented Houses	Employee Houses	Rented Rooms	Un-known	Boarding Houses	Others
IX	Miwa-machi	—	—	3.81	3.32	4.87	2.14	—	—	—
X	Kisarazu-shi	—	—	3.76	2.81	3.51	2.05	—	—	—
	Zone 8 Total	—	—	3.48	2.55	3.13	2.08	—	—	—
9 I	Kamakura-shi	—	—	4.42	3.37	3.30	2.67	—	—	—
II	Ayase-machi	—	—	4.02	2.85	4.74	2.65	—	—	—
	Ebina-machi	—	—	3.99	2.80	3.27	1.93	—	—	—
	Shiroyama-machi	—	—	3.73	2.50	3.49	2.25	—	—	—
III	Akita-machi	—	—	3.62	2.93	3.81	2.67	—	—	—
	Hamura-machi	—	—	3.39	2.72	3.31	2.54	—	—	—
IV	Hannō-shi	—	—	4.15	2.94	3.66	2.48	—	—	—
	Tsurugashima-mura	—	—	3.74	2.77	3.49	1.87	—	—	—
	Hidaka-machi	—	—	4.06	2.66	3.89	2.29	—	—	—
	Kawashima-mura	—	—	3.57	2.56	4.48	2.37	—	—	—
V	Kitamoto-machi	—	—	3.21	2.36	2.83	1.96	—	—	—
	Higawa-machi	—	—	3.41	2.31	2.80	2.10	—	—	—
	Shobu-machi	—	—	3.37	2.44	3.91	2.54	—	—	—
	Kuki-machi	—	—	3.41	2.51	3.50	2.06	—	—	—
	Satte-machi	—	—	3.20	2.25	3.72	1.98	—	—	—
VI	Iwai-machi	—	—	3.46	2.72	3.95	2.07	—	—	—
	Mitsukaidō-shi	—	—	3.72	2.78	3.31	2.29	—	—	—
	Yawahara-mura	—	—	3.89	2.62	4.39	2.19	—	—	—
	Ina-mura	—	—	4.07	3.21	6.42	3.44	—	—	—
VII	Fujishiro-machi	—	—	4.13	2.63	4.03	2.35	—	—	—
	Ryugasaki-shi	—	—	3.80	2.88	3.74	2.09	—	—	—
	Tone-mura	—	—	3.57	2.78	4.36	1.60	—	—	—
	Motono-mura	—	—	4.10	3.15	4.04	2.20	—	—	—
VIII	Sakura-shi	—	—	4.05	3.00	3.71	2.34	—	—	—
	Izumi-machi	—	—	4.21	3.31	6.60	1.49	—	—	—
IX	Shitsu-mura	—	—	3.90	2.54	4.97	2.18	—	—	—
	Nansō-machi	—	—	3.87	3.23	4.06	2.44	—	—	—
	Fukuta-machi	—	—	4.03	3.15	5.42	2.07	—	—	—
X	Kimitsu-machi	—	—	4.36	3.65	4.21	2.48	—	—	—
	Futtsu-machi	—	—	3.53	2.45	3.55	2.02	—	—	—
	Ōsawa-machi	—	—	4.33	3.50	3.81	2.73	—	—	—
	Zone 9 Total	—	—	3.94	3.00	3.44	2.48	—	—	—
10 I	Yokosuka-shi	—	—	3.41	2.55	3.12	2.12	—	—	—
	Zushi-shi	—	—	4.16	3.09	3.87	2.51	—	—	—
	Hayama-machi	—	—	4.46	3.85	3.85	2.67	—	—	—
	Chigasaki-shi	—	—	3.66	2.78	2.91	2.24	—	—	—
	Fujisawa-shi	—	—	4.01	3.06	3.36	2.43	—	—	—
II	Aikawa-machi	—	—	3.96	3.07	4.12	2.25	—	—	—
	Atsugi-shi	—	—	3.62	2.73	3.17	2.23	—	—	—
	Samukawa-machi	—	—	3.73	2.67	3.01	2.01	—	—	—
III	Ōme-shi	—	—	3.61	2.75	3.18	2.34	—	—	—
IV	Sakado-machi	—	—	3.77	2.66	3.70	2.04	—	—	—
	Yoshimi-mura	—	—	4.05	2.75	3.47	1.93	—	—	—
	Moroyama-mura	—	—	3.99	2.78	3.38	2.52	—	—	—
V	Kōnosu-shi	—	—	3.42	2.53	3.41	2.27	—	—	—
	Kisai-machi	—	—	3.37	2.68	3.70	1.65	—	—	—
	Washimiya-machi	—	—	3.27	2.49	3.31	1.75	—	—	—

Table 7. Tatami Space Per Person by Type of Dwelling

(Zone)	(Sector)	District	Ordinary House-holds	Quasi House-holds	Ordinary Households						
					Own Houses	Rented Houses	Employee Houses	Rented Rooms	Un-known	Boarding Houses	Others
V		Kurihashi-machi	–	–	3.17	2.52	2.85	2.14	–	–	–
		Goka-mura	–	–	3.11	2.50	4.55	1.80	–	–	–
VI		Sakai-machi	–	–	3.52	2.95	3.36	2.74	–	–	–
		Sashima-machi	–	–	3.32	2.80	3.47	3.00	–	–	–
		Yatabe-machi	–	–	4.03	2.92	4.49	2.20	–	–	–
VII		Kukizaki-mura	–	–	3.70	2.49	4.00	1.62	–	–	–
		Ushiku-machi	–	–	3.87	2.53	3.78	2.13	–	–	–
		Kawachi-mura	–	–	3.67	3.07	4.40	2.31	–	–	–
		Sakae-machi	–	–	4.05	3.07	3.38	2.38	–	–	–
		Narita-shi	–	–	3.95	2.84	3.62	2.12	–	–	–
VIII		Shisui-machi	–	–	3.78	2.76	4.60	2.70	–	–	–
		Yachimata-machi	–	–	3.65	2.62	3.47	2.15	–	–	–
		Toke-machi	–	–	3.87	2.67	4.71	1.73	–	–	–
IX		Nagara-machi	–	–	4.84	3.39	6.49	2.73	–	–	–
		Obitsu-mura	–	–	4.10	2.97	4.00	2.54	–	–	–
X		Koito-machi	–	–	4.54	2.95	4.33	2.48	–	–	–
		Zone 10 Total	–	–	4.14	3.09	4.31	2.67	–	–	–
		Total for 50 km. Region	–	–	3.31	2.46	2.99	1.93	–	–	–
		National Total	–	–	4.13	2.84	3.20	2.26	–	–	–

1960

(Zone)	(Sector)	District	Ordinary House-holds	Quasi House-holds	Ordinary Households					
					Own Houses	Rented Houses	Employee Houses	Rented Rooms	Boarding Houses	Others
1	I	Chiyoda-ku	–	3.91	4.06	3.23	3.65	2.41	–	–
		Minato-ku	–	4.84	4.24	3.28	3.60	2.39	–	–
		Chūō-ku	–	4.89	3.78	2.82	3.20	2.18	–	–
		Bunkyō-ku	–	4.26	4.10	2.89	3.67	2.28	–	–
		Taitō-ku	–	4.32	3.65	2.53	3.47	2.08	–	–
		Zone 1 Total	–	4.37	3.95	2.89	3.57	2.24	–	–
2	I	Shinagawa-ku	–	3.87	3.67	2.51	3.08	2.08	–	–
	II	Meguro-ku	–	4.22	4.54	2.83	3.70	2.40	–	–
		Shibuya-ku	–	4.22	4.30	3.03	3.79	2.29	–	–
	III	Shinjuku-ku	–	3.98	4.04	2.89	3.52	2.27	–	–
		Nakano-ku	–	4.24	4.29	2.84	3.71	2.29	–	–
	IV	Toshima-ku	–	4.17	3.85	2.56	3.43	2.15	–	–
	V	Kita-ku	–	3.80	3.50	2.41	3.00	2.00	–	–
	VI	Arakawa-ku	–	3.68	3.08	2.10	2.74	1.76	–	–
	VII	Sumida-ku	–	3.74	3.26	2.20	2.79	1.90	–	–
	VIII	Kōtō-ku	–	3.69	3.05	2.16	2.66	1.82	–	–
		Zone 2 Total	–	4.04	3.73	2.55	3.28	2.11	–	–
3	I	Ōta-ku	–	3.93	3.83	2.46	3.30	2.14	–	–
	II	Setagaya-ku	–	4.25	4.78	2.98	3.96	2.40	–	–
	III	Suginami-ku	–	4.30	4.83	3.00	4.23	2.43	–	–
	IV	Itabashi-ku	–	3.91	3.46	2.36	2.96	1.92	–	–
		Nerima-ku	–	4.38	4.10	2.69	3.59	2.16	–	–
	VI	Adachi-ku	–	4.10	3.08	2.26	2.75	1.78	–	–

Table 7. Tatami Space Per Person by Type of Dwelling

(Zone) (Sector)	District	Ordinary House-holds	Quasi House-holds	Ordinary Households					
				Own Houses	Rented Houses	Employee Houses	Rented Rooms	Boarding Houses	Others
VII	Katsushika-ku	—	4.10	3.26	2.38	2.87	1.85	—	—
VIII	Edogawa-ku	—	3.86	3.36	2.27	2.68	1.91	—	—
	Urayasu-machi	—	4.00	2.81	1.83	2.98	1.64	—	—
	Zone 3 Total	—	4.17	3.92	2.56	3.53	2.17	—	—
4 I	Kawasaki-shi	—	3.91	3.38	2.40	2.85	1.98	—	—
II	Komae-machi	—	4.12	4.13	2.81	3.50	2.16	—	—
III	Mitaka-shi	—	4.33	4.19	2.90	3.61	2.12	—	—
	Musashino-shi	—	4.46	4.87	3.18	3.96	2.45	—	—
	Chōfu-shi	—	4.58	3.79	2.70	3.47	2.13	—	—
	Hoya-machi	—	4.42	4.00	3.23	3.61	1.97	—	—
IV	Yamato-machi	—	4.96	3.59	2.50	3.24	2.09	—	—
	Toda-machi	—	4.87	3.36	2.46	3.02	1.90	—	—
V	Warabi-shi	—	4.43	3.36	2.41	3.02	2.02	—	—
	Kawaguchi-shi	—	4.15	3.34	2.28	2.96	1.90	—	—
	Hatogaya-machi	—	5.39	3.40	3.12	3.55	2.05	—	—
VI	Sōka-shi	—	5.17	3.38	2.71	2.97	1.90	—	—
	Yashio-mura	—	4.50	3.29	2.47	2.73	1.64	—	—
	Misato-mura	—	5.17	3.31	2.34	3.46	2.13	—	—
	Matsudo-shi	—	4.57	3.63	2.75	3.63	2.16	—	—
VII	Ichikawa-shi	—	4.28	4.10	2.79	3.58	2.26	—	—
	Zone 4 Total	—	4.18	3.65	2.61	3.15	2.09	—	—
5 I	Tsurumi-ku	—	4.12	3.55	2.44	2.92	2.00	—	—
III	Koganei-shi	—	4.45	4.40	3.03	3.54	2.28	—	—
	Tanashi-machi	—	4.59	3.74	2.89	3.15	2.14	—	—
	Kurume-machi	—	4.66	4.01	3.20	3.76	2.31	—	—
IV	Niza-machi	—	4.76	3.61	2.51	3.42	1.94	—	—
	Kiyose-machi	—	4.75	3.82	2.91	3.91	2.23	—	—
	Adachi-machi	—	5.25	3.67	2.58	4.07	2.47	—	—
	Asaka-machi	—	4.49	3.53	2.94	3.26	2.27	—	—
V	Urawa-shi	—	4.79	4.15	2.99	3.59	2.34	—	—
	Misono-mura	—	5.25	3.42	2.43	4.63	1.50	—	—
	Koshigaya-shi	—	5.43	3.33	2.53	3.60	1.93	—	—
VI	Yoshikawa-machi	—	7.00	3.37	2.60	4.53	1.91	—	—
	Nagareyama-machi	—	5.73	3.76	2.77	3.46	1.99	—	—
VII	Kamagaya-machi	—	4.47	3.46	2.53	3.07	2.41	—	—
VIII	Funahashi-shi	—	4.44	3.76	2.67	3.41	2.15	—	—
	Zone 5 Total	—	4.43	3.56	2.72	3.20	2.14	—	—
6 I	Nishi-ku	—	4.14	3.21	2.50	3.29	1.99	—	—
	Naka-ku	—	4.85	3.54	3.21	4.09	2.15	—	—
	Kanagawa-ku	—	4.02	3.40	2.59	3.22	2.03	—	—
II	Kōhoku-ku	—	4.70	4.13	2.83	3.63	2.32	—	—
	Inagi-machi	—	4.45	3.90	2.45	3.50	2.21	—	—
III	Tama-mura	—	4.80	3.93	2.85	3.89	2.38	—	—
	Fuchu-shi	—	4.72	3.75	3.02	3.13	2.15	—	—
	Kunitachi-machi	—	4.67	4.07	2.92	3.82	2.33	—	—
	Kokubunji-machi	—	4.27	4.11	2.95	3.10	2.18	—	—
	Kodaira-machi	—	4.75	3.92	2.87	3.51	2.24	—	—
	Higashimurayama-machi	—	4.73	3.84	3.30	3.25	3.12	—	—
IV	Tokorosawa-shi	—	5.86	4.00	3.41	3.81	2.37	—	—

Table 7. Tatami Space Per Person by Type of Dwelling

(Zone)	(Sector)	District	Ordinary Households	Quasi Households	Ordinary Households					
					Own Houses	Rented Houses	Employee Houses	Rented Rooms	Boarding Houses	Others
	IV	Miyoshi-mura	—	—	4.05	2.72	13.00	1.92	—	—
		Fujimi-mura	—	4.00	3.85	3.76	2.86	2.32	—	—
	V	Yono-shi	—	4.67	3.81	2.78	3.37	2.15	—	—
		Ōmiya-shi	—	4.92	3.80	2.87	3.47	2.23	—	—
		Iwatsuki-shi	—	5.85	3.58	2.68	3.84	2.14	—	—
	VI	Matsubushi-mura	—	—	3.57	3.00	5.57	2.24	—	—
	VII	Kashiwa-shi	—	4.85	3.68	3.10	3.48	2.07	—	—
		Shōnan-mura	—	7.12	4.30	4.04	5.45	2.12	—	—
		Shirai-mura	—	10.00	4.27	2.35	5.33	2.53	—	—
	VIII	Narashino-shi	—	4.66	3.80	2.83	3.08	2.10	—	—
		Zone 6 Total	—	4.17	3.75	2.91	3.42	2.13	—	—
7	I	Isogo-ku	—	4.56	3.98	2.75	3.27	2.32	—	—
		Minami-ku	—	4.17	3.30	2.42	3.04	2.00	—	—
		Hodogaya-ku	—	4.44	3.59	2.72	3.28	2.05	—	—
	II	Machida-shi	—	4.88	4.01	3.02	3.77	2.24	—	—
	III	Yuki-mura	—	5.00	4.38	2.87	3.16	2.78	—	—
		Hino-machi	—	5.00	3.82	3.44	3.21	2.31	—	—
		Tachikawa-shi	—	5.05	3.78	3.04	2.93	2.25	—	—
		Sunakawa-machi	—	5.92	3.73	2.89	2.69	2.48	—	—
		Yamato-machi	—	4.73	3.69	2.93	3.03	2.15	—	—
	IV	Ōi-mura	—	6.70	3.69	2.62	2.95	2.46	—	—
		Fukuoka-mura	—	5.00	3.63	4.09	3.51	2.34	—	—
	V	Kasukabe-shi	—	5.83	3.47	2.74	3.86	1.97	—	—
		Shōwa-mura	—	6.00	3.46	2.91	3.78	2.42	—	—
	VI	Noda-shi	—	5.61	3.81	2.89	3.98	2.24	—	—
	VII	Abiko-machi	—	5.28	3.85	2.83	3.43	2.16	—	—
		Yachiyo-machi	—	4.82	4.34	3.51	4.23	2.33	—	—
	VIII	Chiba-shi	—	4.66	3.87	2.83	3.53	2.22	—	—
	IX	Goi-machi	—	4.76	4.13	2.70	4.34	2.16	—	—
		Sodegaura-machi	—	6.67	4.30	3.26	4.13	2.51	—	—
		Zone 7 Total	—	4.29	3.74	2.84	3.41	2.15	—	—
8	I	Kanazawa-ku	—	4.76	3.70	2.73	3.35	2.29	—	—
		Totsuka-ku	—	4.75	3.88	3.14	3.42	2.28	—	—
	II	Yamato-shi	—	5.34	3.93	3.45	3.26	2.43	—	—
		Sagamihara-shi	—	5.22	3.93	3.19	3.36	2.22	—	—
		Zama-machi	—	5.72	4.19	3.12	3.31	2.33	—	—
	III	Hachiōji-shi	—	4.89	3.57	2.72	3.54	2.06	—	—
		Akishima-shi	—	5.59	3.59	2.89	3.38	2.23	—	—
		Fussa-machi	—	6.09	3.92	3.50	3.14	2.34	—	—
		Mizuho-machi	—	5.89	3.91	3.23	3.77	2.71	—	—
		Murayama-machi	—	5.45	4.03	2.95	3.22	2.49	—	—
		Musashi-machi	—	6.78	4.15	3.27	3.46	2.84	—	—
	IV	Sayama-shi	—	6.75	4.19	3.01	3.90	2.47	—	—
		Kawagoe-shi	—	5.76	4.07	2.82	3.79	2.28	—	—
		Seibu-machi	—	6.00	4.29	2.98	5.22	2.40	—	—
	V	Ageo-shi	—	5.26	3.89	2.84	3.57	2.04	—	—
		Ina-mura	—	—	4.11	2.43	4.22	2.09	—	—
		Hasuda-machi	—	6.37	4.02	2.79	4.18	1.98	—	—
		Shiraoka-machi	—	4.30	3.69	2.72	4.49	2.15	—	—
		Miyashiro-machi	—	5.75	3.64	2.57	3.05	2.29	—	—

Table 7. Tatami Space Per Person by Type of Dwelling

(Zone)	(Sector)	District	Ordinary Households	Quasi Households	Ordinary Households					
					Own Houses	Rented Houses	Employee Houses	Rented Rooms	Boarding Houses	Others
	V	Sugito-machi	—	4.75	3.64	2.96	4.65	2.39	—	—
	VI	Sekiyado-machi	—	6.42	3.54	3.13	3.67	2.43	—	—
		Moriya-machi	—	7.31	3.95	3.27	4.32	2.45	—	—
	VII	Toride-machi	—	5.42	4.04	2.89	3.39	2.12	—	—
		Inzai-machi	—	6.94	4.39	3.17	3.82	2.42	—	—
		Inba-mura	—	6.00	5.51	5.31	4.74	3.40	—	—
	VIII	Yotsukaidō-machi	—	6.55	4.32	3.07	3.55	2.74	—	—
	IX	Ichihara-machi	—	5.60	3.83	2.80	3.60	2.03	—	—
		Anegasaki-machi	—	5.80	4.20	3.08	5.29	2.15	—	—
		Hirakawa-machi	—	5.38	4.18	3.13	3.71	2.36	—	—
		Miwa-machi	—	6.00	4.44	4.03	3.88	2.07	—	—
	X	Kisarazu-shi	—	7.00	4.29	3.64	3.42	2.76	—	—
		Zone 8 Total	—	6.08	3.93	3.00	3.54	2.27	—	—
9	I	Kamakura-shi	—	5.72	5.02	3.72	3.86	2.40	—	—
	II	Ayase-machi	—	5.90	4.28	3.57	3.63	2.37	—	—
		Ebina-machi	—	4.69	4.21	2.79	3.40	2.42	—	—
		Shiroyama-machi	—	5.54	4.59	2.98	3.24	2.57	—	—
	III	Akita-machi	—	6.77	4.07	3.01	3.98	2.41	—	—
		Hamura-machi	—	6.44	3.97	3.10	2.94	2.34	—	—
	IV	Hannō-shi	—	6.31	4.62	3.27	3.82	2.52	—	—
		Tsurugashima-mura	—	5.50	4.14	2.98	3.84	1.91	—	—
		Hidaka-machi	—	6.95	4.02	3.60	4.58	2.58	—	—
		Kawashima-mura	—	5.33	4.28	3.63	4.91	2.42	—	—
	V	Kitamoto-machi	—	3.64	3.91	2.70	3.60	2.24	—	—
		Higawa-machi	—	5.66	4.05	2.67	2.96	2.01	—	—
		Shobu-machi	—	4.92	3.91	2.77	3.44	2.27	—	—
		Kuki-machi	—	5.79	3.77	2.76	3.86	2.39	—	—
		Satte-machi	—	6.41	3.77	2.45	3.89	2.30	—	—
	VI	Iwai-machi	—	6.67	3.88	3.32	3.72	2.36	—	—
		Mitsukaidō-shi	—	5.07	4.14	3.12	4.21	2.36	—	—
		Yawahara-mura	—	7.43	4.45	3.67	5.06	2.14	—	—
		Ina-mura	—	5.88	4.42	3.32	4.71	3.50	—	—
	VII	Fujishiro-machi	—	6.08	4.56	3.10	5.49	2.17	—	—
		Ryūgasaki-shi	—	5.86	4.33	3.19	4.04	2.36	—	—
		Tone-mura	—	5.75	4.13	3.15	3.67	2.40	—	—
		Motono-mura	—	5.57	4.57	5.19	6.57	2.29	—	—
	VIII	Sakura-shi	—	15.00	4.56	3.25	4.63	2.25	—	—
		Izumi-machi	—	6.00	4.52	4.03	4.70	2.83	—	—
	IX	Shitsu-mura	—	6.17	4.51	3.48	5.51	3.00	—	—
		Nansō-machi	—	4.50	4.38	5.88	4.66	2.72	—	—
		Fukuta-machi	—	5.70	4.24	3.45	3.73	1.74	—	—
	X	Kimitsu-machi	—	6.10	4.94	3.72	4.49	2.25	—	—
		Futtsu-machi	—	5.26	3.99	2.77	3.61	2.59	—	—
		Ōsawa-machi	—	—	4.74	3.81	5.23	2.40	—	—
		Zone 9 Total	—	5.65	4.26	3.25	3.86	2.63	—	—
10	I	Yokosuka-shi	—	5.66	3.84	2.86	3.40	2.41	—	—
		Zushi-shi	—	5.54	4.76	3.22	4.08	2.87	—	—
		Hayama-machi	—	6.07	5.00	4.14	4.34	2.70	—	—
		Chigasaki-shi	—	5.34	4.16	3.05	3.64	2.38	—	—
		Fujisawa-shi	—	5.19	4.51	3.25	3.75	2.53	—	—

Table 7. Tatami Space Per Person by Type of Dwelling

(Zone) (Sector)	District	Ordinary Households	Quasi Households	Ordinary Households					
				Own Houses	Rented Houses	Employee Houses	Rented Rooms	Boarding Houses	Others
II	Aikawa-machi	–	4.83	4.49	3.08	3.85	2.52	–	–
	Atsugi-shi	–	5.38	4.02	2.94	3.68	2.34	–	–
	Samukawa-machi	–	5.63	4.08	2.61	3.61	1.91	–	–
III	Ome-shi	–	5.18	4.08	3.13	3.72	2.64		–
IV	Sakado-machi	–	5.50	4.45	3.07	3.29	2.25	–	–
	Yoshimi-mura	–	2.00	4.36	3.63	3.99	2.82	–	–
	Moroyama-mura	–	3.50	4.49	3.54	4.01	2.69		–
V	Kōnosu-shi	–	7.09	4.07	2.89	4.01	2.35		–
	Kisai-machi	–	7.79	4.08	3.18	5.11	2.48	–	–
	Washimiya-machi	–	6.17	3.88	2.70	3.80	2.42	–	–
	Kurihashi-machi	–	6.65	3.49	2.77	2.93	2.61	–	–
	Goka-mura	–	4.60	3.35	2.99	3.96	3.05	–	–
VI	Sakai-machi	–	6.34	4.01	3.47	3.75	3.14	–	–
	Sashima-machi	–	5.29	3.74	3.42	5.52	1.77	–	–
	Yatabe-machi	–	7.12	4.64	3.55	4.30	2.54	–	–
VII	Kukizaki-mura	–	–	4.05	2.29	6.30	1.89	–	–
	Ushiku-machi	–	6.28	4.35	2.95	3.75	2.37	–	–
	Kawachi-mura	–	5.58	4.42	3.51	3.36	2.34	–	–
	Sakae-machi	–	6.33	4.43	3.26	3.73	2.57	–	–
	Narita-shi	–	6.05	4.02	3.26	3.96	2.51	–	–
VIII	Shisui-machi	–	6.67	3.26	3.49	4.01	2.00	–	–
	Yachimata-machi	–	5.18	4.19	3.05	3.45	2.31	–	–
	Toke-machi	–	6.71	4.50	3.16	4.03	2.80	–	–
IX	Nagara-machi	–	11.50	5.20	4.59	5.51	2.28	–	–
	Obitsu-mura	–	5.50	4.61	4.30	3.78	2.74	–	–
X	Koito-machi	–	4.88	5.14	3.46	6.21	3.25	–	–
	Zone 10 Total	–	5.59	4.19	3.03	3.68	2.48	–	–
	Total for 50 km. Region	–	4.60	4.00	2.70	3.50	2.50	–	–
	National Total	–	5.11	4.71	3.06	3.61	2.50	–	–

Note 1: Tatami space per person is derived by dividing the number of tatami by the number of members in each household.

Note 2: Hyphens (-) in columns indicate the absence of information.

N.B.: *The tatami, a floor mat, is also a unit of measure (about three feet by six feet, or approximately 18 square feet) for the interior of a Japanese home.*

TABLE 8. NUMBER OF ORDINARY HOUSEHOLDS BY NUMBER OF HOUSEHOLD MEMBERS

1950

(Zone)	(Sector)	District	Total Number of Households	Households with Members in Column Headings Below										
				1	2	3	4	5	6	7	8	9	10	Over 11
1	I	Chiyoda-ku	(22,931) 100.0	11.4	13.0	16.6	16.4	14.2	10.8	7.2	4.4	2.7	1.5	1.8
		Minato-ku	(50,204) 100.0	11.1	14.6	18.3	17.5	14.3	10.5	6.4	3.6	2.0	1.0	0.7
		Chūō-ku	(35,899) 100.0	12.6	14.1	16.8	16.0	13.1	10.3	7.1	4.4	2.5	1.5	1.6
		Bunkyō-ku	(44,329) 100.0	10.9	14.8	17.8	17.3	14.4	10.9	6.7	3.7	1.9	0.8	0.8
		Taitō-ku	(55,766) 100.0	8.6	13.9	16.9	16.2	14.0	10.9	8.0	5.0	3.0	1.6	1.9
		Zone 1 Total	(209,129) 100.0	10.7	14.2	17.4	16.7	14.0	10.7	7.1	4.2	2.4	1.3	1.3
2	I	Shinagawa-ku	(68,257) 100.0	9.7	14.7	18.7	18.1	14.9	10.6	6.5	3.6	1.8	0.8	0.6
	II	Meguro-ku	(47,668) 100.0	8.9	14.8	18.6	18.0	15.3	11.2	6.8	3.6	1.6	0.7	0.5
		Shibuya-ku	(42,899) 100.0	10.9	15.2	18.6	17.8	14.6	10.4	6.2	3.5	1.6	0.6	0.6
	III	Shinjuku-ku	(57,944) 100.0	10.2	15.2	18.8	17.9	14.9	10.4	6.4	3.3	1.6	0.7	0.5
		Nakano-ku	(52,169) 100.0	11.7	15.3	18.5	17.7	14.7	10.1	6.3	3.2	1.5	0.6	0.4
	IV	Toshima-ku	(51,428) 100.0	10.0	14.5	19.0	17.8	14.9	10.3	6.9	3.7	1.7	0.7	0.5
	V	Kita-ku	(61,356) 100.0	7.6	13.7	18.5	18.2	15.8	11.5	7.2	4.1	2.0	0.8	0.6
	VI	Arakawa-ku	(44,260) 100.0	7.6	13.0	18.0	17.2	15.1	11.4	7.8	5.0	2.6	1.3	1.0
	VII	Sumida-ku	(50,259) 100.0	6.7	12.3	17.4	17.3	15.5	11.5	8.0	5.1	3.0	1.5	1.7
	VIII	Kōtō-ku	(41,091) 100.0	8.5	13.3	18.9	18.1	15.3	10.8	7.1	3.9	2.2	1.0	0.9
		Zone 2 Total	(517,331) 100.0	9.2	14.2	18.5	17.8	15.1	10.9	6.9	3.9	1.9	0.9	0.7
3	I	Ōta-ku	(93,603) 100.0	9.2	14.0	18.5	18.1	15.2	11.0	6.9	3.8	1.8	0.9	0.6
	II	Setagaya-ku	(95,897) 100.0	9.8	14.4	18.2	18.2	15.2	10.8	6.8	3.5	1.8	0.8	0.5
	III	Suginami-ku	(77,065) 100.0	9.4	14.9	18.6	18.3	15.2	10.9	6.6	3.4	1.6	0.7	0.4
	IV	Itabashi-ku	(50,686) 100.0	8.5	13.1	18.2	18.0	15.8	11.5	7.1	4.1	2.0	1.0	0.7
		Nerima-ku	(26,940) 100.0	8.8	12.2	16.9	18.0	15.2	11.5	7.8	4.8	2.5	1.3	1.0
	VI	Adachi-ku	(58,839) 100.0	7.1	12.1	17.3	17.4	15.5	12.3	8.3	5.0	2.7	1.3	1.0
	VII	Katsushika-ku	(53,678) 100.0	6.7	12.9	17.8	17.6	15.8	11.8	7.9	4.8	2.6	1.2	0.9
	VIII	Edogawa-ku	(45,603) 100.0	7.0	11.9	17.2	17.6	15.5	12.3	8.4	5.1	2.7	1.3	1.0
		Urayasu-machi	(3,052) 100.0	4.3	8.1	15.5	16.4	16.5	13.0	11.2	7.1	4.0	2.5	1.4
		Zone 3 Total	(505,363) 100.0	8.5	13.4	18.0	18.0	15.4	11.4	7.3	4.2	2.1	1.0	0.7
4	I	Kawasaki-shi	(67,386) 100.0	6.2	11.9	17.9	18.4	16.2	12.0	8.0	4.7	2.6	1.2	0.9
	II	Komae-machi	(2,097) 100.0	5.8	14.5	15.5	15.8	17.5	11.3	7.2	5.1	3.8	1.6	1.9
	III	Mitaka-shi	(12,533) 100.0	9.9	12.7	16.0	19.0	16.0	11.7	6.8	4.0	1.8	1.2	0.9
		Musashino-shi	(17,090) 100.0	10.0	13.9	17.8	18.5	15.3	11.2	6.9	3.6	1.6	0.7	0.5
		Chōfu-shi	(7,506) 100.0	8.4	11.7	16.8	17.0	15.1	11.5	8.3	4.8	3.2	1.7	1.5
		Hoya-machi	(3,109) 100.0	7.0	11.6	17.4	16.8	16.5	11.7	8.6	4.9	2.7	1.5	1.3
	IV	Yamato-machi	(2,025) 100.0	7.0	10.0	15.1	14.1	17.2	12.7	8.4	7.5	4.4	1.9	1.7
		Toda-machi	(3,523) 100.0	3.9	8.0	14.3	16.4	16.7	14.5	10.9	7.2	4.2	2.6	1.3
	V	Warabi-shi	(6,390) 100.0	7.0	10.2	16.5	19.5	17.3	12.7	7.7	4.6	2.4	1.0	1.1
		Kawaguchi-shi	(26,466) 100.0	5.4	10.2	16.3	17.1	15.9	13.2	9.3	5.8	3.4	1.7	1.7
		Hatogaya-machi	—	—	—	—	—	—	—	—	—	—	—	—
	VI	Sōka-shi	(5,514) 100.0	4.2	8.7	14.2	16.0	15.1	12.4	10.6	7.3	4.8	3.8	2.9
		Yashio-mura	(2,070) 100.0	2.7	5.5	8.9	11.0	14.0	14.1	13.0	10.9	9.5	5.2	5.2
		Misato-mura	(2,652) 100.0	2.6	4.3	7.8	11.5	12.2	14.5	14.3	11.7	9.5	5.9	5.7
		Matsudo-shi	(10,475) 100.0	5.2	9.7	15.7	16.7	15.4	13.0	10.2	6.3	3.9	2.0	1.9
	VII	Ichikawa-shi	(25,340) 100.0	6.3	11.7	16.9	17.3	16.2	12.5	8.6	5.4	2.8	1.3	1.0
		Zone 4 Total	(194,176) 100.0	6.6	11.3	16.8	17.6	16.0	12.3	8.5	5.2	3.0	1.5	1.2
5	I	Tsurumi-ku	(36,861) 100.0	6.0	12.8	18.9	18.6	16.5	11.9	7.4	4.2	2.1	0.9	0.7

Table 8. Number of Ordinary Households by Number of Household Members

(Zone)	(Sector)	District	Total Number of Households	Households with Members in Column Headings Below										
				1	2	3	4	5	6	7	8	9	10	Over 11
	III	Koganei-shi	(4,672) 100.0	8.1	12.5	15.2	17.2	15.7	11.0	8.3	5.3	2.9	1.5	1.3
		Tanashi-machi	(2,989) 100.0	9.6	10.9	15.5	17.7	16.1	12.5	8.2	4.7	2.4	1.3	1.1
		Kurume-machi	(1,440) 100.0	4.6	7.3	11.0	14.0	14.2	14.2	12.0	9.6	6.5	3.3	3.3
	IV	Niza-machi	(2,046) 100.0	5.3	7.0	13.5	13.8	14.6	14.8	11.0	8.4	6.0	2.6	3.0
		Kiyose-machi	(1,498) 100.0	8.3	13.0	14.5	14.9	13.2	10.7	7.9	7.8	4.7	2.1	2.9
		Adachi-machi	(1,911) 100.0	5.1	8.7	15.0	14.4	15.1	14.2	12.6	7.3	4.6	1.8	1.2
		Asaka-machi	(2,884) 100.0	6.4	8.7	12.8	17.4	15.0	12.9	11.1	7.0	3.9	2.8	2.0
	V	Urawa-shi	(26,223) 100.0	5.2	11.3	16.8	17.5	17.1	13.0	9.0	5.0	2.8	1.3	1.0
		Misono-mura	(1,523) 100.0	3.0	5.2	9.2	11.0	13.5	15.6	15.2	10.2	7.9	4.6	4.6
		Koshigaya-shi	(7,498) 100.0	3.1	6.9	11.3	13.8	14.7	14.9	13.4	9.2	6.1	3.2	3.4
	VI	Yoshikawa-machi	(2,719) 100.0	2.5	4.8	8.9	12.7	13.7	15.0	15.4	11.5	7.9	4.0	3.6
		Nagareyama-machi	(3,269) 100.0	3.3	6.1	12.1	14.4	15.3	14.7	11.9	9.4	6.1	3.9	2.8
	VII	Kamagaya-machi	(1,609) 100.0	3.7	8.7	11.9	14.8	13.4	13.4	11.2	7.7	6.8	4.2	4.2
	VIII	Funahashi-shi	(20,483) 100.0	5.1	11.0	16.2	17.2	15.5	12.4	9.2	5.9	3.7	2.0	1.8
		Zone 5 Total	(117,625) 100.0	5.4	10.8	16.1	17.0	16.0	12.8	9.3	5.8	3.5	1.8	1.5
6	I	Nishi-ku	(19,551) 100.0	8.2	14.5	18.7	17.6	15.1	11.2	7.1	4.2	1.1	1.7	0.6
		Naka-ku	(20,608) 100.0	11.7	14.8	18.0	16.9	14.0	10.4	6.6	3.9	2.0	1.0	0.7
		Kanagawa-ku	(23,686) 100.0	6.7	13.1	18.3	18.0	15.5	11.8	7.8	4.6	2.2	1.2	0.8
	II	Kōhoku-ku	(18,315) 100.0	4.8	9.3	15.2	16.1	15.4	13.2	9.9	7.1	4.6	2.4	2.0
		Inagi-machi	(1,931) 100.0	6.9	9.7	13.4	14.8	15.6	12.0	10.6	8.0	3.9	3.2	1.9
	III	Tama-mura	(1,328) 100.0	4.5	7.5	11.8	15.1	15.3	13.5	11.9	9.8	5.3	3.1	2.2
		Fuchu-shi	(8,430) 100.0	6.4	10.7	15.6	17.6	16.1	12.4	8.8	5.6	3.6	1.7	1.5
		Kunitachi-machi	(3,075) 100.0	8.5	12.3	17.1	17.8	15.9	11.8	6.6	5.3	2.4	1.4	0.9
		Kokubunji-machi	(3,787) 100.0	5.1	9.5	14.9	17.4	17.3	13.9	9.1	5.7	3.8	1.6	1.7
		Kodaira-machi	(4,172) 100.0	5.8	10.5	15.9	17.9	15.0	12.2	8.9	5.5	4.1	2.4	1.8
		Higashimurayama-machi	(2,987) 100.0	5.6	8.6	12.5	15.2	15.1	12.9	11.2	7.9	5.5	3.3	2.2
	IV	Tokorosawa-shi	(9,755) 100.0	4.4	7.9	12.9	14.3	15.9	14.3	11.5	8.4	5.0	3.2	2.2
		Miyoshi-mura	(678) 100.0	2.7	4.1	10.0	12.2	13.8	16.8	13.1	11.4	7.8	6.0	2.1
		Fujimi-mura	(1,832) 100.0	2.3	5.9	10.8	11.8	14.7	15.6	13.6	11.7	7.5	3.8	2.3
	V	Yono-shi	(6,170) 100.0	5.5	10.4	17.0	18.7	17.5	13.1	8.2	4.7	2.4	1.4	1.1
		Ōmiya-shi	(23,901) 100.0	4.4	10.0	15.7	17.9	16.6	13.2	9.5	6.0	3.3	1.9	1.5
		Iwatsuki-shi	(6,025) 100.0	3.0	6.1	11.7	14.2	14.4	14.8	12.1	9.0	6.9	4.1	3.7
	VI	Matsubushi-mura	(1,460) 100.0	3.2	4.7	8.2	12.2	14.0	14.2	14.7	10.7	8.8	6.1	3.2
	VII	Kashiwa-shi	(8,834) 100.0	3.5	8.1	13.8	15.7	15.8	13.9	10.3	7.9	5.3	3.0	2.7
		Shōnan-mura	(1,775) 100.0	3.0	5.1	9.1	13.2	13.3	14.7	12.4	10.4	8.8	6.2	3.8
		Shirai-mura	(1,072) 100.0	3.5	7.2	8.5	10.2	13.3	16.5	14.1	10.3	7.6	4.9	3.9
	VIII	Narashino-shi	(4,856) 100.0	5.7	10.9	16.8	18.5	15.8	12.6	9.1	5.2	2.8	1.7	0.9
		Zone 6 Total	(174,208) 100.0	6.2	11.0	16.0	16.8	15.5	12.5	9.0	6.0	3.5	2.0	1.5
7	I	Isogo-ku	(14,295) 100.0	7.9	13.8	18.4	17.8	15.5	11.9	7.5	3.9	2.0	0.8	0.5
		Minami-ku	(31,605) 100.0	7.5	14.4	18.9	17.7	14.8	11.3	7.4	4.2	2.1	1.0	0.7
		Hodogaya-ku	(15,537) 100.0	5.3	11.1	16.9	17.9	15.9	12.6	9.3	5.4	3.0	1.6	1.0
	II	Machida-shi	(10,123) 100.0	4.8	9.0	14.4	15.9	15.6	13.4	9.9	7.5	4.7	2.5	2.3
	III	Yuki-mura	(1,077) 100.0	2.4	5.7	9.0	11.1	14.8	17.6	13.1	10.6	8.6	3.4	3.7
		Hino-machi	(5,014) 100.0	5.5	9.6	15.3	17.1	16.6	14.3	10.2	5.6	3.3	1.5	1.0
		Tachikawa-shi	(11,439) 100.0	8.9	11.7	16.4	18.3	15.9	12.0	8.0	4.6	2.3	1.2	0.7
		Sunakawa-machi	(2,135) 100.0	4.5	8.1	13.0	15.8	13.5	14.3	10.8	7.9	5.2	3.9	3.0
		Yamato-machi	(2,301) 100.0	2.6	7.0	13.1	16.6	17.0	15.5	12.0	7.0	4.8	3.0	1.4
	IV	Ōi-mura	(793) 100.0	3.7	6.1	11.5	12.7	15.4	14.8	12.4	9.0	6.6	2.9	4.9
		Fukuoka-mura	(1,483) 100.0	4.0	9.5	13.8	16.3	16.7	15.4	10.0	8.0	3.4	1.7	1.2

- 250 -

Table 8. Number of Ordinary Households by Number of Household Members

(Zone)	(Sector)	District	Total Number of Households	Households with Members in Column Headings Below										
				1	2	3	4	5	6	7	8	9	10	Over 11
V		Kasukabe-shi	(2,915) 100.0	5.0	8.5	13.7	16.6	15.5	13.9	10.6	7.8	4.2	2.2	2.0
		Shōwa-mura	(2,585) 100.0	3.3	5.8	11.6	13.3	16.5	14.9	12.0	9.5	5.7	3.8	3.6
VI		Noda-shi	(9,520) 100.0	3.6	7.8	13.4	14.9	15.9	14.0	12.2	8.0	5.2	2.8	2.2
VII		Abiko-machi	(4,019) 100.0	4.8	8.9	14.6	14.7	15.8	13.4	11.0	7.0	4.8	2.3	2.7
		Yachiyo-machi	(2,613) 100.0	3.2	6.3	11.4	13.1	15.0	15.0	12.0	10.3	6.9	3.9	2.9
VIII		Chiba-shi	(35,051) 100.0	5.9	11.8	16.4	16.7	15.6	12.4	8.6	6.1	3.3	1.8	1.4
IX		Goi-machi	(3,606) 100.0	3.8	7.8	12.0	13.2	13.8	15.2	12.7	9.4	6.2	3.3	2.6
		Sodegaura-machi	(2,563) 100.0	3.3	8.2	12.0	13.9	16.0	12.7	12.0	10.2	5.6	3.6	2.5
		Zone 7 Total	(158,674) 100.0	6.0	11.2	16.1	16.7	15.5	12.7	9.2	6.0	3.4	1.8	1.4
8	I	Kanazawa-ku	(12,585) 100.0	7.2	12.3	17.7	19.2	16.9	11.6	7.5	3.9	2.3	0.9	0.5
		Totsuka-ku	(13,218) 100.0	3.6	9.8	14.8	16.6	15.6	13.3	9.9	7.1	4.4	2.7	2.2
	II	Yamato-shi	(3,651) 100.0	5.3	10.3	16.5	19.5	14.8	12.2	9.2	5.4	3.6	1.9	1.3
		Sagamihara-shi	(13,135) 100.0	5.1	8.7	14.5	16.8	15.9	12.8	9.9	7.1	4.3	2.8	2.1
		Zama-machi	(2,221) 100.0	3.8	8.8	13.1	16.6	15.0	14.1	11.5	7.5	4.7	2.7	2.2
	III	Hachiōji-shi	(24,498) 100.0	4.5	9.9	15.3	16.5	16.0	13.5	10.1	6.2	3.5	2.1	2.4
		Akishima-shi	(6,971) 100.0	9.3	11.1	17.0	18.2	16.1	11.5	7.5	4.6	2.4	1.4	0.9
		Fussa-machi	(2,823) 100.0	8.7	11.3	15.0	15.1	15.0	12.8	9.2	5.5	3.6	2.1	1.7
		Mizuho-machi	(1,615) 100.0	3.0	6.6	11.9	13.7	15.6	13.1	12.3	10.1	5.4	4.3	4.0
		Murayama-machi	(1,864) 100.0	3.2	6.4	9.9	12.3	15.7	13.6	12.9	11.6	7.8	4.1	2.5
		Musashi-machi	(4,641) 100.0	4.4	7.2	12.5	14.7	16.7	14.1	11.5	9.5	4.6	2.6	2.2
	IV	Sayama-shi	(5,625) 100.0	3.7	7.2	11.7	14.7	15.0	14.8	11.7	9.3	5.9	3.5	2.5
		Kawagoe-shi	(18,712) 100.0	3.4	8.1	13.3	15.4	16.0	14.8	11.4	8.1	4.7	2.7	2.1
		Seibu-machi	(609) 100.0	2.4	5.4	13.0	14.6	14.9	14.8	12.0	9.4	6.6	3.8	3.1
	V	Ageo-shi	(5,822) 100.0	3.5	7.0	12.5	14.3	15.0	13.2	12.2	8.9	6.3	3.6	3.5
		Ina-mura	(1,176) 100.0	2.4	4.8	8.2	11.1	13.7	15.3	13.5	12.1	9.2	5.0	4.7
		Hasuda-machi	(3,076) 100.0	3.3	6.2	10.7	13.2	15.1	14.4	12.7	9.6	7.0	4.1	3.7
		Shiraoka-machi	(2,724) 100.0	3.3	5.7	10.2	12.7	14.1	15.4	12.0	10.3	7.7	5.1	3.5
		Miyashiro-machi	(1,828) 100.0	2.8	6.9	11.4	12.9	14.6	14.2	13.0	10.0	6.5	4.0	3.7
		Sugito-machi	(3,035) 100.0	2.6	6.4	9.3	12.6	14.5	15.9	13.1	10.9	6.6	4.6	3.5
	VI	Sekiyado-machi	(2,315) 100.0	2.6	4.8	8.7	10.2	13.8	14.2	13.6	11.1	10.3	6.1	4.6
		Moriya-machi	(1,803) 100.0	2.9	7.6	11.5	11.8	14.8	15.7	12.8	9.8	6.3	3.4	3.4
	VII	Toride-machi	(3,831) 100.0	4.4	9.4	13.1	16.6	16.0	13.0	11.2	6.9	4.6	2.9	1.9
		Inzai-machi	(3,457) 100.0	3.4	6.8	10.8	13.8	15.0	14.4	13.1	9.2	6.5	3.6	3.4
		Inba-mura	(1,534) 100.0	3.1	5.3	9.5	12.8	18.2	16.5	17.5	8.9	4.8	2.4	1.0
	VIII	Yotsukaidō-machi	(3,532) 100.0	5.9	9.5	14.0	14.6	16.5	13.8	10.6	7.4	4.2	2.2	1.3
	IX	Ichihara-machi	(2,659) 100.0	3.3	8.1	11.8	14.1	15.6	14.4	11.7	9.6	5.7	3.1	2.6
		Anegasaki-machi	(1,733) 100.0	4.7	9.5	14.1	15.2	15.7	12.5	10.9	7.7	4.4	2.5	2.8
		Hirakawa-machi	(2,437) 100.0	4.2	7.2	10.8	11.8	15.7	15.0	13.4	9.2	6.3	3.1	3.3
		Miwa-machi	(2,045) 100.0	2.9	6.1	10.3	12.9	14.4	16.0	13.7	10.7	6.4	4.1	2.5
	X	Kisarazu-shi	(9,970) 100.0	4.8	9.9	14.6	15.8	15.6	13.7	10.4	7.5	3.7	2.4	1.6
		Zone 8 Total	(165,092) 100.0	4.5	8.8	13.8	15.8	15.7	13.6	10.7	7.5	4.6	2.7	2.3
9	I	Kamakura-shi	(19,137) 100.0	7.1	13.6	17.9	17.9	15.8	11.8	7.6	4.3	2.3	1.0	0.7
	II	Ayase-machi	(1,404) 100.0	3.0	6.3	11.5	14.0	14.7	14.0	11.8	9.9	6.7	4.1	4.0
		Ebina-machi	(2,819) 100.0	3.9	7.5	12.8	13.1	14.5	14.3	13.9	9.1	4.8	3.4	2.7
		Shiroyama-machi	(1,004) 100.0	5.1	6.9	13.8	11.8	14.8	14.0	11.3	8.5	6.7	3.9	3.2
	III	Akita-machi	(2,357) 100.0	3.4	6.3	10.9	13.7	14.9	15.1	13.3	9.5	6.4	3.4	3.1
		Hamura-machi	(1,489) 100.0	4.6	7.4	10.3	13.4	15.9	14.3	11.1	9.7	5.5	3.8	4.0
	IV	Hannō-shi	(8,939) 100.0	3.7	8.1	13.0	15.7	17.5	15.1	11.2	8.0	4.3	2.0	1.4
		Tsurugashima-mura	(1,180) 100.0	1.9	5.5	11.3	14.3	15.3	13.7	14.2	10.3	8.0	3.4	2.1

- 251 -

Table 8. Number of Ordinary Households by Number of Household Members

(Zone)	(Sector)	District	Total Number of Households	Households with Members in Column Headings Below										
				1	2	3	4	5	6	7	8	9	10	Over 11
	IV	Hidaka-machi	(2,918) 100.0	3.1	6.6	11.9	12.8	16.9	16.7	12.1	9.8	5.2	3.0	1.9
		Kawashima-mura	(2,913) 100.0	2.0	3.9	7.9	11.2	14.0	14.3	15.4	12.0	9.3	5.2	4.8
	V	Kitamoto-machi	(2,399) 100.0	3.4	6.8	11.9	13.5	14.6	15.8	11.2	10.0	5.9	3.5	3.4
		Higawa-machi	(3,510) 100.0	3.4	7.2	12.4	14.6	15.0	14.0	12.1	8.5	6.1	3.7	3.0
		Shobu-machi	(3,238) 100.0	2.4	5.3	9.3	12.8	14.1	14.9	13.2	11.5	8.3	4.6	3.6
		Kuki-machi	(3,787) 100.0	2.8	7.4	11.7	14.5	14.3	15.0	12.3	10.5	5.4	3.3	2.8
		Satte-machi	(3,917) 100.0	3.1	6.9	10.1	12.6	15.3	14.6	13.5	9.9	6.7	4.1	3.2
	VI	Iwai-machi	(5,951) 100.0	2.3	5.5	8.7	11.8	14.7	15.3	13.6	11.2	8.6	4.7	3.6
		Mitsukaidō-shi	(8,597) 100.0	3.6	6.7	10.9	13.3	14.8	15.5	12.8	10.0	6.4	3.3	2.7
		Yawahara-mura	(1,499) 100.0	3.8	6.7	9.5	12.1	14.8	14.4	13.4	11.5	7.1	3.9	2.8
		Ina-mura	(1,940) 100.0	2.5	4.5	8.5	11.0	14.0	15.9	15.9	13.0	7.5	3.6	3.6
	VII	Fujishiro-machi	(2,605) 100.0	2.8	5.9	10.1	13.6	15.2	17.4	12.9	10.8	6.3	3.2	1.8
		Ryūgasaki-shi	(6,642) 100.0	4.2	9.3	12.9	15.9	15.8	14.9	11.3	7.8	4.2	2.1	1.6
		Tone-mura	(1,760) 100.0	3.9	7.7	9.8	13.9	15.4	14.2	13.5	9.6	6.3	3.1	2.6
		Motono-mura	(994) 100.0	3.8	5.9	10.0	12.4	16.7	15.6	13.9	10.8	6.1	2.7	2.1
	VIII	Sakura-shi	(6,587) 100.0	4.8	8.5	13.8	14.6	15.3	14.0	11.5	8.1	5.2	2.6	1.6
		Izumi-machi	(1,677) 100.0	2.7	5.7	8.5	13.7	14.0	15.2	12.8	12.6	7.8	4.2	2.8
	IX	Shitsu-mura	(1,712) 100.0	3.5	7.0	9.5	12.3	14.6	14.4	12.6	9.8	7.9	5.1	3.3
		Nansō-machi	(3,647) 100.0	4.0	7.8	11.6	15.0	15.7	15.2	12.3	8.4	5.8	2.3	1.9
		Fukuta-machi	(992) 100.0	3.1	8.3	11.8	14.5	14.4	14.0	13.0	9.5	5.8	2.8	2.8
	X	Kimitsu-machi	(2,609) 100.0	3.7	7.4	11.6	14.8	16.7	15.6	11.9	8.6	4.8	2.6	2.3
		Futtsu-machi	(2,990) 100.0	4.1	7.4	11.4	13.7	13.8	13.2	12.5	9.6	6.5	4.4	3.4
		Ōsawa-machi	(2,849) 100.0	5.2	9.3	13.3	13.9	13.9	12.9	12.9	8.6	5.0	3.2	1.8
		Zone 9 Total	(114,062) 100.0	4.1	8.2	12.4	14.5	15.3	14.4	11.7	8.7	5.5	2.9	2.3
10	I	Yokosuka-shi	(53,812) 100.0	6.1	12.0	18.0	18.6	16.4	12.2	8.2	4.7	2.2	1.0	0.6
		Zushi-shi	(8,073) 100.0	6.1	12.7	17.7	19.2	17.4	12.1	7.3	4.0	2.0	1.0	0.5
		Hayama-machi	(3,231) 100.0	5.2	11.8	14.6	16.6	17.0	13.5	9.9	5.0	3.6	1.8	1.0
		Chigasaki-shi	(10,509) 100.0	4.1	10.7	15.2	17.3	16.1	12.4	10.0	6.5	4.0	2.3	1.4
		Fujisawa-shi	(20,098) 100.0	4.7	10.7	16.0	17.3	16.3	12.3	9.5	5.9	3.6	2.0	1.7
	II	Aikawa-machi	(2,545) 100.0	2.4	6.4	11.4	13.8	14.2	14.3	13.3	10.5	5.8	4.4	3.5
		Atsugi-shi	(7,723) 100.0	2.9	7.2	11.9	13.6	15.4	14.6	12.3	10.2	6.1	3.4	2.4
		Samukawa-machi	(2,069) 100.0	3.0	8.2	13.9	15.1	16.6	14.3	9.8	8.0	5.5	3.1	2.5
	III	Ome-shi	(7,856) 100.0	3.7	8.1	13.2	15.5	15.4	13.7	11.5	8.5	4.7	2.9	2.8
	IV	Sakado-machi	(4,202) 100.0	2.8	4.4	10.8	13.9	15.5	15.9	13.7	11.3	6.0	3.4	2.3
		Yoshimi-mura	(2,655) 100.0	2.8	4.6	8.0	11.9	14.3	16.2	15.6	11.6	7.8	4.0	3.2
		Moroyama-mura	(1,853) 100.0	2.5	5.7	10.8	14.4	16.8	15.5	13.0	9.8	6.4	3.2	1.9
	V	Kōnosu-shi	(5,499) 100.0	3.2	7.3	12.4	14.6	15.2	13.8	11.5	9.0	6.1	3.7	3.2
		Kisai-machi	(2,826) 100.0	2.8	5.6	9.1	12.2	15.1	15.1	14.3	10.7	7.3	4.4	3.4
		Washimiya-machi	(1,596) 100.0	2.7	5.3	9.5	12.1	15.8	15.2	13.5	10.3	7.4	3.7	4.5
		Kurihashi-machi	(2,288) 100.0	4.1	7.4	12.8	14.6	15.7	14.8	12.5	7.8	5.6	2.1	2.6
		Goka-mura	(1,523) 100.0	2.0	3.9	5.7	11.2	14.4	13.2	14.1	12.0	9.3	7.4	6.8
	VI	Sakai-machi	(4,112) 100.0	2.9	6.2	9.8	12.1	14.4	14.4	14.0	10.3	7.5	4.4	4.0
		Sashima-machi	(2,550) 100.0	2.5	5.0	8.0	11.6	13.6	14.7	13.0	13.1	9.0	4.6	4.9
		Yatabe-machi	(3,450) 100.0	3.3	7.2	10.7	13.7	16.1	16.2	13.7	8.6	6.1	2.8	1.6
	VII	Kukizaki-mura	(1,088) 100.0	2.4	5.1	7.6	11.4	15.8	15.4	15.0	11.7	8.8	4.0	2.8
		Ushiku-machi	(2,829) 100.0	4.1	8.6	12.6	14.4	15.4	13.6	13.0	8.6	5.2	2.6	1.9
		Kawachi-mura	(2,445) 100.0	3.8	6.5	10.4	11.7	14.1	14.5	12.6	11.2	7.7	3.7	3.8
		Sakae-machi	(1,787) 100.0	3.6	8.1	10.7	14.9	15.6	14.8	11.6	9.0	7.1	2.4	2.2
		Narita-shi	(8,696) 100.0	5.3	9.6	13.6	14.5	15.2	13.8	11.1	8.2	4.5	2.4	1.8
	VIII	Shisui-machi	(1,167) 100.0	4.3	7.4	13.0	14.0	15.8	14.3	12.0	8.2	5.5	2.7	2.8

Table 8. Number of Ordinary Households by Number of Household Members

(Zone)	(Sector)	District	Total Number of Households	Households with Members in Column Headings Below										
				1	2	3	4	5	6	7	8	9	10	Over 11
VIII		Yachimata-machi	(5,370) 100.0	3.8	8.4	13.4	13.8	14.0	14.0	11.1	8.8	5.9	3.2	3.6
		Toke-machi	(1,240) 100.0	4.9	9.7	12.2	14.1	14.2	13.1	11.0	9.0	5.0	3.7	3.1
IX		Nagara-machi	(1,844) 100.0	3.4	6.6	8.4	15.2	15.4	16.3	13.8	9.1	6.2	2.9	1.7
		Obitsu-mura	(1,403) 100.0	3.3	5.7	12.4	13.4	16.1	16.5	11.7	9.7	5.4	2.9	2.9
X		Koito-machi	(1,175) 100.0	2.9	5.6	8.1	14.0	17.2	14.0	15.4	11.3	5.6	3.3	2.6
		Zone 10 Total	(177,514) 100.0	4.6	9.6	14.5	16.1	15.9	13.3	10.4	7.2	4.3	2.3	1.8
		Total for 50 km. Region	(2,333,231) 100.0	7.4	12.2	16.8	17.0	15.4	12.0	8.4	5.2	2.9	1.5	1.2
		National Total	(16,425,390) 100.0	5.4	10.2	14.8	15.9	15.3	13.1	10.1	6.9	4.2	2.2	1.9
		1955												
1	I	Chiyoda-ku	(20,598) 100.0	4.5	13.1	15.2	16.2	14.2	11.5	8.3	5.5	3.7	2.8	5.0
		Minato-ku	(51,577) 100.0	4.8	15.0	17.3	17.8	15.9	11.6	7.4	4.4	2.4	1.5	1.9
		Chūō-ku	(30,239) 100.0	3.8	14.1	15.7	15.9	14.3	11.7	8.4	5.7	3.6	2.5	4.3
		Bunkyō-ku	(48,517) 100.0	4.7	16.0	17.5	17.9	15.6	11.5	7.4	4.0	2.3	1.4	1.7
		Taitō-ku	(56,811) 100.0	3.7	14.7	15.4	15.2	14.0	11.5	8.5	5.9	3.8	2.7	4.6
		Zone 1 Total	(207,737) 100.0	4.4	14.8	16.4	16.6	14.9	11.6	7.9	5.0	3.1	2.1	3.2
2	I	Shinagawa-ku	(81,572) 100.0	5.2	17.0	18.3	18.1	15.5	11.2	6.8	3.7	2.0	1.1	1.1
	II	Meguro-ku	(55,605) 100.0	4.7	16.3	18.5	19.6	16.4	11.0	6.5	3.5	1.7	0.9	0.9
		Shibuya-ku	(52,338) 100.0	5.2	18.2	18.1	18.8	15.4	10.8	6.4	3.4	1.7	1.0	1.0
	III	Shinjuku-ku	(73,937) 100.0	4.7	17.7	18.5	18.6	15.4	10.6	6.6	3.5	1.9	1.1	1.4
		Nakano-ku	(64,755) 100.0	5.4	17.8	19.1	19.2	15.5	10.7	6.2	3.3	1.5	0.7	0.6
	IV	Toshima-ku	(65,804) 100.0	4.6	17.8	18.4	18.5	15.3	10.9	6.6	3.8	2.0	1.0	1.1
	V	Kita-ku	(76,520) 100.0	3.5	15.9	18.3	18.7	16.6	12.0	7.4	3.7	2.0	1.0	0.9
	VI	Arakawa-ku	(50,730) 100.0	3.5	13.9	16.3	17.0	15.8	12.5	8.4	5.3	3.2	1.9	2.2
	VII	Sumida-ku	(57,507) 100.0	3.0	12.6	16.0	16.3	15.2	12.5	8.9	5.7	3.6	2.5	3.7
	VIII	Kōtō-ku	(55,537) 100.0	3.0	13.6	17.4	18.5	16.6	12.2	8.0	4.7	2.5	1.5	2.0
		Zone 2 Total	(634,305) 100.0	4.3	16.2	18.0	18.4	15.9	11.4	7.1	4.0	2.1	1.2	1.4
3	I	Ōta-ku	(123,708) 100.0	4.1	15.5	18.7	19.5	16.6	11.3	6.9	3.6	1.9	1.0	0.9
	II	Setagaya-ku	(113,187) 100.0	4.1	15.5	18.8	20.1	16.8	11.5	6.7	3.5	1.6	0.8	0.6
	III	Suginami-ku	(88,720) 100.0	4.1	16.4	18.6	19.8	16.5	11.6	6.6	3.3	1.6	0.8	0.7
	IV	Itabashi-ku	(66,513) 100.0	3.2	14.7	18.4	19.6	17.0	12.2	7.3	3.9	1.9	1.0	0.8
		Nerima-ku	(38,464) 100.0	3.0	13.8	18.5	20.8	17.1	11.7	7.4	3.8	2.1	0.9	0.9
	VI	Adachi-ku	(68,822) 100.0	3.7	12.3	17.0	17.6	16.7	13.3	8.8	5.0	2.7	1.6	1.3
	VII	Katsushika-ku	(61,153) 100.0	3.4	12.6	17.3	18.5	16.8	12.9	8.4	4.9	2.5	1.3	1.4
	VIII	Edogawa-ku	(52,733) 100.0	3.2	12.8	16.7	18.0	16.8	13.1	8.7	5.1	2.8	1.5	1.3
		Urayasu-machi	(3,115) 100.0	3.1	8.3	13.6	15.7	17.4	13.4	12.2	7.8	4.1	2.8	1.6
		Zone 3 Total	(616,415) 100.0	3.7	14.5	18.1	19.4	16.8	12.1	7.4	4.0	2.0	1.1	0.9
4	I	Kawasaki-shi	(92,540) 100.0	2.7	13.5	18.3	19.8	17.7	12.2	7.7	4.2	2.1	1.0	0.8
	II	Komae-machi	(2,969) 100.0	3.2	13.6	17.8	18.6	17.7	12.4	7.1	4.4	2.7	1.3	1.2
	III	Mitaka-shi	(14,595) 100.0	3.9	14.1	17.2	20.4	17.5	12.1	7.1	4.0	2.0	1.0	0.7
		Musashino-shi	(20,390) 100.0	3.2	15.7	18.9	20.2	17.1	11.6	6.7	3.4	1.7	0.8	0.7
		Chōfu-shi	(9,247) 100.0	3.4	12.2	17.4	19.2	17.6	12.3	7.8	4.8	2.7	1.4	1.2
		Hoya-machi	(4,950) 100.0	3.0	12.7	17.6	20.8	18.5	12.3	7.7	3.8	2.2	0.8	0.6
	IV	Yamato-machi	(2,625) 100.0	4.5	11.0	16.6	18.2	16.4	13.0	9.1	5.8	2.7	1.6	1.1
		Toda-machi	(4,112) 100.0	2.3	8.7	16.8	17.2	18.3	14.5	9.4	6.7	3.1	1.8	1.2
	V	Warabi-shi	(7,313) 100.0	2.9	11.5	16.8	18.9	19.0	13.7	8.5	4.4	2.4	1.1	0.8
		Kawaguchi-shi	(26,667) 100.0	3.0	10.7	16.0	17.6	16.9	13.6	10.0	5.7	3.2	1.6	1.7
		Hatogaya-machi	(2,852) 100.0	2.6	9.6	15.1	17.3	15.7	15.4	10.8	6.9	4.1	1.4	1.1

Table 8. Number of Ordinary Households by Number of Household Members

(Zone) (Sector)	District	Total Number of Households	Households with Members in Column Headings Below										
			1	2	3	4	5	6	7	8	9	10	Over 11
VI	Sōka-shi	(5,918) 100.0	2.5	8.7	13.4	15.2	16.3	14.9	10.8	8.0	5.1	2.6	2.5
	Yashio-mura	(2,087) 100.0	1.5	5.4	7.5	11.3	11.9	15.5	13.8	12.1	9.3	6.0	5.7
	Misato-mura	(2,667) 100.0	1.1	4.1	6.9	10.4	13.0	14.2	15.8	14.4	9.2	6.0	4.9
	Matsudo-shi	(13,376) 100.0	2.8	11.1	15.9	17.2	16.5	13.2	9.9	6.1	3.7	2.0	1.6
VII	Ichikawa-shi	(27,564) 100.0	3.8	12.6	16.1	18.3	17.2	13.1	8.9	5.1	2.6	1.3	1.0
	Zone 4 Total	(239,872) 100.0	3.0	12.6	17.0	18.9	17.3	12.8	8.4	4.9	2.7	1.3	1.1
5 I	Tsurumi-ku	(42,208) 100.0	2.5	13.6	18.9	20.0	17.5	12.4	7.4	4.0	1.9	1.0	0.8
III	Koganei-shi	(6,297) 100.0	3.5	14.3	17.7	20.1	16.8	11.2	7.8	4.3	2.3	1.1	0.9
	Tanashi-machi	(4,032) 100.0	2.0	11.8	17.4	21.3	19.1	12.7	7.3	4.0	2.2	1.4	0.8
	Kurume-machi	(1,841) 100.0	3.0	9.1	14.2	15.7	15.3	13.4	11.0	9.0	4.7	2.4	2.2
IV	Niza-machi	(2,130) 100.0	3.1	7.4	11.7	14.6	16.5	14.5	12.4	8.4	5.9	3.2	2.3
	Kiyose-machi	(2,022) 100.0	5.8	14.9	16.7	18.2	13.4	10.3	8.1	5.7	3.3	1.6	2.0
	Adachi-machi	(2,059) 100.0	3.3	8.7	13.6	17.0	18.3	14.4	9.8	7.4	4.5	1.8	1.2
	Asaka-machi	(3,256) 100.0	3.5	10.4	13.8	17.5	18.0	13.1	9.2	7.5	4.0	1.9	1.1
V	Urawa-shi	(29,826) 100.0	2.9	12.0	17.3	19.4	17.6	13.4	8.3	4.7	2.3	1.2	0.9
	Misono-mura	(1,521) 100.0	2.2	5.5	7.8	10.3	13.9	15.1	15.8	13.3	7.5	4.5	4.1
	Koshigaya-shi	(7,809) 100.0	2.2	7.1	10.7	12.9	15.8	15.5	12.2	10.0	6.5	3.8	3.3
VI	Yoshikawa-machi	(2,543) 100.0	1.3	4.0	7.2	11.3	12.6	15.6	15.8	13.3	9.3	4.6	5.0
	Nagareyama-machi	(3,359) 100.0	1.9	6.5	10.6	14.9	17.0	14.3	13.1	9.4	5.8	3.8	2.7
VII	Kamagaya-machi	(1,800) 100.0	3.4	6.6	12.3	15.4	14.9	14.0	11.4	7.9	5.9	4.6	3.6
VIII	Funahashi-shi	(22,514) 100.0	3.2	11.3	16.4	17.2	16.7	13.3	9.2	5.9	3.4	2.0	1.4
	Zone 5 Total	(133,207) 100.0	2.8	11.6	16.4	18.3	17.1	13.1	8.9	5.6	3.1	1.7	1.4
6 I	Nishi-ku	(22,070) 100.0	4.1	15.9	18.6	18.8	16.5	11.6	7.0	4.0	1.9	1.0	0.6
	Naka-ku	(22,577) 100.0	6.0	15.6	18.8	18.4	14.9	11.3	7.0	4.0	1.9	1.0	1.1
	Kanagawa-ku	(30,489) 100.0	2.9	14.5	18.8	19.1	16.9	12.7	7.4	4.1	2.0	0.9	0.8
II	Kōhoku-ku	(21,967) 100.0	2.4	10.4	15.6	17.7	17.1	13.7	10.0	6.4	3.5	1.9	1.3
	Inagi-machi	(1,948) 100.0	3.8	10.5	13.4	14.9	16.3	14.5	10.8	8.6	4.4	1.7	1.1
III	Tama-mura	(1,274) 100.0	2.5	7.1	12.4	14.8	17.2	15.7	10.8	9.0	6.2	2.7	1.6
	Fuchu-shi	(11,169) 100.0	3.5	11.4	16.8	19.4	17.0	12.9	8.5	5.2	2.7	1.4	1.2
	Kunitachi-machi	(4,894) 100.0	4.7	14.0	17.8	20.4	17.5	11.2	7.2	3.9	1.7	0.9	0.7
	Kokubunji-machi	(5,028) 100.0	2.3	12.1	15.9	19.1	18.5	13.2	8.5	5.2	2.8	1.4	1.0
	Kodaira-machi	(5,286) 100.0	3.4	10.8	16.2	19.5	18.4	12.5	8.5	4.8	3.2	1.4	1.3
	Higashimurayama-machi	(4,251) 100.0	3.0	10.9	15.2	18.6	16.7	13.3	9.3	5.4	3.9	2.3	1.4
IV	Tokorosawa-shi	(10,408) 100.0	3.5	7.9	12.1	15.0	16.4	14.5	12.0	8.8	5.1	2.6	2.1
	Miyoshi-mura	(684) 100.0	1.8	3.7	10.4	8.8	13.2	16.0	14.5	9.6	11.0	5.6	5.4
	Fujimi-mura	(1,845) 100.0	1.5	5.7	8.7	13.6	14.5	16.9	15.0	11.6	7.6	3.1	1.8
V	Yono-shi	(7,313) 100.0	2.7	11.8	16.8	19.8	18.6	13.5	8.3	4.4	2.2	0.9	1.0
	Ōmiya-shi	(28,908) 100.0	2.4	10.7	15.4	18.7	17.7	14.0	9.3	5.7	3.2	1.6	1.3
	Iwatsuki-shi	(6,043) 100.0	2.2	6.1	10.5	13.4	15.6	15.5	13.4	9.7	6.6	3.6	3.4
VI	Matsubushi-mura	(1,448) 100.0	2.4	4.5	7.3	12.2	13.3	15.4	14.7	12.2	8.3	5.7	4.0
VII	Kashiwa-shi	(8,370) 100.0	2.4	9.2	14.3	15.7	17.1	14.5	10.9	6.7	4.3	2.5	2.4
	Shōnan-mura	(1,771) 100.0	1.8	5.2	8.9	11.2	14.1	16.7	13.7	11.8	8.2	4.7	3.7
	Shirai-mura	(1,395) 100.0	2.3	5.7	8.3	11.5	13.8	15.7	14.3	12.3	8.5	3.9	3.7
VIII	Narashino-shi	(6,387) 100.0	3.5	10.7	16.0	19.3	17.8	13.9	9.0	4.7	2.6	1.6	0.9
	Zone 6 Total	(205,525) 100.0	3.3	12.0	16.2	18.1	16.8	13.2	8.9	5.5	3.1	1.6	1.3
7 I	Isogo-ku	(15,113) 100.0	4.2	14.8	18.8	18.1	17.1	12.7	7.7	3.4	1.8	0.8	0.6
	Minami-ku	(37,202) 100.0	4.7	17.0	18.4	17.7	15.8	11.5	7.2	4.0	1.9	1.0	0.8
	Hodogaya-ku	(20,422) 100.0	2.9	12.4	17.9	19.8	17.1	12.5	8.1	4.8	2.4	1.3	0.8

Table 8. Number of Ordinary Households by Number of Household Members

(Zone) (Sector)	District	Total Number of Households	Households with Members in Column Headings Below										
			1	2	3	4	5	6	7	8	9	10	Over 11
II	Machida-shi	(11,233) 100.0	2.5	9.9	14.9	17.2	17.2	13.4	10.0	6.9	4.2	2.2	1.6
III	Yuki-mura	(1,052) 100.0	1.5	5.2	7.0	11.8	17.2	17.8	15.0	11.8	6.3	3.8	2.6
	Hino-machi	(5,443) 100.0	2.6	10.7	15.0	17.9	18.0	15.1	10.2	5.5	2.7	1.5	0.8
	Tachikawa-shi	(13,075) 100.0	4.3	15.1	17.0	18.6	16.5	12.2	7.7	4.3	2.2	1.1	1.0
	Sunakawa-machi	(2,404) 100.0	3.0	8.7	14.2	16.3	14.5	14.3	12.0	7.0	5.2	3.1	1.7
	Yamato-machi	(2,347) 100.0	1.9	7.2	11.9	16.0	16.7	17.2	11.4	9.2	4.4	2.4	1.7
IV	Ōi-mura	(803) 100.0	1.7	6.6	9.5	13.3	16.7	14.3	13.9	10.0	7.3	4.1	2.6
	Fukuoka-mura	(1,521) 100.0	2.1	9.5	12.8	15.6	19.2	15.6	11.6	7.4	3.7	1.4	1.1
V	Kasukabe-shi	(5,805) 100.0	2.1	7.7	11.7	14.0	15.6	15.1	13.1	9.1	6.1	3.0	2.5
	Shōwa-mura	(2,427) 100.0	1.9	6.4	9.5	13.8	14.4	14.7	13.8	11.2	6.8	3.9	3.6
VI	Noda-shi	(9,864) 100.0	2.5	8.2	13.4	15.7	16.4	14.8	12.0	7.5	5.4	2.4	1.7
VII	Abiko-machi	(4,751) 100.0	3.6	9.4	13.6	16.5	16.3	14.4	10.8	6.8	3.9	2.5	2.2
	Yachiyo-machi	(2,679) 100.0	2.9	6.3	9.4	13.4	15.8	15.8	13.6	11.0	6.6	3.3	1.9
VIII	Chiba-shi	(39,269) 100.0	3.4	12.1	16.4	18.7	16.6	12.9	8.8	5.6	2.9	1.5	1.1
IX	Goi-machi	(3,241) 100.0	2.8	8.1	10.8	13.7	15.7	16.3	13.7	8.8	5.2	2.9	2.0
	Sodegaura-machi	(2,464) 100.0	3.5	7.2	11.6	14.1	16.6	15.2	12.4	9.0	6.0	2.7	1.7
	Zone 7 Total	(180,715) 100.0	3.5	12.3	16.3	17.7	16.5	13.1	9.1	5.6	3.1	1.6	1.2
8 I	Kanazawa-ku	(13,403) 100.0	3.3	12.0	17.5	19.6	18.5	13.8	7.5	4.0	2.0	1.2	0.6
	Totsuka-ku	(16,029) 100.0	2.1	9.8	15.1	19.1	17.7	13.4	9.7	6.0	3.6	1.9	1.6
II	Yamato-shi	(5,369) 100.0	7.0	10.8	16.3	19.5	16.4	12.6	7.8	4.6	2.8	1.3	0.9
	Sagamihara-shi	(16,565) 100.0	3.6	10.8	15.6	17.5	17.5	13.2	9.1	6.1	3.5	1.9	1.2
	Zama-machi	(2,507) 100.0	3.8	10.3	13.4	16.4	15.6	14.6	10.5	7.3	4.0	2.3	1.8
III	Hachiōji-shi	(27,520) 100.0	3.1	10.1	14.7	17.7	17.0	14.0	9.9	6.3	3.6	1.7	1.9
	Akishima-shi	(8,091) 100.0	5.5	12.2	16.2	18.1	18.0	13.1	8.2	4.5	2.4	1.0	0.8
	Fussa-machi	(3,792) 100.0	4.5	14.1	16.7	17.1	15.7	12.4	9.0	5.3	2.3	1.7	1.2
	Mizuho-machi	(1,704) 100.0	3.6	6.9	11.1	12.7	15.3	14.4	13.9	10.0	5.4	3.6	3.1
	Murayama-machi	(1,868) 100.0	1.7	5.2	10.0	12.5	15.1	14.8	15.1	12.4	7.2	3.2	2.8
	Musashi-machi	(4,976) 100.0	4.9	7.1	11.2	15.0	16.3	15.2	12.3	8.9	4.8	2.7	1.6
IV	Sayama-shi	(5,660) 100.0	2.9	6.4	11.7	15.0	16.5	15.9	13.0	9.1	5.3	2.5	1.7
	Kawagoe-shi	(19,474) 100.0	2.3	8.3	12.7	15.8	17.2	15.6	12.3	7.8	4.3	2.1	1.6
	Seibu-machi	(1,564) 100.0	2.8	8.7	11.8	14.5	16.1	15.0	13.7	8.3	4.9	2.4	1.8
V	Ageo-shi	(6,328) 100.0	2.2	7.1	12.0	15.3	17.2	14.7	12.4	8.1	5.3	3.1	2.6
	Ina-mura	(1,135) 100.0	2.5	3.3	7.2	11.3	14.6	17.1	13.8	14.4	7.8	4.9	3.1
	Hasuda-machi	(3,217) 100.0	2.1	6.5	10.8	13.6	15.8	15.8	13.4	10.4	6.2	3.2	2.2
	Shiraoka-machi	(2,692) 100.0	2.2	6.3	10.3	12.3	15.3	15.8	13.7	10.3	6.9	3.8	3.1
	Miyashiro-machi	(1,844) 100.0	1.8	5.8	11.8	11.7	15.7	15.8	12.3	11.1	6.5	4.1	3.4
	Sugito-machi	(2,895) 100.0	2.0	5.3	9.0	11.9	14.5	15.7	14.9	12.4	7.7	4.0	2.6
VI	Sekiyado-machi	(2,211) 100.0	1.9	4.6	8.3	10.1	15.0	14.3	15.0	12.8	9.3	4.9	3.8
	Moriya-machi	(2,151) 100.0	3.3	5.6	10.4	13.5	17.8	16.0	11.8	10.0	6.2	3.5	1.9
VII	Toride-machi	(4,086) 100.0	2.9	9.3	13.5	17.4	17.5	13.7	10.6	6.5	4.5	2.2	1.9
	Inzai-machi	(3,201) 100.0	2.6	7.9	10.1	14.9	15.9	15.6	12.5	9.7	5.4	3.4	2.0
	Inba-mura	(1,488) 100.0	2.3	5.4	8.0	12.8	18.2	19.6	16.5	10.6	4.4	1.4	0.8
VIII	Yotsukaidō-machi	(3,422) 100.0	3.2	9.7	13.8	15.3	17.9	14.3	11.9	7.3	3.7	1.7	1.2
IX	Ichihara-machi	(2,649) 100.0	2.4	7.1	11.6	15.4	16.7	15.3	13.4	8.7	4.8	2.9	1.7
	Anegasaki-machi	(2,106) 100.0	3.6	8.1	11.2	15.3	16.7	15.5	11.7	8.1	4.9	2.9	2.0
	Hirakawa-machi	(2,002) 100.0	2.9	5.7	8.3	12.1	15.4	18.3	14.3	10.8	6.9	2.8	2.5
	Miwa-machi	(1,988) 100.0	2.7	6.3	8.9	12.0	15.7	16.7	14.4	12.4	6.2	2.9	1.8
X	Kisarazu-shi	(10,110) 100.0	3.9	9.5	13.4	15.6	16.8	14.6	10.8	8.5	3.9	1.9	1.1
	Zone 8 Total	(182,047) 100.0	3.2	9.2	13.7	16.6	17.0	14.5	10.8	7.2	4.1	2.1	1.6

Table 8. Number of Ordinary Households by Number of Household Members

(Zone)	(Sector)	District	Total Number of Households	Households with Members in Column Headings Below										
				1	2	3	4	5	6	7	8	9	10	Over 11
9	I	Kamakura-shi	(19,536) 100.0	3.3	13.6	17.9	19.8	17.0	12.5	7.6	4.3	2.2	1.0	0.8
	II	Ayase-machi	(1,390) 100.0	2.4	5.4	9.1	12.4	17.5	15.6	14.4	10.7	5.9	4.2	2.4
		Ebina-machi	(2,960) 100.0	2.6	7.1	12.9	14.1	15.2	15.9	13.5	8.9	5.1	2.9	1.8
		Shiroyama-machi	(883) 100.0	2.5	6.9	11.6	14.7	16.3	15.7	11.0	9.3	6.5	2.6	2.9
	III	Akita-machi	(2,460) 100.0	2.3	7.6	10.5	13.7	15.7	16.5	13.8	10.3	5.0	3.1	1.5
		Hamura-machi	(1,838) 100.0	4.4	9.5	12.8	14.1	14.7	13.8	11.5	8.4	5.0	3.2	2.6
	IV	Hannō-shi	(8,340) 100.0	2.5	9.1	13.0	16.1	17.8	16.3	11.3	7.6	3.6	1.8	0.9
		Tsurugashima-mura	(1,196) 100.0	1.1	5.4	11.6	13.0	16.3	15.3	15.8	11.6	6.3	2.5	1.1
		Hidaka-machi	(2,974) 100.0	1.7	5.9	10.6	14.8	18.1	16.4	15.0	9.0	4.9	2.1	1.5
		Kawashima-mura	(2,872) 100.0	1.5	3.5	7.6	11.2	14.6	18.4	16.1	13.2	7.9	3.7	2.3
	V	Kitamoto-machi	(2,577) 100.0	1.8	6.9	12.0	14.7	16.4	15.3	13.6	9.0	4.9	3.3	2.1
		Higawa-machi	(3,556) 100.0	2.7	6.9	12.1	14.0	16.5	15.3	11.6	10.1	5.3	3.3	2.2
		Shobu-machi	(2,794) 100.0	2.3	5.2	8.7	12.2	14.3	15.5	15.3	11.2	8.2	4.4	2.7
		Kuki-machi	(3,991) 100.0	1.9	7.2	12.2	15.2	15.6	14.3	13.6	9.4	6.0	2.6	2.0
		Satte-machi	(4,096) 100.0	2.8	6.3	10.2	11.1	14.8	15.9	14.1	10.8	7.0	3.8	3.2
	VI	Iwai-machi	(5,832) 100.0	1.8	4.8	7.8	12.4	15.3	15.9	15.5	11.9	8.0	4.0	2.6
		Mitsukaidō-shi	(7,220) 100.0	2.8	6.7	10.2	14.3	16.4	17.1	13.7	9.0	5.6	2.6	1.6
		Yawahara-mura	(2,004) 100.0	1.9	5.8	9.6	12.4	14.8	17.2	16.1	11.0	6.9	3.0	1.3
		Ina-mura	(2,130) 100.0	2.3	5.0	7.9	11.1	15.9	17.9	16.5	11.9	6.2	3.7	1.6
	VII	Fujishiro-machi	(2,276) 100.0	2.1	5.7	10.1	13.2	16.2	17.0	14.3	11.7	5.7	2.7	1.3
		Ryūgasaki-shi	(6,554) 100.0	3.0	8.3	12.7	14.9	18.1	16.1	11.9	7.6	3.9	1.9	1.6
		Tone-mura	(1,734) 100.0	3.6	6.9	9.9	12.6	15.8	16.4	14.3	9.6	5.3	2.8	2.8
		Motono-mura	(973) 100.0	2.8	6.3	8.3	15.0	15.2	17.1	15.2	10.7	5.3	3.0	1.1
	VIII	Sakura-shi	(6,663) 100.0	3.3	8.0	13.0	15.7	16.2	15.6	12.0	8.1	4.2	2.4	1.5
		Izumi-machi	(1,697) 100.0	3.0	5.1	9.6	12.7	16.8	15.6	14.7	10.4	6.8	3.5	1.8
	IX	Shitsu-mura	(1,668) 100.0	2.4	6.5	9.8	12.2	14.3	17.1	14.1	10.7	6.8	3.8	2.3
		Nansō-machi	(3,523) 100.0	3.6	7.9	11.2	14.8	17.0	17.1	13.0	7.9	4.4	1.9	1.2
		Fukuta-machi	(1,413) 100.0	3.3	8.9	10.3	12.9	16.9	15.2	14.0	9.0	5.5	2.2	1.8
	X	Kimitsu-machi	(7,564) 100.0	3.1	8.0	10.6	14.0	17.5	16.5	14.1	8.2	4.5	2.3	1.2
		Futtsu-machi	(2,988) 100.0	2.8	7.2	12.3	12.9	14.6	14.6	13.7	9.0	6.3	3.6	3.0
		Ōsawa-machi	(2,744) 100.0	4.7	9.5	11.7	13.7	14.6	14.9	13.1	8.9	5.1	1.9	1.9
		Zone 9 Total	(113,446) 100.0	2.8	8.1	12.2	14.9	16.3	15.5	12.5	8.6	4.9	2.5	1.7
10	I	Yokosuka-shi	(57,154) 100.0	3.9	12.8	17.0	18.6	17.8	13.3	8.3	4.5	2.1	1.0	0.7
		Zushi-shi	(8,314) 100.0	2.5	13.8	18.3	20.2	17.8	13.3	7.2	3.5	2.0	0.8	0.6
		Hayama-machi	(3,148) 100.0	3.4	11.9	15.5	18.9	16.0	14.2	9.1	5.7	2.9	1.3	1.1
		Chigasaki-shi	(11,625) 100.0	2.5	11.0	15.6	19.1	17.3	14.0	9.3	5.5	3.2	1.5	1.0
		Fujisawa-shi	(22,016) 100.0	2.4	11.5	16.1	19.6	17.4	12.8	8.9	5.3	3.1	1.7	1.2
	II	Aikawa-machi	(2,533) 100.0	2.2	5.7	11.4	14.2	16.3	16.7	13.9	9.6	4.5	3.2	2.3
		Atsugi-shi	(8,010) 100.0	2.0	7.4	11.6	14.0	16.1	15.9	13.5	9.4	5.4	2.9	1.8
		Samukawa-machi	(2,050) 100.0	1.3	7.6	12.4	16.5	18.3	15.9	11.2	7.3	4.6	2.6	2.3
	III	Ōme-shi	(9,922) 100.0	2.6	8.0	12.1	15.5	16.4	15.4	11.8	8.5	4.6	2.5	2.6
	IV	Sakado-machi	(4,235) 100.0	1.9	6.0	10.6	13.2	17.4	17.1	13.8	9.4	6.1	2.9	1.6
		Yoshimi-mura	(2,593) 100.0	2.1	4.4	7.3	10.3	15.3	18.8	17.2	11.6	7.2	3.7	2.1
		Moroyama-mura	(1,870) 100.0	2.4	6.2	11.1	13.4	17.3	17.9	13.6	9.0	5.3	2.2	1.6
	V	Kōnosu-shi	(5,614) 100.0	2.1	7.6	11.9	15.3	16.1	14.8	12.5	8.2	5.9	3.2	2.4
		Kisai-machi	(2,716) 100.0	2.1	5.0	8.1	11.2	15.6	17.0	14.8	11.5	7.6	4.6	2.5
		Washimiya-machi	(1,460) 100.0	2.0	4.3	9.5	12.9	16.1	17.1	13.8	10.7	6.6	4.3	2.7
		Kurihashi-machi	(2,314) 100.0	2.6	7.9	12.5	14.7	16.2	14.7	13.0	8.5	5.1	2.9	1.9
		Goka-mura	(1,498) 100.0	1.4	3.6	6.7	10.8	13.2	14.6	15.8	13.0	9.8	5.3	5.8
	VI	Sakai-machi	(3,990) 100.0	2.6	5.9	9.5	11.9	15.0	15.0	15.0	11.0	7.5	3.7	2.9

Table 8. Number of Ordinary Households by Number of Household Members

(Zone) (Sector)	District	Total Number of Households	Households with Members in Column Headings Below										
			1	2	3	4	5	6	7	8	9	10	Over 11
VI	Sashima-machi	(2,494) 100.0	2.7	4.9	7.2	9.4	14.6	14.8	14.9	14.6	9.0	4.5	3.4
	Yatabe-machi	(3,972) 100.0	2.4	5.9	9.8	14.9	17.7	16.9	14.3	9.3	5.2	2.4	1.2
VII	Kukizaki-mura	(1,081) 100.0	2.6	5.0	7.4	10.5	16.1	17.5	15.0	12.0	6.4	4.4	3.1
	Ushiku-machi	(2,891) 100.0	2.4	7.8	11.7	16.6	17.6	14.8	12.4	8.8	4.0	2.4	1.5
	Kawachi-mura	(2,384) 100.0	3.6	6.2	8.7	12.8	14.4	15.4	13.8	11.3	6.8	3.7	3.3
	Sakae-machi	(1,858) 100.0	2.7	7.4	11.1	14.9	15.4	16.6	13.7	8.9	5.3	2.9	1.1
	Narita-shi	(8,514) 100.0	4.0	8.6	13.0	15.1	16.5	15.8	12.2	7.0	3.9	2.2	1.7
VIII	Shisui-machi	(1,131) 100.0	3.1	7.5	10.3	15.3	15.6	16.5	12.7	8.8	5.0	3.4	1.8
	Yachimata-machi	(4,692) 100.0	3.1	7.8	11.8	15.6	16.2	14.4	12.2	9.0	5.2	2.7	2.0
	Toke-machi	(1,241) 100.0	4.3	7.7	11.0	14.4	17.8	15.0	10.4	10.2	5.0	2.3	1.9
IX	Nagara-machi	(1,691) 100.0	2.5	6.4	9.3	15.1	16.2	16.9	14.7	9.8	5.9	2.2	1.0
	Obitsu-mura	(1,358) 100.0	2.9	6.7	10.4	14.1	17.4	16.9	14.3	7.8	5.7	2.6	1.2
X	Koito-machi	(1,154) 100.0	2.1	5.0	8.2	13.7	18.9	16.1	16.2	10.3	4.6	2.5	1.4
	Zone 10 Total	(185,523) 100.0	3.0	9.9	14.1	16.8	16.9	14.5	10.7	6.8	3.9	2.0	1.4
	Total for 50 km. Region	(2,698,794) 100.0	3.4	13.3	16.8	18.1	16.5	12.6	8.5	5.1	2.8	1.5	1.4
	National Total	(17,254,904) 100.0	3.5	10.7	14.5	16.6	16.6	14.2	10.3	6.5	3.6	1.9	1.6
	1960												
1 I	Chiyoda-ku	(19,907) 100.0	7.7	14.6	15.5	16.4	14.4	11.4	7.9	5.0	3.2	1.9	2.0
	Minato-ku	(57,928) 100.0	10.2	17.5	17.4	17.9	14.0	9.9	5.9	3.2	1.8	1.1	1.1
	Chūō-ku	(28,243) 100.0	6.3	14.6	16.4	16.8	14.5	11.5	7.9	5.1	3.1	1.8	2.0
	Bunkyō-ku	(60,202) 100.0	13.0	19.5	17.2	16.4	13.5	9.0	5.4	2.8	1.6	0.8	0.8
	Taitō-ku	(64,388) 100.0	9.3	18.5	16.0	14.7	12.8	10.2	7.2	4.6	2.9	1.8	2.0
	Zone 1 Total	(230,668) 100.0	10.0	17.7	16.7	16.3	13.7	10.0	6.5	3.9	2.3	1.4	1.5
2 I	Shinagawa-ku	(105,988) 100.0	13.7	20.9	17.8	16.6	12.8	8.4	4.8	2.4	1.3	0.7	0.6
II	Meguro-ku	(71,388) 100.0	11.5	19.5	18.0	18.9	14.2	8.6	4.8	2.3	1.1	0.6	0.5
	Shibuya-ku	(70,407) 100.0	14.7	22.0	17.7	16.8	12.7	7.8	4.3	2.0	1.0	0.5	0.5
III	Shinjuku-ku	(105,549) 100.0	17.4	22.2	16.8	15.8	11.7	7.5	4.1	2.1	1.2	0.6	0.6
	Nakano-ku	(91,739) 100.0	14.5	21.3	18.5	17.6	12.8	7.8	4.0	1.9	0.8	0.4	0.4
IV	Toshima-ku	(97,504) 100.0	16.9	23.4	17.2	15.4	11.4	7.3	4.0	2.1	1.1	0.6	0.6
V	Kita-ku	(106,298) 100.0	12.2	20.1	18.1	17.5	13.7	9.0	4.8	2.4	1.2	0.5	0.5
VI	Arakawa-ku	(62,300) 100.0	8.2	17.3	17.4	16.7	14.3	10.5	6.8	4.0	2.1	1.3	1.4
VII	Sumida-ku	(65,166) 100.0	5.9	15.2	16.8	16.8	14.8	11.4	7.7	4.8	2.9	1.7	2.0
VIII	Kōtō-ku	(74,779) 100.0	6.4	16.7	19.4	18.9	15.3	10.1	6.2	3.2	1.8	1.0	1.0
	Zone 2 Total	(851,118) 100.0	12.7	20.2	17.8	17.0	13.2	8.7	5.0	2.5	1.4	0.8	0.7
3 I	Ōta-ku	(167,718) 100.0	10.5	18.4	18.6	19.0	14.3	9.0	5.0	2.6	1.3	0.7	0.6
II	Setagaya-ku	(158,547) 100.0	10.6	18.4	18.8	19.8	14.2	9.8	4.5	2.0	1.0	0.5	0.4
III	Suginami-ku	(118,494) 100.0	9.2	19.7	18.9	20.3	14.9	8.9	4.4	2.0	0.9	0.4	0.4
IV	Itabashi-ku	(98,020) 100.0	9.0	17.0	19.4	20.2	15.0	9.5	5.1	2.4	1.3	0.6	0.5
	Nerima-ku	(72,597) 100.0	6.8	16.2	20.3	22.8	15.8	9.3	4.7	2.2	1.0	0.5	0.4
VI	Adachi-ku	(89,901) 100.0	4.9	14.6	18.6	19.5	16.4	11.6	6.9	3.8	1.9	1.0	0.8
VII	Katsushika-ku	(84,765) 100.0	6.5	15.2	18.9	19.7	15.7	10.7	6.3	3.4	1.8	0.9	0.9
VIII	Edogawa-ku	(71,771) 100.0	7.5	16.0	18.2	18.5	15.5	10.9	6.6	3.4	1.9	0.8	0.7
	Urayasu-machi	(3,383) 100.0	4.0	9.2	14.6	16.7	17.2	14.8	11.3	6.7	2.8	1.7	1.0
	Zone 3 Total	(865,196) 100.0	8.4	17.3	19.0	20.0	15.2	9.8	5.3	2.6	1.3	0.6	0.5
4 I	Kawasaki-shi	(144,742) 100.0	6.9	16.3	19.7	21.1	15.8	9.9	5.3	2.6	1.3	0.6	0.5
II	Komae-machi	(5,792) 100.0	5.1	16.5	21.6	22.4	15.4	9.6	4.6	2.2	1.4	0.6	0.6

Table 8. Number of Ordinary Households by Number of Household Members

(Zone) (Sector)	District	Total Number of Households	Households with Members in Column Headings Below										
			1	2	3	4	5	6	7	8	9	10	Over 11
III	Mitaka-shi	(22,709) 100.0	5.3	17.9	20.6	21.9	15.9	9.3	4.7	2.4	1.0	0.6	0.4
	Musashino-shi	(29,274) 100.0	7.8	19.7	20.5	20.7	14.6	8.6	4.3	2.2	0.9	0.4	0.3
	Chōfu-shi	(15,424) 100.0	4.3	14.7	20.1	22.5	17.0	10.2	5.4	2.9	1.6	0.7	0.6
	Hoya-machi	(11,286) 100.0	2.9	16.3	24.2	24.1	16.0	8.8	4.2	2.0	0.9	0.3	0.3
IV	Yamato-machi	(3,758) 100.0	5.1	13.5	18.2	21.3	17.8	10.3	6.6	3.8	1.9	0.8	0.7
	Toda-machi	(6,616) 100.0	4.7	12.9	20.0	20.7	16.2	11.4	6.9	3.9	1.7	1.0	0.6
V	Warabi-shi	(11,734) 100.0	4.6	14.8	20.9	21.6	16.6	10.8	5.8	2.7	1.3	0.5	0.4
	Kawaguchi-shi	(36,141) 100.0	4.9	13.4	18.0	19.7	16.8	11.8	7.0	4.1	2.1	1.2	1.0
	Hatogaya-machi	(4,595) 100.0	3.5	12.5	21.0	20.5	16.4	11.1	7.3	4.0	2.3	0.9	0.5
VI	Sōka-shi	(7,623) 100.0	3.2	11.4	15.0	18.4	16.0	13.5	9.0	6.1	3.9	1.9	1.6
	Yashio-mura	(2,188) 100.0	2.3	6.0	8.9	12.1	14.3	15.3	13.6	11.3	7.6	5.0	3.6
	Misato-mura	(2,909) 100.0	1.8	5.3	9.0	12.0	13.5	16.1	15.4	11.0	7.5	4.2	4.2
	Matsudo-shi	(18,925) 100.0	4.6	14.6	18.7	19.5	15.4	11.5	7.2	4.2	2.3	1.1	0.9
VII	Ichikawa-shi	(35,107) 100.0	7.2	14.8	17.9	19.7	16.3	10.8	6.7	3.4	1.7	0.8	0.7
	Zone 4 Total	(358,823) 100.0	6.0	15.6	19.4	20.8	15.9	10.3	5.8	3.2	1.6	0.8	0.6
5 I	Tsurumi-ku	(52,309) 100.0	6.9	15.8	19.0	20.8	16.4	10.3	5.6	2.8	1.3	0.6	0.5
III	Koganei-shi	(10,597) 100.0	5.1	16.9	20.6	22.2	16.2	9.5	5.0	2.5	1.0	0.6	0.4
	Tanashi-machi	(7,168) 100.0	2.5	14.6	21.7	24.0	16.8	11.1	4.6	2.5	1.2	0.6	0.4
	Kurume-machi	(4,438) 100.0	2.6	17.7	23.0	20.8	13.5	8.8	6.0	3.8	2.1	1.0	0.7
IV	Niza-machi	(2,888) 100.0	3.6	9.6	15.4	18.8	17.0	12.6	10.3	6.5	3.3	2.0	0.9
	Kiyose-machi	(3,179) 100.0	7.5	16.5	20.0	20.7	13.4	9.0	5.9	2.9	2.2	1.0	0.9
	Adachi-machi	(2,562) 100.0	3.3	10.7	16.0	19.3	17.7	14.1	8.8	4.9	3.0	1.3	0.9
	Asaka-machi	(5,028) 100.0	5.2	14.8	18.2	20.0	15.9	11.5	6.9	3.8	2.1	0.9	0.7
V	Urawa-shi	(37,485) 100.0	4.2	13.8	18.4	21.9	18.0	11.6	6.4	3.0	1.5	0.7	0.5
	Misono-mura	(1,521) 100.0	2.5	5.0	8.5	11.5	13.2	16.6	15.7	12.2	7.6	3.8	3.4
	Koshigaya-shi	(8,983) 100.0	2.8	7.5	12.0	15.1	15.9	15.1	11.8	8.8	5.3	3.3	2.4
VI	Yoshikawa-machi	(2,645) 100.0	1.9	4.3	7.9	12.2	14.4	15.7	15.7	11.8	8.7	3.9	3.5
	Nagareyama-machi	(5,229) 100.0	2.4	9.6	17.1	19.5	17.5	12.8	9.3	5.7	3.0	1.8	1.3
VII	Kamagaya-machi	(2,733) 100.0	3.7	11.0	17.1	18.4	16.3	10.9	9.1	6.0	4.2	1.9	1.4
VIII	Funabashi-shi	(29,533) 100.0	6.6	14.4	17.5	19.0	15.5	11.4	7.4	4.1	2.1	1.1	0.9
	Zone 5 Total	(176,298) 100.0	5.2	14.1	18.1	20.3	16.4	11.3	6.9	3.8	2.1	1.0	0.8
6 I	Nishi-ku	(24,448) 100.0	5.8	17.6	19.6	19.7	16.2	10.5	5.8	2.6	1.3	0.5	0.4
	Naka-ku	(29,451) 100.0	8.8	19.2	19.8	19.0	14.2	8.9	5.2	2.7	1.2	0.5	0.5
	Kanagawa-ku	(39,787) 100.0	5.7	16.9	19.5	20.8	16.3	10.3	5.8	2.6	1.3	0.5	0.3
II	Kōhoku-ku	(32,556) 100.0	5.1	12.9	17.7	21.4	16.9	11.4	7.0	4.0	1.9	1.0	0.7
	Inagi-machi	(2,269) 100.0	5.0	11.2	14.3	18.3	16.7	14.0	10.2	6.0	2.3	1.3	0.7
III	Tama-mura	(1,713) 100.0	3.5	11.5	15.9	16.8	16.5	14.8	9.0	6.2	3.4	1.2	1.2
	Fuchu-shi	(17,629) 100.0	4.7	14.3	19.0	23.1	16.8	10.5	5.6	3.1	1.7	0.6	0.6
	Kunitachi-machi	(7,613) 100.0	6.0	15.9	20.3	22.6	16.6	9.7	5.0	2.1	1.1	0.4	0.3
	Kokubunji-machi	(8,568) 100.0	3.1	15.9	19.2	23.6	16.9	10.6	5.8	2.8	1.2	0.5	0.4
	Kodaira-machi	(1,132) 100.0	3.3	13.7	21.1	24.8	16.8	9.7	5.8	2.5	1.2	0.7	0.4
	Higashimurayama-machi	(9,079) 100.0	2.9	12.9	22.2	24.3	16.0	10.3	5.8	2.8	1.5	0.7	0.6
IV	Tokorosawa-shi	(13,348) 100.0	2.6	11.9	16.1	17.0	16.4	13.5	10.2	6.5	3.1	1.6	1.1
	Miyoshi-mura	(718) 100.0	1.7	5.0	7.5	11.4	15.0	18.5	16.4	10.6	7.5	3.3	3.1
	Fujimi-mura	(2,260) 100.0	2.1	7.7	11.5	15.8	18.0	16.0	12.7	9.0	4.0	1.9	1.3
V	Yono-shi	(9,083) 100.0	3.7	13.7	18.9	22.3	18.2	11.4	6.2	3.0	1.5	0.6	0.5
	Ōmiya-shi	(36,481) 100.0	3.2	11.6	17.7	22.0	18.2	12.5	7.3	3.8	2.0	1.0	0.7
	Iwatsuki-shi	(6,489) 100.0	2.6	7.3	12.0	15.9	16.4	15.8	12.5	7.9	5.2	2.4	2.0
VI	Matsubushi-mura	(1,494) 100.0	2.2	4.9	9.7	11.8	14.0	16.0	16.8	12.5	5.6	3.9	2.6

Table 8. Number of Ordinary Households by Number of Household Members

(Zone) (Sector)	District	Total Number of Households	Households with Members in Column Headings Below										
			1	2	3	4	5	6	7	8	9	10	Over 11
VII	Kashiwa-shi	(13,350) 100.0	3.4	10.9	18.0	21.6	17.2	11.8	7.8	4.3	2.6	1.4	1.0
	Shōnan-mura	(1,906) 100.0	2.3	6.1	8.1	13.8	15.7	18.0	14.8	10.2	6.0	2.8	2.2
	Shirai-mura	(1,412) 100.0	2.2	5.6	7.7	11.5	17.7	18.4	15.4	10.8	5.5	2.6	2.6
VIII	Narashino-shi	(9,364) 100.0	6.8	12.9	18.4	22.7	16.0	11.1	6.1	3.2	1.4	0.8	0.6
	Zone 6 Total	(280,150) 100.0	4.8	14.2	18.4	20.9	16.6	11.2	6.8	3.6	1.8	20.9	0.8
7 I	Isogo-ku	(17,465) 100.0	4.8	15.4	20.4	21.4	17.0	10.9	5.9	2.5	1.0	0.4	0.3
	Minami-ku	(46,118) 100.0	7.0	17.8	19.8	19.5	15.3	10.2	5.6	2.7	1.2	0.5	0.4
	Hodogaya-ku	(33,458) 100.0	3.4	14.8	20.1	23.4	16.7	10.0	5.8	2.8	1.2	0.5	0.3
II	Machida-shi	(15,009) 100.0	3.2	11.3	17.7	20.8	17.2	12.6	7.9	4.8	2.6	1.2	0.7
III	Yuki-mura	(1,058) 100.0	1.2	5.5	8.3	13.5	15.1	21.3	14.7	10.5	5.4	2.5	2.0
	Hino-machi	(10,167) 100.0	3.2	17.2	21.6	20.5	15.7	11.0	5.8	2.9	1.2	0.5	0.4
	Tachikawa-shi	(15,400) 100.0	7.2	16.6	18.1	19.2	16.5	10.7	6.1	3.0	1.3	0.7	0.6
	Sunakawa-machi	(2,933) 100.0	5.7	10.1	15.5	17.6	17.2	13.3	9.0	6.1	2.8	1.6	1.1
	Yamato-machi	(2,757) 100.0	2.4	8.8	14.2	17.6	18.2	14.8	11.4	6.6	3.4	1.6	1.0
IV	Ōi-mura	(874) 100.0	2.4	7.2	11.6	15.6	16.2	15.8	13.7	7.6	6.1	2.4	1.4
	Fukuoka-mura	(4,242) 100.0	2.9	21.0	26.0	19.7	12.9	8.4	4.3	2.6	1.4	0.5	0.3
V	Kasukabe-shi	(6,452) 100.0	2.6	8.5	13.1	15.3	16.6	15.7	12.0	7.3	4.5	2.4	2.0
	Shōwa-mura	(2,477) 100.0	2.2	5.5	10.6	14.5	14.5	16.2	15.3	9.0	6.9	3.0	2.3
VI	Noda-shi	(10,685) 100.0	3.1	8.9	15.1	17.1	17.4	14.8	10.5	6.7	3.6	1.7	1.1
VII	Abiko-machi	(5,505) 100.0	3.3	10.0	15.8	19.5	17.8	12.9	9.3	5.4	2.8	1.9	1.3
	Yachiyo-machi	(4,474) 100.0	2.8	10.0	16.8	20.2	16.6	13.1	9.4	5.8	2.9	1.7	0.7
VIII	Chiba-shi	(52,779) 100.0	6.2	14.6	18.6	21.0	16.0	10.6	6.4	3.6	1.7	0.8	0.5
IX	Goi-machi	(4,101) 100.0	2.7	8.5	12.0	14.9	18.7	17.2	13.0	7.0	3.4	1.6	1.0
	Sodegaura-machi	(2,527) 100.0	3.8	7.5	11.3	16.9	17.8	15.7	13.6	7.4	3.3	1.9	0.8
	Zone 7 Total	(238,481) 100.0	5.0	14.4	18.6	20.2	16.3	11.4	7.0	3.8	1.9	0.9	0.5
8 I	Kanazawa-ku	(15,816) 100.0	4.0	13.0	18.6	22.5	18.6	11.9	6.3	2.9	1.3	0.6	0.3
	Totsuka-ku	(24,913) 100.0	3.0	13.6	19.2	22.5	16.9	11.0	6.6	3.6	1.9	1.1	0.6
II	Yamato-shi	(9,666) 100.0	10.1	12.2	17.3	21.6	15.7	10.6	6.4	3.3	1.6	0.7	0.5
	Sagamihara-shi	(22,187) 100.0	4.3	12.7	18.3	21.4	17.2	11.9	6.8	3.9	2.0	0.9	0.6
	Zama-machi	(3,255) 100.0	4.2	12.9	17.3	17.4	16.9	12.9	9.1	4.6	2.5	1.5	0.7
III	Hachiōji-shi	(32,380) 100.0	3.7	12.0	16.0	19.3	17.6	13.4	8.4	4.9	2.4	1.5	0.8
	Akishima-shi	(10,006) 100.0	6.4	12.7	17.1	21.6	18.3	11.7	6.3	3.4	1.3	0.7	0.5
	Fussa-machi	(5,033) 100.0	10.6	14.0	16.7	19.2	14.9	10.8	7.3	3.3	1.6	1.0	0.6
	Mizuho-machi	(2,220) 100.0	1.9	7.4	11.8	14.5	18.0	14.9	13.0	9.6	4.9	2.5	1.5
	Murayama-machi	(2,010) 100.0	1.7	5.4	10.5	14.6	15.7	18.1	14.6	10.6	4.9	2.4	1.5
	Musashi-machi	(5,938) 100.0	5.8	8.8	12.9	15.3	17.6	15.4	10.5	7.1	3.9	1.6	1.1
IV	Sayama-shi	(6,218) 100.0	2.8	8.7	12.0	16.8	18.7	16.1	11.4	7.4	3.6	1.6	0.9
	Kawagoe-shi	(21,117) 100.0	2.6	9.2	13.9	18.5	18.6	15.6	10.8	6.3	2.9	1.3	0.3
	Seibu-machi	(1,095) 100.0	1.8	11.2	14.2	18.7	19.9	13.5	10.8	5.3	3.0	1.0	0.6
V	Ageo-shi	(7,416) 100.0	2.5	8.9	13.8	18.5	18.5	14.0	10.3	6.5	3.9	1.7	1.4
	Ina-mura	(1,112) 100.0	1.1	3.5	7.1	12.8	15.3	18.3	17.0	12.1	7.6	3.2	2.0
	Hasuda-machi	(3,752) 100.0	2.3	7.7	12.3	16.7	17.0	15.4	11.9	8.7	4.3	2.3	1.4
	Shiraoka-machi	(2,919) 100.0	2.2	7.2	11.0	14.7	16.5	17.5	12.7	8.6	4.4	3.0	2.2
	Miyashiro-machi	(2,019) 100.0	2.4	6.1	13.0	14.0	16.2	15.5	13.5	8.7	5.6	3.3	1.7
	Sugito-machi	(3,036) 100.0	2.0	5.6	9.8	13.1	15.8	16.4	14.6	12.1	5.8	2.8	2.0
VI	Sekiyado-machi	(2,167) 100.0	2.8	4.5	7.2	11.6	16.5	17.5	16.7	12.2	6.4	3.1	1.5
	Moriya-machi	(2,173) 100.0	3.2	7.0	10.5	16.4	17.8	17.8	12.4	8.2	4.2	1.8	0.7
VII	Toride-machi	(4,674) 100.0	4.2	11.0	15.0	19.1	17.7	14.4	8.3	5.2	2.4	1.8	0.9
	Inzai-machi	(3,203) 100.0	3.2	6.8	9.9	16.9	18.0	16.7	13.4	8.1	3.8	2.1	1.1
	Inba-mura	(1,494) 100.0	2.8	6.2	8.8	14.7	20.2	21.2	14.8	7.0	2.7	1.4	0.2
VIII	Yotsukaidō-machi	(3,449) 100.0	3.7	11.4	15.0	21.0	16.2	14.5	9.2	5.3	2.3	0.8	0.6

Table 8. Number of Ordinary Households by Number of Household Members

(Zone) (Sector)	District	Total Number of Households	Households with Members in Column Headings Below										
			1	2	3	4	5	6	7	8	9	10	Over 11
IX	Ichihara-machi	(2,743) 100.0	3.1	9.0	12.6	16.7	18.7	15.3	12.2	6.4	3.2	1.4	1.4
	Anegasaki-machi	(2,214) 100.0	2.7	10.1	12.8	15.7	17.6	17.0	10.9	6.4	4.1	1.4	1.3
	Hirakawa-machi	(2,000) 100.0	2.8	5.8	8.4	13.4	19.6	18.8	14.3	9.6	4.2	2.0	1.1
	Miwa-machi	(1,779) 100.0	3.7	7.0	9.8	15.0	16.8	19.2	14.0	9.0	3.7	1.1	0.7
X	Kisarazu-shi	(10,928) 100.0	4.4	11.3	15.6	18.5	17.6	13.7	9.5	5.2	2.7	0.9	0.6
	Zone 8 Total	(218,932) 100.0	4.0	11.0	15.5	19.3	17.6	13.6	9.0	5.3	2.6	1.3	0.8
9 I	Kamakura-shi	(22,641) 100.0	4.3	15.6	19.5	21.6	17.0	11.0	5.9	2.8	1.4	0.5	0.4
II	Ayase-machi	(1,541) 100.0	4.8	7.3	11.1	13.8	16.4	18.1	12.6	8.4	4.3	1.5	1.7
	Ebina-machi	(3,358) 100.0	3.5	8.6	13.0	17.3	17.2	15.9	11.5	7.0	3.6	1.6	0.8
	Shiroyama-machi	(1,031) 100.0	3.0	8.8	13.7	15.7	19.2	14.8	10.9	7.1	3.3	2.2	1.3
III	Akita-machi	(2,703) 100.0	2.4	8.2	11.9	15.7	17.4	16.3	14.3	7.1	3.6	1.8	1.3
	Hamura-machi	(2,232) 100.0	3.3	11.1	15.2	17.2	17.3	12.7	10.9	6.7	3.2	1.6	0.8
IV	Hannō-shi	(8,891) 100.0	2.5	9.4	14.3	18.6	19.0	15.8	10.7	5.5	2.5	1.1	0.6
	Tsurugashima-mura	(1,280) 100.0	2.0	7.0	10.8	15.8	19.2	16.2	13.7	7.9	5.7	1.2	0.5
	Hidaka-machi	(3,169) 100.0	2.2	7.0	11.7	17.9	18.6	17.8	13.3	6.6	2.9	1.3	0.7
	Kawashima-mura	(2,819) 100.0	1.2	3.8	7.0	12.5	18.4	21.5	16.5	10.6	5.3	2.0	1.2
V	Kitamoto-machi	(2,985) 100.0	2.2	8.0	13.9	17.5	17.0	15.3	12.4	6.2	4.2	2.0	1.3
	Higawa-machi	(4,112) 100.0	2.8	8.7	13.2	17.5	17.5	14.2	12.1	7.3	3.6	1.6	1.5
	Shobu-machi	(2,817) 100.0	2.5	5.6	8.4	12.7	16.6	18.3	16.5	9.7	6.0	2.4	1.3
	Kuki-machi	(4,389) 100.0	2.2	7.7	11.1	16.7	18.2	15.6	12.9	8.0	4.0	2.2	1.4
	Satte-machi	(4,145) 100.0	2.4	6.6	10.7	13.3	16.8	17.5	14.4	9.0	5.0	2.6	1.7
VI	Iwai-machi	(5,866) 100.0	2.2	4.9	8.7	13.5	17.7	17.6	15.8	10.3	5.8	2.2	1.3
	Mitsukaidō-shi	(7,310) 100.0	3.1	7.6	11.9	16.4	19.0	17.2	12.9	6.9	3.3	1.1	0.6
	Yawahara-mura	(1,983) 100.0	2.3	5.0	9.5	15.2	19.7	19.0	15.4	8.9	3.1	1.4	0.5
	Ina-mura	(2,150) 100.0	2.3	5.2	8.8	13.4	18.7	20.1	16.1	9.1	4.0	1.7	0.6
VII	Fujishiro-machi	(2,348) 100.0	2.5	5.7	11.5	16.1	17.2	17.7	13.0	10.0	4.2	1.4	0.7
	Ryūgasaki-shi	(6,798) 100.0	3.7	9.4	13.8	17.1	18.9	15.9	10.8	5.5	2.9	1.0	1.0
	Tone-mura	(1,717) 100.0	3.5	6.9	10.4	13.6	16.4	18.0	16.1	7.8	3.8	2.0	1.5
	Motono-mura	(960) 100.0	2.7	5.8	9.4	14.0	17.8	20.3	14.9	8.6	4.5	1.8	0.2
VIII	Sakura-shi	(7,348) 100.0	3.9	8.8	13.4	17.8	17.5	16.2	10.6	6.5	3.2	1.2	0.9
	Izumi-machi	(1,718) 100.0	2.3	6.5	9.7	15.2	18.5	18.3	13.4	8.3	4.9	2.0	0.9
IX	Shitsu-mura	(1,711) 100.0	3.1	6.8	10.2	14.3	17.1	17.2	15.1	8.1	4.9	1.9	1.3
	Nansō-machi	(3,504) 100.0	4.9	8.8	11.4	17.0	18.2	17.7	11.8	6.0	2.7	1.1	0.4
	Fukuta-machi	(1,420) 100.0	3.7	9.6	10.9	14.8	18.7	15.3	14.3	6.4	3.6	1.6	1.1
X	Kimitsu-machi	(2,551) 100.0	3.1	8.2	12.0	16.5	18.9	17.3	13.1	6.1	3.3	0.9	0.6
	Futtsu-machi	(3,081) 100.0	2.9	7.2	12.7	14.0	17.4	15.8	13.4	7.9	4.6	2.5	1.6
	Ōsawa-machi	(2,750) 100.0	5.1	9.6	11.8	14.8	16.2	15.7	12.2	8.2	3.8	1.7	0.9
	Zone 9 Total	(121,333) 100.0	3.2	9.2	13.3	17.2	17.8	15.6	11.6	6.5	3.3	1.4	0.9
10 I	Yokosuka-shi	(62,871) 100.0	5.5	14.0	18.1	20.7	17.7	12.2	6.5	3.1	1.4	0.5	0.3
	Zushi-shi	(9,286) 100.0	4.3	15.2	19.1	22.3	17.7	11.0	6.2	2.4	1.2	0.4	0.2
	Hayama-machi	(3,483) 100.0	4.5	13.8	16.3	20.4	16.7	12.9	8.3	4.0	1.7	0.7	0.7
	Chigasaki-shi	(15,005) 100.0	3.1	12.5	18.3	21.6	17.8	12.4	7.2	3.8	1.9	0.9	0.5
	Fujisawa-shi	(27,233) 100.0	3.8	13.1	18.2	21.9	17.2	11.5	6.9	3.9	2.0	0.9	0.6
II	Aikawa-machi	(2,620) 100.0	2.7	7.2	12.7	16.0	17.8	18.8	12.7	6.6	3.3	1.4	0.8
	Atsugi-shi	(8,884) 100.0	2.3	8.3	13.9	16.5	17.1	15.7	12.4	7.2	3.9	1.5	1.2
	Samukawa-machi	(2,175) 100.0	2.6	7.2	11.9	19.1	19.6	16.3	11.3	6.4	2.9	1.7	1.0
III	Ōme-shi	(10,936) 100.0	2.6	9.6	13.9	18.1	17.4	15.0	10.9	6.4	3.3	1.6	1.2

Table 8. Number of Ordinary Households by Number of Household Members

(Zone) (Sector)	District	Total Number of Households	Households with Members in Column Headings Below										
			1	2	3	4	5	6	7	8	9	10	Over 11
IV	Sakado-machi	(4,454) 100.0	2.4	6.7	11.4	16.6	18.9	17.2	12.2	8.3	3.5	1.9	0.9
	Yoshimi-mura	(2,551) 100.0	1.6	3.7	7.8	11.2	18.3	20.4	17.8	9.6	5.7	2.5	1.4
	Moroyama-mura	(1,916) 100.0	2.6	7.4	10.3	16.3	19.4	17.0	14.2	7.3	3.3	1.7	0.5
V	Kōnosu-shi	(6,118) 100.0	2.3	8.5	13.8	17.7	17.7	15.1	10.2	6.9	4.4	1.9	1.5
	Kisai-machi	(2,724) 100.0	2.2	5.2	8.7	14.1	17.0	18.4	14.8	9.4	6.4	2.5	1.3
	Washimiya-machi	(1,495) 100.0	1.5	6.0	8.7	15.2	19.7	18.2	13.8	8.0	4.3	2.7	1.9
	Kurihashi-machi	(2,492) 100.0	3.3	7.8	12.5	17.5	17.3	14.9	12.5	7.6	3.8	1.3	1.5
	Goka-mura	(1,501) 100.0	2.2	3.9	8.2	10.8	13.9	17.4	16.9	12.6	7.1	4.3	2.7
VI	Sakai-machi	(4,024) 100.0	2.6	6.9	9.6	13.6	16.3	16.5	14.7	9.8	5.6	2.6	1.8
	Sashima-machi	(2,503) 100.0	2.4	5.6	6.8	11.2	16.5	17.3	16.3	13.2	6.2	2.9	1.6
	Yatabe-machi	(3,967) 100.0	2.8	6.2	10.5	17.0	19.9	19.2	14.0	6.3	2.7	1.1	0.3
VII	Kukizaki-mura	(1,104) 100.0	2.4	4.8	7.6	12.7	17.2	18.8	16.4	11.1	5.2	2.3	1.5
	Ushiku-machi	(3,192) 100.0	3.0	8.6	12.4	19.3	18.9	15.5	11.2	6.6	3.0	1.0	0.5
	Kawachi-mura	(2,402) 100.0	3.2	6.6	9.6	15.8	16.9	15.7	15.2	9.0	4.7	1.8	1.5
	Sakae-machi	(1,827) 100.0	2.7	7.6	10.0	14.8	19.5	17.6	13.2	8.3	3.9	1.7	0.7
	Narita-shi	(8,720) 100.0	4.0	10.0	14.1	17.6	17.9	15.5	10.1	5.9	2.9	1.2	0.8
VIII	Shisui-machi	(1,170) 100.0	3.7	7.8	10.9	15.6	17.4	18.4	12.5	7.5	3.9	1.5	0.8
	Yachimata-machi	(4,964) 100.0	3.3	8.8	13.2	17.7	17.7	15.7	10.8	6.7	3.4	1.5	1.2
	Toke-machi	(1,364) 100.0	4.3	9.5	12.9	16.9	18.2	15.2	11.1	7.1	3.2	0.7	0.9
IX	Nagara-machi	(1,674) 100.0	3.5	6.9	9.5	14.5	18.7	19.0	15.0	8.1	3.5	1.0	0.3
	Obitsu-mura	(1,321) 100.0	2.6	8.3	10.3	14.3	19.3	16.2	14.2	8.6	3.8	2.0	0.4
X	Koito-machi	(1,147) 100.0	1.7	6.3	11.0	16.0	18.2	19.6	16.2	6.3	3.2	1.2	0.3
	Zone 10 Total	(205,123) 100.0	3.9	11.2	15.5	19.2	17.7	13.9	9.2	5.0	2.6	1.1	0.7
	Total for 50 km. Region	(3,546,122) 100.0	7.9	16.2	17.9	19.0	15.4	10.5	6.3	3.4	1.8	0.9	0.7
	National Total	(19,678,263) 100.0	5.2	12.7	15.9	18.8	17.3	13.1	8.5	4.3	2.3	1.1	0.8

TABLE 9. MEDIAN NUMBER OF HOUSEHOLD MEMBERS IN ORDINARY HOUSEHOLDS

(Zone)	(Sector)	District	1950 Persons	1955 Persons	1960 Persons	(Zone)	(Sector)	District	1950 Persons	1955 Persons	1960 Persons
1	I	Chiyoda-ku	3.53	4.24	3.79	5	I	Tsurumi-ku	3.67	3.57	3.40
		Minato-ku	3.35	3.73	3.27		III	Koganei-shi	3.82	3.72	3.31
		Chūō-ku	3.41	4.02	3.77			Tanashi-machi	3.78	3.89	3.47
		Bunkyō-ku	3.37	3.66	3.02			Kurume-machi	4.92	3.52	4.53
		Taitō-ku	3.66	4.07	3.42		IV	Niza-machi	4.71	4.80	4.15
		Zone 1 Total	3.46	3.87	3.34			Kiyose-machi	3.96	3.70	3.29
								Adachi-machi	4.45	4.40	4.04
2	I	Shinagawa-ku	3.38	3.52	2.87			Asaka-machi	4.31	4.38	3.59
	II	Meguro-ku	3.42	3.54	3.05		V	Urawa-shi	3.95	3.92	3.63
		Shibuya-ku	3.30	2.94	2.67			Misono-mura	5.53	5.70	5.52
	III	Shinjuku-ku	3.33	3.48	2.62			Koshigaya-shi	5.01	5.34	4.79
		Nakano-ku	3.25	3.40	2.77		VI	Yoshikawa-machi	5.68	6.00	5.59
	IV	Toshima-ku	3.38	3.50	2.56			Nagareyama-machi	4.93	4.95	4.08
	V	Kita-ku	3.52	3.79	2.95		VII	Kamagaya-machi	4.82	4.80	3.99
	VI	Arakawa-ku	3.67	3.95	3.42		VIII	Funahashi-shi	4.04	4.15	3.61
	VII	Sumida-ku	3.78	4.13	3.72			Zone 5 Total	4.04	4.10	3.62
	VIII	Kōtō-ku	3.51	3.87	3.39						
		Zone 2 Total	3.45	3.62	2.96	6	I	Nishi-ku	3.47	3.58	3.36
								Naka-ku	3.32	3.28	3.11
3	I	Ōta-ku	3.46	3.60	3.13			Kanagawa-ku	3.66	3.73	3.38
	II	Setagaya-ku	3.42	3.58	3.12		II	Kōhoku-ku	4.30	4.21	3.67
	III	Suginami-ku	3.39	3.55	3.80			Inagi-machi	4.34	4.46	4.08
	IV	Itabashi-ku	3.56	3.70	3.21		III	Tama-mura	4.72	4.78	4.14
		Nerima-ku	3.67	3.71	3.36			Fuchu-shi	3.98	4.02	3.52
	VI	Adachi-ku	3.78	3.97	3.61			Kunitachi-machi	3.68	3.66	3.34
	VII	Katsushika-ku	3.71	3.90	3.48			Kokubunji-machi	4.18	4.04	3.50
	VIII	Edogawa-ku	3.79	3.97	3.45			Kodaira-machi	3.99	4.00	3.48
		Urayasu-machi	4.35	4.54	4.32			Higashimurayama-machi	4.54	4.14	3.50
		Zone 3 Total	3.56	3.71	3.26		IV	Tokorosawa-shi	4.66	4.70	4.14
								Miyoshi-mura	5.56	5.77	5.51
4	I	Kawasaki-shi	3.76	3.74	3.33			Fujimi-mura	5.28	5.34	4.71
	II	Komae-machi	3.90	3.82	3.31		V	Yono-shi	3.92	5.00	3.61
	III	Mitaka-shi	3.60	3.73	3.28			Ōmiya-shi	4.12	4.16	3.80
		Musashino-shi	3.45	3.61	3.10			Iwatsuki-shi	5.05	5.46	4.75
		Chōfu-shi	3.77	3.88	·3.49		VI	Matsubushi-mura	5.55	5.67	5.46
		Hoya-machi	3.85	3.80	3.27		VII	Kashiwa-shi	4.56	4.49	3.85
	IV	Yamato-machi	4.18	3.99	3.61			Shōnan-mura	5.44	5.53	5.22
		Toda-machi	4.44	4.40	3.60			Shirai-mura	5.45	5.54	5.28
	V	Warabi-shi	4.95	4.00	3.85		VIII	Narashino-shi	3.90	4.03	3.53
		Kawaguchi-shi	4.06	4.15	3.70			Zone 6 Total	4.00	4.03	3.60
		Hatogaya-machi	—	4.35	3.63						
	VI	Sōka-shi	4.41	4.63	4.13	7	I	Isogo-ku	3.56	3.67	3.45
		Yashio-mura	5.57	5.81	5.41			Minami-ku	3.53	3.57	3.28
		Misato-mura	5.80	6.02	5.42			Hodogaya-ku	3.93	3.85	3.46
		Matsudo-shi	4.17	4.18	3.35		II	Machida-shi	4.38	4.29	3.85
	VII	Ichikawa-shi	3.87	3.92	3.51		III	Yuki-mura	5.41	5.41	5.30
		Zone 4 Total	3.87	3.48	3.43			Hino-machi	5.18	4.22	3.37
								Tachikawa-shi	3.71	3.74	3.53

Table 9. Median number of Household Members in Ordinary Households

(Zone)	(Sector)	District	1950 Persons	1955 Persons	1960 Persons	(Zone)	(Sector)	District	1950 Persons	1955 Persons	1960 Persons
	III	Sunakawa-machi	4.63	4.54	4.50			Shiroyama-machi	4.85	4.88	4.46
		Yamato-machi	4.63	4.53	4.39		III	Akita-machi	5.06	5.01	4.68
	IV	Ōi-mura	5.03	5.10	4.82			Hamura-machi	4.90	4.63	4.02
		Fukuoka-mura	4.39	4.19	3.00		IV	Hannō-shi	4.54	4.52	4.27
	V	Kasukabe-shi	4.40	4.93	4.63			Tsurugashima-mura	5.13	5.17	4.75
		Shōwa-mura	4.97	5.22	5.17			Hidaka-machi	4.93	4.94	4.61
	VI	Noda-shi	4.64	4.62	4.86			Kawashima-mura	5.68	5.63	5.35
	VII	Abiko-machi	4.44	4.43	4.08		V	Kitamoto-machi	4.99	4.89	4.49
		Yachiyo-machi	5.09	5.12	4.01			Higawa-machi	4.83	4.86	4.45
	VIII	Chiba-shi	3.96	3.97	3.51			Shobu-machi	5.43	5.47	5.13
	IX	Goi-machi	4.96	4.93	4.64			Kuki-machi	4.95	4.87	4.56
		Sodegaura-machi	4.79	4.82	4.59			Satte-machi	5.17	5.31	5.01
		Zone 7 Total	3.99	4.01	3.60		VI	Iwai-machi	5.46	5.50	5.16
								Mitsukaidō-shi	5.03	4.97	4.85
8	I	Kanazawa-ku	3.67	3.88	3.64			Yawahara-mura	5.22	5.25	4.90
		Totsuka-ku	4.32	4.22	3.63			Ina-mura	5.59	5.44	5.08
	II	Yamato-shi	3.92	4.82	3.48		VII	Fujishiro-machi	5.15	5.16	4.82
		Sagamihara-shi	4.31	4.15	3.69			Ryūgasaki-shi	4.49	4.50	4.32
		Zama-machi	4.52	4.36	3.93			Tone-mura	4.95	5.08	4.96
	III	Hachiōji-shi	4.24	4.05	3.94			Motono-mura	5.08	5.20	5.02
		Akishima-shi	3.70	3.88	3.64		VIII	Sakura-shi	4.54	4.62	4.35
		Fussa-machi	3.99	3.86	3.45			Izumi-machi	5.37	5.16	4.88
		Mizuho-machi	4.95	5.03	4.80		IX	Shitsu-mura	5.13	5.31	4.90
		Murayama-machi	5.19	5.37	5.12			Nansō-machi	4.74	4.74	4.43
		Musashi-machi	4.67	4.70	4.41			Fukuta-machi	4.51	4.86	4.59
	IV	Sayama-shi	4.85	3.76	4.52		X	Kimitsu-machi	4.75	4.60	4.54
		Kawagoe-shi	4.61	4.64	4.34			Futtsu-machi	4.73	5.01	4.76
		Seibu-machi	4.98	5.16	4.21			Ōsawa-machi	4.66	4.70	4.50
	V	Ageo-shi	4.84	4.38	4.41			Zone 9 Total	4.71	4.74	4.41
		Ina-mura	5.65	5.65	5.56						
		Hasuda-machi	5.09	5.07	4.65	10	I	Yokosuka-shi	3.75	3.87	3.60
		Shiraoka-machi	5.26	5.23	4.90			Zushi-shi	3.05	3.77	3.58
		Miyashiro-machi	5.10	5.17	4.89			Hayama-machi	4.99	4.02	3.57
		Sugito-machi	5.29	5.60	5.22			Chigasaki-shi	4.13	4.17	3.74
	VI	Sekiyado-machi	5.70	5.71	5.42			Fujisawa-shi	4.09	4.02	3.70
		Moriya-machi	5.06	4.71	4.73		II	Aikawa-machi	5.12	5.01	4.64
	VII	Toride-machi	4.43	4.40	4.04			Atsugi-shi	4.90	4.92	4.66
		Inzai-machi	5.50	4.51	4.73			Samukawa-machi	5.54	4.67	4.47
		Inba-mura	5.07	5.13	4.87		III	Ōme-shi	4.62	4.72	4.34
	VIII	Yotsukaidō-machi	4.36	4.45	4.95		IV	Sakado-machi	5.01	5.05	4.68
	IX	Ichihara-machi	4.81	4.81	4.46			Yoshimi-mura	5.52	5.57	5.30
		Anegasaki-machi	4.42	4.72	4.50			Moroyama-mura	4.98	4.99	4.69
		Hirakawa-machi	5.02	5.31	5.00		V	Kōnosu-shi	4.82	4.82	4.44
		Miwa-machi	5.22	5.27	4.86			Kisai-machi	5.14	5.47	5.16
		Kisarazu-shi	4.30	4.41	3.01			Washimiya-machi	5.31	5.31	4.95
		Zone 8 Total	4.45	4.86	3.77			Kurihashi-machi	4.71	4.76	4.52
								Goka-mura	5.97	5.99	5.64
9	I	Kamakura-shi	3.63	3.48	3.70		VI	Sakai-machi	5.34	5.33	5.06
	II	Ayase-machi	5.05	5.21	4.79			Sashima-machi	5.63	5.76	5.43
		Ebina-machi	4.88	4.88	4.44			Yatabe-machi	4.94	4.25	4.68

Table 9. Median number of Household Members in Ordinary Households

(Zone) (Sector)	District	1950 Persons	1955 Persons	1960 Persons	(Zone) (Sector)	District	1950 Persons	1955 Persons	1960 Persons
VII	Kukizaki-mura	5.51	5.45	5.28	X	Nagara-machi	4.97	5.03	4.84
	Ushiku-machi	4.67	4.65	4.36		Obitsu-mura	4.93	4.92	4.75
	Kawachi-mura	5.25	5.28	4.59	XI	Koito-machi	5.17	5.08	4.82
	Sakae-machi	4.82	4.90	4.76		Zone 10 Total	4.39	4.37	4.02
	Narita-shi	4.46	4.57	4.24					
VIII	Shisui-machi	5.89	4.89	4.70		Total for 50 km. Region	3.79	3.87	3.42
	Yachimata-machi	4.78	4.72	4.40					
	Toke-machi	4.10	4.72	4.35		National Total	4.24	4.31	3.87

Note: The figures are rounded to two decimal places.

TABLE 10. LABOR FORCE, 15 YEARS AND OLDER, BY SEX
(FOR 1950 ONLY, 14 YEAR-OLDS ARE INCLUDED)

1950

(Zone)	(Sector)	District	Total	Labor Force Employed	Labor Force Unemployed	Non-Labor Population	Total	Labor Force Employed M	Labor Force Employed F	Labor Force Unemployed M	Labor Force Unemployed F	Non-Labor Population M	Non-Labor Population F
1	I	Chiyoda-ku	(83,364) 100.0	59.8	1.2	39.0	100.0	42.4	17.4	0.9	0.3	9.2	29.8
		Minato-ku	(157,778) 100.0	55.5	1.8	42.7	100.0	39.7	15.8	1.2	0.6	9.0	33.7
		Chūō-ku	(121,992) 100.0	60.2	1.8	38.0	100.0	42.2	18.0	0.9	0.9	7.6	30.4
		Bunkyō-ku	(139,864) 100.0	53.1	1.9	45.0	100.0	38.0	15.1	1.3	0.6	10.9	34.1
		Taitō-ku	(191,626) 100.0	59.2	1.6	39.2	100.0	42.0	17.2	1.0	0.6	8.1	31.1
		Zone 1 Total	(694,624) 100.0	57.6	1.6	40.8	100.0	40.8	16.8	1.0	0.6	8.9	31.9
2	I	Shinagawa-ku	(205,187) 100.0	53.4	2.2	44.4	100.0	39.6	13.8	1.5	0.7	9.2	35.2
	II	Meguro-ku	(146,637) 100.0	49.3	2.2	48.5	100.0	37.0	12.3	1.5	0.7	11.8	36.7
		Shibuya-ku	(131,973) 100.0	51.7	2.1	46.2	100.0	36.9	14.8	1.5	0.6	10.8	35.4
	III	Shinjuku-ku	(178,873) 100.0	54.0	2.2	43.8	100.0	37.9	16.1	1.5	0.7	10.2	33.6
		Nakano-ku	(153,639) 100.0	48.2	2.5	49.3	100.0	35.9	12.3	1.7	0.8	12.5	36.8
	IV	Toshima-ku	(154,767) 100.0	50.8	2.2	47.0	100.0	37.4	13.4	1.5	0.7	11.4	35.6
	V	Kita-ku	(186,554) 100.0	52.4	2.4	45.2	100.0	39.0	13.4	1.6	0.8	9.7	35.5
	VI	Arakawa-ku	(139,213) 100.0	57.2	1.9	40.9	100.0	42.0	15.2	1.3	0.6	7.7	33.2
	VII	Sumida-ku	(165,489) 100.0	59.3	1.4	39.3	100.0	43.1	16.2	1.0	0.4	7.3	32.0
	VIII	Kōtō-ku	(125,150) 100.0	57.9	1.8	40.3	100.0	45.5	12.4	1.2	0.6	7.0	33.3
		Zone 2 Total	(1,587,482) 100.0	53.4	2.1	44.5	100.0	39.4	14.0	1.4	0.7	9.8	34.7
3	I	Ōta-ku	(279,185) 100.0	51.4	2.1	46.5	100.0	39.5	11.9	1.5	0.6	9.7	36.8
	II	Setagaya-ku	(279,880) 100.0	46.7	2.3	51.0	100.0	35.1	11.6	1.6	0.7	12.8	38.2
	III	Suginami-ku	(234,664) 100.0	47.4	2.0	50.6	100.0	35.5	11.9	1.5	0.5	12.9	37.7
	IV	Itabashi-ku	(150,387) 100.0	51.9	2.3	45.8	100.0	39.1	12.8	1.6	0.7	9.4	36.4
		Nerima-ku	(86,942) 100.0	52.0	1.8	46.2	100.0	36.0	16.0	1.3	0.5	11.8	34.4
	VI	Adachi-ku	(178,849) 100.0	55.2	2.2	42.6	100.0	40.4	14.8	1.6	0.6	8.2	34.4
	VII	Katsushika-ku	(164,568) 100.0	54.6	1.9	43.5	100.0	39.8	14.8	1.4	0.5	9.3	34.2
	VIII	Edogawa-ku	(140,305) 100.0	54.8	2.0	43.2	100.0	40.1	14.7	1.3	0.7	8.5	34.7
		Urayasu-machi	(10,237) 100.0	62.2	0.5	37.3	100.0	43.7	18.5	0.4	0.1	5.5	31.8
		Zone 3 Total	(1,525,017) 100.0	51.1	2.1	46.8	100.0	38.0	13.1	1.5	0.6	10.5	36.3
4	I	Kawasaki-shi	(213,164) 100.0	57.8	1.9	40.3	100.0	43.9	13.9	1.3	0.6	7.3	33.0
	II	Komae-machi	(6,793) 100.0	53.7	2.2	44.1	100.0	38.6	15.1	1.6	0.6	9.2	34.9
	III	Mitaka-shi	(36,370) 100.0	50.4	2.4	47.2	100.0	38.0	12.4	1.7	0.7	10.9	36.3
		Musashino-shi	(51,301) 100.0	47.9	2.1	50.0	100.0	36.3	11.6	1.5	0.6	12.6	37.4
		Chōfu-shi	(23,213) 100.0	52.7	2.4	44.9	100.0	37.9	14.8	1.7	0.7	9.6	35.3
		Hoya-machi	(9,831) 100.0	52.5	2.2	45.3	100.0	36.6	15.9	1.7	0.5	12.1	33.2
	IV	Yamato-machi	(6,904) 100.0	60.0	1.5	38.5	100.0	38.5	21.5	1.1	0.4	8.1	30.4
		Toda-machi	(11,669) 100.0	63.6	1.3	35.1	100.0	40.7	22.9	1.0	0.3	6.8	28.3
	V	Warabi-shi	(19,008) 100.0	52.9	2.3	44.8	100.0	38.2	14.7	1.7	0.6	8.1	36.7
		Kawaguchi-shi	(83,934) 100.0	57.7	1.7	40.6	100.0	41.3	16.4	1.0	0.7	7.3	33.3
		Hatogaya-machi	—	—	—	—	—	—	—	—	—	—	—
	VI	Sōka-shi	(18,730) 100.0	63.7	1.6	34.7	100.0	39.9	23.8	1.2	0.4	7.7	27.0
		Yashio-mura	(8,308) 100.0	75.3	0.7	24.0	100.0	41.1	34.2	0.4	0.3	6.8	17.2
		Misato-mura	(10,841) 100.0	74.5	0.7	24.8	100.0	41.0	33.5	0.4	0.3	6.6	18.2
		Matsudo-shi	(34,858) 100.0	58.5	1.3	40.2	100.0	38.1	20.4	0.9	0.4	9.6	30.6
	VII	Ichikawa-shi	(82,973) 100.0	53.8	1.7	44.5	100.0	36.0	17.8	1.3	0.4	10.2	34.3
		Zone 4 Total	(617,897) 100.0	56.5	1.7	41.8	100.0	40.5	16.0	1.1	0.6	8.0	33.8

Table 10. Labor Force, 15 Years and Older, by Sex
(For 1950 only, 14-year-olds are included)

(Zone)	(Sector)	District	Total	Labor Force Employed	Labor Force Unemployed	Non-Labor Population	Total	Labor Force Employed M	Labor Force Employed F	Labor Force Unemployed M	Labor Force Unemployed F	Non-Labor Population M	Non-Labor Population F
5	I	Tsurumi-ku	(116,698) 100.0	54.6	1.9	43.5	100.0	42.9	11.7	1.3	0.6	8.0	35.5
	III	Koganei-shi	(15,344) 100.0	49.9	2.0	48.1	100.0	36.0	13.9	1.4	0.6	13.6	34.5
		Tanashi-machi	(8,575) 100.0	53.0	2.1	44.9	100.0	38.5	14.5	1.5	0.6	9.4	35.5
		Kurume-machi	(5,432) 100.0	63.9	0.7	35.4	100.0	38.6	25.3	0.6	0.1	8.5	26.9
	IV	Nīza-machi	(7,313) 100.0	69.4	1.0	29.6	100.0	41.7	27.7	0.7	0.3	7.0	22.6
		Kiyose-machi	(8,921) 100.0	50.3	0.7	49.0	100.0	26.6	23.7	0.5	0.2	26.4	22.6
		Adachi-machi	(8,332) 100.0	66.0	1.2	32.8	100.0	40.0	26.0	0.7	0.5	9.7	23.1
		Asaka-machi	(7,569) 100.0	56.7	1.6	41.7	100.0	38.7	18.0	1.0	0.6	8.6	33.1
	V	Urawa-shi	(84,966) 100.0	52.0	1.8	46.2	100.0	36.2	15.8	1.3	0.5	11.5	34.7
		Misono-mura	(6,187) 100.0	77.2	0.2	22.6	100.0	40.7	36.5	0.2	0.0	7.8	14.8
		Koshigaya-shi	(27,404) 100.0	68.8	0.6	30.6	100.0	40.4	28.4	0.4	0.2	7.5	23.1
	VI	Yoshikawa-machi	(10,234) 100.0	75.9	0.3	23.8	100.0	40.6	35.3	0.2	0.1	6.8	17.0
		Nagareyama-machi	(12,101) 100.0	68.7	1.2	30.1	100.0	39.6	29.1	0.9	0.3	8.0	22.1
	VII	Kamagaya-machi	(5,745) 100.0	69.2	0.9	29.9	100.0	39.8	29.4	0.6	0.3	8.3	21.6
	VIII	Funahashi-shi	(67,084) 100.0	55.5	1.8	42.7	100.0	37.2	18.3	1.3	0.5	9.9	32.8
		Zone 5 Total	(519,113) 100.0	55.7	2.5	41.8	100.0	39.1	16.6	1.8	0.7	12.7	29.1
6	I	Nishi-ku	(60,368) 100.0	56.5	2.2	41.3	100.0	41.2	15.3	1.3	0.9	8.2	33.1
		Naka-ku	(65,666) 100.0	53.6	2.3	44.1	100.0	39.6	14.0	1.4	0.9	8.2	35.9
		Kanagawa-ku	(73,992) 100.0	52.5	2.0	45.5	100.0	40.3	12.2	1.1	0.9	9.1	36.4
	II	Kōhoku-ku	(62,359) 100.0	59.1	1.2	39.7	100.0	39.6	19.5	0.8	0.4	8.7	31.0
		Inagi-machi	(6,371) 100.0	61.0	1.7	37.3	100.0	39.5	21.5	1.1	0.6	8.9	28.4
	III	Tama-mura	(5,325) 100.0	59.2	0.7	40.1	100.0	37.3	21.9	0.4	0.3	12.1	28.0
		Fuchu-shi	(31,273) 100.0	47.4	1.6	51.0	100.0	34.9	12.5	0.9	0.7	20.6	30.4
		Kunitachi-machi	(9,769) 100.0	50.8	1.7	47.5	100.0	37.8	13.0	1.1	0.6	12.9	34.6
		Kokubunji-machi	(12,732) 100.0	53.0	1.1	45.9	100.0	35.1	17.9	1.1	0.0	11.9	34.0
		Kodaira-machi	(14,795) 100.0	52.1	1.1	46.8	100.0	35.3	16.8	1.1	0.0	14.1	32.7
		Higashimurayama-machi	(12,425) 100.0	52.2	0.9	46.9	100.0	35.2	17.0	0.7	0.2	16.1	30.8
	IV	Tokorosawa-shi	(34,408) 100.0	63.5	1.4	35.1	100.0	40.2	23.3	1.0	0.4	7.1	28.0
		Miyoshi-mura	(2,883) 100.0	74.9	0.3	24.8	100.0	41.3	33.6	0.3	0.0	7.0	17.8
		Fujimi-mura	(7,174) 100.0	70.8	0.6	28.6	100.0	41.1	29.7	0.4	0.2	6.9	21.7
	V	Yono-shi	(18,903) 100.0	52.2	2.0	45.8	100.0	38.0	14.2	0.2	1.8	9.1	36.7
		Ōmiya-shi	(78,353) 100.0	57.3	1.8	40.9	100.0	38.3	19.0	1.2	0.6	8.9	32.0
		Iwatsuki-shi	(22,551) 100.0	67.0	1.2	31.8	100.0	39.2	27.8	0.9	0.3	7.8	24.0
	VI	Matsubushi-mura	(5,754) 100.0	75.4	0.5	24.1	100.0	40.6	34.8	0.3	0.2	5.2	18.9
	VII	Kashiwa-shi	(30,887) 100.0	64.0	1.3	34.7	100.0	38.6	25.4	0.9	0.4	9.2	25.5
		Shōnan-mura	(7,162) 100.0	76.3	0.3	23.4	100.0	40.0	36.3	0.1	0.2	8.0	15.4
		Shirai-mura	(4,213) 100.0	77.9	0.2	21.9	100.0	41.2	36.7	0.1	0.1	7.5	14.4
	VIII	Narashino-shi	(15,865) 100.0	50.7	2.3	47.0	100.0	34.9	15.8	1.6	0.7	12.5	34.5
		Zone 6 Total	(583,228) 100.0	57.1	1.6	41.3	100.0	39.0	18.1	1.1	0.5	9.6	31.7
7	I	Isogo-ku	(43,501) 100.0	51.6	2.4	46.0	100.0	38.1	13.5	1.5	0.9	8.9	37.1
		Minami-ku	(101,572) 100.0	52.4	2.3	45.3	100.0	38.0	14.4	1.5	0.8	10.5	34.8
		Hodogaya-ku	(50,134) 100.0	54.9	1.9	43.2	100.0	39.8	15.1	1.3	0.6	8.6	34.6
	II	Machida-shi	(34,613) 100.0	58.0	1.4	40.6	100.0	40.2	17.8	0.8	0.6	8.6	32.0
	III	Yuki-mura	(4,281) 100.0	71.4	0.3	28.3	100.0	42.4	29.0	0.2	0.1	5.6	22.7
		Hino-machi	(15,849) 100.0	56.9	1.3	41.8	100.0	40.1	16.8	0.8	0.5	8.3	33.5
		Tachikawa-shi	(34,544) 100.0	51.1	2.6	46.3	100.0	35.7	15.4	1.5	1.1	9.5	36.8
		Sunakawa-machi	(7,340) 100.0	64.3	0.9	34.8	100.0	43.1	21.2	0.6	0.3	6.6	28.2
		Yamato-machi	(7,690) 100.0	58.6	1.4	40.0	100.0	40.8	17.8	1.0	0.4	7.7	32.3
	IV	Ōi-mura	(2,970) 100.0	68.7	0.5	30.8	100.0	40.3	28.4	0.4	0.1	7.2	23.6

Table 10. Labor Force, 15 Years and Older, by Sex
(For 1950 only, 14-year-olds are included)

(Zone)	(Sector)	District	Total	Labor Force Employed	Labor Force Unemployed	Non-Labor Population	Total	Employed M	Employed F	Unemployed M	Unemployed F	Non-Labor Population M	Non-Labor Population F
	IV	Fukuoka-mura	(4,563) 100.0	59.3	1.3	39.4	100.0	41.3	18.0	0.7	0.6	7.5	31.9
	V	Kasukabe-shi	(9,709) 100.0	59.8	1.3	38.9	100.0	38.2	21.6	1.0	0.3	8.0	30.9
		Shōwa-mura	(9,348) 100.0	71.0	0.8	28.2	100.0	40.6	30.4	0.6	0.2	7.2	21.0
	VI	Noda-shi	(33,726) 100.0	66.0	1.1	32.9	100.0	39.0	27.0	0.7	0.4	7.9	25.0
	VII	Abiko-machi	(13,938) 100.0	63.3	1.5	35.2	100.0	37.7	25.6	0.3	1.2	8.6	26.6
		Yachiyo-machi	(10,145) 100.0	76.6	0.6	22.8	100.0	40.5	36.1	0.4	0.2	7.6	15.2
	VIII	Chiba-shi	(117,315) 100.0	55.5	1.8	42.7	100.0	35.8	19.7	1.2	0.6	12.3	30.4
	IX	Goi-machi	(13,684) 100.0	69.7	0.4	29.9	100.0	38.4	31.3	0.3	0.1	9.9	20.0
		Sodegaura-machi	(9,484) 100.0	75.1	0.4	24.5	100.0	39.4	35.7	0.3	0.1	6.4	18.1
		Zone 7 Total	(524,406) 100.0	59.6	1.7	38.7	100.0	38.2	21.4	1.1	0.6	9.7	29.0
8	I	Kanazawa-ku	(36,402) 100.0	50.2	2.3	47.5	100.0	39.5	10.7	1.5	0.8	8.7	38.8
		Totsuka-ku	(45,600) 100.0	58.4	1.5	40.1	100.0	40.3	18.1	0.9	0.6	8.3	31.8
	II	Yamato-shi	(11,177) 100.0	59.3	1.6	39.1	100.0	40.8	18.5	1.1	0.5	7.3	31.8
		Sagamihara-shi	(45,079) 100.0	64.7	1.1	34.2	100.0	42.3	22.4	0.6	0.5	7.6	26.6
		Zama-machi	(7,717) 100.0	61.4	1.2	37.4	100.0	40.9	20.5	0.9	0.3	7.5	29.9
	III	Hachiōji-shi	(84,663) 100.0	57.0	1.2	41.8	100.0	38.6	18.4	0.8	0.4	8.3	33.5
		Akishima-shi	(20,311) 100.0	52.0	2.1	45.9	100.0	40.8	11.2	1.3	0.8	8.0	37.9
		Fussa-machi	(10,054) 100.0	60.7	1.3	38.0	100.0	43.1	17.6	0.8	0.5	6.5	31.5
		Mizuho-machi	(5,891) 100.0	60.0	0.7	39.3	100.0	43.3	16.7	0.3	0.4	5.4	33.9
		Murayama-machi	(7,159) 100.0	56.6	0.8	42.6	100.0	40.3	16.3	0.5	0.3	7.5	35.1
		Musashi-machi	(17,476) 100.0	54.9	0.5	44.6	100.0	40.9	14.0	0.5	0.0	10.8	33.8
	IV	Sayama-shi	(20,586) 100.0	65.6	0.8	33.6	100.0	41.2	24.4	0.5	0.3	6.5	27.1
		Kawagoe-shi	(66,841) 100.0	62.6	0.9	36.5	100.0	39.1	23.5	0.6	0.3	8.4	28.1
		Seibu-machi	(2,268) 100.0	63.9	0.9	35.2	100.0	42.5	21.4	0.4	0.5	6.2	29.0
	V	Ageo-shi	(21,316) 100.0	65.6	1.3	33.1	100.0	39.5	26.1	1.0	0.3	8.2	24.9
		Ina-mura	(4,878) 100.0	75.9	0.5	23.6	100.0	40.9	35.0	0.3	0.2	7.9	15.7
		Hasuda-machi	(12,429) 100.0	63.9	0.8	35.3	100.0	36.6	27.3	0.6	0.2	11.8	23.5
		Shiraoka-machi	(9,433) 100.0	68.9	1.1	30.0	100.0	43.8	25.1	0.9	0.0	9.3	20.7
		Miyashiro-machi	(6,823) 100.0	68.5	0.9	30.6	100.0	40.0	28.5	0.5	0.4	7.9	22.7
		Sugito-machi	(11,607) 100.0	70.4	0.8	28.8	100.0	39.3	31.1	0.6	0.2	7.7	21.1
	VI	Sekiyado-machi	(9,302) 100.0	78.6	0.2	21.2	100.0	40.2	38.4	0.1	0.1	6.6	14.6
		Moriya-machi	(6,709) 100.0	72.1	0.4	27.5	100.0	38.6	33.5	0.3	0.1	8.6	18.9
	VII	Toride-machi	(13,273) 100.0	63.5	1.7	34.8	100.0	37.0	26.5	0.9	0.8	9.1	25.7
		Inzai-machi	(13,094) 100.0	71.9	0.4	27.7	100.0	38.7	33.2	0.3	0.1	9.2	18.5
		Inba-mura	(6,092) 100.0	77.0	0.1	22.9	100.0	39.8	37.2	0.1	0.0	7.9	15.0
	VIII	Yotsukaidō-machi	(12,325) 100.0	65.7	0.9	33.4	100.0	37.7	28.0	0.7	0.2	10.5	22.9
	IX	Ichihara-machi	(6,612) 100.0	66.7	0.8	32.5	100.0	37.5	29.2	0.6	0.2	8.8	23.7
		Anegasaki-machi	(5,916) 100.0	64.6	1.1	34.3	100.0	37.6	27.0	0.6	0.5	8.2	26.1
		Hirakawa-machi	(9,001) 100.0	76.3	0.3	23.4	100.0	39.7	36.6	0.2	0.1	8.2	15.2
		Miwa-machi	(7,900) 100.0	76.2	0.3	23.5	100.0	39.6	36.6	0.2	0.1	7.6	15.9
	X	Kisarazu-shi	(33,570) 100.0	66.6	0.9	32.5	100.0	39.0	27.6	0.6	0.3	7.0	25.5
		Zone 8 Total	(571,561) 100.0	62.0	1.1	36.9	100.0	40.0	22.0	0.7	0.4	9.9	25.0
9	I	Kamakura-shi	(59,446) 100.0	47.3	1.9	50.8	100.0	34.9	12.4	1.3	0.6	11.1	39.7
	II	Ayase-machi	(5,337) 100.0	70.8	0.4	28.8	100.0	43.6	27.2	0.2	0.2	5.5	23.3
		Ebina-machi	(10,140) 100.0	64.5	1.0	34.5	100.0	42.1	22.4	0.6	0.4	6.7	27.8
		Shiroyama-machi	(3,676) 100.0	61.2	1.0	37.8	100.0	40.6	20.6	0.7	0.3	8.3	29.5
	III	Akita-machi	(8,950) 100.0	58.8	0.4	40.8	100.0	31.3	27.5	0.3	0.1	6.8	34.0
		Hamura-machi	(5,490) 100.0	57.6	1.1	41.3	100.0	41.4	16.2	0.7	0.4	7.6	33.7
	IV	Hannō-shi	(31,512) 100.0	60.0	0.8	39.2	100.0	31.2	28.8	0.6	0.2	6.8	32.4

Table 10. Labor Force, 15 Years and Older, by Sex
(For 1950 only, 14-year-olds are included)

(Zone)	(Sector)	District	Total	Labor Force Employed	Labor Force Unemployed	Non-Labor Population	Total	Employed M	Employed F	Unemployed M	Unemployed F	Non-Labor Population M	Non-Labor Population F
	IV	Tsurugashima-mura	(4,398) 100.0	74.8	0.3	24.9	100.0	41.9	32.9	0.3	0.0	7.6	17.3
		Hidaka-machi	(10,692) 100.0	71.8	0.5	27.7	100.0	41.8	30.0	0.2	0.3	6.3	21.4
		Kawashima-mura	(11,874) 100.0	80.3	0.1	19.6	100.0	39.7	40.6	0.1	0.0	6.8	12.8
	V	Kitamoto-machi	(8,529) 100.0	69.6	0.7	29.7	100.0	40.8	28.8	0.4	0.3	7.6	22.1
		Higawa-machi	(12,523) 100.0	64.6	1.4	34.0	100.0	39.3	25.3	1.0	0.4	8.1	25.9
		Shobu-machi	(12,837) 100.0	69.4	0.5	30.1	100.0	39.2	30.2	0.4	0.1	8.8	21.3
		Kuki-machi	(13,775) 100.0	66.0	1.0	33.0	100.0	39.7	26.3	0.7	0.3	8.1	24.9
		Satte-machi	(15,029) 100.0	68.1	0.6	31.3	100.0	38.6	29.5	0.5	0.1	8.1	23.2
	VI	Iwai-machi	(23,305) 100.0	73.7	0.5	25.8	100.0	40.8	32.9	0.2	0.3	6.5	19.3
		Mitsukaidō-shi	(32,253) 100.0	74.0	0.6	25.4	100.0	39.4	34.6	0.4	0.2	7.4	18.0
		Yawahara-mura	(5,802) 100.0	73.8	0.3	25.9	100.0	38.4	35.4	0.1	0.2	8.9	17.0
		Ina-mura	(8,063) 100.0	75.4	0.2	24.4	100.0	38.3	37.1	0.2	0.0	8.6	15.8
	VII	Fujishiro-machi	(10,181) 100.0	73.5	0.6	25.9	100.0	38.8	34.7	0.4	0.2	8.5	17.4
		Ryūgasaki-shi	(22,631) 100.0	66.8	0.7	32.5	100.0	38.7	28.1	0.7	0.0	8.2	24.3
		Tone-mura	(6,667) 100.0	68.2	0.9	30.9	100.0	38.7	29.5	0.4	0.5	7.8	23.1
		Motono-mura	(3,776) 100.0	74.5	0.5	25.0	100.0	40.6	33.9	0.2	0.3	7.3	17.7
	VIII	Sakura-shi	(23,514) 100.0	78.1	0.4	21.5	100.0	37.5	40.6	0.4	0.0	9.2	22.3
		Izumi-machi	(6,706) 100.0	78.9	0.3	20.8	100.0	40.1	38.8	0.1	0.2	7.0	13.8
	IX	Shitsu-mura	(6,616) 100.0	80.0	0.2	19.8	100.0	41.1	38.9	0.2	0.0	6.6	13.2
		Nansō-machi	(13,098) 100.0	74.3	0.3	25.4	100.0	39.6	34.7	0.2	0.1	7.7	17.7
		Fukuta-machi	(6,573) 100.0	74.3	0.5	25.2	100.0	38.4	35.9	0.3	0.2	8.1	17.1
	X	Kimitsu-machi	(9,515) 100.0	69.9	0.7	29.4	100.0	38.2	31.7	0.4	0.3	8.3	21.1
		Futtsu-machi	(11,111) 100.0	64.6	0.2	35.2	100.0	38.8	25.8	0.1	0.1	8.0	27.2
		Ōsawa-machi	(10,036) 100.0	63.9	0.8	35.3	100.0	37.0	26.9	0.6	0.2	8.8	26.5
		Zone 9 Total	(414,055) 100.0	67.3	0.7	32.0	100.0	38.5	28.8	0.5	0.2	8.2	23.8
10	I	Yokosuka-shi	(169,587) 100.0	52.4	1.8	45.8	100.0	40.0	12.4	1.1	0.7	9.3	36.5
		Zushi-shi	(24,641) 100.0	46.6	2.1	51.3	100.0	35.9	10.7	1.5	0.6	10.5	40.8
		Hayama-machi	(10,606) 100.0	52.5	1.6	45.9	100.0	35.6	16.9	1.1	0.5	9.5	36.4
		Chigasaki-shi	(34,592) 100.0	54.7	1.6	43.7	100.0	38.3	16.4	1.0	0.6	9.1	34.6
		Fujisawa-shi	(67,028) 100.0	53.0	1.5	45.5	100.0	36.8	16.2	1.2	0.3	10.3	35.2
	II	Aikawa-machi	(9,822) 100.0	68.4	0.3	31.3	100.0	41.4	27.0	0.1	0.2	5.2	26.1
		Atsugi-shi	(28,536) 100.0	64.3	1.0	34.7	100.0	41.0	23.3	0.6	0.4	7.2	27.5
		Samukawa-machi	(7,161) 100.0	61.4	0.9	37.7	100.0	40.9	20.5	0.6	0.3	8.1	29.6
	III	Ōme-shi	(35,450) 100.0	56.8	0.7	42.5	100.0	39.9	16.9	0.4	0.3	7.5	35.0
	IV	Sakado-machi	(15,542) 100.0	72.3	0.8	26.9	100.0	40.4	31.9	0.5	0.3	7.2	19.7
		Yoshimi-mura	(10,406) 100.0	80.2	0.2	19.6	100.0	41.4	38.8	0.2	0.0	6.5	13.1
		Moroyama-mura	(7,285) 100.0	69.9	0.4	29.7	100.0	39.4	30.5	0.4	0.0	8.4	21.3
	V	Kōnosu-shi	(20,008) 100.0	74.0	0.6	25.4	100.0	38.5	35.5	0.6	0.0	8.4	17.0
		Kisai-machi	(10,974) 100.0	77.1	0.4	22.5	100.0	41.3	35.8	0.3	0.1	6.6	15.9
		Washimiya-machi	(6,237) 100.0	71.7	0.3	28.0	100.0	40.3	31.4	0.2	0.1	7.9	20.1
		Kurihashi-machi	(7,986) 100.0	65.9	1.4	32.7	100.0	38.2	27.7	0.8	0.6	8.1	24.6
		Goka-mura	(6,397) 100.0	77.8	0.2	22.0	100.0	39.2	38.6	0.1	0.1	7.5	14.5
	VI	Sakai-machi	(15,680) 100.0	77.6	0.4	22.0	100.0	38.7	38.9	0.2	0.2	6.3	15.7
		Sashima-machi	(9,962) 100.0	84.1	0.2	15.7	100.0	42.0	42.1	0.1	0.1	5.7	10.0
		Yatabe-machi	(13,057) 100.0	75.8	0.3	23.9	100.0	39.7	36.1	0.2	0.1	7.5	16.4
	VII	Kukizaki-mura	(4,485) 100.0	80.1	0.3	19.6	100.0	41.0	39.1	0.2	0.1	7.3	12.3
		Ushiku-machi	(10,390) 100.0	73.4	0.7	25.9	100.0	40.1	33.3	0.5	0.2	8.5	17.4
		Kawachi-mura	(9,407) 100.0	79.9	0.1	20.0	100.0	40.1	39.8	0.0	0.1	7.4	12.6
		Sakae-machi	(6,576) 100.0	72.5	0.5	27.0	100.0	37.5	35.0	0.4	0.1	8.2	18.8
		Narita-shi	(30,433) 100.0	67.8	0.9	31.3	100.0	37.4	30.4	0.6	0.3	9.0	22.3

Table 10. Labor Force, 15 Years and Older, by Sex
(For 1950 only, 14-year-olds are included)

(Zone)	(Sector)	District	Total	Labor Force Employed	Labor Force Unemployed	Non-Labor Population	Total	Labor Force Employed M	Labor Force Employed F	Unemployed M	Unemployed F	Non-Labor Population M	Non-Labor Population F
	VIII	Shisui-machi	(4,179) 100.0	68.1	0.6	31.3	100.0	38.5	29.6	0.4	0.2	8.5	22.8
		Yachimata-machi	(19,493) 100.0	72.8	0.4	26.8	100.0	40.2	32.6	0.3	0.1	8.5	18.3
		Toke-machi	(4,346) 100.0	72.6	0.8	26.6	100.0	40.1	32.5	0.6	0.2	4.6	22.0
	IX	Nagara-machi	(6,871) 100.0	77.3	0.5	22.2	100.0	39.3	38.0	0.2	0.3	10.5	11.7
		Obitsu-mura	(5,143) 100.0	73.9	0.3	25.8	100.0	39.4	34.5	0.3	0.0	3.6	22.2
	X	Koito-machi	(4,579) 100.0	76.3	0.1	23.6	100.0	40.7	35.6	0.0	0.1	6.6	17.0
		Zone 10 Total	(61,988) 100.0	61.3	1.1	37.6	100.0	39.0	22.3	0.6	0.5	8.5	29.1
		Total for 50 km. Region	(7,539,363) 100.0	56.3	1.8	41.9	100.0	39.2	17.1	1.2	0.6	9.9	32.0
		National Total	(55,583,758) 100.0	64.1	1.3	34.6	100.0	48.2	15.9	0.9	0.4	7.4	27.2

1955

(Zone)	(Sector)	District	Total	Labor Force Employed	Labor Force Unemployed	Non-Labor Population	Total	Labor Force Employed M	Labor Force Employed F	Unemployed M	Unemployed F	Non-Labor Population M	Non-Labor Population F
1	I	Chiyoda-ku	(97,283) 100.0	67.6	0.8	31.6	100.0	46.6	21.0	0.5	0.3	8.0	23.6
		Minato-ku	(191,560) 100.0	60.4	1.4	38.2	100.0	41.5	18.9	1.0	0.4	8.1	30.1
		Chūō-ku	(135,500) 100.0	69.6	0.9	29.5	100.0	47.1	22.5	0.6	0.3	5.8	23.7
		Bunkyō-ku	(178,172) 100.0	58.7	1.3	40.0	100.0	40.4	18.3	0.9	0.4	9.9	30.1
		Taitō-ku	(236,221) 100.0	66.6	1.3	32.1	100.0	45.8	20.8	0.9	0.4	6.1	26.0
		Zone 1 Total	(838,736) 100.0	64.1	1.2	34.7	100.0	44.0	20.1	0.8	0.4	7.7	27.0
2	I	Shinagawa-ku	(273,015) 100.0	58.9	2.0	39.1	100.0	41.8	17.1	1.3	0.7	7.8	31.3
	II	Meguro-ku	(187,471) 100.0	53.5	1.6	44.9	100.0	38.5	15.0	1.1	0.5	11.3	33.6
		Shibuya-ku	(182,763) 100.0	54.3	1.7	44.0	100.0	37.6	16.7	1.2	0.5	10.6	33.4
	III	Shinjuku-ku	(261,925) 100.0	57.4	1.7	40.9	100.0	39.1	18.3	1.2	0.5	10.2	30.7
		Nakano-ku	(214,120) 100.0	52.0	1.8	46.2	100.0	37.5	14.5	1.3	0.5	12.7	33.5
	IV	Toshima-ku	(220,965) 100.0	56.3	1.9	41.8	100.0	39.3	17.0	1.3	0.6	10.0	31.8
	V	Kita-ku	(250,142) 100.0	57.2	2.1	40.7	100.0	40.9	16.3	1.4	0.7	8.4	32.3
	VI	Arakawa-ku	(178,817) 100.0	63.0	1.7	35.3	100.0	45.4	17.6	1.1	0.6	6.2	29.1
	VII	Sumida-ku	(220,267) 100.0	66.3	1.1	32.6	100.0	47.4	18.9	0.7	0.4	5.6	27.0
	VIII	Kōtō-ku	(193,496) 100.0	63.8	1.6	34.6	100.0	48.1	15.7	1.2	0.4	5 .4	29.2
		Zone 2 Total	(2,182,976) 100.0	58.3	1.7	40.0	100.0	41.5	16.8	1.2	0.5	8.8	31.2
3	I	Ōta-ku	(403,579) 100.0	57.0	1.9	41.1	100.0	42.1	14.9	1.3	0.6	8.1	33.0
	II	Setagaya-ku	(383,242) 100.0	50.8	1.6	47.6	100.0	36.5	14.3	1.1	0.5	13.0	34.6
	III	Suginami-ku	(299,177) 100.0	50.7	1.6	47.7	100.0	36.6	14.1	1.1	0.5	12.9	34.8
	IV	Itabashi-ku	(214,621) 100.0	55.8	2.0	42.2	100.0	40.7	15.1	1.4	0.6	9.1	33.1
		Nerima-ku	(131,141) 100.0	53.7	1.7	44.6	100.0	38.9	14.8	1.2	0.5	11.3	33.3
	VI	Adachi-ku	(223,102) 100.0	59.9	1.8	38.3	100.0	42.9	17.0	1.3	0.5	6.8	31.5
	VII	Katsushika-ku	(200,320) 100.0	59.1	1.8	39.1	100.0	41.9	17.2	1.3	0.5	7.7	31.4
	VIII	Edogawa-ku	(174,007) 100.0	59.1	1.7	39.2	100.0	42.2	16.9	1.2	0.5	7.3	31.9
		Urayasu-machi	(10,475) 100.0	63.7	0.4	35.9	100.0	43.0	20.7	0.3	0.1	5.5	30.4
		Zone 3 Total	(2,039,664) 100.0	55.3	1.7	43.0	100.0	40.0	15.3	1.2	0.5	9.8	33.2
4	I	Kawasaki-shi	(300,725) 100.0	59.4	2.1	38.5	100.0	44.0	15.4	1.5	0.6	6.9	31.6
	II	Komae-machi	(10,139) 100.0	54.2	1.7	44.1	100.0	37.9	16.3	1.3	0.4	10.3	33.8
	III	Mitaka-shi	(47,701) 100.0	53.6	1.9	44.5	100.0	39.0	14.6	1.3	0.6	11.8	32.7
		Musashino-shi	(69,137) 100.0	51.8	1.5	46.7	100.0	37.0	14.8	1.0	0.5	12.8	33.9
		Chōfu-shi	(30,910) 100.0	54.3	1.7	44.0	100.0	39.2	15.1	1.3	0.4	10.3	33.7
		Hoya-machi	(15,515) 100.0	54.0	1.9	44.1	100.0	38.4	14.6	1.5	0.4	10.2	33.9
	IV	Yamato-machi	(8,935) 100.0	61.3	1.8	36.9	100.0	40.3	21.0	1.4	0.4	6.9	30.0
		Toda-machi	(13,829) 100.0	66.1	2.2	31.7	100.0	41.7	24.4	1.7	0.5	5.4	26.3
	V	Warabi-shi	(23,207) 100.0	57.6	1.9	40.5	100.0	40.6	17.0	1.3	0.6	6.7	33.8
		Kawaguchi-shi	(88,874) 100.0	61.4	1.6	37.0	100.0	43.1	18.3	1.2	0.4	6.4	30.6

Table 10. Labor Force, 15 Years and Older, by Sex
(For 1950 only, 14-year-olds are included)

(Zone)	(Sector)	District	Total	Labor Force Employed	Labor Force Unemployed	Non-Labor Population	Total	Labor Force Employed M	F	Unemployed M	F	Non-Labor Population M	F
	V	Hatogaya-machi	(9,243) 100.0	60.4	1.4	38.2	100.0	41.6	18.8	1.0	0.4	7.0	31.2
	VI	Sōka-shi	(20,565) 100.0	67.8	0.9	31.3	100.0	42.5	25.3	0.7	0.2	6.0	25.3
		Yashio-mura	(8,451) 100.0	75.9	0.4	23.7	100.0	43.0	32.9	0.3	0.1	5.3	18.4
		Misato-mura	(10,992) 100.0	74.9	0.6	24.5	100.0	41.8	33.1	0.4	0.2	6.1	18.4
		Matsudo-shi	(45,788) 100.0	61.1	1.3	37.6	100.0	39.7	21.4	0.9	0.4	8.9	28.7
	VII	Ichikawa-shi	(95,928) 100.0	57.1	1.3	41.6	100.0	37.7	19.4	1.0	0.3	9.6	32.0
		Zone 4 Total	(799,939) 100.0	58.8	1.7	39.5	100.0	41.4	17.4	1.3	0.4	8.2	31.3
5	I	Tsurumi-ku	(137,767) 100.0	56.8	2.5	40.7	100.0	43.2	14.6	1.8	0.7	7.3	33.4
	III	Koganei-shi	(21,388) 100.0	52.5	2.0	45.5	100.0	37.0	15.5	1.3	0.7	13.1	32.1
		Tanashi-machi	(12,793) 100.0	56.4	1.7	41.9	100.0	39.0	17.4	1.3	0.4	9.1	32.8
		Kurume-machi	(6,460) 100.0	61.3	0.9	37.8	100.0	39.6	21.7	0.7	0.2	8.4	29.4
	IV	Nīza-machi	(7,570) 100.0	70.9	1.3	27.8	100.0	43.0	26.1	0.9	0.4	5.6	22.2
		Kiyose-machi	(10,965) 100.0	57.2	1.3	41.5	100.0	31.4	25.8	0.8	0.5	19.2	22.3
		Adachi-machi	(6,911) 100.0	63.2	1.2	35.6	100.0	40.1	23.1	1.0	0.2	6.8	28.8
		Asaka-machi	(10,581) 100.0	63.0	1.8	35.2	100.0	41.7	21.3	1.3	0.5	6.1	29.1
	V	Urawa-shi	(99,069) 100.0	54.9	1.5	43.6	100.0	37.9	17.0	1.1	0.4	10.4	33.2
		Misono-mura	(6,082) 100.0	76.1	0.6	23.3	100.0	41.3	34.8	0.4	0.2	6.6	16.7
		Koshigaya-shi	(28,608) 100.0	70.3	0.8	28.9	100.0	41.6	28.7	0.6	0.2	6.2	22.7
	VI	Yoshikawa-machi	(10,268) 100.0	76.7	0.4	22.9	100.0	42.1	34.6	0.3	0.1	5.9	17.0
		Nagareyama-machi	(12,398) 100.0	71.6	0.9	27.5	100.0	41.3	30.3	0.6	0.3	6.5	21.0
	VII	Kamagaya-machi	(6,482) 100.0	72.3	1.0	26.7	100.0	42.6	29.7	0.7	0.3	6.5	20.2
	VIII	Funahashi-shi	(78,170) 100.0	60.7	1.5	37.8	100.0	40.6	20.1	1.1	0.2	8.5	29.3
		Zone 5 Total	(455,512) 100.0	59.6	1.7	38.7	100.0	40.6	19.0	1.2	0.5	9.2	29.5
6	I	Nishi-ku	(71,449) 100.0	56.1	2.9	41.0	100.0	40.9	15.2	2.1	0.8	7.5	33.5
		Naka-ku	(78,109) 100.0	60.0	2.5	37.5	100.0	40.6	19.4	1.8	0.7	7.1	30.4
		Kanagawa-ku	(99,285) 100.0	54.8	2.6	42.6	100.0	40.8	14.0	1.9	0.7	8.8	33.8
	II	Kōhoku-ku	(74,979) 100.0	59.1	1.7	39.2	100.0	40.1	19.0	1.3	0.4	8.6	30.6
		Inagi-machi	(6,488) 100.0	61.6	1.8	36.6	100.0	39.6	22.0	1.3	0.5	8.5	28.1
	III	Tama-mura	(5,231) 100.0	60.3	1.0	38.7	100.0	38.2	22.1	0.8	0.2	11.5	27.2
		Fuchu-shi	(40,540) 100.0	50.9	1.8	47.3	100.0	36.9	14.0	1.1	0.7	16.8	30.5
		Kunitachi-machi	(15 ,999) 100.0	53.2	1.8	35.0	100.0	39.3	13.9	1.3	0.5	11.0	34.0
		Kokubunji-machi	(17,991) 100.0	55.6	1.6	42.8	100.0	40.8	14.8	1.1	0.4	11.4	31.4
		Kodaira-machi	(19,895) 100.0	52.7	2.6	44.7	100.0	36.8	15.9	1.9	0.7	13.0	31.7
		Higashimurayama-machi	(16,287) 100.0	54.8	1.6	43.6	100.0	36.7	18.1	1.2	0.4	12.7	30.9
	IV	Tokorosawa-shi	(36,909) 100.0	63.5	1.3	35.2	100.0	40.3	23.2	1.0	0.3	6.9	28.3
		Miyoshi-mura	(2,848) 100.0	76.3	0.5	23.2	100.0	42.7	33.6	0.4	0.1	5.6	17.6
		Fujimi-mura	(7,038) 100.0	76.5	0.7	22.8	100.0	43.4	32.1	0.5	0.2	5.3	17.5
	V	Yono-shi	(23,393) 100.0	56.7	1.8	41.5	100.0	40.0	16.7	1.2	0.6	8.0	33.5
		Ōmiya-shi	(96,605) 100.0	60.7	1.7	37.6	100.0	40.0	20.7	1.2	0.5	7.5	30.1
		Iwatsuki-shi	(22,507) 100.0	69.1	0.9	30.0	100.0	40.6	28.5	0.7	0.2	7.0	23.0
	VI	Matsubushi-mura	(5,724) 100.0	77.7	0.6	21.7	100.0	41.7	36.0	0.5	0.1	5.9	15.8
	VII	Kashiwa-shi	(29,198) 100.0	66.8	1.0	32.2	100.0	40.1	26.7	0.7	0.3	8.3	23.9
		Shōnan-mura	(7,137) 100.0	83.5	0.2	16.3	100.0	42.9	40.6	0.2	0.0	5.6	10.7
		Shirai-mura	(5,518) 100.0	80.9	0.2	18.9	100.0	42.2	38.7	0.1	0.1	6.0	12.9
	VIII	Narashino-shi	(21,669) 100.0	53.7	1.8	44.5	100.0	36.0	17.7	1.3	0.5	13.6	30.9
		Zone 6 Total	(704,799) 100.0	59.0	1.9	39.1	100.0	39.9	19.1	1.4	0.5	8.9	30.2
7	I	Isogo-ku	(47,841) 100.0	53.7	3.1	43.2	100.0	38.1	15.6	2.3	0.8	8.1	35.1
		Minami-ku	(121,899) 100.0	55.4	2.9	41.7	100.0	39.1	16.3	2.1	0.8	8.9	32.8

Table 10. Labor Force, 15 Years and Older, by Sex
(For 1950 only, 14-year-olds are included)

(Zone)	(Sector)	District	Total	Labor Force Employed	Labor Force Unemployed	Non-Labor Population	Total	Labor Force Employed M	Labor Force Employed F	Unemployed M	Unemployed F	Non-Labor Population M	Non-Labor Population F
I		Hodogaya-ku	(66,072) 100.0	56.2	2.4	41.4	100.0	40.5	15.7	1.8	0.6	7.8	33.6
II		Machida-shi	(38,575) 100.0	59.6	1.8	38.6	100.0	40.2	19.4	1.5	0.3	8.1	30.5
III		Yuki-mura	(4,104) 100.0	76.7	0.7	22.6	100.0	42.9	33.8	0.5	0.2	5.9	15.7
		Hino-machi	(17,867) 100.0	59.5	1.8	38.7	100.0	41.1	18.4	1.2	0.6	7.3	31.4
		Tachikawa-shi	(44,597) 100.0	57.8	2.3	39.9	100.0	40.4	17.4	1.5	0.8	7.9	32.0
		Sunakawa-machi	(7,972) 100.0	60.7	1.9	37.4	100.0	41.9	18.8	1.3	0.6	6.1	31.3
		Yamato-machi	(8,095) 100.0	60.2	1.7	38.1	100.0	40.7	19.5	1.3	0.4	7.8	30.3
IV		Oi-mura	(3,134) 100.0	75.5	0.7	23.8	100.0	45.2	30.3	0.5	0.2	4.8	19.0
		Fukuoka-mura	(4,872) 100.0	60.6	1.9	37.5	100.0	41.7	18.9	1.3	0.6	5.9	31.6
V		Kasukabe-shi	(20,837) 100.0	67.6	0.8	31.6	100.0	41.0	26.6	0.6	0.2	7.0	24.6
		Showa-mura	(9,143) 100.0	71.9	0.8	27.3	100.0	40.1	31.8	0.6	0.2	7.7	19.6
VI		Noda-shi	(35,073) 100.0	70.3	1.0	28.7	100.0	40.5	29.8	0.8	0.2	6.3	22.4
VII		Abiko-machi	(16,491) 100.0	67.2	1.0	31.8	100.0	39.4	27.8	0.8	0.2	7.8	24.0
		Yachiyo-machi	(10,130) 100.0	75.7	0.5	23.8	100.0	40.7	35.0	0.3	0.2	6.7	17.1
VIII		Chiba-shi	(135,731) 100.0	58.7	1.6	39.7	100.0	38.4	20.3	1.1	0.5	10.2	29.5
IX		Goi-machi	(12,190) 100.0	71.4	0.8	27.8	100.0	39.7	31.7	0.6	0.2	7.3	20.5
		Sodegaura-machi	(9,068) 100.0	74.5	0.6	24.9	100.0	39.0	35.5	0.4	0.2	8.5	16.4
		Zone 7 Total	(613,691) 100.0	59.8	2.0	38.2	100.0	39.6	20.2	1.5	0.5	8.4	29.8
8 I		Kanazawa-ku	(42,004) 100.0	51.5	3.7	44.8	100.0	38.5	13.0	3.0	0.7	9.1	35.7
		Totsuka-ku	(54,159) 100.0	59.0	2.0	39.0	100.0	41.2	17.8	1.4	0.6	7.3	31.7
II		Yamato-shi	(16,106) 100.0	58.5	2.5	39.0	100.0	38.1	20.4	1.8	0.7	6.6	32.4
		Sagamihara-shi	(54,831) 100.0	59.4	2.2	38.4	100.0	40.3	19.1	1.7	0.5	8.0	30.4
		Zama-machi	(8,738) 100.0	63.1	1.9	35.0	100.0	39.9	23.2	1.3	0.6	6.8	28.2
III		Hachioji-shi	(96,220) 100.0	60.3	1.5	38.2	100.0	39.7	20.6	1.1	0.4	7.7	30.5
		Akishima-shi	(24,683) 100.0	53.9	2.1	44.0	100.0	40.0	13.9	1.5	0.6	7.3	36.7
		Fussa-machi	(12,984) 100.0	61.2	1.6	37.2	100.0	43.5	17.7	1.0	0.6	6.0	31.2
		Mizuho-machi	(6,140) 100.0	63.9	1.0	35.1	100.0	43.5	20.4	0.7	0.3	4.7	30.4
		Murayama-machi	(7,809) 100.0	61.0	0.9	38.1	100.0	39.7	21.3	0.8	0.1	7.9	30.2
		Musashi-machi	(18,408) 100.0	68.9	0.6	30.5	100.0	42.4	26.5	0.5	0.1	5.1	25.4
IV		Sayama-shi	(20,917) 100.0	68.1	1.0	30.9	100.0	41.4	26.7	0.7	0.3	5.9	25.0
		Kawagoe-shi	(69,213) 100.0	65.1	1.0	33.9	100.0	40.4	24.7	0.7	0.3	7.3	26.6
		Seibu-machi	(6,187) 100.0	69.3	1.3	29.4	100.0	38.1	31.2	1.0	0.3	4.9	24.5
V		Ageo-shi	(23,146) 100.0	69.4	1.0	29.6	100.0	40.8	28.6	0.8	0.2	6.6	23.0
		Ina-mura	(4,612) 100.0	77.3	0.8	21.9	100.0	42.2	35.1	0.6	0.2	6.0	15.9
		Hasuda-machi	(12,822) 100.0	65.4	1.0	33.6	100.0	38.0	27.4	0.7	0.3	10.1	23.5
		Shiraoka-machi	(10,060) 100.0	71.0	0.7	28.3	100.0	41.2	29.8	0.5	0.2	7.2	21.1
		Miyashiro-machi	(6,906) 100.0	71.0	1.2	27.8	100.0	40.0	31.0	0.9	0.3	7.5	20.3
		Sugito-machi	(11,060) 100.0	73.1	0.6	26.3	100.0	41.3	31.8	0.4	0.2	6.4	19.9
VI		Sekiyado-machi	(8,602) 100.0	79.6	0.5	19.9	100.0	40.9	38.7	0.4	0.1	5.4	14.5
		Moriya-machi	(7,745) 100.0	74.7	0.6	24.7	100.0	40.1	34.6	0.4	0.2	6.8	17.9
VII		Toride-machi	(14,222) 100.0	66.9	1.2	31.9	100.0	38.9	28.0	0.9	0.3	8.1	23.8
		Inzai-machi	(11,802) 100.0	72.8	0.6	26.6	100.0	39.7	33.1	0.4	0.2	8.3	18.3
		Inba-mura	(5,862) 100.0	79.0	0.1	20.9	100.0	40.1	38.9	0.1	0.0	7.3	13.6
VIII		Yotsukaido-machi	(11,994) 100.0	66.0	1.2	32.8	100.0	38.0	28.0	0.9	0.3	8.9	23.9
IX		Ichihara-machi	(9,560) 100.0	72.5	0.6	26.9	100.0	39.6	32.9	0.4	0.2	7.9	19.0
		Anegasaki-machi	(7,470) 100.0	70.9	0.8	28.3	100.0	40.3	30.6	0.6	0.2	6.5	21.8
		Hirakawa-machi	(7,658) 100.0	79.6	0.7	19.7	100.0	40.8	38.8	0.4	0.3	6.0	13.7
		Miwa-machi	(7,511) 100.0	78.3	0.6	21.1	100.0	40.1	38.2	0.3	0.3	7.3	13.8
X		Kisarazu-shi	(34,593) 100.0	68.9	0.9	30.2	100.0	39.3	29.6	0.6	0.3	6.6	23.6
		Zone 8 Total	(634,024) 100.0	63.8	1.5	34.7	100.0	40.1	23.7	1.1	0.4	6.1	28.6

Table 10. Labor Force, 15 Years and Older, by Sex
(For 1950 only, 14-year-olds are included)

(Zone)	(Sector)	District	Total	Labor Force Employed	Labor Force Unemployed	Non-labor Population	Total	Employed M	Employed F	Unemployed M	Unemployed F	Non-labor Population M	Non-labor Population F
9	I	Kamakura-shi	(65,078) 100.0	50.3	1.8	47.9	100.0	35.6	14.7	1.4	0.4	10.5	37.4
	II	Ayase-machi	(5,326) 100.0	65.7	1.4	32.9	100.0	42.8	22.9	1.0	0.4	5.7	27.2
		Ebina-machi	(10,777) 100.0	65.5	1.3	33.2	100.0	41.2	14.3	1.0	0.3	7.0	26.2
		Shiroyama-machi	(3,288) 100.0	65.9	1.5	32.6	100.0	41.3	14.6	1.2	0.3	6.4	26.2
	III	Akita-machi	(9,253) 100.0	58.2	1.2	40.6	100.0	41.5	16.7	0.8	0.4	7.2	33.4
		Hamura-machi	(6,823) 100.0	63.1	1.1	35.8	100.0	42.8	20.3	0.8	0.3	6.1	29.7
	IV	Hannō-shi	(28,895) 100.0	63.5	1.1	35.4	100.0	40.8	22.7	0.8	0.3	6.3	29.1
		Tsurugashima-mura	(4,576) 100.0	72.0	0.6	27.4	100.0	41.0	31.0	0.4	0.2	8.7	18.7
		Hidaka-machi	(10,936) 100.0	74.2	0.6	25.2	100.0	43.2	31.0	0.4	0.2	5.8	19.4
		Kawashima-mura	(11,398) 100.0	80.9	0.3	18.8	100.0	40.7	40.2	0.2	0.1	6.2	12.6
	V	Kitamoto-machi	(8,885) 100.0	70.7	0.8	28.5	100.0	41.8	28.9	0.7	0.1	6.5	22.0
		Higawa-machi	(12,636) 100.0	65.1	1.7	33.2	100.0	39.6	25.5	1.4	0.3	7.7	25.5
		Shobu-machi	(10,897) 100.0	74.7	0.4	24.9	100.0	40.3	34.4	0.4	0.0	7.4	17.5
		Kuki-machi	(14,180) 100.0	67.6	0.9	31.5	100.0	40.8	26.8	0.6	0.3	7.1	24.4
		Satte-machi	(15,829) 100.0	70.6	0.6	28.8	100.0	39.6	31.0	0.5	0.1	7.1	21.7
	VI	Iwai-machi	(22,280) 100.0	82.1	0.3	17.6	100.0	41.9	40.2	0.2	0.1	5.0	12.6
		Mitsukaidō-shi	(26,402) 100.0	74.1	0.6	25.3	100.0	39.8	34.3	0.5	0.1	6.6	18.7
		Yawahara-mura	(7,730) 100.0	74.2	0.6	25.2	100.0	38.8	35.4	0.4	0.2	7.9	17.3
		Ina-mura	(8,559) 100.0	77.0	0.6	22.4	100.0	39.5	37.5	0.5	0.1	7.6	14.8
	VII	Fujishiro-machi	(8,783) 100.0	74.9	0.5	24.6	100.0	39.2	35.7	0.4	0.1	7.7	16.9
		Ryūgasaki-shi	(22,716) 100.0	71.0	0.8	28.2	100.0	39.6	30.4	0.5	0.3	7.2	26.0
		Tone-mura	(6,458) 100.0	75.1	0.7	24.2	100.0	39.9	35.2	0.4	0.3	7.1	17.1
		Motono-mura	(3,659) 100.0	82.0	0.2	17.8	100.0	40.8	41.2	0.2	0.0	6.8	11.0
	VIII	Sakura-shi	(23,924) 100.0	67.4	1.0	31.6	100.0	37.8	29.6	0.7	0.3	8.9	22.7
		Izumi-machi	(6,459) 100.0	79.9	0.2	19.9	100.0	41.4	38.5	0.2	0.0	5.7	14.2
	IX	Shitsu-mura	(6,408) 100.0	82.8	0.5	16.7	100.0	40.7	42.1	0.3	0.2	6.7	10.0
		Nansō-machi	(12,450) 100.0	76.4	0.6	23.0	100.0	40.1	36.3	0.4	0.2	7.0	16.0
		Fukuta-machi	(4,894) 100.0	77.0	0.6	22.4	100.0	40.9	36.1	0.5	0.1	6.7	15.7
	X	Kimitsu-machi	(9,216) 100.0	75.0	0.7	14.3	100.0	39.7	35.3	0.6	0.1	6.5	7.8
		Futtsu-machi	(11,078) 100.0	70.4	0.4	29.2	100.0	41.4	29.0	0.2	0.2	5.7	23.5
		Ōsawa-machi	(9,609) 100.0	67.2	1.1	31.7	100.0	38.1	29.1	0.7	0.4	7.8	23.9
		Zone 9 Total	(409,402) 100.0	68.2	0.9	30.9	100.0	39.6	28.6	0.7	0.2	7.9	23.0
10	I	Yokosuka-shi	(191,100) 100.0	55.4	3.2	41.4	100.0	39.9	15.5	2.4	0.8	7.8	33.6
		Zushi-shi	(26,556) 100.0	49.4	2.9	47.7	100.0	35.8	13.6	2.2	0.7	9.7	38.0
		Hayama-machi	(10,556) 100.0	50.4	2.6	47.0	100.0	35.4	15.0	2.0	0.6	9.1	37.9
		Chigasaki-shi	(38,157) 100.0	54.9	2.0	43.1	100.0	38.7	16.2	1.5	0.5	8.2	34.9
		Fujisawa-shi	(74,588) 100.0	54.2	1.7	44.1	100.0	37.5	16.7	1.2	0.5	9.3	34.8
	II	Aikawa-machi	(9,483) 100.0	68.5	0.9	30.6	100.0	40.8	27.7	0.6	0.3	5.5	25.1
		Atsugi-shi	(29,309) 100.0	66.5	1.3	32.2	100.0	41.8	24.7	0.9	0.4	6.6	25.6
		Samukawa-machi	(7,148) 100.0	60.0	1.3	38.7	100.0	41.0	19.0	1.0	0.3	7.5	31.2
	III	Ōme-shi	(37,293) 100.0	62.9	0.9	36.2	100.0	40.7	22.2	0.7	0.2	5.7	30.5
	IV	Sakado-machi	(15,561) 100.0	73.2	0.8	26.0	100.0	41.2	32.0	0.7	0.1	6.6	19.4
		Yoshimi-mura	(9,956) 100.0	82.0	0.4	17.6	100.0	42.3	39.7	0.4	0.0	6.0	11.6
		Moroyama-mura	(7,508) 100.0	72.8	0.7	26.5	100.0	40.1	32.7	0.6	0.1	7.9	18.6
	V	Kōnosu-shi	(20,287) 100.0	67.3	1.1	31.6	100.0	39.7	17.6	0.8	0.3	7.5	24.1
		Kisai-machi	(10,506) 100.0	75.8	0.4	23.8	100.0	40.9	34.9	0.3	0.1	6.8	17.0
		Washimiya-machi	(5,631) 100.0	73.5	0.7	25.8	100.0	42.1	31.4	0.5	0.2	6.5	19.3
		Kurihashi-machi	(7,947) 100.0	70.6	0.9	28.5	100.0	40.5	30.1	0.7	0.2	6.0	22.5
		Goka-mura	(5,996) 100.0	81.7	0.5	17.8	100.0	40.6	41.1	0.4	0.1	5.7	12.1
	VI	Sakai-machi	(14,784) 100.0	79.2	0.3	20.5	100.0	41.5	37.7	0.3	0.0	4.9	15.6

Table 10. Labor Force, 15 Years and Older, by Sex
(For 1950 only, 14-year-olds are included)

(Zone)	(Sector)	District	Total	Labor Force		Non-labor Population	Total	Labor Force				Non-labor Population	
				Employed	Unemployed			Employed		Unemployed			
								M	F	M	F	M	F
VI		Sashima-machi	(9,415) 100.0	85.8	0.2	14.0	100.0	43.2	42.6	0.2	0.0	4.5	9.5
		Yatabe-machi	(15,031) 100.0	78.5	0.5	21.0	100.0	41.3	37.2	0.3	0.2	6.3	14.7
VII		Kukizaki-mura	(4,397) 100.0	82.0	0.3	17.7	100.0	41.8	40.2	0.2	0.1	6.3	11.4
		Ushiku-machi	(10,550) 100.0	73.9	0.7	25.4	100.0	39.5	34.4	0.5	0.2	9.5	15.9
		Kawachi-mura	(9,220) 100.0	79.3	0.3	20.4	100.0	39.6	39.7	0.2	0.1	7.1	13.3
		Sakae-machi	(6,857) 100.0	76.4	0.5	23.1	100.0	37.7	28.7	0.4	0.1	6.4	16.7
		Narita-shi	(30,291) 100.0	70.1	0.7	29.2	100.0	38.4	31.7	0.5	0.2	8.1	21.1
VIII		Shisui-machi	(4,100) 100.0	72.1	0.9	27.0	100.0	39.8	32.3	0.8	0.1	7.7	19.3
		Yachimata-machi	(16,801) 100.0	73.2	0.5	26.3	100.0	39.9	33.3	0.4	0.1	7.9	18.4
		Toke-machi	(4,363) 100.0	72.0	0.7	27.3	100.0	39.5	32.5	0.5	0.2	6.8	20.5
IX		Nagara-machi	(6,054) 100.0	75.3	0.4	24.3	100.0	39.1	36.2	0.3	0.1	7.7	16.6
		Obitsu-mura	(4,861) 100.0	76.0	0.5	23.5	100.0	40.1	35.9	0.3	0.2	7.4	16.1
X		Koito-machi	(4,319) 100.0	79.9	0.1	20.0	100.0	41.9	38.0	0.0	0.1	6.0	14.0
		Zone 10 Total	(648,625) 100.0	62.8	1.8	35.4	100.0	39.6	23.2	1.3	0.5	7.6	27.8
		Total for 50 km. Region	(9,327,368) 100.0	59.7	1.7	38.6	100.0	40.9	18.8	1.2	0.5	8.5	30.1
		National Total	(59,476,539) 100.0	66.0	1.3	32.7	100.0	40.2	25.8	0.9	0.4	7.1	25.6
		1960											
1	I	Chiyoda-ku	(98,140) 100.0	70.5	0.3	29.2	100.0	47.6	22.9	0.2	0.1	7.6	21.6
		Minato-ku	(214,959) 100.0	64.1	0.5	35.4	100.0	43.1	21.0	0.3	0.2	7.7	27.7
		Chūō-ku	(134,540) 100.0	73.0	0.3	26.7	100.0	48.9	24.1	0.2	0.1	5.5	21.2
		Bunkyō-ku	(208,128) 100.0	61.2	0.6	38.2	100.0	41.1	20.1	0.3	0.3	10.2	28.0
		Taitō-ku	(258,009) 100.0	70.1	0.5	29.4	100.0	47.1	23.0	0.3	0.2	5.9	23.5
		Zone 1 Total	(913,776) 100.0	67.2	0.4	32.4	100.0	45.1	22.1	0.3	0.1	7.4	25.0
2	I	Shinagawa-ku	(337,284) 100.0	64.3	0.9	34.8	100.0	44.3	20.0	0.4	0.5	7.0	27.8
	II	Meguro-ku	(232,687) 100.0	58.7	0.6	40.7	100.0	41.0	17.7	0.4	0.2	10.1	30.6
		Shibuya-ku	(227,267) 100.0	57.9	0.7	41.4	100.0	38.7	19.2	0.4	0.3	10.3	31.1
	III	Shinjuku-ku	(334,082) 100.0	61.0	0.7	38.3	100.0	40.5	20.5	0.5	0.2	10.1	28.2
		Nakano-ku	(27,784) 100.0	55.6	0.8	43.6	100.0	39.0	16.6	0.6	0.2	12.4	31.2
	IV	Toshima-ku	(289,004) 100.0	60.5	0.9	38.6	100.0	40.7	19.8	0.6	0.3	9.5	29.1
	V	Kita-ku	(320,725) 100.0	61.9	0.8	37.3	100.0	42.7	19.2	0.5	0.3	7.4	29.9
	VI	Arakawa-ku	(216,840) 100.0	66.0	0.7	33.3	100.0	47.1	18.9	0.4	0.3	5.8	27.5
	VII	Sumida-ku	(256,288) 100.0	70.1	0.4	29.5	100.0	50.6	19.5	0.3	0.1	5.1	24.4
	VIII	Kōtō-ku	(262,311) 100.0	67.9	0.5	31.6	100.0	43.2	24.7	0.4	0.1	8.3	23.3
		Zone 2 Total	(2,754,332) 100.0	62.4	0.7	36.9	100.0	43.7	18.7	0.4	0.3	8.1	28.8
3	I	Ōta-ku	(541,951) 100.0	62.6	0.5	36.9	100.0	45.5	17.1	0.4	0.1	7.4	38.1
	II	Setagaya-ku	(508,753) 100.0	54.3	0.6	45.1	100.0	38.1	16.2	0.4	0.2	12.3	32.8
	III	Suginami-ku	(383,139) 100.0	53.6	0.6	45.8	100.0	37.7	15.9	0.4	0.2	12.6	33.2
	IV	Itabashi-ku	(307,965) 100.0	60.3	0.7	39.0	100.0	43.3	20.0	0.5	0.2	8.3	30.7
		Nerima-ku	(226,606) 100.0	55.3	0.6	44.1	100.0	40.0	15.3	0.4	0.2	10.5	33.6
	VI	Adachi-ku	(294,483) 100.0	63.6	0.7	35.7	100.0	44.6	19.0	0.5	0.2	6.3	29.4
	VII	Katsushika-ku	(277,285) 100.0	63.2	0.6	36.2	100.0	43.9	19.3	0.4	0.2	6.9	25.3
	VIII	Edogawa-ku	(233,706) 100.0	63.0	0.6	36.4	100.0	44.6	18.4	0.4	0.2	6.7	25.7
		Urayasu-machi	(11,423) 100.0	64.9	0.6	34.5	100.0	43.6	21.3	0.4	0.2	5.1	29.4
		Zone 3 Total	(2,785,311) 100.0	59.2	0.6	40.2	100.0	43.0	16.2	0.4	0.2	8.5	31.7
4	I	Kawasaki-shi	(463,209) 100.0	63.5	0.6	35.9	100.0	46.7	16.8	0.4	0.2	6.4	29.5
	II	Komae-machi	(18,620) 100.0	55.3	0.5	44.2	100.0	39.5	15.8	0.4	0.1	10.7	33.5
	III	Mitaka-shi	(73,441) 100.0	55.7	0.6	43.7	100.0	40.1	15.6	0.4	0.2	11.2	32.5

Table 10. Labor Force, 15 Years and Older, by Sex
(For 1950 only, 14-year-olds are included)

(Zone)	(Sector)	District	Total	Labor Force Employed	Labor Force Unemployed	Non-Labor Population	Total	Labor Force Employed M	Labor Force Employed F	Labor Force Unemployed M	Labor Force Unemployed F	Non-Labor Population M	Non-Labor Population F
	III	Musashino-shi	(93,394) 100.0	54.8	0.6	44.6	100.0	38.8	16.0	0.4	0.2	11.9	32.7
		Chōfu-shi	(49,937) 100.0	56.1	0.8	43.1	100.0	41.0	15.1	0.4	0.4	8.7	34.4
		Hoya-machi	(33,451) 100.0	56.2	0.6	43.2	100.0	42.0	14.2	0.4	0.2	6.8	36.4
	IV	Yamato-machi	(12,117) 100.0	61.1	0.5	38.4	100.0	46.7	14.4	0.3	0.2	5.2	33.2
		Toda-machi	(21,741) 100.0	67.1	0.4	32.5	100.0	42.1	25.0	0.4	0.0	6.7	25.8
	V	Warabi-shi	(36,889) 100.0	61.0	0.7	38.3	100.0	45.9	15.1	0.2	0.5	5.7	32.6
		Kawaguchi-shi	(121,479) 100.0	64.9	0.4	34.7	100.0	43.9	21.0	0.4	0.0	6.3	28.4
		Hatogaya-machi	(14,415) 100.0	61.2	0.6	38.2	100.0	44.3	16.9	0.5	0.1	5.6	32.6
	VI	Sōka-shi	(26,418) 100.0	69.7	0.6	29.7	100.0	44.9	24.8	0.4	0.2	5.0	24.7
		Yashio-mura	(8,721) 100.0	77.0	0.4	22.6	100.0	43.5	33.5	0.3	0.1	5.6	17.0
		Misato-mura	(11,716) 100.0	77.5	0.3	22.2	100.0	41.3	36.2	0.3	0.0	8.4	13.8
		Matsudo-shi	(61,696) 100.0	62.0	0.5	37.5	100.0	39.6	22.4	0.3	0.2	9.3	28.2
	VII	Ichikawa-shi	(117,382) 100.0	58.8	0.4	40.8	100.0	43.7	15.1	0.4	0.0	7.7	33.1
		Zone 4 Total	(1,164,626) 100.0	61.6	0.5	37.9	100.0	43.1	18.5	0.4	0.1	8.4	29.5
5	I	Tsurumi-ku	(170,370) 100.0	62.2	0.6	37.2	100.0	46.2	16.0	0.4	0.2	6.5	30.7
	III	Koganei-shi	(34,446) 100.0	53.9	0.5	45.6	100.0	38.1	15.8	0.4	0.1	12.4	33.2
		Tanashi-machi	(22,446) 100.0	57.6	0.5	41.9	100.0	40.4	17.2	0.4	0.1	8.4	33.5
		Kurume-machi	(13,553) 100.0	59.4	0.5	40.1	100.0	41.5	17.9	0.3	0.2	7.7	32.4
	IV	Nīza-machi	(9,826) 100.0	68.0	0.7	31.3	100.0	43.0	25.0	0.5	0.2	6.8	24.5
		Kiyose-machi	(13,645) 100.0	54.8	0.7	44.5	100.0	32.3	22.5	0.3	0.4	17.8	26.7
		Adachi-machi	(8,541) 100.0	64.9	0.5	34.6	100.0	42.0	22.9	0.4	0.1	6.6	28.0
		Asaka-machi	(17,347) 100.0	67.1	0.5	32.4	100.0	49.6	17.5	0.4	0.1	5.5	26.9
	V	Urawa-shi	(124,403) 100.0	58.3	0.5	41.2	100.0	39.6	18.7	0.4	0.1	9.4	31.8
		Misono-mura	(6,137) 100.0	81.0	0.2	18.8	100.0	42.2	38.8	0.1	0.1	6.3	12.5
		Koshigaya-shi	(32,768) 100.0	71.6	0.5	27.9	100.0	42.6	29.0	0.3	0.2	5.8	22.1
	VI	Yoshikawa-machi	(10,607) 100.0	82.6	0.1	17.3	100.0	43.7	38.9	0.1	0.0	4.9	12.4
		Nagareyama-machi	(17,677) 100.0	67.0	0.6	32.4	100.0	41.4	25.6	0.5	0.1	7.0	25.4
	VII	Kamagaya-machi	(9,071) 100.0	69.0	0.3	30.7	100.0	44.7	24.3	0.3	0.0	6.3	24.4
	VIII	Funahashi-shi	(98,204) 100.0	61.9	0.6	37.5	100.0	41.4	20.5	0.4	0.2	8.4	29.1
		Zone 5 Total	(589,041) 100.0	61.8	0.5	37.7	100.0	42.4	19.4	0.4	0.1	8.1	29.6
6	I	Nishi-ku	(78,147) 100.0	60.1	0.8	39.1	100.0	42.6	17.5	0.6	0.2	7.2	31.9
		Naka-ku	(94,603) 100.0	62.2	0.9	36.9	100.0	42.0	20.2	0.6	0.3	6.6	30.3
		Kanagawa-ku	(127,196) 100.0	58.7	0.7	40.6	100.0	42.8	15.9	0.5	0.2	8.7	31.9
	II	Kōhoku-ku	(106,448) 100.0	59.8	0.5	39.7	100.0	41.5	18.3	0.4	0.1	8.8	30.9
		Inagi-machi	(7,666) 100.0	64.2	0.6	35.2	100.0	43.0	21.2	0.5	0.1	7.7	27.5
	III	Tama-mura	(7,284) 100.0	57.2	0.4	42.4	100.0	35.7	21.5	0.3	0.1	13.8	28.6
		Fuchu-shi	(59,561) 100.0	54.7	0.6	44.7	100.0	39.0	15.7	0.4	0.2	13.6	31.1
		Kunitachi-machi	(23,808) 100.0	54.4	0.6	45.0	100.0	38.8	15.6	0.4	0.2	10.8	34.2
		Kokubunji-machi	(29,133) 100.0	56.0	0.7	43.3	100.0	41.3	14.7	0.5	0.2	11.1	32.2
		Kodaira-machi	(37,859) 100.0	52.5	0.5	47.0	100.0	37.7	14.8	0.4	0.1	13.6	33.4
		Higashimurayama-machi	(30,138) 100.0	55.7	0.7	43.6	100.0	39.8	15.9	0.5	0.2	10.0	33.6
	IV	Tokorosawa-shi	(45,551) 100.0	65.3	0.5	34.2	100.0	42.5	22.8	0.3	0.2	6.4	27.8
		Miyoshi-mura	(2,868) 100.0	82.3	0.2	17.5	100.0	45.1	37.2	0.2	0.0	4.0	13.5
		Fujimi-mura	(8,142) 100.0	74.8	0.3	24.9	100.0	43.2	31.6	0.2	0.1	5.4	19.5
	V	Yono-shi	(29,366) 100.0	59.2	0.4	40.4	100.0	41.4	17.8	0.3	0.1	7.9	32.5
		Ōmiya-shi	(121,006) 100.0	62.1	0.5	37.4	100.0	41.1	21.0	0.3	0.2	7.6	29.8
		Iwatsuki-shi	(23,783) 100.0	71.3	0.3	28.4	100.0	41.6	29.7	0.3	0.0	6.8	21.6
	VI	Matsubushi-mura	(5,826) 100.0	82.6	0.1	17.3	100.0	43.3	39.3	0.1	0.0	4.9	12.4
	VII	Kashiwa-shi	(43,881) 100.0	63.6	0.5	35.9	100.0	41.0	22.6	0.4	0.1	7.9	28.0

Table 10. Labor Force, 15 Years and Older, by Sex
(For 1950 only, 14-year-olds are included)

(Zone) (Sector)	District	Total	Labor Force		Non-Labor Population	Total	Labor Force				Non-Labor Population	
			Employed	Unemployed			Employed		Unemployed			
							M	F	M	F	M	F
VII	Shōnan-mura	(8,171) 100.0	84.2	0.3	15.5	100.0	48.7	35.5	0.2	0.1	4.8	10.7
	Shirai-mura	(5,516) 100.0	82.8	0.1	17.1	100.0	43.3	39.5	0.1	0.0	5.8	11.3
VIII	Narashino-shi	(30,378) 100.0	55.8	0.5	43.7	100.0	37.6	18.2	0.3	0.2	13.8	29.9
	Zone 6 Total	(926,331) 100.0	60.5	0.6	38.9	100.0	41.3	19.2	0.4	0.2	8.8	30.1
7 I	Isogo-ku	(55,317) 100.0	56.9	0.9	42.2	100.0	40.1	16.8	0.7	0.2	8.1	34.1
	Minami-ku	(144,440) 100.0	58.9	0.9	40.2	100.0	41.3	17.6	0.6	0.3	8.3	31.9
	Hodogaya-ku	(102,808) 100.0	58.2	0.6	41.2	100.0	42.5	15.7	0.4	0.2	7.0	34.7
II	Machida-shi	(49,973) 100.0	59.7	0.8	39.5	100.0	40.5	19.2	0.6	0.2	8.2	31.3
III	Yuki-mura	(4,236) 100.0	75.3	0.4	24.3	100.0	43.7	31.6	0.3	0.1	6.5	17.8
	Hino-machi	(31,140) 100.0	58.8	0.6	40.6	100.0	42.0	16.8	0.4	0.2	7.3	33.3
	Tachikawa-shi	(50,682) 100.0	60.5	1.1	38.4	100.0	40.4	20.1	0.8	0.3	7.6	30.8
	Sunakawa-machi	(9,571) 100.0	62.0	0.8	37.2	100.0	42.2	19.8	0.5	0.3	6.3	30.9
	Yamato-machi	(9,657) 100.0	62.8	0.6	36.6	100.0	41.8	21.0	0.5	0.1	7.8	28.8
IV	Ōi-mura	(3,427) 100.0	76.0	0.2	23.8	100.0	46.5	29.5	0.2	0.0	5.2	18.6
	Fukuoka-mura	(11,825) 100.0	61.6	0.5	37.9	100.0	44.2	27.4	0.4	0.1	5.2	32.7
V	Kasukabe-shi	(23,063) 100.0	69.5	0.3	30.2	100.0	41.6	27.9	0.2	0.1	6.6	23.6
	Shōwa-mura	(9,495) 100.0	73.3	0.2	26.5	100.0	39.7	33.6	0.1	0.1	8.6	17.9
VI	Noda-shi	(37,622) 100.0	72.1	0.5	27.4	100.0	41.3	30.8	0.4	0.1	6.0	21.4
VII	Abiko-machi	(18,825) 100.0	66.6	0.5	32.9	100.0	40.4	26.2	0.4	0.1	7.4	25.5
	Yachiyo-machi	(14,996) 100.0	69.2	0.4	30.4	100.0	40.8	28.4	0.3	0.1	7.3	23.1
VIII	Chiba-shi	(176,168) 100.0	61.2	0.6	38.2	100.0	41.5	19.7	0.4	0.2	9.1	29.1
IX	Goi-machi	(15,113) 100.0	72.1	0.5	27.4	100.0	40.5	31.6	0.3	0.2	7.1	20.3
	Sodegaura-machi	(9,740) 100.0	72.5	0.2	27.3	100.0	38.0	34.5	0.2	0.0	9.9	17.4
	Zone 7 Total	(778,098) 100.0	61.5	0.7	37.8	100.0	41.3	20.2	0.5	0.2	7.9	29.9
8 I	Kanazawa-ku	(51,140) 100.0	55.9	0.7	43.4	100.0	40.5	15.4	0.5	0.2	10.0	33.4
	Totsuka-ku	(80,233) 100.0	61.8	0.5	37.7	100.0	43.5	18.3	0.4	0.1	6.6	31.1
II	Yamato-shi	(28,235) 100.0	59.5	0.8	39.7	100.0	40.3	19.2	0.5	0.3	6.8	32.9
	Sagamihara-shi	(70,349) 100.0	59.9	0.8	39.3	100.0	41.3	18.6	0.6	0.2	7.4	31.9
	Zama-machi	(10,664) 100.0	64.6	0.6	34.8	100.0	42.2	22.4	0.5	0.1	5.2	29.6
III	Hachiōji-shi	(114,115) 100.0	61.3	0.6	38.1	100.0	39.9	21.4	0.4	0.2	8.2	29.9
	Akishima-shi	(30,991) 100.0	56.8	0.9	42.3	100.0	39.5	17.3	0.7	0.2	8.3	34.0
	Fussa-machi	(15,656) 100.0	60.5	0.8	38.7	100.0	39.5	21.0	0.5	0.3	6.4	32.3
	Mizuho-machi	(8,168) 100.0	65.6	0.5	33.9	100.0	43.3	22.3	0.3	0.2	5.2	28.7
	Murayama-machi	(8,424) 100.0	61.0	0.5	38.5	100.0	39.9	21.1	0.5	0.0	8.5	30.0
	Musashi-machi	(21,142) 100.0	67.1	0.5	32.4	100.0	41.5	25.6	0.4	0.1	5.9	26.5
IV	Sayama-shi	(22,937) 100.0	70.0	0.4	29.6	100.0	42.8	27.2	0.4	0.0	5.9	23.7
	Kawagoe-shi	(75,200) 100.0	67.5	0.4	32.1	100.0	41.1	26.4	0.3	0.1	7.1	25.0
	Seibu-machi	(4,611) 100.0	73.1	0.4	26.5	100.0	35.3	37.8	0.4	0.0	4.4	22.1
V	Ageo-shi	(27,042) 100.0	70.3	0.3	29.4	100.0	41.8	28.5	0.2	0.1	6.3	23.1
	Ina-mura	(4,628) 100.0	80.4	0.3	19.3	100.0	42.5	37.9	0.2	0.1	6.7	12.6
	Hasuda-machi	(14,437) 100.0	68.1	0.3	31.6	100.0	39.9	28.2	0.2	0.1	9.1	22.5
	Shiraoka-machi	(10,820) 100.0	71.1	0.4	28.5	100.0	42.1	29.0	0.2	0.2	7.1	21.4
	Miyashiro-machi	(7,454) 100.0	70.7	0.4	28.9	100.0	41.2	29.5	0.3	0.1	7.2	21.7
	Sugito-machi	(11,590) 100.0	75.1	0.4	24.5	100.0	41.5	33.6	0.3	0.1	6.4	18.1
VI	Sekiyado-machi	(8,105) 100.0	80.4	0.2	19.4	100.0	40.8	39.6	0.1	0.1	5.6	13.8
	Moriya-machi	(7,621) 100.0	79.0	0.2	20.8	100.0	40.9	38.1	0.1	0.1	6.2	14.6
VII	Toride-machi	(15,991) 100.0	66.9	0.5	32.6	100.0	39.3	27.6	0.3	0.2	8.2	24.4
	Inzai-machi	(11,984) 100.0	72.5	0.3	27.2	100.0	38.6	33.9	0.2	0.1	9.7	17.5
	Inba-mura	(5,676) 100.0	82.0	0.1	17.9	100.0	40.9	41.1	0.0	0.1	6.1	11.8

Table 10. Labor Force, 15 Years and Older, by Sex
(For 1950 only, 14-year-olds are included)

(Zone)	(Sector)	District	Total	Labor Force		Non-Labor Population	Total	Labor Force				Non-Labor Population	
				Employed	Unemployed			Employed		Unemployed			
								M	F	M	F	M	F
	VIII	Yotsukaidō-machi	(11,399) 100.0	65.0	0.5	34.5	100.0	38.6	26.4	0.4	0.1	8.4	26.1
	IX	Ichihara-machi	(9,930) 100.0	71.7	0.9	27.4	100.0	42.2	29.5	0.4	0.5	6.3	21.1
		Anegasaki-machi	(7,844) 100.0	73.6	0.4	26.0	100.0	41.2	32.4	0.2	0.2	6.2	19.8
		Hirakawa-machi	(7,420) 100.0	79.8	0.2	20.0	100.0	40.5	39.3	0.2	0.0	6.5	13.5
		Miwa-machi	(6,386) 100.0	78.3	0.3	21.4	100.0	40.8	37.5	0.2	0.1	6.7	14.7
	X	Kisarazu-shi	(37,336) 100.0	71.4	0.5	28.1	100.0	41.2	30.2	0.2	0.3	6.3	21.8
		Zone 8 Total	(747,528) 100.0	64.8	0.6	34.6	100.0	41.0	23.8	0.4	0.2	7.3	27.3
9	I	Kamakura-shi	(74,957) 100.0	53.8	0.6	45.6	100.0	37.3	16.5	0.4	0.2	9.8	35.8
	II	Ayase-machi	(5,675) 100.0	69.5	0.4	30.1	100.0	42.7	26.7	0.3	0.1	5.6	24.5
		Ebina-machi	(12,548) 100.0	67.9	0.4	31.7	100.0	41.3	26.6	0.3	0.1	6.5	25.2
		Shiroyama-machi	(3,584) 100.0	64.2	0.6	35.2	100.0	42.0	22.2	0.5	0.1	6.7	28.5
	III	Akita-machi	(10,141) 100.0	61.9	0.4	37.7	100.0	42.5	19.4	0.3	0.1	6.8	30.9
		Hamura-machi	(7,635) 100.0	60.7	0.8	38.5	100.0	40.9	19.8	0.6	0.2	7.4	31.1
	IV	Hannō-shi	(30,758) 100.0	64.7	0.6	34.7	100.0	41.3	23.4	0.4	0.2	6.2	28.5
		Tsurugashima-mura	(4,898) 100.0	74.9	0.2	24.9	100.0	42.2	32.7	0.2	0.0	8.1	16.8
		Hidaka-machi	(11,315) 100.0	76.1	0.2	23.7	100.0	44.3	31.8	0.1	0.1	5.2	18.5
		Kawashima-mura	(10,906) 100.0	80.3	0.2	19.5	100.0	41.2	39.1	0.2	0.0	6.3	13.2
	V	Kitamoto-machi	(10,295) 100.0	69.5	0.3	30.2	100.0	42.1	27.4	0.3	0.0	7.0	23.2
		Higawa-machi	(14,604) 100.0	68.7	0.4	30.9	100.0	41.7	27.0	0.3	0.1	7.0	23.9
		Shobu-machi	(10,731) 100.0	71.9	0.2	27.9	100.0	40.6	31.3	0.1	0.1	7.3	20.6
		Kuki-machi	(15,445) 100.0	68.9	0.3	30.8	100.0	41.8	27.1	0.3	0.0	6.6	24.2
		Satte-machi	(15,739) 100.0	72.1	0.3	27.6	100.0	40.9	31.2	0.2	0.1	7.4	20.2
	VI	Iwai-machi	(21,672) 100.0	83.5	0.1	16.4	100.0	41.9	41.6	0.1	0.0	5.3	11.1
		Mitsukaidō-shi	(25,609) 100.0	75.4	0.2	24.4	100.0	40.3	35.1	0.1	0.1	6.1	18.3
		Yawahara-mura	(7,474) 100.0	76.1	0.2	23.7	100.0	39.1	37.0	0.1	0.1	7.6	16.1
		Ina-mura	(8,422) 100.0	81.7	0.1	18.2	100.0	40.2	41.5	0.1	0.0	6.4	11.8
	VII	Fujishiro-machi	(8,940) 100.0	75.6	0.3	24.1	100.0	39.4	36.2	0.2	0.1	7.8	16.3
		Ryūgasaki-shi	(23,592) 100.0	71.1	0.3	28.6	100.0	39.4	31.7	0.2	0.1	7.4	21.2
		Tone-mura	(6,326) 100.0	78.5	0.3	21.2	100.0	41.1	37.4	0.2	0.1	5.7	15.5
		Motono-mura	(3,689) 100.0	79.5	0.4	20.1	100.0	41.1	38.4	0.2	0.2	6.4	13.7
	VIII	Sakura-shi	(25,898) 100.0	69.4	0.4	30.2	100.0	38.8	30.6	0.3	0.1	8.5	21.7
		Izumi-machi	(6,421) 100.0	79.2	0.2	20.6	100.0	41.3	37.9	0.1	0.1	6.1	14.5
	IX	Shitsu-mura	(6,263) 100.0	80.6	0.3	19.1	100.0	41.1	39.5	0.2	0.1	7.2	11.9
		Nansō-machi	(12,088) 100.0	76.0	0.2	23.8	100.0	39.3	36.7	0.1	0.1	7.7	16.1
		Fukuta-machi	(4,717) 100.0	82.1	0.2	17.7	100.0	41.5	40.6	0.2	0.0	5.6	12.1
	X	Kimitsu-machi	(9,059) 100.0	75.8	0.3	23.9	100.0	39.8	36.0	0.2	0.1	6.5	17.4
		Futtsu-machi	(11,345) 100.0	75.3	0.2	24.5	100.0	42.6	32.7	0.2	0.0	4.7	19.8
		Ōsawa-machi	(9,701) 100.0	71.5	0.3	28.2	100.0	39.3	32.2	0.2	0.1	7.3	20.9
		Zone 9 Total	(430,447) 100.0	69.4	0.4	30.2	100.0	40.2	29.2	0.3	0.1	7.3	22.9
10	I	Yokosuka-shi	(210,136) 100.0	59.1	0.9	40.0	100.0	42.2	16.9	0.7	0.2	7.8	32.2
		Zushi-shi	(29,630) 100.0	53.1	0.8	46.1	100.0	37.0	16.1	0.6	0.2	9.7	36.4
		Hayama-machi	(11,749) 100.0	54.1	0.8	45.1	100.0	36.2	17.9	0.6	0.2	9.4	35.7
		Chigasaki-shi	(48,560) 100.0	57.4	0.6	42.0	100.0	40.4	17.0	0.5	0.1	8.0	34.0
		Fujisawa-shi	(90,992) 100.0	56.4	0.5	43.1	100.0	38.6	17.8	0.4	0.1	9.1	34.0
	II	Aikawa-machi	(9,518) 100.0	74.3	0.2	25.5	100.0	41.3	33.0	0.2	0.0	4.8	20.7
		Atsugi-shi	(32,145) 100.0	66.6	0.5	32.9	100.0	42.3	24.3	0.4	0.1	6.7	26.2
		Samukawa-machi	(8,058) 100.0	66.8	0.4	32.8	100.0	44.2	22.6	0.3	0.1	7.3	25.5
	III	Ōme-shi	(40,758) 100.0	64.8	0.4	34.8	100.0	40.6	24.2	0.3	0.1	6.4	28.8
	IV	Sakado-machi	(16,014) 100.0	73.1	0.3	26.6	100.0	41.5	31.6	0.2	0.1	6.4	20.2

Table 10. Labor Force, 15 Years and Older, by Sex
(For 1950 only, 14-year-olds are included)

(Zone) (Sector)	District	Total	Labor Force Em-ployed	Labor Force Unem-ployed	Non-Labor Population	Total	Labor Force Employed M	Labor Force Employed F	Labor Force Unem-ployed M	Labor Force Unem-ployed F	Non-Labor Population M	Non-Labor Population F
IV	Yoshimi-mura	(9,730) 100.0	81.0	0.1	18.9	100.0	42.7	38.3	0.1	0.0	6.1	12.8
	Moroyama-mura	(7,773) 100.0	70.9	0.2	28.9	100.0	37.2	33.7	0.2	0.0	11.5	17.4
V	Kōnosu-shi	(21,748) 100.0	69.1	0.3	30.6	100.0	41.1	28.0	0.2	0.1	5.3	25.3
	Kisai-machi	(10,228) 100.0	76.0	0.1	23.9	100.0	40.8	35.2	0.1	0.0	7.1	16.8
	Washimiya-machi	(5,620) 100.0	73.9	0.6	25.5	100.0	42.0	31.9	0.3	0.3	5.7	19.8
	Kurihashi-machi	(8,586) 100.0	68.9	0.5	30.6	100.0	40.1	28.8	0.3	0.2	6.8	23.8
	Goka-mura	(5,734) 100.0	80.9	0.1	19.0	100.0	40.5	40.4	0.1	0.0	6.5	12.5
VI	Sakai-machi	(14,454) 100.0	80.9	0.1	19.0	100.0	41.0	39.9	0.0	0.1	5.0	14.0
	Sashima-machi	(9,102) 100.0	87.0	0.2	12.8	100.0	42.4	44.6	0.1	0.1	4.5	8.3
	Yatabe-machi	(14,483) 100.0	80.3	0.3	19.4	100.0	41.4	38.9	0.2	0.1	6.2	13.2
VII	Kukizaki-mura	(4,432) 100.0	79.0	0.1	20.9	100.0	41.4	37.6	0.1	0.0	7.0	13.9
	Ushiku-machi	(11,164) 100.0	72.4	0.5	27.1	100.0	40.0	32.4	0.4	0.1	9.0	18.1
	Kawachi-mura	(8,846) 100.0	81.5	0.1	18.4	100.0	41.0	40.5	0.1	0.0	6.0	12.4
	Sakae-machi	(6,882) 100.0	73.9	0.3	25.8	100.0	38.8	35.1	0.2	0.1	7.6	18.2
	Narita-shi	(30,128) 100.0	69.8	0.5	29.7	100.0	38.4	31.4	0.3	0.2	7.9	21.8
VIII	Shisui-machi	(4,236) 100.0	72.1	0.3	27.6	100.0	40.0	32.1	0.2	0.1	7.6	20.0
	Yachimata-machi	(17,169) 100.0	73.5	0.4	26.1	100.0	39.7	33.8	0.2	0.2	8.1	18.0
	Toke-machi	(4,612) 100.0	68.8	0.3	30.9	100.0	39.8	29.0	0.2	0.1	7.3	23.6
IX	Nagara-machi	(5,892) 100.0	81.5	0.2	18.3	100.0	40.6	40.9	0.1	0.1	6.1	12.2
	Obitsu-mura	(4,664) 100.0	79.4	0.1	20.5	100.0	40.5	38.9	0.1	0.0	6.4	14.1
X	Koito-machi	(4,164) 100.0	82.1	0.1	17.8	100.0	42.1	40.0	0.0	0.1	4.1	13.7
	Zone 10 Total	(707,207) 100.0	64.3	0.6	35.1	100.0	40.7	23.6	0.4	0.2	7.7	27.4
	Total for 50 km. Region	(11,796,697) 100.0	62.2	0.6	37.2	100.0	42.4	19.8	0.4	0.2	8.2	29.0
	National Total	(65,351,895) 100.0	66.9	0.5	32.6	100.0	41.0	25.9	0.3	0.2	7.2	25.4

TABLE 11. GAINFULLY EMPLOYED POPULATION, 15 YEARS AND OLDER, BY INDUSTRY AND SEX
(FOR 1950 ONLY, 14 YEAR-OLDS ARE INCLUDED)

1950

(Zone)	(Sector)	District	Total			Total	Agriculture	Forestry and Hunting	Fisheries and Aquiculture	Mining	Construction	Manufacturing	Wholesale and Retail	Finance and Insurance	Transportation and Communication	Services	Civil Service	Unclassified
			Total	M	F													
1	I	Chiyoda-ku	(49,905) 100.0	70.9	29.1	100.0	0.1	0.0	0.0	0.2	5.4	20.7	36.5	2.3	4.1	21.9	8.4	0.4
		Minato-ku	(87,447) 100.0	71.6	28.4	100.0	0.2	0.0	0.2	0.2	6.8	23.1	26.7	3.5	7.8	21.2	9.9	0.4
		Chūō-ku	(74,559) 100.0	69.1	30.9	100.0	0.1	0.0	0.3	0.2	4.1	21.6	43.2	2.5	6.2	16.7	4.8	0.3
		Bunkyō-ku	(74,328) 100.0	71.6	28.4	100.0	0.1	0.0	0.0	0.2	6.6	28.6	24.5	3.7	6.2	21.2	8.5	0.4
		Taitō-ku	(113,463) 100.0	70.9	29.1	100.0	0.1	0.0	0.0	0.1	5.4	30.3	38.0	1.8	4.0	16.3	3.6	0.4
		Zone 1 Total	(399,702) 100.0	70.8	29.2	100.0	0.1	0.0	0.1	0.1	5.7	25.6	33.8	2.7	5.7	19.1	6.7	0.4
2	I	Shinagawa-ku	(109,670) 100.0	74.2	25.8	100.0	0.3	0.0	0.3	0.2	6.7	36.6	21.4	3.3	8.3	14.6	8.1	0.2
	II	Meguro-ku	(72,281) 100.0	75.0	25.0	100.0	1.2	0.0	0.1	0.3	6.9	29.7	21.3	4.5	7.3	18.3	10.1	0.3
		Shibuya-ku	(68,291) 100.0	71.3	28.7	100.0	0.4	0.0	0.1	0.3	8.6	22.3	24.4	4.9	7.4	21.1	10.2	0.3
	III	Shinjuku-ku	(96,632) 100.0	70.2	29.8	100.0	0.3	0.0	0.1	0.3	8.3	22.6	26.2	4.0	6.8	21.0	9.9	0.5
		Nakano-ku	(74,123) 100.0	74.4	25.6	100.0	1.4	0.1	0.1	0.4	7.1	24.0	22.8	5.4	8.4	19.2	10.9	0.3
	IV	Toshima-ku	(78,570) 100.0	73.6	26.4	100.0	0.4	0.0	0.0	0.2	8.4	27.2	25.5	4.0	8.0	17.2	8.7	0.4
	V	Kita-ku	(97,751) 100.0	74.5	25.5	100.0	0.5	0.0	0.0	0.2	7.0	37.0	19.5	3.2	9.3	13.3	9.7	0.3
	VI	Arakawa-ku	(79,690) 100.0	73.3	26.7	100.0	0.2	0.0	0.0	0.1	7.0	43.8	23.5	1.8	7.6	10.7	5.1	0.2
	VII	Sumida-ku	(98,093) 100.0	72.7	27.3	100.0	0.1	0.0	0.0	0.1	6.0	48.8	23.3	1.3	4.5	12.1	3.3	0.5
	VIII	Kōtō-ku	(72,496) 100.0	78.5	21.5	100.0	0.2	0.1	0.6	0.1	9.2	40.9	22.9	1.3	9.3	10.0	5.1	0.3
		Zone 2 Total	(847,597) 100.0	73.7	26.3	100.0	0.5	0.0	0.1	0.2	7.4	32.0	23.0	3.3	9.6	15.6	8.0	0.3
3	I	Ōta-ku	(143,295) 100.0	77.0	23.0	100.0	1.5	0.0	1.9	0.2	6.0	37.2	19.7	3.4	6.9	15.1	7.9	0.2
	II	Setagaya-ku	(135,267) 100.0	75.2	24.8	100.0	4.8	0.1	0.1	0.4	6.4	23.1	20.9	4.6	8.1	20.2	11.0	0.3
	III	Suginami-ku	(111,085) 100.0	75.0	25.0	100.0	2.7	0.0	0.1	0.6	5.7	23.5	22.9	6.0	7.2	19.7	11.3	0.3
	IV	Itabashi-ku	(77,996) 100.0	75.3	24.7	100.0	5.1	0.0	0.0	0.1	6.2	37.2	17.5	2.7	6.6	13.0	11.2	0.4
		Nerima-ku	(45,195) 100.0	69.3	30.7	100.0	17.1	0.0	0.0	0.2	5.9	22.4	15.1	3.2	6.2	19.9	9.7	0.3
	VI	Adachi-ku	(98,685) 100.0	73.3	26.7	100.0	9.0	0.0	0.0	0.1	6.3	39.5	19.1	1.7	7.9	10.0	5.9	0.5
	VII	Katsushika-ku	(89,808) 100.0	73.0	27.0	100.0	5.1	0.0	0.1	0.1	6.0	45.3	18.0	1.9	6.6	10.6	6.1	0.2
	VIII	Edogawa-ku	(76,867) 100.0	73.5	26.5	100.0	11.4	0.0	1.0	0.2	5.9	38.5	17.7	2.1	7.1	10.5	5.4	0.2
		Urayasu-machi	(6,366) 100.0	70.3	29.7	100.0	20.1	—	26.3	0.0	6.5	9.5	28.1	0.5	1.5	6.2	1.3	0.0
		Zone 3 Total	(784,564) 100.0	74.4	25.6	100.0	6.0	0.0	0.7	0.3	6.1	33.2	19.3	3.4	7.1	15.0	8.6	0.3
4	I	Kawasaki-shi	(123,113) 100.0	76.0	24.0	100.0	12.2	0.0	0.2	0.2	8.3	42.6	12.9	1.0	7.4	9.0	6.0	0.2
	II	Komae-machi	(3,650) 100.0	71.8	28.2	100.0	30.3	—	0.1	0.2	6.4	23.0	11.2	1.5	6.5	14.0	6.4	0.4
	III	Mitaka-shi	(18,350) 100.0	75.4	24.6	100.0	12.5	0.0	0.0	0.3	7.4	26.9	17.3	3.3	7.2	15.2	9.5	0.4
		Musashino-shi	(24,583) 100.0	75.9	24.1	100.0	4.1	0.0	0.0	1.1	6.1	23.5	21.2	5.4	8.4	19.0	10.8	0.4
		Chōfu-shi	(12,227) 100.0	72.0	28.0	100.0	22.7	0.0	0.0	0.6	5.3	24.9	13.6	1.7	5.4	15.5	9.6	0.7
		Hoya-machi	(5,161) 100.0	69.7	30.3	100.0	30.2	0.0	0.0	0.1	7.6	19.8	11.3	2.6	6.8	13.1	7.9	0.6
	IV	Yamato-machi	(4,146) 100.0	64.2	35.8	100.0	40.7	—	—	—	6.3	18.4	11.2	0.6	2.4	10.0	9.2	1.2
		Toda-machi	(7,414) 100.0	63.8	36.2	100.0	45.0	—	0.2	0.1	2.7	30.7	7.6	0.6	3.1	5.1	4.3	0.6
	V	Warabi-shi	(10,062) 100.0	72.3	27.7	100.0	7.9	0.0	0.1	0.1	4.3	45.5	17.6	1.8	5.5	10.3	6.4	0.5
		Kawaguchi-shi	(48,451) 100.0	71.4	28.6	100.0	19.5	0.0	0.1	0.0	3.0	43.7	14.6	1.1	4.5	8.4	4.9	0.2
		Hatogaya-machi	—	—	—	—	—	—	—	—	—	—	—	—	—	—	—	—
	VI	Sōka-shi	(11,924) 100.0	62.6	37.4	100.0	44.5	0.0	0.0	0.0	3.0	24.2	12.2	0.8	4.3	8.3	2.4	0.3
		Yashio-mura	(6,256) 100.0	54.6	45.4	100.0	71.5	0.0	0.1	0.1	2.3	12.9	4.9	0.2	1.7	4.6	1.6	0.1
		Misato-mura	(8,083) 100.0	55.0	45.0	100.0	77.7	0.0	0.1	0.1	1.6	6.6	5.9	0.2	2.7	3.4	1.6	0.1
		Matsudo-shi	(20,379) 100.0	65.2	34.8	100.0	40.5	0.0	0.0	0.1	3.9	15.5	14.6	1.6	6.7	11.3	5.8	0.0
	VII	Ichikawa-shi	(44,639) 100.0	67.5	32.5	100.0	20.9	0.0	0.1	0.2	3.9	29.5	18.6	2.5	4.8	14.6	4.8	0.1
		Zone 4 Total	(348,428) 100.0	71.4	28.6	100.0	20.8	0.0	0.1	0.3	5.7	33.7	14.4	1.7	6.1	10.9	6.1	0.2

Table 11. Gainfully Employed Population, 15 Years and Older, by Industry and Sex
(For 1950 only, 14-year-olds are included)

Total	Agriculture		Forestry and Hunting		Fisheries and Aquiculture		Mining		Construction		Manufacturing		Wholesale and Retail		Finance and Insurance		Transportation and Communication		Services		Civil Service		Unclassified	
	M	F	M	F	M	F	M	F	M	F	M	F	M	F	M	F	M	F	M	F	M	F	M	F
100.0	0.1	0.0	0.0	0.0	0.0	0.0	0.1	0.1	5.1	0.3	16.8	3.9	26.2	10.3	1.5	0.8	3.6	0.5	10.1	11.8	7.2	1.2	0.2	0.2
100.0	0.2	0.0	0.0	0.0	0.2	0.0	0.2	0.0	6.3	0.5	19.2	3.9	17.2	9.5	2.2	1.3	7.0	0.8	10.7	10.5	8.1	1.8	0.3	0.1
100.0	0.1	0.0	0.0	0.0	0.3	0.0	0.1	0.1	3.8	0.3	17.7	3.9	29.2	14.0	1.4	1.1	5.5	0.7	6.8	9.9	4.0	0.8	0.2	0.1
100.0	0.1	0.0	0.0	0.0	0.0	0.0	0.1	0.1	6.2	0.4	22.5	6.1	16.7	7.8	2.4	1.3	5.4	0.8	10.8	10.4	6.9	1.6	0.3	0.1
100.0	0.1	0.0	0.0	0.0	0.0	0.0	0.0	0.1	5.2	0.2	24.6	5.7	25.4	12.6	1.1	0.7	3.6	0.4	7.4	8.9	3.0	0.6	0.3	0.1
100.0	0.1	0.0	0.0	0.0	0.1	0.0	0.1	0.0	5.4	0.3	20.8	4.8	22.9	10.9	1.7	1.0	5.0	0.7	9.0	10.1	5.6	1.1	0.3	0.1
100.0	0.2	0.1	0.0	0.0	0.3	0.0	0.2	0.0	6.4	0.3	28.9	7.7	13.6	7.8	2.2	1.1	7.3	1.0	8.1	6.5	6.7	1.4	0.1	0.1
100.0	1.0	0.2	0.0	0.0	0.1	0.0	0.3	0.0	6.6	0.3	24.5	5.2	14.4	6.9	3.0	1.5	6.5	0.8	10.5	7.8	8.3	1.8	0.2	0.1
100.0	0.3	0.1	0.0	—	0.0	0.1	0.2	0.1	8.1	0.5	17.8	4.5	15.9	8.5	3.5	1.4	6.4	1.0	10.3	10.8	8.2	2.0	0.2	0.1
100.0	0.2	0.1	0.0	0.0	0.0	0.1	0.2	0.1	7.9	0.4	17.8	4.8	16.5	9.7	2.7	1.3	5.7	1.1	10.5	10.5	8.1	1.8	0.4	0.1
100.0	1.0	0.4	0.1	0.0	0.1	0.0	0.3	0.1	6.6	0.5	19.4	4.6	15.5	7.3	3.8	1.6	7.3	1.1	11.3	7.9	8.8	2.1	0.2	0.1
100.0	0.4	0.0	0.0	0.0	0.0	0.0	0.2	0.0	8.0	0.4	21.6	5.6	16.4	9.1	2.7	1.3	7.2	0.8	9.8	7.4	7.2	1.5	0.3	0.1
100.0	0.3	0.2	0.0	0.0	0.0	0.0	0.1	0.0	6.6	0.4	29.0	8.0	12.4	7.1	1.8	1.4	8.3	1.0	7.8	5.5	8.0	1.7	0.2	0.1
100.0	0.2	0.0	0.0	0.0	0.0	0.0	0.0	0.1	6.8	0.2	32.6	11.2	15.7	7.8	0.9	0.9	6.8	0.8	6.0	4.7	4.2	0.9	0.1	0.1
100.0	0.1	0.0	0.0	—	0.0	0.0	0.0	0.1	5.8	0.2	37.2	11.6	15.3	8.0	0.7	0.6	4.0	0.5	6.1	6.0	2.7	0.6	0.4	0.1
100.0	0.2	0.0	0.1	0.0	0.1	0.5	0.0	0.1	8.8	0.4	33.4	7.5	15.1	7.8	0.3	1.0	8.5	0.8	5.5	4.5	4.3	0.8	0.2	0.1
100.0	0.3	0.2	0.0	0.0	0.1	0.0	0.2	0.0	7.1	0.3	26.7	5.3	15.0	8.0	2.2	1.1	6.8	2.8	8.5	7.1	6.6	1.4	0.2	0.1
100.0	1.0	0.5	0.0	0.0	1.6	0.3	0.2	0.0	5.8	0.2	31.0	6.2	13.2	6.5	2.3	1.1	6.1	0.8	8.7	6.4	6.6	1.3	0.1	0.1
100.0	3.2	1.6	0.1	0.0	0.1	0.0	0.4	0.0	6.1	0.3	19.9	4.2	13.8	6.1	3.3	1.3	7.0	1.1	12.2	8.0	8.9	2.1	0.2	0.1
100.0	1.9	0.8	0.0	0.0	0.1	0.0	0.5	0.1	5.3	0.4	19.6	3.9	16.0	6.9	4.4	1.6	6.3	0.9	11.6	8.1	9.1	2.2	0.2	0.1
100.0	2.9	2.2	0.0	0.0	0.0	0.0	0.1	0.0	5.8	0.4	29.7	7.5	11.7	5.8	1.8	0.9	5.8	0.8	7.6	5.4	9.6	1.6	0.3	0.1
100.0	9.8	7.3	0.0	—	0.0	0.0	0.2	0.0	5.6	0.3	16.9	5.5	10.1	5.0	2.2	1.0	5.4	0.8	10.5	9.4	8.0	1.7	0.2	0.1
100.0	4.6	4.4	0.0	0.0	0.0	0.0	0.0	0.1	6.2	0.1	30.5	9.0	12.6	6.5	1.0	0.7	7.0	0.9	5.9	4.1	5.0	0.9	0.5	0.0
100.0	2.7	2.4	0.0	0.0	0.1	0.0	0.1	0.0	5.7	0.3	34.5	10.8	11.4	6.6	1.1	0.8	5.8	0.8	6.3	4.3	5.2	0.9	0.1	0.1
100.0	6.2	5.2	0.0	0.0	1.0	0.0	0.1	0.1	5.5	0.4	30.7	7.8	11.5	6.2	1.2	0.9	6.2	0.9	5.9	4.6	4.4	1.0	0.2	0.0
100.0	8.2	11.9	—	—	23.6	2.7	0.0	—	6.2	0.3	6.6	2.9	19.6	8.5	0.3	0.2	1.3	0.2	3.4	2.8	1.1	0.2	0.0	—
100.0	3.4	2.6	0.0	0.0	0.6	0.1	0.2	0.1	5.8	0.3	26.7	6.5	13.0	6.3	2.3	1.1	6.3	0.8	8.8	6.2	7.1	1.5	0.2	0.1
100.0	7.0	5.2	0.0	0.0	0.2	0.0	0.2	0.0	7.4	0.9	36.2	6.4	7.6	5.3	0.6	0.4	6.6	0.8	5.1	3.9	5.0	1.0	0.1	0.1
100.0	18.2	12.1	—	—	0.1	—	0.2	—	6.3	0.1	19.4	3.6	7.7	3.5	0.9	0.6	5.4	1.1	9.2	4.8	5.4	1.0	0.2	0.2
100.0	7.2	5.3	0.0	0.0	0.0	—	0.2	0.1	6.6	0.8	22.4	4.5	12.0	5.3	2.5	0.8	6.6	0.6	10.0	5.2	7.7	1.8	0.4	0.0
100.0	2.6	1.5	0.0	—	0.0	0.0	0.9	0.2	5.4	0.7	19.8	3.7	14.4	6.8	4.0	1.4	7.6	0.8	11.8	7.2	9.1	1.7	0.3	0.1
100.0	13.8	8.9	0.0	0.0	0.0	0.0	0.5	0.1	4.7	0.6	19.2	5.7	8.9	4.7	1.1	0.6	4.9	0.5	10.4	5.1	7.8	1.8	0.5	0.2
100.0	15.3	14.9	0.0	—	0.0	—	0.1	—	6.9	0.7	16.3	3.5	7.6	3.7	1.8	0.8	5.8	1.0	8.8	4.3	6.7	1.2	0.4	0.2
100.0	20.8	19.9	—	—	—	—	—	—	6.2	0.1	13.9	4.5	6.6	4.6	0.3	0.3	1.9	0.5	5.4	4.6	8.1	1.1	0.8	0.4
100.0	22.5	22.5	—	—	0.1	0.1	0.1	0.0	2.6	0.1	22.9	7.8	5.0	2.6	0.4	0.2	2.8	0.3	3.2	1.9	3.7	0.6	0.5	0.1
100.0	4.5	3.4	0.0	—	0.1	0.0	0.1	0.0	4.2	0.1	33.5	12.0	11.7	5.9	1.1	0.7	4.8	0.7	6.1	4.2	5.6	0.8	0.4	0.1
100.0	10.1	9.4	0.0	0.0	0.1	0.0	0.0	0.0	2.9	0.1	36.5	7.2	9.2	5.4	0.6	0.5	3.8	0.7	4.3	4.1	4.9	0.0	0.2	0.0
100.0	21.9	22.6	0.0	—	0.0	—	0.0	0.0	2.9	0.1	18.4	5.8	8.0	4.2	0.5	0.3	4.0	0.3	4.5	3.8	2.0	0.4	0.2	0.1
100.0	34.2	37.3	0.0	—	0.1	—	0.1	—	2.3	0.0	9.5	3.4	3.1	1.8	0.1	0.1	1.5	0.2	2.4	2.2	1.2	0.4	0.1	0.0
100.0	37.9	39.8	0.0	—	0.1	0.0	0.1	—	1.6	—	5.1	1.5	4.2	1.7	0.1	0.1	2.4	0.3	2.0	1.4	1.3	0.3	0.0	0.1
100.0	21.7	18.8	0.0	0.0	0.0	0.0	0.1	0.0	3.7	0.2	12.6	2.9	9.5	5.1	1.1	0.5	6.2	0.5	6.7	4.6	5.8	0.0	0.0	0.0
100.0	10.7	10.2	0.0	—	0.1	0.0	0.2	0.0	3.7	0.2	20.8	8.7	12.9	5.7	1.8	0.7	4.2	0.6	7.4	7.2	3.8	1.0	0.1	0.0
100.0	11.0	9.8	0.0	0.0	0.1	0.0	0.2	0.1	5.2	0.5	27.1	6.6	9.3	5.1	1.6	0.1	5.4	0.7	6.3	4.6	5.0	1.1	0.2	0.0

Table 11. Gainfully Employed Population, 15 Years and Older, by Industry and Sex
(For 1950 only, 14-year-olds are included)

(Zone) (Sector)	District	Total Total	M	F	Total	Agriculture	Forestry and Hunting	Fisheries and Aquiculture	Mining	Construction	Manufacturing	Wholesale and Retail	Finance and Insurance	Transportation and Communication	Services	Civil Service	Unclassified
5 I	Tsurumi-ku	(63,752) 100.0	79.7	20.3	100.0	2.1	0.0	0.7	0.1	7.5	48.0	15.0	1.3	8.7	10.3	6.2	0.1
III	Koganei-shi	(7,653) 100.0	72.5	27.5	100.0	19.6	0.0	0.0	0.2	5.9	23.6	12.0	2.6	7.5	17.1	11.2	0.3
	Tanashi-machi	(4,545) 100.0	72.8	27.2	100.0	20.5	0.0	—	—	5.4	25.6	16.8	1.5	5.0	14.0	10.8	0.4
	Kurume-machi	(3,471) 100.0	60.4	39.6	100.0	65.8	0.1	—	0.1	2.3	8.0	4.5	0.4	3.8	10.4	4.6	0.0
IV	Nīza-machi	(5,077) 100.0	60.0	40.0	100.0	66.6	—	0.0	0.0	2.1	9.2	5.1	0.2	2.0	5.8	8.8	0.2
	Kiyose-machi	(4,483) 100.0	52.9	47.1	100.0	34.9	—	0.0	0.0	3.0	5.7	5.8	1.4	5.5	35.5	7.9	0.3
	Adachi-machi	(4,060) 100.0	63.1	36.9	100.0	42.9	0.1	—	0.2	3.5	14.8	15.2	0.8	2.9	10.7	8.6	0.3
	Asaka-machi	(4,294) 100.0	68.1	31.9	100.0	34.8	—	0.0	—	6.0	18.9	11.6	0.7	4.1	10.2	13.1	0.6
V	Urawa-shi	(44,195) 100.0	69.7	30.3	100.0	19.9	0.0	0.1	0.3	3.7	23.5	17.1	3.8	7.8	14.0	9.4	0.4
	Misono-mura	(4,776) 100.0	52.9	47.1	100.0	83.9	—	—	—	0.8	3.0	3.6	0.2	1.7	4.5	2.1	0.2
	Koshigaya-shi	(18,847) 100.0	58.7	41.3	100.0	63.8	0.0	0.1	—	2.1	12.7	9.3	0.5	3.3	5.5	2.5	0.2
VI		(7,771) 100.0	53.5	46.5	100.0	75.8	—	0.0	0.0	1.3	7.4	6.9	0.2	1.8	4.8	1.7	0.1
	Nagareyama-machi	(8,318) 100.0	57.6	42.4	100.0	62.7	0.0	0.1	0.1	3.1	12.1	7.5	0.5	5.7	5.8	2.4	0.0
VII	Kamagaya-machi	(3,977) 100.0	57.6	42.4	100.0	72.1	0.1	—	—	2.5	8.2	6.1	0.3	2.5	4.1	4.0	0.1
VIII	Funahashi-shi	(37,230) 100.0	61.4	38.6	100.0	27.6	0.0	3.4	0.2	4.1	20.4	18.2	2.0	6.5	13.0	4.5	0.1
	Zone 5 Total	(222,449) 100.0	68.8	31.2	100.0	28.5	0.0	0.8	0.1	4.6	26.3	13.8	1.7	6.5	11.2	6.3	0.2
6 I	Nishi-ku	(32,391) 100.0	76.8	23.2	100.0	0.3	0.0	0.1	0.1	7.3	30.1	18.8	1.9	13.1	13.5	14.6	0.2
	Naka-ku	(37,081) 100.0	73.3	26.7	100.0	0.6	0.0	1.1	0.1	7.6	13.6	26.4	1.8	12.3	23.4	12.7	0.4
	Kanagawa-ku	(38,863) 100.0	77.2	22.8	100.0	4.7	0.0	1.5	0.1	6.6	30.8	18.8	1.8	11.9	13.1	10.5	0.2
II	Kōhoku-ku	(36,887) 100.0	66.6	33.4	100.0	44.8	0.0	0.0	0.0	3.0	17.6	9.4	1.2	6.3	9.7	7.9	0.1
	Inagi-machi	(3,889) 100.0	64.7	35.3	100.0	54.4	—	0.0	0.5	5.7	11.2	7.3	0.4	3.4	8.5	8.4	0.2
III	Tama-mura	(3,150) 100.0	63.0	37.0	100.0	59.7	—	—	1.3	2.7	9.9	4.1	0.4	4.5	10.4	6.8	0.2
	Fuchu-shi	(14,829) 100.0	73.6	26.4	100.0	25.5	0.0	0.0	0.8	4.6	20.7	11.5	1.1	5.3	17.8	12.3	0.4
	Kunitachi-machi	(4,967) 100.0	74.4	25.6	100.0	21.5	0.0	—	0.2	7.2	15.8	12.5	2.7	5.9	21.1	12.9	0.2
	Kokubunji-machi	(6,680) 100.0	72.7	27.3	100.0	24.6	—	0.0	0.1	4.1	17.1	12.0	2.6	11.4	18.1	9.5	0.5
	Kodaira-machi	(7,637) 100.0	68.6	31.4	100.0	34.8	0.0	—	0.1	3.8	12.2	8.5	1.9	5.6	20.1	12.9	0.1
		(6,459) 100.0	67.7	32.3	100.0	34.2	—	0.0	0.1	5.5	15.3	7.8	1.1	9.3	17.8	8.6	0.3
IV	Tokorosawa-shi	(21,832) 100.0	63.3	36.7	100.0	48.0	0.0	0.0	0.0	2.8	10.8	10.4	0.7	4.8	14.1	8.2	0.2
	Miyoshi-mura	(2,159) 100.0	55.2	44.8	100.0	87.4	—	—	—	0.7	3.1	2.4	0.1	1.0	3.2	2.1	—
	Fujimi-mura	(5,079) 100.0	58.0	42.0	100.0	76.3	—	0.0	0.0	2.3	6.8	4.4	0.2	2.5	3.6	3.7	0.2
V	Yono-shi	(9,858) 100.0	72.9	27.1	100.0	13.6	0.0	0.0	0.1	4.2	36.4	15.8	2.0	9.2	12.1	6.3	0.3
	Omiya-shi	(44,903) 100.0	66.9	33.1	100.0	26.8	0.0	0.0	0.1	3.6	21.5	14.1	1.7	14.6	10.6	6.5	0.5
	Iwatsuki-shi	(15,116) 100.0	58.9	41.1	100.0	62.4	0.1	0.0	0.0	2.2	13.1	8.2	0.6	3.8	6.3	3.1	0.2
VI	Matsubushi-mura	(4,341) 100.0	53.8	46.2	100.0	75.3	0.0	0.1	0.0	1.9	10.4	3.5	0.1	2.5	4.5	1.7	0.0
VII	Kashiwa-shi	(19,766) 100.0	60.3	39.7	100.0	57.0	0.0	0.1	0.1	2.9	10.7	9.5	0.8	7.6	7.4	3.8	0.1
	Shōnan-mura	(5,468) 100.0	52.4	47.6	100.0	83.3	—	0.0	—	0.9	2.2	2.7	0.1	2.6	4.3	3.9	—
	Shirai-mura	(3,281) 100.0	52.9	47.1	100.0	84.4	0.0	—	—	0.7	1.2	4.0	0.1	1.0	4.0	4.6	0.0
VIII	Narashino-shi	(8,040) 100.0	68.8	31.2	100.0	20.9	0.0	2.9	0.1	4.8	20.4	15.6	1.7	13.3	13.7	6.3	0.3
	Zone 6 Total	(332,676) 100.0	68.3	31.7	100.0	29.1	0.0	0.4	0.1	4.6	19.0	14.0	1.4	9.4	13.0	8.8	0.2
7 I	Isogo-ku	(22,460) 100.0	73.8	26.2	100.0	4.9	0.0	1.0	0.1	4.3	21.3	17.2	2.5	15.2	16.8	16.4	0.3
	Minami-ku	(53,237) 100.0	72.5	27.5	100.0	5.6	0.0	0.1	0.1	6.1	21.8	20.1	1.9	12.3	17.8	13.9	0.3
	Hodogaya-ku	(27,504) 100.0	72.6	27.4	100.0	18.6	0.0	0.0	0.1	5.8	29.1	12.2	1.6	10.6	10.8	11.1	0.2
II	Machida-shi	(20,064) 100.0	69.0	31.0	100.0	41.9	0.0	0.0	0.0	5.4	15.2	10.0	1.2	6.7	10.9	8.4	0.3
III	Yuki-mura	(3,059) 100.0	59.3	40.7	100.0	77.1	0.0	—	—	2.0	7.0	2.9	0.1	3.5	4.2	3.1	0.1
	Hino-machi	(9,015) 100.0	70.5	29.5	100.0	32.4	0.0	0.0	0.0	3.3	26.7	9.0	1.0	7.9	11.6	7.8	0.3
	Tachikawa-shi	(17,647) 100.0	73.3	26.7	100.0	3.1	0.0	0.0	0.1	6.2	17.6	22.1	2.2	8.1	19.7	20.3	0.6
	Sunakawa-machi	(4,721) 100.0	67.1	32.9	100.0	49.1	—	0.0	0.1	5.4	6.9	5.9	0.5	3.1	9.1	19.7	0.2
	Yamato-machi	(4,504) 100.0	69.6	30.4	100.0	35.5	0.0	—	—	5.2	16.8	8.6	0.4	6.3	9.4	17.7	0.1
IV	Ōi-mura	(2,041) 100.0	58.6	41.4	100.0	71.1	—	0.1	—	1.8	8.0	6.2	0.2	2.7	4.1	5.6	0.2

Table 11. Gainfully Employed Population, 15 Years and Older, by Industry and Sex
(For 1950 only, 14-year-olds are included)

Total	Agriculture M	Agriculture F	Forestry and Hunting M	Forestry and Hunting F	Fisheries and Aquiculture M	Fisheries and Aquiculture F	Mining M	Mining F	Construction M	Construction F	Manufacturing M	Manufacturing F	Wholesale and Retail M	Wholesale and Retail F	Finance and Insurance M	Finance and Insurance F	Transportation and Communication M	Transportation and Communication F	Services M	Services F	Civil Service M	Civil Service F	Unclassified M	Unclassified F
100.0	1.3	0.8	0.0	0.0	0.1	0.6	0.0	0.1	7.1	0.4	41.4	6.6	9.4	5.6	0.7	0.6	7.9	0.8	5.6	4.7	5.1	1.1	0.1	0.0
100.0	11.4	8.2	—	0.0	0.0	—	0.1	0.1	5.4	0.5	19.0	4.6	7.9	4.1	1.8	0.8	6.9	0.6	10.2	6.9	9.5	1.7	0.3	0.0
100.0	11.3	9.2	0.0		—	—	—	—	4.7	0.7	21.2	4.4	10.9	5.9	1.0	0.5	4.4	0.6	9.1	4.9	9.7	1.1	0.3	0.1
100.0	34.2	31.6	0.1		—	—	0.1	—	2.3	—	6.6	1.4	2.9	1.6	0.2	0.2	3.3	0.5	6.8	3.6	3.9	0.7	0.0	—
100.0	34.5	32.1	—	0.0	0.0	—	0.0	—	2.0	0.1	7.1	2.1	3.0	2.1	0.1	0.1	1.8	0.2	3.6	2.2	7.8	1.0	0.1	0.1
100.0	18.6	16.3	—	0.0	0.0	—	0.0	—	2.8	0.2	4.4	1.3	3.3	2.5	0.9	0.5	5.0	0.5	10.9	24.6	6.8	1.1	0.2	0.1
100.0	20.5	22.4	0.1				0.2	—	3.4	0.1	12.0	2.8	9.5	5.7	0.5	0.3	2.5	0.4	6.3	4.4	7.9	0.7	0.2	0.1
100.0	17.2	17.6		0.0	—		—	—	5.5	0.5	15.8	3.1	7.7	3.9	0.3	0.4	3.8	0.3	5.8	4.4	11.6	1.5	0.4	0.2
100.0	9.8	10.1	0.0	0.0	0.1	0.0	0.2	0.1	3.6	0.1	18.6	4.9	11.2	5.9	2.2	1.6	7.1	0.7	8.3	5.7	8.3	1.1	0.3	0.1
100.0	41.5	42.4	—	—	—	—			0.8	0.0	2.5	0.5	2.0	1.6	0.2	0.0	1.4	0.3	2.6	1.9	1.7	0.4	0.2	0.0
100.0	31.7	32.1	0.0	0.0	0.1	0.0	0.0	—	2.1	0.0	10.1	2.6	6.1	3.2	0.4	0.1	2.9	0.4	3.2	2.3	2.0	0.5	0.1	0.1
100.0	37.2	38.7	—	0.0	0.0	—			1.3	0.0	4.9	2.5	4.4	2.5	0.1	0.1	1.6	0.2	2.4	2.4	1.4	0.3	0.1	0.0
100.0	28.7	34.0			0.1	0.0	0.1	0.0	3.0	0.1	9.8	2.3	4.8	2.7	0.3	0.2	5.3	0.4	3.3	2.5	2.0	0.4	0.0	0.0
100.0	36.2	35.9	0.1		—	—	—	—	2.5	0.0	7.0	1.2	3.5	2.6	0.2	0.1	2.3	0.2	2.4	1.7	3.3	0.7	0.0	0.1
100.0	13.9	13.7	0.0	—	2.9	0.5	0.1	0.1	4.0	0.1	10.6	9.8	11.1	7.1	1.4	0.6	5.8	0.7	7.7	5.3	3.8	0.7	0.1	0.0
100.0	14.3	14.2	0.0	0.0	0.7	0.1	0.1	0.0	4.4	0.2	22.1	4.2	8.7	5.1	1.2	0.5	5.8	0.7	6.3	4.9	5.3	1.0	0.1	0.1
100.0	0.2	0.1	0.0	0.0	0.1	0.0	0.1	0.0	6.9	0.4	24.7	5.4	12.2	6.6	1.1	0.8	12.0	1.1	7.3	6.2	12.0	2.6	0.2	0.0
100.0	0.5	0.1	0.0	0.0	1.1	0.0	0.1	0.0	7.4	0.2	11.6	2.0	19.7	6.7	1.2	0.6	11.2	1.1	9.9	13.5	10.3	2.4	0.3	0.1
100.0	2.7	2.0	0.0	0.0	1.4	0.1	0.1	0.0	6.3	0.3	25.4	5.4	11.8	7.0	1.1	0.7	10.9	1.0	7.7	5.4	8.5	2.0	0.1	0.1
100.0	24.7	20.1	0.0		0.0	0.0	0.0	0.0	2.9	0.1	14.9	2.7	6.2	3.2	0.8	0.4	5.7	0.6	5.4	4.3	6.6	1.3	0.0	0.1
100.0	28.8	25.6			0.0	0.0	0.4	0.1	5.5	0.2	9.1	2.1	4.8	2.5	0.0	0.0	3.1	0.3	5.5	3.0	7.5	0.9	0.0	0.2
100.0	35.0	25.2	—	—	—	—	1.2	0.1	2.6	0.1	6.3	3.6	2.5	1.6	0.3	0.1	3.4	1.1	5.9	4.5	5.7	1.1	0.1	0.1
100.0	15.0	10.5	0.0	0.0	0.0	0.0	0.8	0.0	4.4	0.2	17.5	3.2	7.2	4.3	0.7	0.4	4.7	0.6	12.8	5.0	10.3	2.0	0.2	0.2
100.0	12.9	8.6	0.0		—	—	0.2	0.0	7.0	0.2	12.4	3.4	8.1	4.4	2.2	0.5	5.3	0.6	15.1	6.0	11.0	1.9	0.2	0.1
100.0	14.0	10.6	—	0.0	0.0	—	0.1	0.0	3.9	0.2	13.6	3.5	7.4	4.6	1.9	0.7	10.6	0.8	12.5	5.6	8.3	1.2	0.4	0.1
100.0	19.3	15.5	0.0		—	—	0.1	0.0	3.7	0.1	9.7	2.5	5.7	2.8	1.2	0.7	5.0	0.6	12.7	7.4	11.1	1.8	0.1	0.0
100.0	19.0	15.2	—		0.0	—	0.1	0.0	5.3	0.2	10.9	4.4	5.3	2.5	0.8	0.3	8.5	0.7	10.0	7.8	7.6	1.0	0.2	0.1
100.0	25.1	22.9	0.0	0.0	0.0	0.0	0.0	—	2.7	0.1	7.2	3.6	6.7	3.7	0.5	0.2	4.5	0.3	9.0	5.1	7.4	0.8	0.2	0.0
100.0	46.5	40.9	—	—	—	—	—	—	0.6	0.1	2.4	0.7	1.3	1.1	0.0	0.1	0.9	0.1	1.9	1.3	1.6	0.5	—	—
100.0	39.0	37.3	—		0.0	0.0	0.0	—	2.3	0.0	5.5	1.3	3.2	1.2	0.1	0.1	2.3	0.2	2.2	1.4	3.3	0.4	0.1	0.1
100.0	6.9	6.7	0.0	0.0	0.0	0.0	0.1	—	4.1	0.1	28.1	8.3	10.6	5.2	1.5	0.5	8.6	0.6	7.3	4.8	5.5	0.8	0.2	0.1
100.0	12.2	14.6	0.0		0.0	0.0	0.1	0.0	3.4	0.2	16.5	5.0	8.5	5.6	1.1	0.6	13.4	1.2	6.0	4.6	5.4	1.1	0.3	0.2
100.0	31.3	31.1	0.1		0.0	0.0	—	0.0	2.1	0.1	9.8	3.3	5.8	2.4	0.4	0.2	3.3	0.5	3.5	2.8	2.5	0.6	0.1	0.1
100.0	34.3	41.0	—	0.0	0.1	0.0	0.0	0.0	1.9	0.0	9.1	1.3	2.0	1.5	0.1	0.0	2.2	0.3	2.7	1.8	1.4	0.3	0.0	0.0
100.0	27.0	30.0	0.0		0.1	0.0	0.1	0.0	2.8	0.1	9.2	1.5	5.8	3.7	0.6	0.2	7.1	0.5	4.3	3.1	3.2	0.6	0.1	0.0
100.0	40.3	43.0		0.0	0.0	—	—		0.9	0.0	1.8	0.4	1.6	1.1	0.1	0.0	2.5	0.1	1.7	2.6	3.5	0.4	—	—
100.0	40.9	43.5	0.0		—	—	—	—	0.7	0.0	1.0	0.2	2.6	1.4	0.0	0.1	0.9	0.1	2.4	1.6	4.4	0.2	—	0.0
100.0	9.6	11.3	0.0	—	1.3	1.6	0.1	0.0	4.7	0.1	17.2	3.2	8.9	6.7	1.0	0.7	11.8	1.5	8.5	5.2	5.5	0.8	0.2	0.1
100.0	14.9	14.2	0.0	0.0	0.3	0.1	0.1	0.0	4.4	0.2	15.4	3.6	8.9	5.1	0.9	0.5	8.5	0.9	7.3	5.7	7.4	1.4	0.2	0.0
100.0	2.8	2.1	0.0	—	0.9	0.1	0.1	0.0	4.1	0.2	17.6	3.7	11.0	6.2	1.7	0.8	13.6	1.6	9.0	7.8	12.8	3.6	0.2	0.1
100.0	3.0	2.6	0.0	0.0	0.1	0.0	0.1	0.0	5.9	0.2	17.5	4.3	12.6	7.5	1.1	0.8	11.3	1.0	9.0	8.8	11.7	2.2	0.2	0.1
100.0	10.2	8.4	0.0	0.0	0.0	0.0	0.0	0.0	5.6	0.2	22.8	6.3	7.8	4.4	1.0	0.6	9.5	1.1	6.3	4.5	9.3	1.8	0.1	0.1
100.0	24.4	17.5	0.0	—	0.0	—	0.0	0.0	5.2	0.2	11.9	3.3	6.2	3.8	0.9	0.3	6.0	0.7	6.8	4.1	7.4	1.0	0.2	0.1
100.0	43.2	33.9	0.0		—	—	—	—	2.0	0.0	3.7	3.3	1.5	1.4	0.0	0.1	3.2	0.3	2.9	1.3	2.8	0.3	—	0.1
100.0	18.6	13.8	0.0		0.0	—	0.0	0.0	3.2	0.1	20.7	6.0	5.5	3.5	0.6	0.4	7.3	0.6	7.8	3.8	6.6	1.2	0.2	0.1
100.0	2.2	0.9	0.0		0.0	—	0.1	0.0	5.9	0.3	13.8	3.8	13.4	8.7	1.5	0.7	7.4	0.7	11.1	8.6	17.5	2.8	0.4	0.2
100.0	25.9	23.2	—		—	—	0.1	—	5.1	0.3	5.1	1.8	3.9	2.0	0.3	0.2	2.7	0.4	6.3	2.8	17.6	2.1	0.1	0.1
100.0	19.8	15.7	0.0		—	—	—	—	4.3	0.9	11.0	5.8	5.2	3.4	0.3	0.1	5.7	0.6	6.5	2.9	16.7	1.0	0.1	0.0
100.0	36.5	34.6	—	—	0.1	—	—	—	1.8	0.0	6.2	1.8	3.9	2.3	0.2	0.0	2.4	0.3	2.2	1.9	5.2	0.4	0.1	0.1

Table 11. Gainfully Employed Population, 15 Years and Older, by Industry and Sex
(For 1950 only, 14-year-olds are included)

(Zone) (Sector) District	Total			Total	Agriculture	Forestry and Hunting	Fisheries and Aquiculture	Mining	Construction	Manufacturing	Wholesale and Retail	Finance and Insurance	Transportation and Communication	Services	Civil Service	Unclassified
	Total	M	F													
IV Fukuoka-mura	(2,707) 100.0	68.6	31.4	100.0	40.5	0.1	0.0	—	4.1	13.9	12.8	1.2	9.1	6.7	11.4	0.2
V Kasukabe-shi	(5,805) 100.0	64.0	36.0	100.0	31.4	0.1	0.0	0.0	3.5	22.7	19.0	1.3	5.5	12.1	4.3	0.1
Shōwa-mura	(6,633) 100.0	57.2	42.8	100.0	67.6	0.1	0.0	0.0	3.0	10.7	7.0	0.2	2.6	5.2	3.5	0.1
VI Noda-shi	(22,276) 100.0	58.1	41.9	100.0	51.8	0.0	0.0	0.0	4.3	17.9	10.8	0.6	4.7	7.5	2.4	0.0
VII Abiko-machi	(8,877) 100.0	59.2	40.8	100.0	47.8	0.2	0.3	0.1	3.9	14.5	13.3	1.7	5.9	8.9	3.3	0.1
Yachiyo-machi	(7,766) 100.0	52.9	47.1	100.0	79.3	—	0.0	—	3.3	4.0	4.4	0.1	2.7	4.0	2.1	0.1
VIII Chiba-shi	(65,162) 100.0	64.5	35.5	100.0	31.6	0.1	3.1	0.0	4.7	13.9	14.1	2.0	8.1	14.1	8.2	0.1
IX Goi-machi	(9,408) 100.0	55.9	44.1	100.0	68.6	—	6.8	0.0	1.5	4.1	7.4	0.4	2.6	5.6	3.0	0.0
Sodegaura-machi	(7,120) 100.0	52.5	47.5	100.0	76.4	0.0	6.6	—	1.5	2.8	3.6	0.2	2.1	4.7	2.1	0.0
Zone 7 Total	(300,006) 100.0	66.8	33.2	100.0	30.3	0.0	1.1	0.0	4.7	17.4	13.8	1.5	8.4	12.7	9.9	0.2
8 I Kanazawa-ku	(18,284) 100.0	78.7	21.3	100.0	5.4	0.1	3.3	0.0	5.8	24.0	13.5	1.6	9.9	17.2	19.0	0.2
Totsuka-ku	(26,653) 100.0	69.0	31.0	100.0	38.8	0.0	0.0	0.1	4.0	21.7	7.5	1.0	9.0	9.4	8.4	0.1
II Yamato-shi	(6,624) 100.0	68.9	31.1	100.0	34.7	0.0	0.0	0.1	8.0	14.7	11.2	1.2	6.7	10.4	12.9	0.1
Sagamihara-shi	(27,698) 100.0	68.9	31.1	100.0	43.5	0.0	0.0	0.2	5.3	13.1	7.6	0.6	5.7	11.6	12.2	0.2
Zama-machi	(4,993) 100.0	63.3	36.7	100.0	52.2	0.0	0.2	0.4	4.0	7.6	7.4	0.5	5.1	9.6	12.8	0.2
III Hachiōji-shi	(48,243) 100.0	67.8	32.2	100.0	20.2	0.4	0.0	0.1	4.6	33.7	15.2	1.1	6.5	10.7	7.2	0.3
Akishima-shi	(10,573) 100.0	78.5	21.5	100.0	13.2	0.0	—	0.3	10.1	15.8	10.4	1.1	6.1	19.0	23.3	0.7
Fussa-machi	(6,105) 100.0	71.4	28.6	100.0	15.1	0.1	—	1.0	14.5	13.0	11.0	1.0	3.9	21.7	18.5	0.2
Mizuho-machi	(3,529) 100.0	72.2	27.8	100.0	47.7	—	0.0	0.0	4.3	14.6	8.3	0.6	3.0	9.8	11.7	—
Murayama-machi	(4,075) 100.0	71.1	28.9	100.0	48.7	—	0.0	—	3.7	15.8	5.8	0.3	2.3	11.0	12.0	0.4
Musashi-machi	(11,211) 100.0	63.8	36.2	100.0	47.7	0.0	0.0	0.1	4.6	10.8	7.8	0.6	3.0	14.6	10.8	0.0
IV Sayama-shi	(13,511) 100.0	62.5	37.5	100.0	53.5	0.0	0.0	0.2	3.4	13.9	8.8	0.5	3.3	8.8	7.5	0.1
Kawagoe-shi	(41,856) 100.0	62.4	37.6	100.0	46.3	0.0	0.1	0.2	2.9	17.0	11.8	1.2	5.3	9.3	5.8	0.1
Seibu-machi	(1,450) 100.0	66.4	33.6	100.0	61.2	0.1	—	0.1	3.0	12.4	6.1	0.2	2.0	6.6	8.0	0.3
V Ageo-shi	(13,987) 100.0	60.3	39.7	100.0	58.6	0.0	0.0	0.0	2.8	16.9	6.3	0.5	5.7	5.8	3.1	0.3
Ina-mura	(3,703) 100.0	53.8	46.2	100.0	77.0	0.0	0.0	0.0	1.4	6.4	2.3	0.3	6.8	3.4	2.4	0.0
Hasuda-machi	(7,944) 100.0	58.1	41.9	100.0	63.1	—	0.1	0.0	2.2	9.3	6.3	0.6	6.5	8.9	2.9	0.1
Shiraoka-machi	(7,161) 100.0	57.7	42.3	100.0	69.5	—	0.0	—	1.9	8.4	5.8	0.4	6.4	4.9	2.6	0.1
Miyashiro-machi	(4,677) 100.0	58.3	41.7	100.0	65.9	—	0.0	—	2.3	7.5	5.4	0.7	10.5	5.1	2.4	0.2
Sugito-machi	(8,164) 100.0	55.9	44.1	100.0	68.9	—	0.1	—	1.6	8.1	8.3	0.6	3.9	5.6	2.7	0.2
VI Sekiyado-machi	(7,312) 100.0	51.1	48.9	100.0	82.9	0.1	0.2	—	1.2	2.8	6.1	0.1	1.3	4.1	1.1	0.1
Moriya-machi	(4,838) 100.0	53.5	46.5	100.0	77.1	0.0	0.1	0.0	1.8	5.4	6.2	0.5	2.1	4.4	2.4	—
VII Toride-machi	(8,447) 100.0	58.1	41.9	100.0	50.5	0.0	0.1	0.1	5.2	12.8	13.3	1.0	4.8	8.0	4.2	0.0
Inzai-machi	(9,414) 100.0	53.8	46.2	100.0	74.4	0.0	0.0	—	1.9	4.1	8.7	0.4	2.6	5.7	2.2	0.0
Inba-mura	(4,689) 100.0	51.7	48.3	100.0	85.5	0.0	0.8	—	1.6	1.1	4.2	1.0	1.3	3.2	1.3	—
VIII Yotsukaidō-machi	(8,096) 100.0	57.4	42.6	100.0	63.7	0.0	0.0	0.0	3.2	6.3	7.2	0.9	5.2	8.7	4.7	0.1
IX Ichihara-machi	(6,652) 100.0	54.7	45.3	100.0	71.4	0.0	1.5	—	1.7	5.7	6.3	0.6	2.8	5.9	4.0	0.1
Anegasaki-machi	(3,819) 100.0	57.1	42.9	100.0	67.0	0.0	3.2	0.0	1.4	5.7	8.0	0.8	3.1	8.1	2.7	0.0
Hirakawa-machi	(6,865) 100.0	51.9	48.1	100.0	84.5	0.3	—	0.0	1.6	3.1	2.4	0.2	1.9	4.1	1.9	—
Miwa-machi	(6,019) 100.0	52.0	48.0	100.0	84.4	—	—	0.0	1.3	2.8	3.7	0.1	1.5	4.2	1.8	0.2
X Kisarazu-shi	(22,355) 100.0	58.5	41.5	100.0	52.1	0.1	7.4	0.0	2.8	6.2	11.7	0.7	4.4	9.9	4.7	0.1
Zone 8 Total	(358,947) 100.0	63.7	36.3	100.0	40.6	0.1	6.7	0.1	3.9	15.4	9.6	0.8	5.4	9.7	7.6	0.1
9 I Kamakura-shi	(28,211) 100.0	73.6	26.4	100.0	9.7	0.1	1.6	0.3	4.8	20.6	18.1	3.1	9.2	21.5	10.8	0.2
II Ayase-machi	(3,780) 100.0	61.5	38.5	100.0	71.1	—	—	0.0	4.8	5.8	3.0	0.2	2.7	5.0	7.3	0.1
Ebina-machi	(6,538) 100.0	65.3	34.7	100.0	61.9	0.1	0.1	1.2	3.2	8.8	4.9	0.5	5.1	7.7	6.4	0.1
Shiroyama-machi	(2,248) 100.0	66.4	33.6	100.0	62.2	0.2	0.0	0.1	2.9	7.7	4.6	0.2	7.3	8.3	6.5	0.0
III Akita-machi	(3,161) 100.0	71.9	28.1	100.0	42.0	0.0	0.0	3.3	5.6	11.4	8.4	1.1	5.2	12.2	10.8	0.0
Hamura-machi	(5,260) 100.0	72.3	27.7	100.0	52.9	—	—	1.0	3.0	10.5	5.9	0.5	4.2	9.4	12.5	0.1
IV Hannō-shi	(18,914) 100.0	67.1	32.9	100.0	41.0	2.5	0.1	1.3	3.3	19.5	10.9	0.8	4.7	9.5	6.3	0.1

Table 11. Gainfully Employed Population, 15 Years and Older, by Industry and Sex
(For 1950 only, 14-year-olds are included)

Total	Agriculture		Forestry and Hunting		Fisheries and Aquiculture		Mining		Construction		Manufacturing		Wholesale and Retail		Finance and Insurance		Transportation and Communication		Services		Civil Service		Unclassified	
	M	F	M	F	M	F	M	F	M	F	M	F	M	F	M	F	M	F	M	F	M	F	M	F
100.0	22.3	18.2	0.1	0.0	—	0.0	—	—	3.8	0.3	10.3	3.6	8.6	4.2	0.7	0.5	8.3	0.8	4.0	2.7	10.4	1.0	0.1	0.1
100.0	15.3	16.1	0.1	0.0	0.0	—	0.0	—	3.4	0.1	18.2	4.5	11.5	7.5	0.7	0.6	4.8	0.7	6.5	5.6	3.4	0.9	0.1	0.0
100.0	31.8	35.8	0.1	—	—	—	0.0	—	2.9	0.1	9.2	1.5	4.5	2.5	0.1	0.1	2.3	0.3	3.3	1.9	2.9	0.6	0.1	0.0
100.0	22.5	29.3	0.0	0.0	0.0	0.0	0.0	0.0	3.9	0.4	14.8	3.1	7.0	3.8	0.6	0.0	4.2	0.5	4.1	3.4	1.0	1.4	0.0	0.0
100.0	23.4	24.4	0.2	0.0	0.2	0.1	0.1	—	3.8	0.1	10.0	4.5	6.6	6.7	1.3	0.4	5.5	0.4	5.2	3.7	2.8	0.5	0.1	0.0
100.0	37.4	41.9	—	—	0.0	—	—	—	3.2	0.1	3.3	0.7	2.5	1.9	0.1	0.0	2.3	0.4	2.4	1.6	1.6	0.5	0.0	0.0
100.0	14.8	16.8	0.1	0.0	1.8	1.3	0.0	0.0	4.5	0.2	11.4	2.5	8.6	5.5	1.4	0.6	7.3	0.8	8.0	6.1	6.5	1.7	0.1	0.0
100.0	32.7	35.9	—	—	6.0	0.8	0.0	—	1.4	0.1	3.3	0.8	4.4	3.0	0.2	0.2	2.3	0.3	3.2	2.4	2.4	0.6	0.0	0.0
100.0	34.9	41.5	0.0	—	5.4	1.2	—	—	1.4	0.1	2.3	0.5	2.0	1.6	0.1	0.1	1.9	0.2	2.7	2.0	1.8	0.3	0.0	0.0
100.0	15.0	15.3	0.0	0.0	0.8	0.3	0.0	0.0	4.5	0.2	13.9	3.5	8.6	5.2	1.0	0.5	7.6	0.8	7.1	5.6	8.2	1.7	0.1	0.1
100.0	3.3	2.1	0.1	0.0	2.7	0.6	0.0	—	5.6	0.2	20.6	3.4	8.5	5.0	1.1	0.5	9.0	0.9	10.8	6.4	16.9	2.1	0.1	0.1
100.0	20.9	17.9	0.0	—	0.0	0.0	0.1	—	3.7	0.3	18.2	3.5	4.7	2.8	0.7	0.3	8.2	0.8	5.1	4.3	7.3	1.1	0.1	0.0
100.0	18.2	16.5	0.0	—	0.0	—	0.1	—	7.8	0.2	12.1	2.6	6.9	4.3	0.6	0.6	6.1	0.6	5.8	4.6	11.2	1.7	0.1	0.0
100.0	24.6	18.9	0.0	0.0	0.0	—	0.1	0.1	4.9	0.4	10.8	2.3	4.6	3.0	0.4	0.2	5.2	0.5	7.6	4.0	10.6	1.6	0.1	0.1
100.0	27.6	24.6	—	0.0	0.2	—	0.4	—	3.7	0.3	6.4	1.2	4.4	3.0	0.3	0.2	4.8	0.3	5.1	4.5	10.3	2.5	0.1	0.1
100.0	14.5	5.7	0.4	0.0	0.0	0.0	0.1	0.0	4.5	0.1	19.5	14.2	9.4	5.8	0.7	0.4	5.9	0.6	6.2	4.5	6.4	0.8	0.2	0.1
100.0	9.2	4.0	—	0.0	—	—	0.2	0.1	9.4	0.7	11.7	4.1	7.4	3.0	0.7	0.4	5.5	0.6	13.3	5.7	20.6	2.7	0.5	0.2
100.0	10.9	4.2	0.1	0.0	—	—	1.0	—	13.9	0.6	9.9	3.1	6.7	4.3	0.6	0.4	3.6	0.3	8.0	13.7	16.6	1.9	0.1	0.1
100.0	34.4	13.3	—	—	—	—	0.0	—	4.3	0.0	7.7	6.9	5.2	3.1	0.3	0.3	2.7	0.3	6.5	3.3	11.1	0.6	—	—
100.0	33.7	15.0	—	—	0.0	—	—	—	3.7	0.0	7.8	8.0	4.3	1.5	0.2	0.1	2.1	0.2	7.5	3.5	11.5	0.5	0.3	0.1
100.0	29.6	18.1	0.0	—	—	0.0	0.1	—	4.4	0.2	5.7	5.1	4.9	2.9	0.4	0.2	2.5	0.5	6.4	8.2	9.8	1.0	0.0	0.0
100.0	29.0	24.5	0.0	—	0.0	0.0	0.2	0.0	3.3	0.1	8.6	5.3	5.6	3.2	0.4	0.1	2.9	0.4	5.5	3.3	6.9	0.6	0.1	0.0
100.0	24.3	22.0	0.0	—	0.1	0.0	0.2	0.0	2.8	0.1	11.5	5.5	7.6	4.2	0.8	0.4	4.8	0.5	5.3	4.0	5.0	0.8	0.0	0.1
100.0	38.9	22.3	0.1	—	—	—	0.1	—	3.0	0.0	6.8	5.6	4.0	2.1	0.1	0.1	1.9	0.1	4.1	2.5	7.3	0.7	0.1	0.2
100.0	27.7	30.9	0.0	—	0.0	0.0	0.0	—	2.7	0.1	13.5	3.4	4.3	2.0	0.3	0.2	5.4	0.3	3.5	2.3	2.6	0.5	0.3	0.0
100.0	34.9	42.1	0.0	—	0.0	0.0	0.0	—	1.4	0.0	5.6	0.8	1.2	1.1	0.2	0.1	6.3	0.5	2.3	1.1	1.9	0.5	0.0	0.0
100.0	31.0	32.1	—	—	0.1	0.0	0.0	—	2.1	0.1	7.7	1.6	4.1	2.2	0.4	0.2	6.0	0.5	4.5	4.4	2.2	0.7	0.0	0.1
100.0	33.8	35.7	—	—	0.0	0.0	—	—	1.9	0.0	7.0	1.4	3.6	2.2	0.3	0.1	6.1	0.3	2.8	2.1	2.2	0.4	0.0	0.1
100.0	31.1	34.8	—	—	0.0	0.0	—	—	2.3	0.0	6.1	1.4	3.5	1.9	0.5	0.2	9.8	0.7	3.0	2.1	1.9	0.5	0.1	0.1
100.0	34.1	34.8	—	—	0.1	0.0	—	—	1.5	0.1	6.1	2.0	4.8	3.5	0.4	0.2	3.5	0.4	3.2	2.4	2.1	0.6	0.1	0.1
100.0	39.4	43.5	0.1	—	0.2	0.0	—	—	1.1	0.1	2.3	0.5	3.7	2.4	0.1	0.0	1.1	0.2	2.4	1.7	0.9	0.2	0.0	0.1
100.0	35.6	41.5	0.0	—	0.1	0.0	0.0	—	1.8	0.0	4.6	0.8	3.9	2.3	0.4	0.1	1.9	0.2	3.1	1.3	2.1	0.3	—	—
100.0	21.8	28.7	0.0	0.0	0.1	—	0.1	0.0	4.9	0.3	10.1	2.7	7.9	5.4	0.7	0.3	4.3	0.5	4.7	3.3	3.5	0.7	—	0.0
100.0	36.1	38.3	0.0	0.0	0.0	—	—	—	1.9	0.0	3.6	0.5	4.5	4.2	0.3	0.1	2.3	0.3	3.3	2.4	1.8	0.4	0.0	0.0
100.0	42.3	43.2	0.0	—	0.7	0.1	—	—	1.6	0.0	0.9	0.2	1.8	2.4	0.1	0.9	1.2	0.1	2.1	1.1	1.0	0.3	—	—
100.0	30.7	33.0	0.0	—	0.0	—	0.0	—	2.9	0.3	5.1	1.2	4.2	3.0	0.7	0.2	4.8	0.4	5.2	3.5	3.7	1.0	0.1	0.0
100.0	33.4	38.0	0.0	0.0	0.9	0.6	—	—	1.7	0.0	4.9	0.8	4.0	2.3	0.5	0.1	2.5	0.3	3.6	2.3	3.1	0.9	0.1	0.0
100.0	33.2	33.8	0.0	—	3.0	0.2	0.0	—	1.3	0.1	4.5	1.2	5.3	2.7	0.6	0.2	2.8	0.3	4.5	3.6	1.9	0.8	0.0	0.0
100.0	40.6	43.9	0.2	0.1	—	—	—	—	1.5	0.1	2.4	0.7	1.4	1.0	0.1	0.1	1.8	0.1	2.5	1.6	1.5	0.4	—	—
100.0	41.2	43.2	—	—	—	—	0.0	—	1.2	0.1	2.3	0.5	2.1	1.6	0.1	0.0	1.3	0.2	2.2	2.0	1.5	0.3	0.1	0.1
100.0	24.6	27.5	0.1	0.0	5.5	1.9	0.0	—	2.7	0.1	5.0	1.2	7.2	4.5	0.4	0.3	4.0	0.4	4.9	5.0	4.1	0.6	0.0	0.0
100.0	25.1	15.5	0.1	0.0	0.6	6.1	0.1	0.0	3.8	0.1	10.9	4.5	6.0	3.6	0.5	0.3	4.2	1.2	5.6	4.1	6.7	0.9	0.1	0.0
100.0	5.4	4.3	0.1	0.0	1.4	0.2	0.2	0.1	4.6	0.2	18.0	2.6	12.4	5.7	2.5	0.6	8.2	1.0	11.4	10.1	9.3	1.5	0.1	0.1
100.0	38.6	32.5	—	—	—	—	—	0.0	4.5	0.3	4.6	1.2	1.8	1.2	0.2	0.0	2.4	0.3	2.8	2.2	6.5	0.8	0.1	0.1
100.0	35.8	26.1	0.1	0.0	0.1	0.0	1.1	0.1	3.1	0.1	7.0	1.8	3.0	1.9	0.3	0.2	4.8	0.3	4.4	3.3	5.6	0.8	0.0	0.1
100.0	38.0	24.2	0.2	—	0.0	—	0.1	0.0	2.8	0.1	5.0	2.7	2.7	1.9	0.1	0.1	6.7	0.6	5.1	3.2	5.7	0.8	0.0	—
100.0	28.4	13.6	0.0	—	0.0	—	3.2	0.1	5.5	0.1	6.5	4.9	5.9	2.5	0.7	0.4	4.6	0.6	8.0	4.2	9.1	1.7	0.0	—
100.0	37.0	15.9	—	—	—	—	1.0	0.0	2.9	0.1	6.3	4.2	4.0	1.9	0.3	0.2	3.7	0.5	5.7	3.7	11.3	1.2	0.1	0.0
100.0	24.8	16.2	2.5	0.0	0.1	—	1.3	0.0	3.2	0.1	11.2	8.3	7.5	3.4	0.6	0.2	4.3	0.4	5.7	3.8	5.9	0.4	0.0	0.1

Table 11. Gainfully Employed Population, 15 Years and Older, by Industry and Sex
(For 1950 only, 14-year-olds are included)

(Zone) (Sector)	District	Total Total	M	F	Total	Agriculture	Forestry and Hunting	Fisheries and Aquiculture	Mining	Construction	Manufacturing	Wholesale and Retail	Finance and Insurance	Transportation and Communication	Services	Civil Service	Unclassified
IV	Tsurugashima-mura	(3,288) 100.0	56.1	43.9	100.0	79.7	—	—	0.0	1.9	4.9	3.4	0.2	2.3	4.7	2.9	0.0
	Hidaka-machi	(7,681) 100.0	58.2	41.8	100.0	74.6	0.3	0.0	0.1	2.0	7.0	3.7	0.2	2.6	4.6	4.8	0.1
	Kawashima-mura	(9,539) 100.0	50.5	49.5	100.0	85.6	—	0.1	0.0	2.3	2.6	2.9	0.2	0.8	3.5	1.9	0.1
V	Kitamoto-machi	(5,939) 100.0	58.6	41.4	100.0	65.3	—	0.0	0.0	2.8	11.5	6.3	0.4	5.6	5.5	2.5	0.1
	Higawa-machi	(8,096) 100.0	60.4	39.6	100.0	56.4	0.0	0.0	0.1	2.5	14.7	9.2	0.8	6.0	7.0	3.0	0.3
	Shobu-machi	(7,492) 100.0	57.0	43.0	100.0	72.3	—	0.0	—	1.6	8.2	7.7	0.4	2.5	5.2	2.0	0.1
	Kuki-machi	(9,095) 100.0	60.2	39.8	100.0	57.0	—	—	0.1	2.0	11.6	9.1	0.7	8.8	7.5	3.1	0.1
	Satte-machi	(10,235) 100.0	56.7	43.3	100.0	61.1	0.1	0.0	0.0	2.2	12.3	10.5	0.5	3.3	7.4	2.4	0.2
VI	Iwai-machi	(18,539) 100.0	51.3	48.7	100.0	84.7	0.0	0.1	—	1.1	2.7	5.1	0.1	0.8	4.0	1.3	0.1
	Mitsukaidō-shi	(23,883) 100.0	53.2	46.8	100.0	72.7	0.0	0.1	0.0	2.0	5.7	9.0	0.5	3.0	5.3	1.6	0.1
	Yawahara-mura	(4,282) 100.0	52.0	48.0	100.0	83.4	0.0	0.1	0.0	1.7	2.8	3.8	0.4	1.9	4.2	1.6	0.1
	Ina-mura	(6,080) 100.0	50.7	49.3	100.0	84.9	0.0	—	—	1.5	2.7	3.8	0.2	1.4	3.7	1.7	0.1
VII	Fujishiro-machi	(7,397) 100.0	53.4	46.6	100.0	73.3	—	0.0	0.1	4.1	5.1	6.1	0.3	3.9	4.6	2.5	0.0
	Ryūgasaki-shi	(15,348) 100.0	57.1	42.9	100.0	65.0	0.0	0.0	0.0	2.9	8.7	9.4	0.7	3.2	6.7	3.3	0.1
	Tone-mura	(4,964) 100.0	51.9	48.1	100.0	78.4	—	0.1	—	3.3	4.2	5.1	0.5	1.8	3.6	2.8	0.2
	Motono-mura	(2,949) 100.0	52.0	48.0	100.0	87.5	0.1	0.1	—	1.1	2.1	3.3	0.1	1.4	3.0	1.3	—
VIII	Sakura-shi	(15,698) 100.0	56.1	43.9	100.0	65.3	0.0	0.1	0.0	1.7	6.3	7.9	0.7	6.2	7.5	4.2	0.1
	Izumi-machi	(5,289) 100.0	50.8	49.2	100.0	88.5	—	—	—	0.9	1.6	2.1	0.2	1.9	3.1	1.7	—
IX	Shitsu-mura	(5,291) 100.0	51.4	48.6	100.0	86.4	—	0.0	—	0.7	2.4	2.7	0.1	2.0	3.4	2.3	—
	Nansō-machi	(9,737) 100.0	53.2	46.8	100.0	79.3	0.4	—	—	1.5	3.4	5.7	0.3	1.9	5.5	1.9	0.1
	Fukuta-machi	(2,617) 100.0	54.3	45.7	100.0	78.5	1.2	—	—	1.6	3.8	4.0	0.2	2.4	6.0	2.3	—
X	Kimitsu-machi	(6,655) 100.0	54.6	45.4	100.0	71.4	0.1	5.0	0.0	3.0	4.4	4.8	0.2	2.7	5.9	2.5	—
	Futtsu-machi	(7,177) 100.0	60.0	40.0	100.0	45.5	0.0	27.5	0.0	2.7	5.9	7.4	0.3	3.0	5.9	1.8	0.0
	Ōsawa-machi	(6,414) 100.0	58.0	42.0	100.0	55.2	0.4	10.0	0.1	3.0	6.7	9.6	0.5	3.9	8.1	2.4	0.1
	Zone 9 Total	(271,797) 100.0	58.7	41.3	100.0	62.3	0.2	1.3	0.2	2.6	8.8	8.1	0.7	4.0	7.6	4.1	0.1
10 I	Yokosuka-shi	(88,820) 100.0	76.3	23.7	100.0	7.3	0.0	2.6	0.1	5.8	20.1	13.7	1.1	9.1	17.9	22.3	0.0
	Zushi-shi	(11,476) 100.0	77.1	22.9	100.0	4.5	0.2	2.2	0.2	4.3	21.9	16.8	3.0	9.5	19.0	18.2	0.2
	Hayama-machi	(5,567) 100.0	68.8	31.2	100.0	22.2	0.2	5.3	0.1	4.9	16.4	13.6	2.1	5.3	17.8	12.0	0.1
	Chigasaki-shi	(18,929) 100.0	62.4	37.6	100.0	33.2	0.0	1.7	0.2	3.6	21.6	12.2	1.4	7.5	10.2	8.2	0.2
	Fujisawa-shi	(35,501) 100.0	69.6	30.4	100.0	26.8	0.0	0.7	0.1	4.4	20.2	16.0	2.0	6.9	15.5	7.3	0.1
II	Aikawa-machi	(6,720) 100.0	60.6	39.4	100.0	54.2	0.4	0.1	0.0	3.4	25.8	4.8	0.2	1.7	6.9	2.4	0.1
	Atsugi-shi	(18,368) 100.0	63.8	36.2	100.0	62.1	0.1	0.1	0.4	3.1	8.2	8.1	0.6	4.0	8.4	4.8	0.1
	Samukawa-machi	(4,398) 100.0	66.7	33.3	100.0	51.4	—	—	1.3	2.4	20.9	6.2	0.6	5.0	6.8	5.3	0.1
III	Ōme-shi	(20,168) 100.0	70.2	29.8	100.0	26.0	1.0	—	0.9	5.0	29.4	10.8	1.1	5.0	11.8	8.7	0.3
IV	Sakado-machi	(66,242) 100.0	55.9	44.1	100.0	72.0	0.0	0.0	0.3	2.0	7.3	7.2	0.4	2.2	5.0	3.5	0.1
	Yoshimi-mura	(8,348) 100.0	51.6	48.4	100.0	84.8	—	0.0	—	1.8	3.8	2.7	0.1	1.5	3.2	2.1	0.0
	Moroyama-mura	(5,092) 100.0	56.3	43.7	100.0	70.9	0.1	—	—	2.6	8.9	5.1	0.3	2.2	6.8	3.0	0.1
V	Kōnosu-shi	(13,151) 100.0	58.6	41.4	100.0	53.0	0.0	0.0	0.0	2.3	13.8	10.8	0.6	5.8	9.6	4.0	0.1
	Kisai-machi	(8,464) 100.0	53.5	46.5	100.0	77.8	0.0	0.0	—	1.7	5.9	6.5	0.3	1.9	4.3	1.5	0.1
	Washimiya-machi	(4,451) 100.0	56.6	43.4	100.0	71.6	0.0	0.1	—	1.4	7.6	5.5	0.4	7.1	4.2	2.1	0.0
	Kurihashi-machi	(5,258) 100.0	57.9	42.1	100.0	58.3	0.0	0.0	0.0	4.5	10.1	11.0	0.4	6.8	6.1	2.6	0.2
	Goka-mura	(4,975) 100.0	50.4	49.6	100.0	87.7	—	0.0	—	2.3	2.8	2.1	0.1	1.1	2.6	1.3	—
VI	Sakai-machi	(12,180) 100.0	49.8	50.2	100.0	76.6	0.0	0.0	—	1.2	4.4	7.6	0.3	1.5	5.8	2.5	0.1
	Sashima-machi	(8,381) 100.0	49.9	50.1	100.0	85.8	0.0	—	—	0.8	2.9	4.7	0.1	0.7	3.8	1.2	0.0
	Yatabe-machi	(9,897) 100.0	52.3	47.7	100.0	83.4	0.0	0.0	—	1.1	2.5	4.7	0.2	1.2	4.3	2.5	0.1
VII	Kukizaki-mura	(3,595) 100.0	51.2	48.8	100.0	89.0	0.0	0.3	—	1.1	2.6	2.4	0.1	1.1	2.1	1.3	—
	Ushiku-machi	(7,630) 100.0	54.7	45.3	100.0	77.5	0.1	0.0	0.0	1.7	5.5	5.2	0.2	3.3	4.1	2.3	0.1
	Kawachi-mura	(7,521) 100.0	50.2	49.8	100.0	86.6	—	0.1	—	1.6	1.6	3.8	0.2	1.5	3.4	1.1	0.1
	Sakae-machi	(4,764) 100.0	51.8	48.2	100.0	77.2	0.0	0.1	—	2.2	4.2	6.6	0.2	2.4	5.3	1.7	0.1
	Narita-shi	(20,650) 100.0	55.2	44.8	100.0	64.3	0.1	0.1	0.0	1.7	5.1	11.1	0.5	5.1	9.3	2.6	0.1

Total	Agriculture		Forestry and Hunting		Fisheries and Aquiculture		Mining		Construction		Manufacturing		Wholesale and Retail		Finance and Insurance		Transportation and Communication		Services		Civil Service		Unclassified	
	M	F	M	F	M	F	M	F	M	F	M	F	M	F	M	F	M	F	M	F	M	F	M	F
100.0	41.1	38.6	—	—	—	—	0.0	—	1.9	0.0	3.6	1.3	1.8	1.6	0.2	0.0	2.0	0.3	2.9	1.8	2.6	0.3	0.0	—
100.0	39.3	35.3	0.3	0.0	0.0	—	0.1	0.0	1.9	0.1	4.4	2.6	2.3	1.4	0.1	0.1	2.4	0.2	2.8	1.8	4.5	0.3	0.1	0.0
100.0	39.6	46.0	—	—	0.1	0.0	0.0	0.0	2.3	0.0	2.2	0.4	1.8	1.1	0.1	0.1	0.7	0.1	2.0	1.5	1.7	0.2	0.0	0.1
100.0	30.7	34.6	—	—	0.0	0.0	0.0	0.0	2.8	0.0	9.5	2.0	4.4	1.9	0.3	0.1	5.2	0.4	3.4	2.1	2.2	0.3	0.1	0.0
100.0	27.0	29.4	0.0	—	0.0	0.0	0.0	0.1	2.4	0.1	12.0	2.7	5.8	3.4	0.5	0.3	5.7	0.3	4.3	2.7	2.4	0.6	0.3	0.0
100.0	37.7	34.6	—	—	0.0	0.0	—	—	1.5	0.1	5.3	2.9	5.1	2.6	0.3	0.1	2.3	0.2	3.0	2.2	1.7	0.3	0.1	0.0
100.0	28.3	28.7	—	—	—	—	0.1	0.0	1.9	0.1	9.1	2.5	5.7	3.4	0.5	0.2	8.1	0.7	4.0	3.5	2.4	0.7	0.1	0.0
100.0	30.5	30.6	0.1	—	0.0	0.0	0.0	0.0	2.1	0.1	8.1	4.2	6.6	3.9	0.4	0.1	2.9	0.4	4.1	3.3	1.8	0.6	0.1	0.1
100.0	40.6	44.1	0.0	—	0.1	0.0	—	—	1.0	0.1	2.1	0.6	3.2	1.9	0.1	0.0	0.7	0.1	2.4	1.6	1.1	0.2	0.0	0.1
100.0	34.1	38.6	0.0	—	0.1	0.0	0.0	0.0	2.0	0.0	4.3	1.4	5.5	3.5	0.4	0.1	2.6	0.4	2.8	2.5	1.4	0.2	0.0	0.1
100.0	39.4	44.0	0.0	—	0.1	0.0	—	0.0	1.7	0.0	2.6	0.2	2.1	1.7	0.4	0.1	1.7	0.2	2.4	1.8	1.6	0.0	—	0.1
100.0	40.1	44.8	0.0	—	—	—	—	—	1.2	0.3	2.2	0.5	2.2	1.6	0.2	0.0	1.3	0.1	2.0	1.7	1.5	0.2	0.0	0.1
100.0	33.2	40.1	—	—	0.0	0.0	0.1	0.0	3.8	0.3	4.0	1.1	3.6	2.5	0.3	0.0	3.6	0.3	2.7	1.9	2.1	0.4	0.0	0.0
100.0	30.6	34.4	0.0	—	0.0	0.0	—	—	2.7	0.2	7.2	1.5	6.2	3.2	0.5	0.2	2.9	0.3	4.2	2.5	2.8	0.5	0.0	0.1
100.0	35.3	43.1	—	—	0.1	0.0	—	—	2.9	0.4	3.7	0.5	3.2	1.9	0.3	0.2	1.6	0.2	2.3	1.3	2.5	0.3	0.0	0.2
100.0	43.4	44.1	0.1	—	—	0.1	—	—	1.1	0.0	1.9	0.2	1.3	2.0	0.0	0.1	1.2	0.2	1.9	1.1	1.1	0.2	—	—
100.0	31.3	34.0	0.0	—	0.1	0.0	0.0	0.0	1.6	0.1	5.1	1.2	4.3	3.6	0.5	0.2	5.7	0.5	4.1	3.4	3.3	0.9	0.1	0.0
100.0	42.4	46.1	—	—	—	—	—	—	0.8	0.1	1.5	0.1	1.1	1.0	0.1	0.1	1.6	0.3	1.9	1.2	1.4	0.3	—	—
100.0	41.3	45.1	—	—	0.0	0.0	—	—	0.7	0.0	2.1	0.3	1.5	1.2	0.1	0.0	1.7	0.3	2.1	1.3	1.9	0.4	—	—
100.0	38.7	40.6	0.3	0.1	—	—	—	—	1.4	0.1	2.6	0.8	3.5	2.2	0.2	0.1	1.6	0.3	3.2	2.3	1.6	0.3	0.1	0.0
100.0	37.9	40.6	1.1	0.1	—	—	—	—	1.6	0.0	3.2	0.6	2.8	1.2	0.2	0.0	2.3	0.1	3.2	2.8	2.0	0.3	—	—
100.0	34.0	37.4	0.1	0.0	3.4	1.6	0.0	—	2.2	0.8	3.6	0.8	3.3	1.5	0.1	0.1	2.5	0.2	3.2	2.7	2.2	0.3	—	—
100.0	19.1	26.4	—	0.0	21.7	5.8	0.0	0.0	2.4	0.3	4.7	1.2	4.6	2.8	0.2	0.1	2.6	0.4	3.2	2.7	1.5	0.3	0.0	0.0
100.0	23.9	31.3	0.4	—	9.2	0.8	0.1	0.0	2.9	0.1	5.7	1.0	5.6	4.0	0.3	0.2	3.6	0.3	4.3	3.8	2.0	0.4	0.0	0.1
100.0	30.8	31.5	0.2	0.0	1.1	0.2	0.2	0.0	2.5	0.1	6.7	2.1	5.2	2.9	0.5	0.2	3.6	0.4	4.3	3.3	3.5	0.6	0.1	0.0
100.0	3.3	4.0	0.0	0.0	2.5	0.1	0.0	0.1	5.3	0.5	17.0	3.1	8.1	5.6	0.8	0.3	8.2	0.9	10.7	7.2	20.4	1.9	0.0	0.0
100.0	2.7	1.8	0.2	0.0	2.2	0.0	0.2	0.0	4.0	0.3	18.9	3.0	11.5	5.3	2.3	0.7	8.4	1.1	10.5	8.5	16.1	2.1	0.1	0.1
100.0	8.3	13.9	0.2	0.0	5.0	0.3	0.1	0.0	4.7	0.2	14.8	1.6	9.5	4.1	1.5	0.6	4.5	0.8	9.4	8.4	10.8	1.2	0.0	0.1
100.0	18.2	15.0	0.0	0.0	1.6	0.1	0.1	0.1	3.5	0.1	17.8	3.8	0.3	11.9	1.1	0.3	6.9	0.6	5.5	4.7	7.3	0.9	0.1	0.1
100.0	15.5	11.3	0.0	0.0	0.6	0.1	0.1	0.0	4.3	0.1	16.5	3.7	10.3	5.7	1.6	0.4	6.2	0.7	8.3	7.2	6.1	1.2	0.1	0.0
100.0	35.1	19.1	0.3	0.1	0.1	0.0	0.0	0.0	3.3	0.1	11.6	14.2	2.7	2.1	0.1	0.1	1.5	0.2	3.7	3.2	2.1	0.3	0.1	0.0
100.0	36.7	25.4	0.1	0.0	0.1	0.0	0.3	0.1	2.9	0.2	6.2	2.0	4.9	3.2	0.3	0.3	3.5	0.5	4.7	3.7	4.1	0.7	0.0	0.1
100.0	27.6	23.8	—	—	—	—	1.3	0.0	2.3	0.1	18.2	2.7	3.8	2.4	0.3	0.3	4.6	0.4	3.8	3.0	4.7	0.6	0.1	—
100.0	19.3	6.7	1.0	0.0	—	—	0.8	0.1	5.0	0.0	16.5	12.9	7.7	3.1	0.7	0.4	4.5	0.5	6.7	5.1	7.8	0.9	0.2	0.1
100.0	35.8	36.2	0.0	0.0	0.0	—	0.2	0.1	2.0	0.0	5.5	1.8	4.3	2.9	0.3	0.1	1.8	0.4	2.8	2.2	3.1	0.4	0.1	—
100.0	39.9	44.9	—	—	0.0	—	—	—	1.7	0.1	3.2	0.6	1.6	1.1	0.1	0.0	1.4	0.1	1.9	1.3	1.8	0.3	—	—
100.0	35.8	35.1	0.1	—	—	—	—	—	2.6	0.0	6.1	2.8	3.0	2.1	0.2	0.1	1.9	0.3	3.8	3.0	2.7	0.3	0.1	0.0
100.0	25.0	28.0	0.0	—	0.0	—	—	0.0	2.3	0.0	9.3	4.5	6.8	4.0	0.4	0.2	5.5	0.3	5.8	3.8	3.4	0.6	0.1	0.0
100.0	38.2	39.6	0.0	—	0.0	—	—	—	1.7	0.0	3.9	2.0	4.2	2.3	0.2	0.1	1.7	0.2	2.4	1.9	1.1	0.4	0.1	0.0
100.0	34.4	37.2	0.0	—	0.0	0.1	—	—	1.4	0.0	6.0	1.6	3.7	1.8	0.2	0.2	6.7	0.4	2.4	1.8	1.8	0.3	0.0	—
100.0	26.8	31.5	0.0	—	0.0	—	0.0	—	4.2	0.3	7.9	2.2	6.6	4.4	0.3	0.1	6.4	0.4	3.4	2.7	2.2	0.4	0.1	0.1
100.0	40.8	46.9	—	—	0.0	0.0	—	—	2.2	0.1	2.3	0.5	1.3	0.8	0.1	0.0	1.1	0.0	1.6	1.0	1.0	0.3	—	—
100.0	36.0	40.6	0.0	—	0.0	—	—	—	1.1	0.1	3.7	0.7	2.2	5.4	0.2	0.1	1.3	0.2	3.3	2.5	2.0	0.5	0.0	0.1
100.0	40.7	45.1	0.0	—	—	—	—	—	0.8	0.0	2.1	0.8	2.7	2.0	0.0	0.1	0.6	0.1	2.0	1.8	2.0	0.2	0.0	—
100.0	40.2	43.2	0.0	—	—	—	—	—	1.1	—	2.1	0.4	2.9	1.8	0.2	0.0	1.0	0.2	2.5	1.8	2.2	0.3	0.1	0.0
100.0	42.7	46.3	—	0.0	0.2	0.1	—	—	1.1	0.0	2.2	0.4	1.4	1.0	0.1	—	1.1	0.0	1.3	0.8	1.1	0.2	—	—
100.0	37.3	40.2	0.1	0.0	0.0	—	0.0	0.0	1.7	0.0	4.7	0.8	2.9	2.3	0.1	0.1	3.1	0.2	2.7	1.4	2.0	0.3	0.1	0.0
100.0	41.1	45.5	—	—	0.1	0.0	—	—	1.6	—	1.3	0.3	2.2	1.6	0.1	0.1	0.9	0.6	1.7	1.7	1.1	0.0	0.1	0.0
100.0	36.6	40.6	0.0	—	0.1	—	—	—	2.0	0.2	3.1	1.1	3.1	3.5	0.2	—	2.3	0.1	2.9	2.4	1.4	0.3	0.1	0.0
100.0	30.9	33.4	0.1	0.0	0.1	0.0	0.0	—	1.7	—	4.0	1.1	5.9	5.2	0.4	0.1	4.6	0.5	5.3	4.0	2.1	0.5	0.1	0.0

(Zone) (Sector)	District	Total	M	F	Total	Agriculture	Forestry and Hunting	Fisheries and Aquiculture	Mining	Construction	Manufacturing	Wholesale and Retail	Finance and Insurance	Transportation and Communication	Services	Civil Service	Unclassified
VIII	Shisui-machi	(2,844) 100.0	56.6	43.4	100.0	69.0	0.1	0.2	—	1.4	7.3	6.5	0.3	7.7	4.8	2.7	—
	Yachimata-machi	(14,186) 100.0	55.2	44.8	100.0	76.7	0.1	0.0	—	1.5	5.3	7.3	0.3	2.2	5.0	1.6	0.0
	Toke-machi	(3,157) 100.0	55.1	44.9	100.0	78.0	0.1	0.1	—	2.3	5.2	3.7	0.4	3.7	4.0	2.5	—
IX	Nagara-machi	(5,316) 100.0	50.8	49.2	100.0	85.8	0.1	—	0.4	1.3	2.5	2.8	0.1	1.4	4.0	1.6	—
	Obitsu-mura	(3,801) 100.0	53.4	46.6	100.0	78.8	2.1	0.0	—	1.3	4.9	3.7	0.2	2.6	4.4	2.0	—
X	Koito-machi	(3,494) 100.0	53.4	46.6	100.0	85.0	0.9	—	—	0.8	2.7	3.2	0.2	1.0	4.8	1.4	—
	Zone 10 Total	(378,344) 100.0	64.0	36.0	100.0	45.7	0.1	0.9	0.1	3.4	13.7	10.1	0.9	5.4	10.7	8.9	0.1
	Total for 50 km. Region	(4,244,510) 100.0	69.5	30.5	100.0	20.8	0.1	0.6	0.1	5.4	25.3	17.5	2.1	6.7	13.4	7.7	0.3
	National Total	(35,625,790) 100.0	61.4	38.6	100.0	45.1	1.2	1.9	1.7	4.3	16.0	11.1	1.0	5.1	8.6	3.9	0.1
	1955																
1 I	Chiyoda-ku	(65,728) 100.0	69.0	31.0	100.0	0.0	0.0	0.0	0.2	4.0	21.2	42.6	2.6	3.5	21.4	4.5	0.0
	Minato-ku	(115,612) 100.0	68.7	31.3	100.0	0.1	0.0	0.2	0.2	5.2	23.9	30.0	4.3	7.0	23.1	6.0	0.0
	Chūō-ku	(94,324) 100.0	67.7	32.3	100.0	0.0	0.0	0.2	0.1	3.1	20.1	50.3	2.4	5.3	16.4	2.1	0.0
	Bunkyō-ku	(104,510) 100.0	68.8	31.2	100.0	0.1	0.0	0.1	0.2	5.5	30.4	25.9	4.3	5.2	23.3	5.0	0.0
	Taitō-ku	(157,440) 100.0	68.8	31.2	100.0	0.0	0.0	0.0	0.0	3.7	31.9	38.2	1.9	3.0	18.8	2.5	0.0
	Zone 1 Total	(537,614) 100.0	68.6	31.4	100.0	0.1	0.0	0.1	0.1	4.3	26.5	36.6	3.1	4.8	20.5	3.9	0.0
2 I	Shinagawa-ku	(160,724) 100.0	71.0	29.0	100.0	0.1	0.0	0.2	0.2	6.0	36.6	23.8	3.9	7.2	17.8	4.2	0.0
II	Meguro-ku	(100,300) 100.0	72.0	28.0	100.0	0.6	0.1	0.1	0.3	5.8	30.5	22.8	5.6	7.2	20.9	6.1	0.0
	Shibuya-ku	(99,326) 100.0	69.1	30.9	100.0	0.2	0.0	0.1	0.3	7.2	22.2	26.3	6.1	7.3	24.9	5.4	0.0
III	Shinjuku-ku	(150,413) 100.0	68.1	31.9	100.0	0.2	0.0	0.1	0.3	6.7	23.6	27.8	4.9	6.1	24.5	5.8	0.0
	Nakano-ku	(111,400) 100.0	72.0	28.0	100.0	0.7	0.2	0.1	0.5	6.5	23.5	24.5	6.5	8.1	22.7	6.7	0.0
IV	Toshima-ku	(124,347) 100.0	69.8	30.2	100.0	0.2	0.0	0.1	0.2	6.8	27.6	27.5	4.8	7.2	21.0	4.6	0.0
V	Kita-ku	(143,101) 100.0	71.5	28.5	100.0	0.3	0.0	0.0	0.2	5.7	36.8	22.7	3.9	8.2	16.4	5.8	0.0
VI	Arakawa-ku	(112,588) 100.0	72.1	27.9	100.0	0.1	0.0	0.0	0.1	5.8	46.7	24.0	2.2	6.0	11.9	3.1	0.1
VII	Sumida-ku	(146,134) 100.0	71.4	28.6	100.0	0.1	0.0	0.0	0.0	4.5	52.4	22.5	1.5	3.8	13.2	2.0	0.0
VIII	Kōtō-ku	(123,386) 100.0	75.4	24.6	100.0	0.1	0.1	0.3	0.0	8.0	41.9	23.2	1.6	8.7	12.4	3.7	0.0
	Zone 2 Total	(1,271,719) 100.0	71.2	28.8	100.0	0.2	0.0	0.1	0.2	6.3	34.7	24.5	4.0	6.9	18.4	4.7	0.0
3 I	Ōta-ku	(230,013) 100.0	73.8	26.2	100.0	0.7	0.0	1.6	0.2	5.6	38.3	21.6	4.0	6.5	17.6	3.9	0.0
II	Setagaya-ku	(194,840) 100.0	71.8	28.2	100.0	2.8	0.1	0.1	0.5	6.1	24.1	21.9	6.0	7.7	24.0	6.7	0.0
III	Suginami-ku	(151,571) 100.0	72.7	27.8	100.0	1.6	0.0	0.2	0.8	5.4	23.0	24.4	7.5	7.3	23.4	6.4	0.0
IV	Itabashi-ku	(119,679) 100.0	73.0	27.0	100.0	2.5	0.0	0.0	0.1	5.5	39.1	19.8	3.3	6.7	17.2	5.8	0.0
	Nerima-ku	(770,468) 100.0	72.5	27.5	100.0	9.3	0.0	0.0	0.2	5.4	23.2	18.0	4.9	7.0	21.1	10.9	0.0
VI	Adachi-ku	(133,633) 100.0	71.7	28.3	100.0	5.9	0.0	0.0	0.0	4.8	43.6	20.2	2.0	7.3	11.3	4.9	0.0
VII	Katsushika-ku	(118,394) 100.0	70.8	29.2	100.0	3.1	0.0	0.0	0.1	4.1	47.7	19.0	2.4	6.2	12.6	4.8	0.0
VIII	Edogawa-ku	(102,826) 100.0	71.4	28.6	100.0	7.3	0.0	1.5	0.1	4.4	41.2	19.1	2.6	6.5	12.5	4.8	0.0
	Urayasu-machi	(6,671) 100.0	67.5	37.5	100.0	12.1	0.0	30.6	0.1	1.6	11.2	32.0	0.8	1.5	7.9	2.2	0.0
	Zone 3 Total	(1,128,095) 100.0	72.3	27.7	100.0	3.4	0.0	0.7	0.3	5.2	34.6	21.0	4.3	6.9	17.9	5.7	0.0
4 I	Kawasaki-shi	(178,751) 100.0	74.1	25.9	100.0	6.7	0.0	0.3	0.1	8.7	42.2	15.6	1.6	8.0	13.8	3.0	0.0
II	Komae-machi	(5,495) 100.0	70.0	30.0	100.0	16.2	0.0	0.1	0.3	6.0	24.6	15.7	3.3	6.8	22.3	4.7	0.0
III	Mitaka-shi	(25,586) 100.0	72.7	27.3	100.0	8.2	0.0	0.1	0.3	5.2	29.3	19.2	4.7	7.0	19.9	6.1	0.0
	Musashino-shi	(35,798) 100.0	71.5	28.5	100.0	2.3	0.0	0.1	1.1	5.6	22.5	23.0	6.5	7.6	24.5	6.8	0.0
	Chōfu-shi	(16,777) 100.0	72.3	27.7	100.0	14.4	0.0	0.0	0.5	4.9	24.9	15.8	2.3	9.2	22.7	5.3	0.0
	Hoya-machi	(8,375) 100.0	71.2	28.8	100.0	16.1	0.0	0.0	0.2	5.7	22.9	15.4	3.5	8.4	20.2	7.5	0.1
IV	Yamato-machi	(5,480) 100.0	65.6	34.4	100.0	27.1	0.0	0.0	0.0	7.0	26.2	13.0	1.1	3.5	18.4	3.7	0.0
	Toda-machi	(9,123) 100.0	63.3	36.7	100.0	32.5	0.0	0.1	0.1	3.5	38.0	10.3	1.1	3.7	7.9	2.8	0.0
V	Warabi-shi	(13,357) 100.0	70.5	29.5	100.0	4.8	0.0	0.0	0.1	4.6	44.0	20.4	2.6	5.9	13.3	4.3	0.0
	Kawaguchi-shi	(54,536) 100.0	70.3	29.7	100.0	13.8	0.0	0.0	0.1	3.1	47.8	15.9	1.5	4.2	10.7	2.9	0.0

Table 11. Gainfully Employed Population, 15 Years and Older, by Industry and Sex
(For 1950 only, 14-year-olds are included)

Total	Agriculture		Forestry and Hunting		Fisheries and Aquiculture		Mining		Construction		Manufacturing		Wholesale and Retail		Finance and Insurance		Transportation and Communication		Services		Civil Service		Unclassified	
	M	F	M	F	M	F	M	F	M	F	M	F	M	F	M	F	M	F	M	F	M	F	M	F
100.0	32.8	36.2	0.1	—	0.2	—	—	—	1.3	0.1	6.1	1.2	3.8	2.7	0.3	0.0	6.9	0.8	2.8	2.0	2.3	0.4	—	—
100.0	38.4	38.3	0.1	—	0.0	0.0	—	—	1.5	—	4.6	0.7	4.4	2.9	0.2	0.1	2.0	0.2	2.8	2.2	1.3	0.3	0.0	0.0
100.0	38.3	39.7	0.1	—	0.0	0.0	—	—	2.2	0.1	4.3	0.9	2.3	1.5	0.3	0.1	3.4	0.3	2.1	1.9	2.1	0.4	—	—
100.0	40.5	41.3	0.1	—	—	—	0.4	—	1.3	—	1.8	0.8	1.7	1.1	0.1	—	1.1	0.3	0.6	3.4	1.3	0.3	—	—
100.0	36.4	42.4	1.9	0.2	0.0	—	—	—	1.3	—	4.2	0.7	2.7	1.0	0.2	0.0	2.4	0.2	2.5	1.9	1.8	0.2	—	—
100.0	42.7	42.3	0.9	0.0	—	—	—	—	0.8	—	2.3	0.4	1.8	1.4	0.1	0.1	0.9	0.1	2.8	2.0	1.1	0.3	—	—
100.0	23.2	22.5	0.1	0.0	0.9	0.0	0.1	0.0	3.3	0.1	10.7	3.0	6.2	3.9	0.6	0.3	4.8	0.6	6.1	4.6	7.9	1.0	0.1	—
100.0	10.7	10.1	0.1	0.0	0.5	0.1	0.1	0.0	5.1	0.3	20.1	5.2	11.4	6.1	1.4	0.7	6.0	0.7	7.4	6.0	6.5	1.2	0.2	0.1
100.0	21.9	23.2	1.0	0.2	1.7	0.2	1.5	0.2	4.0	0.3	11.4	4.6	6.8	4.3	0.7	0.3	4.5	0.6	4.6	4.0	3.2	0.7	0.1	0.0
100.0	0.0	0.0	0.0	0.0	0.0	0.0	0.0	0.2	3.7	0.3	16.8	4.4	31.0	11.6	1.6	1.0	3.1	0.4	8.9	12.5	3.9	0.6	0.0	0.0
100.0	0.1	0.0	0.0	0.0	0.1	0.1	0.2	0.0	4.9	0.3	19.4	4.5	19.3	10.7	2.7	1.6	6.2	0.8	10.8	12.3	5.0	1.0	0.0	0.0
100.0	0.0	0.0	0.0	0.0	0.2	0.0	0.1	0.0	2.9	0.2	16.1	4.0	34.4	15.9	1.3	1.1	4.7	0.6	6.2	10.2	1.8	0.3	0.0	0.0
100.0	0.1	0.0	0.0	0.0	0.0	0.1	0.1	0.1	5.3	0.2	23.3	7.1	17.4	8.5	2.7	1.6	4.5	0.7	11.2	12.1	4.2	0.8	0.0	0.0
100.0	0.0	0.0	0.0	0.0	0.0	0.0	0.0	0.0	3.5	0.2	25.8	6.1	25.9	12.3	1.1	0.8	2.7	0.3	7.6	11.2	2.2	0.3	0.0	0.0
100.0	0.1	0.0	0.0	0.0	0.1	0.0	0.1	0.0	4.1	0.2	21.1	5.4	24.9	11.7	1.9	1.2	4.2	0.6	8.9	11.6	3.3	0.6	0.0	0.0
100.0	0.1	0.0	0.0	0.0	0.2	0.0	0.1	0.1	5.8	0.2	28.0	8.6	14.9	8.9	2.5	1.4	6.4	0.8	9.5	8.3	3.5	0.7	0.0	0.0
100.0	0.5	0.1	0.0	0.1	0.1	0.0	0.3	0.0	5.6	0.2	24.2	6.3	15.1	7.7	3.7	1.9	6.2	1.0	11.3	9.6	5.0	1.1	0.0	0.0
100.0	0.2	0.0	0.0	0.0	0.0	0.1	0.2	0.1	6.9	0.3	17.5	4.7	17.1	9.2	4.3	1.8	6.2	1.1	12.2	12.7	4.5	0.9	0.0	0.0
100.0	0.1	0.1	0.0	0.0	0.1	0.0	0.2	0.1	6.3	0.4	18.4	5.2	17.7	10.1	3.3	1.6	5.2	0.9	12.1	12.4	4.7	1.1	0.0	0.0
100.0	0.5	0.2	0.0	0.2	0.1	0.0	0.4	0.1	6.1	0.4	18.7	4.8	16.5	8.0	4.4	2.1	7.0	1.1	12.9	9.8	5.4	1.3	0.0	0.0
100.0	0.2	0.0	0.0	0.0	0.1	0.0	0.2	0.0	6.5	0.3	21.0	6.6	17.3	10.2	3.1	1.7	6.4	0.8	11.3	9.7	3.7	0.9	0.0	0.0
100.0	0.2	0.1	0.0	0.0	0.0	0.0	0.1	0.1	5.5	0.2	27.6	9.2	14.2	8.5	2.3	1.6	7.3	0.9	9.6	6.8	4.7	1.1	0.0	0.0
100.0	0.1	0.0	0.0	0.0	0.0	0.1	0.0	0.0	5.6	0.2	35.3	11.4	15.8	8.2	1.2	1.0	5.3	0.7	6.1	5.8	2.6	0.5	0.0	0.1
100.0	0.1	0.0	0.0	0.0	0.0	0.0	0.0	0.1	4.4	0.1	39.8	12.6	15.1	7.4	0.9	0.6	3.4	0.4	6.0	7.2	1.7	0.3	0.0	0.0
100.0	0.1	0.0	0.1	0.0	0.3	0.0	0.0	0.0	7.8	0.2	33.7	8.2	15.4	7.8	0.9	0.7	8.0	0.7	5.8	6.6	3.3	0.4	0.0	0.0
100.0	0.2	0.0	0.0	0.0	0.1	0.0	0.2	0.0	6.0	0.3	26.7	8.0	15.9	8.6	2.6	1.4	6.1	0.8	9.6	8.8	3.8	0.9	0.0	0.0
100.0	0.5	0.2	0.0	0.0	1.2	0.4	0.1	0.1	5.4	0.2	31.3	7.0	14.0	7.6	2.7	1.3	5.7	0.8	9.6	8.0	3.3	0.6	0.0	0.0
100.0	1.9	0.9	0.1	0.0	0.1	0.0	0.4	0.1	5.8	0.3	19.3	4.8	14.5	7.4	4.1	1.9	6.7	1.0	13.8	10.2	5.3	1.4	0.0	0.0
100.0	1.1	0.5	0.0	0.0	0.1	0.1	0.7	0.1	5.2	0.2	18.6	4.4	16.3	8.1	5.3	2.2	6.3	1.0	13.4	10.0	5.2	1.2	0.0	0.0
100.0	1.5	1.0	0.0	0.0	0.0	0.0	0.1	0.0	5.5	0.0	33.0	9.1	12.7	7.1	2.2	1.1	5.9	0.8	10.4	6.8	4.8	1.0	0.0	0.0
100.0	5.4	3.9	0.0	0.0	0.0	0.0	0.2	0.0	5.2	0.2	17.4	5.8	11.9	6.1	3.5	1.4	6.2	0.8	12.8	8.3	9.9	1.0	0.0	0.0
100.0	3.0	2.9	0.0	0.0	0.0	0.0	0.0	0.0	4.6	0.2	32.9	10.7	13.1	7.1	1.1	0.9	6.4	0.9	6.3	5.0	4.3	0.6	0.0	0.0
100.0	1.6	1.5	0.0	0.0	0.0	0.0	0.0	0.1	3.9	0.2	36.0	11.7	11.7	7.3	1.5	0.9	5.4	0.8	6.8	5.8	4.1	0.7	0.0	0.0
100.0	4.0	3.3	0.0	0.0	1.1	0.4	0.1	0.0	4.2	0.2	32.2	9.0	12.2	6.9	1.5	1.1	5.7	0.8	6.6	5.9	3.8	1.0	0.0	0.0
100.0	5.9	6.2	0.0	0.0	25.0	5.6	0.1	0.0	1.6	0.0	7.9	3.3	20.0	12.0	0.5	0.3	0.0	1.5	0.0	7.9	1.5	0.7	0.0	0.0
100.0	2.0	1.4	0.0	0.0	0.5	0.2	0.2	0.1	5.0	0.2	27.4	7.2	13.6	7.4	2.8	1.5	6.0	0.9	10.1	7.8	4.7	1.0	0.0	0.0
100.0	3.9	2.8	0.0	0.0	0.2	0.1	0.1	0.0	7.9	0.8	34.5	7.7	9.3	6.3	1.1	0.5	7.2	0.8	7.5	6.3	2.4	0.6	0.0	0.0
100.0	9.5	6.7	0.0	0.0	0.1	0.0	0.2	0.1	5.9	0.1	19.3	5.3	10.0	5.7	2.0	1.3	5.9	0.9	13.3	9.0	3.8	0.9	0.0	0.0
100.0	4.7	3.5	0.0	0.0	0.0	0.1	0.2	0.1	5.0	0.2	23.3	6.0	12.4	6.8	3.4	1.3	6.3	0.7	12.6	7.3	4.8	1.3	0.0	0.0
100.0	1.4	0.9	0.0	0.0	0.0	0.1	0.9	0.2	5.4	0.2	18.4	4.1	15.0	8.0	4.5	2.0	6.7	0.9	13.7	10.8	5.5	1.3	0.0	0.0
100.0	8.8	5.6	0.0	0.0	0.0	0.0	0.5	0.0	4.7	0.0	18.6	6.3	10.3	5.5	1.4	0.9	8.3	0.9	14.8	7.9	4.3	1.0	0.0	0.0
100.0	8.7	7.4	0.0	0.0	0.0	0.0	0.2	0.0	5.5	0.2	17.9	5.0	9.9	5.5	2.6	0.9	7.2	1.2	12.9	7.3	6.2	1.3	0.1	0.0
100.0	13.7	13.4	0.0	0.0	0.0	0.0	0.0	0.0	6.3	0.7	19.7	6.5	7.7	5.3	0.7	0.4	3.1	0.4	11.1	7.3	3.3	0.4	0.0	0.0
100.0	15.4	17.1	0.0	0.0	0.1	0.0	0.1	0.0	3.3	0.2	26.9	11.1	6.2	4.1	0.7	0.4	3.3	0.4	4.9	3.0	2.4	0.4	0.0	0.0
100.0	3.0	1.8	0.0	0.0	0.0	0.0	0.0	0.1	4.4	0.2	32.5	11.5	12.6	7.8	1.6	1.0	5.2	0.7	7.9	5.4	3.3	1.0	0.0	0.0
100.0	7.0	6.8	0.0	0.0	0.0	0.0	0.0	0.1	3.0	0.1	37.6	10.2	9.9	6.0	0.9	0.6	3.7	0.5	5.8	4.9	2.4	0.5	0.0	0.0

(Zone) (Sector)	District	Total			Total	Agriculture	Forestry and Hunting	Fisheries and Aquiculture	Mining	Construction	Manufacturing	Wholesale and Retail	Finance and Insurance	Transportation and Communication	Services	Civil Service	Unclassified
		Total	M	F													
V	Hatogaya-machi	(5,581) 100.0	68.9	31.1	100.0	17.3	0.0	0.0	0.0	3.6	34.8	19.2	1.7	7.5	12.2	3.7	0.0
VI	Sōka-shi	(13,947) 100.0	62.7	37.3	100.0	35.3	0.0	0.0	0.1	2.9	30.4	14.8	0.9	5.4	8.2	2.0	0.0
	Yashio-mura	(6,416) 100.0	56.7	43.3	100.0	61.9	0.0	0.0	0.1	2.8	20.3	5.3	0.6	3.2	4.7	1.1	0.0
	Misato-mura	(8,229) 100.0	55.9	44.1	100.0	69.4	0.0	0.1	0.3	2.0	11.6	6.7	0.5	3.8	4.3	1.3	0.0
	Matsudo-shi	(27,994) 100.0	65.0	35.0	100.0	32.7	0.0	0.0	0.4	4.0	17.7	16.0	2.4	7.5	12.9	6.4	0.0
VII	Ichikawa-shi	(54,788) 100.0	66.0	34.0	100.0	15.8	0.0	0.4	0.2	3.8	30.9	20.4	3.5	5.0	16.4	3.6	0.0
	Zone 4 Total	(470,233) 100.0	70.4	29.6	100.0	13.9	0.0	0.2	0.2	5.9	35.2	16.7	2.5	6.7	14.8	3.9	0.0
5 I	Tsurumi-ku	(78,260) 100.0	76.1	23.9	100.0	1.4	0.0	0.5	0.0	8.1	45.9	17.5	1.8	8.6	13.9	2.3	0.0
III	Koganei-shi	(11,238) 100.0	70.5	29.5	100.0	10.9	0.0	0.0	0.3	5.1	26.7	15.5	4.2	7.3	24.0	6.0	0.0
	Tanashi-machi	(7,213) 100.0	69.2	30.8	100.0	12.6	0.1	0.0	0.1	4.0	26.8	19.7	2.8	6.6	20.2	7.2	0.0
	Kurume-machi	(3,960) 100.0	64.5	35.5	100.0	52.5	0.0	0.0	0.1	3.6	12.0	6.8	1.1	5.1	14.6	4.2	0.0
IV	Nīza-machi	(5,370) 100.0	60.6	39.4	100.0	58.5	0.0	0.0	0.1	2.7	13.4	9.0	0.5	2.7	11.0	2.2	0.0
	Kiyose-machi	(6,274) 100.0	54.9	45.1	100.0	22.8	0.0	0.0	0.1	2.2	10.7	10.3	2.8	5.8	38.3	7.0	0.0
	Adachi-machi	(4,371) 100.0	63.4	36.6	100.0	34.3	0.0	0.1	0.1	4.4	20.6	18.1	1.3	3.6	14.5	3.0	0.0
	Asaka-machi	(6,666) 100.0	66.3	33.7	100.0	35.0	0.0	0.1	0.0	3.9	22.8	13.3	1.1	3.5	17.5	2.8	0.0
V	Urawa-shi	(54,388) 100.0	68.9	31.1	100.0	13.9	0.0	0.0	0.3	4.4	24.1	20.3	4.9	7.8	17.0	7.3	0.0
	Misono-mura	(4,630) 100.0	54.2	45.8	100.0	77.7	0.0	0.0	0.0	1.0	6.2	5.8	0.7	1.8	4.9	1.9	0.0
	Koshigaya-shi	(20,111) 100.0	59.2	40.8	100.0	56.1	0.0	0.0	0.0	2.5	16.9	10.6	0.9	4.2	7.1	1.7	0.0
VI	Yoshikawa-machi	(7,875) 100.0	55.0	45.0	100.0	67.9	0.0	0.0	0.0	2.6	10.2	8.4	0.8	3.0	5.4	1.7	0.0
	Nagareyama-machi	(8,882) 100.0	57.6	42.4	100.0	54.3	0.0	0.0	0.1	3.6	16.3	10.0	1.1	5.8	6.6	2.2	0.0
VII	Kamagaya-machi	(4,689) 100.0	58.9	41.1	100.0	64.4	0.0	0.0	0.1	2.5	9.8	8.4	0.6	3.2	6.1	4.9	0.0
VIII	Funahashi-shi	(47,478) 100.0	66.8	33.2	100.0	20.7	0.0	3.6	0.1	3.5	22.6	18.3	2.4	6.2	14.5	8.1	0.0
	Zone 5 Total	(271,405) 100.0	68.1	31.9	100.0	21.8	0.0	0.8	0.1	4.9	27.6	16.2	2.5	6.7	14.6	4.8	0.0
6 I	Nishi-ku	(40,069) 100.0	72.9	27.1	100.0	0.2	0.0	0.0	0.0	7.3	26.9	23.6	2.6	13.6	20.7	5.1	0.0
	Naka-ku	(46,866) 100.0	67.7	32.3	100.0	0.5	0.0	1.0	0.0	6.8	12.5	32.4	2.4	13.1	27.0	4.3	0.0
	Kanagawa-ku	(54,449) 100.0	74.4	25.6	100.0	3.0	0.0	1.2	0.1	7.7	28.7	21.9	2.5	11.9	19.3	3.7	0.0
II	Kōhoku-ku	(44,292) 100.0	67.8	32.2	100.0	33.5	0.0	0.1	0.1	4.0	21.1	12.5	2.1	7.6	15.6	3.4	0.0
	Inagi-machi	(3,996) 100.0	64.3	35.7	100.0	46.2	0.1	0.0	0.3	3.3	15.3	10.5	1.1	3.7	16.5	3.0	0.0
III	Tama-mura	(3,153) 100.0	63.4	36.6	100.0	49.7	0.1	0.0	1.2	3.1	14.8	5.9	0.7	5.2	15.7	3.6	0.0
	Fuchu-shi	(20,639) 100.0	72.4	27.6	100.0	15.3	0.0	0.0	1.0	6.1	21.5	15.0	2.0	6.0	25.5	7.6	0.0
	Kunitachi-machi	(8,510) 100.0	73.9	26.1	100.0	8.9	0.0	0.0	0.4	5.9	16.8	17.3	3.6	8.0	28.6	10.5	0.0
	Kokubunji-machi	(10,006) 100.0	73.3	26.7	100.0	15.0	0.0	0.0	0.2	4.6	17.6	15.1	3.5	14.1	23.0	6.9	0.0
	Kodaira-machi	(10,477) 100.0	70.1	29.9	100.0	22.9	0.0	0.0	0.2	3.8	13.9	11.4	2.7	6.4	25.5	13.2	0.0
	Higashimurayama-machi	(8,932) 100.0	67.0	33.0	100.0	23.3	0.0	0.0	0.1	3.7	18.5	11.6	2.1	11.7	23.2	5.8	0.0
IV	Tokorosawa-shi	(23,441) 100.0	63.4	36.6	100.0	38.2	0.0	0.0	0.0	3.0	13.8	13.1	1.0	5.6	22.8	2.5	0.0
	Miyoshi-mura	(2,174) 100.0	56.0	44.0	100.0	83.5	0.0	0.0	0.0	0.8	4.8	3.6	0.2	1.0	4.7	1.4	0.0
	Fujimi-mura	(5,384) 100.0	56.8	43.2	100.0	69.1	0.1	0.0	0.1	2.5	11.5	6.9	0.5	2.4	5.2	1.7	0.0
V	Yono-shi	(13,272) 100.0	70.5	29.5	100.0	8.0	0.0	0.0	0.2	4.9	36.3	18.1	3.2	9.7	14.3	5.3	0.0
	Ōmiya-shi	(58,614) 100.0	66.0	34.0	100.0	21.8	0.0	0.0	0.3	3.6	24.1	16.2	2.6	13.1	13.7	4.6	0.0
	Iwatsuki-shi	(15,563) 100.0	58.6	41.4	100.0	53.8	0.0	0.0	0.1	2.5	18.4	10.9	1.1	3.8	7.2	2.3	0.0
VI	Matsubushi-mura	(4,447) 100.0	53.7	46.3	100.0	69.8	0.0	0.2	0.0	3.2	12.6	5.1	0.3	3.2	4.4	1.2	0.0
VII	Kashiwa-shi	(19,496) 100.0	60.1	39.9	100.0	48.0	0.0	0.0	0.1	3.4	12.1	12.3	1.5	8.4	11.3	2.9	0.0
	Shōnan-mura	(5,960) 100.0	51.4	48.6	100.0	81.6	0.0	0.0	0.0	1.9	2.4	3.7	0.2	2.1	6.9	1.2	0.0
	Shirai-mura	(4,466) 100.0	52.1	47.9	100.0	84.4	0.2	0.0	0.0	1.3	1.5	4.8	0.1	1.2	5.7	0.8	0.0
VIII	Narashino-shi	(11,633) 100.0	67.0	33.0	100.0	19.4	0.0	1.6	0.0	3.6	24.9	15.3	2.2	12.1	15.0	5.9	0.0
	Zone 6 Total	(415,839) 100.0	67.7	32.3	100.0	21.7	0.0	0.3	0.2	5.0	20.5	17.5	2.2	9.9	18.2	4.5	0.0
7 I	Isogo-ku	(25,709) 100.0	70.9	29.1	100.0	3.9	0.0	1.2	0.0	4.6	21.6	19.9	3.2	14.6	26.6	4.4	0.0
	Minami-ku	(67,488) 100.0	70.6	29.4	100.0	3.7	0.0	0.1	0.1	7.0	23.6	23.0	2.5	12.3	23.4	4.3	0.0

Table 11. Gainfully Employed Population, 15 Years and Older, by Industry and Sex
(For 1950 only, 14-year-olds are included)

Total	Agriculture		Forestry and Hunting		Fisheries and Aquiculture		Mining		Construction		Manufacturing		Wholesale and Retail		Finance and Insurance		Transportation and Communication		Services		Civil Service		Unclassified	
	M	F	M	F	M	F	M	F	M	F	M	F	M	F	M	F	M	F	M	F	M	F	M	F
100.0	9.1	8.2	0.0	0.0	0.0	0.0	0.0	0.0	3.5	0.1	26.1	8.7	12.5	6.7	1.1	0.6	6.2	1.3	7.2	5.0	3.2	0.5	0.0	0.0
100.0	17.0	18.3	0.0	0.0	0.0	0.0	0.0	0.1	2.9	0.0	22.0	8.4	9.3	5.5	0.6	0.3	5.0	0.4	4.3	3.9	1.6	0.4	0.0	0.0
100.0	28.5	33.4	0.0	0.0	0.0	0.0	0.0	0.1	2.8	0.0	15.1	5.2	3.0	2.3	0.3	0.3	3.0	0.2	3.0	1.7	1.0	0.1	0.0	0.0
100.0	32.9	36.5	0.0	0.0	0.1	0.0	0.3	0.0	2.0	0.0	8.6	3.0	4.3	2.4	0.4	0.1	3.5	0.3	2.8	1.5	1.0	0.3	0.0	0.0
100.0	16.2	16.5	0.0	0.0	0.0	0.0	0.3	0.1	3.8	0.2	13.5	4.2	10.1	5.9	1.6	0.8	6.7	0.8	7.5	5.4	5.3	1.1	0.0	0.0
100.0	8.1	7.7	0.0	0.0	0.3	0.1	0.2	0.0	3.6	0.2	22.2	8.7	13.6	6.8	2.4	1.1	4.4	0.6	8.3	8.1	2.9	0.7	0.0	0.0
100.0	7.3	6.6	0.0	0.0	0.1	0.1	0.2	0.0	5.5	0.4	27.8	7.6	10.5	6.2	1.6	0.9	6.0	0.7	8.3	6.5	3.1	0.8	0.0	0.0
100.0	0.8	0.6	0.0	0.0	0.4	0.1	0.0	0.0	7.4	0.7	38.2	7.7	10.8	6.7	1.2	0.6	7.8	0.8	7.6	6.3	1.9	0.4	0.0	0.0
100.0	6.3	4.6	0.0	0.0	0.0	0.0	0.3	0.0	4.8	0.3	20.0	6.7	9.7	5.8	2.8	1.4	6.5	0.8	14.6	9.4	5.5	0.5	0.0	0.0
100.0	7.0	5.6	0.0	0.0	0.1	0.0	0.0	0.0	3.8	0.2	20.1	6.7	11.7	8.0	1.8	1.0	5.6	1.0	12.9	7.3	6.3	0.9	0.0	0.0
100.0	29.0	23.5	0.0	0.0	0.0	0.0	0.0	0.1	3.5	0.1	9.1	2.9	4.5	2.3	0.7	0.4	4.6	0.5	9.5	5.1	3.6	0.6	0.0	0.0
100.0	29.6	28.9	0.0	0.0	0.0	0.0	0.0	0.0	2.7	0.0	9.8	3.6	5.6	3.4	0.3	0.2	2.5	0.2	8.2	2.8	1.9	0.3	0.0	0.0
100.0	11.6	11.2	0.0	0.0	0.0	0.0	0.0	0.1	2.1	0.1	8.3	2.4	6.1	4.2	1.9	0.9	5.4	0.4	13.9	24.4	5.6	1.4	0.0	0.0
100.0	17.1	17.2	0.0	0.0	0.0	0.1	0.1	0.0	4.2	0.2	15.6	5.0	10.9	7.2	0.9	0.4	3.1	0.5	9.0	5.5	2.5	0.5	0.0	0.0
100.0	17.8	17.2	0.0	0.0	0.0	0.1	0.0	0.0	3.8	0.1	17.2	5.6	8.5	4.8	0.8	0.3	3.2	0.3	12.9	4.6	2.1	0.7	0.0	0.0
100.0	6.8	7.1	0.0	0.0	0.0	0.0	0.2	0.1	4.1	0.3	19.1	5.0	13.0	7.3	3.3	1.6	7.0	0.8	9.5	7.5	5.9	1.4	0.0	0.0
100.0	38.2	39.5	0.0	0.0	0.0	0.0	0.0	0.0	1.0	0.0	4.8	1.4	3.4	2.4	0.5	0.2	1.6	0.2	3.1	1.8	1.6	0.3	0.0	0.0
100.0	27.6	28.5	0.0	0.0	0.0	0.0	0.0	0.0	2.5	0.0	12.4	4.5	6.8	3.8	0.7	0.2	3.8	0.4	4.0	3.1	1.4	0.3	0.0	0.0
100.0	31.4	36.5	0.0	0.0	0.0	0.0	0.0	0.0	2.6	0.0	7.6	2.6	5.4	3.0	0.6	0.2	2.9	0.1	3.1	2.3	1.4	0.3	0.0	0.0
100.0	23.0	31.3	0.0	0.0	0.0	0.0	0.1	0.0	3.5	0.1	12.9	3.4	6.3	3.7	0.8	0.3	5.3	0.5	4.0	2.6	1.7	0.5	0.0	0.0
100.0	32.5	31.9	0.0	0.0	0.0	0.0	0.1	0.0	2.3	0.2	7.9	1.9	4.8	3.6	0.5	0.1	2.8	0.4	4.1	2.0	3.9	1.0	0.0	0.0
100.0	10.2	10.5	0.0	0.0	2.6	1.0	0.1	0.0	3.4	0.1	17.3	5.3	11.0	7.3	1.7	0.7	5.5	0.7	7.6	6.9	7.4	0.7	0.0	0.0
100.0	10.8	11.0	0.0	0.0	0.6	0.2	0.1	0.0	4.6	0.3	22.0	5.6	10.1	6.1	1.7	0.8	6.0	0.7	8.1	6.5	4.1	0.7	0.0	0.0
100.0	0.1	0.1	0.0	0.0	0.0	0.0	0.0	0.0	7.0	0.3	21.2	5.7	14.8	8.8	1.6	1.0	12.0	1.6	11.9	8.8	4.3	0.8	0.0	0.0
100.0	0.4	0.1	0.0	0.0	0.9	0.1	0.0	0.0	6.5	0.3	10.3	2.2	19.2	13.2	1.6	0.8	11.9	1.2	13.1	13.9	3.8	0.5	0.0	0.0
100.0	1.7	1.3	0.0	0.0	1.0	0.2	0.1	0.0	7.3	0.4	23.3	5.4	13.8	8.1	1.6	0.9	10.5	1.4	12.0	7.3	3.1	0.6	0.0	0.0
100.0	18.3	15.2	0.0	0.0	0.0	0.1	0.1	0.0	3.8	0.2	17.0	4.1	7.9	4.6	1.5	0.6	6.9	0.7	9.5	6.1	2.8	0.6	0.0	0.0
100.0	24.3	21.9	0.1	0.0	0.0	0.0	0.3	0.0	3.3	0.0	11.6	3.7	6.5	4.0	0.8	0.3	3.4	0.3	11.5	5.0	2.5	0.5	0.0	0.0
100.0	28.1	21.6	0.0	0.1	0.0	0.0	1.2	0.0	3.0	0.1	9.9	4.9	4.1	1.8	0.5	0.2	4.7	0.5	9.0	6.7	2.9	0.7	0.0	0.0
100.0	8.7	6.6	0.0	0.0	0.0	0.0	0.9	0.1	5.9	0.2	17.3	4.2	9.1	5.9	1.3	0.7	5.1	0.9	17.5	8.0	6.6	1.0	0.0	0.0
100.0	6.3	2.6	0.0	0.0	0.0	0.0	0.3	0.1	5.8	0.1	13.0	3.8	10.8	6.5	2.5	1.1	7.1	0.9	18.7	9.9	9.4	1.1	0.0	0.0
100.0	8.5	6.5	0.0	0.0	0.0	0.0	0.1	0.1	4.5	0.1	13.8	3.8	9.3	5.8	2.3	1.2	13.1	1.0	15.5	7.5	6.2	0.7	0.0	0.0
100.0	12.7	10.2	0.0	0.0	0.0	0.0	0.2	0.0	3.7	0.1	10.9	3.0	6.8	4.6	1.9	0.8	5.7	0.7	16.1	10.0	12.1	1.1	0.0	0.0
100.0	12.2	11.1	0.0	0.0	0.0	0.0	0.1	0.0	3.5	0.2	13.2	5.3	7.0	4.6	1.4	0.7	10.6	1.1	13.8	9.4	5.2	0.6	0.0	0.0
100.0	20.1	18.1	0.0	0.0	0.0	0.0	0.0	0.0	3.0	0.0	8.7	5.1	8.0	5.1	0.7	0.3	5.1	0.5	15.8	7.0	2.0	0.5	0.0	0.0
100.0	43.5	40.0	0.0	0.0	0.0	0.0	0.0	0.0	0.8	0.0	3.7	1.1	2.2	1.4	0.2	0.0	0.9	0.1	3.6	1.1	1.1	0.3	0.0	0.0
100.0	33.5	35.6	0.1	0.0	0.0	0.0	0.0	0.1	2.5	0.0	8.3	3.2	4.5	2.4	0.4	0.1	2.3	0.1	3.8	1.4	1.4	0.3	0.0	0.0
100.0	4.1	3.9	0.0	0.0	0.0	0.0	0.2	0.0	4.7	0.2	26.2	10.1	11.6	6.5	2.2	1.0	8.9	0.8	8.3	6.0	4.3	1.0	0.0	0.0
100.0	10.1	11.7	0.0	0.0	0.0	0.0	0.2	0.1	3.5	0.1	17.5	6.6	9.5	6.7	1.6	1.0	12.3	0.8	7.5	6.2	3.8	0.8	0.0	0.0
100.0	26.8	27.0	0.0	0.0	0.0	0.0	0.0	0.0	2.5	0.0	12.7	5.7	6.6	4.3	0.8	0.3	3.3	0.5	4.0	3.2	1.9	0.4	0.0	0.0
100.0	30.9	38.9	0.0	0.0	0.1	0.1	0.0	0.0	3.2	0.0	9.9	2.7	2.9	2.2	0.2	0.1	3.0	0.2	2.5	1.9	1.0	0.2	0.0	0.0
100.0	22.7	25.3	0.0	0.0	0.0	0.0	0.0	0.1	3.2	0.2	9.3	2.8	7.1	5.2	1.0	0.5	7.8	0.6	6.6	4.7	2.4	0.5	0.0	0.0
100.0	37.9	43.7	0.0	0.0	0.0	0.0	0.0	0.0	1.8	0.1	1.8	0.6	1.8	1.9	0.1	0.1	2.0	0.1	4.9	2.0	1.1	0.1	0.0	0.0
100.0	40.8	43.6	0.1	0.1	0.0	0.0	0.0	0.0	1.3	0.0	1.2	0.3	2.8	2.0	0.1	0.0	1.0	0.2	4.1	1.6	0.7	0.1	0.0	0.0
100.0	9.0	10.4	0.0	0.0	0.0	0.0	0.9	0.7	3.5	0.1	19.0	5.9	8.9	6.4	1.5	0.7	10.8	1.3	8.3	6.7	5.1	0.8	0.0	0.0
100.0	11.0	10.7	0.0	0.0	0.3	0.0	0.1	0.1	4.8	0.2	15.8	4.7	10.7	6.8	1.4	0.8	9.0	0.9	10.8	7.4	3.8	0.7	0.0	0.0
100.0	2.2	1.7	0.0	0.0	0.9	0.3	0.0	0.0	4.3	0.3	16.9	4.7	12.2	7.7	2.1	1.1	12.8	1.8	15.9	10.7	3.6	0.8	0.0	0.0
100.0	2.1	1.6	0.0	0.0	0.1	0.0	0.0	0.1	6.7	0.3	17.9	5.7	14.2	8.8	1.6	0.9	11.2	1.1	13.2	10.2	3.6	0.7	0.0	0.0

Table 11. Gainfully Employed Population, 15 Years and Older, by Industry and Sex
(For 1950 only, 14-year-olds are included)

(Zone) (Sector)	District	Total	M	F	Total	Agriculture	Forestry and Hunting	Fisheries and Aquiculture	Mining	Construction	Manufacturing	Wholesale and Retail	Finance and Insurance	Transportation and Communication	Services	Civil Service	Unclassified
I	Hodogaya-ku	(37,149) 100.0	72.0	28.0	100.0	11.6	0.0	0.1	0.0	5.8	31.1	15.8	2.5	11.7	16.7	4.7	0.1
II	Machida-shi	(22,988) 100.0	67.5	32.5	100.0	33.3	0.0	0.0	0.1	4.3	14.1	14.0	1.6	6.7	22.4	3.5	0.0
III	Yuki-mura	(3,147) 100.0	55.9	44.1	100.0	70.7	0.0	0.1	0.1	1.8	8.7	3.8	0.5	3.2	8.1	3.0	0.0
	Hino-machi	(10,624) 100.0	69.2	30.8	100.0	26.1	0.0	0.0	0.4	2.9	29.3	11.2	1.7	7.3	16.8	4.3	0.0
	Tachikawa-shi	(25,764) 100.0	67.0	33.0	100.0	1.8	0.0	0.0	0.2	4.7	15.1	23.5	2.4	7.0	34.3	11.0	0.0
	Sunakawa-machi	(4,841) 100.0	69.0	31.0	100.0	38.3	0.0	0.0	0.1	3.4	11.6	9.4	1.2	3.3	27.3	5.4	0.0
	Yamato-machi	(4,873) 100.0	67.6	32.4	100.0	29.0	0.0	0.0	0.0	3.7	19.6	11.1	0.7	7.0	25.4	3.5	0.0
IV	Ōi-mura	(2,366) 100.0	59.9	40.1	100.0	60.4	0.0	0.0	0.0	1.8	12.0	8.2	0.4	3.2	6.5	7.5	0.0
	Fukuoka-mura	(2,952) 100.0	68.8	31.2	100.0	32.7	0.0	0.0	0.0	4.0	21.4	14.0	1.4	9.1	13.5	3.9	0.0
V	Kasukabe-shi	(14,093) 100.0	60.7	39.3	100.0	45.8	0.0	0.0	0.0	2.9	20.4	13.4	1.3	4.4	8.9	2.9	0.0
	Shōwa-mura	(6,570) 100.0	55.8	44.2	100.0	62.7	0.0	0.0	0.1	3.9	12.4	7.9	0.6	2.6	7.9	1.9	0.0
VI	Noda-shi	(24,671) 100.0	57.7	42.3	100.0	43.3	0.0	0.0	0.0	5.2	20.7	12.5	1.1	5.1	9.7	2.4	0.0
VII	Abiko-machi	(11,087) 100.0	58.6	41.4	100.0	44.1	0.0	0.2	0.0	3.4	15.4	16.3	1.7	6.5	10.0	2.4	0.0
	Yachiyo-machi	(7,667) 100.0	53.8	46.2	100.0	74.3	0.1	0.0	0.0	2.0	6.2	6.3	0.4	3.6	5.1	2.0	0.0
VIII	Chiba-shi	(79,708) 100.0	65.4	34.6	100.0	22.4	0.1	2.6	0.0	4.7	17.5	17.3	2.9	8.5	17.5	6.5	0.0
IX	Goi-machi	(8,703) 100.0	55.6	44.4	100.0	69.2	0.0	1.5	0.0	2.2	5.2	9.2	0.7	3.0	6.9	2.0	0.1
	Sodegaura-machi	(6,758) 100.0	52.3	47.7	100.0	70.8	0.0	9.9	0.0	1.6	1.9	5.6	0.4	2.0	6.1	1.7	0.0
	Zone 7 Total	(367,158) 100.0	72.2	27.8	100.0	23.8	0.0	0.9	0.1	4.8	19.5	16.7	2.1	8.6	18.7	4.8	0.0
8 I	Kanazawa-ku	(21,628) 100.0	74.7	25.3	100.0	3.7	0.1	2.6	—	5.9	23.6	15.7	2.2	8.7	31.5	6.0	—
	Totsuka-ku	(31,968) 100.0	69.8	30.2	100.0	28.2	—	—	0.1	4.9	25.0	10.8	1.7	9.4	15.7	4.2	—
II	Yamato-shi	(9,420) 100.0	65.2	34.8	100.0	19.6	—	—	0.1	5.3	12.8	15.5	1.6	7.4	33.4	4.3	—
	Sagamihara-shi	(32,577) 100.0	67.9	32.1	100.0	32.6	0.1	—	0.5	3.8	9.3	11.3	1.0	5.9	32.0	3.5	—
	Zama-machi	(5,510) 100.0	63.1	36.9	100.0	38.5	—	0.1	0.8	3.5	7.3	10.8	1.1	5.6	29.8	2.5	—
III	Hachiōji-shi	(58,006) 100.0	65.8	34.2	100.0	15.5	0.4	—	0.2	3.9	32.7	17.7	1.6	6.2	17.2	4.6	—
	Akishima-shi	(13,295) 100.0	73.9	26.1	100.0	8.5	—	—	0.7	7.5	15.7	14.5	1.7	6.2	37.6	7.6	—
	Fussa-machi	(7,940) 100.0	71.1	28.9	100.0	10.3	—	—	1.3	15.1	10.3	17.3	1.2	4.9	35.2	4.4	—
	Mizuho-machi	(3,925) 100.0	68.0	32.0	100.0	38.2	—	—	0.1	4.3	19.9	10.6	0.7	3.2	20.2	2.8	—
	Murayama-machi	(4,766) 100.0	65.1	34.9	100.0	40.4	—	—	0.2	3.0	22.7	7.7	0.5	2.3	21.1	2.1	—
	Musashi-machi	(12,684) 100.0	61.6	38.4	100.0	40.5	—	—	0.1	3.6	14.2	10.9	1.0	3.3	22.5	3.9	—
IV	Sayama-shi	(14,253) 100.0	60.7	39.3	100.0	45.3	—	—	0.2	2.9	17.2	11.6	0.9	3.5	16.4	2.0	—
	Kawagoe-shi	(45,066) 100.0	62.1	37.9	100.0	40.2	—	—	0.2	3.3	19.0	14.1	1.7	5.6	12.7	3.2	—
	Seibu-machi	(4,286) 100.0	55.0	45.0	100.0	32.0	—	—	0.3	2.5	36.7	8.6	1.0	3.0	14.5	1.4	—
V	Ageo-shi	(16,058) 100.0	58.8	41.2	100.0	46.7	—	—	0.1	3.1	23.2	9.4	1.1	6.2	7.7	2.5	—
	Ina-mura	(3,566) 100.0	54.6	45.4	100.0	71.0	—	—	—	2.0	8.4	5.1	0.6	7.4	4.0	1.5	—
	Hasuda-machi	(8,389) 100.0	58.0	42.0	100.0	54.7	—	—	0.1	2.9	12.4	9.3	1.0	7.2	10.0	2.4	—
	Shiraoka-machi	(7,146) 100.0	58.0	42.0	100.0	61.2	—	0.1	—	3.5	10.6	8.2	1.1	7.2	6.3	1.8	—
	Miyashiro-machi	(4,905) 100.0	56.3	43.7	100.0	62.1	—	—	—	2.6	9.4	7.2	1.0	9.5	6.1	2.1	—
	Sugito-machi	(8,087) 100.0	56.6	43.4	100.0	64.4	—	0.1	—	2.9	8.9	10.0	1.3	4.0	6.4	2.0	—
VI	Sekiyado-machi	(6,843) 100.0	51.4	48.6	100.0	78.8	—	0.2	—	3.3	3.3	6.5	0.6	1.5	4.7	1.1	—
	Moriya-machi	(5,785) 100.0	53.7	46.3	100.0	72.1	—	—	—	2.4	5.6	8.6	0.8	2.4	6.1	2.0	—
VII	Toride-machi	(9,509) 100.0	58.2	41.8	100.0	41.4	—	—	0.2	4.2	14.7	17.7	1.5	6.0	11.1	3.2	—
	Inzai-machi	(8,589) 100.0	54.5	45.5	100.0	65.0	—	—	—	3.2	4.5	15.0	0.8	2.9	6.9	1.7	—
	Inba-mura	(4,629) 100.0	50.8	49.2	100.0	84.8	—	0.5	—	1.4	1.0	7.0	0.2	1.3	2.9	0.9	—
VIII	Yotsukaidō-machi	(7,915) 100.0	57.6	42.4	100.0	59.5	—	—	—	2.7	7.9	8.7	1.4	5.7	10.0	4.1	—
IX	Ichihara-machi	(6,930) 100.0	54.6	45.4	100.0	65.8	—	2.3	—	2.4	7.6	8.0	0.7	3.3	6.8	3.1	—
	Anegasaki-machi	(5,295) 100.0	56.9	43.1	100.0	64.7	—	4.5	—	1.8	5.8	9.2	0.8	3.4	7.9	1.9	—
	Hirakawa-machi	(6,094) 100.0	51.3	48.7	100.0	83.7	—	—	—	1.9	2.7	3.8	0.3	1.3	4.9	1.4	—
	Miwa-machi	(5,878) 100.0	51.3	48.7	100.0	81.9	0.1	0.1	0.0	1.5	2.4	5.2	0.7	1.7	4.5	1.9	—
X	Kisarazu-shi	(23,828) 100.0	57.1	42.9	100.0	44.2	0.1	8.4	0.1	2.8	5.8	14.9	1.0	4.1	16.0	2.6	—
	Zone 8 Total	(404,770) 100.0	62.9	37.1	100.0	37.8	0.1	0.8	0.2	3.9	16.9	12.6	1.3	5.6	17.3	3.5	—

Table 11. Gainfully Employed Population, 15 Years and Older, by Industry and Sex
(For 1950 only, 14-year-olds are included)

Total	Agriculture		Forestry and Hunting		Fisheries and Aquiculture		Mining		Construction		Manufacturing		Wholesale and Retail		Finance and Insurance		Transportation and Communication		Services		Civil Services		Unclassified	
	M	F	M	F	M	F	M	F	M	F	M	F	M	F	M	F	M	F	M	F	M	F	M	F
100.0	6.6	5.0	0.0	0.0	0.1	0.0	0.0	0.0	5.6	0.2	23.8	7.3	9.7	6.1	1.6	0.9	10.3	1.4	10.5	6.2	3.9	0.8	0.0	0.1
100.0	18.9	14.4	0.0	0.0	0.0	0.0	0.1	0.0	4.0	0.3	10.4	3.7	8.2	5.8	1.1	0.5	6.0	0.7	16.0	6.4	2.8	0.7	0.0	0.0
100.0	35.8	34.9	0.0	0.0	0.1	0.0	0.1	0.0	1.7	0.1	4.8	3.9	2.1	1.7	0.3	0.2	2.9	0.3	5.6	2.5	2.5	0.5	0.0	0.0
100.0	14.2	11.9	0.0	0.0	0.0	0.0	0.3	0.1	2.9	0.0	22.6	6.7	6.6	4.6	1.1	0.6	6.6	0.7	12.2	4.6	2.7	1.6	0.0	0.0
100.0	1.1	0.7	0.0	0.0	0.0	0.0	0.2	0.0	4.5	0.2	11.6	3.5	13.4	10.1	1.7	0.7	6.3	0.7	18.0	16.3	10.2	0.8	0.0	0.0
100.0	22.0	16.3	0.0	0.0	0.0	0.0	0.1	0.0	3.4	0.0	8.4	3.2	5.5	3.9	0.7	0.5	2.7	0.6	21.4	5.9	4.8	0.6	0.0	0.0
100.0	15.9	13.1	0.0	0.0	0.0	0.0	0.0	0.0	3.6	0.1	12.4	7.2	6.2	4.9	0.4	0.3	6.2	0.8	20.2	5.2	2.7	0.8	0.0	0.0
100.0	29.9	30.5	0.0	0.0	0.0	0.0	0.0	0.0	1.8	0.0	8.4	3.6	5.2	3.0	0.4	0.0	2.7	0.5	4.4	2.1	7.1	0.4	0.0	0.0
100.0	17.7	15.0	0.0	0.0	0.0	0.0	0.0	0.0	3.7	0.3	15.7	5.7	9.2	4.8	1.1	0.3	8.4	0.7	9.7	3.8	3.3	0.6	0.0	0.0
100.0	21.1	24.7	0.0	0.0	0.0	0.0	0.0	0.0	2.9	0.0	16.0	4.4	8.3	5.1	0.9	0.4	4.0	0.4	5.2	3.7	2.3	0.6	0.0	0.0
100.0	29.3	33.4	0.0	0.0	0.0	0.0	0.0	0.1	3.7	0.2	9.5	2.9	4.8	3.1	0.4	0.2	2.4	0.2	4.1	3.8	1.6	0.3	0.0	0.0
100.0	17.5	25.8	0.0	0.0	0.0	0.0	0.0	0.0	4.8	0.4	15.7	5.0	7.5	5.0	0.8	0.3	4.5	0.6	5.0	4.7	1.9	0.5	0.0	0.0
100.0	21.4	22.7	0.0	0.0	0.1	0.1	0.0	0.0	3.2	0.2	11.0	4.4	7.8	8.5	1.1	0.6	6.1	0.4	5.9	4.1	2.0	0.4	0.0	0.0
100.0	35.7	38.6	0.1	0.0	0.0	0.0	0.0	0.0	1.9	0.1	4.9	1.3	3.1	3.2	0.3	0.1	3.2	0.4	2.9	2.2	1.7	0.3	0.0	0.0
100.0	10.4	12.0	0.0	0.1	1.6	1.0	0.0	0.0	4.5	0.2	14.5	3.0	10.1	7.2	1.9	1.0	7.6	0.9	9.6	7.9	5.2	1.3	0.0	0.0
100.0	35.3	33.9	0.0	0.0	0.9	0.6	0.0	0.0	2.1	0.1	4.1	1.1	5.2	4.0	0.4	0.3	2.4	0.6	3.6	3.3	1.6	0.4	0.0	0.1
100.0	33.0	37.8	0.0	0.0	6.2	3.7	0.0	0.0	1.6	0.0	1.6	0.3	2.9	2.7	0.3	0.1	1.8	0.2	3.6	2.5	1.3	0.4	0.0	0.0
100.0	17.6	6.2	0.0	0.0	0.6	0.3	0.1	0.0	4.6	0.2	15.0	4.5	10.0	6.7	1.4	0.7	7.7	0.9	11.2	7.5	4.0	0.8	0.0	0.0
100.0	2.3	1.4	—	0.1	2.4	0.2	—	—	5.4	0.5	18.6	5.0	9.0	6.7	1.4	0.8	7.8	0.9	22.6	8.9	5.2	0.8	—	—
100.0	15.7	12.5	—	—	—	—	0.1	—	4.5	0.4	20.1	4.9	6.2	4.6	1.1	0.6	8.5	0.9	9.9	5.8	3.7	0.5	—	—
100.0	10.4	9.2	—	—	—	—	0.1	—	5.1	0.2	10.4	2.4	9.2	6.3	1.2	0.4	6.6	0.8	18.6	14.8	3.6	0.7	—	—
100.0	17.7	14.9	—	0.1	—	—	0.5	—	3.6	0.2	7.3	2.0	6.2	5.1	0.7	0.3	5.4	0.5	23.5	8.5	3.0	0.5	—	—
100.0	21.5	17.0	—	—	0.1	—	0.8	—	3.3	0.2	6.0	1.3	6.2	4.6	0.9	0.2	5.2	0.4	16.9	12.9	2.2	0.3	—	—
100.0	10.1	5.4	0.4	—	—	—	0.2	—	3.8	0.1	19.0	13.7	10.8	6.9	1.1	0.5	5.5	0.7	10.9	6.3	4.0	0.6	—	—
100.0	5.9	2.6	—	—	—	—	0.6	0.1	7.1	0.4	11.4	4.3	8.5	6.0	1.1	0.6	5.4	0.8	27.7	9.9	6.2	1.4	—	—
100.0	6.7	3.6	—	—	—	—	1.2	0.1	14.6	0.5	7.7	2.6	9.8	7.5	0.8	0.4	4.3	0.6	22.1	13.1	3.7	0.7	—	—
100.0	25.9	12.3	—	—	—	—	0.1	—	4.1	0.2	9.9	10.0	6.6	4.0	0.5	0.2	2.8	0.4	15.7	4.5	2.4	0.4	—	—
100.0	25.6	14.8	—	—	—	—	0.2	—	3.0	—	11.2	11.5	4.9	2.8	0.3	0.2	2.0	0.3	16.0	5.1	1.9	0.2	—	—
100.0	23.5	17.0	—	—	—	—	0.1	—	3.5	0.1	6.6	7.6	6.5	4.4	0.7	0.3	2.9	0.4	14.2	8.3	3.6	0.3	—	—
100.0	24.4	20.9	—	—	—	—	0.2	—	2.8	0.1	9.7	7.5	6.8	4.8	0.6	0.3	3.0	0.5	11.6	4.8	1.6	0.4	—	—
100.0	20.7	19.5	—	—	—	—	0.2	—	3.2	0.1	13.1	5.9	8.7	5.4	1.1	0.6	5.0	0.6	7.5	5.2	2.6	0.6	—	—
100.0	19.4	12.6	—	—	—	—	0.3	—	2.5	—	12.0	24.7	5.2	3.4	0.7	0.3	2.8	0.2	11.1	3.4	1.0	0.4	—	—
100.0	21.3	25.4	—	—	—	—	0.1	—	3.1	—	15.7	7.5	5.6	3.8	0.7	0.4	5.8	0.4	4.4	3.3	2.1	0.4	—	—
100.0	31.8	39.2	—	—	—	—	—	—	2.0	—	7.2	1.2	2.4	2.7	0.5	0.1	6.8	0.6	2.6	1.4	1.3	0.2	—	—
100.0	26.0	28.7	—	—	—	—	0.1	—	2.8	0.1	9.6	2.8	5.6	3.7	0.5	0.5	6.9	0.3	4.6	5.4	1.9	0.5	—	—
100.0	29.0	32.2	—	—	0.1	—	—	—	3.4	0.1	8.2	2.4	4.4	3.8	0.7	0.4	6.9	0.3	3.9	2.4	1.4	0.4	—	—
100.0	27.3	34.8	—	—	—	—	—	—	2.5	0.1	7.0	2.4	4.1	3.1	0.7	0.3	9.1	0.4	3.8	2.3	1.8	0.3	—	—
100.0	31.5	32.9	—	—	—	0.1	—	—	2.7	0.2	6.6	2.3	5.9	4.1	0.9	0.4	3.6	0.4	3.8	2.6	1.6	0.4	—	—
100.0	36.8	42.0	—	—	0.1	0.1	—	—	3.0	0.3	2.5	0.8	3.8	2.7	0.5	0.1	1.2	0.3	2.7	2.0	0.8	0.3	—	—
100.0	34.3	37.8	—	—	—	—	—	—	2.3	0.1	4.3	1.3	4.6	4.0	0.6	0.2	2.2	0.2	3.7	2.4	1.7	0.3	—	—
100.0	18.7	22.7	—	—	—	—	0.2	—	3.9	0.3	10.9	3.8	9.1	8.6	1.0	0.5	5.4	0.6	6.1	5.0	2.9	0.3	—	—
100.0	32.8	32.0	—	—	—	—	—	—	3.1	0.1	3.8	0.7	6.4	8.6	0.5	0.3	2.5	0.4	4.1	2.8	1.3	0.4	—	—
100.0	42.7	42.1	—	—	0.4	0.1	—	—	1.3	0.1	0.9	0.1	2.0	5.0	0.1	0.1	1.0	0.3	1.7	1.2	0.7	0.2	—	—
100.0	28.5	31.0	—	—	—	—	—	—	2.5	0.2	6.4	1.5	5.2	3.5	0.9	0.5	5.2	0.5	5.7	4.3	3.3	0.8	—	—
100.0	30.1	35.7	—	—	1.3	1.0	—	—	2.3	0.1	6.5	1.1	4.6	3.4	0.5	0.2	2.8	0.5	4.0	2.8	2.5	0.6	—	—
100.0	33.3	31.4	—	—	3.2	1.3	—	—	1.7	0.1	4.3	1.5	5.3	3.9	0.5	0.3	3.2	0.2	3.9	4.0	1.5	0.4	—	—
100.0	40.0	43.7	—	—	—	—	—	—	1.8	0.1	1.9	0.8	2.2	1.6	0.2	0.1	1.2	0.1	2.8	2.1	1.2	0.2	—	—
100.0	39.2	42.7	0.1	—	0.1	—	—	—	1.5	—	1.9	0.5	2.8	2.4	0.5	0.2	1.3	0.4	2.4	2.1	1.5	0.4	—	—
100.0	21.1	23.1	0.1	—	5.2	3.2	—	0.1	2.7	0.1	4.6	1.2	8.3	6.6	0.7	0.3	3.6	0.5	8.8	7.2	2.0	0.6	—	—
100.0	19.6	18.2	0.1	—	0.5	0.3	0.2	—	3.7	0.2	11.4	5.5	7.3	5.3	0.9	0.4	5.0	0.6	11.3	6.0	2.9	0.6	—	—

Table 11. Gainfully Employed Population, 15 Years and Older, by Industry and Sex
(For 1950 only, 14-year-olds included)

(Zone)(Sector)	District	Total			Total	Agriculture	Forestry and Hunting	Fisheries and Aquiculture	Mining	Construction	Manufacturing	Wholesale and Retail	Finance and Insurance	Transportation and Communication	Services	Civil Service	Unclassified
		Total	M	F													
9 I	Kamakura-shi	(32,766) 100.0	70.7	29.3	100.0	6.6	0.1	0.9	0.2	5.8	20.3	21.8	3.9	9.1	27.1	4.2	—
II	Ayase-machi	(3,499) 100.0	65.2	34.8	100.0	61.6	—	—	0.3	3.1	6.3	6.5	0.9	2.9	16.5	1.9	—
	Ebina-machi	(7,056) 100.0	63.0	37.0	100.0	52.2	—	—	1.3	3.3	12.3	7.4	1.0	5.8	14.4	2.3	—
	Shiroyama-machi	(2,166) 100.0	62.7	37.3	100.0	55.3	—	0.1	1.2	3.9	5.7	7.8	0.5	7.6	15.0	2.9	—
III	Akita-machi	(5,384) 100.0	71.3	28.7	100.0	39.8	—	—	2.1	3.7	13.2	9.9	1.0	4.2	21.8	4.3	—
	Hamura-machi	(4,306) 100.0	67.8	32.2	100.0	28.7	0.1	—	2.5	5.9	14.2	10.5	1.7	5.5	26.3	4.6	—
IV	Hannō-shi	(18,351) 100.0	64.6	35.4	100.0	32.3	2.0	—	1.4	3.6	20.0	15.4	1.6	5.1	16.8	1.8	—
	Tsurugashima-mura	(3,295) 100.0	56.9	43.1	100.0	74.1	—	—	0.1	1.7	7.9	4.6	0.5	2.6	6.6	1.9	—
	Hidaka-machi	(8,115) 100.0	58.2	41.8	100.0	63.5	0.4	—	0.4	3.0	10.8	6.9	1.1	3.4	8.9	1.6	—
	Kawashima-mura	(9,920) 100.0	50.3	49.7	100.0	83.6	—	—	0.1	1.6	4.6	3.9	0.9	0.9	3.4	1.0	—
V	Kitamoto-machi	(6,284) 100.0	59.2	40.8	100.0	56.9	—	—	0.1	3.2	13.4	9.5	0.9	6.7	7.3	2.0	—
	Higawa-machi	(8,224) 100.0	60.9	39.1	100.0	49.3	—	—	—	3.1	17.1	13.0	1.0	6.4	8.0	2.1	—
	Shobu-machi	(8,143) 100.0	53.9	46.1	100.0	68.8	—	0.1	—	1.7	8.9	8.9	0.8	2.7	6.6	1.5	—
	Kuki-machi	(9,586) 100.0	60.3	39.7	100.0	51.5	—	—	—	2.8	13.7	10.7	0.9	9.3	8.8	2.3	—
	Satte-machi	(11,178) 100.0	56.0	44.0	100.0	56.0	—	0.1	—	3.3	13.9	12.2	0.9	3.3	8.2	2.1	—
VI	Iwai-machi	(18,300) 100.0	51.0	49.0	100.0	82.1	—	0.1	—	1.5	2.3	6.8	0.3	1.0	5.0	0.9	—
	Mitsukaidō-shi	(19,576) 100.0	53.7	46.3	100.0	67.8	—	—	—	2.2	5.5	11.6	0.6	3.8	7.2	1.3	—
	Yawahara-mura	(5,732) 100.0	52.3	47.7	100.0	81.4	—	0.1	—	1.8	3.3	5.8	0.4	1.9	4.0	1.3	—
	Ina-mura	(6,593) 100.0	51.3	48.7	100.0	83.3	—	0.1	—	1.4	2.9	5.1	0.6	1.3	3.9	1.4	—
VII	Fujishiro-machi	(6,578) 100.0	52.4	47.6	100.0	70.4	—	—	0.1	2.2	4.9	9.9	0.8	4.4	5.6	1.7	—
	Ryūgasaki-shi	(16,128) 100.0	55.8	44.2	100.0	59.4	—	—	—	2.6	9.1	13.1	0.9	3.8	8.6	2.5	—
	Tone-mura	(4,847) 100.0	53.2	46.8	100.0	73.7	—	0.1	—	3.5	5.3	7.8	0.6	2.3	4.6	2.1	—
	Motono-mura	(3,002) 100.0	49.7	50.3	100.0	85.9	—	0.2	—	1.5	2.9	4.1	0.3	1.6	2.7	0.8	—
VIII	Sakura-shi	(16,130) 100.0	56.1	43.9	100.0	59.6	—	—	—	2.5	7.1	10.1	1.4	6.6	9.4	3.3	—
	Izumi-machi	(5,161) 100.0	51.9	48.1	100.0	85.2	—	—	—	0.8	2.5	4.0	0.4	1.9	3.6	1.6	—
IX	Shitsu-mura	(5,305) 100.0	49.2	50.8	100.0	84.1	0.1	0.1	—	1.3	2.7	3.6	0.7	1.9	4.2	1.3	—
	Nansō-machi	(9,514) 100.0	52.4	47.6	100.0	75.8	0.2	—	—	2.1	3.2	8.0	0.5	1.9	6.8	1.5	—
	Fukuta-machi	(3,770) 100.0	53.1	46.9	100.0	76.6	0.1	—	—	2.1	3.2	6.3	0.8	2.0	7.5	1.4	—
X	Kimitsu-machi	(6,911) 100.0	53.0	47.0	100.0	69.9	0.1	4.2	0.1	2.0	4.2	6.6	0.9	2.6	7.8	1.6	—
	Futtsu-machi	(7,800) 100.0	58.8	41.2	100.0	39.3	—	31.8	0.1	2.2	5.8	10.3	0.5	1.9	7.0	1.1	—
	Ōsawa-machi	(6,456) 100.0	56.7	43.3	100.0	51.6	0.3	8.5	0.2	2.9	8.4	11.1	0.9	3.6	10.8	1.7	—
	Zone 9 Total	(279,376) 100.0	58.0	42.0	100.0	56.0	0.2	1.3	0.3	2.9	9.8	10.8	1.2	4.4	10.9	2.2	—
10 I	Yokosuka-shi	(105,795) 100.0	72.1	27.9	100.0	5.1	—	2.0	0.1	5.4	15.9	19.1	1.5	6.9	33.5	10.5	—
	Zushi-shi	(13,115) 100.0	72.4	27.6	100.0	2.9	0.1	1.1	0.2	5.2	20.8	20.1	3.6	8.8	32.1	5.1	—
	Hayama-machi	(5,322) 100.0	70.2	29.8	100.0	15.8	0.4	3.4	0.1	6.7	17.9	14.8	2.4	6.4	27.8	4.3	—
	Chigasaki-shi	(20,939) 100.0	70.5	29.5	100.0	22.3	—	1.0	0.2	4.2	26.5	14.9	2.4	7.9	16.4	4.2	—
	Fujisawa-shi	(40,452) 100.0	69.1	30.9	100.0	19.7	—	0.5	0.2	4.7	21.1	18.6	2.7	8.1	20.5	3.9	—
II	Aikawa-machi	(6,499) 100.0	59.5	40.5	100.0	47.5	0.2	—	1.1	2.9	27.1	6.3	0.5	1.9	11.1	1.4	—
	Atsugi-shi	(17,156) 100.0	62.8	37.2	100.0	53.3	0.1	—	1.0	3.5	8.7	11.2	1.0	4.4	13.9	2.9	—
	Samukawa-machi	(4,288) 100.0	68.4	31.6	100.0	42.8	—	—	1.6	2.7	23.4	9.5	0.9	5.9	10.0	3.2	—
III	Ōme-shi	(23,472) 100.0	64.7	35.3	100.0	18.4	0.9	—	1.4	4.0	34.2	13.0	1.7	4.8	16.7	4.9	—
IV	Sakado-machi	(11,389) 100.0	56.3	43.7	100.0	66.2	—	—	0.3	2.2	10.2	8.7	0.9	2.5	7.2	1.8	—
	Yoshimi-mura	(8,165) 100.0	51.5	48.5	100.0	81.6	—	—	—	2.2	5.1	3.6	0.6	1.5	4.0	1.4	—
	Moroyama-mura	(5,463) 100.0	55.1	44.9	100.0	61.2	0.3	—	0.1	2.1	10.3	7.0	1.1	2.6	13.8	1.4	0.1
V	Kōnosu-shi	(13,655) 100.0	59.0	41.0	100.0	46.1	—	—	—	2.7	16.7	13.1	1.1	6.5	11.2	2.6	—
	Kisai-machi	(7,964) 100.0	54.0	46.0	100.0	73.1	—	—	—	1.9	7.2	7.6	0.8	2.2	5.2	2.0	—
	Washimiya-machi	(4,138) 100.0	57.3	42.7	100.0	65.2	—	0.1	—	1.8	9.9	8.8	1.0	6.5	5.3	1.4	—
	Kurihashi-machi	(5,612) 100.0	57.3	42.7	100.0	52.5	—	0.1	0.1	4.7	10.4	14.5	0.7	6.9	7.4	2.7	—
	Goka-mura	(4,896) 100.0	49.7	50.3	100.0	86.2	—	—	—	2.3	2.7	3.5	0.3	1.0	2.6	1.4	—
VI	Sakai-machi	(11,709) 100.0	52.4	47.6	100.0	72.6	—	—	—	1.9	4.4	9.4	0.6	1.9	7.1	2.1	—

Table 11. Gainfully Employed Population, 15 Years and Older, by Industry and Sex
(For 1950 only, 14-year-olds included)

Total	Agriculture M	F	Forestry and Hunting M	F	Fisheries and Aquiculture M	F	Mining M	F	Construction M	F	Manufacturing M	F	Wholesale and Retail M	F	Finance and Insurance M	F	Transportation and Communication M	F	Services M	F	Civil Service M	F	Unclassified M	F
100.0	3.9	2.7	0.1	—	0.8	0.1	0.2	—	5.3	0.5	16.9	3.4	14.0	7.8	2.9	1.0	7.9	1.2	15.2	11.9	3.5	0.7	—	—
100.0	36.9	24.7	—	—	—	—	0.2	0.1	2.9	0.2	4.9	1.4	4.2	2.3	0.5	0.4	2.7	0.2	11.5	5.0	1.4	0.5	—	—
100.0	28.8	23.4	—	—	—	—	1.2	0.1	3.0	0.3	7.9	4.4	4.7	2.7	0.7	0.3	5.2	0.6	9.7	4.7	1.8	0.5	—	—
100.0	29.6	25.6	0.1	—	0.1	—	1.1	0.1	3.8	0.1	3.7	2.0	4.7	3.1	0.4	0.1	6.5	1.1	10.5	4.5	2.2	0.7	—	—
100.0	28.0	11.8	—	—	—	—	2.1	—	3.6	0.1	7.9	5.3	6.1	3.8	0.6	0.4	3.7	0.5	15.6	6.2	3.7	0.6	—	—
100.0	18.0	10.7	0.1	—	—	—	2.4	0.1	5.6	0.3	8.8	5.4	6.3	4.2	1.2	0.5	4.7	0.8	16.9	9.4	3.8	0.8	—	—
100.0	16.8	15.5	1.6	0.4	—	—	1.3	0.1	3.6	—	12.0	8.0	9.7	5.7	1.2	0.4	4.6	0.5	11.3	5.5	1.5	0.3	—	—
100.0	37.7	36.4	—	—	—	—	0.1	—	1.7	—	5.9	2.0	2.9	1.7	0.4	0.1	2.3	0.3	4.2	2.4	1.6	0.3	—	—
100.0	32.3	31.2	0.3	0.1	—	—	0.3	0.1	2.9	0.1	7.7	3.1	3.9	3.0	0.7	0.4	3.1	0.3	5.6	3.3	1.4	0.2	—	—
100.0	38.3	45.3	—	—	—	—	0.1	—	1.6	—	3.8	0.8	2.2	1.7	0.6	0.3	0.8	0.1	1.9	1.5	1.0	—	—	—
100.0	26.1	30.8	—	—	—	—	—	0.1	3.2	—	11.0	2.4	5.5	4.0	0.6	0.3	6.4	0.3	4.7	2.6	1.7	0.3	—	—
100.0	23.3	26.0	—	—	—	—	—	—	3.0	0.1	13.8	3.3	8.2	4.8	0.6	0.4	5.9	0.5	4.4	3.6	1.7	0.4	—	—
100.0	33.6	35.2	—	—	—	0.1	—	—	1.7	—	5.4	3.5	5.3	3.6	0.6	0.2	2.5	0.2	3.5	3.1	1.3	0.2	—	—
100.0	24.8	26.7	—	—	—	—	—	—	2.8	—	10.1	3.6	6.5	4.2	0.6	0.3	8.7	0.6	4.9	3.9	1.9	0.4	—	—
100.0	27.7	28.3	—	—	0.1	—	—	—	3.2	0.1	7.9	6.0	7.3	4.9	0.6	0.3	3.0	0.3	4.5	3.7	1.7	0.4	—	—
100.0	39.3	42.8	—	—	—	0.1	—	—	1.4	0.1	1.8	0.5	3.9	2.9	0.2	0.1	0.8	0.2	2.7	2.3	0.9	—	—	—
100.0	31.8	36.0	—	—	—	—	—	—	2.1	0.1	4.1	1.4	6.8	4.8	0.5	0.1	3.4	0.4	3.9	3.3	1.1	0.2	—	—
100.0	39.3	42.1	—	—	—	0.1	—	—	1.7	0.1	2.6	0.7	3.5	2.3	0.3	0.1	1.6	0.3	2.2	1.8	1.1	0.2	—	—
100.0	39.2	44.1	—	—	—	0.1	—	—	1.4	—	2.5	0.4	3.1	2.0	0.4	0.2	1.3	—	2.2	1.7	1.2	0.2	—	—
100.0	31.9	38.5	—	—	—	—	—	0.1	2.1	0.1	3.6	1.3	5.5	4.4	0.5	0.3	4.2	0.2	3.2	2.4	1.4	0.3	—	—
100.0	28.3	31.1	—	—	—	—	—	—	2.5	0.1	7.0	2.1	7.1	6.0	0.6	0.3	3.4	0.4	4.8	3.8	2.1	0.4	—	—
100.0	34.6	39.1	—	—	0.1	—	—	—	3.2	0.3	4.5	0.8	3.7	4.1	0.5	0.1	2.1	0.2	2.7	1.9	1.8	0.3	—	—
100.0	40.1	45.8	—	—	0.1	0.1	—	—	1.4	0.1	2.3	0.6	1.9	2.2	0.2	0.1	1.5	0.1	1.6	1.1	0.6	0.2	—	—
100.0	28.5	31.1	—	—	—	—	—	—	2.2	0.3	5.7	1.4	5.2	4.9	1.0	0.4	5.9	0.7	5.0	4.4	2.6	0.7	—	—
100.0	41.3	43.9	—	—	—	—	—	—	0.8	—	2.0	0.5	2.3	1.7	0.2	0.2	1.6	0.3	2.3	1.3	1.4	0.2	—	—
100.0	37.8	46.3	0.1	—	0.1	—	—	—	1.3	—	2.5	0.2	1.8	1.8	0.5	0.2	1.6	0.3	2.5	1.7	1.0	0.3	—	—
100.0	36.9	38.9	0.1	0.1	—	—	—	—	2.0	0.1	2.3	0.9	4.5	3.5	0.3	0.2	1.6	0.3	3.4	3.4	1.3	0.2	—	—
100.0	36.5	40.1	0.1	—	—	—	—	—	2.0	0.1	2.5	0.7	3.8	2.5	0.5	0.3	2.0	—	4.6	2.9	1.1	0.2	—	—
100.0	31.8	38.1	0.1	—	2.6	1.6	0.1	—	1.9	0.1	3.3	0.9	3.8	2.8	0.6	0.3	2.3	0.3	5.1	2.7	1.4	0.2	—	—
100.0	18.3	21.0	—	—	21.3	10.5	0.1	—	2.1	0.1	4.4	1.4	5.9	4.4	0.3	0.2	1.6	0.3	4.0	3.0	0.8	0.3	—	—
100.0	21.9	29.7	0.3	—	7.3	1.2	0.2	—	2.7	0.2	6.6	1.8	6.3	4.8	0.7	0.2	3.3	0.3	6.0	4.8	1.4	0.3	—	—
100.0	27.2	28.8	0.1	0.1	1.0	0.3	0.3	—	2.8	0.1	7.2	2.6	6.4	4.4	0.9	0.3	3.9	0.5	6.4	4.5	1.8	0.4	—	—
100.0	2.5	2.6	—	—	1.9	0.1	—	0.1	5.1	0.3	13.1	2.8	10.1	9.0	1.0	0.5	6.0	0.9	22.8	10.7	9.6	0.9	—	—
100.0	1.8	1.1	0.1	—	1.0	0.1	0.2	—	4.8	0.4	16.4	4.4	12.7	7.4	2.6	1.0	7.5	1.3	21.2	10.9	4.1	1.0	—	—
100.0	6.6	9.2	0.4	—	3.3	0.1	0.1	—	6.6	0.1	15.7	2.2	9.5	5.3	1.8	0.6	5.3	1.1	17.4	10.4	3.5	0.8	—	—
100.0	12.8	9.5	—	—	1.0	—	0.2	—	4.0	0.2	20.7	5.8	9.5	5.4	1.7	0.7	7.2	0.7	9.9	6.5	3.5	0.7	—	—
100.0	11.7	8.0	—	—	0.4	0.1	0.1	0.1	4.5	0.2	16.6	4.5	11.8	6.8	2.0	0.7	7.2	0.9	11.5	9.0	3.3	0.6	—	—
100.0	28.0	19.5	0.2	—	—	—	1.1	—	2.8	0.1	12.5	14.6	3.5	2.8	0.4	0.1	1.5	0.4	8.3	2.8	1.2	0.2	—	—
100.0	30.7	22.6	0.1	—	—	—	0.8	0.2	3.2	0.1	6.4	2.3	6.2	5.0	0.7	0.3	3.7	0.7	8.7	5.2	2.3	0.6	—	—
100.0	25.2	17.6	—	—	—	—	1.6	—	2.6	0.1	19.0	4.4	5.4	4.1	0.6	0.3	5.2	0.7	5.9	4.1	2.9	0.3	—	—
100.0	13.1	5.3	0.9	—	—	—	1.4	—	3.9	0.1	16.9	17.3	8.2	4.8	1.1	0.6	4.2	0.6	10.7	6.0	4.3	0.6	—	—
100.0	32.3	33.9	—	—	—	—	0.2	0.1	2.2	—	7.4	2.8	5.2	3.5	0.7	0.2	2.2	0.3	4.5	2.7	1.6	0.2	—	—
100.0	37.6	44.0	—	—	—	—	—	—	2.2	—	4.1	1.0	2.2	1.4	0.4	0.2	1.3	0.2	2.6	1.4	1.1	0.3	—	—
100.0	30.4	30.8	0.2	0.1	—	—	0.1	—	2.1	—	6.2	4.1	4.2	2.8	0.8	0.3	2.3	0.3	7.6	6.2	1.1	0.3	0.1	—
100.0	21.7	24.4	—	—	—	—	—	—	2.7	—	10.6	6.1	8.3	4.8	0.9	0.2	6.1	0.4	6.6	4.6	2.1	0.5	—	—
100.0	35.3	37.8	—	—	—	—	—	—	1.9	—	4.6	2.6	4.7	2.9	0.6	0.2	2.1	0.1	3.1	2.1	1.7	0.3	—	—
100.0	31.6	33.6	—	—	—	0.1	—	—	1.7	0.1	7.4	2.5	5.2	3.6	0.8	0.2	6.1	0.4	3.3	2.0	1.2	0.2	—	—
100.0	23.7	28.8	—	—	0.1	—	0.1	—	4.4	0.3	7.6	2.8	7.9	6.6	0.5	0.2	6.5	0.4	4.3	3.1	2.2	0.5	—	—
100.0	39.6	46.6	—	—	—	—	—	—	2.1	0.2	2.0	0.7	2.1	1.4	0.3	—	0.9	0.1	1.6	1.0	1.1	0.3	—	—
100.0	33.9	38.7	—	—	—	—	—	—	1.8	0.1	3.2	1.2	5.9	3.5	0.4	0.2	1.5	0.4	3.9	3.2	1.8	0.3	—	—

Table 11. Gainfully Employed Population, 15 Years and Older, by Industry and Sex
(For 1950 only, 14-year-olds are included)

(Zone)	(Sector)	District	Total	M	F	Total	Agriculture	Forestry and Hunting	Fisheries and Aquiculture	Mining	Construction	Manufacturing	Wholesale and Retail	Finance and Insurance	Transportation and Communication	Services	Civil Service	Unclassified
VI		Sashima-machi	(8,075) 100.0	49.7	50.3	100.0	83.9	0.1	—	—	1.0	2.7	5.9	0.2	0.8	4.5	0.9	—
		Yatabe-machi	(11,795) 100.0	52.6	47.4	100.0	81.0	—	—	—	1.4	2.2	6.2	0.3	1.4	5.7	1.8	—
VII		Kukizaki-mura	(3,607) 100.0	50.9	49.1	100.0	86.2	—	0.1	—	1.7	2.0	4.9	0.3	1.4	2.4	1.0	—
		Ushiku-machi	(7,796) 100.0	53.5	46.5	100.0	73.1	—	—	—	2.0	5.5	8.9	0.5	3.3	5.2	1.5	—
		Kawachi-mura	(7,321) 100.0	50.0	50.0	100.0	84.0	—	0.1	—	2.2	0.9	6.7	0.2	1.3	3.5	1.1	—
		Sakae-machi	(5,240) 100.0	52.0	48.0	100.0	71.9	0.1	—	—	3.6	2.9	12.0	0.7	2.2	5.3	1.3	—
		Narita-shi	(21,247) 100.0	54.8	46.2	100.0	58.0	0.1	—	—	2.4	5.8	13.7	0.8	5.9	11.0	2.3	—
VIII		Shisui-machi	(2,957) 100.0	55.2	44.8	100.0	64.8	0.1	0.1	—	1.7	9.3	7.3	0.9	7.5	5.0	3.3	—
		Yachimata-machi	(12,306) 100.0	54.4	45.6	100.0	69.4	—	—	—	1.8	4.9	12.9	0.5	2.2	6.7	1.6	—
		Toke-machi	(3,140) 100.0	54.9	45.1	100.0	71.9	0.1	—	—	2.5	6.2	8.8	0.6	3.7	4.7	1.5	—
IX		Nagara-machi	(4,558) 100.0	51.9	48.1	100.0	82.4	0.4	—	—	2.0	3.4	3.7	0.5	1.6	4.3	1.7	—
		Obitsu-mura	(3,694) 100.0	52.8	47.2	100.0	77.1	0.4	—	0.3	2.7	4.0	5.2	1.0	1.9	5.9	1.5	—
X		Koito-machi	(3,453) 100.0	52.4	47.6	100.0	81.7	0.4	—	—	1.7	3.6	4.8	0.3	1.3	5.0	1.2	—
		Zone 10 Total	(407,522) 100.0	63.1	36.9	100.0	38.5	0.1	0.7	0.2	3.7	14.1	13.6	1.4	5.2	17.7	4.8	—
		Total for 50 km. Region	(5,553,761) 100.0	68.5	31.5	100.0	14.6	—	0.5	0.2	5.0	27.7	20.5	2.9	6.6	17.5	4.5	0.0
		National Total	(39,261,351) 100.0	60.9	39.1	100.0	37.9	1.3	1.8	1.4	4.5	17.6	13.9	1.6	5.2	11.3	3.5	0.0
		1960																
1	I	Chiyoda-ku	(69,274) 100.0	67.4	32.6	100.0	0.0	0.0	0.0	0.1	3.8	20.5	45.3	2.7	3.5	19.6	4.5	0.0
		Minato-ku	(137,730) 100.0	68.2	31.8	100.0	0.1	0.0	0.1	0.2	5.8	25.9	31.9	4.1	6.7	21.6	3.6	0.0
		Chūō-ku	(98,275) 100.0	67.0	33.0	100.0	0.0	0.0	0.3	0.2	4.1	21.6	43.4	2.5	6.2	16.7	4.8	0.2
		Bunkyō-ku	(127,409) 100.0	67.2	32.8	100.0	0.1	0.0	0.1	0.1	5.6	32.7	27.4	4.4	4.9	21.3	3.4	0.0
		Taitō-ku	(180,977) 100.0	67.1	32.9	100.0	0.0	0.0	0.0	0.0	5.3	35.0	38.3	2.2	2.9	15.3	1.0	0.0
		Zone 1 Total	(613,665) 100.0	67.1	32.9	100.0	0.1	0.0	0.1	0.1	5.0	28.0	38.0	3.2	4.6	18.4	2.5	0.0
2	I	Shinagawa-ku	(217,787) 100.0	68.6	31.4	100.0	0.1	0.0	0.1	0.1	6.4	42.3	23.7	3.5	6.4	15.1	2.3	0.0
	II	Meguro-ku	(136,644) 100.0	69.9	30.1	100.0	0.3	0.0	0.1	0.3	6.1	35.5	22.3	5.0	6.2	19.4	4.8	0.0
		Shibuya-ku	(131,532) 100.0	66.9	33.1	100.0	0.2	0.0	0.0	0.2	8.2	24.1	28.3	5.8	6.7	23.1	3.4	0.0
	III	Shinjuku-ku	(203,650) 100.0	66.5	33.5	100.0	0.1	0.0	0.1	0.2	7.4	25.4	30.3	4.9	5.4	21.5	4.7	0.0
		Nakano-ku	(154,561) 100.0	70.2	29.8	100.0	0.3	0.0	0.1	0.3	8.5	24.8	25.6	7.3	7.3	20.7	5.0	0.1
	IV	Toshima-ku	(174,821) 100.0	67.4	32.6	100.0	0.1	0.0	0.1	0.1	8.4	29.8	29.1	4.9	6.2	18.5	2.8	0.0
	V	Kita-ku	(198,531) 100.0	69.0	31.0	100.0	0.1	0.0	0.0	0.1	7.2	40.0	24.0	4.0	7.3	14.2	3.1	0.0
	VI	Arakawa-ku	(143,198) 100.0	71.4	28.6	100.0	0.1	0.0	0.0	0.0	7.9	48.0	23.3	2.3	5.9	10.8	1.7	0.0
	VII	Sumida-ku	(179,633) 100.0	69.0	31.0	100.0	0.0	0.0	0.0	0.0	5.0	55.0	22.8	1.6	3.6	10.8	1.2	0.0
	VIII	Kōtō-ku	(178,054) 100.0	74.6	25.4	100.0	0.1	0.0	0.2	0.0	9.0	45.8	21.7	1.7	9.6	10.5	1.5	0.0
		Zone 2 Total	(1,718,411) 100.0	69.3	30.7	100.0	0.1	0.0	0.1	0.1	7.4	37.4	25.2	3.9	6.4	16.3	3.1	0.0
3	I	Ōta-ku	(339,235) 100.0	72.6	27.4	100.0	0.3	0.0	0.9	0.1	5.9	47.3	20.2	3.5	5.7	13.9	2.2	0.0
	II	Setagaya-ku	(276,260) 100.0	70.2	29.8	100.0	1.5	0.1	0.1	0.4	6.9	27.9	22.4	6.1	7.1	22.7	4.8	0.0
	III	Suginami-ku	(205,245) 100.0	70.6	29.4	100.0	0.8	0.0	0.1	0.6	7.0	25.4	25.2	7.8	6.7	21.9	4.5	0.0
	IV	Itabashi-ku	(185,875) 100.0	71.8	28.2	100.0	1.1	0.0	0.0	0.1	7.5	44.4	19.4	3.6	6.3	14.2	3.4	0.0
		Nerima-ku	(125,279) 100.0	72.4	27.6	100.0	3.7	0.1	0.0	0.2	7.2	27.6	20.1	6.0	7.4	20.6	7.1	0.0
	VI	Adachi-ku	(187,104) 100.0	70.2	29.8	100.0	3.4	0.0	0.0	0.0	6.9	48.4	19.3	2.3	6.5	10.4	2.8	0.0
	VII	Katsushika-ku	(175,271) 100.0	69.5	30.5	100.0	1.5	0.0	0.0	0.0	5.5	51.8	19.0	2.6	5.5	11.2	2.9	0.0
	VIII	Edogawa-ku	(147,290) 100.0	70.8	29.2	100.0	3.8	0.0	0.9	0.1	6.5	47.2	19.2	2.8	5.9	11.1	2.5	0.0
		Urayasu-machi	(7,418) 100.0	67.1	32.9	100.0	9.4	0.0	20.8	0.0	2.8	22.8	31.6	0.9	2.2	8.1	1.4	0.0
		Zone 3 Total	(1,648,977) 100.0	71.1	28.9	100.0	1.7	0.0	0.4	0.2	6.6	40.1	20.8	4.4	6.3	15.9	3.6	0.0
4	I	Kawasaki-shi	(294,231) 100.0	73.5	26.5	100.0	3.1	0.0	.0.1	0.1	9.8	49.3	14.9	1.9	7.5	11.2	2.1	0.0
	II	Komae-machi	(10,295) 100.0	71.6	28.4	100.0	6.7	0.0	0.1	0.2	7.6	30.4	17.3	4.6	6.0	22.3	4.8	0.0
	III	Mitaka-shi	(40,917) 100.0	71.9	28.1	100.0	3.8	0.0	0.1	0.2	6.6	33.3	19.5	5.5	6.9	19.5	4.6	0.0

Table 11. Gainfully Employed Population, 15 Years and Older, by Industry and Sex
(For 1950 only, 14-year-olds are included)

Total	Agriculture		Forestry and Hunting		Fisheries and Aquiculture		Mining		Construction		Manufacturing		Wholesale and Retail		Finance and Insurance		Transportation and Communication		Services		Civil Service		Unclassified	
	M	F	M	F	M	F	M	F	M	F	M	F	M	F	M	F	M	F	M	F	M	F	M	F
100.0	39.2	44.7	0.1	–	–	–	–	–	0.9	0.1	2.1	0.6	3.3	2.6	0.1	0.1	0.7	0.1	2.6	1.9	0.7	0.2	–	–
100.0	39.4	41.6	–	–	–	–	–	–	1.4	–	1.8	0.4	3.7	2.5	0.2	0.1	1.2	0.2	3.4	2.3	1.5	0.3	–	–
100.0	41.0	45.2	–	–	0.1	–	–	–	1.6	0.1	1.6	0.4	2.6	2.3	0.2	0.1	1.4	–	1.5	0.9	0.9	0.1	–	–
100.0	34.7	38.4	–	–	–	–	–	–	2.0	–	4.1	1.4	4.6	4.3	0.4	0.1	3.2	0.1	3.3	1.9	1.2	0.3	–	–
100.0	39.5	44.5	–	–	0.1	–	–	–	2.1	0.1	0.8	0.1	2.0	4.7	0.2	–	1.1	0.2	1.9	1.6	1.0	0.1	–	–
100.0	35.0	36.9	–	–	–	–	–	–	3.3	0.3	2.1	0.8	5.0	7.0	0.5	0.2	2.1	0.1	2.9	2.4	0.9	0.4	–	–
100.0	27.9	30.1	0.1	–	0.1	–	–	–	2.3	0.1	4.2	1.6	6.7	7.0	0.6	0.2	5.2	0.7	5.9	5.1	0.9	1.4	–	–
100.0	30.6	34.2	0.1	–	–	–	–	–	1.7	–	7.1	2.2	3.9	3.4	0.5	0.4	6.9	0.6	2.8	2.2	2.5	1.8	–	–
100.0	34.6	34.8	–	–	–	–	–	–	1.7	0.1	3.9	1.0	7.1	5.8	0.3	0.2	1.9	0.3	3.5	3.2	1.0	0.6	–	–
100.0	35.1	36.8	0.1	–	–	–	–	–	2.4	0.1	5.1	1.1	4.3	4.5	0.4	0.2	3.5	0.2	2.8	1.9	1.2	0.3	–	–
100.0	39.8	42.5	0.4	–	–	–	–	–	1.9	0.1	2.2	1.2	2.0	1.7	0.2	0.3	1.4	0.2	2.6	1.7	1.4	0.3	–	–
100.0	35.8	31.3	0.3	0.1	–	–	0.2	0.1	2.4	0.3	3.5	0.5	3.4	1.8	0.7	0.3	1.8	0.1	3.6	2.3	1.4	0.1	–	–
100.0	40.0	41.7	0.4	–	–	–	–	–	1.5	0.2	2.9	0.7	2.5	2.3	0.3	–	1.2	0.1	3.0	2.0	1.0	0.2	–	–
100.0	19.3	19.2	0.1	–	0.7	–	0.2	–	3.5	0.2	10.4	3.7	7.8	5.8	1.0	0.4	4.6	0.6	11.3	6.4	4.2	0.6	–	–
100.0	7.4	7.2	–	–	0.4	0.1	0.2	–	4.8	0.2	21.3	6.4	13.1	7.4	1.9	1.0	5.9	0.7	9.7	7.8	3.8	0.7	0.0	0.0
100.0	18.1	19.8	1.0	0.3	1.4	0.4	1.2	0.2	4.2	0.3	12.2	5.4	8.3	5.6	1.1	0.5	4.6	0.6	5.9	5.4	2.9	0.6	0.0	0.0
100.0	–	–	0.0	0.0	0.0	0.0	0.1	0.0	3.4	0.4	15.5	5.0	32.1	13.2	1.6	1.1	3.1	0.4	7.8	11.8	4.0	0.5	0.0	0.0
100.0	0.1	0.0	0.0	0.0	0.1	0.0	0.1	0.1	5.4	0.4	20.2	5.7	21.1	10.8	2.5	1.6	5.9	0.8	9.8	11.8	3.0	0.6	0.0	0.0
100.0	0.0	0.0	0.0	0.0	0.1	0.2	0.0	0.2	3.1	1.0	16.1	5.5	35.6	7.8	1.3	1.2	4.4	1.8	5.4	11.3	1.0	3.8	0.0	0.2
100.0	0.1	0.0	0.0	0.0	0.1	0.0	0.1	0.0	5.2	0.4	23.9	8.8	18.1	9.3	2.7	1.7	4.3	0.6	10.1	11.2	2.7	0.7	0.0	0.0
100.0	0.1	0.0	0.0	0.0	0.0	0.0	0.0	0.0	5.1	0.2	26.2	8.8	24.8	13.5	1.2	1.0	2.6	0.3	6.5	8.8	0.8	0.2	0.0	0.0
100.0	0.1	0.0	0.0	0.0	0.1	0.0	0.1	0.0	4.6	0.4	21.5	6.5	25.0	13.0	1.9	1.3	4.0	0.6	8.0	10.4	2.1	0.4	0.0	0.0
100.0	0.1	0.0	0.0	0.0	0.1	0.0	0.1	0.0	6.0	0.4	30.8	11.5	14.3	9.4	2.1	1.4	5.7	0.7	7.6	7.5	1.8	0.5	0.0	0.0
100.0	0.3	0.0	0.0	0.0	0.2	0.1	0.2	0.0	5.8	0.3	26.7	8.8	14.3	8.0	3.2	1.8	5.2	1.0	10.2	9.2	3.8	1.0	0.0	0.0
100.0	0.2	0.0	0.0	0.0	0.0	0.0	0.2	0.0	7.7	0.5	17.9	6.2	17.5	10.8	4.0	1.8	5.7	1.0	10.9	12.2	2.8	0.6	0.0	0.0
100.0	0.1	0.0	0.0	0.0	0.1	0.0	0.1	0.1	6.9	0.5	18.7	6.7	18.3	12.0	3.1	1.8	4.5	0.9	10.9	10.6	4.0	0.7	0.0	0.0
100.0	0.3	0.0	0.0	0.0	0.1	0.0	0.3	0.0	7.9	0.6	19.1	5.7	16.4	9.2	4.2	3.1	6.3	1.0	11.6	9.1	4.0	1.0	0.0	0.1
100.0	0.1	0.0	0.0	0.0	0.1	0.0	0.1	0.0	7.8	0.6	21.5	8.3	17.6	11.5	3.0	1.9	5.4	0.8	9.6	8.9	2.2	0.6	0.0	0.0
100.0	0.1	0.0	0.0	0.0	0.1	0.0	0.1	0.0	6.8	0.4	28.6	11.4	14.5	9.5	2.2	1.8	6.4	0.9	7.7	6.5	3.1	0.0	0.0	0.0
100.0	0.0	0.1	0.0	0.0	0.0	0.0	0.0	0.0	7.6	0.3	45.3	2.7	15.0	8.3	1.2	1.1	5.3	0.6	5.4	5.4	1.3	0.4	0.0	0.1
100.0	0.0	0.0	0.0	0.0	0.0	0.0	0.0	0.0	4.7	0.3	39.6	15.4	14.6	8.2	0.8	0.8	3.2	0.4	4.9	5.9	9.5	8.3	0.0	0.0
100.0	0.0	0.0	0.0	0.0	0.2	0.0	0.0	0.0	8.4	0.6	35.5	10.3	14.2	7.5	0.9	1.5	8.9	0.7	5.3	5.2	1.2	0.3	0.0	0.0
100.0	0.1	0.0	0.0	0.0	0.1	0.0	0.1	0.0	6.9	0.5	27.5	9.9	15.7	9.5	2.4	0.8	5.7	0.7	8.3	8.0	2.5	0.6	0.0	0.0
100.0	0.3	0.0	0.0	0.0	0.7	0.2	0.1	0.0	5.6	0.3	36.9	10.4	12.9	7.3	2.2	1.3	5.1	0.6	7.0	6.9	1.8	0.4	0.0	0.0
100.0	1.1	0.4	0.1	0.0	0.1	0.0	0.3	0.1	6.4	0.5	21.0	6.9	14.6	7.8	4.1	2.0	6.2	0.9	12.6	10.1	3.8	1.0	0.0	0.0
100.0	0.6	0.2	0.0	0.0	0.1	0.0	0.6	0.0	6.5	0.5	19.7	5.7	14.5	10.7	5.4	2.4	5.7	1.0	14.0	17.7	3.5	1.0	0.0	0.0
100.0	0.7	0.4	0.0	0.0	0.0	0.0	0.0	0.1	6.9	0.6	33.4	10.4	12.3	7.1	2.1	1.5	5.6	0.7	7.9	6.3	2.8	1.6	0.0	0.0
100.0	2.3	1.4	0.0	0.1	0.0	0.0	0.1	0.1	6.8	0.4	20.5	7.1	13.3	6.8	4.2	1.8	6.4	1.0	12.4	8.2	6.3	0.8	0.0	0.0
100.0	1.7	1.7	0.0	0.0	0.0	0.0	0.0	0.0	6.6	0.3	34.9	13.5	12.0	7.3	1.3	1.0	5.7	0.8	5.7	4.7	2.3	0.5	0.0	0.0
100.0	0.8	0.7	0.0	0.0	0.0	0.0	0.0	0.0	5.2	0.3	34.2	17.6	11.6	7.4	1.5	1.1	4.8	0.7	5.8	5.4	2.4	0.5	0.0	0.0
100.0	2.2	1.6	0.0	0.0	0.7	0.2	0.0	0.1	6.2	0.3	38.1	9.1	9.1	10.1	1.5	1.3	5.2	0.7	5.8	5.3	2.0	0.5	0.0	0.0
100.0	5.0	4.4	0.0	0.0	18.7	2.1	0.0	0.0	2.6	0.2	15.2	7.6	18.0	13.6	0.6	0.3	1.8	0.4	4.1	4.0	1.1	0.3	0.0	0.0
100.0	1.1	0.6	0.0	0.0	0.3	0.1	0.2	0.0	6.2	0.4	30.1	10.0	13.3	7.5	2.8	1.6	5.5	0.8	8.7	7.2	2.9	0.7	0.0	0.0
100.0	1.9	1.3	0.0	0.0	0.1	0.0	0.1	0.0	9.0	0.8	37.9	11.4	9.0	5.9	1.2	0.7	6.7	0.8	5.9	5.2	1.7	0.4	0.0	0.0
100.0	4.3	2.4	0.0	0.0	0.1	0.0	0.2	0.0	7.1	0.5	22.8	7.6	11.1	6.2	3.1	1.5	5.3	0.7	13.6	8.7	4.0	0.8	0.0	0.0
100.0	2.4	1.4	0.0	0.0	0.0	0.1	0.2	0.0	6.1	0.5	25.3	8.0	12.7	6.8	3.8	1.7	6.0	0.9	14.8	4.7	3.6	1.0	0.0	0.0

Table 11. Gainfully Employed Population, 15 Years and Older, by Industry and Sex
(For 1950 only, 14-year-olds are included)

(Zone) (Sector)	District	Total	M	F	Total	Agriculture	Forestry and Hunting	Fisheries and Aquiculture	Mining	Construction	Manufacturing	Wholesale and Retail	Finance and Insurance	Transportation and Communication	Services	Civil Service	Unclassified
III	Musashino-shi	(51,150) 100.0	69.7	30.3	100.0	1.1	0.0	0.1	0.7	6.3	25.3	24.6	7.1	7.1	22.7	5.0	0.0
	Chōfu-shi	(27,986) 100.0	72.2	27.8	100.0	6.2	0.0	0.0	0.4	7.0	28.8	18.6	3.6	8.5	22.2	4.7	0.0
	Hoya-machi	(18,804) 100.0	72.9	27.1	100.0	4.8	0.0	0.0	0.0	7.7	28.3	18.3	5.5	8.2	20.4	6.8	0.0
IV	Yamato-machi	(7,386) 100.0	68.9	31.1	100.0	15.9	0.0	0.0	—	8.7	36.8	13.5	1.9	5.3	13.4	4.5	0.0
	Toda-machi	(14,593) 100.0	69.6	30.4	100.0	14.0	0.0	0.0	0.1	6.2	52.4	11.8	1.5	3.9	7.6	2.5	0.0
V	Warabi-shi	(22,488) 100.0	69.1	30.9	100.0	1.7	0.0	0.0	0.1	7.9	45.7	20.2	3.5	6.3	11.2	3.4	0.0
	Kawaguchi-shi	(78,835) 100.0	70.7	29.3	100.0	7.4	0.0	0.0	0.0	5.1	54.4	16.1	1.9	4.2	9.1	1.8	0.0
	Hatogaya-machi	(8,821) 100.0	71.7	28.3	100.0	8.6	0.0	0.0	0.0	5.3	44.4	17.3	3.2	6.9	11.4	2.9	0.0
VI	Sōka-shi	(18,425) 100.0	63.5	36.5	100.0	25.3	0.0	0.0	0.0	4.2	39.1	14.2	1.5	4.2	9.6	1.9	—
	Yashio-mura	(6,717) 100.0	58.3	41.7	100.0	47.6	0.0	0.0	0.0	4.3	30.4	6.5	0.4	2.0	7.4	1.3	0.1
	Misato-mura	(9,077) 100.0	56.2	43.8	100.0	57.8	0.0	0.0	0.4	3.2	19.2	8.2	0.4	3.0	6.7	1.1	0.0
	Matsudo-shi	(38,242) 100.0	64.5	35.5	100.0	21.3	0.0	0.0	0.3	6.9	24.1	18.0	3.3	7.8	12.8	5.5	0.0
VII	Ichikawa-shi	(68,918) 100.0	67.4	32.6	100.0	10.2	0.0	0.2	0.2	4.9	36.0	21.1	3.9	5.1	15.6	2.8	0.0
	Zone 4 Total	(716,885) 100.0	70.9	29.1	100.0	7.4	0.0	0.1	0.2	7.5	41.9	16.9	3.0	6.6	13.4	3.0	0.0
5 I	Tsurumi-ku	(105,907) 100.0	73.8	26.2	100.0	0.9	0.0	0.4	0.0	9.9	50.0	16.3	1.9	8.1	11.0	1.5	0.0
III	Koganei-shi	(18,550) 100.0	70.7	29.3	100.0	4.8	0.0	0.0	0.3	6.8	28.0	18.7	5.3	7.0	23.4	5.7	0.0
	Tanashi-machi	(12,913) 100.0	60.2	39.8	100.0	4.9	0.0	0.0	0.1	6.6	32.2	19.3	4.1	6.6	19.3	6.9	0.0
	Kurume-machi	(8,056) 100.0	69.9	30.1	100.0	21.4	0.0	0.1	0.1	5.8	23.6	13.2	4.8	6.6	19.3	5.1	0.0
IV	Niza-machi	(6,681) 100.0	63.3	36.7	100.0	41.2	0.0	—	0.1	4.3	26.3	10.7	1.3	3.3	10.0	2.8	0.0
	Kiyose-machi	(7,464) 100.0	58.3	41.7	100.0	17.1	0.1	0.0	0.1	5.2	16.9	14.6	2.3	4.9	33.9	4.9	0.0
	Adachi-machi	(5,537) 100.0	64.8	35.2	100.0	23.5	0.0	0.0	0.1	6.3	30.3	18.7	2.2	4.7	11.2	3.0	0.0
	Asaka-machi	(11,644) 100.0	73.9	26.1	100.0	17.3	0.0	0.0	0.1	4.5	30.0	12.0	2.1	4.3	11.2	18.4	0.0
V	Urawa-shi	(72,558) 100.0	67.9	32.1	100.0	9.5	0.0	0.0	0.2	5.8	28.7	20.7	5.5	7.2	16.5	5.9	0.0
	Misono-mura	(4,720) 100.0	54.8	45.2	100.0	71.8	—	—	0.1	2.0	10.7	5.9	0.5	2.3	5.1	1.6	0.0
	Koshigaya-shi	(23,468) 100.0	59.0	41.0	100.0	44.4	0.0	0.0	0.1	3.5	25.3	12.0	0.9	4.1	7.9	1.9	0.0
VI	Yoshikawa-machi	(8,757) 100.0	52.9	47.1	100.0	59.8	0.0	0.0	0.1	3.4	15.1	9.9	0.4	2.4	7.6	1.3	0.0
	Nagareyama-machi	(11,849) 100.0	61.8	38.2	100.0	35.8	0.1	0.0	0.1	5.6	22.5	13.0	2.5	7.5	9.6	3.3	0.0
VII	Kamagaya-machi	(6,255) 100.0	64.8	35.2	100.0	43.9	0.0	0.0	0.0	5.0	18.7	10.6	1.3	4.7	6.3	9.5	0.0
VIII	Funahashi-shi	(60,728) 100.0	67.0	33.0	100.0	14.6	0.0	2.3	0.1	5.7	28.9	19.9	3.1	6.4	14.1	4.9	0.0
	Zone 5 Total	(365,087) 100.0	68.4	31.6	100.0	14.6	0.0	0.5	0.1	6.7	33.7	16.9	3.0	6.5	13.7	4.3	0.0
6 I	Nishi-ku	(46,964) 100.0	70.9	29.1	100.0	0.1	0.0	0.1	0.0	8.8	32.3	24.5	2.6	12.8	15.3	3.5	0.0
	Naka-ku	(58,862) 100.0	67.5	32.5	100.0	0.3	0.0	0.8	0.0	7.5	17.7	34.1	3.0	13.8	19.8	3.0	0.0
	Kanagawa-ku	(74,662) 100.0	72.9	27.1	100.0	1.8	0.0	0.8	0.1	8.4	36.0	21.2	2.7	11.5	14.5	3.0	0.0
II	Kōhoku-ku	(63,677) 100.0	69.4	30.6	100.0	19.2	0.0	0.0	0.1	5.5	33.9	13.7	2.8	8.1	13.4	3.4	0.0
	Inagi-machi	(4,924) 100.0	67.0	33.0	100.0	30.5	0.0	0.0	0.6	8.2	27.8	11.3	1.2	4.5	13.7	2.2	0.0
III	Tama-mura	(4,165) 100.0	62.4	37.6	100.0	28.3	0.1	0.0	0.6	6.9	23.6	7.7	1.6	6.7	21.3	3.2	0.0
	Fuchu-shi	(32,580) 100.0	71.3	28.7	100.0	7.7	0.0	0.1	0.5	6.1	28.0	17.3	2.8	6.8	23.6	7.1	0.0
	Kunitachi-machi	(12,949) 100.0	71.4	28.6	100.0	5.1	0.0	0.0	0.4	6.7	22.3	19.9	4.4	8.8	26.2	6.2	0.0
	Kokubunji-machi	(16,333) 100.0	73.6	26.4	100.0	6.5	0.1	0.0	0.2	6.9	23.2	16.4	4.6	12.8	22.7	6.6	0.0
	Kodaira-machi	(19,876) 100.0	71.9	28.1	100.0	8.8	0.0	0.0	0.2	7.0	26.0	14.0	3.2	7.0	21.0	12.1	0.0
	Higashimurayama-machi	(16,793) 100.0	71.4	28.6	100.0	9.2	—	0.0	0.1	9.3	27.2	13.9	3.3	10.0	20.2	6.8	0.0
IV	Tokorosawa-shi	(29,757) 100.0	65.1	34.9	100.0	26.0	0.0	0.0	0.1	5.5	22.5	14.1	1.7	6.4	21.1	2.7	0.0
	Miyoshi-mura	(2,360) 100.0	49.1	50.9	100.0	74.0	0.0	0.0	0.2	2.0	11.2	5.8	0.4	1.0	4.2	1.4	0.0
	Fujimi-mura	(6,091) 100.0	57.8	42.2	100.0	54.0	0.0	0.0	0.1	4.2	20.8	8.7	1.1	3.4	6.1	1.7	0.0
V	Yono-shi	(17,379) 100.0	69.5	30.5	100.0	4.6	0.0	0.0	0.1	6.3	39.8	18.4	3.9	8.5	14.0	4.4	0.0
	Ōmiya-shi	(75,162) 100.0	66.1	33.9	100.0	14.6	0.0	0.1	0.2	5.2	29.8	17.5	3.0	11.6	12.6	5.4	0.0
	Iwatsuki-shi	(16,938) 100.0	58.4	41.6	100.0	44.8	0.0	0.0	0.1	3.8	25.0	11.3	1.1	4.2	7.3	2.4	0.0
VI	Matsubushi-mura	(4,813) 100.0	52.4	47.6	100.0	62.5	0.1	0.0	0.2	3.0	18.8	6.3	0.2	3.0	4.7	1.2	0.0
VII	Kashiwa-shi	(27,906) 100.0	64.4	35.6	100.0	29.5	0.0	0.0	0.1	6.2	19.1	15.3	2.6	10.3	12.6	4.3	0.0

Table 11. Gainfully Employed Population, 15 Years and Older, by Industry and Sex
(For 1950 only, 14-year-olds are included)

Total	Agriculture		Forestry and Hunting		Fisheries and Aquiculture		Mining		Construction		Manufacturing		Wholesale and Retail		Finance and Insurance		Transportation and Communication		Services		Civil Service		Unclassified	
	M	F	M	F	M	F	M	F	M	F	M	F	M	F	M	F	M	F	M	F	M	F	M	F
100.0	0.7	0.4	0.0	0.0	0.1	0.0	0.6	0.1	5.8	0.5	20.0	5.3	16.0	8.6	4.2	2.9	6.1	1.0	12.2	10.5	4.0	1.0	—	0.0
100.0	4.2	2.0	0.0	0.0	0.0	0.0	0.3	0.1	4.5	2.5	20.7	8.1	12.5	6.1	2.2	1.4	7.5	1.0	14.3	7.9	4.0	0.7	0.0	0.0
100.0	2.9	1.9	0.0	0.0	0.0	0.0	0.0	0.0	7.0	0.7	20.8	7.5	12.0	6.3	3.9	1.6	7.0	1.2	14.0	6.4	5.3	1.5	0.0	0.0
100.0	8.4	7.5	0.0	0.0	0.0	0.0	—	—	8.3	0.4	26.3	10.5	8.7	4.8	1.1	0.8	4.8	0.5	7.3	6.1	4.0	0.5	0.0	0.0
100.0	6.5	7.5	0.0	0.0	0.0	0.0	0.1	0.0	5.9	0.3	39.0	13.4	7.4	4.4	0.9	0.6	3.5	0.4	4.3	3.3	2.0	0.5	0.0	0.0
100.0	1.0	0.7	0.0	0.0	0.0	0.0	0.1	0.0	7.5	0.4	32.3	13.4	12.1	8.1	2.1	1.4	5.5	0.8	6.0	5.2	2.5	0.9	0.0	0.0
100.0	3.7	3.7	0.0	0.0	0.0	0.0	0.0	0.0	4.8	0.3	41.3	13.1	9.8	6.3	1.0	0.9	3.9	0.3	4.7	4.4	1.5	0.3	0.0	0.0
100.0	4.8	3.8	0.0	0.0	0.0	0.0	0.0	0.0	4.8	0.5	33.4	11.0	11.2	6.1	2.2	1.0	6.3	0.6	6.8	4.6	2.2	0.7	0.0	0.0
100.0	11.9	13.4	0.0	0.0	0.0	0.0	0.0	0.0	3.8	0.4	26.9	12.2	8.8	5.4	0.9	0.6	4.2	0.0	5.5	4.1	1.5	0.4	—	—
100.0	20.7	26.9	0.0	0.0	0.0	0.0	0.0	0.0	4.2	0.1	20.9	9.5	4.0	2.5	0.3	0.1	1.8	0.2	5.3	2.1	1.0	0.3	0.1	0.0
100.0	25.3	31.5	0.0	0.0	0.0	0.0	0.4	0.0	3.1	0.1	12.9	6.3	5.1	3.1	0.2	0.2	2.4	0.6	4.9	1.8	0.9	0.2	0.0	0.0
100.0	10.4	9.9	0.0	0.0	0.0	0.0	0.2	0.1	4.3	3.6	17.5	6.6	11.0	7.0	2.2	1.1	7.0	0.8	7.4	5.4	4.5	1.0	0.0	0.0
100.0	5.4	4.8	0.0	0.0	0.2	0.0	0.1	0.1	4.6	0.3	26.0	10.0	14.0	7.1	2.6	1.3	4.4	0.7	7.9	7.7	2.2	0.6	0.0	0.0
100.0	3.9	3.5	0.0	0.0	0.1	0.0	0.1	0.0	7.0	0.5	31.6	10.3	10.6	6.3	1.9	1.1	5.8	0.8	7.5	5.9	2.4	0.6	0.0	0.0
100.0	0.5	0.4	0.0	0.0	0.3	0.1	0.0	0.0	9.0	0.9	39.4	10.6	9.8	6.5	1.2	0.7	7.2	0.9	5.1	5.9	1.3	0.2	0.0	0.0
100.0	3.0	1.8	0.0	0.0	0.0	0.0	0.3	0.0	6.4	0.4	20.8	7.2	11.8	6.9	3.3	2.0	6.2	0.8	14.2	9.2	4.7	1.0	0.0	0.0
100.0	2.8	2.1	0.0	0.0	0.0	0.0	0.1	0.0	6.2	0.4	23.2	9.0	2.1	17.2	2.5	1.6	5.7	0.9	11.7	7.6	5.9	1.0	0.0	0.0
100.0	12.3	9.1	0.0	0.0	0.1	0.0	0.0	0.1	5.3	0.5	16.7	6.9	9.3	3.9	3.4	1.4	5.8	0.8	12.7	6.6	4.3	0.8	0.0	0.0
100.0	21.3	19.9	0.0	0.0	—	—	0.0	0.1	4.2	0.1	17.5	8.8	6.9	3.8	0.9	0.4	2.9	0.4	7.0	3.0	2.6	0.2	0.0	0.0
100.0	8.2	8.9	0.1	0.0	0.0	0.0	0.1	0.0	4.8	0.4	12.4	4.5	8.8	5.8	1.5	0.8	4.4	0.5	14.6	19.3	4.1	0.8	—	—
100.0	11.0	12.5	—	0.0	0.0	0.0	0.1	0.0	6.0	0.3	21.6	8.7	11.7	7.0	1.5	0.7	4.0	0.7	6.4	4.8	2.5	0.5	—	—
100.0	8.5	8.8	0.0	0.0	0.0	0.0	0.1	0.0	4.3	0.2	22.8	7.3	7.5	4.5	1.6	0.5	3.7	0.6	7.5	3.7	17.9	0.5	0.0	0.0
100.0	4.4	5.1	0.0	0.0	0.0	0.0	0.1	0.1	5.4	0.4	21.4	7.3	12.9	7.8	3.4	2.1	6.3	0.9	9.3	7.2	4.7	1.2	0.0	0.0
100.0	35.5	36.3	—	—	—	—	0.0	0.1	2.0	0.0	7.3	3.4	3.3	2.6	0.2	0.3	1.9	0.4	3.3	1.8	1.3	0.3	—	—
100.0	20.4	24.0	0.0	0.0	0.0	0.0	0.0	0.0	3.4	0.1	17.2	8.1	7.3	4.7	0.6	0.3	3.6	0.5	5.0	2.9	1.5	0.4	0.0	0.0
100.0	26.3	33.5	0.0	0.0	0.0	0.0	0.1	0.0	3.1	0.3	9.6	5.5	5.7	4.2	0.3	0.1	2.2	0.2	4.5	3.1	1.1	0.2	—	—
100.0	14.6	21.2	0.1	0.0	0.0	0.0	0.0	0.0	5.1	0.5	16.2	6.3	8.3	4.7	1.8	0.7	6.7	0.8	6.1	3.5	2.8	0.5	0.0	0.0
100.0	22.3	21.6	0.0	0.0	—	0.0	0.0	0.0	4.6	0.4	14.5	4.2	6.5	4.1	0.8	0.5	4.0	0.7	3.7	2.6	8.4	1.1	0.0	0.0
100.0	7.1	7.5	0.0	0.0	1.9	0.4	0.0	0.1	5.3	0.4	21.3	7.6	11.7	8.2	2.0	1.1	5.6	0.8	7.6	6.5	4.3	0.6	0.0	0.0
100.0	7.0	7.6	0.0	0.0	0.4	0.1	0.1	0.0	6.2	0.5	25.3	8.4	10.3	6.6	1.9	1.1	5.8	0.7	7.7	6.0	3.7	0.6	0.0	0.0
100.0	0.1	0.0	0.0	0.0	0.1	0.0	0.0	0.0	8.2	0.6	24.1	8.2	14.7	9.8	1.5	1.1	11.3	1.5	8.1	7.2	2.8	0.7	0.0	0.0
100.0	0.2	0.1	0.0	0.0	0.7	0.1	0.0	0.0	7.1	0.4	13.2	4.5	19.6	14.5	1.9	1.1	12.5	1.3	9.8	10.0	2.5	0.5	0.0	0.0
100.0	1.1	0.7	0.0	0.0	0.8	0.0	0.0	0.1	7.8	0.6	27.6	8.4	13.1	8.1	1.7	1.0	10.2	1.3	8.1	6.4	2.5	0.5	0.0	0.0
100.0	10.4	8.8	0.0	0.0	0.0	0.0	0.0	0.0	5.2	0.3	30.0	3.9	8.6	5.1	1.8	1.0	7.2	0.9	7.6	5.8	2.6	0.8	0.0	0.0
100.0	16.6	13.9	0.0	0.0	—	—	0.6	0.0	8.1	0.1	19.3	8.5	6.9	4.4	0.6	0.6	4.0	0.5	9.1	4.6	1.8	0.4	—	0.0
100.0	16.5	11.8	0.1	0.0	—	—	0.6	0.0	6.6	0.3	15.0	8.6	4.6	3.1	1.0	0.6	5.8	0.9	9.5	11.8	2.7	0.5	—	0.0
100.0	4.6	3.1	0.0	0.0	0.1	0.0	0.5	0.0	5.8	0.3	20.8	7.2	10.3	7.0	1.7	1.1	6.0	0.8	15.3	8.3	6.2	0.9	0.0	—
100.0	3.4	1.7	0.0	0.0	0.0	0.0	0.4	0.0	6.4	0.3	16.3	6.0	12.6	7.3	2.9	1.5	7.8	1.0	16.3	9.9	5.3	0.9	0.0	0.0
100.0	4.2	2.3	0.0	0.1	0.0	0.0	0.1	0.1	6.6	0.3	17.2	6.0	10.2	6.2	2.9	1.7	11.8	1.0	15.0	7.7	5.6	1.0	0.0	0.0
100.0	5.0	3.8	0.0	0.0	0.0	0.0	0.1	0.1	6.6	0.4	19.1	6.9	8.9	5.1	2.1	1.1	6.3	0.7	12.8	8.2	11.0	1.1	0.0	0.0
100.0	5.0	4.2	—	—	0.0	0.0	0.1	0.0	8.7	0.6	19.2	8.0	8.9	5.0	2.1	1.2	8.9	1.1	12.4	7.8	6.1	0.7	0.0	0.0
100.0	13.0	13.0	0.0	0.0	0.0	0.0	0.0	0.0	4.7	0.8	14.6	7.9	8.8	5.3	1.2	0.5	5.8	0.6	14.7	6.4	2.3	0.4	0.0	0.0
100.0	36.2	37.8	—	0.0	—	0.0	—	0.0	2.0	0.0	2.0	9.2	3.6	2.2	0.3	0.1	1.0	0.0	2.9	1.3	1.1	0.3	—	0.0
100.0	25.4	28.6	—	0.0	—	0.0	—	0.0	4.0	0.2	13.7	7.1	5.6	3.1	0.8	0.3	3.0	0.4	3.9	2.2	1.4	0.3	—	0.0
100.0	2.3	2.3	—	0.0	0.0	0.0	0.1	0.0	5.9	0.4	28.4	11.4	11.7	6.7	2.4	1.5	7.7	0.8	7.6	6.4	3.4	1.0	0.0	0.0
100.0	6.6	8.0	0.0	0.0	0.0	0.0	0.1	0.1	4.8	0.4	20.6	9.2	10.1	7.4	1.7	1.3	10.7	0.9	6.7	5.9	4.6	0.8	0.0	0.0
100.0	21.5	23.3	0.0	0.0	0.0	0.0	0.0	0.1	3.6	0.2	16.3	8.7	6.5	4.8	0.7	0.4	3.7	0.5	4.1	3.2	2.0	0.4	0.0	0.0
100.0	25.6	36.8	0.0	0.1	0.0	0.0	0.1	0.1	2.8	0.2	13.9	4.9	3.3	3.0	0.1	0.1	2.9	0.1	2.6	2.1	1.0	0.2	0.0	0.0
100.0	13.4	16.1	0.0	0.0	0.0	0.0	0.1	0.0	5.8	0.4	14.2	4.9	9.1	6.2	1.8	0.8	9.3	1.0	7.1	5.5	3.6	0.7	—	0.0

Table 11. Gainfully Employed Population, 15 Years and Older, by Industry and Sex
(For 1950 only, 14-year-olds are included)

(Zone)(Sector)	District	Total	M	F	Total	Agriculture	Forestry and Hunting	Fisheries and Aquiculture	Mining	Construction	Manufacturing	Wholesale and Retail	Finance and Insurance	Transportation and Communication	Services	Civil Service	Unclassified
VII	Shōnan-mura	(6,876) 100.0	57.9	42.1	100.0	65.1	0.0	0.0	0.0	3.2	5.4	5.3	0.3	2.5	2.7	15.5	0.0
	Shirai-mura	(4,566) 100.0	52.3	47.7	100.0	80.3	0.0	0.0	0.0	2.4	4.6	6.0	0.2	1.7	3.3	1.5	0.0
VIII	Narashino-shi	(16,959) 100.0	67.4	32.6	100.0	10.7	0.0	1.2	0.1	5.1	30.9	15.6	3.2	10.7	16.1	6.4	0.0
	Zone 6 Total	(560,592) 100.0	68.2	31.8	100.0	14.0	0.0	0.3	0.1	6.5	27.8	18.5	2.7	9.8	15.8	4.5	0.0
7 I	Isogo-ku	(31,488) 100.0	70.4	29.6	100.0	2.2	0.0	0.6	0.0	6.8	29.9	20.3	3.7	14.2	18.5	3.8	0.0
	Minami-ku	(85,031) 100.0	70.1	29.9	100.0	2.4	0.0	0.1	0.1	9.1	31.0	23.5	2.6	12.3	15.7	3.2	0.0
	Hodogaya-ku	(59,815) 100.0	73.0	27.0	100.0	5.4	0.0	0.1	0.1	7.1	38.7	16.1	3.0	11.7	13.3	4.5	0.0
II	Machida-shi	(29,834) 100.0	67.9	32.1	100.0	21.0	0.0	0.0	0.1	5.5	26.4	16.3	2.5	7.2	16.7	4.3	0.0
III	Yuki-mura	(3,191) 100.0	58.0	42.0	100.0	57.4	0.2	0.0	0.1	4.0	17.5	5.8	0.7	3.9	8.5	1.9	0.0
	Hino-machi	(18,295) 100.0	71.5	28.5	100.0	10.1	0.0	0.1	0.3	5.1	35.2	14.3	3.9	8.6	17.7	4.7	0.0
	Tachikawa-shi	(30,648) 100.0	66.8	33.2	100.0	1.1	0.0	0.0	0.2	6.5	22.1	28.1	3.1	7.2	26.0	5.7	0.0
	Sunakawa-machi	(5,927) 100.0	68.1	31.9	100.0	25.9	—	0.0	0.1	6.7	23.9	11.5	1.3	4.5	21.3	4.8	0.0
	Yamato-machi	(6,064) 100.0	66.6	33.4	100.0	18.9	0.0	0.0	0.0	6.7	30.3	12.5	1.2	8.2	19.3	2.9	0.0
IV	Ōi-mura	(2,603) 100.0	61.2	38.8	100.0	46.6	0.0	0.0	0.0	5.8	20.8	10.2	0.4	3.1	5.8	7.3	0.0
	Fukuoka-mura	(7,279) 100.0	71.9	28.1	100.0	11.4	0.0	0.0	0.2	7.0	29.6	17.7	5.3	8.8	14.5	5.5	0.0
V	Kasukabe-shi	(16,033) 100.0	59.8	40.2	100.0	37.0	0.0	0.0	0.0	3.5	26.8	15.0	1.4	4.9	8.8	2.6	0.0
	Shōwa-mura	(6,964) 100.0	54.1	45.9	100.0	53.3	0.0	0.0	0.1	3.9	21.1	9.2	0.6	2.8	7.2	1.8	0.0
VI	Noda-shi	(26,891) 100.0	57.8	42.2	100.0	34.2	0.0	0.0	0.3	6.3	25.4	13.9	1.0	5.6	11.4	1.9	0.0
VII	Abiko-machi	(12,533) 100.0	60.7	39.3	100.0	36.6	0.0	0.0	0.1	5.0	19.7	16.1	2.0	7.7	10.4	2.4	0.0
	Yachiyo-machi	(10,374) 100.0	58.9	41.1	100.0	50.8	0.0	0.0	0.1	4.1	13.8	10.7	1.9	6.3	9.3	3.0	0.0
VIII	Chiba-shi	(107,856) 100.0	68.0	32.0	100.0	14.2	0.0	2.1	0.1	6.7	24.0	18.9	3.4	8.2	15.8	6.6	0.0
IX	Goi-machi	(10,896) 100.0	56.1	43.9	100.0	56.7	0.0	5.1	0.0	4.7	9.9	10.1	0.8	3.5	7.2	2.0	0.0
	Sodegaura-machi	(7,058) 100.0	52.5	47.5	100.0	56.9	0.0	19.9	0.2	2.6	3.1	6.7	0.5	2.1	6.0	2.0	0.0
	Zone 7 Total	(478,780) 100.0	67.2	32.8	100.0	15.7	0.0	1.0	0.1	6.6	27.2	18.2	2.7	9.0	15.2	4.3	0.0
8 I	Kanazawa-ku	(28,577) 100.0	72.4	27.6	100.0	1.9	0.0	2.3	0.1	8.4	36.0	16.5	2.5	9.2	18.2	4.9	0.0
	Totsuka-ku	(49,521) 100.0	72.7	27.3	100.0	15.3	0.0	0.1	0.0	6.1	37.3	12.3	2.3	9.5	12.9	4.2	0.0
II	Yamato-shi	(16,800) 100.0	67.8	32.2	100.0	14.1	0.0	0.0	0.1	7.6	25.9	17.6	2.2	8.1	20.4	4.0	0.0
	Sagamihara-shi	(42,117) 100.0	68.1	31.9	100.0	18.9	0.0	0.0	0.9	6.3	25.1	14.0	2.0	7.1	22.3	3.4	0.0
	Zama-machi	(6,883) 100.0	65.4	34.6	100.0	26.1	0.0	0.1	1.5	5.2	20.8	14.0	1.4	6.2	21.3	3.4	0.0
III	Hachiōji-shi	(69,988) 100.0	65.0	35.0	100.0	10.0	0.2	0.0	0.2	5.8	38.2	17.8	2.2	6.8	15.0	3.8	0.0
	Akishima-shi	(17,597) 100.0	69.5	30.5	100.0	4.9	0.0	0.0	0.9	8.7	29.3	15.9	2.2	6.4	25.8	5.9	0.0
	Fussa-machi	(9,469) 100.0	66.4	33.6	100.0	5.2	0.0	0.0	0.6	9.5	18.5	23.9	1.7	5.7	31.9	3.0	0.0
	Mizuho-machi	(5,357) 100.0	66.0	34.0	100.0	31.9	0.0	0.0	0.1	6.0	26.7	12.4	1.0	3.6	16.7	1.6	0.0
	Murayama-machi	(5,132) 100.0	65.4	34.6	100.0	30.4	0.0	0.0	0.0	5.6	32.4	9.4	0.6	3.2	16.5	1.9	0.0
	Musashi-machi	(14,185) 100.0	61.9	38.1	100.0	29.0	0.0	0.0	0.2	5.1	21.0	13.3	0.9	4.2	22.7	3.6	0.0
IV	Sayama-shi	(16,042) 100.0	61.2	38.8	100.0	32.4	0.0	—	0.1	4.3	24.8	12.2	0.9	4.3	15.4	5.6	—
	Kawagoe-shi	(50,772) 100.0	60.8	39.2	100.0	30.7	0.0	0.0	0.2	4.3	26.9	14.9	1.8	6.0	12.3	2.9	0.0
	Seibu-machi	(3,368) 100.0	48.4	51.6	100.0	12.1	0.1	—	0.6	3.4	55.5	8.7	0.5	5.3	12.0	1.8	—
V	Ageo-shi	(19,003) 100.0	59.4	40.6	100.0	30.9	0.0	0.0	0.2	4.2	35.5	10.9	1.3	6.4	8.2	2.4	—
	Ina-mura	(3,724) 100.0	52.8	47.2	100.0	60.0	0.0	—	0.0	2.3	19.4	5.9	0.6	6.9	3.3	1.6	—
	Hasuda-machi	(9,819) 100.0	58.6	41.4	100.0	42.1	—	0.0	0.0	4.4	22.8	10.3	1.0	7.5	8.9	3.0	0.0
	Shiraoka-machi	(7,696) 100.0	59.2	40.8	100.0	50.9	—	0.0	0.0	5.2	16.6	9.5	0.8	8.0	6.8	2.2	0.0
	Miyashiro-machi	(5,330) 100.0	57.6	42.4	100.0	51.0	0.0	—	0.1	3.9	16.8	8.7	1.2	9.7	6.8	1.8	—
	Sugito-machi	(8,698) 100.0	55.3	44.7	100.0	57.8	—	0.0	0.0	2.9	13.8	11.2	1.2	4.7	6.6	1.8	—
VI	Sekiyado-machi	(6,512) 100.0	50.1	49.9	100.0	73.0	0.0	—	0.0	4.7	5.0	7.6	0.3	2.8	6.4	0.2	0.0
	Moriya-machi	(6,026) 100.0	51.7	48.3	100.0	66.9	0.0	0.0	0.1	3.3	7.4	10.2	0.7	3.0	6.2	2.2	0.0
VII	Toride-machi	(10,701) 100.0	58.6	41.4	100.0	34.1	0.0	0.0	0.5	5.4	18.9	17.2	1.8	6.5	12.3	3.3	—
	Inzai-machi	(8,694) 100.0	53.2	46.8	100.0	64.3	0.0	0.1	—	2.7	6.5	14.3	0.6	2.9	7.0	1.4	—
	Inba-mura	(4,657) 100.0	49.8	50.2	100.0	86.0	—	0.2	—	1.6	2.3	3.7	0.3	1.6	3.3	1.0	—

Table 11. Gainfully Employed Population, 15 Years and Older, by Industry and Sex
(For 1950 only, 14-year-olds are included)

Total	Agriculture		Forestry and Hunting		Fisheries and Aquiculture		Mining		Construction		Manufacturing		Wholesale and Retail		Finance and Insurance		Transportation and Communication		Services		Civil Service		Unclassified	
	M	F	M	F	M	F	M	F	M	F	M	F	M	F	M	F	M	F	M	F	M	F	M	F
100.0	29.1	36.0	—	0.0	0.0	0.0	—	0.0	2.9	0.3	3.7	1.7	2.6	2.7	0.2	0.1	2.3	0.2	1.7	1.0	15.4	0.1	—	0.0
100.0	38.6	41.7	—	0.0	—	0.0	0.0	0.0	2.3	0.1	3.4	1.2	3.7	2.3	0.0	0.2	1.3	0.4	1.8	1.5	1.2	0.3	0.0	0.0
100.0	5.0	5.7	0.0	0.0	0.7	0.5	0.0	0.1	4.9	0.2	21.5	9.4	8.9	6.7	1.9	1.3	9.5	1.2	9.4	6.7	5.6	0.8	0.0	0.0
100.0	7.0	7.0	0.0	0.0	0.2	0.1	0.1	0.0	6.1	0.4	20.2	7.6	11.1	7.4	1.7	1.0	8.8	1.0	9.1	6.7	3.9	0.6	0.0	0.0
100.0	1.3	0.9	—	0.0	0.5	0.1	0.0	0.0	6.3	0.5	22.4	7.5	12.1	8.2	2.2	1.5	12.2	2.0	10.3	8.2	3.1	0.7	0.0	0.0
100.0	1.4	1.0	0.0	0.0	0.1	—	0.0	0.1	8.5	0.6	21.2	9.8	14.9	8.6	1.6	1.0	11.1	1.2	8.6	7.1	2.7	0.5	0.0	0.0
100.0	3.2	2.2	0.0	0.0	0.1	—	0.0	0.1	6.7	0.4	29.4	9.3	9.8	6.3	1.8	1.2	10.5	1.2	7.7	5.6	3.8	0.7	0.0	0.0
100.0	12.1	8.9	0.0	0.0	0.0	0.0	0.1	0.0	5.2	0.3	18.5	7.9	9.8	6.5	1.7	0.8	6.4	0.8	10.6	6.1	3.5	0.8	0.0	0.0
100.0	29.7	27.7	0.1	0.1	—	0.0	0.1	0.0	3.7	0.3	11.3	6.2	3.0	2.8	0.4	0.3	3.2	0.7	5.1	3.4	1.4	0.5	0.0	0.0
100.0	6.1	4.0	0.0	0.0	0.1	—	0.2	0.1	4.8	0.3	25.7	9.5	9.0	5.3	2.5	1.4	7.6	1.0	11.7	6.0	3.8	0.9	0.0	0.0
100.0	0.8	0.3	0.0	0.0	0.0	0.0	0.2	0.0	6.1	0.4	15.9	6.2	15.4	12.7	2.0	1.1	6.4	0.8	15.0	11.0	5.0	0.7	0.0	0.0
100.0	15.4	10.5	—	—	—	0.0	0.0	0.1	6.4	0.3	15.6	8.3	6.7	4.8	0.9	0.4	3.8	0.7	15.3	6.0	4.2	0.6	0.0	0.0
100.0	10.4	8.5	0.0	0.0	—	0.0	0.0	0.0	6.1	0.6	19.3	11.0	7.0	5.5	0.7	0.5	7.0	1.2	13.7	5.6	2.4	0.5	0.0	0.0
100.0	22.3	24.3	—	0.0	—	0.0	—	0.0	5.7	0.1	13.4	7.4	6.0	4.2	0.3	0.1	2.5	0.6	4.0	1.8	7.0	0.3	—	0.0
100.0	5.4	6.0	—	0.0	0.0	0.0	0.2	0.0	6.6	0.4	22.0	7.6	11.7	6.0	3.9	1.4	8.0	0.8	9.5	5.0	4.6	0.9	0.0	0.0
100.0	16.8	20.2	0.0	0.0	0.0	0.0	—	0.0	3.3	0.2	18.9	7.9	8.8	6.2	0.9	0.5	4.2	0.7	4.8	4.0	2.1	0.5	0.0	0.0
100.0	23.4	29.9	0.0	0.0	0.0	0.0	0.1	0.0	3.7	0.2	13.9	7.2	5.3	3.9	0.4	0.2	2.5	0.3	3.4	3.8	1.4	0.4	0.0	0.0
100.0	12.6	21.6	0.0	0.0	0.0	0.0	0.3	0.0	5.7	0.6	18.3	7.1	8.2	5.7	0.7	0.3	4.9	0.7	5.5	5.9	1.6	0.3	—	0.0
100.0	17.2	19.4	0.0	0.0	0.0	0.0	0.1	0.0	4.5	0.5	13.6	6.1	8.7	7.4	1.3	0.7	6.9	0.8	6.4	4.0	2.0	0.4	0.0	0.0
100.0	24.1	26.7	0.0	0.0	0.0	0.0	0.1	0.0	3.8	0.3	10.3	3.5	6.4	4.3	1.2	0.7	5.5	0.8	5.1	4.2	2.4	0.6	0.0	0.0
100.0	6.6	7.6	0.0	0.0	1.3	0.8	0.1	0.0	6.2	0.5	19.3	4.7	11.0	7.9	2.2	1.2	7.2	1.0	8.5	7.3	5.6	1.0	0.0	0.0
100.0	27.7	29.0	—	0.0	2.7	2.4	0.0	0.0	4.2	0.5	7.4	2.5	5.4	4.7	0.5	0.3	3.2	0.3	3.5	3.7	1.5	0.5	—	0.0
100.0	27.2	29.7	—	0.0	10.0	9.9	0.1	0.1	2.5	0.1	2.6	0.5	3.2	3.5	0.3	0.2	2.0	0.1	3.1	2.9	1.5	0.5	0.0	0.0
100.0	7.6	8.1	0.0	0.0	0.6	0.4	0.1	0.0	6.4	0.2	19.9	7.3	10.7	7.5	1.7	1.0	7.9	1.1	8.6	6.6	3.7	0.6	0.0	0.0
100.0	1.2	0.7	0.0	0.0	1.8	0.5	0.0	0.1	7.2	1.2	27.8	8.2	9.3	7.2	1.5	1.0	8.1	1.1	11.2	7.0	4.3	0.6	0.0	0.0
100.0	8.4	6.9	0.0	0.0	0.1	—	0.0	0.0	5.6	0.5	28.0	9.3	9.3	3.0	1.5	0.8	8.5	1.0	7.7	5.2	3.6	0.6	0.0	0.0
100.0	7.4	6.7	0.0	0.0	0.0	0.0	0.1	0.0	7.3	0.3	19.1	6.8	9.6	8.0	1.4	0.8	7.3	0.8	12.2	8.2	3.4	0.6	—	0.0
100.0	11.4	7.5	0.0	0.0	0.0	0.0	0.1	0.8	5.8	0.5	18.2	6.9	7.9	6.1	1.3	0.7	6.3	0.8	14.2	8.1	2.9	0.5	0.0	0.0
100.0	14.7	11.4	0.0	0.0	0.1	0.0	1.5	0.0	4.8	0.4	13.8	7.0	7.6	6.4	1.0	0.4	5.4	0.8	13.6	7.7	2.9	0.5	0.0	0.0
100.0	6.6	3.4	0.2	0.0	0.0	0.0	0.2	0.0	5.5	0.3	22.3	15.9	11.0	6.8	1.4	0.8	5.9	0.9	8.7	6.3	3.2	0.6	0.0	0.0
100.0	3.6	1.3	0.0	0.0	0.0	0.0	0.8	0.1	8.1	0.6	19.8	9.5	9.2	6.7	1.3	0.9	5.4	1.0	16.2	9.6	5.1	0.8	0.0	0.0
100.0	4.3	0.9	0.0	0.0	—	0.0	0.6	0.0	8.9	0.6	13.7	4.8	13.7	10.2	1.2	0.5	4.9	0.8	16.7	15.2	2.4	0.6	0.0	0.0
100.0	20.2	11.7	—	0.0	—	0.0	0.1	0.0	5.7	0.3	15.1	11.6	7.2	5.2	0.7	0.3	3.1	0.5	12.6	4.1	1.3	0.3	—	0.0
100.0	19.0	11.4	0.0	0.0	—	0.0	—	0.0	5.5	0.1	18.9	13.5	5.6	3.8	0.4	0.2	2.7	0.5	11.8	4.7	1.5	0.4	—	0.0
100.0	17.1	11.9	0.0	0.0	0.0	0.0	0.2	—	5.0	0.1	11.5	9.5	7.5	5.8	0.6	0.3	3.7	0.5	13.1	9.6	3.2	0.4	0.0	0.0
100.0	7.1	25.3	0.0	—	—	—	0.1	—	4.1	0.2	13.5	11.3	6.9	5.3	0.6	0.3	3.7	0.6	10.1	5.3	5.1	0.5	—	—
100.0	15.2	15.5	0.0	—	0.0	—	0.2	—	4.1	0.2	16.7	10.2	8.8	6.1	1.2	0.6	5.3	0.7	7.0	5.3	2.3	0.6	0.0	—
100.0	7.8	4.3	0.1	0.0	—	—	0.6	—	3.3	0.1	16.6	38.9	4.9	3.8	0.3	0.2	4.8	0.5	8.7	3.3	1.3	0.5	—	—
100.0	14.0	16.9	0.0	0.0	0.0	—	0.2	—	4.0	0.2	22.3	13.2	6.3	4.6	0.8	0.5	5.7	0.7	4.2	4.0	1.9	0.5	—	—
100.0	24.5	35.5	0.0	—	—	—	0.0	—	2.3	—	12.6	6.8	3.3	2.6	0.3	0.3	6.3	0.6	2.2	1.1	1.3	0.3	—	—
100.0	19.6	22.5	—	0.0	—	0.0	0.0	—	4.1	0.3	14.9	7.9	5.6	4.7	0.5	0.3	7.0	0.5	4.6	4.3	2.3	0.7	0.0	0.0
100.0	24.2	26.7	—	0.0	—	0.0	0.0	—	4.8	0.4	11.4	5.2	5.0	4.5	0.5	0.3	7.6	0.4	4.0	2.8	1.7	0.5	0.0	0.0
100.0	23.3	27.7	0.0	0.0	—	—	0.1	0.0	3.8	0.1	10.7	6.1	4.6	4.1	0.8	0.4	9.1	0.6	3.8	3.0	1.4	0.4	0.0	0.0
100.0	27.4	30.4	—	0.0	—	0.0	—	0.0	2.7	0.2	8.9	4.9	6.1	5.1	0.9	0.3	4.4	0.3	3.5	3.1	1.4	0.4	—	—
100.0	32.4	40.6	0.0	0.0	—	0.0	—	0.0	4.3	0.4	3.8	1.2	4.2	3.4	0.2	0.1	1.6	1.2	3.5	2.9	0.1	0.1	0.0	0.0
100.0	29.2	37.7	0.0	0.0	—	0.0	0.1	—	3.2	0.1	5.6	1.8	5.1	5.1	0.6	0.1	2.6	0.4	3.4	2.8	1.9	0.3	0.0	—
100.0	14.9	19.2	0.0	0.0	—	0.0	0.5	—	4.8	0.6	12.9	6.0	9.2	8.0	1.2	0.6	5.8	0.7	6.5	5.8	2.8	0.5	—	—
100.0	31.1	33.4	0.0	—	0.1	—	—	—	2.4	0.3	4.6	1.9	7.0	7.3	0.4	0.2	2.5	0.4	4.0	3.0	1.1	0.3	—	—
100.0	40.7	45.3	—	—	0.1	0.1	—	—	1.5	0.1	1.6	0.7	1.8	1.9	0.2	0.1	1.4	0.2	1.8	1.5	0.7	0.3	—	—

Table 11. Gainfully Employed Population, 15 Years and Older, by Industry and Sex
(For 1950 only, 14-year-olds are included)

(Zone) (Sector)	District	Total	M	F	Total	Agriculture	Forestry and Hunting	Fisheries and Aquiculture	Mining	Construction	Manufacturing	Wholesale and Retail	Finance and Insurance	Transportation Communication	Services	Civil Service	Unclassified
VIII	Yotsukaidō-machi	(7,405) 100.0	59.4	40.6	100.0	44.1	0.0	0.0	0.0	9.4	15.1	10.1	1.6	6.0	6.7	7.0	—
IX	Ichihara-machi	(7,124) 100.0	58.9	41.1	100.0	48.8	—	0.1	0.3	9.7	15.8	10.5	0.8	3.9	7.0	3.1	—
	Anegasaki-machi	(5,770) 100.0	56.0	44.0	100.0	43.8	0.0	20.2	0.0	2.7	7.7	11.0	0.8	3.9	8.2	1.7	—
	Hirakawa-machi	(5,923) 100.0	50.8	49.2	100.0	80.0	0.1	—	—	2.1	3.6	5.3	0.4	1.9	5.1	1.5	0.0
	Miwa-machi	(5,001) 100.0	52.1	47.9	100.0	75.3	—	—	0.1	3.0	5.0	6.8	0.5	2.5	5.1	1.7	0.0
X	Kisarazu-shi	(26,657) 100.0	57.7	42.3	100.0	34.3	0.0	12.5	0.2	3.3	7.2	16.9	1.2	4.3	12.2	7.6	0.0
	Zone 8 Total	(484,548) 100.0	61.2	38.8	100.0	26.8	0.0	1.1	0.3	5.4	26.0	14.1	1.7	6.3	14.6	3.7	0.0
9 I	Kamakura-shi	(40,331) 100.0	69.3	30.7	100.0	4.2	0.1	0.5	0.2	7.1	27.5	21.6	4.1	8.3	23.0	3.4	0.1
II	Ayase-machi	(3,944) 100.0	61.5	38.5	100.0	50.1	0.0	0.0	0.4	4.8	15.8	6.9	0.6	3.7	15.7	2.0	0.0
	Ebina-machi	(8,518) 100.0	60.9	39.1	100.0	36.7	0.0	0.0	2.1	4.1	28.1	9.3	0.9	6.0	10.5	2.3	0.0
	Shiroyama-machi	(2,300) 100.0	65.5	34.5	100.0	38.1	0.1	0.2	3.2	5.9	17.3	8.4	0.7	8.8	13.0	4.3	—
III	Akita-machi	(6,273) 100.0	68.7	31.3	100.0	28.9	0.0	—	2.5	7.2	23.6	10.7	1.3	5.5	17.2	3.1	0.0
	Hamura-machi	(4,638) 100.0	67.2	32.8	100.0	20.8	0.3	0.0	1.2	5.7	25.4	12.0	2.5	7.8	20.2	4.1	—
IV	Hannō-shi	(19,905) 100.0	63.7	36.3	100.0	21.8	2.6	0.0	1.4	4.6	26.3	16.0	1.6	6.2	17.5	2.0	0.0
	Tsurugashima-mura	(3,666) 100.0	56.3	43.7	100.0	58.5	0.0	—	—	4.7	17.1	6.4	0.5	2.7	7.9	2.2	—
	Hidaka-machi	(8,620) 100.0	58.1	41.9	100.0	53.3	0.1	0.0	0.6	5.9	15.9	7.3	0.5	4.0	11.0	1.4	—
	Kawashima-mura	(8,764) 100.0	51.3	48.7	100.0	74.7	0.0	0.0	0.2	2.8	9.8	4.8	0.4	1.3	4.3	1.7	0.0
V	Kitamoto-machi	(7,148) 100.0	60.7	39.3	100.0	40.0	0.0	0.0	0.3	5.4	23.7	11.0	1.2	8.2	8.0	2.2	0.0
	Higawa-machi	(10,032) 100.0	60.8	39.2	100.0	34.1	—	0.0	0.1	4.7	28.8	13.8	1.4	6.9	8.1	2.1	0.0
	Shobu-machi	(7,717) 100.0	56.4	43.6	100.0	59.9	0.0	0.0	0.0	3.0	13.7	9.9	0.7	4.0	6.6	2.2	0.0
	Kuki-machi	(10,641) 100.0	60.7	39.3	100.0	42.3	0.0	0.0	0.0	4.2	18.6	12.3	1.3	10.0	8.9	2.4	0.0
	Satte-machi	(11,357) 100.0	55.6	44.4	100.0	48.8	0.0	0.0	0.0	4.2	17.5	14.5	1.1	3.7	8.5	1.7	0.0
VI	Iwai-machi	(18,091) 100.0	49.4	50.6	100.0	76.2	0.0	0.0	0.0	2.2	4.3	8.3	0.4	1.2	6.1	1.3	—
	Mitsukaidō-shi	(19,317) 100.0	53.4	46.6	100.0	62.7	0.0	0.0	0.1	2.9	6.8	12.8	0.7	4.4	8.0	1.6	0.0
	Yawahara-mura	(5,684) 100.0	51.4	48.6	100.0	77.1	0.0	0.0	0.0	2.8	4.7	6.6	0.5	2.7	4.5	1.3	0.0
	Ina-mura	(6,882) 100.0	49.2	50.8	100.0	75.5	0.0	0.1	0.0	2.4	3.3	6.3	0.2	2.1	8.8	1.3	0.0
VII	Fujishiro-machi	(6,759) 100.0	52.2	47.8	100.0	63.9	0.0	0.0	0.0	3.2	8.0	10.7	0.6	5.4	6.2	2.0	0.0
	Ryūgasaki-shi	(16,777) 100.0	55.4	44.6	100.0	51.9	0.0	0.0	0.0	3.3	13.1	14.2	1.0	4.3	9.8	2.4	0.0
	Tone-mura	(4,978) 100.0	52.2	47.8	100.0	69.2	0.0	0.2	0.1	3.3	7.9	9.0	0.7	2.3	4.8	2.5	0.0
	Motono-mura	(2,934) 100.0	51.7	48.3	100.0	83.0	0.0	0.0	0.0	2.0	3.4	5.0	0.3	2.0	2.8	1.5	0.0
VIII	Sakura-shi	(17,975) 100.0	56.0	44.0	100.0	54.2	0.0	0.1	0.0	3.3	11.5	10.6	1.2	7.1	9.0	3.0	0.0
	Izumi-machi	(5,086) 100.0	51.6	38.4	100.0	81.3	0.0	0.0	0.0	1.8	3.0	4.5	0.5	2.3	4.8	1.8	0.0
IX	Shitsu-mura	(5,046) 100.0	51.0	49.0	100.0	75.7	0.1	0.0	0.0	2.8	6.7	5.3	0.3	2.4	4.5	2.2	0.0
	Nansō-machi	(9,191) 100.0	51.7	48.3	100.0	71.7	0.2	0.0	0.0	2.6	4.0	9.3	0.4	2.3	7.8	1.7	0.0
	Fukuta-machi	(3,869) 100.0	50.6	49.4	100.0	73.0	0.2	0.0	0.1	2.8	5.7	7.0	0.6	2.3	6.6	1.7	—
X	Kimitsu-machi	(6,868) 100.0	52.6	47.4	100.0	63.6	0.0	7.0	0.2	2.7	5.3	8.1	0.6	2.9	7.3	2.3	0.0
	Futtsu-machi	(8,535) 100.0	56.6	43.4	100.0	31.6	0.0	35.9	0.2	2.9	7.2	11.1	0.5	2.1	7.2	1.3	0.0
	Osawa-machi	(6,942) 100.0	54.9	45.1	100.0	44.5	0.3	7.6	0.6	5.2	12.3	12.8	1.2	4.1	9.0	2.4	—
	Zone 9 Total	(298,788) 100.0	57.9	42.1	100.0	47.3	0.2	1.4	0.3	4.1	15.3	12.0	1.3	5.0	10.9	2.2	0.0
10 I	Yokosuka-shi	(124,160) 100.0	71.5	28.5	100.0	3.4	0.0	1.8	0.1	7.0	25.0	18.8	1.7	7.0	21.2	14.0	0.0
	Zushi-shi	(15,742) 100.0	69.6	30.4	100.0	1.7	0.1	0.8	0.2	6.3	29.9	20.1	3.6	8.6	24.5	4.2	—
	Hayama-machi	(6,358) 100.0	66.8	33.2	100.0	11.5	0.2	2.7	0.1	7.6	25.3	17.0	3.2	6.5	21.5	4.4	—
	Chigasaki-shi	(27,844) 100.0	70.4	29.6	100.0	13.8	0.0	0.6	0.2	6.4	34.3	16.2	2.9	7.9	14.1	3.6	0.0
	Fujisawa-shi	(51,310) 100.0	68.4	31.6	100.0	13.0	0.0	0.3	0.2	6.4	29.1	18.9	3.2	7.7	17.9	3.3	0.0
II	Aikawa-machi	(7,073) 100.0	55.9	44.1	100.0	37.7	0.2	0.0	2.8	4.0	34.7	7.4	0.6	2.4	9.0	1.2	—
	Atsugi-shi	(21,422) 100.0	63.5	36.5	100.0	39.5	0.2	0.0	1.4	4.2	18.7	13.4	1.2	5.0	13.4	3.0	—
	Samukawa-machi	(5,380) 100.0	66.2	33.8	100.0	31.0	0.0	0.0	0.9	4.6	36.3	9.0	0.9	6.8	8.0	2.5	0.0
III	Ōme-shi	(26,437) 100.0	62.6	37.4	100.0	11.7	0.8	0.0	1.2	6.2	39.4	14.7	2.0	5.4	15.3	3.3	0.0
IV	Sakado-machi	(11,697) 100.0	56.8	43.2	100.0	53.6	0.0	0.0	0.1	3.8	17.8	10.6	0.8	2.9	8.3	2.1	0.0

Table 11. Gainfully Employed Population, 15 Years and Older, by Industry and Sex
(For 1950 only, 14-year-olds are included)

Total	Agriculture		Forestry and Hunting		Fisheries and Aquiculture		Mining		Construction		Manufacturing		Wholesale and Retail		Finance and Insurance		Transportation and Communication		Services		Civil Service		Unclassified	
	M	F	M	F	M	F	M	F	M	F	M	F	M	F	M	F	M	F	M	F	M	F	M	F
100.0	20.4	23.7	0.0	0.0	0.0	—	0.0	—	3.9	5.5	9.5	5.6	6.3	3.8	1.0	0.6	5.9	0.1	6.2	0.5	6.2	0.8	—	—
100.0	20.8	28.0	—	—	0.0	0.1	0.2	0.1	9.0	0.7	13.0	2.8	5.9	4.6	0.5	0.3	3.4	0.5	3.8	3.2	2.3	0.8	—	—
100.0	22.2	21.6	0.0	—	11.5	8.7	0.0	—	2.4	0.3	5.0	2.7	6.1	4.9	0.6	0.2	3.4	0.5	4.3	3.9	1.3	0.4	—	0.0
100.0	37.4	42.6	0.1	0.0	—	—	—	—	2.0	0.1	2.7	0.9	2.8	2.5	0.2	0.2	1.5	0.4	3.0	2.1	1.1	0.4	0.0	—
100.0	35.4	39.7	—	—	—	—	0.1	—	2.8	0.2	3.5	1.5	3.7	3.1	0.3	0.2	2.0	0.5	2.9	2.2	1.4	0.3	0.0	—
100.0	15.9	18.4	0.0	0.0	7.1	5.4	0.2	—	3.1	0.2	5.4	1.8	8.8	8.1	0.8	0.4	3.8	0.5	5.6	6.6	7.0	0.6	0.0	—
100.0	13.6	13.2	0.0	0.0	0.7	0.4	0.2	0.1	5.1	0.3	15.2	10.8	8.0	6.1	1.1	0.6	5.6	0.7	8.6	6.0	3.1	0.6	0.0	—
100.0	2.5	1.7	0.0	—	0.5	—	0.2	—	6.6	0.5	20.5	7.0	13.6	8.0	2.8	1.3	7.2	1.1	12.5	10.5	2.8	0.6	0.1	—
100.0	28.4	21.7	0.0	—	0.0	—	0.3	0.1	4.6	0.2	11.0	4.8	3.5	3.4	0.5	0.1	3.2	0.5	8.6	7.1	1.4	0.6	0.0	—
100.0	20.8	15.9	0.0	—	0.0	—	2.0	0.1	3.7	0.4	14.6	13.5	5.4	3.9	0.5	0.4	5.2	0.8	6.8	3.7	1.9	0.4	0.0	—
100.0	20.8	17.3	0.1	—	0.2	—	2.9	0.3	5.6	0.3	11.1	6.2	5.0	3.4	0.6	0.1	7.6	1.2	8.1	4.9	3.5	0.8	—	—
100.0	19.5	9.4	0.0	—	—	—	2.2	0.3	6.7	0.5	14.0	9.6	5.9	4.8	0.8	0.5	4.8	0.7	12.2	5.0	2.6	0.5	0.0	—
100.0	12.7	8.1	0.3	—	0.0	—	1.1	0.1	5.5	0.2	16.7	8.7	6.9	5.1	1.5	1.0	6.7	1.1	12.5	7.7	3.3	0.8	—	—
100.0	11.5	10.3	1.9	0.7	0.0	—	1.2	0.2	4.4	0.2	15.9	10.4	9.8	6.2	1.2	0.4	5.4	0.8	10.7	6.8	1.7	0.3	0.0	—
100.0	29.2	29.3	—	0.0	—	—	—	—	4.6	0.1	10.2	6.9	3.3	3.1	0.3	0.2	2.2	0.5	4.8	3.1	1.7	0.5	—	—
100.0	25.9	27.4	0.1	0.0	0.0	—	0.6	—	5.6	0.3	10.1	5.8	4.2	3.1	0.3	0.2	3.5	0.5	6.7	4.3	1.1	0.3	—	—
100.0	34.2	40.5	0.0	0.0	0.0	0.0	0.2	0.0	2.7	0.1	6.4	3.4	2.7	2.1	0.3	0.1	1.1	0.2	2.5	1.8	1.2	0.5	0.0	0.0
100.0	17.2	22.8	0.0	0.0	—	0.0	0.3	0.0	5.1	0.3	16.7	7.0	6.3	4.7	0.8	0.4	7.6	0.6	4.8	3.2	1.9	0.3	0.0	0.0
100.0	15.1	19.0	—	—	0.0	0.0	0.1	0.0	4.4	0.3	20.2	8.6	8.0	5.8	0.9	0.5	6.4	0.5	4.1	4.0	1.6	0.5	0.0	0.0
100.0	29.9	30.0	0.0	0.0	0.0	0.0	0.0	0.0	2.8	0.2	8.3	5.4	5.7	4.2	0.5	0.2	3.5	0.5	3.8	2.8	1.9	0.3	0.0	0.0
100.0	20.0	22.3	0.0	0.0	—	0.0	0.0	0.0	4.1	0.1	12.7	5.9	7.1	5.2	0.8	0.5	9.4	0.6	4.7	4.2	1.9	0.5	0.0	0.0
100.0	23.3	25.5	—	0.0	0.0	0.0	0.0	0.0	4.1	0.1	10.4	7.1	8.1	6.4	0.6	0.5	3.3	0.4	4.4	4.1	1.4	0.3	0.0	0.0
100.0	35.3	40.9	0.0	0.0	0.0	0.0	0.0	0.0	2.0	0.2	2.5	1.8	4.0	4.3	0.3	0.1	1.0	0.2	3.2	2.9	1.1	0.2	—	—
100.0	28.6	34.1	0.0	0.0	0.0	0.0	0.1	0.0	2.8	0.1	4.8	2.0	7.4	5.4	0.5	0.2	3.8	0.6	4.1	3.9	1.3	0.3	0.0	0.0
100.0	35.5	41.6	0.0	0.0	0.0	0.0	—	0.0	2.7	0.1	3.2	1.5	4.0	2.4	0.4	0.1	2.2	0.5	2.3	2.2	1.1	0.2	—	0.0
100.0	34.7	40.8	—	0.0	0.0	0.1	0.0	0.0	2.3	0.1	2.3	1.0	3.5	2.8	0.1	0.1	1.9	0.2	3.4	5.4	1.0	0.3	0.0	0.0
100.0	27.4	36.5	—	0.0	—	0.0	—	0.0	3.0	0.2	5.4	2.6	5.8	4.9	0.3	0.3	5.1	0.3	3.6	2.6	1.6	0.4	—	0.0
100.0	23.7	28.2	0.0	0.0	0.0	0.0	0.0	0.0	3.1	0.2	9.3	3.8	7.9	6.3	0.7	0.3	3.8	0.5	4.8	5.0	2.1	0.3	0.0	0.0
100.0	31.5	37.7	0.0	0.0	0.1	0.1	0.0	0.1	3.0	0.3	6.2	1.7	4.3	4.7	0.4	0.3	2.0	0.3	2.7	2.1	2.0	0.5	—	—
100.0	40.4	42.6	—	0.0	—	0.0	—	0.0	1.9	0.1	2.5	0.9	2.3	2.7	0.2	0.1	1.8	0.2	1.4	1.4	1.2	0.3	—	0.0
100.0	25.6	28.6	0.0	0.0	0.0	0.1	0.0	0.0	2.9	0.4	7.9	3.6	5.4	5.2	0.8	0.4	6.3	0.8	4.7	4.3	2.4	0.6	0.0	0.0
100.0	39.2	42.1	—	0.0	—	0.0	—	0.0	1.7	0.1	2.4	0.6	2.6	1.9	0.3	0.2	2.0	0.3	2.6	2.2	0.8	1.0	—	0.0
100.0	34.3	41.4	0.0	0.1	0.0	0.0	—	0.0	2.8	0.0	4.9	1.8	2.7	2.6	0.2	0.1	1.9	0.5	2.6	1.9	1.6	0.6	—	0.0
100.0	33.9	37.8	0.1	0.1	0.0	0.0	—	0.0	2.4	0.2	2.8	1.2	4.9	4.4	0.3	0.1	1.9	0.4	4.0	3.8	1.4	0.3	0.0	0.0
100.0	32.6	40.4	0.2	0.0	—	0.0	0.1	0.0	2.7	0.1	4.2	1.5	3.3	3.7	0.4	0.2	2.1	0.2	3.6	3.0	1.4	0.3	—	—
100.0	28.5	35.1	0.0	0.0	4.2	2.8	0.2	0.0	2.5	0.2	3.8	1.5	4.5	3.6	0.3	0.3	2.7	0.2	4.1	3.2	1.8	0.5	0.0	0.0
100.0	13.7	17.9	0.0	0.0	22.2	13.7	0.2	0.0	2.7	0.2	5.2	2.0	5.8	5.3	0.4	0.1	1.7	0.4	3.7	3.5	1.0	0.3	0.0	0.0
100.0	18.3	26.2	0.3	0.0	5.3	2.3	0.6	0.0	4.8	0.4	8.6	3.7	6.4	6.4	0.9	0.3	3.6	0.5	4.2	4.8	1.9	0.5	—	—
100.0	22.2	25.1	0.2	0.0	0.9	0.5	0.3	0.0	3.9	0.2	10.3	5.0	6.9	5.1	0.9	0.4	4.4	0.6	6.1	4.8	1.8	0.4	0.0	0.0
100.0	1.7	1.7	0.0	0.0	1.7	0.1	0.1	0.0	6.3	0.7	18.6	6.4	9.7	9.1	1.1	0.6	5.9	1.1	13.2	8.0	13.2	0.8	0.0	0.0
100.0	1.2	0.5	0.1	0.0	0.8	0.0	0.1	0.1	5.7	0.6	22.2	7.7	12.1	8.0	2.4	1.2	7.1	1.5	14.6	9.9	3.3	0.9	—	—
100.0	4.4	7.1	0.2	0.0	2.5	0.2	0.0	0.1	7.2	0.4	19.1	6.2	10.4	6.6	2.2	1.0	5.4	1.1	11.8	9.7	3.6	0.8	—	—
100.0	7.9	5.9	0.0	0.0	0.5	0.1	0.2	0.0	6.0	0.4	25.5	8.8	10.2	6.0	2.0	0.9	7.1	0.8	7.9	6.2	3.1	0.5	0.0	0.0
100.0	7.9	5.1	0.0	0.0	0.3	0.0	0.1	0.1	6.1	0.3	20.8	8.3	11.9	7.0	2.2	1.0	6.7	1.0	9.7	8.2	2.7	0.6	0.0	0.0
100.0	21.6	16.1	0.0	0.2	0.0	0.0	2.4	0.4	3.9	0.1	15.0	19.7	4.1	3.3	0.4	0.2	1.8	0.6	5.7	3.3	1.0	0.2	—	—
100.0	22.2	17.3	0.1	0.1	0.0	0.0	1.3	0.1	4.0	0.2	12.5	6.2	7.8	5.6	0.8	0.4	4.2	0.8	8.1	5.3	2.5	0.5	—	—
100.0	16.5	14.5	—	0.0	—	0.0	0.9	0.0	4.1	0.5	27.4	8.9	5.1	3.9	0.5	0.4	5.5	1.3	4.2	3.8	2.0	0.5	0.0	0.0
100.0	8.3	3.4	0.7	0.1	0.0	0.0	1.1	0.1	6.0	0.2	19.9	19.5	9.2	5.5	1.2	0.8	4.6	0.8	8.9	6.4	2.7	0.6	0.0	0.0
100.0	26.7	26.9	0.0	0.0	0.0	0.0	0.1	0.0	3.7	0.1	10.7	7.1	6.1	4.5	0.5	0.3	2.6	0.3	4.7	3.6	1.7	0.4	0.0	0.0

Table 11. Gainfully Employed Population, 15 Years and Older, by Industry and Sex
(For 1950 only, 14-year-olds are included)

(Zone)(Sector)	District	Total			Total	Agriculture	Forestry and Hunting	Fisheries and Aquiculture	Mining	Construction	Manufacturing	Wholesale and Retail	Finance and Insurance	Transportation and Communication	Services	Civil Service	Unclassified
		Total	M	F													
IV	Yoshimi-mura	(7,881) 100.0	51.4	48.6	100.0	73.1	0.0	0.0	0.0	3.5	10.3	4.6	0.3	1.8	4.9	1.5	0.0
	Moroyama-mura	(5,511) 100.0	52.4	47.6	100.0	53.9	0.1	0.0	0.1	3.2	16.0	7.4	0.7	2.8	14.0	1.8	0.0
V	Kōnosu-shi	(15,015) 100.0	59.0	41.0	100.0	37.8	0.0	0.0	0.1	4.2	23.2	13.9	1.4	7.0	10.0	2.4	0.0
	Kisai-machi	(7,768) 100.0	53.7	46.3	100.0	68.1	0.0	0.1	0.0	2.3	9.3	9.1	0.6	3.2	5.5	1.8	0.0
	Washimiya-machi	(4,154) 100.0	56.8	43.2	100.0	58.0	0.0	0.0	0.0	3.3	14.2	8.9	0.7	7.5	5.2	2.2	0.0
	Kurihashi-machi	(5,907) 100.0	58.2	41.8	100.0	42.3	0.0	0.0	0.0	6.6	16.9	14.1	0.7	8.1	8.5	2.8	0.0
	Goka-mura	(4,639) 100.0	52.1	47.9	100.0	79.9	0.0	0.0	0.2	4.7	4.3	4.4	0.3	1.2	3.4	1.6	0.0
VI	Sakai-machi	(11,606) 100.0	51.1	48.9	100.0	69.1	0.1	0.0	0.0	2.7	4.8	11.2	0.6	2.5	7.1	1.9	0.0
	Sashima-machi	(7,919) 100.0	48.7	51.3	100.0	81.5	0.1	0.0	0.0	1.0	2.6	7.5	0.2	1.0	4.9	1.2	0.0
	Yatabe-machi	(11,637) 100.0	41.6	48.4	100.0	76.8	0.1	0.0	0.0	2.0	2.6	7.2	0.3	1.8	7.3	1.9	0.0
VII	Kukizaki-mura	(3,502) 100.0	52.4	47.6	100.0	82.3	0.0	0.0	0.0	2.4	3.6	5.9	0.4	1.7	2.3	1.4	0.0
	Ushiku-machi	(8,484) 100.0	53.9	46.1	100.0	65.7	0.0	0.0	0.0	2.8	8.1	9.0	0.7	4.2	7.4	2.1	0.0
	Kawachi-mura	(7,209) 100.0	50.3	49.7	100.0	79.3	0.0	0.1	0.0	3.4	2.6	7.5	0.4	1.4	4.0	1.3	0.0
	Sakae-machi	(5,089) 100.0	52.5	47.5	100.0	70.6	0.0	0.3	0.0	4.2	4.9	10.0	0.6	2.5	5.5	1.4	0.0
	Narita-shi	(21,041) 100.0	54.4	45.6	100.0	51.9	0.2	0.0	0.0	3.5	8.1	14.8	1.1	6.6	11.7	2.1	0.0
VIII	Shisui-machi	(3,054) 100.0	55.4	44.6	100.0	55.3	0.0	0.1	0.0	3.2	14.8	8.7	0.7	8.7	6.4	2.1	0.0
	Yachimata-machi	(12,622) 100.0	54.0	46.0	100.0	64.4	0.0	0.0	0.0	2.8	7.9	12.6	0.5	2.9	7.5	1.4	0.0
	Toke-machi	(3,176) 100.0	57.8	42.2	100.0	61.1	0.0	0.0	0.0	3.7	13.8	8.2	0.8	4.3	5.9	2.2	0.0
IX	Nagara-machi	(4,802) 100.0	49.9	50.1	100.0	76.9	0.1	—	0.2	2.5	7.1	4.6	0.3	2.0	5.0	1.3	0.0
	Obitsu-mura	(3,702) 100.0	51.1	48.9	100.0	74.3	0.2	0.0	0.4	3.4	5.7	6.3	0.7	1.6	5.5	1.9	0.0
X	Koito-machi	(3,422) 100.0	51.2	48.8	100.0	78.6	0.3	0.0	0.0	2.2	4.1	5.9	0.7	1.4	5.2	1.6	0.0
	Zone 10 Total	(455,163) 100.0	63.2	36.8	100.0	30.6	0.1	0.6	0.3	5.2	21.3	14.6	1.6	5.7	14.3	5.7	0.0
Total for 50 km. Region		(7,340,896) 100.0	68.0	32.0	100.0	9.5	0.0	0.4	0.2	6.5	33.4	21.1	3.2	6.0	15.4	3.6	0.0
National Total		(43,691,069) 100.0	60.9	39.1	100.0	30.1	1.1	1.5	1.2	6.2	21.9	15.8	1.8	5.6	11.8	3.0	0.0

Table 11. Gainfully Employed Population, 15 Years and Older, by Industry and Sex
(For 1950 only, 14-year-olds are included)

Total	Agriculture		Forestry and Hunting		Fisheries and Aquaculture		Mining		Construction		Manufacturing		Wholesale and Retail		Finance and Insurance		Transportation and Communication		Services		Civil Service		Unclassified	
	M	F	M	F	M	F	M	F	M	F	M	F	M	F	M	F	M	F	M	F	M	F	M	F
100.0	33.7	39.4	0.0	0.0	—	0.0	—	0.0	3.4	0.1	7.1	3.2	2.5	2.1	0.2	0.1	0.4	1.4	2.9	2.0	1.2	0.3	—	0.0
100.0	25.0	28.9	0.1	0.0	—	0.0	0.1	0.0	3.2	0.0	9.0	7.0	3.8	3.6	0.4	0.3	2.5	0.3	6.7	7.3	1.6	0.2	—	0.0
100.0	17.1	20.7	0.0	0.0	0.0	0.0	0.1	0.0	4.1	0.1	14.0	9.2	8.5	5.4	1.0	0.4	6.5	0.5	5.8	4.2	1.9	0.5	—	0.0
100.0	32.6	35.5	—	0.0	0.1	0.0	—	0.0	2.2	0.1	5.7	3.6	5.3	3.8	0.5	0.1	2.9	0.3	3.1	2.4	1.3	0.5	—	0.0
100.0	26.9	31.1	—	0.0	0.0	0.0	—	0.0	3.3	0.0	9.1	5.1	5.2	3.7	0.5	0.2	6.7	0.8	3.1	2.1	2.0	0.2	—	0.0
100.0	18.6	23.7	0.0	0.0	0.0	0.0	0.0	0.0	5.9	0.7	11.8	5.1	7.3	6.8	0.4	0.3	7.7	0.4	4.3	4.2	2.2	0.6	0.0	0.0
100.0	35.9	44.0	—	0.0	0.0	0.0	0.2	0.0	2.1	2.6	2.8	1.5	2.6	1.8	0.2	0.1	1.0	0.2	1.9	1.5	1.2	0.4	—	0.0
100.0	31.1	38.0	0.1	0.0	0.0	0.0	—	0.0	2.5	0.2	3.1	1.7	6.4	4.8	0.4	0.2	2.0	0.5	3.9	3.2	1.6	0.3	—	0.0
100.0	37.5	44.0	0.1	0.0	—	0.0	—	0.0	1.0	0.0	1.8	0.8	4.2	3.3	0.2	0.0	0.7	0.3	2.3	2.6	0.9	0.3	—	0.0
100.0	36.5	40.3	0.1	0.0	—	0.0	—	0.0	1.9	0.1	1.9	0.7	4.0	3.2	0.3	0.0	1.3	0.5	4.0	3.3	1.6	0.3	—	0.0
100.0	39.9	42.4	—	0.0	—	0.0	—	0.0	2.2	0.2	2.8	0.8	3.0	2.9	0.2	0.2	1.7	0.0	1.6	0.7	1.0	0.4	—	0.0
100.0	31.0	34.7	0.0	0.0	0.0	0.0	0.0	0.0	2.7	0.1	6.3	1.8	5.0	4.0	0.5	0.2	3.9	0.3	4.1	3.3	0.4	1.7	0.0	0.0
100.0	36.3	43.0	0.0	0.0	0.1	0.0	—	0.0	3.2	0.2	2.1	0.5	3.8	3.7	0.3	0.1	1.2	0.2	2.2	1.8	1.1	0.2	—	0.0
100.0	34.1	36.5	—	0.0	0.2	0.1	0.0	0.0	3.9	0.3	3.3	1.6	4.7	5.3	0.4	0.2	2.2	0.3	2.7	2.8	1.0	0.4	—	0.0
100.0	24.5	27.4	0.1	0.1	0.0	0.0	0.0	0.0	3.2	0.3	5.3	2.8	7.2	7.6	0.8	0.3	5.4	1.2	6.2	5.5	1.7	0.4	—	0.0
100.0	25.1	30.2	—	0.0	0.1	0.0	—	0.0	2.7	0.5	9.9	4.9	4.5	4.2	0.3	0.4	7.8	0.9	3.3	3.1	1.7	0.4	0.0	0.0
100.0	31.3	33.1	—	0.0	0.0	0.0	0.0	0.0	2.6	0.2	5.4	2.5	7.0	5.6	0.3	0.2	2.4	0.5	3.9	3.6	1.1	0.3	—	0.0
100.0	29.8	31.3	0.0	0.0	0.0	0.0	—	0.0	3.6	0.1	10.4	3.4	4.4	3.8	0.6	0.2	4.0	0.3	3.2	2.7	1.8	0.4	—	0.0
100.0	35.4	41.5	0.1	0.0	—	—	0.2	0.0	2.2	0.3	3.4	3.7	2.7	1.9	0.2	0.1	1.7	0.3	2.9	2.1	1.1	0.2	—	0.0
100.0	32.4	41.9	0.2	0.0	—	0.0	0.3	0.1	3.1	0.3	4.4	1.3	3.7	2.6	0.6	0.1	1.6	0.0	3.3	2.2	1.5	0.4	—	0.0
100.0	37.0	41.6	0.2	0.1	—	—	0.0	0.0	2.0	0.2	3.4	0.7	2.9	3.0	0.5	0.2	1.1	0.3	3.0	2.2	1.1	0.5	—	0.0
100.0	15.1	15.5	0.1	0.0	0.6	0.0	0.2	0.1	4.8	0.4	14.7	6.6	8.2	6.4	1.1	0.5	4.9	0.8	8.4	5.9	5.1	0.6	0.0	0.0
100.0	4.8	4.7	0.0	0.0	0.3	0.1	0.2	0.0	6.1	0.4	24.7	8.7	13.1	8.0	2.1	1.1	5.3	1.3	8.3	7.1	3.0	0.6	0.1	0.0
100.0	13.8	16.3	0.8	0.3	1.2	0.3	1.1	0.1	5.5	0.7	14.7	7.2	9.1	6.7	1.2	0.6	4.9	0.7	6.0	5.8	2.6	0.4	0.0	0.0

TABLE 12. GAINFULLY EMPLOYED POPULATION, 15 YEARS AND OLDER, BY OCCUPATION AND SEX
(FOR 1950 ONLY, 14 YEAR-OLDS ARE INCLUDED)

1950

(Zone) (Sector)	District	Total			Total	Professional and Technical Workers	Managerial Officials	Clerical Workers	Sales Workers	Farmers, Lumbermen and Fishermen	Mining and Quarrying Workers	Transportation and Communication Workers	Craftsmen, Production Process Workers, and General Laborers
		Total	M	F									
1 I	Chiyoda-ku	(49,905) 100.0	70.9	29.1	100.0	7.5	6.2	17.0	23.3	0.1	0.0	1.8	25.7
	Minato-ku	(87,447) 100.0	71.6	28.4	100.0	8.0	6.2	20.9	16.1	0.3	0.0	2.7	30.4
	Chūō-ku	(74,559) 100.0	69.1	30.9	100.0	4.4	6.2	15.0	24.4	0.3	0.0	2.5	27.5
	Bunkyō-ku	(74,328) 100.0	71.7	28.3	100.0	10.9	5.4	21.0	16.7	0.1	0.0	1.9	32.9
	Taitō-ku	(113,463) 100.0	70.9	29.1	100.0	4.7	3.2	10.8	27.2	0.1	0.0	1.5	37.8
	Zone 1 Total	(399,702) 100.0	70.8	29.2	100.0	6.9	5.2	16.4	21.8	0.2	0.0	2.1	31.8
2 I	Shinagawa-ku	(109,670) 100.0	74.1	25.9	100.0	6.9	4.6	20.3	15.0	0.6	0.0	2.1	41.0
II	Meguro-ku	(72,281) 100.0	75.0	25.0	100.0	10.2	8.6	25.1	14.1	1.3	0.0	2.0	29.7
	Shibuya-ku	(68,291) 100.0	71.3	28.7	100.0	9.8	7.0	24.0	16.0	0.4	0.0	2.2	27.6
III	Shinjuku-ku	(96,632) 100.0	70.2	29.8	100.0	9.9	5.9	21.9	16.6	0.3	0.0	1.9	29.6
	Nakano-ku	(74,123) 100.0	74.5	25.5	100.0	11.2	7.1	27.5	15.8	1.4	0.0	2.0	26.0
IV	Toshima-ku	(78,570) 100.0	73.6	26.4	100.0	8.8	5.3	22.0	17.9	0.5	0.0	2.2	33.5
V	Kita-ku	(97,751) 100.0	74.5	25.5	100.0	6.9	3.7	22.3	14.4	0.5	0.0	2.2	42.2
VI	Arakawa-ku	(79,690) 100.0	73.3	26.7	100.0	3.6	2.3	12.3	17.3	0.2	0.0	2.7	54.6
VII	Sumida-ku	(98,093) 100.0	72.8	27.2	100.0	3.7	2.8	10.1	17.5	0.2	0.0	1.9	54.9
VIII	Kōtō-ku	(72,496) 100.0	78.5	21.5	100.0	3.7	2.9	12.8	16.2	1.0	0.0	4.4	50.0
	Zone 2 Total	(847,597) 100.0	73.7	26.3	100.0	7.4	4.9	19.6	16.1	0.6	0.0	2.3	39.5
3 I	Ōta-ku	(143,295) 100.0	76.9	23.1	100.0	7.8	6.6	20.4	13.9	3.4	0.0	2.0	37.6
II	Setagaya-ku	(135,267) 100.0	75.3	24.7	100.0	12.6	8.6	26.9	13.1	4.8	0.0	1.8	24.2
III	Suginami-ku	(111,085) 100.0	75.0	25.0	100.0	12.8	9.3	29.4	15.1	2.7	0.0	1.5	21.3
IV	Itabashi-ku	(77,996) 100.0	75.5	24.5	100.0	6.9	3.3	18.9	13.3	5.1	0.0	2.4	42.9
	Nerima-ku	(45,195) 100.0	69.3	30.7	100.0	9.9	4.4	18.7	11.0	17.0	0.0	1.5	27.1
VI	Adachi-ku	(98,685) 100.0	73.3	26.7	100.0	4.1	1.9	12.9	15.0	8.9	0.0	2.4	48.3
VII	Katsushika-ku	(89,808) 100.0	73.0	27.0	100.0	5.1	2.6	14.5	13.7	5.2	0.0	2.0	49.8
VIII	Edogawa-ku	(76,867) 100.0	73.4	26.6	100.0	5.0	3.2	15.0	13.5	12.4	0.1	2.2	42.3
	Urayasu-machi	(6,366) 100.0	70.3	29.7	100.0	2.3	0.5	2.6	26.6	46.6	0.0	0.6	17.2
	Zone 3 Total	(784,564) 100.0	74.4	25.6	100.0	8.3	5.5	20.2	13.9	6.6	0.0	2.0	35.9
4 I	Kawasaki-shi	(123,113) 100.0	76.0	24.0	100.0	5.4	2.1	14.0	9.9	12.3	0.2	2.2	47.8
II	Komae-machi	(3,650) 100.0	71.8	28.2	100.0	9.7	3.0	15.7	8.7	30.0	0.2	1.6	26.5
III	Mitaka-shi	(18,340) 100.0	75.4	24.6	100.0	9.8	4.8	22.5	12.2	12.5	0.0	1.8	30.1
	Musashino-shi	(24,583) 100.0	76.1	23.9	100.0	13.5	8.0	27.5	13.6	4.1	0.0	1.4	24.0
	Chōfu-shi	(12,227) 100.0	72.2	27.8	100.0	8.2	2.8	16.5	10.1	22.6	0.4	2.5	31.0
	Hoya-machi	(5,161) 100.0	70.0	30.0	100.0	7.9	2.7	15.7	8.6	30.1	—	2.0	27.7
IV	Yamato-machi	(4,146) 100.0	64.2	35.8	100.0	5.5	1.4	8.5	8.6	40.5	—	0.9	28.2
	Toda-machi	(7,414) 100.0	63.6	36.4	100.0	2.3	1.0	7.7	6.6	45.0	0.0	1.4	33.1
V	Warabi-shi	(10,062) 100.0	72.3	27.7	100.0	4.9	2.9	17.3	13.8	7.5	0.0	1.5	46.2
	Kawaguchi-shi Hatogaya-machi	(48,451) 100.0	71.4	28.6	100.0	4.1	2.8	9.9	11.6	19.5	0.0	1.7	45.6
VI	Sōka-shi	(11,924) 100.0	62.6	37.4	100.0	3.1	1.6	6.5	9.7	44.0	0.0	1.3	30.1
	Yashio-mura	(6,256) 100.0	54.6	45.4	100.0	1.9	0.7	2.3	4.3	71.0	0.0	1.0	17.4
	Misato-mura	(8,083) 100.0	54.9	45.1	100.0	1.5	0.4	2.5	4.7	77.6	0.1	1.1	11.1
	Matsudo-shi	(20,379) 100.0	65.2	34.8	100.0	5.1	2.2	12.1	10.9	40.3	0.1	1.8	22.4
VII	Ichikawa-shi	(44,639) 100.0	67.0	33.0	100.0	7.4	5.8	16.3	13.1	20.8	0.0	1.3	28.6
	Zone 4 Total	(348,428) 100.0	71.4	28.6	100.0	6.1	3.2	14.3	10.7	20.9	0.1	1.8	37.2

Table 12. Gainfully Employed Population, 15 Years and Older, by Occupation and Sex
(For 1950 only, 14-year-olds are included)

Service Workers	Unclassified	Total	Professional and Technical Workers		Managerial Officials		Clerical Workers		Sales Workers		Farmers, Lumbermen and Fishermen		Mining and Quarrying Workers		Transportation and Communication Workers		Craftsmen, Production Process Workers, and General Laborers		Service Workers		Unclassified	
			M	F	M	F	M	F	M	F	M	F	M	F	M	F	M	F	M	F	M	F
18.1	0.3	100.0	4.5	3.0	5.8	0.4	11.8	5.2	18.2	5.1	0.1	—	0.0	—	1.8	—	21.5	4.2	7.0	11.1	0.2	0.1
15.1	0.3	100.0	5.7	2.3	6.0	0.2	13.9	7.0	11.1	5.0	0.3	—	0.0	—	2.7	0.0	26.2	4.2	5.5	9.6	0.2	0.1
19.5	0.2	100.0	3.1	1.3	5.7	0.5	9.4	5.6	18.9	5.5	0.2	0.1	0.0	—	2.5	0.0	23.2	4.3	5.9	13.6	0.2	0.0
10.8	0.3	100.0	7.5	3.4	5.2	0.2	14.0	7.0	12.0	4.7	0.1	—	0.0	—	1.9	0.0	26.7	6.2	4.1	6.7	0.2	0.1
14.4	0.3	100.0	3.4	1.3	3.0	0.2	6.8	4.0	20.4	6.8	0.1	—	0.0	—	1.5	0.0	31.5	6.3	4.0	10.4	0.2	0.1
15.3	0.3	100.0	4.7	2.2	4.9	0.3	10.8	5.6	16.3	5.5	0.2	—	0.0	—	2.1	0.0	26.5	5.3	5.1	10.2	0.2	0.1
9.4	0.1	100.0	5.2	1.7	4.4	0.2	13.6	6.7	10.0	5.0	0.5	0.1	0.0	—	2.1	0.0	34.3	6.7	3.9	5.5	0.1	0.0
8.8	0.2	100.0	7.9	2.3	8.5	0.1	17.4	7.7	9.7	4.4	1.0	0.3	0.0	—	2.0	—	24.6	5.1	3.8	5.0	0.1	0.1
12.8	0.2	100.0	7.1	2.7	6.8	0.2	16.4	7.6	10.9	5.1	0.4	0.0	0.0	0.0	2.2	0.0	23.0	4.6	4.3	8.5	0.2	0.0
13.4	0.5	100.0	7.0	2.9	5.6	0.3	14.7	7.2	11.4	5.2	0.3	0.0	0.0	—	1.9	0.0	24.3	5.3	4.7	8.7	0.3	0.2
8.8	0.2	100.0	8.6	2.6	7.0	0.1	19.4	8.1	11.0	4.8	1.0	0.4	0.0	—	2.0	0.0	21.5	4.5	3.9	4.9	0.1	0.1
9.6	0.2	100.0	6.7	2.1	5.2	0.1	14.9	7.1	12.4	5.5	0.4	0.1	0.0	—	2.2	0.0	27.7	5.8	3.9	5.7	0.2	0.0
7.5	0.3	100.0	5.2	1.7	3.6	0.1	14.6	7.7	9.7	4.7	0.4	0.1	0.0	0.0	2.2	0.0	34.6	7.6	4.0	3.5	0.2	0.1
6.9	0.1	100.0	2.5	1.1	2.2	0.1	7.6	4.7	12.1	5.2	0.2	0.0	0.0	0.0	2.7	0.0	42.7	11.9	3.2	3.7	0.1	0.0
8.5	0.4	100.0	2.6	1.1	2.7	0.1	6.1	4.0	12.6	4.9	0.2	0.0	0.0	—	1.9	0.0	43.6	11.3	2.8	5.7	0.3	0.1
8.8	0.2	100.0	2.8	0.9	2.8	0.1	8.4	4.4	11.6	4.6	0.9	0.1	0.0	—	4.3	0.1	43.8	6.2	3.8	5.0	0.1	0.1
9.4	0.2	100.0	5.5	1.9	4.8	0.1	13.1	6.5	11.1	5.0	0.5	0.1	0.0	—	2.3	0.0	32.4	7.1	3.8	5.6	0.2	0.0
8.1	0.2	100.0	6.0	1.8	6.5	0.1	14.2	6.2	9.5	4.4	2.7	0.7	0.0	—	2.0	0.0	32.5	5.1	3.4	4.7	0.1	0.1
7.8	0.2	100.0	10.0	2.6	8.5	0.1	19.1	7.8	9.0	4.1	3.2	1.6	0.0	0.0	1.8	0.0	20.2	4.0	3.4	4.4	0.1	0.1
7.7	0.2	100.0	10.0	2.8	9.2	0.1	21.3	8.1	10.7	4.4	1.9	0.8	0.0	—	1.5	0.0	17.2	4.1	3.0	4.7	0.2	0.0
6.8	0.4	100.0	5.0	1.9	3.2	0.1	13.0	5.9	9.1	4.2	3.0	2.1	0.0	—	2.4	0.0	35.7	7.2	3.8	3.0	0.3	0.1
10.2	0.2	100.0	7.6	2.3	4.3	0.1	13.0	5.7	7.6	3.4	9.7	7.3	0.0	—	1.5	0.0	21.7	5.4	3.8	6.4	0.1	0.1
6.3	0.2	100.0	3.0	1.1	1.9	0.0	8.2	4.7	10.5	4.5	4.6	4.3	0.0	0.0	2.3	0.1	39.4	8.9	3.3	3.0	0.1	0.1
7.0	0.1	100.0	3.8	1.3	2.6	0.0	9.4	5.1	9.3	4.4	2.8	2.4	0.0	0.0	2.0	0.0	39.3	0.5	3.7	3.3	0.1	0.0
6.2	0.1	100.0	3.7	1.3	3.2	0.0	9.7	5.3	9.4	4.1	7.2	5.2	0.1	—	2.2	0.0	34.9	7.4	2.9	3.3	0.1	—
3.6	0.0	100.0	1.5	0.8	0.5	0.0	1.8	0.8	18.9	7.7	31.9	14.7	0.0	—	0.6	—	13.6	3.6	1.5	2.1	0.0	0.0
7.4	0.2	100.0	6.3	2.0	5.4	0.1	14.0	6.2	9.6	4.3	4.0	2.6	0.0	—	2.0	0.0	29.6	6.3	3.4	4.0	0.1	0.1
6.0	0.1	100.0	3.9	1.5	2.1	0.0	9.5	4.5	6.1	3.8	7.1	5.2	0.2	0.0	2.2	0.0	41.9	5.9	2.9	3.1	0.1	0.0
4.4	0.2	100.0	7.7	2.0	2.9	0.1	11.3	4.4	5.4	3.3	18.0	12.0	0.2	—	1.6	—	22.5	4.0	2.0	2.4	0.2	—
6.0	0.3	100.0	7.9	1.9	4.7	0.1	16.7	5.8	8.5	3.7	7.2	5.3	0.2	—	1.8	0.0	25.2	4.9	3.2	2.8	0.2	0.1
7.6	0.3	100.0	10.7	2.8	7.8	0.2	20.8	6.7	9.4	4.2	2.6	1.5	0.0	—	1.4	0.0	19.8	4.2	3.3	4.3	0.3	0.0
5.5	0.4	100.0	6.4	1.8	2.8	0.0	11.7	4.8	7.0	3.1	13.8	8.8	0.4	0.0	2.5	—	24.6	6.4	2.6	2.9	0.4	0.0
4.9	0.4	100.0	6.4	1.5	2.6	0.1	10.8	4.9	5.8	2.8	15.5	14.6	—	—	2.0	0.0	23.3	4.4	3.2	1.7	0.4	0.0
5.6	0.8	100.0	3.3	2.2	1.4	—	5.7	2.8	5.4	3.2	20.6	19.9	—	—	0.9	—	23.5	4.7	2.8	2.8	0.6	0.2
2.3	0.6	100.0	1.6	0.7	0.9	0.1	5.4	2.3	4.3	2.3	22.5	22.5	0.0	—	1.3	0.1	25.7	7.4	1.4	0.9	0.5	0.1
5.4	0.5	100.0	3.6	1.3	2.8	0.1	11.7	5.6	9.4	4.4	4.5	3.0	0.0	—	1.5	—	35.5	10.7	2.9	2.5	0.4	0.0
4.6	0.2	100.0	2.9	1.2	2.7	0.1	6.1	3.8	7.7	3.9	10.1	9.4	0.0	—	1.7	0.0	38.2	7.3	1.9	2.7	0.1	0.1
3.4	0.3	100.0	1.9	1.2	1.5	0.1	4.4	2.1	6.6	3.1	21.8	22.2	0.0	0.0	1.3	0.0	23.2	6.9	1.7	1.7	0.2	0.1
1.2	0.2	100.0	1.3	0.6	0.7	0.0	1.4	0.9	2.8	1.5	33.7	37.3	0.0	—	1.0	0.0	13.0	4.4	0.6	0.6	0.1	0.1
0.9	0.1	100.0	1.0	0.5	0.4	0.0	1.7	0.8	3.4	1.3	37.8	39.8	0.1	—	1.1	0.0	8.8	2.3	0.6	0.3	0.0	0.1
5.0	0.1	100.0	3.6	1.5	2.2	0.0	8.9	3.2	7.0	3.9	20.5	19.8	0.1	—	1.8	0.0	18.7	3.7	2.3	2.7	0.1	0.0
6.6	0.1	100.0	5.1	2.3	5.7	0.1	11.6	4.7	9.3	3.8	10.6	10.2	0.0	0.0	1.3	—	21.1	7.5	2.2	4.4	0.1	0.0
5.5	0.2	100.0	4.5	1.6	3.1	0.1	10.0	4.3	7.1	3.6	11.0	9.9	0.1	0.0	1.8	0.0	31.2	6.0	2.5	3.0	0.1	0.1

Table 12. Gainfully Employed Population, 15 Years and Older, by Occupation and Sex
(For 1950 only, 14-year-olds are included)

(Zone) (Sector)	District	Total			Total	Professional and Technical Workers	Managerial Officials	Clerical Workers	Sales Workers	Farmers, Lumbermen and Fishermen	Mining and Quarrying Workers	Transportation and Communication Workers	Craftsmen, Production Process Workers, and General Laborers
		Total	M	F									
5 I	Tsurumi-ku	(63,752) 100.0	79.8	20.2	100.0	6.7	3.7	16.6	10.6	2.8	0.0	2.9	49.2
III	Koganei-shi	(7,653) 100.0	72.1	27.9	100.0	12.1	3.9	20.3	9.1	19.5	0.0	1.4	27.8
	Tanashi-machi	(4,545) 100.0	72.7	27.3	100.0	7.5	1.9	13.7	14.0	20.8	—	1.7	31.4
	Kurume-machi	(3,471) 100.0	60.5	39.5	100.0	5.9	1.0	7.6	3.5	65.6	—	0.9	12.5
IV	Nīza-machi	(5,077) 100.0	60.0	40.0	100.0	4.1	1.0	4.6	4.3	66.1	—	0.9	16.0
	Kiyose-machi	(4,483) 100.0	52.9	47.1	100.0	22.1	0.7	13.2	4.5	34.7	0.0	0.9	15.8
	Adachi-machi	(4,060) 100.0	63.1	36.9	100.0	5.1	1.7	8.0	11.8	42.6	0.1	0.9	24.8
	Asaka-machi	(4,294) 100.0	68.3	31.7	100.0	4.5	1.5	9.6	8.8	34.7	0.0	2.0	31.6
V	Urawa-shi	(44,195) 100.0	69.7	30.3	100.0	8.8	5.5	22.6	12.2	19.7	0.2	1.1	24.1
	Misono-mura	(4,776) 100.0	52.8	47.2	100.0	2.8	0.7	3.3	2.9	83.5	—	0.3	5.3
	Koshigaya-shi	(18,847) 100.0	58.4	41.6	100.0	2.7	0.9	5.2	7.5	63.4	0.0	0.8	17.1
VI	Yoshikawa-machi	(7,771) 100.0	53.5	46.5	100.0	2.1	0.4	3.0	4.9	75.1	0.0	0.5	12.1
	Nagareyama-machi	(8,318) 100.0	57.6	42.4	100.0	3.1	1.0	6.7	6.0	62.4	0.1	1.1	17.1
VII	Kamagaya-machi	(3,977) 100.0	57.6	42.4	100.0	2.2	0.6	5.0	5.0	72.1	—	0.8	12.4
VIII	Funahashi-shi	(37,230) 100.0	67.1	32.9	100.0	5.6	3.0	13.6	13.4	31.1	0.0	1.3	25.4
	Zone 5 Total	(222,449) 100.0	68.9	31.1	100.0	6.5	3.1	14.3	10.1	29.1	0.0	1.6	29.6
6 I	Nishi-ku	(32,391) 100.0	76.8	23.2	100.0	6.1	3.5	19.0	12.5	0.4	0.0	4.2	44.6
	Naka-ku	(37,081) 100.0	70.2	29.8	100.0	6.0	4.6	14.9	16.1	1.8	0.0	4.3	31.8
	Kanagawa-ku	(38,863) 100.0	76.8	23.2	100.0	6.7	4.1	18.9	12.3	6.2	0.0	3.4	40.6
II	Kōhoku-ku	(36,887) 100.0	66.9	33.1	100.0	5.8	3.2	13.4	6.1	44.7	0.0	1.3	20.3
	Inagi-machi	(3,889) 100.0	64.9	35.1	100.0	4.1	1.1	8.9	5.6	53.7	0.3	1.2	21.4
III	Tama-mura	(3,150) 100.0	63.2	36.8	100.0	5.9	0.9	6.9	3.7	59.1	1.0	0.9	18.1
	Fuchu-shi	(14,829) 100.0	73.7	26.3	100.0	6.9	2.3	16.1	8.3	25.2	0.8	1.7	30.5
	Kunitachi-machi	(4,967) 100.0	74.4	25.6	100.0	9.8	4.5	20.5	8.6	21.0	0.0	1.6	25.1
	Kokubunji-machi	(6,680) 100.0	72.7	27.3	100.0	9.7	4.1	20.1	9.0	24.4	0.0	1.3	25.0
	Kodaira-machi	(7,637) 100.0	68.5	31.5	100.0	12.1	2.9	17.9	5.6	34.6	—	1.5	19.7
	Higashimurayama-machi	(6,459) 100.0	67.7	32.3	100.0	9.4	1.5	12.6	5.8	34.2	0.1	1.8	28.8
IV	Tokorosawa-shi	(21,832) 100.0	63.3	36.7	100.0	3.7	0.9	7.4	8.8	47.6	0.0	1.7	24.8
	Miyoshi-mura	(2,159) 100.0	55.3	44.7	100.0	1.5	0.3	1.9	2.0	87.2	—	0.6	5.3
	Fujimi-mura	(5,079) 100.0	58.0	42.0	100.0	1.9	0.5	3.5	3.3	75.9	—	0.7	12.6
V	Yono-shi	(9,858) 100.0	72.9	27.1	100.0	7.2	4.7	18.5	11.6	13.3	—	1.8	37.6
	Ōmiya-shi	(44,903) 100.0	66.9	33.1	100.0	5.8	2.4	14.9	10.8	26.5	0.0	1.4	32.6
	Iwatsuki-shi	(15,126) 100.0	58.5	41.5	100.0	3.5	1.0	5.9	6.8	61.7	—	0.7	18.0
VI	Matsubushi-mura	(4,341) 100.0	53.8	46.2	100.0	2.6	0.5	3.2	2.9	74.8	—	0.9	13.9
VII	Kashiwa-shi	(19,766) 100.0	60.3	39.7	100.0	4.4	1.4	10.1	7.2	57.1	—	1.1	15.7
	Shōnan-mura	(5,468) 100.0	52.4	47.6	100.0	1.7	0.4	2.2	2.5	83.7	—	0.6	6.4
	Shirai-mura	(3,281) 100.0	52.9	47.1	100.0	2.1	0.2	2.5	3.2	84.2	—	0.4	5.9
VIII	Narashino-shi	(8,040) 100.0	68.8	31.2	100.0	8.0	2.5	17.6	12.7	23.7	—	2.3	28.6
	Zone 6 Total	(332,686) 100.0	68.4	31.6	100.0	5.9	2.8	14.0	9.7	29.2	0.1	2.2	28.7
7 I	Isogo-ku	(22,460) 100.0	73.8	26.2	100.0	7.4	4.3	22.2	11.2	5.8	0.0	3.5	35.6
	Minami-ku	(53,237) 100.0	72.4	27.6	100.0	6.0	2.8	16.1	14.0	5.6	0.0	3.5	40.0
	Hodogaya-ku	(27,504) 100.0	72.6	27.4	100.0	6.2	2.8	16.9	8.3	18.5	0.0	2.2	38.6
II	Machida-shi	(20,064) 100.0	69.0	31.0	100.0	5.7	1.8	11.0	7.6	41.4	—	1.5	25.8
III	Yuki-mura	(3,059) 100.0	59.2	40.8	100.0	2.5	0.4	3.9	2.2	76.7	0.0	0.4	12.6
	Hino-machi	(9,015) 100.0	70.5	29.5	100.0	6.4	1.9	13.7	7.0	32.1	0.0	1.5	32.9
	Tachikawa-shi	(17,647) 100.0	73.4	26.6	100.0	9.5	2.8	18.1	15.3	3.2	0.0	2.8	35.9
	Sunakawa-machi	(4,721) 100.0	67.0	33.0	100.0	2.7	0.4	6.2	4.7	49.1	0.0	1.8	28.1
	Yamato-machi	(4,504) 100.0	69.6	30.4	100.0	4.6	0.8	8.4	7.0	35.6	0.0	2.3	35.6
IV	Oi-mura	(2,041) 100.0	58.5	41.5	100.0	2.0	0.2	4.3	5.6	70.8	—	0.7	14.5

Table 12. Gainfully Employed Population, 15 Years and Older, by Occupation and Sex
(For 1950 only, 14-year-olds are included)

Service Workers	Unclassified	Total	Professional and Technical Workers M	F	Managerial Officials M	F	Clerical Workers M	F	Sales Workers M	F	Farmers, Lumbermen and Fishermen M	F	Mining and Quarrying Workers M	F	Transportation and Communication Workers M	F	Craftsmen, Production Process Workers, and General Laborers M	F	Service Workers M	F	Unclassified M	F
7.4	0.1	100.0	5.0	1.7	3.6	0.1	11.5	5.1	6.8	3.8	1.9	0.9	0.0	—	2.9	0.0	44.7	4.5	3.3	4.1	0.1	0.0
5.7	0.2	100.0	9.5	2.6	3.9	0.0	14.8	5.5	6.0	3.1	11.4	8.1	0.0	—	1.4	—	21.9	5.9	3.0	2.7	0.2	0.0
8.9	0.1	100.0	5.5	2.0	1.9	0.0	9.5	4.2	9.2	4.8	11.4	9.4	—	—	1.7	—	27.2	4.2	6.2	2.7	0.1	0.0
2.7	0.3	100.0	4.2	1.7	1.0	0.0	5.5	2.1	2.2	1.3	34.2	31.4	—	—	0.9	—	10.7	1.8	1.6	1.1	0.2	0.1
2.8	0.2	100.0	3.2	0.9	1.0	—	3.3	1.3	2.5	1.8	34.0	32.1	—	—	0.9	—	13.4	2.6	1.6	1.2	0.1	0.1
7.7	0.4	100.0	6.7	15.4	0.7	—	9.5	3.7	2.7	1.8	18.4	16.3	—	0.0	0.9	—	11.6	4.2	2.2	5.5	0.2	0.2
4.7	0.3	100.0	3.4	1.7	1.7	—	5.7	2.3	7.3	4.5	20.2	22.4	0.1	—	0.9	—	21.2	3.6	2.4	2.3	0.2	0.1
6.6	0.7	100.0	3.5	1.0	1.5	0.0	6.7	2.9	6.0	2.8	16.8	17.9	0.0	—	2.0	—	27.6	4.0	3.6	3.0	0.6	0.1
5.8	0.2	100.0	6.6	2.2	5.5	0.0	16.6	6.0	8.3	3.9	9.7	10.0	0.0	0.2	1.1	0.0	19.3	4.8	2.4	3.4	0.2	0.0
1.1	0.1	100.0	1.8	1.0	0.6	0.1	2.3	1.0	1.7	1.2	41.2	42.3	—	—	0.3	—	4.3	1.0	0.6	0.5	0.1	0.0
2.3	0.1	100.0	1.6	1.1	0.9	0.0	3.6	1.6	5.1	2.4	31.3	32.1	0.0	—	0.8	0.0	14.0	3.1	1.0	1.3	0.1	0.0
1.9	0.0	100.0	1.3	0.8	0.4	0.0	2.1	0.9	3.4	1.5	36.6	38.5	0.0	—	0.5	0.0	8.5	3.6	0.7	1.2	0.0	0.0
2.5	0.0	100.0	2.0	1.1	1.0	0.0	4.8	1.9	3.9	2.1	28.5	33.9	0.1	—	1.1	—	14.7	2.4	1.5	1.0	0.0	0.0
1.9	0.0	100.0	1.4	0.8	0.6	—	3.5	1.5	2.9	2.1	36.2	35.9	—	—	0.8	—	11.0	1.4	1.2	0.7	—	0.0
6.6	0.0	100.0	4.1	1.5	3.0	0.0	9.9	3.7	8.6	4.8	16.7	14.4	0.0	—	1.3	0.0	21.2	4.2	2.3	4.3	0.0	0.0
5.6	0.1	100.0	4.6	1.9	3.1	0.0	10.2	4.1	6.6	3.5	14.8	14.3	0.0	0.0	1.6	0.0	25.4	4.2	2.5	3.1	0.1	0.0
9.3	0.4	100.0	4.5	1.6	3.4	0.1	12.3	6.7	8.3	4.2	0.3	0.1	0.0	—	4.1	0.1	39.3	5.3	4.3	5.0	0.3	0.1
20.3	0.2	100.0	4.0	2.0	4.3	0.3	10.1	4.8	10.7	5.4	1.6	0.2	0.0	—	4.3	—	28.2	3.6	6.8	13.5	0.2	0.0
7.7	0.1	100.0	5.1	1.6	4.1	0.0	12.8	6.1	7.8	4.5	4.3	1.9	0.0	—	3.4	0.0	35.8	4.8	3.4	4.3	0.1	0.0
5.2	0.0	100.0	4.5	1.3	3.2	0.0	9.6	3.8	3.9	2.2	24.3	20.4	0.0	—	1.3	—	17.6	2.7	2.5	2.7	0.0	0.0
3.5	0.2	100.0	3.1	1.0	1.1	—	6.5	2.4	3.9	1.7	27.9	25.8	0.3	0.0	1.2	—	18.5	2.9	2.3	1.2	0.1	0.1
3.3	0.2	100.0	3.4	2.5	0.9	—	4.6	2.3	2.4	1.3	34.2	24.9	1.0	0.0	0.9	—	13.6	4.5	2.1	1.2	0.1	0.1
7.9	0.3	100.0	5.5	1.4	2.3	0.0	11.2	4.9	5.3	3.0	14.8	10.4	0.8	0.0	1.7	—	27.0	3.5	4.9	3.0	0.2	0.1
7.4	1.5	100.0	8.1	1.7	4.4	0.1	15.4	5.1	5.5	3.1	12.7	8.3	0.0	—	1.6	—	21.4	3.7	3.8	3.6	1.5	0.0
6.1	0.3	100.0	8.1	1.6	4.1	0.0	15.0	5.1	5.8	3.2	13.8	10.6	0.0	—	1.2	0.1	21.2	3.8	3.3	2.8	0.2	0.1
5.6	0.1	100.0	8.6	3.5	2.9	0.0	12.6	5.3	3.8	1.8	19.0	15.6	—	—	1.5	—	16.6	3.1	3.4	2.2	0.1	0.0
5.7	0.1	100.0	5.8	3.6	1.5	—	8.8	3.8	4.0	1.8	18.8	15.4	0.1	—	1.8	—	24.0	4.8	2.8	2.9	0.1	0.0
4.9	0.2	100.0	2.3	1.4	0.9	0.0	5.2	2.2	5.8	3.0	24.8	22.8	0.0	—	1.7	—	20.1	4.7	2.4	2.5	0.1	0.1
1.2	—	100.0	1.1	0.4	0.3	—	1.3	0.6	1.1	0.9	45.9	41.3	—	—	0.6	—	4.4	0.9	0.6	0.6	—	—
1.2	0.4	100.0	1.2	0.7	0.5	—	2.4	1.1	2.3	1.0	38.7	37.2	—	—	0.7	—	11.1	1.5	0.7	0.5	0.4	0.0
5.0	0.3	100.0	5.1	2.1	4.7	0.0	13.7	4.8	7.9	3.7	6.9	6.4	—	—	1.8	—	29.9	7.7	2.6	2.4	0.3	0.0
5.3	0.3	100.0	4.2	1.6	2.3	0.1	10.5	4.4	6.9	3.9	12.0	14.5	0.0	—	1.4	0.0	27.0	5.6	2.4	2.9	0.2	0.1
2.3	0.1	100.0	2.3	1.2	1.0	—	4.1	1.8	4.5	2.3	30.6	31.1	—	—	0.7	—	14.2	3.8	1.0	1.3	0.1	0.0
1.1	0.1	100.0	1.8	0.8	0.5	—	2.4	0.8	1.6	1.3	33.8	41.0	—	—	0.9	—	12.1	1.8	0.6	0.5	0.1	0.0
2.9	0.1	100.0	3.0	1.4	1.4	0.0	7.8	2.3	4.3	2.9	27.3	29.8	—	—	1.1	—	13.8	1.9	1.6	1.3	0.0	0.1
2.5	0.0	100.0	1.0	0.7	0.4	0.0	1.8	0.4	1.4	1.1	40.8	42.9	—	—	0.6	—	5.7	0.7	0.7	1.8	0.0	0.0
1.5	0.0	100.0	1.2	0.9	0.2	—	2.0	0.5	2.0	1.2	40.7	43.5	—	—	0.4	—	5.4	0.5	1.0	0.5	—	0.0
4.5	0.1	100.0	5.6	2.4	2.4	0.1	13.2	4.4	7.3	5.4	10.6	13.1	—	—	2.3	0.0	24.9	3.7	2.4	2.1	0.1	0.0
7.2	0.2	100.0	4.3	1.6	2.7	0.1	9.8	4.2	6.3	3.4	14.9	14.3	0.1	0.0	2.2	0.0	24.7	4.0	3.2	4.0	0.2	0.0
9.8	0.2	100.0	5.2	2.2	4.2	0.1	15.4	6.8	7.0	4.2	3.7	2.1	0.0	—	3.5	0.0	29.9	5.7	4.7	5.1	0.2	0.0
11.9	0.1	100.0	4.1	1.9	2.6	0.2	10.7	5.4	9.0	5.0	3.0	2.6	0.0	—	3.5	—	34.1	5.9	5.3	6.6	0.1	0.0
6.4	0.1	100.0	4.4	1.8	2.8	0.0	11.7	5.2	5.3	3.0	10.2	8.3	0.0	—	2.2	0.0	32.0	6.6	3.9	2.5	0.1	0.0
5.0	0.2	100.0	4.2	1.5	1.8	0.0	7.8	3.2	4.9	2.7	24.1	17.3	—	—	1.5	0.0	22.0	3.8	2.5	2.5	0.2	0.0
1.3	0.0	100.0	1.7	0.8	0.4	—	2.8	1.1	1.3	0.9	42.7	34.0	0.0	—	0.4	—	9.0	3.6	0.9	0.4	—	0.0
4.3	0.2	100.0	4.7	1.7	1.9	—	9.6	4.1	4.4	2.6	18.3	13.8	0.0	—	1.5	—	27.3	5.6	2.6	1.7	0.2	0.0
11.9	0.5	100.0	6.4	3.1	2.7	0.1	12.8	5.3	10.0	5.3	2.3	0.9	0.0	—	2.8	—	30.8	5.1	5.2	6.7	0.4	0.1
6.9	0.1	100.0	2.0	0.7	0.4	0.0	4.1	2.1	3.0	1.7	25.9	23.2	0.0	—	1.8	—	24.8	3.3	4.9	2.0	0.1	0.0
5.4	0.3	100.0	3.2	1.4	0.8	—	5.6	2.8	4.1	2.9	19.9	15.7	0.0	—	2.3	—	29.0	6.6	4.4	1.0	0.3	—
1.9	0.0	100.0	1.2	0.8	0.2	—	3.3	1.0	3.4	2.2	36.4	34.4	—	—	0.7	—	12.3	2.2	1.0	0.9	0.0	—

Table 12. Gainfully Employed Population, 15 Years and Older, by Occupation and Sex
(For 1950 only, 14-year-olds are included)

(Zone) (Sector)	District	Total			Total	Professional and Technical Workers	Managerial Officials	Clerical Workers	Sales Workers	Farmers, Lumbermen and Fishermen	Mining and Quarrying Workers	Transportation and Communication Workers	Craftsmen, Production Process Workers, and General Laborers
		Total	M	F									
IV	Fukuoka-mura	(2,707) 100.0	68.3	31.7	100.0	4.0	1.0	11.5	10.1	39.7	—	1.3	27.5
V	Kasukabe-shi	(5,805) 100.0	63.9	36.1	100.0	6.0	2.4	9.3	14.7	31.5	0.0	0.9	30.9
	Shōwa-mura	(6,633) 100.0	57.0	43.0	100.0	3.2	0.7	5.6	5.7	67.0	0.0	0.6	15.3
VI	Noda-shi	(22,276) 100.0	59.0	41.0	100.0	3.7	1.2	7.3	8.5	51.0	—	1.3	23.6
VII	Abiko-machi	(8,877) 100.0	59.2	40.8	100.0	4.6	1.9	9.7	10.9	48.3	0.0	1.1	19.8
	Yachiyo-machi	(7,766) 100.0	53.0	47.0	100.0	2.2	0.5	3.7	3.9	79.2	—	0.7	8.5
VIII	Chiba-shi	(65,162) 100.0	64.5	35.5	100.0	7.8	2.7	16.0	10.5	34.6	0.0	1.6	21.5
IX	Goi-machi	(9,408) 100.0	55.9	44.1	100.0	2.6	0.8	5.3	5.6	75.0	0.0	0.7	7.8
	Sodegaura-machi	(7,120) 100.0	52.5	47.5	100.0	2.6	0.7	3.8	2.9	82.5	—	0.3	6.0
	Zone 7 Total	(300,006) 100.0	66.7	33.3	100.0	6.0	2.3	13.6	10.0	31.3	0.0	2.0	28.1
8 I	Kanazawa-ku	(18,284) 100.0	78.7	21.3	100.0	8.1	3.0	18.6	9.6	8.6	0.0	3.0	40.0
	Totsuka-ku	(26,653) 100.0	69.0	31.0	100.0	6.2	2.2	13.4	5.2	38.6	0.0	1.9	27.1
II	Yamato-shi	(6,624) 100.0	68.9	31.1	100.0	5.4	1.9	12.3	8.5	34.3	—	1.9	28.6
	Sagamihara-shi	(27,698) 100.0	68.9	31.1	100.0	5.5	1.1	9.8	5.5	43.1	0.1	1.8	27.5
	Zama-machi	(4,993) 100.0	63.3	36.7	100.0	5.0	1.4	7.3	5.3	52.0	0.3	1.9	20.1
III	Hachiōji-shi	(48,243) 100.0	67.6	32.4	100.0	4.8	2.7	10.0	11.8	20.6	0.1	1.7	42.2
	Akishima-shi	(10,573) 100.0	78.5	21.5	100.0	5.5	1.8	15.3	8.3	13.0	0.2	2.6	43.9
	Fussa-machi	(6,105) 100.0	71.0	29.0	100.0	5.8	1.5	11.0	8.6	14.9	0.9	2.7	35.5
	Mizuho-machi	(3,529) 100.0	72.2	27.8	100.0	3.4	1.0	4.7	6.4	46.7	0.0	1.7	32.0
	Murayama-machi	(4,075) 100.0	71.1	28.9	100.0	2.9	0.7	3.8	5.3	48.1	—	2.2	33.0
	Musashi-machi	(11,211) 100.0	63.8	36.2	100.0	3.9	0.9	5.9	6.1	47.1	0.0	1.3	25.3
IV	Sayama-shi	(13,511) 100.0	62.8	37.2	100.0	3.3	0.9	6.2	6.8	52.8	0.0	1.3	24.2
	Kawagoe-shi	(41,856) 100.0	62.4	37.6	100.0	4.3	1.5	8.2	9.5	47.0	0.1	1.2	23.9
	Seibu-machi	(1,450) 100.0	66.5	33.5	100.0	2.1	0.7	3.7	5.0	60.6	0.0	1.3	22.6
V	Ageo-shi	(13,987) 100.0	60.2	39.8	100.0	3.1	1.0	7.6	5.1	58.4	0.0	0.9	21.5
	Ina-mura	(3,703) 100.0	53.8	46.2	100.0	3.2	0.6	5.5	1.9	76.1	—	0.7	10.5
	Hasuda-machi	(7,944) 100.0	58.0	42.0	100.0	5.5	0.8	7.0	5.4	62.8	—	0.7	15.7
	Shiraoka-machi	(7,161) 100.0	57.7	32.3	100.0	2.5	0.6	5.8	4.7	69.2	—	0.7	14.3
	Miyashiro-machi	(4,677) 100.0	58.3	41.7	100.0	3.2	1.0	6.7	4.8	65.4	—	1.4	14.9
	Sugito-machi	(8,164) 100.0	55.8	44.2	100.0	2.8	1.0	5.3	7.0	68.1	0.0	0.8	12.8
VI	Sekiyado-machi	(7,312) 100.0	51.0	49.0	100.0	2.0	0.2	2.1	5.5	82.8	—	0.5	5.8
	Moriya-machi	(4,838) 100.0	53.5	46.5	100.0	2.7	0.8	4.2	4.7	76.3	—	0.5	9.5
VII	Toride-machi	(8,447) 100.0	58.1	41.9	100.0	4.6	1.7	9.0	9.9	50.2	0.0	1.0	19.9
	Inzai-machi	(9,414) 100.0	53.7	46.3	100.0	2.9	0.9	4.2	7.1	74.1	0.0	0.4	8.8
	Inba-mura	(4,689) 100.0	51.7	48.3	100.0	1.8	0.3	2.1	3.7	86.9	—	0.4	4.4
VIII	Yotsukaidō-machi	(8,096) 100.0	57.5	42.5	100.0	4.8	1.1	9.9	5.4	63.0	—	0.8	12.4
IX	Ichihara-machi	(6,652) 100.0	54.7	45.3	100.0	2.9	1.0	6.6	5.2	72.7	—	0.5	9.0
	Anegasaki-machi	(3,819) 100.0	58.2	41.8	100.0	4.1	1.1	6.5	7.1	69.4	0.0	0.8	8.2
	Hirakawa-machi	(6,865) 100.0	51.8	48.2	100.0	2.7	0.4	3.6	2.1	84.1	—	0.3	5.9
	Miwa-machi	(6,019) 100.0	51.8	48.2	100.0	2.3	0.6	3.0	2.7	84.1	0.0	0.4	5.5
X	Kisarazu-shi	(22,355) 100.0	58.6	41.4	100.0	3.9	1.4	6.5	9.3	59.1	0.0	1.0	14.0
	Zone 8 Total	(358,947) 100.0	63.6	36.4	100.0	4.5	1.5	8.7	7.5	46.7	0.1	1.4	24.6
9 I	Kamakura-shi	(28,211) 100.0	73.6	26.4	100.0	11.6	7.9	21.0	12.2	11.4	0.0	1.4	24.2
II	Ayase-machi	(3,780) 100.0	61.6	38.4	100.0	2.6	0.5	4.0	2.2	70.4	—	1.5	16.3
	Ebina-machi	(6,538) 100.0	65.2	34.8	100.0	4.9	1.1	7.5	3.7	59.7	0.7	1.4	17.9
	Shiroyama-machi	(2,248) 100.0	66.2	33.8	100.0	4.9	1.0	8.6	2.7	61.7	0.0	0.8	17.3
III	Akita-machi	(3,161) 100.0	72.3	27.7	100.0	3.6	0.9	7.1	4.2	53.2	0.8	2.1	22.6
	Hamura-machi	(5,260) 100.0	71.8	28.2	100.0	4.5	1.3	9.2	5.3	41.5	2.5	1.7	27.7
IV	Hannō-shi	(18,914) 100.0	67.1	32.9	100.0	4.2	2.0	7.2	7.9	43.2	0.9	1.6	28.2

- 308 -

Service Workers	Unclassified	Total	Professional and Technical Workers		Managerial Officials		Clerical Workers		Sales Workers		Farmers, Lumbermen and Fishermen		Mining and Quarrying Workers		Transportation and Communication Workers		Craftsmen, Production Process Workers, and General Laborers		Service Workers		Unclassified	
			M	F	M	F	M	F	M	F	M	F	M	F	M	F	M	F	M	F	M	F
4.8	0.1	100.0	2.7	1.3	1.0	—	8.3	3.2	6.8	3.3	21.5	18.2	—	—	1.3	—	23.2	4.3	3.5	1.3	0.0	0.1
4.2	0.1	100.0	3.6	2.4	2.4	0.0	6.2	3.1	9.1	5.6	15.1	16.4	0.0	—	0.9	—	25.0	5.9	1.5	2.7	0.1	0.0
1.9	0.0	100.0	2.4	0.8	0.7	0.0	4.1	1.5	3.7	2.0	31.4	35.6	0.0	—	0.6	—	13.0	2.3	1.1	0.8	0.0	0.0
3.0	0.4	100.0	2.4	1.3	1.1	0.1	5.1	2.2	5.6	2.9	22.2	28.8	—	—	1.3	—	20.0	3.6	1.3	1.7	0.0	0.4
3.6	0.1	100.0	3.3	1.3	1.8	0.1	7.5	2.2	5.3	5.6	23.3	25.0	0.0	—	1.1	—	15.2	4.6	1.6	2.0	0.1	0.0
1.2	0.1	100.0	1.4	0.8	0.5	—	2.6	1.1	2.3	1.6	37.1	42.1	—	—	0.7	—	7.6	0.9	0.7	0.5	0.1	0.0
5.3	0.0	100.0	5.1	2.7	2.7	0.0	11.4	4.6	6.5	4.0	16.5	18.1	0.0	—	1.6	—	18.3	3.2	2.4	2.9	0.0	0.0
2.2	0.0	100.0	1.7	0.9	0.8	0.0	3.8	1.5	3.5	2.1	38.3	36.7	0.0	—	0.7	—	6.1	1.7	1.0	1.2	0.0	—
1.2	0.0	100.0	1.6	1.0	0.7	—	2.9	0.9	1.6	1.3	39.9	42.6	—	—	0.3	—	5.0	1.0	0.5	0.7	0.0	—
6.6	0.1	100.0	4.1	1.9	2.2	0.1	9.5	4.1	6.3	3.7	15.7	15.6	0.0	0.0	2.0	0.0	23.7	4.4	3.2	3.4	—	0.1
9.0	0.1	100.0	5.8	2.3	3.0	0.0	13.4	5.2	6.0	3.6	6.0	2.6	0.0	—	3.0	—	35.3	4.7	6.1	2.9	0.1	—
5.3	0.1	100.0	4.3	1.9	2.1	0.1	9.6	3.8	3.3	1.9	20.8	17.8	0.0	—	1.9	—	23.5	3.6	3.4	1.9	0.1	—
6.2	0.9	100.0	4.1	1.3	1.9	0.0	8.8	3.5	5.1	3.4	17.9	16.4	—	—	1.9	—	25.0	3.6	3.4	2.8	0.8	0.1
5.0	0.6	100.0	3.7	1.8	1.1	0.0	7.1	2.7	3.4	2.1	24.1	19.0	0.1	0.0	1.8	—	24.1	3.4	3.0	2.0	0.5	0.1
6.5	0.2	100.0	3.9	1.1	1.4	—	5.4	1.9	3.1	2.2	27.3	24.7	0.3	—	1.9	—	16.9	3.2	3.0	3.5	0.1	0.1
5.9	0.2	100.0	3.5	1.3	2.6	0.1	6.9	3.1	7.8	4.0	14.9	5.7	0.1	0.0	1.7	—	27.6	14.6	2.4	3.5	0.1	0.1
8.8	0.6	100.0	4.1	1.4	1.7	0.1	11.0	4.3	6.0	2.3	9.1	3.9	0.2	—	2.6	0.0	37.8	5.9	5.4	3.4	0.4	0.2
18.9	0.2	100.0	4.3	1.5	1.4	0.1	7.3	3.7	5.3	3.3	10.8	4.1	0.9	—	2.7	—	31.8	3.5	6.2	12.7	0.1	0.1
4.1	—	100.0	2.2	1.2	1.0	—	3.1	1.6	4.1	2.3	33.5	13.2	0.0	—	1.7	—	23.9	8.1	2.7	1.4	—	—
3.7	0.3	100.0	1.7	1.2	0.7	—	2.6	1.2	4.0	1.3	33.4	14.7	—	—	2.2	—	24.1	8.9	2.2	1.5	0.2	0.1
9.5	0.0	100.0	2.5	1.4	0.8	0.1	3.8	2.1	4.2	1.9	29.4	17.7	0.0	0.0	1.3	—	18.8	6.5	3.0	6.5	0.0	—
4.5	0.0	100.0	2.2	1.1	0.9	0.0	4.2	2.0	4.4	2.4	28.9	23.9	0.0	0.0	1.3	—	18.4	5.8	2.5	2.0	0.0	0.0
4.3	0.0	100.0	2.8	1.5	1.5	0.0	5.8	2.4	6.3	3.2	24.1	22.9	0.1	0.0	1.2	0.0	18.5	5.4	2.1	2.2	0.0	0.0
3.7	0.3	100.0	1.7	0.4	0.7	—	2.3	1.4	3.6	1.4	38.6	22.0	0.0	—	1.3	—	16.1	6.5	2.0	1.7	0.2	0.1
2.1	0.3	100.0	2.1	1.0	1.0	0.0	5.4	2.2	3.5	1.6	27.2	31.2	0.0	0.0	0.9	0.0	18.7	2.8	1.1	1.0	0.3	0.0
1.5	0.0	100.0	2.6	0.6	0.6	—	4.3	1.2	1.1	0.8	34.2	41.9	—	—	0.7	—	9.3	1.2	1.0	0.5	0.0	—
2.1	0.0	100.0	2.5	3.0	0.8	0.0	5.1	1.9	3.5	1.9	29.7	33.1	—	—	0.7	—	13.6	2.1	2.1	—	0.0	0.0
2.2	0.0	100.0	1.7	0.8	0.6	—	4.6	1.2	2.9	1.8	33.6	35.6	—	—	0.7	—	12.3	2.0	1.3	0.9	0.0	0.0
2.5	0.1	100.0	2.2	1.0	1.0	0.0	5.1	1.6	3.1	1.7	30.8	34.6	—	—	1.4	0.0	13.2	1.7	1.5	1.0	0.0	0.1
2.0	0.2	100.0	1.9	0.9	1.0	0.0	3.4	1.9	4.0	3.0	33.5	34.6	0.0	—	0.8	0.0	10.2	2.6	0.9	1.1	0.1	0.1
1.0	0.1	100.0	1.3	0.7	0.2	—	1.4	0.7	3.3	2.2	39.2	43.6	—	—	0.5	—	4.6	1.2	0.5	0.5	—	0.1
1.3	0.0	100.0	2.0	0.7	0.8	0.0	3.1	1.1	3.0	1.7	35.1	41.2	—	—	0.5	—	8.2	1.3	0.8	0.5	—	—
3.6	0.1	100.0	3.2	1.4	1.6	0.1	6.4	2.6	6.3	3.6	21.6	28.6	0.0	—	1.0	—	16.5	3.4	1.5	2.1	0.0	0.0
1.6	0.0	100.0	2.0	0.9	0.9	0.0	3.0	1.2	3.4	3.7	35.9	38.2	0.0	—	0.4	—	7.5	1.3	0.6	1.0	0.0	0.0
0.4	—	100.0	1.1	0.7	0.3	—	1.7	0.4	1.5	2.2	42.8	44.1	—	—	0.4	—	3.6	0.8	0.3	0.1	—	—
2.5	0.1	100.0	3.1	1.7	1.1	0.0	7.0	2.9	3.1	2.3	30.4	32.6	—	—	0.8	—	10.6	1.8	1.4	1.1	0.0	0.1
2.1	0.0	100.0	2.0	0.9	1.0	0.0	4.7	1.9	3.3	1.9	34.0	38.7	—	—	0.5	—	8.0	1.0	1.2	0.9	0.0	—
2.7	0.1	100.0	3.0	1.1	1.1	—	4.5	2.0	4.6	2.5	36.8	32.6	0.0	—	0.8	—	6.6	1.6	0.8	1.9	0.0	0.1
0.9	—	100.0	1.8	0.9	0.4	0.0	2.8	0.8	1.2	0.9	40.0	44.1	—	—	0.3	—	4.9	1.0	0.4	0.5	—	—
1.2	0.2	100.0	1.4	0.9	0.6	—	2.2	0.8	1.5	1.2	40.8	43.3	0.0	—	0.4	0.0	4.5	1.0	0.3	0.9	0.1	0.1
4.7	0.1	100.0	2.4	1.5	1.4	0.0	4.5	2.0	5.6	3.7	29.8	29.3	0.0	—	1.0	0.0	12.1	1.9	1.7	3.0	0.1	0.0
4.9	0.1	100.0	3.0	1.5	1.5	0.0	6.2	2.5	4.7	2.8	24.7	22.0	0.1	0.0	1.4	0.0	19.5	5.1	2.4	2.5	0.1	0.0
10.0	0.3	100.0	8.7	2.9	7.8	0.1	15.8	5.2	8.0	4.2	6.9	4.5	0.0	—	1.3	0.1	21.2	3.0	3.6	6.4	0.3	0.0
2.4	0.1	100.0	1.7	0.9	0.5	—	2.7	1.3	1.5	0.7	38.2	32.2	—	—	1.5	—	14.0	2.3	1.4	1.0	0.1	0.0
2.9	0.2	100.0	3.5	1.4	1.1	—	5.2	2.3	2.3	1.4	35.5	24.2	0.7	—	1.4	—	13.8	4.1	1.6	1.3	0.1	0.1
3.0	—	100.0	3.3	1.6	0.9	0.1	6.0	2.6	1.6	1.1	37.7	24.0	0.0	0.0	0.7	0.1	14.0	3.3	2.0	1.0	—	—
4.8	0.7	100.0	2.7	0.9	0.9	—	4.8	2.3	3.2	1.0	36.4	16.8	0.8	0.0	2.1	—	17.9	4.7	2.9	1.9	0.6	0.1
6.3	0.0	100.0	3.2	1.3	1.3	0.0	5.8	3.4	3.5	1.8	28.0	13.5	2.5	0.0	1.7	—	22.0	5.7	3.8	2.5	0.0	—
4.8	0.0	100.0	2.7	1.5	2.0	0.0	5.2	2.0	5.5	2.4	27.2	16.0	0.9	0.0	1.6	—	19.7	8.5	2.3	2.5	0.0	0.0

Table 12. Gainfully Employed Population, 15 Years and Older, by Occupation and Sex
(For 1950 only, 14-year-olds are included)

(Zone)	(Sector)	District	Total — Total	Total — M	Total — F	Total	Professional and Technical Workers	Managerial Officials	Clerical Workers	Sales Workers	Farmers, Lumbermen and Fishermen	Mining and Quarrying Workers	Transportation and Communication Workers	Craftsmen, Production Process Workers, and General Laborers
IV		Tsurugashima-mura	(3,288) 100.0	56.0	44.0	100.0	2.9	0.3	3.6	3.1	79.5	—	0.7	7.9
		Hidaka-machi	(7,681) 100.0	58.4	41.6	100.0	2.6	0.6	3.4	3.2	74.2	0.1	0.6	13.5
		Kawashima-mura	(9,539) 100.0	50.1	49.9	100.0	2.0	0.4	2.6	2.5	85.1	0.0	0.3	6.0
V		Kitamoto-machi	(5,939) 100.0	58.6	41.4	100.0	2.9	0.6	6.2	5.0	64.7	—	0.7	17.9
		Higawa-machi	(8,096) 100.0	60.7	39.3	100.0	3.8	0.9	8.9	6.8	56.1	0.0	0.6	20.2
		Shobu-machi	(7,492) 100.0	57.0	43.0	100.0	3.0	0.6	3.5	5.5	71.6	—	0.5	13.2
		Kuki-machi	(9,095) 100.0	60.2	39.8	100.0	4.5	1.1	8.7	7.0	56.4	0.0	0.9	18.3
		Satte-machi	(10,235) 100.0	56.6	43.4	100.0	3.4	0.8	5.2	8.6	60.0	—	0.7	18.4
VI		Iwai-machi	(18,539) 100.0	51.2	48.8	100.0	2.1	0.4	1.9	4.3	84.6	—	0.3	5.5
		Mitsukaidō-shi	(23,883) 100.0	53.2	46.8	100.0	2.7	0.7	3.7	7.3	72.5	0.0	0.6	10.8
		Yawahara-mura	(4,282) 100.0	52.0	48.0	100.0	2.2	0.6	3.2	3.3	82.8	—	0.6	6.6
		Ina-mura	(6,080) 100.0	50.8	49.2	100.0	2.2	0.4	2.7	3.2	84.4	—	0.1	6.1
VII		Fujishiro-machi	(7,397) 100.0	53.4	46.6	100.0	2.3	0.8	4.8	5.4	73.0	0.0	0.5	11.9
		Ryūgasaki-shi	(15,348) 100.0	57.0	43.0	100.0	3.6	1.0	6.4	7.5	64.5	—	0.8	14.0
		Tone-mura	(4,964) 100.0	51.8	48.2	100.0	2.2	0.6	4.3	4.1	78.2	—	0.5	8.4
		Motono-mura	(2,949) 100.0	52.0	48.0	100.0	1.9	0.2	2.7	3.0	87.4	—	0.0	4.0
VIII		Sakura-shi	(15,698) 100.0	56.1	43.9	100.0	4.7	1.2	8.9	6.2	64.9	—	1.1	10.9
		Izumi-machi	(5,289) 100.0	50.8	49.2	100.0	2.0	0.5	2.8	1.7	88.2	—	0.7	3.3
IX		Shitsu-mura	(5,291) 100.0	51.6	48.4	100.0	2.2	0.4	3.9	2.2	85.8	—	0.4	4.3
		Nansō-machi	(9,737) 100.0	53.2	46.8	100.0	3.3	0.5	3.2	3.9	81.7	—	0.4	6.1
		Fukuta-machi	(2,617) 100.0	54.3	45.7	100.0	3.5	0.8	3.5	3.2	79.1	—	0.9	7.5
X		Kimitsu-machi	(6,655) 100.0	54.6	45.4	100.0	3.4	1.1	4.0	3.9	75.7	—	0.7	9.8
		Futtsu-machi	(7,177) 100.0	60.0	40.0	100.0	2.7	0.8	3.4	6.7	72.5	0.0	1.0	10.8
		Osawa-machi	(6,414) 100.0	57.7	42.3	100.0	4.4	1.1	4.7	7.9	65.5	0.0	0.6	13.3
		Zone 9 Total	(271,797) 100.0	58.7	41.3	100.0	4.1	1.6	6.7	6.2	63.3	0:1	0.8	14.1
10	I	Yokosuka-shi	(88,820) 100.0	76.4	23.6	100.0	7.5	2.1	14.8	10.2	9.6	0.0	2.7	40.0
		Zushi-shi	(11,476) 100.0	77.2	22.8	100.0	10.1	7.4	21.3	11.0	6.7	0.0	1.9	31.0
		Hayama-machi	(5,567) 100.0	67.7	32.3	100.0	7.2	6.0	13.4	7.9	28.0	0.0	1.2	24.9
		Chigasaki-shi	(18,929) 100.0	69.9	30.1	100.0	6.1	3.5	14.0	8.8	34.6	0.1	1.2	26.2
		Fujisawa-shi	(35,501) 100.0	69.4	30.6	100.0	7.9	5.3	15.7	11.4	27.4	—	1.4	23.6
	II	Aikawa-machi	(6,720) 100.0	60.6	39.4	100.0	2.9	1.6	3.5	3.9	54.2	0.1	0.5	30.7
		Atsugi-shi	(18,368) 100.0	63.8	36.2	100.0	4.5	1.1	7.0	6.8	61.8	0.2	1.1	14.0
		Samukawa-machi	(4,398) 100.0	66.7	33.3	100.0	4.9	1.4	8.5	5.2	50.9	0.7	1.2	24.3
	III	Ome-shi	(20,168) 100.0	71.3	28.7	100.0	4.6	2.7	9.7	8.0	26.7	0.7	2.0	39.5
	IV	Sakado-machi	(11,242) 100.0	55.9	44.1	100.0	.2.8	0.8	3.8	5.6	71.7	0.3	0.4	12.7
		Yoshimi-mura	(8,348) 100.0	51.5	48.5	100.0	2.4	0.4	2.7	2.3	84.2	—	0.2	6.9
		Moroyama-mura	(5,092) 100.0	56.3	43.7	100.0	4.1	0.9	3.3	3.7	70.9	—	0.6	14.9
	V	Kōnosu-shi	(13,151) 100.0	58.7	41.3	100.0	4.8	0.9	7.3	8.6	52.8	—	0.8	21.3
		Kisai-machi	(8,464) 100.0	53.5	46.5	100.0	2.4	0.6	2.7	4.8	77.4	—	0.5	10.3
		Washimiya-machi	(4,451) 100.0	56.6	43.4	100.0	2.4	0.9	4.8	4.7	71.2	—	1.0	13.5
		Kurihashi-machi	(5,258) 100.0	57.9	42.1	100.0	3.1	0.8	7.0	8.9	58.1	0.0	0.8	18.5
		Goka-mura	(4,975) 100.0	50.4	49.6	100.0	1.4	0.2	2.0	1.9	87.2	—	0.3	6.3
	VI	Sakai-machi	(12,180) 100.0	52.2	47.8	100.0	2.4	0.6	3.5	6.5	76.3	—	0.7	8.0
		Sashima-machi	(8,381) 100.0	50.0	50.0	100.0	1.9	0.2	1.8	4.1	85.4	—	0.2	5.2
		Yatabe-machi	(9,897) 100.0	52.3	47.7	100.0	2.6	0.5	2.9	3.9	83.1	—	0.3	5.4
	VII	Kukizaki-mura	(3,595) 100.0	51.1	48.9	100.0	1.2	0.3	1.8	1.8	89.1	—	0.1	5.1
		Ushiku-machi	(7,630) 100.0	54.7	45.3	100.0	2.8	0.8	4.0	4.4	77.2	0.1	0.6	9.0
		Kawachi-mura	(7,521) 100.0	50.2	49.8	100.0	1.8	0.4	2.6	3.2	86.4	—	0.3	4.0
		Sakae-machi	(4,764) 100.0	51.9	48.1	100.0	2.8	0.8	4.2	5.8	76.7	—	0.5	7.5
		Narita-shi	(20,650) 100.0	55.1	44.9	100.0	3.9	1.1	6.7	8.9	63.9	0.0	1.0	10.0

Table 12. Gainfully Employed Population, 15 Years and Older, by Occupation and Sex
(For 1950 only, 14-year-olds are included)

Service Workers	Unclassified	Total	Professional and Technical Workers		Managerial Officials		Clerical Workers		Sales Workers		Farmers, Lumbermen and Fishermen		Mining and Quarrying Workers		Transportation and Communication Workers		Craftsmen, Production Process Workers, and General Laborers		Service Workers		Unclassified	
			M	F	M	F	M	F	M	F	M	F	M	F	M	F	M	F	M	F	M	F
1.9	0.1	100.0	2.1	0.8	0.3	0.0	2.8	0.8	1.9	1.2	40.6	38.9	—	—	0.7	—	6.4	1.5	1.1	0.8	0.1	0.0
1.7	0.1	100.0	2.0	0.6	0.6	—	2.4	1.0	2.1	1.1	39.1	35.1	0.1	0.0	0.6	—	10.4	3.1	1.0	0.7	0.1	0.0
1.0	0.1	100.0	1.2	0.8	0.4	—	2.0	0.6	1.6	0.9	39.1	46.0	0.0	—	0.3	—	5.0	1.0	0.5	0.5	0.0	0.1
2.0	0.0	100.0	2.0	0.9	0.6	—	4.8	1.4	3.8	1.2	30.4	34.3	—	—	0.7	—	15.3	2.6	1.0	1.0	0.0	0.0
2.4	0.3	100.0	2.6	1.2	0.9	0.0	6.6	2.3	4.8	2.0	26.2	29.9	0.0	0.0	0.6	—	17.6	2.6	1.2	1.2	0.2	0.1
2.1	0.0	100.0	2.1	0.9	0.6	0.0	2.5	1.0	3.6	1.9	37.2	34.4	0.0	—	0.5	0.0	9.5	3.7	1.0	1.1	0.0	0.0
3.0	0.1	100.0	2.7	1.8	1.1	0.0	6.4	2.3	4.4	2.6	27.7	28.7	0.0	—	0.9	—	15.4	2.9	1.5	1.5	0.1	0.0
2.8	0.1	100.0	2.2	1.2	0.8	0.0	3.7	1.5	5.5	3.1	29.8	30.2	—	—	0.7	0.0	12.8	5.6	1.0	1.8	0.1	0.0
0.9	0.0	100.0	1.3	0.8	0.4	0.0	1.4	0.5	2.7	1.6	40.4	44.2	—	—	0.3	0.0	4.3	1.2	0.4	0.5	0.0	0.0
1.7	0.0	100.0	1.7	1.0	0.7	0.0	2.8	0.9	4.5	2.8	33.8	38.7	0.0	0.0	0.6	0.0	8.6	2.2	0.5	1.2	0.0	0.0
0.7	0.0	100.0	1.5	0.7	0.5	0.1	2.8	0.4	1.8	1.5	39.1	43.7	—	—	0.6	—	5.4	1.2	0.3	0.4	—	0.0
0.9	0.0	100.0	1.4	0.8	0.4	0.0	2.1	0.6	1.8	1.4	39.7	44.7	—	—	0.1	—	5.0	1.1	0.3	0.6	0.0	0.0
1.3	0.0	100.0	1.7	0.6	0.7	0.1	3.8	1.0	3.2	2.2	32.8	40.2	0.0	—	0.5	—	9.8	2.1	0.9	0.4	0.0	0.0
2.2	0.0	100.0	2.4	1.2	1.0	0.0	4.8	1.6	5.0	2.5	30.2	34.3	—	—	0.8	—	11.8	2.2	1.0	1.2	0.0	0.0
1.5	0.2	100.0	1.5	0.7	0.6	—	3.3	1.0	2.1	2.0	35.1	43.1	—	—	0.5	—	7.5	0.9	1.0	0.5	0.2	0.0
0.8	—	100.0	1.4	0.5	0.2	—	1.9	0.8	1.0	2.0	43.4	44.0	—	—	0.0	—	3.7	0.3	0.4	0.4	—	—
2.1	0.0	100.0	2.8	1.9	1.2	0.0	6.5	2.4	3.3	2.9	30.9	34.0	—	—	1.1	—	9.2	1.7	1.1	1.0	0.0	—
0.8	0.0	100.0	1.2	0.8	0.5	—	1.9	0.9	0.9	0.8	42.2	46.0	—	—	0.7	—	2.9	0.4	0.5	0.3	—	0.0
0.8	—	100.0	1.5	0.7	0.4	—	2.9	1.0	1.2	1.0	40.9	44.9	—	—	0.4	—	3.7	0.6	0.6	0.2	—	—
0.9	0.0	100.0	2.3	1.0	0.5	0.0	2.5	0.7	2.9	1.0	38.7	43.0	—	—	0.4	—	5.4	0.7	0.5	0.4	0.0	0.0
1.5	0.0	100.0	1.9	1.6	0.8	—	2.7	0.8	2.1	1.1	38.7	40.4	—	—	0.9	—	6.7	0.8	0.5	1.0	—	0.0
1.4	0.0	100.0	2.4	1.0	1.0	0.1	2.9	1.1	2.7	1.2	36.1	39.6	—	—	0.7	—	8.2	1.6	0.6	0.8	—	0.0
2.1	0.0	100.0	1.7	1.0	0.8	0.0	2.5	0.9	4.2	2.5	40.4	32.1	0.0	—	1.0	—	8.7	2.1	0.7	1.4	0.0	—
2.5	0.0	100.0	2.9	1.5	1.1	—	3.4	1.3	4.6	3.3	33.2	32.3	0.0	—	0.6	—	11.2	2.1	0.7	1.8	0.0	0.0
3.0	0.1	100.0	2.8	1.3	1.6	0.0	5.0	1.7	3.9	2.3	31.7	31.6	0.1	0.0	0.8	0.0	11.4	2.7	1.3	1.7	0.1	0.0
13.1	0.0	100.0	5.2	2.3	2.1	0.0	10.5	4.3	6.1	4.1	5.6	4.0	0.0	—	2.7	0.0	35.6	4.4	8.6	4.5	0.0	0.0
10.5	0.1	100.0	7.8	2.3	7.3	0.1	15.9	5.4	7.3	3.7	5.0	1.7	0.0	—	1.9	—	27.0	4.0	4.9	5.6	0.1	0.0
11.3	0.1	100.0	5.7	1.5	5.9	0.1	10.0	3.4	5.0	2.9	13.7	14.3	0.0	—	1.2	—	22.2	2.7	3.9	7.4	0.1	—
5.3	0.2	100.0	4.3	1.8	3.5	0.0	10.5	3.5	5.8	3.0	19.6	15.0	0.1	—	1.2	—	21.9	4.3	2.8	2.5	0.2	0.0
7.2	0.1	100.0	6.0	1.9	5.3	0.0	11.6	4.1	7.1	4.3	15.9	11.5	—	—	1.4	0.0	19.6	4.0	2.4	4.8	0.1	0.0
2.5	0.1	100.0	1.9	1.0	1.6	0.0	2.3	1.2	2.2	1.7	35.0	19.2	0.1	—	0.5	—	16.0	14.7	0.9	1.6	0.1	0.0
3.5	0.0	100.0	3.1	1.4	1.1	0.0	4.9	2.1	4.3	2.5	36.1	25.7	0.2	—	1.1	—	11.4	2.6	1.6	1.9	0.0	0.0
2.9	0.0	100.0	3.7	1.2	1.4	—	6.2	2.3	3.3	1.9	27.3	23.6	0.7	0.0	1.2	—	21.2	3.1	1.7	1.2	0.0	—
5.9	0.2	100.0	3.4	1.2	2.6	0.1	7.0	2.7	6.0	2.0	20.0	6.7	0.7	—	2.0	0.0	25.9	13.6	3.5	2.4	0.2	0.0
1.9	0.0	100.0	1.8	1.0	0.7	0.1	2.7	1.1	3.6	2.0	35.5	36.2	0.2	0.0	0.4	—	10.1	2.6	0.9	1.0	0.0	—
0.9	0.0	100.0	1.7	0.7	0.4	0.0	2.2	0.5	1.2	1.1	39.4	44.8	—	—	0.2	—	6.0	0.9	0.4	0.5	0.0	—
1.5	0.1	100.0	2.5	1.6	0.9	0.0	2.2	1.1	2.3	1.4	35.7	35.2	—	—	0.6	—	11.4	3.5	0.6	0.9	0.1	0.0
3.4	0.1	100.0	3.3	1.5	0.9	0.0	5.3	2.0	5.6	3.0	25.1	27.7	—	—	0.8	—	16.2	5.1	1.4	2.0	0.1	0.0
1.2	0.1	100.0	1.6	0.8	0.6	—	1.9	0.8	3.0	1.8	37.9	39.5	—	—	0.5	0.0	7.5	2.8	0.4	0.8	0.1	0.0
1.5	—	100.0	1.6	0.8	0.8	0.1	3.7	1.1	3.2	1.5	34.2	37.0	—	—	1.0	—	11.4	2.1	0.7	0.8	—	—
2.6	0.2	100.0	2.0	1.1	0.8	0.0	5.2	1.8	5.5	3.4	26.6	31.5	0.0	—	0.8	—	15.6	2.9	1.3	1.3	0.1	0.1
0.7	—	100.0	1.1	0.3	0.2	—	1.4	0.6	1.1	0.8	40.4	46.8	—	—	0.3	—	5.6	0.7	0.3	0.4	—	—
2.0	—	100.0	1.6	0.8	0.6	0.0	2.4	1.1	3.9	2.6	35.6	40.7	—	—	0.7	0.0	6.6	1.4	0.8	1.2	0.0	0.0
1.2	—	100.0	1.1	0.8	0.2	—	1.4	0.4	2.3	1.8	40.5	44.9	—	—	0.2	—	3.9	1.3	0.4	0.8	—	—
1.3	0.0	100.0	1.9	0.7	0.5	0.0	2.2	0.7	2.4	1.5	40.2	42.9	—	—	0.3	—	4.3	1.1	0.5	0.8	0.0	0.0
0.6	0.0	100.0	0.9	0.3	0.3	—	1.5	0.3	1.1	0.7	42.8	46.3	—	—	0.1	—	4.2	0.9	0.2	0.4	0.0	—
1.1	0.0	100.0	2.0	0.8	0.7	0.1	3.4	0.6	2.4	2.0	36.9	40.3	0.1	0.0	0.6	—	8.0	1.0	0.6	0.5	0.0	0.0
1.2	0.1	100.0	1.2	0.6	0.4	0.0	2.0	0.6	1.8	1.4	40.6	45.8	—	—	0.3	—	3.5	0.5	0.4	0.8	0.0	0.1
1.6	0.1	100.0	1.8	1.0	0.7	0.1	3.2	1.0	2.7	3.1	36.4	40.3	—	—	0.5	—	6.0	1.5	0.5	1.1	0.1	0.0
4.5	0.0	100.0	2.4	1.5	1.1	0.0	4.9	1.8	4.8	4.1	30.9	33.0	0.0	—	1.0	—	8.4	1.6	1.6	2.9	0.0	0.0

Table 12. Gainfully Employed Population, 15 Years and Older, by Occupation and Sex
(For 1950 only, 14-year-olds are included)

(Zone) (Sector)	District	Total			Total	Professional and Technical Workers	Managerial Officials	Clerical Workers	Sales Workers	Farmers, Lumbermen and Fishermen	Mining and Quarrying Workers	Transportation and Communication Workers	Craftsmen, Production Process Workers, and General Laborers
		Total	M	F									
VIII	Shisui-machi	(2,844) 100.0	56.7	43.3	100.0	2.8	1.1	7.7	5.1	68.9	—	1.1	11.5
	Yachimata-machi	(14,186) 100.0	55.2	44.8	100.0	2.6	0.6	3.4	6.0	76.3	—	0.6	8.7
	Toke-machi	(3,157) 100.0	55.1	44.9	100.0	1.9	1.1	6.0	3.2	77.3	—	0.9	8.2
IX	Nagara-machi	(5,316) 100.0	50.8	49.2	100.0	2.8	0.4	2.8	2.1	85.3	0.2	0.4	5.1
	Obitsu-mura	(3,801) 100.0	53.4	46.6	100.0	2.6	0.7	4.1	2.9	80.4	—	0.7	7.5
X	Koito-machi	(3,494) 100.0	53.4	46.6	100.0	3.3	0.6	2.3	2.0	85.2	—	0.7	5.1
	Zone 10 Total	(378,344) 100.0	64.0	36.0	100.0	5.1	2.0	9.4	7.6	46.3	0.1	1.4	22.1
	Total for 50 km. Region	(4,244,520) 100.0	69.5	30.5	100.0	6.5	3.7	15.2	12.4	21.2	0.0	1.9	31.3
	National Total	(35,625,790) 100.0	61.4	38.6	100.0	4.5	1.9	8.6	8.4	47.8	1.1	1.2	22.3
	1955												
1 I	Chiyoda-ku	(65,728) 100.0	69.1	30.9	100.0	6.3	7.6	13.3	25.2	0.1	—	2.4	25.0
	Minato-ku	(115,612) 100.0	68.7	31.3	100.0	7.4	7.7	17.8	16.7	0.2	—	3.1	29.2
	Chūō-ku	(894,324) 100.0	68.6	31.4	100.0	3.3	6.8	11.6	28.1	0.1	—	3.5	25.2
	Bunkyō-ku	(104,510) 100.0	68.7	31.3	100.0	9.8	6.4	17.8	17.3	0.1	—	2.3	33.5
	Taitō-ku	(157,440) 100.0	68.8	31.2	100.0	3.9	5.8	8.6	26.3	0.1	—	1.7	36.4
	Zone 1 Total	(537,614) 100.0	68.6	31.4	100.0	6.0	6.7	13.5	22.7	0.1	—	2.5	30.9
2 I	Shinagawa-ku	(160,724) 100.0	71.0	29.0	100.0	6.8	5.3	18.0	15.9	0.5	—	3.1	38.6
II	Meguro-ku	(100,300) 100.0	72.0	28.0	100.0	10.0	8.2	22.3	15.5	0.6	—	2.9	29.4
	Shibuya-ku	(99,326) 100.0	69.1	30.9	100.0	9.7	7.3	21.7	16.4	0.2	—	3.1	26.3
III	Shinjuku-ku	(150,413) 100.0	68.0	32.0	100.0	9.7	6.4	19.7	17.3	0.2	—	2.6	27.9
	Nakano-ku	(111,400) 100.0	72.0	28.0	100.0	11.2	6.9	24.8	17.3	0.7	—	3.1	25.0
IV	Toshima-ku	(124,347) 100.0	69.7	30.3	100.0	8.7	5.6	19.3	18.5	0.2	—	3.2	32.1
V	Kita-ku	(143,101) 100.0	71.4	28.6	100.0	6.8	4.1	19.3	16.1	0.3	—	3.4	40.6
VI	Arakawa-ku	(112,588) 100.0	72.1	27.9	100.0	3.3	3.9	10.0	17.4	0.1	—	3.2	53.8
VII	Sumida-ku	(146,134) 100.0	71.4	28.6	100.0	2.9	5.2	8.4	16.5	0.1	—	2.5	53.8
VIII	Kōtō-ku	(123,386) 100.0	75.4	24.6	100.0	3.1	3.7	10.2	16.1	0.6	—	5.4	50.5
	Zone 2 Total	(1,271,719) 100.0	71.2	28.8	100.0	7.1	5.5	17.1	16.7	0.3	—	3.2	38.4
3 I	Ōta-ku	(230,013) 100.0	73.8	26.2	100.0	7.5	6.2	18.0	15.2	2.2	—	2.9	38.1
II	Setagaya-ku	(194,840) 100.0	71.8	28.2	100.0	13.0	7.9	24.6	14.9	2.8	—	2.6	24.1
III	Suginami-ku	(151,571) 100.0	72.2	27.8	100.0	12.9	8.3	26.8	17.0	1.6	—	2.2	21.1
IV	Itabashi-ku	(119,679) 100.0	73.0	27.0	100.0	6.7	4.2	17.2	14.9	2.5	—	3.6	42.4
	Nerima-ku	(70,468) 100.0	72.6	27.4	100.0	11.1	4.7	19.4	13.1	9.3	—	2.7	26.9
VI	Adachi-ku	(133,633) 100.0	71.6	28.4	100.0	3.8	2.7	10.9	15.5	5.9	—	3.6	50.1
VII	Katsushika-ku	(118,394) 100.0	70.8	29.2	100.0	4.7	3.6	12.8	14.3	3.1	—	3.0	50.2
VIII	Edogawa-ku	(102,826) 100.0	71.4	28.6	100.0	4.9	3.6	13.4	14.4	8.7	0.1	3.3	43.8
	Urayasu-machi	(6,671) 100.0	67.5	32.5	100.0	2.0	0.7	3.2	26.4	42.1	—	1.5	19.2
	Zone 3 Total	(1,128,095) 100.0	72.2	27.8	100.0	8.3	5.5	18.4	15.2	4.1	—	2.9	36.3
4 I	Kawasaki-shi	(178,751) 100.0	74.1	25.9	100.0	6.1	2.2	13.7	11.9	7.1	0.1	3.6	47.1
II	Komae-machi	(5,495) 100.0	69.9	30.1	100.0	13.6	4.5	19.2	10.8	16.1	0.1	2.5	26.9
III	Mitaka-shi	(25,586) 100.0	72.6	27.4	100.0	10.8	5.5	20.9	13.6	8.3	—	2.8	30.4
	Musashino-shi	(35,798) 100.0	71.6	28.4	100.0	13.7	7.4	26.4	15.3	2.3	0.1	2.1	22.4
	Chōfu-shi	(16,777) 100.0	72.2	27.8	100.0	8.5	3.1	16.6	11.7	15.1	0.2	3.9	32.6
	Hoya-machi	(8,375) 100.0	71.2	28.8	100.0	11.3	3.3	17.3	11.7	16.1	—	3.4	29.2
IV	Yamato-machi	(5,480) 100.0	65.6	34.4	100.0	6.3	1.6	11.5	10.3	27.0	—	2.8	32.4
	Toda-machi	(9,123) 100.0	63.3	36.7	100.0	3.1	1.6	8.3	8.5	32.5	0.1	2.0	40.4
V	Warabi-shi	(13,357) 100.0	70.5	29.5	100.0	5.6	2.6	16.3	16.1	4.8	0.0	2.4	45.1

Table 12. Gainfully Employed Population, 15 Years and Older, by Occupation and Sex

(For 1950 only, 14-year-olds are included)

Service Workers	Unclassified	Total	Professional and Technical Workers		Managerial Officials		Clerical Workers		Sales Workers		Farmers, Lumbermen and Fishermen		Quarrying Workers Mining and		Transportation and Communication Workers		Craftsmen, Production Process Workers, and General Laborers		Service Workers		Unclassified	
			M	F	M	F	M	F	M	F	M	F	M	F	M	F	M	F	M	F	M	F
1.8	–	100.0	1.7	1.1	1.1	–	5.9	1.8	2.9	2.2	32.9	36.0	–	–	1.1	–	10.1	1.4	1.0	0.8	–	–
1.8	0.0	100.0	1.5	1.1	0.6	0.0	2.5	0.9	3.7	2.3	38.1	38.2	–	–	0.6	0.0	7.5	1.2	0.7	1.1	0.0	0.0
1.4	–	100.0	1.1	0.8	1.1	0.0	4.4	1.6	2.0	1.2	38.0	39.3	–	–	0.9	0.0	7.0	1.2	0.6	0.8	–	–
0.9	–	100.0	1.9	0.9	0.4	0.0	1.9	0.9	1.2	0.9	40.3	45.0	0.2	0.0	0.4	0.0	4.1	1.0	0.4	0.5	–	–
1.1	–	100.0	1.7	0.9	0.7	0.0	3.5	0.6	1.9	1.0	38.0	42.4	–	–	0.7	0.0	6.4	1.1	0.5	0.6	–	–
0.8	–	100.0	2.3	1.0	0.6	0.0	1.8	0.5	1.0	1.0	43.0	42.2	–	–	0.7	0.0	3.7	1.4	0.3	0.5	–	–
5.9	0.1	100.0	3.6	1.5	2.0	0.0	6.8	2.6	4.7	2.9	23.9	22.4	0.1	0.0	1.4	0.0	18.3	3.8	3.2	2.7	0.0	0.1
7.6	0.2	100.0	4.7	1.8	3.6	0.1	10.5	4.7	8.5	3.9	11.1	10.1	0.0	0.0	1.9	0.0	25.9	5.4	3.2	4.4	0.1	0.1
4.1	0.1	100.0	3.1	1.4	1.8	0.1	6.1	2.5	5.2	3.2	24.3	23.5	1.0	0.1	1.2	0.0	16.9	5.4	1.7	2.4	0.1	0.0
20.1	–	100.0	3.5	2.8	7.1	0.5	8.0	5.3	20.5	4.7	0.1	–	–	–	2.4	–	20.6	4.4	6.9	13.2	–	–
17.9	–	100.0	4.9	2.5	7.2	0.5	10.7	7.1	12.0	4.7	0.2	–	–	–	3.0	0.1	24.8	4.4	5.9	12.0	–	–
21.4	–	100.0	2.0	1.3	6.1	0.7	6.1	5.5	23.7	4.4	0.1	–	–	–	3.4	0.1	20.6	4.6	6.6	14.8	–	–
12.8	–	100.0	6.3	3.5	6.1	0.3	11.0	6.8	12.4	4.9	0.1	–	–	–	2.3	–	26.1	7.4	4.4	8.4	–	–
17.2	–	100.0	2.6	1.3	5.4	0.4	4.4	4.2	20.0	6.3	0.1	–	–	–	1.7	–	29.7	6.7	4.9	12.3	–	–
17.6	–	100.0	3.8	2.2	6.2	0.5	7.8	5.7	17.4	5.3	0.1	–	–	–	2.5	–	25.2	5.7	5.6	12.0	–	–
11.8	–	100.0	4.9	1.9	5.1	0.2	11.0	7.0	10.8	5.1	0.4	0.1	–	–	3.0	0.1	31.3	7.3	4.5	7.3	–	–
11.1	–	100.0	7.4	2.6	8.0	0.2	14.3	8.0	10.7	4.8	0.5	0.1	–	–	2.7	0.2	24.1	5.3	4.3	6.8	–	–
15.3	–	100.0	6.8	2.9	7.0	0.3	14.1	7.6	11.6	4.8	0.2	–	–	–	2.9	0.2	21.5	4.8	5.0	10.3	–	–
16.2	–	100.0	6.6	3.1	6.0	0.4	12.3	7.4	12.3	5.0	0.2	–	–	–	2.5	0.1	22.5	5.4	5.6	10.6	–	–
11.0	–	100.0	8.4	2.8	6.7	0.2	16.2	8.6	12.2	5.1	0.5	0.2	–	–	2.9	0.2	20.5	4.5	4.6	6.4	–	–
12.4	–	100.0	6.4	2.3	5.4	0.2	11.9	7.4	12.7	5.8	0.2	–	–	–	3.1	0.1	25.4	6.7	4.6	7.8	–	–
9.4	–	100.0	5.0	1.8	3.9	0.2	11.5	7.8	10.9	5.2	0.2	0.1	–	–	3.3	0.1	32.3	8.3	4.3	5.1	–	–
8.3	–	100.0	2.2	1.1	3.8	0.1	5.4	4.6	12.4	5.0	0.1	–	–	–	3.1	0.1	41.8	12.0	3.3	5.0	–	–
10.6	–	100.0	1.9	1.0	5.0	0.2	4.4	4.0	11.8	4.7	0.1	–	–	–	2.4	0.1	42.1	11.7	3.7	6.9	–	–
10.4	–	100.0	2.3	0.8	3.6	0.1	5.8	4.4	11.3	4.8	0.5	0.1	–	–	5.3	0.1	42.7	7.8	3.9	6.5	–	–
11.7	–	100.0	5.1	2.0	5.3	0.2	10.5	6.6	11.7	5.0	0.3	–	–	–	3.1	0.1	30.8	7.6	4.4	7.3	–	–
9.9	–	100.0	5.6	1.9	6.1	0.1	11.4	6.6	10.4	4.8	1.7	0.5	–	–	2.8	0.1	32.0	6.1	3.8	6.1	–	–
10.1	–	100.0	10.0	3.0	7.8	0.1	16.1	8.5	10.1	4.8	1.9	0.9	–	–	2.5	0.1	19.3	4.8	4.1	6.0	–	–
10.1	–	100.0	9.8	3.1	8.1	0.2	18.2	8.6	11.8	5.2	1.1	0.5	–	–	2.1	0.1	17.1	4.0	4.0	6.1	–	–
8.5	–	100.0	4.8	1.9	4.1	0.1	10.9	6.3	10.1	4.8	1.5	1.0	–	–	3.4	0.2	34.0	8.4	4.2	4.3	–	–
12.8	–	100.0	8.6	2.5	4.7	–	13.0	6.4	8.9	4.2	5.4	3.9	–	–	2.6	0.1	20.8	6.1	8.6	4.2	–	–
7.5	–	100.0	2.7	1.1	2.6	0.1	6.2	4.7	10.7	4.8	3.0	2.9	–	–	3.3	0.3	39.6	10.5	3.5	4.0	–	–
8.3	–	100.0	3.4	1.3	3.5	0.1	7.5	5.3	9.5	4.8	1.7	1.4	–	–	2.9	0.1	38.4	11.8	3.9	4.4	–	–
7.8	–	100.0	3.5	1.4	3.5	0.1	7.7	5.7	9.7	4.7	5.1	3.6	0.1	–	3.1	0.2	35.3	8.5	3.4	4.4	–	–
4.9	–	100.0	1.1	0.9	0.7	–	1.9	1.3	18.7	7.7	30.6	11.5	–	–	1.4	0.1	11.3	7.9	1.8	3.1	–	–
9.3	–	100.0	6.2	2.1	5.4	0.1	11.8	6.6	10.3	4.9	2.5	1.6	–	–	2.8	0.1	29.1	7.2	4.1	5.2	–	–
8.2	–	100.0	4.6	1.5	2.2	–	8.7	5.0	7.3	4.6	4.3	2.8	0.1	–	3.4	0.2	40.1	7.0	3.4	4.8	–	–
6.3	–	100.0	9.8	3.8	4.4	0.1	12.4	6.8	6.9	3.9	9.5	6.6	0.1	–	2.3	0.2	21.9	5.0	2.6	3.7	–	–
7.7	–	100.0	8.4	2.4	5.3	0.2	14.2	6.7	9.1	4.5	4.8	3.5	–	–	2.6	0.2	24.6	5.8	3.6	4.1	–	–
10.3	–	100.0	10.3	3.4	7.2	0.2	18.0	8.4	10.1	5.2	1.4	0.9	0.1	–	2.0	0.1	18.6	3.8	3.9	6.4	–	–
8.3	–	100.0	6.6	1.9	3.0	0.1	11.0	5.6	7.9	3.8	9.2	5.9	0.2	–	3.7	0.2	26.7	5.9	3.9	4.4	–	–
7.7	–	100.0	9.0	2.3	3.3	–	11.8	5.5	7.6	4.1	8.7	7.4	–	–	2.9	0.5	24.0	5.2	3.9	3.8	–	–
8.1	–	100.0	3.9	2.4	1.6	–	7.0	4.5	6.4	3.9	13.7	13.3	–	–	2.8	–	26.2	6.2	4.1	4.0	–	–
3.5	–	100.0	2.2	0.9	1.6	–	5.3	3.0	5.1	3.4	15.4	17.1	0.1	–	1.9	0.1	29.7	10.7	2.0	1.5	–	–
7.1	–	100.0	4.1	1.5	2.6	–	9.8	6.5	10.8	5.3	2.9	1.9	0.0	–	2.3	0.1	34.5	10.6	3.5	3.6	–	–

Table 12. Gainfully Employed Population, 15 Years and Older, by Occupation and Sex
(For 1950 only, 14-year-olds are included)

(Zone)	(Sector)	District	Total		M	F	Total	Professional and Technical Workers	Managerial Officials	Clerical Workers	Sales Workers	Farmers, Lumbermen and Fishermen	Mining and Quarrying Workers	Transportation and Communication Workers	Craftsmen, Production Process Workers, and General Laborers
	V	Kawaguchi-shi	(54,536)	100.0	70.2	29.8	100.0	3.8	3.0	10.5	12.5	13.7	0.0	2.5	48.3
		Hatogaya-machi	(5,581)	100.0	68.9	31.1	100.0	5.4	1.3	10.0	17.0	17.3	—	4.0	40.0
	VI	Sōka-shi	(13,947)	100.0	62.7	37.3	100.0	2.9	2.2	6.3	11.0	35.1	0.0	2.8	34.7
		Yashio-mura	(6,416)	100.0	56.7	43.3	100.0	1.7	0.7	2.2	5.0	61.9	0.1	1.6	25.8
		Misato-mura	(8,229)	100.0	55.9	44.1	100.0	1.7	0.3	2.7	5.6	69.4	0.1	1.7	17.3
		Matsudo-shi	(27,994)	100.0	64.9	35.1	100.0	5.4	2.2	12.4	12.1	32.7	0.0	3.3	24.0
	VII	Ichikawa-shi	(54,788)	100.0	66.0	34.0	100.0	7.7	6.0	16.3	15.0	16.2	0.0	1.9	29.2
		Zone 4 Total	(470,233)	100.0	70.3	29.7	100.0	6.8	3.3	14.5	12.5	14.2	0.1	2.9	38.3
5	I	Tsurumi-ku	(78,260)	100.0	76.1	23.9	100.0	6.7	3.5	15.0	12.7	1.8	0.0	4.0	48.1
	III	Koganei-shi	(11,238)	100.0	70.4	29.6	100.0	13.3	4.4	21.0	12.5	11.0	0.0	2.3	28.3
		Tanashi-machi	(7,213)	100.0	68.6	31.4	100.0	9.5	2.5	14.9	14.9	12.7	—	3.0	32.2
		Kurume-machi	(3,960)	100.0	64.5	35.5	100.0	7.1	1.6	9.4	5.3	52.8	—	2.3	17.4
	IV	Nīza-machi	(5,370)	100.0	60.6	39.4	100.0	3.5	1.2	5.1	6.3	58.4	—	1.8	20.2
		Kiyose-machi	(6,274)	100.0	54.9	45.1	100.0	20.8	0.9	16.6	8.0	22.9	—	1.7	17.7
		Adachi-machi	(4,371)	100.0	63.4	36.6	100.0	5.3	1.9	9.7	15.2	34.1	0.0	1.8	26.6
		Asaka-machi	(6,666)	100.0	66.3	33.7	100.0	3.7	1.4	7.7	11.2	34.8	0.0	2.9	30.8
	V	Urawa-shi	(54,388)	100.0	68.9	31.1	100.0	9.6	5.4	22.6	15.2	14.0	0.0	2.0	24.1
		Misono-mura	(4,630)	100.0	54.2	45.8	100.0	2.7	0.5	3.4	5.2	76.1	—	0.8	10.0
		Koshigaya-shi	(20,111)	100.0	59.2	40.8	100.0	3.1	0.9	5.5	8.8	55.6	0.0	1.4	21.7
	VI	Yoshikawa-machi	(7,875)	100.0	54.9	45.1	100.0	2.1	0.5	2.8	6.9	67.8	0.0	1.4	15.7
		Nagareyama-machi	(8,882)	100.0	57.6	42.4	100.0	3.2	1.2	7.2	7.6	54.1	0.0	2.4	21.5
	VII	Kamagaya-machi	(4,689)	100.0	58.9	41.1	100.0	2.7	1.0	4.9	6.2	64.2	—	1.6	14.4
	VIII	Funahashi-shi	(47,478)	100.0	66.8	33.2	100.0	5.5	3.1	12.8	13.3	24.5	—	2.4	25.8
		Zone 5 Total	(271,405)	100.0	68.0	32.0	100.0	6.9	3.2	14.2	12.1	22.5	0.0	2.6	30.8
6	I	Nishi-ku	(40,069)	100.0	72.9	27.1	100.0	6.1	4.2	17.1	15.9	0.2	0.0	6.3	39.3
		Naka-ku	(46,866)	100.0	67.7	32.3	100.0	5.6	4.2	14.4	19.0	1.5	—	5.6	28.8
		Kanagawa-ku	(54,449)	100.0	74.4	25.6	100.0	7.5	4.0	17.6	15.1	3.9	0.0	4.6	38.7
	II	Kōhoku-ku	(44,292)	100.0	67.8	32.2	100.0	7.6	3.6	14.1	8.7	33.5	0.0	2.8	23.5
		Inagi-machi	(3,996)	100.0	64.3	35.7	100.0	4.5	1.6	8.3	8.2	45.9	0.4	2.7	23.8
	III	Tama-mura	(3,153)	100.0	63.4	36.6	100.0	7.3	1.3	6.8	4.3	50.2	0.9	3.2	22.2
		Fuchu-shi	(20,639)	100.0	72.4	27.6	100.0	7.6	2.7	16.2	11.3	16.9	0.6	3.2	31.2
		Kunitachi-machi	(8,510)	100.0	73.9	26.1	100.0	11.8	4.2	24.2	12.7	9.0	0.2	2.5	25.0
		Kokubunji-machi	(10,006)	100.0	73.3	26.7	100.0	11.3	3.7	21.7	11.1	14.9	0.0	3.4	25.7
		Kodaira-machi	(10,477)	100.0	69.9	30.1	100.0	12.2	3.0	16.4	8.9	22.8	0.0	2.3	20.6
		Higashimurayama-machi	(8,932)	100.0	67.0	33.0	100.0	10.9	1.9	14.9	9.3	23.3	—	3.1	29.7
	IV	Tokorosawa-shi	(23,441)	100.0	63.4	36.6	100.0	4.3	1.5	8.0	10.7	37.9	0.0	2.9	27.4
		Miyoshi-mura	(2,174)	100.0	56.0	44.0	100.0	1.3	0.4	2.3	2.9	83.5	—	0.8	7.6
		Fujimi-mura	(5,384)	100.0	56.8	43.2	100.0	1.9	0.7	3.9	5.5	68.9	—	1.2	16.6
	V	Yono-shi	(13,272)	100.0	70.5	29.5	100.0	8.0	4.8	19.2	13.6	8.0	0.0	2.8	37.7
		Omiya-shi	(58,614)	100.0	65.9	34.1	100.0	5.8	2.6	14.6	12.6	21.7	0.0	2.9	32.6
		Iwatsuki-shi	(15,563)	100.0	58.6	41.4	100.0	3.8	0.9	5.9	8.3	53.7	0.0	1.0	23.4
	VI	Matsubushi-mura	(4,447)	100.0	53.7	46.3	100.0	2.6	0.2	2.7	4.4	69.8	—	1.6	17.6
	VII	Kashiwa-shi	(19,496)	100.0	60.0	40.0	100.0	5.1	1.5	10.1	9.7	48.2	0.0	2.7	18.2
		Shōnan-mura	(5,960)	100.0	51.4	48.6	100.0	1.5	0.4	2.4	4.1	80.4	—	0.9	7.0
		Shirai-mura	(4,466)	100.0	52.1	47.9	100.0	1.9	0.2	1.7	4.2	84.6	—	0.6	4.8
	VIII	Narashino-shi	(11,633)	100.0	67.1	32.9	100.0	7.5	3.1	15.6	12.5	20.8	—	3.9	30.6
		Zone 6 Total	(415,839)	100.0	67.7	32.3	100.0	6.5	3.1	14.1	12.4	22.0	0.1	3.6	29.3
7	I	Isogo-ku	(25,709)	100.0	71.0	29.0	100.0	7.7	4.3	19.9	13.8	5.0	0.0	6.1	33.0

- 314 -

Table 12. Gainfully Employed Population, 15 Years and Older, by Occupation and Sex
(For 1950 only, 14-year-olds are included)

Service Workers	Unclassified	Total	Professional and Technical Workers		Managerial Officials		Clerical Workers		Sales Workers		Farmers, Lumbermen and Fishermen		Mining and Quarrying Workers		Transportation and Communication Workers		Craftsmen, Production Process Workers, and General Laborers		Service Workers		Unclassified	
			M	F	M	F	M	F	M	F	M	F	M	F	M	F	M	F	M	F	M	F
5.7	—	100.0	2.6	1.2	2.9	0.1	6.1	4.4	8.2	4.3	6.9	6.8	0.0	0.0	2.4	0.1	38.9	9.4	2.2	3.5	—	—
5.0	—	100.0	3.6	1.8	1.3	—	5.8	4.2	11.4	5.6	9.0	8.3	—	—	3.4	0.6	31.8	8.2	2.6	2.4	—	—
5.0	—	100.0	1.8	1.1	2.1	0.1	3.7	2.6	7.3	3.7	16.9	18.2	0.0	—	2.7	0.1	25.9	8.8	2.3	2.7	—	—
1.0	—	100.0	1.2	0.5	0.7	—	1.1	1.1	2.9	2.1	28.3	33.6	0.1	—	1.6	—	20.2	5.6	0.6	0.4	—	—
1.2	—	100.0	1.2	0.5	0.3	—	1.6	1.1	3.6	2.0	32.8	36.6	0.1	—	1.7	—	13.9	3.4	0.7	0.5	—	—
7.9	0.0	100.0	3.8	1.6	2.2	—	8.1	4.3	7.9	4.2	15.9	16.8	0.0	0.0	3.0	0.3	19.4	4.6	4.6	3.3	0.0	—
7.7	—	100.0	5.3	2.4	5.9	0.1	10.6	5.7	10.2	4.8	8.4	7.8	0.0	—	1.9	—	20.9	8.3	2.8	4.9	—	—
7.4	0.0	100.0	5.0	1.8	3.2	0.1	9.3	5.2	8.1	4.4	7.4	6.8	0.1	0.0	2.8	0.1	31.2	7.1	3.2	4.2	0.0	—
8.2	0.0	100.0	5.0	1.7	3.4	0.1	9.5	5.5	7.9	4.8	1.2	0.6	0.0	—	3.8	0.2	41.9	6.2	3.4	4.8	0.0	—
7.2	—	100.0	10.1	3.2	4.3	0.1	13.9	7.1	8.0	4.5	6.4	4.6	0.0	—	2.2	0.1	22.1	6.2	3.4	3.8	—	—
10.3	—	100.0	6.9	2.6	2.4	0.1	9.4	5.5	9.0	5.9	7.0	5.7	—	—	2.7	0.3	25.0	7.2	6.2	4.1	—	—
4.1	—	100.0	5.1	2.0	1.5	0.1	6.7	2.7	3.3	2.0	29.1	23.7	—	—	2.3	—	14.3	3.1	2.2	1.9	—	—
3.5	—	100.0	2.7	0.8	1.2	—	3.5	1.6	3.4	2.9	29.6	28.8	—	—	1.8	—	16.1	4.1	2.3	1.2	—	—
11.4	—	100.0	7.2	13.6	0.9	—	12.2	4.4	4.5	3.5	11.9	11.0	—	—	1.6	0.1	13.8	3.9	2.8	8.6	—	—
5.4	—	100.0	3.4	1.9	1.9	—	5.8	3.9	9.5	5.7	17.0	17.1	0.0	—	1.8	—	21.8	4.8	2.3	3.1	—	—
7.5	—	100.0	2.8	0.9	1.4	—	4.7	3.0	7.4	3.8	17.7	17.1	—	—	2.9	—	25.0	5.8	4.4	3.1	—	—
7.1	—	100.0	7.1	2.5	5.3	0.1	15.4	7.2	10.0	5.2	6.9	7.1	0.0	0.0	1.9	0.1	19.5	4.6	2.8	4.3	—	—
1.3	—	100.0	1.8	0.9	0.5	—	2.3	1.1	3.2	2.0	37.4	38.7	—	—	0.7	0.1	7.5	2.5	0.8	0.5	—	—
3.0	—	100.0	2.1	1.0	0.8	0.1	3.5	2.0	5.8	3.0	27.5	28.1	—	—	1.3	0.1	16.9	4.8	1.3	1.7	—	—
2.8	—	100.0	1.3	0.8	0.5	—	1.8	1.0	4.6	2.3	31.3	36.5	—	—	1.4	—	12.8	2.9	1.2	1.6	—	—
2.8	—	100.0	2.2	1.0	1.2	—	5.0	2.2	4.7	2.9	22.8	31.3	—	—	2.4	—	17.8	3.7	1.5	1.3	—	—
5.0	—	100.0	2.0	0.7	1.0	—	3.2	1.7	3.6	2.6	32.2	32.0	—	—	1.5	0.1	11.8	2.6	3.6	1.4	—	—
12.6	—	100.0	3.9	1.6	3.1	—	8.3	4.5	8.2	5.1	13.2	11.3	—	—	2.3	0.1	20.2	5.6	7.6	5.0	—	—
7.7	0.0	100.0	4.9	2.0	3.1	0.1	9.3	4.9	7.7	4.4	11.3	11.2	—	—	2.5	0.1	25.5	5.3	3.7	4.0	—	—
10.9	0.0	100.0	4.3	1.8	4.1	0.1	10.3	6.8	10.3	5.6	0.1	0.1	—	—	6.1	0.2	33.4	5.9	4.3	6.6	—	—
20.9	—	100.0	3.9	1.7	3.9	0.3	8.6	5.8	12.3	6.7	1.3	0.2	—	—	5.4	0.2	25.2	3.6	7.1	13.8	—	—
8.6	—	100.0	5.6	1.9	3.9	0.1	11.0	6.6	9.8	5.3	2.7	1.2	—	—	4.5	0.1	33.1	5.6	3.8	4.8	—	—
6.2	—	100.0	6.0	1.6	3.6	—	9.5	4.6	5.3	3.4	18.2	15.3	—	—	2.8	—	19.5	4.0	2.9	3.3	—	—
4.6	—	100.0	3.2	1.3	1.2	0.4	5.3	3.0	5.1	3.1	24.3	21.6	0.4	—	2.6	0.1	19.4	4.4	2.8	1.8	—	—
3.8	—	100.0	3.7	3.6	1.3	—	4.3	2.5	3.0	1.3	28.2	22.0	0.9	—	2.9	0.3	16.9	5.3	2.3	1.5	—	—
10.3	—	100.0	5.7	1.9	2.6	0.1	10.5	5.7	7.1	4.2	10.0	6.9	0.5	0.1	2.9	0.3	27.0	4.2	6.1	4.2	—	—
10.4	—	100.0	9.2	2.6	4.1	0.1	17.4	6.8	8.2	4.5	6.4	2.6	0.2	—	2.5	—	20.6	4.4	5.3	5.1	—	—
8.2	—	100.0	8.7	2.6	3.6	0.1	15.6	6.1	7.1	4.0	8.5	6.4	—	—	3.2	0.2	22.1	3.6	4.5	3.7	—	—
13.8	—	100.0	8.0	4.2	3.0	—	11.1	5.3	5.4	3.5	12.5	10.3	—	—	2.2	0.1	17.0	3.6	10.7	3.1	—	—
6.9	—	100.0	6.0	4.9	1.9	—	10.0	4.9	5.8	3.5	12.3	11.0	—	—	3.0	0.1	24.0	5.7	4.0	2.9	—	—
7.3	—	100.0	2.7	1.6	1.5	—	5.1	2.9	6.6	4.1	19.9	18.0	—	—	2.8	0.1	21.6	5.8	3.2	4.1	—	—
1.2	—	100.0	0.9	0.4	0.4	—	1.4	0.9	1.7	1.2	43.7	39.8	—	—	0.8	—	6.3	1.3	0.8	0.4	—	—
1.3	—	100.0	1.2	0.7	0.7	—	2.5	1.4	3.7	1.8	33.3	35.6	—	—	1.2	—	13.5	3.1	0.7	0.6	—	—
5.9	—	100.0	5.7	2.3	4.7	0.1	12.7	6.5	8.9	4.7	4.2	3.8	—	—	2.7	0.1	28.6	9.1	3.0	2.9	—	—
7.2	—	100.0	4.1	1.7	2.5	0.1	9.4	5.2	7.7	4.9	10.0	11.7	—	—	2.8	0.1	26.2	6.4	3.2	4.0	—	—
3.0	—	100.0	2.5	1.3	0.9	—	3.9	2.0	5.2	3.1	26.7	27.0	—	—	1.0	—	17.3	6.1	1.1	1.9	—	—
1.1	—	100.0	1.7	0.9	0.2	—	2.0	0.7	2.5	1.9	30.7	39.1	—	—	1.5	0.1	14.6	3.0	0.5	0.6	—	—
4.5	—	100.0	3.5	1.6	1.5	—	7.1	3.0	5.6	4.1	22.6	25.6	—	—	2.6	0.1	14.8	3.4	2.3	2.2	—	—
3.3	—	100.0	1.0	0.5	0.4	—	1.6	0.8	1.6	2.5	37.5	42.9	—	—	0.9	—	6.1	0.9	2.3	1.0	—	—
2.0	—	100.0	1.2	0.7	0.2	—	1.2	0.5	2.4	1.8	40.9	43.7	—	—	0.5	0.1	4.3	0.5	1.4	0.6	—	—
6.0	—	100.0	5.2	2.3	3.0	0.1	10.3	5.3	7.4	5.1	9.9	10.9	—	—	3.8	0.1	24.4	6.2	3.1	2.9	—	—
8.9	0.0	100.0	4.7	1.8	3.0	0.1	9.1	5.0	7.8	4.6	11.3	10.7	0.1	—	3.5	0.1	24.2	5.1	4.0	4.9	—	—
10.2	—	100.0	5.3	2.4	4.2	0.1	12.5	7.4	8.5	5.3	3.1	1.9	—	—	5.7	0.4	26.9	6.1	4.8	5.4	—	—

Table 12. Gainfully Employed Population, 15 Years and Older, by Occupation and Sex
(For 1950 only, 14-year-olds are included)

(Zone)(Sector)	District	Total			Total	Professional and Technical Workers	Managerial Officials	Clerical Workers	Sales Workers	Farmers, Lumbermen and Fishermen	Mining and Quarrying Workers	Transportation and Communication Workers	Craftsmen, Production Process Workers, and General Laborers
		Total	M	F									
I	Minami-ku	(67,488) 100.0	70.6	29.4	100.0	6.4	3.3	14.8	16.0	3.8	0.0	4.7	38.2
II	Hodogaya-ku	(37,149) 100.0	72.0	28.0	100.0	7.0	3.1	17.2	11.2	11.6	0.0	4.4	38.5
	Machida-shi	(22,988) 100.0	67.5	32.5	100.0	6.5	2.3	11.7	10.9	33.3	0.0	2.9	26.1
III	Yuki-mura	(3,147) 100.0	55.9	44.1	100.0	2.2	0.3	4.2	3.1	71.1	0.2	1.5	16.0
	Hino-machi	(10,624) 100.0	69.2	30.8	100.0	6.4	2.2	13.4	8.9	26.1	0.3	2.8	34.5
	Tachikawa-shi	(25,764) 100.0	70.0	30.0	100.0	7.1	3.3	14.7	15.6	2.1	0.1	3.5	30.3
	Sunakawa-machi	(4,841) 100.0	69.0	31.0	100.0	3.5	0.7	8.0	7.8	38.0	0.1	2.8	30.0
	Yamato-machi	(4,873) 100.0	67.6	32.4	100.0	5.3	1.0	8.2	9.3	28.7	—	3.4	37.9
IV	Ōi-mura	(2,366) 100.0	59.9	40.1	100.0	2.0	0.5	4.7	6.5	60.3	—	1.2	17.7
	Fukuoka-mura	(2,952) 100.0	68.8	31.2	100.0	5.4	0.8	10.7	11.7	32.7	0.0	2.2	31.2
V	Kasukabe-shi	(14,093) 100.0	60.6	39.4	100.0	4.4	1.4	7.2	10.9	45.6	0.0	1.5	25.9
	Shōwa-mura	(6,570) 100.0	55.8	44.2	100.0	3.4	0.5	4.4	6.6	62.1	—	1.3	18.5
VI	Noda-shi	(24,671) 100.0	57.6	42.4	100.0	3.9	1.3	7.9	9.8	43.0	—	2.1	27.8
VII	Abiko-machi	(11,087) 100.0	58.6	41.4	100.0	4.3	1.6	9.6	13.9	43.7	—	2.1	21.1
	Yachiyo-machi	(7,667) 100.0	53.7	46.3	100.0	2.0	0.9	4.5	5.2	73.8	—	1.8	10.0
VIII	Chiba-shi	(79,708) 100.0	64.2	35.8	100.0	8.6	3.0	16.2	12.7	25.0	0.0	3.1	23.7
IX	Goi-machi	(8,703) 100.0	55.6	44.4	100.0	2.8	1.0	5.1	7.8	70.5	0.0	1.2	8.7
	Sodegaura-machi	(6,758) 100.0	52.3	47.7	100.0	2.6	0.7	3.7	4.3	80.6	0.0	0.7	5.6
	Zone 7 Total	(367,158) 100.0	66.1	33.9	100.0	6.3	2.6	13.4	12.2	24.5	0.0	3.4	28.9
8 I	Kanazawa-ku	(21,628) 100.0	74.7	25.3	100.0	8.7	2.9	17.2	12.0	6.3	0.0	4.3	38.4
	Totsuka-ku	(31,968) 100.0	69.7	30.3	100.0	7.0	2.0	14.7	8.1	28.2	0.0	3.7	30.2
II	Yamato-shi	(9,420) 100.0	65.1	34.9	100.0	7.0	2.1	12.6	12.2	19.6	0.0	4.0	25.8
	Sagamihara-shi	(32,577) 100.0	66.8	33.2	100.0	5.8	1.4	11.8	9.0	32.4	0.2	3.7	27.9
	Zama-machi	(5,510) 100.0	63.1	36.9	100.0	4.7	1.7	9.5	8.4	38.5	0.3	3.2	22.7
III	Hachiōji-shi	(58,006) 100.0	65.8	34.2	100.0	5.2	3.8	10.7	13.6	15.9	0.2	2.7	40.7
	Akishima-shi	(13,295) 100.0	73.8	26.2	100.0	5.9	1.8	14.1	11.9	8.4	0.5	3.9	39.9
	Fussa-machi	(7,940) 100.0	71.1	28.9	100.0	5.8	2.1	11.1	12.0	10.0	1.0	4.0	36.3
	Mizuho-machi	(3,925) 100.0	68.0	42.0	100.0	3.0	1.3	5.1	9.1	38.0	0.1	2.4	34.1
	Murayama-machi	(4,766) 100.0	65.1	34.9	100.0	4.2	1.2	3.6	6.9	40.3	—	2.6	36.8
	Musashi-machi	(12,684) 100.0	61.5	38.5	100.0	3.5	1.0	5.6	8.5	40.5	0.1	2.0	26.2
IV	Sayama-shi	(14,253) 100.0	60.7	39.3	100.0	3.0	1.2	6.2	9.2	45.0	0.1	2.4	26.9
	Kawagoe-shi	(45,066) 100.0	62.1	37.9	100.0	4.8	1.9	8.8	11.7	39.9	0.1	2.2	25.5
	Seibu-machi	(4,286) 100.0	55.0	45.0	100.0	1.8	1.7	5.2	7.7	31.9	0.1	2.3	43.8
V	Ageo-shi	(16,058) 100.0	58.8	41.2	100.0	3.4	1.4	8.1	7.5	46.5	0.0	1.8	28.3
	Ina-mura	(3,566) 100.0	54.6	45.4	100.0	3.5	0.7	5.1	4.2	70.7	—	1.0	13.4
	Hasuda-machi	(8,389) 100.0	58.0	42.0	100.0	5.2	1.0	7.3	8.0	54.7	0.0	1.6	19.1
	Shiraoka-machi	(7,146) 100.0	57.9	42.1	100.0	2.6	0.7	5.6	6.7	61.4	—	1.8	18.6
	Miyashiro-machi	(4,905) 100.0	56.3	43.7	100.0	3.5	1.1	6.5	6.0	61.8	—	2.8	15.5
	Sugito-machi	(8,087) 100.0	56.5	43.5	100.0	3.5	1.0	5.2	8.6	63.8	—	1.6	14.1
VI	Sekiyado-machi	(6,842) 100.0	51.4	48.6	100.0	2.1	0.4	2.1	6.3	78.9	—	0.9	8.1
	Moriya-machi	(5,785) 100.0	53.7	46.3	100.0	3.0	0.7	3.7	7.3	72.0	—	0.8	10.8
VII	Toride-machi	(9,509) 100.0	58.2	41.8	100.0	5.2	1.9	9.3	14.6	41.2	—	2.0	20.3
	Inzai-machi	(8,589) 100.0	54.5	45.5	100.0	3.2	0.8	4.2	13.5	64.9	—	1.1	9.6
	Inba-mura	(4,629) 100.0	50.8	49.2	100.0	1.6	0.4	1.9	6.4	85.0	—	0.5	3.7
VIII	Yotsukaidō-machi	(7,915) 100.0	57.6	42.4	100.0	4.8	1.1	9.5	6.9	59.2	—	1.9	13.5
IX	Ichihara-machi	(6,930) 100.0	54.8	45.2	100.0	3.3	1.0	6.7	6.3	67.9	—	1.2	11.0
	Anegasaki-machi	(5,295) 100.0	56.9	43.1	100.0	3.3	0.7	5.1	7.9	69.0	—	1.6	9.5
	Hirakawa-machi	(6,094) 100.0	51.3	48.7	100.0	2.2	0.6	3.1	2.8	83.2	—	0.6	6.0
	Miwa-machi	(5,878) 100.0	51.3	48.7	100.0	2.4	0.9	3.4	4.6	81.8	0.0	0.5	5.3
X	Kisarazu-shi	(23,828) 100.0	57.1	42.9	100.0	3.8	1.0	6.4	11.6	52.3	0.1	2.0	15.0

Table 12. Gainfully Employed Population, 15 Years and Older, by Occupation and Sex
(For 1950 only, 14-year-olds are included)

Service Workers	Unclassified	Total	Professional and Technical Workers		Managerial Officials		Clerical Workers		Sales Workers		Farmers, Lumbermen and Fishermen		Mining and Quarrying Workers		Transportation and Communication Workers		Craftsmen, Production Process Workers, and General Laborers		Service Workers		Unclassified	
			M	F	M	F	M	F	M	F	M	F	M	F	M	F	M	F	M	F	M	F
12.8	—	100.0	4.4	2.0	3.2	0.1	9.1	5.7	10.3	5.7	2.2	1.6	—	—	4.6	0.1	31.4	6.8	5.4	7.4	—	—
7.0	0.0	100.0	5.1	1.9	3.1	—	11.0	6.2	7.0	4.2	6.6	5.0	—	—	4.2	0.2	31.1	7.4	3.9	3.1	—	—
6.3	—	100.0	4.7	1.8	2.2	0.1	7.5	4.2	6.4	4.5	18.8	14.5	—	—	2.8	0.1	21.7	4.4	3.4	2.9	—	—
1.4	—	100.0	1.5	0.7	0.3	—	2.8	1.4	1.6	1.5	35.6	35.5	0.2	—	1.5	—	11.6	4.4	0.8	0.6	—	—
5.4	—	100.0	4.9	1.5	2.2	—	8.9	4.5	5.4	3.5	14.1	12.0	0.2	0.1	2.6	0.2	27.8	6.7	3.1	2.3	—	—
23.3	—	100.0	4.7	2.4	3.0	0.3	9.1	5.6	10.0	5.6	1.2	0.9	0.1	—	3.4	0.1	25.6	4.7	12.9	10.4	—	—
9.1	—	100.0	2.5	1.0	0.7	—	4.8	3.2	4.7	3.1	21.9	16.1	0.1	—	2.6	0.2	25.5	4.5	6.2	2.9	—	—
6.2	—	100.0	3.5	1.8	1.0	—	4.8	3.4	5.2	4.1	15.8	12.9	—	—	3.3	0.1	29.6	8.3	4.4	1.8	—	—
7.1	—	100.0	1.1	0.9	0.5	—	3.2	1.5	4.0	2.5	29.8	30.5	—	—	1.2	—	13.7	4.0	6.4	0.7	—	—
5.3	—	100.0	4.0	1.4	0.8	—	7.2	3.5	7.8	3.9	17.5	15.2	0.0	—	2.2	—	26.0	5.2	3.3	2.0	—	—
3.1	0.0	100.0	2.9	1.5	1.4	0.0	4.7	2.5	6.9	4.0	21.0	24.6	0.0	—	1.4	0.1	21.0	4.9	1.3	1.8	0.0	—
3.2	—	100.0	2.1	1.3	0.5	0.0	3.0	1.4	4.0	2.6	28.9	33.2	—	—	1.2	0.1	15.0	3.5	1.1	2.1	—	—
4.2	—	100.0	2.3	1.6	1.2	0.1	5.3	2.6	5.7	4.1	17.4	25.6	—	—	2.0	0.1	22.0	5.8	1.7	2.5	—	—
3.7	—	100.0	3.3	1.0	1.6	0.0	6.9	2.7	6.2	7.7	21.3	22.4	—	—	2.0	0.1	15.8	5.3	1.5	2.2	—	—
1.8	—	100.0	1.1	0.9	0.8	0.1	3.0	1.5	2.5	2.7	35.3	38.5	—	—	1.8	—	8.3	1.7	0.9	0.9	—	—
7.7	—	100.0	5.7	2.9	3.0	0.0	10.9	5.3	7.5	5.2	12.0	13.0	0.0	—	2.9	0.2	20.1	3.6	2.1	5.6	—	—
2.9	—	100.0	1.8	1.0	1.0	0.0	3.2	1.9	4.6	3.2	35.9	34.6	0.0	—	1.0	0.2	7.1	1.6	1.0	1.9	—	—
1.8	—	100.0	1.7	0.9	0.7	—	2.5	1.2	2.2	2.1	39.2	41.4	0.0	—	0.6	0.1	4.8	0.8	0.6	1.2	—	—
8.7	0.0	100.0	4.3	2.0	2.5	0.1	8.6	4.8	7.4	4.8	12.1	12.4	0.0	0.0	3.2	0.2	23.9	5.0	4.1	4.6	0.0	0.0
10.2	—	100.0	6.0	2.7	2.8	0.1	11.5	5.7	7.0	5.0	4.6	1.7	0.0	—	4.2	0.1	32.2	6.2	6.4	3.8	—	—
6.1	—	100.0	5.1	1.9	2.0	0.0	9.9	4.8	4.8	3.3	15.6	12.6	0.0	—	3.6	0.1	25.1	5.1	3.6	2.5	—	—
16.7	—	100.0	5.2	1.8	2.0	0.1	8.7	3.9	7.6	4.6	10.4	9.2	0.0	—	3.8	0.2	21.7	4.1	5.7	11.0	—	—
7.8	0.0	100.0	3.9	1.9	1.3	0.1	7.9	3.9	5.2	3.8	17.5	14.9	0.2	0.0	3.6	0.1	24.0	3.9	3.2	4.6	0.0	—
11.0	—	100.0	3.4	1.3	1.7	—	5.4	4.1	4.7	3.7	21.7	16.8	0.3	—	3.2	—	18.8	3.9	3.9	7.1	—	—
7.2	0.0	100.0	3.6	1.6	3.7	0.1	6.5	4.2	8.4	5.2	10.5	5.4	0.1	0.1	2.6	0.1	27.3	13.4	3.1	4.1	0.0	—
13.6	—	100.0	4.4	1.5	1.8	0.0	8.9	5.2	7.6	4.3	5.8	2.6	0.5	0.0	3.8	0.1	34.0	5.9	7.0	6.6	—	—
17.7	—	100.0	3.9	1.9	2.0	0.1	6.6	4.5	7.3	4.7	6.6	3.4	1.0	0.0	4.0	—	32.2	4.1	7.5	10.2	—	—
6.9	—	100.0	1.8	1.2	1.3	0.0	3.2	1.9	5.8	3.3	25.6	12.4	0.1	—	2.2	0.2	23.5	10.6	4.5	2.4	—	—
4.4	—	100.0	1.7	2.5	1.2	0.0	2.3	1.3	4.6	2.3	25.6	14.7	—	—	2.5	0.1	24.6	12.2	2.6	1.8	—	—
12.6	—	100.0	2.3	1.2	1.0	0.0	3.5	2.1	5.4	3.1	23.4	17.1	0.1	—	1.9	0.1	17.1	9.1	6.8	5.8	—	—
6.0	—	100.0	2.0	1.0	1.2	0.0	3.9	2.3	5.6	3.6	24.0	21.0	0.1	0.0	2.3	0.1	18.6	8.3	3.0	3.0	—	—
5.1	—	100.0	3.3	1.5	1.8	0.1	5.7	3.1	7.3	4.4	20.3	19.6	0.1	0.0	2.1	0.1	19.2	6.3	2.3	2.8	—	—
5.5	—	100.0	1.2	0.6	1.7	—	3.1	2.1	4.8	2.9	19.4	12.5	0.1	0.0	2.3	0.0	18.9	24.9	3.5	2.0	—	—
3.0	0.0	100.0	2.3	1.1	1.4	0.0	5.3	2.8	4.4	3.1	21.2	25.3	—	—	1.8	0.0	21.0	7.3	1.4	1.6	0.0	—
1.4	—	100.0	3.1	0.4	0.7	—	3.9	1.2	2.0	2.2	31.4	39.3	0.0	—	1.0	0.0	11.8	1.6	0.7	0.7	—	—
3.1	0.0	100.0	2.7	2.5	0.9	0.1	4.7	2.6	4.9	3.1	26.0	28.7	—	—	1.6	—	16.0	3.1	1.2	1.9	0.0	—
2.6	—	100.0	1.8	0.8	0.7	0.0	4.0	1.6	3.6	3.1	29.0	32.4	—	—	1.8	0.0	15.7	2.9	1.3	1.3	—	—
2.8	—	100.0	2.5	1.0	1.1	0.0	4.5	2.0	3.5	2.5	27.2	34.6	—	—	2.8	0.0	13.2	2.3	1.5	1.3	—	—
2.2	—	100.0	2.3	1.2	1.0	0.0	3.3	1.9	5.1	3.5	30.8	33.0	—	—	1.6	0.0	11.3	2.8	1.1	1.1	—	—
1.2	—	100.0	1.4	0.7	0.4	—	1.4	0.7	3.7	2.6	36.8	42.1	—	—	0.8	0.1	6.4	1.7	0.5	0.7	—	—
1.7	—	100.0	2.1	0.9	0.7	0.0	3.0	0.7	3.6	3.7	33.9	38.1	—	—	0.8	—	8.7	2.1	0.9	0.8	—	—
5.5	—	100.0	3.6	1.6	1.8	0.1	6.4	2.9	7.4	7.2	18.6	22.6	—	—	2.0	0.0	16.1	4.2	2.3	3.2	—	—
2.7	—	100.0	2.4	0.8	0.8	—	2.7	1.5	5.4	8.1	32.9	32.0	—	—	1.0	0.0	8.3	1.3	1.0	1.7	—	—
0.5	—	100.0	1.1	0.5	0.4	—	1.4	0.5	1.6	4.8	42.5	42.5	—	—	0.4	0.1	3.1	0.6	0.3	0.2	—	—
3.1	—	100.0	2.9	1.9	1.1	0.0	6.3	3.2	4.0	2.9	28.1	31.1	—	—	1.9	0.0	11.6	1.9	1.7	1.4	—	—
2.6	—	100.0	2.4	0.9	1.0	—	4.2	2.5	3.5	2.8	31.3	36.6	—	—	1.2	0.0	9.6	1.4	1.4	1.2	—	—
2.9	—	100.0	2.1	1.2	0.7	—	3.6	1.5	4.5	3.4	36.2	32.8	—	—	1.6	—	7.2	2.3	1.0	1.9	—	—
1.5	—	100.0	1.3	0.9	0.5	0.1	2.3	0.8	1.5	1.3	39.6	43.6	—	—	0.5	0.1	5.0	1.0	0.6	0.9	—	—
1.1	—	100.0	1.5	0.9	0.9	—	2.2	1.2	2.4	2.2	39.1	42.7	0.0	—	0.5	—	4.3	1.0	0.4	0.7	—	—
7.8	—	100.0	2.2	1.6	1.0	0.0	4.0	2.4	6.5	5.1	26.2	26.1	0.1	—	1.9	0.1	12.4	2.6	2.8	5.0	—	—

Table 12. Gainfully Employed Population, 15 Years and Older, by Occupation and Sex
(For 1950 only, 14-year-olds are included)

(Zone)	(Sector)	District	Total		M	F	Total	Professional and Technical Workers	Managerial Officials	Clerical Workers	Sales Workers	Farmers, Lumbermen and Fishermen	Mining and Quarrying Workers	Transportation and Communication Workers	Craftsmen, Production Process Workers, and General Laborers
		Zone 8 Total	(404,769)	100.0	62.9	37.1	100.0	4.8	1.8	9.2	10.0	38.5	0.1	2.6	26.4
9	I	Kamakura-shi	(32,766)	100.0	70.7	29.3	100.0	12.3	7.6	18.9	15.0	7.4	0.0	2.5	24.7
	II	Ayase-machi	(3,499)	100.0	65.2	34.8	100.0	2.9	0.5	5.5	4.1	61.4	—	2.6	18.1
		Ebina-machi	(7,056)	100.0	63.0	37.0	100.0	4.9	0.9	7.6	6.0	52.2	0.4	3.0	20.8
		Shiroyama-machi	(2,166)	100.0	62.6	37.4	100.0	4.6	0.8	8.9	5.4	54.7	1.1	2.3	19.1
	III	Akita-machi	(5,384)	100.0	71.3	28.7	100.0	4.4	1.2	7.8	8.0	39.4	1.1	3.6	26.6
		Hamura-machi	(4,306)	100.0	67.8	32.2	100.0	5.4	1.5	9.9	8.8	28.0	1.3	2.8	31.6
	IV	Hannō-shi	(18,351)	100.0	64.2	35.8	100.0	4.5	1.8	7.4	12.2	35.6	0.6	2.6	28.9
		Tsurugashima-mura	(3,295)	100.0	56.9	43.1	100.0	3.1	0.4	4.3	4.2	73.7	0.0	1.4	11.0
		Hidaka-machi	(8,115)	100.0	58.2	41.8	100.0	3.1	0.6	4.7	5.4	63.9	0.2	1.4	17.7
		Kawashima-mura	(9,220)	100.0	50.3	49.7	100.0	2.1	0.5	2.1	3.6	83.3	0.0	0.4	7.1
	V	Kitamoto-machi	(6,284)	100.0	59.2	40.8	100.0	3.5	0.7	6.7	7.9	56.6	—	1.9	19.9
		Higawa-machi	(8,224)	100.0	60.9	39.1	100.0	4.3	1.2	8.0	10.3	49.0	0.0	1.6	21.9
		Shobu-machi	(8,143)	100.0	53.9	46.1	100.0	3.0	0.7	3.0	7.8	68.5	—	1.0	13.5
		Kuki-machi	(9,586)	100.0	60.3	39.7	100.0	4.3	1.1	8.0	9.2	50.9	—	2.8	20.3
		Satte-machi	(11,178)	100.0	56.0	44.0	100.0	3.5	1.2	4.9	9.9	55.3	—	1.3	20.3
	VI	Iwai-machi	(18,300)	100.0	51.0	49.0	100.0	2.2	0.4	1.9	5.7	82.0	—	0.4	5.9
		Mitsukaidō-shi	(19,576)	100.0	53.7	46.3	100.0	3.0	0.7	4.0	10.3	67.2	—	1.3	11.1
		Yawahara-mura	(5,732)	100.0	52.3	47.7	100.0	2.1	0.4	2.8	5.0	81.0	—	0.7	6.8
		Ina-mura	(6,593)	100.0	51.3	48.7	100.0	2.0	0.2	2.7	4.7	83.1	—	0.4	5.9
	VII	Fujishiro-machi	(6,578)	100.0	52.3	47.7	100.0	2.6	0.6	5.3	8.4	70.3	0.0	1.4	9.8
		Ryūgasaki-shi	(16,128)	100.0	55.8	44.2	100.0	3.8	0.9	6.2	11.0	59.2	—	1.3	14.2
		Tone-mura	(4,847)	100.0	53.2	46.8	100.0	2.3	0.5	4.6	6.8	73.4	—	0.8	9.7
		Motono-mura	(3,002)	100.0	49.7	50.3	100.0	1.6	0.4	2.4	7.3	82.7	—	0.2	4.7
	VIII	Sakura-shi	(16,130)	100.0	56.1	43.9	100.0	5.2	1.3	8.6	8.3	59.4	0.0	2.0	11.9
		Izumi-machi	(5,161)	100.0	51.9	48.1	100.0	2.1	0.6	3.0	3.1	84.9	—	0.8	4.5
	IX	Shitsu-mura	(5,305)	100.0	49.2	50.8	100.0	2.2	0.5	3.2	3.1	84.3	—	0.8	5.0
		Nansō-machi	(9,514)	100.0	52.4	47.6	100.0	3.6	1.1	3.2	6.5	75.8	—	0.5	7.0
		Fukuta-machi	(3,770)	100.0	53.1	46.9	100.0	3.5	0.7	3.7	4.5	76.2	0.0	1.1	8.3
	X	Kimitsu-machi	(6,911)	100.0	53.0	47.0	100.0	3.4	0.9	4.5	5.1	74.1	0.0	1.0	9.2
		Futtsu-machi	(7,800)	100.0	58.8	41.2	100.0	2.4	0.7	2.8	9.3	70.6	0.1	1.3	10.0
		Ōsawa-machi	(279,376)	100.0	56.7	43.3	100.0	4.2	1.0	5.0	10.0	59.8	0.2	1.7	14.2
		Zone 9 Total	(279,376)	100.0	58.0	42.0	100.0	4.4	1.6	6.7	8.7	57.5	0.1	1.6	15.3
10	I	Yokosuka-shi	(105,795)	100.0	72.1	27.9	100.0	7.0	2.2	12.8	13.2	6.9	0.0	4.0	33.6
		Zushi-shi	(13,115)	100.0	65.5	34.5	100.0	10.4	6.7	20.6	13.9	4.0	—	3.0	29.8
		Hayama-machi	(5,322)	100.0	70.2	29.8	100.0	7.8	6.2	14.4	11.0	19.5	—	2.3	27.3
		Chigasaki-shi	(20,939)	100.0	70.5	29.5	100.0	7.1	3.9	15.6	11.3	23.0	0.1	2.8	29.8
		Fujisawa-shi	(40,452)	100.0	70.1	29.9	100.0	9.0	5.7	16.1	14.2	20.0	0.0	2.4	24.0
	II	Aikawa-machi	(6,499)	100.0	59.5	40.5	100.0	3.0	2.1	4.4	5.4	47.0	1.0	1.3	32.9
		Atsugi-shi	(19,490)	100.0	62.8	37.2	100.0	5.0	1.5	7.6	8.4	54.5	0.4	2.3	15.4
		Samukawa-machi	(4,288)	100.0	68.4	31.6	100.0	4.6	1.3	10.0	7.7	42.0	0.6	2.8	27.1
	III	Ome-shi	(23,472)	100.0	64.7	35.3	100.0	4.4	3.4	8.7	10.4	19.1	0.8	2.7	43.3
	IV	Sakado-machi	(11,389)	100.0	56.3	43.7	100.0	3.0	0.7	4.3	7.3	66.1	0.2	1.1	14.6
		Yoshimi-mura	(8,165)	100.0	51.5	48.5	100.0	2.4	0.4	2.9	3.1	81.3	—	0.5	8.5
		Moroyama-mura	(5,463)	100.0	55.1	44.9	100.0	6.7	1.1	4.6	5.5	61.8	0.0	1.0	16.3
	V	Kōnosu-shi	(13,655)	100.0	59.0	41.0	100.0	5.0	1.3	7.6	10.8	46.1	0.0	2.0	23.0
		Kisai-machi	(7,964)	100.0	54.0	46.0	100.0	2.5	0.4	3.6	7.1	72.6	0.0	1.3	11.1
		Washimiya-machi	(4,138)	100.0	57.3	42.7	100.0	2.8	0.8	4.5	8.0	65.4	—	1.8	14.6
		Kurihashi-machi	(5,612)	100.0	57.3	42.7	100.0	3.7	1.1	6.9	11.8	52.6	—	1.7	18.3

- 318 -

Table 12. Gainfully Employed Population, 15 Years and Older, by Occupation and Sex
(For 1950 only, 14-year-olds are included)

Service Workers	Unclassified	Total	Professional and Technical Workers		Managerial Officials		Clerical Workers		Sales Workers		Farmers, Lumbermen and Fishermen		Mining and Quarrying Workers		Transportation and Communication Workers		Craftsmen, Production Process Workers, and General Laborers		Service Workers		Unclassified	
			M	F	M	F	M	F	M	F	M	F	M	F	M	F	M	F	M	F	M	F
6.6	0.0	100.0	3.3	1.5	1.8	0.0	6.0	3.2	5.9	4.1	20.0	18.5	0.1	0.0	2.5	0.1	20.1	6.3	3.2	3.4	0.0	—
11.6	—	100.0	9.3	3.0	7.4	0.2	12.9	6.0	9.4	5.6	4.7	2.7	0.0	—	2.3	0.2	20.9	3.8	3.8	7.8	—	—
4.9	—	100.0	2.0	0.9	0.5	0.0	2.9	2.6	2.4	1.7	36.8	24.6	—	—	2.5	0.1	15.0	3.1	3.1	1.8	—	—
4.2	—	100.0	3.6	1.3	0.9	0.0	4.8	2.8	3.9	2.1	28.5	23.7	0.4	0.0	2.9	0.1	15.8	5.0	2.2	2.0	—	—
3.1	—	100.0	3.5	1.1	0.8	—	5.7	3.2	3.1	2.3	29.2	25.5	1.0	0.1	2.0	0.3	15.8	3.3	1.5	1.6	—	—
7.9	—	100.0	3.0	1.4	1.2	0.0	4.8	3.0	4.9	3.1	27.7	11.7	1.0	0.1	3.6	—	20.4	6.2	4.7	3.2	—	—
10.7	—	100.0	4.1	1.3	1.4	0.1	6.4	3.5	5.6	3.2	17.6	10.4	1.3	0.0	2.7	0.1	24.8	6.8	3.9	6.8	—	—
6.4	0.0	100.0	3.0	1.5	1.8	0.0	4.8	2.6	7.7	4.5	20.3	15.3	0.6	0.0	2.5	0.1	20.6	8.3	2.9	3.5	0.0	—
1.9	—	100.0	2.1	1.0	0.4	—	2.9	1.4	2.7	1.5	37.6	36.1	0.0	—	1.4	—	8.7	2.3	1.1	0.8	—	—
3.0	—	100.0	2.0	1.1	0.5	0.1	3.2	1.5	3.1	2.3	32.5	31.4	0.2	—	1.4	0.0	13.7	4.0	1.6	1.4	—	—
0.9	—	100.0	1.4	0.7	0.5	0.0	1.6	0.5	2.0	1.6	38.0	45.3	0.0	—	0.4	—	5.9	1.2	0.5	0.4	—	—
2.8	—	100.0	2.4	1.1	0.7	0.0	5.1	1.6	4.9	3.0	25.7	30.9	—	—	1.9	—	16.9	3.0	1.6	1.2	—	—
3.7	—	100.0	3.1	1.2	1.2	0.0	5.5	2.5	6.7	3.6	23.0	26.0	0.0	—	1.5	0.1	18.2	3.7	1.7	2.0	—	—
2.5	—	100.0	1.9	1.1	0.7	0.0	2.3	0.7	4.7	3.1	33.3	35.2	—	—	0.9	0.1	9.0	4.5	1.1	1.4	—	—
3.4	—	100.0	2.5	1.8	1.1	0.0	5.7	2.3	5.5	3.7	24.6	26.3	—	—	2.7	0.1	16.6	3.7	1.6	1.8	—	—
3.6	—	100.0	2.2	1.3	1.2	0.0	3.3	1.6	6.0	3.9	27.3	28.0	—	—	1.3	0.0	13.5	6.8	1.2	2.4	—	—
1.5	—	100.0	1.3	0.9	0.4	—	1.5	0.4	3.3	2.4	39.0	43.0	—	—	0.4	0.0	4.5	1.4	0.6	0.9	—	—
2.4	—	100.0	2.0	1.0	0.7	0.0	2.9	1.1	6.1	4.2	31.3	35.9	—	—	1.2	0.1	8.7	2.4	0.8	1.6	—	—
1.2	—	100.0	1.5	0.6	0.4	—	2.3	0.5	2.8	2.2	39.0	42.0	—	—	0.6	0.1	5.3	1.5	0.4	0.8	—	—
1.0	—	100.0	1.3	0.7	0.2	—	2.2	0.5	2.7	2.0	39.1	44.0	—	—	0.4	—	5.0	0.9	0.4	0.6	—	—
1.6	—	100.0	1.9	0.7	0.5	0.1	3.9	1.4	4.3	4.1	31.5	38.8	0.0	0.0	1.4	0.0	8.0	1.8	0.8	0.8	—	—
3.4	—	100.0	2.5	1.3	0.9	0.0	4.4	1.8	6.1	4.9	28.0	31.2	—	—	1.2	0.1	11.4	2.8	1.3	2.1	—	—
1.9	—	100.0	1.7	0.6	0.5	—	3.3	1.3	3.1	3.7	34.2	39.2	—	—	0.8	0.0	8.4	1.3	1.2	0.7	—	—
0.7	—	100.0	1.1	0.5	0.4	—	1.7	0.7	1.8	5.5	40.2	42.5	—	—	0.2	—	4.0	0.7	0.3	0.4	—	—
3.3	0.0	100.0	3.3	1.9	1.3	0.0	5.8	2.8	4.2	4.1	28.4	31.0	0.0	—	1.9	0.1	9.8	2.1	1.4	1.9	0.0	0.0
1.0	—	100.0	1.4	0.7	0.6	0.0	2.0	1.0	1.6	1.5	41.1	43.8	—	—	0.7	0.1	3.9	0.6	0.6	0.4	—	—
0.9	—	100.0	1.5	0.7	0.5	—	2.0	1.2	1.6	1.5	38.0	46.3	—	—	0.8	—	4.4	0.6	0.4	0.5	—	—
2.3	—	100.0	2.2	1.4	1.0	0.1	2.2	1.0	3.6	2.9	36.8	39.0	—	—	0.5	0.0	5.4	1.6	0.7	1.6	—	—
2.0	—	100.0	2.3	1.2	0.7	—	2.6	1.1	2.4	2.1	36.2	40.0	0.0	—	1.1	—	6.8	1.5	1.0	1.0	—	—
1.8	—	100.0	2.3	1.1	0.9	0.0	3.1	1.4	2.8	2.3	34.3	39.8	0.0	—	1.0	0.0	7.7	1.5	0.9	0.9	—	—
2.8	—	100.0	1.7	0.7	0.7	0.0	1.9	0.9	5.3	4.0	39.2	31.4	0.1	—	1.2	0.1	7.7	2.3	1.0	1.8	—	—
3.9	—	100.0	2.6	1.6	0.9	0.1	3.2	1.8	5.7	4.3	29.5	30.3	0.1	0.1	1.7	—	11.7	2.5	1.3	2.6	—	—
4.1	0.0	100.0	3.1	1.3	1.6	0.0	4.6	2.1	5.1	3.6	28.3	29.2	0.1	0.0	1.5	0.1	12.1	3.2	1.6	2.5	—	0.0
20.3	—	100.0	4.6	2.4	2.1	0.1	8.1	4.7	7.4	5.8	4.2	2.7	0.0	—	3.8	0.2	29.2	4.4	12.7	7.6	—	—
11.6	—	100.0	7.9	2.5	6.6	0.1	13.9	6.7	8.5	5.4	2.8	1.2	0.0	—	2.7	0.3	18.1	11.7	5.0	6.6	—	—
11.5	—	100.0	6.0	1.8	6.0	0.2	9.9	4.5	6.7	4.3	10.3	9.2	—	—	2.2	0.1	24.6	2.7	4.5	7.0	—	—
6.4	—	100.0	5.2	1.9	3.8	0.1	10.9	4.7	7.3	4.0	13.6	9.4	0.1	—	2.7	0.1	23.9	5.9	3.0	3.4	—	—
8.6	0.0	100.0	6.7	2.3	5.6	0.1	11.2	4.9	8.9	5.3	12.0	8.0	0.0	0.0	2.3	0.1	19.4	4.6	4.0	4.6	0.0	—
2.9	—	100.0	2.2	0.8	2.1	0.0	2.8	1.6	3.1	2.3	27.6	19.4	1.0	—	1.2	0.1	18.1	14.8	1.4	1.5	—	—
4.9	—	100.0	3.7	1.3	1.4	0.1	4.9	2.7	5.1	3.3	30.4	24.1	0.4	0.0	2.1	0.2	12.6	2.8	2.2	2.7	—	—
3.9	—	100.0	3.4	1.2	1.2	0.1	6.8	3.2	4.5	3.2	24.6	17.4	0.6	0.0	2.7	0.1	22.7	4.4	1.9	2.0	—	—
7.2	—	100.0	3.1	1.3	3.3	0.1	5.5	3.2	6.9	3.5	13.9	5.2	0.8	0.0	2.5	0.2	25.6	17.7	3.1	4.1	—	—
2.7	—	100.0	2.1	0.9	0.7	0.0	2.9	1.4	4.5	2.8	32.2	33.9	0.1	0.1	1.1	0.0	11.4	3.2	1.3	1.4	—	—
0.9	—	100.0	1.8	0.6	0.4	0.0	2.1	0.8	1.8	1.3	37.3	44.0	—	—	0.5	—	7.3	1.2	0.3	0.6	—	—
3.0	—	100.0	3.3	3.4	1.0	0.1	3.1	1.5	3.3	2.2	31.1	30.7	0.0	—	0.9	0.1	11.2	5.1	1.2	1.8	—	—
4.2	—	100.0	3.5	1.5	1.2	0.1	5.3	2.3	7.0	3.8	21.9	24.2	0.0	—	2.0	0.0	16.5	6.5	1.6	2.6	—	—
1.4	—	100.0	1.7	0.8	0.4	—	2.7	0.9	4.5	2.6	35.1	37.5	0.0	—	1.2	0.1	7.8	3.3	0.6	0.8	—	—
2.1	—	100.0	2.1	0.7	0.8	0.0	3.3	1.2	4.7	3.3	31.5	33.9	—	—	1.8	—	12.1	2.5	1.0	1.1	—	—
3.9	—	100.0	2.6	1.1	1.0	0.1	4.6	2.3	6.5	5.3	24.0	28.6	—	—	1.6	0.1	15.2	3.1	1.8	2.1	—	—

Table 12. Gainfully Employed Population, 15 Years and Older, by Occupation and Sex
(For 1950 only, 14-year-olds are included)

(Zone)	(Sector)	District	Total			Total	Professional and Technical Workers	Managerial Officials	Clerical Workers	Sales Workers	Farmers, Lumbermen and Fishermen	Mining and Quarrying Workers	Transportation and Communication Workers	Craftsmen, Production Process Workers, and General Laborers
			Total	M	F									
V		Goka-mura	(4,896) 100.0	49.7	50.3	100.0	1.3	0.4	2.1	3.2	85.9	—	0.3	6.3
VI		Sakai-machi	(11,709) 100.0	52.3	47.3	100.0	3.0	0.7	3.5	8.0	72.3	—	0.9	8.6
		Sashima-machi	(8,075) 100.0	49.7	50.3	100.0	2.2	0.3	1.5	5.3	83.7	—	0.4	5.3
		Yatabe-machi	(11,795) 100.0	52.6	47.4	100.0	2.9	0.5	2.7	5.4	80.6	—	0.6	5.7
VII		Kukizaki-mura	(3,607) 100.0	50.9	49.1	100.0	1.2	0.3	1.7	4.4	86.3	—	0.6	5.0
		Ushiku-machi	(7,796) 100.0	53.5	46.5	100.0	2.7	0.7	3.9	7.7	72.9	—	1.0	9.4
		Kawachi-mura	(7,321) 100.0	50.0	50.0	100.0	2.0	0.3	2.1	5.2	83.7	—	0.6	4.6
		Sakae-machi	(5,240) 100.0	52.0	48.0	100.0	2.5	0.6	3.9	10.7	71.6	—	1.0	7.4
		Narita-shi	(21,247) 100.0	54.8	45.2	100.0	4.7	1.1	7.1	10.5	57.7	—	2.1	11.1
VIII		Shisui-machi	(2,957) 100.0	55.1	44.9	100.0	2.2	1.2	7.1	6.5	64.9	—	3.0	13.1
		Yachimata-machi	(12,306) 100.0	54.4	45.6	100.0	2.7	1.1	3.2	9.0	69.4	—	1.0	10.1
		Toke-machi	(3,140) 100.0	54.9	45.1	100.0	2.1	0.8	5.2	5.3	71.7	—	1.4	11.9
IX		Nagara-machi	(4,558) 100.0	52.0	48.0	100.0	2.8	0.5	3.0	2.7	82.7	0.1	0.4	6.9
		Obitsu-mura	(3,694) 100.0	52.8	47.2	100.0	2.6	0.7	3.6	4.1	77.5	0.2	1.0	8.8
X		Koito-machi	(3,453) 100.0	52.4	47.6	100.0	2.8	0.7	2.6	3.8	81.6	—	1.0	5.9
		Zone 10 Total	(407,552) 100.0	63.1	36.9	100.0	5.4	2.3	9.4	10.2	39.1	0.1	2.3	22.4
		Total for 50 km. Region	(5,553,760) 100.0	68.5	31.5	100.0	6.7	4.3	14.5	14.4	15.0	0.0	2.9	32.4
		National Total	(39,261,351)100.0	60.9	39.1	100.0	4.9	2.1	8.7	10.7	40.3	0.9	2.2	24.1
		1960												
1	I	Chiyoda-ku	(69,274) 100.0	67.4	32.6	100.0	5.7	7.5	14.2	24.7	0.0	0.0	3.1	24.9
		Minato-ku	(137,730) 100.0	67.2	32.8	100.0	7.1	7.0	18.1	15.8	0.0	0.1	3.9	30.8
		Chūō-ku	(98,275) 100.0	66.9	33.1	100.0	3.2	5.5	12.6	28.1	0.1	—	3.7	26.1
		Bunkyō-ku	(127,409) 100.0	67.1	32.9	100.0	8.9	5.9	19.4	16.5	0.1	0.0	3.3	33.4
		Taitō-ku	(180,977) 100.0	67.0	33.0	100.0	3.8	4.6	10.2	23.6	0.1	—	2.5	39.4
		Zone 1 Total	(613,665) 100.0	67.1	32.8	100.0	5.7	5.9	14.7	21.2	0.1	0.0	3.2	32.5
2	I	Shinagawa-ku	(217,787) 100.0	68.6	31.4	100.0	5.9	4.3	17.9	13.8	0.4	0.0	4.1	42.6
	II	Meguro-ku	(136,644) 100.0	69.8	30.2	100.0	9.7	6.8	22.4	13.6	0.4	0.0	3.7	32.7
		Shibuya-ku	(131,532) 100.0	66.9	33.1	100.0	9.5	6.4	22.4	15.3	0.2	0.0	4.0	27.1
	III	Shinjuku-ku	(203,650) 100.0	66.5	33.5	100.0	9.3	5.4	20.6	15.8	0.1	0.0	3.6	28.4
		Nakano-ku	(154,561) 100.0	70.3	29.7	100.0	10.6	5.5	25.4	16.0	0.4	0.0	4.1	27.3
	IV	Toshima-ku	(174,821) 100.0	67.4	32.6	100.0	8.0	4.3	21.1	16.8	0.2	0.0	4.1	32.7
	V	Kita-ku	(198,531) 100.0	68.9	31.1	100.0	5.9	3.2	20.1	14.7	0.1	0.0	4.6	41.7
	VI	Arakawa-ku	(143,198) 100.0	71.3	28.7	100.0	2.8	3.2	10.7	15.0	0.1	0.0	4.3	55.6
	VII	Sumida-ku	(179,633) 100.0	69.0	31.0	100.0	2.6	3.7	9.4	14.7	0.1	0.0	3.5	56.7
	VIII	Kōtō-ku	(178,054) 100.0	74.6	25.4	100.0	2.7	3.3	11.0	13.5	0.1	0.0	6.9	56.7
		Zone 2 Total	(1,718,411) 100.0	69.3	30.7	100.0	6.8	4.5	17.9	14.9	0.2	0.0	4.3	40.1
3	I	Ōta-ku	(339,235) 100.0	72.6	27.4	100.0	6.4	5.2	18.2	12.2	1.1	0.0	3.9	44.2
	II	Setagaya-ku	(276,260) 100.0	70.2	29.8	100.0	12.3	7.0	25.9	14.0	1.5	0.0	3.8	25.9
	III	Suginami-ku	(205,245) 100.0	72.2	27.8	100.0	12.4	7.2	28.4	15.8	0.8	0.4	3.3	22.0
	IV	Itabashi-ku	(185,875) 100.0	71.8	28.2	100.0	5.2	3.5	18.2	13.0	1.2	0.0	4.7	46.2
		Nerima-ku	(125,279) 100.0	72.4	27.6	100.0	11.5	4.8	23.2	13.6	3.7	0.0	4.5	28.2
	VI	Adachi-ku	(187,104) 100.0	70.2	29.8	100.0	3.5	2.2	12.4	13.1	3.4	0.0	4.9	53.6
	VII	Katsushika-ku	(175,271) 100.0	69.5	30.5	100.0	4.4	3.1	14.0	12.9	1.6	0.0	4.2	52.2
	VIII	Edogawa-ku	(147,290) 100.0	70.8	29.2	100.0	4.1	3.0	14.1	12.6	4.6	0.0	4.7	49.3
		Urayasu-machi	(7,418) 100.0	67.1	32.9	100.0	1.9	1.0	5.1	22.3	30.6	0.0	2.6	31.9
		Zone 3 Total	(1,648,977) 100.0	71.0	29.0	100.0	7.7	4.8	19.6	13.4	2.1	0.0	4.1	39.7

Table 12. Gainfully Employed Population, 15 Years and Older, by Occupation and Sex

(For 1950 only, 14-year-olds are included)

Service Workers	Unclassified	Total	Professional and Technical Workers M	F	Managerial Officials M	F	Clerical Workers M	F	Sales Workers M	F	Farmers, Lumbermen and Fishermen M	F	Mining and Quarrying Workers M	F	Transportation and Communication Workers M	F	Craftsmen, Production Process Workers, and General Laborers M	F	Service Workers M	F	Unclassified M	F
0.5	–	100.0	0.9	0.4	0.4	–	1.6	0.5	1.8	1.4	39.3	46.6	–	–	0.3	–	5.1	1.2	0.3	0.2	–	–
3.0	–	100.0	1.9	1.1	0.7	0.0	2.5	1.0	4.8	3.2	33.6	38.7	–	–	0.8	0.1	6.8	1.8	1.2	1.8	–	–
1.3	–	100.0	1.3	0.9	0.3	0.0	1.1	0.4	2.7	2.6	39.3	44.4	–	–	0.3	0.1	4.2	1.1	0.5	0.8	–	–
1.6	–	1 0.0	2.0	0.9	0.5	0.0	1.9	0.8	3.1	2.3	39.2	41.4	–	–	0.6	0.0	4.7	1.0	0.6	1.0	–	–
0.5	–	100.0	0.9	0.3	0.3	–	1.4	0.3	2.2	2.2	41.1	45.2	–	–	0.6	–	4.1	0.9	0.3	0.2	–	–
1.7	–	100.0	2.0	0.7	0.7	–	2.9	1.0	3.7	4.0	34.7	38.2	–	–	1.0	0.0	7.7	1.7	0.8	0.9	–	–
1.5	–	100.0	1.2	0.8	0.3	–	1.6	0.5	2.5	2.7	39.2	44.5	–	–	0.6	0.0	4.1	0.5	0.5	1.0	–	–
2.3	–	100.0	1.6	0.9	0.6	0.0	2.6	1.3	4.5	6.2	34.9	36.7	–	–	1.0	–	6.1	1.3	0.7	1.6	–	–
5.7	–	100.0	3.0	1.7	1.0	0.1	4.8	2.3	5.4	5.1	27.5	30.2	–	–	2.1	0.0	9.1	2.0	1.9	3.8	–	–
2.0	–	100.0	1.5	0.7	1.1	0.1	4.7	2.4	3.4	3.1	29.7	35.2	–	–	2.8	0.2	10.8	2.3	1.1	0.9	–	–
3.5	–	100.0	1.6	1.1	1.0	0.1	2.1	1.1	5.3	3.7	34.5	34.9	–	–	1.0	0.0	7.9	2.2	1.0	2.5	–	–
1.6	–	100.0	1.6	0.5	0.8	–	3.7	1.5	2.9	2.4	35.0	36.7	–	–	1.3	0.1	8.9	3.0	0.7	0.9	–	–
0.9	–	100.0	1.8	1.0	0.5	–	2.2	0.8	1.4	1.3	40.1	42.6	0.1	–	0.4	0.0	5.1	1.8	0.4	0.5	–	–
1.5	–	100.0	1.7	0.9	0.7	–	3.0	0.6	2.5	1.6	36.1	41.4	0.2	0.0	0.9	0.1	7.2	1.6	0.5	1.0	–	–
1.6	–	100.0	2.1	0.7	0.7	–	1.8	0.8	1.9	1.9	39.6	42.0	–	–	1.0	0.0	4.7	1.2	0.6	1.0	–	–
8.8	0.0	100.0	3.8	1.6	2.2	0.1	6.3	3.1	6.0	4.2	19.9	19.2	0.1	0.0	2.2	0.1	17.9	4.5	4.7	4.1	0.0	–
9.8	0.0	100.0	4.8	1.9	4.1	0.2	9.2	5.3	9.7	4.7	7.7	7.3	0.0	0.0	2.8	0.1	26.1	6.3	4.1	5.7	0.0	0.0
6.1	0.0	100.0	3.3	1.6	2.1	0.0	5.7	3.0	6.5	4.2	20.2	20.1	0.8	0.1	2.1	0.1	17.8	6.3	2.4	3.7	0.0	0.0
19.9	0.0	100.0	3.0	2.7	6.8	0.7	7.6	6.6	19.3	5.4	0.0	0.0	0.0	–	2.9	0.2	20.2	4.7	7.6	12.3	0.0	0.0
17.2	0.0	100.0	4.5	2.6	6.5	0.5	10.4	7.7	10.9	4.9	0.0	0.0	0.1	–	3.5	0.4	25.6	5.2	5.7	11.5	0.0	0.0
20.7	0.0	100.0	1.8	1.4	4.8	0.7	6.3	6.3	22.3	5.8	0.1	0.0	0.0	0.0	3.4	0.3	21.3	4.8	6.9	13.8	0.0	0.0
12.5	0.0	100.0	6.0	2.9	5.6	0.3	11.3	8.1	11.7	4.8	0.1	0.0	0.0	0.0	2.9	0.4	25.4	8.0	4.1	8.4	0.0	0.0
15.8	0.0	100.0	2.4	1.4	4.2	0.4	4.8	5.4	17.1	6.5	0.1	0.0	0.0	–	2.3	0.2	31.0	8.4	5.1	10.7	0.0	0.0
16.7	0.0	100.0	3.6	2.1	5.4	0.5	7.9	6.8	15.7	5.5	0.1	0.0	0.0	0.0	2.9	0.3	25.9	6.6	5.6	11.1	0.0	0.0
11.0	0.0	100.0	4.1	1.8	4.1	0.2	10.1	7.8	9.1	4.7	0.4	0.0	0.0	–	3.6	0.5	33.2	9.4	4.0	7.0	0.0	0.0
10.7	0.0	100.0	7.2	2.5	6.6	0.2	13.7	8.7	9.2	4.4	0.3	0.1	0.0	–	3.2	0.5	25.5	7.2	4.1	6.6	0.0	0.0
15.1	0.0	100.0	6.5	3.0	6.1	0.3	13.7	8.7	10.4	4.9	0.2	0.0	0.0	–	3.4	0.6	21.	5.5	5.0	10.1	0.0	0.0
16.8	0.0	100.0	6.1	3.2	5.1	0.3	12.2	8.4	10.8	5.0	0.1	0.0	0.0	–	3.1	0.5	22.4	6.0	6.7	10.1	0.0	0.0
10.7	0.0	100.0	7.8	2.8	5.4	0.1	15.8	9.6	11.1	4.9	0.3	0.1	0.0	0.0	3.5	0.6	21.7	5.6	4.7	6.0	0.0	0.0
12.8	–	100.0	5.7	2.3	4.1	0.2	12.3	8.8	11.4	5.4	0.1	0.1	0.0	0.0	3.5	0.6	25.4	7.3	4.7	8.1	0.0	0.0
9.7	–	100.0	4.2	1.7	3.1	0.1	11.5	8.6	9.8	4.9	0.1	0.0	0.0	0.0	4.0	0.6	31.9	9.8	4.3	5.4	0.0	0.0
8.3	0.0	100.0	1.8	1.0	3.0	0.2	5.4	5.3	10.3	4.7	0.1	0.0	0.0	0.0	3.8	0.5	43.7	11.9	3.2	5.1	0.0	0.0
9.3	0.0	100.0	1.6	1.0	3.6	0.1	4.4	5.0	10.2	4.5	0.1	0.0	0.0	–	3.2	0.3	42.6	14.1	3.3	6.0	0.0	0.0
5.8	0.0	100 0	1.8	0.9	3.1	0.2	5.9	5.1	9.3	4.2	0.1	0.0	0.0	–	6.5	0.4	44.9	11.8	3.0	2.8	0.0	0.0
11.3	0.0	100.0	4.6	2.2	4.3	0.2	10.4	7.5	10.1	4.8	0.2	0.0	0.0	0.0	3.8	0.5	31.4	8.7	4.3	7.0	0.0	0.0
8.8	0.0	100.0	4.7	1.7	5.0	0.2	11.1	7.1	8.1	4.1	0.9	0.2	0.0	0.0	3.4	0.5	36.2	8.0	3.2	5.6	0.0	0.0
9.6	0.0	100.0	9.2	3.1	6.8	0.2	16.7	9.2	9.4	4.6	1.1	0.4	0.0	–	3.2	0.6	20.2	5.7	3.6	6.0	0.0	0.0
9.7	0.0	100.0	9.3	3.1	7.1	0.1	18.8	9.6	10.9	4.9	0.7	0.1	0.4	0.0	2.8	0.5	18.6	3.4	3.6	6.1	0.0	0.0
8.0	0.0	100.0	4.4	0.8	3.4	0.1	11.0	7.2	8.7	4.3	0.7	0.5	0.0	–	4.2	0.5	35.7	10.5	3.7	4.3	0.0	0.0
10.5	0.0	100.0	8.6	2.9	4.7	0.1	15.3	7.9	9.4	4.2	2.4	1.3	0.0	–	3.8	0.7	22.2	6.0	6.0	4.5	0.0	0.0
6.9	0.0	100.0	2.4	1.1	2.1	0.1	6.9	5.5	8.6	4.5	1.8	1.6	0.0	0.0	4.3	0.6	40.9	32.7	3.2	3.7	0.0	0.0
7.5	0.1	100.0	3.0	1.4	3.0	0.1	8.0	6.0	8.4	4.5	0.9	0.7	0.0	–	3.7	0.5	39.1	13.1	3.4	4.1	0.0	0.1
7.6	0.0	100.0	2.8	1.3	2.9	0.1	7.8	6.3	8.3	4.3	2.9	1.7	0.0	–	4.1	0.6	38.8	10.5	3.2	4.4	0.0	0.0
4.6	0.0	100.0	1.0	0.9	0.9	0.1	2.3	2.8	15.2	7.1	24.2	6.4	0.0	–	2.4	0.2	19.4	12.5	1.7	2.9	0.0	–
8.6	0.0	100.0	5.6	2.1	4.6	0.2	12.2	7.4	9.0	4.4	1.4	0.7	0.0	0.0	3.6	0.5	31.0	8.7	3.6	5.0	0.0	0.0

Table 12. Gainfully Employed Population, 15 Years and Older, by Occupation and Sex
(For 1950 only, 14-year-olds are included)

(Zone)	(Sector)	District	Total			Total	Professional and Technical Workers	Managerial Officials	Clerical Workers	Sales Workers	Farmers, Lumbermen and Fishermen	Mining and Quarrying Workers	Transportation and Communication Workers	Craftsmen, Production Process Workers, and General Laborers
			Total	M	F									
4	I	Kawasaki-shi	(294,231) 100.0	73.4	26.6	100.0	5.4	2.1	15.2	9.6	3.4	0.0	4.6	52.4
	II	Komae-machi	(10,295) 100.0	71.6	28.4	100.0	13.4	4.3	23.3	11.1	6.7	0.0	3.9	29.9
	III	Mitaka-shi	(40,917) 100.0	71.9	28.1	100.0	11.7	4.8	24.7	12.8	3.8	0.0	4.0	31.1
		Musashino-shi	(51,150) 100.0	70.9	29.1	100.0	14.0	6.2	29.3	14.7	1.1	0.0	3.3	22.1
		Chōfu-shi	(27,986) 100.0	72.2	27.8	100.0	10.1	3.3	20.0	12.0	6.5	0.1	6.7	33.3
		Hoya-machi	(18,804) 100.0	72.9	27.1	100.0	13.1	3.8	24.4	12.8	5.0	0.0	4.9	28.6
	IV	Yamato-machi	(7,386) 100.0	68.9	31.1	100.0	5.4	1.9	13.2	9.3	15.8	0.0	5.1	41.6
		Toda-machi	(14,593) 100.0	69.6	30.4	100.0	3.3	2.1	11.3	8.8	13.9	0.2	4.1	52.3
	V	Warabi-shi	(22,488) 100.0	69.3	30.7	100.0	4.7	2.5	18.6	14.2	1.7	0.1	4.1	46.9
		Kawaguchi-shi	(78,835) 100.0	70.7	29.3	100.0	3.2	3.3	12.6	10.9	7.0	0.0	3.8	53.7
		Hatogaya-machi	(8,821) 100.0	71.7	28.3	100.0	6.3	2.4	15.5	13.0	8.5	0.0	5.4	44.5
	VI	Sōka-shi	(18,425) 100.0	63.5	36.5	100.0	3.2	2.1	9.3	10.3	25.1	0.0	4.1	41.6
		Yashio-mura	(6,717) 100.0	58.3	41.7	100.0	1.5	1.0	3.8	5.1	47.7	0.0	3.2	36.3
		Misato-mura	(9,077) 100.0	56.2	43.8	100.0	1.6	0.6	3.8	5.9	57.9	0.3	3.4	25.1
		Matsudo-shi	(38,242) 100.0	66.6	33.4	100.0	6.2	2.8	16.2	11.7	21.4	0.2	4.8	29.5
	VII	Ichikawa-shi	(68,918) 100.0	67.4	32.6	100.0	7.4	5.9	19.5	14.0	10.6	0.0	3.1	32.2
		Zone 4 Total	(716,885) 100.0	70.9	29.1	100.0	6.7	3.2	17.1	11.1	7.5	0.1	4.3	43.0
5	I	Tsurumi-ku	(105,907) 100.0	74.3	25.7	100.0	5.3	3.1	16.0	10.5	1.2	0.0	5.0	52.0
	III	Koganei-shi	(18,550) 100.0	70.7	29.3	100.0	14.0	4.9	26.4	12.2	5.0	0.0	3.9	26.6
		Tanashi-machi	(12,913) 100.0	70.2	29.8	100.0	9.6	3.0	21.0	13.2	5.0	0.0	4.4	34.3
		Kurume-machi	(8,056) 100.0	69.9	30.1	100.0	12.5	3.1	21.4	9.3	21.7	—	4.4	22.9
	IV	Nīza-machi	(6,681) 100.0	63.3	36.8	100.0	3.7	1.5	8.6	7.1	41.2	—	3.7	30.4
		Kiyose-machi	(7,464) 100.0	59.0	41.0	100.0	19.8	1.5	16.6	10.5	17.3	—	3.9	23.1
		Adachi-machi	(5,537) 100.0	64.8	35.2	100.0	4.8	1.9	12.6	13.6	23.5	0.1	3.6	34.8
		Asaka-machi	(11,644) 100.0	73.9	26.1	100.0	3.8	1.9	11.3	8.4	17.4	0.0	3.9	31.9
	V	Urawa-shi	(72,558) 100.0	67.9	32.1	100.0	9.1	5.1	24.0	13.7	9.6	0.0	3.1	28.3
		Misono-mura	(4,720) 100.0	54.8	45.2	100.0	2.3	0.5	4.1	4.7	71.5	0.1	2.0	13.7
		Koshigaya-shi	(23,468) 100.0	59.5	40.5	100.0	2.9	1.1	6.8	8.3	44.4	0.0	3.0	30.6
	VI	Yoshikawa-machi	(8,757) 100.0	52.7	47.3	100.0	2.0	0.6	3.6	7.2	60.0	0.0	2.4	21.6
		Nagareyama-machi	(11,849) 100.0	61.8	38.2	100.0	5.3	2.1	13.3	9.6	35.9	0.1	3.9	26.1
	VII	Kamagaya-machi	(6,255) 100.0	64.8	35.2	100.0	2.8	1.3	9.4	7.8	43.8	—	3.6	23.3
	VIII	Funahashi-shi	(60,728) 100.0	67.0	33.0	100.0	5.7	3.0	15.3	13.5	17.4	0.0	4.0	31.2
		Zone 5 Total	(365,087) 100.0	68.4	31.6	100.0	6.8	3.2	16.7	11.3	15.2	0.0	4.0	35.4
6	I	Nishi-ku	(46,964) 100.0	70.9	29.1	100.0	5.2	4.1	18.3	14.0	0.0	—	7.2	41.4
		Naka-ku	(58,862) 100.0	67.5	32.5	100.0	6.5	4.9	17.4	17.4	1.0	0.0	6.5	28.8
		Kanagawa-ku	(74,662) 100.0	72.9	27.1	100.0	6.7	4.0	19.0	12.9	2.5	0.0	5.7	41.1
	II	Kōhoku-ku	(63,677) 100.0	69.5	30.5	100.0	8.0	3.8	18.6	8.8	19.3	0.0	4.0	31.5
		Inagi-machi	(4,924) 100.0	67.0	33.0	100.0	3.8	1.3	9.4	7.0	30.6	0.4	4.8	38.0
	III	Tama-mura	(4,165) 100.0	62.4	37.6	100.0	8.5	1.2	10.5	5.1	28.7	0.1	5.6	31.7
		Fuchu-shi	(32,580) 100.0	71.3	28.7	100.0	8.6	2.5	20.4	11.1	9.0	0.2	4.9	33.0
		Kunitachi-machi	(12,949) 100.0	71.4	28.6	100.0	12.7	3.7	27.5	12.1	5.2	0.1	4.4	25.5
		Kokubunji-machi	(16,333) 100.0	73.6	26.4	100.0	11.9	3.7	25.4	10.6	6.6	—	6.0	27.6
		Kodaira-machi	(19,876) 100.0	71.9	28.1	100.0	10.6	2.7	21.6	9.7	8.9	0.0	4.6	30.1
		Higashimurayama-machi	(16,793) 100.0	71.4	28.6	100.0	10.6	2.4	21.5	9.9	9.3	—	5.5	33.7
	IV	Tokorosawa-shi	(29,757) 100.0	65.1	34.9	100.0	5.0	1.6	13.9	10.4	26.1	0.0	4.2	33.4
		Miyoshi-mura	(2,360) 100.0	54.8	45.2	100.0	1.3	0.5	3.1	3.7	74.5	—	1.2	14.7
		Fujimi-mura	(6,091) 100.0	57.8	42.2	100.0	3.3	0.9	7.2	6.1	54.4	—	2.0	24.3
	V	Yono-shi	(17,379) 100.0	69.5	30.5	100.0	7.0	4.2	21.9	12.0	4.6	0.0	4.0	40.7
		Ōmiya-shi	(75,162) 100.0	66.1	33.9	100.0	5.5	2.6	18.0	11.7	14.6	0.0	3.8	36.2

Table 12. Gainfully Employed Population, 15 Years and Older, by Occupation and Sex
(For 1950 only, 14-year-olds are included)

Service Workers	Unclassified	Total	Professional and Technical Workers		Managerial Officials		Clerical Workers		Sales Workers		Farmers, Lumbermen and Fishermen		Mining and Quarrying Workers		Transportation and Communication Workers		Craftsmen, Production Process Workers, and General Laborers		Service Workers		Unclassified	
			M	F	M	F	M	F	M	F	M	F	M	F	M	F	M	F	M	F	M	F
7.3	0.0	100.0	3.9	1.5	2.0	0.1	9.5	5.7	5.8	3.8	2.1	1.3	0.0	0.0	4.1	0.5	42.8	9.6	3.2	4.1	0.0	0.0
7.4	0.0	100.0	9.8	3.6	4.2	0.1	15.1	8.2	6.8	4.3	4.2	2.5	0.0	-	3.5	0.4	24.3	5.6	3.7	3.7	0.0	-
7.1	0.0	100.0	8.8	2.9	4.6	0.2	16.2	8.5	8.7	4.1	2.4	1.4	0.0	0.0	3.3	0.7	24.7	6.4	3.2	3.9	0.0	0.0
9.3	0.0	100.0	10.4	3.6	6.0	0.2	19.8	9.5	9.7	5.0	0.8	0.3	0.0	0.0	2.7	0.6	17.8	4.3	3.7	5.6	0.0	0.0
8.0	0.0	100.0	7.6	2.5	3.2	0.1	12.9	7.1	8.1	3.9	4.4	2.1	0.1	-	6.1	0.6	25.8	7.5	4.0	4.0	0.0	0.0
7.4	0.0	100.0	10.0	3.1	3.7	0.1	16.5	7.9	8.8	4.0	3.0	2.0	0.0	-	4.1	0.8	22.6	6.0	4.2	3.2	0.0	0.0
7.7	-	100.0	3.0	2.4	1.9	0.0	8.0	5.2	6.2	3.1	8.4	7.4	0.0	-	4.7	0.4	32.4	9.2	4.3	3.4	-	-
3.9	0.1	100.0	2.3	1.0	2.1	0.0	6.7	4.6	5.6	3.2	6.4	7.5	0.2	-	3.7	0.4	40.7	11.6	1.9	2.0	0.0	0.1
7.2	0.0	100.0	3.4	1.3	2.5	0.0	11.2	7.4	8.9	5.3	1.1	0.6	0.1	-	3.6	0.5	35.4	11.5	3.1	4.1	-	0.0
5.5	0.0	100.0	2.1	1.1	3.1	0.2	6.7	5.9	6.9	4.0	3.7	3.3	0.0	0.0	3.4	0.4	42.7	11.0	2.1	3.4	0.0	0.0
4.4	0.0	100.0	4.6	1.7	2.3	0.1	9.4	6.1	9.0	4.0	4.7	3.8	0.0	-	4.4	1.0	35.2	9.3	2.1	2.3	0.0	0.0
4.3	0.0	100.0	2.2	1.0	2.1	0.0	5.3	4.0	6.6	3.7	11.9	13.2	0.0	-	3.9	0.2	29.8	11.8	1.7	2.6	0.0	-
1.4	0.0	100.0	0.9	0.6	1.0	-	1.9	1.9	3.1	2.0	20.7	27.0	0.0	-	2.9	0.3	27.2	9.1	0.6	0.8	-	0.0
1.4	0.0	100.0	1.1	0.5	0.6	-	2.1	1.7	3.3	2.6	26.2	31.7	0.3	0.0	3.2	0.2	18.8	6.3	0.6	0.8	-	0.0
7.2	0.0	100.0	4.4	1.8	2.7	0.1	10.1	6.1	7.3	4.4	10.5	10.9	0.2	0.0	4.2	0.6	23.1	6.4	4.1	3.1	0.0	0.0
7.3	0.0	100.0	5.0	2.4	5.7	0.2	12.4	7.1	9.6	4.4	5.8	4.8	0.0	-	2.7	0.4	23.5	8.7	2.7	4.6	0.0	0.0
7.0	0.0	100.0	4.8	1.9	3.1	0.1	10.7	6.4	7.1	4.0	4.0	3.5	0.1	0.0	3.8	0.5	34.3	8.7	3.0	4.0	0.0	0.0
6.9	0.0	100.0	3.8	1.5	3.0	0.1	9.6	6.4	6.3	4.2	0.8	0.4	0.0	0.0	4.5	0.5	43.6	8.4	2.7	4.2	0.0	0.0
7.0	0.0	100.0	10.3	3.7	4.8	0.1	17.0	9.4	7.9	4.3	3.1	1.9	0.0	-	3.2	0.7	21.0	5.6	3.4	3.6	0.0	0.0
9.5	0.0	100.0	7.2	2.4	3.0	0.0	13.4	7.6	8.4	4.8	2.9	2.1	0.0	-	3.7	0.7	26.1	8.2	5.5	4.0	-	
4.7	0.0	100.0	9.5	3.0	3.1	0.0	14.7	6.7	6.8	2.5	12.5	9.2	-	-	3.8	0.6	17.1	5.8	2.4	2.3	0.0	0.0
3.8	0.0	100.0	2.7	1.0	1.5	0.0	5.6	3.0	4.5	2.6	21.0	20.2	-	-	3.5	0.2	22.0	8.4	2.5	1.3	0.0	0.0
7.3	-	100.0	6.4	13.4	1.5	0.0	11.5	5.1	6.2	4.3	8.4	8.9	-	-	3.5	0.4	17.7	5.4	3.8	3.5	-	-
5.1	-	100.0	3.2	1.6	1.8	0.1	7.9	4.7	8.3	5.3	11.0	12.5	0.1	-	3.2	0.4	27.0	7.8	2.3	2.8	-	-
21.4	0.0	100.0	2.7	1.1	1.8	0.1	7.3	4.0	5.6	2.8	8.6	8.8	0.0	-	3.5	0.4	25.7	6.2	18.7	2.7	-	0.0
7.1	0.0	100.0	6.5	2.6	5.0	0.1	15.5	8.5	8.9	4.8	4.6	5.0	0.0	0.0	2.6	0.5	21.9	6.4	2.9	4.2	0.0	0.0
1.1	0.0	100.0	1.4	0.9	0.5	-	2.3	1.8	2.6	2.1	35.1	36.4	0.1	-	1.7	0.3	10.5	3.2	0.6	0.5	-	0.0
2.9	-	100.0	1.9	1.0	1.1	0.0	3.9	2.9	5.0	3.3	20.8	23.6	0.0	-	2.7	0.3	22.8	7.8	1.3	1.6	-	-
2.6	-	100.0	1.1	0.9	0.6	-	1.8	1.8	4.1	3.1	26.2	33.8	0.0	0.0	2.2	0.2	15.6	6.0	1.1	1.5	-	-
3.7	0.1	100.0	3.9	1.4	2.1	0.0	9.1	4.2	6.1	3.5	14.9	21.0	0.1	-	3.4	0.5	20.4	5.7	1.8	1.9	0.0	0.1
8.0	0.0	100.0	2.1	0.7	1.3	0.0	6.2	3.2	4.6	3.2	22.2	21.6	-	-	3.3	0.3	18.8	4.5	6.3	1.7	0.0	-
9.9	0.0	100.0	4.0	1.7	2.9	0.1	9.5	5.8	8.0	5.5	9.6	7.8	0.0	-	3.4	0.6	24.5	6.7	5.1	4.8	0.0	0.0
7.4	0.0	100.0	4.7	2.1	3.1	0.1	10.5	6.2	7.0	4.3	7.6	7.6	0.0	0.0	3.5	0.5	28.3	7.1	3.7	3.7	0.0	0.0
9.8	0.0	100.0	3.4	1.8	3.9	0.2	10.5	7.8	8.6	5.4	0.0	0.0	-	-	6.6	0.6	33.9	7.5	4.0	5.8	0.0	0.0
17.5	0.0	100.0	4.5	2.0	4.6	0.3	10.4	7.0	10.6	6.8	0.9	0.1	0.0	-	6.0	0.5	23.8	5.0	6.7	10.8	0.0	0.0
8.1	0.0	100.0	4.8	1.9	3.9	0.1	11.7	7.3	8.1	4.8	1.8	0.7	0.0	-	5.3	0.4	33.7	7.4	3.6	4.5	0.0	0.0
6.0	0.0	100.0	6.2	1.8	3.7	0.1	12.2	6.4	5.5	3.3	10.5	8.8	0.0	-	3.5	0.5	25.2	6.3	2.7	3.3	0.0	0.0
4.7	0.0	100.0	2.6	1.2	1.3	0.0	5.1	4.3	4.0	3.0	16.6	14.0	0.4	0.0	4.3	0.5	30.0	8.0	2.7	2.0	-	0.0
8.6	-	100.0	4.2	4.3	1.2	-	6.0	4.5	3.0	2.1	16.7	12.0	0.1	-	4.9	0.7	23.4	8.3	2.9	5.7	-	-
10.3	0.0	100.0	6.3	2.3	2.5	0.0	12.9	7.5	6.7	4.4	5.7	3.3	0.2	0.0	4.3	0.6	26.7	6.3	6.0	4.3	0.0	0.0
8.8	0.0	100.0	9.6	3.1	3.6	0.1	18.6	8.9	7.6	4.5	3.5	1.7	0.1	0.0	3.7	1.7	20.5	5.0	4.2	4.6	0.0	-
8.2	0.0	100.0	9.2	2.7	3.5	0.2	17.2	8.2	6.8	3.8	4.3	2.3	-	-	5.4	0.6	23.0	4.6	4.2	4.0	0.0	0.0
11.8	0.0	100.0	7.4	3.2	2.6	0.1	14.5	7.1	6.2	3.5	5.2	3.7	0.0	-	4.1	0.5	23.3	6.8	8.6	3.2	-	-
7.1	0.0	100.0	6.9	3.7	2.3	0.1	14.9	6.6	6.5	3.4	5.1	4.2	-	-	4.9	0.6	26.6	7.1	4.2	2.9	0.0	0.0
5.4	0.0	100.0	3.2	1.8	1.5	0.1	8.9	5.0	6.5	3.9	13.1	13.0	0.0	-	3.9	0.3	25.2	8.2	2.8	2.6	0.0	0.0
1.0	-	100.0	0.7	0.6	0.5	-	1.7	1.4	2.0	1.7	36.8	37.7	-	-	1.1	0.1	11.2	3.5	0.8	0.2	-	-
1.8	0.0	100.0	2.4	0.9	0.9	-	4.3	2.9	3.7	2.4	25.7	28.7	-	-	1.9	0.1	17.9	6.4	1.0	0.8	-	-
5.6	0.0	100.0	4.5	2.5	4.1	0.1	13.9	8.0	8.0	4.0	2.3	2.3	0.0	-	3.4	0.6	30.9	9.8	2.4	3.2	-	0.0
7.6	0.0	100.0	3.7	1.8	2.5	0.1	11.2	6.8	7.0	4.7	6.5	8.1	0.0	-	3.3	0.5	28.0	8.2	3.9	3.7	0.0	0.0

Table 12. Gainfully Employed Population, 15 Years and Older, by Occupation and Sex
(For 1950 only, 14-year-olds are included)

(Zone) (Sector)	District	Total			Total	Professional and Technical Workers	Managerial Officials	Clerical Workers	Sales Workers	Farmers, Lumbermen and Fishermen	Mining and Quarrying Workers	Transportation and Communication Workers	Craftsmen, Production Process Workers, and General Laborers
		Total	M	F									
V	Iwatsuki-shi	(16,938) 100.0	58.4	41.6	100.0	3.2	0.9	7.2	8.3	44.9	0.0	2.5	30.2
VI	Matsubushi-mura	(4,813) 100.0	52.4	47.6	100.0	2.1	0.6	3.4	4.9	62.6	—	2.6	22.5
VII	Kashiwa-shi	(27,906) 100.0	64.4	35.6	100.0	6.1	2.6	16.2	10.3	29.4	0.0	4.7	25.0
	Shōnan-mura	(6,876) 100.0	57.9	42.1	100.0	1.0	0.4	2.1	4.9	64.6	—	1.4	10.4
	Shirai-mura	(4,566) 100.0	52.3	47.7	100.0	1.8	0.4	2.0	5.1	80.3	—	1.4	7.6
VIII	Narashino-shi	(16,959) 100.0	67.4	32.6	100.0	7.1	2.8	19.2	11.4	12.1	0.0	5.6	34.9
	Zone 6 Total	(560,592) 100.0	68.2	31.8	100.0	6.8	3.2	17.7	11.5	14.1	0.0	4.9	33.3
7 I	Isogo-ku	(31,488) 100.0	70.4	29.6	100.0	6.8	4.6	21.5	12.5	2.7	0.0	7.2	35.8
	Minami-ku	(85,031) 100.0	70.1	29.9	100.0	5.6	3.4	16.6	13.9	2.4	0.0	6.2	42.0
	Hodogaya-ku	(59,815) 100.0	73.0	27.0	100.0	7.2	3.2	20.5	10.2	5.4	0.0	5.9	40.9
II	Machida-shi	(29,834) 100.0	67.9	32.1	100.0	7.4	2.5	15.4	10.9	21.1	0.0	4.2	32.0
III	Yuki-mura	(3,191) 100.0	58.0	42.0	100.0	2.2	0.3	5.5	3.6	58.2	0.0	2.9	24.8
	Hino-machi	(18,295) 100.0	71.5	28.5	100.0	10.4	2.8	22.6	9.5	10.4	0.2	4.5	34.1
	Tachikawa-shi	(30,648) 100.0	66.8	33.2	100.0	7.1	3.0	16.8	16.8	1.2	0.2	4.9	32.4
	Sunakawa-machi	(5,927) 100.0	68.1	31.9	100.0	3.0	1.3	10.6	7.8	26.0	0.0	4.9	37.8
	Yamato-machi	(6,064) 100.0	66.6	33.4	100.0	4.4	1.2	11.7	9.4	18.9	0.0	4.7	43.8
IV	Ōi-mura	(2,603) 100.0	61.2	38.8	100.0	1.7	0.8	4.6	7.6	46.8	—	2.5	28.5
	Fukuoka-mura	(7,279) 100.0	71.9	28.1	100.0	11.1	3.2	23.8	12.6	11.4	0.0	4.9	28.0
V	Kasukabe-shi	(16,033) 100.0	59.8	40.2	100.0	4.2	1.5	8.5	11.2	37.0	0.0	2.8	31.5
	Shōwa-mura	(6,964) 100.0	54.1	45.9	100.0	3.3	0.7	5.2	6.9	53.3	0.0	2.0	26.3
VI	Noda-shi	(26,891) 100.0	57.8	42.2	100.0	3.9	1.6	8.4	10.1	34.1	0.1	3.4	33.1
VII	Abiko-machi	(12,533) 100.0	60.7	39.3	100.0	4.4	1.9	11.5	13.1	35.8	0.0	3.7	24.6
	Yachiyo-machi	(10,374) 100.0	58.9	41.1	100.0	4.8	2.0	11.4	8.1	50.8	0.1	3.6	15.8
VIII	Chiba-shi	(107,856) 100.0	67.8	32.2	100.0	7.7	3.0	17.1	11.7	16.2	0.0	4.5	30.3
IX	Goi-machi	(10,896) 100.0	56.1	43.9	100.0	2.8	0.8	6.3	7.8	61.7	0.0	2.5	14.7
	Sodegaura-machi	(7,058) 100.0	52.5	47.5	100.0	2.7	0.7	4.3	5.1	77.0	0.0	1.4	7.2
	Zone 7 Total	(478,780) 100.0	67.1	32.9	100.0	6.4	2.8	16.0	11.6	16.6	0.0	4.9	33.6
8 I	Kanazawa-ku	(28,577) 100.0	72.4	25.6	100.0	7.4	2.9	18.8	10.8	4.1	0.0	5.1	42.7
	Totsuka-ku	(49,521) 100.0	70.5	29.5	100.0	7.4	2.4	18.8	8.0	15.4	—	4.4	38.1
II	Yamato-shi	(16,800) 100.0	67.8	32.2	100.0	6.5	2.4	15.1	11.6	14.2	0.0	4.8	34.7
	Sagamihara-shi	(42,117) 100.0	68.9	31.1	100.0	6.8	1.9	15.6	9.8	19.0	0.5	4.9	33.8
	Zama-nachi	(6,883) 100.0	65.4	34.6	100.0	5.1	2.0	14.2	9.9	25.8	0.4	4.9	29.7
III	Hachiōji-shi	(69,988) 100.0	65.0	35.0	100.0	5.5	3.3	13.1	12.2	10.3	0.1	4.1	44.5
	Akishima-shi	(17,507) 100.0	69.5	30.5	100.0	5.3	1.8	16.1	11.4	5.0	0.3	5.7	42.2
	Fussa-machi	(9,469) 100.0	65.3	34.7	100.0	4.9	2.3	13.0	14.4	5.2	0.4	5.2	34.5
	Mizuho-machi	(5,357) 100.0	66.0	34.0	100.0	2.6	1.0	6.3	9.9	31.8	0.1	4.1	38.4
	Murayama-machi	(5,132) 100.0	65.4	34.6	100.0	3.8	1.2	6.0	7.8	30.6	—	3.6	43.3
	Musashi-machi	(14,185) 100.0	61.9	38.1	100.0	3.3	1.5	7.4	9.0	29.3	0.1	3.9	34.0
IV	Sayama-shi	(16,042) 100.0	61.2	38.8	100.0	2.6	1.3	7.7	8.9	32.5	0.1	3.8	34.2
	Kawagoe-shi	(50,772) 100.0	60.8	39.2	100.0	4.6	1.8	10.6	11.1	30.7	0.1	3.3	32.6
	Seibu-machi	(3,368) 100.0	48.4	51.6	100.0	1.8	2.2	8.0	6.4	12.3	0.3	4.0	60.8
V	Ageo-shi	(19,003) 100.0	59.4	40.5	100.0	3.4	1.6	10.3	7.9	31.0	0.0	3.1	39.2
	Ina-mura	(3,724) 100.0	52.8	47.2	100.0	1.5	0.9	6.0	3.9	59.9	—	3.2	23.3
	Hasuda-machi	(9,819) 100.0	58.6	41.4	100.0	4.3	1.0	9.5	7.4	42.1	—	2.9	29.8
	Shiraoka-machi	(7,696) 100.0	59.2	40.8	100.0	2.4	0.9	7.7	6.8	51.0	—	2.8	25.7
	Miyashiro-machi	(5,330) 100.0	57.6	42.4	100.0	3.2	0.8	8.5	6.4	51.0	0.0	3.9	23.3
	Sugito-machi	(8,698) 100.0	55.3	44.7	100.0	3.0	0.7	6.1	9.0	57.9	—	2.5	18.5
VI	Sekiyado-machi	(6,512) 100.0	50.8	49.2	100.0	2.3	0.4	2.3	6.8	73.1	—	1.7	11.2
	Moriya-machi	(6,026) 100.0	51.7	48.3	100.0	2.4	0.6	4.4	8.1	66.5	0.1	1.5	14.4

Table 12. Gainfully Employed Population, 15 Years and Older, by Occupation and Sex

(For 1950 only, 14-year-olds are included)

Service Workers	Unclassified	Total	Professional and Technical Workers		Managerial Officials		Clerical Workers		Sales Workers		Farmers, Lumbermen and Fishermen		Mining and Quarrying Workers		Transportation and Communication Workers		Craftsmen, Production Process Workers, and General Laborers		Service Workers		Unclassified	
			M	F	M	F	M	F	M	F	M	F	M	F	M	F	M	F	M	F	M	F
2.8	—	100.0	2.0	1.2	0.9	0.0	4.4	2.8	4.7	3.6	21.5	23.4	0.0	—	2.1	0.4	21.5	8.7	1.3	1.5	—	—
1.3	—	100.0	1.3	0.8	0.6	0.0	1.9	1.5	2.7	2.2	25.5	37.1	—	—	2.5	0.1	17.4	5.1	0.5	0.8	—	—
5.7	0.0	100.0	4.1	2.0	2.5	0.1	11.2	5.0	6.1	4.2	13.5	15.9	0.0	—	4.0	0.7	20.3	4.7	2.7	3.0	—	0.0
15.2	—	100.0	0.7	0.3	0.4	—	1.4	0.7	1.9	3.0	29.1	35.5	—	—	1.3	0.1	8.3	2.1	14.8	0.4	—	—
1.4	0.0	100.0	1.1	0.7	0.4	—	1.3	0.7	2.9	2.2	38.5	41.8	—	—	1.1	0.3	6.2	1.4	0.8	0.6	0.0	0.0
6.9	0.0	100.0	5.4	1.7	2.7	0.1	12.5	6.7	6.5	4.9	5.9	6.2	0.0	—	4.9	0.7	25.9	9.0	3.6	3.3	—	0.0
8.5	0.0	100.0	4.8	2.0	3.1	0.1	11.2	6.5	7.1	4.4	7.1	7.0	0.0	0.0	4.4	0.5	26.4	6.9	4.1	4.4	0.0	0.0
8.9	0.0	100.0	4.7	2.1	4.5	0.1	13.2	8.3	7.4	5.1	1.7	1.0	0.0	—	6.3	0.9	28.5	7.3	4.1	4.8	0.0	—
9.9	0.0	100.0	3.6	2.0	3.2	0.2	9.7	6.9	8.6	5.3	1.4	1.0	0.0	—	5.6	0.6	33.5	8.5	4.5	5.4	0.0	0.0
6.7	0.0	100.0	5.2	2.0	3.2	0.0	13.1	7.4	6.0	4.2	3.3	2.1	0.0	—	5.3	0.6	33.1	7.8	3.8	2.9	0.0	0.0
6.5	—	100.0	5.3	2.1	2.4	0.1	9.9	5.5	6.6	4.3	12.1	9.0	0.0	—	3.7	0.5	24.4	7.6	3.5	3.0	—	—
2.5	0.0	100.0	1.6	0.6	0.3	—	3.0	2.5	2.1	1.5	30.2	28.0	0.0	—	2.4	0.5	17.5	7.3	0.9	1.6	—	0.0
5.5	0.0	100.0	8.1	2.3	2.7	0.1	14.8	7.8	6.1	3.4	6.3	4.1	0.1	0.1	3.8	0.7	26.5	7.6	3.1	2.4	0.0	—
17.6	0.0	100.0	4.5	2.6	2.8	0.2	9.9	6.9	9.9	6.9	0.8	0.4	0.1	0.1	4.3	0.6	26.4	6.0	8.1	9.5	0.0	0.0
8.6	—	100.0	1.9	1.1	1.2	0.1	6.1	4.5	4.5	3.3	15.3	10.7	0.0	—	4.3	0.6	29.2	8.6	5.6	3.0	—	—
5.9	—	100.0	2.9	1.5	1.2	0.0	6.7	5.0	5.0	4.4	10.5	8.4	0.0	—	4.2	0.5	32.4	11.4	3.7	2.2	—	—
7.5	—	100.0	1.2	0.5	0.8	0.0	2.6	2.0	4.1	3.5	22.5	24.3	—	—	2.0	0.5	21.4	7.1	6.6	0.9	—	—
5.0	0.0	100.0	8.6	2.5	3.2	0.0	16.3	7.5	9.0	3.6	5.5	5.9	0.0	—	4.5	0.4	21.9	6.1	2.9	2.1	0.0	0.0
3.3	0.0	100.0	2.7	1.5	1.4	0.1	4.8	3.7	6.6	4.6	16.9	20.1	0.0	—	2.3	0.5	23.8	7.7	1.3	2.0	0.0	0.0
2.3	—	100.0	1.6	1.7	0.7	0.0	3.0	2.2	3.8	3.1	23.4	29.9	0.0	—	1.8	0.2	18.9	7.4	0.9	1.4	—	—
5.3	—	100.0	2.3	1.6	1.6	0.0	5.5	2.9	5.6	4.5	12.6	21.5	0.1	—	3.0	0.4	25.3	7.8	1.8	3.5	—	—
5.0	—	100.0	3.4	1.0	1.8	0.1	7.6	3.9	6.5	6.6	17.3	18.5	0.0	—	3.2	0.5	18.8	5.8	2.1	2.9	0.0	0.0
3.4	0.0	100.0	3.2	1.6	1.9	0.1	8.0	3.4	4.6	3.5	24.2	26.6	0.1	—	3.1	0.5	12.3	3.5	1.5	1.9	0.0	0.0
9.5	0.0	100.0	5.1	2.6	2.8	0.2	10.9	6.2	6.7	5.0	7.9	8.3	0.0	—	3.9	0.6	25.5	4.8	5.0	4.5	0.0	0.0
3.4	—	100.0	1.6	1.2	0.8	—	3.7	2.6	4.3	3.5	30.2	31.5	0.0	—	2.2	0.3	12.0	2.7	1.3	2.1	—	—
1.6	0.0	100.0	1.5	1.2	0.7	0.0	2.7	1.6	2.2	2.9	37.4	39.6	0.0	—	1.3	0.1	6.0	1.2	0.7	0.9	—	0.0
8.1	0.0	100.0	4.3	2.1	2.7	0.1	10.0	6.0	6.8	4.8	8.1	8.5	0.0	0.0	4.3	0.6	26.9	6.7	4.0	4.1	0.0	0.0
8.2	0.0	100.0	5.1	2.3	2.8	0.1	11.7	7.1	6.1	4.7	3.0	1.1	0.0	—	4.5	0.6	34.6	8.1	4.6	3.6	0.0	—
5.5	0.0	100.0	5.4	2.0	2.3	0.1	12.5	6.3	4.6	3.4	8.4	7.0	—	—	3.9	0.5	30.1	8.0	3.3	2.2	0.0	—
10.7	—	100.0	4.3	2.1	2.3	0.1	9.7	5.4	6.4	5.2	7.5	6.7	0.0	—	4.3	0.5	28.5	6.2	4.8	5.9	—	—
7.7	0.0	100.0	4.7	2.1	1.8	0.1	9.9	5.7	5.7	4.1	11.5	7.5	0.4	0.1	4.4	0.5	27.0	6.8	3.5	4.2	0.0	0.0
8.0	0.0	100.0	3.6	1.5	1.8	0.2	8.3	5.9	5.3	4.6	14.7	11.1	0.4	—	4.4	0.5	22.8	6.9	4.1	3.9	0.0	0.0
6.9	0.0	100.0	3.5	2.0	3.0	0.3	7.8	5.3	7.6	4.6	6.9	3.4	0.1	0.0	3.4	0.7	29.6	14.9	3.1	3.8	0.0	0.0
12.2	0.0	100.0	3.5	1.8	1.7	0.1	10.5	5.6	7.0	4.4	3.7	1.3	0.3	0.0	4.7	1.0	32.8	9.4	5.3	6.9	—	0.0
20.1	0.0	100.0	2.8	2.1	2.1	0.2	7.6	5.4	8.5	5.9	4.4	0.8	0.3	0.1	4.7	0.5	28.6	5.9	6.3	13.8	0.0	0.0
5.8	0.0	100.0	1.5	1.1	1.0	—	3.6	2.7	5.6	4.3	20.2	11.6	0.1	—	3.6	0.5	26.6	11.8	3.8	2.0	0.0	—
3.7	0.0	100.0	1.4	2.4	1.2	0.0	3.3	2.7	4.8	3.0	19.2	11.4	—	—	3.2	0.4	29.8	13.5	2.5	1.2	0.0	0.0
11.5	—	100.0	1.9	1.4	1.4	0.1	4.1	3.3	5.3	3.7	17.2	12.1	0.1	—	3.5	0.4	23.2	10.8	5.2	6.3	—	—
8.9	0.0	100.0	1.7	0.9	1.2	0.1	4.2	3.5	4.8	4.1	17.3	15.2	0.1	—	3.4	0.4	22.9	11.3	5.6	3.3	0.0	—
5.2	0.0	100.0	3.0	1.6	1.8	0.0	6.3	4.3	6.6	4.5	15.0	15.7	0.1	—	2.8	0.5	23.0	9.6	2.2	3.0	0.0	0.0
4.2	0.0	100.0	1.2	0.6	2.1	0.1	3.9	4.1	3.7	2.7	7.9	4.4	0.3	—	3.5	0.5	23.4	37.4	2.4	1.8	0.0	0.0
3.5	—	100.0	2.2	1.2	1.6	0.0	6.2	4.1	4.5	3.4	14.1	16.9	0.0	—	2.7	0.4	26.6	12.6	1.5	2.0	—	—
1.3	—	100.0	1.2	0.3	0.9	—	4.2	1.8	2.2	1.7	24.4	35.5	—	—	2.8	0.4	16.4	6.9	0.7	0.6	—	—
3.0	0.0	100.0	2.1	2.2	0.9	0.1	5.9	3.6	4.0	3.4	19.5	22.6	—	—	2.5	0.4	22.2	7.6	1.5	1.5	0.0	—
2.7	0.0	100.0	1.6	0.8	0.9	0.0	5.1	2.6	3.4	3.4	24.4	26.6	—	—	2.4	0.4	20.2	5.5	1.2	1.5	—	0.0
2.9	0.0	100.0	2.1	1.1	0.8	0.0	5.0	3.5	3.5	2.9	23.1	27.9	0.0	—	3.6	0.3	17.9	5.4	1.6	1.3	0.0	0.0
2.3	0.0	100.0	1.9	1.1	0.7	0.0	3.4	2.7	5.0	4.0	27.3	30.6	—	—	2.3	0.2	13.5	5.0	1.2	1.1	0.0	—
2.2	—	100.0	1.5	0.8	0.4	—	1.5	0.8	3.5	3.3	32.3	40.8	—	—	1.5	0.2	9.3	1.9	0.8	1.4	—	—
2.0	—	100.0	1.8	0.6	0.6	0.0	2.8	1.6	3.5	4.6	29.0	37.5	0.1	—	1.4	0.1	11.6	2.8	0.9	1.1	—	—

Table 12. Gainfully Employed Population, 15 Years and Older, by Occupation and Sex
(For 1950 only, 14-year-olds are included)

(Zone) (Sector)	District	Total	M	F	Total	Professional and Technical Workers	Managerial Officials	Clerical Workers	Sales Workers	Farmers, Lumbermen and Fishermen	Mining and Quarrying Workers	Transportation and Communication Workers	Craftsmen, Production Process Workers, and General Laborers
VII	Toride-machi	(10,701) 100.0	58.6	41.4	100.0	5.3	1.8	11.5	13.2	33.3	0.2	3.5	25.6
	Inzai-machi	(8,694) 100.0	53.2	46.8	100.0	3.1	1.2	5.2	11.8	63.7	—	2.0	10.7
	Inba-mura	(4,657) 100.0	49.8	50.2	100.0	1.4	0.4	1.6	4.8	84.7	—	1.2	5.2
VIII	Yotsukaidō-machi	(7,405) 100.0	59.4	40.6	100.0	5.3	1.2	10.8	8.2	44.3	—	2.9	20.0
IX	Ichihara-machi	(7,124) 100.0	58.9	27.1	100.0	3.1	1.2	7.9	7.7	49.0	0.3	2.6	24.7
	Anegasaki-machi	(5,770) 100.0	56.0	44.0	100.0	3.0	0.8	5.5	7.8	64.1	0.0	2.4	12.9
	Hirakawa-machi	(5,923) 100.0	50.8	49.2	100.0	2.2	0.7	3.4	4.2	80.1	—	1.2	6.9
	Miwa-machi	(5,001) 100.0	52.1	47.9	100.0	2.3	0.9	4.3	5.2	75.1	0.1	1.4	9.6
X	Kisarazu-shi	(26,657) 100.0	57.7	42.3	100.0	3.9	1.3	6.9	11.7	47.1	0.1	2.7	14.7
	Zone 8 Total	(484,548) 100.0	63.2	36.8	100.0	5.0	1.9	11.8	9.9	27.9	0.1	3.8	32.8
9 I	Kamakura-shi	(40,331) 100.0	69.3	30.7	100.0	11.5	7.2	21.1	13.5	4.7	0.0	3.4	29.0
II	Ayase-machi	(3,944) 100.0	61.5	38.5	100.0	2.3	0.9	7.1	4.3	50.5	0.0	3.5	24.7
	Ebina-machi	(8,518) 100.0	60.9	39.1	100.0	4.0	1.2	9.5	6.3	36.6	0.5	4.9	33.4
	Shiroyama-machi	(2,300) 100.0	65.5	34.5	100.0	4.1	1.3	11.6	5.6	38.1	1.5	5.3	28.5
III	Akita-machi	(6,273) 100.0	68.6	31.4	100.0	3.5	1.1	10.0	8.0	29.1	1.3	5.8	35.7
	Hamura-machi	(4,638) 100.0	67.2	32.8	100.0	5.0	1.5	12.7	9.2	20.7	0.5	4.8	38.3
IV	Hannō-shi	(19,905) 100.0	63.7	36.3	100.0	4.6	1.8	9.5	11.2	26.0	0.6	4.0	35.5
	Tsurugashima-mura	(3,666) 100.0	56.3	43.7	100.0	2.6	0.6	5.2	5.4	58.6	—	2.2	23.0
	Hidaka-machi	(8,620) 100.0	58.1	41.9	100.0	2.5	0.6	5.5	5.5	53.6	0.4	2.3	26.0
	Kawashima-mura	(8,764) 100.0	51.3	48.7	100.0	1.9	0.4	3.6	3.7	74.6	0.1	1.2	13.4
V	Kitamoto-machi	(7,148) 100.0	60.7	39.3	100.0	3.8	1.3	9.9	8.2	40.2	0.1	3.6	29.4
	Higawa-machi	(10,032) 100.0	60.8	39.2	100.0	3.6	1.4	11.5	9.7	34.1	0.0	3.2	32.9
	Shobu-machi	(7,717) 100.0	56.4	43.6	100.0	2.9	0.7	5.3	7.9	59.6	0.0	2.4	18.8
	Kuki-machi	(10,641) 100.0	60.7	39.3	100.0	4.5	1.0	9.0	9.3	42.3	—	3.6	26.6
	Satte-machi	(11,357) 100.0	55.6	44.4	100.0	3.5	1.2	6.3	10.6	48.8	—	2.5	23.6
VI	Iwai-machi	(18,091) 100.0	50.1	49.9	100.0	2.4	0.4	2.3	6.4	76.4	0.0	1.0	9.2
	Mitsukaidō-shi	(19,317) 100.0	53.4	46.6	100.0	3.0	0.9	5.0	9.6	62.7	0.0	2.1	13.8
	Yawahara-mura	(5,684) 100.0	51.4	48.6	100.0	1.9	0.5	3.3	5.3	77.0	—	1.6	9.2
	Ina-mura	(6,882) 100.0	49.2	50.8	100.0	1.7	0.3	3.2	5.3	75.4	0.0	1.3	9.1
VII	Fujishiro-machi	(6,759) 100.0	52.2	47.8	100.0	2.4	0.8	6.3	8.8	63.5	0.0	2.4	13.8
	Ryūgasaki-shi	(16,777) 100.0	55.4	44.6	100.0	3.7	1.1	7.9	10.5	51.8	—	2.3	18.2
	Tone-mura	(4,978) 100.0	52.2	47.8	100.0	1.9	0.7	5.3	8.7	67.6	0.1	1.7	12.2
	Motono-mura	(2,934) 100.0	51.7	48.3	100.0	1.3	0.4	2.8	6.8	80.3	—	1.1	6.3
VIII	Sakura-shi	(17,975) 100.0	55.9	44.1	100.0	4.5	1.1	9.7	7.6	54.2	0.0	3.2	16.4
	Izumi-machi	(5,086) 100.0	52.2	47.8	100.0	1.9	0.5	4.0	3.0	81.8	—	1.7	5.9
IX	Shitsu-mura	(5,046) 100.0	51.0	49.0	100.0	2.4	0.5	3.9	3.7	75.8	—	1.9	10.6
	Nansō-machi	(9,191) 100.0	51.7	48.3	100.0	4.0	1.1	3.6	6.7	71.8	—	1.5	8.9
	Fukuta-machi	(3,869) 100.0	50.6	49.4	100.0	3.2	0.8	3.7	5.2	73.4	0.1	1.4	10.6
X	Kimitsu-machi	(6,868) 100.0	52.6	47.4	100.0	3.4	0.9	4.8	5.9	70.6	0.2	2.0	10.2
	Futtsu-machi	(8,535) 100.0	56.6	43.4	100.0	2.3	0.9	3.5	9.2	66.8	0.1	1.7	12.6
	Ōsawa-machi	(6,942) 100.0	54.9	45.1	100.0	3.9	1.6	5.7	10.0	52.2	0.5	3.2	19.0
	Zone 9 Total	(298,788) 100.0	57.9	42.1	100.0	4.4	1.8	8.5	8.7	48.8	0.1	2.7	20.8
10 I	Yokosuka-shi	(124,160) 100.0	71.5	28.5	100.0	5.9	1.9	14.1	11.9	5.1	0.1	4.9	36.0
	Zushi-shi	(15,742) 100.0	69.9	30.1	100.0	10.1	6.1	22.0	12.9	2.5	0.3	4.2	32.1
	Hayama-machi	(6,358) 100.0	66.8	33.2	100.0	8.5	5.6	16.4	11.6	14.3	—	3.5	30.1
	Chigasaki-shi	(27,844) 100.0	70.4	29.6	100.0	7.3	4.2	17.9	11.0	14.3	0.0	3.5	35.9
	Fujisawa-shi	(51,310) 100.0	68.4	31.6	100.0	8.5	5.7	18.1	12.9	13.3	0.0	3.6	30.1
II	Aikawa-machi	(7,073) 100.0	55.8	44.1	100.0	2.6	2.3	5.0	5.5	38.1	1.3	3.2	39.7
	Atsugi-shi	(21,422) 100.0	63.5	36.5	100.0	5.2	1.6	10.0	9.5	39.7	0.6	3.8	24.5

Table 12. Gainfully Employed Population, 15 Years and Older, by Occupation and Sex
(For 1950 only, 14-year-olds are included)

Service Workers	Unclassified	Total	Professional and Technical Workers		Managerial Officials		Clerical Workers		Sales Workers		Farmers, Lumbermen and Fishermen		Mining and Quarrying Workers		Transportation and Communication Workers		Craftsmen, Production Process Workers, and General Laborers		Service Workers		Unclassified	
			M	F	M	F	M	F	M	F	M	F	M	F	M	F	M	F	M	F	M	F
5.6	—	100.0	3.4	1.9	1.7	0.1	7.6	3.9	6.3	6.9	14.6	18.7	0.2	—	3.1	0.4	19.1	6.5	2.6	3.0	—	—
2.3	0.0	100.0	2.0	1.1	1.2	0.0	2.9	2.3	5.0	6.8	31.1	32.6	—	—	1.7	0.3	8.4	2.3	0.9	1.4	—	0.0
0.7	—	100.0	0.9	0.5	0.4	—	1.0	0.6	1.6	3.2	40.5	44.2	—	—	1.0	0.2	4.0	1.2	0.4	0.3	—	—
7.3	—	100.0	2.8	2.5	1.2	0.0	6.6	4.2	4.1	4.1	20.2	24.1	—	—	2.7	0.2	16.0	4.0	5.8	1.5	—	—
3.5	0.0	100.0	1.9	1.2	1.1	0.1	4.6	3.3	4.1	3.6	20.8	28.2	0.3	—	2.3	0.3	22.2	2.5	1.6	1.9	0.0	0.0
3.5	—	100.0	2.0	1.0	0.8	0.0	3.2	2.3	4.0	3.8	32.9	31.2	—	—	2.0	0.4	9.7	3.2	1.4	2.1	—	—
1.3	0.0	100.0	1.6	0.6	0.6	0.1	2.0	1.4	2.0	2.2	37.4	42.7	—	—	1.0	0.2	5.7	1.2	0.5	0.8	0.0	0.0
1.1	0.0	100.0	1.5	0.8	0.8	0.1	2.4	1.9	2.6	2.6	35.6	39.5	—	0.1	1.2	0.2	7.6	2.0	0.4	0.7	0.0	—
11.6	—	100.0	2.2	1.7	1.2	0.1	4.1	2.8	5.8	5.9	23.1	24.0	0.1	0.0	2.4	0.3	11.9	2.8	6.9	4.7	—	—
6.8	0.0	100.0	3.2	1.8	1.8	0.1	7.3	4.5	5.6	4.3	14.4	13.5	0.1	0.0	3.3	0.5	24.2	8.6	3.3	3.5	.0.0	0.0
9.6	0.0	100.0	8.5	3.0	7.0	0.2	13.8	7.3	8.1	5.4	2.9	1.8	0.0	—	2.8	0.6	22.9	6.1	3.3	6.3	0.0	0.0
6.7	0.0	100.0	1.6	0.7	0.8	0.1	3.8	3.3	2.3	2.0	28.3	22.2	0.0	—	3.4	0.1	19.4	5.3	1.9	4.8	0.1	0.0
3.6	0.0	100.0	2.8	1.2	1.1	0.1	5.4	4.1	3.4	2.9	20.8	15.8	0.5	—	4.4	0.5	20.6	12.8	1.9	1.7	—	0.0
4.0	—	100.0	2.8	1.3	1.2	0.1	6.9	4.7	3.1	2.5	21.0	17.1	1.3	0.2	4.5	0.8	22.7	5.8	2.0	2.0	—	—
5.5	0.0	100.0	2.2	1.3	1.0	0.1	5.6	4.4	4.7	3.3	19.4	9.7	1.1	0.2	5.4	0.4	25.8	9.9	3.4	2.1	0.0	—
7.3	—	100.0	3.1	1.9	1.5	—	7.7	5.0	5.0	4.2	12.7	8.0	0.4	0.1	4.1	0.7	29.3	9.0	3.4	3.9	—	—
6.8	0.0	100.0	2.8	1.8	1.8	0.0	5.8	3.7	6.7	4.5	15.0	11.0	0.6	—	3.5	0.5	24.8	10.7	2.7	4.1	0.0	—
2.4	—	100.0	1.8	0.8	0.5	0.1	2.8	2.4	2.8	2.6	29.2	29.4	—	—	2.0	0.2	16.1	6.9	1.1	1.3	—	—
3.6	—	100.0	1.6	0.9	0.6	0.0	3.0	2.5	3.1	2.4	26.2	27.4	0.3	0.1	1.9	0.4	20.0	6.0	1.4	2.2	—	—
1.1	0.0	100.0	1.2	0.7	0.4	—	1.8	1.8	1.8	1.9	34.4	40.2	0.1	—	1.0	0.2	10.1	3.3	0.5	0.6	0.0	0.0
3.5	0.0	100.0	2.6	1.2	1.3	0.0	6.6	3.3	4.7	3.5	17.5	22.7	0.1	—	3.3	0.3	22.9	6.5	1.7	1.8	—	—
3.6	0.0	100.0	2.3	1.3	1.3	0.1	7.0	4.5	5.7	4.0	15.1	19.0	0.0	0.0	3.0	0.2	24.8	8.1	1.6	2.0	0.0	—
2.4	—	100.0	1.9	1.0	0.7	0.0	3.3	2.0	4.7	3.2	29.7	29.9	0.0	—	2.0	0.4	13.1	5.7	1.0	1.4	—	—
3.7	0.0	100.0	2.6	1.9	0.9	0.1	5.9	3.1	5.2	4.1	20.1	22.2	—	—	3.2	0.4	21.0	5.6	1.8	1.9	0.0	0.0
3.5	—	100.0	2.1	1.4	1.1	0.1	3.5	2.8	5.6	5.0	23.3	25.5	—	—	2.4	0.1	16.4	7.2	1.2	2.3	—	—
1.9	—	100.0	1.5	0.9	0.4	0.0	1.7	0.6	3.4	3.0	35.4	41.0	0.0	—	0.9	0.1	6.2	3.0	0.6	1.3	—	—
2.9	—	100.0	1.9	1.1	0.9	0.0	3.4	1.6	5.3	4.3	28.4	34.3	0.0	—	1.7	0.4	10.8	3.0	1.0	1.9	—	—
1.2	—	100.0	1.3	0.6	0.5	—	2.4	0.9	2.8	2.5	35.6	41.4	—	—	1.3	0.3	7.2	2.0	0.3	0.9	—	—
3.7	0.0	100.0	1.0	0.7	0.3	—	1.9	1.3	2.5	2.8	34.8	40.6	0.0	—	1.1	0.2	6.8	2.3	0.8	2.9	0.0	0.0
2.0	—	100.0	1.6	0.8	0.8	0.0	4.1	2.2	4.3	4.5	27.3	36.2	0.0	—	2.2	0.2	10.9	2.9	1.0	1.0	—	—
4.5	—	100.0	2.5	1.2	1.1	0.0	5.0	2.9	5.6	4.9	23.8	28.0	—	—	1.9	0.4	14.0	4.2	1.5	3.0	—	—
1.8	0.0	100.0	1.2	0.7	0.7	—	3.2	2.1	3.2	5.5	31.3	36.3	0.1	—	1.5	0.3	10.0	2.2	1.0	0.8	—	0.0
1.0	—	100.0	0.9	0.4	0.4	0.0	1.8	1.0	2.0	4.8	40.2	40.1	—	—	0.8	0.3	5.3	1.0	0.3	0.7	—	—
3.3	—	100.0	2.8	1.7	1.1[1]	0.0	5.9	3.8	3.5	4.1	25.4	28.8	0.0	—	2.7	0.5	12.9	3.5	1.6	1.7	—	—
1.2	0.0	100.0	1.2	0.7	0.5	—	2.4	1.6	1.5	1.5	39.4	42.4	—	—	1.6	0.1	5.0	0.9	0.6	0.6	—	—
1.2	0.0	100.0	1.5	0.9	0.5	—	2.2	1.7	1.8	1.9	34.4	41.4	—	—	1.6	0.2	8.4	2.2	0.6	0.6	—	0.0
2.4	0.0	100.0	2.2	1.8	1.0	0.1	2.3	1.3	3.4	3.3	33.9	37.9	—	—	1.3	0.2	6.7	2.2	0.9	1.5	—	0.0
1.6	—	100.0	2.0	1.2	0.7	0.1	2.7	1.0	2.0	3.2	33.0	40.4	0.1	—	1.3	0.1	8.4	2.2	0.4	1.2	—	—
2.0	0.0	100.0	2.2	1.2	0.9	0.0	3.1	1.7	2.9	3.0	32.7	37.9	0.2	0.0	1.8	0.2	8.1	2.1	0.7	1.3	0.0	0.0
2.9	—	100.0	1.3	1.0	0.9	0.0	2.1	1.4	4.6	4.6	36.0	30.8	0.1	0.0	1.4	0.3	9.1	3.5	1.1	1.8	—	—
3.9	—	100.0	2.3	1.6	1.5	0.1	3.4	2.3	4.8	5.2	23.9	28.3	0.4	0.1	2.8	0.4	14.5	4.5	1.3	2.6	—	—
4.2	0.0	100.0	2.9	1.5	1.8	0.0	5.3	3.2	4.7	4.0	23.5	25.3	0.1	0.0	2.4	0.3	15.6	5.2	1.6	2.6	0.0	0.0
20.1	0.0	100.0	3.6	2.3	1.8	0.1	8.3	5.8	6.6	5.3	3.1	1.8	0.1	0.0	4.2	0.7	29.1	6.9	14.7	5.4	0.0	0.0
9.8	—	100.0	7.5	2.6	6.0	0.1	13.5	8.5	7.5	5.4	2.0	0.5	0.3	—	3.4	0.8	25.7	6.4	4.0	5.8	—	
10.0	—	100.0	6.0	2.5	5.5	0.1	10.6	5.8	6.7	4.9	7.1	7.2	—	—	2.9	0.6	24.1	6.0	3.9	6.1	—	—
5.9	0.0	100.0	5.2	2.1	4.1	0.1	12.3	5.6	6.9	4.1	8.3	6.0	0.0	—	3.2	0.3	27.8	8.1	2.6	3.3	0.0	—
7.8	0.0	100.0	6.1	2.4	5.6	0.1	12.1	6.0	7.9	5.0	8.2	5.1	0.0	—	3.0	0.6	22.7	7.4	2.8	5.0	0.0	0.0
2.3	—	100.0	1.7	0.9	2.2	0.1	2.7	2.3	2.8	2.7	21.6	16.5	1.2	0.1	2.6	0.6	19.9	19.8	1.1	1.2	—	—
5.1	0.0	100.0	3.7	1.5	1.5	0.1	6.0	4.0	5.6	3.9	22.2	17.5	0.6	0.0	3.2	0.6	18.5	6.0	2.2	2.9	0.	...

Table 12. Gainfully Employed Population, 15 Years and Older, by Occupation and Sex
(For 1950 only, 14-year-olds are included)

(Zone) (Sector)	District	Total			Total	Professional and Technical Workers	Managerial Officials	Clerical Workers	Sales Workers	Farmers, Lumbermen and Fishermen	Mining and Quarrying Workers	Transportation and Communication Workers	Craftsmen, Production Process Workers, and General Laborers
		Total	M	F									
II	Samukawa-machi	(5,380) 100.0	66.2	33.8	100.0	3.8	1.1	10.5	5.9	30 8	0.4	3.4	40.3
III	Ōme-shi	(26,437) 100.0	62.6	37.4	100.0	4.7	2.6	11.2	10.3	12.9	0.7	4.0	47.3
IV	Sakado-machi	(11,697) 100.0	56.8	43.2	100.0	3.4	0.9	6.2	7.4	53.6	0.1	2.0	23.3
	Yoshimi-mura	(7,881) 100.0	52.7	47.3	100.0	2.4	0.4	3.6	3.8	73.1	0.0	1.1	14.7
	Moroyama-mura	(5,511) 100.0	52.4	47.6	100.0	7.6	0.8	5.4	6.0	54.4	0.1	1.8	21.0
V	Kōnosu-shi	(15,015) 100.0	59.6	40.4	100.0	4.6	1.4	8.9	10.5	38.2	0.0	3.0	29.7
	Kisai-machi	(7,768) 100.0	53.7	46.3	100.0	2.5	0.6	4.3	7.0	68.1	0.0	2.3	13.4
	Washimiya-machi	(4,154) 100.0	56.8	43.2	100.0	2.4	0.8	6.5	7.0	58.1	—	2.8	20.7
	Kurihashi-machi	(5,907) 100.0	58.6	41.4	100.0	3.7	1.1	9.5	10.7	42.4	—	2.9	25.4
	Goka-mura	(4,639) 100.0	50.1	49.9	100.0	1.3	0.5	3.2	3.2	80.0	0.2	0.9	9.9
VI	Sakai-machi	(11,606) 100.0	51.1	48.9	100.0	2.8	0.7	3.6	8.9	69.1	—	1.9	9.8
	Sashima-machi	(7,919) 100.0	48.7	51.3	100.0	2.2	0.5	1.7	6.1	81.5	—	0.8	5.7
	Yatabe-machi	(11,637) 100.0	51.6	48.4	100.0	2.9	0.7	2.9	5.8	76.9	—	1.5	7.5
VII	Kukizaki-mura	(3,502) 100.0	52.4	47.6	100.0	1.2	0.3	2.9	5.1	82.0	—	0.9	6.8
	Ushiku-machi	(8,084) 100.0	55.2	44.8	100.0	3.4	0.9	5.5	7.1	65.7	0.0	2.1	12.8
	Kawachi-mura	(7,209) 100.0	50.3	49.7	100.0	1.7	0.4	2.8	6.1	79.2	—	1.4	7.2
	Sakae-machi	(5,089) 100.0	52.5	47.5	100.0	2.4	0.6	4.9	8.6	69.9	0.0	1.8	9.7
	Narita-shi	(21,041) 100.0	54.9	45.0	100.0	4.3	1.3	8.4	10.7	51.7	—	3.3	14.5
VIII	Shisui-machi	(3,054) 100.0	55.4	44.6	100.0	2.3	0.9	8.5	6.8	55.7	—	3.7	19.5
	Yachimata-machi	(12,622) 100.0	54.0	46.0	100.0	2.9	1.1	4.0	9.1	64.6	—	2.1	13.2
	Toke-machi	(3,176) 100.0	57.8	42.2	100.0	2.4	1.0	6.4	6.3	61.1	0.0	3.0	17.8
IX	Nagara-machi	(4,802) 100.0	49.9	50.1	100.0	2.7	0.6	3.3	3.4	77.2	0.1	1.3	10.6
	Obitsu-mura	(3,702) 100.0	51.1	48.9	100.0	2.3	1.0	4.5	4.4	74.6	0.3	1.6	10.2
X	Koito-machi	(3,422) 100.0	51.2	48.8	100.0	2.7	1.0	3.2	3.9	79.5	—	2.0	6.1
	Zone 10 Total	(455,163) 100.0	63.2	36.8	100.0	5.3	2.3	11.3	10.0	31.3	0.1	3.4	27.4
	Total for 50 km. Region	(7,340,896) 100.0	68.2	31.8	100.0	6.5	3.9	16.6	13.2	9.9	0.0	4.1	36.2
	National Total	(43,691,069) 100.0	60.9	39.1	100.0	5.0	2.2	10.2	10.8	32.5	0.8	3.4	28.6

Table 12. Gainfully Employed Population, 15 Years and Older, by Occupation and Sex
(For 1950 only, 14-year-olds are included)

Service Workers	Unclassified	Total	Professional and Technical Workers		Managerial Officials		Clerical Workers		Sales Workers		Farmers, Lumbermen and Fishermen		Mining and Quarrying Workers		Transportation and Communication Workers		Craftsmen, Production Process Workers, and General Laborers		Service Workers		Unclassified	
			M	F	M	F	M	F	M	F	M	F	M	F	M	F	M	F	M	F	M	F
3.7	0.1	100.0	2.4	1.4	1.1	—	6.3	4.2	3.1	2.8	16.3	14.5	0.4	—	3.2	0.2	31.8	8.5	1.5	2.2	0.1	0.0
6.3	0.0	100.0	2.9	1.8	2.5	0.1	6.7	4.5	6.5	3.8	9.4	3.5	0.7	0.0	3.4	0.6	27.8	19.5	2.7	3.6	0.0	—
3.1	0.0	100.0	2.2	1.2	0.8	0.1	3.4	2.8	4.1	3.3	26.8	26.8	0.1	—	1.8	0.2	16.3	7.0	1.3	1.8	0.0	—
0.9	0.0	100.0	1.7	0.7	0.4	0.0	2.1	1.5	2.0	1.8	33.6	39.5	0.0	—	1.0	0.1	11.6	3.1	0.3	0.6	—	0.0
2.9	—	100.0	3.0	4.6	0.7	0.1	3.2	2.2	3.2	2.8	25.6	28.8	0.1	0.0	1.5	0.3	13.9	7.1	1.2	1.7	—	—
3.7	0.0	100.0	3.2	1.4	1.3	0.1	5.8	3.1	6.2	4.3	17.5	20.7	0.0	—	2.7	0.3	21.3	8.4	1.6	2.1	0.0	0.0
1.8	—	100.0	1.6	0.9	0.6	0.0	2.7	1.6	4.1	2.9	32.7	35.4	0.0	—	2.1	0.2	9.3	4.1	0.6	1.2	—	—
1.7	—	100.0	1.6	0.8	0.8	0.0	4.5	2.0	4.0	3.0	26.7	31.4	—	—	2.6	0.2	15.7	5.0	0.9	0.8	—	—
4.3	0.0	100.0	2.3	1.4	1.0	0.1	6.1	3.4	5.4	5.3	18.7	23.7	—	—	2.6	0.3	20.7	4.7	1.8	2.5	0.0	—
0.8	—	100.0	0.9	0.4	0.5	—	1.9	1.3	1.7	1.5	35.9	44.1	0.2	0.0	0.8	0.1	7.8	2.1	0.4	0.4	—	—
3.2	—	100.0	1.9	0.9	0.7	0.0	2.4	1.2	4.8	4.1	31.3	37.8	—	—	1.4	0.5	7.4	2.4	1.2	2.0	—	—
1.5	—	100.0	1.4	0.8	0.5	—	1.2	0.5	3.1	3.0	37.4	44.1	—	—	0.6	0.2	4.1	1.6	0.4	1.1	—	—
1.8	—	100.0	2.0	0.9	0.6	0.1	1.8	1.1	3.0	2.8	36.5	40.4	—	—	1.3	0.2	5.7	1.8	0.7	1.1	—	—
0.8	—	100.0	1.0	0.2	0.3	—	1.9	1.0	2.4	2.7	39.8	42.2	—	—	0.9	—	5.7	1.1	0.4	0.4	—	—
2.5	—	100.0	2.4	1.0	0.9	0.0	3.7	1.8	3.9	3.2	31.1	34.6	0.0	—	1.9	0.2	10.5	2.3	0.8	1.7	—	—
1.2	—	100.0	1.2	0.5	0.4	—	1.8	1.0	2.9	3.2	36.4	42.8	—	—	1.2	0.2	6.0	1.2	0.4	0.8	—	—
2.1	—	100.0	1.5	0.9	0.6	0.0	2.9	2.0	3.5	5.1	34.1	35.8	0.0	—	1.5	0.3	7.8	1.9	0.6	1.5	—	—
5.8	0.0	100.0	2.4	1.9	1.2	0.1	5.7	2.7	5.5	5.2	24.4	27.3	—	—	2.3	1.0	11.3	3.2	2.1	3.7	0.0	0.0
2.5	0.1	100.0	1.5	0.8	0.8	0.1	4.7	3.8	3.3	3.5	25.5	30.2	—	—	3.3	0.4	14.9	4.6	1.3	1.2	0.1	0.0
3.0	0.0	100.0	1.8	1.1	0.9	0.2	2.4	1.6	4.8	4.3	31.5	33.1	—	—	1.8	0.3	9.8	3.4	1.0	2.0	0.0	0.0
2.0	—	100.0	1.5	0.9	1.0	0.0	4.1	2.3	3.2	3.1	30.0	31.1	0.0	—	2.8	0.2	14.1	3.7	1.1	0.9	—	—
0.8	0.0	100.0	1.7	1.0	0.6	—	2.2	1.1	1.8	1.6	35.7	41.5	0.1	—	1.1	0.2	6.4	4.2	0.3	0.5	0.0	0.0
1.1	0.0	100.0	1.4	0.9	1.0	0.0	3.2	1.3	2.1	2.3	32.8	41.8	0.3	0.0	1.5	0.1	8.3	1.9	0.5	0.6	—	—
1.6	—	100.0	1.8	0.9	1.0	—	1.9	1.3	1.8	2.1	37.6	41.9	—	—	1.9	0.1	4.7	1.4	0.5	1.1	—	—
8.9	—	100.0	3.5	1.8	2.2	0.1	7.0	4.3	5.5	4.5	15.8	15.5	0.1	0.0	2.9	0.5	20.8	6.6	5.4	3.5	0.0	0.0
9.4	0.2	100.0	4.5	2.0	3.7	0.2	10.0	6.6	8.6	4.6	5.1	4.8	0.0	0.0	3.6	0.5	28.5	7.7	4.0	5.4	0.2	0.0
6.5	0.0	100.0	3.2	1.8	2.1	0.1	6.4	3.8	6.3	4.5	15.7	16.8	0.8	0.0	3.0	0.4	20.8	7.8	2.6	3.9	0.0	0.0

PART III

POPULATION FLUIDITY OF TOKYO METROPOLITAN COMPLEX

TABLE 13

REGIONAL SOURCES OF DAYTIME POPULATION INFLUX OF WORKERS AND STUDENTS OVER 15 YEARS OLD

Zone	Sector	Region	Total Daytime Workers & Students	Regional Sources of Daytime Workers & Students			Total Workers & Students in Region	Total Workers & Students in Daytime Influx	Total Workers & Students in Daily Outflow
				Region	Number	Percent			
1	I	Chiyoda-ku	633597	Suginami-ku	64685	10.2	79219	568912	14534
				Setagaya-ku	75994	12.0			
				Nakano-ku	40677	6.4			
				Shinjuku-ku	31404	5.0			
				Ōta-ku	29324	4.6			
				Toshima-ku	23366	3.7			
				Kita-ku	20916	3.3			
				Bunkyō-ku	20484	3.2			
				Shibuya-ku	19976	3.2			
				Nerima-ku	18173	2.9			
				Itabashi-ku	17022	2.7			
				Shinagawa-ku	16247	2.6			
				Meguro-ku	15265	2.4			
				Minato-ku	14878	2.3			
				Kawasaki-shi	12845	2.0			
				Katsushika-ku	10426	1.7			
				Musashino-shi	10106	1.6			
				Edogawa-ku	9662	1.5			
				Adachi-ku	9474	1.5			
				Taitō-ku	9429	1.5			
				Kōtō-ku	9023	1.4			
				Urawa-shi	7965	1.3			
				Arakawa-ku	7746	1.2			
				Ichikawa-shi	7217	1.1			
				Sumida-ku	6587	1.0			
				Mitaka-shi	6425	1.0			
				Chūō-ku	5268	0.8			
				Ōmiya-shi	4862	0.8			
				Chiba-shi	4750	0.7			
				Funahashi-shi	4709	0.7			
					3972	0.6			

- 335 -

TABLE 13

REGIONAL SOURCES OF DAYTIME POPULATION INFLUX OF WORKERS AND STUDENTS OVER 15 YEARS OLD—Continued

Zone	Sector	Region	Total Daytime Workers & Students	Regional Sources of Daytime Workers & Students			Total Workers & Students in Region	Total Workers & Students in Daytime Influx	Total Workers & Students in Daily Outflow
				Region	Number	Percent			
1	I	Minato-ku	351466	Tsurumi-ku	3637	0.6	243125	50382	
				Kawaguchi-shi	3431	0.5			
				Kamakura-shi	3351	0.5			
				Fujisawa-shi	3159	0.5			
				Matsuda-shi	3126	0.5			
				Kanagawa-shi	2926	0.5			
				Kōhoku-ku	2859	0.5			
				Koganei-shi	2791	0.4			
				Hodogaya-ku	2615	0.4			
				Chōfu-shi	2594	0.4			
				Kashiwa-shi	2508	0.4			
				Others	61723	9.9			
				Suginami-ku	108341	30.8			
				Setagaya-ku	23036	6.6			
				Ōta-ku	21125	6.0			
				Shinagawa-ku	20550	5.8			
				Meguro-ku	18028	5.1			
				Shibuya-ku	12037	3.4			
				Nakano-ku	10760	3.1			
				Shinjuku-ku	10326	3.1			
				Kita-ku	9618	2.7			
				Kawasaki-shi	7684	2.2			
				Toshima-ku	7192	2.0			
				Nerima-ku	6826	1.9			
				Itabashi-ku	5103	1.5			
				Bunkyō-ku	4997	1.4			
				Adachi-ku	4671	1.3			
				Katsushika-ku	3714	1.1			
				Taitō-ku	3686	1.0			
					3277	0.9			

TABLE 13

REGIONAL SOURCES OF DAYTIME POPULATION INFLUX OF WORKERS AND STUDENTS OVER 15 YEARS OLD—Continued

Zone	Sector	Region	Total Daytime Workers & Students	Regional Sources of Daytime Workers & Students — Region	Number	Percent	Total Workers & Students in Region	Total Workers & Students in Daytime Influx	Total Workers & Students in Daily Outflow
1	I	Chūō-ku	518225	Araka-ku	3244	0.9	107799	427433	17007
				Edogawa-ku	3139	0.9			
				Kōtō-ku	3135	0.9			
				Tsurumi-ku	2701	0.8			
				Musashino-shi	2476	0.7			
				Urawa-shi	2419	0.7			
				Chūō-ku	2309	0.7			
				Kōhoku-ku	2041	0.6			
				Sumida-ku	1960	0.6			
				Kanagawa-ku	1866	0.5			
				Ōmiya-shi	1755	0.5			
				Ichikawa-shi	1745	0.5			
				Mitaka-shi	1678	0.5			
				Kamakura-shi	1637	0.5			
				Kawaguchi-shi	1547	0.4			
				Fujisawa-shi	1545	0.4			
				Hodogaya-ku	1525	0.4			
				Others	33713	9.6			
				Suginami-ku	90792	17.5			
				Setagaya-ku	47603	9.2			
				Ōta-ku	29119	5.6			
				Nakano-ku	20668	4.0			
				Shinjuku-ku	19664	3.8			
				Kita-ku	19163	3.7			
				Toshima-ku	16531	3.2			
				Shinagawa-ku	15725	3.0			
				Shibuya-ku	15507	3.0			
				Kōtō-ku	14112	2.7			
					13786	2.7			

TABLE 13

REGIONAL SOURCES OF DAYTIME POPULATION INFLUX OF WORKERS AND STUDENTS OVER 15 YEARS OLD—Continued

Zone	Sector	Region	Total Daytime Workers & Students	Regional Sources of Daytime Workers & Students			Total Workers & Students in Region	Total Workers & Students in Daytime Influx	Total Workers & Students in Daily Outflow
				Region	Number	Percent			
				Minato-ku	12720	2.5			
				Meguro-ku	12349	2.4			
				Bunkyō-ku	11757	2.3			
				Nerima-ku	11476	2.2			
				Itabashi-ku	10701	2.1			
				Katsushika-ku	8921	1.7			
				Edogawa-ku	8825	1.7			
				Taitō-ku	8741	1.7			
				Adachi-ku	8570	1.7			
				Kawasaki-shi	7071	1.4			
				Arakawa-ku	6794	1.3			
				Ichikawa-shi	6300	1.2			
				Sumida-ku	6177	1.2			
				Urawa-shi	6040	1.2			
				Musashino-shi	5745	1.1			
				Funahashi-shi	3718	0.7			
				Chiyoda-ku	3615	0.7			
				Mitaka-shi	3532	0.7			
				Chiba-shi	3520	0.7			
				Ōmiya-shi	3339	0.6			
				Kamakura-shi	2869	0.6			
				Kawaguchi-shi	2862	0.6			
				Tsurumi-ku	2697	0.5			
				Kanagawa-ku	2507	0.5			
				Fujisawa-shi	2423	0.5			
				Others	52220	9.8			
1	I	Bunkyō-ku	198402	Toshima-ku	85559	43.1	152921	112843	67362
				Suginami-ku	11174	5.6			
					10002	5.0			
				Itabashi-ku	8519	4.3			

TABLE 13

REGIONAL SOURCES OF DAYTIME POPULATION INFLUX OF WORKERS AND STUDENTS OVER 15 YEARS OLD—Continued

Zone	Sector	Region	Total Daytime Workers & Students	Regional Sources of Daytime Workers & Students			Total Workers & Students in Region	Total Workers & Students in Daytime Influx	Total Workers & Students in Daily Outflow
				Region	Number	Percent			
1	1	Taitō-ku	277751	Kita-ku	8079	4.1	199441	122898	44588
				Shinjuku-ku	6609	3.3			
				Nerima-ku	5822	2.9			
				Nakano-ku	4998	2.5			
				Setagaya-ku	4934	2.5			
				Taitō-ku	3896	2.0			
				Arakawa-ku	3144	1.6			
				Adachi-ku	2816	1.4			
				Ōta-ku	2678	1.3			
				Shibuya-ku	2552	1.3			
				Katsushika-ku	2286	1.2			
				Sumida-ku	2144	1.1			
				Meguro-ku	1931	1.0			
				Edogawa-ku	1915	1.0			
				Shinagawa-ku	1882	0.9			
				Kōtō-ku	1852	0.9			
				Chiyoda-ku	1608	0.8			
				Minato-ku	1502	0.8			
				Urawa-shi	1343	0.7			
				Ichikawa-shi	1339	0.7			
				Others	19795	10.0			
				Adachi-ku	154853	55.8			
				Arakawa-ku	10137	3.7			
				Kita-ku	9021	3.2			
				Katsushika-ku	8793	3.2			
				Suginami-ku	6837	2.5			
				Sumida-ku	6331	2.3			
				Toshima-ku	5833	2.1			
				Bunkyō-ku	5201	1.9			
					5092	1.8			

TABLE 1.3

REGIONAL SOURCES OF DAYTIME POPULATION INFLUX OF WORKERS AND STUDENTS OVER 15 YEARS OLD—Continued

Zone	Sector	Region	Total Daytime Workers & Students	Regional Sources of Daytime Workers & Students			Total Workers & Students in Region	Total Workers & Students in Daytime Influx	Total Workers & Students in Daily Outflow
				Region	Number	Percent			
				Edogawa-ku	3796	1.4			
				Itabashi-ku	3673	1.3			
				Setagaya-ku	3340	1.2			
				Shinjuku-ku	3338	1.2			
				Nakano-ku	3222	1.2			
				Nerima-ku	2774	1.0			
				Kōtō-ku	2636	0.9			
				Ōta-ku	2613	0.9			
				Urawa-shi	2360	0.8			
				Ichikawa-shi	2299	0.8			
				Shinagawa-ku	1934	0.7			
				Setagaya-ku	1903	0.7			
				Ōmiya-shi	1785	0.6			
				Matsudo-shi	1757	0.6			
				Kawaguchi-shi	1652	0.6			
				Others	26571	9.6			
2	I	Shinagawa-ku	246337	Ōta-ku	146393	59.4	245389	99944	98996
				Meguro-ku	22259	9.0			
				Setagaya-ku	9948	4.0			
				Kawasaki-shi	9122	3.7			
				Suginami-ku	7324	3.0			
				Minato-ku	5484	2.2			
				Shibuya-ku	3419	1.4			
				Nakano-ku	3324	1.3			
				Shinjuku-ku	2840	1.2			
				Kita-ku	2564	1.0			
				Toshima-ku	1937	0.8			
				Tsurumi-ku	1925	0.8			
				Itabashi-ku	1806	0.7			
					1620	0.7			

TABLE 1.3

REGIONAL SOURCES OF DAYTIME POPULATION INFLUX OF WORKERS AND STUDENTS OVER 15 YEARS OLD—Continued

Zone	Sector	Region	Total Daytime Workers & Students	Regional Sources of Daytime Workers & Students			Total Workers & Students in Region	Total Workers & Students in Daytime Influx	Total Workers & Students in Daily Outflow
				Region	Number	Percent			
				Nerima-ku	1480	0.6			
				Kōhoku-ku	1158	0.5			
				Kanagawa-ku	1072	0.4			
				Others	22662	9.3			
2	II	Meguro-ku	132407	Setagaya-ku	74815	56.5	164834	57592	90019
				Shinagawa-ku	11701	8.8			
				Ōta-ku	6237	4.7			
				Kawasaki-shi	5931	4.5			
				Suginami-ku	4230	3.2			
				Shibuya-ku	4177	3.2			
				Nakano-ku	3246	2.5			
				Shinjuku-ku	2840	1.5			
				Minato-ku	1908	1.4			
				Toshima-ku	1716	1.3			
				Kōhoku-ku	1215	0.9			
				Nerima-ku	1199	0.9			
				Others	956	0.7			
					12236	9.9			
2	II	Shibuya-ku	179949	Setagaya-ku	76411	42.5	162385	103538	85974
				Suginami-ku	18556	10.3			
				Nakano-ku	13583	7.5			
				Meguro-ku	8236	4.6			
				Shinjuku-ku	7529	4.2			
				Ōta-ku	5795	3.2			
				Kawasaki-shi	4537	2.5			
				Minato-ku	3184	1.8			
				Toshima-ku	3174	1.8			
					3049	1.7			

TABLE 1.3

REGIONAL SOURCES OF DAYTIME POPULATION INFLUX OF WORKERS AND STUDENTS OVER 15 YEARS OLD—Continued

Zone	Sector	Region	Total Daytime Workers & Students	Regional Sources of Daytime Workers & Students			Total Workers & Students in Region	Total Workers & Students in Daytime Influx	Total Workers & Students in Daily Outflow
				Region	Number	Percent			
2	III	Shinjuku-ku	314913	Shinagawa-ku	2797	1.6	243586	180274	108947
				Nerima-ku	2298	1.3			
				Itabashi-ku	2231	1.2			
				Kita-ku	1945	1.1			
				Bunkyō-ku	1403	0.8			
				Musashino-shi	1363	0.8			
				Mitaka-shi	1255	0.7			
				Chōfu-shi	1243	0.7			
				Kōhoku-ku	1065	0.6			
				Taitō-ku	860	0.5			
				Fuchū-shi	756	0.4			
				Edogawa-ku	702	0.4			
				Others	18679	9.8			
				Suginami-ku	134639	42.8			
				Nakano-ku	30481	9.7			
				Setagaya-ku	20974	6.7			
				Toshima-ku	13749	4.4			
				Shibuya-ku	10030	3.2			
				Nerima-ku	9383	3.0			
				Kōtō-ku	7877	2.5			
				Itabashi-ku	7416	2.4			
				Kita-ku	6018	1.9			
				Bunkyō-ku	5550	1.8			
				Ōta-ku	5314	1.7			
				Meguro-ku	4337	1.4			
				Shinagawa-ku	4272	1.4			
				Musashino-shi	3326	1.1			
				Minato-ku	3092	1.0			
				Kawasaki-shi	2500	0.8			
				Mitaka-shi	2269	0.7			
					2113	0.7			

TABLE 13

REGIONAL SOURCES OF DAYTIME POPULATION INFLUX OF WORKERS AND STUDENTS OVER 15 YEARS OLD—Continued

Zone	Sector	Region	Total Daytime Workers & Students	Regional Sources of Daytime Workers & Students — Region	Number	Percent	Total Workers & Students in Region	Total Workers & Students in Daytime Influx	Total Workers & Students in Daily Outflow
				Taitō-ku	2012	0.6			
				Adachi-ku	1777	0.6			
				Katsushika-ku	1769	0.5			
				Edogawa-ku	1685	0.5			
				Chōfu-shi	1684	0.5			
				Arakawa-ku	1668	0.5			
				Others	30978	9.6			
2	III	Nakano-ku	186912	Suginami-ku	145169	77.7	285713	41743	140544
				Shinjuku-ku	14119	7.6			
				Nerima-ku	3392	1.8			
				Setagaya-ku	3183	1.7			
				Shibuya-ku	1916	1.0			
				Others	1773	0.9			
					17360	9.3			
2	IV	Toshima-ku	188174	Itabashi-ku	99309	52.8	204948	88865	106639
				Nerima-ku	11940	6.3			
				Kita-ku	9210	4.9			
				Suginami-ku	7513	4.0			
				Shinjuku-ku	6749	3.6			
				Nakano-ku	5216	2.8			
				Setagaya-ku	4401	2.3			
				Bunkyō-ku	3568	1.9			
				Shibuya-ku	3497	1.9			
				Arakawa-ku	2040	1.1			
				Adachi-ku	1689	0.9			
				Ōta-ku	1580	0.8			
				Meguro-ku	1481	0.8			
				Urawa-shi	1389	0.7			
				Taitō-ku	1352	0.7			
					1288	0.7			

TABLE 13

REGIONAL SOURCES OF DAYTIME POPULATION INFLUX OF WORKERS AND STUDENTS OVER 15 YEARS OLD—Continued

Zone	Sector	Region	Total Daytime Workers & Students	Regional Sources of Daytime Workers & Students — Region	Number	Percent	Total Workers & Students in Region	Total Workers & Students in Daytime Influx	Total Workers & Students in Daily Outflow
				Katsushika-ku	1154	0.6			
				Kawagoe-shi	1136	0.6			
				Shinagawa-ku	1100	0.6			
				Omiya-shi	1034	0.5			
				Kawaguchi-shi	994	0.5			
				Tokorosawa-shi	971	0.5			
				Minato-ku	893	0.5			
				Others	18674	10.0			
2	V	Kita-ku	168073	Itabashi-ku	110780	65.9	224596	57293	113816
				Toshima-ku	6428	3.9			
				Adachi-ku	4517	2.7			
				Arakawa-ku	4001	2.4			
				Kawaguchi-shi	3933	2.3			
				Urawa-shi	3862	2.3			
				Ōmiya-shi	2992	1.8			
				Nerima-ku	2949	1.8			
				Suginami-ku	2171	1.3			
				Bunkyō-ku	2077	1.2			
				Warabi-shi	1742	1.0			
				Katsushika-ku	1520	0.9			
				Nakano-ku	1353	0.8			
				Taitō-ku	1321	0.8			
				Shinjuku-ku	1270	0.7			
					1171	0.7			
				Others	15986	9.5			
2	VI	Arakawa-ku	147813	Adachi-ku	105243	71.2	156966	42570	51713
				Kita-ku	8387	5.7			
				Katsushika-ku	5720	3.9			
					2930	2.0			

TABLE 1.3

REGIONAL SOURCES OF DAYTIME POPULATION INFLUX OF WORKERS AND STUDENTS OVER 15 YEARS OLD—Continued

Zone	Sector	Region	Total Daytime Workers & Students	Regional Sources of Daytime Workers & Students — Region	Number	Percent	Total Workers & Students in Region	Total Workers & Students in Daytime Influx	Total Workers & Students in Daily Outflow
				Taitō-ku	2521	1.7	195305	75467	41323
				Toshima-ku	1582	1.1			
				Itabashi-ku	1378	0.9			
				Suginami-ku	1037	0.7			
				Bunkyō-ku	1014	0.7			
				Matsudo-shi	955	0.7			
				Sumida-ku	842	0.6			
				Nerima-ku	836	0.6			
				Urawa-shi	802	0.5			
				Others	14571	9.7			
2	VII	Sumida-ku	229449	Katsushika-ku	153982	67.1	193351	81470	50368
				Edogawa-ku	13162	5.7			
				Kōtō-ku	9371	4.1			
				Adachi-ku	7742	3.4			
				Ichikawa-shi	5343	2.3			
				Taitō-ku	3334	1.5			
				Suginami-ku	2526	1.1			
				Kita-ku	2208	1.0			
				Arakawa-ku	2153	0.9			
				Funahashi-shi	2122	0.9			
				Chiba-shi	2024	0.9			
				Bunkyō-ku	1828	0.8			
					1188	0.5			
				Others	22466	9.8			
2	VIII	Kōtō-ku	224453	Edogawa-ku	142983	63.7			
				Katsushika-ku	15922	7.1			
				Sumida-ku	5687	2.5			
				Ichikawa-shi	4953	2.2			
					4081	1.8			

TABLE   13

REGIONAL SOURCES OF DAYTIME POPULATION INFLUX OF WORKERS AND STUDENTS OVER 15 YEARS OLD—Continued

Zone	Sector	Region	Total Daytime Workers & Students	Regional Sources of Daytime Workers & Students			Total Workers & Students in Region	Total Workers & Students in Daytime Influx	Total Workers & Students in Daily Outflow
				Region	Number	Percent			
3	I	Ōta-ku	334609	Suginami-ku	3452	1.5	386096	94631	146118
				Funahashi-shi	3090	1.4			
				Chiba-shi	2939	1.3			
				Adachi-ku	2772	1.2			
				Kita-ku	2430	1.1			
				Chūō-ku	2006	0.9			
				Nakano-ku	1818	0.8			
				Shinjuku-ku	1817	0.8			
				Setagaya-ku	1792	0.8			
				Arakawa-ku	1649	0.7			
				Ōta-ku	1639	0.7			
				Taitō-ku	1636	0.7			
				Toshima-ku	1629	0.7			
				Bunkyō-ku	1362	0.6			
				Others	21296	9.5			
				Kawasaki-shi	239978	71.7			
				Shinagawa-ku	18599	5.6			
				Setagaya-ku	14048	4.2			
				Tsurumi-ku	7097	2.1			
				Meguro-ku	5536	1.7			
				Suginami-ku	5220	1.6			
				Kōhoku-ku	3577	1.1			
				Kanagawa-ku	2594	0.8			
				Minato-ku	2512	0.8			
					1973	0.6			
				Others	33475	9.8			
3	II	Setagaya-ku	223178	Suginami-ku	154071	69.0	351488	69107	197397
				Meguro-ku	9606	4.3			
				Shibuya-ku	6688	3.0			
				Kawasaki-shi	5440	2.4			
				Ōta-ku	4908	2.2			
				Nakano-ku	4529	2.0			
					3427	1.5			

TABLE 1.3

REGIONAL SOURCES OF DAYTIME POPULATION INFLUX OF WORKERS AND STUDENTS OVER 15 YEARS OLD—Continued

Zone	Sector	Region	Total Daytime Workers & Students	Regional Sources of Daytime Workers & Students — Region	Number	Percent	Total Workers & Students in Region	Total Workers & Students in Daytime Influx	Total Workers & Students in Daily Outflow
				Shinjuku-ku	3137	1.4			
				Shinagawa-ku	2940	1.3			
				Chōfu-shi	2014	0.9			
				Komae-machi	1673	0.7			
				Toshima-ku	1573	0.7			
				Minato-ku	1394	0.6			
				Others	21778	10.0			
3	III	Suginami-ku	146201	Nakano-ku	97343	66.6	393806	48858	296463
				Setagaya-ku	8461	5.8			
				Musashino-shi	5492	3.8			
				Nerima-ku	3309	2.3			
				Shinjuku-ku	3185	2.2			
				Mitaka-shi	2286	1.6			
				Shibuya-ku	2280	1.6			
				Toshima-ku	2065	1.4			
				Koganei-shi	1094	0.7			
				Meguro-ku	1041	0.7			
				Hachiōji-shi	920	0.6			
				Fuchu-shi	915	0.6			
				Ōta-ku	868	0.6			
				Tachikawa-shi	851	0.6			
				Kodaira-machi	806	0.6			
				Others	14479	9.7			
3	IV	Itabashi-ku	177310	Kita-ku	123146	69.5	213559	54164	90413
				Toshima-ku	8330	4.7			
				Nerima-ku	7069	4.0			
				Kawagoe-shi	6356	3.6			
				Toda-machi	2270	1.3			
				Suginami-ku	2129	1.2			
				Nakano-ku	2065	1.2			
				Shinjuku-ku	1666	0.9			
				Bunkyō-ku	1633	0.9			
					1582	0.9			

TABLE 13

REGIONAL SOURCES OF DAYTIME POPULATION INFLUX OF WORKERS AND STUDENTS OVER 15 YEARS OLD—Continued

Zone	Sector	Region	Total Daytime Workers & Students	Regional Sources of Daytime Workers & Students — Region	Number	Percent	Total Workers & Students in Region	Total Workers & Students in Daytime Influx	Total Workers & Students in Daily Outflow
				Kawaguchi-shi	1192	0.7			
				Yamato-machi	1145	0.6			
				Asaka-machi	1133	0.6			
				Others	17594	9.9	151648	27262	91439
		Nerima-ku	87471	Suginami-ku	60209	68.8			
				Itabashi-ku	4066	4.7			
				Toshima-ku	2906	3.3			
				Nakano-ku	2569	2.9			
				Shinjuku-ku	2439	2.8			
				Hoya-machi	1649	2.0			
				Tokorosawa-shi	1125	1.3			
				Kita-ku	907	1.0			
				Setagaya-ku	881	1.0			
				Tanashi-machi	865	1.0			
				Asaka-machi	536	0.6			
				Musashino-shi	455	0.5			
					403	0.5			
				Others	8461	9.6			
3	VI	Adachi-ku	167615	Katsushika-ku	134014	80.0	204843	33601	70829
				Arakawa-ku	4679	2.8			
				Kita-ku	4067	2.5			
				Kusaka-shi	2665	1.6			
				Matsudo-shi	1367	0.8			
				Koshigaya-shi	1335	0.8			
				Taitō-ku	1249	0.7			
				Sumida-ku	1224	0.7			
					1128	0.7			
				Others	15887	9.4			
3	VII	Katsushika-ku	150042	Adachi-ku	118421	78.9	193774	31621	75353
				Edogawa-ku	3996	2.7			
					3929	2.6			

TABLE 1.3

REGIONAL SOURCES OF DAYTIME POPULATION INFLUX OF WORKERS AND STUDENTS OVER 15 YEARS OLD—Continued

Zone	Sector	Region	Total Daytime Workers & Students	Regional Sources of Daytime Workers & Students — Region	Number	Percent	Total Workers & Students in Region	Total Workers & Students in Daytime Influx	Total Workers & Students in Daily Outflow
				Sumida-ku	2997	2.0			
				Matsudo-shi	1976	1.3			
				Ichikawa-shi	1921	1.3			
				Funahashi-shi	1565	1.0			
				Chiba-shi	1171	0.8			
				Others	14066	9.4			
3	VIII	Edogawa-ku	123038		95100	77.3	163467	27938	68367
				Katsushika-ku	4589	3.5			
				Ichikawa-shi	3821	3.1			
				Kōtō-ku	3702	3.0			
				Sumida-ku	2020	1.6			
				Funahashi-shi	1839	1.5			
				Others	11967	10.0			
		Urayasu-machi	5588		5434	97.2	7800	154	2266
				Others	154	2.8			
4	I	Kawasaki-shi	338785		231108	68.2	326188	107677	95080
				Tsurumi-ku	17087	5.6			
				Ōta-ku	14033	4.1			
				Kōhoku-ku	7402	2.2			
				Kanagawa-ku	6487	2.0			
				Setagaya-ku	6174	1.8			
				Hodogaya-ku	4877	1.4			
				Shinagawa-ku	4507	1.3			
				Minami-ku	3936	1.2			
				Yokosuka-shi	3216	1.0			
				Meguro-ku	2978	0.9			
				Totsuka-ku	2701	0.8			
				Others	34279	9.5			

TABLE 13

REGIONAL SOURCES OF DAYTIME POPULATION INFLUX OF WORKERS AND STUDENTS OVER 15 YEARS OLD—Continued

Zone	Sector	Region	Total Daytime Workers & Students	Regional Sources of Daytime Workers & Students			Total Workers & Students in Region	Total Workers & Students in Daytime Influx	Total Workers & Students in Daily Outflow
				Region	Number	Percent			
4	II	Komae-machi	7299	Setagaya-ku	4355	59.7	12323	2944	7968
				Chōfu-shi	595	8.2			
				Kawasaki-shi	419	5.7			
				Machida-shi	332	4.5			
				Suginami-ku	200	2.5			
				Fuchū-shi	161	2.2			
				Hachiōji-shi	151	2.1			
				Mitaka-shi	126	1.7			
				Shibuya-ku	75	1.0			
				Sagamihara-shi	67	0.9			
				Inagi-machi	62	0.8			
					61	0.8			
				Others	698	9.9			
4	III	Mitaka-shi	39119	Suginami-ku	20570	52.6	49787	18549	29217
				Musashino-shi	3448	8.8			
				Hachiōji-shi	2456	6.3			
				Chōfu-shi	876	2.2			
				Nakano-ku	854	2.2			
				Koganei-shi	796	2.0			
				Tachikawa-shi	789	2.0			
				Fuchū-shi	760	1.9			
				Setagaya-ku	708	1.8			
				Kodaira-machi	541	1.4			
				Akishima-shi	492	1.3			
				Kokubunji-machi	443	1.1			
				Hoya-machi	434	1.1			
				Nerima-ku	376	1.0			
				Tanashi-machi	337	0.9			
				Hino-machi	336	0.9			
					333	0.9			

TABLE 13

REGIONAL SOURCES OF DAYTIME POPULATION INFLUX OF WORKERS AND STUDENTS OVER 15 YEARS OLD—Continued

Zone	Sector	Region	Total Daytime Workers & Students	Regional Sources of Daytime Workers & Students			Total Workers & Students in Region	Total Workers & Students in Daytime Influx	Total Workers & Students in Daily Outflow
				Region	Number	Percent			
				Kunitachi-machi	299	0.9			
				Shinjuku-ku	285	0.8			
				Others	3986	9.9			
4	III	Musashino-shi	48143	Suginami-ku	22865	47.5	64644	25278	41779
				Mitaka-shi	6007	12.5			
				Koganei-shi	2752	5.7			
				Nakano-ku	1348	2.8			
				Setagaya-ku	1089	2.3			
				Nerima-ku	996	2.1			
				Hachiōji-ku	994	2.1			
				Hoya-machi	911	1.9			
				Tachikawa-shi	874	1.8			
				Fuchu-shi	720	1.5			
				Kokubunji-machi	662	1.4			
				Kodaira-machi	628	1.3			
				Tanashi-machi	628	1.3			
				Shinjuku-ku	527	1.1			
				Higashimurayama-machi	518	1.1			
				Akishima-shi	471	1.0			
				Shibuya-ku	409	0.8			
				Chōfu-shi	354	0.7			
				Hino-machi	329	0.7			
					321	0.7			
				Others	4740	9.7			
		Chōfu-shi	25282	Setagaya-ku	16157	63.9	32873	9125	16716
				Suginami-ku	1673	6.6			
				Mitaka-shi	1051	4.2			
					769	3.0			

TABLE 13

REGIONAL SOURCES OF DAYTIME POPULATION INFLUX OF WORKERS AND STUDENTS OVER 15 YEARS OLD—Continued

Zone	Sector	Region	Total Daytime Workers & Students	Region (Regional Sources)	Number	Percent	Total Workers & Students in Region	Total Workers & Students in Daytime Influx	Total Workers & Students in Daily Outflow
		Hoya-machi	8670	Fuchū-shi	503	2.0	21954	2602	15886
				Nakano-ku	422	1.7			
				Hachiōji-shi	421	1.7			
				Shibuya-ku	350	1.4			
				Musashino-shi	323	1.3			
				Komae-machi	302	1.2			
				Kawasaki-shi	282	1.1			
				Shinjuku-ku	267	1.1			
				Inagi-machi	244	1.0			
				Others	2518	9.8			
4	IV	Yamato-machi	7528	Itabashi-ku	4029	53.5	8278	3499	4249
				Kawagoe-shi	760	10.1			
				Asaka-machi	443	5.9			
				Nerima-ku	382	5.0			
				Kita-ku	376	5.0			
				Toshima-ku	145	1.9			
				Adachi-machi	139	1.8			
				Suginami-ku	118	1.6			
				Fujimi-mura	107	1.4			
				Niza-machi	106	1.4			
				Fukuoka-mura	93	1.2			
					84	1.1			

TABLE 1.3

REGIONAL SOURCES OF DAYTIME POPULATION INFLUX OF WORKERS AND STUDENTS OVER 15 YEARS OLD—Continued

Zone	Sector	Region	Total Daytime Workers & Students	Regional Sources of Daytime Workers & Students			Total Workers & Students in Region	Total Workers & Students in Daytime Influx	Total Workers & Students in Daily Outflow
				Region	Number	Percent			
4	V	Toda-machi	10790	Sakado-machi	64	0.9	15698	2318	7226
				Others	682	9.2			
		Warabi-shi	13349	Kawaguchi-shi	8472	78.5	25275	3709	15635
				Warabi-shi	426	3.9			
				Itabashi-ku	379	3.5			
				Kita-ku	294	2.7			
					240	2.2			
				Others	979	9.2			
		Kawaguchi-shi	81472	Urawa-shi	9640	72.2	85915	20819	25262
				Kawaguchi-shi	771	5.8			
				Ōmiya-shi	617	4.6			
				Toda-machi	501	3.8			
				Kita-ku	350	2.6			
					227	1.7			
				Others	1243	9.3			
				Urawa-shi	60653	74.4			
				Ōmiya-shi	2905	3.6			
				Warabi-shi	2416	3.0			
				Hatogaya-machi	2301	2.8			
				Kita-ku	2043	2.5			
					1967	2.4			
				Toda-machi	1028	1.3			
				Others	8159	10.0			
		Hatogaya-machi	4760	Kawaguchi-shi	4162	87.4	9649	598	5487
				Others	373	7.8			
					225	4.8			

TABLE 13

REGIONAL SOURCES OF DAYTIME POPULATION INFLUX OF WORKERS AND STUDENTS OVER 15 YEARS OLD—Continued

Zone	Sector	Region	Total Daytime Workers & Students	Regional Sources of Daytime Workers & Students			Total Workers & Students in Region	Total Workers & Students in Daytime Influx	Total Workers & Students in Daily Outflow	
				Region	Number	Percent				
4	VI	Kusaka-shi	16611		13634	82.1	19899	2977	6265	
				Koshigaya-shi	662	4.0				
				Adachi-ku	415	2.5				
				Kasukabe-shi	306	1.8				
				Others	1594	9.6				
		Yashio-mura	5688		5303	93.2	6960	385	1657	47.7
				Others	385	6.8				
		Misato-mura	7399		7208	97.4	9540	191	2332	57.9
				Others	191	2.6				
		Matsudo-shi	28317		23292	82.3	43327	5025	20035	21.4
				Kashiwa-shi	816	2.9				
				Nagareyama-machi	438	1.5				
				Katsushika-ku	367	1.3				
				Ichikawa-shi	353	1.2				
				Abiko-machi	280	1.0				
				Others	2771	9.8				
4	VII	Ichikawa-shi	55909		40786	72.9	81000	15183	40214	
				Funabashi-shi	2741	4.9				
				Chiba-shi	2269	4.1				
				Edogawa-ku	1924	3.4				
				Katsushika-ku	1346	2.4				
				Matsudo-shi	1001	1.8				
				Sumida-ku	501	1.0				
				Others	5401	9.5				
5	I	Tsurumi-ku	122328		70558	57.7	118381	51770	47823	
				Kawasaki-shi	10964	9.0				
				Kanagawa-ku	6476	5.3				

TABLE 13

REGIONAL SOURCES OF DAYTIME POPULATION INFLUX OF WORKERS AND STUDENTS OVER 15 YEARS OLD—Continued

| Zone | Sector | Region | Total Daytime Workers & Students | Regional Sources of Daytime Workers & Students | | | Total Workers & Students in Region | Total Workers & Students in Daytime Influx | Total Workers & Students in Daily Outflow |
				Region	Number	Percent			
				Hodogaya-ku	3683	3.0			
				Kōhoku-ku	3595	2.9			
				Ōta-ku	3582	2.9			
				Minami-ku	3212	2.6			
				Totsuka-ku	2188	1.8			
				Nishi-ku	2181	1.8			
				Yokosuka-shi	2040	1.7			
				Naka-ku	1453	1.2			
				Others	12396	9.8			
5	III	Koganei-shi	16186	Suginami-ku	7391	45.7	23164	8795	15773
				Meguro-ku	1090	6.7			
				Hachiōji-shi	531	3.3			
				Musashino-shi	530	3.3			
				Kodaira-machi	473	2.9			
				Kokubunji-machi	453	2.8			
				Nerima-ku	405	2.5			
				Tachikawa-shi	395	2.4			
				Fuchū-shi	383	2.4			
				Mitaka-shi	380	2.4			
				Setagaya-ku	335	2.1			
				Nakano-ku	290	1.7			
				Akishima-shi	253	1.6			
				Higashimurayama-machi	243	1.5			
					230	1.4			
				Kunitachi-machi	195	1.2			
				Hino-machi	167	1.0			
				Bunkyō-ku	145	0.9			
				Ōme-shi	135	0.8			
				Shinjuku-ku	122	0.8			

TABLE 13

REGIONAL SOURCES OF DAYTIME POPULATION INFLUX OF WORKERS AND STUDENTS OVER 15 YEARS OLD—Continued

| Zone | Sector | Region | Total Daytime Workers & Students | Regional Sources of Daytime Workers & Students | | | Total Workers & Students in Region | Total Workers & Students in Daytime Influx | Total Workers & Students in Daily Outflow |
				Region	Number	Percent			
		Tanashi-machi	12239	Ōta-ku	120	0.7	15180	6295	9236
				Sunakawa-machi	118	0.7			
				Shibuya-ku	107	0.7			
				Yamato-machi	99	0.6			
				Others	1790	9.9			
				Tokorosawa-shi	5994	48.6			
				Hoya-machi	759	6.1			
				Suginami-ku	743	5.8			
				Nerima-ku	548	4.5			
				Higashimurayama-machi	479	3.9			
					477	3.9			
				Kodaira-machi	340	2.8			
				Musashino-shi	293	2.4			
				Sayama-shi	279	2.3			
				Kurume-machi	270	2.2			
				Nakano-ku	204	1.7			
				Kawagoe-shi	182	1.5			
				Mitaka-shi	166	1.4			
				Shinjuku-ku	122	1.0			
				Koganei-shi	108	0.9			
				Toshima-ku	86	0.7			
				Ōta-ku	83	0.7			
				Others	1156	9.6			
		Kurume-machi	4331	Tokorosawa-shi	3672	84.8	9322	659	5650
				Nerima-ku	96	2.2			
				Hoya-machi	85	2.0			
					62	1.4			
				Others	386	9.6			

TABLE 13

REGIONAL SOURCES OF DAYTIME POPULATION INFLUX OF WORKERS AND STUDENTS OVER 15 YEARS OLD—Continued

Zone	Sector	Region	Total Daytime Workers & Students	Regional Sources of Daytime Workers & Students — Region	Number	Percent	Total Workers & Students in Region	Total Workers & Students in Daytime Influx	Total Workers & Students in Daily Outflow
5	IV	Niza-machi	5850	Adachi-machi	4553	77.8	7261	1297	2708
				Asaka-machi	221	3.8			
				Itabashi-ku	143	2.5			
				Tokorosawa-shi	106	1.8			
				Kawagoe-shi	95	1.6			
				Suginami-ku	64	1.1			
				Fujimi-mura	62	1.1			
					59	1.0			
				Others	547	9.3			
		Kiyose-machi	5723	Tokorosawa-shi	4705	82.2	8192	1018	3487
				Nerima-ku	188	3.3			
				Kurume-machi	134	2.3			
					126	2.2			
				Others	570	10.0			
		Adachi-machi	4810	Fujimi-mura	3313	69.0	6140	1497	2827
				Suginami-ku	151	3.1			
				Kawagoe-shi	127	2.6			
				Asaka-machi	124	2.6			
				Niza-machi	105	2.2			
				Itabashi-ku	98	2.0			
				Setagaya-ku	84	1.7			
				Toshima-ku	68	1.4			
				Urawa-shi	67	1.4			
				Nerima-ku	56	1.2			
				Yamato-machi	52	1.2			
				Meguro-ku	43	0.9			
					42	0.9			
				Others	480	9.8			

- 357 -

TABLE   13

REGIONAL SOURCES OF DAYTIME POPULATION INFLUX OF WORKERS AND STUDENTS OVER 15 YEARS OLD—Continued

Zone	Sector	Region	Total Daytime Workers & Students	Regional Sources of Daytime Workers & Students			Total Workers & Students in Region	Total Workers & Students in Daytime Influx	Total Workers & Students in Daily Outflow
				Region	Number	Percent			
5		Asaka-machi	10978	Itabashi-ku	7673	69.6	12534	3341	4897
				Kawagoe-shi	425	3.9			
				Niza-machi	369	3.4			
				Yamato-machi	346	3.2			
				Nerima-ku	336	3.1			
				Adachi-machi	260	2.4			
				Suginami-ku	174	1.6			
				Toshima-ku	149	1.4			
				Kita-ku	109	1.0			
					96	0.9			
				Others	1077	9.5			
	V	Urawa-shi	61446	Ōmiya-shi	44125	71.8	85019	17321	40894
				Yono-shi	4556	7.4			
				Kawaguchi-shi	2438	4.0			
				Warabi-shi	1168	1.9			
				Kawagoe-shi	815	1.3			
				Kawagoe-shi	608	1.0			
				Ageo-shi	589	1.0			
				Iwatsuki-shi	496	0.8			
				Kita-ku	469	0.8			
				Others	6182	10.0			
		Misono-mura	4044		4015	99.3	5058	25	29
				Others	29	0.7			
		Koshigaya-shi	20468		18704	91.4	25045	1764	6341
				Yoshikawa-machi	279	1.4			
				Kusaka-shi	272	1.3			
				Matsubushi-mura	218	1.1			

TABLE 13

REGIONAL SOURCES OF DAYTIME POPULATION INFLUX OF WORKERS AND STUDENTS OVER 15 YEARS OLD—Continued

Zone	Sector	Region	Total Daytime Workers & Students	Regional Sources of Daytime Workers & Students — Region	Number	Percent	Total Workers & Students in Region	Total Workers & Students in Daytime Influx	Total Workers & Students in Daily Outflow
				Kasukabe-shi	212	1.0			
				Others	783	3.8			
5	VI	Yoshikawa-machi	7685		7476	97.3	9146	209	1670
				Others	209	2.7			
5		Nagareyama-machi	7711		7290	94.5	12982	421	5692
				Others	421	5.5			
5	VII	Kamagaya-machi	5015		4288	85.5	6689	727	2401
				Funahashi-shi	247	4.9			
				Others	480	9.6			
5	VIII	Funahashi-shi	49339		39338	79.7	69069	10001	29731
				Chiba-shi	2269	4.6			
				Narashino-shi	1724	3.5			
				Ichikawa-shi	1448	2.9			
				Others	4560	9.3			
6	I	Nishi-ku	58250		24592	42.2	52444	33658	27852
				Hodogaya-ku	5528	10.0			
				Minami-ku	4339	7.4			
				Kanagawa-ku	3901	6.7			
				Totsuka-ku	2280	3.9			
				Naka-ku	2201	3.8			
				Kōhoku-ku	2168	3.7			
				Yokosuka-shi	1783	3.1			
				Isogo-ku	1652	2.8			
				Kanazawa-ku	1090	1.9			
				Kawasaki-shi	1088	1.9			
				Tsurumi-ku	859	1.5			

TABLE 13

REGIONAL SOURCES OF DAYTIME POPULATION INFLUX OF WORKERS AND STUDENTS OVER 15 YEARS OLD—Continued

Zone	Sector	Region	Total Daytime Workers & Students	Regional Sources of Daytime Workers & Students			Total Workers & Students in Region	Total Workers & Students in Daytime Influx	Total Workers & Students in Daily Outflow
				Region	Number	Percent			
				Ōta-ku	627	1.2			
				Others	6142	9.9			
6	I	Naka-ku	119740	Minami-ku	45322	37.9	65286	74418	19964
				Nishi-ku	16000	13.0			
				Isogo-ku	6933	5.8			
				Kanagawa-ku	6595	5.5			
				Hodogaya-ku	6374	5.3			
				Kōhoku-ku	6213	5.2			
				Yokosuka-shi	4017	3.4			
				Totsuka-ku	3670	3.1			
				Kawasaki-shi	2819	2.4			
				Kanazawa-ku	2776	2.3			
				Tsurumi-ku	2752	2.3			
				Fujisawa-shi	2389	2.0			
				Kamakura-shi	1703	1.4			
				Others	1614	1.3			
					10563	9.1			
		Kanagawa-ku	82953	Kōhoku-ku	41786	50.4	86345	41167	44559
				Minami-ku	5480	6.6			
				Hodogaya-ku	4473	5.4			
				Tsurumi-ku	3928	4.7			
				Kanagawa-ku	3424	4.1			
				Kawasaki-shi	3291	4.0			
				Totsuka-ku	2451	3.0			
				Naka-ku	2332	2.8			
				Yokosuka-shi	2273	2.7			
				Isogo-ku	1920	2.3			
				Kanazawa-ku	1539	1.9			
					1321	1.6			

TABLE 1.3

REGIONAL SOURCES OF DAYTIME POPULATION INFLUX OF WORKERS AND STUDENTS OVER 15 YEARS OLD—Continued

Zone	Sector	Region	Total Daytime Workers & Students	Regional Sources of Daytime Workers & Students			Total Workers & Students in Region	Total Workers & Students in Daytime Influx	Total Workers & Students in Daily Outflow
				Region	Number	Percent			
				Ōta-ku	999	1.2			
				Others	7736	9.3			
6	II	Kōhoku-ku	51666	Kanagawa-ku	31526	61.0	74046	20140	42520
				Kawasaki-shi	1855	3.6			
				Setagaya-ku	1783	3.5			
				Ōta-ku	1633	3.2			
				Meguro-ku	1466	2.8			
				Suginami-ku	1139	2.2			
				Tsurumi-ku	1112	2.2			
				Minami-ku	859	1.7			
				Hodogaya-ku	714	1.4			
				Nishi-ku	682	1.3			
				Sagamihara-shi	654	1.3			
				Shinagawa-ku	625	1.2			
				Shibuya-ku	520	1.0			
				Naka-ku	475	0.9			
				Minato-ku	448	0.9			
				Machida-shi	441	0.9			
				Nakano-ku	373	0.7			
					331	0.6			
				Others	5030	9.6			
	II	Inagi-machi	3409	Fuchū-shi	2791	81.9	5465	618	2674
				Setagaya-ku	85	2.5			
				Kawasaki-shi	80	2.4			
				Tachikawa-shi	61	1.8			
					60	1.8			
				Others	332	9.6			

- 361 -

TABLE 1.3

REGIONAL SOURCES OF DAYTIME POPULATION INFLUX OF WORKERS AND STUDENTS OVER 15 YEARS OLD—Continued

Zone	Sector	Region	Total Daytime Workers & Students	Regional Sources of Daytime Workers & Students			Total Workers & Students in Region	Total Workers & Students in Daytime Influx	Total Workers & Students in Daily Outflow
				Region	Number	Percent			
6	III	Tama-mura	2720		2404	88.4	4570	316	2172
				Yuki-mura	77	2.8			
				Others	239	8.8			
		Fuchū-shi	33850		19305	57.0	37213	14545	17908
				Hachiōji-shi	1372	4.1			
				Kokubunji-machi	943	2.8			
				Tachikawa-shi	853	2.5			
				Suginami-ku	818	2.4			
				Chōfu-shi	710	2.1			
				Setagaya-ku	646	1.9			
				Kunitachi-machi	615	1.8			
				Koganei-shi	607	1.8			
				Hino-machi	585	1.7			
				Akishima-shi	505	1.5			
				Tama-mura	487	1.4			
				Inagi-machi	424	1.3			
				Kodaira-machi	418	1.2			
				Musashino-shi	357	1.1			
				Mitaka-shi	333	1.0			
				Higashimurayama-machi	276	0.8			
				Kawasaki-shi	253	0.7			
				Nakano-ku	247	0.7			
				Ōme-shi	243	0.7			
				Sagamihara-shi	237	0.7			
				Yamato-machi	198	0.6			
				Yuki-mura	195	0.6			
				Others	3223	9.6			

TABLE 1.3

REGIONAL SOURCES OF DAYTIME POPULATION INFLUX OF WORKERS AND STUDENTS OVER 15 YEARS OLD—Continued

Zone	Sector	Region	Total Daytime Workers & Students	Regional Sources of Daytime Workers & Students			Total Workers & Students in Region	Total Workers & Students in Daytime Influx	Total Workers & Students in Daily Outflow
				Region	Number	Percent			
		Kunitachi-machi	13518	Suginami-ku	5878	43.5	16141	7640	11263
				Tachikawa-shi	1397	10.3			
				Musashino-shi	614	4.5			
				Kokubunji-machi	470	3.5			
				Fuchū-shi	422	3.1			
				Hachiōji-shi	410	3.0			
				Mitaka-shi	386	2.9			
				Akishima-shi	299	2.3			
				Koganei-shi	297	2.3			
				Nakano-ku	249	1.8			
				Setagaya-ku	246	1.8			
				Ōme-shi	232	1.7			
				Hino-machi	222	1.6			
				Shinjuku-ku	165	1.2			
				Nerima-ku	127	0.9			
				Higashimurayama-machi	97	0.7			
				Fussa-machi	95	0.7			
				Sunakawa-machi	93	0.7			
				Machida-shi	84	0.6			
				Ōta-ku	81	0.6			
				Hamura-machi	72	0.5			
				Yamato-machi	72	0.5			
				Toshima-ku	68	0.5			
				Meguro-ku	61	0.4			
				Shibuya-ku	60	0.4			
				Others	1261	9.6			
		Kokubunji-machi	14579	Suginami-ku	6951	47.7	19812	7628	12861
					960	6.6			
				Hachiōji-shi	498	3.4			

TABLE 1.3

REGIONAL SOURCES OF DAYTIME POPULATION INFLUX OF WORKERS AND STUDENTS OVER 15 YEARS OLD—Continued

Zone	Sector	Region	Total Daytime Workers & Students	Regional Sources of Daytime Workers & Students			Total Workers & Students in Region	Total Workers & Students in Daytime Influx	Total Workers & Students in Daily Outflow
				Region	Number	Percent			
		Kodaira-machi	15864	Kodaira-machi	492	3.4	24774	5053	13963
				Koganei-shi	459	3.1			
				Tachikawa-shi	421	2.9			
				Musashino-shi	416	2.9			
				Fuchū-shi	379	2.6			
				Mitaka-shi	312	2.1			
				Kunitachi-machi	259	1.8			
				Akishima-shi	237	1.6			
				Higashimurayama-machi	216	1.5			
				Nakano-ku	206	1.4			
				Setagaya-ku	186	1.3			
				Yamato-machi	164	1.1			
				Shinjuku-ku	128	0.9			
				Ōme-shi	126	0.9			
				Hino-machi	125	0.9			
				Itabashi-ku	113	0.8			
				Tokorosawa-shi	108	0.7			
				Toshima-ku	107	0.7			
				Sunakawa-machi	103	0.7			
				Murayama-machi	94	0.6			
				Nerima-ku	86	0.6			
				Others	1433	9.8			
				Suginami-ku	10811	68.1			
				Kokubunji-machi	522	3.3			
				Higashimurayama-machi	429	2.7			
					429	2.7			
				Hachiōji-shi	282	1.8			
				Yamato-machi	216	1.4			

TABLE 1.3

REGIONAL SOURCES OF DAYTIME POPULATION INFLUX OF WORKERS AND STUDENTS OVER 15 YEARS OLD—Continued

Zone	Sector	Region	Total Daytime Workers & Students	Regional Sources of Daytime Workers & Students — Region	Number	Percent	Total Workers & Students in Region	Total Workers & Students in Daytime Influx	Total Workers & Students in Daily Outflow
				Koganei-shi	216	1.4			
				Tokorosawa-shi	208	1.3			
				Tachikawa-shi	202	1.2			
				Fuchū-shi	163	1.0			
				Nakano-ku	126	0.9			
				Musashino-shi	123	0.8			
				Setagaya-ku	105	0.7			
				Murayama-machi	101	0.6			
				Akishima-shi	100	0.6			
				Nerima-ku	93	0.5			
				Mitaka-shi	85	0.4			
				Ōme-shi	85	0.4			
				Hino-machi	84	0.4			
				Others	1484	9.8			
		Higashimurayama-machi	7963		6622	83.2	18536	1341	11914
				Tokorosawa-shi	264	3.3			
				Yamato-machi	137	1.7			
				Suginami-ku	82	1.0			
				Nerima-ku	61	0.8			
				Others	797	10.0			
6	IV	Tokorosawa-shi	27704		20762	74.9	32404	6942	11642
				Sayama-shi	934	3.4			
				Kawagoe-shi	819	3.0			
				Hannō-shi	719	2.6			
				Musashi-machi	712	2.6			
				Higashimurayama-machi	452	1.6			
				Nerima-ku	227	0.8			
				Hidaka-machi	169	0.6			

TABLE 1.3

REGIONAL SOURCES OF DAYTIME POPULATION INFLUX OF WORKERS AND STUDENTS OVER 15 YEARS OLD—Continued

Zone	Sector	Region	Total Daytime Workers & Students	Regional Sources of Daytime Workers & Students			Total Workers & Students in Region	Total Workers & Students in Daytime Influx	Total Workers & Students in Daily Outflow
				Region	Number	Percent			
6	V			Fuchū-shi	167	0.6			
				Others	2743	9.9			
		Miyoshi-mura	2002		1991	99.5	2482	11	491
				Others	11	0.5			
		Fujimi-mura	4308		4221	98.0	6437	87	2216
				Others	87	2.0			
		Yono-shi	15857		8727	55.0	20080	7130	11353
				Omiya-shi	2834	17.9			
				Urawa-shi	1666	10.5			
				Ageo-shi	295	1.9			
				Iwatsuki-shi	235	1.5			
				Hasuda-machi	206	1.3			
				Kōnosu-shi	182	1.1			
				Kawagoe-shi	174	1.1			
				Others	1538	9.7			
		Ōmiya-shi	61571		49226	79.9	85001	11345	35775
				Urawa-shi	1860	3.0			
				Ageo-shi	1250	2.1			
				Yono-shi	1137	1.9			
				Iwatsuki-shi	847	1.4			
				Kawagoe-shi	556	0.9			
				Hasuda-machi	527	0.9			
				Others	5168	9.9			
		Iwatsuki-shi	14578		13777	94.5	18379	801	4602
				Others	801	5.5			

TABLE 1.3

REGIONAL SOURCES OF DAYTIME POPULATION INFLUX OF WORKERS AND STUDENTS OVER 15 YEARS OLD—Continued

Zone	Sector	Region	Total Daytime Workers & Students	Regional Sources of Daytime Workers & Students			Total Workers & Students in Region	Total Workers & Students in Daytime Influx	Total Workers & Students in Daily Outflow
				Region	Number	Percent			
6	VI	Matsubushi-mura	3971		3891	98.0	5005	80	2144
				Others	80	2.0			
6	VII	Kashiwa-shi	20453	Nagareyama-machi	17952	87.8	31301	2506	13349
					552	2.7			
				Others	1954	9.5			
6		Shōnan-mura	6406		6204	96.8	7174	202	970
				Others	202	3.2			
		Shirai-mura	4317		4306	99.8	4812	11	506
				Others	11	0.2			
	VIII	Narashino-shi	17159	Funahashi-shi	9702	56.5	21186	7457	11484
				Chiba-shi	1456	8.5			
				Ichikawa-shi	1342	7.8			
				Sakura-shi	531	3.1			
				Suginami-ku	350	2.0			
				Yachiyo-machi	329	1.9			
				Edogawa-ku	285	1.7			
				Narita-shi	225	1.3			
				Katsushika-ku	178	1.0			
				Setagaya-ku	168	1.0			
				Nakano-ku	161	0.9			
				Ōta-ku	151	0.9			
				Shinjuku-ku	138	0.8			
				Kōtō-ku	126	0.7			
				Sumida-ku	100	0.6			
				Shisui-machi	86	0.5			
				Kita-ku	79	0.5			
				Others	78	0.5			
					1674	9.8			

TABLE 1.3

REGIONAL SOURCES OF DAYTIME POPULATION INFLUX OF WORKERS AND STUDENTS OVER 15 YEARS OLD—Continued

Zone	Sector	Region	Total Daytime Workers & Students	Regional Sources of Daytime Workers & Students — Region	Number	Percent	Total Workers & Students in Region	Total Workers & Students in Daytime Influx	Total Workers & Students in Daily Outflow
7	I	Isogo-ku	20142	Minami-ku	13716	68.1	36126	6426	22410
				Naka-ku	2019	10.0			
				Kanazawa-ku	804	4.0			
				Nishi-ku	714	3.5			
				Yokosuka-shi	515	2.6			
					489	2.4			
				Others	1885	9.4			
		Minami-ku	62393	Isogo-ku	45611	73.1	94827	16782	49216
				Naka-ku	2367	3.8			
				Nishi-ku	1880	3.0			
				Hodogaya-ku	1801	3.0			
				Kanazawa-ku	1647	2.6			
				Yokosuka-shi	1344	2.2			
				Kanagawa-ku	1260	2.0			
					1240	2.0			
				Others	5243	8.3			
		Hodogaya-ku	37266	Nishi-ku	25983	69.7	66905	11283	40922
				Totsuka-ku	1731	4.6			
				Minami-ku	1531	4.1			
				Kanagawa-ku	1478	4.0			
				Yamato-shi	1000	2.7			
				Kōhoku-ku	685	1.8			
				Naka-ku	624	1.7			
					503	1.4			
				Others	3731	10.0			
7	II	Machida-shi	21939	Sagamihara-shi	18017	82.1	34531	3922	46514 / 21.1
				Setagaya-ku	1044	4.8			
					432	2.0			

TABLE 1.3

REGIONAL SOURCES OF DAYTIME POPULATION INFLUX OF WORKERS AND STUDENTS OVER 15 YEARS OLD—Continued

Zone	Sector	Region	Total Daytime Workers & Students	Regional Sources of Daytime Workers & Students — Region	Number	Percent	Total Workers & Students in Region	Total Workers & Students in Daytime Influx	Total Workers & Students in Daily Outflow
7	III			Hachiōji-shi	397	1.8			
				Others	2049	9.3			
		Yuki-mura	2279	Yuki-mura	2263	99.3	3423	16	1160
				Others	16	0.7			
		Hino-machi	16372	Hino-machi	8901	54.4	20710	7471	11809
				Hachiōji-shi	3621	22.1			
				Tachikawa-shi	483	3.0			
				Suginami-ku	337	2.1			
				Akishima-shi	224	1.4			
				Machida-shi	208	1.3			
				Fuchū-shi	178	1.1			
				Kunitachi-machi	156	1.0			
				Musashino-shi	145	0.9			
				Yuki-mura	133	0.8			
				Mitaka-shi	117	0.7			
				Koganei-shi	116	0.7			
				Kokubunji-machi	113	0.7			
				Others	1640	9.8			
		Tachikawa-shi	45250	Tachikawa-shi	20398	45.1	34984	24858	14586
				Akishima-shi	3019	6.7			
				Hachiōji-shi	2492	5.5			
				Suginami-ku	1489	3.3			
				Kunitachi-machi	1433	3.2			
				Sunakawa-machi	1331	2.9			
				Hino-machi	1161	2.6			
				Fuchū-shi	1057	2.3			
				Ōme-shi	1015	2.2			
				Kokubunji-machi	810	1.8			

TABLE 1.3

REGIONAL SOURCES OF DAYTIME POPULATION INFLUX OF WORKERS AND STUDENTS OVER 15 YEARS OLD—Continued

Zone	Sector	Region	Total Daytime Workers & Students	Regional Sources of Daytime Workers & Students — Region	Number	Percent	Total Workers & Students in Region	Total Workers & Students in Daytime Influx	Total Workers & Students in Daily Outflow
				Musashino-shi	756	1.7			
				Kodaira-machi	734	1.6			
				Fussa-machi	696	1.5			
				Yamato-machi	666	1.5			
				Murayama-machi	627	1.4			
				Koganei-shi	576	1.3			
				Higashimurayama-machi	572	1.3			
				Mitaka-shi	563	1.2			
				Akita-machi	434	1.0			
				Nakano-ku	420	0.9			
				Kōnosu-shi	391	0.9			
				Iwatsuki-shi	341	0.8			
				Others	4275	9.3			
		Sunakawa-machi	4347	Tachikawa-shi	2902	66.8	6553	1415	3651
				Akishima-shi	288	6.6			
				Yamato-machi	124	2.9			
				Hachiōji-shi	104	2.4			
				Kokubunji-machi	103	2.4			
				Murayama-machi	74	1.7			
				Kunitachi-machi	69	1.6			
				Nerima-ku	62	1.4			
				Setagaya-ku	61	1.4			
				Kodaira-machi	55	1.3			
				Ōme-shi	55	1.3			
					47	1.1			
				Others	373	9.1			
		Yamato-machi	4374	Murayama-machi	164	3.7	6790	1140	3556
				Tachikawa-shi	135	3.1			

TABLE 1.3

REGIONAL SOURCES OF DAYTIME POPULATION INFLUX OF WORKERS AND STUDENTS OVER 15 YEARS OLD—Continued

Zone	Sector	Region	Total Daytime Workers & Students	Regional Sources of Daytime Workers & Students			Total Workers & Students in Region	Total Workers & Students in Daytime Influx	Total Workers & Students in Daily Outflow
				Region	Number	Percent			
				Tokorosawa-shi	99	2.3			
				Akishima-shi	85	1.9			
				Higashimurayama-machi	80	1.8			
				Sunakawa-machi	76	1.7			
				Hachioji-shi	68	1.6			
				Others	433	10.0			
7	IV	Ōi-mura	2298		2100	91.4	2770	198	670
				Others	198	8.6			
7		Fukuoka-mura	2949		2524	85.6	7936	425	5412
				Kawagoe-shi	233	7.9			
				Others	192	6.5			
7	V	Kasukabe-shi	14834		12322	83.1	17432	2512	5110
				Hannō-shi	428	2.9			
				Ōmiya-shi	401	2.7			
				Sugito-machi	260	1.4			
				Others	1423	9.9			
7		Shōwa-mura	6181		5713	92.4	7420	468	1705
				Others	468	7.6			
7	VI	Noda-shi	26088		23800	91.2	28749	2288	4949
				Others	2288	8.8			
7	VII	Abiko-machi	9686		8674	89.6	13885	1012	5211
				Kashiwa-shi	271	2.8			
				Others	741	7.6			

TABLE 1.3
REGIONAL SOURCES OF DAYTIME POPULATION INFLUX OF WORKERS AND STUDENTS OVER 15 YEARS OLD—Continued

Zone	Sector	Region	Total Daytime Workers & Students	Regional Sources of Daytime Workers & Students — Region	Number	Percent	Total Workers & Students in Region	Total Workers & Students in Daytime Influx	Total Workers & Students in Daily Outflow
7	VIII	Yachiyo-machi	7529		7397	98.2	11305	132	3908
				Others	132	1.8			
		Chiba-shi	111655		91288	81.8	122868	20367	31580
				Funahashi-shi	1739	1.6			
				Yotsukaidō-machi	1586	1.4			
				Ichihara-machi	1333	1.2			
				Narashino-shi	1304	1.2			
				Kisarazu-shi	1222	1.1			
				Sakura-shi	1204	1.1			
				Goi-machi	1142	1.0			
				Others	10837	9.6			
7	IX	Goi-machi	10871		9726	89.5	11836	1145	2110
				Ichihara-machi	307	2.8			
				Others	838	7.7			
		Sodegaura-machi	7085		6912	97.6	7864	173	952
				Others	173	2.4			
8	I	Kanazawa-ku	26140		15435	59.0	34150	10705	18715
				Yokosuka-shi	3476	13.3			
				Isogo-ku	1436	5.5			
				Minami-ku	1299	5.0			
				Zushi-shi	585	2.2			
				Kanagawa-ku	460	1.8			
				Hodogaya-ku	376	1.4			
				Nishi-ku	366	1.4			
				Naka-ku	357	1.4			
				Others	2350	9.0			

TABLE 13

REGIONAL SOURCES OF DAYTIME POPULATION INFLUX OF WORKERS AND STUDENTS OVER 15 YEARS OLD—Continued

Zone	Sector	Region	Total Daytime Workers & Students	Regional Sources of Daytime Workers & Students			Total Workers & Students in Region	Total Workers & Students in Daytime Influx	Total Workers & Students in Daily Outflow
				Region	Number	Percent			
8		Totsuka-ku	38569		26523	68.8	55108	12046	28585
				Kamakura-shi	2081	5.4			
				Yokosuka-shi	1811	4.7			
				Fujisawa-shi	1279	3.3			
				Hodogaya-ku	900	2.3			
				Minami-ku	697	1.8			
				Zushi-shi	588	1.5			
				Chigasaki-shi	515	1.3			
				Yamato-shi	463	1.2			
				Others	3712	9.7			
	II	Yamato-shi	12284		9433	76.8	18840	2851	9407
				Sagamihara-shi	428	3.5			
				Fujisawa-shi	312	2.5			
				Atsugi-shi	298	2.4			
				Machida-shi	270	2.2			
				Totsuka-ku	259	2.1			
				Ebina-machi	217	1.8			
				Others	1067	8.7			
		Sagamihara-shi	36464		29001	79.5	47860	7463	18859
				Machida-shi	1791	5.0			
				Hachiōji-shi	497	1.4			
				Kōhoku-ku	400	1.1			
				Shiroyama-machi	393	1.1			
				Yamato-shi	389	1.1			
				Zama-machi	384	1.1			
				Others	3609	9.7			

TABLE 1.3

REGIONAL SOURCES OF DAYTIME POPULATION INFLUX OF WORKERS AND STUDENTS OVER 15 YEARS OLD—Continued

Zone	Sector	Region	Total Daytime Workers & Students	Regional Sources of Daytime Workers & Students			Total Workers & Students in Region	Total Workers & Students in Daytime Influx	Total Workers & Students in Daily Outflow
				Region	Number	Percent			
8	III	Zama-machi	7478	Sagamihara-shi	4333	57.9	7628	3145	3295
				Atsugi-shi	1164	15.6			
				Yamato-shi	261	3.5			
				Machida-shi	237	3.2			
				Ebina-machi	219	3.0			
				Setagaya-ku	126	1.7			
				Totsuka-ku	90	1.2			
				Hodogaya-ku	77	1.0			
				Aikawa-machi	76	1.0			
				Minami-ku	72	1.0			
				Others	64	0.9			
					759	10.0			
		Hachiōji-shi	66670	Hino-machi	55899	83.8	77945	10771	22046
				Machida-shi	1290	1.9			
				Sagamihara-shi	1025	1.5			
				Tachikawa-shi	962	1.4			
				Setagaya-ku	790	1.2			
				Others	134	0.9			
					6570	9.3			
		Akishima-shi	14860	Tachikawa-shi	9167	61.7	20039	5693	10872
				Fussa-machi	700	4.7			
				Hachiōji-shi	499	3.4			
				Ōme-shi	424	2.9			
				Akita-machi	400	2.7			
				Sunakawa-machi	369	2.5			
				Hamura-machi	253	1.7			
				Murayama-machi	206	1.4			
				Mizuho-machi	200	1.3			
					194	1.3			

TABLE 13

REGIONAL SOURCES OF DAYTIME POPULATION INFLUX OF WORKERS AND STUDENTS OVER 15 YEARS OLD—Continued

Zone	Sector	Region	Total Daytime Workers & Students	Regional Sources of Daytime Workers & Students — Region	Number	Percent	Total Workers & Students in Region	Total Workers & Students in Daytime Influx	Total Workers & Students in Daily Outflow
				Kunitachi-machi	186	1.3			
				Suginami-ku	183	1.2			
				Musashino-shi	180	1.2			
				Hino-machi	180	1.2			
				Kodaira-machi	137	0.9			
				Fuchū-shi	133	0.9			
				Others	1449	9.7			
		Fussa-machi	11988	Ōme-shi	6581	54.9	10546	5407	3965
				Akita-machi	801	6.7			
				Akishima-shi	737	6.1			
				Hamura-machi	662	5.5			
				Mizuho-machi	556	4.6			
				Tachikawa-shi	460	3.9			
				Hachiōji-shi	301	2.5			
				Itsukaichi-machi	241	2.0			
				Musashi-machi	236	2.0			
				Murayama-machi	184	1.5			
				( )	119	1.0			
				Others	1110	9.3			
		Mizuho-machi	3790	Others	3552	93.7	5799	238	2247
				Others	238	6.3			
		Murayama-machi	3814	Mizuho-machi	3357	88.0	5568	457	2211
				Mizuho-machi	81	2.2			
				Others	376	9.8			
		Musashi-machi	15083	Sayama-shi	11330	75.1	15263	3753	3933
				Sayama-shi	1109	7.4			
				Hannō-shi	960	6.4			

TABLE 13

REGIONAL SOURCES OF DAYTIME POPULATION INFLUX OF WORKERS AND STUDENTS OVER 15 YEARS OLD—Continued

Zone	Sector	Region	Total Daytime Workers & Students	Regional Sources of Daytime Workers & Students			Total Workers & Students in Region	Total Workers & Students in Daytime Influx	Total Workers & Students in Daily Outflow
				Region	Number	Percent			
8	IV	Sayama-shi	14036	Tokorosawa-shi	678	4.5	17241	2014	5219
				Others	1006	6.6			
		Kawagoe-shi	47820	Kawagoe-shi	12022	85.7	55863	6067	14110
				Musashi-machi	540	3.8			
				Others	458	3.3			
				Others	1016	7.2			
		Seibu-machi	2866	Sakado-machi	41753	87.3	3582	453	1169
				Kawashima-mura	988	2.1			
				Others	805	1.7			
				Others	4274	8.9			
8	V	Ageo-shi	16614	Hannō-shi	2413	84.7	20665	2145	6196
				Others	243	8.5			
				Others	210	6.8			
		Ina-mura	2874	Ōmiya-shi	14469	87.1	3999	115	1240
				Others	526	3.2			
				Others	1619	9.7			
		Hasuda-machi	7277	Others	2759	96.0	10803	459	3985
				Others	115	4.0			
		Shiraoka-machi	5570	Others	6818	93.7	8403	146	2979
				Others	459	6.3			
				Others	5424	97.4			
				Others	146	2.6			

TABLE 13

REGIONAL SOURCES OF DAYTIME POPULATION INFLUX OF WORKERS AND STUDENTS OVER 15 YEARS OLD—Continued

Zone	Sector	Region	Total Daytime Workers & Students	Regional Sources of Daytime Workers & Students			Total Workers & Students in Region	Total Workers & Students in Daytime Influx	Total Workers & Students in Daily Outflow
				Region	Number	Percent			
		Miyashiro-machi	3985	Others	3741 / 244	93.9 / 6.1	5783	244	2042
8	VI	Sugito-machi	7784	Others	7083 / 701	91.0 / 9.0	9349	701	2266
		Sekiyado-machi	6046	Others	6004 / 42	99.3 / 0.7	6769	42	765
		Moriya-machi	5353	Others	5270 / 83	98.4 / 1.6	6451	83	1181
8	VII	Toride-machi	9200	Fujishiro-machi / Others	7955 / 411 / 834	86.5 / 4.5 / 9.0	12051	1245	4096
		Inzai-machi	8855	Others	8252 / 603	93.2 / 6.8	9528	603	1276
		Inba-mura	4549	Others	4516 / 33	99.3 / 0.7	4892	33	376
8	VIII	Yotsukaidō-machi	5421	Others	5130 / 291	94.6 / 5.4	8452	291	3322
8	IX	Ichihara-machi	5947	Others	5493 / 454	92.4 / 7.6	7832	454	2339
		Anegasaki-machi	5009	Others	4910 / 99	98.0 / 2.0	6265	99	1355

TABLE   13

REGIONAL SOURCES OF DAYTIME POPULATION INFLUX OF WORKERS AND STUDENTS OVER 15 YEARS OLD—Continued

Zone	Sector	Region	Total Daytime Workers & Students	Regional Sources of Daytime Workers & Students			Total Workers & Students in Region	Total Workers & Students in Daytime Influx	Total Workers & Students in Daily Outflow
				Region	Number	Percent			
		Hirakawa-machi	5695		5590	98.2	6303	105	713
				Others	105	1.8			
		Miwa-machi	4625		4554	98.5	5338	71	784
				Others	71	1.5			
8	X	Kisarazu-shi	29752	Kimitsu-machi	26293	88.4	28981	3459	2688
					638	2.1			
				Others	2821	9.5			
9	I	Kamakura-shi	33621		22813	67.9	48392	10808	25579
				Fujisawa-shi	1956	5.8			
				Totsuka-ku	1899	5.6			
				Yokosuka-shi	1771	5.3			
				Zushi-shi	1045	3.1			
				Chigasaki-shi	794	2.4			
				Others	3343	9.9			
9	II	Ayase-machi	4576		2917	63.7	4276	1659	1359
				Yamato-shi	579	13.7			
				Atsugi-shi	177	3.9			
				Ebina-machi	164	3.6			
				Zama-machi	154	3.4			
				Fujisawa-shi	121	2.6			
				Others	464	9.1			
		Ebina-machi	6720		5871	87.4	9326	849	3455
				Atsugi-shi	383	5.7			
				Others	466	6.9			
		Shiroyama-machi	1465		1434	97.9	2540	31	1106
				Others	31	2.1			

TABLE 1.3

REGIONAL SOURCES OF DAYTIME POPULATION INFLUX OF WORKERS AND STUDENTS OVER 15 YEARS OLD—Continued

Zone	Sector	Region	Total Daytime Workers & Students	Regional Sources of Daytime Workers & Students			Total Workers & Students in Region	Total Workers & Students in Daytime Influx	Total Workers & Students in Daily Outflow
				Region	Number	Percent			
9	III	Akita-machi	3773	Others	3477 296	92.2 7.8	6909	296	3432
		Hamura-machi	2542	Ōme-shi Others	2188 139 215	86.1 5.5 8.4	5226	354	3038
9	IV	Hannō-shi	18956	Hidaka-machi Others	16571 695 1690	87.4 3.7 8.9	21735	2385	5164
		Tsurugashima-mura	3018	Others	2876 142	95.3 4.7	4116	142	1240
		Hidaka-machi	7052	Others	6871 181	97.4 2.6	9215	181	2344
		Kawashima-mura	7743	Others	7681 62	99.2 0.8	9412	62	1731
9	V	Kitamoto-machi	4801	Others	4583 218	95.5 4.5	7854	218	3271
		Higawa-machi	8454	Ageo-shi Konosu-shi Others	7228 288 148 792	85.5 3.4 1.8 9.3	11168	1226	3940
		Shōbu-machi	6956	Others	6793 163	97.7 2.3	8367	163	1574

TABLE 1.3

REGIONAL SOURCES OF DAYTIME POPULATION INFLUX OF WORKERS AND STUDENTS OVER 15 YEARS OLD—Continued

Zone	Sector	Region	Total Daytime Workers & Students	Regional Sources of Daytime Workers & Students			Total Workers & Students in Region	Total Workers & Students in Daytime Influx	Total Workers & Students in Daily Outflow
				Region	Number	Percent			
		Kuki-machi	8884	Shiraoka-machi	7686	86.5	11613	1198	3927
				Shōbu-machi	152	1.7			
				Satte-machi	137	1.6			
					126	1.4			
				Others	783	8.8			
		Satte-machi	10445	Others	9717	93.0	12253	728	2536
					728	7.0			
9	VI	Iwai-machi	18337	Others	18117	98.8	18938	220	821
					220	1.2			
		Mitsukaidō-shi	19425	Others	19376	99.7	20656	49	1280
					49	0.3			
		Ina-mura	6740	Others	6518	96.7	7360	222	842
					222	3.3			
		Yawahara-mura	5225	Others	5156	98.7	6168	69	1012
					69	1.3			
		Fujishiro-machi	5870	Others	5643	96.1	7446	227	1803
					227	3.9			
9	VII	Ryūgasaki-shi	17244	Others	16100	93.4	18464	1144	2364
					1144	6.6			
		Tone-mura	4371	Others	4334	99.2	5324	37	990
					37	0.8			
		Motono-mura	2768	Others	2733	98.7	3147	35	414
					35	1.3			

TABLE 1.3

REGIONAL SOURCES OF DAYTIME POPULATION INFLUX OF WORKERS AND STUDENTS OVER 15 YEARS OLD—Continued

Zone	Sector	Region	Total Daytime Workers & Students	Regional Sources of Daytime Workers & Students			Total Workers & Students in Region	Total Workers & Students in Daytime Influx	Total Workers & Students in Daily Outflow
				Region	Number	Percent			
9	VIII	Sakura-shi	16465	Others	14877 1587	90.4 9.6	20135	1587	5258
		Izumi-machi	4795	Others	4746 49	99.0 1.0	5419	49	673
9	IX	Shitsu-mura	4467	Others	4438 29	99.4 0.6	5344	29	906
		Nansō-machi	9485	Others	9238 247	97.4 2.6	9911	247	673
		Fukuta-machi	3577	Others	3521 56	98.4 1.6	4117	56	596
9	X	Kimitsu-machi	6204	Others	6078 126	98.0 2.0	7444	126	1366
		Futtsu-machi	8328	Others	8112 216	97.4 2.6	9009	126	897
		Ōsawa-machi	6507	Others	6234 273	95.8 4.2	7528	273	1294
10	I	Yokosuka-shi	119276	Kanazawa-ku Others	105446 3158 10672	88.4 2.6 9.0	139937	13830	34491
		Zushi-shi	10938	Yokosuka-shi Atsugi-shi	6258 1837 452	57.2 17.8 4.1	18880	4680	12622

TABLE 1.3

REGIONAL SOURCES OF DAYTIME POPULATION INFLUX OF WORKERS AND STUDENTS OVER 15 YEARS OLD—Continued

Zone	Sector	Region	Total Daytime Workers & Students	Regional Sources of Daytime Workers & Students — Region	Number	Percent	Total Workers & Students in Region	Total Workers & Students in Daytime Influx	Total Workers & Students in Daily Outflow
				Hayama-machi	447	4.1			
				Kanazawa-ku	433	4.0			
				Kamakura-shi	404	3.7			
				Others	1107	9.1			
		Hayama-machi	3163		2870	90.7	7557	293	4687
				Others	293	9.3			
		Chigasaki-shi	18594		16087	86.5	31986	2507	15899
				Fujisawa-shi	1129	6.1			
				Others	1378	7.4			
		Fujisawa-shi	46054		34786	75.5	59994	11268	25208
				Chigasaki-shi	2778	6.0			
				Kamakura-shi	2398	5.2			
				Totsuka-ku	977	2.1			
				Yamato-shi	870	1.9			
				Others	4245	9.3			
10	II	Aikawa-machi	6459		6293	97.4	7521	166	1228
				Others	166	2.6			
		Atsugi-shi	21050		17811	84.6	23688	3239	5877
				Ebina-machi	684	3.2			
				Sagamihara-shi	539	2.6			
				Others	2016	9.6			
		Samukawa-machi	4956		3882	78.3	5953	1074	2071
				Chigasaki-shi	448	9.0			
				Fujisawa-shi	176	3.6			
				Others	450	9.1			

TABLE 1.3

REGIONAL SOURCES OF DAYTIME POPULATION INFLUX OF WORKERS AND STUDENTS OVER 15 YEARS OLD—Continued

Zone	Sector	Region	Total Daytime Workers & Students	Regional Sources of Daytime Workers & Students			Total Workers & Students in Region	Total Workers & Students in Daytime Influx	Total Workers & Students in Daily Outflow
				Region	Number	Percent			
10	III	Ōme-shi	277225		22959	84.3	29020	4266	6061
				Okutama-machi	825	3.0			
				Hamura-machi	524	1.9			
				Akita-machi	317	1.3			
				Others	2599	9.5			
		Sakado-machi	9729		9316	95.8	12747	413	3431
				Others	413	4.2			
		Yoshimi-mura	6790		6790	100.0	8388	0	1598
				Others	0	0			
		Moroyama-mura	4691		4600	98.1	5943	91	1343
				Others	91	1.9			
10	V	Kōnosu-shi	12589		11733	93.2	16558	856	4825
				Others	856	6.8			
		Kisai-machi	7070		7053	99.8	8434	17	1381
				Others	17	0.2			
		Washimiya-machi	3355		3290	98.1	4466	65	1176
				Others	65	1.9			
		Kurihashi-machi	4435		4326	97.5	6470	109	2144
				Others	109	2.5			
		Goka-mura	4379		4336	99.0	4874	43	538
				Others	43	1.0			

TABLE 1.3

REGIONAL SOURCES OF DAYTIME POPULATION INFLUX OF WORKERS AND STUDENTS OVER 15 YEARS OLD—Continued

Zone	Sector	Region	Total Daytime Workers & Students	Regional Sources of Daytime Workers & Students			Total Workers & Students in Region	Total Workers & Students in Daytime Influx	Total Workers & Students in Daily Outflow
				Region	Number	Percent			
10	VI	Sakai-machi	12239		11916	97.4	12194	323	278
				Others	323	2.6			
		Sashima-machi	7853		7853	100.0	8192	0	339
				Others	0	0			
		Yatabe-machi	11774		11492	97.6	12387	282	895
				Others	282	2.4			
10	VII	Kukizaki-mura	3269		3250	99.4	3735	19	485
				Others	19	0.6			
		Ushiku-machi	7215		7044	97.6	8706	171	1662
				Others	171	2.4			
		Kawashi-mura	7042		7029	99.8	7648	13	619
				Others	13	0.2			
		Sakae-machi	4804		4695	97.7	5593	109	898
				Others	109	2.3			
		Narita-shi	20926		19836	94.8	23292	1090	3456
				Others	1090	5.2			
10	VIII	Shisui-machi	2320		2259	97.4	3386	61	1127
				Others	61	2.6			
		Yachimata-machi	12642		12413	98.2	13738	229	1375
				Others	229	1.8			

TABLE 13

REGIONAL SOURCES OF DAYTIME POPULATION INFLUX OF WORKERS AND STUDENTS OVER 15 YEARS OLD—Continued

Zone	Sector	Region	Total Daytime Workers & Students	Regional Sources of Daytime Workers & Students			Total Workers & Students in Region	Total Workers & Students in Daytime Influx	Total Workers & Students in Daily Outflow
				Region	Number	Percent			
10		Toke-machi	2598	Others	2577 21	99.2 0.8	3573	21	996
10	IX	Nagara-machi	4323	Others	4323 0	100.0 0	5174	0	851
		Obitsu-mura	3630	Others	3458 272	95.3 4.7	3948	172	490
10	X	Koito-machi	3531	Others	3396 135	96.2 3.8	3669	135	273

APPENDIX

LIST OF MUNICIPAL MERGERS IN THE TOKYO METROPOLITAN COMPLEX
(50-KILOMETER RADIUS)

APPENDIX
LIST OF MUNICIPAL MERGERS IN THE TOKYO
METROPOLITAN COMPLEX (50-KILOMETER RADIUS)

Zone	Sector	(1950)	(1955)	(1960)
1	I	Chiyoda-ku	Chiyoda-ku	Chiyoda-ku
		Minato-ku	Minato-ku	Minato-ku
		Chūō-ku	Chūō-ku	Chūō-ku
		Bunkyō-ku	Bunkyō-ku	Bunkyō-ku
		Taitō-ku	Taitō-ku	Taitō-ku
2	I	Shinagawa-ku	Shinagawa-ku	Shinagawa-ku
	II	Meguro-ku	Meguro-ku	Meguro-ku
		Shibuya-ku	Shibuya-ku	Shibuya-ku
	III	Shinjuku-ku	Shinjuku-ku	Shinjuku-ku
		Nakano-ku	Nakano-ku	Nakano-ku
	IV	Toshima-ku	Toshima-ku	Toshima-ku
	V	Kita-ku	Kita-ku	Kita-ku
	VI	Arakawa-ku	Arakawa-ku	Arakawa-ku
	VVII	Sumida-ku	Sumida-ku	Sumida-ku
	VIII	Kōtō-ku	Kōtō-ku	Kōtō-ku
3	I	Ōta-ku	Ōta-ku	Ōta-ku
	II	Setagaya-ku	Setagaya-ku	Setagaya-ku
	III	Suginami-ku	Suginami-ku	Suginami-ku
	IV	Itabashi-ku	Itabashi-ku	Itabashi-ku
		Nerima-ku	Nerima-ku	Nerima-ku
	VI	Adachi-ku	Adachi-ku	Adachi-ku
	VII	Katsushika-ku	Katsushika-ku	Katsushika-ku
	VIII	Edogawa-ku	Edogawa-ku	Edogawa-ku
		Urayasu-machi	Urayasu-machi	Urayasu-machi
4	I	Kawasaki-shi	Kawasaki-shi	Kawasaki-shi
	II	Komae-mura	Komae-mura	Komae-mura
	III	Mitaka-machi	Mitaka-shi	Mitaka-shi
		Musashino-shi	Musashino-shi	Musashino-shi
		Chōfu-machi	Chōfu-shi	Chōfu-shi
		Jindai-machi		
		Hoya-machi	Hoya-machi	Hoya-machi
	IV	Yamato-machi	Yamato-machi	Yamato-machi
		Toda-machi	Toda-machi	Toda-machi
		Misasa-mura	Misasa-mura	
	V	Warabi-machi	Warabi-machi	Warabi-machi
		Kawaguchi-shi	Kawaguchi-shi	Kawaguchi-shi
		Angyō-mura	Angyō-mura	
		(Hatogaya-machi)	(Hatogaya-machi)	Hatogaya-machi[1]

LIST OF MUNICIPAL MERGERS IN THE TOKYO
METROPOLITAN COMPLEX (50-KILOMETER RADIUS)

Zone	Sector	(1950)	(1955)	(1960)
4	VI	Sōka-machi	Sōka-machi	Sōka-shi
		Yatsuka-mura		
		Shinden-mura		
		Kawayanagi-mura		
		Hachijō-mura	Hachijō-mura	Yashio-mura
		Shiadome-mura	Shiadome-mura	
		Yahata-mura	Yahata-mura	
		Hikonari-mura	Hikonari-mura	Misato-mura
		Tōwa-mura	Tōwa-mura	
		Waseda-mura	Waseda-mura	
		Matsudo-shi	Matsudo-shi	Matsudo-shi
	VII	Ichikawa-shi	Ichikawa-shi	Ichikawa-shi
		Gyōtoku-machi		
		Minamigyōtoku-machi	Minamigyōtoku-machi	
5	I	Tsurumi-ku	Tsurumi-ku	Tsurumi-ku
	III	Koganei-shi	Koganei-shi	Koganei-shi
		Tanashi-machi	Tanashi-machi	Tanashi-machi
		Kurume-machi	Kurume-machi	Kurume-machi
	IV	Katayama-mura	Niza-machi	Niza-machi
		Owada-machi		
		Kiyose-machi	Kiyose-machi	Kiyose-machi
		Shiki-machi	Adachi-machi	Adachi-machi
		Muneoka-mura		
		Asaka-machi	Asaka-machi	Asaka-machi
		Uchimagi-mura		
	V	Urawa-shi	Urawa-shi	Urawa-shi
		Tsuchiai-mura		
		Ōkubo-mura		
		Noda-mura	Noda-mura	Misono-mura
		Daimon-mura	Daimon-mura	
		Totsuka-mura	Totsuka-mura	
		Koshigaya-machi	Koshigaya-machi	Koshigaya-shi
		Sakurai-mura		
		Nigata-mura		
		Masubayashi-mura		
		Ōbukuro-mura		
		Ogishima-mura		
		Oewa-mura		
		Ōsagami-mura		
		Gamō-mura		
		Osawa-machi		

Zone	Sector	(1950)	(1955)	(1960)
5	VI	Yoshikawa-mura	Yoshikawa-machi	Yoshikawa-machi
		Miwanoe-mura		
		Asahi-mura		
		Nagareyama-machi	Nagareyama-machi	Nagareyama-machi
		Yagi-mura		
		Shinkawa-mura		
	VII	Kamagaya-mura	Kamagaya-mura	Kamagaya-machi
	VIII	Funahashi-shi	Funahashi-shi	Funahashi-shi
		Ninomiya-mura		
		Toyotomi-mura		
6	I	Nishi-ku	Nishi-ku	Nishi-ku
		Naka-ku	Naka-ku	Naka-ku
		Kanagawa-ku	Kanagawa-ku	Kanagawa-ku
	II	Kōhoku-ku	Kōhoku-ku	Kōhoku-ku
		Inagi-mura	Inagi-mura	Inagi-machi
	III	Tama-mura	Tama-mura	Tama-mura
		Fuchū-mura	Fuchū-shi	Fuchū-shi
		Nishifu-mura		
		Tama-mura		
		Yaho-machi	Kunitachi-machi	Kunitachi-machi
		Kokubunji-machi	Kokubunji-machi	Kokubunji-machi
		Kodaira-machi	Kodaira-machi	Kodaira-machi
		Higashimurayama-machi	Higashimurayama-machi	Higashimurayama-machi
	IV	Tokorosawa-machi	Tokorosawa-shi	Tokorosawa-shi
		Yanase-mura		
		Mikajima-mura		
		Miyoshi-mura	Miyoshi-mura	Miyoshi-mura
		Tsuruse-mura	Tsuruse-mura	Fujimi-mura
		Nanbata-mura	Nanbata-mura	
		Mizutani-mura	Mizutani-mura	
	V	Yono-machi	Yono-machi	Yono-shi
		Ōmiya-shi	Ōmiya-shi	Ōmiya-shi
		Sashiōgi-mura		
		Mamiya-mura		
		Uemizu-mura		
		Katayanagi-mura		
		Iwatsuki-mura	Iwatsuki-shi	Iwatsuki-shi
		Kawatōri-mura		
		Kashiwazaki-mura		
		Wado-mura		
		Nīwa-mura		
		Jionji-mura		
		Kawai-mura		

LIST OF MUNICIPAL MERGERS IN THE TOKYO
METROPOLITAN COMPLEX (50-KILOMETER RADIUS)

Zone	Sector	(1950)	(1955)	(1960)
	VI	Matsubushiryō-mura Kanasugi-mura	Matsubushiryō-mura	Matsubushi-mura
	VII	Kashiwa-machi Tsuchi-mura Tanaka-mura Kogane-mura Tomise-mura	Kashiwa-shi[2]	Kashiwa-shi
		Kazahaya-mura Tega-mura	Shōnan-mura	Shōnan-mura
		Shirai-mura	Shirai-mura	Shirai-mura
	VIII	Tsudanuma-machi	Narashino-shi	Narashino-shi[3]
7	I	Isogo-ku Minami-ku Hodogaya-ku	Isogo-ku Minami-ku Hodogaya-ku	Isogo-ku Minami-ku Hodogaya-ku
	II	Machida-machi Minami-mura Sakai-mura Tadao-mura Tsurukawa-mura	Machida-machi Sakai-mura Tadao-mura Tsurukawa-mura	Machida-shi
	III	Yuki-mura Hino-machi Nanao-mura Tachikawa-shi Sunakawa-mura Yamato-mura	Yuki-mura Hino-machi Nanao-mura Tachikawa-shi Sunakawa-machi Yamato-machi	Yuki-mura Hino-machi Tachikawa-shi Sunakawa-machi Yamato-machi
	IV	Ōi-mura Fukuoka-mura	Ōi-mura Fukuoka-mura	Ōi-mura Fukuoka-mura
	V	Kasukabe-machi Kawabe-mura Minamisakurai-mura Tomida-mura Hōshubana-mura	Kasukabe-shi Shōwa-mura	Kasukabe-shi Shōwa-mura
	VI	Noda-shi Fukuda-mura Kawama-mura Abiko-machi Fusa-mura Kōhoku-mura	Noda-shi Fukuda-mura Kawama-mura Abiko-machi	Noda-shi Abiko-machi

LIST OF MUNICIPAL MERGERS IN THE TOKYO
METROPOLITAN COMPLEX (50-KILOMETER RADIUS)

Zone Sector	(1950)	(1955)	(1960)
IV	Irumagawa-machi	Sayama-shi	Sayama-shi
	Iruma-mura		
	Horikane-mura		
	Okutomi-mura		
	Mizutomi-mura		
	Kashiwabara-mura		
	Kawagoe-shi	Kawagoe-shi	Kawagoe-shi
	Yoshino-mura		
	Furuya-mura		
	Yamada-mura		
	Minamifuruya-mura		
	Takashina-mura		
	Fukuhara-mura		
	Nakuwashi-mura		
	Kasumigaseki-mura		
	Daitō-mura		
	Higashikaneko-mura	Seibu-machi	Seibu-machi
V	Ageo-machi	Ageo-machi	Ageo-shi
	Hirakata-mura		
	Haraichi-machi		
	Ōya-mura		
	Kamihira-mura		
	Ōishi-mura		
	Ina-mura	Ina-mura	Ina-mura
	Hasuda-machi	Hasuda-machi	Hasuda-machi
	Kurohama-mura		
	Hirano-mura		
	Shinozu-mura	Shiraoka-machi	Shiraoka-machi
	Hikatsu-mura		
	Ōyama-mura		
	Monma-mura	Miyashiro-machi	Miyashiro-machi
	Suka-mura		
	Sugito-machi	Sugito-machi	Sugito-machi
	Takano-machi		
	Teigō-mura		
	Tomiya-mura		
	Sakurai-mura	Izumi-mura	
	Toyooka-mura		
VI	Sekiyado-machi	Sekiyado-machi	Sekiyado-machi
	Futagawa-mura		
	Kimakase-mura		

LIST OF MUNICIPAL MERGERS IN THE TOKYO
METROPOLITAN COMPLEX (50-KILOMETER RADIUS)

Zone	Sector	(1950)	(1955)	(1960)
7	VII	Ōwada-mura	Yachiyo-machi	Yachiyo-machi
		Matsumi-mura		
		Aso-mura		
	VIII	Chiba-shi	Chiba-shi	Chiba-shi
		Kotehashi-mura		
		Makuwari-machi		
		Oihama-machi		
		Shina-mura		
		Honda-machi		
	IX	Goi-mura	Goi-machi	Goi-machi
		Tōkai-mura		
		Chigusa-mura		
		Nagaura-mura	Sodegaura-machi	Sodegaura-machi
		Shōwa-machi		
		Negata-mura		
8	I	Kanazawa-ku	Kanazawa-ku	Kanazawa-ku
		Totsuka-ku	Totsuka-ku	Totsuka-ku
	II	Yamato-machi	Yamato-machi	Yamato-machi
		Sagamihara-machi	Sagamihara-shi	Sagamihara-shi
		Zama-machi	Zama-machi	Zama-machi
		Hachiōji-shi	Hachiōji-shi	Hachiōji-shi
		Yokoyama-mura		
		Onkata-mura		
		Kawaguchi-mura		
		Kazumi-mura		
		Yui-mura		
		Motohachiōji-mura		
		Asakawa-machi	Asakawa-machi	
		Shōwa-machi	Akishima-shi	Akishima-shi
		Haijima-machi		
		Fussa-machi	Fussa-machi	Fussa-machi
		Mizuho-machi	Mizuho-machi	Mizuho-machi
		Murayama-machi	Murayama-machi	Murayama-machi
		Toyooka-machi	Toyooka-machi	Musashi-machi
		Kaneko-mura	Kaneko-mura	
		Miyadera-mura	Miyadera-mura	
		Fujisawa-mura	Fujisawa-mura	
		Motosayama-mura	Motosayama-mura	

LIST OF MUNICIPAL MERGERS IN THE TOKYO
METROPOLITAN COMPLEX (50-KILOMETER RADIUS)

Zone	Sector	(1950)	(1955)	(1960)
8	VI	Moriya-machi	Moriya-machi	Moriya-machi
		Ōno-mura		
		Ōisawa-mura		
	VII	Toride-machi	Toride-machi	Toride-machi
		Omonma-mura		
		Terahara-mura		
		Inatoi-mura		
		Takai-mura		
		Omori-machi	Inzai-machi	Inzai-machi
		Kioroshi-machi		
		Funaho-mura		
		Eiji-mura		
		Rokugō-mura	Inba-mura	Inba-mura
		Munekata-mura		
	VIII	Chiyoda-machi	Yotsukaidō-machi	Yotsukaidō-machi
		Asahi-mura		
	IX	Yamato-machi	Ichihara-machi	Ichihara-machi[4]
		Kituma-mura		
		Ichihara-mura	Ichihara-mura	
		Anegasaki-machi	Anegasaki-machi	Anegasaki-machi
		Nakagawa-mura	Hirakawa-machi	Hirakawa-machi
		Hiraoka-mura		
		Tomioka-mura		
		Shisai-mura	Miwa-machi	Miwa-machi
		Yōrō-mura		
		Unakami-mura	Unakami-mura	
	X	Kisarazu-machi	Kisarazu-shi	Kisarazu-shi
		Kamatari-mura		
		Kaneda-mura		
		Nakagō-mura		
9	I	Kamakura-shi	Kamakura-shi	Kamakura-shi
	II	Ayase-machi	Ayase-machi	Ayase-machi
		Ebina-machi	Ebina-machi	Ebina-machi
		Arima-mura		
		Kawajiri-mura	Shiroyama-machi	Shiroyama-machi[5]
		Shōnan-mura		
		Misawa-mura		
	III	Tasai-mura	Akita-machi	Akita-machi
		Higashiakiru-mura		
		Nishiakiru-mura		
		Nishitama-mura	Hamura-machi	Hamura-machi

LIST OF MUNICIPAL MERGERS IN THE TOKYO
METROPOLITAN COMPLEX (50-KILOMETER RADIUS)

Zone	Sector	(1950)	(1955)	(1960)
9	IV	Hannō-machi	Hannō-shi	Hannō-shi
		Haraichiba-mura	Haraichiba-mura	
		Higashi-agano-mura	Higashi-agano-mura	
		Agano-mura	Agano-mura	
		Tsurugashima-mura	Tsurugashima-mura	Tsurugashima-mura
		Komagawa-mura	Hidaka-machi	Hidaka-machi
		Koma-mura		
		Takahagi-mura	Takahagi-mura	
		Nakayama-mura	Kawashima-mura	Kawashima-mura
		Ikusa-mura		
		Mihonoya-mura		
		Idemaru-mura		
		Yatsuhu-mura		
		Omino-mura		
	V	Kitamotoyado-mura	Kitamoto-machi	Kitamoto-machi
		Higawa-machi	Higawa-machi	Higawa-machi
		Kanō-mura		
		Kawataya-mura		
		Shōbu-machi	Shōbu-machi	Shōbu-machi
		Obayashi-mura		
		Sanga-mura		
		Kayama-mura		
		Ōyama-mura		
		Kuki-machi	Kuki-machi	Kuki-machi
		Ōta-machi		
		Ezura-mura		
		Kiyoku-mura		
		Satte-machi	Satte-machi	Satte-machi
		Miyuki-mura		
		Kamitakano-mura		
		Yoshida-mura		
		Gongendōgawa-mura		
		Yoshiro-mura		
	VI	Iwai-machi	Iwai-machi	Iwai-machi
		Nakagawa-mura		
		Nanagō-mura		
		Kamiōmi-mura		
		Ijima-mura		
		Yumata-mura		
		Nanae-mura		
		Nagasu-mura		

LIST OF MUNICIPAL MERGERS IN THE TOKYO
METROPOLITAN COMPLEX (50-KILOMETER RADIUS)

Zone	Sector	(1950)	(1955)	(1960)
		Nagasu-mura		
9	VI	Mitsukaidō-machi	Mitsukaidō-shi	Mitsukaidō-shi
		Toyooka-mura		
		Sugahara-mura		
		Ōharawa-mura		
		Mizuma-mura		
		Goka-mura		
		Ōno-mura		
		Sakate-mura		
		Yahara-mura		
		Mase-mura		
		Uchimoriya-mura	Uchimoriya-mura	
		Sugao-mura	Sugao-mura	
		Jūwa-mura	Yawahara-mura	Yawahara-mura
		Fukuoka-mura		
		Kokinu-mura		
		Mishima-mura	Ina-mura	Ina-mura
		Yaida-mura		
		Yutaka-mura		
		Obari-mura		
		Itabashi-mura		
	VII	Sōma-machi	Fujishiro-machi	Fujishiro-machi
		Rokugō-mura		
		Sannō-mura		
		Takasu-mura		
		Kuga-mura		
		Ryūgasaki-machi	Ryūgasaki-shi	Ryūgasaki-shi
		Nareshiba-mura		
		Ōmiya-mura		
		Yahara-mura		
		Nagato-mura		
		Kawarashiro-mura		
		Kitamonma-mura		
		Fukawa-machi	Tone-mura	Tone-mura
		Fumi-mura		
		Monma-mura		
		Higashimonma-mura		
		Motono-mura	Motono-mura	Motono-mura
	VIII	Sakura-machi	Sakura-shi	Sakura-shi
		Usui-machi		
		Shitsu-mura		

LIST OF MUNICIPAL MERGERS IN THE TOKYO
METROPOLITAN COMPLEX (50-KILOMETER RADIUS)

Zone	Sector	(1950)	(1955)	(1960)
		Negō-mura		
		Yatomi-mura		
		Wada-mura		
		Shirai-mura	Izumi-machi	Izumi-machi
		Sarashina-mura		
	IX	Shitō-mura	Shitsu-mura	Shitsu-mura
		Urutsu-mura		
		Uchida-mura	Nansō-machi	Nansō-machi
		Heizō-mura		
		Toda-mura		
		Tsurumai-machi		
		Ushiku-machi		
		Makuta-mura	Fukuta-machi	Fukuta-machi
		Tanioka-mura		
	X	Kimitsu-machi	Kimitsu-machi	Kimitsu-machi
		Sadamoto-mura		
		Sunami-mura		
		Futtsu-machi	Futtsu-machi	Futtsu-machi
		Aohori-machi		
		Ino-mura		
		Sanuki-machi	Ōsawa-machi	Ōsawa-machi
		Ōnuki-machi		
10	I	Yokosuka-shi	Yokosuka-shi	Yokosuka-shi
		Zushi-machi	Zushi-shi	Zushi-shi
		Hayama-machi	Hayama-machi	Hayama-machi
		Chigasaki-shi	Chigasaki-shi	Chigasaki-shi
		Koide-mura		
		Fujisawa-shi	Fujisawa-shi	Fujisawa-shi
		Goshomi-mura		
		Shibuya-mura		
	II	Aikawa-machi	Aikawa-machi	Aikawa-machi
		Takamine-mura		
		Nakatsu-mura	Nakatsu-mura	
		Atsugi-machi	Atsugi-shi	Atsugi-shi
		Koaya-mura		
		Echi-mura		
		Nanmōri-mura		
		Tamagawa-mura		
		Aikawa-mura		
		Mutsuai-mura		

Zone	Sector	(1950)	(1955)	(1960)
		Shizuka-mura		
		Nagata-mura		
		Sashima-mura		
		Morito-mura		
		Kutsukake-mura	Katsukake-machi	Sashima-machi
		Oigosuge-mura	Fusato-mura	
		Sakasaiyama-mura		
		Yatabe-mura	Yatabe-machi	Yatabe-machi
		Onokawa-mura		
		Katsuragi-mura		
		Shimana-mura		
VII		Kukizaki-mura	Kukizaki-mura	Kukizaki-mura
		Ushiku-mura	Ushiku-machi	Ushiku-machi
		Okada-mura		
		Okuno-mura		
		Namaita-mura	Kawachi-mura	Kawachi-mura
		Genseida-mura		
		Mizuho-mura		
		Kanaezu-mura	Kanaezu-mura	
		Fukama-mura	Fukama-mura	Sakae-machi
		Ajiki-machi	Ajiki-machi	
		Narita-machi	Narita-shi	Narita-shi
		Tōyama-mura		
		Toyozumi-mura		
		Kuzumi-mura		
		Nakagō-mura		
		Habu-mura		
		Kōzu-mura		
VIII		Shisui-machi	Shisui-machi	Shisui-machi
		Yachimata-machi	Yachimata-machi	Yachimata-machi
		Hyūga-mura		
		Kawakami-mura		
		Toke-machi	Toke-machi	Toke-machi
		Nagara-mura	Nagara-machi	Nagara-machi[6]
		Mizukami-mura		
		Hiyoshi-mura		
		Obitsu-mura	Obitsu-mura	Obitsu-mura
		Koito-mura	Koito-machi	Koito-machi
		Naka-mura		

LIST OF MUNICIPAL MERGERS IN THE TOKYO
METROPOLITAN COMPLEX (50-KILOMETER RADIUS)

Zone	Sector	(1950)	(1955)	(1960)
		Ogino-mura	Ogino-mura	
10	II	Samukawa-machi	Samukawa-machi	Samukawa-machi
	III	Osogi-mura	Ōme-shi	Ōme-shi
		Naruki-mura		
		Yoshino-mura		
		Mita-mura		
		Kasumi-mura		
		Chōfu-mura		
		Ome-machi		
	IV	Sakado-machi	Sakado-machi	Sakado-machi
		Miyoshino-mura		
		Suguro-mura		
		Nissai-mura		
		Ōya-mura		
		Higashiyoshimi-mura	Yoshimi-mura	Yoshimi-mura
		Minamiyoshimi-mura		
		Kitayoshimi-mura		
		Nishiyoshimi-mura		
		Moroyama-mura	Moroyama-mura	Moroyama-mura
		Kawakado-mura		
	V	Kōnosu-machi	Kōnosu-shi	Kōnosu-shi
		Mida-mura		
		Tamamiya-mura		
		Mamuro-mura		
		Kasahara-mura		
		Jōkō-mura		
		Kisai-machi	Kisai-machi	Kisai-machi
		Tanadare-mura		
		Togaya-mura		
		Kōguki-mura		
		Takayanagi-mura		
		Washimiya-machi	Washimiya-machi	Washimiya-machi
		Sakurada-mura		
		Kurihashi-machi	Kurihashi-machi	Kurihashi-machi
		Shizuka-mura	Shizuka-mura	
		Toyota-mura	Toyota-mura	
		Goka-mura	Goka-mura	Goka-mura
	VI	Sakai-machi	Sakai-machi	Sakai-machi

LIST OF MUNICIPAL MERGERS IN THE TOKYO
METROPOLITAN COMPLEX (50-KILOMETER RADIUS)

NOTES

1. (Zone 4, Sector V) In 1955 Hatogaya-machi was part of Kawaguchi-shi, but in 1960 it was a separate municipality again.

2. (Zone 6, Sector VII) In the 1955 census Fuse-mura is treated as part of Kashiwa-shi and Abiko-machi, but the 1950 census report includes all data for Fuse in those for Kashiwa.

3. (Zone 6, Sector VIII) The 1950 census report does not include in the data for Narashino-shi those for the partially merged portion of Makuwari-machi.

4. (Zone 8, Sector IX) The area of Ichihara-machi differs in 1955 and 1960.

5. (Zone 9, Sector II) All data for Misawa-mura in 1950 are included in those for Shiroyama-machi although the former municipality was only partially merged with the latter.

6. (Zone 10, Sector IX) All data for Mizukami-mura in 1950 are included in those for Nagara-machi although the former municipality was only partially merged with the latter.